ACCOUNTING STANDARDS IN EVOLUTION

Ross M. Skinner
J. Alex Milburn

Toronto

Canadian Cataloguing in Publication Data

Milburn, J. Alex (John Alexander), 1938-
        Accounting standards in evolution

2nd ed.
First ed. written by Ross M. Skinner.
ISBN 0-13-088015-9 (college)
ISBN 0-13-088846-X (trade)

1. Accounting – Standards – Canada. I. Skinner, Ross M. Accounting standards in
evolution. II. Title.

HF5635.S4813 2001   657'.02'18   C00-930315-4

0-13-088015-9 (college)
0-13-088846-X (trade)

Vice President, Editorial Director: Michael Young
Acquisitions Editor: Samantha Scully
Marketing Manager: James Buchanan
Developmental Editor: Laurie Goebel
Production Editor: Mary Ann McCutcheon
Copy Editor: Shirley Corriveau
Production Coordinator: Janette Lush
Page Layout: Heidi Palfrey
Permissions Research: Susan Wallace-Cox
Art Direction: Julia Hall
Cover Design: Liz Harasymczuk
Cover Image: Chris McElcheran/Masterfile

1 2 3 4 5   05 04 03 02 01

Printed and bound in USA.

Contents

Chapter 17 Financial Instruments 328

Chapter 18 Recognition of Asset Impairment; Statement Presentation of Accounting Adjustments and Extraordinary, Unusual and Peripheral Gains and Losses 367

Chapter 19 Business Combinations 396

Chapter 23   Disclosure Issues   496

Chapter 24   Accounting for Changing Prices   532

PART III: A CONCEPTUAL FRAMEWORK AND STANDARD SETTING   571

Chapter 25   A Conceptual Framework for Financial Reporting   572

Chapter 26   The Establishment of Accounting Standards   594

PREFACE

The first edition of this book, authored by Ross Skinner, was issued in 1987. The preface to that edition stated three principal objectives:

The first [objective] is to recount in an organized fashion the standards that govern financial reporting today. The second is to explain why they take the form that they do—that is, to explore the general theory underlying today's standards and the particular thinking that has influenced the form taken by individual standards. The third is to evaluate the standards and underlying theory critically—to appraise strengths and weaknesses with a view to stimulating discussion and possible improvement.

I have attempted to remain faithful to these objectives in updating the book, and in replacing, modifying, and extending parts of it to reflect the sense of, and reasons for, changes that have taken place since 1987.

The preface to the 1987 edition emphasized also that accounting standards have evolved over time and will continue to evolve—hence the title of this book. This must be so if accounting standards are to keep pace with changes in the business environment and in society's expectations for financial information.

Much has happened since 1987. The pace of change has been accelerating as a result of the effects of the globalization of capital markets, revolutionary advances in information technology and in investment and risk management theories and practices, among other factors. These developments have severely challenged significant aspects of the traditional historical cost-based accounting model. Many new accounting standards have been issued in recent years that have effectively extended or replaced parts of the model to try to meet these challenges.

The piecemeal, issue-by-issue approach to accounting standard setting has resulted in an uneven development, and a patchwork of standards—what some have described as a "mixed attribute model". This has created a confusing picture for accounting students and practitioners alike. It is difficult to detect a unifying theory from existing standards and practices. The temptation may be to focus on a literal interpretation of specific standards, without trying to develop a broader framework of understanding. Such a narrow objective can only serve to diminish the usefulness of accounting as an economic information system, and to diminish the role of accountants as experts in enhancing the information value of financial reports. One may easily lose one's way in the forest of detailed accounting rules if one does not have the context that comes from understanding how accounting has come to be what it is, its conceptual underpinnings, its limitations, and something of the forces of change and opportunities for improvement.

The current times have been described as an "information age". Much of the current emphasis would seem to be on developments in information technology rather than on information content, however. Accounting and accounting standard setting is primarily concerned with the content (the relevance and reliability) of financial information. The benefits of advanced technology for the rapid processing and communication of large quantities of accounting data can be fully realized only if that data have relevant information value. It is hoped that this book will contribute to promoting a better understanding of financial accounting as a crucial information discipline.

It is a strong belief of the authors that an understanding of the past development of ideas will help us in the present and the future. All of us have our ingrained mind-sets, and it is instructive to look back and see how much of previous conventional wisdom has proven to be ill suited to changing conditions. This is why Part I of this book contains a brief excursion through the history of accounting. Accountants would do well to study the history of their discipline and how it has responded to changes in its environment. Chapters 2 and 3 are very little changed from the original edition, while Chapter 4 on developments in the twentieth century has been extended to briefly examine the effects of developments in academic thinking and research on the information value of accounting, as well as recent steps taken towards internationalization of accounting standards and standard setting.

Part II examines the state of current accounting standards. Financial accounting has been rooted in the transactions-based historical cost model. Even at the height of its influence this model did not come close to providing satisfactory answers to many very important accounting questions. Its inadequacies became increasingly clear from the late 1960s. The analyses of specific issues in Part II trace the bases for this, and the efforts of accounting standard setters to address the problems—in part by placing emphasis on a more rigorously reasoned conceptual framework that gives predominance to decision usefulness and economic concepts of assets and liabilities. There is also evidence of the increasing influence of modern capital markets and finance theories as, for example, standard setters struggle with the implications of present value concepts, and with the effects of complex business transactions to debundle, rebundle and diversify risks and combine and restructure business enterprises.

The traditional historical cost model concentrated on product-handling industries and was poorly adapted to the financial reporting needs of such important sectors as financial institutions, investment companies, service industries, and extractive industries. In recent years efforts have been made to incorporate all types of enterprises within a common conceptual framework, reasoning that similar transactions should be accounted for similarly regardless of the industry setting. This edition of the book has deleted the chapters on extractive industries and financial institutions that appeared in the 1987 edition, and has attempted to include important material that was in those chapters within discussions of pertinent accounting subject areas.

The final chapter of Part II (Chapter 24) chronicles efforts made to replace or revise historical cost-based accounting so as to better portray the effects of changing prices in financial reports. Those efforts failed, for several reasons. A major reason was that no one model could be demonstrated to be superior, and all have serious conceptual and practical problems. Interest in these models largely disappeared when inflation levels dropped in the mid 1980s—but standard setters may do well to consider the lessons of this experience so as to be prepared should a repetition of inflation or fundamental price instability reappear in the future. Chapter 24 represents a condensation of material that made up four chapters of the 1987 book. At the same time it introduces some new ideas in suggesting that developments in capital markets and finance-based thinking may have significant implications for redefining concepts of capital maintenance.

The focus of this book is on Canada and Canadian GAAP. But, since the early 1900s Canadian accounting has been much influenced by U.S. practice and standards. Thus the book examines U.S. developments in some depth as these have affected the thinking and development of Canadian practice and standards. As can be seen from the discussion of particular issues in Part II, Canadian standard setters have been independent and selective in taking different positions from the U.S. on a number of matters, despite the fact that the CICA conceptual framework is essentially the same as that of the U.S. The examination of particular accounting issues in Part II offers critical analyses of factors (political, conceptual and practical) that have given rise to some significant differences in accounting between the two countries. The globalization of capital markets, increasing integration of business on a North American basis, and the predominance of U.S. capital markets, are having profound effects on Canadian GAAP, and give question as to the usefulness of separate Canadian standards in the longer term. The examination of particular issues in Part II has been expanded to assess the influence of the international dimension by including some comparative analyses of significant IASC standards. In Part III, the broader implications of U.S. influences and increasing demands for internationalization of accounting standards are examined.

The gaps and weaknesses of existing financial accounting stimulate accountants to ponder whether a better conceptual framework could be articulated. The first chapter of Part III (Chapter 25) examines the need for a conceptual framework. It then builds upon the literature in this field to suggest a structure of thought, and some possibilities for the improvement of the explicit framework. It notes that certain changes in thinking underlying developments discussed in Part II have resulted in some de facto changes in the conceptual underpinnings of financial accounting that have yet to be incorporated in the formal conceptual framework.

The final chapter of Part III (Chapter 26) deals with the process of accounting standard setting. The standard setting process must demonstrate its competence and its independence from preparer and other vested interests if it is to have credibility. As well, the record suggests that standard setting requires some measure of legal support to be workable. To receive such support it must be seen to be acting in the public interest and to be performing effectively. The CICA's performance as the authoritative financial accounting standard setter in Canada has been credible to date. Some serious challenges have arisen in the past few years, however. This chapter examines these challenges and proposals that have been made to address them.

Part IV contains chapters on accounting for not-for-profit organizations and governments. These chapters have been expanded, reflecting major developments since 1987.

This book reflects developments as of about the end of 1998, and it indicates those areas in which significant changes were in process at that time.

The completion of this book owes much to the support and assistance of a number of people and organizations. I am grateful in particular to Walter Ross, Ian Hague, Gordon Richardson and his students at the University of Waterloo, and Paul Evans and his colleagues and students at York University, for their reviews and helpful comments on significant parts of the book. The chapter on government was written by Stephenie Fox, with help from Ron Salole, with little input from me, as I have little expertise in this area. Without their work this chapter would not exist. I am also indebted to Kerry Danyluk who prepared initial drafts of the chapter on not-for-profit organizations and provided helpful comments on the chapter on income taxes. I also appreciate the support of Ernst and Young through the early stages of the work. Paul Evans and Gordon Richardson must also be singled out for their support for this book at a critical time in its preparation. I would also like to especially thank Bob Rutherford and the Canadian Institute of Chartered Accountants for providing me with office support and access to its library facilities. Finally, I thank Roberta Terzolo and Sylvia Ego for their dedication and proficiency in word processing many drafts and countless corrections.

Ross M. Skinner
J. Alex Milburn

ABBREVIATIONS

Following is a list of abbreviations used in this book.

Accounting and Business Terms

ACM	Actuarial cost method
CCA	Capital cost allowance
CCA	Current cost accounting
COP	Current operating profit
CRVA	Current realizable value accounting
CVA	Current value accounting
DCF	Discounted cash flow
EPS	Earnings per share
EV	Economic value
FIFO	First in, first out
GAAP	Generally accepted accounting principles
IAS	International Accounting Standard (IASC)
LIFO	Last in, first out
LOCAM	Lower of cost and market value
NRV	Net realizable value
R&D	Research and development
RC	Replacement cost
RCA	Replacement cost accounting
SAR	Stock appreciation right
SCF	Statement of cash flow
SFAS	Statement of financial accounting standards (U.S., FASB)
VF	Value to the firm

Institutions and Associations

AAA	American Accounting Association
AIA	American Institute of Accountants (former name of AICPA)
AICPA	American Institute of Certified Public Accountants
AcSB	Accounting Standards Board (CICA)
APB	Accounting Principles Board (U.S., 1959 to 1973)
CAP	Committee on Accounting Procedure (U.S., 1939 to 1959)
CICA	Canadian Institute of Chartered Accountants
CIPREC	Canadian Institute of Public Real Estate Companies
EIC	Emerging Issues Committee (CICA)
EITF	Emerging Issues Task Force (FASB)
FASB	Financial Accounting Standards Board (U.S., 1973–)
IASC	International Accounting Standards Committee
IFAC	International Federation of Accountants
NYSE	New York Stock Exchange
OSC	Ontario Securities Commission
PSAB	Public Sector Accounting Board (CICA)
SEC	Securities and Exchange Commission (U.S.)
SIC	Standing Interpretations Committee (IASC)

References to Professional Literature

The content of this book does not take into account professional recommendations subsequent to:

- Release No. 97 of the *CICA Handbook*, dated October 1998.
- EIC 90 of the CICA Emerging Issues Committee of the CICA, dated December 1998.
- IAS 39 of the IASC, dated December 1998.
- Statement of Financial Accounting Standards No. 134 by the FASB, dated October 1998.

INTRODUCTION

Accounting is a practical occupation. It has little point unless it serves a purpose. Some people—a small minority—find some satisfaction in the symmetry of a balanced set of accounts. But for most people the value in accounting lies in the information it conveys.

That information may be simple—perhaps no more than a record of wealth, of property owned and debts owed. A mere record of wealth at a particular date, however, is no more than an inventory. Compare inventories of wealth at two different dates and one has additional information—an indication of managerial stewardship, especially important when management is separated from ownership. Add a record of inflows and outflows of cash, goods, and services in the period; thereby a basis is laid for control of the steward and his subordinates. Analyze the inflows and outflows in terms of causes and effects, and one has an explanation of the sources of gain or loss. Consider the relationship of past gains and losses to conditions prevailing when they were incurred, and one has a basis for predicting consequences of future actions.

Thus, accounting results may furnish information useful for decision making by management or by others with an interest in the reporting entity. Take this one step further to aggregate the financial information reported by significant entities or subsets of entities within a society, and one may have information relevant to social policies. Entity accounting data may also be used as instruments of social policy—as in the application of income and other taxes, price regulation, and so on.

Two conditions give rise to accounting in its various forms. The first is the existence of some need for information that may be satisfied by accounting records. The second is the development of means and techniques for satisfying such needs. By way of analogy, we know that certain problems theoretically solvable by mathematical methods could not in practice be attempted until the computational power of the computer became available. Just so can we say that applications of accounting were limited to listings of goods until coined money became avail-

1

able and was adopted as a unit of account. It is evident that if we seek an explanation of why we account as we do, we should first look to economic history for the answer.

Our review of history starts with a paradox. Accounting in some form can be traced back in various civilizations for over six thousand years. In our own Western civilization accounting has been widespread for over five hundred years. Yet it is only in the last seventy-five to one hundred and fifty years that accountants have felt a need to work out a theory of accounting. The explanation of this paradox is simple. Successful accomplishment in any activity requires understanding of the task and mastery of techniques required to carry it out. Where the task is clear, interest is restricted to techniques. So long as the accounting goal was merely to keep records, accounting instruction concentrated on "how to do it." When a financial reporting objective—an information communication goal—was added to the record-keeping function, the task of accounting became more difficult, and a theory to guide its methods became necessary.

Since roughly 1850, accounting has increasingly been used to provide information for decisions rather than merely to provide a record of property owned and transactions in property. Two branches of accounting have emerged in that period distinguishable by the type of decision made. *Management accounting* is concerned with the production and interpretation of information that will be useful for an entity's internal decisions about investment, production, pricing, marketing, and so on. *Financial reporting*, on the other hand, is concerned with the production and interpretation of information for use by persons outside the entity. One very important purpose of financial reporting is to facilitate decisions by outside parties whether to invest in the entity or provide credit to it.

The stress on the information uses of accounting transforms it from a mere technique (albeit one of considerable practical importance) into a discipline that needs to be understood at a conceptual level. We need to know not just how to account but why we account. This is particularly true of financial reporting. Management of an entity is in the fortunate position of being able to specify the information it wants to aid efficient operation. Good management accounting, thus, rests upon an appreciation of the information needed to optimize management performance. Financial accounting, in contrast, addresses a much more diffuse audience—all those outside an entity who have some legitimate interest in its financial progress and well-being.

Determination of who those people are, and the selection and measurement of the information that is beneficial for them to receive, require a conceptual framework that was lacking in 1850. Gradually, over the next century, customary modes of financial reporting emerged, and were eventually dignified by the name "generally accepted accounting principles." From roughly 1930 on, societies of professional accountants, frequently urged on by governments or government agencies, attempted to codify such principles in order to remove inconsistencies and conflicts within them and to encourage improvement in financial reporting. Over a period of time the constitution of the committees created for this purpose has been modified so as to be more widely representative and independent. At the same time the committees' recommendations have been increasingly recognized as being authoritative, so that it has become possible to describe these committees or boards as standard-setting bodies and their recommendations as standards of financial reporting. In effect, the determination of accounting principles by a process of acceptance has been largely superseded by organized standard-setting efforts.

The primary purposes of this book are to trace the development of present-day accounting standards and practices in Canada, and to describe and evaluate them in conceptual terms. In so doing, we must recognize the substantial influence of U.S. standards and practices, and most recently implications of the internationalization of the capital marketplace. Part I of the book is devoted to a history of the evolution of financial accounting, from a collection of recording techniques rationalized by the invention of double entry to a sophisticated communication device using the medium of financial statements and reports. Part II discusses existing accounting standards for business enterprises as influenced by history and current thought, and evaluates them on their merits. Part III assesses the conceptual framework for financial reporting, reviews pertinent accounting research, and concludes with a discussion of the institutions needed to develop and maintain effective accounting standards. Part IV reviews accounting standards for not-for-profit organizations and governments.

THE HISTORICAL DEVELOPMENT OF ACCOUNTING

THE RECORD-KEEPING FUNCTION OF ACCOUNTING

Accounting is concerned in essence with wealth. Wealth, that is to say an accumulation of goods beyond immediate human needs, is the basis of civilization. It is not surprising, then, to find some form of accounting associated with the most ancient of recorded civilizations.

Three periods in the development of accounting can be discerned. In the first, from 4000 B.C. up to A.D. 1300, the record-keeping aspect was predominant. Accumulations of wealth require control and for this some form of accounting is essential. The second period, from about 1300 up to 1850, was marked by the spread of commerce. With widespread commerce the need for adequate records grew. The distinguishing feature of this period was that accounting records became capable of dealing with masses of data and summarizing them so as to facilitate the business carried on. This period may still be called a record-keeping stage, but the advances implicit in the technique of double entry mark the era as one of systematized bookkeeping rather than one of mere record keeping. The double-entry technique was further important in that it was capable of extension and refinement so as to meet the needs of the third era from 1850 to the present.

The groundwork for this final period was laid by the vast surge of economic activity in the preceding century known as the Industrial Revolution. The emergence of large-scale enterprise required the mobilization of large capital sums, which in turn led to the separation of the functions of ownership and management and to increasing use of the legal institution of the limited liability company. In time, accounting played its part by becoming a source of information about costs and profits to assist management. Accounting statements became a means of communicating information to investors, creditors, and others who were separate from internal management but entitled to reports on enterprise progress. The development of accounting as an information source is described beginning in Chapter 3.

PRECONDITIONS OF ACCOUNTING

Certain attainments of civilization were necessary before even the simplest accounting record could exist. Further advances in skills and institutional arrangements were necessary for advanced forms. The following were among the more important preconditions for accounting with any degree of sophistication.

Literacy

People must be able to read and write in order to keep records of any length. Thus, in the earliest civilizations accounting was largely limited to those institutions, such as the church and government, that represented repositories of the literary arts or could afford to employ clerks drawn from the limited section of the population that could read and write. There were, however, some ways to cope with the problem of illiteracy. In Babylonia scribes were used to make records of contracts, receipts, etc. These could be said to be the earliest public accountants. In pre-Norman England and in medieval times generally, accountability was fulfilled largely by oral communication of activities and results. An audit—literally a hearing—was performed mainly by evaluating the reasonableness of such reports.

An Efficient Numbering System

Any accounting record beyond the simplest lists and records of individual transactions entails addition and subtraction. Widespread facility in these skills, in turn, depends upon an adequate numbering system. The Arabic numbering system, familiar to us, did not become widely known in European civilizations until at least the thirteenth century A.D. Even then, the use of Roman numerals in record keeping continued to be common for many years.

The Arabic system has "place-value," meaning that its numbers can be arrayed in columns. Thereby, addition or subtraction is made easy by beginning with the extreme right-hand column and moving progressively to the left. To achieve place-value within the usual decimal base it was necessary to have nine numerical symbols for the figures one to nine and a zero cipher which could be combined with each of the other numbers to yield ten, twenty, and so on. Many ancient numbering systems had no zero and had a varying number of numerical symbols.[1] The Romans used seven basic symbols; one of the major Greek systems had twenty-eight. With few symbols, numbers were long. In Roman notation the number 3,878 is written MMMDCCCLXXVIII. With a greater number of symbols the typical length of numbers can be reduced, but at the expense of making the system harder to learn. The impediment to arithmetical operations caused by lack of place-value could be overcome in computations by the use of the abacus, which was common in ancient civilizations. The important point for accounting, however, was that without place-value in written figures there was no incentive to put figures in columns and to separate the record of opposites (cash receipts and payments; amounts receivable and payable). Thus, the primitive numbering systems in the ancient world meant primitive accounting.

Writing Materials

Until comparatively recently, extensive account keeping depended upon supplies of inexpensive writing material. Paper was invented in China in the second millennium B.C. but was not introduced to Europe until the twelfth or thirteenth centuries A.D. Before the availability of paper a variety of writing materials was used to keep accounts. The Babylonian civilizations relied on clay tablets. Egypt benefited from the use of a much less cumbersome material—papyrus—from at least 3000 B.C., and potsherds were also often used for brief accounts after the conquest by Alexander the Great in the fourth century B.C. From that time, for about one thousand years, papyrus became the main writing material for important documents in Greek and Roman civilization. Some temple or government accounts were even inscribed on stone or other durable material, but wooden tablets coated with wax were widely used for everyday accounts. These were convenient because they could be erased and reused. Parchment was also used to some extent and became the more common material toward the end of the Roman Empire. However, not until the introduction of paper was there a relatively inexpensive and convenient writing material. As a consequence, accounting and documentation in the ancient world were cramped and limited.

Money

The idea of coinage, that is the issuance of pieces of valuable metal stamped by government authority as a guarantee of purity and weight, was conceived in China in the second millennium B.C. Coined money came into use in the Mediterranean world around the seventh century B.C. The existence of a standard medium of exchange was vital to any advanced development of accounting, for without it accounts could consist only of records of individual contracts and inventories of property by quantities. Once money had become available as a "unit of account," it was possible to represent diverse kinds of property by numbers and thus, by a process of valuation, derive totals for capital, profits, and so on.

The invention of coined money, however, did not result in widespread improvements in accounts for many hundreds of years. The existence of many states and principalities, each with its own coinage, presented a problem in recording accounts using any one currency as the unit of account. (The problem of foreign currency translation is indeed an ancient one.) In addition, the valuation process required when money is used as a common unit of account depends to a considerable extent on the existence of widespread market exchange values. It was difficult to express accounts in terms of money when most transactions were the result of barter. Thus the realization of the full potential for accounting from the invention of money had to await the commercial expansion that marked the end of the Middle Ages.

THE AGE OF RECORD KEEPING

We must now examine how accounting developed to satisfy the need for records. From the earliest times there was a need for a record of incomplete transactions. A narrative description of transactions, set down in chronological order, was the natural form of record. Frequently, when a loan was made or credit given or accepted, space was left below the original transaction record to record its ultimate completion. These simple records of transactions, however, did not provide the summarization and classification of data necessary for usefulness in the management of affairs. This lack of summarization is the primary reason why we classify the ancient age of record keeping separately from the age of bookkeeping that began about A.D. 1300.

Accounting for Control

Apart from the record-keeping aspect, the major use of accounts in the initial era was that of control. Substantial accumulations of wealth always require administration. This meant that property owners had to employ servants to look after their affairs, and those so entrusted needed to be made accountable for property passing through their hands. Governments, in particular (perhaps because the rulers, unlike today, had a personal interest in the result) took care to control tax receipts and keep accurate records of other receipts and disbursements. Perhaps the most sophisticated government accounting system was achieved in China during the Chao Dynasty (1122–256 B.C.). The system in use exhibited a full accounting cycle, marked by budgeting, responsibility accounting by funds, interim and annual reporting, audit, and a triennial examination of the effectiveness of each government agency.[2]

Whether the entity was a government, a religious institution, a private estate, or simply a household, the elements of control were the same. These were the creation of records of transactions (with varying degrees of support documentation), sometimes a separation of functions so as to achieve internal control, and an audit. The audit, in essence, was a review of the records by the owner, or by officials sufficiently informed to assess their probable accuracy. In the absence of detailed documentation, the principal audit technique was that of interrogation.

This accounting framework persisted through the Middle Ages and beyond. English manorial accounting has given us a name for it—stewardship accounting—from the title of the official responsible for the business affairs of the manor. A "Charge and Discharge" statement was developed as the form of the steward's account. This statement recorded the amount the steward was charged for, namely property in his hands at the beginning of the period and any natural increase in property. Amounts deemed to be discharges of his responsibility included expenses of the manor, payments to the owner of the manor, and losses of property from natural causes. The steward remained accountable for any balance not discharged. Chatfield points out that it was in the steward's interest to minimize the receipts for which he was responsible and maximize the report of expenses and losses. To this he attributes the origin of the doctrine of conservatism in accounting.[3]

The stewardship form of accounting persisted long after the widespread adoption of double-entry accounting for commercial use. Indeed, in important aspects it underlies fund accounting by governments and not-for-profit-organizations today. It is also interesting to note that in earliest times there was little difference in objectives and concepts between public sector and private sector accounts. It was the desire to compute costs and profits that set accounting for private enterprises on a separate path.

THE EVOLUTION OF BOOKKEEPING

By A.D. 1300 most of the conditions for accounting progress had been fulfilled. Paper was becoming available. Coined money was in common use as a medium of exchange. The Arabic numerical notation was being introduced. Finally, the development of Mediterranean commerce enhanced the demand for good records. In the two centuries before 1300 the Crusades had opened up the Middle East to trade, and silks, spices, and other Eastern products created a demand for European goods in exchange. Italy was in the best position to take advantage of the trading opportunities, and Venice and Genoa established themselves as entrepôts in the trade between Europe and the East. Italians, especially the Florentines, also became the world's bankers. In all this they were helped by advances in business organization, such as the invention of bills of exchange and the use of credit. The time was ripe for the first major advance in accounting.

- The widespread development of credit and banking made it convenient to have continuous records of amounts due to and from other parties, rather than separate records for each transaction entered into and its settlement. In these individual accounts it was convenient and natural to separate opposites—loans and repayments, deposits and withdrawals. The resulting "bilateral form" of account reflected the concept of duality in the form of debits and credits.

- The Italians developed the practice of trading through overseas consignment agents. An agent is accountable to his principal for the goods consigned to him and proceeds from their sale. The balancing of goods unsold and sales proceeds (represented either by accounts receivable or cash collected) with the obligation to the principal also provided a natural illustration of the concept of duality embodied in double entry.

- As the form of business evolved from a series of isolated ventures to a continuing enterprise, a new concept of a business as an entity with an existence separate from that of its owners began to take root. When a long-term business was conducted in partnership form, accounting for capital also gained in importance because each partner had to be credited with his proper share of profits.

Thus we can see the elements of double-entry bookkeeping drawing together as a natural outcome of early business conditions. The concept of capital, required in the case of continuing partnerships, confirmed the basic equilibrium of double entry. The maintenance of equilibrium, in practice, required the opening of nominal accounts for revenues and expenses. This represented in the long run the great potential of the double-entry system, namely its ability to distinguish and analyze the elements of profit and loss and thus explain the change in capital from time to time.

Early Forms of Bookkeeping

This potential was not realized immediately. Early trading firms typically operated in separate ventures. Records of venture costs and receipts had been kept together well before the introduction of double entry. It was natural to continue with the venture as the focus of accounts in a double-entry system, particularly since ship captains or other parties were frequently entitled to share in the profits of individual ventures. In contrast, the need for periodic reckonings of profit of the business as a whole was much smaller for many businesses. Typically, a ledger was not closed and balanced except on special occasions such as the death of a partner. Owners were able to keep on top of their businesses by dint of personal contact, following the results of ventures, and reading the ledgers themselves.

There were some exceptions. Surviving records of banking and manufacturing companies of Florence provide evidence of a more advanced technique. The Medici bank, for example, required annual balance sheets (essentially listings of account balances) from its nine branches in Italy and abroad and used these as a means of control, especially watching for doubtful accounts receivable and excessive loans.[4] Examples can also be found of financial statements displaying such accrual techniques as prepayments, depreciation accounting, and allowances for taxes and contingencies.

Double-entry accounting is associated with the name of Friar Luca Pacioli and his treatise on bookkeeping. This was one of five sections in his book *Summa de Arithmetica, Geometria, Proportioni et Proportionalita*, published in 1494. This date is more than one hundred and fifty years after the time of the earliest surviving set of accounts identified as a complete double-entry system. It is evident that Pacioli did not invent the system; rather, he described it as actually practised in his day. Since much of his experience was in Venice, his treatise reflected practices of that centre and came to be known as "the method of Venice." In particular, it described venture accounting, and, although Pacioli recommended annual balancing to help detect errors, he never mentioned periodic financial statements. The contribution of Pacioli was that he made knowledge of the method of Venice widespread. The *Summa* was translated into several languages, and foreign accounting treatises for hundreds of years tended to be copies of Pacioli's work or copies of copies.

From the fifteenth century on, the advantage in trading and commerce moved from the Mediterranean to the Atlantic as discoveries widened the horizons of Western civilization. Spain and Portugal led in the sixteenth century, to be succeeded by England and the Low Countries as maritime power shifted northward. The method of Venice followed the spread of commerce. Although, inevitably, adaptations and improvements were made over the course of time, the record-keeping uses of accounts remained primary.

THE ORGANIZATION OF ENGLISH
TRADE AND COMMERCE A.D. 1300–1800

The five centuries from 1300 to 1800 saw an expansion of trade and commerce that created a need for new forms of business organization. That same expansion also eventually created a need for financial reports to organize the information from a set of accounts and to provide a succinct means of conveying information to parties at interest. In fact, the development of financial reporting is closely linked with the emergence of the modern business corporation, with its limited liability and transferable shares. Since financial reporting traditions in the English-speaking countries have their origin in the development of the corporation in England in the nineteenth century, we turn now to a description of the organization of English commerce leading up to that century.

Forms of Business Organization

Apart from the individual proprietorship, several forms of organization of commercial activity can be traced from early times in England. A form of partnership existed in the thirteenth and fourteenth centuries in the "Societas," firms of Italian financiers operating in England. The basic concept of the corporation as an artificial person was also recognized in the common law at that time, although not in connection with commercial activity. The church, the town, and the guild were all recognized as entities independent of their members, capable of owning property in their own right and having perpetual existence. Members, being separate persons in law from the corporation, had no direct claim on its property nor any personal liability for its debts.

The extension of this concept to business ventures did not take place until later, and at first only on a restricted basis. Most large corporations up to the end of the seventeenth century were established by royal charter, such as the Russia Company (1555), the East

India Company (1600), and the Hudson's Bay Company (1670). (These are short forms of the companies' names; their full legal names were much longer.) Often these charter companies were given monopolies to trade in a certain area or in certain products and in some cases took on obligations in return, such as the promotion of colonization. They did not necessarily receive all the attributes that characterize corporations today; for example, the privilege of limited liability for shareholders was not invariable.

Such a company might evolve over a period of time from a loose umbrella covering a recurring series of self-liquidating ventures to a permanent entity possessed of substantial assets in the form of ships, trading posts, and inventories. The East India Company, for example, originally raised capital (the joint stock) for each voyage separately. At the end of each voyage the property was divided among the subscribing venturers. As the company acquired more permanent property, it became increasingly difficult to identify assets with individual voyages, and it became necessary to allocate them (and hence profits) among voyages. Beginning in 1613 the problem of allocation was lessened by raising capital subscriptions for four-year terms, one quarter to be paid up each year. In 1657 the principle of permanently invested capital and transferable shares was adopted. As a result, future distributions no longer represented divisions of assets at the conclusion of a venture, but rather "dividends" paid from profits.[5] The change, however, did not mean the end of venture or voyage accounting. It was still possible to base profit computation on the results of completed voyages together with allowances for administrative expenses and asset valuations outside the voyage accounts.

Some chartered companies were "regulated," meaning that membership was restricted to merchants who had been apprenticed to the trade. This limitation hampered the raising of capital, so that their companies tended to lose out over time to companies organized on the joint-stock principle. The term "joint stock" simply referred to the contribution of the members to finance the company which, depending on the participation arrangements, might take the form of cash or assets (such as ships) for use in the venture.

The great majority of business ventures, of course, were not carried on by chartered corporations. The idea of contributions to a joint stock—in effect, a pooling of assets—was adopted by unincorporated companies as well as corporations. English privateering activity in the late 1500s, for example, was largely carried on by joint-stock companies. In effect, these were informal extended partnerships, and their exact legal status was nebulous. At first, most such companies were engaged in foreign trading activity. Later, as domestic enterprise grew in scale, the joint-stock concept was adopted for such diverse activities as mining, water supply, insurance, and banking.

The South Seas Bubble

Transfers of interests in joint-stock companies were permitted, and in time a market for shares developed. Stock jobbers (dealers in stocks) were active in the market, and company promoters used the market to raise capital. Commercial publication of share prices commenced in 1692. As in any unregulated market there was some fraud and deceit, and share prices fluctuated widely. Scott reports that, for the most part, company flotations before 1700 were reasonable speculations.[6] Failures, nevertheless, tended to be blamed on what was called the "pernicious art of stock jobbing" and cast a shadow on the whole concept of joint-stock companies.

From 1690 to 1720, periods of boom and crisis succeeded each other in the market, culminating in a major crash in 1720. The crash is associated with the South Seas Company, which was organized in 1711. At that time the market price of government debt was severely depressed. The company had two objectives: one was to obtain a government monopoly on trade in South America; the other was to acquire government debt cheaply, thereby establishing a firm base of assets. The idea was that the company would accept all unfunded government debt (debt that did not have a specific revenue source earmarked for its repayment) at par in subscription for its shares. The theory was that ownership of that debt by the company would provide it with an undoubted "fund of credit" against which it could borrow to finance its activities.

This plan was implemented, and the company operated relatively uneventfully for several years. But in 1719, a company promotion boom began in England on a highly speculative basis. Shares in new companies were issued with as little as one-eighth of one percent paid up on the par value. As the boom progressed, the stated objects of many of the companies became increasingly improbable, so that skeptical observers referred to them as "bubble companies."

The promoters of the South Seas Company evidently decided to take advantage of the speculative fever. In early 1720 they successfully competed with the Bank of England (then privately owned) to win the right to undertake a new scheme involving the national debt. The scheme called for the company, as before, to buy in outstanding government debt (this time funded debt) in return for subscriptions to its shares. If, for example, the South Seas stock stood at a premium of twenty-five percent over par, it would issue *eight* £100 par value shares for each £1,000 bond, crediting capital account with £1,000. But since £1,000 represented the par value of *ten* shares, the government permitted the company to make up the difference by selling two extra shares to the public. The company paid the government a bonus on selling these shares, and recorded the remainder of the proceeds as gain.

This government-abetted scheme for share price inflation through treating capital proceeds as income met with ill-deserved success. The company's shares advanced rapidly in price as soon as it obtained the right to undertake the debt conversion operation. This meant that it had to issue substantially fewer shares for each £1,000 bond acquired and consequently had more bonus shares to sell independently for its and the government's gain. That very success created problems, however, for there was not enough cash in the country available for investment to buy up the bonus shares. The answer to that problem was simple. The shares were sold for very little cash down; credit was extended for the remainder of the price, the shares themselves being accepted as security.

Yet cash was still tight, especially since so many other companies were selling shares at the same time. To eliminate this competition the company encouraged Parliament to pass the so-called "Bubble Act." This act, effective June 24, 1720, prohibited the offering of shares for public subscription by companies that did not have a charter or that had a charter for activities other than those for which it was raising money. Two months later, the South Seas Company instigated legal action against four other companies for contravention of the Bubble Act. The result was unfortunate. A rapid fall in the price of shares of the companies attacked resulted in margin calls. These triggered liquidation of shareholdings, thereby putting pressure on the share prices of all companies, including the South Seas Company. In the space of less than two months the company's shares fell from a peak price of £1,000 to £180. The rapid collapse of the boom left the fledgling capital market, as so often since, sadder but not permanently wiser.

The Stagnation of Accounting

The aftermath of the bubble period was a prolonged distrust of joint-stock companies. It was felt that the extravagant promotions proved that investors not personally involved in company activity would fail to invest wisely. Moreover, managers of such companies were bound to be inefficient since their own financial interest was not at stake. The dominant thinking in Parliament was that joint-stock companies should be discouraged, and incorporation granted only in cases where capital requirements were very large and limited liability essential. Types of enterprise qualifying under these criteria included such public works as canals, bridges and docks, companies undertaking long and continuing risks such as life insurance, financial institutions such as banks, and companies engaged in foreign trade. The result of this thinking, together with strict enforcement of the Bubble Act, was to hamper the issuing of capital at the very time when the new enterprises springing up might have found a developed capital market most useful. Thus the new textile companies, mines, foundries, metal-working companies, and potteries remained largely in private hands until well into the nineteenth century.

There was little in this history to forward the development of financial reporting. Company charters could contain clauses requiring regular audit and financial reporting to shareholders. Clauses might also state that dividends were to be paid only out of profits and specify the nature of reserves that could be withheld from distributable profits. None of these clauses, however, were standardized nor mandatory. As for business in private hands, the old accounting traditions were sufficient, and little organized thought was given to accounting's potential as a source of information for management and decision making. Chatfield sums up the state of eighteenth-century accounting as follows:

> [T]he eighteenth century merchant still valued it [double-entry bookkeeping] chiefly for its ability to bring order to his accounts. Most problems we associate with profit finding and asset valuation concerned him hardly at all. Without the paraphernalia of accruals, matching, or periodic reckonings, his venture accounts measured the results of particular operations, while paging through the ledger gave him some idea of overall activity. But he developed neither a clear concept of income nor systematic procedures for judging the success or failure of his business over a period of time. Public investment in firms was rare, a tradition of accountability to outsiders was lacking, and financial statements were of minor importance. It was the Industrial Revolution, not the bookkeeping innovations preceding it, which drew out accountancy's analytical potential.[7]

SUMMARY

As a practical art, accounting responds to needs. The existence of wealth creates a need for records to serve as a control over those entrusted with it. Trade creates a need for records of unsettled transactions. We therefore find some form of accounting records associated with early civilization—as far back as six thousand years ago.

Record keeping requires both skills and facilitating conditions. Clerks must be literate; an efficient numbering system and cheap writing material are necessary for extensive records; and a standard of value in the form of money is essential to any large-scale records because of the need for some common unit of account.

The spread of commerce after the Crusades vastly increased the importance of good business records. As the leaders in trade and banking the Italians pioneered advances in record keeping, and the concept of double entry evolved naturally out of the need for records of continuing business relationships. For the most part, however, such relationships did not include the provision of capital for a business on a long-term basis by parties not involved in running it. Instead, outside financing tended to be for individual ventures, resulting in profit reporting on a venture-by-venture basis, rather than for regularly established periods of time.

Double entry, in its venture accounting version, accompanied the spread of commerce throughout Europe. As the scale of business activity grew, a need developed for a better capitalized and more permanent form of business organization than the trading ventures typical of early commerce. The English corporation authorized by royal charter provided one means of meeting this need. The evolution of private joint-stock enterprises into companies with transferrable shares, plus the development of a market for exchange of shares around 1700, represented another. The collapse of the South Seas Bubble in 1720 and the consequent restrictive legislation, however, set back for a century the development of this logical means of raising capital. Accounting might have been expected to free itself from the traditional venture accounting approach more quickly had it not been for this restriction on the form of business organization. As it was, accounting remained largely frozen in its previous mold until well into the nineteenth century.

REFERENCES

[1] For a full and interesting discussion see G.E.M. de Ste. Croix, "Greek and Roman Accounting," in *Studies in the History of Accounting*, ed. A.C. Littleton and B.S. Yamey (London: Sweet & Maxwell, 1956), pp. 14–74, especially from p. 50 on.

[2] See M. Chatfield, *A History of Accounting Thought*, rev. ed. (Huntington, N.Y.: Robert E. Krieger Publishing Co., 1977), pp. 8–9.

[3] Ibid., p. 29.

[4] See R. de Roover, "The Development of Accounting Prior to Luca Pacioli According to the Account-books of Medieval Merchants," in *Studies in the History of Accounting*, ed. Littleton and Yamey, pp. 151–52.

[5] Chatfield, *A History of Accounting Thought*, pp. 79–80.

[6] W.R. Scott, *The Constitution and Finance of English, Scottish and Irish Joint-Stock Companies to 1720*, 3 vols. (Cambridge: Harvard University Press, 1912; reprint ed., New York: Peter Smith, 1951), chap. 18.

[7] Chatfield, *A History of Accounting Thought,* p. 61.

EMERGENCE OF THE FINANCIAL REPORTING FUNCTION

The quickening in the pace of economic development from about 1750 on has become known as the Industrial Revolution. This era saw the transformation of manufacturing from a localized activity producing simple goods into large-scale production, centralized in factories, and using paid labour. This change was fundamental. Where formerly much of business, especially foreign trade, was carried on in the form of separate ventures, now the characteristics of continuous production, a large workforce, and large capital investment were more compatible with the modern accounting concept of the "going concern."

As the scale of enterprise grew and with advances in technology, particularly the application of steam power, the limitations on company financing caused by restrictions on incorporation became increasingly unsatisfactory. In 1825 the English Bubble Act was repealed. The act of repeal made it possible to spell out the degree of limitation of liability in company charters, but that still left the status and powers of joint-stock companies in doubt. In 1837, incorporation became easier as the system of incorporation by letters patent was adopted. The Joint Stock Companies Act of 1844 went further by granting a general power to incorporate by registration. An 1855 act permitted all registered companies to obtain limited liability. At that date it could be said that the corporation in its modern legal form had evolved.

Large-scale, continuing enterprise meant changes in relations with investors where an enterprise was widely owned. Where, previously, profit sharing could be accomplished merely by dividing up the assets of completed ventures, a more regular process of distribution was now called for. Dividends could only be paid with assets deemed surplus to business needs. This did not mean that dividends could be paid only out of profits, although there was obviously some connection. A firm exploiting a wasting asset such as a coal mine, for example, might reasonably pay out all receipts in excess of those required for its running expenses and for maintaining the operation until the workings were exhausted. In any event, cash available for dividends would be greater when times were good than when they were bad. Inevitably, there was an association in the public mind between dividends and profitability, with the result that the size of dividends paid might well affect the value of an interest in a company. Obviously, in the absence of financial reporting the opportunities for manipulation of public opinion through manipulation of dividends were very great. Thus, the first major opportunity for accounting to serve a wider interest than that of owner-managers arose with the transformation of business activity into going concerns.

THE CORPORATION AND FINANCIAL REPORTING

The Companies Act of 1844 introduced two significant requirements. First, a "full and fair" balance sheet was to be presented to each ordinary meeting of shareholders. Second, auditors were to be appointed and their report on the balance sheet was to be read at the meeting. In the same year the Joint Stock Banking Act required that banks incorporated under it provide an annual audited balance sheet and profit and loss account. In the following year, the Companies Clauses Consolidation Act, applicable to the public-utility type of corporation chartered by special act of Parliament, included audit and financial reporting requirements in model clauses of company regulations. The act also provided that no dividend should be paid by those companies out of capital.

These acts represented the first acknowledgement of a public interest in financial reporting and audit. The legislation, however, proved ineffective. It did not specify the minimum contents of the balance sheet; it said nothing about the basis of valuation of assets and liabilities; and it did not set out in detail the auditor's duties. It did not even require that the statutory balance sheet relate to the date of the shareholders' meeting. It was easy to evade the intent of the legislation, even to the point of filing identical statements year after year or fabricating them for the purpose of filing with the registrar.

When legislation on companies was next revised in 1855 and 1856, the issue was faced as to whether to strengthen the regulation of accounts and audit or to drop the mandatory requirements. The laissez-faire attitude of the times apparently persuaded Parliament that financial reporting could be left as a matter to be settled between a company and its shareholders. The mandatory reporting and audit provisions were dropped, not to be revived until 1900. The 1856 Joint Stock Companies Act, however, encouraged good financial reporting with a model set of company articles, including enlightened provisions with respect to the accounts to be kept, the audit, and the forms of the balance sheet and the statement of income and expenditure to be laid before the annual general meeting. The model articles also provided that dividends should not be payable except out of profits. The directors, however, might set aside reserve funds out of profits to meet possible contingencies, for equalizing dividends, or for repairing and maintaining the works. The reference to reserves may have been unfortunate in that it did not answer the question whether the provision for such reserves might be deducted in determining reported profits and, if so, whether the provisions needed to be disclosed.

Many companies did provide audited financial statements to shareholders as suggested by the model articles in the 1856 and subsequent acts. In addition, legislation passed during the nineteenth century to regulate special types of companies such as banks, insurance companies, railroads, and gas companies usually required the provision of audited financial statements, sometimes semiannually rather than annually. Thus, company accountants and auditors had to wrestle with questions of valuation of assets and computation of profits.

Legislation or an individual company's articles might require a full and fair financial statement and might prohibit the payment of dividends except out of profits, but it was left to the accountant and management to say what those terms meant.

It must be remembered that there was no cohesive public accounting profession much before 1880. The Edinburgh Society of Accountants became the first "chartered accountants," receiving a royal charter in 1854. Local societies were formed in a number of centres in ensuing years, and in 1880 a merger of English societies resulted in the Institute of Chartered Accountants in England and Wales. Up until that time accountants often offered a variety of services such as that of appraiser, actuary, and estate executor, in conjunction with public accounting. Bankruptcies and liquidations constituted their chief source of work. Since there was often a whiff of fraud about business failures, it was natural to appoint individuals with such skills to make special investigations or to conduct audits of companies on behalf of creditors or shareholders. Nevertheless, auditing, as such, was not their main line of business, and no established body of knowledge had been built up covering audit reports on financial statements. The medieval tradition of the audit as a check against fraud and error led to detailed checks of the recorded transactions. But there were no understood audit requirements specifically designed to support reports on the fairness of financial statements.

BASES OF NINETEENTH-CENTURY FINANCIAL REPORTS

In the face of this void in accounting theory, financial reporting for corporations developed on an ad hoc basis. There were two distinct strands of development. The so-called "double-account" basis of accounting and financial reporting was associated with large, public-service companies. Other types of enterprise, which were generally denied the right to incorporate until after the repeal of the Bubble Act, continued the accounting tradition of privately owned business in previous centuries. This tradition, although never highly codified, called for the production of a balance sheet (if any financial report at all was required) reporting assets and liabilities valued on whatever basis seemed reasonable.

The requirement of the English legislation that corporations produce financial reports led to the notion that the answers to questions of accounting rested with the law, and with the courts on matters of detail. It was possible to deduce the existence of a "capital maintenance" doctrine under the law, and that provided some guidance to accounting evolution. By the end of the century, however, decisions of the courts had destroyed that doctrine. Financial reporting for corporations was left where it started out—without any real theory to guide it.

The "Double-Account" Form of Financial Statement

As already noted, the Companies Clauses Consolidation Act of 1845 set out audit and financial reporting requirements for the public-utility type of company incorporated by special act of Parliament. The fundamental concept of the special act companies was that capital subscribed was to be spent in construction of a facility to be maintained in the public service permanently. All necessary expenditures to operate and maintain the facility were to be met from revenue so as to ensure perpetual service. This led naturally to a division in the balance sheet. The "capital" section recorded the presumed permanent fixed capital assets and capital subscribed, while the "revenue" section recorded the assets and liabilities associated with day-to-day operations, or "circulating capital" as it was called. Similarly, a distinction was made between profits, representing the excess of operating revenues over operating expenditures, and "capital" gains and losses, being the results of any disposition of capital assets.

The problems associated with the double-account system are particularly well illustrated in railroad accounting. The railway age in Great Britain could be said to begin about 1830 with the successful development of the steam locomotive. There was a burst of railway promotion in 1835 and 1836 and again in the mid-1840s. In those years, about one thousand companies were promoted and five thousand miles of track completed. In only a few years, however, railway shares fell out of favour among investors, and many companies found it necessary to institute enquiries into alleged fraud or abuse in the previous promotional period. Construction booms and periods of financial stringency alternated for the next two decades.

The double-account concept applied to the new railways led to questions that can be categorized under two main headings: (1) How should one distinguish between expenditures chargeable to capital and those chargeable to revenue account? and (2) Is a provision for depreciation of capital assets a necessary charge in determining operating profits?

Distinguishing Capital and Revenue Expenditures

Under the first heading there were several practical questions (some of them with a very modern sound).

- What should be done with interest paid on loans (and, until prohibited in 1847, on shareholders' capital) during construction? Most companies charged such interest to capital. Some, but not all, companies divided interest between revenue and capital when some branch lines were still under construction.

- Might capital expenditures be charged to revenue account? In the late 1840s, when railway shares were out of favour with investors, several companies "closed their capital accounts." This meant that capital expenditure had to be written off to revenue account unless specially authorized by the shareholders. Such policies usually had to be abandoned in a few years since they made major line extensions or other capital improvements impossible, or they prevented a regular dividend policy, or both. Nonetheless, the fact that the accounting for capital expenditure was considered optional indicated that the accounting was regarded more as a matter of financial policy than as a matter of proper profit and asset reporting.

- Might a portion of the cost of capital asset replacements be charged to capital? On this question practice varied among companies. At least some companies capitalized the cost of betterments (although this created the problem of distinguishing between normal repairs and betterments). Beyond this, some companies also accepted the idea of capitalizing the increase in cost of a replacement over the original capitalized cost of the asset replaced, even though no betterment was involved. Other companies charged all replacements to revenue account.

- Might current repairs be capitalized? Although there could be little rationale for such a practice, it does not appear to have been uncommon, at least in the early years of railway promotion.

Depreciation

Initial consideration of depreciation was confused by a conflict between two interpretations of the reason for depreciation accounting. On the one hand, depreciation would be conceived of as a necessary charge against revenue in order to allow for the regular consumption of capital through use. On the other hand, depreciation accounting could be regarded as merely the name given to the process of valuing capital assets. From the latter perspective, there was no depreciation unless there was a decline in the market value of the asset. In one extreme case, fixed assets were written up rather than depreciated, with the credit being carried to the revenue account.

The valuation notion was superseded at a fairly early date, to be replaced by the idea of depreciation as a means of (1) providing on a regular basis for the inevitable decline in serviceability of capital assets and (2) creating a fund for their replacement. Since rolling stock clearly had limited life, a depreciation provision was at first thought desirable for it. But then, since rolling stock was replaced regularly, it was felt the cost of replacements could be absorbed as they occurred and depreciation accounting was not required. Opinions about depreciation accounting for rails developed in the opposite direction. At first it was thought that proper maintenance would make rails last so long that depreciation was not worth consideration. Then opinion shifted. Since rails were replaced only at extended intervals, a depreciation fund was seen as desirable for them.

Unfortunately, a depreciation provision was seen more as a matter of business policy than as a principle of accounting. This view probably was encouraged by statutory references to reserve funds "for maintaining and repairing the works"—something that directors might (or might not) set aside along with reserves for contingencies and for equalizing dividends. Some companies dropped depreciation provisions in the promotional period of the mid-1840s, but many companies commenced them after the shakeout in the late 1840s. In a few years most discontinued them again, having found them inadequate to meet replacements. The general contention of railroad management was that the soundest course was to charge replacements against revenue when required. This, of course, made it crucial that a proper distinction be made between new construction and replacement expenditures—a distinction which it may be doubted was actually achieved in practice. Also, replacement accounting encouraged management to smooth reported results simply by varying the amount of replacement expenditures. In the extreme, replacements too long postponed could lead to the failure of the railroad, a fate that was not uncommon.

Clearly the accounting practices of the railways were inconsistent to the point of chaos. The situation was so unsatisfactory that Parliament, in the Regulation of Railways Act of 1868, was moved to impose uniform financial reporting and audit provisions on the railways, notwithstanding its general reluctance to interfere with the internal affairs of companies. The reporting system that was adopted confirmed the double-account system but did nothing to solve the question of the distinction between capital and revenue. In fact, the system probably encouraged the use of replacement accounting instead of depreciation accounting. Thus the inconsistencies and inadequacies of railroad accounting continued.[1]

Financial Reporting for Ordinary Companies

For other, less capital-intensive enterprises, there was no special theory to guide financial reporting. Rather, the natural approach was to provide a valuation of individual assets and liabilities. The important statement was a listing of these valuations—a balance sheet. Accumulated profits (the amount divisible among partners or owners) was represented by the excess of net assets over the capital committed previous to the reporting date. The chief problems were to provide fair valuations for the balance sheet items and see that none was omitted. The growth in scale of enterprise increased this difficulty, and the emerging accounting profession had to ponder several vexing questions.

- How might values be found for inventory? When productive processes became extended it was no longer possible to refer to market prices for substantial portions of the inventory. The problem was met by the development of cost accounting, largely in the last quarter of the century.[2] Costs useful for management purposes could be adopted as a reasonable basis of valuation for financial accounting as well.

- Was it reasonable to take into account fluctuations in the market value of working capital items? There was no "realization" rule in previous accounting traditions, and accountants did not think it wrong in principle to record assets at market value even though such value was above cost. But values that went up could also come down. Moreover, in those days dividends paid were closely associated with the amount of profits reported. A realization test not only would lessen uncertainty about valuations but also would ensure that profits reported were in liquid form, thereby facilitating payment of the dividend suggested by the profit figure. For such practical reasons, accountants in time came to advocate the rule of valuation at lower of cost and market.

- How about fluctuations in value of fixed assets and investments? Again, since the previous tradition was a valuation tradition, accountants could not say that revaluation of fixed assets was wrong. They did, however, come to the view that to be continually writing such assets up and down was not a useful practice in a going concern and could be misleading. Their conservative instinct was satisfied by the idea that long-term assets need only be written down for value changes that appeared to be relatively permanent.

- Was it necessary to provide for depreciation with respect to the wearing out of long-term assets used in production? Accountants were quick to adapt the valuation idea to a belief in a depreciation provision. Much of the discussion revolved around practical questions. How was it possible to estimate useful life? Should depreciation be heavy when repairs and maintenance were light? The discussion was at a level that would not be out of place today, and an excellent theoretical exposition on depreciation was published as early as 1890.[3]

- Should goodwill be valued and should purchased goodwill be amortized? Instinctively, accountants were against the valuation of goodwill. Sentiment was mixed on the question of amortization.

- Was it proper to create reserves out of profits and subsequently restore them to profits for the purpose of equalizing reported profits and dividend payments? If so, what disclosure must be given? It is probably fair to say that not all accountants were opposed to the desire to report profit figures indicative of long-term earning power. But there was a natural concern about the obvious dangers of misrepresentation. Unfortunately, the very wording of the model articles in the 1856 and 1862 companies acts seemed to encourage such reserves, and judicial dicta in dividend cases certainly did not discourage them.

Profit Measurement and the Doctrine of Capital Maintenance

It is clear from the literature of the time that English accountants took a very legalistic view of financial reporting. The requirements to provide full and fair reports and to ascertain profits distributable as dividends were embodied in companies acts or clauses in a company's articles. Therefore the form and content of financial statements was ultimately a matter for the law to decide. (An alternative interpretation—that what was a fair financial report, or what was profit, should be determined on economic principles—seems not to have been considered.)

The historical business tradition, stemming from the days when business consisted of a series of ventures, was that profits should be distributed when determined. It became English practice for company shareholders to approve the final dividend at the annual general meeting of the company. It was desirable, therefore, that the financial statements presented to the annual meeting should display the surplus that was distributable.

There were grounds for believing that the law did control the amount distributable as dividends. One of the long-standing concerns about the granting of limited liability to companies had been that creditors might be damaged by fraudulent or negligent dissipation of company assets. A possible answer to this lay in the existence of shareholders' capital as a margin of safety, but this was effective only so long as the capital was maintained. It could be inferred that the law required such capital maintenance as the price of limited liability. First, limited companies had to state in their initial Memorandum of Association the amount of their proposed registered capital, while companies without limited liability did not have to do so. Second, while a limited liability company might subsequently increase or consolidate the existing capital, it was prohibited from reducing it. Finally, since a company's Memorandum of Association declared that capital was to be applied to the purposes of the business, it was reasoned it would be beyond the power of the directors to return it to the shareholders. This reasoning was reinforced by the specific provisions respecting reduction of capital introduced into the 1867 and 1877 companies acts. If dividends were permitted to reduce capital, these provisions would have been unnecessary and meaningless.

Early court cases dealing with the legality of dividends upheld the capital maintenance doctrine. These cases also held that valuations upon which directors made their dividend decisions must be neither negligently made nor fraudulent and, in a sketchy way, began to give some guidance on valuation questions. By the last quarter of the nineteenth century, the emerging accounting profession might reasonably consider its task to be that of achieving a better definition of distributable profits within the framework of the law. The prevailing thinking is illustrated by an excerpt from a paper read by Ernest Cooper in 1888 to the CA Students Society of London:

> Numerous questions arise upon the valuation of assets. . . . One matter I think it is of great importance for auditors as well as directors to bear carefully in mind [is] that the law itself or knowledge of the law in regard to accounts of Companies is . . . in an extremely imperfect state. Many practices of Companies in regard to their accounts, I think we may assume, will in course of time, come up for consideration by the Judges, with whom, of course, and not with accountants, must rest the ultimate decision of doubtful points arising upon accounts.[4]

Collapse of the Capital Maintenance Doctrine

Three cases in the short period of ten years rudely disrupted the accountants' understanding of the state of the law. The first and most important of these was the case of *Lee v. Neuchatel Asphalte Co.* decided by the Court of Appeal in 1889.[5] The company was formed in 1873 to exploit a mining concession held for a limited period of years. The articles of the company provided that profits should be applied to dividends, except that before recommending any dividend the directors might set aside, out of profits, a reserve fund for contingencies, dividend equalization, or repairing or maintaining works connected with the business. The question in the case was whether there could be said to be distributable profits without provision for exhaustion of the capital asset (the mining concession).

The judges who decided the case agreed upon the result but for contradictory reasons. Cotton L.J. noted that the capital subscribed included the mining concession. No provision for exhaustion was required because the concession was still held and had increased in value. Lopes L.J. stressed the inherently wasting character of the mining concession and held there was no obligation to recoup the cost of such wasting assets before distribution of dividends.

The opinion of Lindley L.J. was the most sweeping of the three rendered. There was nothing in the companies acts "about how dividends are to be paid, nor how profits are to be reckoned; all that is left . . . to the commercial world." Similarly there was nothing requiring capital to be made up if lost. "If they [businessmen] think their prospects of success are considerable, so long as they pay their creditors, there is no reason why they should not go on and divide profits . . . although every shilling of the capital may be lost." There was nothing in the acts to show "what is to go to capital account or what is to go to revenue account. . . . Businessmen very often differ in their opinion about these things." All that the previous cases had decided was that "You must not have fictitious accounts. If your earnings are less than your current expenses, you must not cook your accounts so as to make it appear that you are earning a profit, and you must not lay your hands on your capital to pay dividends."

The decision in the case of *Verner v. The General and Commercial Investment Trust (Limited)*[6] followed naturally from the reasoning in Neuchatel. The company was organized to make investments in stocks and debentures but not to operate as a trader or broker. Its investments were speculative in character and, at the time of the case, market value was below cost by £246,000. (Total issued capital was £600,000.) Current investment receipts, however, exceeded administration expenses and debenture interest expense, so that there were liquid funds from which a dividend could be paid. It was held that since the company still held the assets in which its capital had been invested, the dividend could not be said to be paid out of capital. It was not necessary to recoup the loss in value of such assets before payment of dividends. What was necessary was that the dividend could be paid without reduction of the amount of "circulating capital" (presumably at the beginning of the fiscal year). This was the same as saying that there had to be an excess of receipts over ordinary expenses in the given year out of which the dividend could be paid.

The final case was *in re National Bank of Wales Limited.*[7] In this case it had been found upon liquidation of the bank that substantial advances made to customers and certain directors were worthless. It was apparent in hindsight that profits in certain years had been deliberately overstated because of the failure to write off or make provision for bad and doubtful accounts. A director of the bank, John Cory, was sued by the liquidator for restitution of funds on the grounds (*inter alia*) that dividends had wrongfully been paid out of capital while he was a director. On appeal, it was held that the dividends were not paid out of capital on the peculiar reasoning that the capital was already lost by reason of the fact the debts were bad. On further appeal to the Privy Council, the decision was upheld on different grounds. The issue of whether dividends had been paid out of capital was thus left unresolved. Two judges went out of the way to disassociate themselves from some of the sweeping generalizations of the Appeal Court. Unfortunately, however, they did not clearly indicate their own views, stating merely that the question was difficult and had to be dealt with case by case.

These three cases effectively destroyed the capital maintenance doctrine in law and with it the accountants' assumption that the law provided a conceptual framework for accounting. The literature of the last decade of the nineteenth century reflects accountants' consternation, as evidenced by the following extract from another paper by Ernest Cooper.

> Six years ago . . . I read a paper at a Meeting of your Society entitled 'What is Profit of a Company?'
>
> . . . It seems as though the state of matters in regard to Profit, which in 1888 was doubt and uncertainty, is in 1894 something like confusion.
>
> Unless I am misinformed, Counsel and Solicitors are in doubt how to advise upon questions connected with preparing Balance Sheets and ascertaining Profit.
>
> . . . It has been held that Directors paying a Dividend do so at their peril if they have not a Balance Sheet showing the true state of the Company (*Rance*'s case, 6 Ch. 104). They expose themselves to the terrible penalties that Judges have attached to Sec. 165 of the Companies Act of 1862. . . . Within the last few months a Judge has stated that Auditors are sufficiently Officers of a Company in his view to bring them within this section. If he be right, the already sufficient responsibilities and anxieties of an Auditor will be extended beyond those known to any trade or profession.[8]

SUMMARY

The new enterprises that developed in the Industrial Revolution were of a different character from the trading ventures of earlier centuries. The new industries required increasingly large amounts of capital, employed a large workforce, and operated continuously. Venture accounting was no longer suitable for them, but it was not necessarily clear what should succeed it.

Although long delayed by the disillusionment caused by the South Seas Bubble, reform of corporations legislation eventually took place in the nineteenth century to meet the needs of the new enterprises. The legislation created or enhanced a demand for financial reports, a demand that accountants and accounting theory were quite unprepared to meet.

In the absence of a cohesive theory, financial reporting developed in an ad hoc fashion. A particular form of reporting had grown up in one sector—that of capital-intensive companies providing essential public services in transportation and public utilities. This reporting system—the double-account system—emphasized the distinction between the supposedly permanent capital investment and the operating costs to run it. This distinction was artificial; few forms of investment are permanent, and there is no clear dividing line between assets with a short and a long life. As a result, the system faced difficulty in classifying costs incurred as between capital and revenue accounts. Neither was there a good understanding of the need to recognize depreciation of capital assets. When depreciation was recognized at all, it was thought of more as an expedient to facilitate replacement than as a requirement for measuring profit and financial position.

With respect to other forms of business, accountants tended to think of financial statements as a report on valuations. Practical problems, however, suggested modification of the simple valuation approach. As production processes became more complicated, cost was easier to compute than value to account for inventory in nonmarketable form. As for fixed assets, mere fluctuations in value seemed irrelevant to a going concern. The need for depreciation was also in question here. Finally, the proper accounting for reserves held back from distributable profits was an open question.

Accountants looked to the courts to provide precedents that would help them resolve financial reporting issues. The belief that it was illegal to reduce capital provided support both for conservatism in valuations of circulating assets and for appropriate provisions for depreciation of capital assets or for other losses. Three cases respecting the legality of dividends toward the end of the nineteenth century shattered that belief. Without it, accountants were left with no real theory of financial reporting. They knew that assets and liabilities had to be reported and valued and profit had to be measured, but they had been left with no theory as to how to do it.

REFERENCES

1 See the summing up by H. Pollins, "Aspects of Railway Accounting Before 1868," in *Studies in the History of Accounting*, ed. A.C. Littleton and B.S. Yamey (London: Sweet & Maxwell, 1956), especially pp. 353–54.

2 For an excellent history see M.C. Wells, *Accounting for Common Costs* (Urbana, Ill.: Center for International Education and Research in Accounting, 1978).

3 O.G. Ladelle, "The Calculation of Depreciation," in *The Late Nineteenth Century Debate over Depreciation, Capital and Income*, ed. R.P. Brief (New York: Arno Press, 1976). (First published in *The Accountant*, November 29, 1890, and December 6, 1890.)

4 E. Cooper, "What Is Profit of a Company?" in *Late Nineteenth Century Debate*, ed. R.P. Brief. (First published in *The Accountant*, November 10, 1888, pp. 740–46.)

5 *Lee v. Neuchatel Asphalte Company* (1889) 41 Ch.D. 1. (Reprinted in *Late Nineteenth Century Debate*, ed. R.P. Brief.)

6 *Verner v. The General and Commercial Investment Trust* (Limited) (1894) 63 Ch.D. 456. (Reprinted in *Late Nineteenth Century Debate*, ed. R.P. Brief.)

7 *In re National Bank of Wales Limited* (1899) 2 Ch.D. 629 and *Dovey v. Cory* (1901) AC. 477.

8 E. Cooper, "Chartered Accountants and the Profit Question," in *Late Nineteenth Century Debate*, ed. R.P. Brief. (First published in *The Accountant*, November 24, 1894, pp. 1033–43.)

FINANCIAL ACCOUNTING IN THE TWENTIETH CENTURY

To this point our description of the modern history of accounting has been limited to developments in the United Kingdom. This is legitimate since the situation in North America was very similar. The accounting profession developed first in England and Scotland, and many accountants from there visited the Americas to audit the accounts of enterprises financed by British capital. A considerable number remained to mingle with local accountants in establishing the profession in North America.

In spite of the fact that corporations legislation in the United States typically had nothing to say about financial reporting or audit, the development of accounting in that country in the nineteenth century was very similar to that in England. Chatfield points out one difference.[1] Relatively more of the financing of American companies consisted of short-term bank credit rather than the issuance of capital stock. Bankers looked to working capital as the prime security for their loans. Accordingly, audits for credit purposes naturally concentrated on the balance sheet position and, in particular, on working capital rather than on profit. The idea of conservatism in the valuation of working capital was thus reinforced.

The leading edge of advances in accounting shifted from England to the United States in the twentieth century. The U.S. emerged from World War I as a creditor nation and undoubtedly the most powerful of the world's economies. Its new status was reflected in a burgeoning capital market that enhanced the need for sound financial reporting. At the same time, American universities were the first to recognize accounting as an academic study, and it became a principal subject in the early business schools. Acceptance of accounting as an academic discipline introduced a more conceptual and critical approach to its study, which balanced and enriched its pragmatic orientation.

EMERGENCE OF AN HISTORICAL COST-MATCHING MODEL

As described in the previous chapter, the collapse of the capital maintenance doctrine left financial reporting with little conceptual basis. Storey recounts that the void was filled by the proposition that most business undertakings had become going concerns and, therefore, their assets should be reported in a balance sheet at "going-concern value."[2] That value depended upon the nature of the asset. Under the going-concern proposition, those assets *with which* business was carried on—the fixed assets—should be valued at cost reduced by an appropriate allowance for consumption of utility over their useful lives. Fluctuations in market or realizable value could be ignored because the fixed assets of a going concern would not be sold. On the other hand, assets such as inventory and accounts receivable *in which* the business was conducted —the "floating" or "circulating" assets —should be valued at realizable value because realization was the whole purpose for which those assets were held.

The going-concern concept provided a satisfactory guide to practice except in one respect. Conservative accountants did not like the idea of reporting inventory at realizable values above cost when realization lay in the future. It was, therefore, widely accepted that a valuation basis of the lower of cost and realizable value was preferable.

Accountants' beliefs as to the basis of good accounting in the early twentieth century can be summarized in the following statements:

* The balance sheet is the most important financial report.
* The balance sheet is basically a statement of asset values and liabilities.
* Cost is a satisfactory basis of valuation for assets held for use or sale, except that depreciation of fixed assets should be allowed for and inventory should be written down to realizable value if below cost.

These beliefs did not answer all questions. Accountants were confused about whether capital gains or losses were part of income and about the definition of income in general. They did not know whether, or how, to account for goodwill. In addition, they were in no position to impose their ideas of accounting theory upon managements of companies, especially in the absence of any clear legal support. The following aspects of practice were particularly troublesome:[3]

* Many companies periodically would write up (or, less frequently, write down) their fixed assets on the basis of appraisals. So long as the balance sheet was regarded as a valuation statement, this was hard to resist.
* Many company managements resisted the idea that depreciation was a necessary expense of earning income and must be recorded systematically. Management tended to look on depreciation as a discretionary reserving of profits against ultimate replacement of plant. Such reserves could be varied in amount depending on whether times were good or bad.
* Some prosperous companies considered it proper to create "secret reserves" by understating assets or overstating liabilities, with consequent reduction in profits reported. Although the practice was conservative, its arbitrary aspects concerned anyone interested in fair financial reporting. The situation was even worse if, in some subsequent year, the reserves were released, thereby overstating profits reported at that time. That result was definitely unconservative, but management could always argue that reserves were intended to protect "against a rainy day." If it was proper to create them, it must be proper to use them when the rainy day arrived.

As time passed, the contradictions and inconsistencies in corporate financial reporting became less and less tolerable, and the forces making for change became more insistent. Some of the forces for change in the United States were as follows:

- The income tax legislation of the early part of the century created a need for good accounting records and provided a stimulus to some change in theory. Basically it shifted attention from the balance sheet to measurement of income. It was advantageous for tax purposes to establish that income arose only upon realization and also to accept the necessity for depreciation as a charge in determining income earned. The need for an objective basis for taxation also emphasized actual transactions, rather than valuations, as a basic groundwork for financial reporting. Thereby impetus was given to the adoption of the cost principle for valuation of assets.

- Certain government agencies became interested in good financial reporting as an aid to the granting of credit and thereby to the expansion of business and investment. At the request of the Federal Trade Commission, the American Institute of Accountants (AIA) prepared a guide to audit entitled *Uniform Accounting*. This 1917 statement suggested formats for the balance sheet and income statement. It was reissued with revisions and under new titles in 1918 and again in 1929 and 1936, the final version being entitled *Verification of Financial Statements*.

- The New York Stock Exchange (NYSE), as the primary market for publicly traded securities, also was influential. Listed companies were required to submit financial statements to shareholders from the early 1920s, although these did not have to be audited until 1933.

Although constructive, these efforts might well be characterized as "too little and too late." There was little accounting progress during the prosperous 1920s. Then the stock market crash of 1929 and the ensuing Great Depression provided a much more compelling impetus toward the improvement of financial reporting. Rightly or wrongly, inadequate financial reporting received some of the blame for the market excesses before the crash and the subsequent losses. An AIA Committee on Co-operation with the NYSE was formed in 1930. In 1933 it recommended six accounting principles. Five of these were accepted by the NYSE; the unfortunate exception was the suggestion that companies should disclose the accounting methods employed by them—a most desirable rule given the alternatives possible in accounting practice. These five, plus one other, were formally adopted by the AIA membership in 1934.[4] These so-called "basic principles" in fact represented attempts to curb the worst excesses of 1920s accounting and came nowhere near to providing a rounded framework for good accounting practice.

A more powerful stimulus for change was conceived in 1933. In that year, the federal government enacted the Securities Act to regulate the issuance of new securities to the public. In the following year, the Securities and Exchange Act was enacted to regulate trading in public securities markets, and the Securities and Exchange Commission (SEC) was set up as the regulating body. The threat of government intervention galvanized the U.S. accounting profession to organized action to promote improvements in accounting principles. The SEC resolved by a narrow margin to devote its efforts to regulation of disclosure in prospectuses and annual financial statements and to rely on the profession for improvements in accounting measurements.

The pressure for reform faced the U.S. accounting profession with a dilemma. There was no body with both the power and capability to mandate comprehensive change in financial reporting. The SEC had been given authority over the financial reporting of public companies but lacked the means, on its own, to enforce a whole new model of financial reporting. Corporation management, which has the responsibility to prepare financial reports, is invariably interested primarily in its own situation and lacks the energy to consider an overall theory of financial reporting. Moreover management, almost inevitably, is inclined to favour accounting practices that do not overly restrict its freedom to report as it thinks best. Auditors and the professional societies of accounting have ample reason to desire a well-defined accounting theory and clear-cut guidelines based upon it. But auditors (at least, the auditors of the 1930s and 1940s) also lacked the power and perhaps the will to develop and enforce a well-defined accounting theory and tight accounting standards. The responsibility for financial reports lay in the first instance with management. The auditor was in no position to say what must be done—merely what might not be done under pain of a qualified report. Moreover, many auditors and accountants believed that, in view of the complexity and variety in forms of business enterprise, rules of general application could not be set out except in the most abstract terms.

The practical result of this was that the U.S. accounting profession, with continual prodding by the SEC, tried to achieve reform in little steps rather than by dramatic changes. From the outset the position was adopted that prescription of all-embracing accounting rules was undesirable. Rather, each corporation should adopt those reporting practices best suited to its individual circumstances, provided those practices were "generally accepted" and/or had "substantial authoritative support." (The latter phrase was used by the SEC in 1938 to describe accounting practices that would be acceptable in financial statements filed with it.)

The primary need seen by the American Institute was to narrow areas of difference and inconsistency in accounting practices and to further the development and recognition of generally accepted accounting principles. For this purpose, reference to the institute membership as a whole, as was done in 1934, was too cumbersome, and occasional special committees were not sufficient. In 1939, a standing Committee on Accounting Procedure (CAP) was set up with the objective of issuing bulletins to the membership on accounting matters.

In spite of the notion of the overriding importance of what came to be known as generally accepted accounting principles (GAAP), the fact that a committee could express preferences and give guidance logically implied that there was some underlying accepted theory of accounting. In its introductory bulletin the CAP pointed to a demand for greater uniformity in accounting, and to increased emphasis on the income statement with "a tendency to regard the balance sheet as the connecting link between successive income statements."[5]

This concept of the primacy of the income statement filled the vacuum left by the loss of faith in balance sheet valuations. It was observed in the depression period that stock prices responded more to reported income than to balance sheet book values. But income had to be defined in a certain way to avoid the valuation problem. Income tax law, by which income was seen basically as an excess of measurable receipts over expenses, provided a possible answer. Income was to be based on actual business transactions. It should not be considered earned until revenue was "realized" and costs pertaining thereto were matched. This implicit conceptual framework was supported by academic writing of the time—in particular, the American Accounting Association's *Tentative Statement of Accounting Principles Underlying Corporate Financial Statements*, issued in 1936. The same ideas were strongly encouraged by the SEC.

Further support for the emphasis on the income statement came in 1940, with the publication by the American Accounting Association of a monograph by W.A. Paton and A.C. Littleton. In their preface the authors said:

> We have attempted to weave together the fundamental ideas of accounting rather than to state standards as such. The intention has been to build a framework within which a subsequent statement of corporate accounting standards could be erected. Accounting theory is here conceived to be a coherent, coordinated, consistent body of doctrine which may be compactly expressed in the form of standards if desired.[6]

This work was broadly in tune with the thinking of the times. Merely by its existence as a well-reasoned exposition, it was to be enormously influential. Its important feature was that it was not merely an organized recital of accounting practice. Instead, it provided an approach to building a conceptual framework that was followed, with variations, in many subsequent publications.

Paton and Littleton suggested that the most important accounting responsibility of a modern corporation was to provide information to investors, present and prospective, who were not familiar with its affairs as insiders. They further suggested that a large corporation was a quasi-public institution having broad responsibilities: to employees for fair wages and working conditions, to customers for fair prices and good service, and to government and to society for taxes. Because of this broad accountability and the need to avoid bias in favour of one interest or another, a consistent framework of accounting standards was needed. Standards were seen as statements giving broad guidance to the presentation of accounting facts. Standards were not intended to be detailed rules. They should, however, be orderly and internally consistent; they should be in harmony with observable conditions; and they should be impartial.

The basic concepts suggested by the authors and some of the implications they deduced from them are listed below.

- A business undertaking is an entity in its own right, separate from its proprietors or investors or other interested parties.

- Continuity of enterprise is the typical experience; hence, accounting may normally assume a "going concern."

- The continuity characteristic of business makes "earning power" the most significant determinant of enterprise value. Hence the income statement is the most important accounting report.

- Money-price is the common denominator by which diverse objects can be expressed homogeneously in the accounts. Unity is achieved in accounting because all transactions are expressed in "price aggregates." Hence, the concepts of cost, revenue, asset, liability, etc. are all aspects of the single subject matter—the exchange transaction.

- Business activity consists of transforming inputs (materials, labour, etc.) into outputs representing new combinations with new utilities. Input costs can be seen as "attaching" to outputs. Hence assets can be recorded at cost, leaving the recognition of value added from activity until "realization." At that time, the gain can be objectively measured.

- Costs measure effort and revenues measure accomplishment. Ideally, income reported would represent revenues realized less the costs contributing to the revenues. For practical reasons it is not possible to trace all costs to revenue. Hence, some costs must be matched with time periods rather than directly with realized revenue.

- Accounting should be based on verifiable, objective evidence to the extent possible.

Inevitably there were many who disagreed with some of the detailed prescriptions of Paton and Littleton, but the broad framework of ideas was appealing. Both the emphasis on the income statement and the idea that accounting was a process of allocation of objectively determined price aggregates, guided by the ideal of matching cause and effect, appealed to accountants seeking some theoretical justification for avoiding the slippery process of value estimation.

FROM GAAP TO ACCOUNTING STANDARDS

Committees or boards of professional accountants laboured to give guidance to the goal of better accounting. The American lead in appointing a standing committee was followed shortly by other countries. The English Institute of Chartered Accountants in 1942 appointed a committee to issue technical recommendations. The Committee on Accounting and Auditing Research of the Canadian Institute of Chartered Accountants commenced work in 1946.

U.S. Experience—CAP and APB

The United States experience has gone through three distinct periods. Each of the first two periods ended with a sense of disillusionment and a determination to do better. Both times a strong element in the disillusionment was a sense that the committee or board involved had spent most of its time "fighting brush fires" and that its recommendations lacked any substantial conceptual base. In each case the succeeding board was given a mandate to engage in more basic research and build a "conceptual framework," within which individual recommendations were expected to fit in a logical, internally consistent fashion.

The CAP lasted twenty years. In that period it issued fifty-one bulletins, including eight on accounting terminology. Many important issues were dealt with, including such subjects as allocation of income tax cost, treatment of costs associated with pension plans, and accounting for business combinations. In retrospect, it is clear that the committee's work suffered from a strong belief in "general acceptance." The belief that accounting standards could not be imposed but must develop through acceptance made the committee timid, so that very often its opinions were expressed as preferences rather than positive recommendations. Often, also, practice in a particular area would stretch criteria suggested by the CAP. For example, in business combinations the committee suggested that "pooling of interests" accounting was appropriate when equity interests of both combining parties continued after a merger and when all the circumstances indicated that it was a real sharing of interests not simply an acquisition of one party by the other. If one combining interest was "minor," it was to be presumed the merger was not a pooling. Nevertheless, over a period of time, practice came to accept pooling accounting when one of the combining interests was even less than 5 percent of the other. As a result of these problems, in the end it could be said that the committee failed to achieve its objective of reducing inconsistency in practice.

The proposed solution was to bring theory and research to bear on the problems of practice. The CAP was replaced by the Accounting Principles Board (APB) in 1959. It was to be supported by a Director of Research and a greatly expanded program of research studies. The first charge upon the research division was to draw up a new conceptual framework and suggest its broad implications for financial accounting. This was seen as involving two phases. There was to be identification of a few postulates of accounting—observations to be taken as given. Then, broad principles were to be enunciated, flowing from and consistent with the postulates.[7]

The attempt was not a success. The statement of postulates seemed innocuous—almost a statement of self-evident concepts lacking any strong guidance for practical standards. The statement of broad principles suffered from a different criticism—it gave unwelcome guidance. Both statements were thought by the APB to be "too radically different from present generally accepted accounting principles for acceptance at this time."[8] In addition, there was considerable doubt whether the proposals in the studies could be implemented without accounting becoming too subjective. The board commissioned a new study to catalogue accounting principles that were thought to be generally accepted, with the idea that this might give a lead to further research better adapted to the needs of practice.[9] A few years later, the board itself issued a statement organizing and summarizing what it considered to be the existing status of GAAP.[10]

In the meantime, having rejected the proposed new conceptual framework, the APB was forced to take up where the CAP had left off. Almost immediately it ran into heavy weather. The Revenue Act of 1962 introduced a new tax concession in order to stimulate economic activity—the investment tax credit. Accounting for the tax reduction resulting from this credit raised completely new issues. There was a sharp split in opinion among board members as to the best accounting, and its recommendation received only the minimum support required for issuance under its voting rules. That split in opinion was duplicated in industry. The SEC refused to support the majority recommendation of the board. Thus, the board was faced with a situation where its implicit conceptual framework was inadequate, general acceptance could not be found for *any* single position, and its authority was under attack. It was forced to retreat and accept a diversity of accounting methods for the tax credit.

Thereafter, for a time the board seemed to settle down. Research studies on more specific subject areas began to appear. Although their recommendations were not always followed in board pronouncements, at least they helped the board to arrive at reasoned conclusions on the issues. Over a period of some twelve years the board issued thirty-one "Opinions." Many of the subjects had previously been dealt with by the CAP. However, given greater background research in the complex issues, the board was able to provide more positive and more detailed guidance. At least part of the reason for more detailed and specific rules was the desire to avoid the erosion of standards that previously had resulted from the stretching of criteria expressed in general terms.

The complexity of the issues dealt with by the APB had certain consequences. One was a lack of unanimity within the board itself on many issues. Compromises often had to be made to obtain the two-thirds majority necessary to approve issuance of an opinion. In addition, the variety in possible views increased the opportunity for parties with a vested interest to lobby board members on behalf of their point of view. On occasion, lobbying also went over the heads of the APB in attempts to persuade the SEC and Congress that they should overrule the board. The politicized atmosphere surrounding certain highly charged issues revealed an apparent weakness in the composition of the board. The majority of the members of the board were partners of auditing firms. It appeared to cynical observers that they were open to pressures from important clients that might affect the independence of their opinions. The compromises necessary to obtain agreement on complex questions reinforced that impression, even though there was never any solid evidence to support it. Moreover, the compromises emphasized the absence of a thorough conceptual framework to support the board's opinions.

In an attempt to solve this problem, the institute, by now renamed the American Institute of Certified Public Accountants (AICPA), decided to make a more formal effort to get back to first principles. A study on the objectives of financial statements was commissioned. About the same time the profession relinquished its sole responsibility for the appointment of the standard-setting board and joined with other private sector associations to sponsor a new board—the Financial Accounting Standards Board (FASB). This new board was urged to arrive at some agreed-upon conceptual framework with all deliberate speed.

U.S. Experience—Adding Weight to GAAP

In the course of this history a little-noted evolution took place. As previously indicated, the CAP did not regard itself as legislating accounting principles; it merely provided informal guidance. The ultimate test of a principle was general acceptance. This attitude continued through the early years of the APB. However, the investment tax credit debacle was very damaging to the APB's prestige and threatened its claim to give informed guidance. The reaction in the profession was to close ranks. In 1964, Council of the AICPA attempted to add weight to the APB's opinions by adopting a resolution that institute members should ensure that any departure from the board's opinions be specifically disclosed, either in footnotes to the financial statements or in the audit reports of members. A few years later, the authority of the APB's opinions was further strengthened. The AICPA's Code of Ethics was amended to make it a contravention of ethics to issue an unqualified audit report on financial statements not in conformity with a specific APB recommendation, unless the departure was necessary to make the statements not misleading.

After the APB was dissolved, the FASB was recognized as its successor for the purpose of application of the code of ethics. The FASB was further strengthened by an announcement of the SEC in 1973 that it would regard accounting practices contrary to FASB promulgations as lacking in substantial authoritative support. As a result of these developments, the opinions of the APB and then the FASB became much more than guidance to good practice: they became effectively the only acceptable practice. This was a change of overwhelming importance. General acceptance, as a justification of an accounting principle, was valid only where the boards had not made a specific recommendation. When a board opinion was issued, it became a rule of practice. Accounting *standards*, arrived at by a quasi-legislative procedure, thus tended to replace accounting *principles*, recognized as a result of general acceptance.

U. S. Experience—The FASB

The FASB was formed in 1973 and continues to the present day. It differs from the APB in several important respects. First, it is independent of the accounting profession per se. Second, while the APB was made up of unpaid part-time appointees, the seven FASB members are well-paid full-time positions. This, and much increased staff support, has enabled a more rigorous examination of issues. The FASB's elaborate due process procedures, including public meetings and formal hearings, ensure high visibility and extensive input. They have also resulted in the process being more overtly political in nature.[11]

The FASB has issued statements, interpretations of statements, and technical bulletins at a rate much accelerated over that of the APB. Not surprisingly, the outpouring of standards has led to periodic complaints about "standards overload." The complaints have been reinforced by the fact that the board has continued the APB tradition of highly detailed rule making. On the other hand, concerns began to be voiced that the elaborate due process procedures took too long. It was put forward that there needed to be an interpretive function to deal expeditiously with current issues. In response, an Emerging Issues Task Force was established in 1984. It is chaired by the FASB's Director of Research and its membership consists of accountants drawn from national public accounting firms and industry.

Great importance was assigned to the development of a conceptual framework. Six Statements of Financial Accounting Concepts were issued over the period from 1978 to 1985. These concepts statements put in place a rigorously reasoned statement of objectives based on decision usefulness and the primacy of investor interests. They also set out qualitative characteristics of useful financial information built on basic concepts of relevance and reliability. But, perhaps most important, they signalled a fundamental shift from the traditional revenue-expense matching principles to a more disciplined "asset and liability" view. This conceptual reorientation resulted from a growing realization that revenue-expense matching theory is open ended and circular if it is not grounded in sound economic concepts of "assets" and "liabilities." Traditional revenue-expense matching resulted in deferred debits and credits on the balance sheet that could not be justified in any real world economic sense. They were simply balances awaiting allocation to income.

The FASB's decision usefulness objective and its asset and liability view were consistent with developing academic conclusions on the essential arbitrariness of cost and revenue allocations, and the importance of an informational value basis for financial accounting (to be examined in the following section).

FASB concepts statements have had a significant influence on accounting standards (as we will see in analyzing specific issues in Part II). They have provided the model for conceptual frameworks of standard-setters in other jurisdictions, including Canada. However, the FASB conceptual framework is far from a complete product. Consensus on basic premises proved to be difficult to attain and that difficulty increased as the statements progressed closer to providing principles for actual accounting. A number of observers have expressed disappointment that the FASB, despite its prodigious efforts, was unable to achieve agreement on fundamental recognition and measurement concepts. This inability of the FASB to produce a more fully developed conceptual framework reflected the unsettled state of evolving accounting theory and a fundamental lack of consensus within the accounting community.

PRESSURES FOR IMPROVEMENTS IN FINANCIAL REPORTING

An Information Value Perspective

In the late 1960s and early 1970s leading accounting academics started down a new path. They had become increasingly critical of conventional income measurement thinking. The normative theorizing that characterized the development of accounting thought to that time did not seem to bear up well to the close scrutiny of rigorous research methods. The American Accounting Association published two closely reasoned studies that concluded that allocations at the heart of the cost-matching theory of income are, in concept, wholly arbitrary — mere calculations with no verifiable measurement substance.[12] At the same time a new "informational perspective" began to emerge, based on the efficient market literature emanating from finance economics. The efficient market hypothesis (EMH) focuses on the relationship between accounting information and security prices. Under efficient market conditions share prices may be expected to respond to reported accounting earnings if such earnings have information value to investors.[13] An extensive body of evidence has been developed over the past thirty years on security price effects and information value implications of reported earnings and other disclosures.[14] Among the more important findings:

- There is a significant, although not one to one, positive correlation between security price changes and reported earnings changes. Further, measures of risk in securities prices appear to be significantly correlated with variability in accounting earnings. Thus, accounting earnings seem to have information content. While this should be of comfort to accountants, the evidence indicates that reported earnings represent only a small part of the information relevant to price determination. Some have read this as an indication that earnings have not been well measured.[15]

- Security prices act as if investors see through accounting method changes that do not have cash flow consequences to the enterprise. As an example, EMH price-effects studies have indicated that securities prices do not move in response to changes in reported earnings that are attributable solely to changes in depreciation methods. This has been interpreted to mean that security prices respond in a relatively sophisticated manner to accounting information. This evidence is not unequivocal, however. There are a number of unexplained findings with respect to situations in which security prices behave in ways that seem not entirely consistent with sophisticated efficient markets.[16]

The EMH literature is concerned with the role of financial reporting to facilitate investor decision making. Financial statements are considered to have value if they contain cost-effective information that is relevant to estimating expected return or the variability of return for individual securities and portfolios of securities. To be cost-effective, the information should not be available as cheaply from other sources. The form of presentation (whether, for example, an item of information is incorporated in the financial statement measurements themselves or only in the notes) is considered relevant only to the extent that it makes the information more or less costly to prepare and analyze.

By the 1980s, two additional schools of thought that are broadly compatible with the informational perspective were attracting attention. They are Agency Theory and Positive Accounting Theory.

Agency theory takes a stewardship interpretation of financial accounting. It is concerned with the demand for accounting information within a relationship under which a *principal* (for example, an investor of capital in an enterprise) entrusts its welfare (capital investment) to an *agent* (management of the enterprise). The demand for financial accounting occurs when the principal cannot directly observe the activities of the agent (known as the "moral hazard" problem) and contracts for the payment of return on capital to be based in whole or in part on financial accounting data. The contract will be designed to provide the agent with the incentive to manage the enterprise in the best interests of the principal. An example would be a bonus plan that rewards management for achieving higher income returns for the principal. The value of accounting information may then be judged in terms of its usefulness in facilitating efficient contracting with respect to incentives and risk/reward sharing between management and investor interests.[17] It is commonly advocated that information should be hard, in the sense of being objective and verifiable, in order to have value for contracting purposes. If it is soft, that is, open to manipulation by management, it will be inefficient for contracting purposes because it cannot be relied upon by the principal. But, presumably the information must also bear a predictable relationship to the reality it is purporting to depict (the economic objective the principal wants the agent to achieve). (Thus we see the potential need for trade-off between objectivity and representational faithfulness.)

Positive Accounting Theory (PAT) is closely aligned with Agency Theory.[18] Once contracts based on accounting information are in place, PAT is interested in the accounting choices management will make within the degrees of freedom it may have within generally accepted accounting principles. The early PAT literature was concerned with opportunism in explaining management behaviour in attempting to present financial information that would put the best light on its stewardship. We will see many potential opportunities for this in later chapters of this book. For example, the historical cost model may enable management to enhance reported income by selling winners (assets that have gone up in value) and holding losers; fuzzy concepts of "liabilities" and "equity" may enable in-substance debt (in the form of mandatorially redeemable preferred shares, for example) to be classified as equity; various "off-balance sheet" financing schemes may be created; and so on. In a broad sense, PAT has been concerned with explaining accounting practice as a function of the efforts of competing interests who are affected by accounting and who are assumed to want to influence the choice of financial reporting methods.[19] A basic conclusion some draw from this theory is that the search for "best" accounting methods is essentially a "social choice" issue, requiring an assessment of the effects of accounting alternatives on various stakeholders. PAT researchers are therefore interested in the process of accounting standard setting.

In summary, these informational value perspectives have had two basic themes:

1. That financial accounting should place less emphasis on trying to determine a single best earnings figure and more on providing disclosures that have cost-effective information content.

2. That accounting standards should be developed with attention to their economic and social effects, which is seen to require political processes for achieving trade-offs among participant interests.

The informational value theories have very significantly influenced academic accounting thinking over the past two to three decades. One result has been a concentration of research efforts on the effects of accounting information, and another has been a de-emphasis of accounting measurement theory as a field of academic interest.

Fully consistent with the informational value philosophy is the clear trend over the past twenty years or so to much expanded disclosures in financial reporting. This is evident in standards developed during this period requiring, among other things, disclosure of accounting policies, industry segments information, data on cash flows, and most recently, certain information pertaining to financial risk exposures. As well, securities regulators have instituted requirements for management discussion and analysis.

The informational value perspective has clearly added a very important dimension to the consideration of accounting issues. There are, however, concerns that the perspective is incomplete. Standard setters have complained that to date most informational value research has focused on the effects of accounting standards some years after they have been issued. They claim that this has not been of much help to them in respect of forward-looking issues.[20] But the concern goes deeper than this. Empirical research on, for example, the stock price effects of reported income or other selected accounting disclosures can be help-ful in assessing whether those disclosures may have value to investors. But it cannot *of itself* provide a coherent theory of accounting that can serve as a basis for reasoning for-ward to resolve accounting issues. The premise that selection among accounting alterna-tives is a social choice decision has not given accounting standard setters much with which to work. It is well recognized that social welfare issues are impossible to solve by deductive methods, which has led some to conclude that such issues must be addressed by political processes involving the interaction of competing interests. Where, accounting practition-ers may ask, is the accounting expertise in this?

Perhaps the most concerning aspect of the informational value philosophy has been its de-emphasis of financial accounting as a measurement system. This has left a large void in the development of accounting thought. Underlying the informationalist's lack of inter-est in accounting as a measurement system has been a belief that entity income and finan-cial position are indeterminate within a very large range.[21] This belief is in conflict with traditional accounting thinking, which has been founded on the presumption that "account-ing principles rest on principles of economics," and that there are basic economic realities from which valid and useful financial accounting principles can be deduced.[22] It is implicit within this that financial statements can be expected to have information value to the extent that they are reasonable representations of those recognized economic realities.

There has been some evolution of the traditional view of accounting over the years, in the face of irrefutable evidence as to the deficiencies of traditional historical cost-matching accounting. Most will accept that revenue-matching and allocation precepts that were appro-priate to the simpler times of the 1940s and 50s are inadequate to today's needs. It may also be recognized that trade-offs based on consideration of predominant user interests and soci-ety values will be necessary when appropriate accounting cannot be reasoned from basic accounting principles. Many are not prepared, however, to abandon accounting as measure-ment discipline or the foundations of the traditional model. Rather they may be expected to try to adapt, extend or even re-engineer, aspects of the traditional model. They may reason that, in attempting to improve financial accounting, one should start with accepted economic prin-ciples and rational decision models and reason forward within them as far as practicable. In this spirit a noted accounting scholar observed that ". . . our traditional accounting methods have been deficient and their deficiencies give rise to conflicts between economic interests that could be avoided if accounting's theoretical foundations were more soundly based." [23]

The FASB, the CICA Accounting Standards Board, and standard setters generally are continuing to work to try to improve accounting standards within this context. In explaining the FASB's concern to develop a conceptual framework, Storey observed that ". . . the FASB concluded that accounting did possess a core of fundamental concepts that were nei-ther subject to nor dependent on the moment's particular transitory consensus." [24]

Thus the informational value and measurement schools have approached accounting from opposite poles. The latter has tried to work within an accounting model and adapt it to changing conditions, while informational value advocates have worked from without, attempt-ing to judge accounting by its social value and economic consequences. An informational value academic might be viewed as a social scientist interested in assessing accounting information in terms of its value to society. An accounting measurer may be analogous to an engineer who is primarily concerned with the engine itself (that is, with the underlying accounting model). The engineer is presumably interested in understanding the specifications of the model, exactly how it works, what it is capable of, what its limitations are, and how it might be most efficiently designed to fulfill certain presumed purposes. Both the social scientist and engineering perspectives are relevant.

Two additional academic schools of thought have recently attracted attention. They are the Feltham-Ohlson valuation theory, and signalling theory. According to the Feltham-Ohlson model, the market price of owners' equity of an entity is equal to the accounting book value of its owners' equity plus "subjective goodwill."[25] Since "subjective goodwill" is, for the most part, not recorded in financial statements, the market value of owners' equity is equal to accounting book value of owners' equity plus the present value of future "abnormal earnings." Abnormal earnings is defined as accounting earnings minus an appropriate charge for the cost of capital multiplied by opening book owners' equity. The Feltham-Ohlson model is considered of importance because it defines a structure for relating accounting data and the value of an enterprise. It is also noteworthy that it places importance on balance sheet and income accounting numbers.

Signalling theory relates to management's attempts to convey information about the quality of an enterprise that may be highly subjective or unobservable by normal accounting methods (for example, the goodwill and earnings prospects of an enterprise). The theory assumes a form of asymmetric information called adverse selection. The idea is that inferior enterprises will have the incentive to misrepresent their "quality" so as to obtain the same cost of capital as superior enterprises. The difficult task, then, for a high-quality enterprise is to signal its superiority in a credible way that distinguishes it from inferior enterprises. Signalling theory might be thought of as an extension beyond PAT, in that it would theorize the use of accounting choices to try to convey information about future earnings prospects. Signalling theorists are concerned with the information content of discretionary disclosures, and with understanding the forces that may determine when management will voluntarily disclose information and when it may be expected to try to withhold it. Research in this area is considered to have important implications for accounting standard setting (in assessing what accounting and disclosure should, and should not, be made mandatory). As well, it may help securities regulators focus their financial reporting compliance and enforcement policies.[26]

External Pressures and Expectations Gaps

The above struggles within accounting should be viewed within the context of a society that has been undergoing fundamental change. The world has entered an "information age" of global capital markets, and there are profound implications in this for financial reporting.[27] Although the shape of these implications is still far from clear, the following areas of development seem likely to be relevant to understanding current pressures on financial accounting.

- Revolutionary advances in information technology have changed the ways in which business is being done. Sophisticated real time technology is enabling enterprises to engage in elaborate and complex exchanges and business arrangements which are challenging traditional transactions-based accounting concepts. For example, economic exchanges may involve partial transfers of ownership and various sharings of risks and benefits, rather than being outright sales or purchases in the traditional sense. Developments in these areas have severely challenged accounting criteria for distinguishing sales from financings in certain securitization and other complex asset-transfer transactions discussed in Chapter 7, and some leasing and sale-leaseback transactions discussed in Chapter 13.

- Advances in computer technology and its accessibility is enabling preparers and users to handle complex information bases and perform data manipulations that could not have been accommodated on a cost-effective basis even a few years ago. This is increasing business' capability for implementing more complex accounting and for updating calculations for such factors as interest, inflation, and other risk and market effects. The problems of information overload are accordingly lessened in some degree.

- Developments in information technology and in finance theories have led to major changes in capital markets. A broadening array of derivative financial instruments (including futures, forwards, options and swaps) has revolutionized portfolio investment, hedging and risk-taking strategies. As well, ready markets now exist for selling or "securitizing" previously nonmarketable assets such as loans, mortgages, and other forms of receivables. Recent business failures attest to the fact that a company's fortunes can change quickly, with decision and planning horizons much reduced in many areas. These developments have given rise to questions as to the relevance of traditional historical cost accounting for financial instruments.

- There have been concerns about corporate governance and accountability and calls for both (1) broader measures of management performance and the effects of corporate activities than have been provided by conventional financial statements, and (2) accountability to a wider community of stakeholders beyond investors. As an example, enterprises are being forced to assume greater responsibilities for the effects of their activities on the environment.

One might be tempted to be pessimistic in assessing the implications of these developments for financial reporting. They may seem overwhelming. Some have expressed concerns that they may be rendering obsolete financial accounting as we know it. Clearly there is an increasing demand for information beyond conventional financial statements. But the demand for relevant and reliable reporting of enterprise financial position and results of operations (including income determinations) is not abating. From the perspective of agency theory, for example, effective financial accountability to external stakeholders may be considered essential to obtain their cost-effective participation in providing capital and other resources to corporate entities.

It was noted above that the informational value perspective has heralded significant changes in financial reporting thought, but that its de-emphasis of accounting as a measurement system has left a void. This point is underlined when one assesses external expectations of financial accounting. Accountants continue to be held accountable under the law (as evidenced by securities and corporations legislation and court decisions) for financial statements that *present fairly* a reporting entity's *financial position* and *results of operations*. These italicized words are what the law demands and the auditor reports on in the standard short-form auditor's opinion. Investors and other external stakeholders clearly expect financial statement figures to be fair representations. Numbers described as "accounts receivable," or "inventories," or "sales revenues," or "operating expenses," are expected to be reasonable measures of those items. Public accountants are sued, and generally lose credibility, where these expectations are not met. Informed users of financial information may accept that there are limitations in the ability of financial statements to represent economic income and financial condition. But the public may reasonably expect that these limitations should be within tolerable and understandable bounds.

The past decade has witnessed a number of spectacular business failures where it has been alleged that reported income and/or balance sheet amounts did not adequately signal imminent problems. Supplementary note disclosures are considered essential, but are not accepted as a substitute for fairly measured financial statement figures. Significant public concerns have been raised, and various studies have indicated that user expectations have not been fully met.[28]

In attempting to put these changes and challenges in perspective, it is well to note that many of the institutions in our society have been held up to scrutiny and criticism in recent years, as they have struggled to adjust to the times. It should be no surprise that financial accounting, which plays a key informational role in the capital marketplace, should also be the subject of serious attention.

THE ACCRUAL ACCOUNTING EVOLUTION

It is instructive to consider how financial accounting has changed in response to the pressures cited above. Certainly many accounting pronouncements have been issued in recent years, but do they amount to any substantive change in the basic model set out in the 1940 Paton and Littleton monograph referred to earlier in this chapter?

One's first reaction might be no—that the fundamental concepts of historical cost matching still stand. In support of this it might be observed that most now agree that the "experiment" with supplemental current cost and general price level disclosures of the late 1970s and early 1980s failed, and that few are advocating any wholesale overthrow of historical cost accounting. But such a reaction would be simplistic and incomplete. While basic elements of the Paton and Littleton model can still be found within the foundations upon which modern financial accounting is constructed, there has been a process of significant development and extension from these basic concepts.

We have already commented on the influence of the informational value perspective, and the expansion of disclosures provided in financial reports. In addition to this, three significant areas of development in recognition and measurement stand out.

1. The centre of the Paton and Littleton framework was the exchange transaction. Transactions were to be recorded at their transaction values (costs) leaving recognition of value added from corporate activities until "realization." Over the years an expanding accrual concept has been gradually transforming these traditional concepts. This is evident in the growing number of standards that require the recording of certain effects of current events in advance of transaction realization. The following examples will help make the nature and extent of this development clear.

   • Long-term monetary assets and liabilities denominated in a foreign currency had once been commonly carried at their historical cost transaction values until they were realized or settled. Now they are required to be translated at current exchange rates (see Chapter 21).

   • The traditional deferral method of income tax allocation for timing differences between accounting and taxable income has been replaced by (1) a more comprehensive "temporal differences" methodology, and (2) the "liability method" under which deferred taxes are recognized at current tax rates (see Chapter 16).

- There is acceptance for accounting for portfolio investments of investment enterprises at current market values. The FASB has recently extended the use of fair value accounting for marketable securities and derivatives (see Chapter 17). This evidences an extension of the traditional historical cost principle of recognizing value added on *realization* towards one based more on *realizability*.

- GAAP now require best estimate-based expense/liability accruals for certain expected future costs such as retirement benefits and environmental reclamation as the activities take place that are considered to have caused these costs to be incurred. Previously they were normally recognized only when the payments were made (see discussion at Chapter 8).

2. There has been a renewed emphasis on the balance sheet. More specifically, there is less tolerance for accepting cost-revenue matching residuals on the balance sheet if they do not meet in-substance definitions of "assets" and "liabilities." Here the FASB conceptual framework definitions of these terms have been a significant reference point. This renewed attention to the balance sheet does not represent an abandonment of income measurement, but is more in the nature of a check on it. It reflects the view that if revenue and expense allocations are to make sense, the resulting balance sheet accruals should also make sense, that is, be justifiable as real assets or liabilities.

3. While there are still glaring exceptions, time value of money is increasingly being factored into accounting standards where there is a significant delay in receipt or payment of future benefits or outlays. A notable recent example is accounting for loan impairments (see Chapter 18). That time is money is a reality that can no longer be ignored in modern business, and therefore in accounting for business activities.

These changes have been taking place in an uneven, piecemeal fashion—so much so that it may be difficult to detect a coherent theory connecting the existing mix of inconsistent standards and practices. Such major inconsistencies are the unfortunate but inevitable consequence of an issue-by-issue standard-setting process during a period of rapid change. Nevertheless, if one stands back and considers the cumulative results of accounting standards put in place in recent years, it is possible to detect some sense of a developing, evolving accounting theory. (We will examine potential implications of these and other changes for the theory of accounting in Part III, in light of the specific issues of accounting and accounting standards examined in Part II.)

It is suggested that the above described developments indicate that an evolution has progressed to the point that financial reporting may no longer be adequately described as "historical cost-matching accounting." A better working label may be simply "accrual accounting." The 1985 FASB Concepts Statement No. 6 describes accrual accounting thus:

> Accrual accounting attempts to record the financial effects on an entity of transactions and other events and circumstances that have cash consequences for the entity in the periods in which those transactions, events, and circumstances occur rather than only in the periods in which cash is received or paid by the entity. (par. 139)

This is an open-ended definition. It has no precise meaning because it depends critically on the period in which the effects of transactions, events and circumstances may be deemed to "occur" and the FASB Concepts Statement gives no guidance on how this is to be determined. But it is not a meaningless concept. Its recognition of events and circumstances beyond traditional completed "transactions" represents an extension of the Paton and Littleton model. As well, it accurately depicts an evolving accounting system. One might visualize accrual accounting as a continuum of possibilities, beginning with slight modifications of cash basis accounting and expanding outwards towards the recognition of rights and obligations earlier and earlier in the business process of commitment and realizability. As such, "accrual accounting" may only be understood through reference to the development of accounting practices and standards within a particular society at a particular time—which is the subject of Part II.

THE CANADIAN EXPERIENCE

The issues, pressures and directions outlined above, have been framed largely in terms of the U.S. environment because it is there that they have, for the more part, originated. They apply generally to Canada as well, however, although there are some important differences. These relate to the authoritative framework for Canadian GAAP, and to distinctions of perspective that are rooted in differences in Canada's economic and political environment.

Authoritative Framework

There has been the same transition of professional statements in Canada as in the U.S. In the early years, they merely represented guidance to good practice; now they have become mandatory standards. The mechanism of the evolution, however, has been somewhat different. From an early date, the Canadian profession followed the practice of making recommendations with respect to financial disclosure provisions to the legislature concerned, whenever companies acts were in the process of revision. The most noteworthy success along these lines came in 1953 when the revised Ontario Corporations Act incorporated the provisions of the first CICA bulletin on financial disclosure virtually in their entirety. As companies acts in the other provinces and in the federal jurisdiction came under review, there was a tendency to follow suit, so that the legal impact of the CICA recommendations on financial disclosure spread through much of the country.

The next step in the transition from generally accepted principles to accounting standards came in 1968 when the *CICA Handbook* was adopted. The CICA on its own volition (but following the precedent established by the AICPA council) adopted a recommendation that any departure from its recommendations should be specifically disclosed in notes to the financial statements or, failing that, in the auditor's report. The obvious intention was to encourage adherence to CICA recommendations. The CICA committee, however, did not suggest or intend that other accounting practices, if properly supported, could not be considered acceptable, and disclosure of a departure from the recommendations was not considered tantamount to qualification of the audit report.

This understanding was upset by forces outside the profession. In 1972, the securities administrators of several Canadian provinces announced National Policy No. 27. This stated that the securities administrators would regard *CICA Handbook* pronouncements as "generally accepted accounting principles" as that term was used in either securities legislation or companies legislation. Although the policy statement did not say that CICA pronouncements were the *only* generally accepted accounting principles, commission actions have led to that conclusion. In a number of cases, commissions have required compliance with CICA recommendations. As a result of this policy, the *CICA Handbook* has, in effect, taken on the status of law with respect to most filings under the jurisdiction of provincial securities acts. In 1975, the same result was brought about with respect to annual financial statements for companies under federal jurisdiction, as a result of the inclusion of a reference to the *CICA Handbook* in the regulations to the Canada Business Corporations Act. Many provinces have also amended their companies legislation to this effect.

The Standard-Setting Process

The CICA standard-setting authority has undergone several restructurings over the years, and a further restructuring is contemplated as this is written. In 1968, membership in the committee was broadened to include representatives of other bodies interested in financial reporting, and the former series of bulletins was transformed into a "Handbook" with a logically organized structure. In 1973 the accounting committee was split off from auditing and organized into sections so as to enlarge the number of subjects that could be under consideration at any one time. Steps were also taken to obtain broader exposure of proposed committee recommendations before their adoption was voted upon.

In 1991, the committee was renamed the Accounting Standards Board and trimmed from twenty-two to thirteen members. As well, projects began to be assigned to task forces, rather than board sections. A task force has the responsibility, with CICA staff support, to see a project through from initial research and development of a statement of principles, to preparation of an exposure draft, and ultimately, preparation of a final Handbook standard. Task forces report to the board at each stage, and the board assumes responsibility for issuing exposure drafts and final standards.

This task force approach has several advantages. Members of a task force can be selected on the basis of their interest and expertise in the particular subject area. It also provides continuity through the two to three year average term of a project. Such continuity cannot be provided by board members themselves who serve three-year terms with one-third membership turnover each year. In sum, the restructuring was aimed at improving productivity and, at the same time, reducing somewhat the burden on board members. Board and task force members continue to be unpaid volunteers.

Thus the standard-setting authority and process is quite different from that of the FASB. This reflects a smaller standard-setting budget. As well, it is notable that the function of standard setting is still under the sponsorship of the Chartered Accountancy profession, rather than being carried on under the aegis of an independent foundation as is the case in the United States.

In 1986 an independent commission was set up by the CICA to investigate concerns of a widening gap between the public expectations of auditing and what auditors were accomplishing. The commission's report (known as the *Macdonald Report*) was issued in 1988.[29] It confirmed the existence of an expectations gap and concluded that it was attributable in significant part to accounting. Thus a number of its recommendations were aimed at strengthening accounting standards and the standard-setting process.

One of its recommendations was that more timely guidance be provided on new and emerging issues in order to "nip bad accounting practice in the bud." As a result the Emerging Issues Committee (EIC), modelled on the Emerging Issues Task Force in the United States, was established in 1989 to provide quick practical advice on such issues. It is not permitted to take positions that would modify or conflict with *CICA Handbook* standards. It has issued more than ninety consensus views (called "abstracts"). Many of these abstracts have been interpretations of existing Handbook standards. This interpretive role may be even more important in Canada than in the U.S. given the less detailed nature of *CICA Handbook* recommendations.

These abstracts do not have the formal authority of Handbook recommendations. In practice, however, they carry considerable weight because they represent the consensus view of a group of respected, knowledgeable accountants. Thus it is very difficult for companies to justify alternative treatments. The Ontario Securities Commission has made the authority of EIC abstracts even stronger by requiring reporting issuers to comply with them.

Securities regulators in Canada, led by the dominant Ontario Securities Commission, have been content for the most part to leave accounting standard setting to the CICA. But the commissions exert a significant influence on GAAP in practice as a result of their reviews of issuer financial statements in prospectuses and annual reports, and the positions they take on accounting and disclosure matters that come to their attention as a result of these reviews. Commissions' staff are in a position to see emerging problems and the Chief Accountant of the Ontario Securities Commission brings many issues to the EIC as an observer member of that committee.

Until the early 1990s, banks and insurance companies had not been subject to *CICA Handbook* standards and GAAP. Not-for-profit organizations were brought within GAAP and the *CICA Handbook* in 1989 (see Chapter 27). These three classes of entities have characteristics that set them apart, and their accounting and disclosure practices have differed in significant respects from the normal accrual accounting of other types of organizations. They have all now been brought within the ambit of the *CICA Handbook* and GAAP [30] but the struggle to account appropriately for their unique characteristics is ongoing. Life insurance companies have been permitted to continue certain of their past practices pending further study.

In 1992 new federal legislation governing financial institutions, including banks, insurance companies and trust and loan companies, provides the Superintendent of Financial Institutions, Canada, with the authority to specify accounting standards for public reporting that could contravene GAAP.[31] At present the superintendent's requirements simply supplement GAAP and do not conflict with CICA standards.

Overall, the *CICA Handbook* standards and accounting standard-setting process have served Canada well. But in recent years a number of problems have arisen principally as a result of changes in the external business and investment environment. These have necessitated that the CICA standard-setting process and its objectives be re-thought—and the Task Force on Standard Setting was commissioned to examine these issues. [32]

The relevant forces of change have included (1) the pull of the U.S. capital markets and accounting standards, and (2) the broader implications of the globalization of capital markets and the recognition of the need for internationally harmonized accounting standards. A brief discussion of each of these areas appears in the two following sections of this chapter. (A more in-depth analysis is deferred to Chapter 26, Part III.) There are other important considerations as well. These include:

- the complexity of the modern business and investment environments. Can a volunteer board be expected to cope with these matters on a timely and effective basis?

- the interdependence and representativeness of a standard-setting process that is directed by one professional accounting organization (the CICA). It has been found necessary in the U.S. and in a number of other countries to establish accounting standard-setting authorities that are independent of professional accounting organizations.

- the much increased cost of accounting standard setting and its necessary supporting activities (research, monitoring, compliance and education). Who should bear these costs?

These issues and their implications for accounting standard setting in Canada may be best addressed in light of the analysis of accounting issues in Part II. Thus their further consideration is deferred to a separate chapter on the establishment of accounting standards in Part III.

CANADA–U.S. GAAP DIFFERENCES

Not surprisingly, Canadian accounting standards have tended to cover much the same subjects as those of the U.S. More often than not American standards have addressed issues before the CICA, and these standards have frequently been the basis for the development of Canadian recommendations. In 1988 the *CICA Handbook* adopted a brief statement of financial statement concepts which is generally modelled on the much more in-depth FASB Concepts Statements.[33] As well, there has been a measure of consultation between the standard-setting bodies. Thus, it may be expected that Canadian standards will have arrived at similar conclusions to those of the U.S. For the most part, this has been the case, but as we will see in Part II, there are some notable areas of difference.

Some have expressed concern at this, feeling that, in view of the linkages between the U.S. and Canadian capital markets, Canadian financial reporting practice should not be different from that of the United States. This sentiment is generally supported by a number of Canadian companies registered with the SEC, who dislike being forced by the SEC to reconcile differences between Canadian accounting practices followed in their financial statements and corresponding U.S. practices. A survey by the Ontario Securities Commission found that Canadian SEC registrants have been reporting a significant number of differences with material impacts on reported earnings. [34]

Certainly, the reason for having an independent Canadian standard-setting function in the first place must be that the Canadian environment is different and that it is important to ensure that the Canadian context is factored into Canadian standards. As well, consistent with the informational value school claim that accounting standard selection has a social value context, it may be noted that U.S. accounting standards are influenced by different political and vested-interest balancing considerations than those of Canada. Thus they may be expected to arrive at some answers that would not be considered appropriate within the Canadian context.[35]

These issues are assuming increasing practical importance in a globally competitive marketplace. Some Canadian SEC registrants, wholly owned subsidiaries of U.S. companies and multinational companies complain about the burden of keeping track of U.S. and Canadian differences. This has put a heavy onus on the CICA to justify differences.

A related issue has been the intrusion of U.S. accounting standards and practices into Canadian GAAP. Questions often arise as to whether a particular U.S. standard or practice may be accepted as being in accordance with Canadian GAAP. Historically, U.S. literature and practice have been recognized as authoritative support for Canadian practice in cases where there is no conflict with a Canadian standard. Not infrequently a U.S. standard may be issued on a subject where there is no Canadian standard. The question then arises whether the U.S. accounting can be accepted as Canadian GAAP, even though it may have no precedent in Canadian practice. This has given rise to some questions in the past.[36] Presumably, such questions should now be referred to the EIC.

The Canadian recommendations are normally shorter and less detailed than the American. In part this simply reflects the fact that the all-volunteer Canadian board does not have the resources to explore every subject to the same extent as does the FASB. In part also, it reflects a Canadian policy to leave more room for the exercise of professional judgment as to the best accounting in each situation. There are both advantages and disadvantages to the policy. It can be easier to see the framework of principles behind more generally stated recommendations; also, it is certainly easier to adapt to special circumstances if one is not confined by a rigid set of rules. On the other hand, professional judgment cannot operate in a vacuum. There needs to be a clear depiction of the concepts underlying an accounting standard as a basis for consistent professional judgment. The problem has been that accounting standards are often compromises with no clear conceptual base, so that they may be open to different interpretations failing highly specified rules. (This may, in part, explain why the EIC has issued over ninety abstracts in less than ten years.)

THE INTERNATIONAL DIMENSION

Accounting standards have developed within national settings, influenced by local laws and institutions. But users of financial reports are not confined within national borders. Capital flows across borders, and investing and capital funding decisions have become more international in scope. Since investors worldwide need to compare and make sense of prospectuses and annual reports of companies from different parts of the world, common standards of financial reporting are highly desirable. Multinational companies, for their part, would find their financial reporting function less costly and less of a nuisance if the accounting results of all their operating units could be kept on the same basis.

The International Accounting Standards Committee (IASC) was established in 1973. It was initially sponsored by professional accounting bodies in nine countries, including Canada. Its members now include professional accounting bodies in over one hundred countries. The internationalization of the accounting profession was carried a step further with the formation of the International Federation of Accountants (IFAC) in 1977. The two bodies agreed to cooperate and, in effect, the IASC acts as the delegated representative of the IFAC with respect to accounting standards. The purpose of the IASC has been "to formulate and publish in the public interest, accounting standards to be observed in the presentation of financial statements and to promote their worldwide acceptance and observance."[37] The actual standard-setting business of the IASC is conducted by a board that has sixteen members, of which Canada is one.

By the late 1980s the IASC had developed an impressive number of standards on a wide range of issues. Its standards were not, however, having much influence in reducing differences between countries. There are substantial difficulties in the way of international harmonization. Different countries have different tax and corporations legislation and different forms of government regulation. There is a question as to the degree to which local accounting standards *should* change to meet an international harmonization goal. Standards designed for use in well-developed, public capital markets may be considered less valuable where there is no such market. Standard setters and securities regulators from countries with open capital markets, including Canada, the U.S., and the UK press for international standards that reflect best estimate accruals and broad disclosures, that is, that would codify prevalent practices in their countries. On the other hand, countries like Germany and Japan have accounting systems in place that emphasize discretionary conservatism and limited disclosures; naturally they have been concerned that the IASC has been moving too fast in adopting the "Anglo-Saxon" accounting model. Through the 1980s, international standards reflected a degree of compromise. Considerable flexibility was allowed in order to avoid losing the support of important constituent members. But the globalization of capital markets, and pressures from investor and preparer interests, have been changing this. The International Organization of Securities Commissions (IOSCO) has been strongly encouraging an effort to improve international accounting standards to better facilitate comparability between financial statements of international companies domiciled in different countries. The SEC and the Ontario and Quebec Securities Commissions are influential members of IOSCO. In the late 1980s, the IASC carried out an ambitious program to substantially reduce accounting alternatives in existing standards. In 1995, an agreement was made with IOSCO under which the IASC would carry out a work program to further develop its standards so that they would comprise an agreed-upon comprehensive core of standards. In return, IOSCO agreed that upon completion of this program, it would consider endorsing IASC standards for cross-border capital raising and for listing of securities in all global markets. IASC standards would then become the international benchmark standards.

The IASC completed the last project in its work program at the end of 1998. While this is a very significant accomplishment, it now remains for IOSCO to carry out a review of the body of standards to determine whether they merit endorsement.

The IASC activities have recently been expanded to include a separate committee to issue interpretations of the IASC standards.

The IASC is presently reviewing its purposes, strategies and processes. Changes in the international environment have placed a serious strain on its resources. It has relied extensively on the work of volunteers, and some question whether this can continue to provide an effective base. It also sees its purposes to be changing. Its main role has been as a harmonizer in developing international standards, largely by selecting from among existing national standards. It views its role going forward as more of an initiator of new ideas and a coordinator of national interests—with a goal of bringing about convergence between national and global accounting standards.

A strategy working party was formed and has issued a discussion paper. [38] It has proposed a bicameral structure:

- The group that would develop standards would be representative of, and financed by, leading national standard-setting bodies. One of the perceived problems with the current IASC Board is that its national representatives are professional accounting bodies, which in many countries do not have the responsibility for national standard setting. In particular, in the U.S., the sponsoring body is the American Institute of Certified Public Accountants (AICPA) which has no control over the actions of the FASB or the SEC, the bodies that set the standards in the U.S.

- This standard-setting group would be accountable to a board that would be broadly representative of national, business, regulatory and user interests.

These proposals are highly controversial. Some are concerned that the oversight board would result in delaying and over-politicizing the process, and that it might result in inferior compromised standards. Others are concerned that too much power not be given to the standard-setting group, which may be expected to be dominated by major developed countries.

In the meantime, Canadian securities regulators face difficult decisions with regards to the appropriate accounting standards requirements for foreign companies issuing securities in Canadian markets. On the one hand, there is concern to protect Canadian investor interests by ensuring that they have financial information on these companies that meet Canadian GAAP standards. On the other hand, there are increasing demands from some sectors of the investment community for better access to foreign investment opportunities. They claim that foreign companies will be discouraged from participating in Canadian capital markets if they have to adjust financial statements prepared according to their local standards to meet Canadian requirements.[39]

Some recent research has indicated that international companies may be less likely to list their shares on exchanges with more stringent requirements.[40] Others warn against simplistic interpretation of such findings. The chairperson of the FASB has taken issue with those who would relax U.S. accounting and reporting requirements for foreign companies that want access to the U.S. capital markets. He expressed some concern that the development of international standards based on compromise may degenerate into "a search for the lowest common denominator," and may serve to inhibit real improvement in financial reporting.[41]

The chief impact of international standards on Canadian standards to date has probably resulted from the interaction that occurs when the same subject is being studied by both Canadian and international standard setters. There has also been some impetus for the CICA Accounting Standards Board to consider significant areas of difference. Overall, the impact of IASC standards on Canadian practice has not been very noticeable. The Toronto Stock Exchange has encouraged listed companies either to state that their accounting policies comply with international standards or to disclose differences therefrom. Relatively few companies are doing so. But this is changing as IASC standards command a greater influence around the world. The Canadian standard-setting function is in the unenviable position of trying to harmonize its standards with both those of the FASB and IASC. This is particularly difficult because FASB and IASC standards currently differ in some significant respects. [42]

Other international bodies have come into existence in recent years. One of these is the "G4+1," which includes representatives of standard-setting bodies in Australia, Canada, New Zealand, the UK and the U.S., plus the IASC as an observer. These bodies share very similar conceptual frameworks and objectives of accounting information. The G4+1 has carried out a number of studies seeking common solutions to financial reporting issues. Canada is also a member of the AFTA Committee for Co-operation in Financial Reporting Matters. ("AFTA" refers to the American Free Trade Association, and members of this committee are Canada, Chile, Mexico and the U.S.) Thus far, its efforts have largely related to efforts at identifying and understanding differences in accounting between these countries. [43]

SUMMARY

Financial accounting entered the twentieth century with little in way of a theoretical basis. The balance sheet was considered the most important statement and was considered a valuation statement. The use of cost as a starting point for valuation, however, was supported on practical grounds.

The introduction of income tax created greater interest in the measurement of income and gave a practical impetus to the development of the realization rule for revenue recognition and to the recognition of depreciation accounting. Certain government agencies and the

New York Stock Exchange also made efforts to improve the standard of financial reporting. The depression of the 1930s and the formation of the Securities and Exchange Commission provided a considerably stronger impetus for improvement. The accounting profession was faced with the need to become more forceful in its ideas and actions or risk subordination to government regulation of financial reporting.

By this time the groundwork had been laid for a more comprehensive theory of financial accounting based on the deemed primacy of the income statement. The theory that came to be known as "historical cost accounting" was expounded in academic writing which proved to be highly influential in shaping accounting practice. Essential elements of this theory were the propositions (1) that accounting should be based on price aggregates resulting from bargained exchanges, and (2) that income can be appropriately measured by recognizing revenue when realized and matching incurred costs with recognized revenue. It was thought that matching could be achieved largely by means of attaching costs to cost objects, such as inventory or fixed assets, that are written off as sold or consumed. Although no statement of the historical cost theory was officially adopted by the practising profession at the time, the influence of the theory permeated the detailed recommendations of professional committees from the 1930s onward.

The profession attempted to make progress through a program of gradualism. It was believed that a comprehensive set of rules for accounting would be far too inflexible to meet the variety of circumstances encountered in business, and that generally suitable accounting practices would emerge, with a little guidance from the profession, by a process of general acceptance. A standing Committee on Accounting Procedure was established in 1939 in the United States to make recommendations designed to achieve greater uniformity in practice. Similar bodies were established subsequently in Canada and in a number of other countries.

The American experience was that such bodies tended to get caught up in individual issues and, perhaps, did not "see the forest for the trees." There were, as a result, recurring cries for more attention to be paid to the theoretical basis of financial reporting. It was found also that a committee recommendation did *not* automatically become generally accepted. Some recommendations were stretched so far beyond their intent as to produce absurd results. Because of this, recommendations tended to become more detailed and more categorical. External authority was added to professional recommendations through required disclosure of departures from them and through SEC support. Finally, the Financial Accounting Standards Board was set up independent of the profession in 1973.

The FASB initially placed great importance on establishing a conceptual framework as a basis from which to reason forward in developing accounting standards. But the results, despite its prodigious efforts, were somewhat disappointing because it was unable to achieve consensus on fundamental recognition and measurement concepts.

Meanwhile, leading accounting academics were becoming increasingly critical of traditional cost-matching accounting. They began to abandon interest in accounting as a measurement discipline, concluding that efforts to determine accounting earnings were doomed to be an unproductive, largely arbitrary exercise. Instead, they embraced an "informational value" perspective which originated in efficient markets literature emanating from finance economics. It is concerned with the idea that under efficient market conditions share prices may be expected to respond to reported accounting numbers if those numbers have information value to investors. This has led to a concentration on empirical research on share price effects of accounting income and other disclosures. Two other compatible schools of thought developed—agency theory which, as applied to financial accounting, is concerned with judging accounting in terms of its ability to facilitate efficient contracting between management and capital providers, and positive accounting theory, which holds that the selection of accounting principles and practices is a social choice issue involving trade-offs between affected interests.

This informational value perspective has undoubtedly added an important dimension to accounting thought. The significant trend toward expanded disclosures in financial reports over the past twenty years or so is consistent with this thinking. However, in tending to de-emphasize accounting as a measurement discipline, it has left a void. Many international accountants accept that the Paton and Littleton model of the 1940s has significant deficiencies, but, rather than discard it, they are inclined to try to adapt, expand, or even re-engineer parts of the model to fit modern needs. They believe that sound financial accounting can be reasoned forward from basic economic principles and rational decision models. Certainly the FASB, and accounting standard-setting bodies in Canada and other countries, continue to work to try to improve accounting standards within this context.

Traditional financial accounting is being severely challenged by developments arising out of what has been described as the "information age." In particular, revolutionary advances in information technology and capital markets are changing the portfolio management strategies of investors and the ways in which transactions and business arrangements are constructed to transfer and share risks. The implications for financial accounting are profound. Certainly they indicate no abatement in the need for fair and reliable financial reporting, with expanded disclosures, of financial position and results of operations of business and not-for-profit entities.

The FASB has responded to these challenges with a profusion of standards, interpretations and guidance on particular issues. The inevitable consequence of an issue-by-issue standard-setting process is inconsistencies within GAAP, and it may seem difficult to detect any coherent underlying theory. But some significant evolutionary changes in accounting theory are becoming evident from recent standards. A broadening concept of accrual accounting is extending and displacing certain of the elements of classical historical cost accounting theory—in particular, expanded concepts of exchange transactions and for recognition of future events, as well as greater prominence given to market realizability, to the time value of money, and to the need to justify balance sheet residuals of the income measurement process as true "assets" and "liabilities."

Canadian experience has not been as turbulent as the American, although it has been subject to the same general influences and challenges. Standard setting has remained under the wing of the chartered accountancy profession, and its authority has been reinforced by official recognition under securities and corporations legislation. There has been the same tendency to proliferation of standards (not surprisingly since the same economic influences exist in Canada as in the United States). Canadian GAAP continue to be very similar to those of the U.S., although there is a long list of potentially significant differences on particular issues. Some have been questioning whether they all reflect real differences in circumstances and have information value.

While the CICA standard-setting process has served Canada well, a number of significant problems are now becoming apparent. At the root of these problems is the pull of U.S. capital markets and accounting standards, and broader pressures for international harmonization, as well as issues of independence, complexity of accounting issues, and the cost of standard setting. The CICA Task Force on Standard Setting has made some recommendations for changes in the focus and process of accounting standard setting in Canada, but at the time of writing, it is not clear what will ultimately emerge.

The International Accounting Standards Committee was founded in 1973 and is now sponsored by over one hundred countries. The committee has made significant progress in developing a comprehensive body of standards and in reducing the alternatives permitted in those standards.

REFERENCES

1   M. Chatfield, *A History of Accounting Thought*, rev. ed. (Huntington, N.Y.: Robert E. Krieger Publishing Co., 1977), pp. 1–7.

2   R.K. Storey, "Revenue Realization, Going Concern and Measurement of Income," *The Accounting Review*, April 1959, pp. 232–38.

3   These and other shortcomings were denounced in W.Z. Ripley, *Main Street and Wall Street* (Boston: Little, Brown & Co., 1927).

4   The six principles, in brief, were:

   • Unrealized profit should not be credited to income.

   • Charges belonging in income account should not be charged to capital surplus.

   • Surplus of a subsidiary earned before acquisition is not part of consolidated earned surplus.

   • When a company has acquired its own stock and not cancelled it, dividends on that stock do not form part of its income.

   • Amounts receivable from officers, employees, and affiliated companies must be shown separately in the balance sheet.

   • If stock is issued to acquire property and some stock is donated back to the company, the par value of the stock issued cannot be treated as cost of the property nor can proceeds from the resale of the stock be credited to surplus.

   The full text of these principles may be found in American Institute of Accountants, Committee on Accounting Procedure, *Restatement and Revision of Accounting Research Bulletins*, Accounting Research Bulletin No. 43 (New York: AIA, 1953).

5   American Institute of Accountants, Committee on Accounting Procedure, *General Introduction and Rules Formerly Adopted*, Accounting Research Bulletin No. 1 (New York: AIA, 1939), subsequently consolidated in Introduction and Chapter 1 of *Restatement and Revision of Accounting Research Bulletins*, Accounting Research Bulletin No. 43 (New York: AIA, 1953).

6   W.A. Paton and A.C. Littleton, *An Introduction to Corporate Accounting Standards*, Monograph No. 3 (AAA, 1940), p. ix.

7   The resulting publications were M. Moonitz, *The Basic Postulates of Accounting*, Accounting Research Study No. 1 (New York: AICPA, 1961) and R.T. Sprouse and M. Moonitz, *A Tentative Set of Broad Accounting Principles for Business Enterprises*, Accounting Research Study No. 3 (New York: AICPA, 1962).

8   AICPA, APB, *Statement by the Accounting Principles Board*, APB Statement No. 1 (New York: AICPA, 1962).

9   P. Grady, *Inventory of Generally Accepted Accounting Principles for Business Enterprises*, Accounting Research Study No. 7 (New York: AICPA, 1965).

10   AICPA, APB, *Basic Concepts and Accounting Principles Underlying Financial Statements of Business Enterprises*, APB Statement No. 4 (New York: AICPA, 1970).

11   See, for example, P.B.W. Miller and R.J. Redding, *The FASB: The People, the Process and the Politics*, 2nd ed. (Homewood, Illinois: Irwin, 1988).

12   A.L. Thomas, *The Allocation Problem in Financial Accounting Theory*, Studies in Accounting Research No. 3 (AAA, 1969) and *The Allocation Problem: Part Two*, Studies in Accounting Research No. 9 (AAA, 1974).

13   Market Efficiency has been defined simply in these terms: "A Securities Market is efficient if security prices 'fully reflect' the information available." E. Fama, "Efficient Capital Markets: A Preview of Theory and Empirical work," *Journal of Finance*, May 1970, pp. 383–417. A good discussion of the concept of market efficiency appears in W.H. Beaver, *Financial Reporting: An Accounting Revolution*, 2nd ed. (Englewood Cliffs, N.J.: Prentice-Hall, 1989), chap. 6. He expands the definition to frame it in terms of universal access to information, as follows: "The market is efficient with respect to some specified information system, if and only if, security prices act *as if* everyone observes the information system" (p. 135).

14   Ibid., chap. 5.

15   See B. Lev, "On the Usefulness of Earnings and Earnings Research: Lessons and Directions from Two Decades of Empirical Research," *Journal of Accounting Research*, 1989 Supplement, pp. 153–92.

16   Beaver briefly analyzed research on market efficiency anomalies in *Financial Reporting: An Accounting Revolution*, pp. 142–44. For a recent study that presents and analyses evidence of certain apparent market efficiency anomalies, see V.L. Bernard and J.K. Thomas, "Evidence that Stock Prices Do Not Reflect the Implications of Current Earnings for Future Earnings," *Journal of Accounting and Economics*, 1990, pp. 305–40.

17   For an overview of the theory and some analysis of its general implications for financial accounting, see D.B. Thornton, "A Look at Agency Theory for the Novice," *CA Magazine*, November 1984, pp. 90–97 and January 1985, pp. 93–100, and sources cited therein.

18   For an elaboration of agency and positive accounting ideas, see *Ethics and Positive Accounting Theory* (Waterloo: University of Waterloo Centre for Accounting Ethics, 1995).

19   See R.L. Watts and J.L. Zimmerman, *Positive Accounting Theory* (Englewood Cliffs, N.J.: Prentice-Hall, 1986). For an overview of the theory and empirical evidence and criticisms of it, see L.A. Boland and I.M. Gordon, "Practice in a Positive Light," *CA Magazine*, July 1992, pp. 37–41.

20   This was a concern expressed by the chairperson of the FASB. See D.R. Beresford, "The Need for More Relevant Research," *Status Report*, FASB Financial Accounting series, May 31, 1991, pp. 2–3.

21 W.H. Beaver described it this way: ". . . the information-oriented researchers perceived that the theory of income measurement under imperfect and incomplete markets had reached a point of diminishing returns . . ." See "Challenges in Accounting Education," *Issues in Accounting Education*, Fall 1992, p. 139.

22 G.J. Staubus, "The Market Simulation Theory of Accounting Measurement," *Accounting and Business Research*, Spring 1986, p. 118.

23 D. Solomons, *Making Accounting Policy: The Quest for Credibility in Financial Reporting* (New York: Oxford University Press, 1986), p. 246.

24 R.K. Storey, "The Framework of Financial Accounting Concepts and Standards," in D.R. Carmichael, S.B. Lilien and M. Mellman, *Accountants' Handbook*, 7th ed. (New York: John Wiley and Sons, Inc, 1991), p. 1.40.

25 For an example of their theory, see G.A. Feltham and J.A. Ohlson, "Valuation and Clean Surplus Accounting for Operating and Financial Activities," *Contemporary Accounting Research*, Spring 1995, pp. 689–731.

26 For a summary and examples of this research and its implications, see G.D. Richardson, "Signals and Signs," *CA Magazine,* March 1998, pp. 37–39.

27 See, for example, R.K. Elliott, "The Third Wave Breaks on the Shores of Accounting," *Accounting Horizons*, June 1992, pp. 61–85.

28 With respect to Canada, see *Report of the Commission to Study the Public's Expectations of Audits* (Toronto: The Canadian Institute of Chartered Accountants, 1988).

29 Ibid.

30 See CICA "Introduction to Accounting Recommendations," par. 2, *CICA Handbook* (Toronto: CICA).

31 The reporting implications of this legislation are well discussed in CICA, Assurance and Related Services Guideline, "Auditor's Report on the Financial Statements of Federally Regulated Financial Institutions," in *CICA Handbook*, AuG 14 (Toronto: CICA, 1992).

32 CICA, *CICA Task Force on Standard Setting—Final Report* (Toronto: CICA, 1998).

33 CICA, "Financial Statement Concepts," *CICA Handbook,* Section 1000 (Toronto: CICA).

34 Office of the Chief Accountant of the Ontario Securities Commission, *Study of Differences Between Canadian and United States Generally Accepted Accounting Principles* (Toronto: Ontario Securities Commission, 1993).

35 See, for example, the brief discussion of Canadian/U.S. differences in the CICA Research Study, *Corporate Reporting: Its Future Evolution* (Toronto: CICA, 1980), chap. 10.

36 Difficulties arose, for example, when the FASB adopted a standard on interest capitalization (Standard No. 34) in 1989. It introduced some highly pragmatic rules that conflicted with normal Canadian practice at that time, and there was considerable debate whether the standard could be adopted in whole or in part as Canadian GAAP. A more recent illustration is the complex set of FASB rules for accounting for derivatives and hedges (Standard No. 133), many of which have no precedent in Canadian practice.

37 See IASC, *Preface to Statements of International Accounting Standards* (London: IASC, 1978), par. 2.

[38] Strategy Working Party of the International Accounting Standards Committee, *Shaping IASC for the Future* (London: IASC, 1998).

[39] Canadian securities regulators have adopted a policy that allows very large foreign multinational companies to issue existing securities in Canada on the basis of financial information filed with certain major foreign exchanges without reconciling their financial statements to Canadian GAAP. See National Policy No. 53, *Foreign Issues Prospectus and Continuous Disclosure Systems*, 1994.

[40] See, for example, G.C. Biddle and S.M. Saudagaran, "Foreign Stock Listings: Benefits, Costs, and the Acounting Policy Dilemma," *Accounting Horizons*, September 1991, pp. 69–80.

[41] D.R. Beresford, "Internationalization of Financial Reporting Standards: A Challenge to the Profession," *Status Report*, FASB Accounting Series, November 1992, pp. 9–10.

[42] See FASB, *The IASC–U.S. Comparison Project: A Report on the Similarities and Differences Between IASC Standards and U.S. GAAP*, ed. C. Bloomer (Norwalk: FASB, 1996).

[43] See *Significant Differences in GAAP in Canada, Chile, Mexico and the United States: An Analysis of Accounting Pronouncements as of June 1998* (Toronto: CICA, 1998).

2

ACCOUNTING STANDARDS TODAY

ACCRUAL ACCOUNTING

Part I has described how the need for communication through financial reports evolved in the middle of the nineteenth century and how accountants and managements groped their way over a long period toward forms of reports acceptable for that purpose. The notions of capital maintenance and going concern provided some guidance in dealing with the difficult questions of valuation of assets and liabilities, but an articulated theory of financial reporting did not emerge until well on in the twentieth century. From the 1930s onward the application of the theory has developed and been continuously modified to meet new situations.

The objective of Part II of this book is to describe today's accounting standards and explain how they fit within accrual accounting concepts that have evolved from historical cost accounting theory. This chapter begins with a recapitulation of the basic tenets. We then consider some gaps in the theory and areas that need clarification. The groundwork is then laid for succeeding chapters. Since the basic data for accrual accounting are provided by exchange transactions, we analyze and classify the types of transactions engaged in by an entity and other events that may affect its financial position and results of operations. We then discuss the nature of the issues that must be addressed in the course of taking the input provided by transactions and other events, and interpreting it so as to arrive at the figures for assets, liabilities, revenues, and expenses that appear in financial reports.

ELEMENTS OF ACCRUAL ACCOUNTING

The theory that developed in the 1930s and has been refined and extended in succeeding decades rests on the following assumptions:

- Measurement of results of operations for a period has been accepted as the primary goal of financial reports. Observation of reactions of the capital markets and other interested parties to accounting reports suggests that information as to income earned in a period has particular significance for investment and other decisions. Balance sheet information has, however, assumed increased importance as an indicator of financial feasibility, risks assumed, and quality of earnings.

- Assets and liabilities are measured initially at their cost or transaction value, which is generally the amount of cash or fair value of assets or liabilities exchanged therefor. They are carried at those cost or transaction values until such time as an accountable event occurs. Accountable events include the transfer to others of the risks and rewards of ownership, settlement of a liability, the use of an asset in a productive activity, and changes in certain external conditions. Accountable changes in external conditions include situations in which the values of assets have fallen below amounts currently realizable or recoverable from future operations.

- Revenue from productive activity is to be recognized as being earned when (1) reasonable assurance exists as to the amount of consideration to be received, and (2) the commitments undertaken by the enterprise in return for the revenue have been substantially fulfilled. Assets recorded when revenue is recognized are measured at estimated realizable value.

- Costs incurred for assets for use in a productive activity are to be recognized as expenses as the usefulness of the asset expires. When an item of inventory is sold, it is obvious that its usefulness to the vendor has expired and expense (the cost of goods sold) must be recognized. In other cases the expense recognition point is far from obvious. The problem of expense recognition has often been expressed as the problem of "matching" costs with revenues. This description is appropriate to recognition of cost of goods sold and other sales-related costs but not to the treatment of other types of costs. Hence the more general term "expense recognition" is preferable.

- Windfalls (the receipt of unearned benefits) are recognized only when realized or virtually certain of realization. Casualties (costs or losses incurred without compensating benefit) are recognized generally when they become probable and can be measured with reasonable reliability, although there has recently been some acceptance of the notion that probability should enter into the measurement of an obligation rather than being considered a condition for its recognition.

This accounting system may be broadly described as "transaction-based accounting" since exchange transactions provide the source figures for assets, liabilities, revenues, and expenses. This orientation to bargained transactions provides the foundation for the claim that the system is "objective." It is a reasonable assumption that a bargained transaction between an entity and outsiders represents good evidence of the value of the good or service received by the entity at or near the time of the transaction.

In the course of the accounting, however, initially recorded figures are subject to a variety of adjustments.[1] Various costing methods may be used to calculate the total cost of an asset manufactured internally. Depreciation or amortization is recorded to allow for gradual consumption of the utility of assets held for use over a period of time. A judgment-based allowance for uncollectible amounts reduces the transaction figure for accounts receivable. Write-downs of other assets under the rule of "lower of cost and market" are made in various circumstances. As well, liabilities for future expenditures may require accrual when the contracted exchange takes place over an extended period of time, as when employees provide their services to an entity in return for future pensions. Such judgment-based adjustments and accruals must be taken into account in assessing the overall objectivity of the transactions-based system.

In addition, the gain in objectivity is attained at the expense of some loss of completeness. Because revenue recognition rules are tied to external transactions, an enterprise generally cannot take account of the value added by its productive activity before such revenue transactions occur. The development of capital markets has enabled transactions-based figures in the form of representative market values to serve as an objective basis for earlier recognition of certain financial instruments. But other improvements in the well-being of an enterprise cannot be recognized. For example, the discovery of mineral or oil and gas reserves by a company in the extractive industries, the natural growth of timber reserves in a forest products company, or internally generated "goodwill," are not taken into account under the transactions-based accrual system. Finally, historical cost theory, as customarily applied, does not allow for the fact that the value of the currency in which transactions are measured changes over time as a result of inflation or deflation.

UNCLEAR AREAS

There are certain matters on which accounting theorists have not reached a consensus and which have not been extensively addressed by authoritative accounting recommendations. To begin with, financial reports deal with the resources and operations of a specific reporting entity. We need to ask what criteria determine how we define the entity that is to report. Second, we have noted that one of the most important objectives of accounting is to measure income. If we are going to measure income, it would seem we need to have a clear idea of what income is. Finally, it may be useful to examine what is, or ought to be, the impact of uncertainty on accounting measurements, since uncertainty about the future is pervasive in the real world.

The Concept of the Accounting Entity

The core function of financial reporting is to report wealth and changes in wealth over time. We cannot begin to account, however, unless we have a clear definition of the entity for which we are accounting. There are two aspects to the question of entity. The first is that of defining the boundaries of the entity itself. What criteria are there to tell us what resources and what transactions belong to the entity furnishing a financial report? The second aspect is that of determining what is the focus of interest in the report. To use the common expression, what is the bottom line? If we aim to report income and wealth, we must ask whose income and whose wealth we are reporting.

The Boundaries of an Entity

In a modern society, wealth is owned by individuals, business partnerships or associations, business corporations, nonprofit organizations, and governments. It would be natural to look to ownership as the determining factor in defining an accounting entity. But, while ownership is an important factor, it is not the only factor. We have little difficulty in visualizing Kovac's Fruit Store as an entity in its own right apart from the Kovac family. The essential point, in this example, is that we can recognize the fruit store as a separate function or activity. The transactions in which it engages—the buying and selling of fruit, the payment of wages and other operating expenses—can be distinguished from the personal transactions of Mr. Kovac. This capability of separation is the key to an accounting entity. Economic resources and obligations can be identified with the entity, and we can define boundaries so that records may be designed to keep track of flows of resources across its boundaries.

To a considerable degree, the choice of accounting entity is a matter of convenience. In fact, there may be overlaps in defined entities. While a group of companies is treated as one entity in consolidated financial statements, a single corporation within the group can also be reported on as an entity, and its separate statements are relied upon for income tax, credit agreements, or other purposes.

Flexibility in choice of entity is obviously desirable for special purposes. One would expect some theory, however, to tell us how the entity should be defined for the purpose of financial reports to the public. Unfortunately, no such theory exists in complete form. The question has been tackled in the context of consolidation accounting for business enterprises. Until very recently, little attention had been paid to not-for-profit organizations. The problem of entity definition is still more acute in government, where an activity may be treated as a separate entity simply because of the structure of the legislation authorizing it.

The Focus of Interest in Financial Reports

We must also ask what is to be the primary focus of interest in entity financial statements. Consider Kovac's Fruit Store. The person primarily interested in its financial statements will be Mr. Kovac himself. (Of course, his banker, and perhaps others, will be interested as well.) He will want to know details about his investment in the business and what has been its profit and cash flow. In other words, the person who has most at stake in the success of the business is the proprietor, and his interest is "proprietary." Consequently, the focus of interest in the income statement will be the profit accruing to the proprietor after all other claims on revenues are satisfied. The focus of interest in the balance sheet will be the residual left over after all claims on assets are deducted.

Compare Kovac's Fruit Store with a large multinational corporation. Many people besides its shareholders have a major stake in the activities and well-being of such a corporation. Its management and employees often have a more enduring stake than an individual small shareholder, who may buy in today and sell out in six months. The financial interest of bondholders, bankers, and other creditors may be almost as great as that of the shareholders and usually will be concentrated in fewer hands. The taxation authorities of several countries have a stake in the corporation's activities and its reporting of them. The communities in which its plants are located have a stake in whether it operates in a safe and socially responsible fashion. Realistically, the shareholders of such a corporation are only one of a number of constituencies that have an interest in the corporation.

In the light of this, many accounting theorists think that a nonproprietary ("entity") view should govern financial reporting. Under the so-called "entity" viewpoint, the principal accounting focus of interest is upon the financial resources entrusted to the entity itself and the changes in them over the accounting period, not upon the interests of the various constituencies. Reporting the distribution of entity operating income among its claimants, including the income tax authorities, various classes of creditors, and the several classes of shareholders, is considered a secondary activity.

The point of view taken—proprietary or entity—can affect the way the accounting is performed, including the form of presentation of the financial statements.[2] Some examples are as follows:

- A corporation may receive a government subsidy that induces it to undertake investment in plant that it would not otherwise undertake. From a proprietary point of view, the investment involved is the net amount after the subsidy, and that net amount should be recorded as the cost of the plant. From an entity point of view, the assets under the corporation's control have been increased by a plant with a certain gross cost, and arguably that is what it should account for.

- From a proprietary point of view, interest paid on debt and income taxes represent expenses because they reduce the income available for the proprietary interest. From an entity point of view, taxes and interest represent distributions of its income from operations like dividends, rather than expenses required to earn entity income.

- A corporation may purchase or redeem outstanding debt securities for less or more than their carrying value on the books. From the proprietary point of view, a gain or loss has been realized that forms part of the reported income for the proprietor(s). From an entity point of view, there is no gain or loss but merely a rearrangement of claims upon it.

By and large, today's accounting standards for business enterprises adopt the proprietary point of view. This may be partly attributable to the evolution of accounting from the position where its primary objective was a report to owners. The emphasis is reinforced by the major influence upon accounting of regulation in the interests of full and fair disclosure to the capital markets. As a practical matter the financial information prepared on the proprietary basis and suitable for security holders is sufficiently transparent that it may not result in any significant loss of financial information that it is relevant to other stakeholders.

Nonbusiness organizations are a different matter. As noted, there exists no strong theory to indicate what ought to be the boundaries of the reporting entity for them.

The Meaning of Income in Accounting

Most of us have some idea of income in our minds and may feel no strong need for explanation of the concept. Simply from the derivation of the word, one might think that income is something that comes in and hence should be observable (perhaps as a flow of cash). A little thought, however, serves to dispel that notion. If a person receives cash on loan, he or she does not have income. On the other hand, the salary received in cash by an employee may well be less than his or her income because of various deductions made by the employer or because some income is received as nonmonetary benefits or perks.

Thus the concept of income is more complicated than might appear at first sight. Indeed, we have different implicit concepts for income from labour and income from capital. If you buy a fixed-term annuity, for example, you divide the annuity payments that come in into two portions, one representing return of the capital invested and the remainder considered to be income. On the other hand, if you invest time and effort in a professional education such as medicine, you do not divide the subsequent net proceeds from your practice into a portion representing return of your investment and a remainder representing income. The moral of this is that income is subject to different definitions which may depend on perceived purposes and effects and what is considered to be feasible of reasonable measurement. Thus, if we say that income determination is a primary objective of accounting, we ought to make explicit what we mean by the term *income*. In logic, it has to be defined before we can measure it.

Formal attempts to define income, especially in the works of economic theorists, almost always involve some notion of capital maintenance. A popular ideal definition of income for a business (adapted from economic theory) is that income for a period is that amount that can be distributed by a business and yet leave it as well off at the end of the period as it was at the beginning. There are severe problems in making this ideal operational.

- In the first place, well-offness is a subjective concept. It depends upon expectations as to the future and expectations can change with time. If one's resources have not changed but expectations as to future cash inflows from them have changed over a period, it must be decided whether that change in expectations is or is not part of the income to be measured for the period.

- In any event, expectations in themselves cannot be directly measured. Any practical measurement of income must look for objective surrogates for expectations. An obvious choice of surrogate lies in market values for resources and claims upon them. Since market values are based on collective expectations, any income measurement based on market values necessarily includes the effect of changes in collective expectations.

- Market values for assets that represent claims to money consist of the present value of the future money claims discounted at a market rate of interest. Market values of other assets, being largely based on expectations of future cash flows, are also affected indirectly by going rates of interest. The general level of interest rates can change over a period. Hence, some changes in market values over a period will be attributable to changes in interest rates rather than to changes in the assets' collective ability to generate cash flows. If income measurement is based on market values, it will necessarily include the impact of changing interest rates. Some people, at least, have preferred a definition of income based solely on changes in prospects for distributable cash flows, exclusive of the impact of changing interest rates.

- It is common knowledge that the value of a business as a whole will be different from the sum of the values of its identifiable assets less liabilities. If one wishes a measure of well-offness, it is the value of the business as a whole that is relevant (except when sale of the net assets individually would bring more than the business, in which case the business ought to be liquidated). Any estimation of the value of a business as a going concern is considered too subjective for purposes of income measurement. The customary recourse—that is, valuing the assets and liabilities individually to arrive at a measure of well-offness—means that the measurement of income is less than ideal. (This problem is known as the "aggregation problem" and will be encountered repeatedly in accounting contexts.)

- Measures of net resources, and hence income, are necessarily made in monetary terms so that one can arrive at one total representing a whole portfolio of different kinds of resources. But the real value of money—that is, its purchasing power or command over goods—itself changes over time. Thus, increases in values in monetary terms over a period do not necessarily correspond with real increases in well-offness. Some believe that income ought to be defined in real terms. That is to say, any measure of income based on nominal valuations in money ought to be deflated or inflated to compensate for changes in the purchasing power of money. Measurement of changes in purchasing power, however, itself creates a number of difficult conceptual and practical problems.

The problems in measurement of what might be considered an ideal definition of income have been such that the ideal has clearly not been influential in the development of accounting practice. The traditional historical cost accounting theory did not go much beyond the idea that income is the excess of revenues over the expenses of earning those revenues. To measure income for a period one must decide what are the revenues for a period and the expenses applicable to those revenues. The result of this focus was to define income in terms of conventions for recognizing revenues and expenses that had little relationship to the ideal concept of income. This pragmatic approach leaves room for much confusion as to what really are the essential concepts of income, revenue, and expense.

In the first place, there has been confusion as to when income emerges in the course of business activity. Under the ancient venture accounting tradition, there was no income until the venture was completed. Later, when business became more continuous in character, Adam Smith, the father of classical economics, suggested that income should be considered to arise upon realization through sale. In contrast, the valuation approach to accounting for ordinary nineteenth century business enterprise stipulated no such requirement for income recognition.

The emphasis on realization through the mid twentieth century was primarily supported by considerations of convenience and income tax advantage, rather than by theoretical considerations. George O. May wrote:

> Manifestly, when a laborious process of manufacture and sale culminates in the delivery of the product at a profit, that profit is not attributable, except conventionally, to the moment when the sale or delivery occurred.[3]

It was recognized that realization is not an essential characteristic of accounting income but may be abandoned when considered appropriate. A striking example was provided by the treatment of long-term construction contracts. It was generally conceded that significant distortion in reported income can occur if income recognition is left until the date of completion of such a contract, so that the realization principle could be disregarded in this case.

The traditional revenue and expense approach, which was applied with a certain predisposition to smooth out volatility, resulted in the deferral of various debits and credits to be reflected in income of future years. Because of the articulation of the balance sheet and income statement, these deferred items were necessarily treated as assets or liabilities for amortization on more or less arbitrary bases. This attracted criticism. Just what was the real nature of these assets and liabilities? It was often hard to say and because of this they were dubbed by one writer as "what-you-may-call-its"—a fair description.[4] This revenue and expense orientation thus de-emphasized the balance sheet leaving it to consist of residuals from the income measurement process.

With the development of the FASB conceptual framework, a contrasting approach was developed under the name of the "Asset and Liability viewpoint."[5] Under this viewpoint no cost may be deferred unless there is strong evidence that the asset recorded probably will result in receipt of a benefit in the future. Similarly no credit may be deferred unless there is good evidence it represents a probable future sacrifice. This increased concern to justify the balance sheet effects has helped to place some boundaries around the recognition of income. In recent years the emphasis has been on recording income as the risks and benefits of the good or service are transferred to the buyer, subject to having reasonable assurance as to the amount of consideration to be received and the amount of costs to be incurred to earn the income. But this has not provided a clear concept of income. Rather, income measurement continues to be a function of a mix of concepts, conventions and assumptions for recognizing and measuring different types of revenues, expenses, assets and liabilities, and it is not clear that either the "Revenue and Expense" or "Asset and Liability" viewpoints is predominant in accounting standards and practice.

In short, although people may have some implicit notions about income, the lack of an agreed definition has encouraged inconsistent accounting and has made it difficult to arrive at cohesive accounting standards.

Accounting Conflicts Stemming from Uncertainty

The results of transactions must be classified—asset or expense, revenue or liability. The essence of assets and liabilities rests in the fact that they represent expectations of future benefit or future sacrifice. Accountants must take a position in the face of uncertain outcomes.

As noted above, in the early period of the historical cost model there was an attempt to hide behind the revenue-expense matching objective to defer debits or credits to future periods without much attention to whether they met asset or liability tests of expected future benefit or sacrifice. Although this is largely in the past, there continue to be significant differences in accountants' attitudes on just how the ideal of matching should be reconciled with uncertainty. Some have instinctively wished to minimize uncertainty and would "expense all costs when incurred unless they can be clearly shown to have future benefit."[6] Others strive to carry forward all costs that may be associated with future revenues in order to effect a full matching of cost efforts with revenue accomplishments.

As a result, some standards seem to be greatly influenced by the matching ideal while others are very much influenced by the desire to minimize the use of estimates and allocations by sticking as close as possible to cash accounting. Capitalization of interest standards and the concentration in the United States on full absorption inventory costing in preference to direct costing represent victories for deferral and allocation. Standards requiring immediate expensing of research costs (and in the U.S., development costs also) because of lack of assurance as to commercial results is an example of the "stick-to-cash" attitude. In Canada, deferral of development costs is permitted only if several tests are met indicating a considerable degree of certainty as to future benefit. The debate in the late 1970s and early 1980s over "successful efforts" versus "full cost" accounting for deferred exploration and development costs in the oil and gas industry well illustrated the divergence of views.

Conflicts stemming from uncertainty have been most directly evident in determining asset recoverable values, future cost liabilities (such as for pensions and warranties), and windfall gains and losses. In each such situation the accountant must select a single number from a potentially wide range of possible outcomes.[7] Should accounting aim for best estimates at the risk of considerable error, or should it bias standards toward more conservative possibilities? The development of accounting standards has suffered from a tug-of-war between these two points of view. CICA and FASB concepts statements acknowledge that there is a place for the convention of conservatism in attempting to ensure that net assets and income are not overstated, but that it should not encompass their deliberate understatement.[8] These concept statements evidence a significant change in philosophy from that of discretionary conservatism that is still apparent in some countries, notably Germany and Japan. Nevertheless, although there has been some evolution in thinking over the years, conservative attitudes and practices are still quite common in North America.

There has been a distinct trend in recent years for standards to call for "best estimate" measures of liabilities and asset recoverability allowances, but there continues to be strong resistance in some quarters to the volatility that can result therefrom. Thus we have seen, for example, the development of pension accounting requirements that provide for best estimate-based liability estimates while allowing deferred income recognition of experience gains and losses.

The concept of "best estimates" is not well defined. In some cases it may be interpreted to mean expected value (that is, the probability-weighted average of possible outcomes), while in others it may be seen to mean mode (that is, most likely value) or some other measure of central tendency. The differences between these measures can be substantial in particular circumstances. Few accounting standards even acknowledge these issues. In practice best estimates may range from verging on intentional understatement of net assets (for example, some pension liability estimates that are influenced by traditional actuarial funding assumptions) to being very unconservative (for example, some provisions for contingent losses—see analysis in Chapter 8).

Representative markets will, of course, impound available information on possible outcomes into a single market price at a point in time. Such a price can be expected to reflect discounts or premiums for various risks since investors tend to be risk averse. Some believe that the objective of financial accounting should be to reflect market-equivalent values, and that fair value surrogates should be developed when representative market values do not exist. They might look to finance literature and capital markets thinking on interest rates, risks and contingency pricing models for guidance in so doing.

In sum, although there has been a noticeable movement over the years toward best estimate-based accounting in the face of uncertainty, it is far from consistently applied and the concept itself has not been clearly defined.

Disclosure of uncertainty and risk has attracted considerable attention in the past few years. The mathematics of statistics tell us that a number purporting to represent a probabilistic distribution may be considered to have two essential elements—a measure of its central tendency (expected value, mode etc.) and some indication of the dispersion or variability about that measure. Thus a full and fair presentation of assets and liabilities under uncertainty should include information on the resulting variability. This is a difficult task because it will rarely be susceptible of useful quantification but may mostly have to be expressed in some blend of numerical and qualitative terms. Several standards in the past few years, more in the U.S. than in Canada, have attempted to provide more meaningful disclosures of uncertainties and exposures to risk, but these efforts must be considered to be still at an early stage of development.

The Matching Problem

The core of accrual accounting is the idea that bargained transaction amounts can be attributed to periods so as to measure income. The idea of matching is customarily expressed in terms of matching costs with recognized revenues. It should be appreciated, however, that revenue recognition conventions are merely devices for attributing revenues to accounting periods. Thus, a more general description of accrual accounting is that it measures income for a period by attributing (matching) both revenue transactions and cost transactions to periods.

There are problems in attributing one event to a time period or associating events with each other. Four types of attribution may be identified.[9]

- One-to-one attribution. There is little or no problem in associating single events or transactions when one can observe the link between them. For example, if one buys a single pig, there is no problem in saying that the cost of the pig is $X, the observed purchase price. If one sells the same pig for $Y, it is similarly obvious what the revenue from the sale is. It logically follows that the profit from the sale of the pig is $Y minus $X.

- Many-to-one attribution. There is also little problem in attributing many subjects or events to one object if there is a connection directly traceable between each of the subjects and the object. For example, if one can observe materials being cut for a product and labour being expended in its fabrication, we can say that the materials and labour are attributable to the product and its cost cannot be less than the sum of the costs of the material and labour.

- One-to-many attribution. There is, however, a severe problem in attributing one subject to several objects. Suppose the pig purchased for $X is butchered and the various parts sold. It is well known that there is no way to demonstrate what is the cost of a side of bacon or any other product of that pig. There is one "joint" cost of all the meat and other products obtained from the pig, and there is no way to prove what is the cost of a particular portion of the meat. There are several conventions that can be devised for attributing a cost. For example, if the pig weighed 200 kilograms at purchase, one could say that the cost per kilogram is $X/200 and if a piece of bacon weighs 2 kilograms, its cost is $2X/200. The "joint costing" approach would attribute cost to a particular portion of meat by saying that its cost is determined by computing the percentage of its sale price to the total sale price of all the products from the pig and applying that percentage to the total cost of the pig. A "by-product costing" approach would assume that the cost of the less important products was equal to the revenue realizable from them, leaving a net cost to be assigned to the other, more important products on some other basis. The point is that one or more of these conventions may seem to be reasonable in particular circumstances but none can be proven to be correct to the exclusion of any other approach.

- Many-to-many attribution. It must be obvious that if the partitioning of one subject among many objects is impossible to measure, the attribution of many subjects jointly to many objects will be equally impossible to demonstrate. As an example, factory overhead will consist of many types of cost—indirect labour, power, heat, repairs and maintenance, depreciation, and so on. Attribution of these costs to the many products produced by the factory requires costing conventions. Many conventions may look more or less reasonable; none can be proved to be superior to any competitor.

The problem is fundamental and pervasive. One-to-many and many-to-many attributions are present in all situations in which inputs are combined to produce outputs over time. The objective of any active business operation is to combine various inputs (labour, materials, plant and equipment, management expertise, etc.) in such a way that the sum of the revenue inflows will exceed the sum of the cost outflows to yield an income return for the effort, expertise and capital invested. The individual inputs lose their identity in the process of being transformed into products or services. We cannot see how much of the cost of a particular input, say, an item of equipment, is attributable to a particular item of output. About all we can say nonarbitrarily is that the item of equipment contributed, along with many other inputs, to the generation of revenues over its useful life.

The central question is whether the matching objective is so flawed that it can serve no useful purpose and should be discarded for something else. There would seem to be good reasons for believing that cost and revenue allocations can be useful, and that there is no obviously better "something else" with which to replace them. There is a basic economic premise at the root of the matching objective. It is that one has to make economic sacrifices to achieve economic benefits. An economic good is defined by the fact that its production required a past sacrifice and by the expectation that it will yield future satisfactions. The past sacrifice may be interpreted as its cost, while the future satisfactions are the economic benefits expected to result from its consumption, use or sale. This concept of an economic good is at the heart of the accepted definition of an "asset" in financial accounting. An "asset" is defined in terms of expected future economic benefits to result from past transactions or events. The very important point here is that the fundamental premise of sacrifices to achieve benefits is consistent not only with a revenue-matching objective, but also with the concept of assets (and liabilities, being the inverse of assets).

Let us examine the attribution problem from the perspective of the asset-liability view. An item of equipment purchased to be used as a necessary part of a revenue-generating process clearly qualifies as an asset. It has resulted from a past transaction and it embodies expected future benefits through its use in helping to generate future revenues. But which future revenues are attributable to it? Future revenues will result from a multiplicity of factors, some of which have occurred in the past (such as know how, inventory on hand, fixed assets, etc.) and some of which must occur in the future (such as future employee efforts, selling efforts and economic conditions). In other words, future revenues will be the result of the interaction of past and future factors, and we are faced with the many-to-many attribution problem. The accepted definition of "assets" establishes certain necessary conditions in stipulating that future benefits should result from past events or transactions. But it does not establish sufficient conditions for recognition and measurement purposes because it does not provide a basis for linking past events with particular future economic benefits. Thus, we seem to end up with the same attribution problem whether we approach it from a revenue-expense matching or an asset-liability perspective, within current accepted concepts.

Under cost-based accrual accounting inputs are recorded at historical cost to be expensed as they are considered to be used in a revenue-generating process (subject to write-downs for impairment). Some have argued that the attribution problem would be resolved if input assets were carried at current values. The difficulty with this is that an operating activity transforms inputs into outputs, and it is the output revenues that are the object of the activity. Under incomplete and imperfect markets there is no necessary connection between changes in the current cost or realizable value of input assets and the future revenues to be generated from the sale of future outputs.

In summary, there would seem to be no ready answers to the fundamental attribution problem. Present day accrual accounting encompasses various conventions for allocating costs and revenues to reporting periods. These imply various presumptions as to relationships between past events and future benefits expectations. It has been observed that "an accrual can be viewed as a form of forecast about the future,"[10] and that ultimately the value of a particular accrual may lie in the information it provides as to management's expectations. A depreciation provision that reflects managements' careful evaluation of probable asset useful lives and future pattern of revenue benefits may be presumed to have more information and income measurement value than one that simply presents "boilerplate" allocation rules. Thus it seems important to understand allocation bases and the presumptions they contain with respect to the relations between the past and future. Standards should at least aim to eliminate what is not rational (for example, intertemporal allocations that do not incorporate reasonable assumptions as to the time value of money). They might also strive to require internal consistency. Reasoning forward within the rational expectations thinking of modern economics and capital markets finance may hold out some promise for improving the information value of accrual accounting.[11] It is important to develop disclosures that better portray the future expectations that may be implicit in accruals and the extent of economic indeterminacy.

ACCRUAL ACCOUNTING THEORY AND GENERALLY ACCEPTED ACCOUNTING PRINCIPLES

The discussion so far in this chapter might be taken to suggest that problems in accounting all result from limitations, short comings or ambiguities in cost-based accrual accounting theory. Things are not quite as simple as that.

It will be recalled from Chapter 4 that accounting standard-setting bodies have developed from a tradition that holds that the ultimate test of accounting policies is general acceptance. While their pronouncements now establish requirements, rather than being mere recommendations or statements of preference, the tradition of the importance of general acceptance remains powerful. For one thing, authoritative standards are still far from comprehensive in their coverage. The *CICA Handbook* holds that when a matter is not covered by a CICA recommendation, generally accepted accounting principles include practices and procedures that are "accepted by virtue of their use in similar circumstances by a significant number of entities in Canada."[12] We have also observed in Chapter 4 the "positive accounting theory" presumption that accounting standards and practice reflect trade-offs between those parties whose interests are affected by accounting outcomes. Certainly management and various external stakeholder interests can bring significant pressures to bear on the development of standards and practice. These pressures are seldom based on an enlightened appreciation of accrual accounting theory. Thus it is far from clear that accounting theory will necessarily be the controlling influence on a proposed standard.

The present situation is that the test for the use of an accounting method ostensibly remains general acceptance rather than conformity with fundamental financial accounting theory. The term "general acceptance" is used in audit reports and has been adopted by legislation or regulation governing financial reporting. Use of the term has been a source of some confusion. In a new situation there may be no generally accepted principle. Failing a clearly applicable standard, if different entities adopt different policies, there may be no basis for determining which is generally accepted. (In practice, it is not impossible that all will be considered generally accepted.) On the other hand, a recommendation of a standard-setting body is automatically deemed generally accepted to the exclusion of other practices, no matter how unpopular that recommendation may be.

This situation has provided part of the reason why some have urged the development of an explicit conceptual framework for financial reporting—so that the theory we have can be made as clear as possible. This, it is hoped, would facilitate a more enlightened understanding of the concept of "general acceptance" and, perhaps, reduce the danger that accounting will be too much influenced by short-term self-interest and political pressures.

THE IMPLEMENTATION OF ACCRUAL ACCOUNTING

As has been indicated, accrual accounting relies, in the first instance, upon transactions to furnish measurements of assets, liabilities, revenues, and expenses. It also relies mainly upon transactions to signal when assets, liabilities, revenues, and expenses are to be recognized. Transactions with outsiders, however, are not sufficient to provide information on all changes in financial position that ought to be recorded. Production activity and market conditions may have significant impact on the well-being of an entity in advance of transactions with outsiders. Other events, some fortuitous, may also have significant impact on entity resources. The following tabulation is an attempt to provide a classification of the transactions, events and activities that result in changes in entity resources.[13] This classification provides a background for discussion in the remainder of Part II of this book.

I. Transactions and events that give rise to inflows or outflows of assets and liabilities to or from the entity.

A. Exchange transactions with other parties in which each party receives and gives up something of value.

1. Operating transactions. These consist of purchases, sales, and barters of goods or services (including services rendered for wages) in the normal course of active operations. In purchase and sale transactions there is generally an active party who performs by delivering goods or services and a passive party whose obligation is simply to make payment.

2. Intercorporate investment transactions. These consist of purchases and sales of investments acquired to obtain control or significant influence over the strategic operating, financing and investing activities of an enterprise.

3. Portfolio investment transactions. These consist of purchases or sales of financial instruments acquired for passive investment income or hedging purposes, where the purchaser does not acquire a right to manage or significantly influence the investee. Also included is the receipt of investment returns in the form of interest, etc.

4. Financing transactions. These are borrowings from or loans to others. The essential element of a financing transaction is the promise of one party to pay cash to the other in future.

5. Settlement transactions. These are collections or repayments flowing from obligations arising out of other transactions or events. In most cases they consist of payment of cash in satisfaction of a previously incurred obligation.

6. Advance payments. These are payments made as full or partial settlement of obligations not yet incurred.

B. Nonreciprocal transfers to or from other parties.

1. Capital transactions. These are contributions or withdrawals of capital by owners, or payments of a return (e.g. dividends) to owners.

2. Other. These include taxes, grants, gifts, thefts, fines, settlements of threatened or actual lawsuits, and so on.

II. Transactions and events that give rise to changes in assets and liabilities held.

A. Productive activities. These include manufacturing, processing, distribution, packaging, trading, growing things, extraction of minerals, and service activities of all kinds. They also include the discovery of valuable assets where discovery activities are planned.

B. Changes in values of assets and liabilities as a result of market, foreign exchange or interest rate conditions.

III. Completely fortuitous events involving creation or destruction of assets or changes in their value while held.

A. Windfalls. These consist of completely unplanned accessions of assets or changes in the value of assets owned. An example would be discovery of valuable gravel deposits under land acquired for other purposes.

B. Casualties. These are fortuitous losses of assets or incurrences of liabilities. Examples would include loss or damage to assets from fire, flood, earthquakes, etc.

Inspection of this classification of transactions, events and activities helps one to visualize the problems in representing them faithfully in financial reports. Those problems will be of two sorts—determining when to recognize them and choosing appropriate measurement bases.

- In general, these problems are least difficult in exchange transactions (category I, A, above) particularly when the exchange involves an immediate payment of cash. Exchange events are usually readily observable, and the consideration usually provides an appropriate measurement basis. There are, however, some significant exceptions. Measurement issues arise in respect of nonmonetary exchanges, basket or compound instrument purchases (in allocating the consideration between the component parts), and when payment is delayed (raising questions of discounting to reflect the time value of money and related risks). There can be both recognition and measurement problems in recording continuous (as opposed to discrete) exchanges. An example of a continuous transaction is the commitment by an entity to provide future pensions in return for current employee services.

- Nonreciprocal transfers (category I, B) may or may not be easy to account for. Capital transactions are straightforward if the transfer is in cash. Depending on their particular circumstances, other nonreciprocal transfers may present problems in timing of recognition as well as measurement.

- In analyzing activities giving rise to changes in assets and liabilities held (category II), inputs to a productive process should be distinguished from financial instruments and other assets held for sale. As noted earlier, there are major conceptual and practical difficulties in determining when to recognize the results of productive activities and how to allocate input asset transaction values to those activities, because inputs interact in combination to produce outputs. Cost-based accrual principles do not recognize changes in the value of input assets on hand except to reflect write-downs for impairment. But financial instruments and other assets held for sale represent separable rights to future benefits and thus are more readily amenable, in theory at least, to individual valuation. Changes in their values may be easy to measure when representative markets exist. Often, however, there will not be complete and representative markets for a particular asset. As well, whether or not a change in market conditions (for example, a change in the market value of a financial instrument) should be recognized is commonly argued to depend on management's intent to trade or hold for the long term. Applying a management intent condition gives rise to both conceptual and practical difficulties.

- Windfalls (category III, A) may be difficult to measure. It may also be difficult to know when to recognize them.

- Casualties (category III, B) are likely to be easy to recognize because the loss is observable. Measurement, however, may involve a difficult valuation process.

The broad issues may be summarized as follows:

- What determines when transactions and other events should receive initial recognition in the accounts? In other words, when does an accountable event occur? How are these events to be measured for the purpose of recording them? These matters are the subject of Chapter 6.

- What are the conditions that justify recognition of revenue and gains? These issues are discussed in Chapter 7.

- On what basis are costs incurred to be recognized as expenses? This question resolves itself into two subquestions.

  - Where a productive process has occurred so that the assets acquired in transactions with outside parties (including labour and overhead services among assets acquired) have been transformed or partially transformed into a product or service suitable for sale, how shall the costs of the factors of production be assigned or aggregated into the cost of the work in process or finished product?

  - On what basis shall the cost of product or other costs not treated as product costs be recognized as expenses because their capacity for contribution to future revenue has expired or partially expired?

    We must also consider how expenses should be recognized when obligations are undertaken in present operations that will probably result in costs in future periods. Chapter 8 deals with expense and loss recognition and measurement issues.

It will be observed that these broad decision areas are expressed largely in terms of an entity that manufactures, processes, or distributes a product or service. Traditional accounting theory has concentrated largely on this type of entity and has had little to say about nonbusiness organizations. Some types of financial institutions, extractive companies, real estate companies, investment enterprises, brokers, and traders all have accounting problems for which the traditional historical cost model has somewhat limited relevance. As a result, the accounting practices of these entities tended to develop through general acceptance within the industries themselves. In recent years more attention has been paid to their unique aspects but it is still difficult to fit some of their accounting practices within any recognized conceptual framework of accounting.

Chapter 9 covers certain balance sheet issues. Succeeding chapters deal with recognition and measurement matters specific to certain common types of assets, obligations, and circumstances, as well as the statement of changes in financial position and presentation and disclosure issues. Since current GAAP ignore price changes of assets and liabilities while held (except for certain financial instruments), theories of accounting for changes in the values of assets and liabilities are reserved for separate discussions in Chapter 24. Chapters 27 and 28 deal with questions relating to the unique features of not-for-profit organizations and governments.

SUMMARY

The outlines of a historical cost-matching theory were clear by the 1930s. Since that time, it has evolved and developed into a broader theory of accrual accounting, to meet new situations. The elements are belief in the primary importance of income measurement but with an increased recognition of the complementary importance of the balance sheet asset and liability values; reliance on transaction value as the primary basis of reporting assets and liabilities but with an expanding recognition of accruals for accountable events; recognition of revenue as earned based on substantial completion of effort and reasonable assurance of collection of proceeds; and recognition of expense as benefits from costs incurred are consumed.

Certain substantive matters remain unclear within these broad outlines of accrual accounting. There are no clear criteria for defining the boundaries of the reporting entity. Nor is there agreement on the appropriate focus of interest as the basis for preparing financial statements. In business accounting, there tends to be a "proprietary" focus. Some writers feel that focus is inappropriate for large corporations because many parties besides shareholders have a stake in such an entity. The suggested alternative is the net resources entrusted to the corporation and resource flows before distributions to the various stakeholders.

A very serious deficiency is the lack of any clear accounting theory as to how income should be defined. For example, traditional accounting practice had stressed that income should be "realized," but the exceptions allowed prove that this is a rule of convenience rather than a fundamental characteristic of the concept of income. Increased concern to justify balance sheet effects has helped to place some boundaries around traditional revenue-expense matching practices, but it has not provided a clear concept of income. As a result, it has been difficult to achieve cohesive standards for the recognition of earned revenue and income.

Conflicts stemming from uncertainty lie at the root of many accounting issues. Some would try to avoid uncertainty problems by expensing all costs when incurred unless there is a very high degree of assurance of future benefit. Others adopt much less conservative attitudes and promote liberal approaches to balance sheet deferrals in order to achieve full cost matching with revenues. Accounting standards represent an inconsistent mix of these opposing philosophies, with some standards being much influenced by matching objectives and others by a desire to minimize the need for estimates. There has been a distinct trend over the years for accounting standards to call for best estimates as the basis for measuring asset recoverable values and future cost liabilities, but there continue to be strong pockets of resistance to the volatility that can result therefrom. Further, the concept of "best estimates" is not well defined so that it is open to a wide range of interpretation. It has come to be recognized that full and fair presentation of assets and liabilities under uncertainty requires supporting information on variability of estimates and exposure to risk. Standard setters have been attempting to develop more useful disclosures in this area but efforts to date are still at a fairly early stage.

Even without uncertainty, the assignment of results of transactions to accounting periods—the implementation of the matching objective—suffers from a severe problem. Frequently in accounting a single subject must be allocated among several objects. There is no single method for making such an allocation that can be shown to be superior to all possible competing methods. Allocation methods may seem intuitively reasonable, but the superiority of one over another cannot be scientifically demonstrated. Accounting standard setters are faced with a choice when allocations are required. Either no standard allocation method is provided, in which case there is a high probability that different entities will use different methods in similar circumstances; or a standard allocation method is adopted in the interests of promoting comparability, but it is inevitably arbitrary. Recent attention has focused on the information value of competing allocation methods and, in particular, on the information they may convey with respect to management's expectations within rational capital markets thinking.

The primary objective of this chapter has been to review the basic elements of accrual accounting theory as it has developed and discuss some major unclear areas. We should not, however, let this focus cause us to forget that accounting has developed within a tradition that places much importance on general acceptance. General acceptance may be defined only in part by reference to accounting theory. It is also much influenced by pragmatically developed practices and pressures from those affected by accounting outcomes. Thus there is an ambiguity in general acceptance and its relationship to accounting theory which tends to make the setting of consistent standards more difficult than it would otherwise be.

In the face of these theoretical and practical difficulties, the task of accounting standards has been to devise workable ways to implement the broad outlines of cost-based accrual theory. Standards must address these questions: When should transactions and other events first be recognized in the accounts and how should they be measured? When should revenue be recognized? How should costs incurred be attached to cost objects such as inventory or fixed assets? On what basis should expense be recognized as the benefits from such cost objects are consumed? How should expense be recognized for costs to be incurred in future because of obligations arising from present activities?

REFERENCES

[1]   An interesting historical cost interpretation of the role of exchange events as the essential data of accounting, and the partitioning of their cost measures, is contained in W.J. Schrader, R.E. Malcom, and J.J. Willingham, " A Partitioned Events View of Financial Reporting," *Accounting Horizons*, December 1988, pp. 10–20.

[2]   It is an oversimplification to talk of only two points of view with respect to the accounting entity. Meyer identified some eight different concepts in three broad categories. See P.E. Meyer, "The Accounting Entity," *Abacus*, December 1973, pp. 116–26. In addition, the significance of the fundamental view taken of the entity to the form of accounting to be adopted is often debatable. For examples of conflicting reasoning, compare opinions expressed in T.A. Lee, "The Accounting Entity Concept, Accounting Standards, and Inflation Accounting," *Accounting and Business Research*, Spring 1980, pp. 176–86, with those expressed in F.A. Bird, L.F. Davidson, and C.H. Smith, "Perceptions of External Accounting Transfers Under Entity and Proprietary Theory," *The Accounting Review*, April 1974, pp. 233–44. See also H.P. Hill *Accounting Principles for the Autonomous Corporate Entity* (Westport, CT: Quorum Books, A Division of Greenwood Press Inc., 1987).

[3]   G.O. May, *Financial Accounting: A Distillation of Experience* (New York: Macmillan Co., 1943; reprint ed., Houston: Scholars Book Co., 1972), p. 30.

[4]   R. T. Sprouse, "Accounting for What-You-May-Call-Its," *Journal of Accountancy*, October 1966, pp. 45–53.

[5]   For a more extended discussion of these two viewpoints, see FASB Discussion Memorandum *Conceptual Framework for Financial Accounting and Reporting: Elements of Financial Statements and Their Measurement* (Stamford: FASB, 1976), pp. 37–40.

[6]   H.W. Bevis, *Corporate Financial Reporting in a Competitive Economy* (New York: Macmillan Co., 1965), pp. 97–100.

7   W.H. Beaver illustrates the range of possible answers that could be derived in a simple setting involving an accounts receivable allowance for uncollectible accounts as part of his discussion of the role of accrual accounting from an informational perspective in *Financial Reporting: An Accounting Revolution*, 2nd ed. (Englewood Cliffs, N.J.: Prentice Hall, 1989), pp. 98–101.

8   See FASB, *Qualitative Characteristics of Accounting Information*, Statement of Financial Accounting Concepts No. 2 (Stamford: FASB, 1980) pars. 91–97; and CICA, "Financial Statement Concepts," *CICA Handbook*, Section 1000 (Toronto: CICA), par. 21(d).

9   The discussion in this section is stimulated by the published work of Arthur L. Thomas. His most complete exposition of the problems with matching is to be found in the series Studies in Accounting Research published by the American Accounting Association. His two studies (Nos. 3 and 9 in the series) are entitled *The Allocation Problem in Financial Accounting Theory* (AAA, 1969) and *The Allocation Problem: Part Two* (AAA, 1974). Anyone wishing a simpler expression of his ideas may see papers by him entitled "The FASB and the Allocation Fallacy," *Journal of Accountancy*, November 1975, pp. 65–68; "Matching: Up from Our Black Hole," in *Accounting for a Simplified Firm Owning Depreciable Assets: Seventeen Essays and a Synthesis Based on a Common Case*, ed. R.R. Sterling and A.L. Thomas (Houston: Scholars Book Co., 1979) pp. 11–33; and *Joint-Cost Allocation Revisited*, Occasional Paper No. 20 (Lancaster, England: International Centre for Research in Accounting, University of Lancaster, 1980). Exchanges of differing views between Thomas and two commentators are to be found in *The Accounting Review* (L.G. Eckel, "Arbitrary and Incorrigible Allocations," *The Accounting Review*, October 1976, pp. 764–77, and A.L. Thomas, "Arbitrary and Incorrigible Allocations: A Comment," *The Accounting Review*, January 1978, pp. 263–69), and in *CA Magazine* (S. Himmel, "Financial Allocations Justified," *CA Magazine*, October 1981, pp. 70–73 and A.L. Thomas, "Why Financial Allocations Can't Be Justified," *CA Magazine*, April 1982, pp. 28–32). Thomas' analysis led him to the conclusion that the matching concept is so incapable of implementation as to be meaningless. This is a more extreme conclusion than that reached by the authors of this book.

10   W.H. Beaver, *Financial Accounting: An Accounting Revolution*, p. 98.

11   See, for example, J.A. Milburn, *Incorporating the Time Value of Money Within Financial Accounting*, CICA Research Study (Toronto: CICA, 1988), chaps. 9–11.

12   CICA, "Financial Statement Concepts," *CICA Handbook*, Section 1000, pars. 60–61.

13   This classification scheme is adapted from L.T. Johnson and R.K. Storey, *Recognition in Financial Statements: Underlying Concepts and Practical Conventions* (Stamford: FASB, 1982), chap. 8.

INITIAL RECOGNITION AND MEASUREMENT

A first question in accounting is what constitutes an accountable event, that is, an event that should be recognized and measured in financial statements? Since accrual accounting is a transactions-based system, this question becomes first and foremost what constitutes a "transaction" that should be recognized in the accounts? Income accounting provides a set of rules for allocating revenues and expenses to accounting periods, and in the process these rules affect the recognition and measurement of various assets and liabilities. Transactions, however, often take place before it is appropriate to recognize any revenue or expense consequences. Accordingly, there must be accounting standards to govern the initial recognition and measurement of "accountable events" quite separate from standards for measuring income. Discussion of these initial standards is the purpose of this chapter.

INITIAL RECOGNITION OF TRANSACTIONS

An exchange transaction involves obtaining something from another party in return for giving something up. Some transactions may not be exchanges, that is, they may not be reciprocal, but may result in obtaining a benefit from another party without giving anything up (a gift or a grant, for example), or conversely may result in giving something up without obtaining any compensating benefit (taxes, fines, or a lawsuit settlement, for example). Transactions and market-determined prices resulting therefrom provide essential evidence of economic activities and values. It is the monetary values resulting from transactions, and the contractual arrangements within which they take place, that comprise the source data for financial accounting.

Initial recognition principles in financial accounting are concerned primarily with recording what has been acquired or sacrificed. Recognition issues focus on when these benefits or sacrifices should be reflected in the accounts. It is notable that "assets" and "liabilities" are defined in accounting in terms of the expected future economic benefits or sacrifices to result from past transactions and events. Accordingly, it is appropriate to consider initial recognition issues from the perspective of whether an asset has been acquired or liability incurred.

With respect to assets the historical tradition was that the accounts provided a summary of property owned. The emphasis on ownership provided a recognition rule—recognize a transaction at the time that legal title to the asset is obtained. In modern accounting the strict emphasis on legal position has been reduced in favour of applying a broader economic test, whether the entity has obtained control of resources from which future economic benefits may be obtained (see *CICA Handbook*, par. 1000.29–.31). From a user point of view, the important characteristic of an asset is not whether the entity has legal title to it, but whether the entity bears the risks and is in a position to reap the rewards of its possession.

In common situations this may be a readily observable physical act, such as when delivery of a good takes place. From the purchaser's point of view, it is generally convenient to recognize the transaction when a commodity is actually delivered because delivery provides firm evidence of the vendor's performance. That recognition point also makes sense since it is the time when the purchaser has the opportunity to use the commodity and should become accountable for it. From the vendor's point of view, the most convenient time to record a sale may be the point of shipment, although the product risk and reward may not pass until delivery. Nevertheless, the point of shipment from the plant may be a satisfactory practical basis for recognizing a sale transaction where risks related to delivery are determinable and are not major. In short, ideally the exchange should be recognized at the time of effective transfer of control, when the risk and reward associated with the thing are exchanged. In practice, the recognition point may be modified slightly from the ideal to facilitate convenient and consistent reporting.

A performance test can also be applied with respect to the typical acquisition of services. For example, if an independent consultant is engaged to render a report, a logical recognition point would be the delivery of the report. On the other hand, if the consulting process is a lengthy one that takes place in stages, the obligation is more appropriately recognized progressively as the service is rendered.

In simple financing and investment transactions by industrial, commercial, and service enterprises—for example, the issuance of debt securities or the making of loans—there is usually little lapse of time between the effective date of the contract and the transfer of funds. Therefore, although recording at the contract date is technically correct, a delay until cash is paid or received may be of little significance unless a reporting period-end intervenes. However, with the development of sophisticated financial instruments, including derivatives, that can have highly volatile values, it is important that the principle be clear. The principle is being formalized in the accounting standards in several jurisdictions. For example, the IASC has recently issued a standard that includes this provision: "An enterprise should recognize a financial asset or financial liability when, and only when, it becomes a party to the contractual provisions of the instrument."[1]

Capital transactions that are the subject of a contract, such as share capital issues or reductions, are likewise recorded when the entity becomes party to the contract. (In an unincorporated entity, where capital contributions and withdrawals are decided upon informally, recognition would be given only as they occur.) Dividends are recognized when they become an enforceable debt which will generally be at the declaration date.

Various types of taxes should be recognized not later than the date on which they become legally payable. Income tax accounting standards, however, require recognition of accrued taxes earlier as the obligation builds up (as is discussed in Chapter 16).

The above describes relatively straightforward recognition situations. In the modern world, however, complex interrelated contractual arrangements and transactions are common. These can give rise to difficult questions related to defining transactions, determining when control and relevant risks and benefits have been transferred and, from a liability stand-point, when an entity has become obligated as a result of past events. The following discussion identifies some key areas in which difficulties arise.

Future Expenditures

When an entity's current actions are likely to result in future expenditures, there is acceptance of the principle that these future expenditures should be realistically estimated and recognized as obligations currently. But major questions arise in attempting to implement this principle. These questions relate to determining what possible future events should be given current recognition, that is, should be considered to result from past events or transactions. Several situations may be identified:

- Ongoing operating activities may involve the receipt of goods or services in exchange for commitments that are likely to result in future expenditures. These commitments may be the result of explicit contracts, or legislative requirements, or they may be constructive obligations that can be inferred from society values or ethical or moral considerations. For example, the sale of goods may obligate the vendor to incur future expenditures to hon-our warranties if the goods should prove to be faulty. As another example, it is accepted that employers should recognize an obligation for future pensions to employees under a defined benefit plan as the employees provide their services, and that this might involve a constructive commitment to employees beyond what is legally enforceable. Also, enti-ties are now expected to recognize obligations for likely future expenditures to restore prop-erties for environmental damage caused by past operating activities. In each of these cases, an entity is expected to recognize a liability by anticipating probable future trans-actions/claims to result from its past activities. (The issues in making such provisions are addressed in Chapter 8, and with respect to pensions in Chapter 14.)

- On the other hand, more or less fortuitous nonreciprocal transfers, such as losses result-ing from earthquakes, fires, floods or lawsuits are generally not anticipated. Rather they are recognized in the period in which the underlying loss event takes place and it is probable that future expenditures or an impairment of existing assets will result. (These are known as contingent losses and are discussed in Chapter 8.)

- Traditional conditions for recognition of a liability are that future outcomes related to past events be probable and capable of reasonable estimation and measurement. There has been concern that inability to meet these conditions may be claimed on the merest pretext so as to minimize provisions for future costs and losses that are attributable to past events and transactions. This concern has crystallized into a conceptual issue in recent years. In particular, there is increasing acceptance in accounting for financial obligations that measurability and probability of future cash outlays resulting from contractual com-mitments should be treated as matters of measurement, *not* recognition.[2] To illustrate, if an enterprise has a contractual commitment to pay party A if party B should default on a loan, it has an obligation that it cannot avoid if an event that is beyond its control should occur. This obligation would have some price or value in the capital marketplace even if the probability of default is remote. In other words, the enterprise would have to pay some amount to have someone else assume this burden. That amount would depend on the likelihood of B's default and measurement uncertainty. The amount would be small if the likelihood of B's default is considered to be remote. Presumably, the amount would be based on the perceived probability of default multiplied by the expected outlay that would be required in the event of default.

The implications of this principle for recognition and measurement of contingent claims have not been thoroughly thought through and applied in financial accounting. The *CICA Handbook* Statement of Concepts continues to state that an item should be recognized if, "(a) the item has an appropriate basis of measurement and a reasonable estimate can be made of the amount involved; and (b) for items involving obtaining or giving up of future benefits, it is probable that benefits will be obtained or given up" (par. 1000.44). It goes on to note the inevitable consequence of this—that "it is possible that an item will meet the definition of an element [that is, meet the definition of a 'liability' or 'asset'] but still not be recognized in the financial statements because it is not probable that future economic benefits will be obtained or given up or because a reasonable estimate cannot be made of the amount involved" (par. 1000.45). This traditional conceptual framework condition would seem to be obsolete, at least in respect of financial obligations. (This issue is discussed further in respect of accounting for contingencies in Chapter 8.)

- In some cases there are difficulties in determining when a past event has taken place that should trigger the recognition of a future expenditure. For example, should an entity recognize a liability in respect of an offer to provide early retirement incentives to employees at the time management formulates the plan to make the offer, when it makes the offer, or only as employees accept the offer?[3] A conceptual study of the significance of future events for recognition and measurement in financial accounting was undertaken by the G4+1 group of standard setters, using case studies of a representative cross-section of situations.[4]

- In the past it had customarily been assumed that it was not important to recognize an obligation if it could be expected to give rise to an asset with reasonably offsetting cash flow impacts. As an example, it had been general practice for there to be no recognition of the expected future cost to settle an outstanding lawsuit if there were reasonable grounds for expecting that it would be covered by insurance. In reality, however, the liability claim and the asset recoverability are separate and distinct if the entity is responsible to meet the liability regardless of its recoverability from its insurer. In other words, there may be no legal right of offset. In recent years, increased emphasis on the balance sheet and on conveying more useful information on exposure to risks have led to redefining of criteria for netting assets and liabilities. (See further discussion at Chapter 9.)

Future Benefits

Future benefits are the other side of the future expenditures issue. The question is whether past events or transactions have resulted in rights to future benefits that warrant recognition. Whether the rights to future benefits have been received may turn, as noted above, on performance and when the principal efforts to earn the benefits have taken place. Whether such benefits are sufficiently assured (which includes their measurability), is often open to judgment. A more conservative approach is generally taken to the recognition of windfall gains than to ongoing revenue-generating activities. Windfalls are normally recognized only when realized or virtually certain of realization. (Revenue and gain recognition issues are considered in Chapter 7 and asset versus expense classification of costs in Chapter 8.)

Financial Commitments and Options

We have noted that accounting has been moving towards recognition of certain events and transactions at an earlier stage in the process of acquiring rights to future benefits and assuming obligations with respect to future expenditures. We have noted the principle that a financial instrument be recognized at the moment of becoming party to the underlying contract. It is from that moment that the enterprise is subject to the benefits, obligations, and risks inherent in that instrument. Application of this principle will result in the recognition of all financial commitments and options, including some that may not have been readily identified as such in the past (for example, credit guarantees and commitments to extend lines of credit at fixed interest rates).

In the modern world, the risks and benefits inherent in a particular set of assets may be separated out ("debundled") and distributed among various parties. For example, an enterprise may transfer its loans receivable portfolio to another party, but retain some or all of the credit risk (by providing some degree of guarantee against default) and continue to service the loans (collect payments on behalf of the transferee). Perhaps a third party will take on the interest risk (through an interest rate swap). There are major difficulties in determining whether such asset transfer transactions should be treated as sales, and more generally, what recognition should be given by the transferor and transferee to the various rights and commitments that have been transferred and retained. Issues relating to complex asset transfer transactions (including securitizations) are addressed in Chapter 7.

Executory Contracts

It is also pertinent to examine carefully nonfinancial contracts and what may indicate whether rights and obligations exist that should be recognized. Even a short-term contract for the purchase of a good may involve several events. A purchase order is placed or a contract signed which may or may not be cancellable under general or specific conditions. The good is manufactured, perhaps to the customer's specifications and then shipped and delivered. The purchaser may have a period to test the good and decide whether to keep it. Finally the purchaser makes payment. Even at this stage there may be some right of return or some degree of continuing risk on the part of the vendor. At what point in this progression of events does an entity attain sufficient rights to benefits and attendant risks and responsibilities to warrant recognition in its accounts? Each step in the process conveys some rights and obligations and modern contracts are almost infinitely variable in their terms and may involve some ongoing sharing of risks and rights.

In accounting, a contract under which neither party has performed, or one in which the portion of the contract obligation remaining unperformed by each party is equal, is known as an executory contract. There is no doubt that the existence of executory contracts can be significant to an entity's financial position. A company with sufficient orders on hand to give assurance of activity that will cover its fixed costs is usually (assuming the order prices are compensatory) in a better position than one with little work ahead of it. Moreover, non-cancellable contracts at fixed prices transfer the risk of price fluctuations to the purchaser.[5]

The question of executory contracts is important because of the significance in business of long-term contractual arrangements. The following points seem important from the point of view of the purchaser under a long-term contract:

- The contract will usually involve a minimum monetary commitment year by year, for example, under basic rental clauses or "take-or-pay" clauses for products. These minimum commitments are very similar to fixed commitments for debt charges and thus are an important factor in assessing the solvency of an enterprise.

- Some contracts are for the services of an asset in being—typically in the case of long-term leases. If such leases cover virtually the whole useful life of the asset, there is very little difference in economic significance between them and an instalment purchase of the asset. Yet not only is the balance sheet portrayal different between an owned asset and a leased asset that is not capitalized, the expense recognition is typically different as well, since depreciation and interest connected with an owned asset are rarely equivalent to rental on a leased asset (see Chapter 13).

- Long-term contracts for product are often akin to a long-term commodity speculation. In addition, if the contract is long enough, it may be sufficient to recoup the whole cost of a plant built by the vendor to produce the product and may consume the whole useful life of such plant. In that case, the contract for the product in substance buys the plant just as much as would a direct lease of the plant for its full economic life.

Similarly, the existence of a long-term contract has important economic significance to the vendor of products or services.

Given that commitments under long-term contracts can be so significant, the question for accounting standards is not whether financial statements should in some way disclose their significance but rather how that disclosure may best be achieved—whether by formal recognition of the contract rights and obligations among the assets and liabilities of the entity or by other means. The possibilities seem to be the following:

- At one end of the scale, the present value of all contractual rights and obligations could be recognized as assets and liabilities as soon as they become firm and noncancellable. This would be in accordance with a fundamental definition of an asset as an expectation of future benefit arising from present conditions based on a past transaction (the contract) and of a liability as an expectation of future required sacrifices arising from the contract. Since contract rights and obligations are part of financial position in this widest sense, it could be argued that they should be recorded in the balance sheet. Disclosure in a footnote would not carry the same weight. In addition, valuation of rights under unperformed contracts would force consideration of the need for provisions for loss. Such need can easily be overlooked when commitments are not formally recorded.[6]

- Against this position, it may be argued that it would be confusing to mix up in one statement assets that are employed in earning a return and other assets that have yet to become available to the purchaser. An intermediate position, then, would be to recognize contract rights and obligations with respect to assets actually in being and rendering service. This would support the practice of capitalizing leases that are in substance purchases of assets. It could also support a practice of capitalizing the rights to property use inherent in all leases.

- At the other end of the scale would be a policy of reliance on disclosure with respect to all contractual rights and obligations that are unperformed, rather than the formal incorporation of capitalized present values in the balance sheet. This policy would avoid the difficulty of determining which contracts should be capitalized and the almost inevitable inconsistency in capitalizing some and not others that are quite similar. Proponents of the efficient markets hypothesis would reason that disclosure (including quantification of capitalized values if desired) could be just as effective as inclusion in the balance sheet in providing information to the capital markets.

From the late 1970s standards in Canada and the U.S. have required capitalization of leases that could be considered equivalent to purchases of assets. It has proved very difficult to draw a reasonable line between capital and operating leases. Such a line must inevitably be arbitrary within some range, and standard setters have had to develop numerous interpretations and supplementary rules in response to efforts on the part of reporting business interests to as much as possible keep lease liabilities off the balance sheet. (See further discussion at Chapter 13.). The FASB has made explicit the requirement for disclosure of unconditional purchase obligations for goods or services, including disclosure of the minimum amounts required to be paid under such contracts and their timing. Disclosure is also required of actual amounts paid (including any excess over minimum requirements) in periods covered by the financial report.[7]

It should be noted that under the disclosure-only alternative, an enterprise would at least have to consider the need to make provisions for losses in the event of an "onerous contract," that is, a "contract in which the unavoidable costs of meeting the obligations under the contract exceed the economic benefits expected to be received from it."[8] While this general impairment principle may be clear, it has not been implemented on a consistent basis.

RECOGNITION OF EVENTS THAT OCCUR SUBSEQUENT TO THE DATE OF THE FINANCIAL STATEMENTS

Questions arise as to the recognition in financial statements of events that occur after the end of the period but before the financial statements are finalized. Examples of such post-balance sheet events:

- A bankruptcy of a debtor occurring after the year-end suggests that the allowance for uncollectible accounts with respect to amounts owing by that debtor at the year-end is inadequate.

- There is a sharp decline in price of a major inventory commodity that indicates that inventory on hand at the year-end will realize less than its recorded cost at that date.

- A division of the business or a significant portion of productive assets is sold after the period-end.

Whether and how such post-balance sheet events should be accounted for in period-end statements depends upon a fundamental distinction in their nature. Certain subsequent events, such as the first above, cast light on the estimates made in accounting for assets and liabilities in respect of conditions existing at the year-end. The bankruptcy normally provides confirming evidence of the debtor's inability to pay at the year-end. It is natural and logical that the subsequent information be taken into account to make sure the estimates in the financial statements are the best possible. On the other hand, other subsequent events, such as the last-mentioned above, have nothing to do with the position at the year-end. Such events cannot be used to change the accounting otherwise required for assets and liabilities that do exist at the year-end. They may, however, be of such importance that they should be disclosed in the notes to financial statements to make the statements as useful as possible.

The second situation above might seem to be more problematic. On the one hand, the subsequent decline in commodity prices provides clear evidence that the inventory will realize less than its cost. However, on the other hand, if the cause of the decline is an abrupt change in external market prices after the year-end, then it may be considered to be a subsequent event that did not reflect conditions existing at the year-end.[9] Again, disclosure may be required.

Some may argue that an entity's reported results of operations and year-end position would be portrayed more usefully for readers in the above situations if the sale of the division and the loss of inventory value were formally recorded in the accounts at the year-end. Nevertheless, accounting principles do not permit recognition of subsequent events that are not reasonably attributable to conditions existing at the year-end. One reason for this is that it would be difficult to know where to stop if some subsequent events were recognized in financial statements but not others. Inclusion of a subsequent transaction may seem useful in one case, but other cases would be less clear and confusion would inevitably result.

Disclosure is important in these cases. Where subsequent events have a significant impact on financial position or future operations, such events not only may, but should, be disclosed.[10] In most cases, such disclosure is given by footnote to the financial statements. Where, however, the subsequent events represent a significant departure from normal operating transactions and their impact is extreme, it would be good practice to provide pro forma figures incorporating the effect of the subsequent transactions, either in a footnote or in an extra column beside the historical transaction figures.

MEASUREMENTS ON INITIAL RECOGNITION

The generally accepted principle is that transactions should be recorded at their fair value on initial recognition. "Fair value" is customarily defined as the amount at which an asset would be exchanged, or a liability settled, between knowledgeable, willing parties in an arm's-length transaction. This idea of fair value underlies accounting's reliance on bargained exchanges as the initial basis of measurement of assets and liabilities. In addition, the exchange value has the great advantage for accounting purposes of being verifiable.

The importance of getting a proper measurement of the exchange value cannot be overstated. If the consideration in a sale transaction is not fairly measured, profit will be directly misstated as a result. Likewise, if the cost of an asset acquired in a purchase transaction is not fairly stated, all subsequent measurements using that cost figure will be distorted.

The majority of transactions are at arm's length and the consideration given or received is normally cash or monetary assets or liabilities bearing competitive rates of interest. In these circumstances, the use of the exchange price for initial measurement is the most satisfactory general rule. But some transactions do not call for a cash price or a price fairly equivalent to a cash price. In some cases, payment is delayed and the contract does not call for a reasonable rate of interest to compensate for the delay. Some transactions involve an exchange of nonmonetary consideration. In certain situations the consideration may have to be allocated between several assets and/or liabilities (basket transactions). Finally, some transactions are not at arm's length. Each of these circumstances gives rise to questions as to appropriate measurement on initial recognition. These questions are discussed in succeeding sections.

Delayed Payment Transactions

Where a contract provides that there shall be a discount from the contract price for payment in cash within a certain short period, it is obvious that the fair value of the rights exchanged under the contract is the cash amount after discount, not the contract price. In such cases the best accounting treatment is to record sales revenues and purchase costs as the net cash figure. If the discounts happen not to be taken by the purchaser, the extra amount ultimately paid should be recorded as an item of financial revenue (by the vendor) or financial expense (by the purchaser).

Where payment is not called for within a short period of time after performance and the contract does not provide a reasonable rate of interest on the contract price for the delay in cash payment, it is clear that the transaction is not fairly measured at the contract price. The task then becomes one of finding a fair valuation for the transaction.

• A note payable or other debt security given by the purchaser as consideration may have an observable market value that can be used to value the transaction.

• It may be that the goods or services sold in the transaction can be independently valued. There may, for example, be an established market for such goods or services from which a current price can be obtained. Alternatively, the vendor may offer the goods for sale both for a cash price and on delayed credit terms. If so, the cash price (if that price is taken by a sufficient number of purchasers to evidence that it is realistic) can be used to value the credit transaction.

• If neither of these approaches provides a reliable value, the debt can be valued by "imputing" the interest rate that would be negotiated on an arm's-length basis for a debt instrument of equivalent quality. Factors to be considered in selecting the imputed interest rate would include the credit standing of the debtor as evidenced by the interest rate paid on other borrowings, and the repayment and other terms of the debt including the collateral given.

On occasion, cash may be exchanged for an interest-free loan. The rational assumption in such situations is that the difference between the fair value of the loan and the cash exchanged represents some additional right or privilege conveyed to the borrower, which in logic should be separately accounted for in accordance with its substance.

Fair valuing delayed payment consideration is required within GAAP with exceptions for certain situations that are considered to have some extenuating characteristics.[11] In Canada exceptions have included interest-free loans from governments and to employees. The differences between the fair values of these loans and the cash exchanged presumably represent government grants and employee remuneration respectively. Perhaps the error in not accounting separately for these differences is not serious if they are effectively earned over the terms of the loans. Some liabilities for future expenditures may not be discounted for the time value of money. For example, in the U.S. the SEC has not accepted discounted provisions for future environmental costs unless their timing is clearly determinable (see discussion in Chapter 8). On the other hand, defined benefit pensions are highly uncertain future outlays which are discounted, but here there is a well-established actuarial methodology.

When a monetary asset or liability is recorded at a figure different from its stated principal amount because of delayed payment terms, it will be necessary to amortize the difference over the period to payment, so that the asset or liability will be recorded at face value at maturity. The accepted way to do this is called the "effective-yield" method. The imputed interest rate is applied to the opening book value of the asset or liability each period and interest revenue or expense is recognized. When the transaction has been valued directly by either of the first two methods above (that is, not using an imputed interest rate), it will be necessary to calculate the effective interest rate implied by the difference between the contract price and the cash-equivalent valuation used in the accounting.

Transactions and Nonreciprocal Transfers That Are Nonmonetary

Nonmonetary exchanges are commonly known as "barter" transactions. In such transactions the fair values of the things exchanged are not evident from the transaction itself, as would be the case if cash were the consideration. The old joke about the child who sold her dog for $50,000 and took back two $25,000 cats in payment illustrates the point.

The general rule is that a barter transaction should be recorded at the fair value of the thing acquired or the fair value of the thing disposed of, whichever can be estimated more reliably. There may be various indicators of fair value. The best indicator, of course, would be a market price derived from an active market for freely exchangeable goods. In the absence of such market prices, regular price quotations by the buyer or seller for goods or services similar to those involved in the exchange may furnish evidence of value. Such evidence, however, is not always persuasive. For example, a television station might sell unused advertising time to a newspaper in return for advertisements displayed in the paper. Neither party might be willing to buy advertising from the other independently at normal rates, but each may think it worthwhile to incur the little additional extra cost in running an advertisement for the other in return for what it gets. In such a case, a valuation of the transaction at a figure as low as the incremental cost of running the advertisement may reflect the economics of the situation.

Nonreciprocal transfers such as the receipt or disbursement of a gift or dividend in kind may also be nonmonetary. Once again, fair value recording of the transaction is necessary to achieve fair presentation.

Transfers involving the issuance or reacquisition of share capital are similar to exchanges in that the share capital issued or reacquired can be viewed as being sold or bought. Thus, when such transfers involve the exchange of shares for nonmonetary consideration, the fair value of the transaction may be evidenced by quoted market values for the shares at or about the time of the transaction. Some caution is required if a sizable block of shares is involved, since quoted values for small numbers of shares traded on an exchange may be an unreliable indicator of the price at which a large block of shares would trade.

There are certain exceptions to the general rule that nonmonetary transactions and transfers should be recorded at fair value:[12]

- Where the asset given up is part of the operating assets of the enterprise, consideration must be given to the possibility of conflict with the accepted rules for the measurement of income. In particular, income is usually not recognized until near the culmination of an earning process. For example:

- If a product held for sale is swapped for other inventory or rights to acquire other inventory in the same line of business, the transaction should not be recognized at fair value and revenue should not be recorded.

- Assets held for use in the production of goods or services by an enterprise are rarely written down and never written up to fair values. If, therefore, such productive assets were simply exchanged for assets of the same general type, performing the same function in the same line of business, it would be quite inconsistent to record fair values at that time since nothing would have changed insofar as the basic operations were concerned (see *CICA Handbook*, pars. 3830.08–09).

- Where nonmonetary assets are spun off to owners as part of a plan of reorganization, liquidation, or division of a going concern (and not merely as a dividend) the nonreciprocal transfer is accounted for on the basis of the recorded values of resources transferred, not fair value (see *CICA Handbook*, pars. 3830.11–.12).

In addition, where fair value is not determinable within reasonable limits—that is, when there is a major uncertainty about the realizability of any fair value figure that might be assigned—the transfer is recorded at the carrying value of the asset given up by the entity for the lack of any better alternative.[13]

The fact that the exchange of productive property for similar productive property does not generate a gain or loss prompts a question. Suppose productive property is destroyed or expropriated and the insurance or expropriation proceeds are, after an interval but as soon as possible, reinvested in replacement property. The receipt of proceeds is a monetary transaction, but from the standpoint of the entity the conversion into money is involuntary and is rectified by restoration of the previous position as soon as possible. Except for this involuntary event, no gain or loss would have been recorded and the productive plant carrying value would have been unaffected. Such a situation forces a choice between two accounting standards that appear to be relevant:

- On the one hand, it can be argued that involuntary conversions of productive plant should not be considered realizations if reinvestment of the monetary proceeds in similar plant occurs. So far as possible, the business has been continued as it would have been if there were no interruption. Therefore, the historical record of results and the trends from year to year will best be portrayed by accounting that ignores the involuntary interruption.

- On the other hand, it can be argued that the general rule is that monetary exchanges provide evidence of fair value that should not be ignored in accounting. It is always desirable that the figures for assets and liabilities be as close to a current fair value as possible. Under accrual accounting, recognition of changes in fair value is delayed in practice until transactions provide objective evidence of the change. But there is no justification for delaying recognition beyond that point.

The latter viewpoint is the one that is accepted.[14]

The CICA Emerging Issues Committee has been called upon to consider when nonmonetary exchanges of equity interests in business enterprises may be considered to be exchanges of similar productive assets that do not result in a culmination of an earnings process (and thus would be recorded at book values rather than fair values). It has ruled that an entity that issues its own shares as consideration for a business acquisition should measure the transaction at fair value, even if the acquiror and acquiree operate in the same line of business using similar productive assets.[15] It has also set out detailed rules for determining when an exchange of equity investments, or productive assets for equity investments, may be considered to be a nonmonetary exchange of similar productive assets.[16] These matters are considered in more depth in Chapter 19 on business combinations.

Basket Transactions

Transactions in which more than one right or thing is bought or sold for a single negotiated price are known generally as "basket" transactions. Whether the transaction is a purchase or sale, there is an accounting problem in attributing a price to the several things bought or sold. Since this is a "one-to-many" attribution, there is no single demonstrably correct answer to this problem (see Chapter 5).

The problem is that the price negotiated for the basket of assets will rarely be exactly equal to the sum of estimates of fair value for each asset individually. Depending on the circumstances, any of the following approaches to attribution of the total price could appear reasonable:

- The total price might be divided up among individual items in proportion to the estimated fair value of the individual items.

- A purchaser who bought the basket with the aim of keeping some assets and disposing of others for whatever they would fetch might attribute estimated realizable value to the latter (or actual realized value if known soon enough) and allocate the remaining purchase price to the assets to be retained, in proportion to their fair values.

- When a purchase price (including the value of liabilities assumed, if any) is less than the sum of estimated fair values, a purchaser might assign the estimated fair value as the cost of assets whose values are the most reliably measurable and reduce or eliminate the estimated fair values of other assets so that the total values assigned make up the total purchase price.

- When the purchase price of the assets of a business purchased as a going concern exceeds the sum of estimated fair values of identifiable assets purchased (less values of liabilities assumed where applicable), the excess will be assigned to general goodwill.

In the ordinary basket transaction, the vendor does not usually have an accounting problem since no purpose is served by ascertaining the gain or loss on each individual item sold and there is therefore no need to allocate the sale price. A vendor or issuer of securities does, however, need to allocate the price when the things sold represent different types of future claims. This occurs when a company sells different securities for one price. A conceptually similar problem exists when securities with hybrid characteristics (for example, convertible debentures) are sold.

- Different types of securities may be issued as a unit for one price, for example 100 preferred shares with 10 common shares or a $1,000 debenture with 10 common shares. In such a case, the consideration should be divided in accordance with the relevant fair value of each security at the date of issuance. This accounting rule is reinforced in Canada by legal requirements that the shares be issued for a consideration equal to their fair value.

- Securities (usually debentures or preferred shares) may also be issued with detachable warrants entitling the holder to buy a given number of common shares at a stated price for a given period. The holders of these warrants have a call upon the company for common shares and that call has a value. Faithful representation requires that the proceeds from issuance be allocated to the warrants and the other securities in accordance with the fair value of each type of security at the date of issue.[17]

• Securities (usually debentures or preferred shares) may also be issued that are convertible into other securities (usually common shares) on stated terms. The holders of such convertible securities thus have two rights—the right to receive interest and payment of principal at maturity (or equivalent rights for preferred shares) and the right to convert into common shares. The latter right has a value in itself which is evidenced by the fact that the convertible security will be issuable at a lower yield rate (i.e., at a higher price) than would another security of the same issuer similar in all respects except for the conversion privilege. The exercise of one right, however, extinguishes the other. In particular, exercise of the conversion privilege extinguishes the right to receive further payments on the debt or preferred shares. One view is that because the conversion rights are not separable from the security, the consideration received for convertible securities should be entirely assigned to the debt or preferred share category so long as the conversion right has not been exercised. This view has been accepted in practice in the U.S,[18] and until recently in Canada. The result of this practice is that the cost to service the convertible security in terms of interest or dividend yield is understated. An alternative (and better) view is that the conversion privilege has a distinct value, that such value can be estimated with reasonable reliability, and that faithful representation of the security issued requires the separation of proceeds into amounts attributable to its separate elements. This latter view has now been adopted by the CICA and IASC in respect of issuers of financial instruments that contain both a liability and an equity component. An issuer of such securities is now required to separate the liability and equity elements as at the date issued, and classify the liability component with liabilities and the equity component in equity.[19] This standard and its basis for application are discussed in Chapter 9.

Related-Party Transactions; Economic Dependence

In the real world, parties to exchanges are not always independent; there may be some relationship between them that gives them a common interest. This fact casts doubt on the assumption that exchange prices are always good indicators of fair value.

Where a relationship between parties affects their dealings, transactions between them are said to be not at arm's length. In accounting, parties are said to be "related" if one party has the ability to control or significantly influence the operating and financial decisions of the other, or if each of the parties is subject to the control or significant influence of another party.[20]

When parties are related, accounting must be concerned with the possibility that their transactions are not priced on the same basis that they would be if their dealings were fully at arm's length. Another way of putting this is to say that the substance of the transactions may not be fully indicated by their form. Thus, an overly high price for goods or services sold by one party to another may, in substance, embody a gift or subsidy from the buyer to the vendor.

The definition of relationship in terms of *ability* to control or *significantly* influence another party means that it will not always be clear whether parties are related. One party may be able to control another without having a legal right to do so. And significant influence is, of course, a matter of degree. In practice the most difficult situations to judge will be those where an individual has some form of control or influence over another individual or a corporation. The inclusion of the term "significant influence" in the general definition of the term "related party" indicates that individual shareholdings that represent less than legal control of a corporation may give rise to related-party status. In the United States a "principal owner," defined as someone (whether an individual or corporation) who owns over 10% of the voting interest, is deemed to be related to a corporation.[21] The *CICA Handbook* provides examples of related-party relationships, and it emphasizes the importance of the degree of influence which one party may exert on another (see pars. 3840.04–.06).

The *CICA Handbook* has had a related-party disclosure standard in place since 1979. In 1995, it issued a significantly expanded standard that addresses measurement as well as providing for some additional disclosures. The definition of a "related party" is not much changed. As with the original standard, the new standard does not apply to management compensation arrangements in the normal course of operations. (Additional considerations apply to such arrangements, and these are addressed in Chapter 14.)

Measurement

Since the basic objective of the transactions-based accrual system is to report transactions at fair value, one might think that amounts involved in transactions with related parties should be adjusted, where necessary, to prices that would be equivalent to those that would be arrived at between willing buyers and sellers bargaining on an arm's-length basis. Yet, even if revaluations were made so as to identify subsidy elements in related-party transactions, the possibility would remain that, without the existence of related parties, different transactions might have taken place. Also, some transactions that did take place might not have occurred. To adjust the actual record for transactions that would have taken place but did not because of the related-parties situation, or that did take place but would not have in the absence of the relationship, would be speculative in the extreme. As well, such adjustments would obscure the picture of the activity of the entity as it actually took place and ignore the fact that resources owned and claims upon them are all based on the transactions that actually took place.

Not surprisingly, the CICA Accounting Standards Board concluded, consistent with standards and practices throughout the world, that accountants should not attempt to restate related-party transactions to fair value. Under the Canadian standard, most related-party transactions will be measured at their exchange amounts (that is, the amounts of consideration paid or received as agreed between the related parties). However, the standard provides that a transaction that is not in the normal course of operations should be measured at its carrying value unless the transaction results in a substantive change in the ownership interests in the item transferred, and the exchange amount is supported by independent evidence (pars. 3840.18 and .26). To understand the reason for this rule, it is to be remembered that GAAP do not permit capital assets to be written up to reflect upraised values (see Chapter 11). It would clearly be unacceptable to effectively accomplish a write-up by "selling" such assets to a subsidiary in which there is little or no outside ownership. In setting out this rule, the *CICA Handbook* Section 3840 has tried to codify best practice.

Some rather obtuse guidance is provided on when transactions may be considered to be in the normal course of operations.[22] Its essence may be best embodied in the idea that "a related- party transaction is presumed not to be in the normal course of operations when it is not of a type that is usually, frequently or regularly undertaken by the enterprise for the purpose of generating revenue." (See par. 3840.22).

The *CICA Handbook* also provides that, as a general rule, a change in the ownership interest in the item transferred should be presumed to be substantive when the transaction results in a related party having acquired or given up at least 20% of the total ownership interest in the item (par. 3840.31). Major productive assets may be transferred in the form of subsidiary company shares. Some difficult issues have arisen in applying this rule to the combination of business units under common control. These issues are discussed in Chapter 19, under the heading, "Non-Arm's-Length Business Combinations."

Where a related-party transaction is measured at its carrying amount, any difference between the carrying amounts of the items exchanged, together with any related tax effects, are to be treated as a charge or credit to equity. Paragraph 3840.16 sets out this example: Suppose an enterprise transfers an asset with a carrying amount in its accounts of $1,000 to a related party in exchange for a property carried at $700 in the books of the related party. In this case, the enterprise would record the property received at $700 and charge the "loss" of $300 to equity. It is reasoned that the difference represents a capital distribution or contribution.

Where a related-party transaction is measured at its exchange amount, gains and losses will have to be allocated between the controlling and noncontrolling interests, as is illustrated in Appendix B to Section 3840.

Disclosure

Users of financial reports need information about related parties and transactions with them in order to be able to assess the extent to which the reported results of an enterprise may have been affected by control or influence relationships. As an important part of such an assessment, users will want to understand the potential for variability in the design and pricing of related-party transactions. Disclosure could be designed to cover one or all of the following: the fact that relationships with other parties exist that could have an impact on transactions of the reporting entity; the identity and relationships of parties who are related to the reporting entity; and practical details about transactions that have actually occurred with related parties.[23]

There has been some debate on the desirability of disclosing the existence of parties controlling or controlled by the reporting entity or controlled in common with it. Certainly identification of controlling interests or, at least, disclosure of their existence could be of considerable importance, particularly in the case of public companies. Controlling interests may affect the results of an enterprise in ways that go beyond related-party transactions, for example, by restricting access to certain markets and allocating sales between entities under common control. The IASC requires disclosure of control relationships whether or not there have been transactions between the related parties.[24] The Canadian standard does not require disclosure of control relationships in the absence of actual transactions between the reporting entity and interests controlled by it or controlling it. A common reason provided for not requiring this disclosure is that the legal permissibility of nominee shareholdings in Canada makes it impossible to enforce it. This reason may seem rather weak; if one cannot identify controlling interests, then surely it must not be possible to identify and disclose transactions with those interests. Yet transactions with controlling interests are to be disclosed.

In any event, *CICA Handbook* disclosures focus only on information about related-party transactions and the parties to those transactions. It requires:

- a description of the transactions, including those for which no amount has been recorded, and the relationship between the transacting parties;

- the recorded amount of the transactions classified by financial statement category, and amounts due to and from related parties along with their terms and conditions;
- the measurement basis (whether carrying value or exchange amount);
- contractual obligations with related parties and contingencies involving related parties (see paragraphs 3840.43–.54).

As noted earlier, compensation arrangements with management, expense allowances, and the like are exempted from financial statement disclosure in the *CICA Handbook*. However, legislation requires that certain details of management remuneration and directors' fees be disclosed in proxy information circulars sent to shareholders.[25]

Several matters warrant comment with respect to implementing effective disclosures.

- The standard notes that services may be rendered to related parties without compensating charge or without any charge at all. It emphasizes that such services are related-party transactions even if they have not been given accounting recognition. Examples include the use of a patent or licence for no charge, or the provision of management services. Such transactions are to be identified and explained. To be useful, such descriptions should convey the significance or extent of the transactions to the reporting enterprise.

- Enterprise managements may be expected to be motivated to make reassuring statements about related-party transactions. In particular, they may wish to indicate that they are priced on an "arm's-length equivalent" basis. Such statements attempt to minimize any concerns that investors may have as to the potential for contrived transactions, or for artificial pricing of these transactions. When transactions with related parties are made on the same terms as transactions with unrelated parties under similar conditions, the fact that they are on a basis equivalent to arm's-length transactions is considered proper disclosure. If, however, there are no similar independent transactions to provide objective evidence, it should be considered improper to make such a representation (see paragraph 3840.55).

- It may be expected that materiality tolerances of users will be less for related-party transactions than for arm's-length transactions. The CICA standard (paragraph 3840.45) makes a weak statement to this effect, but there is no useful guidance in authoritative literature on this point.

- As noted above, the CICA standard calls for the disclosure of the basis (carrying amount or exchange amount) used to measure related-party transactions. It also notes the desirability of more in-depth information on the basis for determining the exchange amounts in respect of transactions that are not in the normal course of operations. Disclosure of the effects of any significant changes in basis upon which such transactions are made from one period to another is also desirable, and is required in the U.S.[26]

- The possibility of manipulation of accounting results by means of related-party transactions cannot be ignored. Disclosures may not be enough in rare cases in which the purported form of a related-party transaction masks its substance. Suppose, for example, that the entire inventory of an entity were sold to a related party just before the year-end and a gain recorded. Unless there was a basic change in the manner of carrying on the business (which would be apparent within a short period of time after the sale), the transaction may be a sham that should not be accounted for in accordance with its form. There are too many possible forms of sham transactions to permit accounting rule making that addresses every one. Accountants must apply common sense and professional judgment in examining transactions with related parties to decide whether financial statements incorporating their effects can be considered fairly presented, even with extensive disclosure.

Economic Dependence

Major customers or suppliers or other parties having a business relationship with an entity may be in a position to exert significant influence upon it. Such parties are not considered to be related parties solely by virtue of economic dependence. Nevertheless, Canadian standards require explanatory disclosure where operations depend upon a significant volume of business with another party.[27]

SUMMARY

Since accrual accounting relies mainly on exchange transactions to provide data entering into the accounts, it is vital to understand when a transaction should first be recognized in the accounts and how it should be measured.

Historically, since a balance sheet was regarded as a statement of property owned and legal claims, it was thought that the proper test for initial recognition was the legal position. When was title transferred in an asset purchase? When did a liability become legally enforceable? Today, we think more in terms of accounting's objective of providing useful information. We wish to know what assets are actually on hand, capable of being managed for profit. We also wish to know what claims exist that may significantly affect the liquidity of the entity. In general terms, then, the governing rule is that a transaction should be recognized at the time the purchaser controls the rights and assumes the risks of the asset that is the subject of the transaction or at the time an entity is effectively obligated to make future sacrifices as a result of past events or transactions.

In the modern world of complex contractual arrangements and legal requirements there are some difficult questions as to when rights and risks should be considered to have been acquired and when an entity should recognize that it has a liability. There has been increased emphasis on the balance sheet concepts of "assets" and "liabilities," and on conveying more useful information on exposure to risks. In particular, there has been more rigorous attention to the idea that probable future expenditures (such as those related to environmental reclamation) should be recognized as liabilities as an entity performs the acts or receives the benefits that constructively obligates it to pay them.

Every sizable entity is, at all times, enmeshed in a web of contractual relationships with other parties that are not yet fully performed. The existence of these executory contracts can have a significant effect on the well-being of an entity. Three possible approaches to reporting the existence of these contracts can be visualized. First, amounts involved in the contracts could be discounted to a present value and that value recorded as both an asset and liability in the balance sheet. Second, a capitalization policy could be followed when the contract covers an asset in being, whose services are currently being enjoyed by one of the contracting parties. Finally, information about executory contracts could be provided in a supplementary note to the financial statements. In today's practice, the third approach is predominant. Capitalization of amounts in long-term contracts is followed in the single case of long-term leases of property, when the lease is deemed virtually equivalent to an instalment purchase of the property.

It is often asked whether a significant transaction or event that takes place after a fiscal period-end, but before the financial statements are issued, should be reflected in those financial statements. If a subsequent event casts light on the probable accuracy of estimates made in valuing assets and liabilities that are presented or disclosed in the period-end financial statements, the estimates should be adjusted in accordance with the new information. On the other hand, when a subsequent event is independent of the conditions that existed in the previous period, no adjustment should be made to the period-end financial statements. Financial statements are intended to be a record, as factual as possible, of what has actually occurred up to the reporting date. Significant subsequent events for which the financial statements are not adjusted should be disclosed as part of the supplementary financial information provided.

Since transactions provide the basic input to accounting, it is obvious that their measurement should be realistic in relation to bargained "fair" values at the time of the exchange. Measurement difficulties may be encountered in several situations.

- If the settlement date of a transaction is delayed for a significant period, good accounting requires that the nominal amount of the transaction be discounted unless the contract provides for interest at a commercial rate.

- Nonmonetary exchanges or barter transactions also require estimation of the equivalent cash value involved in the transaction. That value is usually established by reference to the fair value of the thing given up or the fair value of the thing received in the exchange, whichever is more clearly evident. There are two exceptions to this fair value rule: (1) if the values of neither of the things exchanged can be measured with a reasonable degree of satisfaction, or (2) if the assets exchanged represent similar productive assets, so that the exchange cannot be regarded as the culmination of an earnings process.

- Certain types of exchanges are called basket transactions, because they involve the purchase or sale of several things for one price. These transactions present a problem in allocating the purchase or sale price among its components. In business combinations, accounting standards spell out the basis in some detail. Convertible securities give rise to, perhaps, the most difficult questions. Here, only one security is sold for a single price, but the security contains rights beyond those embodied in a nonconvertible security. Unless the conversion right is separately accounted for, the effective interest cost or dividend yield on a convertible security will be understated. A major step was taken recently when Canada and the IASC adopted standards that require separate accounting by the issuer for the debt and equity components of convertible securities.

Transactions between related parties create a considerable problem for fair transaction measurement. When one party is able to exercise significant influence over another, it is often not possible to tell whether the transaction is fairly priced or even whether it would have taken place at all in the absence of the relationship. Some argue that related-party transactions should be measured at fair values and that the adjusted values (where adjustment is necessary) should form the basis of the accounting. A CICA standard confirms that such remeasurements should not be attempted. It provides that related-party transactions that are not in the normal course of operations should be measured at their carrying amounts unless they result in a substantive change in the ownership of the transferred item. Otherwise, related-party transactions should be measured at their exchange amounts. Accounting standards place considerable emphasis on the disclosure of the existence, nature and amounts of transactions with related parties.

REFERENCES

[1] IASC, *Financial Instruments: Recognition and Measurement*, IAS 39 (London: IASC, 1998), par. 27. Some practical considerations apply in respect of recognition on the trade date versus the settlement date for "regular way" purchases and sales. See par. 30.

[2] See, for example, discussion in IASC, Steering Committee on Financial Instruments, *Accounting for Financial Assets and Financial Liabilities*, A Discussion Paper (London, IASC, 1997), pp. 57–60.

[3] Canadian and U.S. GAAP have had different answers to this question. Under Canadian GAAP an employer is expected to provide for all forms of special employee termination benefits at the time the decision to implement the program is made by management (See CICA Emerging Issues Committee, *Special Termination Benefits*, EIC Abstract 23 (Toronto: CICA, 1991). In the U.S. a liability is to be recognized when the employees accept the offer (See FASB, *Employers' Accounting for Settlements and Curtailments of Defined Benefit Pension Plans and for Termination Benefits*, Statement of Financial Accounting Standards No. 88 (Stamford: FASB, 1985), par. 15.

[4] L.T. Johnson, *Future Events: A Conceptual Study of Their Significance for Recognition and Measurement* (Norwalk: FASB, 1994).

[5] It is important to understand what this may mean. In transferring the risk of price fluctuations by entering into a noncancellable contract at a fixed price, the seller will take on the reverse risk to that of the purchaser. For example, if the price goes up during the contract period, the purchaser will gain (because it has the promise of goods that are worth more than it must pay for them), while the seller is made worse off (in the sense that it must sell goods for a price that is less than the market price). However, the seller may not be exposed to this price risk if it has already acquired the good, or the inputs to manufacture the good, at the lower price.

[6] The case for recognition of noncancellable purchase commitments and attendant issues are discussed in M.R. Gujarathi and S.F. Biggs, "Accounting for Purchase Commitments: Some Issues and Recommendations," *Accounting Horizons*, September 1988, pp. 75–82.

[7] See FASB *Disclosure of Long-term Obligations*, Statement of Financial Accounting Standards No. 47 (Stamford: FASB, 1981).

[8] This quotation is from IASC, *Provisions, Contingent Liabilities and Contingent Assets*, IAS 37 (London: IASC, 1998), par. 10, and pars. 66–69. The *CICA Handbook* does not have a similar specific requirement, although it may be reasoned from the general principle that one should provide for known losses.

[9] See CICA, "Subsequent Events," *CICA Handbook*, Section 3820 (Toronto: CICA). Whether a subsequent event relates to conditions existing at the previous period-end may be open to interpretation in some situations. But generally a change in external market prices would be considered to reflect the conditions at the time the change occurs. *CICA Handbook*, Section 3820, par. 09, for example, notes that financial statements would not be adjusted for a decline in the market value of investments or changes in foreign exchange rates occurring between the date of the financial statements and the date they are finalized.

[10] Ibid., pars. 3820.10 and 3820.12.

11 In the United States, a valuation approach has been required for delayed payment transactions, with some specified exceptions, since 1971 by APB, *Interest on Receivables and Payables*, Opinion No. 21 (New York: AICPA, 1971). In Canada there has been no equivalent official recommendation. In its absence, occasional examples may be encountered of delayed payment amounts of the types covered by the U.S. standard being recorded at face value rather than fair value. The practice, however, cannot be regarded as generally accepted.

12 These exceptions are set out in CICA, "Non-monetary Transactions," *CICA Handbook*, Section 3830 (Toronto: CICA), which was effective in 1990. It was patterned after APB, *Accounting for Nonmonetary Transactions*, Opinion No. 29 (New York: AICPA, 1973).

13 This may be reasoned within the general recognition principle that an item should have an appropriate basis of measurement that is capable of reasonable estimate. See CICA, "Financial Statement Concepts," *CICA Handbook*, Section 1000 (Toronto: CICA), par. 44.

14 Involuntary conversions are discussed in FASB, *Accounting for Involuntary Conversions of Nonmonetary Assets to Monetary Assets: An Interpretation of APB Opinion No. 29*, FASB Interpretation No. 30 (Stamford: FASB, 1979).

15 CICA Emerging Issues Committee, *Measurement of Cost of a Business Acquisition Effected by Issuing Shares*, EIC Abstract 62 (Toronto: CICA, 1995).

16 CICA Emerging Issues Committee, *Non-Monetary Transactions—Application of CICA 3830.09*, EIC Abstract 67 (Toronto: CICA, 1996) and *Non-Monetary Transaction in which the Transferor Receives an Equity Interest in the Transferee*, EIC Abstract 81 (Toronto: CICA, 1997).

17 See APB, *Accounting for Convertible Debt and Debt Issued with Stock Purchase Warrants*, Opinion No. 14 (New York: AICPA, 1969), pars. 12–15.

18 The Accounting Principles Board reversed itself on this issue between Opinion No. 10 (*Omnibus Opinion—1966*) and Opinion No. 14 (*Accounting for Convertible Debt*). The arguments are discussed in paragraphs 1–11 of the latter Opinion. The FASB is currently considering the issues of distinguishing debt and equity and is expected to propose that the debt and equity components of compound debt instruments be separated and classified as liabilities and equity on the basis of their respective fair values at the date of issuance.

19 CICA, "Financial Instruments—Disclosure and Presentation," *CICA Handbook*, Section 3860 (Toronto: CICA, 1995), par. 24. This standard was the result of a joint project with the IASC, which adopted an almost identical standard. See IASC, *Financial Instruments: Disclosure and Presentation*, IAS 32 (London: IASC, 1995), par. 23.

20 CICA, "Related Party Transactions," *CICA Handbook*, Section 3840 (Toronto: CICA), pars. .03–.05.

21 FASB, *Related Party Disclosures*, Statement of Financial Accounting Standards No. 57 (Stamford: FASB, 1982), par. 24e.

22 See CICA, "Related Party Transactions," pars. 3840.18–.24 and CICA Emerging Issues Committee, *Identification of Related Party Transactions in the Normal Course of Operations*, EIC Abstract 83 (Toronto: CICA, 1997).

23 These different aspects are thoroughly reviewed in Chapters 7 to 9 of a CICA Research Study by A.K. Mason, *Related Party Transactions* (Toronto: CICA, 1979).

24 IASC, *Related Party Disclosures,* IAS 24 (London: IASC, 1984 [reformatted in 1994]), par. 20.

25 Ontario Securities Commission regulations require extensive disclosures in proxy information circulars of all forms of remuneration of individual senior executives. See "Statement of Executive Compensation," Ontario Securities Act R.R.O. Regulation 1015, Form 40, in P.G. Findlay, *Consolidated Ontario Securities Act and Regulations 1996*, 25th ed. (Scarborough: Carswell Thompson, 1996). These were modelled on similar SEC requirements.

26 FASB, *Related Party Disclosures*, par. 2c.

27 CICA, "Economic Dependence," *CICA Handbook*, Section 3841 (Toronto: Canada).

RECOGNITION OF REVENUES AND PERIPHERAL SALES AND REALIZATIONS

In an exchange economy, the goal of productive activity is to sell a product or service for more than its cost of production. As explained in Chapter 5, present-day accounting measures income as the difference between costs (sacrifices) and revenues (benefits). On this basis, if one visualizes a business in the form of a single venture, income over its entire lifetime will be the difference between cash receipts (excluding capital paid in) and cash disbursements (excluding capital withdrawn or return on capital, such as dividends, paid out).[1] It is natural, therefore, to think of revenue as an inflow of assets (ultimately cash) in exchange for the product of the enterprise.

This discussion oversimplifies matters. An enterprise may receive cash other than in exchange for product or service, or as a capital contribution. For example, if some asset were destroyed by fire, the insurance proceeds would not represent payment for the productive activity of the enterprise. It is still true that over the lifetime of an enterprise the excess of cash receipts over cash disbursements (excluding cash associated with capital transactions) will equal the net gain. But that net gain will consist of (1) the excess of revenues from productive activity over costs of earning those revenues, and (2) miscellaneous gains or losses on events or activities that are not part of the main activity of the enterprise.

When we speak of the lifetime of an enterprise from initial cash investment to ultimate cash realization, it is possible to talk solely about movements in cash. When we account for a period shorter than the enterprise lifetime, we have a problem. At any given point of time the enterprise will have delivered product or services for which it has not yet received payment. Conversely, it may have received payment for which it has not yet satisfied its obligation to deliver. It will also have incurred other costs and acquired rights or things that may reasonably be expected to be rewarded by the receipt of cash in a future exchange transaction. Moreover, it may not yet have paid for goods or services it has received. Thus, estimation of income for a period is considerably more difficult than determination of income for a completed business lifetime. Such estimation requires that noncapital cash inflows of past, present, and future periods be assigned to periods in which they are "earned." Similarly, noncapital cash outflows of past, present, and future periods must be assigned to the period in which any benefit from them is used up. That is, the goal of income accounting under the transaction-based model is to provide rules for assigning revenues and expenses from operating transactions and gains and losses from peripheral activities to accounting periods.

Because income accounting associates cash flows with time periods, it automatically results in recognizing assets and liabilities. For example, a cash receipt today associated with revenue of a future period must be recorded as unearned revenue—a liability to deliver product or service in the future. A cash disbursement today associated with revenue of future periods must be recorded as an asset—an expectation of future benefit. In other words, asset and liability recognition (and changes in assets and liabilities previously recognized) can result from income accounting conventions as well as the conventions governing initial recognition of assets and liabilities discussed in the previous chapter.

The first part of this chapter will discuss the recognition of revenues that result from the ordinary activities of an enterprise. Such revenues include both sales of goods or services arising out of active business operations, and passive interest, dividend, and royalty returns. A section at the end of the chapter will refer to recognition of sales and other realizations that are not part of normal income-generating activities.

RECOGNITION OF EARNED REVENUES

It was once customary to think of recognition of revenue and income as being synonymous with *realization*. One of the dictionary meanings of the term "realize" is the conversion of property into money. That definition emphasizes both the idea of an exchange and of a liquid asset received in exchange (strictly speaking, cash itself).

Historically, conservatism and the desire for certainty reinforced the emphasis in accounting on exchange for a liquid asset. The exchange test reduced uncertainty as to the amount of revenue to be recognized. It also reduced uncertainty as to the amount of expenses incurred to earn the revenue, since frequently most of a vendor's work was performed before the product was sold. The liquid asset criterion also meant that proceeds would be more easily measurable. The result of all these influences tended to focus attention on point of sale as the criterion par excellence for revenue recognition. Thus, in 1934, the membership of the American Institute of Accountants formally adopted the following rule:

> Unrealized profit should not be credited to income account ... Profit is deemed to be realized when a sale in the ordinary course of business is effected, unless the circumstances are such that the collection of the sale price is not reasonably assured.[2]

This simple rule seemed quite satisfactory for the majority of situations for many years. Where it was not—notably in the case of long-term construction contractors—generally accepted practice developed alternatives that dealt with the particular problem. In the later 1960s and early 1970s, this happy situation began to break down. Several contributing causes can be discerned.

- The rule that revenue was earned at point of sale was essentially based on a stereotype of a business making a standardized product for a mass market, on a more or less regular basis, with few obligations after sale. That image had never fitted construction contractors, and it became less and less realistic as a description of much modern business activity. The growth of the service sector of the economy alone saw to that.

• In the business stereotype, sale came near the end of the business activity, when most costs had been incurred. Measurement uncertainties were thereby minimized. In some industries, business practices changed and developed so this was no longer true. The sale might come early on, leaving substantial obligations on the vendor for future performance. Worse, the sale itself might involve significant uncertainties as to collection. In these circumstances, sale was not a good basis for triggering revenue recognition.

• In many types of business, one sales price might cover several products or services. Even a business manufacturing a straightforward product was apt to have to provide increasingly complex warranties or other services. One price received for a bundle of products or services raises the question whether one revenue recognition point is satisfactory or whether allocation of revenue to work performed is required.

By 1970, some modification of previously accepted ideas had occurred. It was no longer believed that revenue could be recognized only in exchange for a liquid asset. (The treatment of barter transactions described in Chapter 6 illustrates this point.) It was also felt that a sale was not, by itself, sufficient for revenue recognition—there had to be performance by the vendor as well. The accepted rule was stated by the Accounting Principles Board (APB) as follows:

> Revenue is generally recognized when both of the following conditions are met: (1) the earning process is complete or virtually complete, and (2) an exchange has taken place.[3]

The traditional exception for long-term contractors was also acknowledged.

Since 1970 practice has continued to develop, and considerable study has been given to special situations. The result has been the development of further exceptions to the sales basis of revenue recognition, some inconsistencies between rules applied in different situations, and some difficulty in seeing a common rationale for revenue recognition.

A general *CICA Handbook* standard was adopted in 1986, based on an earlier IASC standard.[4] It states that revenue recognition should be based on certain performance conditions. With respect to revenues realized through the sale of goods, performance is tied to the transfer of significant risks and rewards of ownership to the buyer. This in turn requires that "all significant acts have been completed and the seller retains no continuing managerial involvement in, or effective control of, the goods transferred ...."[5] For service transactions and long-term contracts the percentage-of-completion or completed contract basis should be followed depending on which method best relates revenue to the work accomplished. In all cases, there should be reasonable assurance as to the measurement of the consideration to be received and its ultimate collection. These recommendations are not explained or elaborated, and so are really little more than starting point objectives. In applying these objectives to particular circumstances, three broad approaches to the recognition of revenue may be identified.

The first may be called the "critical event" approach.[6] Under this approach, the revenue from product sale or service is recognized in full at the time of one selected critical event. (The 1934 American Institute rule indicated that sale was ordinarily deemed to be that critical event. The above-noted CICA standard recognizes this as the point at which the significant risks and rewards of ownership are ordinarily considered to be transferred to the buyer, subject to collectibility and measurement conditions being met.) Certain accounting results flow from this approach. Certain assets, such as accounts receivable or accrued revenue, are recognized and measured at the amount of revenue received or to be received. Any costs previously recorded as assets that are deemed applicable to that revenue must be written off. Costs to be incurred after the critical event that are applicable to the revenue must be estimated, and expense and liability recorded.

The second approach to revenue recognition is the "accretion" approach. Under this approach, revenue is deemed to be earned over the whole period of productive activity and is recognized gradually on some basis that relates to accomplishment. The asset recognized is accrued revenue, measured at a reasonable proportion of the ultimate amount of revenue to be received. Costs that are deemed to be associated with the ultimate product or service sold are generally written off when incurred, since the accrued revenue stands as the asset recorded in their place. Other costs, such as costs of capital assets, are written off as their benefits are consumed in operations.

A third approach represents an extension of the other two. When one sale price conveys several distinguishable benefits to the customer, the total revenue is allocated among the distinctive products or services. Then, the amount allocated to each such product or service is recognized as earned on either the critical event or accretion approach.

The feasibility of each of these approaches depends to a considerable extent upon the time when a revenue transaction takes place. If a transaction is not contracted until late in the production cycle, recognition usually must be based upon the critical event approach (with some small possibility of revenue allocation to after-sale activities). If the revenue-producing contract is entered into early, however, any of the three approaches—critical event, revenue accretion, or revenue allocation—becomes possible.

The Critical Event Approach

As just explained, when a revenue transaction does not occur until late in the productive cycle of a business, the critical event approach is almost always followed. The reason is that until that time the amount of revenue can rarely be estimated with reasonable confidence, and hence the income cannot be measured satisfactorily. This clue suggests that the basic criterion for selection of the precise critical event is the removal of uncertainty. That criterion usually suggests point of sale as the critical event for revenue recognition when the revenue transaction occurs late in the cycle of productive activity, but other critical events are conceivable. These will be reviewed first in the following discussion.

Revenue Recognition at Completion of Production

Long-standing practice has sanctioned the recognition of revenue and profit before sale (at the time of completion of inventory ready for sale) in a limited number of situations. As a matter of mechanics this is accomplished by valuing the completed inventory at net realizable value while writing off production costs.

Early accounting literature provided two justifications for this practice. First, in a few cases (precious metals were cited as an example) where there were no substantial selling costs and the price was stable, there could be relative certainty as to the amount of revenue and profit as soon as production was completed and its cost was known. Second, in some industries more than one product was produced by a common production process or from common materials, and in this situation the joint-costing problem (a one-to-many attribution) meant that presumed cost figures for inventory were highly arbitrary.

Today, there is hardly any industry—certainly not the production of precious metals—that can confidently count upon receipt of a fixed predetermined price for all its output (in the absence of long-term sales contracts). Market conditions are generally too volatile for this. There are, however, enterprises—including precious metal producers—with products consisting of interchangeable units that are readily marketable at quoted representative market prices. In such cases, selling is not a major activity of the business, so that the significant acts of performance have taken place on completion of production. The modern argument for recognition of revenues at net realizable values at this point is that any subsequent gain or loss on sale must reflect changes in market conditions that are logically attributed to the periods in which they occur.

In practice, end-product inventory is valued at estimated realizable values in a small minority of situations. In Canada, these include some base metal mining companies. (To the extent possible in these cases, the net realizable value of production on hand at a year-end is based on amounts actually realized after the year-end.) Reflecting revenue at the point of completion of production is inconsistent with the *CICA Handbook* revenue recognition requirement that a seller transfer the significant risks and rewards of ownership to a buyer. Some mining companies carrying inventories at market are avoiding the problem by treating the write-up of inventory to net realizable value as a separate income statement credit that is not included in revenue per se. While this approach may get around the problem technically, if it is accepted that reflecting revenue at point of production is valid in some situations, then it would appear that the CICA revenue recognition requirement is inadequate or incomplete. In the United States, the general practice of mining companies is to value product at some estimate of cost, and many Canadian companies follow suit.

Recognition of revenue at completion of production has merit in those industries where expenditure of effort is not necessarily highly correlated with value of production from one period to the next. Such conditions are found, for example, in agriculture. The chief limitation on the method's use lies in the difficulties in reasonably predicting values for product.[7]

Finally, it may be noted that the logical basis for recognizing revenue on completion of production—that the product is readily marketable at representative quoted market prices—may be extended to marketable portfolio investments. Where securities markets are reasonably efficient, quoted market values are realizable without any significant effort or selling activity. There is now widespread acceptance for treating changes in market prices rather than the point of sale as the "critical event" for recognizing income on marketable financial instruments, at least those that are held for "trading purposes." These issues will be discussed in Chapter 17.

Revenue Recognition at Completion of a Venture

There are times when an enterprise is undertaken, costs are incurred, and revenues come in, but whether the final result will be a profit or loss is shrouded in uncertainty until near the end of the venture. In circumstances such as these, the businessperson may revert to one of the earliest forms of accounting—"venture" accounting or "voyage" accounting. Under this approach, all costs and revenues of the venture are entered in one account and carried forward as a net figure in the balance sheet (subject to write-downs if losses appear probable). The accumulated venture balance is not closed out until the venture is completed and all revenues and costs are known. This form of accounting was widely used in trading ventures from the Middle Ages onward. The "completed contract" method of accounting for contractors may be regarded as a variant of it. In general, the venture basis of accounting has application where the business carried on naturally consists of a small number of projects and where the final total cost or revenue associated with any project is highly speculative, so that early experience gives no assurance as to the final result.

Revenue Recognition at Point of Sale

Point of sale is a satisfactory point for revenue recognition in a large number of situations because, when sale occurs, the amount of revenue can usually be estimated with fair certainty. Also, costs applicable to the revenue are largely known. A further idea implicit in the selection of sale as the recognition point is that of customer satisfaction. Consider the case of a standard product made under conditions in which costs are well controlled and highly predictable. From the standpoint of the vendor the hardest job may be to get the order; once that is done one may be able to estimate profit with a high degree of certainty. In spite of that, many accountants feel that profit is not earned and therefore revenue should not be recognized until the vendor has delivered the product or service the customer is buying. This is the idea implicit in one of the tests stated by APB Statement No. 4, quoted previously, that "the earnings process is complete or virtually complete."

Comments made in Chapter 6 as to recognition and measurement of transactions are relevant to sales transactions. That is, the criterion for recognition should be performance rather than the legal test of transfer of title. Also, the sales revenue to be recognized should allow for trade and quantity discounts, cash discounts, and discounts for substantial delay in collection.

Recognition of revenue as earned requires the coincident recognition of expenses of earning that revenue, so that a proper income figure emerges. Costs that are directly related to sales (for example, cost of goods sold and sales commissions) must be identified and written off. A suitable basis must also be in place for writing off other costs incurred before sale that are not directly traceable to particular sales (for example, costs of capital assets used in administration). Finally, expense must be recognized for after-sale costs, such as warranties. Such provisions can present difficulty since the amount of after-sale costs is not known but rather must be estimated. In spite of this difficulty, recognition of any material amount of such costs at the time that revenue is recognized is required for fair income reporting.

Uncertainties with respect to recognition of revenue at point of sale include uncertainty whether all receivables will be collected, uncertainty as to the possibility of returns by customers, and uncertainty as to the amount of claims for substandard or damaged goods. Gross revenue recorded should be reduced by allowances for all these possibilities, based on informed estimates and past experience.

The Impact of Major Uncertainty

Ordinarily, as just described, allowances are made for the possibilities of return, nonpayment, etc., in recording revenue. Upon occasion, however, the inability to estimate with reasonable assurance the dollar impact of transactions that will not be consummated is justification for delaying recognition of earned revenue beyond the usual recognition point.[8] The accounting reaction to such uncertainty may take various forms.

- A sale for accounting purposes is supposed to transfer substantially all the benefits and risks pertaining to ownership of the property. If the sales contract is so loosely drawn or the business policy of the vendor is so flexible that the transaction does not, in substance, transfer ownership, the transaction may be more like an option or consignment than a sale. In these circumstances, the sale transaction is simply not accounted for. Any cash received is treated merely as a deposit that may be applied when recognition of the transaction becomes justified.

- Where the principal uncertainty concerns collectibility, the traditional approach has been to recognize the sale but defer recognition of the profit. This may be achieved by one of three methods:

  - The instalment basis of accounting calls for transfer of previously deferred profit to income as cash is received, in the proportion that the cash receipt bears to the total sale price. Some writers suggest this procedure is illogical in that it determines the amount of profit to be taken up on each instalment on the basis of a total sale price that is uncertain of collection. With respect to any individual transaction, this objection is correct. The objective of the procedure, however, is merely to restrain recognition of profit to allow for some unknown percentage of uncollectibles and, when applied to sales transactions in the aggregate, may (or may not) arrive at a reasonable result.

  - The cost-recovery basis of accounting is still more conservative than the instalment basis. Under cost recovery, all cash collections are credited against the asset account until the cost of the asset sold is completely recaptured. Thereafter, further cash collections are all profit. The fact that, under this method, profit recognition does not take place until well after sale, makes it rather unsatisfactory from the standpoint of income measurement, and it is rarely encountered in practice.

  - In the case of sales of services, if no costs have been deferred as an inventory of work done on service contracts, the above two methods of delayed profit recognition cannot be used. In their place, under conditions of great uncertainty, revenue might be recorded on a simple cash collection basis, rather than when billed.

The Emerging Issues Committee has considered a situation in which an entity sells assets where the large part of the consideration is a note receivable and the seller has recourse only against the assets sold. It concludes that a gain on the sale should be recognized only to the extent it is realized and there is reasonable assurance of collection. A gain is considered to be realized when there is a "substantial commitment" on the part of the purchaser. This may be evidenced by cash payment in excess of 15 percent of the purchase price, or by certain other means. The intent and ability of the purchaser to honour its obligations must also be demonstrated.[9]

It is obvious that after-sale costs present another difficulty in that their amount cannot be completely known at the point of sale. The more demanding that after-sale activities are and the further in the future that they will occur, the greater the uncertainty. Uncertainty will also be greater in new situations—for example, uncertainty as to warranty costs for a new-technology product. Severe difficulties in estimation of after-sale costs (if, for example, it is thought the variance in possible warranty costs could be enough to wipe out the profit) may be grounds for postponement of recognition of revenue and profit on the whole transaction.

The Accretion Approach

The simplest example of the accretion approach is furnished by accounting practice with respect to investments carrying a fixed rate of interest. Where interest is an important element of enterprise income, especially in the case of financial intermediaries or other entities holding large investment portfolios, the standard practice is to recognize interest revenue as it accretes over time. Wherever material, revenue will be recorded on the effective-yield method whereby interest at the rate stated in the security is modified by amortization of any premium or discount from face value implicit in its acquisition price. The key to the use of the accretion approach in this case is the promise of a fixed return on a time basis. Revenue from other investments, such as dividends on stocks, is customarily not recorded until entitlement to it arises. (One could argue that accretion of dividends on secure preferred stocks would provide a fairer presentation.)

A second major example of the accretion approach is furnished by accounting practice with respect to long-term construction contracts. An accretion basis of accounting for such contracts developed quite early, for at least two reasons:

- When contracts were long-term in nature and irregular in their incidence, waiting until completion to recognize revenue and profit provided a misleading picture of activity and results of operations.

- Because a contract price was arrived at before work was done, one major uncertainty that ordinarily dictates delay in revenue recognition was not present. (It may be noted, however, that because of the possibility of "change notices," "extras," performance bonuses, or penalties, etc., the total revenue that will be received on a contract is rarely completely certain.)

As a result it became accepted practice for long-term construction contractors to record revenue on the so-called "percentage-of-completion" basis. Originally the percentage-of-completion method was considered only as an acceptable alternative to the completed contract method. Now, both Canadian and U.S. literature suggest that the percentage-of-completion method should be used unless there are inherent hazards outside normal business risks that make estimates on particular contracts unreliable.[10]

Depending on the circumstances of the business and the contract, one of several approaches can be used to measure the contractor's performance. These can be classified broadly as "output methods" and "input methods."[11] Output methods base the amount of revenue to be recorded on some measure of accomplishment. Costs incurred to accomplish the measured output are identified and matched with revenue; thus it is essential to keep cost records that can be related to accomplishment. Input methods look at costs or efforts expended and express them as a percentage of total estimated costs or efforts to arrive at the percentage of contract revenue to be recognized. A more detailed discussion follows.

Output Methods

- If a contract specifies a price per unit produced or delivered, revenue recognition on the basis of units shipped is similar to normal procedures for recognition at point of sale.

- Contracts that pay on the basis of units of work done, for example, quantities of pavement laid or earth excavated or dredged, can also be dealt with on a unit basis.

- It may be possible to specify milestones in contract achievement for the purposes of revenue recognition—for example, stages of construction of a building—and revenue can be recognized based on architects' or engineers' certificates. If this method is used, however, there must be confidence that the revenue accrued at each milestone represents a fair recompense for that stage of work. The payment called for by the contract for each stage is not necessarily a good measure of accomplishment. Contract payments may be loaded at the front end to assist the financing of the contractor.

Input Methods

- A very commonly used indicator is that of costs incurred on the contract. Total revenues are estimated, total costs are estimated, and revenue earned is recognized as that percentage of total estimated revenue that the actual costs incurred to date represent of total estimated costs. For the purpose of this calculation it is important to exclude from actual costs those that do not represent actual performance, such as payments made to subcontractors who have not yet performed. The cost basis of measurement may also be modified when it is felt that some costs do not provide good indicators of performance. For example, if it is felt that materials acquisition or subcontracting do not involve the same effort as work performed directly by the contractor, they may be excluded from costs used in measuring percentage of performance. Alternatively, a low margin of profit may be applied to them.

- Another way to refine percentage-of-completion methods is to base percentages of completion on what are regarded as key indicators, such as labour hours, labour dollars, machine hours, etc.

There is a method of revenue recognition that falls between the percentage-of-completion approach and the completed contract approach. Under the completed contract approach, no revenue is recognized at all until the contract is complete or substantially complete. Correspondingly, no contract costs are written off until that time. Period costs that cannot be clearly related to contracts, however, continue to be written off. As a result, in any period when contract completions are unusually high or low, period costs may appear very much out of line with the apparent volume of business activity as indicated by contract costs recognized as expenses. To avoid this, a contractor who cannot recognize contract profit under the percentage-of-completion method, perhaps because of considerable uncertainty as to the total amount of revenue or costs, but who has some assurance that there will be no loss may use a percentage-of-completion accounting approach with a zero estimate of profit. In this way, a reasonable impression of activity on contracts is portrayed in the income statement, but the principle that profit should not be recognized in the face of inherent uncertainty is respected.

This discussion is not exhaustive. A number of variations on these revenue recognition methods may make sense in particular contract situations. For example, some enterprises may not recognize revenue and profit on contracts until they are some distance into the contract, when estimates of total costs and revenues have become more reliable. The important point of principle, however, is that where an earnings process is extended over a long period, revenue recognition at a critical event simply fails to portray reasonably the activities going on. This point is most obvious in relation to contracting enterprises but is applicable in concept to any type of enterprise. There has been a tendency for the accretion approach to revenue recognition to become more widely used whenever the amount of revenue can be established at the outset.

A transaction to "sell" assets may be in substance a lease rather than a sale. This may be the case where a manufacturer guarantees the resale value of equipment to the purchaser, so that the difference between the proceeds received by the manufacturer and the residual value guarantee should be considered to be the equivalent of lease payments. This treatment would amount to an accretion method as revenue would be recorded as lease income over the period to the exercise date of the guarantee (assuming it is an operating lease).[12]

The Revenue Allocation Approach

Earlier, reference was made to the necessity for making provision for after-sale costs (such as warranty costs) when revenue is recognized at a critical event. The existence of after-sale costs gives rise to a conceptual question in revenue recognition. Should all the sale revenue be recorded at the point of sale and provision made simply for the future costs to be incurred? Or should the sales price itself be apportioned, part to be assigned as revenue of the period of sale and part to be deferred to the future period, in an amount sufficient to allow a profit to be reported in that period on the work done by the vendor in fulfilling his obligation? More generally, can there be multiple revenue recognition points tied to distinguishable segments of the vendor's performance?

Application of the accretion concept represents one response to the problem of revenue recognition when major activity occurs after the sale price is established. But, in complex situations, allocation of revenue represents an alternative that may be exercised in conjunction with an accretion approach or a critical event approach. For example, suppose in the real estate industry a condominium project were sold with the sale price covering property management services for a stated period after sale. Because of the absence of separate compensation for the property management function, the sale price should be allocated between the two functions. In this case, the sale price allocated to the property management function would be recognized as revenue on the accretion approach as that function was performed. The sale price allocated to the condominium units would, in Canada, be recognized when the purchaser is in a position to occupy the unit—a critical event.

Basis of Revenue Allocation

A serious problem in any scheme for allocation of revenue is that of pricing the various functions to which revenue is allocated. No general criteria have been stated in accounting standards. Bases of allocation have been developed for individual situations that are not necessarily consistent in terms of their underlying concepts.

It would seem, a priori, that the best basis for allocation of revenue to functions would be prices established by the marketplace for those functions if they are independently performed. Unfortunately, such prices are likely to be available only in a minority of situations. Something equivalent may be available for financial service companies, however. For example, if a company is making a loan or investment that entails certain associated tasks, a market rate of interest may be capable of being observed that can be taken as the price for the pure function of "renting" the money.

If independently established prices are not available, it may be possible to simulate them by estimating what would provide a reasonable margin over costs of providing each function, given the capital investment required for performance of the function and the risks involved. Caution needs to be exercised to ensure that revenue allocated to functions performed first is estimated such that a reasonable profit remains for later functions.

In a number of cases, revenue is allocated to some functions in an amount equal to the cost of performing them, leaving the remainder of the revenue to be allocated to later functions. This cost-recovery basis of allocation is similar in concept to by-product costing for inventory. There could be two motives for such an approach. First, allocation on a cost-recovery basis to functions performed in the early stages may be desired to be conservative, leaving the profit element to be recognized in later stages closer to the culmination of the earning process. Second, the cost-recovery basis may be used for functions that are considered secondary in character, reserving profit recognition for the activities that are considered more important.

If a cost-recovery approach is adopted, a decision must be made as to whether the revenue allocated will be equal to directly traceable costs only or may be calculated on a full costing basis, that is, including an allowance for fixed overheads. In a number of cases only directly traceable costs are included—a conservative approach.

It may be noted that the same result, from the standpoint of income reported, can be obtained in relation to secondary functions by simply deferring the costs in question until the major revenue recognition point(s) without any revenue allocation to the minor activity. There is no obvious basis for preferring one of these expedients over the other; both are found in practice in different contexts.

Treatment of Initial Fees

The practice in some industries of charging an initial fee at the inception of service and subsequently continuing service fees may in some cases interrelate with the question of revenue allocation. One danger needs to be guarded against. It may be that an initial fee and continuing service charges are enough, taken together, to fairly compensate the service provided, but the continuing service charge alone is inadequate to be fair compensation for continuing service efforts. In effect, part or all of the initial charge is required to recompense the continuing activity.

An initial fee may be charged to cover initial costs required to provide a customer with access to continuing service. An example of such a charge might be an installation charge for cable TV. When the fee is reasonable in relation to the costs and effort involved in providing access, there should be no objection to recognizing revenue from the charge and writing off the related costs at completion of the work for which the fee is charged. It should be clear, however, that the fees for continuing service will be adequate so that it can stand on its own feet.[13]

In another case, an initial fee may be charged merely to help the service provider finance the requisite capital investment. Such might be the case, for example, in a sports or fitness club. The accounting for that initial fee would depend upon its nature. If the fee is refundable when a member withdraws, it should be treated as a deposit. If it is not refundable it may logically be taken into income, but if the fee is paid on a once-and-for-all basis a precise indicator of the appropriate revenue recognition period is lacking. In those circumstances, amortization over the average duration of a membership would seem to be appropriate.

Some Specific Industry Situations

The following paragraphs review revenue recognition standards and practices in several significant industry settings, demonstrating issues that arise in applying the revenue recognition approaches discussed above.

Fees Associated with Lending Activities

Since the 1970s lenders have been charging a variety of fees for services related to financing and lending activities. These fees have grown to comprise a significant proportion of the revenues of many of these organizations. A diversity of revenue recognition practices developed, and the piecemeal efforts of the accounting profession to deal with them through the mid-1980s well illustrate many of the revenue allocation issues discussed above. The FASB stepped in and established accounting and disclosure standards for these fees and related costs in 1986 and the CICA followed with an Accounting Guideline that, for the most part, adopted the FASB conclusions.[14] Three broad groups of fees may be identified:

- Loan origination fees are charged to the borrower for services related to originating, refinancing or restructuring loans. These include application, processing and underwriting fees. The CICA and FASB standards reject arguments that these are revenues for performing distinct and separate services. They reason that revenue is not earned merely by the acquisition of a loan and that such fees, less directly related costs, are an integral part of the loan return that should be recognized as an adjustment of interest yield on an effective interest basis over the life of the loan.

- Commitment fees are separate charges for entering into agreements that obligate the financial institution to make a loan or pay off a financial obligation of another party if certain events occur. Examples are standby fees and fees for providing guarantees and letters of credit. Such charges are to be amortized on a rational and systematic basis over the commitment period when the institution has good reason to expect that the commitment will not be called upon and will not result in a loan. Otherwise they must be deferred and recognized as an integral part of the interest return of the related future loan or as revenue when the commitment expires unexercised.

- Syndication fees are charges for arranging or managing the syndication of a loan. These are to be recognized on completion of the loan arrangements provided that any portion of the loan retained by the institution bears an interest yield that is not less than the average yield to be earned by the other lenders involved in the financing.

Franchising

A franchise arrangement commonly calls for payment of an initial franchise fee and continuing fees. The former may cover the right to use the franchise name and various set-up services provided by the franchisor, such as help in site selection, management training and facility design. The latter may also cover the right to use the franchise name as well as continuing services by the franchisor.

In the past, problems have been encountered in accounting for initial fees because it was not clear when the fee was earned by the franchisor; sometimes fees were not payable in full immediately, and there was doubt as to their ultimate collectibility; and finally, inadequate financial statement presentation and disclosure of initial fees might conceal their nonrecurring nature. As franchising spread as a form of business, franchisors commonly recognized revenue from initial franchise fees at the time of sale, although other recognition bases were used to some extent, such as recognition at time of cash collection or when the franchisee opened for business. After some experience it became clear that recognition at time of sale was too early in many cases. Present recommended practice is as follows:[15]

- First, it must be considered whether continuing franchise fees are likely to be sufficient in relation to future services to be provided by the franchisor. If not, an appropriate portion of the initial fee should be deferred and amortized over the life of the franchise so as to cover continuing services with a reasonable profit allowance.

- In addition, if any part of the fee is for tangible property, that part must be separated out and treated as revenue from the sale of assets.

- The remainder of initial franchise fees is to be recognized when the franchisor has substantially performed all services called for, any obligation to refund cash or forgive receivables has expired, and no other conditions or obligations exist. There is a presumption that substantial performance will not have been completed before the franchisee has opened for business.

- In unusual cases where the collection period for franchise fees is extended and collectibility cannot be estimated with reasonable assurance, revenue is to be recognized on either the instalment or the cost-recovery basis.

- Should the franchisor have an option to purchase a franchisee business and there is an understanding or probability that it will do so, initial franchise fee revenue is to be completely deferred to be applied against the franchisor's investment in the outlet if, as, and when it occurs.

The Real Estate Industry

Enterprises in the real estate industry often engage in transactions of great complexity that provide practical tests of the general principles of revenue recognition. There are several major problem areas. First, a sales transaction in form may be little different from an option. The buyer may have so little stake in the property that he or she may feel free to "walk away" from it if its value drops or other difficulties occur. Second, a vendor may retain obligations in connection with property sold so that it remains exposed to some risks pertaining to the property. Third, a vendor may undertake commitments to perform other services after sale as part of the inducements for the sale. Fourth, one contract may cover not only the transfer of property but also the responsibility to construct improvements. The response to these various conditions may take the form of postponement of recognition of sale, making provision at time of sale for future service costs, or, in some fashion, apportioning the sale price so that revenue and profit are recognized in instalments or by stages of completion.

In Canada, accounting problems of the real estate industry have been studied and recommendations made by the Canadian Institute of Public Real Estate Companies (CIPREC).[16] With respect to revenue recognition, the recommendations are along the following lines:

- Revenue from land sales is recognized when the vendor has fulfilled all its obligations, which is normally at the time title passes. However, land may be sold under an agreement whereby possession is obtained by the purchaser, but title does not pass until the purchase price has been fully paid. Revenue may be recognized in such a case where all other significant obligations have been met. Vendor obligations will typically include such matters as registering a plan of subdivision and letting contracts for land servicing. At the time of revenue recognition the purchaser should have made a significant down payment in cash, or given consideration of equivalent value, or have given a strong covenant, so that there is a high degree of assurance that the purchaser is committed to the property.

The appropriate revenue recognition date will often be indicated by the date when interest begins to run on the purchaser's unpaid balance. Substantial uncertainties as to future costs to be incurred, the financial capability of the purchaser, or a variety of other factors, may suggest that recognition of the sale should be postponed.

- Recognition of a sale may be precluded by factors indicating that the vendor has retained effective control and the risks of ownership of the underlying property. The vendor may retain control by having a right or obligation to repurchase the property (for example, an option to repurchase at less than fair value). The vendor may retain the risks of ownership by providing the purchaser with a cash flow guarantee or a promise to support the leasing operations of the property for other than a short period for which the related costs can be reasonably estimated.

- Sales of houses and commercial or industrial buildings are normally recognized when title passes at closing. Sales of condominium units may be recognized when arrangements are made to permit and require the purchaser to buy, finance, and occupy the unit, even though it may not be possible for legal title to pass until some later date.

- Where a real estate company constructs a building for a single purchaser, percentage-of-completion accounting would be permissible, just as it would be for any general contractor.

In the United States, a much more detailed set of accounting standards has been enunciated for transactions involving real estate.[17] These standards provide a considerable variety of rules for revenue recognition, depending on the circumstances, but are so worded as to leave less room for judgment than do the CIPREC recommendations.

Computer Software

The computer software business has experienced spectacular growth and continuing innovation and development under highly competitive conditions. Companies in the industry have been offering a wide variety of products ranging from off-the-shelf programs to highly customized software and support services. The business has also featured complex marketing arrangements. Products and related services may be sold, leased or licensed with some rights and risks being retained by software developers. Sales contracts frequently provide generous warranties, rights to future program enhancements and ongoing services. As a result, the recognition of revenues can be open to a broad range of interpretation and judgment. It was difficult to determine to what extent the diverse practices that developed during the 1980s reflected real differences in circumstances or simply differences in companies' conservative or aggressive accounting predispositions.[18]

With the strong encouragement of the FASB and the SEC, the AICPA developed an earlier issues paper into a Statement of Position (SOP) in 1991. Subsequently a number of practice issues arose that were not adequately addressed in the SOP. Further consideration led to its replacement in 1997, and further amendment in 1998.[19] The guidance provided in these statements amounts to authoritative status in the U.S. The current statement, as amended, provides that revenue be recognized on delivery and acceptance of developed software, if there is a clearly defined arrangement with the customer, the vendor's fee is fixed or determinable, and collectibility is probable.

Revenue recognition is complicated where, as is commonly the case, there are multiple elements to a software arrangement with a customer, some of which are to be delivered at future dates. The statement requires that the revenue should be allocated to the various elements based on defined objective evidence of fair value. If sufficient evidence does not exist to enable this allocation, all revenue is to be deferred until the earlier of the point at which objective evidence does exist, or all elements have been delivered (with some exceptions, for example, post-customer support programs). No revenue is to be recognized if the portion allocable to delivered elements is subject to forfeiture or refund if any of the undelivered elements are not delivered. If an arrangement to deliver a software system requires significant production, modifications or customization, percentage-of-completion accounting may be appropriate if there are clearly determined stages of progress. This pronouncement is highly complex and detailed, so much so that an AICPA software revenue recognition task force has been set up to address applications issues.

There is no authoritative literature on the subject in Canada, and Canadian accounting practices have been much influenced by the AICPA statements. A few public Canadian software companies that are SEC registrants have referred to adherence to them in their accounting policy notes.

Revenue from Service Transactions

In the past few decades the performance and sale of services has formed an increasing percentage of business activity. Yet much of accounting literature is still written as though business activity mainly consisted of the manufacture and sale of tangible products. Accordingly, there has been a tendency for accounting practices for service industries to develop and become generally accepted within the narrow context of the industry itself, with little concern for consistency with what is done in other industries. Some of the inconsistencies in practices for recognition of initial fees, described earlier, represent examples.

The essential problem in service industries, as in any other business, is to relate revenues with the periods in which they are deemed earned and associate costs appropriately with either recognized revenues or time periods. As observed throughout this chapter, in some cases an appropriate cost-revenue association is achieved by timing revenue recognition (through accretion approaches) to coincide with the incurrence of related costs, while in other cases it is more appropriate to defer or anticipate costs (i.e., account for them as inventories or liabilities for future expenditures) so that they are expensed at the point of revenue recognition. Applying these approaches to achieve reasonable revenue-cost association presents particular problems for the service sector because the natural association of costs of goods sold with sales revenue that is found in manufacturing industries is lacking in many service industries. Consider an advertising agency that earns commissions on advertising placed. Where services such as research, art work, copywriting, and production are not covered by specific charges, how are they to be associated with commissions revenues? What are the implications for revenue recognition?

In view of the wide variety of service activities, it is not surprising that a variety of revenue recognition methods is found. The following discussion is largely based on suggestions in an FASB "Invitation to Comment."[20]

- Many service activities consist of the performance of a single act, for example, repair of appliances or sale of property by a real estate broker. The only possible revenue recognition point in such a case is that of point of sale, which often will coincide with or be close to cash collection. In such cases, direct sale costs are often incurred virtually instantaneously with the sale (for example, sale commissions), while other costs bring no benefit unless there are sales. Accordingly, it usually makes sense to charge all costs to expense as they are incurred. If, however, costs are incurred that are directly related to revenue that will be recognized in future, they may be deferred.

- By extension, if the service activity performed consists of a series of acts, but one act among them represents the culmination of performance and is much more significant than other acts, revenue can be recognized at the time of the culminating act, usually the point of sale or execution of service. All costs that cannot be directly related to future revenue are expensed.

- In contrast, when the service activities are well defined and revenue is known or capable of estimation within reasonable limits, an accretion basis of revenue recognition becomes both feasible and the most faithful representation of the activity portrayed. If, for example, the service consists largely of making facilities available for a fee (as in a club or health spa), it makes sense to recognize revenue as earned on a time basis and write off all costs as incurred.

- Some services, such as maintenance and repair of appliances or office equipment, may also be offered for a flat fee for a given contract period. Revenue from service contracts would normally be recognized ratably over the life of the contract in the absence of a better basis of recognition. Common sense should govern, however. For example, if the typical contract term is three years and experience indicates that the costs of repair service tend to increase over the three years, it would be sensible to recognize contract revenue in a rising pattern over its duration.[21]

- In other situations, the service performed may be more variable over time. If revenue tends to vary with direct effort it may be possible to accrue revenue as performance proceeds. In a public accounting firm, for example, if recovery rates per hour can be reasonably estimated, earning activity is fairly portrayed by valuing hours accumulated in work in process at estimated recoverable amounts (allowing an appropriate discount for expected delays in collection) and writing off costs as incurred. In effect, inventory is carried at estimated realizable value. This approach may also be applicable in legal firms and some consulting practices.[22] In situations that are basically similar but where revenue recoveries are more difficult to estimate, the approach may be varied by valuing work in process at a cost rate per hour. Putting some value on work in process, where billing and realization is delayed, is likely to provide a better portrayal of income and financial position than would a system of writing off all costs when incurred and recognizing revenue only when billed.

- In still other situations, services are contracted for in advance covering specified work— for example, architectural or engineering project services. In such cases, accounting that is very similar to that described previously for construction contractors may be followed.
  - When a sales value can be assigned reasonably objectively to specific activities, revenue may be recognized as the activities are performed.
  - Alternatively, the direct costs of contract performance may be accumulated and revenue recognized in the proportion that performance costs to date bear to total estimated cost on the service contract. (Reference is made here to the accumulation of direct costs, whereas in construction contract accounting, a considerable amount of indirect costs is likely to be accumulated by contracts. The difference may be explained by the

facts that (1) in service industries a high proportion of cost will be salary costs that can be treated as direct, and (2) remaining costs are likely to be of a general and administrative nature whose allocation to contracts would be arbitrary at best.)

- The usual condition holds that revenue recognition should be postponed if collectibility cannot be estimated with reasonable certainty.

RECOGNITION OF TRANSACTIONS IN ENTERPRISE ASSETS AND LIABILITIES

It has become common for enterprises to engage in transactions to realize cash from the sale, sale-leaseback, collateralization or securitization of its financial and capital assets; or to defease or restructure its liabilities. There are various financing, risk management and accounting (off-balance sheet financing and gain recognition) motivations for these transactions. Financial intermediaries have been designing increasingly sophisticated, and often highly complex, transactions that can be tailored to allocate benefits, risks and obligations among various parties in many different ways.

These transactions are apart from the normal revenue-generating activities of an enterprise, but they involve quite similar questions to those we have addressed in relation to revenue recognition. In general, what are the appropriate principles for recognition of these transactions as sales (assets) or settlements (liabilities), and for consequential recognition of gains and losses? The traditional concept of "realization" calls for sales recognition of assets if cash, or other consideration that is reasonably assured of collection, has been exchanged and the substantial risks and benefits of ownership have been transferred—and for liabilities to be treated as extinguished on the basis of repayment of the obligation. These conventional concepts were not designed with today's sophisticated transactions in mind, and they are open to inconsistent application and abuse.

Of course, recognition of gains and losses at the time of realization has always given entity management some ability to manage reported income, by selling selected assets or settling particular liabilities in order to record gains or losses at strategic times. This ability is an inevitable consequence of a historical cost-based accounting model. The dangers of financial statement users being misled by this are moderated somewhat by disclosures that distinguish the effects of nonrecurring, nonoperating transactions (see Chapter 18). Serious consideration is being given by the FASB, the IASC and other standard setters to the possibilities of measuring financial assets and financial liabilities on a current, fair value basis, with immediate recognition of changes in value in income (see discussion at Chapter 17). This would eliminate this income management possibility in respect of financial assets and liabilities.

Perhaps a more serious concern is that traditional concepts are open to wide interpretation and manipulation in determining whether particular transactions constitute realized sales of assets or settlements of liabilities. There are many examples. A borrowing arrangement collateralized by an enterprise's receivables may be slightly "re-engineered" to appear to be a sale of the receivables. A transfer of assets to a third party may be consummated in a manner that leaves the vendor exposed to some risks in relation to the transferred assets, so that it is open to opinion whether sufficient risks and benefits have been transferred to qualify it as a sale. Financial assets, such as stocks and bonds, may be "loaned," or sold subject to repurchase agreements, and conventional realization concepts may provide little or no basis for deciding whether they constitute sales realizations.

The basic issues, and the responses of accounting standard setters to date, are demonstrated by the situations discussed below.

Distinguishing Sales from Debt Financing

Some transactions that are structured as sales of capital assets or receivables in exchange for cash may really be debt financings. Questions arise as to the appropriateness of sales treatment if the transferor retains some of the risks and benefits associated with the transferred assets. Under traditional recognition concepts the issue becomes one of defining how much and what types of risks and benefits may be retained by the transferor and still legitimately treat the transfer as a sale.

Sale-Leaseback Transactions

Certain of the issues are well illustrated by sale-leaseback transactions. Suppose an entity A sells its plant which has a net book value of $600,000 to an independent party for $1 million cash, and simultaneously leases some or all of the plant back for a portion of its estimated remaining useful life. Has a sale taken place, and if so, is it appropriate to recognize the $400,000 gain in income? Alternatively, has A simply borrowed $1 million, with the future lease payments being the principal and interest repayments of that debt? The accounting under these two alternatives can be dramatically different. In the U.S., the FASB has disallowed sales treatment for sale-leasebacks involving real estate if there is any "continuing involvement" by the transferor in the property beyond a simple fixed-term lease. Such "continuing involvement" is very broadly defined to include any obligation or option to repurchase the property or any direct or indirect guarantee of the buyer-lessor's investment or return on the property.[23] There is no similar pronouncement in Canada, and in practice sales treatment has been permitted on a less restricted basis.[24]

If the transaction is considered to be a sale, then one must examine the implications of the leaseback under lease accounting standards, which standards are similar in Canada and the U.S.[25] (Lease accounting issues are the subject of Chapter 13.) These standards set out criteria for determining when a lease should be considered equivalent to the purchase of the underlying assets by the lessee (a "capital lease"). If the leaseback in the example above is considered to be a capital lease, it would be treated by A as a repurchase of the asset at $1 million in exchange for an equivalent amount of debt, being the lease obligation. Alternatively, if A is not considered to have effectively repurchased the asset through the leaseback, the plant asset would be removed from the balance sheet and the lease would be treated as an operating lease. This would result in no liability being set up for the lease obligation; rather the lease payments would simply be expensed as they become due. In either case, the gain would not be recognized immediately in income (unless only a minor portion of the plant was leased back), but would be amortized to income over the lease term, or over the estimated useful life of the plant if accounted for as a capital lease. This is because a sale and simultaneous leaseback are interdependent transactions, with the result that the sale price of the property will not necessarily be a realistic indicator of its fair value. If the vendor-lessee is a good credit risk, the sale price in the agreement could be more than the fair value of the property, in which case the lease payments would be commensurately increased. Thus the gain is considered to be realized over the term of the leaseback or, if a capital lease, as the leased asset is used.

Transfers of Receivables and Like Assets

Companies in certain industries build up portfolios of amounts receivable, which may be collectible in instalments with interest. These range from retail and credit card receivables to mortgages on real estate. It has become quite common for entities to exchange some or all of their portfolios of receivables for cash in order to free up cash for other investments. It is clear that such a transaction can be regarded as a completed sale, and a gain or loss recorded, if the vendor has no continuing involvement in, or obligation in respect of the transferred assets. What, however, is the position if the vendor does have some continuing involvement or obligation? Examples of continuing involvement include full or partial guarantees of the collectibility of transferred receivables, conditional or unconditional agreements to reacquire the assets, options written or held, and servicing agreements (to look after collection of receivable payments and remit them to the transferee). Such arrangements can be complex and take a variety of forms. They often involve securitizations, under which special-purpose entities or trusts are set up to hold the financial assets for the beneficial interests of unit holders. Other examples include securities lending arrangements, repurchase agreements ("repos") and a number of possible factoring arrangements.

In 1983 the FASB issued a standard that ruled that a transfer of receivables with recourse should be treated as a realized sale under certain conditions. These were that the transferor did not have any option to repurchase the receivables, that the purchaser could not require the transferor to repurchase them (other than under the recourse provisions), and that the transferor could reasonably estimate the allowance required for uncollectible accounts.[26] This standard was open to criticism from a number of perspectives. It was essentially a pragmatic set of rules that did not have any clear conceptual basis. Some believed that the existence of an option should not rule out sales treatment if the option could be reasonably priced; others argued that an option should only rule out sales treatment if it is exercisable at less than the fair value of the receivables at the date of transfer. Some argued that a transferor entity's retention of credit risk through the recourse provisions leaves it exposed to the primary risk associated with the receivables, so that it should not be treated as a sale, but rather, should simply be treated as a loan.

The FASB readdressed the issues and put in place a new standard (SFAS 125) in 1996.[27] It holds that if an enterprise surrenders control over financial assets, the transfer shall be accounted for as a sale, with any interests or risks retained by the transferor being separately valued and recorded in the transferor's books. Thus, where the transferor assumes certain financial obligations as part of the transfer agreement (for example, a default guarantee), or obtains certain rights (for example, a right to receive defined "excess cash flows" that may be generated by the assets), these are to be separately recognized as liabilities or assets of the transferor and measured at their fair value at the date of the transaction. It may be noted that this approach is analogous to the revenue allocation approach discussed earlier, where the sales price is apportioned among component parts.

In concept the principle is simple and straightforward. As well it is consistent with the concept of an "asset" in financial accounting, defined as economic resources *controlled* by the enterprise. It is also seen to be a more precise and powerful principle than the traditional "risks and rewards" approach, which does not recognize the effects of apportioning risks among parties.

Difficulties arise, however, in implementing the principle where the rights or obligations retained by the transferor are so significant that they may seem to negate the premise that the transferor has really surrendered control of the transferred assets. SFAS 125 holds that the transferor has surrendered control if, and only if, all of the following conditions are met:

- The transferred assets have been put beyond the reach of the transferor and its creditors, even in bankruptcy.
- The transferee obtains control of the assets, including the right to pledge or exchange the assets (or, if the transferee is a special-purpose entity, the holders of the beneficial interests in that entity have the right to pledge or exchange those interests).
- The transferor is not both entitled and obligated to repurchase or redeem the assets before their maturity, or is not entitled to repurchase or redeem transferred assets that are not readily obtainable (SFAS 125, paragraph 9).

The application of these conditions to the wide variety of asset transfer transactions in the U.S. has required a highly intricate and complex set of supporting rules. A number of questions have arisen in practice, and the FASB is currently in the process of developing some adjustments to, and interpretations of, certain of these conditions. The more major of these adjustments relate to determining when some accounts in a portfolio of transferred receivables may be subsequently returned to the transferor without upsetting treatment as a sale, and what recognition should be given to assets held as collateral in respect of a transfer treated as a loan when the secured party has the right to sell or repledge the collateral. These illustrate the tangle of detail and complexity of many transfer transactions that make the concept of control difficult to apply. The implications of these difficulties are significant because transfer transactions are frequently constructed to exploit accounting ambiguities in order to achieve a desired accounting result.

An IASC study of accounting for financial instruments has also addressed these issues.[28] It supports the principle that asset transfer transactions be treated as sales if control is surrendered, and it rejects the traditional risks and rewards approach.[29] However, it questions two of the FASB conditions:

- Whether the transferred assets must be beyond the reach of a bankruptcy trustee or receiver in the event the transferor should become bankrupt—which in most situations will be a very remote contingency, and
- Whether the inability of a transferee to sell or pledge transferred assets should necessarily, in all cases, mean that the transferor has not surrendered control.[30]

An international joint working group of accounting standard setters has been set up to further consider these issues (among other issues of accounting financial instruments) in an effort to come up with a harmonized international standard. This joint working group includes the CICA, the FASB, the IASC, the U.K. Accounting Standards Board, and representatives of five other standard-setting jurisdictions.

In the meantime, the IASC has put in place a standard on financial instruments that adopts a control-based approach, with much briefer and more broadly defined conditions than those of the FASB.[31] This standard has been developed by the IASC as an interim step, pending further consideration of the issues by the international joint working group.

In Canada there is no *CICA Handbook* standard that directly addresses this issue. In 1989, the Emerging Issues Committee adopted a position which it has attempted to reason forward from the *CICA Handbook* standard on revenue recognition. As a result it is based on the transfer of the risks and rewards of ownership.[32] The EIC concluded that for a transfer of receivables to be recognized as a sale, the transferor must have transferred the significant risks and rewards of ownership of the receivables, as well as having reasonable assurance regarding the measurement of the consideration received. Implementation of this position requires some basis for determining what constitutes "significant risks and rewards," which determination must be arbitrary in significant degree. The EIC abstract states that any recourse provided by a transferor must be reasonable in relation to the losses expected to be incurred on the receivables, and that it is unlikely that a sale could be justified if the total recourse exceeded 10 percent of the proceeds received—a very wide range in that typical loss experience on quality receivables would rarely be expected to exceed 3 or 4 percent under normal conditions. This CICA approach is clearly inconsistent with the FASB standard and developing international thinking. Currently the CICA has a project underway to address what is viewed to be the most troublesome form of financial asset transfer in Canada—securitization. It is proposing to replace the EIC abstract with a guideline that is consistent with SFAS 125.

Debt Extinguishment

The treatment of gain or loss on extinguishment of debt when such extinguishment is accomplished with the proceeds of a new issue of debt is a question that has divided accountants for many years. Debt refunding may become attractive for various reasons. For example, it may be thought that interest rates will rise in future and therefore extending the maturity date of existing debt is desirable. If interest rates at the date of refunding are below the interest rate on the outstanding debt, a premium will be required to redeem that outstanding debt (in the absence of a right to call it). In such a case, some accountants have felt it erroneous to record a loss on the debt redemption when the refunding operation as such is considered desirable. Moreover, it is pointed out that if the loss were deferred and amortized over the remaining term of the debt redeemed, that amortization, together with the interest costs (at the lower rate) on the new debt, would merely approximate the interest costs that would have been paid had the old issue been left outstanding. Accepted accounting practice on this issue has varied over the years. It has come to be accepted, however, that bygones should be bygones and gain or loss with respect to an issue of debt that is retired should not be deferred.[33]

A further question arises that is analogous to that addressed above in respect of transfers of assets: what is the appropriate accounting for debt extinguished if the debtor retains some obligations with respect to it? Suppose, for example, a debtor is legally released from the primary obligation on real estate debt because that obligation is assumed by the purchaser of mortgaged property, but the original debtor remains secondarily liable. In such a case, it is reasoned that the debtor's position has changed from that of being a direct debtor to that of an entity subject to a contingent liability as guarantor. Thus, the debt is treated as extinguished when the debtor ceases to be primarily liable, and a gain or loss on the extinguishment should be recorded. The guarantee is then treated as a contingent liability to be recognized and measured in accordance with the CICA standard on contingencies (*CICA Handbook*, Section 3290). This, it is to be noted, requires recognition only if it is likely that the guarantee will be exercised. It may be reasoned that, in concept, such a guarantee should be initially recorded at its fair value.[34]

There have also been considerable differences in views and practice in determining when a modification of the terms of a debt instrument may be sufficiently significant to justify treatment as a settlement of the old debt and issuance of new debt.[35]

In-Substance Defeasance

Suppose a debtor sets aside securities in trust to meet all obligations with respect to outstanding debt. May the trust assets be offset against the outstanding debt for balance sheet presentation purposes, and may a gain be recognized for the difference between the carrying value of the trust securities and the recorded amount of the debt? The FASB described this as "in-substance defeasance." In 1983 it ruled that, with proper disclosure, the transaction may be accounted for as though the debt were extinguished; accordingly, gain could be recognized. To qualify for such treatment, however, the chance of the debtor being called upon to make good on the debt, other than from the trust assets, had to be remote. To ensure this, the assets would have to be irrevocably placed in the trust, be monetary assets in the same currency as the debt, and be essentially risk-free. Also, cash flows from the trust assets would have to approximately coincide in timing and amount with scheduled interest and principal payments on the debt.[36] In-substance defeasance has been accepted in practice in Canada under the same conditions established by the FASB, but there have been few applications.

The FASB reconsidered the matter, and in 1996 determined that "in-substance defeasance" arrangements are not sufficient to warrant de-recognition of a liability. It now requires that the debtor should report both the asset in the trust and the liability on its balance sheet.[37] This revised position is reasoned from the fact that the debtor is not released from the primary obligation under a debt agreement merely by setting assets aside in a trust. If the assets in the trust prove insufficient for some reason, the debtor must make up the difference. Also in practice it was found that there is virtually no such thing as an irrevocable trust, and in a number of cases these trusts have been revoked and the defeasance reversed.

SUMMARY

In the early days of the historical cost accounting model, revenue recognition did not present serious problems. The basic idea that revenue should be recognized only when realized—that is, when an exchange transaction was consummated in which the consideration was a liquid monetary asset—seemed capable of dealing with the vast majority of situations. Recognition of revenue with respect to a single contract extending over a long period of time was considered a special case that could be dealt with by a special approach—percentage-of-completion accounting.

As the variety in forms of business organization and revenue transactions has grown, experience has shown that several revenue recognition approaches are needed to permit faithful representation of business activity. The criteria governing when each approach should be adopted are, in some respects, still unclear. The following are the main ideas.

Three possible approaches may be taken to revenue recognition: the critical event approach, the revenue accretion approach, and the revenue allocation approach. The approach that is taken in a particular circumstance is significantly influenced by the point in the cycle of productive activity at which a revenue contract is entered into.

When a sale contract is not made until most productive effort has taken place, revenue is ordinarily recognized at the time of a "critical event." The criteria governing the selection of that critical event are that it should represent the time when the significant risks and rewards from ownership of the asset sold have been transferred to the purchaser and there is not significant remaining uncertainty as to the consummation of the sale, collectibility of the consideration, or remaining costs to be incurred to fulfill the vendor's obligations.

Normally that critical event is the point of delivery by the vendor under a sales contract, provided there is little doubt as to acceptance by the customer. Other critical event recognition points are used in a minority of cases.

If some costs required to fulfill a contract obligation will be incurred after the critical event recognition point, a liability for them must be accrued in order to provide a proper measure of income. Indeed, when major efforts remain to take place after an initial revenue recognition point, it may be better to follow the revenue allocation approach, allocating the total contract revenue between an amount to be recognized at the initial recognition point (such as sale) and a remainder to be recognized upon completion of the subsequent activities or as they are performed, in accordance with the circumstances.

Great uncertainty as to consummation of sales transactions, collectibility of proceeds, or amount of future costs to be incurred to satisfy post-sales obligations causes postponement of the critical event or deferment of the net income recorded on the sale. If the amount of returns or future costs is unpredictable but could be large, the critical event should be postponed. If the uncertainty relates to future collectibility, the sale may be recognized but its income results deferred, to be recognized subsequently on the instalment or cost-recovery basis.

When a sale contract is settled before an extended production or service process, great uncertainty as to costs may lead to postponement of revenue recognition until some subsequent critical event (such as completion of the work—the completed contract basis of recognition). Frequently, however, it will be appropriate to recognize some revenue as work proceeds, either on the accretion approach or the revenue allocation approach.

The accretion approach is used when revenue can be related to some reasonable indicators of progress. Such indicators may consist of output measures, in which case it is necessary to be able to relate costs incurred to the several outputs. Indicators may also be input measures—measures of effort or costs.

The revenue allocation approach requires the identification of several functions covered by the single contract price and allocation of some revenue to each function. The revenue allocated to each function is recognized either on the critical event basis or the accretion basis, as seems most appropriate. Ideally, the amount of revenue allocated to each function is based on prices for the function if it were performed independently. If such prices are not available, the allocation becomes based more on judgment. One expedient is to allocate to minor functions only sufficient revenue to cover costs traceable to performance of those functions.

Treatment of an initial fee charged when a continuing relationship is set up with a customer depends upon the circumstances. When the initial fee is for identifiable services and is reasonable in amount, it may be recognized as though it were a separate revenue transaction. In other cases, the initial fee may be a separate charge that simply provides additional revenue to cover continuing service cost. In such cases, the fee, if not refundable, can be recognized as revenue over the estimated service period for the customer or club member in question. In still other cases, an initial fee may cover some specific initial services but may be unreasonably high in relation to the value of those services, so that it appears, in substance, to be merely a different way of charging for continuing services. If the fee for continuing services does not appear to be adequate compensation, some or all of the initial fee should be deferred for amortization against revenue recognized over the estimated period of continuing service.

Revenue from property owned, such as interest and dividends on securities, royalties, and rentals, is recognized on different bases, depending on the circumstances. Revenue from interest and rentals, for example, is recognized on the accretion approach in proportion to time elapsed. Revenue from dividends is recognized on a critical event basis—the event being the declaration of the dividend. Revenue from royalties is recognized as it accrues in accordance with the terms of the rental agreement.

Sales and other transactions to realize or refinance a company's working assets or to settle or extend its debt can give rise to special considerations. Traditionally such transactions, and attendant gains and losses, have been recognized on realization, except that losses amounting to impairment may require earlier recognition. The development of sophisticated financing arrangements and risk management strategies have exposed significant limitations in the traditional realization convention. For example, questions arise when an entity enters into sale-leaseback arrangements with respect to its productive assets, or sells receivables with recourse. When, or under what conditions, do such transactions amount to a sale, with consequent recognition of gains or losses, and when might they be simply debt financings? Analogous questions arise with respect to whether debt has effectively been extinguished under various circumstances in which the original debtor retains some obligations or risks with respect to it. Such issues have been the subject of considerable attention by standard setters in recent years. The FASB has recently developed a standard for transfers of financial assets that provides for sales treatment if control over the assets is surrendered, with separate recognition of any rights or obligations that have been retained by the transferor. This standard sets out highly complex conditions to define when control should be considered to have been surrendered.

REFERENCES

[1] This proposition is demonstrated by R.K. Storey, "Cash Movements and Periodic Income Determination," in *Financial Accounting Theory: Issues and Controversies*, ed. S.A. Zeff and T.F. Keller (New York: McGraw-Hill Book Co., 1964), pp. 46–53. Storey points out that the proposition is true only if profit is deemed satisfactorily measured by the net increment in cash. If profit were deemed to be the excess of purchasing power received over purchasing power invested and prices were not stable over the period of measurement, the proposition would no longer be true.

[2] American Institute of Accountants, Committee on Accounting Procedure, "Rules Adopted by Membership," Chapter 1A in *Restatement and Revision of Accounting Research Bulletins*, Accounting Research Bulletin No. 43 (New York: AIA, 1953), par. 1.

[3] AICPA, APB, *Basic Concepts and Accounting Principles Underlying Financial Statements of Business Enterprises*, APB Statement No. 4 (New York: AICPA, 1970), par. 150.

[4] CICA, "Revenue," *CICA Handbook*, Section 3400 (Toronto: CICA). See also IASC, *Revenue*, IAS 18 (London: IASC, Revised 1993).

[5] *CICA Handbook*, Section 3400, par. 07.

[6] The term "critical event" was coined in an article by J.H. Myers, "The Critical Event and Recognition of Net Profit," reprinted in *Financial Accounting Theory*, ed. Zeff and Keller, pp. 54–59.

[7] See CICA Research Study, *Accounting and Financial Reporting by Agricultural Producers* (Toronto: CICA, 1986), pp. 15–17. The study group supported the lower of

cost or market method of inventory valuation, but reasoned that market value less estimated disposition costs might be appropriate in relatively rare circumstances when there is a readily determinable and realizable market price, the goods are available for immediate delivery, and there are relatively insignificant and predictable costs of disposal.

8   See FASB, *Revenue Recognition When Right of Return Exists*, Statement of Financial Accounting Standards No. 48 (Stamford: FASB, 1981). SFAS 48 emphasizes as well the requirement that risks in connection with the property sold be effectively transferred.

9   CICA, Emerging Issues Committee, *Gain Recognition in Arm's-length and Related Party Transactions When the Consideration Received Includes a Claim on the Assets Sold*, EIC 79 (Toronto: CICA, 1997). EIC 79 only covers sales that are *not* in the normal course of business, but one might reason by analogy to transactions with similar characteristics that are in the normal course. However, in the real estate industry, usually revenues, not just gains, would be deferred in the types of situations outlined in EIC 79 for sales in the normal course. See Canadian Institute of Public Real Estate Companies, *Recommended Accounting Practices for Real Estate Investment and Development Companies* (Toronto: CIPREC, 1998), pars. 402.1 and 402.10.

10   See *CICA Handbook*, Section 3400.15, and AICPA, *Accounting for Performance of Construction-Type and Certain Production-Type Contracts*, Accounting Standards Division Statement of Position No. 81-1 (New York: AICPA, 1981), especially pars. 23–25. The AICPA statement provides a useful discussion of all aspects of contract accounting.

11   This is now the subject of an EIC abstract. CICA, Emerging Issues Committee, *Construction Contractors—Revenue Recognition When the Percentage of Completion Method Is Applicable*, EIC 78 (Toronto: CICA, 1997).

12   CICA, Emerging Issues Committee, *Revenue Recognition on Sales With a Guaranteed Minimum Resale Value*, EIC 84 (Toronto: CICA, 1998).

13   In American practice, cable-TV hook-up revenue is recognized only to the extent that it reflects direct selling costs. Any remainder of the hook-up charge is deferred to be amortized over the estimated average lifetime of a subscriber connection. Initial subscriber installation costs are capitalized and depreciated in a normal fashion. Costs of disconnecting and reconnecting are charged to expense when incurred. See FASB Statement of Financial Accounting Standards No. 51, *Financial Reporting by Cable Television Companies* (Stamford: FASB, 1981).

14   See CICA Accounting Guideline "Fees and Costs Associated with Lending Activities," October 1987, in *CICA Handbook* (Toronto: CICA); and FASB, *Accounting for Non Refundable Fees and Costs Associated with Originating or Acquiring Loans and Initial Direct Costs of Leases*, Statement of Financial Accounting Standards No. 91 (Norwalk: FASB, 1986).

15   See CICA Accounting Guideline, "Franchise Fee Revenue," July 1984, in *CICA Handbook* (Toronto: CICA). See also FASB, *Accounting for Franchise Fee Revenue*, Statement of Financial Accounting Standards No. 45 (Stamford: FASB, 1981).

16   Canadian Institute of Public Real Estate Companies, "Revenue and Profit Recognition on Sales of Real Estate," *Recommended Accounting Practices for Real Estate Investment and Development Companies*, Section 400 (Toronto: CIPREC, 1998).

17 See FASB, *Accounting for Sales of Real Estate*, Statement of Financial Accounting Standards No. 66 (Stamford: FASB, 1982).

18 See, for example, R. Schattke, "Accounting for Computer Software: The Revenue Side of the Coin," *Journal of Accountancy*, January 1988, pp. 58–70.

19 AICPA, *Software Revenue Recognition*, SOP 97-2 (New York: AICPA, 1997), and AICPA, *Modification of SOP 97-2, "Software Revenue Recognition," With Respect to Certain Transactions*, SOP 98-9 (New York: AICPA, 1998).

20 See FASB Invitation to Comment, *Accounting for Certain Service Transactions* (Stamford: FASB, October 23, 1978).

21 By way of analogy see FASB, *Accounting for Separately Priced Extended Warranty and Product Maintenance Contracts*, Technical Bulletin No. 90-1 (Nowalk: FASB, 1990).

22 The Emerging Issues Committee Concluded that a law firm should recognize its fee revenue as it provides services using the percentage of completion method. CICA, Emerging Issues Committee, *Law Firms—Revenue Recognition*, EIC 65 (Toronto: CICA, 1995).

23 FASB, *Accounting for Leases: Sale-Leaseback Transactions Involving Real Estate; Sales-Type Leases of Real Estate*, Statement of Financial Accounting Standards No. 98 (Norwalk: FASB, 1988).

24 See discussion of real estate sale-leaseback transactions under Canadian GAAP, and an example illustrating basic issues and alternatives, in CICA Research Report, *Leasing Issues* (Toronto: CICA, 1989), pp. 8.4–8.8.

25 CICA, "Leases," *CICA Handbook*, Section 3065 (Toronto: CICA), in particular, pars .65–.70; and FASB, *Accounting for Leases*, FASB Statement No. 13 as Amended and Interpreted (Norwalk: FASB, 1998).

26 FASB, *Reporting by Transferors for Transfers of Receivables with Recourse*, Statement of Financial Accounting Standards No. 77 (Stamford: FASB, 1983).

27 FASB, *Accounting for Transfers and Servicing of Financial Assets and Extinguishments of Liabilities*, Statement of Financial Accounting Standards No. 125 (Norwalk: FASB, 1996).

28 IASC, *Accounting for Financial Assets and Financial Liabilities,* A Discussion Paper (London: IASC, 1997), chap. 3.

29 The IASC Discussion Paper also considered a standard developed by the U.K. Accounting Standards Board, *Reporting the Substance of Transactions*, FRS 5 (London: The Accounting Standards Board Limited, 1994). It is based on the risks and benefits approach, but with some modifications for certain special cases. The IASC discussion paper contains an analysis of the U.K. standard—see IASC, *Accounting for Financial Assets and Financial Liabilities*, pp. 70-72.

30 Ibid., pp. 63–64 and 66–70.

31 IASC, *Financial Instruments: Recognition and Measurement*, IAS 39 (London: IASC, 1998), pars. 35–56.

32 CICA Emerging Issues Committee, *Transfers of Receivables*, EIC 9 (Toronto: CICA, 1989).

[33] AICPA, APB, *Early Extinguishment of Debt*, APB Opinion No. 26 (New York: AICPA, 1972). Lacking a standard in Canada, practice has developed with reference to this standard.

[34] The IASC has recently concluded that a guarantee arising on the extinguishmental debt or its transfer to another party should be recognized at its fair value. See IASC, *Financial Instruments: Recognition and Measurement*, IAS 39, par. 64.

[35] See CICA, Emerging Issues Committee, *Debtor's Accounting for a Modification or Exchange of Debt Instruments*, EIC 88 (Toronto: CICA, 1998).

[36] FASB, *Extinguishment of Debt: An Amendment of APB Opinion No. 26*, Statement of Financial Accounting Standards No. 76 (Stamford: FASB, 1983).

[37] FASB, *Accounting for Transfers and Servicing of Financial Assets and Extinguishments of Liabilities*, par. 16.

EXPENSE RECOGNITION; LOSSES AND CONTINGENCIES

In the previous chapter we introduced the subject of periodic income measurement by reviewing accounting standards for recognition of revenue. In this chapter we begin consideration of standards for matching costs with revenues (or with accounting periods) in order to arrive at a net period income figure. To put that in another way, we are about to address the subject of recognition of "expense."

Let us begin with some comments on terminology.

- In a purchase transaction, the purchaser gives "consideration" in exchange for the goods or services acquired. The consideration represents the sacrifice in the transaction, which may consist of payment of money or the giving up of some other valuable commodity or the assumption of a liability.

- The term "cost" represents the value of the consideration given. In a fair exchange it may be presumed that it will also approximate the value of the thing acquired. Cost is also used in somewhat different senses. For example, in addition to the sense of acquisition cost, it may be used to mean manufactured cost, that is, the sum of acquisition costs of material, labour, and overhead that is deemed (by the costing system in use) to be required to produce a commodity.

- The term "expenditure" is used to describe the payment of cash or equivalent or the incurrence of a contractual liability to purchase goods and services. Expenditure is often used almost interchangeably with cost to mean the value of consideration.

- The term "expense" refers to the consumption of the benefit obtained from goods or services owned. In historical cost accounting, expense is measured by the cost of the goods or services consumed. Cost is also used on occasion to mean the same thing as expense. Thus we may speak of cost of operations for a period instead of expense for a period.

Expenditures are made to acquire benefits in the form of goods or services. With a few exceptions (expenditure on land is one), the benefits received from expenditures are sooner or later entirely consumed. As those benefits are consumed we wish to recognize expense. With respect to profit-oriented enterprises, goods and services may be presumed to be consumed in revenue-generating processes. (The special circumstances of not-for-profit organizations are considered in Chapter 27.) The objective of cost-based accrual accounting for profit-oriented enterprises is to recognize the cost of goods and services as expenses at the moment when the related revenue is recognized. Revenue recognition is the trigger point, and we have already noted the relationship between the timing of revenue recognition and the accrual of related expenses in Chapter 7. The measurement of income as the difference between recognized revenues and the expenses incurred to achieve those revenues is consistent with what could be described as a fundamental "economic law"—that one must make economic sacrifices to obtain economic satisfactions. An economic good is defined by the fact that its acquisition required a past sacrifice (its cost) and by the expectation that its consumption will yield a future satisfaction (ultimately revenues). The economic presumption of sacrifice to achieve benefits underlies the traditional "matching" objective in financial accounting. This concept of an economic good, and its presumption of sacrifice to achieve benefits, is also at the heart of the concept of "assets" in financial accounting, as probable future economic benefits to result from past events or transactions. In other words, the fundamental "economic law" is consistent not only with the revenue-expense matching objective, but also with the balance sheet concept of "assets" (and "liabilities").

In this chapter we wish to discuss standards for recognition of expenses and losses, bearing in mind this basic revenue-expense matching objective. We shall divide our discussion into three sections:

- *Goods and services costs as assets or expenses.* The relationship between cost inputs and revenue outputs varies from direct and traceable to highly indirect and untraceable. All goods and services inputs must be acquired on or before their contribution to revenue generation. The accounting question then is whether costs to acquire particular inputs should be considered to be assets (that is, be expected to contribute to the achievement of revenues in future periods), or simply should be expensed as they are incurred. Recognition as assets requires methods for associating costs with particular "cost objects" (assets), and bases for recognizing the consumption of asset benefits in future periods. Our discussion of these matters in this chapter will be general. In Chapters 10 to 13 we shall delve more thoroughly into the subjects of inventory accounting, tangible capital asset accounting, intangible asset accounting, and expense recognition with respect to those assets.

- *Accrued liabilities and related expenses.* In a number of cases an entity receives goods or service benefits in return for an obligation to make future expenditures. Such undertakings to make future expenditures are liabilities for accounting purposes just as much as are contractual liabilities. In some of these cases, the obligation will be a direct result of the recognition of revenues. An example is a liability for warranty costs, which costs are recognized as an expense at the moment the revenue from the related product is recorded. In other cases obligations to make future expenditures may not be directly related to the recognition of revenues. These include obligations to pay future pensions in respect of past employee services, and liabilities for future expenditures to restore properties for environmental damage. In some cases the resulting incurred costs may be appropriately treated as assets rather than as immediate expenses. The recording of accrued liabilities that entail future expenditures, and related measurement and expense recognition issues, are discussed in this chapter. We shall, however, reserve detailed exploration of the complex issues in accounting for pensions and other retirement benefits for Chapter 14.

- *Contingencies.* Upon occasion an entity discovers it has or may have an obligation to make payments, which may or may not be attributable to specific aspects of its operations, but which were not previously foreseen. Although the obligation, in some sense, must have arisen out of operations prior to the date of discovery, no benefit from the payment will be discernible at the time of discovery. When recognized, therefore, the amount charged against income does not represent an expense recognized in relation to benefit consumed, but simply a loss. The obligation to make payment is also a liability for accounting purposes but, to the extent it is uncertain, is customarily known as a contingent liability. The recognition of losses, and contingencies in general, is the subject of a separate section of this chapter.

We shall end the chapter with a discussion of a particularly difficult area of expense/loss recognition—accounting for environmental costs.

GOODS AND SERVICES COSTS AS ASSETS OR EXPENSES

Recognition of expense with respect to goods and services acquired involves several decisions. These are: (1) the subdivision of costs between "period costs" and costs attaching to assets, (2) the selection of "cost objects" to be recorded as assets, (3) the choice of methods for attaching costs to assets, and (4) the choice of methods for measuring expense to be recognized with respect to assets sold or assets whose usefulness has otherwise expired.

Recognition of Expense for Period Costs

The first decision occurs at the time the initial cost to acquire a good or service is recognized. Some costs, such as sales commissions, will be clearly applicable to revenue currently being recognized as earned and thus should be recorded as expense immediately. Most other transaction costs will be incurred in the hope and expectation of contributing to future revenue. Ideally, all costs in such transactions would be carried forward as costs of identifiable product or service projects and be recognized as expense when revenue therefrom is recognized. Unfortunately, this ideal is unattainable for several practical reasons. For example, planning and research activities, although clearly applicable to hoped-for future revenue, may well not be capable of association with existing products or service categories. In this situation, there is likely to be considerable uncertainty as to whether these expenditures will benefit future operations. In addition, many services acquired, such as administrative services, although necessary, have a very indirect connection with specific earned revenues. Finally, many expenditures will have transitory benefits and will be recurring in nature, so that expense figures reported for a going concern will be very little different if they are written off as incurred, rather than deferred and matched with earned revenues on some more precise basis. For these several reasons—uncertainty of future benefit, remoteness from direct productive activity, or short-lived character of benefit—it is accepted that many expenditures should be recognized as expense as soon as incurred. The costs involved are known as "period costs" because they are written off in the period they are incurred.

In addition to outlays with transitory or uncertain benefits, there are costs from which benefit may be perceived over a future period but which should nevertheless be written off when incurred. For example, many companies in the 1980s adopted early retirement plans whereby employees were offered incentives to retire within a certain period. It was easy to see future benefit from this policy—reduction in payroll costs after the retirement, reducing the drag of older employees on productivity, greater flexibility in promotion policy, and so on. Yet the costs of the program should be recognized as expense immediately, rather than be deferred.[1] The benefit that the entity gains from the program lies in the liquidation of an obligation it has to existing employees. The cost of paying someone not to work is not a positive contribution to future operations. There is a simple test to distinguish whether such an expenditure relates to the future or the past. If a new company would not have to make the same expenditure as an existing company, the latter's cost is a legacy from the past, not an investment in the future. Ideally, it should have been accrued over the service period of the employees taking early retirement. Since it was not, it must be written off when it finally becomes clear that it will be incurred.

Selection of Cost Objects

If a cost is not to be treated as a period cost, a second decision arises. The cost in question must be associated with some cost object that will be recorded as an asset. The question is: What are the criteria that guide the selection of cost objects?

- The most obvious cost object, of course, is a tangible good to be sold or made into a good to be sold in future.
- Where the product of the business is service rather than a tangible good, it may still be possible, if costs can be associated with particular revenue contracts, to record an asset category similar in nature to tangible inventory. Thus a consulting engineering or architectural firm may accumulate salary costs as contract work in process for specific jobs or clients.
- Other tangible goods may be acquired for use rather than for sale. Plant and equipment are examples. Rarely is there doubt that the cost of such items should be treated as an asset and carried forward for matching against future revenues.
- Payments are often made to suppliers of goods or services in advance of the receipt of those items. The fact that something is yet to be received ordinarily justifies the treatment of prepayments (prepaid insurance, prepaid rent, etc.) as assets.
- Purchases may consist of intangible property such as a licence or legal right. If the intangible is well defined and benefit from its use can be controlled, it is just as clearly a potential source of future revenue as any tangible productive asset like machinery and equipment.
- If, however, the cost incurred does not give rise to a well-defined contractual or property right, the case is more doubtful. Consider costs incurred for advertising and promotion. Undoubtedly the expenditure is incurred in the hope that future revenue will be enhanced. But how successful will the promotion be? And how long will the benefit last? The fuzziness of the matching concept is epitomized by the name frequently given to such intangible cost objects. When carried forward, they are often called simply "deferred costs" rather than by a name, like plant and equipment or prepayments, or patent rights, that independently describes the nature of the asset.

Deferred costs provide the best example of the problem of allocation of expenditures to periods of benefit. In principle there is no difference, for the purpose of income measurement, between the cost of a tangible asset that contributes to the production of future revenue and any other expenditure that has the same result. Yet accountants are instinctively wary of treating the latter as assets. The primary reason for this is the uncertainty as to whether such expenditures will contribute to the production of revenues. To lessen that concern, some accountants have advocated that costs be carried forward only with respect to assets that are severable from the enterprise.

Costing of Assets

After the selection of cost objects, there remains the problem of assignment of costs to the cost objects. For something acquired in an exchange transaction, the cost is simply the sacrifice made in the exchange. In most cases that sacrifice can be measured in terms of the amount payable in the transaction.

This uncomplicated concept of cost does not carry through to the "cost" of an asset emerging from a productive process. The accountant thinks of the cost of a manufactured product as being the sum of the acquisition costs of all its components. That description begs the question of what are the components of a manufactured product. Some costs, such as raw materials, are traceable directly to individual units of product. Some costs vary in amount with the volume of production but cannot be traced directly to individual products. Some costs are required to provide productive capacity but are fixed in amount even though the volume of production varies quite widely. In general, only a minority of costs are traceable directly to units of product, and other costs must be *allocated* on some basis to provide a figure of cost per unit of product.

For accounting purposes the historical cost of an asset that is fabricated rather than purchased outright in an exchange transaction is the sum of the acquisition costs of the components deemed to have entered into the asset under the costing system in force. Obviously the significance of such a figure of cost depends upon the validity of the costing system. Possible costing elements are reviewed below.

- For tangible goods there is always the cost of materials embodied in the good. Although the actual material embodied represents an absolute minimum cost figure, there may be a question whether the cost of scrap material resulting from trimming or production errors should be included as part of the cost of the good. Possibly an allowance for a standard amount of scrap may be counted as part of the product cost with any excess being treated as expense. A general concept of prudent costs may be applied, which is that only those costs that could be expected to be incurred by reasonably prudent management should be eligible to be carried forward.

- In some instances there is a further problem when a single source of raw material eventually gives rise to a number of products. Examples of such "joint" products include a variety of refined products derived from crude oil, a number of metals obtained from complex ore bodies, and various cuts of meat, hides, and other products obtained from a single animal slaughtered. In all these cases, as soon as more than a single output emerges from the production process, material costs cannot be traced to individual outputs because tracing the costs to a product involves a one-to-many allocation (as discussed in Chapter 5).

- Labour that is directly expended in fabrication of a product can be visualized as embodied in it, just as are materials. The direct costs of material and labour are known as "prime costs," as distinguished from other costs of production known as "overhead costs."

- Certain types of overhead costs tend to vary with the volume of production, while other types are relatively fixed in amount over a considerable range of production. Still others may be described as "semi-variable"—that is, they may have both fixed and variable components, or they may increase in steps at given volume points but remain relatively constant between steps. If the amount of a given cost is highly correlated with the quantity of production, this is evidence that the cost is caused by the act of production and therefore can legitimately be counted as a product cost. Moreover, the higher the correlation with production volume, the more likely it is that reasonable ways can be found to trace the costs to the product.

- Fixed overhead costs are often described as "capacity costs," in that the costs are incurred in order to provide the facilities or capacity to produce or render service, while additional variable costs must ordinarily be incurred to make the product. Some capacity costs, such as the cost of plant and equipment, may be described as "sunk costs" or unavoidable costs since, once incurred, they are unalterable. Other capacity costs, such as regular maintenance costs or rentals, are recurring and may be more controllable. By definition, fixed costs cannot be traced to the output of production processes. As a consequence, if they are to be attached to cost objects such as inventory or self-constructed capital assets, some relatively arbitrary allocation basis must be found.

- Overhead costs are customarily classified as manufacturing, selling, and general and administrative costs. In principle, the attachment of costs to cost objects should not depend on how the cost is described but rather on whether a relationship can be established between it and the cost object. In practice, however, it is usually assumed that a cost that is described as general and administrative is inherently indirect and cannot reasonably be associated with such cost objects as inventory or self-constructed capital assets. Occasional exceptions to this rule are justified, for example, in accumulating costs applicable to contracts in process where the contract price specifically allows for recovery of general and administrative costs.

- Thus far, only costs incurred in consideration for the acquisition of goods or services have been described. These are distinguishable by their nature from costs of financing or cost of capital, that is, payments made or other rewards given to suppliers of capital for the use of their funds. In accounting (with the exception of regulated industries), only costs associated with outstanding debt are treated as "financing costs." Such financing costs include not only interest at the stipulated rate but also amortization of costs of issue and premium or discount in the issue price of the debt.

What then are the criteria that are, or ought to be, used to attach costs to cost objects? The most obvious criterion is that of causation. If it can be shown that a cost had to be incurred to produce the cost object, then it is logical that such cost should be deemed to be a cost *of* the object. The strength of the demonstration that a cost had to be incurred, however, varies with the circumstances. In some cases—for example, the prime costs of material and direct labour—we can observe that the cost is necessary to the product, for without it there is no product. When it can be shown that a given cost varies in step with the volume of production, the proof of a causal connection is also strong. Commonly, however, a given cost (for example, power) contributes to a variety of products; hence, it is difficult to allocate the cost incurred among individual units of product. Often the problem can be lessened by making additional measurements (for example, metering power usage by production runs). It then becomes a cost/benefit question whether the additional measurement is worthwhile.

When a cost does not vary with volume of output, the problem becomes much more difficult. Simple reasoning may tell us that costs of capacity to produce must precede production, so that one can say the former is a cause of the latter. However, it is not possible to establish direct causation between specific output and the capacity cost, and there is no way to demonstrate how much of the capacity cost is related to individual products. Frequently allocations are based on some indicator of intensity of activity—such as direct labour cost, hours worked, or machine hours consumed. Less frequently allocation may be based on value of output—as when joint costs are allocated in proportion to the selling price or net contribution margin of the products. Many modern manufacturing operations have become overhead intensive and, in particular, have only a minor direct labour element. There are indications that traditional overhead allocations based on overall volume measures, like direct labour hours, do not provide reasonable product cost figures in these situations, and more specific activity-based alternatives are being put forward for internal management purposes (see discussion in Chapter 10).

Two major issues have arisen with respect to techniques for attaching costs to cost objects. First, there is the question whether costs allocated to a given object should be restricted to variable costs (direct costing), or whether they should include an allocated portion of fixed overhead costs (absorption costing or full costing). Second, there is the question whether financing costs may be attributed to a cost object. In practice, the answer to both these questions is "it depends." That answer will be discussed in greater detail in subsequent chapters.

Recognition of Expense As Assets Are Consumed

Once costs are attached to cost objects, some system must be in place to recognize expense as the benefit from the asset is consumed. With respect to product costs there must be a partitioning of costs between those applicable to revenue currently being recognized and those applicable to revenue yet to be recognized. In the ordinary case of sale of goods, this means that costs must be identified with goods as they are produced, so that subsequently there can be a division between cost of goods sold and cost of goods still on hand.

In the case of tangible or intangible capital assets held for use rather than sale, there is no periodic disposition of part of the asset to provide a basis for distinguishing between costs to be written off and costs that retain their asset status. Because of this, some scheme of amortization of assets' costs must be adopted to portray the periodic consumption of their usefulness. That scheme will inevitably be arbitrary in some degree but it is supposed to meet the test of being "systematic and rational." (The issues are addressed in Chapters 11 and 12.) Costs carried forward as prepayments are simply written off as the prepaid service is received.

Particular attention must be given to the need for special write-downs of asset carrying values if they become impaired so that they can no longer be expected to contribute to, or be recoverable from, future revenue-generating activities. (Asset impairment issues are considered in Chapter 18.)

The reduction of asset carrying values by depreciation, amortization, or reduction of amounts prepaid is not necessarily synonymous with recognition of expense. Some portion of the amounts written off may be classified as overhead costs that will, under the costing system in force, be allocated to cost of inventory or other assets currently being produced.

ACCRUED LIABILITIES AND RELATED EXPENSES

We observed the general principle in Chapter 6 that a liability should be recognized at the time an entity becomes obligated to make future sacrifices as a result of past events or transactions. Difficult questions arise in attempting to apply this principle to common types of accrued liabilities. In addressing these questions a distinction is made between obligations for future expenditures in the normal course of operations of an enterprise and provisions for losses that are contingent on the outcome of one or more future events. There is much confusion in drawing this distinction in both authoritative literature and practice. Nevertheless, the estimation and measurement of "contingent losses" give rise to some different considerations that have been the subject of different standards, so that they are examined in a separate section of this chapter.

In accounting for normal ongoing operating activities, the objective is to recognize and measure an obligation to make future expenditures at the moment the entity receives the related good or service benefits. Three sets of issues arise in attempting to operationalize this objective:

- There are fundamental conceptual questions as to whether certain types of future events should be factored into the recognition and measurement of an accrued obligation.
- Some basic estimation issues need to be addressed.
- There is the question whether the amount of expected future expenditures should be discounted to a present value at the reporting date.

Which Future Events?

The receipt of some benefits (such as employee services, or revenues on the sale of a product) may obligate an employer to make certain future outlays (such as post-retirement benefits for employee services, or product warranty costs). Certain of these future outlays may be contingent on future events taking place. (An employee may have to work a minimum length of time to qualify for a pension, or a product may have to fail and a customer initiate a claim for a warranty expenditure to be incurred.) In respect of normal course activities, it has become accepted in principle, although with some exceptions in practice, that one should not wait for claims to be made in order to recognize the liability. Rather, an obligation should be recognized when the related benefit is recognized and its measurement should reflect best estimates of the expenditures that can reasonably be expected to be incurred.

But before we can address the estimation and measurement problems, we must agree on exactly what it is that should be measured. In some simple situations, the future expenditures may be precisely determinable from a fixed formula. In most cases, however, some assumptions must be made as to future economic conditions. In common circumstances, an entity will be exposed to risks of changes in future conditions that could substantially affect the future expenditures. For example, a warranty provision may be subject to future price increases in labour or replacement parts. In other cases, there may be exposure to changes in future income tax rates, interest rates, or foreign exchange rates.

There is much inconsistency in practice, and as between standards, with respect to whether such future events should be factored in, and if so how. We will see this question arising time and again in examining specific application issues in subsequent chapters. There would seem to be some movement towards acceptance that estimates of accrued liabilities should be based on the extension of current economic conditions—that the effects of future changes from current conditions (future changes in interest rates, or yet-to-be-legislated changes in income tax rates, for example) are future events that are properly reflected in the future periods in which they occur. On the other hand, there are differences of view as to whether, or when and how, expected future improvements in productivity or technology should be factored into the measurement of some obligations, for example, obligations for environmental remediation. The significance of future events for recognition and measurement is beginning to be recognized as a generic matter, in need of study as an issue in itself.[2]

Allowing for Future Price Changes

A particularly important subset of this issue is whether future inflation or specific price change expectations should be reflected in measuring obligations that are exposed to these risks.

Consider a hypothetical example. Operations today result in an obligation to perform specific work five years hence. If that work were performed today, it would cost $1 million. Suppose the current rate of inflation is 6%. If these current inflationary conditions are presumed to extend for the next five years, and future prices of this work are presumed to reflect general inflation, the cost to discharge this obligation at the end of five years would be expected to rise to approximately $1,340,000. Thus, a provision of $1 million, without further adjustment, would clearly be inadequate. Some questions arise. Should the accrual take into account current general levels of inflation? Alternatively, might an estimate of future expenditures reflect some estimate of future changes in the specific prices of the particular good or service if current conditions indicate that these may be expected to increase at a different rate than general levels of inflation?

This issue is linked to the question of discounting future expenditures to determine their present values, and thus this discussion will be further developed in considering that issue below.

Estimation Issues

Once it has been determined how future expenditures should reflect future events, the problem becomes a pure estimation problem. Sometimes it is one of estimating how many people will qualify for future payment. For example, this question arises with respect to pension or other employee benefits that are payable only if employees survive or fulfill certain vesting conditions. Such costs to be recorded depend on estimation of these probabilities and often will be calculated by actuaries. Sometimes the problem also involves estimates of the future costs of making good on the obligation. For example, estimates of future warranty costs require not only estimates of how many claims will be made, but also estimates of the cost of satisfying the claims. Engineering judgments may be required in these estimates. Sometimes estimates are required of major work that must be done in future, for example, making good the environmental damage resulting from current operations. Estimates of such future costs may be based on previous experience but can be very difficult when extensive experience is lacking as in the case of decommissioning costs for nuclear reactors.

Various references in accounting literature suggest that where the probable amount of future costs cannot be "reasonably estimated," a liability need not be recorded.[3] Instead, disclosure could be made of the existence of the liability where it may be material. This state of affairs is unsatisfactory. First, the decision whether an amount can be reasonably estimated is subjective, and there is danger that judgment might be biased by a desire to omit liabilities in order to present a better picture of financial condition. Second, the omission of any estimate of a material liability necessarily means that reported income and shareholders' equity are misstated. If the liability actually exists, the one thing that is known for sure is that its amount is not zero. If the uncertainty is so great that an estimate cannot be made within reasonable limits and the possible amounts are material to the financial position or income reported, the general rule is that profit on the related business transactions should not be recognized but rather should be deferred until such time as the costs are reasonably determinable. (The relationship of revenue recognition to future cost determinability was addressed in Chapter 7.)

Estimation problems arise whenever there is a range of possible outcomes. This is the essence of uncertainty. The possibility that amounts can be estimated only within a range is a very serious one for accrual accounting in general. Accounting standards that deal with accruals for future expenditures tend to call for "best estimates" which is defined in terms of "likely" outcomes. Unfortunately, these are not well-defined concepts in financial accounting.

Often the estimation problem is mitigated by the law of large numbers. That is, when a single risk may have a wide range of possible outcomes, it will nevertheless be found that the outcomes of a large number of similar risks will average out to a figure that is predictable within a narrow range. Thus, it is possible to estimate fairly accurately the survival contingencies (and based on this, the pension costs) of a large employee group. But if one executive or a small group of executives is given entitlement to a pension, the ultimate cost may vary over a wide range. Current pension accounting standards require the recording of expense based on the expected value of the accrued obligation in this case. As we shall see, however, standards for the recognition of "contingent losses" with varying likelihoods of occurrence and ranges of outcomes have permitted a minimum estimate.

When a range exists as to the probable future expenditures related to a recognized benefit, and no estimate within the range is more likely than any other, rational measurement theories would focus on the central estimate in the range rather than its minimum estimate. In the case where a probability distribution of estimated expenditures follows a normal curve, the central estimate would also be the likely estimate. A more difficult situation occurs when a probability distribution is skewed, that is, when a range of possible outcomes is quite wide but the probabilities are concentrated at one end of the range. In such a case, the median estimate will not be the most probable estimate.

A major question in financial accounting relates to whether a liability accrual should reflect some provision for adverse deviations, that is, for the possibility that the future expenditures will exceed best estimates. Traditionally, there has been a view that accountants should be conservative in the face of uncertainty, and allow for some prudent margin of safety. The *CICA Handbook* attempts to distinguish between appropriate conservatism (where the objective is to ensure that liabilities are not understated), and unacceptable negative bias, (which would involve the deliberate overstatement of liabilities).[4] This can be a slippery slope, because there has been no clear theory to guide these judgments.

This issue may be visualized from the perspective of finance theory, as one of determining how risk should be represented in measuring an obligation. Risk may be defined simply as the exposure to loss, that is, to the chance that outcomes will be worse than expected. It is well documented that human beings tend to be risk averse. By this it is meant that we tend to place greater weight on the possibilities of doing worse than expected than on the possibilities of doing better. As a result, investors tend to demand a higher rate of expected return the higher the perceived risk. This is evident in securities prices and market risk-adjusted interest rates. In other words, it may be expected that a fair market measure of an obligation to make uncertain future outlays will reflect a provision for adverse deviation in the form of an adjustment for risk. In recent years there have been major advances in the development of market-based option pricing models. These models attempt to factor in the contingencies, and related volatility of value, represented by the underlying instrument.

Accounting standard setters are beginning to look to capital market prices and contingency pricing models for help in developing measures of cost that appropriately reflect risk. As an example, the FASB has recently proposed utilizing option pricing models in measuring management compensation that takes the form of stock options (see Chapter 14). However, in the majority of circumstances requiring accruals for future expenditures there are no directly equivalent market prices or reliable pricing surrogates, and lacking these, measurement adjustments for risk continue to be highly subjective.

The appropriate financial statement representation of an uncertain obligation may be considered to have two dimensions. The first is the single estimate measure that is recorded in the financial statements. The second is the dispersion of possible outcomes around that estimate. A very significant challenge for accounting is to provide useful disclosure of this dispersion, that is, of the exposure to measurement variability. This is a subject of discussion in Chapter 23. More research could be done to help standard setters better understand how the dispersion of possible outcomes could be best communicated.

Discounting the Liability

When an obligation will not need to be satisfied until sometime in the future, it is natural to ask whether the estimated cost of that obligation should be discounted when it is first recognized in the accounts. It was noted in Chapter 6 that discounting is required in measuring purchase or sale transactions carrying delayed payment terms. The same logic supports the application of a discount factor to amounts of future expenditures to be recognized in connection with current operations. However, while a discounting methodology is applied in some cases, for example in pension cost accounting (see Chapter 14), it has not been applied to the measurement of liability provisions in a number of other areas (notably provisions for future income taxes (see Chapter 16) and highly uncertain provisions for environmental costs, to be discussed later in this chapter). Of course the period to maturity of many accruals may be sufficiently short that the discount factor is unimportant.

If an accrual of future expenditures is to be discounted when first recognized, a discount rate must be selected. One's initial reaction might be that this should be the rate of interest accessible to the entity through borrowing on the basis that incurring an obligation to be liquidated in the future is in effect the same as borrowing. But the risks to the entity are not identical to borrowing because the entity is assuming the additional risk that the amounts of future expenditures will be greater than the estimates predicted. Thus, it may be appropriate to reduce the rate to reflect this risk. Whatever the rate selected, the liability initially recognized on a discounted basis would have to be accreted at that rate until maturity to cover the estimated expenditures at that time.

It was suggested in the previous section that a proper estimate of the future expenditures comprising an accrued liability should take into account inflationary/price change impacts on those expenditures between the recognition date and the future payment date. This issue is closely related to that of selecting the appropriate interest rate to discount the expenditures. It is well established in economic theory that the market rate of interest at any particular time represents the combination of a "real" interest rate and the anticipated rate of inflation over the term for which the interest rate is quoted. Thus, if the annual interest rate is 10% and the anticipated annual inflation rate is 6%, the real interest rate may be calculated as $(1.10/1.06) - 1 = 0.037736$ or 3.77%.

This serves to demonstrate an important point: it would be illogical to discount future expenditures that are not adjusted for expected future price effects using an actual (nominal) rate of interest which includes an anticipated rate of inflation. Such a present value determination would understate the obligation. In other words, if the liability is to be discounted at a current market rate of interest, the estimates of future expenditures must include estimated future inflationary/price change effects through the period until the expenditures will be made.

The trouble with this is that many may be reluctant to try to estimate future price-adjusted expenditures to be incurred some considerable time in the future. As an alternative, an accountant may ask for an estimate of the amount that would be incurred if the obligation were discharged immediately, and then discount this amount at the estimated real rate of interest. To illustrate, let us return to the example in which operations today result in an obligation to perform specific work five years hence. Suppose that, if that work were performed today, it would cost $1 million. The accountant would then discount the $1 million amount at the real rate. If this rate was presumed to be 3.77%, the present value of this amount paid in five years would be $831,000. Subsequently, that figure would be accreted at the nominal rate of interest (10%) in order to accrue to a future expenditure of about $1,340,000 in five years, which would presume a rate of inflation of 6%.

This alternative calculation does not avoid the need to estimate future inflation. Rather, the onus is transferred to the accountant to make an assumption as to the expected rate of inflation (in this example 6%) in order to derive the estimated "real" rate of interest of 3.77%. In the absence of indexed securities trading in the market there will be no extrinsic evidence as to the real rate of interest; only the nominal rate of interest can be observed. Nevertheless, there have been economic studies that have estimated the historical medium-to-long-term real interest rates in Canada as being in the neighbourhood of 3%. In any event, it would be far better accounting to make an accrual for future cost based on discounting at any reasonable estimate of real interest rates than it would be to ignore the liability altogether. In addition, as the obligation comes closer to maturity it is always possible to modify the amount of the accrual as its probable ultimate amount becomes less uncertain.

Accounting Practice

Despite the undisputed theory of accrual accounting requiring recognition of liabilities for future sacrifices attributable to recognized benefits, practice has almost always lagged in making the necessary accruals. Sometimes the explanation has been that no one seriously thinks of the financial consequences at the time that new activities give rise to obligations. Initially, also, it may be that the amounts are immaterial. Hence, the expenses may be accounted for on the cash basis because it is easier to do so, and because it makes little difference to the financial position and results reported. Subsequently, as the business grows or the underlying activities assume greater importance, the unaccounted-for liability becomes more material in the balance sheet. Even then, it may be rationalized that since the increase in the liability in any given year is immaterial to the income reported, it need not be accrued.

Finally, when the undisclosed liability becomes uncomfortably large, it is possible for a business to look at the financial reports of other companies, ascertain that they too do not accrue for the same type of obligation and, therefore, argue that it is "generally accepted" to account for such obligation on a cash basis, no matter what accounting theory says. In that situation, the only effective way to rectify accounting practice across the board is to have accounting standard setters address the issue and state that the cash basis of accounting for the cost in question should no longer be considered acceptable. Unfortunately, by that time many companies have a strong vested interest in nondisclosure of the accumulated obligation, and many imaginative arguments may be made as to why the liability cannot be accurately estimated, how costly it will be to account for it on the accrual basis, or what serious economic consequences will follow from any requirement to implement proper accrual accounting.

Warranty Costs

An early example of the failure to apply accrual accounting in a new situation is provided by warranty obligations. When products were simple and the rule of "caveat emptor" prevailed in commercial practice, costs of product claims after sale were small. Gradually, however, companies began introducing product warranties, first in the area of consumer durables and then more broadly. The legal background also gradually changed to provide more protection to buyers, so that today few suppliers of goods are not at risk with respect to future claims for inadequate product quality. Some companies made provision for estimated future warranty costs as soon as they adopted a formal warranty policy. Others did not, and the failure was widespread throughout the 1950s and later. Over a long period of time, however, accrual accounting for warranty costs gained ground, so that today we can say that provision for warranty obligations is required both by accounting theory and generally accepted practice. In this case, the general practice has been to base the provision on estimates of future costs, not discounted.

Employee Benefits

Several questions in liability accounting have originated with fringe benefits promised to employees. A long-standing example is provided by vacation pay. Long before there were any legal requirements on the subject, many companies adopted policies of providing paid vacations to employees who met minimum service requirements and were still employed at the time that vacations might be taken. For companies with a calendar year-end and a vacation qualification year stretching from, say, May 1 to April 30, that meant that many employees had earned, through their service to the fiscal year-end, the greater part of the vacations to which they would become entitled the following May 1.

It could be argued, of course, that if an employee does not continue in service until the following April 30, he or she will receive nothing, in which case there is no liability at the preceding December 31. The other view is that the vacation policy was adopted by the employer as part of the employee compensation package. The employee earns his or her vacation by service throughout the vacation qualification year; therefore, the liability should be accrued over that period. The fact that some employees may not qualify for vacation because of subsequent termination does not mean that a vacation liability is not accruing. An allowance for vacations that will not be taken can be built into the calculation of the accrual. That is, the problem is one of measurement of the liability, not a question whether a liability exists. In past practice, some companies accounted for vacation pay on an accrual basis but many accounted for it only on a cash basis—probably because it was considered immaterial, but possibly also because of a belief that it was not a recordable liability.

In 1980 the FASB addressed the issue of accounting for payments for "compensated absences." By this term the board meant to include all payments by employers to active employees for periods in which they do not render service, such as vacation periods, periods when they are absent because of illness, and paid holidays.[5] The standard requires that a liability be accrued for employees' compensation for future absences if the employees' right to receive compensation for future absences is attributable to services already rendered, the obligation relates to rights that vest or accumulate, payment of the compensation is probable, and the amount can be reasonably estimated. In 1992, the FASB extended the application of this standard to post-employment benefits provided by an enterprise in respect of, for example, disability, layoff, or death.[6] The standard (SFAS 112) applies to all types of post-employment benefits other than those provided through a pension or post-retirement benefit plan (which are covered by separate standards as noted in the following section). An employer would recognize an obligation for post-employment benefits that do not meet the above conditions when it is probable that a liability has been incurred and the amount can be reasonably estimated. There has been no similar standard in Canada. However, in 1999 the CICA adopted a similar set of requirements.[7]

Benefits to Retired Employees

Over the years many employers adopted policies, formal or informal, of providing welfare benefits for retired employees such as dental or medical benefits or death benefits. Unless administered in conjunction with a company pension plan, the cost of such benefits has usually been recorded on a cash basis rather than an accrual basis. Since it is clear that benefits to retired employees must be attributable to service performed before retirement, it would seem that accrual accounting should be performed for such benefits, just as it is for pension benefits. The FASB has addressed this matter, and developed a standard that requires full accrual accounting parallel to that required for pensions.[8] No comparable standard has existed in Canada, and most Canadian companies have recorded the cost only as cash payments are made to retirees.[9] However, in 1999 the CICA adopted a standard consistent with that of the FASB (see Chapter 14).

At one time these benefits were thought to be fringe benefits with a relatively minor cost. Until the FASB focused attention on them, few companies had bothered to try to quantify their accrued obligations. When they did many were in for a rude surprise; by any reasonable estimate the unrecorded liabilities in the U.S. corporate sector were immense.[10] In

Canada, the availability of medical coverage under government plans should mean that the problem of post-retirement welfare benefits is less severe than in the U.S. However, in recent years provincial governments have been attempting to control the costs of their programs by limiting coverage, with the result that increased obligations are being assumed by some Canadian companies to provide supplementary benefits.

The subject of employer accounting for costs and liabilities under pension and other post-retirement benefits is a difficult one. The issues are so complex that the subject deserves a chapter to itself (see Chapter 14).

CONTINGENCIES

In the previous section we worked with the principle that a liability should be accrued in respect of future expenditures arising out of normal operations at the moment when the entity obtains the related good or service benefits. An additional class of liability accruals needs to be considered. An entity may become subject to liabilities that are not related to any discernible benefit, but are simply losses. While such liabilities must in some sense have arisen out of risk conditions resulting from past activities, they would not have been expected, or considered to be measurable events, of that past period. Standards for accounting for such unforeseen losses are known under the title of accounting for contingencies. As will be seen in the following discussion, the concept of a contingency is not very clearly defined.

In the discussion that follows the focus will be on recognizing and measuring contingent loss liabilities. Provisions for certain losses are effected through recording impairments in asset values. Particular issues related to reflecting losses through asset write-downs are developed in Chapter 18.

The Meaning of a Contingency

The Canadian definition of a contingency is as follows:

> A contingency is defined as an existing condition or situation involving uncertainty as to possible gain or loss to an enterprise that will ultimately be resolved when one or more future events occur or fail to occur. Resolution of the uncertainty may confirm the acquisition of an asset or the reduction of a liability or the loss or impairment of an asset or the incurrence of a liability.[11]

A similar definition is found in the FASB Statement of Financial Accounting Standards No. 5.[12] Some observations on this definition are as follows:

- There is an emphasis on a condition or situation *existing* at the financial reporting date that has potential for gain or loss. The term "existing" implies that contingencies requiring accounting consideration arise solely from business done to date, the assets and liabilities associated therewith, and transactions to which an entity is committed at the reporting date. Mere intentions to undertake future risks do not represent accounting contingencies.

- The reference to uncertainty as to possible gain or loss adds little by itself. Any human activity is uncertain. The definition goes on to speak of uncertainty "that will ultimately be resolved" by future events. Since uncertainties with respect to individual aspects of activity must be resolved eventually, it is not clear what these words add to the definition.

Is this definition helpful? One test is to see how clearly it applies to particular situations. For example, both the *CICA Handbook* and FASB Statement No. 5 attempt to distinguish between uncertainties that meet the definition of contingencies and normal uncertainties in accounting estimates. Both state that amounts owing for services received are not contingencies even though the amount owing has to be estimated. Consistent with this, the CICA material suggests that provisions for warranties "are not usually regarded as contingencies." In contrast, the FASB suggests that these are contingencies, since a claim must be made to fix the obligation and presumably this is the future event that resolves the contingency. Similarly, the CICA material suggests that losses from doubtful accounts are not contingencies, whereas the FASB statement says that they are, since there is initially doubt as to the collectibility of the accounts.

The common definition of the CICA and the FASB seems to conceal an unstated difference in concept. The CICA concept seems to be that uncertainties associated with revenues and expenses recognized in the course of normal business merely constitute, so to speak, normal estimation difficulties. The FASB concept is much broader and seems to embrace all uncertainties created by the possibility of future actions by parties outside the entity, even though an estimate of the effects of such actions is part of the normal process of revenue and expense accounting.

At the heart of this apparent difference is the question as to what may be considered an existing loss contingency condition. To demonstrate this issue, suppose an entity is exposed by its past activities to possible claims by outside parties. Does this exposure constitute an existing loss contingency condition, or must a claim be made, or a claimable event occur, for the condition to exist? Authoritative literature and practice provide different answers to this question. Let us examine warranties which, as observed above, are included in contingencies by the FASB but excluded by the CICA. It has been demonstrated in the previous section of this chapter that the recognition of the sale of a product accompanied by a warranty is considered to be the trigger point for recognizing a warranty obligation. An entity is required to estimate how many of the items sold have defects that will lead to claims, and it must accrue for the obligation to satisfy them. In other words, future warranty claims are anticipated in respect of sold products. The provision is considered to be an expense of normal operations, not a loss.

On the other hand, exposure to possible future losses are generally not considered to pass the "existing condition" threshold until a specific loss event takes place (for example, a fire, or a plane crash, or an oil spill), or in some circumstances, until a legal claim is made against the reporting entity. Mere exposure to risk of loss is not considered to be an accountable contingency.

What distinguishes these situations? It may be reasoned that a true loss situation is outside the normal run of business activities and could not be expected to be reasonably anticipated as a foreseeable consequence of its operating activities. The argument is that an entity has no obligation or asset impairment in respect of random events (such as a fire, a plane crash, or an oil spill) until such an event takes place. Thus there would seem to be a distinction based on the difference between *expenses* and *losses* that may provide a basis for determining when an accounting contingency should be considered to exist. However, this distinction is not made in the FASB standard, and is not made entirely clear in the CICA standard. Furthermore, what may be an unforeseeable loss in one situation or industry, might be a foreseeable expense that should be provided for at the time of revenue recognition in another. The distinction can be important because it can affect the timing and measurement of an obligation.

Accounting Treatment of Contingent Losses

Once a loss contingency condition has arisen (for example, the reporting entity has been sued), there is then the question whether this condition will materialize into an actual loss that should be accrued.

Implicit within the accounting standards dealing with loss contingencies is a division of uncertainty into two categories, namely event uncertainty—what is the probability of the adverse future event (for example, of the reporting entity receiving an unfavourable judgment in the lawsuit)—and measurement uncertainty—what will be the loss if the adverse event occurs. Determination of the accounting treatment depends upon judgments on both these matters.

Event Uncertainty

Under the first category a judgment must be made as to the probability of occurrence of the adverse event. According to the *CICA Handbook* (paragraph 3290.06) the probability of an event may be deemed to be (1) likely, which is defined to be a high chance of occurrence, (2) unlikely, which is a slight chance of occurrence, or (3) not determinable. The third subdivision presumes that there are situations in which no judgment as to probability can be made (presumably on the grounds that there is no evidence or experience upon which to base a judgment).

Measurement Uncertainty

A judgment must be made as to whether the amount of loss, if it is considered likely to occur, is reasonably capable of estimation. There are several possible situations. The amount of loss could be one particular figure with little chance of variance, plus or minus. The amount of possible loss could fall into a wider range but with one figure within that range clearly more probable than others. The amount of possible loss could fall into a wide range with no one figure within that range considered more likely than any other. It is even conceivable that there could be two reasonably possible figures of loss, widely separated in amount. For example, it might appear that a lawsuit is likely to be lost, but the likely damages could differ substantially depending on whether actions of the plaintiff are deemed to have contributed to the loss.

The prescribed accounting treatment in Canada, based on the foregoing judgments, is as follows:

- If a loss is considered likely and its amount is reasonably capable of estimation
    - Accrue the estimated amount of loss where a point estimate of loss has been made;
    - If one particular estimate of loss within the possible range is considered a better estimate than any other, accrue that amount, and disclose, by footnote to the financial statements, the exposure to loss above the amount accrued; or
    - Accrue the *minimum* estimate of loss where there is a range of possible loss but no amount appears a better estimate than any other, and disclose the exposure to loss above the amount accrued.
- If a recovery related to the loss is likely (for example, a recovery from a third party with respect to a guarantee), the loss to be accrued is reduced by the likely recovery amount.

- If a loss is considered likely but its amount is not reasonably capable of estimation, disclose the existence of the contingent loss and state that an estimate of loss cannot be made.

- If a loss is possible but its likelihood is not determinable, disclose the existence of the contingent loss and its amount or the fact that its amount is not determinable.

This standard is confusing, incomplete and biased towards nonrecognition of losses. To start with, defining "likely" as high chance of occurrence means there will be no accrual in many situations in which there is a better than even chance that material losses will occur. More than this, allowing enterprises to judge probabilities to be "indeterminable" invites avoidance of accruals. All judgments about future events are inherently uncertain and hence could be said to be "not determinable." If one assumes that judgments can be made, it is hard to believe that a knowledgeable person has no idea whatsoever of the possible outcomes of existing conditions.

The FASB description of probabilities of event occurrence might seem clearer than the Canadian. The FASB does not have an "indeterminable" category, but rather defines the range of possibilities into events that are "probable," "reasonably possible," and "remote." It is, however, doubtful that this classification has led to the earlier recognition of contingent losses than the Canadian standard. Evidence indicates that the FASB terms are open to a wide range of interpretation in practice and that it has been common for there to be no provision for contingent losses until their probability of occurrence is clearly determinable and is high.[13]

The usefulness of the guidance provided by these standards may be further lessened by the use of verbal descriptions of degrees of probability. The CICA's definition states that a future event is likely if its chance of occurrence is high and unlikely if its chance of occurrence is slight. The reference to "chance of occurrence" clearly implies that a judgment as to degree of probability is to be made. Would everyone agree with the meaning and, specifically, the degree of probability of such terms as "likely," "high chance of occurrence," "unlikely," and "slight chance of occurrence"? Research indicates that people tend to disagree over quite a wide range as to probabilities to be assigned to verbal descriptions.[14]

A second major area of concern relates to the measurement of a "likely" loss. The requirement to use the lowest figure in a range of equally likely possibilities is contrary to the long-standing tradition of conservatism. We have noted above that in accruing for ongoing obligations arising in the normal course, there is now wide recognition for the principle that such obligations should reflect "best estimates" of the most likely amount. While the concept of "best estimates" is not well defined, reasoning within established literature in economic statistics, it seems inadequate to accrue only the minimum estimate rather than a central estimate in the range.

The problem, however, is that no single number may be truly representative of a loss contingency where there is a wide range of reasonably possible outcomes. In this case, limitations of deterministic accounting may be mitigated by supporting disclosures. The *CICA Handbook* (paragraph 3290.22) calls for disclosure of the exposure to loss in excess of the amount accrued, or a statement that such estimate cannot be made. In addition, where a loss might be significant in relation to the whole financial position, it would be good practice to make disclosure even though the probability of such loss is slight. Unfortunately, a number of enterprises simply indicate that amounts of such exposures are not determinable.

The CICA initiated a project to improve the existing *CICA Handbook* standard in 1990. A task force was appointed and proposals exposed for comment early in 1993.[15] A revised standard was approved in principle by the Accounting Standards Board in 1994. This revised standard would require recognition of a contingent loss if it is considered to be more likely than not to occur. An enterprise would not be able to avoid recognition on the grounds of inde-terminability; it would have to decide whether a future loss-confirming event was more likely than not to occur. All contingent losses passing this test for recognition would be measured at management's "best estimate," which amount would have to be within a "range of reasonably possible amounts." The revised standard would also require expanded dis-closures, including the nature of the contingency, whether a provision had been made, and the amount of the provision (unless disclosure of the amount would have a significant adverse effect on the resolution of the contingency, in which case an explanation would be given of the reason for its nondisclosure). The standard strove for earlier and more realistic provisions for contingent losses, while still leaving considerable room for judgment in apply-ing largely undefined concepts of probability estimation and "best estimate" measurement.

In the late stages of the development of this revised standard, the Canadian Bar Association (CBA), led by a contingent of prominent litigators, voiced its strong objections. Specifically, it asserted that the indeterminacy of legal proceedings made it virtually impossible to make "more-likely-than-not" assessments of outcome, and that any assessment that a loss was likely on this basis would be tantamount to admission of liability. The disclosure of even the fact that a provision had been made could, in its view, have serious adverse consequences for an enter-prise in signalling this to the other party in a legal suit. There may be doubt as to whether the proposed accounting and disclosures could really pose a serious risk of adversely influencing the outcome of litigation, but the CBA took the view that such risk was intolerable, and out-weighed any benefit to investors of earlier recognition and fuller disclosure. The CBA linked its concerns to a joint policy statement of the CBA and CICA, under which legal counsel for an enterprise provides the auditors with confirmation of management's assessment of any lit-igation pending against the enterprise.[16] The CBA indicated that it may not be able to provide this confirmation under the proposed revised *CICA Handbook* standard. Such confirmation let-ters are viewed by auditors as essential audit evidence. In the end, the CICA Accounting Standards Board capitulated to these concerns and the revised standard was not released.[17]

The IASC has recently issued a standard on provisions and contingencies that has effec-tively adopted the recognition and measurement positions abandoned by the CICA.[18] The IASC standard defines a "provision" as a liability of uncertain timing or amount. Provisions are to be recognized on the balance sheet when an enterprise (1) has, or is more likely than not to have, a present obligation as a result of a past event, (2) it is more likely than not that an outflow of resources will be required to settle the obligation, and (3) a reliable esti-mate can be made of the amount. The standard presumes that a reliable estimate can be made except in rare cases where an enterprise cannot determine a range of possible out-comes. The IASC standard then limits its definition of "contingent liabilities" to comprise only those situations that do not meet the above criteria for recognition as liabilities.

Provisions are to be measured at the "best estimate" of the expenditure required to set-tle them. Generally this is considered to be the amount that an enterprise would rationally pay to settle the obligation or transfer it to a third party. The IASC standard requires that provisions be measured on a discounted present value basis where the time value of money is material, but it gives little supporting guidance.

The IASC standard sets out fairly extensive disclosures, but, "in rare cases" where these disclosures can be expected to "prejudice seriously" the position of an enterprise in a dispute with other parties, the enterprise can disclose as little as the general nature of the dispute and the reason why additional disclosures are not made.

Gain Contingencies

Unlike the case of loss contingencies, a gain contingency is not accrued in the financial statements, but is to be recognized only when realized. The reason given for the asymmetrical treatment of contingent gains and losses is that accrual of contingent gains would offend the realization convention (*CICA Handbook*, paragraph 3290.18). In place of recognition by accrual, the *CICA Handbook* calls for footnote disclosure of the existence of likely contingent gains, prohibits disclosure of unlikely contingent gains, and permits but does not require disclosure of contingent gains where their likelihood is not determinable. As with loss contingencies, footnote disclosure, if given, should include an estimate of the amount or a statement that an estimate cannot be made.

The abandoned revised CICA standard on contingencies, referred to above, would have provided for the accrual of virtually certain contingent gains.[19]

Some Issues in Contingency Accounting and Disclosure

Probability of Future Outflows—A Recognition Condition or a Measurement Matter?

We have observed that a contingent liability is not recognized if a future outflow of resources is not "likely" (however that is defined). This position is fundamentally at odds with accepted accounting for financial liabilities where the probability of future payout is considered to be a matter of measurement, not recognition. For example, a written financial option may be "out of the money," that is, there may be a low probability that the option will be exercised and the writer required to make any payout. Nevertheless, the option is an existing financial liability of the issuer which must be recognized and valued. In a fair market, a financial liability that has a high probability of future payout will have a higher value than one for which the probability of payout is low. But both will have a nonzero fair value. (The recognition and measurement of financial instruments of this nature are discussed in Chapter 17.)

The application of this logic to a contingent liability may be demonstrated by an example. Suppose enterprise A has provided a guarantee to a third party that enterprise B will repay a borrowing of $1 million. Suppose B's financial condition is such that there is considered to be a 10% chance that it will default. If this credit guarantee is considered to be a contingent liability, no provision would be made by A because a future payout is not likely. However, enterprise A has an existing obligation which it cannot avoid if B should be unable to repay the borrowing. The "expected value" of A's obligation under the guarantee is the probability of default (10%) multiplied by the amount of the borrowing ($1 million) or $100,000, ignoring the time value of money. The fair value of this obligation (the amount that A would presumably have to pay another party to assume this obligation) is, therefore, presumably in the order of $100,000. There is a strong case that this credit guarantee should be recognized and measured at $100,000, not simply ignored.

A contingent liability arising under a lawsuit has a significant additional uncertainty, because one must first establish whether it is likely that the enterprise is liable, that is, has a present obligation. If it is determined that it does, then under the "expected value" logic, the liability would be recognized and measured as above, even if the probability of payout is considered to be remote.

To date, accounting standard setters have not addressed the fundamental inconsistency between the recognition and measurement of contingent liabilities and financial liabilities such as options.

Reserves for Contingencies

Some decades ago some entities followed the practice of creating and maintaining arbitrary "reserves for contingencies" that were defended on the proposition that any entity is faced with the possibility of unforeseeable losses merely by being in business. It was then claimed that the possibility of unasserted claims was covered and no special disclosure was required should their assertion become probable. This accounting is no longer accepted, because such reserves cannot meet the definition of a liability and their arbitrary creation is too open to abuse.

Reserves for Self-Insurance

Some entities also used to create "reserves for self-insurance" by charges against income. The reasoning was that an enterprise that did not carry normal insurance because its risks were sufficiently spread to "self-insure" would show a different pattern of income from companies that did insure, even though their financial position and income potential were essentially the same. The noncomparability would arise because the income reported by the self-insurer would appear better (through the lack of insurance premium expense) in periods when no losses were incurred but would appear worse in other periods when losses were incurred, even though over a period of years the two practices balanced out.

These reserves have long been considered unacceptable. It is generally recognized that reserves for self-insurance understate the equity position when no loss has occurred. This is obviously so, since a company would be free to place insurance at any time, thereby removing the need for the reserve. It is further felt that recording charges to income for self-insurance costs (considered equivalent to insurance premiums) is "what if" accounting that does not correspond with the facts. Authoritative statements encourage, but do not require, that an entity make disclosure of its exposure if it does not carry insurance against a material risk that normally would be covered.

Reserves for Catastrophes

Many casualty insurance companies at one time followed the practice of maintaining "reserves for catastrophes," on reasoning somewhat similar to that used by noninsurance companies to justify reserves for self-insurance. The reasoning was that some types of insurance losses may be bunched at particular times by reason of a single event (a catastrophe), such as a hurricane striking a populated but unprotected area. Such catastrophic losses occur irregularly so that loss amounts are not level from year to year. Premiums, on the other hand, are designed to cover such losses on average over a period of years. It used to be argued that a better portrayal of income is achieved by accruing reserves in years when losses are light and drawing them down in heavy loss years. This practice has also been discontinued on the grounds that the reserves did not represent real liabilities.

Offsetting Recoveries

Not infrequently a company may incur a loss which may be recoverable in whole or in part from a third party, for example an insurer or a guarantor. As noted earlier, the existing CICA standard on contingencies provides that a loss to be accrued is reduced by a likely recovery amount. There is some discomfort with this treatment. It is inconsistent with the recognition criteria for contingent gains; a likely contingent gain is recognized if it reduces the amount accrued for a related contingent loss, but not otherwise. From a balance sheet perspective, recovery from a third party is subject to separate risks (in particular, the credit risks of the insurer or the guarantor) so that there will be no legal right of setoff against the liability for the loss. Canadian standards now require that a financial asset and a financial liability not be offset on the balance sheet unless the enterprise has a legally enforceable right of setoff and intends to settle on a net basis or to realize the asset and settle the liability simultaneously.[20] Thus it would be expected that the gross amount of the asset representing the amount of likely recovery and the liability for likely loss should each be reflected on the balance sheet. However, under the contingency standard the likely loss and likely recovery may be offset in the income statement.

Disclosure of Risks and Uncertainties, and Possible Adverse Consequences of Disclosure

It is uncontentious that general risks attributable to the business carried on are not required to be described in financial statements. This is a common sense conclusion. Uncertainty is pervasive, and the user of financial statements ought to be presumed to have sufficient acquaintance with the world to know that. That being said, it is a different situation when a general business risk threatens to become an immediate claim or risk. Accounting standards do list as contingencies such items as threat of expropriation of assets, threatened litigation, possible claims and assessments. Where a general business risk has resulted in a foreseeable claim or loss, management must exercise its judgment as to whether the risk is sufficiently slight to permit ignoring it or whether it must be disclosed and/or a loss accrued.

Standards for the disclosure of risks and uncertainties have been expanded in recent years. An AICPA Statement of Position was issued in 1994, after a two-year comment period. It requires information on the nature of an enterprise's operations, the use of significant estimates in preparation of its financial statements, certain significant estimates, and the enterprise's vulnerability to certain risk concentrations. An enterprise is required to identify circumstances in which it is at least reasonably possible that estimates will change in the near term (one year) with potential material effects on its financial statements.[21] The CICA subsequently issued a much less extensive standard on disclosure of measurement uncertainties.[22]

The CICA's withdrawal of its revised standard on contingencies, described earlier, demonstrates the difficult trade-off between the rights of investors to receive information on material risks and contingencies, and the concerns that disclosures of sensitive situations could have adverse consequences for the reporting enterprise. It is often feared that disclosure of a loss contingency may increase the probability of its occurrence. For example, where a risk exists that an outside party may assert a claim against an entity and it is thought that such a claim, if asserted, would be successful, management must weigh the probability of assertion of the claim. If it is probable that the claim will be made, and if the potential loss accrual is unusual and sufficiently material, it may be difficult to disclose that fact without alerting possible claimants to their position. Moreover, when accrual is not made for the full loss exposure, the disclosure called for by the contingency standards may also alert possible claimants. Unfortunate though this result may appear to the reporting entity, existing accounting standards leave little alternative to disclosure of at least the existence and nature of the contingency, in the interests of fair financial reporting.

These disclosure issues are further discussed in Chapter 23.

Accounting upon Resolution of a Contingency

Since contingencies, by definition, are related to "an existing condition," it is natural to ask whether losses recognized upon the subsequent resolution of a contingency or adjustments of any initial accruals should be accounted for as prior period adjustments. The FASB has long prohibited prior period adjustment treatment. It reasons that it would be inconsistent to prohibit initial accrual of a loss on the grounds that it is not considered to be a measurable event at that time and then, on resolution of the contingency, attribute the loss to that earlier period.[23] In other words, it may be expected that the resolution of a contingency will be the result of new information, and thus should not be accorded prior period treatment.

Until recently the *CICA Handbook* provided that resolution of a contingency would qualify for prior period adjustment treatment if certain conditions were considered to be met. There was no clear guidance on the application of these conditions, and there was great difficulty in practice in distinguishing contingencies that should and should not be treated as prior period adjustments. The most troublesome of these conditions was to judge whether the resolution of a contingency was attributable to subsequent "economic events" (in which case it did not qualify for prior period treatment). The CICA standard was changed in 1996 to prohibit prior period adjustments for other than errors and accounting policy changes.[24]

Critique and Summary of Contingency Accounting

It is evident from the foregoing that accounting standards dealing with contingencies have not succeeded in eliminating confusion. The first difficulty arises in trying to distinguish contingent gains and losses from ongoing expense and revenue accruals. It might be argued that since uncertainty is pervasive, attempts to fit it into these categories are likely to be confusing. Nevertheless, it may be possible to deal with uncertainty in standards for revenue and cost recognition and provide a separate standard for uncertain losses and gains as the CICA has attempted. The key difference in accounting that may follow from this distinction lies in what constitutes an existing condition that should necessitate an accrual. The "existing condition" leading to an ongoing liability accrual is the receipt of a particular good or service benefit, which requires anticipation of related future events (such as warranty claims that may be expected to arise as a result of a sale). With respect to a contingency, the assumption is that future loss and gain events (such as material catastrophes or windfall gains) are not foreseeable, so that the existing qualifying condition for accrual does not occur until a specific loss or gain event takes place. It is not until then that an asset right or liability obligation exists. This differentiation may be sustainable in concept at least, although distinguishing between gain/loss and cost/revenue items can be expected to be difficult in particular situations.

What seems far more difficult to sustain are different standards that require best estimate provisions for a liability arising from ongoing liability accruals, while providing only for accrual of the minimum estimate for contingent losses within a range, and only where this amount is "reasonably determinable" and there is a high chance of occurrence. Current contingency standards seem less and less likely to lead to a fair presentation of income and financial position in a world where business enterprise is increasingly bound up in obligations and commitments to be satisfied in the future.

It is submitted that recording the expected value of a contingent loss obligation, and recording a gain or loss for the difference between the expected and actual outcome when it occurs, would be better accounting than ignoring the obligation initially on the grounds of uncertainty. Disclosure could then be concentrated on the possible variance of the estimate.

Whatever the decision on loss accrual, there remains the problem of providing adequate disclosure of the range of possible loss. More research is necessary on, for example, representations of uncertainties in statistical mathematics, to assist standard setters in giving guidance on how sensitivities to risk and ranges of possible outcomes can be best communicated. A priori, it seems desirable to convey some idea of the range of possible loss, and of the most likely loss when that figure departs significantly from the central point of the range.

ENVIRONMENTAL COSTS

Reasoning within the theory developed earlier in this chapter, an enterprise would be expected to provide for measurable obligations to make future expenditures to clean up environmental damage that has occurred and for which it is responsible. Such obligations may arise as a result of ongoing revenue-generating activities (such as a mining operation that will have to make future expenditures for site restoration), or as a result of an accident (such as a chemical spill).

Until fairly recent years, few enterprises paid close attention to environmental restoration costs. Primarily this was because they were not held to a high degree of accountability for the environmental consequences of their actions. But times have changed. Tougher legislation, reflecting a heightened public awareness and concern, has forced enterprises to assume increased responsibility for the impact of their operations on the environment. This, in turn, has led to pressures on the accounting profession to develop improved standards for the recognition and measurement of environmental obligations, and for disclosure of related contingencies and risks.

Providing for environmental expenses and losses is subject to particularly difficult estimation and measurement problems. To start with, laws assigning responsibilities for past environmental damage are still evolving, and in many areas restoration technology is in an early state of development. It may be difficult for an enterprise to assess the extent of its responsibilities and what may constitute acceptable remedial efforts, thus making subjective estimates of future expenditures even more uncertain. Nevertheless, empirical research has demonstrated that capital markets put considerable importance on estimating enterprises' environmental liabilities and risks. Even quite crude measures of environmental risk exposures appear to have information value in explaining equity market prices. There is also some evidence suggesting that significant, measurable environmental liabilities are not recognized in enterprise financial statements.[25]

In both the U.S. and Canada, standards on contingencies have provided the general framework for the recognition, measurement and disclosure of environmental costs. Accounting for these costs has, therefore, been subject to all the previously discussed shortcomings of contingent loss provisioning. To date, considerably more attention has been made to improve reporting of environmental risks and obligations in the U.S. than in Canada. In response to increasing concerns as to the potential immensity of unrecognized environmental liabilities, the SEC and FASB each issued interpretations aimed at achieving timely and realistic provisioning and fair disclosures within the general requirements of the FASB contingencies standard (Statement No. 5).[26] These may be summarized as follows:

- The SEC expects registrants to make all reasonable efforts to obtain the necessary information to develop appropriate estimates of incurred costs and losses, including retention of experts if necessary. Liability estimates should reflect all currently available facts and be based on existing technologies and presently enacted laws. Measurements are to incorporate the likely effects of inflation.

- Environmental liabilities are to be evaluated independently of any potential claims for recovery. A claim for recovery is to be recognized only if it is probable of realization. (It had not been uncommon for enterprises to offset reasonably possible, but not necessarily probable, recoveries against probable liabilities.) The SEC does not accept offsetting of asset recovery claims against liability accruals on the balance sheet.

- Discounting of expenditures to be incurred in future periods is acceptable only if the timing and amounts of future payments are "reliably determinable." This would require site-specific plans and bases of determination with which knowledgeable third parties could be expected to concur.

- The SEC has indicated that environmental liabilities will often be of such significance that detailed disclosures beyond those typically provided under FASB Statement No. 5 will be necessary.

The AICPA subsequently issued a statement of position that provides more specific guidance on the application of these general requirements.[27]

There is some evidence of increased recognition and disclosure of environmental obligations by U.S. enterprises in recent years, which is considered to be attributable, at least in part, to SEC pressures.[28]

In some cases, the costs of future environmental site restoration will qualify as capital assets. As an example, one of the first steps in developing an open pit mine is to strip away the overburden in order to enable access to the ore. The act of removing the overburden may be considered to obligate the company to future site restoration. Accordingly, the theoretically correct accounting treatment would be to record the liability and recognize the cost as part of the capital investment to develop the mine that will be recovered from future ore sales. However, in practice it has been common in both the U.S. and Canada for companies not to set up the asset and liability, but simply accrue for the estimated restoration costs as an expense over the useful life of the mine.

In 1996, the FASB issued an exposure draft on accounting for obligations associated with the closure or removal of long-lived assets such as those in the preceding paragraph, as well as, for example, nuclear plant decommissioning costs.[29] It proposed that obligations for future closure, removal and site reclamation be recognized as liabilities when incurred, which may be on acquisition, construction or development of the asset. These liabilities would include "constructive obligations" that could be inferred from an entity's actions or representations, as well as evident legal liabilities. Recognized environmental obligations would be measured at the present value of estimated cash flows discounted at the risk-free rate in effect when the liabilities were incurred. Estimates of cash flows would factor in the effects of inflation and advances in technology that are expected to be available in the near term. The offsetting debit would be recognized as an increase in the cost of the long-lived asset associated with the obligation. Certain changes in the subsequent measurement of the liability would also be capitalized, and depreciation would be revised prospectively. The FASB is reconsidering certain of these issues and is contemplating a second exposure draft.

In Canada, the only CICA pronouncement that is specific to environmental costs states that:

> When reasonably determinable, provisions should be made for future removal and site-restoration costs, net of expected recoveries, in a rational and systematic manner by charges to income.[30]

This brief recommendation does not say anything that could not have been reasonably deduced from established general principles and standards. It has, however, forced enterprises to focus specifically on environmental costs and, in so doing, it has made it difficult for them to avoid making some systematic provisions for these costs.

While the recommendation may have resulted in more accruals, it has been deservedly criticized for its ambiguity and incompleteness. In particular, it may be read to permit an existing obligation for site restoration to be accrued over some more or less arbitrary future period, rather than recognized when the damage is done. As well, its general assertion that provisions be "net of expected recoveries" is open to broad interpretation and abuse. [31]

Once an environmental cost has been recognized, the next question is whether it should be immediately written off as a current income item or carried forward as an asset. Generally costs that are incurred to rectify past damage would not be expected to meet the "probable future benefits" test to qualify for treatment as an asset. However, it has been claimed that some environmental costs have unique characteristics that may justify capitalization in certain circumstances, for example, when they can be considered to be a necessary cost to achieve future benefits expected to result from a property. As well, it has become accepted that costs incurred to improve the safety of a property or to mitigate future environmental contamination should be capitalized even though they may not enhance the future service potential of the property. Some argue that capitalization policies for environmental costs should be liberal so as not to penalize enterprises by requiring them to expense costs that have been incurred to help protect or restore the environment. These issues are examined in Chapter 11 on capital assets.

Sustainability and Financial Accounting

Financial accounting as presently developed endeavours to reflect only costs that are to be borne by the reporting enterprise. It makes no attempt to record additional costs that enterprise activities may inflict upon society in using up or contaminating "free" community resources such as air and water. Some advocate that the accounting model should be expanded to reflect the *total cost* to society of an economic enterprise's activities—that is, measure the extent to which enterprise activities are meeting or compromising a society goal of "sustainable development."[32] ("Sustainable development" is defined as development "that meets the needs of the present without compromising the ability of future generations to meet their own needs.")[33]

Accountants can play a useful part in working with other disciplines to develop improved systems for monitoring and reporting environmental impacts of corporate and government enterprises. It is evident that disclosure of environmental performance by business enterprises is important to investors and other stakeholders—and that capital markets assign a higher cost of capital to enterprises that are not considered to be forthright in providing reliable information.[34] However, it is outside the purpose of financial accounting to measure environmental effects for which an enterprise is not financially accountable. Financial accounting is intended to reflect the financial effects on the entity itself of its economic activities. If society places no market price on a resource used by an entity, then it has no financial cost to that entity. Financial accounting should not be attempting to record costs that society does not price and charge to reporting enterprises.

Rather than trying to alter the existing purposes of financial accounting, it may be better for society to work to develop clear laws and market incentives that convert externality effects into internal costs to be incurred by corporate enterprises. There has been some significant movement in this direction, as a result of environmental legislation (leading to accountable obligations for costs to be borne by entities) and in the development of market-based incentives in some countries (for example, tradable pollution credits). Financial accounting for environmental obligations will continue to be a very difficult, subjective undertaking, particularly as environmental laws defining property rights and responsibilities continue to change and evolve. The greater the uncertainty of environmental obligations of particular enterprises, the more important it is for financial accounting to develop disclosures that effectively indicate risk exposures.[35]

SUMMARY

Measurement of periodic income under accrual accounting requires that expenditures on goods and services be recognized as expense in those periods when the benefit from the goods and services is received. A particular reporting period may be benefited by expenditures made in prior periods, expenditures of the current period, or expenditures that will not take place until future periods. When a benefit is received in the current period in return for an obligation to be satisfied by future expenditures, the necessary expense recognition is achieved by "accruing" the liability. For accounting purposes, that accrual is as much a liability at a particular reporting date as is the contractual liability for goods and services already received.

In this chapter we dealt first with the treatment of incurred costs as assets or expenses. Several stages are involved in the process of expense recognition.

- First, "period costs" incurred are written off to expense as the expenditure takes place. The justification is that their benefit is short-lived or that reasonable assurance is lacking as to benefits after the reporting date attributable to the expenditure.

- Second, for deferrable costs, "cost objects"—what we customarily think of as assets—must be identified.

- Third, costing methods must be adopted to associate costs incurred with cost objects. A long-standing debate exists over whether a "full costing" or "absorption costing" approach should be adopted or whether costs attached to assets should be confined to costs that are fairly directly traceable to the object—the "direct costing" approach. There has also been some division of opinion whether financing costs, such as interest, may be treated as part of the cost of an asset while it is being constructed or made ready for service. It is now accepted that financing costs may be attached to assets when a connection can be traced.

- The final stage is the recognition of expense as an asset's benefit is used up. For inventories, this requires a method for allocating costs previously attached to the inventories as between costs applicable to goods sold or scrapped and costs applicable to goods still on hand. For other assets that are largely consumed in use rather than being sold, some "systematic and rational" basis must be adopted for amortizing cost to expense over the asset's useful life.

When a liability accrues in a period—that is, when operations of a period have benefited in return for an obligation to make expenditures in future—the measurement of the cost and the accrued liability can be difficult. First, one must ask what assumptions should be made about future economic conditions. In particular, there is the question as to how future inflation and price changes should be reflected in measuring obligations that are exposed to these risks. The question also arises whether the future expenditures should be discounted in recognizing costs currently. Theory provides a yes answer to this latter question, and the selection of an interest rate has significant implications for the inclusion of expected price changes in the estimates of future expenditures.

Once it has been determined what should be measured, the problem becomes one of estimation. In theory, accruals of future expenditures should be based on "best estimates" or "expected values." However, under uncertainty there will always be a range of possible outcomes and accounting has no generally accepted theory for the selection of single point estimates from ranges of possibilities. There is also the age-old question as to how risk, that is, the possibility of adverse deviations from expectations, should be reflected in an estimate. Contingency pricing models in finance economics and capital markets hold some promise, although their implications for accounting obligation accruals remain largely unexplored.

Not infrequently, an entity may discover that it may have an obligation to make future payments that will not give rise to any discernible benefits. When first noticed, they often appear to be only possible, not a certainty—in which case they are known as contingencies. There is some confusion in accounting literature as to whether any accrual that is not for a fixed amount or any judgment-based allowance, such as an allowance for doubtful accounts, is a contingency. A narrower concept of a contingency distinguishes it from normal estimation problems such as those just described. Within this narrower view, a contingency is thought of as a condition involving the possibility of gain or loss that had its origin in previous operations but that was not foreseen when those operations and activities took place. This latter concept appears to be at the basis of the CICA standard on contingencies.

Recognition of a liability and consequent loss with respect to a contingency (once it is realized that it exists) depends upon a judgment as to how likely the loss is and whether a reasonable estimate can be made of its amount. The guidance given in accounting standards as to both of these judgments is poorly worded and is biased towards nonrecognition of the loss. This shortcoming may be partially overcome by required disclosure, but even here more thought needs to be given to effective ways to convey to statement readers the range of possible outcomes of the contingency.

In contrast to contingent losses, recognition of a contingent gain is not to take place before realization. Disclosure of the contingent asset before recognition is restricted to the more likely cases.

Accruals for uncertain future expenditures to restore environmental damage may be seen as an application of accounting for contingencies. They do, however, give rise to some particularly difficult estimation and asset-expense recognition issues.

REFERENCES

[1]   See CICA, Emerging Issues Committee, *Special Termination Benefits*, EIC 23 (Toronto: CICA, 1991); and FASB, *Employers' Accounting for Settlements and Curtailments of Defined Benefit Pension Plans and for Termination Benefits,* Statement of Financial Accounting Standards No. 88 (Stamford: FASB, 1985).

[2]   L.T. Johnson, *Future Events: A Conceptual Study of Their Significance for Recognition and Measurement* (Norwalk: FASB, 1994). This was a joint study of the G4+1 standard-setting bodies.

3   See CICA, "Financial Statement Concepts," *CICA Handbook,* Section 1000 (Toronto: CICA), par. 44. It indicates that for an item to be recognized in financial statements, it should be the case that "a reasonable estimate can be made of the amount involved."

4   Ibid., par. 21(d).

5   See FASB, *Accounting for Compensated Absences,* Statement of Financial Accounting Standards No. 43 (Stamford: FASB, 1980).

6   FASB, *Employers' Accounting for Postemployment Benefits,* Statement of Financial Accounting Standards No. 112 (Norwalk: FASB, 1992).

7   CICA, "Employees' Future Benefits," *CICA Handbook,* Section 3461 (Toronto: CICA).

8   FASB, *Employers' Accounting for Postretirement Benefits Other Than Pensions,* Statement of Financial Accounting Standards No. 106 (Norwalk: FASB, 1990).

9   See CICA, Emerging Issues Committee, *Post Retirement Benefits Other Than Pensions,* EIC 5 (Toronto: CICA, 1989). It identified "pay-as-you-go" accounting as an acceptable alternative in Canada, and required disclosure of post-retirement benefit plans and accounting policies for these plans.

10 See, for example, D.G. Searfoss and N. Erickson, "The Big Unfunded Liability: Postretirement Healthcare Benefits," *Journal of Accountancy,* November 1988, pp. 28–39.

11 CICA, "Contingencies," *CICA Handbook,* Section 3290 (Toronto: CICA), par. 02.

12 FASB, *Accounting for Contingencies,* Statement of Financial Accounting Standards No. 5 (Stamford: FASB, 1975).

13 For example, it has been asserted that, in the application of FASB Statement No. 5, "'probable'… has, in the case of banks, come to mean 'virtually certain'…" See United States General Accounting Office, *Failed Banks: Accounting and Auditing Reforms Urgently Needed,* Report to Congressional Committees (Washington: United States GAO, 1991), p. 26.

14 See, for example, G.R. Chesley, "Interpretation of Uncertainty Expressions," *Contemporary Accounting Research,* Spring 1986, pp. 179–99; and G.R. Chesley and H.A. Wier, "The Challenge of Contingencies: Adding Precision to Probability," *CA Magazine,* April 1985, pp. 38–41. A summary of research evidence on the range of numerical values assigned to verbal expressions of probability values appears at J.E. Boritz, CICA Research Report, *Approaches to Dealing with Risk and Uncertainty* (Toronto: CICA, 1990), pp. 23–24.

15 CICA, *Contingent Gains and Losses,* Exposure Draft (Toronto: CICA, 1993).

16 CICA, "Communications With Law Firms Regarding Claims and Possible Claims," *CICA Handbook* (Toronto: CICA).

17 The only public notice of this was one paragraph in the CICA Accounting Standards Board brochure, *FYI,* of December 31, 1996.

18 IASC, *Provisions, Contingent Liabilities and Contingent Assets,* IAS 37 (London: IASC, 1998).

19 CICA, *Contingent Gains and Losses,* Exposure Draft, par. 09.

20 CICA, "Financial Instruments—Disclosure and Presentation," *CICA Handbook,* Section 3860 (Toronto: CICA), pars. 3860.34–.35 and .41.

21 AICPA, Accounting Standards Executive Committee, *Disclosure of Certain Significant Risks and Uncertainties,* SOP 94-6 (New York: AICPA, 1994).

22 CICA, "Measurement Uncertainties," *CICA Handbook,* Section 1508 (Toronto: CICA).

23 FASB, *Prior Period Adjustments,* Statement of Financial Accounting Standards No. 16 (Stamford: FASB, 1977), par. 37.

24 This was done by withdrawing the *CICA Handbook* section on "Prior Period Adjustments," (former Section 3600).

25 See M.E. Barth and M.F. McNichols, "Estimation and Market Valuation of Environmental Liabilities Relating to Superfund Sites," *Journal of Accounting Research,* Supplement 1994, pp. 177–209; and D. Cormier and M. Magnan, "Investors' Assessment of Implicit Environmental Liabilities: An Empirical Investigation," *Journal of Accounting and Public Policy,* Summer 1997, pp. 215–241.

26 See FASB, Emerging Issues Task Force, *Accounting for Environmental Liabilities,* EITF Abstract No. 93-5 (Norwalk: FASB, 1993); and SEC, *Accounting and Disclosures Related to Loss Contingencies,* Staff Accounting Bulletin No. 92, 17 CFR Part 211 (June, 1993).

27 AICPA, Accounting Standards Executive Committee, *Environmental Remediation Liabilities,* SOP 96-1 (New York: AICPA, 1996).

28 For a brief overview of research findings, and references to important studies, see American Accounting Association's Financial Accounting Standards Committee, "Response to IASC Exposure Draft, 'Provisions, Contingent Liabilities and Contingent Assets'," *Accounting Horizons,* June 1998, p. 197. This paper, pp. 192–200, contains a useful review of research relating to the information value of the recognition and disclosure of provisions and contingencies, including significant research on environmental costs and obligations.

29 FASB, *Accounting for Certain Liabilities Related to Closure or Removal of Long-Lived Assets,* Proposed Statement of Financial Accounting Standards (Norwalk: FASB, 1996).

30 CICA, "Capital Assets," *CICA Handbook,* Section 3060 (Toronto: CICA, 1990), par. 39.

31 For a critical analysis of these issues see CICA Research Report, *Environmental Costs and Liabilities: Accounting and Financial Reporting Issues* (Toronto: CICA, 1993), chap. 4.

32 See, for example, D.B. Rubenstein, "Lessons of Love," *CA Magazine,* March 1991, pp. 35–41.

33 World Commission on Environment and Development, *Our Common Future* (New York and London: Oxford University Press, 1987), p. 8.

34 American Accounting Association, "Response to IASC Exposure Draft, 'Provisions, Contingent Liabilities and Contingent Assets'," *Accounting Horizons,* June 1998, pp. 192–200.

35 For a discussion of the role of financial accounting in relation to the environment and market forces, see D.B. Thornton, "Green Accounting and Green Eyeshades," *CA Magazine,* October 1993, pp. 34–40. In particular he draws on established economic literature to make the point that property rights and obligations must be clearly delineated for market prices to work effectively in allocating scarce resources.

FINANCIAL POSITION AND CAPITAL

We observed, in Chapter 4, two distinct shifts during this century in the relative emphasis placed on the balance sheet versus the income statement. Entering the twentieth century the focus was on the balance sheet. This shifted to the income statement with the development of the historical cost-matching theory in the 1930s and '40s—so much so that the balance sheet became, in part, a collection of residuals left over from the revenue-expense matching process. Over time growing dissatisfaction with the increasingly apparent limitations of classical revenue-expense matching gave rise to another shift. The FASB concepts statements developed in the mid-1970s placed primary emphasis on reasoning within economic substance definitions of "assets" and "liabilities," and this framework significantly influenced thinking in Canada and other countries.

This renewed attention to the balance sheet has come to be interpreted in quite a different light from that of the traditional "revenue-expense" versus "asset-liability" debate. The classical view had been that one could not expect to get both the balance sheet and income statements right—that one had to choose between an income determination model (based on revenue-expense matching) and some balance sheet asset-liability valuation model. If one tried to mix asset-liability and revenue-expense models, then the balance sheet and income statements would not articulate with one another. The modern view would seem to be that this is not an either-or matter, but that the goal of developing a representationally faithful income statement should be complementary to that of developing a representationally faithful balance sheet. We observed, in Chapter 5, that the fundamental economic premise that sacrifices (costs) must be incurred to achieve benefits (revenues) is at the heart of both revenue-expense matching and in-substance concepts of "assets" and "liabilities." The implication is that one should expect that, if the results of revenue-expense matching are to make economic sense, the balance sheet "residuals" (revenue and cost accruals) should be justifiable as real assets and liabilities.

The complementary nature of financial position and income might be best appreciated by visualizing a business enterprise as simply a cash-generating machine for accounting purposes. This is not a revolutionary idea. It simply reflects a fundamental premise of the conceptual framework for financial accounting—that it is the "ability of the enterprise to generate favourable cash flows" that is of primary interest to investors, creditors and other external user interests.[1] Accounting income may then be seen as a measure of the excess of revenues (represented by inflows of cash or claims to cash or equivalents) over expenses incurred to achieve those revenues (represented by current and past outflows of cash or obligations to pay cash or equivalents in future periods). Income or earning power is usually the most significant determinant of a business enterprise's value. Of course the ability of an enterprise to generate favourable cash flows is not indicated solely by reference to its income numbers. One must, among other things, also understand the enterprise's stock of resources that constitutes its investment base for generating the income flows. Investors and others require information on financial position as a basis for assessing return on investment and risk.

Consistent with the depiction of a business enterprise as a cash-generating machine for accounting purposes, its assets and liabilities must be visualized in terms of their probable ultimate future contribution to, or claim on, future cash flows. Again, this is not a new idea, but one that is fully consistent with currently accepted conceptual framework statements. Both FASB and CICA concepts statements indicate that the value of an asset lies in its ability "to contribute directly or indirectly to future net cash flows."[2]

This helps us understand the central informational role of the statement of finance position, still commonly referred to as the balance sheet. The FASB Concepts Statement No. 1 concluded that investors and others have primary interest in information relevant to evaluating "the amounts, timing and uncertainty of prospective net cash inflows to the related enterprise" (paragraph 37). Within this context a primary purpose of the balance sheet is to present assets, liabilities and capital classified by components that convey information on liquidity (that is, nearness to cash) and exposure to various risks. In a more general sense, the balance sheet can be expected to be looked to by users to help evaluate financial capability, adaptability and solvency. It may also be used as a check on the quality of reported earnings, by reference, for example, to how "soft" enterprise assets may be, that is, how tenuous and uncertain may be the relationship of various types of enterprise assets to the generation of future cash flows.

In this chapter we will first discuss three issues following from these general balance sheet objectives as they pertain to assets and liabilities:

- The portrayal of liquidity, with particular reference to the classification of current assets and liabilities.

- The presentation of risk exposures, and particularly, accounting questions that arise when one considers how an enterprise's risk exposures may be affected by matched or mismatched assets and liabilities and various hedging strategies.

- Considerations related to the incompleteness of balance sheet representations and concerns with respect to off-balance sheet items.

Finally, we will examine accounting for capital and the problem of distinguishing debt from equity.

ASSETS AND LIABILITIES

Current Assets and Liabilities

As recounted in Chapter 3, nineteenth-century English accounting developed the idea of circulating capital as consisting of those assets that go through a continuing cycle of purchase, manufacturing, and sale together with the liabilities that finance them. The subdivision of the balance sheet between circulating capital and other long-term capital proved to be of some significance for credit granting purposes. Bankers of early industries found it convenient to have a subdivision of assets between those that would be realized in cash in the normal course of operations and those that would not, and a subdivision of liabilities between those that would be paid out of such realizations and those that would not. This notion of circulating capital was, however, designed simply to differentiate between different characteristics of assets held and not primarily to measure their liquidity. There was some confusion in this because it tended to be assumed that liquidity was indicated by the balance sheet description of an asset. Thus inventory was current, regardless of how long it might be in process. Plant and equipment was noncurrent, even though it might make a considerable contribution to current cash flow.[3]

The Committee on Accounting Procedure of the AICPA introduced the idea of an "operating cycle" in an extensive consideration of current assets and liabilities in its Bulletin No. 30 issued in 1947.[4] It defined operating cycle as the average period that elapses between the time materials are acquired for inventory and the time the product is sold and cash collected upon the sale. Thus it is a cash-to-cash cycle. This idea clearly stems from the notion of "circulating capital." The committee inserted a one-year test for current assets as well. Assets would be treated as current if they were expected to be realized within the operating cycle or within one year. Current liabilities were then defined as obligations that would require the use of existing resources properly classified as current assets or that would require the creation of other current liabilities.

In practice what has resulted is that, for the most part, an asset is classified as current if it is expected to contribute to cash flow within twelve months. A liability is classified as current if it is expected to be liquidated within twelve months. The operating cycle test becomes operative only when the cash-to-cash cycle with respect to goods sold (or services rendered) takes longer than twelve months.[5] Under that provision, inventories in certain industries may be treated as current even though the investment in them will be tied up for much longer than one year. Instalment accounts receivable may also be classified as current if that is the normal basis upon which goods are sold. The twelve month test could be considered to be moderately useful for the purpose of indicating solvency. The operating cycle criterion considerably diminishes that utility.

The reference to assets expected to be sold or consumed also created some difficulties. Under a strict application of the test, marketable securities not intended to be sold would be excluded from current assets. Yet, if it is desired to use the current asset figure as an indication of liquidity, holdings of marketable securities are certainly pertinent. The *CICA Handbook* standard seems to indicate that such securities should be classified as current.[6] However, there is some confusion in this, as it is common for enterprises to classify investments that are not held for trading purposes outside current assets even though the bulk of the portfolio may be readily marketable.[7] Thus, in practice, what is included in current assets may be affected by management's intentions.

An intention test may also be applied to exclude from the current category short-term obligations that are intended to be refinanced. In this case, however, there is a question whether that intention can be fulfilled. Accordingly, accounting standards permit classification of such obligations as long-term only if contractual arrangements exist that ensure refinancing on a basis that pushes the maturity date beyond twelve months. In Canada, also, practice permits certain debts that are short-term in form to be classified as noncurrent (for example, demand bank loans that are designated as term loans) provided the lender acknowledges its intention to permit the loan to remain outstanding beyond twelve months.

If one is concerned with the potential cash requirements to liquidate debt, there is another point of some significance. Suppose an entity borrows $1 million at 10% maturing in ten years with interest payable annually. It thus commits itself to the payment of $100,000 each year for ten years and $1 million at the end of the ten-year period. Customarily, no part of the $1 million is shown as a current liability until the end of the ninth year. Yet, at the issue date, the present value at 10% of the interest payments accounts for approximately $614,000 of the liability and the present value of the payment on principal ten years hence is only $386,000. The present value of the first year's interest payment alone is $91,000. One can argue that current liabilities should include a figure of $91,000 or $100,000 with respect to such debt if the real desire is to portray its requirements for cash in the short term.[8]

It can be seen then that the concepts of current assets and current liabilities lack clarity and that there are anomalies in their interpretation. The concepts might be improved if the focus was put on the evaluation of entity liquidity and the rule condensed into one based upon (1) expectations of cash realization in operations within a short time period, such as a year, and (2) capability of being realized upon within short notice. Even such simple criteria are not without difficulties, however. All assets represent expectations of future cash inflows in a sense, or they would not been shown as assets. Yet it is not practicable to quantify realistically the contribution to cash over a year of such assets as plant and equipment and goodwill. In any event, the picture shown by a statement of position is static. It tells very little about the cash flow from operations to be expected over the next year or period of years.

On balance, it might be more sensible if the classification of assets and liabilities between current and noncurrent were abandoned. As a substitute, more information could be given as to the maturity dates of monetary assets and liabilities shown in the balance sheet, including disclosure of past-due amounts. This, together with improved cash flow information would provide the analyst with a better perspective on the liquidity of an enterprise. A more informative basis of classification, both in the balance sheet and the income statement would be operating assets and liabilities, more or less passive investments, and financing. This classification fits the format now prescribed for the statement of cash flows (see Chapter 22). Within these categories in the balance sheet, assets and liabilities could be listed in order of liquidity.

Asset and Liability Risk Attributes and Relationships

An enterprise's exposure to risk will be affected by how its assets and liabilities work together. Certain of the risks inherent in a particular asset may be counter-balanced by offsetting risks of other assets or liabilities. On the other hand, in some cases a mismatched mix of assets and liabilities may magnify an entity's exposure to particular risks. As an example of the latter, an entity may be exposed to serious liquidity risk if it has assets that are locked in, so that they will generate cash flows only over a long term, financed by debt that must be repaid over the short term. This mismatch should be apparent from a fairly presented balance sheet and supporting note disclosures within the requirements of existing GAAP.

Certain asset and liability risk matches or mismatches may be obscured or confused by accounting that recognizes the assets and liabilities at different times, or that measures them on different bases. As an example, a Canadian company might borrow in U.S. dollars but not consider itself exposed to U.S./Canadian dollar exchange rate fluctuations because it has a contract to sell its product in U.S. dollar amounts that will be sufficient to meet its scheduled debt payments. In other words, the company would consider the exchange currency risk inherent in the liability to be effectively hedged by the future sales. The difficulty is that the debt appears on the balance sheet at the end of the current period but the future sales will not be recognized for accounting purposes until the future periods in which they are considered to be earned.

A number of serious questions arise in financial accounting in determining what may be considered an effective hedge, and how the offsetting effects may be appropriately accounted for and disclosed. These issues are discussed in Chapter 17, on financial instruments, and in Chapter 21 on foreign currency translation.

The effects of potentially counter-balancing exposures to risk may be confused by measurement inconsistencies. For example, the stream of future cash payments called for by a particular debt may be counter-balanced in whole or in part by assets with more or less matched expected future cash inflows. But, if the assets and liabilities are measured on different bases, the accounting may yield anomalous results. To illustrate, suppose an entity has incurred debt of $1 million to be repaid in equal annual installments of principal and interest at the end of each of the next five years, with the interest rate being 10%. This works out to a five year annuity of about $264,000. Suppose it has acquired a minimum risk government bond with the exact same cash flows over the same five-year period. Finally, suppose that the investment is accounted for at current market values, while the debt is accounted for on an amortized cost basis. If interest rates fell to, say, 7% at the beginning of the second year, the government bond market value would be adjusted to approximately $894,000, and a gain would be recorded. The accounting value of the debt on an amortized cost basis would continue to be its present value at 10%, or about $836,000. This accounting result of identical cash streams being recorded at significantly different values is obviously troublesome.[9] This same mismatch could occur where both the asset and the liability are carried on a cost basis, if they were acquired at different times when different interest rates were in effect. To illustrate, suppose the debt in the above example was issued at the 10% rate at the beginning of year 1, and the government bond acquired for $894,000 at the 7% rate at the beginning of year 2.

The measurement mismatch is clear in these simple cases, but it may not be so obvious where an entity has many assets and liabilities of different types purchased at different times.

In sum, it would seem that accounting must consider not only the merits of a particular accounting measurement or recognition basis for a particular transaction or event, but must also keep in mind implications with respect to the risk interrelationships of assets and liabilities.

These issues have assumed much increased importance and difficulty over the past ten years or so for several reasons. These include the globalization of markets and business activities, a marked increase in the volatility of foreign currencies and interest rates and commodity prices, and the availability of sophisticated financial instruments to facilitate risk management strategies. These developments have focused attention on enterprise vulnerability to risks and on the need for effective risk management, not only with respect to financial institutions, which are particularly vulnerable, but also with respect to many commercial enterprises and not-for-profit organizations. It is clear that, in order to be able to understand an enterprise's financial position and its risk exposures, an investor requires information on the essential terms, risk attributes, and uncertainties inherent in its particular mix of assets and liabilities. There have been some significant improvements in disclosure standards, for example, of financial instruments and financial risk management strategies[10] and, in the U.S., with respect to contingent liabilities (as reported in Chapter 8). However, it is well recognized that GAAP have not kept pace with the increased level of sophistication of risk management and hedging activities. In particular, issues relating to the recognition, measurement and disclosure of financial instruments and hedging activities have been the subject of intensive study by accounting standard setters in recent years. These issues are a particular focus of Chapter 17 on financial instruments.

Off-Balance Sheet Issues

No discussion of the balance sheet would be complete without considering what assets and liabilities are not recognized. We have previously observed that accrual accounting, being transactions based, does not purport to reflect the full economic wealth of an enterprise. It omits, for example, the discovery value of a mine, the knowledge and talents of employees, and internally generated goodwill. These omissions are inherent in the limitations of the accounting model and in what it is feasible to recognize and reliably measure—and we will not pursue them here.

A particular class of "off-balance sheet" items does warrant our attention, however. Some significant assets and liabilities go unrecorded as a result of weaknesses in the existing accounting model that accounting standard setters may be expected to address. Three areas of practice may be identified: (1) offsetting of assets and liabilities, (2) certain applications and interpretations of asset and liability recognition and extinguishment principles, and (3) the exclusion from consolidated financial statements of significant assets and liabilities over which the reporting enterprise has some beneficial interest and responsibility.

Offsetting of Assets and Liabilities

In 1966, APB Omnibus Opinion No. 10 stated that "it is a general principle of accounting that the offsetting of assets and liabilities in the balance sheet is improper except where a right of setoff exists." [11] Exactly what a "right of setoff" meant was not defined, however. In the 1980s new forms of financing transactions gave rise to questions and several accounting pronouncements and practices were developed that began to blur the principle. In 1988 a FASB technical bulletin attempted to clarify the term. It defined a right of setoff as "a debtor's legal right, by contract or otherwise, to discharge all or a portion of the debt owed to another party by applying against the debt an amount that the other party owes to the debtor." [12] It set out four conditions, all of which must be met for a right of setoff to exist. Three of these are clear from the above definition. The other condition is that the reporting party must intend to setoff. This latter condition was not explained, and four years later the FASB allowed an exception in permitting netting on the basis of "master netting arrangements." [13] Financial institutions that undertake many financial instrument transactions with each other commonly enter into these arrangements. A master netting agreement will provide that, in the event of default by one party with respect to any financial instrument subject to the agreement, the other party has the right to settle all outstanding instruments with the defaulting party on a net basis. The FASB position is that exchange contracts under master netting agreements with the same counterparty may be offset. This position was taken in response to pressures from the securities industry. One FASB member dissented, noting that the conditions for offsetting call for the right of setoff to be unconditional and the reporting party must intend to setoff. As he observed, "under a master netting arrangement, both the ability and intent to setoff are conditional." [14]

Besides this exception, the FASB has left in place a number of previously issued standards that permit offsetting under conditions that may not meet the four setoff conditions. These include leveraged leases, the offsetting of pension assets and liabilities held in a separate fund and, as we observed in Chapter 8, some netting permitted in accounting for contingent losses.

Canadian practice had tended to follow U.S. practice and standards until the CICA and IASC put in place virtually identical standards on disclosure and presentation of financial instruments. They were the product of a joint IASC/CICA project that began in 1989. These standards include a requirement that a financial asset and a financial liability may be offset only when there is a legally enforceable right to setoff and the reporting entity either intends to settle on a net basis or to realize the asset and settle the liability simultaneously. It makes no exception for netting on the basis of master netting arrangements. [15]

Asset and Liability Recognition and Extinguishment Principles

Another major area of difficulty arises from principles related to recognition and discontinuing recognition of assets and liabilities. Ambiguities and uncertainties with respect to these principles and their application have opened the door to various degrees of exploitation for the purpose of enhancing reporting income and/or achieving off-balance sheet treatment. The following summarizes the more significant areas of difficulty identified in earlier chapters:

- The general nonrecognition of executory contracts—with particular reference to lease transactions and problems in distinguishing between operating leases and leases which are tantamount to the purchase of capital assets (discussed in Chapter 6 and to be further addressed in Chapter 13);

- Difficulties in ascertaining when a transfer of assets for cash or equivalent may be a sale and when it may be a debt financing—with particular reference to sale-leasebacks of capital assets and securitizations of receivables and like assets (discussed in Chapter 7);

- Problems in determining whether certain transactions have resulted in the extinguishment of debt—with particular reference to whether a reporting entity has retained primary or secondary responsibility for the obligation and with respect to the effectiveness of "in-substance" defeasance (discussed in Chapter 7); and

- A variety of problems related to the recognition of liabilities for future expenditures that are the result of past events or transactions—with particular reference to post-employment benefits, environmental reclamation, and contingent losses (discussed in Chapter 8).

Accounting standards have been developed to address some of these situations. At the same time, however, increasingly sophisticated transactions continue to challenge these standards and it may be expected that there will always be some grey areas that will allow some significant "off-balance financing." Standard setters have resorted, with only limited success, to drawing more or less arbitrary lines in a number of these situations (for example in attempting to distinguish a capital lease from an operating lease). Not surprisingly, enterprise managements and their advisors have become adept at developing transactions that just fit inside or outside the lines, depending on the accounting they might wish to achieve. In these cases, the role of disclosure is crucial so as to enable informed readers to assess for themselves the effects of these borderline transactions on financial position, liquidity and risk.

Consolidation and Control

The final class of off-balance sheet issues involves determining the entities that should be included in the consolidated financial statements of a corporate group. The traditional accounting had been that a parent company should consolidate its subsidiaries, with some exceptions. An entity was defined to be a subsidiary of another entity (the parent) if the parent owned directly or indirectly a majority of the shares carrying the right to elect the majority of its board of directors. In recent years it has become fairly common for some assets and liabilities to be placed in entities that are technically not "subsidiaries," with the express purpose of removing them from the balance sheet of the reporting enterprise. This, it has been alleged, has been used with other off-balance sheet accounting schemes noted above to hide some of the real assets and liabilities of a corporate group.

In 1991 the CICA issued a standard that attempted to broaden the basis for consolidation by broadening the concept of "control."[16] In particular, it recognizes that an enterprise may control another enterprise other than by holding a majority of its voting shares. It is not clear that this pronouncement is having a significant effect in changing practice, however. It leaves much room for judgment. What is clear is that there are new forms of risk sharing business arrangements that are not readily assessable in terms of traditional concepts of control. It has become common for special purpose companies or trusts to be created to hold assets and liabilities and to carry out certain tasks—for example, to hold a capital lease or a portfolio of receivables financed by nonrecourse debt and to utilize the cash flows from the assets to service the debt. Such entities may be set up so that no one actively controls them on a continuing basis; rather they may be effectively preprogrammed to carry out their function, perhaps with some guarantees by the initiating parties. These and other forms of business arrangements, such as joint ventures and various cooperative activities, give rise to difficult questions as to whether or when their assets and liabilities should be recorded in the balance sheets of the investor-venturer enterprises. These subjects are addressed in Chapter 20.

ACCOUNTING FOR CAPITAL

Capital Transactions

One principle that has always been agreed upon in accounting is that there is a fundamental distinction between the nature of capital transactions and income transactions. No matter how narrowly or how broadly the concept of income is defined, there will be some "capital transactions" that lie outside it.

It is necessary, however, to have a clear idea of what constitutes a capital transaction. The following are the principal types:[17]

- First are transactions in which capital is contributed to an entity or withdrawn from it. In a business corporation this would include the subscription of capital in return for shares. It would also include forfeiture of shares by a shareholder, redemption of shares according to the terms of their issue, or purchase by the corporation of its own shares on the open market.

- Payments of costs and expenses in connection with the issuance of capital are likewise regarded as capital transactions. Gains and losses on redemption of capital or on purchase and resale of shares are excluded from income since they are part of a capital transaction.

- Payment of a return on capital, such as dividends, is also a capital transaction.

- Under Canadian tax law, part of the income tax paid by a Canadian controlled private company is refundable to the company in an amount equal to a specified percent of any dividend paid by the company (up to the amount of refundable tax previously paid). The effect is that if a company pays a dividend equal in amount to its income after tax (excluding the refundable tax), then most of the refundable tax will be recovered. One way of looking at the refundable tax is that it is not an income tax on the company, but rather an advance payment of tax that will become payable by the shareholder if and when income earned by the company is passed on to the shareholder in the form of dividends. The CICA has therefore recommended that the refundable tax paid by the company be treated as a capital transaction and charged against retained earnings—that is, as a payment not to shareholders but on account of shareholders.[18]

- In those rare cases where a business combination is treated as a pooling of interests, the theory is that the merged company is in substance a continuation of all the preceding companies entering into the merger. As a result, the previous financial histories of the combining companies are added together as representing the history of the pooled entity, and the assets and liabilities of each component at the time of the combination are added together at their existing carrying values to form the statement of financial position of the combined entity. There are always some expenses directly attributable to any combination and the question arises of how these should be reported. Since they are attributable to the combination, they are clearly not part of the income history of any component before combination. On the other hand, since the combined entity is considered to be merely a continuation of the previous components, neither do the expenses represent a cost of earning income after the combination. The solution adopted to this dilemma is to treat the expenses as capital transactions and charge them directly to retained earnings.[19]

- Provisions or releases of "reserves" on a discretionary basis are also regarded as capital in nature (that is, as appropriations of retained earnings) and hence do not affect reported income.[20]

- On occasion a company that is in financial difficulties may go through a reorganization in which creditors and shareholders accept a reduction in their rights and claims upon the company, and assets are written down to values considered more realistic in the situation. A quasi-reorganization is similar except that it does not involve the creditors. Instead, it takes place after a formal approval by the shareholders, usually involving a reduction of legal capital. Write-downs or other losses related to circumstances that existed prior to a reorganization or quasi-reorganization would be accounted for in the income statement for that period. Revaluation adjustments resulting from a reorganization are accounted for as capital transactions. Adjustments to restate share capital, and any costs to effect a reorganization or quasi-reorganization, are applied first to eliminate retained earnings (deficit). The balance is then applied against contributed surplus or placed in a separately identified shareholders' equity account. Consistent with treatment as a "fresh start," retained earnings is accumulated from the date of a financial reorganization or quasi-reorganization. To show that the enterprise has had a "fresh start," disclosure is made that the balance in retained earnings (or deficit) was accumulated since the date of the reorganization/quasi-reorganization for a period of at least three years after the readjustment. [21]

It is evident that a clear concept of capital is an essential underpinning to the concept of a capital transaction. The concept of capital is very broad under the entity theory—consisting of all financing provided to an entity. The concept of capital under the proprietary viewpoint is limited to capital furnished by the proprietor or partners in an unincorporated entity, or to equity shares in a corporation. Historically, and until very recently, accountants largely looked to the law to define the distinction between equity and debt in applying the proprietary concept. A broader economic interpretation is that capital should be defined to be residual equity—for example in a corporation, share capital that carries a right to participation in residual income and residual assets on liquidation after all fixed amount claims of other security holders are satisfied.

Distinguishing Debt from Equity

The traditional proprietary viewpoint under the influence of legal concepts of corporation capital has the following consequences.

- Issuance and redemption or repurchase of debt securities are not considered capital transactions. Consequently, expenses and discounts or premiums on issue of such securities are absorbed in income (by amortization) along with interest costs. Also, gains and losses on retirement or early redemption are reported as income.

- In contrast, issuance of preferred and common shares and costs thereof, and gains and losses on their redemption or repurchase, are considered capital transactions.

The legal basis for the distinction between debt and equity became increasingly unsatisfactory as capital structures became more sophisticated and enterprises began issuing hybrid debt-equity instruments. Their legal description as shares or debt may camouflage their true nature. For example, preferred shares that are retractable on specific dates at the option of the holder, and "term preferred" shares that have a fixed redemption date, are much more consistent in substance with debt than with equity capital. Looking at the other side of the coin, debt that is convertible into common shares may have most of the attributes of equity when the issuer has the ability to force conversion and no retraction privilege exists.

Not surprisingly, the emphasis we see on the balance sheet for depiction of in-substance assets and liabilities has led to pressures to abandon capital classification based on a legal form for one that reflects the economic substance of the distinction between liabilities and equity. In 1995, the CICA adopted a standard that requires that an issuer of a financial instrument classify it on its balance sheet in accordance with the substance of its contractual provisions on initial recognition based on conceptual definitions of financial liabilities and equity.[22]

A companion requirement is that a compound financial instrument, that is one that has both a maturity date and a right to convert into an equity instrument, should be separated into its liability and equity parts on initial recognition with each part accounted for according to its respective characteristics. The most common example is debt that is convertible into the issuing enterprise's common shares at the option of the holder. Such an instrument would be considered to comprise two parts: a financial liability (the contractual obligation to pay cash) and an equity instrument (a call option granting the holder the right to convert into common shares). The question is how to measure each of these components. One approach is to determine the fair value of the debt component at the date of issue by discounting the contracted cash flows at the current market interest rate for stand-alone debt of that term and risk. The value of the equity (option) component would then be the difference between the proceeds received for the whole instrument and the fair value of the debt component. Another possibility would be to estimate the fair value of each component standing alone and then adjust these amounts on a pro rata basis so that the sum of the values of the components equals the total consideration received for the instrument as a whole.[23]

The treatment of interest, dividends and gains and losses must, of course, be consistent with the balance sheet classification of the related debt and equity instruments. If, for example, a term preferred share were to be classified as a liability, its "dividends" should be accrued, appropriately on an effective interest basis, and reported as a deduction from income. Likewise, a gain or loss arising on the refinancing or redemption of a particular instrument would be reflected in income or as an equity adjustment according to the debt or equity classification of the instrument.[24]

The standard's requirement for in-substance balance sheet classification has proved to be difficult to implement in respect of certain types of securities that may seem to have both debt and equity characteristics. The more contentious questions that have arisen are discussed below:

- A number of enterprises have issued securities in the form of debt that can be settled on maturity, at the option of the issuer, either in cash or in common shares of the issuer of equivalent market value to the debt. In substance, there is no residual equity risk in these instruments, because the holder will either receive cash or an equivalent value in shares. Thus it would seem reasonable to conclude that the instrument should be classified as debt. However, the *CICA Handbook* states that a "financial liability" involves a contractual obligation to deliver cash or other financial assets to the holder, or to make an exchange of financial instruments on terms that are potentially unfavourable. In this case, since the issuer has the right to settle the principal portion of the instrument by distributing its equity, it does not meet the definition of a financial liability.

  After much deliberation, the EIC concluded that the present value of the principal component of the security is equity, while the present value of the future interest stream of cash payments is a liability.[25] The IASC Standing Interpretations Committee reached a similar conclusion, but the IASC board subsequently amended its standard to require such instruments to be classified and accounted for as financial liabilities.[26]

- Some issued securities impose an obligation to pay cash or equivalent at a future time only if a particular event occurs. An example would be a preferred share that is redeemable by the holder for a fixed amount of cash if its market value has fallen below that amount. Should this preferred share be classified as debt or equity by the issuer? The EIC concluded that it should be classified as debt on initial recognition if, at that date, it is probable that the event will occur requiring settlement in cash or equivalent.[27] A subsequent change in expectations would not result in any change in this classification. However, if the initial probability assessment turns out to be incorrect, it will be necessary to account for that effect when the outcome becomes known.

- Some organizations, such as partnerships and cooperatives, issue financial instruments that provide for payments to holders of a pro rata share of the residual equity of the issuer. These financial instruments may require redemption in specific circumstances, such as the death of the holder, that are certain to take place. The fact that they are ultimately payable may seem to make them financial liabilities. However, since the holder only shares in the residual equity on repayment, they are considered to be equity (*CICA Handbook*, paragraph 3860.23). An EIC abstract addressed a more complex situation where a cooperative issues shares that are redeemable by the holder at a fixed amount, but which entitle the holder to a pro rata share of the cooperative's net assets in the event of its liquidation or wind-up.[28]

- Estate freeze tax planning arrangements have commonly involved the exchange of all the common shares of a private owner-managed enterprise for so-called "high-low" preference shares. Typically these preference shares are mandatorily redeemable on demand by the holder for cash or equivalent in the amount of the fair value of the common shares at the date of the transaction. This transaction allows the owner of the business (the common shareholder) to freeze the value of his or her estate at the date of the transaction, and nonvoting participating shares may be issued at nominal value to, say, his or her children so that they will benefit from subsequent increases in the value of the business.

  It was with considerable consternation that private company owner/managers and their advisers discovered the implications of the new *CICA Handbook* standard for the recognition and measurement of these preference shares. Previously these shares had been routinely included in equity at the carrying value of the common shares for which they were exchanged. An EIC Abstract concluded that, under the new standard, these shares are in substance debt (because they are mandatorily redeemable on demand by the holder). More than this, it concluded that they should be measured on issuance at the fair value of the common shares at the date of the transaction.[29] Since this fair value includes internally generated goodwill of the business, in most cases recording the liability at this amount will mean that it will exceed (perhaps by a very significant amount) the carrying value of the business' assets, and thus cause the enterprise to be in a reported deficit position.

  Not surprisingly, very strong objections were made against this accounting by affected private company owner/managers and their advisors. They made various arguments to the effect that this classification as a liability and its measurement at the fair value of the common shares exchanged did not reflect the substance of these transactions, and further, that this accounting would undermine sound tax management practices and give rise to significant adverse consequences. The EIC, supported by the Accounting Standards Board, has remained firm in its opinion. However, the board did decide to delay the implementation of these provisions for nonpublic enterprises (other than cooperatives, life insurance enterprises and banks) until years beginning on or after January 1, 2000, in order to study the issues further.[30]

  In evaluating this situation, it seems clear that these "high-low" preference shares meet the definition of a financial liability. There might, however, be some merit in an argument that measurement at the fair value of the common shares exchanged overstates the fair value of the liability—if it is probable that the holder will not demand payment for some considerable number of years (perhaps not until he or she dies). There is precedent for taking into account probable future payment behaviour in pricing some financial instruments, for example in pricing mortgages that are subject to prepayment options, and in pricing portfolios of credit risk receivables when they are securitized. The EIC reasons that in being payable on demand, the high-low shares are analogous to demand loans that are typically valued at their face value on issuance even though the holder may not be expected to demand payment for some years.

Overall, preparers and accountants were not well prepared to implement this standard, and initially, at least, reacted very negatively to it. The above implementation problems, while constituting a small proportion of debt and equity instruments, strengthened their view that the standard was not well conceived. One reason why the standard has been difficult to assimilate in Canada may be that it opened up a new difference with U.S. GAAP. The FASB has had the possibility of developing an in-substance distinction between debt and equity on its agenda for some years.[31] However, it has yet to develop its intentions into a standard. It has recently resurrected its project and now appears likely to issue an exposure draft that is generally consistent, in most respects, with that of the CICA standard, although the FASB proposals may differ on some matters—for example, with respect to the classification of a security in the form of debt that can be settled by the issuer at maturity in common shares of equivalent fair value to that of the security. The CICA will consider the FASB standard, and may adjust the *CICA Handbook* requirements to eliminate differences with it.

Minority (Noncontrolling) Interest

If a parent company owns less than 100 percent of a subsidiary's common shares, it nevertheless accounts for 100 percent of the carrying value of the subsidiary's assets and liabilities in its consolidated statements, together with a figure of "minority interest" (now referred to as "noncontrolling interest" in the *CICA Handbook*) representing the proportionate share of the outside shareholders in the book value of the subsidiary's net assets. Is that minority interest equivalent to capital of the parent company (perhaps like a special kind of preferred share)? Such an interpretation is reasonable in theory, and it has recently been proposed by the FASB (see further discussion in Chapter 20). However, it is not at present a generally accepted accounting principle. If it were, the issue of shares by the subsidiary to a minority interest would be regarded as a capital transaction, not giving rise to gains or losses to be reported as income. Instead, present practice is to treat such dispositions in consolidated statements as de facto dispositions of the parent company's investment in the subsidiary giving rise to an income gain or loss.[32]

Accounting for Proprietary Equity

Balance Sheet Portrayal

Under the proprietary viewpoint, all income is considered to accrue to the common equity, subject to the claims of prior ranking capital. We can see, then, that the total ownership interest recorded in a balance sheet (the difference between assets and liabilities) comes basically from two sources—capital transactions and accumulated retained income. How then is capital portrayed in a balance sheet?

There are two partially conflicting ideas that influence the presentation. One (and this is the older, more traditional idea) is that the balance sheet of a corporation should show its legal capital. The legal capital is the amount that cannot be reduced (except by losses) without formal proceedings. By inference, an excess of net assets over legal capital must be distributable in the absence of other impediments.

The other idea is that the balance sheet presentation of capital should preserve the record of the source of the capital. That is to say, there should be a basic distinction between capital arising from capital transactions and capital arising from the accumulation of income not distributed.

Accounting standards favour the second concept—that elements of capital should be classified by source rather than by legal status.[33] Implementation of this preference, however, is not necessarily clear-cut.

- Cash dividends paid are customarily charged against retained earnings. The common view is that dividends represent a distribution of earnings. It is possible in law, however, to pay dividends out of contributed surplus. Any accounting rule that required that dividends be charged to retained earnings would be tantamount to saying that for accounting purposes a corporation cannot return capital even though in law it may. Provided the directors explicitly determine that a dividend represents a distribution of contributed surplus and provided the shareholders are informed that it is not a distribution of earnings, there seems to be no basis for objection to treatment of the dividend in accordance with its legal form.

- Stock dividends, unlike ordinary dividends, do not involve any disposition of the net assets of an entity. If one is interested in portraying the source of the net assets (capital transactions or retained earnings), does it make sense to change that portrayal where there has been no change in the assets? To justify the change, one has to visualize a notional payment of cash on the dividend and concurrent subscription for additional stock by the shareholders. Since it is not at all sure that shareholders would reinvest given the choice, this interpretation seems somewhat fanciful (see further discussion of stock dividends below).

- When a company redeems or purchases shares for cancellation (a capital transaction), the cost must be allocated among whatever components of shareholders' equity are shown in the balance sheet. Various bases of allocation are described in the *CICA Handbook*.[34] A method is favoured that would reduce capital attributed to the same class of shares, pro rata, absorb any excess against contributed surplus to the extent it arises from transactions in the same class of shares, and charge any remaining excess to retained earnings.

- When a company issues shares, there usually are some expenses of issue that are treated as a capital transaction because they are a necessary incidental to raising capital. The preferable accounting treatment would be to show the net proceeds of issue after expenses as the capital attributable to the issue. The legal capital, however, is often the consideration actually received from the shareholders. It has been customary not to report capital issued for cash at an amount less than the legal capital. Accordingly, share issue expenses are commonly written off directly to retained earnings.

In view of these uncertainties in classification, one is bound to question whether it is all worthwhile. Is any user's decision influenced by the division between reported capital and accumulated retained earnings? Does any financial ratio depend upon that split? It has been argued that the reader will be able to tell from the split whether capital has been raised largely from capital contributions or whether retained earnings have been significant. Even if this were true, is it important? A history of earnings and dividends for the last five to ten years, usually readily available, has far more significance to the financial statement user than any accumulated retained earnings figure in the balance sheet. It is suggested that the portrayal of capital in a balance sheet would be improved by the following principles:

- Disclose the amount of residual equity that is free from restriction on distribution, and the nature and extent of any significant restrictions. Such disclosures should include the legal capital of the corporation and any restrictions in the legal capacity of the corporation to make dividend distributions—covenants in loan agreements, etc. Legal capital may be significantly different from reported accounting share capital, for example when there has been a pooling-of-interests or a reverse takeover. It is important that such differences be disclosed, but adequate disclosure has sometimes been overlooked in practice.

- Provide a statement or statements tracing the changes in all items of residual equity over the reporting period from capital issues, repurchases, or retirements; from exercise of warrants, options, or conversion privileges; from earnings for the period; from dividends declared; and from any other capital transactions.

- Disclose additional information deemed relevant in the same way as at present, including the number of shares outstanding and changes therein, all terms and conditions attaching to preferred shares, details of commitments to issue shares upon exercise of outstanding conversion, option, or warrant rights, and details of any share transactions for noncash consideration.

The following comments deal with a few specific situations in accounting for capital.

Stock Splits and Stock Dividends

A stock split clearly has no significance other than to the number of shares outstanding. Each shareholder has exactly the same proportionate interest in the company after the split as he or she had before. There is no reason, therefore, to change the balance sheet display of capital for a stock split other than to adjust the figures given for the number of shares outstanding.

A common shareholder's proportionate interest in a company is likewise unaffected by a dividend paid entirely in stock. Stronger arguments are made for accounting recognition in this case, however, and greater consideration is required.

- Consider the (rare) case of a dividend paid in stock (either additional preferred shares or common shares) on a preferred share. In this case the relative interests of the preferred and common shareholders are clearly altered by the dividend. Proper accounting would therefore require crediting capital of the appropriate category for the fair value of the stock issued and charging retained earnings.

- Now consider the case where a dividend in the form of preferred stock is paid to common shareholders. The claim of each shareholder upon the assets of the company is not altered by the dividend, since what a shareholder gains through holding preferred shares he or she loses in his or her residual equity claim. The form of the shareholder's interest has, however, changed. It would seem right in this case, then, to credit preferred share capital for the fair value of the shares issued and reduce common equity. There could be a theoretical argument that all the elements of common equity should be reduced proportionately, but in practice the entire dividend would be charged to retained earnings.

- We come now to the most common case—that of a dividend in common stock paid to the common shareholders. Here the effect is exactly the same as a split of common stock. Yet the accounting practice is different. Why? The only authoritative statement is found in the U.S. Accounting Research Bulletin No. 43.[35] There it was argued that a shareholder looks upon stock dividends as a distribution of corporate earnings in an amount equivalent to the fair value of the shares. That impression is reinforced (it was said) because little change in the market value of the shares may be observable after the dividend. Accordingly, the fair value of shares issued as a stock dividend should be capitalized where those conditions hold. The bulletin suggested that stock dividends in an amount less than 20 or 25 percent of the outstanding shares were unlikely to materially affect their market value. (It may be doubted that conclusion would be valid today.) Until the 1980s, stock dividends had been relatively rare in Canada and practice did not necessarily follow American precedent. It had been common to capitalize a stock dividend at the minimum amount permitted by law.

In the 1980s in Canada stock dividends became more common for tax reasons. A number of companies split their common shares into two classes that are freely interchangeable, one of which pays dividends in cash and the other of which pays dividends in stock having a market value equivalent to the cash dividends. In these cases, the stock dividend is invariably capitalized at its cash equivalent value. The fact that shareholders have the right to choose between a cash and stock dividend makes the latter in substance equivalent to payment of a cash dividend.

Treasury Stock Purchases

Legislation in most jurisdictions in Canada now require that corporations purchasing their own shares must cancel them, or restore them to the category of authorized but unissued, thereby reducing stated capital. (There continue to be a few situations in which a corporation may temporarily hold some of its own shares without immediately cancelling them, for example, some of its shares may be owned by an entity that is acquired by the corporation.) CICA recommendations, which predate this legislation, call for the cost of unretired shares to be deducted from the total of shareholders' equity, with no gain or loss being recorded until they are cancelled.[36]

Employee Loans to Purchase Shares

Some corporations have loaned money to employees, officers or directors to purchase the corporations' shares. It may be questioned whether the borrowers are really at risk to repay the loans if the price of the shares declines. The answer to this question depends on the terms of a particular loan, and management's intent and ability to enforce repayment. If, as may be expected in many situations, the substance of the arrangement is such that the borrowers really are not at risk, the loan should not be treated as an asset but rather deducted from shareholders' equity.[37] When deducted from shareholders' equity any interest received, net of related income taxes, would be treated as a reduction of dividends paid rather than reflected in income.

Other Adjustments to Owners' Equity

We have described how recorded capital is affected directly by capital transactions and indirectly by income transactions that end up in the retained earnings account. We are left with some odds and ends that do not fit under this dichotomy. By and large they represent the fruit of compromise—an agreement that some changes in assets and liabilities should be recorded, but ducking the issue of whether the change is capital or income in character. Since they represent compromises, not much can be said about their logic.

- Appraisal increase credits represent a hangover from a time when it was acceptable in some circumstances to revalue capital assets. The practice is now forbidden in Canada. The accounting for such credits is still set out in the *CICA Handbook*, applicable to those few corporations that may have recorded appraisals when the practice was accepted. [38]

- In the United States, there is a somewhat similar practice with respect to investments in certain marketable equity and debt securities that are categorized as "available for sale." For balance sheet purposes these securities are required to be measured at their current fair values. Unrealized holding gains and losses, however, are to be kept out of reported income and instead reported as a net amount in what is described as "other comprehensive income" (see Chapter 17).

- Translation of the accounts of a foreign subsidiary for purposes of inclusion in a parent company consolidation is discussed in Chapter 21. When the subsidiary is considered to be a "self-sustaining" operation, its assets and liabilities are translated for the purposes of the parent company's consolidated financial statements using the current exchange rate at the balance sheet date. If the exchange rate changes over the course of the year, a gain or loss results from this translation process and the accumulated amount is carried as a separate line component in shareholders' equity. Gains and losses on translation of foreign investees carried on the equity basis of accounting are similarly treated.

- U.S. standards require that the liability recognized with respect to a pension plan be not less than the excess of the present value of pension obligations measured by the accumulated benefit method over the fair value of the pension fund assets. That minimum liability recognized is to be balanced by an intangible asset up to the amount of any prior service cost from a plan amendment not yet recognized in income. An excess of the minimum liability over the latter amount is to be recorded as a separate component (a reduction) of shareholders' equity.

- Under U.S. and recent international standards gains and losses on financial instruments that are considered to be hedges of risks related to future transactions are classified outside regular income. (This presentation is discussed in Chapter 17.)

The list of gains and losses that may be classified as some form of equity adjustment, or in a performance statement other than the regular income statement, has lengthened in recent years. The presentation issues are addressed in Chapter 18.

SUMMARY

The role of the statement of financial position, or balance sheet, is complementary to that of the income statement. Income or earning power is usually the most significant determinant of a business enterprise's economic value. Earning power is not, however, indicated only by an enterprise's reported income numbers; investors also require information on its financial position as an important basis for assessing return on investment and risk.

The balance sheet has assumed an enhanced status since the mid-1970s. There has been increased attention to whether balance sheet deferrals resulting from revenue-expense matching meet in-substance definitions of "assets" and "liabilities." External users may be expected to look to the balance sheet for information on financial capability, adaptability and solvency— which is, in essence, information on liquidity (that is, nearness to cash) and exposure to risks.

Assets and liabilities have been classified as current or long-term as an indicator of liquidity for over one hundred years. In spite of the durability of the concept of current assets and liabilities, the objectives of, and basis for, the classification are confused and its significance is limited. The portrayal of liquidity could be accomplished more effectively by other means—for example, through improved disclosures of significant types of monetary assets and liabilities and better cash flow information.

An enterprise's exposure to risk may depend not only on the risk characteristics of its individual assets and liabilities, but also on how these risks are matched or mismatched with each other. The statement of financial position and supporting note disclosures can provide valuable insights on this. The effects of matched or mismatched asset and liability positions may be confused, however, by accounting recognition and measurement differences. For example, assets may be measured on a different basis than liabilities with offsetting risks.

There is also concern that balance sheet representations are limited by systematic exploitations of weaknesses in the accrual accounting model that have allowed certain events and transactions to be kept off the balance sheet. One area of attention is the offsetting of assets and liabilities, and here standard-setting efforts have made headway in reducing exceptions in practice to the general rule that an asset and a liability may be netted only when there is legal right of setoff. A second area concerns problems observed in earlier chapters in the application of transaction recognition standards, based on the conveyance of rights and risks, to securitizations of receivables, executory contracts (such as leases), and debt extinguishments. A third popular "off-balance sheet" technique has involved placing debt in entities that escape subsidiary consolidation rules; these issues are addressed in a later chapter.

Finally, we turn to accounting for capital. It has long been understood that there must be a clear distinction between capital and income transactions, and between capital (equity) and debt, under the proprietary theory. Historically, accounting has classified capital according to the legal form of an instrument. This has not been satisfactory from an economic substance standpoint. Preferred shares, for example, frequently contain provisions that make them more like debt than equity. A recent CICA standard has put in place requirements for classification between debt and equity on the basis of the in-substance definitions of "liabilities" and "equity." Several difficult questions have arisen in implementing this standard in respect of instruments that have debt and equity characteristics.

Some confusion exists as to the presentation of owners' equity in the balance sheet—particularly the shareholders' equity of a corporation. Should the legal capital (the amount that cannot be distributed to owners without formal proceedings for reduction of capital) be shown separately, or should capital be classified by source—that is, distinguishing between capital contributed and accumulated retained earnings? Accounting standards generally espouse the latter idea, but there are difficulties. For example, a capitalized stock dividend transfers accumulated earnings to capital. On the other hand, an ordinary dividend may in some circumstances be charged to a contributed capital account.

It is doubtful that there is much significance to the subclassification of shareholders' equity. The significant figure is the total claim on the net assets of the business of each class of capital. It is also useful to know that portion of the residual equity that could not be distributed by way of dividends, for example because it is legal capital or because of covenants in trust indentures.

REFERENCES

1   FASB, *Objectives of Financial Reporting by Business Enterprises*, Statement of Financial Accounting Concepts No. 1 (Stamford: FASB, 1978), par. 25. The CICA's much briefer statement of concepts, issued in 1988, is consistent with this in stating that, "Investors and creditors of profit oriented enterprises are interested … in predicting the ability of the entity to earn income and generate cash flows …." CICA, "Financial Statement Concepts," *CICA Handbook*, Section 1000 (Toronto: CICA), par. 12.

2   See CICA, "Financial Statement Concepts," Section 1000, par. 30.

3   The confusion is well described in L.C. Heath, *Financial Reporting and the Evaluation of Solvency*, Accounting Research Monograph No. 3 (New York: AICPA, 1978), chaps. 3 and 4.

4   This bulletin was subsequently reproduced as Chapter 3A in American Institute of Accountants, Committee on Accounting Procedure, *Restatement and Revision of Accounting Research Bulletins*, Accounting Research Bulletin No. 43 (New York: AIA, 1953).

5   This is explicit in CICA, "Current Assets and Current Liabilities," *CICA Handbook*, Section 1510 (Toronto: CICA).

6   The CICA standard refers to current assets as those that are "ordinarily realizable" within one year or the normal operating cycle. *CICA Handbook*, Section 1510, par. 01. See also CICA, "Temporary Investments," *CICA Handbook*, Section 3010 (Toronto: CICA), par. 02, which states that investments should be included in current assets "if capable of reasonably prompt liquidation."

7   A recently revised IASC standard takes the position that marketable securities should be classified as current assets only if they are *expected* to be realized within twelve months. IASC, *Presentation of Financial Statements*, IAS 1 (London: IASC, Revised 1997), par. 59.

8   This point is convincingly made in R. Ma, "Liability Measurement: The Case of the Lessee's Obligation," in *External Financial Reporting: Essays in Honour of Harold Edey*, ed. B. Carsberg and S. Dev. (Englewood Cliffs, N.J.: Prentice-Hall International in cooperation with London School of Economics and Political Science, 1984), pp. 81–89.

9   As an example, this mismatching can arise in accounting for pension plans. General purpose financial statements of pension plans are required to measure investments at current market values which, it is recognized, may be inconsistent with the basis on which the accrued pension obligation of the plan has been determined. See CICA, "Pension Plans," *CICA Handbook*, Section 4100 (Toronto: CICA), par. 17.

10 In particular, see CICA "Financial Instruments—Disclosure and Presentation," *CICA Handbook*, Section 3860 (Toronto: CICA, 1995), pars. .43–.95.

11 APB, *Offsetting Securities Against Taxes Payable*, in Omnibus Opinion No. 10 (New York: AICPA, December 1966), par. 7.

12 FASB, *Definition of a Right of Setoff*, FASB Technical Bulletin No. 88-2 (Stamford: FASB, 1988), par. 2.

13 FASB, *Offsetting of Amounts Related to Certain Contracts, an Interpretation of APB Opinion No. 10 and FASB Statement No. 105*, FASB Interpretation No. 39 (Norwalk: FASB, 1992). This replaced FASB, *Definition of a Right of Setoff*, FASB Technical Bulletin No. 88-2, carrying forward its definition and four conditions, but making an exception for master netting arrangements.

14 FASB, *Offsetting of Amounts Related to Certain Contracts*.

15 CICA, "Financial Instruments—Disclosure and Presentation," par. 34; and IASC, *Financial Instruments—Disclosure and Presentation*, IAS 32 (London: IASC, Revised 1998), par. 33.

16 CICA, "Subsidiaries," *CICA Handbook*, Section 1590 (Toronto: CICA).

17 See CICA, "Capital Transactions," *CICA Handbook*, Section 3610 (Toronto: CICA).

18 See CICA, "Income Taxes," *CICA Handbook*, Section 3465 (Toronto: CICA, 1997), pars. .71–.78. These paragraphs replace CICA, "Corporate Income Taxes—Additional Areas," *CICA Handbook* Section 3471 (Toronto: CICA). It is to be noted that, if it is unlikely that the taxes will be recovered (i.e., that sufficient dividends will be paid in the foreseeable future), the tax payments are charged to income.

19 CICA, "Business Combinations," *CICA Handbook,* Section 1580 (Toronto: CICA), par. .72.

20 See CICA, "Reserves," *CICA Handbook*, Section 3260 (Toronto: CICA).

21 See CICA, "Comprehensive Revaluation of Assets and Liabilities," Section 1625; and "Surplus," *CICA Handbook*, Section 3250 (Toronto: CICA).

22 CICA "Financial Instruments—Disclosure and Presentation," pars. 3860.18–.23. The IASC has adopted the same requirements, see IASC, *Financial Instruments—Disclosure and Presentation*, IAS 32, pars. 18–22.

23 CICA, Financial Instruments—Disclosure and Presentation," pars. 3860.29–.30.

24 Ibid., par. 3860.31.

25 CICA, Emerging Issues Committee, *Financial Instruments that May Be Settled at the Issuer's Option in Cash or its Own Equity Instruments*, EIC 71 (Toronto: CICA, 1996). The EIC classification gives rise to a number of questions relating to how to account subsequently for the component parts. The EIC's answers to these questions are controversial in themselves.

26 IASC, *Financial Instruments: Recognition and Measurement*, IAS 39 (London: IASC, 1998), par. 11.

27 CICA, *Presentation of a Financial Instrument When a Future Event or Circumstance May Affect the Issuer's Obligations*, EIC 70 (Toronto: CICA, 1996).

28 CICA, *Presentation of Members' Shares in a Co-operative Organization as Liabilities or Equity*, EIC 72 (Toronto: CICA, 1996).

29 CICA, *Recognition and Measurement of Financial Instruments Presented as Liabilities or Equity Under CICA 3860*, EIC 69 (Toronto: CICA, 1996).

30 For a review and analysis of the arguments see P. Martin, "Liability or Equity?" *CA Magazine*, November 1996, pp. 30–33.

31 For a full discussion of the issues see FASB Discussion Memorandum, *Distinguishing Between Liability and Equity Instruments and Accounting for Instruments with Characteristics of Both* (Norwalk: FASB, 1990).

32 CICA, "Consolidated Financial Statements," *CICA Handbook*, Section 1600 (Toronto: CICA), pars. .42–.46.

33 See CICA, "Surplus," Section 3250.

34 See CICA, "Share Capital," *CICA Handbook*, Section 3240 (Toronto: CICA), pars. 13–18.

35 American Institute of Accountants, Committee on Accounting Procedure, "Stock Dividends and Stock Split-Ups," in *Restatement and Revision of Accounting Research Bulletins*, Accounting Research Bulletin No. 43 (New York: AIA, 1953), chap. 7B.

36 See "Share Capital," Section 3240, pars. 6–11.

37 See CICA Emerging Issues Committee, *Share Purchase Loans*, EIC 44, (Toronto: CICA, 1993).

38 See "Capital Assets," *CICA Handbook*, Section 3060 (Toronto: CICA), par. 64.

INVENTORY AND COST OF SALES

Inventory accounting presents some debatable issues both in the aspect of costing the asset and in the aspect of determining cost of sales. In the former category there is a long-standing controversy over the merits of direct costing as against full absorption costing. This issue has never been conclusively settled, and has received no serious attention in the last three or four decades. In the latter category there has been the issue of what is the proper cost flow assumption for determining cost of sales—first in, first out (FIFO) or last in, first out (LIFO). This issue, likewise unsettled, took on greater importance under the inflationary conditions beginning in the 1970s, since inflation tends to widen the impact of choice of one method over the other.

These two issues, (1) cost attachment to inventory, and (2) costing methods for determining cost of sales, constitute the subject matter of this chapter. Provisions for impairment of inventory and the application of "lower of cost and market" approaches are deferred to Chapter 18, which gathers together all asset impairment issues.

COST ATTACHMENT TO INVENTORY

Years ago it was quite common to find manufactured goods costed at "prime cost"—that is, including the cost of materials and direct labour only. Of course, at that time manufacturing processes were simple and such costs constituted a high percentage of total costs. With increasing mechanization and complexity of production processes, overhead costs became more and more important, a trend that has continued. It was natural that systems would be developed for attaching overhead costs to products. From the 1920s through the 1940s there was much innovation and development of costing systems. Probably these systems were developed primarily for purposes such as assisting in product-pricing decisions. Once available, however, they could be, and were, used for financial reporting purposes as well.

These cost systems were devised and adopted by individual businesses or industries, so that it was inevitable that there would be differences between them. When professional accounting societies began making recommendations to guide financial reporting practice, an important goal was to narrow the gap between prime costing methods and highly developed costing systems that provided an "absorption" of overhead costs pertaining to manufacturing. It was relatively easy to conclude that the exclusion of all overheads from a cost calculation was likely to result in a figure quite unrepresentative of the sacrifice and effort in the ordinary process of manufacture. It was less easy to obtain agreement beyond that.

Full Absorption Costing vs. Direct Costing—The Traditional Debate

For more than twenty years from about 1940, a vigorous debate raged between supporters of "full absorption costing" and those of "direct costing." The absorption-costers held, in general, that every cost that could be identified as being necessary for production must find its way into the unit cost figure for individual products. The direct-costers, in contrast, saw a distinction between costs of providing capacity to produce, which were essentially fixed over wide ranges of production, and actual costs of production, which tended to vary with the volume of production activity. The important arguments are summarized below.

On Behalf of Direct or Variable Costing

- Costs that are already fixed are not pertinent to management operating decisions as to volume of production or price of product. Management is interested in information on the cost and revenue effects of its decisions. Since its decisions can have no effect on costs that are already fixed, it is argued it is unlikely that it will be useful to include fixed costs in figures reported as assets.

- A division of costs between fixed and variable is necessary to find the volume break-even point in a business. By the same token, a division between variable costs of goods sold and fixed manufacturing and other costs will provide a better portrayal of margins achieved on sales and hence will produce an income statement more useful for financial analysis.

- Revenue is recognized in most cases upon completion of performance. Income accounting requires that costs applicable to the completed performance be written off when revenue is recognized, and that costs carried forward in inventory be restricted to those clearly identifiable with future revenue. If fixed costs are included in inventory, one will find that during years of inventory build-up less than twelve months' fixed costs will be included in cost of sales, while in years when inventory is reduced, more than twelve months' fixed costs will be absorbed. As a result, periodic profits reported will not reflect the results of completed performance only but will also be affected by inventory build-ups and draw-downs. This confuses the financial report and even provides an opportunity to manipulate profits by building up inventory when it is desired to bolster the reported results.

On Behalf of Full Absorption Costing

- The full absorption case rests essentially on the proposition that costs that are necessarily incurred in production should be reflected in the cost assigned to products in inventory.

If this is not done, a shift in production technology from a variable cost to a fixed cost (say, a substitution of machinery for labour) will have the strange result that the apparent product cost will go down by the full amount of the variable cost eliminated.

- In rebuttal to the direct costing argument—it is argued that there is nothing wrong with reported profit being influenced by inventory build-up. Profit is earned by all activity, not just by sale. It would be bad management to build up inventory if it could not be sold, since carrying unsold inventory costs money. Hence, if a company is producing rapidly and building up inventory, it is a fair assumption that its prospects are good, and this can reasonably be reflected in reported profits. If expectations change such that the recorded cost may not be recoverable, then the "lowest of cost and market" rule (to be discussed in Chapter 18) is applied.

A concept called "relevant costing" was put forward in 1962.[1] It is based on the proposition that a cost incurred should be treated as an asset only if it has a favourable effect on expected future costs or future revenues. On this basis, variable costs would always be carried forward since, if they had not been expended, it would be necessary to incur them again to have product for sale. The future economic benefit from fixed costs is more debatable. If future orders can be readily filled from future production, then fixed costs incurred in the past, such as depreciation, have no favourable effect on future revenues and should not be carried forward. On the other hand, if product must be on hand to make sales possible (for example, because current production cannot meet demand), then all costs incurred and associated with the product may legitimately be treated as part of the inventory asset. Since most businesses require a certain stock of inventory at all times to avoid lost revenue from stockouts, it would seem that most of the time the relevant costing basis would require recognition of fixed costs in inventory with respect to at least part of the inventory. It might be provided that each business should establish minimum inventory quantities suitable to its circumstances. Then fixed costs would be included in inventory only up to the minimum quantities established, with variable costing being applied to inventory held above those quantities. This proposal is consistent with the second sentence in the following recommendation on inventory costing from the *CICA Handbook*:

> Usually expenditures arising out of abnormal circumstances, such as re-handling of goods and idle facilities, are not included. Similarly, in some cases, a portion of fixed overhead is excluded where its inclusion would distort the net income for the period by reason of fluctuating volume of production.[2]

Activity-Based Costing

Traditional methods for allocating overhead costs to multiple products have been criticized in managerial accounting literature over the past five to ten years. The conventional practice has been to allocate overheads to products on the basis of a measure of overall volume or effort. A frequently used measure has been direct labour hours or dollars. For example, if a company produces products A and B and a unit of A requires on average two hours of direct labour while a unit of B requires one hour, allocated overheads would be assigned on the basis of units produced weighted by an A:B per unit absorption of 2:1. In selecting direct labour as the allocation basis the presumption must be that the amount of labour necessary to make a product bears a strong relationship to overhead usage—that a product requiring more direct labour is also likely to require more supervisory time (indirect labour), lead to more machinery wear and tear (depreciation), and result in higher utilities costs. This was probably a reasonable presumption in earlier times when manufacturing operations were labour intensive, products were relatively simple and product lines limited. Such conditions are unlikely to prevail today. Many modern manufacturing operations have become overhead intensive, with the direct labour component replaced to a significant extent by automated computer-controlled machinery and processes. There are strong indications that traditional general overhead allocation measures, such as direct labour hours, may no longer provide reasonable product cost figures in such situations. For example, product B might utilize much more machinery set-up time, engineering support efforts, packing activity, etc. than product A—so that allocating these costs between A and B on the basis of a 2:1 direct labour ratio will not yield realistic product costs. With the growth of overhead costs relative to material and direct labour costs, the concern is that traditional overhead allocation bases may seriously distort unit costs. [3]

Activity or transaction costing has been put forward as an internal management product costing solution to the potential distortions of traditional overhead allocation methods. [4] Activity-based costing first assigns costs to particular activities, or component processes. The cost of each activity is then allocated to products based on how much of its service is considered to be used or caused by each product. For example, costs of a product scheduling activity might be assigned on the basis of number of production runs, while purchasing function costs may be allocated based on number of purchase orders, etc. The key to the implementation of this concept lies in identifying distinct overhead activities and in determining a representative measure of each activity's relationship to products. As defined in managerial accounting literature activity-based costing takes a long-term view of cost behaviour and does not differentiate costs as between fixed and variable in terms of volume of output.

What little evidence exists indicates that activity-based costing is not widely used in practice, although there are signs of increasing receptivity to the basic ideas. [5] It has been developed for internal management purposes, and it is not clear whether it is having any influence on product costing for external accounting purposes. Certainly there is nothing in GAAP that would preclude different pools of indirect costs being allocated on different bases to determine product costs. To date there has been no consideration of the issues by financial accounting bodies. [6]

Accounting Standards and Impressions of Practice

There has been considerable criticism in managerial accounting literature over the past fifteen years to the effect that traditional cost accounting practices lack relevance for modern managerial decision-making purposes. [7] In contrast, accounting cost attachment concepts have received little serious attention from financial accountants over the past thirty to forty years. Cost allocation concepts have been largely abandoned as a field considered to have potential for theoretical development in financial accounting. This has been the case since the 1960s, when allocations were demonstrated to be inherently arbitrary and therefore presumed to be lacking in intrinsic information content. [8] (We have observed and commented on this in Chapter 4.)

The principal authoritative literature may be found in Accounting Research Bulletin No. 43 of the AICPA, issued in 1953, and *CICA Handbook* Section 3030, which has not undergone any change since the late 1960s. On the matter of assignment of overhead costs to inventory, both the American and Canadian pronouncements contain some rather vague language. It has been stated that the intention of Bulletin 43 was to prescribe full absorption costing only. A different interpretation, however, can be drawn from what it actually says: "exclusion of all overheads from inventory costs does not constitute an accepted accounting procedure."[9]

Unfortunately, there would seem to be no recent surveys of inventory-costing practice to prove what are generally accepted applications of the authoritative recommendations. There is virtually no useful information on overhead costing practices in financial statement accounting policy notes. Nevertheless, there are some indications that at least some U.S. manufacturing firms may not treat all indirect production costs as components of inventory cost, notwithstanding the emphasis in the United States on full absorption costing.[10] (The Tax Reform Act of 1986, which brought further pressure for full absorption costing, may have changed this picture.) There is no reliable evidence of current practice in Canada. It would seem, however, that direct costing is accepted to be within GAAP in Canada. The following are some impressions as to prevailing Canadian practice.

- It is clear that costing inventory at prime cost is contrary to generally accepted accounting principles if variable overhead costs are significant in amount, as they usually are. There probably are cases where a direct costing approach is rigorously followed. Much more common, however, are cases where some indirect productive costs, but not others, are allocated to inventory. Depreciation on manufacturing plant and equipment has been a common exclusion from allocated costs. In general, it would seem likely that there is much variation in practice from one enterprise to another.

- It is now generally recognized that it is wrong to calculate an indirect cost figure per unit of inventory on the basis of the actual amount of such costs for a period divided by the actual quantity of inventory units produced, regardless of whether production is high or low. Such a practice has the nonsensical result of showing a high per-unit cost when volume of production is low and a low cost when production is high, in spite of the fact that the cost is largely fixed. To avoid this, it is necessary to determine a standard or representative per-unit cost from time to time, based on an estimate of the normal or planned production capacity of the plant. Then, in periods when production is low, the amount of indirect costs allocated to inventory will be less than the actual incurred costs, and the difference (the cost "unabsorbed") will be written off as a period expense attributable to unused capacity. Occasionally, in periods of abnormally high activity, actual overhead costs may be "over-absorbed" using the standard rate per unit for allocation to inventory. In such cases it is accepted that the amount over-absorbed should be apportioned between inventory on hand at the end of the period and cost of goods sold.

- It is permissible, where indirect or fixed overhead costs are allocated to inventory, to allocate such overheads only with respect to minimum quantities and to include variable overhead costs only in inventory above the minimum.

- Very few enterprises would consider any costs initially classified as general and administrative to be included in overheads allocated to inventory, because such costs are generally thought to be too remote from the production process. If, however, it can be shown that a given administration cost is caused by manufacturing activity and some reasonable basis for associating it with inventory can be found, there is no theoretical reason why it should not be allocated to inventory.

What rule should be adopted if it were desired to standardize practice? The answer might depend upon the objective. One possible aim might be to report an inventory cost as close as possible to its fair value. If so, full absorption costing would generally be preferable. Another aim might be to minimize distortion of income reported. If so, there would be at least some cases in which a full costing approach would be better than direct costing. Those cases can be identified by irregularity in the pattern of revenue recognition. If revenue is recognized on the critical event basis at or near completion of earning activity and the business is such that these completion dates occur at irregular intervals (for example, in businesses that do work to order rather than producing standard goods with a fairly steady pattern of sales), it is best to associate as much cost as possible with work in process. This will avoid the misleading picture conveyed by substantial overhead cost write-offs in periods when productive activity on incomplete projects is at a high level but little revenue is being recognized on completed projects. Of course, in these same circumstances distortion of income may be even more effectively avoided by adopting the accretion approach to revenue recognition (as discussed in Chapter 7).

On the other hand, a direct costing approach saves work and is more easily defended against the charge that the allocation of overheads to individual products is arbitrary. It is also less likely to create problems in income reporting when inventory is overstocked.

Interest as an Element of Inventory Cost

Full discussion of the possible allocation of financing costs to cost objects is reserved for the next chapter, since the question arises most frequently in connection with self-constructed capital assets. In principle, if financing costs can be directly traced to inventory, there is no reason why they should not be deferred as part of the cost accumulated in inventory up to the time it is ready for sale. In practice, as discussed below, interest may be inventoried by land developers and by contractors.

Inventory Costing—Contractors

This section on cost attachment may be concluded with brief reference to certain specialized industry practices. It has already been noted that when revenue recognition is irregular, a full cost approach is desirable. This is borne out by the practice of contractors who do not use the accretion (percentage-of-completion) basis of revenue recognition. In some cases contract prices may be established so as to cover specific named costs plus an allowance for profit or margin. In those cases contract costing should at least accumulate costs that are specifically designated for recovery in the contract price. Such costs may include an allowance for general and administrative costs which will accordingly be inventoried.

May costs be carried forward in contract work in process if they are not covered in the scheduled costs reimbursable? That depends on the circumstances. Provided there are reasonable bases for allocation of a given cost to the contract and provided the contract price allows sufficient margin to recover such costs, there is no reason for not inventorying them. Where contracts are not fully financed by purchaser prepayments, there will normally also be some interest costs if the contract is of any duration. It will usually be possible to trace interest costs to the contracts causing it, and it is therefore appropriate to treat such interest as a contract cost.

Costing Real Estate Inventories

Real estate developers who buy land, service it, obtain approval of plans of subdivision, and sell lots or lots and houses together are carrying on an activity with some similarity to the manufacture of a product. Correspondingly, the land acquired for this purpose, whether raw or developed, is similar to the inventory of a manufacturer. Because real estate projects are long in development and revenue from sale is irregular, a full costing basis is highly appropriate for them. Accounting practices recommended by the Canadian Institute of Public Real Estate Companies include the following. Pre-acquisition costs incurred in seeking out land for development may be initially treated as deferred charges. Then when land is acquired, an appropriate portion of the deferred charges may be capitalized as part of the land cost. (If the acquisition effort is abandoned, the deferred costs should be written off at that time.) General and administrative costs that are directly attributable to acquisition, development, and construction activities are capitalized, as are carrying costs (interest and real estate taxes) during the development and construction period. Interest capitalized is restricted to actual interest, whether directly incurred for the project or allocated out of the general interest cost borne by the company. Imputed interest on equity may not be capitalized. It is also recommended that the cost of issues of bonds and debentures that finance specific developments should be included in the costs of those developments.[11]

FINDING COST OF GOODS SOLD OR OF GOODS CONSUMED IN MANUFACTURING

Inventory costing conventions attribute costs incurred to goods on hand. When the goods are made to order, costs are likely to be assigned to individual units or job lots. When goods are made for stock, costs are likely to be allocated to production runs, from which unit costs can be derived by dividing the run cost by the quantity produced. However unit cost is determined, there are likely to be differences in the unit cost assigned to goods produced at different times. When goods are sold, the question arises: What is the correct figure to be recognized as cost of goods sold? A similar question occurs with respect to raw materials or supplies bought at different times. When they are put into production or consumed in production the question is: What cost figure should be entered in the costing system for raw material or supplies consumed?

One set of cost-flow assumptions visualizes costs incurred as attaching to specific physical flow of goods. Other cost-flow assumptions consider the physical flow unimportant, but rather give priority to writing off inventory costs against revenues on bases thought to best portray the income earned on completed transactions.

Expense Recognition Based on Physical Flow of Goods

Specific Identification

The most easily understood method of finding cost of sales is that of "specific identification." If the cost of each unit of inventory has been determined and particular goods sold are specifically identified, the cost to be written off seems obvious. This method is invariably used when goods in inventory are costly and individual in character. That is, it is used generally for luxury items or "big ticket" items, such as art objects, jewellery, automobiles in the hands of dealers, and so on. Its use makes sense because both the cost and the sale price will be highly influenced by individual features of the thing sold. By specific identification the vendor is enabled to pinpoint successes and failures in acquisition of goods and, thereby, improve his or her judgment. Specific identification is also used for goods made to the customer's order. Once again, special features ordered by the customer may have influenced the cost, and it is useful for the vendor to be able to compare actual results with those expected when a price was quoted on the job.

FIFO

Where goods dealt in are interchangeable or easily replaceable (the majority of business situations), the arguments for specific identification are no longer convincing. For many goods, one unit is indistinguishable from another so that specific identification is not a practical possibility.

In the case of perishable goods, it can safely be assumed that an attempt will be made to dispose of the earliest goods received or produced before later goods. Thus it can be assumed that costs applicable to unsold goods on hand are the latest costs incurred, and that therefore the write-off of costs from inventory should be on the FIFO convention. Even when goods are not very perishable, it might be presumed that management will generally tend to move goods on a first in, first out basis. Thus the FIFO convention is widely used, basically because in most cases it is likely to conform to the natural physical flow of goods. (There may be some situations where plant layout does not conduce to a FIFO movement of nonperishable goods. Even so, the FIFO convention may be used simply because it makes reported results more comparable to those of other entities.)

Expense Recognition Based on Other Cost-Flow Assumptions

Average Cost

The interchangeable character of many types of inventory leads to another cost-flow assumption. Where a collection of identical or nearly identical goods has been acquired at varying prices, it seems reasonable to think of a total cost applicable to all the units held and an average price per unit. That average cost can then be written off as units are sold or consumed. When more goods are acquired for inventory, their cost is added to the pool of costs remaining in inventory, and a new average is struck. This method has some appeal as a reflection of the homogeneous character of goods in inventory. It involves more computational work than FIFO, however, and often will produce results little different from FIFO. It is also widely used.

Base Stock

A radically different approach was developed around 1900 under the name of the "base stock" method. The concept underlying this method was that any ongoing business must hold minimum quantities of inventory that do not vary greatly in composition from one period to the next. One could say, then, that these basic quantities are more akin to a fixed asset than to inventory that will be sold or consumed. If so, it was considered undesirable to attach different costs to the base amount from time to time, just as it would be undesirable to continuously revalue fixed assets held. To initiate this method, inventory held was divided into two components. The fixed component consisted of defined minimum quantities valued at cost at the date of initiation of the method or at an arbitrary figure deemed likely to be as low as cost might drop to at any time in future. Quantities in excess of the defined minimum quantities were considered to be true inventory, to be accounted for by using any of the accepted cost-flow assumptions.

The base stock method was criticized on various grounds. Valuation of the fixed component at arbitrary, low prices was said to be a departure from the historical cost principle. The selection of basic quantities was also arbitrary. In addition, there was no automatic mechanism whereby the defined base stock could change as different goods were added to inventory and others were phased out. As a result, the method was really only workable for a business engaged in processing a stable commodity, such as lead, copper, or sugar. On top of this, the method was disallowed early on for taxation purposes in the United States (and later in the United Kingdom and Canada) which greatly reduced its practical appeal.

LIFO

The place of base stock was taken by the LIFO cost-flow assumption. LIFO is quite similar to base stock in its practical effect, although supported by a different theory. The concepts underlying LIFO, as it was originally conceived, are as follows. There are certain businesses, for example, base metal processors, oil refiners, and tanners, that process a primary commodity that is subject to wide swings in price over short periods of time. To protect itself against such price gyrations, a business may try to set selling prices so as to recover the current replacement cost of the commodity plus what is, in effect, a processing charge to reward the business for its effort. It may be argued that the most appropriate cost figure to match against the selling price, therefore, is a current cost, and the latest cost incurred provides the best approximation to a current cost. Since costs recognized as cost of sales are always the latest costs, it follows that inventory on hand is carried at the earliest cost incurred (at or subsequent to the effective date of adoption of the LIFO method).

There are a number of practical flaws in the LIFO method.

- If prices are changing rapidly in either direction, the cost of the most recent purchase may not be very close to the current cost at the time of sale. The method works best, therefore, when an enterprise reorders at regular and frequent intervals and maintains inventory quantities at a fairly constant level, rather than speculating in price movements by stocking up when prices are low and vice versa.

- Sometimes it may be impossible to maintain inventory quantities at a level amount for reasons beyond the control of the enterprise. For example, a strike in the plants of a major supplier may cause a reduction in the stock of the enterprise. Under such conditions "involuntary liquidation" of inventory occurs, and goods sold are costed at prices increasingly remote in time so that they bear no relation to current prices. Thus the method fails in its objective.

- The same results can occur when an enterprise phases out some existing products or lines of business in a "voluntary liquidation." Old costs are matched against current revenues.

- The LIFO method was intended to cope with the distorting effect of *fluctuations* in acquisition prices of inventory. The idea was that, as acquisition prices rose, LIFO would reflect the higher costs of sales sooner than FIFO; the converse would occur when prices fell, but over a complete cycle of price movement the amount charged to cost of sales would be the same under the two methods. This idea ignored the possibility of a continuing upward trend in prices, such as has been experienced over much of the last sixty years. When the long-term price trend is rising, LIFO tends to charge more to expense than does FIFO, and correspondingly the valuation of inventory on hand tends to be lower. The net result is that income reported by companies using the LIFO method is not comparable, even over a complete business cycle, with that reported by companies under the FIFO method. Also, the inventory figure reported in the balance sheet of companies using LIFO tends to be grossly undervalued in terms of current conditions.

In brief, the LIFO idea represents an attempt to make the figure of cost of sales a better representation of the current sacrifice involved to earn revenue than is achieved by other cost-flow assumptions. That objective is worthwhile, but it is not always attained because of the problem of inventory liquidation. In addition, LIFO provides a very poor representation of the worth of inventory on hand for balance sheet purposes. In essence, LIFO is an attempt to adopt replacement cost accounting for the income statement but not for the balance sheet. That peculiar characteristic was forced by the need to argue that the method represented merely a variant of the historical cost system. In fact, because the inventory carrying values in the balance sheet may represent costs incurred many years ago, the method is fundamentally incompatible with other applications of historical cost accounting, as well as being an inadequate substitute for replacement cost accounting. Nevertheless, it is possible to argue that, with all its conceptual faults, the use of LIFO accounting for inventory produced a better representation of income in the inflationary period of the 1970s and early 1980s than did any other available method.

There are two approaches to the implementation of LIFO. The older, "specific goods" approach prices goods on hand at the end of the year at the cost figure at which the same or similar goods were carried at the beginning of the year, up to the quantities held in the previous year. Any addition to quantities held over the previous year-end, or goods held that were not in stock at the previous year-end, are costed at their acquisition price in the current year. The similarity of goods held at the beginning and end of the fiscal year is crucial to the successful application of the specific goods method. A business that is continually changing from one product to another is, in effect, making voluntary liquidations of the discontinued products, so that older costs, rather than current costs, are charged to cost of sales with respect to such products.

This liquidation problem is reduced under the application of "dollar value" LIFO, but the extent of the reduction may depend upon the specific way it is applied. To implement dollar value LIFO, it is first necessary to divide the inventory into pools of costs, for the purpose of developing price ratios applicable to each pool that measure the change between current-year cost and base-year cost. (Base year is the year of adoption of LIFO.) Pools of costs may include all inventories in a "natural business unit." Alternatively, "multiple pools" may be developed by product line, with separate pools for raw material, work-in-process, and finished goods in each product line. To lessen the exposure to the voluntary liquidation problem, it is desirable to have as few pools as possible, and for this purpose the natural business unit approach is generally preferable.

There are many other points of detail that arise in the application of the LIFO method. Since LIFO is little used in Canada because its use is not generally permitted for tax purposes, these are not reviewed here. Those interested may refer to U.S. literature and U.S. tax regulations for further information.[12]

Accounting Standards and Evaluation of Practice

Existing accounting standards in Canada and the United States have not changed significantly in over forty years, and generally accept all of the cost determination methods discussed above. The *CICA Handbook* Section 3030 states that the most suitable method will depend on the circumstances and "should be one which results in the fairest matching of costs against revenues regardless of whether or not the method corresponds to the physical flow of goods" (par .09). It provides no guidance on how to determine the "fairest matching." This, as is evident from the above discussion, is a matter of opinion. The fact is that no one of these methods can be proved to be superior in accounting theory with respect to goods that are not differentiable. Thus it may be expected that the selection of method will be influenced by other factors. LIFO is much more prevalent in the U.S. than Canada because U.S. tax legislation permits it while it is generally not allowed by Canadian tax authorities. A considerable body of research in the U.S. has focused on how managers choose an inventory cost attribution method and on stock price reactions to LIFO adoptions. Various management incentive and signalling theories have been advanced to explain why large numbers of U.S. companies continue to use FIFO and thus forego potentially large tax savings that could be achieved by using LIFO. Stock market reactions to adoptions of LIFO have been inconclusive, indicating a mixture of interacting factors. On the whole, this research seems not to have contributed very much to the advancement of financial accounting. [13]

Certain Aspects of Costing Sales under Contracts

Apart from general issues involved in the choice of cost-flow assumptions, special problems may be found in particular industries. Industries that contract to produce a quantity of high-value products, such as aircraft or aircraft components, may use an accounting method that falls between the completed contract method and percentage-of-completion accounting. That is to say, revenue may be recognized and applicable costs written off for each unit of product shipped, rather than only upon completion of the contract. In effect, the product unit is treated as though it were a small contract in itself, accounted for on the completed contract basis.

There is no problem in this if the costing system is capable of providing a cost figure for each unit completed and that cost is recognized as the cost to be matched with the unit sale proceeds. There is, however, a more sophisticated basis of costing units sold that may be applied in industries to which the "learning curve" applies. The learning curve is a phenomenon first observed in airframe manufacturing but applicable to other industries as well. What has been observed is that in a demanding manufacturing process the direct labour required and perhaps some other manufacturing costs as well tend to decrease for each succeeding unit of production in a reasonably predictable fashion over an extended period of time. As a result of this learning effect, the first units produced in a production series will have a considerably higher cost, and later units a considerably lower cost, than the average for the whole production run. Based on this phenomenon, some companies relieve the inventory of accumulated costs at an estimated average cost per unit for each unit completed, rather than at the actual cost. As the production run progresses, the actual experience is checked to see if the forecast productivity gains are actually being achieved, and adjustments are made to the costing-out rate where necessary.

There are some dangers with this system.

- If revenue billable for succeeding units in the production run is reduced to reflect the learning effect, it is wrong to cost units completed on this method. Recognition of the learning curve can be in revenue or in costs but not both.

- If there are interruptions to the production schedule, the learning effect is also interrupted. Should such interruptions occur, through strikes or for other reasons, it is vital that recalculations be made of costs expected over the future of the contract, and that loss be recognized, so that the revised chargeout rate per unit (the revised average cost) can absorb all the costs carried forward in inventory.

This description has been written in terms of an average chargeout rate for a specific contract. There are industries (again the aircraft industry is an example) where a given product may be expected to be manufactured over an extended period of years under a number of individual contracts for different customers. Thus the learning effect may continue through several contracts, including contracts not yet signed at the time early contracts are commenced. In this situation, an entity may adopt the "program costing" approach. An assumption is made as to the total number of units that will be produced under all contracts in the program, future as well as present, and an estimated average cost is struck assuming the learning effect. This average cost is used as a chargeout rate from the beginning. Since all the productivity gains will not be realized within the early contracts, it is obvious that such a chargeout rate will not absorb all costs incurred in those contracts, and some will remain in inventory to be absorbed as part of the cost of future contracts.

Clearly the risk of error is much higher under program costing. First, the number of units to be sold in the program can only be an estimate, rather than being a number determined by a contract. Second, there is the possibility that sales prices in later, follow-on contracts may have to be reduced because of competition, etc. Third, in a very long program there could be a time when costs level off and this must be allowed for. Finally, the risk of interruption or delays in the production schedule disrupting the learning curve is greater the longer the program. The method should be used, therefore, only with the utmost caution.[14]

In recent years there has been some evidence that learning curves may be tending to be flatter as direct labour is replaced by automated manufacturing systems.[15]

Costing Retail Land Sales

Determining costs of units of land sold out of a land subdivision also presents complicated problems.

- It is necessary to estimate all costs that will be incurred under the developer's obligation to complete work for the subdivision as a whole. Any future carrying costs to be capitalized must also be estimated in order to arrive at a total estimated pool of costs for the subdivision.

- Proceeds of land sold or to be sold at less than fair value pursuant to agreements with governments are treated as reductions of the pool of costs. Hence, any future proceeds of this nature must be estimated.

- Should there be any servicing costs incurred for the joint benefit of later stages in a large development (for example, oversized sewers or water mains), the extra cost expended for the benefit of the later stages is removed from the pool and deferred, to be charged against such stages.

- The net pool of costs must then be apportioned to units sold. If all units are alike, the unit cost is calculable by straight division. If the land is basically sold for one type of use (for example, residential or commercial) but the sizes of the units vary, costs may be allocated on an area or foot-front basis. Where the units for sale have a different value, however, a more satisfactory way to apportion costs is on the "net-yield" basis, whereby the amount of cost assigned to each unit sold is proportional to its sale price, expressed as a percentage of the anticipated total proceeds from all units.

- The expectation may be that sales prices for units to be sold later will be higher than those sold earlier. If this is the case, but the market value used in the calculation of costs per unit sold is a current value rather than an estimate of ultimate proceeds, it may be reasonable to omit future estimated carrying costs from the pool of costs being allocated. The justification would be that future increases in sales realization (not taken into account in the calculation) are expected to cover future carrying costs.

SUMMARY

Costing assets and subsequently finding ways to recognize expense as the asset value is consumed represent the key questions in inventory accounting. There have been next to no advances in standards or financial accounting thought on these matters for many years.

Full absorption costing provides a balance sheet carrying value closer to fair value than does direct costing. It is particularly suitable in a business with an irregular pattern of revenue recognition. A modification of this method, to restrict capitalization of fixed overheads to minimum inventory quantities, has some theoretical merit. Direct costing, on the other hand, has some practical merits. It is simpler to apply and can be helpful in analyzing factors that have influenced operating results. In practice, inventory costing methods used by enterprises often represent compromises between the two approaches, rather than being entirely one or the other.

Overhead costs have typically been allocated between products on the basis of an overall volume measure, usually direct labour hours or dollars. This basis of allocation has come in for considerable criticism in management accounting literature in recent years. Critics point out that use of overhead activities in the production of particular products may bear little relationship to direct labour hours or dollars in modern manufacturing operations. A concept known as activity costing has been put forward as a more logical basis, and seems to merit consideration. The concept does not appear to be in wide use at present, however, (although little hard evidence of practice is available) and it has yet to receive attention in financial accounting literature.

Several methods of costing goods sold are found in practice. When goods are produced to order, costs are usually accumulated by order or by job and there is little problem in associating costs with revenue. The same is frequently true in the case of contracts for services. Likewise, when goods sold represent high value items with individual characteristics, the costing system usually provides for specific identification of costs with individual inventory items.

The difficult problems in recognition of cost of goods sold arise when the inventory consists of interchangeable items. In such cases, when goods on hand have been acquired at different costs, some assumption as to flow of cost factors must be made when the goods are sold to permit recognition of expense.

A common assumption is that the cost to be recognized as cost of goods sold consists of the earliest costs in inventory (the FIFO assumption). The assumption has appeal because it is probably consistent with the physical movement of goods in most businesses.

A second widely accepted assumption is that an average of costs accumulated for all units of goods that are "fungible" or interchangeable represents a reasonable figure of cost to be recognized as each unit is sold. This assumption has appeal because the use of an average figure seems compatible with the interchangeable character of the goods.

A third assumption (the LIFO assumption) recognizes the most recent cost incurred as the cost to be assigned to cost of goods sold. The rationale for this is that the most recent cost is the best representation of the sacrifice made to earn revenue. Unfortunately, the actual application of LIFO is such that it often does not succeed in matching a current cost against revenue recognized. The problem is that LIFO is supposed to be an application of historical cost accounting, and it is difficult, perhaps impossible, to ensure that some historical cost can be found that is equivalent to a current cost. There is, in fact, an inherent conflict between the conceptual justification of LIFO and the historical cost accounting theory.

Specialized inventories present special problems in costing work in process and determining the cost of units sold. These problems are resolved within the general framework of inventory accounting while having regard to the special characteristics of the industry.

REFERENCES

[1]   G.H. Sorter and C.T. Horngren, "Asset Recognition and Economic Attributes—The Relevant Costing Approach," *The Accounting Review*, July 1962, pp. 391–99.

[2]   CICA, "Inventories," *CICA Handbook*, Section 3030 (Toronto: CICA), par. 03.

[3]   See for example, J.K. Shank and V. Govindarajan, "The Perils of Cost Allocation Based on Production Volumes," *Accounting Horizons*, December 1988, pp. 71–79.

[4]   This is not a brand new concept. See G.J. Staubus, *Activity Costing and Input-Output Accounting* (Homewood, Ill.: Richard D. Irwin, 1971).

[5]   See for example, R.E. Malcom, "Overhead Control Implications of Activity Costing," *Accounting Horizons*, December 1991, pp. 69–78. See also The Society of Management Accountants, *Activity-Based Costing*, Management Accounting Issues Paper 3 (Hamilton: The Society of Management Accountants of Canada, 1993). This survey of Canadian organizations indicated that only 15 percent of responding enterprises had implemented activity-based costing, while an additional 15 percent were assessing it. It concluded that activity-based costing was in the early stages of development in Canada.

[6]   For a brief analysis of a number of issues that could arise in attempting to adapt activity-based costing to external financial accounting purposes, see N. Hartnett, J. Lowry and R. Luther, "Is ABC Feasible for External Reporting?" *Accountancy*, May 1994, p. 74.

[7]   See for example, H.T. Johnson and R.S. Kaplan *Relevance Lost: The Rise and Fall of Management Accounting* (Boston: Harvard Business School Press, 1987).

[8]   For an interesting opinion on the state of production cost accounting and the factors that have inhibited its development, see G.J. Staubus, "The Dark Ages of Cost Accounting: The Role of Miscues in the Literature," *The Accounting Historians Journal*, Fall 1987, pp. 1–18.

[9]   American Institute of Accountants, Committee on Accounting Procedure, "Inventory Pricing," chap. 4 in *Restatement and Revision of Accounting Research Bulletins*, Accounting Research Bulletin No. 43 (New York: AIA, 1953), par. 5.

10   See E.W. Noreen and R.M. Bowen, "Tax Incentives and the Decision to Capitalize or Expense Manufacturing Overhead," *Accounting Horizons*, March 1989, pp. 29–42.

11   See Canadian Institute of Public Real Estate Companies, *Recommended Accounting Practices for Real Estate Investment and Development Companies*, Section 200 (Toronto: CIPREC).

12   Numerous LIFO accounting and disclosure issues have been covered in an issues paper prepared by the Task Force on LIFO Inventory Problems, Accounting Standards Division of the AICPA, and presented by the Accounting Standards Executive Committee to the Financial Accounting Standards Board: *Identification and Discussion of Certain Financial Accounting and Reporting Issues Concerning LIFO Inventories* (New York: AICPA, November 30, 1984). The paper still represents the U.S. profession's most authoritative source on LIFO issues and the SEC has recognized it as such. See FASB Emerging Issues Task Force, "LIFO Accounting Issues," EITF Abstract 84-24 in *EITF Abstracts* (Norwalk: FASB, 1993).

13   For examples of recent research in this area, see B.E. Cushing and M.J. LeClere, "Evidence on the Determinants of Inventory Accounting Policy Choice," *The Accounting Review*, April 1992, pp. 355–66; S. Bar-Yosef and P.K. Sen, "On Optimal Choice of Inventory Accounting Method," *The Accounting Review*, April 1992, pp. 320–36; J.R.M. Hand, "Resolving LIFO Uncertainty: A Theoretical and Empirical Re-examination of 1974–75 LIFO Adoptions and Non-adoptions," *Journal of Accounting Research*, Spring 1993, pp. 21–49; and M. Frankel and R. Trezevant, "The Year-End LIFO Inventory Purchasing Decision: An Empirical Test," *The Accounting Review*, April 1994, pp. 382–98. The latter article provides evidence that U.S. firms using LIFO are more likely to purchase extra inventory at year-ends than firms using FIFO, and that permitting LIFO for tax purposes may lead to inventory management inefficiencies.

14   For a general discussion of accounting methods relying on the learning curve see N. Baloff and J.W. Kennelly, "Accounting Implications of Product and Process Start-Ups," *Journal of Accounting Research*, Autumn 1967, pp. 131–43 and W.J. Morse, "Reporting Production Costs That Follow the Learning Curve Phenomenon," *The Accounting Review*, October 1972, pp. 761–73.

15   See D.B. Pattison and C.J. Teplitz, "Are Learning Curves Still Relevant?" *Management Accounting*, February 1989, pp. 37–40.

TANGIBLE CAPITAL ASSETS AND DEPRECIATION

This is the first of two chapters dealing with accounting for assets held for use in operations rather than for sale. In this chapter we deal with property, plant, and equipment. These have traditionally been called "fixed assets," but are now more commonly referred to as "tangible capital assets." In the next chapter we discuss accounting for intangible assets.

The accounting problems for tangible capital assets reduce to two basic issues: how to find the cost of assets and how to recognize expense as the benefits from the costs incurred expire. The latter problem does not apply to an asset such as land so long as its continued economic usefulness remains a reasonable presumption. Issues relating to impairment and the recognition of losses on capital asset write-downs are not covered in this chapter, but are deferred to Chapter 18.

COST ATTACHMENT

The fundamental principle for costing property, plant, and equipment is clear. All costs actually incurred and necessary for the acquisition of the asset and making it ready to serve should be capitalized. The difficulties come in the practical application of this principle.

Assets Purchased Externally

The majority of tangible capital assets are purchased from external sources. The chief element of cost, then, is the invoiced price less any applicable cash or trade discounts. The chief costing problem lies in ensuring that costs incidental to acquisition and costs of making the asset capable to serve are capitalized. With respect to land and buildings, such costs include any costs of options to buy the property that were exercised, commissions if any, legal fees, land survey costs, etc. With respect to equipment, costs include all customs duties and taxes, transportation inward, insurance in transit, foundations and installation costs, and other charges for testing and preparation.

Assets Purchased as Replacements

Certain questions arise when an asset replaces one previously owned. If the previous asset is traded in on the new one, the only objective figure in the exchange is the cash paid out over and above the trade-in allowance. Often a trade-in allowance is inflated, with a compensatory inflation in the contract price for the new asset. When it is suspected this may have happened, a realistic trade-in price should be substituted in the accounting to avoid inflating the cost of the new asset and misstating the gain or loss on the asset traded in. When a realistic trade-in value cannot be estimated, the entity may adopt the neutral procedure of recognizing no gain or loss on the asset disposed of. This will mean that the new asset will be costed at the sum of the cash price paid and the net book value of the asset traded in.

A second question relates to the costs of removal of the asset replaced. Although some accounting literature suggests that removal costs may be added to the cost of the replacement asset (or any excess of removal costs over salvage may be so added), this is clearly wrong in principle. The cost of restoring a site to its original condition represents a cost applicable to the service of the asset retired. Only the cost that would be necessarily incurred to install a new asset, whether or not it replaced a previous asset, is properly capitalized.

Additions and Renovations

Difficult practical problems can arise when additions or renovations are made to an existing asset (most often a building).

*   The cost of a straight *addition* to a building should, of course, be capitalized. Unfortunately, an addition often involves damage to the existing structure that must be made good. Ordinarily it can be accepted that virtually all such restoration cost may be capitalized since it is a necessary consequence of management's decision to undertake the addition. The work, however, may restore the existing premises to a better condition than they were in previously (for example, simply by leaving them in a freshly painted condition). In general, if work has been done that would have been done in any event (e.g., repainting) and the work would have been treated as expense, an appropriate estimate of that part of the cost of the addition should be written off.

*   An improvement that enhances the service potential of a capital asset is called a *betterment*.[1] For example, air-conditioning added to a building would be a betterment. Costs necessarily incurred for betterments should be capitalized.

*   Costs may be incurred that increase *the capacity* of an asset for service without increasing the quality of service. Such costs are similar in economic effect to an addition. Sometimes the increased capacity is represented by an increased volume capability and sometimes by an extension of service life at the existing capacity. Where costs incurred to extend service life are capitalized, care should be taken to adjust the depreciation rate accordingly. A possible alternative would be to leave the rate unchanged but charge the additional cost against the previously accumulated depreciation.

- Improvements are often difficult to distinguish from major repairs. In fact, one project may have characteristics of both. In such a case, it is necessary to apportion the cost based on informed estimates.

- In addition, in some situations a major repair may be viewed as a replacement. For example, a new roof may be viewed as a repair to a building or a new asset in itself. The proper accounting for such major repairs will depend upon the depreciation policy, as will be described subsequently under the heading "Interrelationship between Depreciation and Other Costs of Plant Service."

Environmental Costs

An entity may incur significant costs on existing property, plant or equipment to reduce future environmental damage that would otherwise be caused by their operation. Such costs may be incurred voluntarily or may be required by law. Questions arise as to whether expenditures for this purpose can qualify for capitalization. Costs incurred, for example, to rebuild a smoke stack to reduce air pollution or to remove asbestos from a building may not improve the asset's life expectancy, capacity or efficiency. In these cases it may seem that one would have to conclude that the expenditures cannot qualify as betterments from the entity's perspective, and should be expensed. But some regard this as too narrow a view. They hold that investments in future environmental improvements should be presumed to reflect to the future benefit of the entity and be capitalized. Certainly costs to incorporate current environmental standards into the structure of a new building would be treated as part of the initial capital cost of that building.

In the U.S., the FASB Emerging Issues Task Force has concluded that costs incurred to achieve improved safety or that result in mitigating future environmental contamination of existing property, plant and equipment may be capitalized.[2] This has been viewed as support for acceptance of this practice in Canada, since there is no authoritative literature on the issue here. A CICA Research Report contains an analysis of the issues but reaches no conclusions.[3]

Expenditures for the improvement of *future* environmental impacts must be carefully distinguished from costs to rectify *past* environmental damage caused by a reporting entity's activities. The latter will normally require treatment as an expense or loss. But if a property is acquired with the knowledge that certain costs will have to be incurred to restore it for environmental damage in order to make it ready to serve, then such costs are capitalized as incurred. It may be presumed that the acquisition price of the property would have been reduced accordingly. Of course, if the actual costs subsequently incurred exceed amounts that were reasonably expected at the time of acquisition, the excess should be written off.

Self-Constructed Assets

The primary attribute of cost—that it represents a sacrifice of money or money's worth—is reasonably evident when management makes an outside purchase. Such purchase costs can also be taken as evidence of value received, since management has discretion whether or not to incur them. The situation is less clear when an entity constructs plant or equipment for its own account. The doubt has manifested itself (as was true for inventory) in debates over the merits of direct costing versus full costing and over the propriety of including interest as part of an asset cost.

Basis of Costing

The general arguments for and against direct or variable costing and for and against full costing need not be repeated here. Arguments in favour of capitalizing the full cost of fixed productive capacity may be somewhat less compelling in respect of plant and equipment construction than inventories, however. In particular, a decision to produce an asset for one's own use may be justified by the existence of excess capacity, that is, on the expectation that its value in use will exceed the variable cost of its production. The conservative view, then, is that only variable costs should be capitalized with respect to self-constructed assets unless the decision to construct them has caused the loss of other valuable production.

Practice with respect to capitalization of costs of self-constructed assets varies. Those companies that rarely construct capital assets for their own use are likely to follow a variable costing approach or relevant costing (see Chapter 10). Those companies that regularly produce their own capital assets may well follow their normal inventory costing procedures. Doubts as to the value of capital assets produced in such a situation would probably be smaller since the assets are likely to be similar to assets produced for sale. As with inventories, allocation of general and administrative costs to the asset is rare. Exceptions are found in industries that are continually building for their own account. Some public utilities or real estate companies, for example, may be said to be in the business of construction as well as their primary business. In such cases, self-constructed assets may include an allocation or direct charging of such costs as those of the engineering department, construction office, and appropriate other general and administrative costs.

Construction Inefficiencies

Costs of self-constructed assets (or assets acquired under a cost-plus contract) lack the certainty in amount provided by a fixed price contract. Accordingly there is greater danger that such an asset may not be worth its cost, especially in the case of projects involving technically difficult construction. Accounting literature generally warns that abnormal costs owing to inefficiency or bad luck should not be capitalized. Examples of such costs might include extra costs attributable to strikes, fires, flood, etc. In practice, however, it may be difficult to quantify such costs or losses. For example, a variety of extra costs may be caused by construction delays. Yet some such delays may be no surprise in a complex project. It seems unreasonable to require that costs of routine inefficiency (which would be covered by an allowance for contingencies in a contractor's bid) must be identified and written off. Even strike costs may be offset in part if it is reasonable to assume that it would have been necessary to pay higher employment costs without the strike. In short, the identification of costs of inefficiency is subject to reasonable judgment, and immediate write-off needs to be considered only where major problems in construction have occurred.

Capitalization of Financing Costs

When an asset is self-constructed (or when a major asset is acquired from a contractor), it is normally necessary to make payments to meet costs before the asset is ready for service. Financing must be obtained for such payments and costs (interest, etc.) will be incurred on such financing. Several questions arise in relation to such financing costs. May they be considered part of the cost of the asset financed? If so, on what basis are they to be attached to the asset? If costs of debt during construction are treated as part of the asset cost, should there be a cost imputed to the use of equity capital as well?

The early view in accounting, for the most part, was that debt costs were a necessary expense of borrowing and no more. Interest was payable for the use of money for a period and consequently was required to be treated as an expense in the period it accrued. The contrary view was that one should look to how the borrowed money was used in order to decide how to account for the interest costs. If borrowed money was used in construction, the cost of that borrowing during the construction period could be recovered from revenues only after the plant went into service. Accordingly, a proper matching required that such interest cost be treated as part of the plant cost, so that it would become part of depreciation expense matched against plant revenues.

Until 1979 there was no authoritative accounting guidance on the subject of capitalization of interest. In the absence of such guidance, practice was mixed. Most companies did not capitalize interest costs in any circumstances. There was a tendency, however, for companies engaged in major construction projects to capitalize interest with respect to such projects. Where interest was capitalized, in general it was restricted to interest directly traceable to the project.

In 1979, the FASB issued Statement of Financial Accounting Standards No. 34, *Capitalization of Interest Cost*, to standardize U.S. accounting in this area. The standard introduced the following ideas.

- Interest cost is a necessary part of the cost of acquiring an asset if a period of time is required to get it ready for use. Therefore, interest not only may be capitalized during that period, it must be capitalized.

- In practice, rigorous application of the test that interest should be capitalized during any period of acquisition or construction would necessitate capitalization of interest in many situations (for example, where inventories are long in production or maturation). Because of the turnover of assets, a change to a policy of capitalization of interest would often have little impact on income reported. The board therefore concluded that capitalization of interest should take place only with respect to an asset that represents a discrete project for which costs are separately accumulated and where the amount of interest is likely to be significant. In the case of inventory, interest capitalization is restricted to industries such as heavy contractors, shipyards, etc.

- The basic objective of interest capitalization is to record the sacrifice involved in construction. That sacrifice may be reasoned to include not only the additional interest cost on borrowing caused by the project but also any additional return foregone because the construction project was undertaken. The benefit of such other return would, in the absence of construction, accrue to the equity. Although such sacrifice is undoubtedly part of the economic cost of the asset, the board concluded that capitalization of such a return would be outside the transaction-based cost model. The reasoning was that the cost would have to be "imputed," rather than being a cost resulting from an exchange transaction.

- The board found a compromise answer, however. It observed that in the absence of construction the funds tied up in it would be available to retire existing debt. Interest on that debt represents the result of an exchange transaction. Therefore it is legitimate to capitalize, as a cost of construction, not only interest on debt incurred subsequent to the date construction commences, but also the "avoidable" cost of interest on debt that has been incurred previous to construction but that theoretically might be paid off were it not for the construction. The total amount capitalized is not permitted to exceed total debt interest recorded, in order to maintain the premise that only costs actually incurred in an exchange transaction may be capitalized.

The standard is quite flexible with respect to the precise manner of determining the interest to be capitalized. An average rate of interest can be used, calculated on a judgment-based selection of borrowings deemed applicable. Alternatively, the standard permits the use of interest on borrowing specifically deemed to be for the construction. In that case, interest with respect to any excess of construction expenditures over deemed specific borrowings is to be capitalized at the average rate for all other borrowing deemed to be applicable.

As is apparent, the board's conclusions were highly pragmatic. Moreover, the logic is necessarily strained by the board's unwillingness to modify what it conceives to be the framework of the cost-based accrual model. The recommendations were in serious conflict with normal practice in Canada up to 1979. Since U.S. precedents tend to be accepted in Canada (in the absence of a contrary CICA recommendation), the FASB recommendations have been adopted by some Canadian companies, thereby enlarging the existing diversity in practice in this area. The *CICA Handbook* currently states that the cost of a capital asset may include interest costs that are "directly attributable to the acquisition, construction, or development activity." It provides no additional guidance on the issue.[4] In practice, this has been interpreted to permit adoption of the U.S. interest capitalization standard. *CICA Handbook* Section 3850 requires disclosure of the amount of interest capitalized in the reporting period.

A criticism may be made of any capitalization method that restricts amounts capitalized to actual interest incurred. The asset cost recorded will differ depending upon the way it is financed. The use of equity financing results in no cost capitalization. In contrast, the higher the percentage of debt, the more the cost of the asset will appear to be.

The only way to avoid these criticisms completely, while still maintaining the principle that an asset's acquisition cost includes the cost of financing it, is to recognize an imputed cost with respect to equity capital and capitalize an overall cost of capital with respect to all asset acquisition expenditures. Some accountants argue forcefully that such a procedure would provide a better representation of the economics of investment.[5] It is acknowledged, however, that adoption of that procedure would raise consequential questions as to the treatment of the credit arising from capitalization (is it income?) and as to the treatment of costs of capital bound up in holding assets as opposed to merely constructing them. In present practice an overall cost of capital figure is capitalized only by regulated public utilities and in a few analogous situations, and then only during the construction or acquisition period. This divergence from normal GAAP is justified on the basis that it conforms to the way that regulators calculate the rate base upon which a return on capital is calculated for recovery (along with other costs) from tariffs for service.

The general rule is that capitalization of interest should cease as soon as the asset is substantially complete and capable of operation at a reasonable level of capacity. That means that testing and trial runs should be complete.

EXPENSE RECOGNITION—DEPRECIATION

Except in the case of land, the usable life of any tangible capital asset must come to an end sooner or later. An ultimate limit is imposed by deterioration of the asset through wear and tear or exposure to the elements. Thus there is a physical boundary to asset life. More important, however, is the boundary imposed by obsolescence. An asset may continue to be perfectly fit for its original intended use and yet have lost all its value except as scrap. Obsolescence may be caused by technological advances whereby some other asset will perform the function better. It may also be caused by shifts in the business environment. Demand for the output of the asset may disappear, or changes in volume may make some other scale of production facility less costly per unit of output.

Because property, plant and equipment have limited lives, their cost (less ultimate net salvage, if any) is an expense required to earn income over its useful life. Determination of income for a period less than the asset lifetime requires some decision as to how much of that expense is applicable to each period under review. This is accomplished by depreciation accounting.

Unfortunately, authoritative literature contains no articulated theory of depreciation. There is little more than the following definition, which dates back to the 1940s:

> ... depreciation accounting [is] a system of accounting which aims to distribute the cost or other basic value of tangible capital assets, less salvage (if any), over the estimated useful life of the unit (which may be a group of assets) in a systematic and rational manner. It is a process of allocation, not of valuation.[6]

The *CICA Handbook* endorses this definition, observing that "amortization should be recognized in a rational and systematic manner appropriate to the nature of a capital asset with a limited life and its use by the enterprise."[7] The use of any conventional depreciation method makes the allocation "systematic." The important question, however, is what makes depreciation rational?

We might begin an assessment of depreciation accounting by recalling a fundamental premise of the conceptual frameworks of both the FASB and CICA—that all assets are presumed to be acquired by profit-oriented enterprises with the expectation that they will contribute, directly or indirectly, to the generation of future cash flows. For fixed assets the future cash flows will result from the revenue-generating processes to which they are expected to contribute. Thus, it would be logical to expect that depreciation should reflect a capital asset's contribution to the generation of revenues.

But here we run into the fundamental "one-to-many" allocation arbitrariness problem discussed in Chapter 5. To put this problem in perspective, it is useful to compare a financial asset (for example, a loan receivable) with a capital asset (such as a machine used in a production process). The relationship of a loan receivable to future cash flows is unique and direct, because the loan contract will specify an identifiable stream of future cash flows. The problems are to estimate their timing and amounts and to determine the effective interest rate so as to arrive at the appropriate carrying value and interest accruals. The relationship of the cost of a machine to future cash flows is much less direct. The machine will contribute over its useful life, along with many other inputs, to a revenue-generating process. The various inputs work together to produce revenues in total. The inputs lose their identity in this process, so that it is impossible to determine nonarbitrarily which costs contributed to particular items of revenue.

The "one-to-many" and "many-to-many" allocation problems were formally documented in the late 1960s. Since then many accountants have tended to dismiss depreciation accounting as an arbitrary exercise verging on the useless. Typical is this observation in a well-respected accounting text:

The definition of depreciation as a systematic and rational method of allocating costs to periods is purely syntactic. The resulting allocation has no real-world connotations.

Its advice: "... absent tax reasons, use the simplest method at all times—usually straight-line depreciation."[8]

Efficient-markets based empirical research has been concerned with the effects of differences in depreciation methods on stock market prices. The hypothesis underlying this research is that efficient markets see through such differences as having no information content (so that they can be expected to have no stock market price effects), except if the changes carry some cash flow consequences (if, for example, they affect an enterprise's taxes payable, or management compensation or perhaps, less directly, induce some sort of "political" costs). The results of this research are generally consistent with this hypothesis, although there are some anomalies and unanswered questions.[9]

Depreciation accounting has received little attention from standard setters since the 1940s. With the possible exception of regulated public utilities, practice has, for the most part, become a rather perfunctory exercise of mechanically applying traditional depreciation methods. Useful life and salvage value determinations tend to be based on accepted conventions rather than on rigorously developed evidence and estimates. This lack of attention to depreciation accounting serves to reinforce the view that there is little information value in it.

It is instructive to examine depreciation accounting from an informational value perspective. Academic literature seems to accept that cost allocations *could* have information value, even if they are arbitrary, if they indicate something of management's expectations with respect to a business' earnings and future cash flow generating ability.[10] For this to be the case depreciation would have to be calculated in a way that is logically related to managements' rational expectations for the generation of future cash flows. This suggests a perspective for examining the components of depreciation expense—specifically, how are salvage values, useful lives and depreciation patterns determined and what is, or could be, their logical relationship to cash flow generating expectations?

Salvage Value as a Factor in the Depreciation Base

The base for calculation of depreciation, according to the standard definition, is historical cost less "salvage." Several comments may be made.

- First, the proceeds obtainable from a capital asset depend upon the date at which it is disposed of and generally decline with age. The salvage figure obviously should be an estimate of proceeds at the actual date of disposal. Thus the estimate of salvage must correlate with the estimate of asset life.

- The actual salvage proceeds, of course, will be affected by price changes between the date an asset is acquired and its disposal date. Does an estimate of salvage require a forecast of inflation over the period to disposal of the asset? It will be remembered that it was reasoned in Chapter 8 that a proper estimate of future expenditures comprising an accrued liability should take into account future inflation/price change effects. Otherwise the liability will be underaccrued. Accountants have been reluctant to apply this reasoning to the estimation of future capital asset salvage values, presumably because the effect is to augment these values. It is even conceivable that estimated inflation-adjusted salvage proceeds could exceed the original cost of a long-lived asset, so that no depreciation at all would be recognized. Many accountants reject this result, and believe it best to avoid basing depreciation on subjective estimates of inflation rates far into the future. They counsel that it is better to be conservative and, where possible, base estimates of salvage values on the disposal values of comparable assets at the date of the acquisition.

On the other hand, the result of ignoring future inflation expectations is that a potentially large gain will be recorded upon disposal of a capital asset if salvage values do in fact rise as a result of inflation. Some defend this result, arguing that it is better to reflect a "holding gain" at the end of an asset's useful life than to reduce depreciation so that it is far removed from the current cost to render its service. Others object that this is not defensible within a cost-based accrual model—that it results in the overstatement of depreciation expense through an asset's useful life, and so is inconsistent with the professed allocation-of-cost purposes of depreciation accounting. Further, such accounting might be expected to have reduced information value since it will not reflect best estimates of future salvage values.

A related issue further complicates this debate. It was observed in Chapter 8 that the pricing of future cash flows to reflect the effects of inflation is inextricably linked to the question of discounting them to determine their present values. This linkage results from the fact that market interest rates are composed of a "real" rate and an expected rate of inflation. Thus the question whether future cash flows should factor in future inflation effects cannot be addressed rationally without addressing how the time value of money is to be reflected in the accounting. Unfortunately, the implications of the time value of money have not been factored into traditional depreciation accounting—and we will return to this issue in examining depreciation patterns later in this chapter.

Existing accounting standards do not address how salvage values should be priced. This, plus a general lack of explanatory disclosures in financial statements, means that it can be quite unclear what estimates of salvage values may purport to represent.

- Must costs of removal of the asset be offset against estimated salvage proceeds? In general, the answer is yes. The cost of restoring the surroundings to the conditions they were in before the asset was acquired is logically part of the cost of the asset services, and should be recognized as expense in its service period.

- What should be done if removal costs exceed salvage proceeds? Should the depreciation charge be increased so that accumulated depreciation at the end of the asset life will be enough to absorb both the write-off of the asset cost and the cost of removal in excess of salvage? Where the excess removal costs are small, such a procedure may be perfectly satisfactory as a practical matter. There are situations, however, where removal costs are major. In such cases it would be technically better accounting to provide for the expected future cash outflow as a liability, rather than as an accumulation of depreciation. The subject of accruals for future expenditures is discussed in Chapter 8.

In many situations the amount of net salvage will be immaterial, and extreme efforts to attain precision in estimates are not warranted in view of the more important uncertainty as to useful life. In practice, careful consideration of salvage amounts is largely restricted to public utility companies.

The Meaning and Estimation of Useful Life

As already suggested, the useful life of an asset comes to an end as a result of physical deterioration or for economic reasons. But many types of assets pass through several hands before being abandoned or scrapped at the end of their physical or economic life. From the standpoint of the first owner, however, an asset's useful life is over when he or she sells it. One is left with the rather ordinary conclusion that the "useful life" over which cost less net salvage value is to be allocated cannot be longer than the period of ownership. May it be shorter? It may be if the owner fails to recognize that the economic value of the asset has expired. For example, an asset may be taken out of service and held, ostensibly as standby, even though the likelihood of future reactivation is small. Indeed, if management is not alert, an asset may sometimes remain in service and yet contribute nothing to net cash returns.

The estimation of length of useful life, therefore, reduces to an estimate of how long the asset will be held, subject to caution concerning the possibility of complete obsolescence prior to the end of the normal holding period. Since the asset retirement date lies in the future, the estimate may not be more than an informed guess. Past experience with similar types of assets provides some guidance. Where the main cause of retirement is physical deterioration, the past experience may be a good guide. Studies of certain categories of public utility plant, for example, have yielded statistics that show that retirements take place in relatively well-defined patterns, and "survival curves" are constructed on much the same principle as mortality tables used in life insurance. Asset lives for assets that are more individual in character and more subject to obsolescence are less predictable. Helpful industry-wide studies are sometimes available. An entity must also bear in mind its own replacement policy, the possible impact of its maintenance policy on length of life, and the possibility of acceleration in the rate of obsolescence in the future. In the end, however, estimates require judgment. Once made, estimates of useful life and salvage should be reviewed regularly and amended when necessary. Conditions change, and depreciation accounting should adapt to those changes.

The foregoing represents the theory with respect to estimation of useful lives. Practice is somewhat different. Apart from public utilities, most companies pay little attention to the estimation of useful lives but rather tend to follow past practices and accepted norms. Historically, much of practice can be traced to the influence of income taxation. The imposition of a tax on business income in the second decade of the 1900s was a great stimulus to depreciation accounting. When it came to saving taxes businesspeople could see the merits of the concept of depreciation, even though many had been unenthusiastic when it was simply a question of financial reporting. Changes in the tax system in 1949 freed depreciation for financial accounting purposes from any requirement to reflect "capital cost allowances" claimed for tax purposes. Nevertheless, for many years thereafter depreciation rates continued to be consistent with short asset lives. It is not certain, however, that the application of traditional use-life assumptions are still generally conservative under the conditions of accelerating change witnessed in recent years.

A recent *CICA Handbook* recommendation has attempted to reduce the scope for overly optimistic amortization by requiring that annual depreciation provisions be based on the greater of cost less scrap value over the total expected life of a capital asset and the cost less residual value over the estimated useful life to the reporting entity. This makes little sense conceptually and it seems to have had little impact in practice. The Handbook also indicates that useful life estimates should not exceed forty years except where a longer life is clearly demonstrated.[11]

Depreciation Patterns—Conceptual Analysis

Given estimates of salvage value and useful life, the final step in depreciation accounting is to select a pattern for allocation of the depreciable base over the estimated useful life. Depreciation accounting is defined as a "systematic and rational" allocation process, but no criteria for rational allocation methods are set out in authoritative accounting literature. In practice a variety of depreciation patterns have gained acceptance and may be applied virtually interchangeably, even though the resulting figure of depreciation may be quite different depending on the method adopted. The following discussion reviews some suggestions as to criteria of rationality.

Depreciation Based on Asset Contributions to Net Revenue

We begin with the elementary observation noted earlier that investment in property, plant, and equipment is made in the expectation that asset services will contribute to the generation of a net cash inflow over a period of years. It seems logical to conclude from this that depreciation expense reported should be in some way proportional to the "net revenue contribution" (NRC) expected from the asset—that is, the revenue to be received from the asset's output less related expenses. Unfortunately, as observed earlier, it is impossible to make objective estimates of NRCs—that is, of the net revenue contributions of specific asset inputs.

But let us stand back and ask what may be known or predictable and what assumptions might be reasonable. Revenues result from the *combined* contributions of all of the capital assets devoted to a particular process and all the other inputs that work together to produce and sell the good or service outputs of that process. Knowing nothing else, the most reasonable assumption may be that each dollar of unamortized capital asset cost (net of salvage value) is equivalent in terms of its contribution to revenue generation. If this assumption is accepted, then depreciation pattern selection becomes a matter of estimating the pattern of revenues to be generated over the useful life of a capital asset by the *whole* revenue-generating process to which the asset contributes. The overall pattern would be adjusted for the unique contribution characteristics of the particular capital asset—for example, any expected decline in the pattern of its productivity over its useful life, or the pattern of anticipated future repair and maintenance costs. This approach to selecting an appropriate depreciation pattern must involve highly subjective estimates. It would not, however, be a wholly arbitrary policy decision, but would be an estimation process based on a reasonable all-input-dollars-are-equal attribution assumption. [12]

There are at least two ways in which a depreciation pattern could be based upon such a forecast of the pattern of NRCs of a revenue-generating process. [13] Under the simplest approach, the depreciation pattern is the pattern of forecasted NRCs over the life of the asset. Thus, if NRCs were expected to be constant over the asset lifetime, the depreciation pattern would be straight-line. Consequently, the operating profit margin after depreciation recorded would be an unchanging percentage of net revenues period by period (assuming actual NRCs turned out to be as forecast).

There is a profound conceptual problem with this approach, because it gives no recognition to the time value of money. Consistent with the economics of investment, NRCs to be received in the more distant future are less valuable than those to be realized in the nearer future. The economic significance of future NRCs at any point in time may be measured by their discounted present value; therefore, a logical depreciation pattern would be one that results in the net carrying value of the asset declining in step with the present value of the estimated future NRCs. Such a depreciation pattern is said to be "time-adjusted." On this basis, if the NRCs are expected to be constant over the asset's lifetime, the reported net carrying value of the asset would decline in the same fashion as does the value of an annuity—slowly at first and with increasing rapidity as time passes.

The idea of determining expenses on a present value basis is perhaps most easily seen and accepted when the expenses reflect expenditures to be made in future periods (for example, the discounting of future pension benefits in determining pension expense of the current reporting period). The concept of time value of money is just as applicable to expenditures made in advance of appropriate expense recognition. In other words, economic value is, in logic, time-adjusted whether one is consuming an economic benefit in advance of paying for it (a liability) or is paying for an economic benefit in advance of consuming it (an asset).

The rigorous implementation of time value adjusted depreciation would require addressing the equivalent issues to those raised in Chapter 8 with respect to discounting future expenditures to determine liability accruals. These pertain to the selection of an appropriate interest rate to discount the NRCs and the closely linked question of whether the pattern of future NRCs should be adjusted to take into account inflationary/price change impacts. The accounting profession has yet to give serious attention to these issues.

Depreciation Based on the Decline in Asset Market Value

It has been said that depreciation is intended to provide a rational allocation of asset cost over its service life; it is not intended as a valuation of the asset. This proposition needs some examination. Since the cost of an asset is normally a market price at the date of acquisition and salvage proceeds represent a market price, one is entitled at least to ask why a depreciation pattern consistent with the decline in market value for used assets would not be rational.

One traditional concern has been that market values fluctuate. Since a fixed asset is acquired for use and not for sale, it is argued such fluctuations are irrelevant. In addition, there might be a general inflationary or deflationary trend in prices that would be reflected in market values. Such effects, it may be argued, should not be reflected in a historical cost accounting system.

These arguments carry some weight without being totally conclusive. It is possible to conceive of a typical decline in asset value with use and age that would occur in the absence of temporary price fluctuations or inflationary or deflationary price trends. Depreciation based on such a decline may be little different from a depreciation pattern based on the present values of NRCs, where there are representative market prices for used assets that reflect typical use and revenue return expectations.

A serious practical objection to basing depreciation on market values for used assets lies in the lack of available information as to typical used market values. The difficulty is twofold. For some, perhaps many, types of assets there is no representative market from which price information can be derived. Such exchanges of used assets as take place represent isolated deals. For other types of assets relatively active markets exist but there is no organized source of information concerning the prices at which exchanges are taking place. It is apparent that considerable research would be necessary to provide an adequate base of information to support depreciation patterns that could be deemed to simulate typical market value declines.[14]

Depreciation Based on Physical Output

A third approach to depreciation accounting is to make the periodic asset cost write-off proportional to the consumption of its capacity to serve. The application of this method requires estimates of quantities of output over the asset life rather than net revenue contributions. Since output should produce net revenue, however, the difference in thinking between this approach and that which recognizes depreciation expense proportional to undiscounted NRCs may be more apparent than real. If the net sales price of a unit of output is expected to be constant over the asset's life, the two methods are essentially the same.

Recognition of depreciation expense on the basis of physical output is subject to two criticisms. First, it is not a fully sufficient representation of the economic benefits of production, that is, of output sales revenues and price effects. Second, it weights current and future production equally so that no recognition is given to the time-value-of-money expectation that future benefits have less economic value than current benefits.

Summary of Criteria for Rational Depreciation

After discussing possible objectives for depreciation accounting, Lamden, Gerboth, and McRae suggested the following criteria for a rational depreciation method:[15]

- The depreciation allocation should be proportional to some measure of the asset's contribution to the business (an NRC approach).
- The depreciation allocation should be proportional to the incidence of events contributing to the exhaustion of asset usefulness (a service-capacity approach).
- Depreciation should result in measuring the decline in asset value in conformity with the values a rational purchaser would assign to the remaining service potential of the asset from time to time over its life (an asset valuation approach).
- The depreciation allocation should tend to equalize the sum of depreciation and other asset-related costs year by year (an NRC approach).
- The depreciation allocation should result in reporting, other things being equal, a constant rate of return on the net recorded investment in the asset (a time-adjusted NRC approach).

As may be seen, these criteria merely summarize the various approaches discussed above. The authors recognized that the objectives contain a significant degree of conflict. These conflicts remain unaddressed by authoritative accounting standards. The traditional criteria for rational depreciation are long overdue for in-depth reconsideration. In particular, it must be questioned whether depreciation criteria that do not factor in the time value of money can be accepted as rational in any real sense.

Conventional Depreciation Patterns

Conventional depreciation patterns may be classified as straight-line methods, unit-of-output methods, declining-charge methods, and increasing-charge methods.

The Straight-Line Pattern

The simplest and most common depreciation pattern is the straight-line pattern. The annual depreciation amount is found by dividing the estimated number of periods of useful life into the depreciation base (cost less net salvage).

The straight-line pattern is sometimes thought to be justified on the grounds that it will result in recording a constant margin on net revenue. In fact, that result is unlikely to be achieved. There are probably relatively few instances in which the revenue contribution of an asset does not decline with age (owing to increasing operating inefficiencies, greater downtime, etc.) while its repair and maintenance costs go up with age. In any event, constant margin on net revenues is deficient as a fully rational measurement objective because it ignores the time value of money. A more likely justification for the straight-line pattern is that it represents a compromise between the conflicting arguments favouring decreasing-charge and increasing-charge methods. It also has the virtue of simplicity in calculation.

Unit-of-Output Pattern

The pattern known by the name of "unit-of-output" depreciation is also essentially a straight-line method. The amount of depreciation for each unit of output is found by dividing the depreciable base by the estimated quantity of output over the asset's useful life.

The unit-of-output pattern has been considered to be most appropriate where the quality of service of an asset does not deteriorate with use, maintenance costs do not increase, and the useful life of the asset is largely determined by rate of usage rather than passage of time.

Decreasing-Charge Patterns

There are at least three variations of decreasing-charge patterns. Under the "diminishing-balance" method, a rate of depreciation is struck that is applied to the opening carrying value of the asset for each period (cost less depreciation accumulated in previous periods) so as to reduce the carrying value to estimated salvage value at the end of the asset's life. As the net undepreciated balance declines progressively, so does the amount of the periodic depreciation charge.

The "sum-of-the-years'-digits" method is a method whereby the depreciation for a particular year of an asset's life is a fraction of the depreciable base. The denominator of the fraction is the sum of the digits in the asset's expected life. The numerator is the reverse digit to the actual year in the life. That is to say, in the first year of a ten-year life asset the numerator is ten, in the second year it is nine, and so on. This method is rarely found in Canada but is more common in the United States because of its acceptance for tax purposes there.

The "double-declining-balance" pattern is a diminishing-balance method where the depreciation rate set (applicable to the progressively declining undepreciated balance) is double what would appear to be the appropriate straight-line rate. The simple doubling of the straight-line rate is arbitrary. It became customary because that is the basis adopted for tax purposes when the capital cost allowance system was introduced in 1949. This method never completely writes off the asset and thus is bound to contain some error when applied to assets that have no net positive salvage value. It is conceivable that some other arbitrarily selected rate (say 150% of straight-line rates) might produce results that would appear more reasonable for some types of assets.

Increasing-Charge Patterns

There are two increasing-charge depreciation methods that are essentially the same mathematically but are explained by somewhat different processes of reasoning.

The *annuity method* depreciation provision consists of two parts. The first is an annuity over the useful life of the asset with a present value equal to its depreciable cost. This is considered to be the "rent" that would have had to be paid if the asset were not owned. The second part reflects the benefits of ownership by a credit for interest or return on capital tied up in the asset. The equal annual charge and the decreasing credit for interest return on the book value of the asset result in a net charge that is increasing over time. The two components might be separated or combined in the financial statements.

A provision for depreciation under the *sinking-fund method* similarly consists of two components. The basic component is the level annual sum that would have to be deposited in a sinking fund to accumulate at interest to the amount of the depreciable base at the end of an asset's life. The second component is the charge for interest on the increasing balance of the notional sinking fund each year. The concept is that maintenance of capital requires recognition of asset consumption (the level annual sum) plus the interest foregone on the outstanding capital balance (book value) of the asset.

In spite of the differences in concept, it may be noted that if the same interest rate is used, the net depreciation charge under both the annuity and sinking-fund methods will be the same. Each method assumes a constant rate of return on the undepreciated asset balance and level NRCs over the asset's useful life.

The practical effects of these increasing-charge methods is that the longer the asset life and the higher the interest rate assumed, the more the depreciation provision will be concentrated in the latter portion of the life. For example, at 5% and 10% rates of interest, 31% and 42% respectively of the cost of a 25-year asset remain to be amortized in the last 5 years of its life. This increases to 42% and 62% respectively to be amortized in the last 10 years of a 50-year asset. It is apparent, then, that increasing-charge depreciation methods are extremely vulnerable to errors in life estimates for such longer asset lives.

In practice, increasing-charge depreciation methods are little used in Canada except in the case of rental properties of real estate companies, and a few utility companies. The CIPREC manual suggests an arbitrary limitation of the interest assumption to 4–6%.[16] These methods are virtually never seen in the U.S. as the SEC has generally refused to accept them.

Time-Adjusted Interpretation of Conventional Depreciation Patterns

With the exception of the increasing charge methods, the depreciation methods *as conventionally interpreted* above do not take into account the time value of money. It should be emphasized, however, that with the exception of the unit-of-output method, these methods may be interpreted within a time-adjusted context. To demonstrate this and its logical implications, let us examine the straight-line method. We have observed that the conventional, non-time-adjusted, interpretation of straight-line depreciation is that it is premised on a level pattern of net revenues. The example in Table 11-1 illustrates that the rather unrealistic result is that the asset seems to be increasingly profitable as it ages because the reported rate of return on the decreasing asset book value increases each year.[17] In contrast, the

Table 11-1	Net Revenue Patterns Implicit in Straight-line Depreciation on a Non-Time-Adjusted and a Time-Adjusted Basis

(Capital asset costing $1,000 with a 3-year life and no salvage value purchased with the expectation of a 10% annual rate of return)

	Period 1	Period 2	Period 3
A. Conventional (non-time-adjusted) straight-line depreciation			
Implied net revenue contribution (3-year annuity at 10%)	$ 402	$402	$402
Depreciation	333	333	333
Net income	69	69	69
Net book value of assets, beginning of year	$1,000	$667	$333
Rate of return on asset	6.9%	10.3%	20.7%
B. Time-adjusted straight-line depreciation			
Depreciation	333	333	333
Expected return at 10% of opening book value:			
year 1 ($1,000 × .10)	100		
year 2 ($667 × .10)		67	
year 3 ($333 × .10)			33
Implied net revenue contribution	$ 433	$400	$366

time-value-of-money assumption is that the rate of return on investment should be expected to be constant.[18] As Table 11-1 illustrates, under this assumption, the expected pattern of NRCs implicit in straight-line depreciation is declining.

Table 11-2 presents an example of an asset costing $10,000 with a useful life of five years and with salvage value of $778 at the end of that period. Three different patterns of NRCs over its life are shown along with the depreciation patterns required to produce a constant return on investment over the lifetime of the asset.

This calculation shows that, even if the objective of reporting a constant rate of return on the asset is accepted, that objective does not imply the choice of one depreciation pattern in particular. It all depends on the pattern of the asset's NRCs over its life. Moreover, even though NRC patterns can never be known with certainty, a calculation such as the foregoing, showing the NRCs implied by each depreciation pattern, can be an aid to judgment. For example, few assets are likely to have level NRCs over their whole life. Thus the annuity pattern will almost always be unreasonable. The straight-line calculation, in contrast, appears more likely. The declining-balance pattern also could be applicable for some assets, although the rate of decline in implied NRCs shown in this table looks extreme.

What should govern the choice of interest rate in a time-adjusted interpretation of depreciation? Various approaches may be put forward, including internal rate of return, cost-of-

Table 11-2	Patterns of Depreciation That Will Yield a Constant Rate of Return on an Asset, Given Different Rates of Decline in Net Revenue Contributions

| | Period | | | | |
	1	2	3	4	5
Annuity Pattern					
Net revenue contribution	$ 2,511	$2,511	$2,511	$2,511	$2,511
Depreciation	1,511	1,662	1,828	2,011	2,212
Net income	1,000	849	683	500	299
Net book value of asset, beginning of year	$10,000	$8,489	$6,828	$5,000	$2,989
Rate of return on asset	10%	10%	10%	10%	10%
Straight-Line Pattern					
Net revenue contribution	$ 2,844	$2,660	$2,475	$2,291	$2,106
Depreciation	1,844	1,844	1,844	1,844	1,844
Net income	1,000	816	631	447	262
Net book value of asset, beginning of year	$10,000	$8,156	$6,311	$4,467	$2,622
Rate of return on asset	10%	10%	10%	10%	10%
Declining-Balance Pattern (40% rate)					
Net revenue contribution	$ 5,000	$3,000	$1,800	$1,080	$648
Depreciation	4,000	2,400	1,440	864	518
Net income	1,000	600	360	216	130
Net book value of asset, beginning of year	$10,000	$6,000	$3,600	$2,160	$1,296
Rate of return on asset	10%	10%	10%	10%	10%

capital rates and market-based asset return rates. If accounting is to be based on rational expectations, there would seem to be merit, in concept at least, in selecting a market rate of interest appropriate to the term of investment adjusted for the risks inherent in the particular capital asset and the underlying revenue-generating process.

As a final point on depreciation patterns, it should be noted that the patterns described above are not the only possible ones. Those patterns have become established because each embodies a simple mathematical formula that undeniably makes the pattern "systematic" (if not necessarily "rational"). There is no logical reason, however, why they should not be adapted or combined if the result appears more rational than that yielded by conventional patterns. For example, a declining-balance pattern could be adopted for the first fraction of an asset's life, with a switch to straight-line for its remaining years, or vice versa.

Summary Critique of Depreciation Patterns and Practice

Several points arising out of the foregoing discussion may be worth some emphasis. It is clear that depreciation accounting has long been neglected, and that practice continues to be based on old conventions that do not stand up well to contemporary concepts of "assets" and their ultimate basis in future cash flow expectations. The selection of depreciation methods in practice is treated, for the most part, as a matter of management policy, with little attention paid to conceptual considerations and estimation parameters.

This is unfortunate because there are indications that the significance, and therefore information value, of depreciation accounting would be improved, perhaps substantially, through more rigorous attention to reasoning from rational expectations. This would entail explicitly factoring in the time value of money, and basing estimates of salvage value, useful life and pattern of net revenue benefits on reasonable expectations and on assumptions that are internally consistent and in keeping with expectations.

Interrelationship between Depreciation and Other Costs of Plant Service

Acquisition cost and salvage proceeds are not the only costs or cost recoveries associated with the services of plant and equipment. There are ancillary costs required to obtain their services, including running costs, repairs and maintenance, and costs pertaining to ownership. Income accounting, in principle, requires that *all* the costs of plant and equipment services be accounted for in a systematic and rational fashion. That broader objective may be achieved by logical treatment of ancillary costs on their own, or by modifying depreciation accounting to take the pattern of other costs into consideration. Either way, their essential interconnection should not be ignored.[19]

Major repairs or replacements illustrate the interconnection. As mentioned earlier, often components of a larger unit require renovation or replacement one or more times during the lifetime of the major unit. Roofs, wiring, and plumbing require renewal in buildings. Steel-making furnaces require relining. Ships require quadrennial as well as annual surveys. All these represent costs of obtaining property services that occur irregularly and may distort average costs of operation if written off to expense as incurred. What expense recognition method would be "systematic and rational" for them?

On the one hand, if such a cost is in respect of the replacement of a component of an existing capital asset, there is logic in removing the cost and accumulated depreciation of the replaced component and capitalizing the replacement. Examples of separable components could include the elevators within a building or the engines of an aircraft. This accounting would require separating cost components on initial acquisition and applying different depreciation rates to each in order to recognize their different useful lives. The approach has the practical difficulty that the costs of the separate components may not be easily determinable at the date of first acquisition. As an alternative, when a structure has major components that require renewal before the end of the life of the structure itself, the depreciation rate may be established at a higher figure than would be applicable to the shell alone. When components are replaced, the cost may be charged against the accumulated depreciation, with the expectation that after these charges the depreciation accumulated will be an appropriate amount in respect of the structure as a whole.

On the other hand, one may take the view that periodic major repair or renewal costs must be incurred to maintain the existing capital asset so that it will achieve its estimated useful life, capacity for productivity, and salvage value. Within this context various approaches have been found in practice.

- The depreciation pattern of the capital asset may be selected to take into account the expected repair and maintenance pattern, for example, by weighting depreciation more to the earlier years if repairs and maintenance costs are expected to increase with the age of the asset. In this case repair and maintenance costs would simply be expensed as incurred.

- A provision for major periodic repairs or replacement of components may be separated from depreciation accounting by charging expense and crediting a provision (liability account). This has been an accepted practice with respect to the cost of relining steel furnaces and the cost of quadrennial surveys for ships. This method is open to question because of the difficulty in justifying expected future replacements or repairs as true liabilities in the balance sheet of the current period.

- Alternatively, major repairs or component replacement costs have on occasion been accounted for by deferring them when incurred and amortizing the deferred cost over the period to the next expected repair date or the end of service life of the related asset. This approach avoids the need for estimates of future costs. Both this method and the previous one are deficient in that provision for major repairs is missed out for one period in their service life. Under the previous method there is no provision in the final period before scrapping. Under this method there is no provision in the first period after acquisition. It may also be questioned whether capitalization of major repairs (or the cost of a replacement without removing the undepreciated amount of the replaced component) meets the concept of an "asset," since it is not a "betterment" as discussed earlier in this chapter.

- Finally, major repairs and replacements may simply be written off when incurred, without any allowance in the selection of the depreciation patterns, if their probable amount in any particular year is unlikely to be such as to severely distort the recorded total of expenses.

Some Implementation Issues in Depreciation Accounting

A number of practical points in depreciation accounting are discussed below.

Commencement of Depreciation

An initial question is, at what time following the acquisition of the asset should depreciation accounting begin? If depreciation is calculated on the unit-of-production basis (implying that wear and tear is the chief cause of loss of useful life), depreciation obviously begins when the asset begins to render service. In the majority of cases, however, where depreciation will take place over time even if not used, the answer is somewhat different. The theory is that depreciation should begin when the asset is capable of rendering service, whether it does so or not. As a practical matter, companies follow two or three shortcuts with respect to depreciation on new assets routinely acquired. A half-year's depreciation may be written in the year of addition and one-half year's at the end, or a full-year's depreciation in the first year and none in the year of disposal, or the reverse. These shortcut approaches are acceptable only when their deviation from a policy of accruing depreciation on new assets from their individual ready-to-serve dates is immaterial.

Depreciation on large capital projects begins after completion of testing and trial runs—that is, it coincides with the date when interest capitalization ceases. Any incidental revenue before that ready-to-serve date should be treated as a reduction of asset cost. An exception is indicated where a major asset inevitably goes through a load build-up period. In such a case there are good grounds for phasing in the full depreciation accrual, simply to fulfill the objective of relating depreciation to the asset's net revenue contribution. Such a procedure has some precedent in major new public utility construction but is less likely to be justified in the plant expansion of ordinary industries. When adopted, the depreciation build-up should be proportional to the faster of the actual or planned load build-up. The failure of load to grow as planned is not an excuse for failure to accrue depreciation.

Depreciation on Idle Plant

May depreciation be suspended when plant is idle by reason of a strike or other causes? If depreciation were primarily a function of wear and tear, the argument for suspension would be a strong one. However, to the extent that obsolescence is the primary factor in determining economic life, an asset loses value whether or not it is used. Thus, it is the normal practice to continue the standard depreciation write-off during the period of idleness. If plant units are taken out of service and held as standby, depreciation is also continued. Depreciation may be discontinued on plant taken out of service with a view to sale. In this situation such plant held for realization should be segregated from the plant in use on the balance sheet, its value should be written down to estimated realizable value, and that valuation should be kept under review as time passes to see whether further write-downs are necessary.

Individual Asset vs. Group Depreciation

There may be some question whether assets are considered as a group or individually for depreciation purposes. Ordinarily, assets are classified in similar-life groups to facilitate the calculation of depreciation. That does not necessarily imply that the accumulated depreciation is not, in principle, applicable to individual assets. It is common practice, when an individual asset is disposed of, to calculate the depreciation that must have been accumulated with respect to it and to recognize gain or loss for the difference between the asset's net book value and proceeds on disposal. An alternative approach is to consider the accumulated depreciation as being applicable to the entire group or class of assets, in which case no gain or loss would be recognized on disposal of an individual asset. Instead, the asset cost would be written off against the accumulated depreciation account and the proceeds of disposal would be credited to that account. Especially when there are only a few assets in a class or group, however, care must be taken to see that the balance of accumulated depreciation after a disposal is not unreasonably high or low in relation to the cost and remaining lives of assets still in service. The group or "bulk" reserve approach, as it is called, is found most frequently in conjunction with a declining-balance depreciation pattern but may be applied to other patterns as well.

Probabilistic Depreciation

A company that owns a number of assets of the same general type is likely to find that some last longer and some expire earlier than the best estimate of life expectancy. For example, suppose a company buys eight assets for $1,000 each that will probably be retired (with no net salvage) at year-ends shown in the following list: year 8, one asset; year 9, two; year 10, two; year 11, two; and year 12, one. Since the average probable life is ten years the normal straight-line depreciation write-off would be $800 per annum. In fact, however, with perfect foreknowledge annual depreciation should be as follows: The eight-year asset, $125; the nine-year assets, $222.22; the ten-year assets, $200; the eleven-year assets, $181.82; and the twelve-year asset $83.33. Thus the straight-line depreciation for the group as a whole should be: for the first eight years, $812.37; in year nine, $687.37; in year ten, $465.15; in year eleven, $265.15; and in year twelve, $83.33. If this pattern of higher depreciation in the first several years tailing off towards the end is correct for a group of assets, then it must also be correct for a single asset, given the uncertainty that always exists as to estimated useful life. In the normal situation a refinement to use such "probabilistic depreciation" would probably be immaterial when weighed against the range of judgment possible in choice of depreciation method and the estimates of all kinds entering into the depreciation calculation. In cases where depreciation judgments are made more scientifically, however, the adjustment to probabilistic depreciation may properly be taken into account.[20]

Depreciation Adjustments

In theory, estimates of useful lives used for depreciation purposes should be kept under regular review to see whether changes in them should be made. The question arises, if a change in useful life is indicated, should a recalculation of previously accumulated depreciation be made and an adjustment made to income account currently, or as a prior period adjustment? The answer is no. The estimation process in accounting is inherently uncertain. Changes made in estimates may themselves prove to be in error. Accordingly, the generally accepted approach is that changes in estimates should not result in a restatement of previously reported results. Instead, a change in estimate should be made through current income if it applies to a short-life asset or liability (e.g., a changed estimate affecting profit reported on a contract in process) or prospectively if it applies to a longer-life asset or liability. Thus the suggested practice would be to adjust the depreciation rate so as to cause the depreciable base to be fully provided for at the end of asset lives as re-estimated. An exception would be made if it were estimated that depreciation as newly calculated could not be recovered from net revenues over the remaining lives. In such a case, an immediate write-down to recoverable values would be called for.

APPRAISALS OF CAPITAL ASSETS

The recording of capital assets in balance sheets on the basis of appraised value rather than cost was common before the development and spread of the historical cost model in the 1930s and 1940s. The gradual acceptance of cost-based accounting and the active opposition to appraisals by the SEC led to the virtual disappearance of the use of appraisals in the United States. An important factor in such disappearance, also, was undoubtedly the lack of confidence by accountants in the reliability of appraisals. It was not until 1965, however, that the Accounting Principles Board in the U.S. was prepared to state positively that property, plant, and equipment should not be written up by an enterprise to reflect appraisal or current values above cost.[21]

In some other countries, notably the United Kingdom, the practice of making regular valuations of property, plant, and equipment for financial statement purposes continues to be common.

In Canada the CICA Committee on Accounting and Auditing Research clearly tried to discourage the use of an appraisal basis for valuation for fixed assets when it said, "The writing up of fixed asset values should not occur in ordinary circumstances."[22] That statement originated in Bulletin 11 issued in 1955, at which time CICA recommendations did not have the influence they have today. In 1955, over 25 percent of the companies covered in a survey of financial reporting practice by public Canadian companies disclosed some or all property valued on an appraisal basis. That percentage steadily declined over the years after 1955, levelling off to a figure of about 5 percent in the late 1970s.[23] The practice was prohibited altogether from 1989. In that year, the CICA Emerging Issues Committee concluded that it should be considered appropriate to write capital assets up to appraised value only when the entire balance sheet is revalued as part of a reorganization.[24] In 1990 the *CICA Handbook* ruled that all capital assets should be carried on a cost basis, with no exceptions.[25] In 1992 comprehensive revaluation of assets and liabilities was explicitly limited to situations in which (1) a parent may push down its cost values to a subsidiary in which it has acquired virtually all of the equity interests, or (2) an enterprise in financial difficulties has undergone a reorganization resulting in a change in control.[26] Neither of these situations is considered a departure from historical cost, as the "revaluation values" reflect the bargained costs to the acquiring interests.

The justification, if any, for appraisal write-ups of capital assets is found in the presumption that the resulting figures are more relevant than amortized historical costs. Particularly in the case of long-lived property, historical costs can become quite unrepresentative of current economic values. On the other hand, the accountant's traditional suspicion of appraisal values is not without foundation. Appraisals may be conducted for many purposes and may use different criteria of value—current market value, long-term fair value, physical capacity to serve, and so on. If appraisals were to be used in accounting, the basis of appraisal value would need to be defined. For property, plant, and equipment held for use, the basis presumably should be the reproduction cost of the property less allowance for physical and functional depreciation (i.e., obsolescence). Difficulties in estimating such a depreciated current cost and related conceptual issues are discussed in Chapter 24.

SUMMARY

As with inventory, there are two basic issues in accounting for tangible capital assets—determining the cost of the assets, and finding a basis for recognition of expense as their value is consumed.

Most capital assets are acquired by external purchase. The principal problem for such assets is to make sure that costs incidental to the acquisition are capitalized. When improvements are made to existing assets, there also can be difficulties in differentiating betterments from repairs; these are resolved in accordance with the facts of the case. Self-constructed assets present some conceptual problems with respect to capitalization of overheads and of financing costs during construction. All variable costs of construction including variable overheads should be capitalized, but there is some inconsistency in practice beyond that. Canadian practice accepts that costs of debt financing construction may be capitalized but does not require it. At one time, the amount of financing cost capitalized was restricted to the increase in interest costs incurred during the construction period. An FASB recommendation broadened the basis of capitalization by permitting capitalization of all interest that would be "avoidable" if construction had not taken place.

Measurement of periodic income requires recognition of depreciation expense on a systematic and rational basis over the estimated useful life of all property, plant, and equipment. The amount to be recognized as depreciation over that lifetime (the depreciation base) is the original cost less the expected net salvage proceeds on disposal after deducting any costs of removal.

Depreciation patterns are supposed to recognize expense over an asset's useful life in a "systematic and rational" pattern. Patterns used in practice generally follow some mathematical formula such as the straight-line basis. Accordingly, a depreciation pattern can be said to be "systematic." Unfortunately, it is more difficult to ensure that a pattern is rational. While there are fundamental difficulties relating to the arbitrariness of one-to-many allocations, it seems that the rationality, and consequent information value, of depreciation provisions could be improved substantially by more rigorous attention to the development of consistent estimation bases reflecting management expectations and incorporation of the logical consequences of the time value of money. In practice, entities tend to follow customary depreciation patterns with little attention being paid to conceptual considerations and estimation bases.

Logically, all costs associated with the service of a capital asset should be recognized as expense in a systematic and rational fashion over the asset's useful life. Depreciation accounting, however, normally deals only with the original cost less salvage. Other costs that are associated with plant service but that occur irregularly should be dealt with on a basis compatible with depreciation accounting, if material. A variety of ways exist, for example, to spread the cost of major repairs and renewals over a reasonable period.

In Canada, carrying values of fixed assets can no longer be restated on the basis of appraisals. Restatement on the basis of appraisals is essentially inconsistent with the historical cost model of accounting, just as is LIFO accounting for inventory.

REFERENCES

[1] A CICA recommendation, issued in 1990, defines a "betterment" in terms of the enhancement of a capital assets' service potential. It states that "service potential may be enhanced when there is an increase in the previously assessed physical output or service capacity, associated operating costs are lowered, the life or useful life is extended, or the quality of output is improved." See CICA, "Capital Assets," *CICA Handbook*, Section 3060 (Toronto: CICA), par. 29.

[2] FASB Emerging Issues Task Force, *Capitalization of Costs to Treat Environmental Contamination*, EITF Abstract No. 90-8 (Norwalk: FASB, 1990).

[3] CICA Research Report, *Environmental Costs and Liabilities: Accounting and Financial Reporting Issues* (Toronto: CICA, 1993), chap. 3.

[4] See CICA, "Capital Assets," Section 3060, par. 26. The only other mention of interest capitalization issues in CICA authoritative literature is in an Emerging Issues Committee Abstract that concludes that it is not a generally accepted practice to capitalize interest costs on investments in takeover targets. See CICA Emerging Issues Committee, *Capitalization of Interest Costs on Investments in Potential Takeover Targets*, EIC 12 (Toronto: CICA, 1990).

5 See, for example, R.N. Anthony, *Tell It Like It Was: A Conceptual Framework for Financial Accounting* (Homewood, Ill.: Richard D. Irwin, 1983).

6 American Institute of Accountants, Committee on Accounting Procedure, *Restatement and Revision of Accounting Research Bulletins*, Accounting Research Bulletin No. 43, chap. 9C (New York: AIA, 1953), par. 5.

7 CICA, "Capital Assets," Section 3060, par. 31.

8 E.S. Hendriksen and M.F. van Breda, *Accounting Theory*, 5th ed. (Homewood, Ill: Richard D. Irwin, 1992), p. 528.

9 See, for example, W.H. Beaver, *Financial Reporting: An Accounting Revolution*, 2nd ed. (Englewood Cliffs, N.J.: Prentice-Hall, 1989), pp. 112–16. He observed that, while empirical evidence on depreciation method differences seem consistent with the view that depreciation lacks information value, other efficient-markets research that indicates that accounting income provides a better explanation of stock prices than cash flows (i.e., than income before depreciation and other noncash accruals) could be interpreted otherwise.

10 See, for example, Beaver, *Financial Reporting: An Accounting Revolution*, pp. 98–101.

11 CICA, "Capital Assets," Section 3060, pars. 31–32.

12 For an in-depth discussion of this approach to depreciation accounting within a discounted time-value-of-money perspective, see J.A. Milburn, CICA Research Study, *Incorporating the Time Value of Money Within Financial Accounting* (Toronto: CICA, 1988), chaps. 9–13.

13 The differences between the two approaches are well described in O. Johnson, "Two General Concepts of Depreciation," *Journal of Accounting Research*, Spring 1968, pp. 29–37.

14 One early attempt to estimate typical declines in used asset values is found in Chapter 5 of G. Terborgh, *Realistic Depreciation Policy* (Chicago: Machinery and Allied Products Institute, 1954). A later work is Study No. 7 in the series Studies in Accounting Research of the American Accounting Association, C.R. Beidleman, *Valuation of Used Capital Assets* (AAA, 1973). An examination of used market prices for selected types of equipment in the categories of railroad cars, fork lift trucks and machine tools indicated that: (1) asset useful lives were significantly longer than those customarily used for accounting purposes, (2) salvage could be quite significant in amount, and (3) value tended to drop off in a gentle declining-balance pattern. Significantly, the statistical significance of Beidleman's observations was improved when market prices were deflated by price indexes. It should be remembered, of course, that past results are only a guide to the future. A quickening in the pace of technological advance could be expected to change both asset lives and the rate of decline in asset values.

15 C.W. Lamden, D.L. Gerboth, and T.W. McRae, *Accounting for Depreciable Assets*, Accounting Research Monograph 1 (New York: AICPA, 1975).

16 Canadian Institute of Public Real Estate Companies, *Recommended Accounting Practices for Real Estate Companies* (Toronto: CIPREC, September 1990), Section 512.

17 The use of straight-line depreciation on long-term capital assets that are financed largely by long-term debt gives rise to what has been referred to as the "front-end load" effect. The combination of depreciation and interest expense can result in an essentially profitable

operation reporting losses in early years and increasing profits in later years. This effect has periodically troubled utility rate regulators and others, particularly in times of high borrowing rates. This has been a stimulus for the adoption of sinking fund depreciation in the real estate industry in Canada because real estate rental properties have been typically financed in significant part by long-term debt. For a discussion of the "front-end load" effect in a regulatory environment, see *Pipeline Regulation and Inflation: An Evaluation of Tariff Levelling*, R.M. Morrison and R.J., Shultz, eds. (Montreal: National Energy Board and the Centre for the Study of Regulated Industries, 1983).

18 The constant-return-on-investment assumption is open to question, given that market interest rate "yield curves" contradict it. Under normal market conditions yield curves are a rising function, that is, money invested for a longer term normally commands a higher rate of interest than money invested for a shorter term. The yield curve is constantly changing with changes in capital market conditions, including inflation expectations. Time-value-of-money-adjusted depreciation models could accommodate this additional sophistication, although the calculations would be more complex.

19 For a lucid explanation, See W.T. Baxter, *Depreciation* (London: Sweet & Maxwell, 1971).

20 Literature on this subject includes two articles by Y. Ijiri and R.S. Kaplan, "Probabilistic Depreciation and Its Implications for Group Depreciation," *The Accounting Review*, October 1969, pp. 743–56, and "Sequential Models in Probabilistic Depreciation," *Journal of Accounting Research*, Spring 1970, pp. 34–46. See also F.C. Jen and R.J. Huefner, "Depreciation by Probability-Life," *The Accounting Review*, April 1970, pp. 290–98, and R.A. Friberg, "Probabilistic Depreciation with a Varying Salvage Value," *The Accounting Review*, January 1973, pp. 50–60. Terborgh, *Realistic Depreciation Policy,* chap. 8, identified the problem with an average service life assumption in 1954.

21 AICPA, APB, *Status of Accounting Research Bulletins*, APB Opinion No. 6 (New York: AICPA, 1965), par. 17.

22 The origin of this recommendation may be found in Bulletin No. 11, *Surplus*, issued in 1955 by the Committee on Accounting and Auditing Research of the CICA. That bulletin said, "Unless replacement cost accounting becomes generally acceptable, the writing up of fixed asset values should not occur in ordinary circumstances and should be discouraged. It is recognized that there may be exceptions ... [in enumerated circumstances]."

23 See the biennial surveys published by the CICA under the title *Financial Reporting in Canada* (Toronto).

24 CICA Emerging Issues Committee, *Appraisals*, EIC 6 (Toronto: CICA, 1989 [withdrawn 1994]).

25 CICA, "Capital Assets," Section 3060, par. 18.

26 CICA, "Comprehensive Revaluation of Assets and Liabilities," *CICA Handbook*, Section 1625 (Toronto: CICA).

12

INTANGIBLES

A second category of assets held for use rather than sale may be described under the general title "intangibles." Under this heading we include "deferred charges," specific types of intangibles such as patent rights or franchises, and general intangible value commonly known as "goodwill." The accounting use of the term "intangible assets" is somewhat narrower than one might expect from the ordinary meaning of the words. From their dictionary meaning, for example, we might think that accounts receivable or investments in securities are intangible assets since they have no corporeal existence beyond writing on a piece of paper. In accounting, however, the term intangible asset is generally reserved for assets that contribute to the generation of operating income and excludes financial assets, such as accounts receivable and portfolio investments.

THE NATURE, CLASSIFICATION AND RECOGNITION OF INTANGIBLES

If one accepts the general definition of an asset as any right or condition that carries with it an expectation of future benefit, it is clear that intangibles can be assets just as much as tangibles like inventory or plant and equipment. A patent in a drug company or a brand name in a cosmetic company are as important to the production of revenue as any of the physical assets. Intangibles have assumed much increased importance as service and knowledge-based industry has become a major segment of the Canadian economy. Some of the most significant resources of many modern enterprises are intangible. These intangible resources include skilled employees, technological know-how, licensing agreements, distribution networks, franchises, patents and brand names, among others. Present accounting is criticized in some quarters because financial statements do not recognize most of these resources and make no attempt to reflect their value to the enterprise.[1]

Again, we must go back to the basic principles and premises of the accrual model in order to explain why this is so, and to have a starting point for considering existing accounting standards and practices. As with tangible capital assets, intangibles are to be recognized at their cost to the reporting entity, and the objective is to expense them as they contribute to revenue benefits. The basic issues in accounting for intangibles are as follows:

- Intangibles that have been acquired, or internally developed, at a cost to the reporting entity must be identified, and the costs that are reasonably traceable to them determined.

- It must then be assessed whether these costs can be linked to reasonably assured future benefits, as the basis for determining whether they should be charged to expense in current or future periods.

In order to address these issues, and place them in perspective, it is instructive to examine the nature of intangibles, how they may arise, and how they may be classified within existing accrual accounting.

There are a large number of intangible factors that may enhance an entity's well-being. Table 12-1 sets out typical sources of intangible benefit to an entity. As noted in the second column, certain of these sources may be embodied as separate identifiable intangible assets (franchises, licenses, etc.). The right-hand column lists some activities of an entity that may help to create intangible benefits. These activities entail the incurrence of costs, some of which might be recognized as "deferred cost" assets by a reporting entity. The sources of intangible benefits set out in the left-hand column that are not reflected as specific intangibles or deferred cost assets comprise general "goodwill."

Examination of this table leads to the question: for accounting purposes, which of these intangibles should be classified as deferred charges, which as identifiable intangibles, and

Table 12-1 Intangibles

Source of Intangible Value	Embodiment of Intangibles	Activity Creating Intangibles

Favourable attitudes
  Customer loyalty
  Supplier loyalty
  Employee loyalty
  Good governmental relationship
  Good credit standing
		Advertising
		Circulation promotion
		  (publishers, cable TV)
		Charitable and community
		  activity
		Skilled management
		Successful business operation

Competitive advantage Exclusive rights to do business	Franchises, licences Patents, copyrights, agreements	Lobbying R&D

Desirable products
  Brand recognition
	Trademarks	Marketing, product-launch
		  activities

Technological know-how
  Secret manufacturing processes
  Skilled workforce
		Development activities
		R&D
		Staff training

Going concern value		Organization, start-up activities

which as general goodwill? For example, if institutional advertising builds goodwill, should the asset be classified as deferred advertising or goodwill? If research efforts result in a patentable product, is the asset research cost or patents?

The Concept of Goodwill

One hundred years ago, business goodwill was thought of very much as its name suggests—the advantage to a business of kindly feelings toward it, especially on the part of customers. Originally, goodwill was thought to pertain directly to the personality and skill of the owner. Later it was realized that to a considerable degree goodwill attached to the business itself and represented part of its value that could be realized if the business was sold. In addition, the concept of goodwill tended to broaden beyond that of mere customer loyalty. If goodwill represented a value transferable with the business, it was natural to think of it as comprehending all intangible factors that could lead to profits above those that might normally be expected from investment in the tangible assets of the business.

Recognition that goodwill existed posed a problem for accountants. Were there circumstances in which goodwill should be recognized as an asset of the business? How could it be measured if it was recognized? Once goodwill was defined as representing the totality of intangible factors beneficial to a business, a means of estimating its value became possible. The future level of profitability of the business could be forecast, and then a fair return on the fair value of the tangible assets of the business could be estimated. Subtracting the latter figure from the forecast profits left a figure of excess or "super" profits, which could be presumed to be attributable to intangible goodwill. Discounting these expectations of excess profits (for as long as they could be expected to persist) would yield a present value that could be considered to be the value of goodwill. Of course, such a value estimate is highly subjective.

Even when the balance sheet was thought of as a listing of values, accountants were never predisposed in favour of recording goodwill in the accounts. Recognition of the value of goodwill as it grew would be to take credit for unrealized profit, and, in any event, the method of valuation was very speculative. General acceptance of the transactions-based historical cost system settled the question. Since goodwill could not be associated with an exchange transaction, it could not be recognized.

There is one major exception to that general statement. Whenever one business purchases another, it inevitably pays for any goodwill that may exist, along with other assets. In such a basket purchase of assets the total purchase cost (including the value of liabilities assumed) must be assigned to individual assets acquired to enable subsequent accounting. Accounting standards call for estimation of the fair value of all the identifiable assets acquired, and assignment of the excess of the total purchase price over the sum of such fair values to goodwill. (The opposite case, where the sum of fair values of identifiable assets exceeds the total purchase price, will be discussed later in this chapter.)

The present situation, then, is that goodwill is defined as the summation of all intangible factors that add value to a business, except for identifiable intangibles and deferred charges to be discussed below. However, goodwill as such is not accounted for under the cost-based accrual system except on occasions when it is purchased in a business combination transaction.

Identifiable Intangibles

As the middle column of Table 12-1 illustrates, some aspects of overall intangible value take specific forms. Typically, those specific intangibles are associated with a legal or contractual right. As such, they can often be bought or sold separately from the particular business entity. For example, a company might patent a process and sell the patent to another company for exploitation, perhaps retaining a royalty right. Because such intangibles can be bought, there are occasions when they will be recognized as assets under historical cost accounting, just as is a purchased tangible asset.

There are two inconsistencies in accounting for intangibles: (1) an inconsistency between the treatment of purchased identifiable intangibles and the treatment of internally developed identifiable intangibles, and (2) a possible inconsistency between the treatment of identifiable intangibles acquired in a business combination and those purchased separately.

The first inconsistency may be illustrated by patents. If a valuable patent is purchased from another party its cost will be capitalized, to be amortized over its period of usefulness. If the same patent is developed through internal research efforts, most of the costs of that research are likely to be written off as incurred. (See subsequent discussion of research and development costs.) The explanation for this anomaly is evident. In contrast to the case of self-constructed tangible assets, there is much less certainty that a valuable intangible asset can be created by internal effort, at least until advanced stages of that effort.

CICA Handbook Section 3060 provides that an entity capitalize "directly attributable costs" incurred to construct or develop capital assets, and it defines "capital assets" to include "intangible property" (listing as examples, brand names, copyrights, franchises, licenses, patents, subscription rights and trademarks). This recommendation cannot be expected to result in the capitalization of many significant self-developed intangible property costs, however. In the first place, most costs necessary to the development of an intangible, such as a patent or brand name, will be incurred long before the creation of a valuable asset is sufficiently assured to warrant capitalization. Such costs can be expected to be evaluated for deferral according to their activity—in other words as R&D or advertising costs, etc.—rather than as patent or brand name intangibles. Second, internal costs are rarely directly attributable to the development of intangible property. But the possibility exists in some cases. For example, might some costs of the circulation department of a magazine publisher be directly attributable to the development or betterment of a subscriptions list intangible?

It is to be noted that the IASC also provides for the capitalization of internally generated intangibles under criteria similar to that of the *CICA Handbook*. However, it explicitly rules out recognition of "internally generated brands, mastheads, publishing titles, customer lists and items similar in substance," on the grounds that these cannot be reasonably distinguished "from the cost of developing the business as a whole" (that is, from general goodwill).[2]

The second inconsistency likewise may be traced to practical causes. Accounting standards for business combinations that are accounted for as basket purchases call for the total purchase cost to be allocated among individually identifiable assets, with any excess over the sum of their fair values being reported as goodwill. It can be argued that it is logical that an identifiable intangible asset acquired in a business combination should be recognized on the same basis as one acquired by individual purchase. Implementation of this instruction, however, can encounter practical problems stemming from confusion as to just what is an identifiable intangible. Most businesses do have some patent, franchise, or contract rights that unquestionably have value. But there rarely, if ever, are markets for such highly individual intangible assets. Thus, such assets may not be capable of reliable direct valuation. Neither can the total purchase price for all assets be allocated to individual assets in proportion to their contribution to net cash flows because the attribution of cash flows to individual assets requires a one-to-many allocation that is impossible to make. For these reasons, many purchasers do not make a serious attempt to allocate costs in a business combination to specific intangible assets but rather lump all intangibles under the heading of goodwill.

Others, however, have interpreted the word "identifiable" differently. Some reason that if one can put a name to an intangible factor, that is enough to consider it as identifiable. Thus, "circulation lists" of a publisher or "licences" of a cable TV company may receive all or most of the allocation of cost that otherwise would be described as goodwill. In reality, the essential character of such intangibles may be indistinguishable from that of goodwill—both contribute to the superior earning power of the enterprise.[3] Yet the accounting for them may be different depending upon what they are called.[4] Until 1990, there had been some incentive in Canada for acquirers in business combinations to assign value to specific intangibles as they did not always require amortization while purchased goodwill did. Now all intangibles require amortization, although different rates may be appropriate to different types of intangibles as compared with general goodwill.

Deferred Charges

It often happens that a business incurs material amounts of costs on an irregular basis that are expected to benefit one or more future periods as well as the current period. It has been generally accepted that in some such situations costs may be "deferred" for amortization against future periods of benefit. In a sense, such deferred costs represent identifiable aspects of the composite intangible that is goodwill. They are identifiable by the common sense test that they require a significant expenditure that is reasonably expected to bear fruit in future periods.

Since expectations become progressively less certain of realization as the forecast time span lengthens, deferred charges are almost invariably amortized over a relatively short period. Some accountants may see a distinction between deferred charges and goodwill on this basis. Deferred costs are expected to bring relatively short-term benefits; goodwill is generally more long-lasting. The distinction, however, is not sharply marked.

To sum up the foregoing discussion on the nature of intangibles:

- Many intangible factors may contribute to the earnings and success of the business. The term goodwill is now used in accounting to comprehend the value of all intangible factors favourable to a business (apart from specific identifiable factors).

- Goodwill builds up or declines in value in a business almost insensibly. Certain costs may appear designed to build goodwill—e.g., advertising, some staff training expenses, etc.—but goodwill is likely to be built as much by quality of product and service as by direct outlays. As a practical matter it is impossible to value goodwill objectively in the absence of a sale of the business. It is also impossible to identify all costs that contribute to the development of goodwill and only to goodwill. Accordingly, the cost-based accrual model does not attempt to cost and record goodwill built up internally. If certain cost outlays appear likely to result in future benefits, those costs may be recorded as "deferred charges"—e.g., deferred advertising—but they are not called goodwill because at best they are only a part of the overall goodwill. Goodwill as such is recorded only when purchased as part of the assets of a business acquired.

- Some specific intangibles representing legal or contractual rights may be bought or sold separately—for example patents. In such cases the transaction cost will form the basis for accounting. In a few cases it may be possible to build up internal costs that are directly attributable to developing a specific intangible.

- Specific identifiable intangible factors acquired in a business combination are supposed to be accounted for separately from goodwill. This requirement creates a problem not encountered when a specific intangible is purchased by itself. First, there is the question of what is meant by an identifiable intangible. Second, there is the problem of assigning part of the overall purchase cost to identifiable intangibles when there is no market for such intangibles. For these reasons, present accounting practice for so-called identifiable intangibles is inconsistent and unsatisfactory.

ACCOUNTING FOR RECOGNIZED INTANGIBLES

As with other costs laid out to earn income, two basic questions have to be resolved in accounting for an intangible: What is its cost, and on what basis should it be recognized and written off? These will be covered in the discussion below of individual classes of intangibles.

Deferred Charges

It is not possible to catalogue all the different types of costs incurred for services that may carry intangible benefits over several future periods. The types mentioned below represent those that are commonly considered for deferment, but the comments are not exhaustive.

Advertising

Advertising expenditures, in some industries at least, have a direct relationship to future sales. It is natural, therefore, to consider the deferment of advertising costs for write-off over some period of expected future benefit. In fact, it is acknowledged that for interim financial reporting purposes, a proper portrayal of income may require some spreading of advertising expenses over the fiscal year.[5] Nevertheless, the carryforward of deferred advertising costs at a fiscal year-end has been relatively rare in Canada. In part, that is because the period of future benefit would normally be short and the amounts deferrable relatively immaterial. There may also be a feeling that advertising is a normal cost of business maintenance that should be expensed as incurred. Finally, the period of benefit is uncertain, and the study required to improve estimates of the duration of benefit from advertising may be felt to be not worth the trouble.[6] Cost deferment has tended to occur, therefore, only in relation to relatively expensive programs that are undertaken irregularly—say a new product launch—and then the amortization period will be short.

In the United States the AICPA developed a Statement of Position (SOP) effective from June 1994 which, with one significant exception, requires that all advertising costs be expensed either as the costs are incurred or at the time the advertising first appears.[7] The exception is "direct response" advertising, which is advertising directed to specific potential customers soliciting their orders on particular products or services. An example is a direct mail-order catalogue. The incremental costs of direct response advertising are to be capitalized where a company can demonstrate, using directly equivalent past experience, a clear link between the advertising and sales to customers. The company must maintain documentation that identifies customer orders and the specific advertising that elicited the orders (for example, coded order forms, coupons, phone logs, etc.). These capitalized costs are to be amortized based on the ratio of actual to future estimated revenues attributable to the advertising. This accounting would presumably be acceptable under Canadian GAAP, as it is not in conflict with any authoritative Canadian standard or principle. The SOP also calls for disclosure of advertising costs capitalized and expensed. Only a few companies disclose these costs in Canada.

Product Development

Product development costs are incurred regularly in many industries in significant amounts. Often they are expensed when incurred because they are regarded simply as necessary costs of staying in business. If there is any variation in the level of development costs, however, an entity may wish to follow a policy of deferral and amortization in order to portray income more effectively. In the automobile industry, for example, tooling and development for new models may be accumulated at the time of model change for amortization over the new model production period. Similarly, in other consumer durable industries, major product development costs may be deferred for amortization over product life cycles of varying lengths. Product development costs, as here described, are to be distinguished from development costs of new products (to be discussed subsequently) as that term is used in the phrase "research and development."

Process Improvement

Occasionally a company may undertake a major program that is primarily to make the workflow and handling more efficient, rather than to add new equipment. Since such a program may be costly and undertaken only infrequently, it may be felt that it is proper to spread the cost over several fiscal periods. Any such costs deferred should be restricted to costs directly traceable to the program and should not represent maintenance or repairs deferred from previous years. They should clearly enhance service potential of the existing plant, and not include any costs related to disposing of inefficient plant or otherwise downsizing or rationalizing operations for excess capacity (what some refer to as restructuring costs). These latter costs reflect impairments rather than additions to value and thus should be recognized as expenses or losses in the current period.

The period of amortization of capitalized process improvement costs is likely to be arbitrary, but it is generally acknowledged it should be short in view of the intangible nature of the benefit. A three-year amortization period has been common.

The Emerging Issues Committee has recently taken the position that costs of "business process re-engineering" should be expensed as incurred. Process re-engineering is defined as "the effort to reengineer the entity's business processes to increase efficiency and effectiveness."[8] The EIC abstract goes on to note, however, that costs incurred to acquire or construct property or equipment of a business process re-engineering project, as well as computer software intended for internal use, may be capitalized if the criteria for capitalization in *CICA Handbook* Section 3060 are met. This abstract may seem somewhat circular. However, it may effectively force businesses to expense costs of process improvements except where they are attributable to identifiable tangible or intangible capital assets.

Start-Up Costs

Any enterprise that grows in discrete units will often experience a reasonably well defined set of "start-up" costs with each new unit. For example, a financial institution opening a new branch, a motel chain opening a new motel, and a fast food chain opening a new restaurant may all have a well-developed pattern of promotional activities to start business flowing. As well, they may incur salary and travel costs of an opening project team, costs to recruit and train new staff, and so on. Some but not all enterprises in this position accumulate and defer such start-up costs. The CICA Emerging Issues Committee concluded that pre-operating costs may be deferred if they are related directly to a new facility, would not have been incurred in the absence of its start-up, and are probable of recovery from its future operations.[9] Since the period of benefit is indefinite, the amortization period selected is essentially arbitrary. The Emerging Issues Committee concluded that anything beyond five years would generally be considered excessive.

A different position has been reached in the U.S.. A recent AICPA Statement of Position has concluded that all costs of start-up activities, including organization costs, should be expensed as incurred.[10] This position is reasoned to be consistent with the FASB standard on R&D costs (discussed in a later section of this chapter). Prior to this SOP, some U.S. companies capitalized start-up costs while others expensed them.

Initial Losses

Initial losses are a feature of many project start-ups, as much as special start-up costs. The fact is that when a branch is opened, a new plant constructed, or a new venture undertaken, it often takes some time to reach a profitable level of activity. Moreover, in planning the project such initial losses may well have been allowed for in the project evaluation. In an economic sense, then, start-up period losses might be regarded as part of the investment necessary to get a project up and running. At one time there was some support for deferring start-up losses for write-off against subsequent hoped-for profits, and two or three Canadian companies adopted this practice in the 1960s. The practice did not catch on, however, and it is now generally accepted that deferral of losses, whether start-up or otherwise, is not permissible.

Financing Costs

When an entity raises financing in the form of debt or capital stock, various costs are normally incurred, including legal fees, prospectus costs, commissions to selling agents, and so on. The benefit from these costs is obviously the use of funds obtained through the financing. Costs related to debt financing are deferred and the amortization accomplished, along with that of any discount or premium on the issue, on the "effective-yield" method. That is, interest and amortization expense together are recognized as expense at a constant yield rate on the balance of debt and unamortized costs outstanding.

Issue costs related to capital stock are normally written off against retained earnings or netted against share capital at the time they are incurred. *CICA Handbook* Section 3610 requires that they be treated as capital items, not charged against expense. In the past an acceptable alternative was to carry them unamortized as a deferred asset. This would seem no longer to be accepted, as all intangibles now require amortization (under *CICA Handbook* Section 3060).

Recently a question arose as to the appropriate accounting treatment of "initial offering costs" incurred by closed-end investment funds. Such funds carry their investments on a market value basis. Some of these enterprises had been deferring these costs and in amortizing them either to income or retained earnings. An OSC Staff Accounting Communiqué took issue with this practice. It took the view that such costs should be accounted for as capital transactions, and accordingly, charged directly to retained earnings when incurred since they have no future realizable value.[11] A similar position has been taken in the U.S.[12]

Research and Development (R&D)

There is no better example of a cost incurred for future benefit, nor is there a better example of the difficulty in accounting for intangibles. The difficulties begin with definitions. Research costs are defined for accounting purposes as investigatory costs undertaken in the hope of gaining new scientific or technical knowledge. They include costs up to the stage where new products or processes or significant improvements to existing products and processes are conceived of as being feasible. Development activities are concerned with the translation of ideas into usable results. They include testing and evaluation of alternative possibilities, design, construction and testing of prototypes and pilot plants, and (in Canada but not in the United States) market research delineating the potential market before commercial production. In practice, some difficulty may be experienced in distinguishing between costs of research and costs of development since the activities tend to run into each other.

Costs of R&D are to be determined by approaches that are generally similar to those used in costing inventory—including the allocation of overheads where applicable. In Canada, tangible capital assets and specific intangibles acquired for a single R&D project and with no expected alternative use are to be capitalized. Depreciation written thereon over the life of the project is to be classified as R&D. In the United States, if the capital asset or intangible has no future use beyond the project for which it is acquired, its entire cost is to be classified as R&D upon acquisition.

Historically, views have varied on the appropriate accounting treatment of R&D costs. Income accounting theory calls for their deferment for amortization over periods of presumed future benefit, and a minority of companies followed this practice up through the early 1970s. Many companies did not, however, because they considered the benefits from research costs especially, and from new product or process costs to a degree, to be speculative. If only three projects out of ten will prove successful, many accountants and businessmen have felt that no costs should be carried forward since the odds on any individual project are that it will fail. They have been unimpressed with an argument that all costs may be properly carried forward because it is necessary to try ten projects to get three successes. The unpleasant surprise when losses have to be recognized on large unsuccessful projects would, in their view, outweigh the unpleasantness of regular absorption of costs not related to current income. Even when projects are successful, the appropriate period for amortization and its pattern (declining-balance or straight-line) might be considered little better than educated guesses. Finally, many established companies looked on R&D costs as part of the regular recurring costs of maintaining the business that should be absorbed regularly, much like general and administrative costs.

With this background of generally conservative attitudes, and facing a lack of uniformity in practice, accounting standard setters examined the issues in the 1970s. The FASB espoused the extreme position by requiring that all R&D costs be written off to expense at the time they are incurred.[13] The CICA has been somewhat less conservative in recommending that development costs (but not research costs) be deferred under certain conditions.[14] The conditions are that it be "demonstrated" that the product or process is technologically feasible, the enterprise intends to continue to the stage of selling or using the output, the market for it or use for it is clearly defined, and the enterprise is able to obtain the resources necessary to complete the project.

Thus the CICA has attempted to adhere a little more closely to the theory of income accounting. In practice, however, the tests for deferral of development costs tend to be difficult to meet, with the consequence that not many Canadian companies are deferring significant development costs. In particular, in many cases much of the development activity is directed at establishing technical feasibility and in defining potential markets, and, given the conditions noted above, these costs will not qualify for deferral.

It is necessary to amortize any costs that have been deferred coincident with the start of commercial production, preferably on the basis of projected sales or use of the product or process. Also required is a regular review of the unamortized balance and write-off of any portion deemed not recoverable.

Despite the apparent differences between U.S. and Canadian standards, most costs clearly incurred for future benefit will be charged to expense immediately in both countries. The standards thus properly call for full disclosure of amounts of R&D costs incurred and written off. Ontario Securities Commission experience has been that many Canadian companies that successfully develop new products do not capitalize any of the costs of developing them, and that some companies that do capitalize these costs "appear least likely to be able to satisfy the criteria for deferral."[15]

The issues continue to be debated, and there is increasing dissatisfaction with the existing standards in some quarters. Several academic studies in recent years have provided evidence of a significant relationship between R&D expenditures and subsequent earnings benefits and stock market prices.[16] Some claim that the required expensing of most R&D puts high-tech companies at a disadvantage in competing for capital with, for example, Canadian oil and gas and mining companies, which can capitalize exploration costs on a much more liberal basis.[17] The comparison with oil and gas and mining exploration is not a perfect analogy, however, as the recoverability of exploration costs may be more clearly associated with tangible benefits in the form of provable reserves that have determinable values.

Computer Software Costs

The difficulty in defining cut-off points for determination of costs to be written off and costs to be capitalized is well illustrated by the experience in applying R&D standards to the production of computer software. The problem here is that, although some steps in the production of computer software are like R&D, they also are an integral part of the production of the product.

After extended deliberation the FASB issued a standard to guide practice in 1985.[18] The standard provides decision rules (1) to distinguish costs deemed to be research and development from those deemed to be production costs, and (2) to distinguish between initial production costs to be recorded as a capital asset (and subsequently amortized) and other recurring production costs to be treated as inventory. Costs are to be written off as research and development expense up to the time that technological feasibility is established. The primary indicator of technological feasibility is the completion of detail program design in accordance with product specifications. However, if further development features are high-risk because they incorporate novel or untried functions, the uncertainties must have been resolved by coding and testing beyond the program design stage. It must also be established that the enterprise has the necessary capability to produce the product. In cases where productive plans do not include a detail program design stage, technological feasibility is not considered established until there exists a tested working model consistent with the product design.

After technological feasibility is deemed established, costs of producing the software documentation and training materials are to be capitalized. If the software is to become part of another product or process, however, capitalization is not to begin until that other product or process has emerged from the R&D stage. Capitalization of cost ceases and amortization begins when the product is available for general release. Amortization for a period is to be based upon the ratio of current revenue from the product to the total of current and anticipated future revenue. The figure of amortization is not to be less, however, than a figure arrived at by spreading the unamortized balance of cost equally over the estimated remaining life of the product.

Purchased software acquired for sale or lease is to be accounted for on a basis consistent with internally developed software. That is, if the technological feasibility of the purchased software is not established, the cost must be written off. An exception is made if some or all of the cost of that software may be attributed to an alternative future use. In that case, the appropriate portion of the cost may be capitalized and amortized over the period of use.

The 1985 standard did not address costs incurred for the development of computer software for *internal use*. This was not seen to be a significant issue at that time and most enterprises simply expensed these costs as incurred. However, these costs have grown in significance and diverse practices have developed. An AICPA SOP on accounting for the costs of computer software intended for internal use was issued in 1998.[19] It provides for capitalization from the point when the application development stage, as defined, is reached. It also provides guidance on capitalizable costs.

In Canada computer software costs are accounted for under the general R&D *CICA Handbook* standard. As noted in the previous section, it provides that development costs may not be carried forward unless the product is feasible technically (which is not defined), and also meets tests of market and financial feasibility. A number of Canadian companies have adopted the FASB definition of technological feasibility for computer software, thereby leading to a degree of cross-border harmonization of accounting practice in this area.

There have been some criticisms of the U.S. standard. These have been concerned mainly with the point at which technological feasibility should be considered determinable, whether it may be subject to manipulation depending on how the development process is defined, and whether the line should be drawn at an earlier stage thus allowing for greater deferral of costs.[20]

Development-Stage Companies

The problem of cost deferment is at its most acute in entities that are in a pre-operating stage (including enterprises formed to explore for minerals or oil and gas that have not yet gone into production). Since there is no revenue from operations, it is an elementary observation that all costs are being incurred in the hope of future benefit. Traditional accounting practice in Canada accepted this observation and permitted all costs to be treated as deferred charges (other than costs that could be assigned to specific assets such as capital assets or inventory acquired in anticipation of operations). Any incidental revenue received during the pre-operating period would normally be credited against the single amount carried forward as deferred pre-operating costs. Sometimes this practice has varied (not very logically) by excluding general and administrative costs or interest expense from the deferred pre-operating costs.

The total deferred costs would continue to accumulate (without an effective recoverability test since recoverability is usually virtually impossible to estimate in the pre-operating stage) until the enterprise commenced operations and reached a commercial operating level. It has generally been recognized that there should be a control, however, to the effect that if operations take longer than expected to reach a commercial or profitable level, deferment of net costs should cease and the transition to normal profit and loss accounting should be made.

There are several difficulties with this traditional basis of accounting. The first is the difficulty just mentioned in establishing the transition point from the development-stage accounting to regular income accounting. The second is the problem of disposing of the deferred pre-operating costs. In the mining industry, the exploration and any preliminary development costs are assigned to areas of interest and are written off if and when a decision is made to abandon efforts in the area. (Abandonment may be signalled by allowing claims to lapse, but a write-off of exploration costs may be required before that date since the effective interest in a area may lapse yet claims be maintained in good standing on a purely speculative basis.) A CICA study of mining exploration companies generally favoured carrying such costs forward as assets until there is an intention to abandon the company's interest.[21] Where exploration and development costs in an area are carried through to production, amortization (depletion) begins on a unit-of-production basis. Selection of a unit rate of amortization is usually difficult since mineral reserves may not be adequately delineated at the outset. In companies outside the extractive field, there is neither a basis for write-off of pre-operating costs before production nor any particularly logical basis for amortization after commercial operations commence.

If development-stage accounting is logical at all, it should be logical for major new projects of established operating companies as well as for new companies. There is nothing to stop a going concern from embarking on a new business venture that, if undertaken by an entirely new company, would be accounted for using development-stage accounting. Some going concerns in fact, used to follow accounting equivalent to development-stage accounting when undertaking completely new projects. They must now meet the conditions for deferral of pre-operating costs set out in EIC 27, discussed earlier under the heading "StartUp Costs." (EIC 27 states that it does not deal with accounting issues of an entity that is itself in the development stage.)

In short, it can be said that accounting for ventures in the development stage is shot through with inconsistencies and anomalies and is difficult to fit into the normal income accounting framework. The FASB addressed these inconsistencies shortly after it dealt with research and development costs.[22] In essence, the board decided to eliminate distinctive accounting practice for development-stage enterprises and apply to them the same accounting standards applicable to operating enterprises. Because of the normal inability to establish recoverability of pre-operating costs and because much of the activity of development-stage enterprises consists of raising financial resources, planning, and research and development, the board's decision meant that most costs for such enterprises, except for tangible assets, would be written off when incurred.

In these circumstances, the board called for special disclosure in the financial statements. The statements are to be described as those of an entity in the development stage and are to describe the nature of the development-stage activity. The deficit is to be described as having been accumulated in the development stage. The financial statements are to show separately the cumulative amounts of revenue, expense, etc., since the inception of the enterprise. An analysis of shareholders' equity from inception is to be provided showing, *inter alia,* dates and details of each issue of equity securities, distinguishing those issued for cash and those issued for other consideration, the nature of any noncash consideration, and the basis for assigning dollar amounts to it. In this fashion, the board has avoided the well-nigh impossible task of determining whether costs incurred in the development-stage activities have produced equivalent value so as to justify their asset status.

There is no standard on the subject in Canada, and the range of traditional practices described above has been accepted. Some companies have selectively applied certain aspects of the U.S. standard. Development-stage enterprises are specifically exempted from the CICA R&D standard (see paragraph 3450.01). This lack of guidance and consequential accounting inconsistencies have been a source of significant concern to securities regulators for some years. In response to these concerns, the CICA commissioned a research report, which was completed in 1996.[23] This report recommended accounting parallel to that of the FASB—that is, that enterprises in the development stage should be subject to the same accounting standards of recognition and measurement as operating enterprises. It made some recommendations on how asset impairment standards should be applied to such enterprises, with particular reference to mining exploration companies. It also recommended some special disclosures about enterprises in the development stage and their activities.

At the time this is written, the CICA Accounting Standards Board has indicated its intention to issue (1) an exposure draft proposing to withdraw exclusion of development-stage enterprises from the requirements for accounting R&D costs and pre-operating costs, and (2) an accounting guideline adopting the basic recommendations of the above-noted research report.

Identifiable Intangibles

As already described, identifiable intangibles may be acquired by purchase or developed through internal effort. In general, only directly traceable costs, such as legal fees for patent applications, should be capitalized for self-developed identifiable intangibles.

Amortization of the cost of purchased or internally developed identifiable intangibles should, in theory, take place over their economic life. In some cases, as in patents, the duration of the legal life puts a maximum on the economic life of the asset. The economic life may nevertheless be shorter than the legal life, and amortization should be over a shorter period if past experience with similar assets or other evidence so indicates. In other cases a legal right, such as a licence, may be of short duration, but if the right is renewable without charge and normally without difficulty, the economic life may be longer. Until 1990, generally accepted accounting principles in Canada did not require the amortization of intangible assets with an indefinite life. This was inconsistent with the required amortization of purchased goodwill, and with GAAP in the U.S. where it has been held that no intangible asset has an indefinite life. CICA proposals to require amortization for all specific intangibles were met with opposition, particularly from the communications industry. It argued that the cost of acquired intangibles like customer circulation lists and cable TV licences do not lose value because they are maintained by current expenditures. Amortization would, it claimed, result in a double charge against income. The reply to this is that any existing intangible must be expected to deteriorate over time as, for example, customers on a subscriptions list eventually die or move away. Thus it should be amortized based on this expected attrition. As well, as we observed earlier, *CICA Handbook* Section 3060 provides that internal costs incurred to replace or improve such assets would be capitalized if they are directly attributable to the development of the intangible property. But, as we discussed, the problem with this is that the bulk of costs incurred are likely to be too general to be directly attributable to intangible assets like customer lists, and thus are unlikely to meet the test for capitalization.

In the end the CICA concluded that all intangibles should be amortized. As in the U.S., amortization is generally to be over a maximum of forty years where a shorter life is not indicated.[24] (See discussion in the following section of concerns that forty years is too long a period.)

Goodwill

From the earlier discussion it will be apparent that goodwill is accounted for only in the situation when one entity purchases another. The problem, then, is what to do with the cost of the goodwill purchased. The problem has been debated for more than three-quarters of a century, and no one yet has come up with an answer satisfactory to everyone. There are three main proposals for accounting for goodwill purchased in a business combination. The basis for each and the objections to each are set out briefly below.

- Possibly the simplest approach would be to write off purchased goodwill at the date of acquisition against any surplus account that is available—in most cases retained earnings. The argument for this is that the end result would be consistent with the treatment of internally generated goodwill. The latter is not accounted for (and any cost incurred in generating it is written off). Hence the former should be written off as well. It is sometimes argued, also, that goodwill is not an asset of the entity: the entity cannot manage goodwill or realize upon it by selling it. Rather, goodwill is an asset only to the owners of the enterprise and should be accounted for by them rather than by the entity.[25] The objection to these arguments is that if management of an entity has paid for goodwill in acquiring a going concern business, it has bought it as an asset, and should be accountable for it.[26] If goodwill is not of permanent life, its cost should be recognized as an expense against income. Otherwise the performance of the management will be made to look unduly favourable. A management that builds a business and bears the start-up costs and probable period of losses or low profits will suffer in comparison with a management that buys a business as a going concern with an established level of profitability.

  Also, in common situations the write-off of goodwill against surplus on acquisition will not be practicable, or at the least will be disadvantageous, because the acquirer will not have enough surplus to absorb the write-off or because of the severe effect on its debt/equity ratio.

- A directly opposite approach is to capitalize the cost of purchased goodwill and leave it unamortized unless or until the business to which it is related is sold or the goodwill appears to be losing or have lost its value. The argument for this is that purchased good-will may be expected to be maintained by current operations. Amortizing it against income may thus result in double counting of expense—in incurring the expense to maintain it on top of the goodwill asset amortization. It may be claimed that true account-ability lies in recognizing a write-down charge against income only when there is a real loss in its value. One difficulty with this idea is that the determination of loss of value is likely to be highly judgmental and unreliable. There is the distinct possibility that an entity will discover, too late, that it has a worthless asset on its balance sheet. A related objection stems from the normal expectation that the *original* goodwill acquired in a business combination cannot last forever. Not to amortize purchased goodwill on the grounds that it is being maintained is effectively to substitute internally generated good-will for the purchased goodwill, which is inconsistent with not capitalizing internally gen-erated goodwill in other situations. In addition, management may be tempted to bias the allocation of the purchase price of a business towards goodwill and away from other assets if goodwill does not have to be amortized.

• An intermediate position is that in which goodwill is capitalized upon acquisition but then is amortized over a period deemed appropriate in the circumstances, but with an outside limit. This approach involves acceptance of the proposition that no intangible asset lasts forever. Indeed, if one considers the fact that an acquired business is likely to have made a variety of outlays with future intangible benefit, that the value of those intangible ben-efits is probably reflected in the overall goodwill payment, and that the duration of some of those elements is quite short, a fairly rapid amortization of goodwill would be justi-fied. As a practical matter the period and pattern for amortization is usually likely to be arbitrary. Many entities may be expected to choose to amortize purchased goodwill over the maximum permitted by accounting standards even though common sense may indicate that its economic life will be much shorter in most cases.[27] The chief virtue of this approach may be that it gets a dubious asset off the balance sheet, while a long amortization period tends to ensure that the reported income effect in any one year is min-imized. Securities regulators have expressed concern about overly long amortization periods for goodwill and other intangibles. The Ontario Securities Commission, for example, has indicated that it will challenge companies using forty years, or even shorter periods, to provide evidence that these periods represent a reasonable expectation for use-ful life in their particular circumstances.[28]

As noted, U.S. and Canadian standards require capitalization of purchased goodwill and amortization by the straight-line method over its estimated life, not to exceed forty years. The IASC has recently issued a standard that states that there is a rebuttable assump-tion that goodwill amortization should not exceed twenty years from initial recognition.[29]

Negative Goodwill

Inspection of the earlier display of factors that may be advantageous to a business suggests that a number of factors may be disadvantageous almost as easily as advantageous. For exam-ple, a management may be incompetent rather than efficient. A workforce may be untrained, surly, and uncooperative rather than skilled and hard working. Because of these negative intangible factors, it is as easy for a business to realize less than a normal return on its tangible assets as it is to earn above average returns. Hence it is not inappropriate to think of "negative goodwill" as the summation of all the adverse intangible factors bearing on a business, just as we think of positive goodwill as the summation of favourable factors.

As with positive goodwill, negative goodwill may manifest itself when a business is purchased by another entity. If the situation were considered the mirror image of that of positive goodwill, one would expect that the identifiable assets and liabilities acquired should be recorded at their individual fair values and the difference between the sum of these fair values and the purchase price be recorded as a deferred credit, to be amortized to income over the period during which the adverse factors are expected to persist.

Although this proposed treatment is not illogical, there are two other possibilities. It may be that the purchaser of the business was a good negotiator or was lucky and made a "bargain purchase." That is to say, the acquirer genuinely may have acquired a business with good prospects for less than it was worth. Some might discount this possibility on the grounds that independent parties acting in their own interest are likely to strike a fair price without undue advantages to one side or the other. No doubt this is so in the majority of cases, but any accountant with wide experience will know it is not true universally. True bargain purchases do happen (just as people sometimes pay too much to acquire a business). If it could be proved that a business has been purchased at a bargain, some might argue that the logical treatment would be to take the credit for negative goodwill into income immediately in the period of purchase. This treatment is, of course, inconsistent with the general maxim that an enterprise does not earn profits just by buying assets—i.e. that a purchase transaction establishes the cost of the items acquired.

There is a third possible explanation for negative goodwill: that it results from an overvaluation of the net assets of the business acquired. Valuation of the individual assets of a going concern is a difficult art because many of them are in a semi-manufactured state or in a used condition and there rarely are good markets for such assets from which prices can be derived. Thus the apparent negative goodwill may simply be the amount of asset overvaluation, or liabilities undervaluation. If so, the credit balance might be handled by subtracting it from the valuations placed on the assets, or increasing the valuation of assumed liabilities.

Thus, there are three possible treatments for negative goodwill: (1) treat it as a price allowance because of subnormal profit expectations and bring it into income over the period in which the profits are expected to remain subnormal, (2) treat it as the result of a bargain purchase and credit it to income immediately upon acquisition, or (3) treat it as resulting from valuation errors and deduct it from the estimated fair values of the individual identifiable assets, probably beginning with those for which the valuation is most uncertain.

North American accounting standards for business combinations have chosen the third of these approaches. If the initial valuation of assets of an entity acquired indicates negative goodwill, the CICA recommends that the credit be used to reduce the valuations previously assigned to identifiable nonmonetary assets, allocating the reduction among individual assets according to circumstances.[30] The American standard limits the application of the credit to noncurrent assets (excluding long-term investments in marketable securities) and treats any excess as a deferred credit.[31] These recommendations generally espouse the most conservative procedure. They also tend to limit manipulation of accounting for business combinations since any overvaluation of nonmonetary assets acquired beyond a certain point will be cancelled out by the credit back of negative goodwill. A rigorous application, however, can lead to misleading portrayal of financial position and results of operations in the case of a true bargain purchase. The complete elimination of property, plant, and equipment values, as sometimes occurs, is often indisputably wrong by any sensible judgment. The Canadian practice of taking any further reduction against inventory values has an absurd effect on the cost of sales figure in the next accounting period.

A recent IASC standard has taken a different approach. Negative goodwill (measured as the excess at the date of a business combination of the acquirer's interest in the fair values of the identifiable assets and liabilities over the cost of the acquisition) is to be presented as a deduction from the assets of the consolidated enterprise in the same balance sheet category as positive goodwill. To the extent that it can be reliably identified with future expected losses or expenses in the acquirer's plan for the acquisition, such negative goodwill is to be amortized as these future losses and expenses are recognized. Otherwise, it is to be amortized over the weighted average useful life of the acquired depreciable capital assets, with any excess recognized immediately in income.[32]

SUMMARY

Intangibles do not represent a homogeneous class of asset. To understand the accounting for intangibles it is first necessary to review the types of assets that are accounted for.

- The term "goodwill" may be envisaged to stand for the totality of intangible factors that add value to a business enterprise. It is not a specifically recognizable asset like other assets, but rather an omnibus term embracing a wide variety of beneficial intangible factors.

- In some cases, specific embodiments of intangible value are identifiable because they represent valuable rights, usually legal or contractual, that can be controlled by the entity. Identifiable intangibles such as patents, licences, franchises, royalty agreements, etc. can often be bought and sold, sometimes separately from the business carried on.

- In several other cases, one can be reasonably sure that some fairly well defined expenditure will be repaid by intangible rewards in future, although those rewards are inseparable from the business carried on. Thus, advertising may produce customer loyalty, and costs of opening a new branch or sales outlet may result in building a base of customers. Such assets essentially represent components of overall goodwill.

Certain inconsistencies in the accounting for intangibles result partly from differences in their inherent character, partly from difficulty in measuring their cost, and partly from confusion as to their appropriate classification.

- Overall goodwill is created as much, if not more, by the efficient operation of a business as it is by any identifiable expenditure. Accordingly, the valuation of goodwill created through regular operations is a highly subjective exercise. However, when one business acquires another, part of the purchase consideration inevitably relates to the goodwill of the latter; hence it is not possible to avoid accounting for purchased goodwill.

- Even though the growth of overall goodwill is not accounted for, it is generally accepted that costs incurred to create certain subcomponents of goodwill may be "deferred" for future write-off at a time closer to that when the benefit from the expenditure is received. This practice is more limited by U.S. standards than Canadian.

- While purchase costs of identifiable intangibles that can be separated from a business are capitalized, internal costs to produce a similar specific intangible are unlikely to be capitalized because it is difficult to trace those costs to the intangible right. In one case, that of patent rights, today's accounting standards prohibit capitalization of most of the research and development costs required to produce the ultimate asset.

- Standards for accounting for acquisition of a business require that *identifiable* intangibles acquired with the business be allocated a portion of the cost of purchase, separate from any residual cost attributed to goodwill. Unfortunately, because of the lack of markets for such specialized assets there is rarely objective evidence upon which to base an allocation of cost to them. Thus, in practice there may be little or no allocation to specific intangibles.

- On the other hand, owing to the lack of a rigorous definition of what is an "identifiable" intangible, it is possible in the case of some business purchases to call some or all of the general goodwill of a business acquired by some other name, such as circulation lists, and thereby treat it as an identifiable intangible.

Today's practice with respect to intangibles may be summarized as follows:

- Purchase costs for identifiable intangibles that are bought and sold individually are capitalized. Since 1990, all such costs must be amortized over the expected useful life of the intangible (which may be shorter than its legal existence), or over not more than forty years if the asset is considered to have an indefinite life.

- Certain types of expenditures that clearly carry significant intangible future benefits may be recorded as assets and described as "deferred" costs in the balance sheet. There is no clear basis for differentiating what types of costs should be deferred. Some practices have evolved, and some standards have been developed, for certain types of activities (for example, advertising, R&D, new activity start-up, development-stage companies, and computer software), with some inconsistencies as between these standards and practices. Frequently the period of future benefit from such expenditures is indeterminate. Accordingly, the period over which they are amortized to income may be determined mostly by practice and convention. The period of amortization of deferred costs is usually relatively short.

- When one business acquires another, any cost identified as the cost of purchased goodwill is recorded as an asset and is supposed to be written off over its period of benefit but, in any event, over a period not exceeding forty years. The judgment as to duration of the benefit from purchased goodwill is almost always arbitrary.

- In a business combination, the sum of the fair values of the assets acquired sometimes exceeds the sum of the purchase price paid and liabilities assumed. In different situations there are different possible explanations for the existence of such "negative goodwill." To improve consistency in the accounting, however, the standard approach in North America is to reduce the values that otherwise would be assignable to assets acquired, thereby eliminating the figure of negative goodwill.

REFERENCES

[1] Concerns that current financial reporting provides inadequate information on intangible assets of business enterprises have recently attracted the attention of a number of accounting academics, practitioners and standard setters. See B. Lev, "Announcing the Foundation

of the Intangibles Research Center at the Vincent C. Ross Institute of Accounting Research," *Accounting Horizons*, March 1997, pp. 136–38.

2   IASC, *Intangible Assets*, IAS 38 (London: IASC, 1998), pars. 39–55.

3   An Emerging Issues Committee Abstract provides that an intangible factor should be "separately identifiable" to be treated as a specific intangible asset in a business acquisition. It indicates, as an example, that "where the previous owners of the acquired business have entered into a noncompetition agreement, the benefit of such an agreement should be recognized as an identifiable asset and amortized over a period not exceeding the term of the agreement." See CICA, Emerging Issues Committee, *Costs Incurred on Business Combinations*, EIC 42 (Toronto: CICA, 1992).

4   The debate over the separate valuation of specific intangibles goes back some years. See J.R. Campbell and J.D. Taylor, "Valuation of Elusive Intangibles," *CA Magazine,* May 1972, pp. 39–46, and J.L. Vaughan, Jr., "Give Intangible Assets Useful Life," *Harvard Business Review*, September–October 1972, pp. 127–32. In more recent years the issues are well illustrated by the controversy in the U.S. over whether there is a separately identifiable intangible asset related to commercial banks' core deposits. This has involved the FASB, the SEC, bank regulatory agencies and tax courts. For a discussion of these issues see W.T. Harrison, Jr. and D.P. Hollingsworth, "The Core Deposit Intangible Asset," *Accounting Horizons*, September 1991, pp. 38–49. Tax advantages provide at least part of the motivation for separate accounting for specified intangibles in the U.S.

5   See Accounting Principles Board, *Interim Financial Reporting,* APB Opinion No. 28 (New York: AICPA, 1973), par. 16d.

6   For a contrary view, see D.L. Flesher, *Accounting for Advertising Assets* (University, Miss.: Bureau of Business and Economic Research, School of Business Administration, University of Mississippi, 1979). The author suggests that deferral and amortization of advertising costs could make a material difference to the figures reported where marketing is the major activity of an entity. Methods of estimating the duration of benefit from advertising based on past experience are also described. The methods, however, are not wholly convincing.

7   AICPA, Accounting Standards Executive Committee, *Reporting on Advertising Costs*, Statement of Position 93-7 (New York: AICPA, 1993).

8   CICA Emerging Issues Committee, *Accounting for the Costs of a Business Process Reengineering Project*, EIC 86 (Toronto: CICA, 1998). This abstract was patterned on FASB Emerging Issues Task Force, *Accounting for Costs Incurred in Connection with a Consulting Contract or an Internal Project that Combines Business Process Reengineering and Information Technology Transformation*, EITF 97-13 (Norwalk: FASB, 1997).

9   CICA Emerging Issues Committee, *Revenues and Expenditures During the Pre-operating Period*, EIC 27 (Toronto: CICA, 1991).

10   AICPA, Accounting Standards Executive Committee, *Reporting on the Costs of Start-Up Activities,* Statement of Position 98-5 (New York: AICPA, 1998).

11   Ontario Securities Commission, "Initial Offering Costs of Closed-end Investment Funds," Staff Accounting Communiqué 52-708, in *OSC Bulletin,* December 5, 1997, p. 6414.

[12] Such costs are treated as start-up or organization costs, see AICPA, *Reporting on the Costs of Start-Up Activities,* Statement of Position 98-5 (New York: AICPA, 1998).

[13] FASB, *Accounting for Research and Development Costs,* Statement of Financial Accounting Standards No. 2 (Stamford: FASB, 1974).

[14] CICA, "Research and Development Costs," *CICA Handbook*, Section 3450 (Toronto: CICA). The IASC standard is similar to that of Canada. See IASC, *Intangible Assets,* IAS 38 (London: IASC, 1998), pars. 39–50.

[15] Ontario Securities Commission, Office of the Chief Accountant, "1994/1995 Financial Statement and MD&A Review Program," *OSC Bulletin,* July 7, 1995, p. 3116.

[16] In particular, see T. Sougiannis, "The Accounting Based Valuation of Corporate R&D," *The Accounting Review,* January 1994, pp. 44–68. The author examined reported accounting earnings and R&D expense numbers for a sample of U.S. companies over the period 1975 to 1985. His findings were that, on average, a one dollar increase in R&D expenditures led to a two dollar increase in profits over a seven-year period, and that stock market price effects were consistent with investors acting as if they adjusted accounting earnings to try to undo the immediate expensing of R&D. A further paper put forward empirical evidence that stock market prices did not fully reflect the value of the unbooked assets, raising questions about the full efficiency of stock prices and the possibility of improving the information value of financial statements through improved accounting and disclosure of R&D. See B. Lev and T. Sougiannis, "The Capitalization, Amortization and Value-Relevance of R&D," Paper presented at AAA/FASB Financial Reporting Research Conference, December 3–5, 1992, Harvard University. Another study found a statistically significant decline in "earnings usefulness" (based on a measure of the stock return responsiveness to reported earnings), of companies forced to switch from capitalizing to expensing R&D expenditures at the time FASB Statement 2 went into effect. See M.L. Loudder and B.K. Behn, "Alternative Income Determination Rules and Earnings Usefulness: The Case of R&D Costs," *Contemporary Accounting Research*, Fall 1995, pp. 185–205.

[17] See, for example, B.A. Brennan, "Mind Over Matter," *CA Magazine,* June 1992, pp. 21–24.

[18] See FASB *Accounting for the Costs of Computer Software to Be Sold, Leased, or Otherwise Marketed*, Statement of Financial Accounting Standards No. 86 (Stamford: FASB, 1985).

[19] AICPA Accounting Standards Executive Committee, *Accounting for Costs of Computer Software Developed or Obtained for Internal Use,* Statement of Position 98-1 (New York: AICPA, 1998).

[20] See, for example, T.L. Fox and R.M. Ramsower, "Why FASB 86 Needs Revision," *Journal of Accountancy*, June 1989, pp. 93–98.

[21] CICA Research Study, *Accounting and Financial Reporting By Junior Mining Companies* (Toronto: CICA, 1988), chap. 5.

[22] See FASB *Accounting and Reporting by Development Stage Enterprises,* Statement of Financial Accounting Standards No. 7, (Stamford: FASB, 1975).

[23] CICA Research Report, *Accounting and Reporting for Enterprises in the Development Stage* (Toronto: CICA, 1996).

24 CICA, "Capital Assets," *CICA Handbook*, Section 3060 (Toronto: CICA), par. 32. The U.S. standard is AICPA, APB, *Intangible Assets*, APB Opinion No. 17 (New York: AICPA, 1970), par. 29.

25 See G.R. Catlett and N.O. Olson, *Accounting for Goodwill*, Accounting Research Study No. 10 (New York: AICPA, 1968).

26 For an analysis of the literature with respect to why goodwill is considered to be an asset, see L.T. Johnson and K.R. Petrone, "Is Goodwill an Asset?," *Accounting Horizons*, September 1998, pp. 293–303.

27 The CICA Survey of 200 Canadian public company annual reports indicates that, of 107 companies reporting goodwill in their 1997 financial statements, 35 amortized it over the maximum allowed period of 40 years. C. Byrd and I. Chen, *Financial Reporting in Canada*, 23rd ed. (Toronto: CICA 1998), p. 268.

28 Ontario Securities Commission, Office of the Chief Accountant, "1994/1995 Financial Statement and MD&A Review Program," in *OSC Bulletin,* July 1995, p. 3115.

29 IASC, *Business Combinations,* IAS 22 (London: IASC, Revised 1998), par. 44.

30 CICA, "Business Combinations," *CICA Handbook*, Section 1580 (Toronto: CICA), par. 44.

31 AICPA, APB, *Business Combinations,* APB Opinion No. 16 (New York: AICPA, 1970), par. 87.

32 IASC, *Business Combinations,* IAS 22, pars. 59–64.

Chapter 13

LEASES

From the post-World War II period the practice of leasing capital assets, rather than owning them, has expanded many times over. Several factors have contributed to this growth. As a substitute for ownership, a lease generally provides all of the financing for an asset. Thus a lessee can conserve its equity for the purpose of financing working capital or other assets. A lessor often has a stronger credit rating than a lessee and may be willing to share the benefits of lower financing costs. A lessor may also be able to utilize tax benefits in connection with the property leased, whereas a lessee may not have enough taxable income to do so immediately or may be a nontaxable entity. More generally, modern leases may be designed to divide the various risks, benefits and obligations related to the underlying property between the lessor, lessee and, often other parties, to fit their respective risk preferences, use needs and capabilities. Finally, to the extent that lease financing is "off-balance sheet," lessees have felt their financial position appears stronger, with consequent favourable impact on their credit rating and cost of capital.

Accountants have long felt concern that accounting for leased property in accordance with its legal form might not portray the economic substance of an entity's financial position. More specifically, these have been the concerns:

- Fixed payments due under a lease commitment can be equally onerous to payments due on debt. The essential question is: What is the nature of a liability for accounting purposes? Should the term "liability" for accounting purposes be assumed to include any obligation that requires a fixed series of payments in future?

- A lease contract may be the equivalent of a conditional or installment sale of the asset leased. This is often obvious where the lessee has an option to purchase the asset at the termination of the lease for consideration that is clearly a bargain. It may also be indicated when the lease contains bargain renewal options or where its noncancellable term covers what may reasonably be expected to be the economic life of the asset. If a lease is in substance an asset purchase, failure to show the asset in the balance sheet may conceal the full investment risk of the company and will certainly distort any comparisons of rate of return on assets with other companies. This distortion is compounded by the different accounting for the expenses of leased and purchased assets. Suppose, for example, that an asset having a five-year life with no expected salvage value can be bought for $5,000 or rented for $1,278 a year, payable in advance. (The present value of these five annual payments of $1,278 discounted at 14% is $5,000.) If the asset is bought out of the proceeds of debt bearing interest at 14%, and if depreciation is on the straight-line basis, the first year's ownership cost will be $1,000 in depreciation (an operating expense) and $700 in interest (a financial expense). This contrasts with the rental expense of $1,278 under the lease alternative, which would be reported entirely as an operating expense. Under the ownership alternative the interest expense will decline as the debt is paid off, and thus the total ownership costs will show a declining pattern. The rental expense, however, would remain constant. If, therefore, leasing and purchasing are merely two different ways to get exactly the same thing—the use of the asset over its economic life—the difference in manner of reporting the costs is questionable.

The initial response of the profession to these concerns was to call for expanded disclosure of lease commitments by lessees. In addition, capitalizing the initial present value of the lease payments as an asset and obligation was recommended where it was clearly evident that the lease was in substance a purchase.[1] Practice was slow to accept that recommendation. Preparers of financial statements were reluctant to lose the supposed advantages of off-balance sheet financing. As a result, later accounting standards for lease accounting attempted to be much more specific as to the criteria that mark a lease as being in substance a purchase and sale of property.

The existing *CICA Handbook* standard was issued in 1978.[2] It was based on, and for the most part is consistent with, a much more complex and comprehensive FASB standard issued two years earlier.[3] The U.S. standard has been amended seventeen times and has been the subject of numerous interpretations, technical bulletins and EITF abstracts. The CICA standard has undergone only very minor amendments, although recently leasing issues have been the subject of several EIC abstracts, mostly confirming acceptance of FASB amendments and interpretations. When the *CICA Handbook* is silent or unclear on a particular matter, reference is often made to the FASB material for guidance.

The concept underlying present lease standards—that leases that are in substance purchases and sales of property should be so accounted for—is not the only possible concept. Some accountants have suggested that the purchase-equivalent character of a lease is not the important one in terms of business economics. An entity acquires an asset not for the joys of ownership but rather for the service it will yield. The essential characteristic of a leased asset is its ability to render valuable service, and that is provided (for a limited period) by short-term leases as well as leases that cover the economic life of the property. By this reasoning, then, it would be appropriate to recognize the present value of lease rentals (less any portion of the rentals required to cover lessor services) as an asset and obligation at the inception of all leases. Such an approach would also have the practical merit of avoiding the necessity of spelling out criteria for the identification of leases to be capitalized—criteria that are inevitably difficult to implement.

Lease Accounting Terminology

Under present standards, leases that transfer "substantially all benefits and risks incident to ownership of the property leased" are given the following names:

- From the viewpoint of the lessee such a lease is called a "capital lease."[4]
- From the viewpoint of a lessor who simply buys an asset for the purpose of leasing—that is, an investor in leases—such a lease is called a "direct financing lease."
- From the viewpoint of a lessor who is a manufacturer or dealer in particular types of assets and who uses leases as a medium for disposing of assets for profit, such a lease is called a "sales-type lease."

The three categories will be referred to collectively hereafter as "ownership leases." A lease that does not qualify as an ownership lease is called an "operating lease" by both lessor and lessee.

Several special terms have been defined to facilitate implementation of lease accounting standards. These are described below.

Bargain purchase option This is an option granted to the lessee to purchase the property leased that appears, at the inception of the lease, to be so favourable that its exercise ultimately is reasonably assured.

Contingent rentals These are rentals whose amount is determined by factors other than the passage of time. A definition is provided for contingent rentals because a rental that may or may not have to be paid is not considered sufficiently certain to be included in amounts recorded for lease assets and obligations capitalized in a balance sheet. Contingent rentals may be based on percentages of sales, or intensity of use of the property leased. Lease payments dependent upon factors that are measurable at the inception of the lease, such as the Consumer Price Index or the prime bank lending rate, are to be regarded as a fixed rental based on the index or rate existing at the lease inception. Changes in rentals resulting from subsequent variations in such index or rate are regarded as contingent.[5]

Executory costs These are costs pertaining to the property leased that will be paid in future, such as property taxes, insurance, or costs of cleaning and maintenance. Unless the lessee bears such costs, rentals must cover them, and only the net rental after deduction of such costs, and perhaps a profit element thereon, can be considered payment for use of the property.

Initial direct costs These are costs, such as commissions and legal fees, that are incurred by the lessor at the inception of a lease and are directly traceable to the negotiation and execution of the lease.

Interest rate implicit in the lease This is the discount rate required to be applied to (1) "minimum lease payments" (defined below) excluding any portion attributable to executory costs and profit thereon, and (2) any estimated residual value of the leased property that is not included in minimum lease payments, so that the sum of the discounted present value of these two items is equal to the fair value of the property leased at the inception of the lease.

Lease term This is the noncancellable term of the lease plus further periods for which the terms and conditions of the lease establish reasonable assurance at its inception that the lessee will exercise renewal privileges for those periods. The lease term as defined, however, does not extend beyond the date upon which a bargain purchase option becomes exercisable.

Lessee's incremental borrowing rate This is the hypothetical rate of interest the lessee would have had to pay if it had purchased, rather than leased, the property and borrowed the money necessary to pay for it. For the purpose of estimating that hypothetical rate it is assumed that the debt is repayable over a term similar to that of the lease, and with security to the lender equivalent to that which the lessor possesses under the lease.

Minimum lease payments From the lessee's point of view, minimum lease payments comprise minimum rentals called for by the lease over its term together with (1) any guarantee given by the lessee or a related party of the residual value of the property reverting to the lessor at the end of the lease term, and (2) any penalty payable by the lessee for failure to renew or extend the lease at the end of its term. From the lessor's point of view, minimum lease payments comprise the foregoing plus any guarantee of residual value that is provided by a financially capable third party who is unrelated to both the lessor and lessee.

Criteria for Identification of Ownership Leases

How does one identify a lease that conveys substantially all the benefits and risks incident to ownership? Several criteria are given in the standards.

- If, in all probability, the lessee will ultimately obtain title to the property in accordance with the terms of the lease, it is obviously an ownership lease. That occurs when the lease actually conveys title at the end of the lease term, or when it grants an option to buy the property at some time during the lease that appears to be such a bargain that its exercise is reasonably assured.

- If the lease term is such that the lessee may expect to obtain substantially all of the economic benefits from the property, even though it will not result in transfer of title, the lease is also to be considered an ownership lease. For this purpose, it is suggested that a lease that covers 75% of economic life in terms of elapsed time will usually be considered to convey substantially all of the asset's economic benefits.

- If the lease provides the lessor with assurance of recovery of its investment in the leased property together with some return on investment over and above the recovery, the lease is also to be considered an ownership lease. Such assurance is considered to be provided when the present value of the minimum lease payments at the inception of the lease (excluding any portion of the rentals required to cover "executory costs") equals substantially all (usually taken as 90% or more) of the fair value of the leased property.

The last of these three tests is the most complicated. In order to apply it a lessor must calculate the "interest rate implicit in the lease." The end result of this test is that, for the lessor, a lease may be considered to convey substantially all the benefits and risks of ownership if the present value of the unguaranteed residual value at the lease inception does not exceed 10% of the fair value of the property. The application of the test by the lessee differs from that of the lessor. If the lessee's "incremental borrowing rate" is lower than the interest rate implicit in the lease, or if it is not possible to ascertain or make a reasonable estimate of the rate implicit in the lease, the incremental borrowing rate is used.

It may be noted that, if the first criterion is met, it is unnecessary to consider the other criteria. The latter two tests are applicable only to leases that leave a residual property right to the lessor. Both of the last two criteria are attempting to measure whether the unguaranteed residual right is so significant that the lease should not be considered as a substantial transfer of the risks and rewards to the lessee. If either is met, the lease is to be treated as an ownership lease.

ACCOUNTING FOR OWNERSHIP LEASES

Lessor Accounting

It should be noted first that, for lessor accounting only, a lease must pass two further tests in order to be accounted for as an ownership lease.

- If the lessor has exposure to further costs—for example, by way of guarantee of asset performance or guarantee against obsolescence—that are not collectible from the lessee or others, the amount of such costs must be capable of reasonable estimation so that provision may be made for them in recording income.

- Similarly, the credit risk should be normal in the circumstances so that reasonable allowances for uncollectibility can be made. (This test is puzzling in the sense that the normality of the credit risk is virtually impossible to judge and of doubtful relevance. The equivalent FASB condition is the ordinary revenue collectibility test—that the collectibility of the minimum lease payments is reasonably predictable. This is the interpretation usually given to the CICA test.)

As a result, it is possible that a lease that is treated as a capital lease by the lessee will be treated as an operating lease by the lessor.

Direct Financing Leases

The basic idea in accounting for a direct financing lease is that the lessor is considered to have conveyed the property, except for any residual value retained, to the lessee and to have in its place a receivable from the lessee. Initially the lease asset is recorded at the net investment in the underlying property. (Thus if a lessor bought a piece of equipment for $50,000 and immediately leased it by a direct financing lease, the initial lease asset would be recorded at $50,000, which will be its fair value.) This initial lease asset amount represents the discounted present value of the sum of (1) the minimum lease rentals over the term of the lease less the portion thereof deemed to relate to executory services, and (2) any estimated residual value of the lessor in the property at the end of the lease. The discount rate is the rate that equates these future rentals and estimated residual value cash flows with the initial lease asset amount. The rate is, then, the interest rate implicit in the lease, with one adjustment for initial direct costs to be explained shortly.

Income from a direct financing lease is treated as the equivalent of interest income to be recognized over the lease term so as to yield a constant rate of return on the unamortized balance of the lease asset. In other words, the accounting is simply that of any fixed interest bearing investment, such as an annuity or a long-term bond, accounted for in accordance with the effective interest method.

The application of this accounting must reflect certain special attributes of lease arrangements, however. The most typical of these are discussed below.

- Initial direct costs require particular attention because they are generally recoverable by the lessor from the lease rental payments. The standards provide that such costs should be expensed as incurred and an equal amount of unearned lease income recognized as earned immediately, so as to offset the expense. Obviously, if this is done, the income recognition rate must be reduced accordingly so that there can be recognition of a constant rate of return for the lease term.

- On occasion, a lessor may be entitled to an investment tax credit on the acquisition of the property to be leased. It is accepted that the present value of such credits should be deducted from the fair value of the property in computing the rate of interest implicit in the lease.

- At the inception of the lease, the portion of the net investment attributable to any estimated future residual value accruing to the lessor is that future amount discounted at the income recognition rate. To illustrate, suppose a lease with an eight-year term, an estimated residual value of $10,000, and an implicit interest rate in the lease of 9.7%. In this case, the portion of the initial net investment in the lease attributable to the residual value is the present value of $10,000 at 9.7% for eight years, which is a approximately $4,770. Since the accounting ends up with $10,000 on the books at the end of the lease term, it is obvious that the original amount of $4,770 is "accreted" at the interest rate of 9.7%. The standards require that the estimate of residual value be reviewed regularly and that, if a reduction in the estimate is made, an appropriate adjustment should be made to the net carrying value of the lease so that it will represent the reduced expected residual value discounted at the income recognition rate. An upward adjustment is not to be made, however, reflecting the traditional aversion to recording what may be considered to be contingent gains.

- Where a lessor has the responsibility to pay executory costs, an estimate must be made of the payments to be incurred. If the service giving rise to the executory costs is significant, the lessor should also allow a profit margin thereon on a reasonable basis. The total of the estimated costs and profit margin each period should be deducted from the gross rentals for the purpose of calculating the interest rate implicit in the lease and determining the minimum lease rentals making up the lease asset receivable at the inception of the lease. It is then necessary, subsequently, to split rentals received between the portion to be treated as a reduction of minimum lease payments receivable and the remainder to be treated as service revenue.

In summary, then, apart from the possible recognition of profit in relation to the executory costs, the total income from the lease is attributed to accounting periods on the basis of the calculated constant rate of return, which is consistent with the view of a lease as a financing vehicle. It will be noted that no profit is to be attributed to the effort involved in negotiating the lease or arranging realization of the residual value. That result occurs because the prescribed accounting allows only for the recovery of costs in the treatment of initial direct costs and in the calculation of estimated residual value. This illustrates once again a point made in Chapter 7 on revenue recognition—that when income is earned in different activities undertaken over more than one period, the allocation of income to periods may be arbitrary to some degree.

Income Tax Considerations

Since the constant rate of return is a pretax rate of return, an appropriate income tax charge must be accounted for. Assuming the lessor continues to be taxed on the basis of asset ownership, his actual taxes payable will be considerably affected by the timing of capital cost allowance. It will be necessary, therefore, to use tax allocation accounting to maintain the standard rate of tax expense in relation to the pretax income reported from the lease.

In Canada (but not under U.S. or IASC standards), a different basis of accounting for a lease is also available that takes account, in its approach to income recognition, of the income tax advantages of leasing. The essential concept is that the lessor is interested in after-tax returns. Accordingly, it is more faithful to the economics of leasing to calculate the effective after-tax rate of return on the lease investment and recognize income at that rate rather than use a pretax rate.

On this basis the after-tax cash flows to result from a lease are scheduled out period by period for its term. This involves adjusting the periodic rental and residual value amounts by the income tax that will be payable or recoverable each period based on capital cost allowance deductions to be taken for tax purposes. The after-tax rate of interest implicit in the lease is then determined by equating this after-tax cash flow stream with the initial lease amount. The after-tax lease income for each period is then found by applying this constant after-tax rate to the unamortized balance of the investment. In order to adopt this accounting, the lessor must be reasonably assured of obtaining the capital cost allowances on the leased property and of having enough taxable income to absorb the tax deductions arising from the lease.

Clearly the method using the after-tax rate is a more faithful representation of the economics of the lease. Properly understood, a rate of return is an expression stating the relationship between cash flows and cash investment on a basis allowing for the time value of money. Since an entity's well-being depends upon the return it can retain after tax, the relevant rate of return should not ignore the impact of tax law upon the timing of cash flows.

There is a problem, however, in fitting income recognition based on an after-tax rate of return into an accounting presentation framework that traditionally shows tax expense separate from other revenues and expenses. Moreover, even though the calculation of the after-tax return is based on the net investment in the lease—that is, the net investment after deducting deferred taxes—the *CICA Handbook* specifically requires that deferred taxes be presented separately in the balance sheet. How may this be done? One approach is to gross up the scheduled after-tax return using the standard tax rate. To illustrate this, suppose the after-tax return on a direct financing lease for a period is $4,000, and that the standard income tax rate is 45%. In this case income before tax would be calculated to be ($4,000/0.55) = $7,273 on a pretax basis. Income tax expense would be the difference of $3,273 (which is, of course, 45% of $7,273). This income tax expense figure would be divided between the actual taxes payable and deferred taxes depending on the timing difference effects in the period. It is evident that this calculation of pretax income based on the standard rate is highly artificial, as is the calculation of deferred tax which is dependent upon that pretax figure. It results in an undiscounted deferred tax figure stacked up on a discounted after-tax income amount, with the pretax income figure being the "plug."

An alternative basis of accounting could be developed that would effectively calculate deferred taxes on a discounted basis so as to result in internally consistent pretax and after-tax rates of return. The approach involves determining the constant percent of pretax income that will be sufficient to fund all anticipated tax payments under the lease assuming the after-tax rate of return on the lease. The tax expense recorded in a period will then be that percent of pretax income plus an amount equivalent to interest on the deferred tax balance. On this basis the effective tax rate reported on a direct financing lease will be less than the standard tax rate where the timing of deductions for capital cost allowances is accelerated in the early periods of the lease. This reflects the benefit of being able to defer the payment of taxes on the rental receipts.[6]

As noted, this alternative method calculates deferred taxes on a discounted basis—a practice that is prohibited by the *CICA Handbook*. However, when the lease accounting is based on the use of an after-tax rate of return, it is only consistent in logic that every element in the net investment in the lease, including the deferred taxes, should be reported on a discounted basis. The presentation previously described, under which the figure of undiscounted deferred tax was backed into, is artificial and inconsistent with the economics of the lease.

Sales-Type Leases

Not infrequently the lessor will be the manufacturer of the asset leased (for example an airplane manufacturer) or a wholesaler or retailer (for example, an automobile dealer). In such a case an ownership lease priced at the sales value (fair market value) of the property will exceed its cost to the lessor. The result of such a lease is the effective sale of the property, as well as the provision of financing to the lessee. In a sales-type lease the present value of minimum lease payments (after allowance for executory costs and related profit) is recorded as an asset and credited to sales revenue. The previous carrying value of the property leased, less the present value of any unguaranteed residual value therein, is written off as cost of sales. Thus the initial investment in the lease recorded in the balance sheet consists of the present value of the minimum lease payments and the present value of the unguaranteed residual value, just as in the case of the direct financing lease. The subsequent accounting is exactly the same as for the direct financing lease except that an amount equal to initial direct costs is not transferred from unearned to earned income at the lease inception. The reason is that with sales-type leases initial direct costs are deemed to represent costs that should be set off against profit to be recorded on the sale of the property, rather than against the income subsequently recorded from the lease.

The lessor under both direct financing and sales-type leases discloses in the financial statements the net investment in the leases and finance income therefrom. Disclosure is also to be made of the accounting basis used in recognizing income. If the balance sheet is classified, the current portion of the investment in the lease is classified as a current asset.

Lessee Accounting

The lessee under a capital lease must record the lease as though it had bought an asset and undertaken a debt equal to the purchase price. As noted earlier, the deemed purchase price is the capitalized value of the minimum lease payments less the amount deemed applicable to executory services, determined by discounting them at the lower of the interest rate implicit in the lease (if known to the lessee) and the lessee's incremental borrowing rate.

Depreciation is written on the capital value of the leased asset using the lessee's customary depreciation methods. When the lease is capitalized because it transfers title to the asset, or probably will do so at the end of the lease term, the depreciation period will be the assumed useful life of the asset, consistent with the lessee's depreciation policy for similar owned assets. If the lease is capitalized because it fits either of the other two criteria for capitalization—that is, it covers more than 75% of the estimated economic life of the asset, or the present value of minimum lease payments exceeds 90% of fair value—the asset must be fully amortized over the lease term even though that term is shorter than its estimated useful life. It may be, however, that amortization of the asset need not reduce the asset to zero at the end of the lease term. The minimum lease payments that form the basis of the amount capitalized include the amount of any guarantee of the residual value by the lessee or a related third party. That means that, at the end of the lease term, the accounts will still show a liability for this guarantee. If the asset retains that much residual value to the lessor, the lessee will not be called upon to make good on the guarantee. Hence, amortization of the asset need only reduce its carrying value at the end of the lease term to the estimated residual value; when the lessor realizes the residual value, the lessee can offset the carrying value against the recorded liability for the guarantee.

Rental payments, excluding the portion accounted for as executory costs, will be accounted for partly as interest on the debt obligation and partly as repayment of principal. The interest portion will be calculated at the rate assumed in capitalizing the asset. In this way, the debt will be amortized down to the residual guarantee amount by the rental payments.

Financial statement disclosure is required with respect to assets capitalized under leases and their amortization, in a manner broadly consistent with disclosure given to fixed assets. Disclosure is also required of capitalized lease obligations separate from other long-term obligations and of details of future minimum lease payments for each of the next five years and in aggregate. Where a classified balance sheet is presented, the current portion of long-term lease obligations must be classified among current liabilities.

Operating Leases

In contrast to ownership leases, accounting for operating leases contains few problems. In most cases rentals payable are equal amounts per period over the lease term, and will be accounted for as revenue (by the lessor) and expense (by the lessee) on a straight-line basis consistent with the payment terms. Even if rentals are not constant over the lease, the standards suggest that revenue and expense should be recognized on the straight-line basis unless circumstances indicate that another method is more appropriate. (For example, if the asset's service declines sharply with age, a declining rental would be perfectly logical.)

Initial direct costs incurred by a lessor with respect to an operating lease should be deferred and amortized in proportion to revenue recognition. The lessor must disclose rental income recorded for the year and the cost and accumulated depreciation of property held for leasing. The *CICA Handbook* Section 3065 encourages additional disclosure, such as information as to the amount of contingent rentals received or paid. The FASB standard *requires* all the additional disclosure that is merely suggested by the *CICA Handbook*.

Because of the commitment aspect, lessees disclose future minimum lease payments required on operating leases for each of the next five years and in aggregate (excluding, if desired, leases that are for less than one year at the date of their inception).

PROBLEMS IN LEASE ACCOUNTING

Distinguishing Capital Leases

At best existing lease accounting standards have been only a qualified success. It is clear that most lessees prefer not to recognize the capitalized value of leases in their balance sheet. First, it puts debt on the balance sheet that they fear may be adverse to their credit rating. Second, it tends to require greater charges to income in earlier years of the lease than the straight rental amount. Finally, the more complicated accounting makes work.

If the standards were to say simply that leases should be capitalized where they convey substantially all the benefits and risks of ownership of the property, they would be too vague to be implemented uniformly and, in view of the resistance by financial statement preparers, would be unlikely to achieve their objective. Accordingly, the standards have attempted to lay down quantitative criteria for capitalization. Unfortunately, these criteria simply provide signposts for those who are minded to avoid capitalization of their leases.[7] Many leasing transactions are routinely structured to just fail to meet the criteria for capitalization specified in the standards.[8]

Following are some common interpretations of the criteria used to try to avoid capital lease treatment by lessees.

- A lease may be structured so that significant rental payments meet the definition of "contingent rentals," thus avoiding their inclusion in minimum lease payments for the purpose of computing the 90% test (i.e., the test for capitalization based on the present value of minimum lease payments exceeding 90% of the fair value of the lease property). These "contingent rentals" may be based on levels of asset usage or output that are virtually certain to be achieved, and thus may be the equivalent in substance of minimum lease payments.

- It may be determined that fixed purchase or renewal options are not bargains by reference to prices prevailing at the inception of a lease without any consideration of the likelihood of future price increases to result from inflation during the option period. As an example, a fixed price option to purchase a building at the end of ten years may not be considered a bargain in relation to what a comparable ten year old building is worth currently. But it may be reasonably expected to be a bargain in ten years under even very modest inflationary conditions.

- Minimum lease payments are to be discounted at the lower of the incremental borrowing rate and the rate implicit in the lease, if known by the lessee, in computing the 90% test. Commonly the implicit rate will be the lower of the two. It may, for example, be reduced as a result of tax advantages ceded by the lease to the lessor. In practice, little effort may be made to estimate the implicit rate. Further the incremental borrowing rate selected may include a risk premium that is on the high side of a reasonable range given the security provided by the underlying leased property.

- The CICA standard requires that the lease term assumed in carrying out the tests for capitalization include all periods for which failure to renew would impose a penalty on the lessee that would be sufficiently large to make renewal reasonably assured. No supporting guidance is provided, and, in practice, only prohibitively large monetary penalties may be considered significant enough to warrant concluding that a lease term will be extended. (An addition to the original FASB standard provides a detailed definition of "penalties" and makes it clear that they include any economic detriment that could be suffered by a lessee if the lease is not renewed, including costs to vacate or discontinue use of the leased property, adverse tax consequences, etc., taking into account such factors as the importance of the property to the lessee's business and the availability of comparable replacement property.)[9]

- Partial residual value guarantees by lessees are not risk-weighted, with the result that most of an estimated residual value could be excluded from the minimum lease payments for the purposes of computing the 90% test, even though the lessee may be effectively assuming most of the real risk of loss. As an example, a lessee might guarantee the lessor against loss on the first $2,500 of an estimated residual value of $10,000. This may constitute most of the real risk if there is very little possibility of the residual value of the property falling below $7,500.

This list is far from complete, but is illustrative of the room for interpretation that is available to lessees who are determined to achieve operating lease accounting.[10] The key 90% test is very sensitive to relatively small adjustments in the determination of minimum lease payments, the interest rate used to discount them, and the estimated fair value of the leased property.

It is generally conceded that there can be no clear concept as to what constitutes a lease that is substantially equivalent to ownership of property. A lease will always be different in some respects from outright ownership. Any criteria that attempt to distinguish an ownership lease must draw essentially arbitrary lines, and as a result, will be open to literal interpretation.

As observed earlier, some have questioned whether purchase equivalency is a relevant concept for determining whether a lease asset and obligation should be recognized. A compelling case may be made that it is an outdated concept given developments in modern lease contracting. Many leases for large dollar items (such as airplanes, buildings, trucking fleets, etc.) are highly complex contracts designed to apportion the rights, obligations and risks attaching to capital assets amongst the lessor, lessee and other participating interests. As we have seen, a lease may deal with many rights, risks and responsibilities—including tax benefits, use benefits, residual values, interest and inflation risks, responsibility for the maintenance of production capability through the use period, and even, in some cases, some sharing of the risks and rewards related to the value of the output to be achieved from the use of the underlying property. The modern lease is a very flexible instrument that can be designed in an almost infinite variety of ways to accommodate the lessor, lessee and, in some cases, other parties who participate in assuming certain risks and responsibilities. An enterprise may enter into a lease involving a major productive facility with the object of obtaining only those use rights and assuming only those obligations and risks that it feels are suited to its expertise and financial capabilities. Other rights, risks and obligations may be put to other parties who can assume them more efficiently and economically.

Existing standards, which hold that a lessee has acquired no asset and assumed no liability unless the lease has transferred substantially all of the risks and benefits of ownership related to the underlying leased property, clearly are not in tune with the reality of sophisticated leases that may apportion the risks and benefits in such a way that no party ends up with the substantial ownership of the original asset.

Some propose that the answer is to capitalize all noncancellable leases.[11] They argue that, if a lessee has obtained the right to the use of property in return for a commitment to make fixed payments, it has acquired an asset and assumed a liability, whether or not the lease agreement has passed substantially all the risks and rewards of the underlying property to the lessee. It may also be pointed out that the essential basis for determining the transaction values of these assets and liabilities is well established by existing lease standards, which provide for measuring a capital lease at the present value of expected cash flows set out in the lease contract.[12] It is acknowledged that, if such lease assets do not represent all the risks and rewards of conventional capital asset ownership, it would be important for there to be full disclosure of their essential attributes.

Capitalization, with appropriate description and disclosure, of all material noncancellable leases would clearly be more consistent with the economics. In support of this there is evidence that investors evaluate enterprise equity risk on the basis that debt has been adjusted to capitalize operating leases.[13] Certainly such accounting can be squared with the existing broad concepts of "assets" and "liabilities"—as probable economic benefits/sacrifices to result from past events or transactions. It would also have the advantage of enabling separate accounting for lease assets and lease liabilities, (which can be expected to have equal carrying values only at the commencement of a lease). Finally, it would do away with the need for arbitrary criteria for distinguishing ownership from operating leases, and with all the time and energy spent in attempting to fit leases to those criteria.

On the other hand, while the logic may seem compelling, the capitalization of all non-cancellable leases would not be without problems. To begin with, what exactly is a non-cancellable lease? How should contingent rents and options for renewal be treated? Leases subject to cancellation can also have value, just as lease renewal and purchase options and rights to contingent rents can have value. In addition, should some distinction be made between leases for assets that are actually in place and being used (plant and equipment, etc.) and contracts pertaining to future services (for example, contractual commitments to maintain a leased premises through its useful life in return for fees which may be fixed in amount or may be contingent on future conditions)? As an extension of this question, how would capitalization of non-cancellable leases be reconciled with accounting for other commitments, such as take-or-pay contracts and, perhaps, some types of long-term employment contracts?

In summary, significant issues need to be addressed before an effective general lease capitalization standard could be put in place. A number of authors have put forward the idea, but to date there has been no in-depth study of it.[14]

It is interesting to note that there has been resistance in Europe to any capitalization of leases where legal ownership in the property rests with the lessor. It is argued that, since the North American rules are arbitrary leading to structuring of leases to avoid the rules, they do not lead to comparable, useful financial statements. Better, it is claimed, to treat all leases as operating and instead provide disclosures of information on the characteristics of major leases.[15] The IASC has, however, put in place an accounting standard consistent with the U.S. and Canadian standards.[16]

Other Implementation Issues

A variety of questions come up in the course of lease accounting because of the special circumstances of particular leases or because of changes that can be negotiated in lease agreements after their initiation. The more significant of these questions are dealt with here briefly. It is to be noted that guidance provided in FASB material is generally looked to where a matter is not covered in CICA literature.

Renewals, Modifications, and Terminations of Leases

Renewals, extensions, or changes in the provisions of an existing lease are considered to give rise to a new lease. The classification of that new agreement (as an operating or ownership lease) is established in accordance with the criteria previously explained. When a previous ownership lease is reclassified as an operating lease, the net investment in the lease (in the case of a lessor) or related asset and obligation (in the case of a lessee) are written off. The lessor would also reinstate the leased asset among the recorded tangible assets at the lower of its original cost, fair value, or present carrying amount of the investment in the lease. Thus, the lessor might have to recognize a loss on the lease change. The lessee could show either a loss or gain on write-off of the lease asset and obligation.

Where the classification of an ownership lease does not change, asset and obligation balances related to the original lease are not written off, but rather are adjusted to take account of the new lease provisions in order to be appropriately amortized over the remaining term of the new lease.

The termination of an ownership lease before conclusion of the original agreement is dealt with in the same manner as changes from ownership leases to operating leases. That is, previous balances relating to the lease asset are written off the books, the lessor reinstates the property among his tangible recorded assets, and the net adjustment is carried to income.[17] It may be noted here that FASB instructions for dealing with lease changes are far more comprehensive and complicated than those in the *CICA Handbook*. As a result, practice in Canada may differ in some situations.

Sale or Assignment of Lease Rights or Leased Property by Lessor

When a lessor assigns its interest in an ownership lease or sells the property so leased, accounting for the transaction follows the normal course. When the property leased is sold, the entire net investment in the lease and residual value (if any) is written off against the sales proceeds. When the lease rentals are sold without sale of the property, the write-off against sales proceeds excludes any residual property values on the books. Usually, sale of property that has been leased out on an operating lease would also be treated as a normal sale.

Questions arise in some situations as to whether a transfer of an ownership lease, or property leased out, to other parties is really a sale. If the lessor vendor retains substantial risks of ownership (e.g., by an agreement to reacquire property upon certain events) it is not accounted for as a sale. Instead, the proceeds are recorded as an amount borrowed, and accounted for accordingly.[18] Considerations pertaining to the sale or financing treatment of transfers of receivables ("securitizations") were discussed in Chapter 7, and would apply as well to lessor ownership lease receivables.

Subleases

When a lessee subleases property, it looks upon the sublease agreement as would any lessor and accounts for it in accordance with the approaches already described. The fact that there is a sublease does not affect the lessee's accounting for the obligation it has to the primary lessor. However, when a lease is amended with the participation of the lessor, so that the sublessee becomes the primary obligor, it is reasonable (and the FASB specifically recommends) that the lessee treat the original lease as terminated, and account for any secondary obligation it may retain on the same basis as any other contingency.

Sale-Leaseback Transactions

This involves the sale of a property with the purchaser concurrently leasing the same property back to the seller. Sale-leaseback arrangements have been examined in Chapter 7, in considering situations in which transactions constructed as sales may in substance be debt financings. If a leaseback to the vendor-lessee covers virtually the entire economic life of the property (as it often does), it is evident that the purchaser-lessor does not really have the risks and rewards of the property. Rather, its position is more like that of a lender to the lessee on the security of the property.

If the transaction is considered a sale, the vendor-lessee's accounting requires particular attention. Under current lease standards the lessee accounts for the lease obligation and lease asset following the approaches already described. Because of the uncertainty as to the significance of the sale price, however, the vendor-lessee does not recognize profit or loss on the sale. Instead, the nominal profit or loss is deferred and amortized to income. When the lease is treated as a capital lease it is amortized on the following basis:

- If the lease is for land only, the amortization is on a straight-line basis over the term of the lease. The end result of this accounting is strange and probably unintended by the standard setters. The land sold and leased back is in the possession of the vendor-lessee uninterruptedly. As a result of this accounting, however, by the end of the lease term it has been written up or down by the difference between the ostensible sale price and its prelease carrying value, with the credit or debit going to income over the period of the lease. (This result may cause one to reconsider whether the transaction should have been considered to be a sale in the first place.)

- If the lease covers land and buildings, amortization is proportionate to the depreciation of the buildings.

- If the lease covers other depreciable assets, the amortization is proportionate to their depreciation.

If the lease is treated as an operating lease, the amortization is in proportion to rental payments over the term of the lease. If the leaseback covers only a minor portion of the property sold, specific rules specify that a portion of a gain might immediately be taken into income.[19]

The lessor's accounting in a sale and leaseback transaction contains no modifications of the normal lease accounting rules.

The Leveraged Lease

This is a lease involving three parties—the lessee, the lessor, and a third party financier whose payment comes from the lessee rentals but who has no recourse against the general credit of the lessor for nonpayment. In the United States such an arrangement can be designed to have substantial tax advantages to the lessor. In essence, a U.S. lessor is entitled to credits and capital cost allowance on the leased property for tax purposes that result in greatly accelerated after-tax cash inflows in the early years of the lease. The lessor's net equity in a lease (the lease asset less the nonrecourse debt) rapidly declines in the early years, typically to a negative balance. In later years net cash outflows will occur as increasing tax payments are required. Finally, a net cash inflow may be received on the realization of any residual value in the property.

Separate conventional accounting by the lessor for the pretax rental income on the lease asset, interest on the debt and income tax will typically produce reported losses in the early years of the lease and rising reported profits in later years. The FASB concluded that such accounting results misrepresent the true economics of this arrangement and that it should be accounted for on a combined basis. It requires that the net income to be achieved over the term of the lease (that is, lease income after deducting income tax to be paid and interest on the debt) should be allocated as a constant rate of return on the net investment balance (the lease asset net of the nonrecourse debt) in the periods in which that balance is positive. The investment is to be shown net of the nonrecourse debt on the balance sheet, with an adjustment to break out the deferred income tax balance to meet tax allocation accounting requirements.

The FASB obviously concluded that these leveraged lease arrangements are so unique they justify radical departure from the normal accounting to be followed by lessors under U.S. GAAP. This uniqueness might be questioned. The effects of this particular combination of extensive tax deferral and leverage within a direct financing lease may be quite extreme, but the basic tax and leverage elements are present in some degree in many lease arrangements.

As explained earlier, under Canadian GAAP lessors can adopt an after-tax approach to accounting for finance leases that goes part way towards the FASB accounting. But the treatment of interest on the debt as a reduction of lease income, to be allocated on the basis of the net lease equity when positive, is an extension beyond the provisions of the *CICA Handbook* standard, and is in conflict with accepted principles of accounting for debt and debt interest. Netting nonrecourse debt against the lease asset on the balance sheet is inconsistent with normal standards for offsetting assets and liabilities (as discussed in Chapter 9). This does not mean that the FASB accounting for leveraged leases makes no sense in the circumstances. The unsatisfactory accounting results from following the basic lease standard in this situation are, perhaps, indicative of basic problems with existing lease and tax allocation accounting.

Until the early 1990s, leveraged leases as defined in the U.S. had not been possible in Canada, because the accelerated tax write-offs were not permitted. However, a change in administrative policy by Canadian tax authorities appears to have made such arrangements a viable possibility in some situations. As soon as this became known, questions began to arise as to whether the FASB accounting could be applied in Canada. The CICA Emerging Issues Committee concluded that the FASB accounting is acceptable under Canadian GAAP for leveraged leases meeting all the conditions specified by the FASB standard, except that the investment in a leveraged lease cannot be offset against the related debt on the balance sheet if the conditions required for offsetting (in *CICA Handbook* Section 3860) are not met.[20]

Lease Inducements

A lessor may provide concessions or benefits to a lessee as inducements for the lessee to sign a lease. These may take a variety of forms including an up-front cash payment to the lessee, a rent-free period, reimbursement of the lessee's moving or leasehold improvement costs, or the assumption by the lessor of the lessee's pre-existing lease. GAAP treat such inducements as the equivalent of reduced rent, so that their exchange value should be recognized and systematically allocated over the term of the new lease.[21] Thus any costs incurred by the lessor on behalf of the lessee, such as would arise on the assumption of the lessee's old lease, must be estimated and provided for. The lessee would charge the costs as a loss relating to the old lease, with the credit being spread as a reduction of rent under the new lease. This may require some "what if" estimates by the lessee of the loss that it would have had to bear to terminate a lease or sublet the old premises. The rationale for this accounting is straightforward. The expectation must be that the lessor understands the rental market and will adjust upward the future cash rents to compensate for the estimated costs of inducements provided to a lessee.

Some argue that the costs of terminating an old lease should be treated as an asset in circumstances where a new and better lease arrangement has been achieved. This argument is most commonly heard in times of falling rents, when it may be a wise economic decision to absorb the costs to abandon the remaining term of an old uneconomic lease in order to take advantage of current market conditions to achieve a cheaper longer term lease in perhaps new and improved premises. This argument does not wash on close inspection, however. The loss on the old lease is not a benefit to, or betterment of, the new lease, any more than the unamortized cost of old abandoned plant could be seen as part of the cost of the new and improved plant. The issue arises with respect to operating leases in part because there has been virtually no practice of writing down existing ongoing leases where current market rents for equivalent space are appreciably lower. In theory, proper accounting would recognize the loss on an uneconomic lease when it becomes uneconomic, and not wait until it is abandoned for a new lease.

Accounting for Real Estate Leases

Real estate leases in many cases are more significant to the financial position and results of operations of an entity than any other class of lease. At the same time, they present the most difficulties in following lease accounting standards.

One complication is the separation of any components of the lease that do not represent real estate property. Thus, if equipment is included in property leased, an estimate of the rentals applicable to it must be made, difficult though that may be. These estimated rentals and the equipment leased are accounted for as though they constituted a separate and distinct lease. A second complication lies in the estimate of amounts included in the lease for executory costs. If the latter costs involve significant effort by the lessor, it is reasonable to assume that an allowance for profit should be included in the estimates—that is, the estimate of executory costs should produce a figure equivalent to what the lessee would have to pay to have the services performed by a third party.

Leases of land and buildings together for periods of, say, forty or fifty years also present complications. If title is transferred at the end of the lease, or there is a bargain purchase option, the lessee will account for the lease as an ownership lease. In such a case there must be an allocation of the capitalized value of the asset between the portions attributable to the land and the building in order that depreciation accounting may be based on the latter only. This allocation is made in proportion to the fair values of the two components at the inception of the lease.

When title transfer does not take place at the end of a lease of land and buildings there will often be cases where substantially all the benefits and risks of building ownership have been transferred, but, because of its perpetual life, the same is not true of the land. In such cases there must be some standard approach to classification of the lease. When the fair value of the land is minor in relation to the total fair value of the leased property at the lease inception (the FASB suggests where land value is less than 25% of the whole), the land and building are considered as a single unit for the purpose of classifying the lease, and the economic life of the building is taken as the economic life of the unit. Accordingly, if the lease is classified as an ownership lease the lessee will depreciate the whole asset over the lease term. The lessor will account for the lease as for any other lease involving a single asset.

When the fair value of the land is significant in relation to the total fair value of the leased property at the inception, the two components are considered separately for the purposes of lease classification and accounting. For this purpose, the net rentals are allocated to the two components. This enables classification of the building component of the lease either as ownership or operating lease and accounting for it accordingly. The land component is accounted for as an operating lease. The *CICA Handbook* recommendation is that the net rentals be allocated between land and building components in proportion to their fair values. This is not logical since the rental applicable to the building must cover both return on investment and depreciation of the asset, while the rental applicable to the land need cover a fair return only. The FASB avoids this objection by stipulating that the fair annual rental for the land is to be taken as a product obtained by multiplying its fair value by the lessee's incremental borrowing rate. The remainder of the minimum lease payments is then attributed to the building.[22]

SUMMARY

Leases were traditionally considered to be executory contracts. As such, lease rentals were recognized as revenue or expense only as the lessee used the assets leased, which usually coincided fairly closely with rental payment dates. With the great expansion of the leasing industry doubts began to be expressed that this accounting was satisfactory. While a long-term lease could have much the same economic effect as a purchase of an asset wholly financed by debt, the two transactions might be accounted for very differently.

To avoid this, accounting standards have been developed with the general intent that leases that transfer "substantially all the benefits and risks of ownership" (referred to here as "ownership leases") should be accounted for differently from other "operating leases." The standards have provided criteria for making the distinction between the two types of leases. These have had to be spelled out in quantitative terms to make them workable.

A lessor who has put property out under an ownership lease is considered to have sold the property or at least sold most of the valuable rights inherent in it. Accordingly, lessor accounting is designed to show as an asset not the property itself, but rather the present value of lease rentals receivable (together with any residual property value after the lease expiration). Income accounting follows the approach ordinarily used for interest-bearing investments. This means that the implicit rate of interest provided by the lease rentals must be calculated. That return can be calculated on a pretax or after-tax basis and, in Canada, either rate may be used to govern income recognition, even though the resulting pattern of income over the lease lifetime may be quite different. A lessor who is an investor in ownership leases is said to enter into "direct financing leases." A lessor who is a manufacturer or dealer in the property leased may record a profit when property is rented under an ownership lease; such leases are called "sales-type leases."

A lessee who rents property under an ownership lease (called a "capital lease" in this case) records the present value of the lease rentals as though it were tangible property purchased, financed by debt. Again, an interest rate must be selected to make this calculation, and for this purpose the lessee will use its "incremental borrowing rate," unless it knows the interest rate implicit in the lease and it is lower. Normal depreciation accounting and debt accounting procedures are followed thereafter with respect to the assets and liabilities recorded.

Many technical problems are encountered as a result of changes in leases, subleases, sale and leaseback transactions, "leveraged leases," and so on.

At best, lease accounting standards have been a qualified success. There has been basic resistance to them from those who desire to preserve the presumed advantages of off-balance sheet financing. This is reinforced by the apparent complexity of the lease accounting standards. The decision to restrict capitalization to those leases that are substantially equivalent to ownership forced very detailed rule making upon the standard setters, because "substantially equivalent" is such a fuzzy concept. When rules are detailed and are literally interpreted, it is easy to frustrate their intention by structuring transactions so that they just fail to meet criteria specified in the rules. Lease accounting has suffered from this problem in practice, particularly in the case of real estate leases.

This problem gives rise to consideration of possible alternatives. We observed in Chapter 6 that accrual accounting has evolved beyond recognition based on completed transactions and legal ownership towards a general economic test based on the transfer of rights and benefits, and exposure to associated risks. The modern lease is a very flexible instrument that can be designed to apportion various rights, risks and obligations related to an underlying property among lessee, lessor, and often other participants, such that no one party may end up with the substantial ownership of the original asset. An alternative concept, put forward in the literature, is that all non-cancellable leases should be capitalized – that is, that each of the participant interests should recognize as assets and liabilities the particular rights acquired and obligations assumed as a result of a non-cancellable lease contract. If the essence of an asset lies in the future services it can provide, it may be reasoned that leased rights are just as much an asset as those acquired in the outright purchase of a property, and that the commitment to pay for these rights is just as much a liability. This concept is simpler in its essence than the purchase equivalency concept embodied in today's standards, but would present its own implementation problems. Chief among these would be the problems of measuring the exchange value equivalents of various options, contingent rents, guarantees and residual values that make up the modern lease contract.

REFERENCES

[1]   See recommendations in American Institute of Accountants Committee on Accounting Procedure Bulletin No. 38, *Disclosure of Long-term Leases in Financial Statements of Lessees* (New York: AIA, 1949), subsequently consolidated in Chapter 14 of *Restatement and Revision of Accounting Research Bulletins*, Accounting Research Bulletin No. 43 (New York: AICPA, 1953). See also APB Opinion No. 5, *Reporting of Leases in Financial Statements of Lessee* (New York: AICPA, 1964).

2 CICA, "Leases," *CICA Handbook*, Section 3065 (Toronto: CICA).

3 FASB, *Accounting for Leases*, Statement of Financial Accounting Standards No. 13 (Stamford: FASB, 1976). A codification of FASB pronouncements issued through October 1998 is available. See FASB, *Accounting for Leases: FASB Statement No. 13 as Amended and Interpreted* (Norwalk: FASB, 1998).

4 Outside North America these leases are normally referred to as "finance leases." See IASC, *Leases*, IAS 17 (London: IASC, 1983, Revised 1997), par. 3.

5 This was clarified in CICA Emerging Issues Committee, *Minimum Lease Payments and Contingent Rentals*, EIC 19 (Toronto: CICA, 1990).

6 This approach to lease reporting on an after-tax basis reflects the approach to discounting deferred taxes developed in J.A. Milburn, *Incorporating the Time Value of Money Within Financial Accounting*, CICA Research Study (Toronto: CICA, 1988), chaps. 17–19.

7 Research has shown that some businesses shifted their pattern of asset acquisition from leasing to buying as a result of the introduction of lease capitalization standards. It has also indicated that some leases were renegotiated and that significant numbers of leases have been structured to avoid the necessity of capitalization. See A.R. Abdel-khalik, *The Economic Effects on Lessees of FASB Statement No. 13, Accounting for Leases* (Stamford: FASB, 1981). See also R.F. Selby, "Controlling the Financial Impact of Long-term Leases," *CA Magazine*, May 1979, pp. 28–31; R.F. Selby, "Real Estate Leases: An Accounting Dilemma," *CA Magazine,* October 1980, pp. 53–56; and R. Dieter, "Is Lessee Accounting Working?" *The CPA Journal*, August 1979, pp. 13–19.

8 This does not mean that no leases end up being accounted for as capital leases. A survey of annual reports of 200 public Canadian companies indicated that in 1997, 71 of the companies had at least some capital leases. CICA, *Financial Reporting in Canada 1998*, 23rd ed. (Toronto: CICA, 1998), p. 282.

9 FASB, *Accounting for Leases*, Statement of Financial Accounting Standards No. 98 (Norwalk: FASB, 1988).

10 These and other issues are identified and discussed in CICA Research Report, *Leasing Issues* (Toronto: CICA, 1989).

11 This idea has been put forward for consideration by the "G4+1" working group of standard-setting bodies in Australia, Canada, New Zealand, U.K. and U.S. (the IASC has observer status). See W. McGregor, *Recognition by Lessees of Assets and Liabilities Arising Under Lease Contracts* (Norwalk: FASB, 1996). The suggestion has also been made by the major representative body of financial analysts, the Association for Investment Management and Research (AIMR), *Financial Reporting in the 1990s and Beyond* (Charlottesville, VA: AIMR, 1993).

12 Estimations have been made of the balance sheet and income effects of capitalizing operating leases from note disclosures of operating leases in U.S. company financial statements. See E.A. Imhof, Jr., R.C. Lipe, and D.W. Wright, "Operating Leases: Impact of Constructive Capitalization," *Accounting Horizons*, March 1991, pp. 51–63 and E.A. Imhof, Jr., R.C. Lipe, and D.W. Wright, "Operating Leases: Income Effects of Constructive Capitalization," *Accounting Horizons*, June 1997, pp. 12–32.

13 See K.M. Ely, "Operating Lease Accounting and the Market's Assessment of Equity Risk," *Journal of Accounting Research*, Autumn 1995, pp. 397–415.

14 A discussion of some issues appears in McGregor, *Recognition by Lessees of Assets and Liabilities Arising Under Lease Contracts*, 1996, chap. 4. See also CICA Research Report, *Leasing Issues*, 1989, chap. 12.

15 See, for example, H. Schulz, "Accounting for Lease Contracts: Leaseurope's Perspective," in *World Leasing Yearbook, 1993* (London: Euromoney Publications, 1993), pp. 42–43.

16 IASC, *Leases*, IAS 17 (London: IASC, 1983, Revised 1997).

17 CICA Emerging Issues Committee, *Lessor Accounting for a Lease Cancellation*, EIC 61 (Toronto: CICA, 1995).

18 CICA Emerging Issues Committee, *Seller's Retention of Substantial Risks of Ownership—Application of CICA 3065.61*, EIC 85 (Toronto: CICA, 1998).

19 The FASB rules have been accepted in CICA Emerging Issues Committee, *Accounting for Sales with Leasebacks*, EIC 25 (Toronto: CICA, 1991).

20 CICA Emerging Issues Committee, *Leveraged Leases*, EIC 46 (Toronto: CICA, 1993, Revised 1995).

21 See CICA Emerging Issues Committee, *Accounting for Lease Inducements by the Lessee*, EIC 21 (Toronto: CICA, 1991).

22 This and certain other detailed issues in lease accounting are discussed in R. Brault, N. Chlala, and L. Ménard, "Accounting for Leases: Why Canadian Standards Don't Measure Up," *CA Magazine*, December 1985, pp. 42–51. Some of the issues the authors raised have since been the subject of CICA Emerging Issues Committee abstracts.

EMPLOYEE COMPENSATION—

PENSIONS AND OTHER POST-EMPLOYMENT BENEFITS; STOCK-BASED COMPENSATION

NOTE: This chapter is drafted based on standards existing as of the end of 1998. In March 1999, the CICA replaced its 1987 pension accounting Section 3460 with a significantly changed and more comprehensive standard—"Employee Future Benefits" (*CICA Handbook* Section 3461). The new standard is effective for years beginning on or after January 1, 2000, with earlier adoption encouraged. The 1999 CICA standard is intended to harmonize Canadian GAAP with U.S. GAAP on most major matters relating to accounting and disclosure by employer enterprises for all forms of post-employment benefits. The new CICA standard makes some significant changes to its 1987 standard on pension costs and obligations, and it also covers other post-employment benefits not previously addressed in the *CICA Handbook*. In particular, it covers other retirement benefits such as health care and life insurance, and other post-employment benefits including disability income benefits, severance benefits and compensated absences.

This chapter addresses the development of major theories and issues with reference to the 1987 CICA standard and U.S. standards, with some brief reference to differences with IASC requirements. The chapter does not attempt to analyze the 1999 CICA standard, other than to note in square brackets the major areas of change (which, for the most part, are to adopt developed FASB positions).

We have observed in earlier chapters that a fundamental principle of accrual accounting is that costs should be recognized at the moment when the reporting entity receives the related goods or services. The application of this principle to accruals for vacation pay and retired employees' benefits was briefly discussed in Chapter 8. We will now extend that discussion to address the complex issues involved in accounting for pensions and other post-employment benefits. These will comprise the first part of this chapter.

Pensions and other post-employment benefits are sometimes described as deferred wages because they represent employee remuneration that is paid in periods *after* employees provide their services to the employer. Another form of employee remuneration involves providing benefits to employees in expectation of future employee services. There are some difficult questions as to when, and in some cases whether, a cost of such benefits should be recognized and how it should be measured and allocated to expense. Stock-based compensation is of particular concern in this regard, and is the subject of the second part of this chapter.

PENSIONS AND OTHER POST-EMPLOYMENT BENEFITS

Pension Costs and Obligations

Pension plans adopted by employers are of two broad types: "defined contribution" plans and "defined benefit" plans. Under a defined contribution plan, the amount contributed by the employer is established by a set formula such as a percentage of the employee's salary. The amount accumulated for each employee over the years, together with investment earnings added, provides a fund from which an annuity can be bought at retirement. The amount of the annuity depends on the earnings achieved on contributions before retirement and the rates at which annuities can be bought at retirement. Thus, the employee does not have assurance as to the amount of pension to be received.

In contrast, under a defined benefit plan the employer provides a formula for calculating the pension benefits to be paid after retirement. The formula is usually related to years of service and often also to wage levels while employed. The employer is then expected to provide the promised benefits. Usually regular contributions to a separate pension fund will be required under federal or provincial pension legislation to ensure that money will be available at retirement. Completely unfunded plans are possible, however, for some types of arrangements.

For the most part, defined contribution plans do not present particular accounting problems. If the formula calls for employer contributions on a regular predetermined basis, the expense each period is simply the required contribution with respect to that period. The accounting problems that arise with respect to defined benefit plans will be discussed in the remainder of this part.

There are three dominant types of defined benefit plans, classified according to the formula by which the pension benefits are calculated. "Flat-benefit" plans promise employees a given amount of monthly benefit after retirement for each year of service. "Career-average" plans promise a unit of benefit expressed as a percentage of salary for each year worked. Thus, for service in a particular year an employee earns an annual pension of, say, 2% of salary in that year. Alternatively it could be said that the employee earns a pension of 2% of total earned salary over his or her career, or 2% times average salary during the career times the number of years of service—hence the name "career-average."

Finally, there are plans that base the benefit upon salary in the last year of the employee's service or the average of the last three or five or ten years or perhaps an average of the three or five mostly highly paid years in his or her career. Thus, the benefit formula could be 1.5% of average salary in the last five years of service times the number of years of service. These "best-pay" or "final-pay" plans will be referred to under the latter name hereafter. Final-pay plans were originally devised for executives who might be expected to experience a steep rise in earnings over their careers and who would therefore find a pension based on average career earnings to be much lower than their earnings level just prior to retirement. With the inflationary trends over much of the past thirty years, the same could be said of the pattern of most employees' earnings over their lifetime, and final-pay plans have become much more common.

The Evolution of Pension Accounting

The Nature of an Employer's Obligation for Pensions

If one goes back far enough in history one finds that the grant of a pension was usually a mark of favour by an monarch or nobleman to an artist or other retainer. Favours given can be withdrawn and this *ex gratia* characteristic carried over to pensions when first granted by corporations. Since there was no firm commitment, it was natural that pension payments should be treated as expense on a "pay-as-you-go" basis.

That pensions paid to retired employees are mere acts of beneficence lacks credibility in a business setting. The idea grew that a pension policy adopted by a business should be considered part of the consideration for services of employees—a form of wage that was deferred to the employee's post-retirement years. When pension plan terms came to be included as a subject in collective bargaining, that view could hardly be denied—at least for those plans. It soon came to be recognized that other plans also, at least indirectly, represented a bargain struck between the employees and employers in the market for labour services. Consider a businessperson who has no pension plan hiring clerical help. He or she may well hear a desirable candidate say: "I'd like to work for you but I can't afford to pass up the pension and other benefits I can get from X corporation." If people act in their own best interests, the businessperson has no option but to provide competitive fringe benefits or else pay a higher direct wage.

Even if pensions are regarded as a form of deferred wage explicitly or implicitly bargained with the employees, there remains the question of exactly what is the bargained transaction. It has been customary for many funded pension plans to contain a clause to the effect that the employer is entitled to terminate the plan. In that event the legal liability may be limited to amounts that have been contributed to the pension fund, although legislation in a number of jurisdictions now makes the employer liable for certain minimum amounts if the fund is insufficient. Almost all plans also contain a clause to the effect that an employee's entitlement to receive benefits under the plan formula does not "vest" (i.e., does not become an absolute right) until he or she has put in a prescribed number of years of service. Because of these considerations, accountants with a legalistic bent of mind took one of two positions—that an obligation for pensions should be recognized only to the extent of the employer's legal liability, or that no cost should be recorded until vesting occurs.[1]

Most accountants came to reject these positions, reasoning that, since a pension is regarded as part of employee compensation, it follows that cost should be recognized as the employee puts in service. It may be that some employees will not receive their pensions because their employment is terminated before vesting. But this is a problem in *estimating* the amount of the employer's liability that can be solved on the basis of past experience and judgment, just like the problem of estimating future warranty costs.

The important contribution of accounting standards adopted in the 1960s was the recognition of this point. At that time it was argued that, once adopted, a business could not easily abandon a pension plan. Since accounting assumes a business will continue as a going concern in the absence of evidence to the contrary, it must also be assumed that it will need satisfied employees; hence, its pension arrangements cannot be unilaterally terminated notwithstanding that it may have the technical right to do so.

The Development of Accounting Standards

Until the mid-1960s the interest of accounting authorities had been restricted to the narrow question of the treatment of "past service" costs. When a plan was first adopted it was customary to grant some benefit entitlement to long-service employees in respect of their years of service before the plan came into force. Such "past service" had a cost, and employers normally made supplemental payments into the new pension fund over a period of perhaps ten years to cover that cost. These costs were accorded a variety of treatments ranging from making an immediate change to retained earnings to expensing them as they were paid or funded. In the United States, the Committee on Accounting Procedure of the American Institute of Accountants reasoned that an employer would not voluntarily assume an obligation for past service unless future benefit was expected. Thus, it concluded that the cost should be written off as expense over current and future years when the benefit might be deemed received.[2]

Standards issued in the mid-1960s introduced some order into the accounting for other major issues besides past-service costs.[3] These pronouncements fell far short of solving all the problems, however. In particular, flexibility was allowed in the choice of actuarial methods and assumptions, which allowed numerous inconsistencies in accounting to grow over time.

In considering these standards it is important to understand the role of actuarial science. Accountants have traditionally relied upon actuaries to furnish estimates of pension cost for a period. Actuaries, in turn, developed such estimates primarily to guide the rate or amounts of contributions to be made to funds set up for payment of future benefits. The main concern of actuaries has been that the necessary fund be built up by the time employees retire. It does not matter how much is contributed in a particular year, provided the actuarial costing method used meets the retirement fund objective and the minimum funding requirements of the applicable federal or provincial pension plan regulators. As well, income tax legislation places some limits on excessive employer deductions for funding contributions, and these must also be considered. With these constraints in mind, an actuary works with management to design a pension funding program to best fit an entity's financial capabilities and objectives. Actuaries are not concerned that consistent actuarial cost methods be followed. Hence, actuarial science has not provided a measurement theory that is fully appropriate to meeting the accounting objective of measuring income for a period. In particular, the existence of a wide variety of actuarial costing methods led periodic pension expense figures based on actuarial funding determinations to lack comparability from company to company.

Practice in recognizing pension obligations and periodic pension cost up to the mid-1980s relied almost completely upon the amounts funded as determined by customary actuarial methods, even though it had long been understood that the objective of setting aside assets in a pension fund and that of measuring pension cost for a period are quite different. This situation changed with the introduction of standards in Canada and the United States that took effect in 1987.[4] These two standards are referred to hereafter as the 1987 standards. As will be seen, the FASB standard is more progressive on a number of issues than the 1987 CICA standard. [The new 1999 CICA standard referred to at the beginning of this chapter has adopted the

FASB positions on most of these areas of difference.] The principal features of these 1987stan-dards will be explained in the following section on issues in pension accounting.

Recent Pension Experience

A brief history of pension plans since 1950 helps one understand the issues. In the early 1950s pension plans were costed assuming that investment returns of 3.5% to 4.5% could be achieved. At that time interest yields on Government of Canada securities were around 3 to 3.5%, so that the pension cost interest assumption was closely in tune with current invest-ment yields. Throughout the 1950s and early 1960s interest rates tended to creep up. The result was a tendency for a surplus over obligations to build up in pension plans. These surpluses permitted relatively painless improvements in benefits, including more widespread adoption of final-pay benefit formulas.

Then, in the late 1960s, inflation began to gallop and continued to do so through much of the 1970s. Increases in wage and salary rates meant continuous and strong increases in the amounts of pension obligations under final-pay plans. Investment returns, on the other hand, lagged. Although over the long term the nominal rate of return on investments may tend to increase or decrease so as to remain above the inflation rate, in the short term a significant proportion of fund assets were locked into low yields on fixed-return securities. In addi-tion, inflation tended to depress the market values of both bonds and stocks. Thus, pension funds found themselves with obligations soaring and asset values increasing slowly or even declining, so that huge deficits began to appear in actuarial valuations of final-pay plans. Flat-benefit and career-average plans were in better shape, except that their fixed formula ben-efits began to look inadequate in the face of inflation. Hence there was a tendency to update benefits, and resulting large past service obligations had to be dealt with.

From 1950 on there had been a tendency for actuaries to revise their interest assumptions for valuation purposes following, but lagging behind, changes in market interest rates. In the 1970s that tendency became more marked in the face of huge unfunded positions opening up in plan valuations.

In the first half of the 1980s the picture changed again. The rate of inflation declined and the rate of wage and salary increases for a time fell below the rate of inflation. Interest rates, how-ever, stayed well above the rate of inflation so that funds could achieve rates of return well above the rates assumed for actuarial valuation purposes. In the early 1980s, the typical actu-arial interest rate assumption had increased to the neighbourhood of 6.5%; at the same time, yield rates on Government of Canada long-term bonds were around 15%. The interest rate assump-tion had clearly come adrift from any correspondence with current market conditions. The result was an in-built tendency for large surpluses to appear in successive plan valuations.

These surpluses could, of course, be used to improve pension benefits, and to some extent they were. But employers had always assumed that, alternatively, surpluses could be applied to reduce their future contributions, or could even be withdrawn for use in the busi-ness. The 1987 pension standards presumed that any pension surplus accrues to the benefit of the employer sponsor of a plan, and accordingly provided that it be amortized as a reduc-tion of pension expense. This simply reflected the expectation that an employer's pension obligation is fully defined by the pension contract with employees—so that employees should expect to have no entitlement to surplus assets in an overfunded plan (just as employer sponsors are expected to make up any deficiencies in an underfunded plan).

Employers were in for a shock, however, when beginning in the mid-1980s employees in Canada began to challenge this belief. At the same time several of the larger provincial pension authorities placed moratoriums on the withdrawal of surplus by employers from ongoing plans. Pension authorities did not prohibit companies from drawing down surpluses by reducing their annual contributions, but some companies found that they were severely constrained in their ability to do this by the fine print in the terms of their plans. Thus, the question of entitlement to surplus assets became confused, and several court cases indicated that the answer is likely to turn on the specific provisions of the particular plan and, perhaps, evidence of other related agreements with employees. Curiously, it would appear that the employer's right to pension surpluses has not been similarly challenged in the U.S.

For these and other reasons, many companies began to rethink their pension arrangements in Canada. Some have replaced their defined benefit plans with defined contribution arrangements, thus putting the risks of pension adequacy to employees.[5] Most larger companies have continued their defined benefit plans, but the uncertainties as to surplus entitlement may provide an incentive for them to have their actuaries develop funding assumptions so as to result in contribution levels that minimize the surplus asset cushions in pension plans. The economic downturn in the early 1990s resulted in some companies fully or partially settling or curtailing their plans, giving rise to questions on the determination and recognition of gains and losses.

Issues in Pension Accounting

One observation may help in understanding these issues. Pension cost for a period has traditionally been thought of as a single amount. In reality, it is made up of several components. These may be considered in two groups.

- The first group comprises the basic elements of a pension cost calculation. One must first estimate what benefit payments will be made in the future with respect to members of the plan. Then, since it is agreed that the benefit payments to be made in the future must be discounted, a discount (interest) rate must be selected. Finally some method must be adopted for attributing the total estimated benefits that ultimately will be paid to the periods in which they are earned. The following components of pension expense result:
  - A service cost component—i.e., the present value of benefits considered to be earned by plan members for service during the year. (It would not be unreasonable to restrict the term "pension cost for the period" to this component alone.)
  - The interest cost to be added to the liability for pension benefits previously accrued. This is the selected discount rate multiplied by the accrued liability.
  - In a funded plan, the return on pension fund assets for the year, which is a credit offset against the above two cost components.
- The second group is made up of possible adjustments, as follows:
  - The amount of cost attributed to the year with respect to any plan changes that have granted benefit entitlements to employees for service prior to the changes (known as past service cost).
  - The amount recognized in the year for experience gains and losses or for adjustments resulting from changes in actuarial assumptions.

 – The amortization, required by accounting standards, of any initial unrecognized underfunded or overfunded position outstanding at the time the standards came into effect.
(These are known as "transitional adjustments.")

The pension expense figure for a period, then, is the total of these components.

 The issues will be discussed under the following headings:

* Specification and estimation of future benefit payments
* Attribution of cost to years of service, and the choice of an actuarial cost method (ACM)
* The choice of an interest rate
* Accounting for pension fund investments
* Accounting for experience gains and losses and changes in actuarial assumptions
* Accounting for past-service cost
* Transitional adjustments
* Recognition of a minimum pension liability
* Limits on pension surplus recognition
* Curtailments and settlements of pension obligations; special termination benefits
* Disclosure
* Multiemployer defined benefit plans
* An evaluation.

Specification and Estimation of Future Pension Benefits

The general principle that a liability should be accrued currently for future pension costs
attributable to current employee service raises the question of what future pension amounts
are so attributable. There are three aspects to this question. First, what is the substance of the
pension commitment, and might it go beyond the formula specified in the formal plan?
Second, what future events should be factored into the determination and, in particular,
should future salary levels be projected for a final-pay plan? Third, is some degree of conservatism appropriate in the estimation of the amount of such benefits in view of the uncertainty of the many variables?

 The standard answer to the first of these questions has been that the benefit formula
stated in the pension plan provides the basis for estimating the future liability for service up
to a particular plan valuation date. That answer seems logical on the face of it. If a pension
plan is regarded as a contract for deferred wages, one would think that the terms of the contract must govern the liability.

 It can be observed, however, that employers often amend plans to improve benefits.
When they do, it is quite customary to grant improvements in benefits in respect of past
service. Not infrequently, improvements in benefits are extended to plan members who
have already retired. How can benefit improvements attributed to past service be explained?
There are two possible answers. The first is that even though the benefit improvement is
calculated by reference to past service, it really is given as part of the consideration for
future service. The second is that there is an unwritten understanding between employer
and employees—a sort of implied contract—that when plan benefits are improved there
will be no discrimination between members' service before and after the date of the amend-

ment. As an example, is it unreasonable that an employee might expect, and the employer might feel some obligation to grant, an increase in a pension that has been severely eroded by inflation? In fact, surveys have indicated that a majority of employers have increased pensions to retired employees in inflationary conditions (although normally by a percentage that is below the rate of inflation).[6]

The essential question is: If pension entitlements represent deferred wages, what is the employees' and employer's understanding of the entitlement involved? The pension plan provides a formula expressed in nominal dollars. But perhaps there is an understanding as well that the employer will supplement the pension if needed so that it will really perform its function of supporting the employee's living standard after retirement. If so, that future sacrifice on the part of the employer is actually attributable to the service of the employee while employed, and should be allowed for in the accrual at that time. The trouble is, of course, that there is no clear and unequivocal commitment on the part of the employer to maintain the purchasing power of pension income. Clearly, accounting for unstated moral obligations is very difficult—any assumption as to what an individual employer will do in future, in the absence of a contractual or statutory obligation, can be very much a guess.

Probably because of this uncertainty, the 1987 accounting standards took the position that the plan formula ordinarily is the basis for estimating pension benefits earned at a valuation date. The FASB standard acknowledges the possibility that an employer may have a commitment to future amendments (as evidenced by a past history of making such amendments). If so, the accounting is to be based on that substantive commitment and its existence and nature is to be disclosed.[7] The CICA standard could be interpreted to allow the same accounting. It defined a pension plan as any arrangement "contractual or otherwise." The reference to "otherwise" could permit accruals for future benefit improvements based on evidence similar to that suggested by the FASB. However, the wording of these standards does not seem strong enough to force recognition of probable future amendments, even though a plan has a regular history of amendments.

The second question (what future events should be factored into the liability estimate?) was discussed in respect of accrued liabilities generally in Chapter 8. It was suggested there that an accrued liability should assume the continuation to the future of conditions existing at the date of the accrual (for example, assume the continuation of current interest rates and general levels of inflation implicit in those rates), while the effects of future changes from existing conditions (future changes in interest rates, tax rates, etc.) are most appropriately reflected as events of the future periods in which they occur. It was noted, however, that this is not a clearly defined or agreed upon principle. One major issue of this type in pension accounting is whether future salary levels should be projected for final-pay plans, and the above suggested principle would seem open to different interpretations. On the one hand, it could be argued that the accrued pension liability should be calculated based on employee salary levels at the time of the accrual (i.e., with no projection), on the grounds that future increases in salaries are independent future events. This answer is troubling from a practical standpoint because it results in significantly skewing pension expense towards the final years of an employee's service. As an example, if an employee in a final-pay plan retires after thirty-five years of service and receives a salary increase in the last year, the current service component of pension expense in the final year could increase by a factor of thirty-five times the effect of the salary increment. A conceptual argument for projecting future salary levels could be that one should assume a continuation of past promotions and inflation adjustments based on current economic conditions.[8]

The issue of whether or not to project future salary levels for final-pay plans has been hotly debated over the years. The 1987 standards ended up prescribing the use of projected benefit methods for both career average and final-pay plans. It is not clear why it was considered logical to require salary projection for career-average plans since the career-average formula has no reference to future salary levels.

The third question centres on the estimation problem and whether a degree of conservatism is appropriate. In order to calculate future benefits payable to pension plan members, estimates must be made of a number of variables. Mortality in the employee group must be estimated. Some estimate must also be made of the ages at which employees will choose to retire. Withdrawals before retirement from causes other than death, such as employee disability or resignation, must be estimated. Withdrawals must also be separately characterized as between those that occur before vesting and after vesting. Salary escalation must be estimated for final-pay plans. All these estimates are customarily known as "actuarial assumptions." (The interest rate used to discount estimated future payments is also customarily referred to as an actuarial assumption. However, since it is different in character and purpose from other actuarial assumptions, it will be discussed under a separate heading below.)

Actuarial assumptions differ in nature, one from another. The fundamental assumption of mortality rates and the assumption of disability rates depend largely on physical constraints inherent in human beings and on the physical environment. Experience over time and observation of trends enable quite reliable long-term predictions. Assumptions as to retirement ages are less reliable, being dependent on social trends and conditions specific to the employer that may change from time to time. Assumptions of turnover in employment are likewise affected, but to a greater degree, by both these factors. The actuary can look to experience in the past in the particular workforce, but cannot be confident that the future will be similar to the past. Even less certainty can be felt about the so-called economic assumptions. These include the assumption of salary escalation required when actuarial cost methods incorporating salary projection are used, and the several assumptions required to predict the level of governmental pensions where plan benefits are integrated with government benefits.

It is generally thought that actuaries have tended to err on the conservative side in their assumptions.[9] The 1987 standards stated that for accounting measurement purposes each assumption is to be a "best estimate" of the most likely future result. The standards give few specifics, however, as to how to determine best estimates. The assumptions are described as reflecting management's judgment. Although, no doubt, management will rely on actuarial advice, the final responsibility is management's.

Attribution of Cost to Years of Service

The objective is to attribute the cost of future retirement benefits to the years in which the employee renders the service that gives rise to the benefits. The first task is to define the service period. For most retirement plans an employee may be considered to be earning his or her pension from the date of hire to the date of retirement. However, there are some plans where credit for service may not begin until after the date of hire, and in some cases an employee may have earned full entitlement to retirement benefits prior to retirement. The 1987 CICA standard was silent on this issue, presuming attribution to the full working life of an employee. [The 1999 CICA standard contains complex provisions for determining the attribution period.]

The next task is to allocate the expected full obligation to individual years within the attribution period. To derive a pension cost attributable to employee service in a given period, there must be some way of assessing how much of the full pension obligation at retirement is attributable to work done in that particular year. In straight mathematical terms, there are a great many possible ways to assign a discounted amount to periods so that it will accumulate with interest to the full estimated liability at employee retirement dates. Actuaries have developed a variety of standard patterns for the allocation of future costs to service years, usually known as "actuarial valuation methods" (ACMs). Some common ACMs used in calculating the current service cost component of pension expense (also known as "normal cost") are described below.

- One family of ACMs is called *"accrued benefit" methods* (also known as "unit credit" or "single premium" methods). The basic idea underlying this family is that benefits earned to date by employees can be derived from the plan benefit formula. Those accrued benefits can be valued at their discounted present value at the financial reporting date, and the increase in that accrued liability over the period is the pension cost to be allocated to the period.

  The first method in the accrued benefit family of methods, known as the "accumulated benefit" method, is based directly on current entitlements under the pension formula. For example, in a career-average plan, the pension entitlement might increase by 2% of the current year's salary each year. Thus the pension cost for the year is simply the present value of a pension of 2% of the year's salary, taking into account mortality probabilities, withdrawal before vesting, etc.

  Two methods in the accrued benefit family depart from strict adherence to rights currently earned under the pension formula. Both methods "project" the change in earned entitlement amounts that will occur in future as a result of increases in salary before retirement. Then those projected entitlement amounts (less allowances for decrements) are allocated to years of service on one of two bases. An equal amount may be assigned to each year of service or, an amount may be assigned based on the proportion that the current year's salary is of the anticipated career salary. The method by which the projected benefit is allocated evenly over years of service (before discounting) is known as the "projected benefit method prorated on services" and the other as the "projected benefit method prorated on salaries."

- A second family of ACMs is known as *"level contribution" methods*. (A common actuarial description for this family is "projected benefit" or "level premium" methods. They are *not*, however, the same as the "projected methods" just described.) The level contribution family of methods does not go through the step of finding an amount of benefits deemed to be earned or accrued at a financial reporting date and valuing that obligation. Rather, it takes the estimated benefit to be earned over an employee's career and spreads the discounted cost thereof over the service period, as a level cost for each year or as a level percentage of salary. Various actuarial approaches within this family of methods are known as "entry age normal," "individual level premium," "attained age normal," and "aggregate."

The choice of ACM can have a significant effect on the amount of pension liability and periodic pension expense recorded. It can be generalized that, as long as there are some plan members who have not yet retired, the accumulated liability determined under a level contribution approach will always be higher than that under an accrued benefit approach (given the use of the same interest assumption). This follows from the fact that level contribution ACMs charge more to expense in the early years of an employee's career so that other ACMs must always be in a position of needing to catch up.

The question is: Is one method more rational than another for the purpose of measuring income? Or might it be that different ACMs are appropriate for different types of plans? The answer seems straightforward for flat benefit and career-average plans, because the benefit entitlement earned by an employee or employee group for a given year's service is unequivocally determinable from estimates that are directly derived from the pension formula. Actuarial assumptions are required as to future events that will affect the ultimate benefit payouts, but the cost for any year is the discounted present value of the best estimates of those future payouts. This reasoning leads to the use of the accumulated benefit ACM (the pure form of the accrued benefit family of methods) for both the flat-benefit plan and the career-average plan. In spite of the "career-average" name given to the latter type of plan, its formula actually gives a specific discrete benefit (e.g., 2% of the current year's salary) for each year of service.

The treatment of the final-pay plan is more debatable. If it is determined that future salary levels should be projected (see discussion in the preceding section), then the choice comes down to one of the accrued benefit with projection methods or one of the level contribution methods. While some argue that there is an appealing logic underlying the accrued benefit approach, others hold the view that a number of methods may be equally defensible in reasonably allocating pension cost to periods of employee service. They argue that level contribution ACMs are as good as any other, and that the level percentage of payroll method is intuitively appealing.[10]

The 1987 standards have prescribed the use of the accumulated benefit ACM for flat-benefit plans and the projected benefit method prorated on services for career-average and final-pay plans. The fact that the plan formula is relied upon to provide the unit of benefit to be attributed to each year of service was influential in this decision. As noted earlier, there does not seem to be any logic, other than conservatism, in requiring salary projection for career-average plans.

The Choice of Interest Rate

Actuaries have tended to think of the interest assumption as an assumption of what monies set aside in the pension fund can earn over the long term. This thinking is tied into the funding objective that has traditionally been the main concern of actuaries. They have had no independent theory as to the interest assumption applicable to an *unfunded* pension obligation, but merely a general (and sound) conviction that obligations not payable until the future are less burdensome than obligations payable currently.

In estimating the future rate of return on investments, actuaries have traditionally taken a long view. Pension obligations stretch far into the future. The funds required to meet those obligations will come partly from assets on hand, but also very largely from reinvestment of earnings. Thus, the discount rate assumed depends only in part on the apparent rate of return on existing pension fund assets. To a considerable degree it depends on the returns available on funds that will be reinvested in future, which is very largely a guess. For these reasons actuaries have traditionally used an interest assumption considered to be representative of long-term rates of return, and have expected to change it only infrequently. Stability in the interest assumption has practical advantages, since it tends to stabilize the employer's contributions to the pension fund with respect to the current service of employees.

But the actuarial approach conceals an economic fact that is important to accounting. If the benefit earned in a year is a fixed dollar amount determined by the pension formula, the real cost *does* vary from year to year depending on the level of interest rates. The variation in real cost could easily be seen if an employer followed a practice of buying deferred annuities to cover each employee's pension entitlement as it was earned. The cost of the annuities bought each year would vary directly with current interest rates available in the marketplace.

As well, since the estimates of long-run rates of return must be subjective judgments, it should be no surprise that, historically, there have been wide variations in the interest assumptions used by actuaries for different plans. Although some of the disparity might be attributed to different yields on assets held by different plans, such differences do not provide a complete explanation. In addition, from around 1970 onward, changes in the interest assumption became much more common, even though the rate was supposed to be long-term. The frequency of changes was no doubt largely in response to the increased volatility of interest rates. Thus, acceptance of the actuary's long-run interest assumption has meant acceptance of the effects of periodic, subjectively determined, changes in the rates. As a result, figures of pension expense and unfunded obligation (where reported) were not comparable between companies and were inconsistent between years within a single company.

The effects of variability in interest rate selection and of changes in rates can be very significant. There is a long-standing actuarial rule of thumb that a change of 1% in the interest assumption will change the expense recognized for a typical plan population in the neighbourhood of 20% to 25%. This percentage might be about a third lower for plans valued under the accrued benefit method. In final-pay plans, changes in the interest assumption might well be accompanied by an offsetting change in the salary escalation assumption. If so, the impact of the interest rate change would be cut roughly in half. (The offset is not complete because a change in the salary escalation adjustment only applies up to employees' retirement dates, while a change in the interest assumption affects the calculations after retirement as well.)

The FASB made a radical break with past tradition in SFAS No. 87. It introduced two interest rate assumptions in place of the traditional assumption of one long-term rate. First, the discount rate to be used in valuing the obligation and calculating the interest expense related to that obligation is to be a best estimate of the interest rate that would be implicit in the price of annuities purchased to settle the obligation if such annuities were purchased at the valuation date. That is to say, the rate is a current rate and may be expected to vary from one annual valuation date to another. Second, there is to be a determination of an expected long-term rate of return on plan assets. That rate of return is to be applied to a "market-related" valuation of plan assets to determine the investment earnings component of pension cost in the next reporting period. Certain accounting consequences of this change in interest rate treatment are important.

- The valuation of the accrued pension obligation and the current-service cost component of periodic pension cost are more volatile than under previous accounting practice because of the regular re-estimation of the current interest rate obtainable for settlement of the obligation.

- The interest cost component of periodic pension cost will also be affected. However, in this case the volatility will be dampened by the effect of changes in the interest assumption on the valuation of the obligation. The higher the rate, the lower the value of the obligation, and vice versa. Thus, if the interest assumption is raised, the higher rate will be applied to a lower obligation figure.

- Because the expected rate of return on assets is supposed to be a long-term rate one might expect that it will be changed infrequently. If a stable rate of return were applied to pension fund assets valued at market value, the volatility in market values of assets from year to year would also introduce a corresponding volatility into the investment return component of periodic pension cost. To reduce this effect, the FASB decided that "market-related" values of assets shall be used for this purpose, rather than fair values at the valuation date. The meaning of the term "market-related" will be discussed in the following section on accounting for pension fund investments.

The interest rate used to discount the pension obligation ideally should be estimated by ascertaining interest rates implicit in current prices for annuity contracts that could settle the obligation. Alternatively, annuity rates may be estimated by looking to returns currently available on high-quality fixed-income investments over the term to maturity of the obligation. Such rates may be reasoned to be consistent with the goal of basing assumptions on best estimates, since they reflect efficient market expectations with respect to *general* interest risk factors. They will not, however, necessarily reflect the *specific risks* of a particular employer's pension obligations—for example, the default risk of the underfunded plan of an overextended employer, or the risk of adverse deviation assumed by the employer (i.e., the risk that actual pension benefit payments will exceed the estimates). Issues related to the estimation of specific risk factors are in need of study.

In practice, it appears that at least some U.S. companies may not have been very rigorous in applying the settlement rate requirement, and were not adjusting their discount rates to reflect current interest rate conditions. Several years ago when interest rates fell significantly, one would have expected that a realistic application of the FASB current settlement rate requirement would have produced significant increases in accrued pension obligation figures (the result of discounting estimated future pension payments at a lower interest rate), with consequent increases in the current service cost component of pension expense and the incurrence of experience losses. The SEC challenged a number of companies that seemed not to have appropriately adjusted their pension discount rates. It has made it clear that, when the general level of interest rates rises or declines, it expects the pension obligation discount rate to be appropriately adjusted.

The CICA 1987 standard parted company with the FASB in dealing with the interest assumption. The intent of the CICA standard seemed to be to cling to the traditional actuarial approach. Although it called for assumptions reflecting management's best estimates, it stated: "The assumptions would take into account the actual experience of the plan and, in recognition of the long-term nature of the plan, expected long-term future events, without giving undue weight to recent experience." [11] That description sounds very much like the traditional actuarial approach to the choice of interest rate. [12] In practice, however, the *CICA Handbook* section's best estimates assumption requirement has been interpreted to be sufficiently general to permit either a traditional long-run or settlement rate basis. [13] [The 1999 CICA standard has now adopted a similar position to that of the FASB.]

Accounting for Pension Fund Investments

When a plan is funded, the accepted accounting treatment for the employer is to net the pension fund assets against the accrued pension obligation, and to reduce pension expense by a measure of the return on pension fund assets. The thinking in support of this treatment is that the pension fund assets are held as a separate trust apart from the employer's business to be managed on behalf of the plan members. One might infer from this accounting treatment that the funding liquidates the liability of the employer or that right of setoff exists (as discussed in Chapter 9). But neither is the case. In the normal course the employer retains the residual responsibility for the payment of the benefits. The assets set aside in the fund will be applied to meet that responsibility, but if they are lost or the fund makes a lower return than expected, the employer makes up the difference.

Because of this effect on the financial position of the employer, there is a strong argument that the gross pension obligation and the pension fund assets should both be displayed in the balance sheet of the employer.[14] In this way, the full liability for which the employer enterprise is ultimately responsible would be clearly disclosed, and the pension fund assets for which it bears the ultimate risk (and shares the rewards) would be displayed also.[15] A segregation of the assets and obligations to indicate the dedication of the former to the latter would, of course, be desirable.

While there is sense in this broad presentation, accounting standards continue to accept the traditional net approach to the determination of employer pension cost and liabilities. Nevertheless, in order to make the pension expense determination, we must examine the separate parts and how they relate to each other. At issue here then is the valuation of the pension fund assets that is used in determining the investment return component of pension expense.

We must first emphasize the need for compatibility between the valuation of pension fund assets and the valuation of the pension plan obligation. This may be illustrated by a hypothetical case. Suppose it is estimated that the portion of a plan's obligations maturing twenty years hence will amount to $100,000. Suppose high-quality zero coupon bonds are held with a principal amount receivable in twenty years of $100,000. The position, thus, is completely in balance. As long as the estimated obligation remains unchanged and the bonds are still held, it will remain so. Suppose further that the bonds have just been acquired at a cost of $21,455—that is, on an 8% yield basis—and that the obligation has been discounted at 8% as well, so that the current valuations correctly reflect the fully funded position. Now consider how the fund assets and obligations are to be valued at the next valuation date. In the normal course the valuation of the obligation will be accreted at 8% to amount to $23,171 because it is one year closer to maturity. But suppose also that interest rates have fallen from 8% to 6% in the intervening period. If the discount rate is dropped to 6% the obligation will now be valued at $31,185. But if the bonds held are valued at amortized cost they will only amount to $23,171, and the valuation will show a net experience loss of $8,014. To avoid this result the bonds need to be valued at current market price rather than amortized cost. Since bonds sell on a yield basis their current market value should have appreciated to the $31,185 figure.

The lesson is that if pension obligations are discounted at current interest rates, the correct basis of valuation for interest-bearing investments will be current market value. The connection is less direct for investments that do not carry fixed interest rates. Nevertheless, the fair market value for such investments will adjust for interest rate changes according to the nature of their future cash flows. Thus the valuation of all forms of investment at current market value is quite appropriate if liabilities are valued at current interest rates.

What if pension obligations are discounted at long-term average rates of return rather than at interest rates current at the valuation date? In such a case, a valuation of pension fund assets at current market values would be inconsistent, but the appropriate alternative is not obvious. Presumably the assets should be stated at a figure consistent with the long-term yield expected to be obtained from them. For a portfolio of fixed-interest securities, the traditional accounting basis of amortized cost or the "deferral and amortization" approach (see discussion in Chapter 17) could be considered appropriate. For equity securities, the objective would be a carrying value that reflects the expected long-term return (with such return including anticipated capital gains). But this would seem more in the nature of a subjective forecast than a measure of value. A compromise that retains some tie to actual experience is to value such securities at a moving average of market values over a recent period of years. If there is a long-term trend in the prices of securities held, such a moving average will give it some recognition, with a lag determined by the length of the averaging period.

The 1987 CICA standard called for the use of "market-related values" for pension fund assets. That term was defined to allow either current market value (or an approximation thereto when market prices are not available) or a value that is adjusted to market over a period not to exceed five years.

Once the market-related values of pension fund assets at the beginning and end of a period are determined, total investment income (that is dividend and interest income plus the market-related value determination of unrealized gains less losses) can be computed. One might expect that this investment income would be treated as the investment return component of pension expense. This is, after all, the accounting measure of the actual return earned on the assets in the period. Instead, as noted earlier, the investment return component of pension expense is determined by applying the assumed long-run rate of return to the opening market-related value of fund assets as adjusted for contributions and withdrawals of funds during the period. This may be envisaged as a normalized expected return. The difference between this and the accounting measure of the actual investment return is treated as an experience gain or loss, which is deferred and amortized to future periods as explained in the following subsection. Some argue, with good reason, that this results in an unnecessary smoothing that serves to distort actual net pension expense.[16]

The FASB standard has taken a somewhat different approach. The pension obligation is to be revalued at current interest rates each year. This suggests that pension fund assets should be valued at market value at the same date, and, in fact, they are so valued for the purpose of measuring the fund surplus or deficiency at the valuation date. However, the return on investment component of pension cost is to be based on an assumed long-term rate of return applied to market-related values of the assets. To reconcile the use of current values in the valuation position and of market-related values for income measurement purposes, the FASB has determined that the difference between the actual return on fund assets and the investment return component of periodic pension cost shall be treated as an experience gain or loss, recognition of which is delayed. The FASB compromise is an uneasy one. The FASB believes that current fair values of fund assets are more relevant than any other possible basis of valuation, but it has been unwilling to extend that belief into a requirement that the investment return component of pension expense reflect the unrealized gains and losses that result from valuation at fair value. [The 1999 CICA standard has adopted the FASB position.]

Accounting for Experience Gains and Losses and Changes in Actuarial Assumptions

Actuarial assumptions represent estimates of what the experience will be on average with respect to the various factors affecting pension costs, not what experience will be in any given short period. Some assumptions (especially the economic assumptions) are little more than educated guesses based on past experience, and could prove to be substantially in error over the whole period required to discharge the pension obligations to an existing employee group. For these reasons any valuation of pension plan liabilities and assets will show differences between their actual amounts at the valuation date and the amounts they would have been had the assumptions proved to be exactly fulfilled in the period since the last valuation. These differences are known as "experience gains and losses."

All actuarial assumptions are tentative. It is not surprising, therefore, that they may be changed. The result, of course, is an increase or decrease in the calculated value of the plan obligations, and consequently an increase or decrease in plan surplus or deficit. Assumptions might be different for the future than for the past and yet both be well founded. Alternatively, changes in assumptions may result from the fact that previous assumptions have not been borne out by experience. It might seem desirable that the effects of a change to correct inappropriate assumptions of the past should be absorbed as quickly as possible. The whole matter is so nebulous, however, that both the CICA and the FASB have decided there need be no distinction between the treatment of changes in actuarial assumptions and of experience gains or losses.

The 1987 CICA standard took the straightforward but arbitrary position that experience gains and losses and the effect of changes in actuarial assumptions shall be amortized to income over the expected average remaining service life of the employee group, which will usually be in the range of ten to twenty years. The standard suggested that a shorter amortization period may be appropriate in some circumstances, but gave no clue as to what those circumstances could be.

The FASB standard requires amortization only if experience gains or losses exceed 10% of the greater of the accrued pension obligation and the market-related value of plan assets. If an excess exists, amortization is to begin based on the average remaining service period of active plan members. This corridor formula establishes a minimum only. An enterprise is permitted to use any consistently followed systematic method of amortization, except that the minimum amount calculated under the corridor formula must be recognized in any year that it exceeds the systematic amortization amount. [The 1999 CICA standard has adopted this accounting.]

Some are highly critical of any deferral of experience gains and losses. They argue that, since actuarial assumptions are supposed to be best estimates and the latest actuarial evaluation should provide the best data, any experience gain or loss should be recognized as part of the pension cost immediately it is determined. They ask, what information value can there be in these deferrals and arbitrary amortization? The FASB itself expressed the belief that it would be preferable conceptually for there to be no delay in recognizing experience gain or losses, but it concluded that this would be too great a change from past practice.[17]

On the other hand, a plausible case may be put forward for not recognizing variances from subjective best estimates of future long-term pension payments where the variances fall within a tolerable probability range. Realistically, the best that can be done is to develop estimates that are within a range of reasonably possible outcomes. It may be argued that it follows from this that accounting standards should accept some reasonable range of experience differences from best estimates without requiring adjustment of current pension expense. To require that such differences be immediately reflected in income could be viewed as introducing artificial fluctuations and distortions. Differences within a reasonable range of estimation variability might then be carried forward without amortization, or they might be gradually absorbed into income over a sufficiently long period that they will have no material effect in any one year. Thus either the FASB 10% corridor approach or the more conservative 1987 CICA approach of long-term amortization may be justifiable under this argument. In logic, however, it seems difficult to justify anything other than immediate recognition of differences outside the zone of reasonable estimation variance. Disclosure of the obligation value based on best estimates, the accepted estimation variance, and the amount of unamortized experience differences would be highly desirable.

Accounting for Past-Service Cost

When a pension plan is initially adopted, or when a plan is amended to improve benefits, it is customary to award some entitlement to benefits to members at the time of the adoption or amendment, based on their service previous to that date. Thus, no further performance is required from such employees to earn those benefits. The proper accounting for such "past-service" benefits has been a matter of considerable debate. Should a liability be recorded with respect to the benefit entitlements granted, or at least the vested portion thereof, at the date of grant? How should the cost of past-service benefits be matched to accounting periods?

The answer to the question whether liability recognition is required at the date of adoption or amendment logically rests upon the accepted accounting definition of a liability. Some argue that the liability should be recognized because it represents a probable future sacrifice attributable to past transactions or events, the event in this case being the employer's grant of the past-service entitlement.[18] Others question this, noting that entities regularly sign contracts that call for future payments but do not record the liability until there is performance by the other party. Has there been performance in the case of the grant of past-service benefits? The fact that the benefit is calculated on the basis of *past* service suggests that performance has occurred and the liability should be recognized. The same logic might dictate that the cost be written off immediately. The opposing argument is that past service, in spite of its name, is really granted with respect to the future service of the employee group. If the expense should be recognized in future, it is argued that the liability accrual need not be recognized until then.

The 1987 CICA standard accepted the latter position. The FASB position straddles the two arguments. The FASB pension standard holds that when a plan amendment grants past-service, the employees have performed all the services required to be entitled to benefits. Therefore, there is a substantive liability. But it also believes that employers obtain future economic benefits from such plan amendments. In other words, by granting past service benefits the employer has bought an intangible asset akin to goodwill. The FASB, however, decided to continue the past practice of accruing past service as an expense and a liability over the assumed future period to be benefited. While the FASB does not require recognition of a liability for past service and a corresponding intangible asset at the time of a plan introduction or amendment, under certain conditions (to be discussed subsequently) a minimum liability is to be recognized with respect to all the unfunded obligations of the plan. The obligation for past service is a factor in the calculation of that minimum liability. [The CICA 1999 standard has *not* been changed to require any recognition of a minimum liability and offsetting intangible asset for past-service cost.]

Obviously, if the cost of past-service benefits is attributed to future service periods, it remains necessary to decide over how many periods the cost should be recognized. The "future economic benefits" to the employer are thought to stem chiefly from the incentive effect of plan amendments upon the employee. Logically the cost recognition period should relate to the length of time in which the incentive effect of the plan adoption or amendment persists. Unfortunately, there is no available evidence as to the typical duration of the incentive or as to how it diminishes with time.

The 1987 standards suggest that it is reasonable to relate the past-service cost associated with a plan initiation or amendment to the remaining service life of the employee group covered at the time of the initiation or amendment. The standards differ somewhat in their recommendations as to how this might be done. The FASB method prescribes minimum amortization reflecting the estimated service lives of active employees to the dates when they are fully eligible for pension benefits. This will be a declining pattern since the number of existing employees remaining with the company can be expected to decline over time. To reduce computations, however, the FASB is prepared to accept any consistently applied amortization method that absorbs the cost of the past service more rapidly.

The CICA 1987 standard called for amortization of the past-service cost in a "rational and systematic" manner over an appropriate period, normally the expected *average* remaining service life of the employee group. This is more conservative than the FASB in the sense that the average remaining service life will be shorter than the full remaining service period of existing employees, although as noted, the FASB permits faster amortization. [The 1999 CICA standard has been harmonized with that of the FASB.]

In addition, CICA and FASB standards contemplate that there may be circumstances, such as a history of regular plan amendments, that indicate that the period of economic benefit from an amendment is shorter than the remaining service life of an employee group. In these circumstances, amortization ought to be accelerated. In practice few employers have adopted shorter amortization periods.

For most plans the average remaining service life will fall in the range of ten to twenty years. Such a period seems likely to be far longer than the period over which the motivational impact of most plan amendments could ever be expected to last.

A wholly different interpretation of past service from that taken by the CICA and FASB standards could be put forward. This has its roots in the suggestion noted earlier that the substantive plan may be different from the formal pension contract, and more specifically, that an employer may recognize a constructive obligation to amend the plan in future to help maintain its purchasing power in the event of inflation. It has been noted that many employers have a record of regularly making such amendments. If this broader perspective is taken, then an employer's best estimate of most likely pension payments should build in future improvements to pensions to reflect future inflation expectations. Then, except in respect of fundamental changes in a plan, if past-service adjustments differ from expectations, they are in essence experience gains or losses. Under this approach deferral of unexpected past-service adjustments resulting from ongoing improvements would not have to be premised on the dubious expectation that they have long-term benefit to future periods.

Transitional Adjustments

Ordinarily, when a change in accounting basis is made, it is desirable to make a retroactive adjustment to results previously reported in order to show trends in the figures on the new basis of accounting. It was considered impractical to insist on this for pension accounting. Accordingly, the 1987 standards adopted a compromise. The amounts of the pension obligation and of the plan assets were required to be calculated on the 1987 basis of accounting. The net underfunded or overfunded position shown on the new basis of calculation was to be compared with the net accrued pension liability or prepaid pension asset recognized under the previous basis of accounting. The difference became an unrecognized transition asset or liability to be amortized over future years. [Transitional adjustments to the 1999 CICA standard will be allowed on either a prospective basis, with amortization normally over the average remaining service period of active employees, or retroactively, with restatement of prior periods encouraged.]

Recognition of a Minimum Liability

Because the cost of past-service amendments is recognized on an amortized basis, and the same is true for net experience losses and any net liability arising as a result of transitional adjustments, the unfunded obligation with respect to pensions will not normally be fully reflected in any figure of net pension asset or liability recorded in the employer enterprise's balance sheet. Such delayed recognition of part of the pension obligation has been traditional in pension accounting, and is continued in the Canadian 1987 standard.

The FASB has taken a small step toward recognition of a minimum liability in some circumstances. Details of the calculation will not be set out here other than to say it is based on the use of an "accumulated benefit" ACM for all plans, which minimizes the amount of the liability. If the gross obligation so calculated exceeds the amount of the plan assets, a minimum liability is to be recorded in the balance sheet. An intangible asset is recognized to balance the minimum liability up to the amount of any remaining unamortized balance of past-service cost. If the minimum liability figure exceeds such unamortized past-service cost, the difference (with adjustment for deferred taxes) is to be charged as a separate reduction of shareholder's equity.

It seems doubtful that this complicated accounting conveys worthwhile information.[19] [The 1999 CICA standard does *not* adopt this accounting.]

Limits on Pension Surplus Recognition

We have previously noted that, beginning in the early 1980s, pension plans began to report large experience gains, leading to increasing plan surpluses. At the same time in Canada many employers found themselves seriously restricted in their ability to benefit from these surpluses by some provincial pension regulatory authorities, and in some cases by the terms of their own plans.

The 1987 standards did not contemplate this possibility. They implicitly presumed that any pension surplus accrues to the benefit of the employer sponsor of a defined benefit plan. Based on this presumption, as we have seen, the standards call for amortization of experience gains as a reduction of pension expense. In some cases, the surpluses grew so large that experience gain amortization plus the pension fund normalized investment return exceeded the other pension cost components, resulting in negative pension expense. In a number of other cases the amount of reported pension expense was less than amounts contributed to pension funds. The result was that almost immediately the 1987 standards went into effect, many employers were reporting increasing pension assets on their balance sheets. The recognition of these assets effectively presumed employer entitlement to the surplus assets in the pension fund. The obvious question then arose whether these debits on the balance sheet were really valid recognizable assets if an employer had no ability to use the underlying pension fund surplus other than to increase perhaps already generous employee pension benefits.

The very first EIC Abstract attempted to deal with this problem.[20] It held that an employer should recognize a pension asset only to the extent that it represents an expected future benefit, and it sets out an approach to determining a cap on the amount of a pension asset that should be recorded. The cap is set as the amount of any surplus that an employer could withdraw (which has been nil for ongoing plans registered in Quebec and Ontario) plus the present value of future draw-downs of surplus that the employer could expect to achieve through eliminating or reducing future contributions to the plan. The abstract suggests a rough surrogate for the latter present value determination where an employer has the right to eliminate any future contributions as long as a surplus exists. This is determined simply by dividing the estimated annual service cost component of pension expense by the long-run rate of return assumed in determining the investment return component of pension expense. The logic of this rule-of-thumb surrogate may be illustrated by an example. Suppose a plan has an annual current service cost of $1,000 and that the assumed long-run rate of return is 8%. Assume further that, although the employer is prohibited from withdrawing a surplus from the plan, it has the right to eliminate any contributions to the plan while the surplus exists. What is the maximum benefit of this right to the employer? The EIC suggests that, at maximum, the employer could effectively draw down $1,000 of the surplus each year in perpetuity by eliminating the current service cost contribution that it would have to make if there was no surplus. The present value of $1,000 per year in perpetuity is $12,500 ($1,000/.08). Looked at in another way, $12,500 is the amount that invested at 8% will yield an annual return of the potential $1,000 annual contribution saving.

This rule of thumb only works, in logic, if it is assumed that there will be no change in the existing status of the workforce covered by the plan—in other words, that it will always have exactly the same makeup of employees at the same levels of experience and pension entitlement. While this condition will never be fully met, the surrogate does serve as a quickly determinable, and perhaps not unreasonable, pension asset limit where an employer has a reasonable stable workforce and unlimited right to take "contribution holidays" as long as any surplus exists.

This has not been an easy rule to interpret and apply. In particular, the cap can change significantly if the annual current service cost or assumed interest rate change. Additional complex guidance has had to be issued to try to deal with adjustments of the cap.[21] These surplus entitlement issues do not seem to have arisen in the U.S. [The basic concept of the CICA EIC abstract is embodied in the new 1999 standard.]

Curtailments, Settlements and Special Termination Benefits

The accounting methods discussed so far assume, in essence, that a pension plan, once adopted, continues in a routine fashion indefinitely. In particular, the delay in recognition of experience gains and losses, of past-service cost, and of the transition asset and liability are founded on the view that the pension plan will continue to operate on a steady keel, so that it is legitimate to smooth out the reporting of its financial consequences. While this assumption is not unreasonable most of the time, there are occasions when sharp discontinuities occur in pension plans, including the ultimate discontinuity of plan termination.

There are two significant types of discontinuity in pension plans—a plan "settlement" and a "curtailment."

- A settlement is any irrevocable event by which the employer is relieved of the primary obligation to pay some or all of the promised benefits.

- A curtailment is an event that significantly reduces the expected years of future service of employees or eliminates the expectation of earning future benefits for a significant number of employees. A curtailment might result from a plant closing with resulting termination of employment or from adoption of an early retirement program that significantly reduces the future years of service of the employees taking early retirement.

If a plan is terminated and the accrued obligation has been transferred to other parties, both a curtailment and a settlement have taken place.

A settlement consists of the discharge of some or all of an employer's obligation existing under a pension plan. The consideration for that discharge may differ from the amount of obligation as previously calculated, so that a question of gain or loss recognition arises. In contrast, when a curtailment occurs there is no settlement of the liability, but there is nevertheless likely to be a change in the calculated amount of the pension obligation. For example, employees who terminate their employment before the expected retirement date may lose some unvested benefits that have been allowed for in the liability calculation. Also, in a final-pay plan, their ultimate pensions will be based upon salaries at the time of the termination, rather than the presumably higher salaries they would have received had they stayed until normal retirement age. The recalculation of the pension obligation as a result of a curtailment thus also raises the question of gain or loss recognition.

Gain or loss calculated on the basis of a comparison of the calculated obligation before and after the events of settlement or curtailment does not tell the whole story. We must remember that the amount of the obligation as calculated immediately before the settlement or curtailment may have been affected by events that have not yet been reflected in the accounts. For example, the calculated obligation may have been increased by a plan amendment granting past-service benefits, the cost of which has not yet been fully amortized against income. Similarly, there may exist an unrecognized balance of transition asset or liability, or an unrecognized balance of experience gain or loss. These unrecognized balances have a bearing on the amount of gain or loss to be recognized upon a settlement or curtailment.

The FASB's requirements are much more detailed than those of the CICA 1987 standard for the accounting treatment of settlements and curtailments.[22]

- We will first examine the accounting for settlements. A settlement may result from direct transfers of assets to employees to discharge the obligation to them, or from the purchase of annuities to meet the obligation. For the employer to be discharged as obligor under an annuity contract, the contract should make a third party insurer directly and unconditionally responsible to the pensioners for the pension payments. In other words, if an employer buys annuities from an insurance company, but the annuities are payable to the employer who remains responsible for remitting the amounts to the pensioners, the employer has not really settled the liability. It is not clear that accounting practice in Canada has observed this subtle but important distinction. As well, an annuity may be participating or nonparticipating. Some participating annuities may make the employer subject to additional payment for adverse experience, or otherwise expose the employer to continuing risks with respect to satisfaction of the obligation. If they do, the purchase of those annuities cannot be regarded as a settlement. More limited participation rights do not prevent settlement accounting. The FASB is not explicit as to where the dividing line should be drawn. The CICA 1987 standard provides no guidance on the matter of distinguishing participating annuities.

The FASB requires that the gain or loss to be recognized upon complete settlement of a pension plan obligation be comprised of (1) any difference between the calculated amount of the obligation before settlement and the consideration given for the settlement; (2) any unamortized experience gain or loss accumulated right up to immediately before the settlement; and (3) any transition *asset* remaining unamortized at the settlement date. Two aspects of this calculation are notable. First, it is assumed that settlement of the employer's obligation for pension benefits without termination of the plan or curtailment of future employee service should not affect any future benefits the employer may have expected from past-service costs undertaken previously because the employees remain with the company. Thus, unrecognized past service is not to be taken into account when recording gain or loss on settlement. Second, an unrecognized transition *liability* is not an element to be taken into account in computing settlement gain or loss. The FASB arbitrarily assumes that any such liability is likely to be caused in large part by the grant of past-service benefits prior to the date of transition and should be treated as such.

The 1987 CICA standard is not explicit on the determination of a settlement gain or loss. The rather loose wording of *CICA Handbook* paragraph 3460.53 seems to indicate that unamortized past-service cost, as well as all unamortized experience and transitional gains and losses should be taken into account in computing gain or loss upon settlement.

A settlement may cover only part of an employee's existing pension obligation. For example, annuities might be purchased to cover vested benefits only, or to cover benefits accrued based on present salaries but not on projected salaries. If the settlement is partial, the second and third elements of gain or loss listed above (experience gain or loss and unamortized transition asset) are to be prorated according to the reduction in the calculated amount of the pension obligation resulting from the settlement. In order to reduce the effort required to comply with this accounting, the FASB has conceded that employers may adopt a policy (to be followed consistently) of not recognizing gain or loss where the cost of a year's settlements is less than the sum of the service cost and interest components of periodic pension cost for that year.

- Let us now turn our attention to accounting for curtailments. When a curtailment occurs, two aspects must be considered. First, the fact that the number of years of future service of employees is curtailed means that benefits previously expected from past-service plan amendments are no longer to be expected. Therefore, the FASB requires that a loss be recognized with respect to any unamortized past-service cost in the proportion that the reduction in expected future years of service is of the previously expected total future years of service. Any transition liability still unrecognized at the curtailment date is considered tantamount to past service and therefore is to be treated on the same basis— i.e., as a loss is to be recognized.

Second, a curtailment will usually result in a change (often a reduction) in the measured amount of the pension obligation. In isolation, that change can be considered a gain or a loss. However, this apparent gain or loss may be related to an offsetting unrecognized experience loss or gain that arose in a prior period. As an example, suppose that in year one the assumed rate of salary escalation in respect of a final-pay plan was increased, resulting in an increase in the pension obligation and an experience loss to be recognized over a number of future years. Suppose that in year two a curtailment takes place that significantly reduces the expected years of service of the employee group in this plan. The result of the curtailment is that the accrued pension obligation is reduced and an apparent gain arises because a provision for future salary escalation is no longer needed in respect of the curtailed years of service. This apparent gain is in part a reversal of the unrecognized experience loss that arose in year one. This possibility led the FASB to conclude that apparent gains arising on the remeasurement of plan obligations due to a curtailment should be adjusted by any net unamortized experience loss. The FASB sets out detailed instructions to implement this.

These FASB instructions regarding computation of gain or loss with respect to curtailments are complex and based on intricate reasoning. In contrast, the 1987 CICA standard said simply that gains or losses are to be recognized on curtailments, "including any unamortized amounts related to previous plan amendments, changes in assumptions and experience gains and losses" (paragraph 3460.53). It provided no guidance on how such gains or losses are to be determined. Various approaches could be taken with very different reported results. In view of this confusion, an entity could not be criticized for following the FASB standard in this area, without being considered to have departed from Canadian GAAP.

[The 1999 CICA standard adopts the approach to curtailments and settlements set out in the FASB standards.]

An employer may offer employees termination benefits. These may take different forms, including lump-sum payments, periodic future payments, or enhanced pension benefits. The FASB differentiates between "contractual termination benefits" (a scheme of benefits agreed upon to take effect if certain events occur, such as a plant closing), and "special termination benefits" (benefits offered to employees for a short period of time). It specifies that a loss with respect to contractual termination benefits should be provided for when payment becomes probable and the amount is reasonably capable of estimation. A liability and loss for special termination benefits in respect of voluntary terminations is to be recognized when the employees accept the offer and the amount can be reasonably estimated.[23] Involuntary terminations are to be recognized when management approves a detailed plan and communicates it in sufficient detail to employees.

The CICA Emerging Issues Committee took a different view to the recognition of voluntary special termination benefits. It concluded that a best estimate of the cost should be provided for at the date management makes the commitment to implement a special terminations program.[24] It might be noted that some argue for a middle ground, that is, that a liability arises when management makes an irrevocable offer to employees. [The 1999 CICA standard adopts the FASB position.]

Situations that give rise to payments of termination benefits may also give rise to curtailment accounting with respect to the pension plan.

Disclosure

The 1987 FASB standard prescribes extensive disclosures for defined benefit plans. In 1998 the FASB revised and standardized these disclosures for pensions and other post-retirement plans.[25] It added some disclosures with respect to changes in obligations and plan assets, and permitted some reduction of disclosures by nonpublic companies. Otherwise the 1998 disclosures are substantially the same as those of the 1987 standard. The more significant features of these disclosures are summarized below.

- A reconciliation of the beginning and ending balance of (1) the benefit obligation and (2) the fair value of plan assets, with separate disclosures of the principal components of the changes in the period.

- The funded status of the plans, and amounts recognized and not recognized in the statement of financial position, including unamortized amounts of past-service costs, actuarial gains and losses and transitional adjustments; and the amount of net post-retirement benefit prepaid assets or accrued liabilities.

- The amount of net benefit cost recognized in the period, separately disclosing its components (service cost, interest cost, expected return on plan assets, the amounts of amortization for experience gains and losses, past-service costs and transitional amounts), and the amount of gains and losses on any settlements or curtailments.

- Key assumptions with respect to the assumed discount rate, rate of compensation increase (for pay-related plans), and expected long-term rate of return on plan assets.

- Information about assumed health care trend rates where applicable to health care retirement plans.

- The effect of a one percentage point change in the assumed health care trend rates.

- Information on substantive commitments assumed, any alternative methods used to amortize past-service cost, and termination benefits recognized.

- If applicable, details concerning securities of the employer and related parties held by the pension plan and details of annual benefits covered by annuities issued by the employer and related parties.

This information may be aggregated for all an enterprise's retirement benefit plans, provided that disclosure is made of the aggregate obligation and aggregate fair value of plan assets for plans with benefit obligations in excess of plan assets.

A reduced set of disclosures is required for nonpublic entities.

For defined contribution plans disclosure is to be made of the amount of the cost recognized and of any significant changes affecting comparability of information for periods presented.

For defined benefit plans, the 1987 CICA standard, in sharp contrast to the FASB standard, required only that disclosure be given of the present value of accrued pension benefits and, separately, the value of pension fund assets. (Presumably "value" refers to market-related values used in the accounting, but that is not made clear.) The standard suggests that companies "may wish to disclose" certain additional items. For defined contribution plans, disclosure of the present value of any future past-service contributions to be made by the employer is all that was required.

The FASB disclosures add greatly to the information available and to the understanding of statement readers who have some familiarity with the working of pension plans. It is apparent that serious analysts soon equipped themselves to grasp the significance of the disclosures.[26] The disclosure required by the CICA, in contrast, was notable only for its brevity. This was all the more disturbing when it is considered that the discount rate used to calculate the pension obligation and the current-service cost—a key assumption—was a softer figure under the CICA standard than under the FASB's. The inadequate CICA disclosure is inconsistent with the general principle that disclosure should be made when material accounting estimates are subject to a high degree of judgment. [The 1999 CICA standard has adopted disclosures similar to those of the FASB standard, but with some exceptions. In particular, the new CICA standard only encourages, but does not require, disclosure of the effects of a one percentage point change in assumed health care costs.]

Multi-Employer Defined Benefit Plans

A multi-employer plan will cover employees of several, perhaps many, unrelated employers. Usually these plans are administered by a board on behalf of the employers and plan members. Employers are assessed for annual contributions to fund the plan. There is no segregation of plan assets or pension obligations by individual employers. As a result, accounting standards provide that employers generally account for multi-employer plans as if they were defined contribution plans, so that an employer simply expenses the required contribution each period.

An Evaluation

The problem of accounting for pension costs and obligations represents a severe test of the practicality of recognizing and measuring future costs attributable to past and present operations. The 1960s accounting standards were founded on the belief that actuarial science provided answers to the measurement problem. The renewed interest in the problem in the 1980s was associated with the realization that actuarial funding approaches were in significant respects inconsistent with accounting concepts and objectives. Extensive discussion and research preceded the 1987 standards and identified the key issues. With this background, the standards setters arrived at a number of decisions.

- The basic concept that pension benefits are attributable to service rendered during an employee's working career and that accordingly the liability should be recognized then, was reaffirmed. Unfortunately, since plan improvements after retirement will normally not be anticipated in the accounting, this objective cannot be fully achieved.

- There was some acknowledgment of the proposition that an employer might have an unwritten commitment to make benefit improvements, and, if so, the cost recognized for a period could be based upon expected benefit improvements. This was not strongly urged, however, and most enterprises continue to look only to promises currently embodied in their pension plan formulas as a basis for the accounting.

- Standard methods were adopted for allocation of employee entitlements to future benefits under a plan to the periods in which they are deemed earned. Although the reasons for choosing one actuarial cost method over another remain debatable, the decision to select just one among possible alternatives represented a major break from past tradition, and this improves the comparability of accounting from one enterprise to another.

- The requirement that actuarial assumptions be "best estimates" was also an important break from past tradition, as funding assumptions that were the bases of pension accounting in the past were subject to varying degrees of conservative bias. There is still, however, considerable range for judgment.

- A normal basis for recognition of the cost of amendments to pension plans was put in place. This normal basis almost certainly extends the amortization period long beyond the possible benefit from amendments.

- The CICA and FASB 1987 standards provided for somewhat different bases for treatment of experience gains and losses and of the effect of changes in actuarial assumptions. There is no obvious reason to prefer one basis over the other since it is difficult to be other than arbitrary in this area.

- The FASB made the most radical break from previous tradition in its prescription of an interest rate reflecting current conditions to be used in valuing the gross pension obligation and calculating the interest accrual thereon. To be consistent with this basis of valuing the pension obligation, the FASB prescribed a current fair value basis for pension fund assets. It, in effect, adopted current value accounting for the off-balance-sheet figures of pension plan assets and liabilities. To limit volatility, the FASB adopted an uneasy compromise for measurement of the investment return component of pension expense.

- In effectively allowing either a settlement rate or a long-run rate of return approach to the determination of pension obligations, the 1987 CICA standard permitted a wide range of valuations. The CICA choice of "market-related value" was, perhaps, reasonable relative to a long-run return measure of a pension obligation.

- The FASB significantly advanced disclosures with respect to pension plans and their accounting. The disclosure requirements of the CICA 1987 standard, in contrast, were grossly inadequate [but this is rectified in the 1999 CICA standard].

The FASB has stated its belief that its standard is probably not the final step in pension accounting. That belief is almost certainly correct, although it is doubtful that accounting for a cost so dependent upon estimates of future events can ever be made a matter of routine.

Post-Retirement Benefits Other Than Pensions

Employers commonly provide various types of retirement benefits besides pensions. The most significant of these have been health care benefits. There is no doubt but that, in logic within the accrual model, a liability for these costs should be accrued as employees earn these benefits by providing their services, just as for pensions. They were not included in the 1987 pension standards, however, pending consideration of some additional issues.

The large majority of companies have followed the traditional practice of expensing the cost of these benefits only as they are paid, despite the compelling logic of accrual accounting. To understand this practice, some historical background may be helpful. Most employers awarded various post-retirement benefits apart from pensions over the years on a more or less piecemeal basis, without closely monitoring and managing the obligation and costs. They had been assumed at the start to be but minor fringe benefits. FASB proposals to require measurement and accrual of these costs forced many U.S. employers to face up to the fact that these benefits had grown to become substantial commitments, incremented by rapidly accelerating health care costs and aging workforces. In short, the FASB's initiative focused attention on a serious problem, and it led many companies to reassess their plans and to take steps to try to change them so as to limit and control their costs. The problem has been thought to be less severe in Canada, because of extensive government medical plans.

Evidence indicates, however, that increasing obligations have been assumed by Canadian companies as provincial governments have attempted to limit the coverage of their programs.[27]

The FASB put a standard in place on accounting for post-retirement benefits (SFAS 106), effective for most U.S. companies in 1993.[28] Small nonpublic companies and plans outside the U.S. were given a two-year deferral. The FASB standard requires full accrual accounting parallel to that required for pensions, but it differs in some significant respects where the board concluded that there were compelling reasons for differences. The following discussion will concentrate on SFAS 106, and the major areas of difference from the 1987 pension standard.

Specification of Benefits—The Substantive Plan

SFAS 106 is consistent with the 1987 pension standard in suggesting that in some situations the substantive plan may differ from the formal written plan—that established practices or representations to employees may lead to the presumption that benefits will be increased to reflect, for example, inflation effects beyond what is specified in the written plan. Employers argued that they should also be permitted to make reasonable assumptions for scaling back plan benefits in reaction to estimated increases in future health care costs. To illustrate, a written plan might specify a $100 deductible from the annual amount an employer will pay in respect of a retired employee's health costs. This deductible might be expected to be increased with future cost increases. The FASB recognized that a plan may be considered to include expected cost sharing with employees provided that this is evidenced by a consistent past practice and the employer has the ability, and has clearly communicated to plan members its intent, to institute cost sharing provisions if certain conditions exist (for example, if health care costs exceed a certain level).

Benefit Estimation Issues

There is an additional dimension of uncertainty in estimating certain post-retirement future benefits other than pensions. Pension accounting requires the estimation of cash benefits to be paid, while accounting for other post-retirement benefits requires estimation of the cost of services to be provided to retirees. The level of future payments under a health care plan will depend not only on members' ages, life expectancies and inflation, but also on factors affecting health care costs. These factors are not amenable to very reliable estimation based on historical data or trends. Some argue that sound estimates of future health care costs suitable for accounting recognition are just not possible, so that financial statements should simply reflect pay-as-you-go accounting supplemented by information about post-retirement benefit plans and factors that bear on the future direction of the underlying costs.[29] The FASB did not accept this argument. It concluded that reasonable estimates of the obligation can be developed and that failure to recognize the obligation could severely impair the usefulness and credibility of financial statements. With respect to health care plans, it requires best estimates of future claim costs, reduced by the expected effects of coverage by government plans and any cost sharing provisions with employees. This is to be determined by reference to past claims experience of the employer and other similar plans (perhaps by reference to the experience of insurers and benefit consultants) adjusted by an estimated future health care cost trend rate. This trend rate shall be an individual rate determined for each plan reflecting the plan's design and demographics. It is to be noted that these estimates are not based on the continuation of existing conditions, but require consideration not only of estimates of future health care cost inflation, but also of future changes in health care utilization and expected future technological advances. Future benefit coverage by governmental programs is, however, assumed to be as provided by existing laws.

In sum, one might well conclude that the estimation of future health care costs can be no more than an educated guess. Nevertheless, in accepting the responsibility for a health care plan for retirees, it is reasonable to expect that an employer should be held accountable for a best estimate of the liability that has accrued.

Attribution of Cost to Years of Service

Consistent with the 1987 pension standard, SFAS 106 requires a benefit/years of service approach to allocating cost to periods. Unlike pensions, however, some health plans have not made benefits a function of years of service, but rather have promised the same retirement benefits to all employees who meet the basic eligibility conditions. SFAS 106 states that an equal amount of the expected post-retirement benefit obligation for an employee (before discounting) shall be attributed to each year of service, except where a plan formula attributes a greater share of expected benefits to early years of service.

The beginning of the attribution period will generally be the date an employee is hired. The service cost component of the expense is to be fully accrued when the employee has met all the conditions necessary to receive all of the benefits of the plan, which for many U.S. plans is a date prior to retirement. This was a controversial issue, with many arguing that the attribution period should extend to an employee's retirement date regardless of the term to full eligibility. However, the board reasoned that a plan's substantive formula should determine the accounting for the underlying exchange transaction with employees, and that no benefit could be expected for any period beyond the date when an employee's additional service will not change benefit entitlement.

Funding the Obligation

Tax rules in the U.S., and in Canada, do not provide employers with any incentive to prefund post-retirement benefits that are not part of a pension plan. As a result few of these other post-retirement plans are prefunded, so that the accrued obligation is generally not offset by any assets unconditionally restricted to the payment of the obligation and there is, therefore, generally no investment return component in the post-retirement plan expense calculation. Since there is no deduction by an employer for tax purposes until the benefits are paid, a deferred tax temporary difference arises. This may lead to a large deferred tax debit on the balance sheet where the accrued post-retirement benefit obligation is large and the deferred tax debits are not offset by deferred tax credits arising from other timing differences. The question then is whether there is sufficient assurance that enough taxable income will be generated in future periods to enable these deferred tax debits to be treated as assets on the balance sheet. In the U.S., employers argued that, if they had to provide for the obligation, they should not be unduly constrained by deferred tax asset accounting rules from recognizing the related tax debits as assets. This may have been a major factor in the FASB relaxing its recognition criteria for the recognition of tax debits as assets—a subject that will be examined in Chapter 16.

In the rare case where a post-retirement plan fund does exist, the FASB calls for the same bases for determining the long-run rate of return and plan asset valuation as in its 1987 pension standard.

Plan and Experience Adjustments

SFAS 106 provides for the same forward amortization of the cost of plan amendments related to past service and experience gains and losses as the 1987 pension standard, with two exceptions.

- A plan amendment might reduce, rather than increase, the accumulated post-retirement benefit obligation. In this case, the reduction is to be applied to reduce any unamortized prior-service cost and any unrecognized transition obligation, and only the remaining credit amortized to future periods.

- In some cases, an employer may decide to temporarily deviate from the substantive plan, for example, to forgive increased retiree contributions called for by the cost sharing provisions of a plan in respect of past claims. When this happens, the resulting gains or losses are to be recognized immediately.

Some Other Differences from SFAS 87

- The FASB elected not to require recognition of the minimum liability as required by the pension accounting standard.

- Settlements and curtailments are to be accounted for as set out in the 1987 pension standard, except that any gain arising on settlement should be reduced by any unrecognized transition obligation.

Previous to the 1999 CICA standard, no standard comparable to SFAS 106 existed in Canada. Thus Canadian companies could follow pay-as-you-go accounting, and most did so. Accrual accounting as required by SFAS 106 was certainly acceptable under Canadian GAAP.[30] However, it seems that most Canadian enterprises were not prepared to adopt proper accrual accounting for these benefits until required to do so. [The 1999 CICA standard puts requirements in place that are generally the same as those of SFAS 106.]

Other Post-Employment Benefits

To this point in this chapter we have discussed standards for accounting for *post-retirement* benefits. They do not cover benefits provided to former or inactive employees after employment but before retirement. These benefits include supplemental employment benefits, severance benefits, disability benefits and continuation of health care benefits and life insurance. FASB Statement 112 filled this gap.[31] It requires employers to recognize the obligation to provide post-employment benefits of all kinds if the obligation is attributable to employees' services already rendered, employees' rights to those benefits accumulate or vest, payment of the benefits is probable, and the amount of the benefits can be reasonably estimated. If these conditions are not met, the employer would account for them when it is probable that a liability has been incurred and the amount can be reasonably estimated.

There has been no similar *CICA Handbook* standard, although the FASB accounting could be reasoned to be appropriate, if not required, under Canadian GAAP. [The 1999 CICA standard sets out requirements similar to those in SFAS 112.]

IASC Standards

The IASC revised its standard on employee benefits (IAS 19) in 1998.[32] It is based on the same principles as the FASB and 1999 CICA standards, with a few differences in application.

- Pension obligations are to be discounted at a current market interest rate, but are determined by reference to the high-quality corporate bond rate (rather than the current settlement or government rate). Thus the rates used in applying IAS 19 may be expected to be marginally higher than under the FASB and 1999 CICA standards.

- Past-service costs are to be amortized to expense on a straight-line basis over the average period until the benefits become vested (rather than over the average remaining service life of active employees). This will normally result in immediate expensing of past-service costs related to retired employees and a significant proportion of active employees, since their accrued pension benefits for services rendered will normally have vested.

- Expected investment return on plan assets is to be based on their fair value (rather than "market related value").

- There are some differences in the bases of determining gains and losses on curtailments and settlements, and on the conditions for recognizing terminations. The IASC standard is much less specific than the FASB and 1999 CICA standards.

STOCK-BASED COMPENSATION

Typically, compensation plans for key employees are in some way related to the company's stock. Putting company shares in the hands of employees is one way of stimulating them to identify the company's interests with their own. Making their compensation related to changes in the market value of the company stock may have even more direct motivational effect. If these compensation plans represent a form of incentive to employees, one must naturally consider what their cost is to the employer. Under the principles developed in this chapter, expense ought to be recognized by the company in relation to that cost, and the obligation ought to be recognized at the time the employee service is rendered. Unfortunately, it has proved very difficult to arrive at a basis for making such recognition.

We shall begin our discussion by describing several common types of plans and consider how they benefit employees. We will then consider whether, in each case, such benefits represent a measurable cost that is or ought to be recognized for accounting purposes. This provides a basis for identifying issues and evaluating existing GAAP and recent, controversial FASB proposals.

Survey of Employee Stock or Stock-Price-Related Plans

Stock Bonuses

A simple way to achieve stock ownership by employees who are deemed significant contributors to a company's success is to pay performance bonuses in the form of stock rather than cash. The benefit to the employee is obviously the value of the stock. The cost to the company is not a direct cash cost, but rather the sacrifice of the opportunity to sell the shares for cash, and the resultant dilution of other shareholders' interest in the company. Since stock issued must be recognized at fair market value at the issue date, the cost of the compensation must be recorded and would be expensed (usually immediately) just as would a cash bonus.

Noninterest-Bearing Stock Purchase Loans

Employees receive benefits if shares are issued to them and they are given loans to pay for them that are noninterest bearing or carry an interest rate that is low by normal commercial standards. On the surface, the benefit is the receipt of a low-interest or no-interest loan. The benefit to the employee and cost to the company can be quantified by discounting the loan. The difference between the face amount of the loan and its discounted value would represent a measure of the inherent compensation expense. It might be argued that the ownership of company stock motivates employees over the period elapsing till they are entitled to take the stock down and sell it, so that the compensation expense should be deferred and recognized over that period. In Canada, companies have generally not discounted these employee loans, which has the same net effect on income as if the loans were discounted and the compensation expense element amortized over the terms of the loans to offset the imputed interest expense. It has been proposed that such loans should be discounted and the employee remuneration element accounted for explicitly.[33]

    This superficial view of the employee benefit is not completely correct in some situations. There have been occasions when companies whose stocks have declined in price have forgiven employee loans on account of stock purchases. It may be, therefore, that a stock purchase "loan" is really not intended to involve a risk to the employee if the share price declines. (Some plans are formally structured to avoid the risk of share price decline by allowing employees to subscribe for convertible preferred shares that will have a floor redemption price even though the common stock declines in price.) If that is the plan's substance, recording the stock as issued against a loan receivable is misleading. The CICA EIC has concluded that the appropriate presentation in this case is to credit the capital stock account (as is required because the stock is legally issued) and to treat the "loan" as a separately disclosed deduction from shareholders' equity.[34] But more than this, if the stock purchase plan does not involve any risk to the employee for price decline during the term of the "loan," it may be viewed as simply a means of giving the employee a call on the stock, which will be exercised only if the price goes up. In other words, the plan may be akin to a stock option plan, giving rise to additional issues to be discussed below.

Employee Stock Options

The most popular form of stock-related incentive compensation is the simple stock option. Typically, an employee is given an option for a limited period, say five to ten years, to acquire stock in the company at an exercise price that is usually close to the market price at the date the option is granted. The option right is not assignable and is usually contingent upon the employee's continued employment with the company. Since the option exercise price is usually at, or only slightly below, the market value at the date the option is granted, there is normally little, if any, assured benefit to the employee from the plan. Nevertheless, the employee who is granted the option undoubtedly receives something of value. What he or she receives is the right to profit if the shares appreciate in value during the option period. As in the case of a stock bonus plan, the cost to the company of a stock option lies in the sacrifice of the opportunity to sell the shares for cash at the current market price instead of the exercise price and the dilution of the shareholders' equity as a result. The employer incurs the cost of providing the option in exchange for expected employee services. In Canada usually no attempt is made to recognize compensation cost in connection with employee stock option plans.

Phantom Plans and Stock Appreciation Rights

A "phantom" stock plan simulates the effect of a stock option without actually requiring the issuance of stock. Instead of granting the employee an option on a given number of shares, the company will credit him or her with an equivalent number of phantom shares. At any time after the employee's rights become exercisable, the value of the phantom shares may be computed, and the employee is permitted to request payment for his or her accumulated rights.

In a variation of the phantom plan, "stock appreciation rights" (SARs) are granted to the employee giving him or her a right to receive the appreciation in price of a given number of shares over the plan period. Phantom plans and SARs differ from the plans they simulate in that their cost is eventually represented by a real cash outflow rather than by dilution of the equity of other shareholders. Accordingly, it is not possible to avoid accounting for the associated cost. Thus there is a fundamental conflict between accounting for phantom plans and for other types of stock-related incentive plans.

Accounting for Stock-Price-Related Plans

Canadian standard setters have simply not addressed these discrepancies. U.S. standard setters have been more venturesome. The basic U.S. standard dates back to an APB Opinion in 1972 (Opinion 25).[35] This standard did not call for any value to be recognized in respect of employee stock options apart from any excess of the quoted market value of the underlying shares over the price to be paid by the employees at the date the options were granted.

Much has changed since Opinion 25 was issued. Stock options and other forms of stock-based compensation have become much more common and are increasingly sophisticated and varied in form. As well, stock option pricing models are much more advanced and are widely available and used by employers and compensation consultants in determining employee compensation packages. Against this background Opinion 25 is criticized for producing anomalous results and for providing little guidance on how to account for new forms of stock compensation plans. A number of FASB interpretations, technical bulletins and EITF abstracts have been issued over the years, but these merely give guidance within the principles of Opinion 25. The board added a project to its agenda to reconsider accounting for stock-based compensations in 1984. The complex and controversial nature of the issues, and other priorities, have inhibited progress. But in 1993 the board issued an exposure draft dealing with all forms of stock-based compensation. It proposed some fundamental changes.[36]

Following is a discussion of the major issues, dealing first with a straightforward employee stock option plan, and then turning to cash compensation based on stock appreciation rights.

Stock Options

Let us envisage an example of a typical employee stock option. Suppose a key employee is granted an option at the beginning of year one to buy 100 of the company shares at $10 each, which is the market price of the shares at that date (the grant date). Suppose that the terms of the plan require the employee to remain with the company for three years before he or she can acquire the stock, (the vesting period), and that the option expires if it is not exercised within five years. The initial conceptual question is whether there is any cost to the employer that should be recognized for such an option. This question is interrelated with a second question, as to when this determination should be made—i.e., at the grant date, the vesting date, or the exercise date (or variations thereof), and with a third question of how the measurement should be made. Let us examine the issues as they relate to each of the three dates.

- There are persuasive arguments that this option should be recognized at the grant date. This is the date at which the contract between employer and employee is made and both parties commit themselves to it. The employer has exchanged a commitment to issue 100 shares at $10 and to forego any increase in the value of those shares for up to five years. GAAP require that stock options issued for other goods or services (for example to acquire a plant or equipment or the shares of another business) be recorded at their fair value as representing part of the cost incurred for these goods or services. The issuance of stock options to acquire employee services is a similar transaction. Something of value, a stock option, is exchanged for something else of value, employee services. Recognition at the grant date necessitates determining the fair value of the option at that date, which value is considered to be an employer cost incurred for employee services. The stock option value is presumably the value that both parties have in mind in entering into the contract, that is the value based on the stock price and expectations at the grant date. There are some problems in arriving at a fair value, however. Employee stock options have restrictions at the grant date that do not exist for normal traded options. In particular, they are generally subject to vesting requirements and cannot be sold, but can only be exercised. As a result, there are no directly equivalent market prices to establish their value. But this may not be an insurmountable problem, and the suggestion is that the models long used in finance theory for estimating the value of traded options be used, modified to allow for the reduction in value of employee options resulting from the restrictions contained within them.[37]

- Some argue that the recognition of the grant date is not appropriate because the option is really only a commitment by an employer to issue shares *if* employees render future services during the vesting period. It may be reasoned, in other words, that it is merely an executory contract (like a purchase or sales commitment) which is not recognized until goods or services are delivered. Acceptance of this argument would presumably result in an accrual of a cost over the vesting period based ultimately on the value of the option at the end of the vesting period.[38] The option would be more reliably valued at the end of the vesting period than it would be at the grant date, but the cost shown throughout the vesting period could be very volatile depending on the stock price through that period.

- Finally, there is the exercise date. It has the advantage of being a simple measurement, based on the excess of the exercise price over the option price. Some advocate this measure on the grounds that this is the realized effect of the option and argue that it is appropriate to defer measurement until realization when there are significant uncertainties in valuation at earlier stages. This answer seems to have little conceptual merit, however. Once the employee has the right to exercise the option, his or her position is like that of an investor and the variation in the value of the option after that date cannot reasonably be considered to be compensation expense.

What is notable in this analysis is that all three alternatives would logically result in an employee remuneration cost, based on the fair value of the transaction defined at each of the dates. But APB Opinion 25 arrived at none of these positions. The APB decided that the compensation should be determined at the grant date, but that the option itself should not be valued. Rather, as observed above, the compensation value is simply to be determined on the basis of its "intrinsic value," i.e., the difference between the market value of the stock and the exercise price at the grant date. Since almost all options are granted at or near the current market price, this has meant that generally no expense is recognized. This answer is clearly wrong in theory, but Opinion 25 was based largely on practical grounds.

The FASB exposure draft made the major leap in proposing that employee stock options be recognized at their fair value at their grant dates. The board's research led it to conclude that mathematical models now enable a reasonable valuation of traded stock options, and that readily available software for personal computers reduces the computations to a "fill-in-the-blanks" exercise. The exposure draft proposed specific adjustments to reduce these values for the nontransferability and the vesting restrictions of employee stock options. It also proposed that companies whose options relate to shares that are not publicly traded should measure employee stock options at a "minimum value" that omits any value for expected market volatility. In essence, the minimum value is based on the presumption that an option is worth at least the value of the right to defer payment of the exercise price until the end of the option term.

The final question concerns the allocation of the cost that is recognized to periods when it is deemed earned by the employee. This is governed by the facts of the case, and little guidance was provided by the Opinion 25. Option rights could be deemed to have been awarded as compensation for past services only, in which case the expense would be recognized in full at the date of grant. When a cost is recognized with respect to current and future services, however, the unamortized amount thereof is not carried as an asset but rather is deducted from shareholder's equity. The FASB exposure draft would recognize amounts attributable to the future as a prepaid compensation asset, which would be amortized over the periods to which the employees are considered to perform the services in exchange for their remuneration. The service period would generally be presumed to be the vesting period. Awards for past service would continue to be expensed in the period granted.

Stock Appreciation Rights

Subsequent to APB Opinion 25, plans based on SARs multiplied and it became necessary for the FASB to develop rules for their treatment.[39] The FASB decided that the liability for SARs must be accrued over the service period covered by the plan (presumed to be the period until the rights vested in the absence of any other indication). The amount to be accrued at any given time is be based on the worth of the SARs if they were to be exercised at the current market price, and the cost resulting from recording that target is to be prorated over the service period.

Reliance on the current market price for recognition of the accrued liability necessarily means wide fluctuations in its amount as the stock price fluctuates. That, in turn, means wide fluctuations in expense to be recognized each period. Indeed, if there were a sharp drop in stock price from one reporting period to another, the expense recorded could be negative. The resulting fluctuations in reported expense figures have naturally drawn criticism. But even more serious is the discrepancy between the treatment of ordinary stock options and SARs, because the compensation is measured at the grant date for stock options and ultimately at the exercise date for SARs. The problem is not easy to solve.

On the one hand it could be argued that the fundamental inconsistency should be overcome by valuing SARs as at the grant date. If employee stock options can be reasonably valued, then presumably so can SARs at the grant date. Of course, at the exercise date the stock price will normally be different from that expected at the grant valuation date. Suppose it is much higher. What is the nature and explanation of the extra amount that must be paid by the company? There are two possible explanations.

- One explanation is that the higher stock price is attributable to the employee's efforts, so that the full high cash payments would be treated entirely as compensation expense. If this explanation is accepted, however, one must consider its significance for the treatment of incentive stock options. Unless the grant of a stock option to an employee can be shown to be substantially different in character from that of the grant of SARs (which seems unlikely) their accounting ought to be consistent. To achieve this it would be necessary to recognize compensation expense for the full excess of the market price of shares optioned at the exercise date over the exercise price of the option.

- An alternative hypothesis is that changes in the share price after the grant date are affected by so many events that it is unreasonable to attribute them to the efforts of one or more specific employees. The compensation element would then be restricted to the value that the employee and employer together see in it at the date the right is granted. This accounting would be consistent with accounting for ordinary employee stock options if the latter were valued as an option and not merely by taking the difference between the exercise price and the grant date share price. The ordinary stock option, when exercised, is recorded at the option price received and results in no further charge to income when exercised. To create consistency between option accounting and accounting for SAR payments in this case, the excess of the SAR payment over compensation expense recognized at the grant date would be written off as a capital transaction. The result would be the same as if stock had actually been issued at the grant date price and immediately repurchased by the company for cancellation at the current market price.

It may be unlikely that either of these possible accounting approaches would enlist general support at this time. Yet it seems that one of them would have to be adopted to cure the present conceptual inconsistencies between accounting for ordinary stock options and accounting for SARs.

The FASB exposure draft would perpetuate the different accounting outcomes on the basis of whether an award is considered to be a liability or an equity instrument.

- If an award is to be settled in cash or other assets, or if employees can compel such settlement, it would be considered to be a liability to the employer. Liabilities would be valued each period based on the current stock price measure of the award, and the effect of changes would be reflected in remuneration expense. This then would continue to require accounting for most SARs at their exercise price.

- If an award is to be settled through the issuance of company shares, or the employer has the choice, it would be measured at the grant date and subsequently accounted for as capital by the company. Thus employee stock options would fit into this category.

Overall, the major change proposed by the 1993 FASB exposure draft was that the fair value of stock options at their grant dates be recognized as an employee remuneration cost. This proposal met with strong opposition, led by management interests. Objections were based on various traditional conceptual arguments, practical measurability issues and cost-benefit concerns. There was a loud outcry by objectors alleging that many companies, particularly new companies in high-tech industries, would be greatly disadvantaged by the proposed accounting. Many of these companies cannot afford to pay high cash salaries to executives, and instead provide a significant proportion of executive remuneration through stock option plans. They claimed that recognition of costs for these options would result in lower stock prices and higher costs of capital, which in turn would make it much more difficult for them to develop and compete in the marketplace. It may be suggested that these fears are overblown and that, if an option makes economic sense, recording the cost should not affect the benefit other than making management more accountable for it. As to the concerns for practical measurability, advocates of the FASB proposals argued that the uncertainty is no greater than that inherent in many other accruals commonly made in financial accounting.[40]

The FASB, under strong pressure from business and ultimately from powerful U.S. political interests, backed down. In 1995 it issued a standard that encourages entities to adopt the fair value-based method of accounting proposed in the exposure draft for all employee stock option plans. But it continues to allow the intrinsic value-based method provided for in APB Opinion 25. However, it requires entities electing to remain with accounting under Opinion 25 to provide pro forma disclosures of net income and earnings per share as if the fair value method had been applied.[41]

In 1996 the FASB embarked on a project to address a number of difficult issues relating to the implementation and interpretation of Opinion 25. It is expected to issue an exposure draft proposing guidance on these issues in 1999.

As noted above, in Canada generally no attempt is made to recognize compensation costs for employee stock options. With respect to SARs, the EIC has ruled that phantom stock option plans that are to be paid out in cash should be accrued and accounted for as an expense.[42] There are no other authoritative standards in place in Canada and, contrary to U.S. GAAP, practice appears to accept recording no compensation expense in respect of SARs if either party can elect to have the appreciation paid in cash or in company shares. If paid in cash, the appreciation is treated as a reduction of capital. Thus employers in Canada can easily structure stock-based compensation (options or SARs) so as to avoid the necessity of recognizing any expense charge. This seems to be flagrantly at odds with logically supportable accrual accounting concepts.

SUMMARY

Recognition of a cost and a liability for future payments under a pension plan presents a challenging set of problems in a difficult accounting area—that of making appropriate provision for uncertain future cash payments resulting from obligations arising out of current operations.

A key factor in understanding the conceptual issues and arriving at conclusions on them is the realization that periodic pension cost, as customarily reported, is an amalgam of several conceptually distinct measurements, including (1) the cost attributable to current service of the employees for the period, (2) interest added to pension obligations previously rec-

ognized, (3) earnings recognized on investments held in any separate pension fund, (4) cost
to be recognized from plan changes that grant benefit entitlements for past service, and (5)
adjustments to previously recorded figures to allow for experience different from that upon
which previous measurements were based and for changes in estimates of the future.

The principal issues in pension cost accounting are summarized below.

- The first requirement is an estimate of the future benefit payments that will arise from
employee service over their careers. In principle, accounting standards recognize that
future benefits paid may result from unwritten commitments by the employer, and these
may be greater than those embodied in a formal pension plan document. In practice,
however, the accounting is likely to be based only on the express plan formula as it
exists from time to time.

- In view of the very long lapse of time between employee service and payment of benefits, estimates of future benefits and of future returns attainable on pension plan investments are subject to considerable uncertainty. Accounting standards hold that estimates
should be "best estimates," rather than having a conservative bias. Because of the wide
range possible in judgments as to some of these variables, the requirement to use best estimates may be expected to have only modest effects on standardizing practice.

- Some method is required for allocating the discounted amount of future benefit payments
to years in which they are deemed earned by employees. There are a large number of
actuarial cost methods that provide for such allocation, many of which can meet the test
of being rational and systematic. To promote uniformity in practice, accounting standards
have adopted one stated method to be applied to each particular pension plan formula.

- In the selection of a discount rate to be applied in recognizing the present cost of future
benefits, the CICA has permitted traditional actuarial practice of basing the rate on
some estimate of the long-run average rate of return on fund investments. The FASB
standard requires that the pension obligation be revalued each year at a discount rate
reflecting current conditions, and that cost attributed to employee service in the ensuing year be discounted using the same rate. [The 1999 revised CICA standard adopts the
FASB position.]

- The CICA has prescribed valuation of pension fund assets at market-related values—a
basis allowing for some smoothing of the effect of fluctuations in market value—which
can be considered compatible with the use of an estimated long-term average rate of
investment return for discounting the plan obligation. The FASB prescribes the use of
a current fair value for valuing pension fund assets which is compatible with the use of
a discount rate reflecting current conditions in valuing the pension fund obligation. In an
uneasy compromise, however, the FASB bases the calculation of the investment return
component of annual pension cost upon an estimate of long-term rate of return, and this
is applied to a separate valuation of pension fund assets, on the basis of market-related
values. [The 1999 revised CICA standard adopts the FASB position.]

- Periodic revaluations of pension plan obligations reveal experience gains and losses.
In view of the fact that valuations of pension plan obligations themselves rest upon
assumptions as to future experience, and that future experience is likely to deviate in
some respect from the assumptions, it is not thought necessary to continuously adjust pension obligations and costs recognized as indicated by the latest valuation data. However,
to avoid the possibility of a growing divergence between the position revealed by suc-

cessive valuations and the obligation accounted for, some amortization of differences is required. The basis of amortization is necessarily highly arbitrary.

- Since plan amendments granting benefit improvements for past service are usually not anticipated in the accounting, there must be some basis for recognizing their cost when they do occur. CICA and FASB accounting standards provide that amortization should be in relation to the expected remaining service life of the employee group in the normal situation. (A recent IASC standard requires immediate expensing except where the past service benefits are not vested.)

- Because adjustments to measured plan obligations resulting from plan amendments and experience gains and losses are not given immediate recognition, there will be occasions when something akin to an "off-balance sheet liability" exists. The FASB requires recognition of a minimum amount of liability for pension but not other post-retirement plans, offset by an intangible asset and, on occasion, a direct reduction of shareholder's equity. Since the minimum liability is calculated on a different basis from that used to measure the pension obligation for other purposes, it is doubtful that this accounting has much information value. The CICA standard does not require this minimum liability determination.

- In Canada employers face restrictions in their access to pension plan surpluses, which surpluses became large for many plans in the mid-1980s. As a result supplementary guidance has been developed setting a cap on the amount of a pension asset that may be recognized in an employer's balance sheet based on its presumed ability to draw down surplus assets of the plan.

- Discontinuities in pension plans resulting from significant curtailments in expected future employee service, or settlements in whole or in part of plan obligations, give rise to recalculation of the amount of pension obligations and immediate recognition of gain or loss. The FASB standard gives detailed guidance as to how this should be done. [The 1999 CICA standard adopts the FASB approach.]

- The FASB prescribes extensive disclosure in connection with pension plans and the accounting performed for them. This disclosure provides great help to a skilled statement analyst in understanding the significance of pension plan commitments and costs. The disclosure required by the CICA standard, in contrast, has been minimal. [The 1999 CICA standard adopts disclosures similar to those of the FASB.]

The FASB has also developed a standard on accounting for post-retirement benefits other than pensions, the most significant being health care costs. It provides for accrual of the best estimate of the future payments as employees provide their services, just as for pensions. There are some differences resulting from the unique characteristics of these costs. In particular, estimation is required of the future health care cost trend rate and the service cost is to be accrued over the period to which employees become fully eligible to receive the benefits, which may predate their retirement. [The 1999 CICA standard puts in place similar requirements for post-retirement benefits other than pensions.]

Stock-based compensation for key employees represents a form of future obligation undertaken in return for services. The obligation and the related expense have traditionally not been recognized at the time an option is granted or over the period that it matures. Canadian accounting standards have ignored the problem, while U.S. standards have addressed it but have not provided a satisfactory answer. One of the difficulties has been that of developing an objective measure of the compensation at the time it is earned by the employee. This issue has grown more pressing with the development of compensation plans that reward the employee in the same way as stock options but pay that reward in cash rather than stock. When cash is paid, some accounting must be given for the full payment, including that portion of the reward attributable to appreciation in the stock price after the compensation award was granted. This is fundamentally in conflict with accounting for stock options, where the appreciation in stock prices after the date of grant is ignored.

An FASB exposure draft proposed fair valuation of employee stock options at the grant date with the resulting cost being treated as compensation expense, usually over the vesting period. This was strongly opposed by management interests. The FASB has ended up with a standard that encourages fair value accounting but allows traditional accounting if pro forma income disclosures are provided of the effects of applying the fair value method.

REFERENCES

[1]   See the argument of L. Lorensen and P. Rosenfield in "Vested Benefits—A Company's Only Pension Liability," *Journal of Accountancy*, October 1983, pp. 64–76.

[2]   American Institute of Accountants, Committee on Accounting Procedure, *Pension Plans—Accounting for Annuity Costs Based on Past Services*, Accounting Research Bulletin No. 36 (New York: AIA, 1948), subsequently consolidated in *Restatement and Revision of Accounting Research Bulletins*, Accounting Research Bulletin No. 43 (New York: AIA, 1953), chap. 13A.

[3]   See AICPA, APB, *Accounting for the Cost of Pension Plans*, APB Statement No. 8 (New York: AICPA, 1970); and CICA, Committee on Accounting and Auditing Research, *Accounting for the Costs of Pension Plans*, Bulletin No. 21 (Toronto: CICA, 1965). The CICA Bulletin became *CICA Handbook* Section 3460 in 1969.

[4]   See "Pension Costs and Obligations" *CICA Handbook*, Section 3460 (Toronto: CICA), and FASB, *Employers' Accounting for Pensions*, Statement of Financial Accounting Standards No. 87 (Stamford: FASB, 1985). The *CICA Handbook* Section 3460 replaced the previous standard in the same section (see note 3) in 1986. See also J.L. Amble and J. M. Cassel, *A Guide to Implementation of Statement 87 on Employers' Accounting for Pensions* (Stamford: FASB, 1986).

[5]   See D.A. Robertson and T.R. Archibald, *Survey of Pension Plans in Canada*, 9th ed. (Toronto: Financial Executives Institute Canada, 1993), pp. 32–33.

[6]   Ibid., pp. 42–45. See also analysis of this issue in R.M. Skinner, *Pension Accounting: The Problem of Equating Payments Tomorrow with Expenses Today* (Toronto: Clarkson Gordon, 1980), chap. 10.

[7]   FASB, *Employers' Accounting for Pensions*, par. 41.

[8]   Some research evidence in the U.S. indicates that investors include expectations of future salary progression in assessing the value of the employer's shares. See M.E. Barth, "Relative Measurement Errors Among Alternative Pension Asset and Liability Measures," *The Accounting Review*, July 1991, pp. 433–63; and H.F. Mittelstaedt and P.R. Regier, "The Market Response to Pension Plan Terminations," *The Accounting Review*, January 1993, pp. 1–27.

9 A study using 1980 pension plan data indicated that, at that time, on a best estimate basis there were very large unrecognized surpluses in many Canadian private sector pension plans. D.D. Ezra, *The Struggle for Pension Fund Wealth* (Toronto: Pagurian Press Limited, 1983).

10 These propositions concentrate entirely on pension cost in isolation. But pension costs are only one element in the total compensation of employees. Total compensation will be established by negotiation in the labour market. An exploratory conceptual analysis makes some suggestions as to how this market might work. It proposes that different ACMs would be logical under different scenarios. Unfortunately, the empirical research necessary to determine which scenario(s) applies in the real world has not been performed. See J.E. Pesando and C.K. Clarke, *Economic Models of the Labour Market: Their Implications for Pension Accounting*, Studies in Canadian Accounting Research (Toronto: Canadian Academic Accounting Association, 1983). For a condensed version of the study by the authors, see "Economic Models of the Labour Market and Pension Accounting: An Exploratory Analysis," *The Accounting Review*, October 1983, pp. 733–48.

11 *CICA Handbook*, Section 3460, par. 16.

12 This intention of the CICA Accounting Standards Committee was confirmed by R.M. Callard, "Pension Accounting Evolution," *CA Magazine*, April 1986, pp.61–67. The author, who was the CICA staff on the project, noted that the committee disagreed with the FASB decision to require the settlement rate, concluding that "on an ongoing basis, it would be appropriate to discount benefit obligations using a long-term assumption."

13 The Robertson and Archibald, Financial Executives Institute Canada study, *Survey of Pension Plans in Canada*, pp. 62–63 states that approximately 50% of the companies it surveyed reported that their best estimate assumptions for accounting purposes differ from their assumptions used for funding purposes, with a primary area of difference being the interest rate assumed.

14 See, for example, J.L. Treynor, P.J. Regan, and W.W. Priest, Jr., *The Financial Reality of Pension Funding under ERISA* (Homewood, Ill.: Dow Jones-Irwin, 1976).

15 There is some evidence in the U.S. that investors may include pension assets and liability figures disclosed in employer enterprise financial statement rates as if they were on the face of the employer's balance sheet. See discussion of this issue in T.W. Scott, "Costing the Gold Watch," *CA Magazine*, September 1992, pp. 39–45, and the research cited in this article.

16 See discussion of this issue in Skinner, *Pension Accounting: The Problem of Equating Payments Tomorrow with Expenses Today*, and Pesando and Clarke, *Economic Models of the Labour Market: Their Implications for Pension Accounting*.

17 FASB, *Employers' Accounting for Pensions*, par. 107.

18 See, for example, T.S. Lucas and B.A. Hollowell, "Pension Accounting: The Liability Question," *Journal of Accountancy*, October 1981, pp. 57–66.

19 Some research based on U.S. stock market price effects suggests that investors place higher value on pension asset and liability figures disclosed in financial statement notes than they do on the amounts recorded in the balance sheet. See M.E. Barth, "Relative Measurement Errors Among Alternative Pension Asset and Liability Measures."

[20] CICA Emerging Issues Committee, *Pension Surplus Recognition*, EIC 1 (Toronto: CICA, 1989).

[21] This guidance was provided as extensions to CICA, *Pension Surplus Recognition*, EIC 1, and in CICA, *Pension Accounting Issues: Questions and Answers* (Toronto: CICA, 1996).

[22] FASB, *Employers' Accounting for Settlements and Curtailments of Defined Benefit Pension Plans and for Termination Benefits*, Statement of Financial Accounting Standards No. 88 (Stamford: FASB, 1985). See also J.L. Amble and J. M Cassel, *A Guide to Implementation of Statement 88* (Stamford: FASB, 1988).

[23] FASB, *Employers' Accounting for Settlements and Curtailments of Defined Benefit Pension Plans and for Termination Benefits*, par. 15.

[24] CICA Emerging Issues Committee, *Special Termination Benefits*, EIC 23 (Toronto: CICA, 1991).

[25] FASB, *Employers' Disclosures About Pension and Other Postretirement Benefits*, Statement of Financial Accounting Standards No. 132 (Norwalk: FASB, 1998).

[26] This is evidenced in the U.S. by the market-based research footnoted throughout this chapter. See also, M.E. Barth, W.H. Beaver and W.R. Landsman, "A Structural Analysis of Pension Disclosures Under SFAS 87 and Their Relation to Share Prices," *Financial Analysts Journal*, January–February 1993, pp. 18–26.

[27] Morneau Coopers & Lybrand, and Financial Executives Institute Canada, *Report on Post-employment Benefits in Canada* (Toronto: Financial Executives Institute Canada, 1994).

[28] FASB, *Employers' Accounting for Post-retirement Benefits Other than Pensions*, Statement of Financial Accounting Standards No. 106 (Norwalk: FASB, 1990).

[29] See, for example, D.L. Gerboth, "Accruing the Costs of Other Post-employment Benefits—The Measurement Problem," *The CPA Journal*, November 1988, pp. 36–44.

[30] See CICA, Emerging Issues Committee, *Post Retirement Benefits Other than Pensions*, EIC 5 (Toronto: CICA, 1989). It indicated that at least three methods were acceptable in Canada—accrual for the actuarially determined cost based on current service, accrual when an employee retires, and pay-as-you-go accounting.

[31] FASB, *Employers' Accounting for Postretirement Benefits*, Statement of Financial Accounting Standards No. 112 (Norwalk: FASB, 1992).

[32] IASC, *Employee Benefits*, IAS 19 (Revised) (London: IASC, Revised 1998).

[33] CICA, *Financial Instruments*, Re-exposure Draft (Toronto: CICA, 1994), par. 077. The CICA Accounting Standards Board did not proceed to develop the recognition and measurement proposals in this re-exposure draft into *CICA Handbook* standards (see discussion at Chapter 17).

[34] CICA Emerging Issues Committee, *Share Purchase Loans*, EIC 44 (Toronto: CICA, 1993).

[35] AICPA, APB, *Accounting for Stock Issued to Employees*, Opinion No. 25 (New York: AICPA, 1972).

[36] FASB, *Accounting for Stock-Based Compensation*, Exposure Draft (Norwalk: FASB, June 1993).

[37] See, for example, J.J. Weygandt, "Valuation of Stock Option Contracts," *The Accounting Review*, January 1977, pp. 40–51; R.J. Sokol, "Using Classic Financial Tools to Analyze Deferred Compensation," *CA Magazine*, February 1983, pp. 52–57; T.W. Foster III, P.R. Koogler, and D. Vickrey, "Valuation of Executive Stock Options and the FASB Proposal," *The Accounting Review*, July 1991, pp. 595–610.

[38] See FASB Exposure Draft, *Accounting for Stock-based Compensation*, pars .86–.88. It also discusses "service date" and "service expiration date" alternatives to the vesting date which have somewhat different implications for when an employee may be considered to have rendered the services related to a stock option award. See pars. 81–94.

[39] See FASB, *Accounting for Stock Appreciation Rights and Other Variable Stock Option or Award Plans: An Interpretation of APB No. 15 and 25*, Interpretation No. 28 (Stamford: FASB, 1978).

[40] See, for example, "Considering the Options," *The Economist*, July 30, 1994, pp.70–71.

[41] FASB, *Accounting for Stock-Based Compensation*, Statement of Financial Accounting Standards No. 123 (Norwalk: FASB, 1995).

[42] CICA Emerging Issues Committee, *Phantom Stock Option Plans*, EIC 37 (Toronto: CICA, 1992).

GOVERNMENT
ASSISTANCE

In a modern state no enterprise can avoid the pervasive influence of government. It has been said that the power to tax is the power to destroy. It might also be said that the kindly sun of government beneficence can breathe life into new enterprise and restore the failing. No one can doubt that government taxation, direct and indirect, and government assistance, also direct and indirect, are material to the financial well-being of an enterprise.

As previously described, cost-based accrual accounting rests upon a foundation of bargained transactions in which the accounting entity knows what it is getting in return for payments made and knows what it is sacrificing in return for payments received. The absence of free bargaining in most transactions with government means that the general theory of the accrual system provides little guidance for their accounting. As a result, accounting standards have developed largely on an individual issues basis. In this chapter we deal with issues in two broad areas of government relations: accounting for direct government assistance to business and accounting for indirect government assistance through the income tax system.

ACCOUNTING FOR DIRECT GOVERNMENT ASSISTANCE

Direct assistance may take at least two different forms. First, governments may make outright grants or subsidies. Second, governments may provide assistance by providing service at less than market rates—for example, providing loans at low interest rates. Or a government may simply refrain from charging a normal tax on particular enterprises—for example, a municipality may agree not to charge taxes for a period to new industry locating within its boundaries. Variations of these basic types of direct assistance are also possible. For example, a grant may be repayable if qualifying conditions are not fulfilled, or a loan may be made forgivable upon fulfillment of given conditions.

Conceptual Questions

Prior to the 1960s a business entity rarely received contributions from anyone who did not have a financial interest in it. Typically, any contributions received without an obvious quid pro quo represented donations from shareholders—people who were benefited by the financial well-being of the business. Accordingly, the logical accounting treatment was to treat such contributions as capital receipts; they clearly were not part of any earning process.

The key conceptual question with respect to government assistance is whether it too should be treated as a capital receipt or whether, in some fashion, it should be a factor in income accounting. The following arguments have been made in favour of treating government assistance as a capital contribution:

- The costs incurred by an entity represent the results of bargained exchanges. It would be wrong to distort the portrayal of actual amounts paid for goods and services by offsetting grant proceeds against them.

- Government grant programs have tended to be temporary and subject to change. It would be preferable to portray operating results on a stand-alone basis to help evaluation of the long-term viability of the entity.

- Government grants are paid gratuitously and are in no sense earned. Therefore they should not affect reported income.

- Government grants can be regarded merely as capital financing, because they reduce the need to raise capital from other sources.

The arguments in favour of taking grant proceeds into account in income determination are as follows:

- Accounting traditionally is concerned with reporting the results of the commitment of resources by the owners of the entity. It is the *net* cost of assets and the *net* expenses borne by the owners that is of interest in evaluating the success or otherwise of their investment. It does not distort what actually happened to show net costs in this way. As for portrayal of long-term viability, management will make future investment decisions in the light of conditions prevailing in the future. There is no requirement to replace existing investment if it is not profitable. Therefore, there is no requirement to show the results of existing investment as if it had not been subsidized merely because future replacement of investment might not be eligible for subsidy.

- Government assistance is not truly gratuitous since an entity must take certain actions or fulfill certain conditions to qualify for assistance. Fulfillment of the qualifications for assistance usually involves costs that are taken into account in the determination of income. From the viewpoint of reporting on the progress of the enterprise itself, it is important to take the assistance into account as well as the costs. The conditions imposed for the receipt of government assistance normally provide adequate guidance for recognizing the impact of the assistance on income. The assistance should be recognized in income in step with the expenses that are offset or the revenues that are subsidized by the government program.

Grants and Subsidies

The question of accounting for government assistance was first addressed in Canada in 1967 in the context of government grants to subsidize qualified investment in plant and equipment. The CICA recommendation was two-pronged. If an enterprise would have made a qualified investment even without the stimulus of the grant, it was to be treated as contributed capital (not income). On the other hand, if the enterprise would not have made the investment without the grant, the grant proceeds were to be credited against the cost of the assets subsidized. In this way their carrying value would not be above the amount of sacrifice voluntarily made by the entity, and thus could be presumed to be the equivalent of an economic value evidenced by a bargained transaction.

This solution proved to be unworkable. The accounting treatment depended upon what management claimed was a determining factor in its decision. Since the grant was available in any case, management had to exercise its imagination as to whether it would have made the investment without the grant. In practice, the basis of accounting adopted seemed to conform more to the end result desired rather than to what appeared to be the economics of the situation.

As a result, the CICA re-examined the question some years later, and issued *CICA Handbook* Section 3800 in 1975. By that time the variety of government assistance programs had greatly increased, so that it was necessary to consider more than just investment subsidies. This time it was decided to follow the proprietary theory completely. From the standpoint of an owner deciding whether to make an investment or incur some other expenditure, it is the *net* cost that is relevant to the decision whether the expenditure is worthwhile. If government assistance is available, it is logical to take it into account in the expenditure decision. It follows that the best accounting for proceeds from government assistance is to offset them against the cost or costs with which they are associated. The credit for the assistance received then flows into income automatically, as the net cost is recognized in expense in accordance with normal income determination rules.

Implementation of this approach to accounting for government assistance requires determination of the essential nature of the assistance. That nature is normally indicated by the conditions imposed for qualification for assistance.

- If the assistance is intended to supplement revenue, it should be credited to revenue (as an item of other income) as conditions for receipt of assistance are fulfilled.

- If the assistance is designed to subsidize costs that will be treated as period costs, it should be offset against them as they are expensed. Assistance received in advance of the expensing of related costs should be treated as a deferred credit to be matched with actual cost outlays as they are written off to expense in future.

- If assistance is tied to expenditure on capital assets, two treatments are permissible. The amount of assistance may be deducted directly from the recorded cost of the capital assets and depreciation based on the net amount. Alternatively, the assistance amount may be treated as a deferred credit and amortized to income in step with depreciation written on the related assets.

In practice it is not always easy to distinguish just how a particular type of government assistance should be reflected in income. When a grant is tied to a particular type of cost, there is a strong presumption that the grant should be reflected in income in step with the recognition of that cost as expense. For example, if a grant is a percentage of expenditures on scientific research or pollution control, it is clear that the purpose of the program is to reduce the cost of making those particular expenditures. If a grant is a percentage of investment in plant and equipment in a particular location, it is clear that the appropriate treatment of the grant is a reduction of capital asset costs. Even though the program's objective may be to create employment in a particular area, the fact is that it achieves that aim by reducing the cost of investment in that area.

The situation is more obscure when eligibility for government assistance is not conditional upon specific monetary expenditure by the entity within a clearly defined time period. For example, a grant intended to stimulate employment might be conditioned upon achieving a given level of employment and maintaining it for at least three years. One might argue in such a case that the grant could be amortized to income over the three years, since it becomes unconditional at the end of that time. On the other hand, if fixed investment had to be made to create those jobs, and especially if that investment could not readily be disposed of if the venture were closed down, one might argue that, in substance, qualification for the government assistance put the entity at risk over the lifetime of the investment. Hence, the case may be made that the grant should be reflected in income over that lifetime.

Since there is a wide variety in terms and conditions possible in government assistance programs, it is very difficult to suggest accounting rules appropriate to every circumstance. In general, however, whenever doubt exists it can be suggested that, if it appears that achievement of the government support required a long-term investment, then the credit arising from the receipt of that support is best amortized over the lifetime of the venture.[1]

Conditions applicable to government assistance programs may also introduce an element of uncertainty into the accounting. If the entity has fulfilled the important conditions required to achieve the objectives of the program, and has reasonable assurance of fulfilling the remaining conditions, it is considered proper to accrue the estimated amount of assistance receivable and begin accounting for its income effect. Similarly, if assistance has been received but may be required to be repaid if the entity does not continue to fulfill certain conditions, income accounting may proceed provided there is reasonable assurance those continuing conditions will be met. Finally, certain assistance may be provided in the form of loans that will be forgiven over a period of time if the entity continues to fulfill specific conditions. Assuming there is reasonable assurance at the outset that the conditions will be fulfilled, the forgivable loan is tantamount to a grant, and may be so accounted for so long as the qualifying conditions continue to be fulfilled.

In assessing an entity's operations it is useful to know the extent to which income and financial position reported have been affected by government assistance, and especially the extent to which support currently being credited to income account will be discontinued in future without compensating reduction in costs or in revenues. The *CICA Handbook* Section 3800 calls for disclosure of a considerable amount of detail with respect to grants received, their terms and conditions, and any contingent liability for repayment.

If a grant does not reduce the tax basis of a capital asset but its amount is credited against the carrying value of the asset on the books, the total capital cost allowance claimable over the asset's life will exceed its initial carrying value. Under a different government program a grant might reduce the tax basis of the asset. A difference between the initial tax and accounting basis for the asset will create difficulty for the operation of tax allocation accounting (to be discussed in the next chapter).

Concessionary Arrangements

Subsidies may be given by different levels of government in many different ways. For example, a senior government might make low-cost financing available for entities setting up business in a depressed area. Or, a municipality may commit itself to remission of taxes for a fixed period to induce industry to locate within its boundaries. It is extremely difficult to account for such forms of government assistance in a manner that is consistent with the treatment given outright grants or subsidies.

Consider a municipality that gives a business a ten-year remission of real property taxes. The form of assistance is a tax remission, but the purpose is to induce investment in the community. It is normally at the point of the initial investment decision that the availability of the assistance affects management decision making. It would be logical, therefore, to capitalize the present value of the government assistance as an asset at the time the invest-ment is undertaken, and treat the offsetting credit as a reduction in capital asset cost or deferred credit, just as if the municipality had given a direct subsidy.

In practice this degree of sophistication in accounting is not attempted, no doubt partly because of the difficult estimates that would be required of capitalized value and appropri-ate amortization period. Government assistance received by way of concessions is normally accounted for just as it is received. For example, realty tax expense is simply not recorded if none is charged under a concessionary arrangement. Accordingly, where government concessions are material to results reported, it is important to disclose their amount and the future period for which they will continue.

GOVERNMENT ASSISTANCE THROUGH THE INCOME TAX SYSTEM

One particular form of concessionary assistance occasionally used in Canada in the past has been the so-called "income tax holiday." For example, new mines used to be free from income tax for the first three years after the beginning of commercial production. In such a case it would have been difficult, if not impossible, to place a value on the concession at the commencement of operations. In contrast, another program briefly in effect in the early 1970s allowed a new enterprise in a depressed area the choice of a stated subsidy against cap-ital asset costs or a three-year income tax holiday. In that case, a company electing the tax holiday could have recorded an asset for the amount equal to the capital asset subsidy it might have had—crediting capital asset cost for the value of the subsidy—and subsequently recorded a gain or loss on its decision, depending upon whether the tax avoided under the holiday exceeded or fell short of the recorded asset. No one adopted this decision-oriented—and possibly embarrassing to management—basis of accounting.

These two different income tax concessions stimulate consideration of a conceptual question. Suppose a government program gives an enterprise a choice between an outright grant or taking an equivalent amount as a reduction in taxes payable. In this case the tax reduction, if taken, is in substance a grant. Thus, if a given program grant would be treated as a reduction in capital asset cost, an equivalent tax reduction taken under the same program should in concept be credited to capital assets. Correspondingly, the tax expense for the period would be recorded as if there had not been a tax reduction.

The case is more debatable when government assistance is available *only* in the form of a credit against income taxes payable. In that case there are two necessary conditions to receipt of the assistance—fulfillment of the program qualifications, and the earning of taxable income. This is a specific example of a general problem in accounting. When two or more events are necessary to one outcome, which event shall be regarded as predominant so as to form the basis of accounting recognition of the outcome?

In this situation, two competing views have been held. Under one viewpoint, the expense for income tax is whatever amount results from the law and regulations adopted by the government. If the government permits special tax reductions in special circumstances, these represent merely "a selective reduction in tax rate." The reduction should "flow through" to net income reported in the year when the reduction is effective. Under the other viewpoint, it is pointed out that the receipt of the tax concession is almost always conditional upon the taxpayer undertaking other actions. Thus, the tax reduction ought to be accounted for as a direct offset to the costs incurred in the other transactions undertaken to meet the government conditions.

This fundamental question in tax accounting has arisen in the context of accounting for individual tax incentives and has been answered, either through the development of practice or through specific accounting standards, in ways that have not always been consistent. We discuss a few specific cases below.

Tax Incentives through Deductions from Taxable Income

Tax Incentives through Extra Expense Allowances

Extra tax deductions from taxable income have sometimes been provided by simply factoring up a cost that otherwise would be deductible at its actual amount. For example, Canadian tax law at one time allowed a deduction for scientific research expenditures of 150% of their actual cost. So long as such expenditures are written off in the accounts in the same year as the tax deduction is taken, the "flow-through" and government grant approaches to accounting for the tax saving will have the same effect on net income after tax. Under the flow-through approach, tax expense is reported in the income statement at its actual reduced amount and the research expenditures that gave rise to the extra tax reduction are reported as expenses at their actual amount. Alternatively, the tax reductions resulting from the extra deductible amount could be treated on a basis equivalent to a government grant. To accomplish this the amount of the tax reduction would have to be calculated and reported income tax increased, while the actual expense that qualified for the extra tax reduction would be reduced. In practice, this refinement in accounting would not normally be performed. Flow-through accounting is likely to be followed automatically although, in view of the lack of impact on the reported income figure, it may be doubted that much thought has been given to the desirability of a different form of presentation.

Tax Incentives through Extra Capital Cost Allowances

The situation is less straightforward when an extra tax allowance is granted for capital expenditures. For example, some years ago a qualified investment within a given period gave rise to a right to claim capital cost allowance (CCA) based on 115% of the cost of the asset. This provision was intended to stimulate capital investment. Accounting for the incentive on a basis fully consistent with that for direct capital assistance would have required that an amount equivalent to the present value of the extra capital cost allowance be credited against the asset account (or treated as a deferred credit) and be brought into income in step with depreciation on the asset. Because of the extra record-keeping complications that this would cause, however, the general practice was simply to allow the tax reduction from the extra capital cost allowance to flow through to income.[2]

The CICA has since issued a standard for treatment of investment tax credits (see next section), and a flow-through treatment in a situation similar to that just described would be inconsistent with this standard.

Investment Tax Credits

One of the most hotly debated issues in accounting has been that of the treatment of tax credits allowed in consideration for investment in qualifying assets. This debate was first joined in the United States in 1962. The Internal Revenue Code permitted an "investment credit" against taxes payable equal to a percentage of the cost of certain depreciable assets acquired after 1961. The immediate question was, when should the reduction be taken into income?

Some felt that it could be treated as income immediately—the flow-through basis. Others thought that since it stemmed from investment in depreciable assets, it should be reflected in income in step with depreciation written on the assets. There was also a modification of the flow-through method. As originally enacted, any tax credit taken reduced the tax basis (undepreciated capital cost in Canadian terms) of the assets. It was identical in effect, therefore, to a 100% claim of CCA up to the amount of the tax credit without corresponding depreciation being written in the accounts. Under tax allocation principles (see next chapter) the difference in timing of the reduction of tax and book values should lead to recognition of a deferred tax credit recorded at the current rate of tax. Thus, it was proposed that the amount of the investment credit should be apportioned: 52% (the then-current rate of tax) should be credited to deferred taxes and 48% could flow through immediately to income.

The opinion of American accountants on this issue was sharply divided. A majority of the Accounting Principles Board favoured the deferral and amortization approach to recognizing the credit in income. However, two phenomena previously almost unknown were to frustrate a standard embodying the majority opinion. Deferral and amortization was strongly opposed by certain industrial interests. A lobby was organized to go over the heads of the board to the Securities and Exchange Commission in an attempt to persuade the commission not to enforce the board's opinion. Deferral and amortization was also opposed by the U.S. Treasury Department on the grounds that such an accounting rule would reduce the incentive to business to take advantage of the program and thereby would tend to frustrate its aims. This was the first important occasion on which an argument was made that accounting standards should be determined, not necessarily by the criterion of fair presentation, but rather by the criterion of their expected "economic consequences."

The significance of an economic consequences argument in this case should be understood. If the flow-through method provided the most faithful presentation of the effect on income and wealth of the investment credit, then there was no need to argue that it had favourable economic consequences. It would be justified on its own merits. It is only when the flow-through method was *not* the best method to achieve accounting objectives (or if it had to be concluded that there was no basis for determining the best method) that possible economic consequences needed to be marshalled in its support. In effect, the Treasury Department was taking the cynical position that fair financial accounting should take second place to the presumed economic policy objectives of government.

The economic consequences argument might be examined on its own merits. In deciding on capital expenditures, most enterprises go through a "capital budgeting" exercise to determine whether the proposed expenditures meet certain criteria. For example, incremental cash receipts and outlays that are forecast as a result of operation of a proposed capital asset may be discounted by, say, the current weighted-average cost of capital to see whether the net present value equals or exceeds the cost of the proposed asset. If it does not, the investment may be expected to be rejected.

Even a modest investment credit may be sufficient to cause the present value of cash flows to exceed the cash outlay and lead to acceptance of the project. In other words, the availability of government assistance changes the economics of the project and should stimulate investment *regardless of the accounting.* Some might argue that some managements may be sufficiently incompetent as not to make such an analysis. Or, it might be felt that management with incentive compensation contracts tied to reported accounting earnings would be motivated to make uneconomical investments merely to take advantage of the boost in earnings from flow-through accounting. If either of these is correct, prohibition of flow-through accounting would dampen the potential stimulative effect of the investment tax credit. It is hard to believe, however, that sound public policy can be based upon inducing unsound private decisions.

These considerations were not strongly urged in 1962 or even since that time. Under political pressure, the Securities and Exchange Commission failed to support the Accounting Principles Board in its proposed accounting standard and forced the board to adopt a permissive stance.[3] A subsequent effort by the board in 1971 met with further lobbying that culminated in a congressional prohibition of any attempt to prescribe a single method of accounting in the financial reports of entities to be filed with government agencies. [4] As a result, accounting practice for the investment tax credit in the United States is still optional.

Investment tax credits were introduced in Canada a few years after their introduction in the United States. The CICA gave consideration to their accounting in connection with projects on income tax accounting and government grant accounting. Each time it backed off making a recommendation, in view of the controversy on the subject so evident in the United States. Finally it became clear that standards for accounting for direct government assistance were open to serious attack unless logical consistency could be achieved between the accounting for government assistance effected through the tax system and directly.[5] In essence the CICA adopted, in a standard issued in 1985, the following convincing reasoning:

- The cost-based accrual accounting system calls for accrual accounting when cash flows fall into periods other than those to which they may be reasonably attributed in accordance with their underlying economic causes.
- It is inconsistent with the accrual model of accounting to record gains merely because assets have been acquired.
- Government assistance pinpointed to specific situations and rendered through the tax system is not fundamentally different in character from direct government grants.
- Accordingly, investment tax credits should be deducted from the related investment in capital assets or treated as deferred credits to be amortized to income on the same basis as the related assets.[6]

SUMMARY

This chapter deals with accounting aspects of government assistance to private enterprise by way of direct grants or subsidies or assistance granted on special conditions through reductions in income tax.

The basic issue in accounting for direct government assistance is whether such assistance should be treated as a capital contribution, or whether it should enter into income accounting. Today's accounting standards are firmly based upon the proprietary viewpoint; thus, any contributions from parties other than shareholders must be reflected in income sooner or later. That settled, the accounting resolves itself into a question of how government assistance should be reflected in income.

- All selective government assistance is granted based on conditions to be fulfilled by the grantee. Fulfillment of these conditions normally involves costs to the grantee. A logical basis for accounting for the government assistance, therefore, is to reflect it in income at the same time as the related costs are written off. This can be achieved by crediting the grant proceeds against the costs in the first instance leaving only the net cost to be written off as expense, or by treating the grant proceeds as a deferred credit when first received and amortizing that credit to income in step with the expensing of the related costs.

- Assistance granted by government is not always expressed as conditional upon monetary expenditure. It may be based upon attainment by the grantee of some nonmonetary objective. In such a case, judgment must be exercised as to the proper basis for recognition of the assistance proceeds in income. If the grant has the result of involving the enterprise in capital investment, as often it will, it would be logical to amortize the grant in step with the amortization of the investment.

- Governments may provide assistance through remission of normal taxes, rather than through a direct payment to the grantee. Logically, the value of such assistance should be treated in the same fashion as a direct subsidy. In practice it is not. The expense reported is simply lower than it otherwise would be. Where this is the case, it is important that financial statements disclose the existence and amount of the special assistance and its termination date.

Government assistance may also be given indirectly by selective tax deductions or tax credits, rather than by direct grant. The grantee in such a case must have taxable income to take advantage of the assistance. Because of this, there has been debate whether the benefit of the tax concession should be reported in income as the tax reductions are achieved—the so-called "flow-through" basis of accounting—or whether the income tax expense should be "normalized" to the figure it would have been without the special concessions. The credit resulting from the normalization entry is then treated in the same fashion as would a credit from direct government assistance. This latter position has been accepted in Canada in the case of accounting for the investment tax credit, effective in 1985. To be logical, any other form of special concession granted through the income tax system should henceforth be treated in a compatible fashion.

REFERENCES

[1] This problem is discussed in "Accounting for Government Assistance," *CICA Handbook,* Section 3800 (Toronto: CICA), par. 12. The guidance given by that paragraph is quite general and it is possible that it might be interpreted differently from the opinions here expressed.

[2] See "New CCA Base: 115% of Cost," *Canadian Chartered Accountant*, March 1971, pp. 152–53.

[3] See AICPA, APB, *Accounting for the "Investment Credit,"* APB Opinion No. 2 (New York: AICPA, 1962) and *Accounting for the "Investment Credit,"* APB Opinion No. 4 (New York: AICPA, 1964).

[4] See AICPA, APB, *Acceptable Methods of Accounting for Investment Credits Under 1971 Act*, AICPA Accounting Interpretations of APB Opinion No. 4, Interpretation No. 3 (New York: AICPA, 1972).

[5] See R.H. Crandall, "Government Intervention—The PIP Grant Accounting Controversy," *Cost and Management*, September–October 1983, pp. 55–59. This article was reprinted in "Commentary," ed. R.T. Sprouse, *Accounting Horizons*, September 1988, pp. 110–16.

[6] See CICA, "Investment Tax Credits," *CICA Handbook*, Section 3805 (Toronto: CICA).

INCOME TAX

Accounting for income tax of corporations has been a contentious subject since the early 1950s. The debate has revolved around the question of income tax allocation. Is income tax a cost whose recognition as expense can be allocated between periods, like other costs, for the better portrayal of income? If allocation is performed, what is its conceptual basis, and how is it to be implemented?

A few accounting writers have suggested that income tax is not an *expense* of earning income but rather is a *distribution* of income after it has been earned. From this they argue that distributions are what they are and cannot be allocated. To support the argument, it is pointed out that income tax is not voluntarily undertaken, and is not in any direct way a payment for services. Rather than being laid out to earn profits, it is an appropriation of profits. These observations are true, and it is certainly open to someone to define income tax as a distribution and not an expense. That, however, would not end the matter so long as one objective of accounting is to report how much income accrues to the owners of a company. If, for example, pretax income this year contains elements that will be taxed next year, what is the best way to measure the owners' share in that income? Should only the actual tax payable be deducted this year, or should the additional tax that will probably be payable next year because of transactions that are reported as part of this year's income also be deducted? The allocation of income tax expense among accounting periods, it is clear, stems from the proprietorial emphasis in generally accepted accounting principles. Income tax is generally considered a cost of doing business that management is accountable for effectively managing. Only after provision has been made for it is income available to owners or for reinvestment in the business.

The complex subject of income tax allocation will be discussed on the basis of the following natural progression of issues:

- The idea of allocating income tax between periods begins with defining the differences between accounting and taxable income, and considering to what extent these differences may be expected to reverse in future periods. The first question is whether the tax effects of timing or temporary differences should be allocated between periods on either a comprehensive or partial basis. This requires addressing a complex series of arguments that have been debated over many years.

- A second set of issues relates to the measurement of the tax effects of differences that it is determined should be allocated. There are three contenders, known generally as the deferral, asset and liability (formerly known as the accrual method), and net-of-tax methods. We shall discuss each of these. As well, there is the fundamental question whether deferred tax balances should be reported on a discounted basis.

- Deferred tax debits, including tax loss carryforwards, require additional consideration as to whether, or under what circumstances, they may qualify for recognition as assets.

- Finally, intraperiod tax allocation, balance sheet classification, and disclosure matters are addressed. (Refundable taxes are discussed in Chapter 9.)

Before addressing these issues, it would seem useful to provide a historical overview and perspective.

A Historical Perspective

The first authoritative accounting statement to suggest what we now know as interperiod tax allocation was issued in the U.S. in 1944.[1] By the time it was issued, the emphasis on "matching" revenues and costs to achieve a proper measure of income was resulting in recognition of an increased number of deferred charges in the balance sheet. Usually, costs treated as deferred charges were claimable for tax purposes only in the year incurred. Consequently, if income taxes were charged to income without allocation between accounting periods, tax expense reported would appear unnaturally low in relation to pretax income when deferred charges were incurred, and unnaturally high in subsequent periods when the deferred charges were written off. The statement recommended that an amount equal to the tax reduction attributable to the deferred cost should be added to the actual tax payable for the year to arrive at a proper expense figure, and credited to the deferred charge account. Thereafter, the deferred charge, net of the tax reduction, would be amortized in the normal fashion.

The year 1954 saw the beginning of a long debate over tax allocation in both Canada and in the United States. In the latter country, the Revenue Act of 1954 gave permission for the use of accelerated patterns of depreciation (such as the sum-of-the-years' digits method) for tax deduction calculations. In Canada, the declining-balance basis for capital cost allowance (that is, an accelerated write-off pattern) had been adopted with the new Income Tax Act in 1949. A Canadian company was not permitted, however, to take advantage of the faster tax write-offs unless it also wrote depreciation of the same amount in its books. That requirement was rescinded in 1954. In that year, then, in both countries the possibility arose of significant continuing differences between depreciation written on the books and depreciation (or capital cost allowance) claimed for tax purposes. The acceleration of depreciation allowances for tax purposes simply meant that less tax would be paid in the early years of an asset's life and more in the later years. In these circumstances it was asked: Would it not be best from an accounting point of view to "defer" the tax reduction resulting from tax allowances in excess of book depreciation on assets, and to credit those tax reductions back against tax expense in those future years when tax allowances were less than book depreciation? In this way, one could match the tax effect of capital cost allowances with depreciation written in the accounts.

This question was far more important in Canada than in the United States. The new tax system applied the declining-balance basis to all assets, not just to assets acquired after the effective date of the new law as in the United States. In addition, Canadian taxpayers could claim capital cost allowance on the cost of all assets to which title had been acquired (including the cost of assets still under construction). Thus, without interperiod tax allocation, reported tax expense in Canada could be reduced and reported profits increased by the mere act of acquiring assets. To the CICA that idea was repugnant. In Bulletin No. 10, the CICA Accounting and Auditing Research Committee expressed a strong preference for interperiod tax allocation to solve this problem. In the United States the Committee on Accounting Procedure took up a compromise position at first, but a few years later the committee changed its mind and recommended the position preferred in Canada.

A substantial minority of companies were not convinced by the argument for interperiod tax allocation. As a result, conflicting accounting presentations continued for some years. Then, in 1967, by which time official institute recommendations had acquired more authority, both the CICA and the U.S. Accounting Principles Board issued new statements.[2] The statements withdrew sanction for the flow-through or "taxes payable" method of recording income tax expense and prescribed a "comprehensive tax allocation" approach. The basis of that approach was the "deferral" method, under which timing differences were to be deferred at tax rates in effect in the year the differences originate with no subsequent adjustment of accumulated balance sheet deferred tax debits or credits to reflect changes in tax rates.

The debate did not die with these pronouncements. A wide variety of strongly held views continued to appear in the literature. Many authors set out arguments in favour of "flow-through" accounting or various forms of partial allocation. A major criticism of the deferral method of comprehensive tax allocation was that it resulted in "dangling debits and credits" in the balance sheet that did not represent true "assets" and "liabilities." This concern assumed greater importance with the adoption by the FASB, and later the CICA, of conceptual frameworks that emphasized the balance sheet and in-substance concepts of assets and liabilities. As well, some expressed dissatisfaction with the rules for asset recognition of deferred tax debits (based on "reasonable assurance" of realization) and loss carryforwards (based on "virtual certainty" of realization).

The FASB undertook a fundamental reconsideration of accounting for income taxes in the early 1980s and, after much debate, issued SFAS 96 in 1989. SFAS 96 reaffirmed comprehensive tax allocation, but from a balance sheet perspective. It made three major changes:

- It expanded the concept of timing differences to encompass virtually all temporary differences between the accounting and tax bases of assets and liabilities.

- It replaced the deferral method with the accrual method, under which deferred tax balance sheet amounts are adjusted to reflect changes in tax rates and laws, with adjustments made directly through income.

- It required complex scheduling of the reversal of temporary differences to future years, and it permitted no recognition of deferred tax debit balances that could not be demonstrated to offset against reversing deferred tax credit balances in future years. The thinking was that the recovery of deferred tax debits that did not offset against reversing credits must depend on the enterprise earning future income and that the earning of future income should not be anticipated.

The standard was strongly resisted from the moment it was issued. The board found itself inundated with requests to change the criteria for the recognition and measurement of deferred tax assets and to reduce the complexity of scheduling future reversals of temporary differences. The FASB bowed to these pressures and suspended the effective date of SFAS 96 in order to reconsider these issues. Early in 1992 the board replaced SFAS 96 with SFAS 109.[3] SFAS 109 retained the asset and liability approach (the expanded concept of temporary differences and the accrual method), but it reduced the complexity of the standard and changed the basis for recognizing deferred tax debits and loss carryforwards as assets to one based on whether it is more likely than not that the amounts will be realized.

In Canada the CICA issued an exposure draft in 1988 which proposed to adopt the accrual method of comprehensive tax allocation and the broader concept of temporary differences, but it proposed not to change its existing rules for recognizing deferred tax debits and loss carryforwards. The responses to the exposure draft were critical and diverse, indicating that the CICA could expect to find it difficult to arrive at a new standard that would have broad support. In light of this and the controversy that had emerged over SFAS 96 in the U.S., the CICA decided to shelve the project.

However, as time passed, Canada was left virtually alone in the world in continuing to require the deferral method. It issued a new exposure draft in 1996 that proposed a standard modelled very closely on SFAS 109. The standard was issued as *CICA Handbook* Section 3465 in 1997, to be effective with retroactive application for years beginning on or after January 1, 2000.[4] Earlier application is encouraged.

INTERPERIOD TAX ALLOCATION— COMPREHENSIVE, PARTIAL OR FLOW-THROUGH?

Comprehensive Tax Allocation

Comprehensive tax allocation has been based upon the idea that most revenues earned by a business are included in taxable income sooner or later, and most costs incurred are allowed as deductions sooner or later. There are, however, differences in the timing of recognition of some revenues and expenses for accounting and tax purposes. These differences can make actual taxable income for a given year differ sharply from the accounting income reported for that year. Thus, the actual tax payable may not be a fair presentation of the real burden of taxes on that reported accounting income. To resolve this, the idea of comprehensive tax allocation is that (with the exception of a few items) each dollar of revenue reported for accounting purposes can be considered as bearing a tax charge, and each dollar of expense reported for accounting purposes can be considered as being entitled to a tax reduction. To the extent there are differences in any given year in the timing of recognition of revenues and expenses for accounting and tax purposes, the resulting income tax effects (whether an increase or decrease in tax) are deferred (and treated as deferred tax assets or liabilities in the balance sheet), to be brought back into the figures of tax expense in future years when the timing differences reverse.

To understand the concept of comprehensive tax allocation fully, we need to examine first the causes of differences between accounting income before tax and taxable income.

Timing Differences

A timing difference between accounting and taxable income can be classified on the basis of whether it relates to a revenue item or to an expense item, and also whether the recognition of the item for accounting purposes precedes or follows its recognition for tax purposes. This provides four different categories. Table 16-1 sets out a number of examples in each category. The table also expands on the character of each timing difference listed, and lays the groundwork for some points to be discussed subsequently.

Table 16-1   Summary of Accounting/Tax Timing Differences

Type of Timing Difference	Related Asset/ Liability (1)	Cause of Reversal (2)	Reversal Predictable or Indefinite? (3)	Future Effect on Tax (4)
A. Revenue/income recorded before taxed				
Installment sales	Installment accounts receivable	Cash collection	Predictable	Tax payable when cash collected
Percentage-of-completion contract income	—	Completion of contract	Predictable	Tax payable when contract complete
Unremitted profits of foreign investee	Equity accounted investment; nil in consolidation	Remittance of profits	Indefinite	Tax payable when profits remitted
B. Expense recorded before tax deduction				
Warranty costs	Warranty liability	Specific costs incurred	Predictable	Tax deduction when costs incurred
Deferred compensation	Compensation liability	Compensation paid	Predictable	Tax deduction on payment
LIFO cost of sales in excess of FIFO	Inventory	FIFO exceeds LIFO	Indefinite	Tax deduction if reversal
C. Expense recorded after tax deduction				
Some prepayments or deferred charges	Prepaid or deferred asset	Asset amortized	Predictable	Tax payable on future net cash recovery from asset
Capital cost allowance in excess of depreciation	Depreciable assets	Depreciation catches up to capital cost allowance	Predictable (for individual assets)	Tax payable on future net cash recovery from asset
D. Revenue/income recorded after taxed				
Intercompany profits eliminated on consolidation	—	Goods sold to outsiders	Predictable	Tax reduced by previous step-up in asset tax basis
Customer prepayments on subscriptions or contracts	Unearned revenue	Revenue recognition requirements fulfilled	Predictable	Tax reduced to extent of expenses to be incurred to earn revenue.

- Column (1) lists the related asset or liability for each timing difference. For example, revenue from installment sales is taxed at a different time from that at which it is recognized in the accounts. The installment account receivable is the asset recorded when the revenue is recognized. Accordingly, that receivable is the asset that is related to the deferred tax recorded. It will be noted that no related asset or liability is shown in Table 16-1 for certain types of timing difference. This may occur when the tax legislation and accounting give different timing recognition to a cash-generating event. For example, suppose an enterprise recognizes contract income on a percentage completion basis, and that it is also paid on that basis, so that it has cash in hand for work completed to date. This income may not be taxable until the contract is complete, so that there is a timing difference but no asset or liability to relate it to.

- Column (2) sets out the causes of reversal of the timing difference. Several timing differences occur because the taxation system clings to a cash basis for recognition of certain revenues and expenses while accounting is on an accrual basis. If the accounting accrual precedes the cash effect, the reversal occurs when the cash transaction takes place (for example, when warranty costs are actually paid). If the cash effect precedes the accounting accrual, the reversal occurs when the accounting accrual entry is made (for example, when a deferred cost is amortized to expense). Other timing differences reverse when the income measurement convention used for accounting purposes catches up with that used for tax purposes or vice versa.

- Column (3) indicates whether the timing of reversal is predictable or is indefinite. In most cases, it is predictable. However, in a few cases, as in the case of the use of LIFO accounting for financial reporting and FIFO for tax purposes, the time of reversal (if any) is indefinite. Some question whether tax allocation is appropriate when the timing of reversal is indefinite. These situations are the exception rather than the rule, and they will be discussed separately a little later in this section.

- Column (4) describes how future tax will be affected by reversals of timing differences.

Temporary Differences

Temporary differences embody all timing differences as described above plus certain additional differences between the tax and accounting bases of assets and liabilities. The broader concept of temporary differences results from a balance sheet orientation under which it is assumed that all reported amounts for assets and liabilities will ultimately be recovered and settled, respectively. Based on this assumption, any difference between the tax basis of an asset or liability and the amount at which it is recorded on the balance sheet will result in taxable or deductible amounts in the future period(s) when the asset or a liability is recovered or settled. Certain events create differences between the tax and accounting basis of an asset or a liability without creating timing differences, per se. For example, an enterprise may acquire a capital asset at a cost that is more or less than its tax deduction base. This is a common result in a business acquisition where the fair values attributed to the assets and liabilities of a purchased entity at the date of acquisition differ from their tax values.

The recently replaced CICA tax allocation standard applied only to timing differences, while the new standard applies to temporary differences, with a few exceptions (the most notable being goodwill on which amortization is not deductible for tax purposes).[5]

Let us examine how the concept of temporary differences would apply to a difference between the tax and accounting bases of an acquired asset. Suppose that a depreciable capital asset is acquired for $600 with a tax deduction basis of zero. To determine the temporary difference deferred tax effect, we must first determine the asset's equivalent pretax value (say P). If the tax rate is 40%, P = $600 + (.4) (P), which is $1,000. An adjustment is then made to debit the capital asset and credit deferred tax liability for $400. The rationale for this entry is that the $600 amount paid for this asset is less than it would have been if it had tax deduction value. Its net-of-tax cost of $600 is restated to an equivalent pretax value ($1,000), and the $400 deferred tax liability represents the deferred tax effect of the difference between the asset's accounting base of $1,000 and its tax base of zero.[6] This is not a fully satisfactory adjustment, because it does not take into account the time value of money. In order to reflect the true value of the tax nondeductibility, one would discount the future tax deductions that have been foregone at an appropriate competitive interest rate. This is a problem with the *measurement* of temporary differences, which we will briefly consider later in this chapter.

In the case of a business combination accounted for as a purchase, the determination is simpler. The values assigned to identifiable assets and liabilities acquired are to be based on their pretax fair values (determined as if the tax basis was the same as the fair value). Any difference between that fair value and the tax basis is then a temporary difference and its tax effect is recognized on acquisition as a deferred tax liability or asset (see paragraphs 3465.16–17, which include an example). Again the deferred tax balance arising is overstated because it is not discounted for the time value of money. This affects the amount of goodwill, which is the "plug" in a business acquisition.

Accounting for Deferred Taxes When Reversal Is Indefinite

As indicated, there are a few situations where the timing of reversal is indefinite. Income earned by foreign subsidiaries or investees is recognized by the investor under consolidation or equity accounting when earned by the foreign entity, but withholding tax (and domestic income tax when applicable) is not payable until earnings are remitted. Sometimes also a company obtains tax deductions with respect to the capital cost of an asset that will not be charged off to income unless it is sold. For example, if interest is capitalized as part of the cost of land acquired that is not held for sale, and that interest reduces taxes, the reversal of the timing difference will not occur unless the land is sold.

Some question whether deferred taxes should be recorded even under a comprehensive allocation basis in these cases. In practice, such cases are dealt with on a situation-specific basis. In Canada, deferred tax is to be recognized in respect of unremitted earnings of subsidiaries and joint ventures except where, "it is apparent that this difference will not reverse in the foreseeable future" (paragraph 3465.37). The thinking is that the parent company controls or has joint control over the dividend policy of the investee and thus is in a position to determine that profits will not be distributed in the foreseeable future, in which case it will make no provision for the tax that would be payable if profits were to be remitted (paragraphs 3465.40–.41). A deferred tax liability would, however, be recorded for a temporary difference of this nature related to an equity-accounted investee, because the investor cannot control the timing of any dividends (paragraph 3465.42). On the other hand, Canadian practice has been to provide for deferred taxation with respect to a temporary difference arising from claiming interest for tax purposes that is capitalized as part of the cost of land not held for sale.

In the U.S., SFAS 109 requires that deferred taxes be provided on any excess of taxable unremitted earnings of domestic subsidiaries and equity accounted investees arising after the effective date of the standard. It reasons that management's ability to determine if and when such earnings will be remitted does not eliminate the existence of a deferred tax liability. The taxing authority has a claim that precludes shareholders from ever realizing a portion of these earnings, so that this amount should not be included in shareholders' equity. The FASB standard does not, however, require provision for deferred taxes on the unremitted earnings of foreign subsidiaries or foreign corporate joint ventures that are "essentially permanent in nature," in part because of the potential complexity of the calculations.[7]

Objections Voiced to Comprehensive Tax Allocation

The debate over the allocation of tax expense raged over many years. Participants in the debate typically argued from different premises and, not surprisingly, arrived at different conclusions. The accounting literature cited in the bibliography provides extensive examination of the debate. The principal arguments of those who have objected to comprehensive tax allocation will be reviewed here, proceeding from the simplest to the more complex.

There is no real relationship between accounting and taxable income. Some writers have argued that there is no real functional relationship between the basis for determining how much income taxes a company will pay and the accounting measure of income. They argue that the tax law is so full of provisions designed to provide administrative convenience or special incentives that it has lost all connection with accounting income.

The strength of this argument depends upon the facts. It is conceivable that accounting and income taxation could lose touch. For example, if the tax law were to adopt a new definition of income (perhaps more explicitly designed to avoid the taxation of real capital in the guise of income during inflation) while accounting clung to the historical cost model, the two systems might be very difficult to reconcile. Or, if the tax system made a large number of modifications over the years to the definition of taxable revenues and taxable deductions, such changes might, on a cumulative basis, add up to a system recognizably different from the accounting model.

It is doubtful that history to date supports such a conclusion. In Canada, evidence of the similarity of the two systems is provided by the fact that the computation of taxable income in a corporate tax return begins with the words "income shown by the financial statements" and continues with the adjustments (relatively few in number) to arrive at taxable income. It could not be set up in this way if there were not a large degree of common ground between the two systems.

Income tax allocation obscures management performance. A few accountants have argued that reporting tax expense as the amount actually payable accurately portrays management's skill or otherwise in minimizing taxes. This is a shallow argument. Unless future years' income tax rates are expected to be higher than the current year's rates by more than the after-tax rate of interest obtainable, management would be foolish not to claim every possible deduction it can for tax purposes as early as possible. Thus, ordinarily there is no real skill involved in making the right choices in filing income tax returns, to the extent that choices exist at all. (Many differences between tax and accounting income are prescribed by law and are not a matter of choice.)

Income taxes are indivisible. Some have argued from the premise that taxes paid result from a process of applying a statutory tax rate to a figure of *net* taxable income. Therefore, they reasoned that no individual revenue or individual cost can be related in isolation to the figure of tax expense. It is contrary to the nature of income tax to attribute parts of it to individual items of revenue or cost recognized for accounting purposes (notwithstanding that it can often be shown that had the enterprise not incurred a particular cost or become entitled to proceeds from a particular revenue transaction, the net tax would have been a different figure).[8]

This is basically an argument against *any* allocation in accounting reports. If it is wrong to discover a relationship between net taxable income and certain costs and revenues, and hence between taxable income and the periods in which those costs and revenues are reported, it must be equally wrong to, say, discover a relationship between the cost of a capital asset and the period in which it renders service. That capital asset cost is just as indivisible as is income tax expense. To argue that income tax allocation is illegitimate because it requires a division of cost is to argue that a very high percentage of existing accounting conventions are illegitimate.

Taxes payable accounting assists the prediction of future cash flows. Others have argued that investors and other users of financial statements are interested in future cash flows and will be better served by reporting taxes at the amount assessable, since that represents cash payable in or soon after the fiscal year.

The implicit assertion in this claim is that future cash flows will look like cash flows in the most recent period—an argument that is unsubstantiated and extremely dubious. Taxes payable accounting makes it appear as though accelerated deductions for capital cost allowances, for example, eliminate taxes rather than just postponing their effects. One may doubt that this aids prediction.

The argument is either illogical or incomplete. If one year's actual cash flows are the best evidence of future cash flows, why not just present a cash statement? Why not, for example, write off investment in plant on a cash basis? If the answer is that capitalization and amortization of plant cost provide a better estimate of average future cash flows to be expected, how does one distinguish between plant cost allocation and income tax allocation in this respect? In short, this argument, like the one preceding, is really saying that the whole present system of income accounting is wrong and should be changed to a cash basis statement.

Income tax allocation assumes future events. A number of opponents of tax allocation have argued that a reversal of a timing difference does not have a tax effect unless there is taxable income at the time of the reversal. The existence of taxable income at that time will depend (largely) on future revenues and future costs. Therefore the tax effect of the reversal is contingent upon future events, and thus that reversal impact is not properly an asset or liability before that time. Until that time the asset or liability is contingent only.[9]

To evaluate this argument, consider the nature of liabilities. The amount of warranty costs depends upon future events. The amount of pension cost also depends upon future events. The crucial question for accounting is *which* event triggers recognition of revenues, costs, and associated assets and liabilities. Once that is decided, the rest of the problem is measurement. Opponents of tax allocation have noted that in no other case is the occurrence of the future event dependent upon future revenue earning activity of the company.[10] Warranty claims are made and pensions are payable regardless of whether the enterprise makes a profit in the future. There is a conclusive answer to this argument in at least insofar as deferred tax credits are concerned. The realization of virtually every asset carried at cost or some derivative of cost in the balance sheet—assets such as inventory, plant and equipment, and various intangibles—is dependent upon future transactions and, if income cannot be assumed, the assets are written down.

This argument is particularly apropos in relation to capital assets, because the most controversial and most material aspect of tax allocation accounting relates to the temporary differences between depreciation on capital assets and capital cost allowances. Consider depreciable plant carried in the balance sheet at, say, $10 million whose undepreciated capital cost for tax purposes has been reduced to, say, $6 million. The plant book value of $10 million implies an expectation that at least $10 million can be recovered from future revenues over and above amounts required to cover other costs of earning that revenue. If that expectation is fulfilled, taxable income over that period will be at least $4 million (because capital cost allowance claims with respect to the plant are restricted to $6 million). There are, of course, uncertainties since the future is always uncertain. But at least we can say this. If we knew that future revenue activities could recover only $6 million from the present plant, then we should have increased depreciation to date and thereby we would have eliminated the timing difference. If we knew the future operations would recover $10 million with respect to the plant, we could be sure the reversal of the timing difference would generate taxable profit and, for the reasons given above, it is logical to relate that tax cost to the earlier periods when the excess capital cost allowance was taken.

Deferred tax debits and their relationship to the future earning of income give rise to some additional considerations that we will address later in this chapter.

Many "temporary" differences never reverse. The application of tax allocation requires some kind of judgment as to when temporary differences reverse. A clear basis for determining when a reversal occurs is therefore necessary. For example, if revenue is recognized on installment sales before it is taxed, does that difference reverse when the revenue enters into taxable income (e.g., when cash is collected), or may the assumption of reversal be nullified by a subsequent originating difference?

Comprehensive tax allocation is based on the presumption that future originating temporary differences do *not* nullify scheduled reversals of existing temporary differences. Most have accepted this in relatively clear-cut situations, as in the installment sales example. It has been controversial, however, in relation to more complex situations, and in particular when it comes to reversal of differences between booked depreciation and amortization of plant for tax purposes. Since income tax amortization of plant is typically limited to cost, it is clear that, for a single asset, tax amortization in excess of book depreciation must have completely reversed by the time the asset is fully depreciated. Yet most opponents of comprehensive tax allocation have argued that reversals do not take place because one can normally count upon excess tax amortization on new plant assets being available to offset the reversal on older assets.

The argument that temporary differences with respect to amortization of capital assets do not normally reverse is simple. Most companies are going concerns. Most going concerns are continually replacing their capital assets and a majority are growing—i.e., adding to their net capital stock. In addition, with exceptions in some individual industries, even if inflation is moderate new assets are likely to cost more than those they replace. For all these reasons, the net amount claimable for tax purposes is likely to rise over the long term, and net reductions in the excess of amounts claimed over depreciation written are likely to occur rarely and not in significant amounts. In these circumstances, if tax allocation accounting is followed, the balance of deferred tax credits will tend to show a steady increase. From this some claim that the "liability" for deferred taxes is not a true liability because it is never paid off.

Even if it is conceded that the total amount of deferred tax credits should not normally be expected to decrease in a going concern enterprise, it is irrelevant unless it can be shown that it is proper in accounting for tax effects to lump together assets not yet acquired with assets held. Accounts payable may be expected not to decrease in a steady state company, but that is not a sufficient reason for removing them from the balance sheet.

One might address the issue of whether it is proper that the tax deductibility of future assets should offset the reversal of existing temporary differences by posing a simple question. Ask any rational businessperson whether he or she would pay as much for an asset that is not claimable for tax purposes as he or she would for a physically identical asset that is deductible. The answer will surely be no. Then ask if it would change his or her opinion if it was known that the enterprise would be purchasing additional pieces of equipment that would be fully tax deductible. Again, if he or she is rational, it would not. The point is that there is no connection between the first purchase decision and subsequent decisions. There is no basis whatsoever for assuming that the tax status of the second and subsequent assets has anything to do with the first. The payment of taxes on the reversal of an accelerated capital cost/depreciation temporary difference is avoided only by making a future economic sacrifice in lieu of payment, that is, by expending resources on new capital assets in the future and sacrificing part of their tax deduction value to offset the reversing temporary difference. It is fundamentally in error to take into account future transactions that are not the consequence of past transactions in any way.

In the last analysis, the answer to the tax allocation controversy should be sought in the economics of business and investment. If it is true that no rational businessperson would pay as much for an asset that is not deductible for tax purposes as he or she would for one that is deductible, why should not some expense be recognized in the period when an asset is stripped of part of the value received in exchange for the cost incurred? Opponents of tax allocation have never answered this question.

Tax allocation is essentially arbitrary and thus adds no information value. Some have argued that depreciation accounting is crude and arbitrary to start with, so that requiring tax allocation for timing differences between tax and accounting depreciation on top of this is simply adding complexity without improving the information value of financial accounting.

It might be useful to approach this argument by going back and examining the basis for depreciation on capital assets. Why is there a temporary difference in the first place? While depreciation accounting is, as we have seen in Chapter 11, an imprecise and highly arbitrary process, it is, nevertheless, a selective process that must meet certain criteria. Depreciation must have some claim to being "systematic and rational," and must reflect realistic estimates of an asset's useful life and residual value. This may leave a wide range of choice, but it is not unlimited. One would expect the company simply to use the tax basis of depreciation for accounting purposes where it provides a reasonable measure of the expense within these criteria.

It may be expected, then, that deferred tax differences exist only where there is a good economic income measurement reason for accounting income to be different from taxable income. In other words, if differences exist in the first place, it must be because the underlying accounting allocation (for example the depreciation provision) is a better representation than the tax allocation (capital cost allowance claim), and the difference has significant implications for the measurement of tax expense.

If this reasoning is valid, then the accounting should be expected to add information value. We might then ask whether there is empirical evidence that supports or refutes this expectation. There have been a few studies of this, and the results indicate that tax allocation accounting does indeed have information value.[11] One study provides empirical evidence that net deferred tax liabilities disclosed under SFAS 109 have value-relevant information in excess of that of its deferral method predecessor, APB Opinion No. 11.[12]

Partial Tax Allocation

Few opponents of comprehensive tax allocation favour a complete flow-through, or taxes payable, approach. Most accept that some temporary differences between accounting income and taxable income warrant recognition through tax allocation procedures. There is no consensus among them, however, on exactly how such "partial allocation" should be implemented.

A Canadian research study discusses a number of bases for implementing partial allocation, and favours an approach that would recognize deferred tax only with respect to nonrecurring (probably more accurately described as irregularly occurring) temporary differences.[13] Underlying most approaches to partial tax allocation is a belief in one or more of the arguments against comprehensive tax allocation discussed in the preceding section. Some proponents combine these arguments with some others. For example, some reason that, while reversal of depreciation-related differences may take place sometime in the future, they are so distant that their discounted present value is insignificant.

A partial allocation approach has been in place in the United Kingdom for some years. A Statement of Standard Accounting Practice was issued effective in 1979 and then revised in 1985.[14] The standard calls for recognition of deferred taxes in relation to originating timing differences based on forecasts of whether a liability or asset will "crystallize" within a foreseeable period. Future asset acquisitions are taken into account in assessing the likelihood of a crystallization of liability. The foreseeable period may be relatively short—say, three to five years—if timing differences recur regularly but may need to be extended if significant reversals in subsequent years are a reasonable possibility. Timing differences are to be looked at on a combined basis in judging whether net reversals are likely. The accrual approach is to be used in recognizing deferred tax assets or liabilities so that these have to be revalued with changes in tax rates.

There has been wide ranging criticism of the U.K. standard and the U.K. Accounting Standards Board is contemplating abandoning partial tax allocation.

The IASC also permitted partial tax allocation, but in 1996 it issued a revised standard that requires comprehensive tax allocation along the lines of SFAS 109 and the new CICA standard.[15]

Summary Evaluation

The preceding discussion strongly suggests that the conceptual arguments in favour of comprehensive tax allocation are convincing. The major objections have effective counter arguments at every point. In fact, debate of this issue, which had been highly controversial for many years, seems now to have abated as the basic concept of comprehensive tax allocation has been reaffirmed in the U.S., and subsequently by the IASC and CICA. The significant issues now seem to relate largely to the following matters of interpretation and application.

- Should the traditional concept of timing differences be broadened to encompass all temporary differences between the tax and accounting bases of assets and liabilities? In principle, this follows naturally from a balance sheet perspective. The issues here seem to come down to whether there should be exceptions for certain items (such as goodwill) on pragmatic grounds.

- We have observed that there are a few situations where the timing of reversals is indefinite, and the question is whether they should be subject to tax allocation accounting. We have noted that, in Canada, accounting varies depending upon the type of temporary difference.

- Some question whether deferred tax debits qualify as assets, and this will be addressed in a separate section later in this chapter.

Acceptance of the principle of comprehensive tax allocation by standard setters does not of itself resolve the matter. Many people continue to be confused as to the true nature of deferred tax amounts appearing in the balance sheet and there continues to be debate as to how they should be measured and presented. Deferred tax assets and liabilities in the balance sheet should be explainable in terms of real economic phenomena. This leads us into a discussion of the measurement and presentation issues, which are the subject of the following part.

INTERPERIOD TAX ALLOCATION— MEASUREMENT AND PRESENTATION ISSUES

Over the years three ways to implement tax allocation have been suggested—the deferral, asset and liability (accrual), and net-of-tax methods. Each of these methods suggests a different concept of the deferred tax balances that appear in the balance sheet.

The Deferral Method

Under this method the tax effect of a timing difference is computed at the tax rates in the year a temporary difference originates without subsequent adjustment of the accumulated tax allocation debit or credit balance to reflect changes in tax rates. No particular effort is made to explain what is the nature of the resulting deferred tax debit or credit in the balance sheet.

The deferral method was adopted in Canada and the United States in 1967. In the 1960s, it was generally accepted that if matching in the income statement were achieved, one need not be concerned with justifying what the resultant deferred charges or credits in the balance sheet may represent. Correct matching would automatically mean that deferred charges represented future benefits in some sense, and deferred credits represented some form of future sacrifice or disadvantage. Since that time, accounting theorists have placed increasing emphasis on a balance sheet point of view. They have been sharply critical of these deferred charges and credits on the grounds that they are uninterpretable because they do not reflect the present value of expected future cash flows. Deferral method balances do not embody these properties because no account is taken of the rates at which the tax balances may be expected to be drawn down, and there is no provision for discounting expected future cash flows for the time value of money.

As noted earlier, the CICA has now replaced this time honoured method with an "asset-liability" method consistent with that adopted by the FASB, and recently by the IASC. (In order to emphasize the distinction between the deferral and asset and liability methods, the *CICA Handbook* suggests that the term "deferred taxes" be replaced by the term "future income taxes." This suggested terminology is not used in this book because it may seem to suggest taxes that relate to future rather than current reporting periods.)

The Asset-Liability Method

Under the asset-liability method, a recorded deferred tax liability is held to represent the future tax burden that is attributable to temporary differences, while a recorded deferred tax asset is held to represent future tax advantages attributable to temporary differences. Since those advantages or that burden will be realized in the future, their amounts depend upon the tax rates that will exist in future. Accordingly, it is held that the balances should be calculated originally and subsequently recalculated based on best estimates of tax rates that will exist in future when the temporary differences reverse, i.e., when the deferred tax balances are settled or realized.

The asset-liability method gives rise to some applications questions:

- What is the best estimate of the tax rate(s) that will exist in the future period(s) when a temporary difference reverses? SFAS 109 requires that the estimate reflect the provisions of enacted tax law. The effects of future changes in tax law are not to be anticipated. The CICA standard has been modified to fit the legislative process in Canada. It is common practice for federal and provincial governments to announce changes and make them effective before they are formerly "enacted," that is, receive final royal assent. In these cases, tax rate or law changes may be considered substantively enacted at the earlier date when they are, for all intents and purposes, part of the operating tax law (paragraph 3465.58).

- The objective is to measure a deferred tax asset or liability using the substantively enacted rate expected to apply when the asset or liability is effectively realized or settled. This may require some presumptions as to the timing of temporary difference reversals, and may require some estimates as to how the reversing difference will be taxed or deductible—for example, whether it may qualify for capital gains tax rates. Such estimates should be consistent with reasonable, prudent and feasible, tax strategies. Where taxes are based on graduated tax rates, an enterprise may face a more or less arbitrary determination of the effective tax rate to be applicable to reversing temporary differences in future years. SFAS 109 provides that the average graduated tax rate for the estimated amount of annual taxable income in future years be used (see paragraphs 18 and 236). The CICA does not provide any effective guidance (see paragraph 3465.62).

The effect of a change in tax laws or rates is to be included in income from continuing operations in the period in which the change took place (paragraph 3465.64). However, if a change in the deferred tax balance is the result of a change in control of the enterprise or in shareholder status, and such change is directly related to the shareholders' actions or the injection of new capital, the effect is recorded as a capital transaction. Otherwise, effects of changes in tax status resulting from the enterprise's decisions are included in income tax expense (see paragraph 3465.68).

The Net-of-Tax Method

This method focuses attention not so much on the future tax effects of temporary differences as on the valuation of assets and liabilities associated with temporary differences. For example, if provision is made for future warranty costs in recording income from goods sold but the costs are not deductible until paid, it is suggested that the amount of provision can be reduced because of the expectation of an offsetting tax deduction. Or, if capital cost allowance is taken in excess of normal depreciation in the accounts, additional depreciation would be written because the prospects for the after-tax cash return from an asset are reduced by using up its tax deduction potential. From this explanation it can be seen that the net-of-tax method is not really a *tax* allocation process. Rather, it is a modification of other accounting conventions to allow for the effects of income tax treatment on asset and liability valuation. That is to say, the tax expense line in the income statement would remain at the amount of tax payable for the year. An amount *equal to* the tax charges and tax reductions caused by temporary differences would be taken into account as an adjustment to normal depreciation expense, warranty cost provision, etc., recorded elsewhere in the income statement. (Some accountants, however, would prefer to apply the net-of-tax method differently. In order to preserve the normal percentage relationship between pretax income and tax expense reported in the income statement, they would "normalize" the tax expense figure for charges and credits associated with temporary differences. The offsetting credits and debits, however, would be taken as adjustments to the associated asset and liability accounts in the balance sheet. Although it is obviously illogical to debit tax expense and credit accumulated depreciation, for example, it is argued that such a presentation would improve reader understanding of the fundamental elements of income and financial position.)

The net-of-tax method has been ruled out by accounting standards in Canada, the U.S., and IASC.

The Use of Discounting in Tax Allocation Accounting

Over the years a number of writers have suggested that deferred tax balances resulting from tax allocation accounting should be reported on a discounted basis.[16] Accounting standard setters have never pursued this possibility in any depth. It seems likely that the long-standing controversies over the basic merits of tax allocation, and the deferral/accrual/net-of-tax measurement issues, have made standard setters wary of introducing yet another complication.

Nevertheless, the failure to use discounting may well significantly reduce the fairness of the portrayal of income tax expense under the tax allocation approach. We have seen one example of the anomalous effect of not discounting deferred taxes in our earlier discussion of temporary differences—specifically, the application of tax allocation accounting to differences between the tax and accounting bases of an acquired asset. Lengthy postponement of tax liabilities is equivalent to a significant reduction in the effective tax rate.

Several issues would have to be addressed in working out a conceptually sound and workable approach to discounting deferred taxes.

- Discounting is consistent in concept with the asset-liability approach to tax allocation since it is based upon anticipation of the impact on future taxes payable of temporary difference reversals. Discounting does not appear to be consistent with the deferral approach. Some argue that discounting also has no place in net-of-tax accounting. We have seen, however, that time-adjusted depreciation patterns described in Chapter 11 embrace an interest factor, indicating that net-of-tax accounting and explicit recognition of an after-tax interest factor are not incompatible.[17]

- Application of discounting techniques would require a solution to two conceptual issues. The first involves finding a rationale for selection of an interest rate. The second is to find a rationale for determination of the periods in which reversing differences will become taxable or deductible (in view of the fact that capital cost allowance on many assets will exceed depreciation for several years before it reverses). These issues seem likely to be resolvable, although the solutions may add considerable complexity to deferred tax computations.

- A further conceptual obstacle is that the accounting profession has yet to incorporate the time value of money into depreciation and amortization accounting (as we have seen in Chapter 11). It is not reasonable to expect to develop a rational approach to discounting deferred taxes in respect of differences between the tax and accounting bases of capital assets (the primary source of temporary differences) unless it is constructed upon a rational time-adjusted approach to capital asset depreciation.[18]

CICA standards, along with those of the FASB and IASC, prohibit discounting of deferred taxes (see paragraph 3465.57).

DEFERRED TAX ASSETS

Deferred tax debits may be considered to include both deductible temporary differences and loss carryforwards. The basic question in respect of each of these is whether they should be considered to be assets. Their essential claim to asset value (putting aside the possibility that they may be recovered by being offset against future reversals of existing deferred tax credits) is their potential for reducing future income taxes that would otherwise be payable on future income. Their realization, in other words, depends on the earning of future profits. There is a strong argument in logic that, since the earning of future profits is an event to be reported in future periods, any claim that is dependent on future profits cannot be considered to qualify as an asset until those future profits are earned.

We have previously observed that other items treated as assets (including inventories, capital assets, and intangibles) are also carried forward on the expectation of future revenues in excess of costs. But there is a vital difference between these assets and deferred tax debits. The former are productive assets in the sense that their costs are carried forward in the expectation that they will contribute to a profitable revenue-generating process. A deferred tax debit does not represent a contributing input to the production of future income. It is simply passively dependent upon the earning of future income. (One may differentiate deferred tax debits that could be realized through sale in the marketplace, because they would then be realizable at going market values independently of the enterprise earning future income. They would then take on attributes more akin to those of a financial instrument. At present, however, realization by other than earning future taxable income is not a practical possibility, except in unusual circumstances.)

In the U.S., the FASB reasoned in SFAS 96 that deferred tax debits that are not recoverable by offset against reversing deferred tax credits should not be recorded as assets. But, as we have noted, the board subsequently reconsidered and concluded in SFAS 109 that deferred tax debits do qualify as assets if it is more likely than not that they will be realized.

The fundamental conundrum here is that, once again, we have a situation where a single result —the future tax reduction—is dependent upon two conditions: (1) the prepayment of tax or the incurrence of a loss that gives an enterprise the right to a future tax deduction, and (2) the subsequent earning of taxable profits. Both conditions must be met for a deferred tax debit to have value. Its dependence upon earning future taxable profits would rule out it being an asset unless the dominant accountable event is considered to be the initial event of prepayment of tax or incurrence of loss. Today's tax allocation standards have taken this position. An asset is recognized with respect to rights to future tax reductions provided there is sufficient assurance as to their realizability (i.e., as to the earning of sufficient future income).

Under the old standard (which remains effective through 1999), the *CICA Handbook* required differentiation between deferred tax timing debits and loss carryforwards. Deferred tax timing debits were to be recorded as assets if they met a "reasonable assurance" recoverability test, while loss carryforwards had to meet a much more stringent "virtual certainty test." This added considerable complexity and uncertainty to the accounting, because the two types of deferred tax debits are not independent of one another. Tax loss carryforwards can be increased or decreased by electing to claim or not to claim optional deductions such as capital cost allowances.

The new standard adopts the basis in place in the U.S., under which a deferred tax asset is defined to include both deductible temporary differences and loss carryforwards, and the same "more-likely-than-not" realizability test is applied to both (paragraph 3465.24). This greatly simplifies the accounting from that of the pre-existing CICA standard.

An enterprise would consider prudent and feasible tax planning strategies that it could expect to take to realize deferred tax debits in determining the amount that is more likely than not to be realized (see paragraph 3465.26). Brief guidance is given on assessing favourable and unfavourable evidence to support a judgment as to whether some portion or all of a deferred tax debit warrants recognition as an asset (paragraphs 3465.27-.29).

An enterprise is to reassess recognized and unrecognized deferred tax debits at each balance sheet date. If conditions have changed so that it is now more likely than not that sufficient taxable income will be available to allow a previously unrecognized amount to be realized, it is recognized. The current income tax expense for that year is reduced by this amount (except in certain business combination and financial reorganization situations (see paragraphs 3465.46-.55)). On the other hand, if an enterprise's situation has deteriorated so that some or all of a previously recognized deferred tax asset is no longer considered to be more likely than not to be realized, it is written down and the charge is included in current income tax expense.

Thus there is increased potential for volatility as a result of perceived changes in a company's prospects than under the old standard, which required realization of previously unrecognized deferred tax timing differences or loss carryforward benefits before they could be recognized. Disclosure is required of the amount and expiry dates of unused tax losses and income tax reductions, and the amount of deductible temporary differences, for which no deferred tax asset has been recognized (paragraph 3465.91(f)).

OTHER ISSUES

Intraperiod Allocation

Any tax effects (reduction or increase) associated with gains or losses arising from discontinued operations or extraordinary items (as these are defined in the *CICA Handbook*), or in respect of other items charged or credited to shareholders' equity, or certain other special items, are to be reported together with those items (paragraphs 3465.63 and .65–.69). The *CICA Handbook* does not specify how the allocation to these items is to be determined, but the general approach has been to compute the amount of the tax effect attributable to such special items on a "with-and-without" basis—that is, by calculating what the tax expense would have been without the special items and comparing that figure to the actual tax expense. In the U.S, SFAS 109 is very specific. Income tax is first determined in respect of income from continuing operations, and the tax expense or benefit over and above this is apportioned first by determining the effect of any special net loss items, and then the amount that remains is apportioned ratably to net gain items.[19]

Unusual revenues, expenses, gains or losses reported in the income statement that do not qualify as "discontinued operations" or "extraordinary items" are to be reported on a before-tax basis in the income statement, with applicable taxes included in the normal income tax provision. Separate disclosure of the income tax effects related to such items may be useful information, however, and might be disclosed in the notes to the financial statements.[20]

Balance Sheet Classification of Deferred Taxes

The *CICA Handbook* (paragraph 3465.87) suggests that deferred tax balances should be classified as current or noncurrent depending upon the classification of the asset or liability to which they relate. Column (1) of Table 16-1 indicates that deferred tax cannot always be related to a specific asset or liability. Where this is the case, it is accepted that one should look directly to the estimated date of settlement or realization and classify the deferred tax as current if this will occur within one year of the financial reporting date, and noncurrent if not. Where the settlement or realization date of deferred tax with respect to a particular type of temporary difference is indefinite, any deferred tax provided would normally be classified as noncurrent.

Disclosure with Respect to Income Tax Generally

For a variety of reasons, tax expense reported for a period may differ from the figure one would expect based on pretax accounting income. The actual tax rate may differ from the normal rate, for example, because of the small business deduction, because income is earned abroad and taxed at different rates, or as a result of the impact of tax rate changes on deferred tax balances. Losses may be incurred that are not subject to tax allocation because of lack of sufficient assurance, and so on. Taxes payable will also usually differ from tax expense reported because of temporary differences between taxable and accounting income. An analyst may well wish to know what are the causes of the differences in both these categories. The analyst may base his or her assessment of the quality of the reporting entity on predictions of one or both of income and operating cash flow in the next few years. It makes a difference to those predictions whether differences in both categories are likely to persist. For example, if changes in income tax or other legislation are likely to occur, an analyst estimating future after-tax income will need information to help estimate the impact of these events. Or, if the analyst is trying to estimate the operating cash flow available to meet debt commitments in the near future, temporary difference effects that will sharply reverse within that period are relevant to that analysis.

In order to meet these information needs, public enterprises, as well as life insurance enterprises, deposit-taking institutions and cooperatives, are required to disclose the following information (see paragraphs 3465.92–.95):

- The nature and effects of temporary differences and unused tax losses and income tax reductions that comprise deferred tax assets and liabilities.
- The major components of income tax expense.
- A reconciliation of the effective income tax rate or expense recorded to the statutory income tax rate or dollar amount.

Rate-Regulated Enterprises

Rate-regulated enterprises are not required to recognize deferred income tax liabilities or assets to the extent that these amounts can be expected to be included in the approved rate charged to customers in the future, and are expected to be recoverable from future customers (paragraph 3465.102).

SUMMARY

Accounting for income tax has been a controversial subject for many years. The essential problem stems from the fact that income that is subject to tax in a period is not calculated in exactly the same way as is income for the same period in accordance with accounting standards. To a high degree each calculation is based on the same material—transactions engaged in by the entity. But the two calculations may allocate the revenues and expenses flowing from these transactions to different periods. This fact gives rise to the basic question: should income tax be allocated among periods to correspond with the way that revenues and expenses that make up taxable income are reported as elements of accounting income?

It is easiest to see and accept that interperiod tax allocation is justified when an identifiable revenue or expense is recognized in a clear-cut fashion in one period for accounting purposes and in another for the purposes of taxation, especially when the lapse of time between recognition for the two purposes is short. The major debate over the years has been in respect of timing differences between accounting and tax that are recurring or reverse only over an extended period of time during which they may be expected to be replaced by other originating differences. Some have advocated that there should be only "partial allocation" for certain types of timing differences. In particular, many objections have been made to tax allocation for timing differences represented by the excess of capital cost allowance taken for tax purposes over depreciation written on plant for accounting purposes. Among other things, it has been argued that a going concern entity can be expected to acquire new plant assets that will entitle it to more capital cost allowances with the likely result that, in the aggregate, the timing differences will never reverse. As a result, the balance of deferred tax credit will never decline, and cannot be regarded as a true liability. The heart of this argument lies in the assumption that it is proper to offset capital cost allowances on plant yet to be acquired against deficiencies in capital cost allowances on assets currently held. This assumption is fundamentally in error.

The arguments in favour of a comprehensive tax allocation system now seem to be accepted by most accountants. The debate on the basic concepts of comprehensive tax allocation has now largely abated, and it is required by most standard setters around the world (with the notable exception of the U.K.). Accounting standard setters have recently been focusing on matters of interpretation and application, the more important being the following:

- The expansion of the traditional concept of timing differences to encompass additional temporary differences between accounting and tax bases of assets and liabilities. The reasoning here is that any difference between the tax basis of an asset or liability and the amount at which it is recorded on the balance sheet will ultimately result in taxable or deductible amounts in the future period(s) when the asset is recovered or the liability settled. This expanded concept of "temporary differences" is consistent with an increased emphasis on the balance sheet in financial accounting.

- The circumstances under which deferred tax debits (including temporary or timing difference debits and loss carryforwards) qualify as assets. Deferred tax debits are associated with future reductions in taxes. For the most part their value can be realized only if the entity earns taxable profits in the future. If one believes that an asset should never be recorded that can be realized only by means of profits arising from subsequent transactions, deferred tax debits should not be recorded (unless covered by recorded deferred tax credits). Today's standards do not reflect this thinking. Rather, they hold that deferred tax debits should be recognized as assets if there is sufficient assurance of their recoverability. A two-part standard had been in place in Canada. It required "virtual certainty" of recovery for the recognition of loss carryforwards and a lesser hurdle of "reasonable assurance" in respect of timing difference debits. This has now been replaced by a standard that applies the same "more-likely-than-not" recoverability test to all deferred tax debits.

- The measurement of tax allocation effects. The fact that recorded deferred tax assets and liabilities stand for real impacts on future taxes payable suggests that they should be measured at future tax rates to the extent possible. That means adoption of the accrual, or "asset-liability," approach to tax allocation, rather than the traditional deferral approach. Following the lead of the FASB, the CICA has recently adopted an asset-liability method, under which deferred tax balance sheet amounts are adjusted to reflect changes in substantially enacted tax rates and laws, with adjustments made through income. In economic terms, a strong case can be made for discounting the future tax impacts, but a number of perceived conceptual and practical problems stand in the way.

Other issues discussed in the chapter include intraperiod allocation, balance sheet classification and disclosures.

REFERENCES

1   American Institute of Accountants, Committee on Accounting Procedure, *Accounting for Income Taxes*, Accounting Research Bulletin No. 23 (New York: AIA, 1944), subsequently consolidated in Chapter 10B of *Restatement and Revision of Accounting Research Bulletins*, Accounting Research Bulletin No. 43 (New York: AIA, 1953).

2   CICA, "Corporate Income Taxes," *CICA Handbook*, Section 3470, superseded in 1998 (Toronto: CICA); and AICPA, Accounting Principles Board, *Accounting for Income Taxes*, APB Opinion No. 11, superseded in 1992 (New York: AICPA, 1967).

3   FASB, *Accounting for Income Taxes*, Statement of Financial Accounting Standards No. 109 (Norwalk: FASB, 1992).

4   CICA, "Income Taxes," *CICA Handbook*, Section 3465 (Toronto: CICA).

5   Ibid., pars. 3465.22–23.

6   It may not be often that an asset will be acquired that is not part of a business combination where the carrying amount on acquisition will be different from its tax basis. But such situations can arise. See discussion of this accounting and the considerations involved in it in CICA, Accounting Standards Board, *Background Information and Basis for Conclusions: Income Taxes, Section 3465* (Toronto: CICA, 1999), pars. .34–.39.

7   FASB, *Accounting for Income Tax*, SFAS 109, pars. 169–174.

8   This argument along with others is reviewed in T.H. Beechy, *Accounting for Corporate Income Taxes: Conceptual Considerations and Empirical Analysis* (Toronto: CICA, 1983), chap 2.

9   See P. Rosenfield and W.C. Dent, "No More Deferred Taxes," *Journal of Accountancy*, February 1983, pp. 44–55.

10   See Beechy, *Accounting for Corporate Income Taxes,* chap. 2, par. 51.

11   See, for example, D. Givoly and C. Hayn, "The Valuation of the Deferred Tax Liability: Evidence from the Stock Market," *The Accounting Review*, April 1992, pp. 394–410; and J.K. Cheung, G.V. Krishnan and C. Min, "Does Interperiod Tax Allocation Enhance Production of Cash Flows?" *Accounting Horizons*, December 1997, pp. 1–15.

12   B.C. Ayers, "Deferred Tax Accounting Under SFAS No. 109: An Empirical Investigation of its Incremental Value-Relevance Relative to APB No. 11," *The Accounting Review*, April 1998, pp. 195–212.

13   Beechy, *Accounting for Corporate Income Taxes,* chaps. 2 and 11.

14   Institute of Chartered Accountants in England and Wales, *Accounting for Deferred Tax*, rev., Statement of Standard Accounting Practice No. 15 (London: ICAEW, 1978, revised 1985).

15   IASC, *Accounting for Taxes on Income*, International Accounting Standard 12 (London: IASC, Revised 1996).

16   For an early example, see H.A. Black, *Interperiod Allocation of Corporate Income Taxes*, Accounting Research Study No. 9 (New York: AICPA, 1966).

17   A discounted net-of-tax approach to depreciation accounting is demonstrated in J.A. Milburn, *Incorporating the Time Value of Money Within Financial Accounting* (Toronto: CICA, 1988), chap. 18.

18 Ibid., chaps. 17–19. This study indicates that the effects of discounting deferred taxes arising from capital cost allowance/depreciation timing differences may be quite different from what one might initially expect intuitively, where depreciation is assumed to be determined on a time-adjusted basis.

19 FASB, *Accounting for Income Taxes*, pars. 35–38.

20 CICA Emerging Issues Committee, *Net of Tax Presentation and Supplementary Earnings Per Share Figures*, EIC 40 (Toronto: CICA, 1992).

Chapter

C h a p t e r

FINANCIAL

INSTRUMENTS

To this point in Part II we have concentrated on the accounting issues associated with active business operations. In this chapter we turn our attention to financial investing and risk management activities. While operating assets are acquired to be used to produce goods or services for sale, financial assets are of a more passive nature. The investor's actions are limited to decisions to buy, sell or hold, and to financial risk and cash flow management and cash collection activities. *Primary financial assets* include cash, all forms of receivables, and debt and equity securities (other than equity securities held for the purpose of controlling or significantly influencing the operations of the investee, which are the subject of a later chapter).

In recent years, the possibilities for investment, financing, hedging, and speculation have been greatly expanded by the emergence of a wide variety of options and forward contracts. These are known as *secondary or derivative* instruments because their value is based on, or "derived" from, price changes of specified primary instruments, or changes in specified rates, indices or other variables. Frequently, decisions to acquire derivatives are determined in relation to the investor's holdings of other investments and liabilities. They are often used to hedge financial risks. It follows that accounting for derivatives cannot be considered in isolation from accounting for primary financial assets and liabilities. The term "financial instruments" is used to encompass all financial assets and liabilities, including financial derivatives.[1] Financial instruments comprise most of the assets and liabilities of financial institutions and a significant proportion of the assets and liabilities of most operating enterprises.

The accounting for financial instruments has been the subject of much concern in recent years, as it has become evident that GAAP have not kept pace with developments in the capital marketplace. Two closely related issues predominate: measurement (whether, or in what circumstances, a market or fair value basis of accounting should replace traditional historical cost accounting), and accounting for hedges and related risk management practices. As well, standard setters are challenged to improve the presentation and disclosure of financial instruments, exposures to financial risks, and income effects.

We will begin by considering accounting for primary financial instruments. We will then turn to consider the dimensions added by derivatives, and the demand for hedge accounting adjustments to correct for the apparent mismatches that occur when gains and losses on financial instruments designated as hedges are recognized in income in different periods than gains and losses arising on the items hedged. Finally, we will consider related disclosure issues.

PRIMARY FINANCIAL INSTRUMENTS

Three categories of primary financial instruments may be identified apart from cash itself: receivables (including accounts receivable, notes and loans), portfolio investments, (including debt and equity securities), and financial liabilities. Traditionally, these three classes of instruments have been accounted for separately with little attempt made in accounting standards or in practice to consider the need for consistency of accounting as between them. Yet, from risk/return and cash flow management standpoints, an enterprise may be expected to consider them together. For example, many enterprises manage interest rate risk on an overall basis for all financial assets and liabilities. Thus, it is of importance to consider the logical consistency of accounting as between categories of financial instruments.

The initial recognition and measurement of primary financial instruments is generally straightforward, usually reflecting clearly evident market transactions. Questions may arise in particular circumstances, however. The key areas in which difficulties may arise have been discussed in an earlier chapter on initial recognition issues (Chapter 6), and on related issues arising on derecognition (Chapter 7).

The major questions to be considered in this chapter relate to measurement in periods subsequent to initial recognition. Historically, the accounting basis has been cost. But this has been changing. The comparative merits of cost, or lower of cost and market (LOCAM), versus a current market or fair value basis of accounting have been the subject of much debate over the years. This debate has greatly intensified in recent years with the expansion of well-developed, but highly volatile, securities markets, and the increased acceptance of sophisticated market-based portfolio and risk management concepts.

There is an important, but subtle, difference between the terms "market value" and "fair value." "Fair value" is the broader term; it means the amount at which a financial instrument could be expected to be exchanged between knowledgeable, willing parties in an arm's-length transaction. Strictly speaking, "market value" refers more narrowly to the price obtainable in an active market. "Fair value" will generally be the quoted market price, where such is available, but may be determinable by other means where an active market does not exist. The terms are often used interchangeably in the literature, but we will generally refer to fair value, except when referring to quoted market prices.

In Canada, authoritative literature on financial assets differentiates receivables, temporary investments, and long-term (portfolio) investments.

Receivables

The receivables category includes trade accounts receivable, notes receivable, and consumer and commercial loans. Receivables are generally accounted for at cost less allowances for uncollectible accounts. Accounting for impaired loans within the cost model is deferred to Chapter 18.

Temporary Investments

Short-term or "temporary" investments are defined as "transitional or current in nature, such as short-term investments made to obtain a return on a temporary basis," and it is required that they be "capable of reasonably prompt liquidation."[2]

It is not always clear whether particular investments should be classified as temporary or as long-term portfolio investments. Liquidity is a prerequisite for investments classified as temporary. Some investments, such as treasury bills, call loans, and short-term deposits are liquid because they have early maturity dates or are callable. Others are liquid because active markets exist for them, for example, publicly traded shares and debt securities. The classification of these latter securities rests upon management intention, which is open to interpretation and some potential for abuse. If management has no fixed intention with respect to a liquid security that could be held for the long term, should it be classified as current because there is no firm intention to hold it, or should it be classified as long-term because there is no firm intention to sell it? Some enterprises classify all liquid investments as current, in order to maximize reported working capital and working-capital ratio. Others may have a policy to classify all investments as long-term, leaving only temporary investments of cash that is surplus to current business needs to be classified as current. Because of this uncertainty in basis of classification, it is possible that a management could decide to reclassify some of its investment portfolio as short-term should it appear that reported working capital needed bolstering. Conversely, cases have occurred where investments have been reclassified from the current to the long-term category in order to avoid a write-down to market under the more stringent valuation rules applicable to temporary investments. In the U.S., SFAS 115 requires strict classification of marketable securities for measurement purposes, as will be discussed in the following section.

The *CICA Handbook* specifies that temporary investments are not to be carried above market value (paragraph 3010.06). It does not rule out accounting for temporary investments on the basis of current market values, although the traditional valuation basis has been the lower of cost and market. There may be no market for certain short-term investments, but their early maturity or other facilities for realizing upon the asset usually mean that cost will approximate market. For other securities, "market" means the figure realizable at the financial reporting date and is not affected by changes in market quotations subsequent to that date. The LOCAM test may be applied by individual security or by the whole portfolio classified as temporary investments. If securities have been written down, and their market value subsequently recovers, practice is mixed with respect to reversal of the write-downs.

Long-Term (Portfolio) Investments

CICA Handbook Section 3050 (paragraph .18) states simply that "the cost method should be used in accounting for portfolio investments." It is generally accepted that portfolio investments need not necessarily be written down when market value is below cost. Presumably the basis for this is the belief that recognition of fluctuations in market value of an investment held for the long term would not improve reporting of income. If the value of one or more individual securities has suffered an impairment that is other than temporary, however, those individual securities are to be written down. It is a matter for judgment when that condition exists. The words "other than temporary" unfortunately are sufficiently vague to allow for considerable variability in judgment. As well, when a write-down appears necessary, judgment is involved in determining the amount of the writedown. Once a long-term investment is written down, the reduced carrying value cannot be written up again before disposal. Issues related to reflecting impairment will be discussed in Chapter 18. It is sufficient to note here that the impairment tests for long-term portfolio investments are less stringent than they are for temporary investments.

The recommendation of paragraph 3050.18 to use the cost method for portfolio investments is only part of the story. The *CICA Handbook* section excludes "investments held by companies that account for security holdings at market values in accordance with the practices in their industry" (paragraph 3050.01). In practice, investments are being accounted for on a fair value basis by some major classes of financial institutions and some not-for-profit organizations. Unfortunately, clear criteria have not been developed to distinguish the substance of these situations from those in which portfolio investments are carried on a cost basis. The following describes some of these situations and something of the reasoning that may underlie the accounting.

- In some cases investments are accounted for on a fair value basis because the nature of the entity's business is such that their ready realizability is considered to be of supreme importance to any assessment of its financial position. The volatile nature of the business of investment dealers and brokers, for example, makes the cashable status of their assets and liabilities by far the most relevant financial information for them. Only fair values provide a good portrayal of liquidity and solvency of the enterprise. These organizations recognize realized and unrealized gains and losses through income. A cost-based portrayal of income from their investments is of little interest since, for the most part, income from investments while held will be overshadowed by gains and losses in trading.

  Cashable values are also important to open-end investment funds (mutual funds) because participants have a right to redemption of their position at current net asset values upon very short notice. It is instructive to note, however, that closed-end investment funds also commonly use market value accounting, indicating that market values are considered important for investment companies even when liquidity is not the prime concern.

- In other cases, the predominant sentiment has been directly opposite. When the investments in a portfolio are likely to be held for the long term, a traditional school of thought has been that earnings from investments should be reported on a smooth basis from year to year—representative of the long-term rate of return—rather than reporting a figure that fluctuates widely from period to period because of realized and unrealized gains and losses. But there has been a widening diversity of views and practice. Some examples:

  – A large endowment fund or pool of trust funds in a charitable or educational entity pays out its income each year to support the activities for which the funds were donated or collected. The traditional view has been that an accounting basis that provides a smooth measure of income facilitates budgeting for such activities. But frequently these investments are actively managed, and funds allocated on a fair value basis. In 1988 *CICA Handbook* Section 3050 was amended to provide that pooled investment funds of not-for-profit organizations that have market-based unit values that are used to allocate income to participants be exempted from requirements to use cost-based accounting.

– A life insurance company has policy obligations that will require the disbursement of funds over many years into the future. These obligations are valued by discounting actuarial estimates of future payments using interest rates intended to represent attainable long-run investment returns with a margin for safety.[3] A large portion of the investments held to fund the obligations consist of fixed-interest securities. If interest rates rise significantly, the market values of these fixed-interest securities will decline. Thus, a loss would be shown on a fair value basis of accounting. It would be inconsistent to value assets at fair value without also revaluing policy obligations at current interest rates. The traditional response has been that regular revaluation of both assets and liabilities would increase the accounting cost, and might confuse readers of the statements because of the volatility of figures reported, without providing a significantly better portrayal of operations.[4]

– Similar arguments may be made for pension plans. But in 1990 the CICA adopted a standard on pension plans that took the opposite view. It requires that investments be measured at fair values in pension plan financial statements. To be consistent with this, pension plan obligations would logically need to be valued at market-equivalent values, using "best estimate" assumptions discounted at an appropriate current risk-adjusted interest rate. However, the standard permits pension plan obligations to be determined using estimated long-run, rather than current market-based, interest rates.[5]

– Banks and other deposit-taking institutions have strongly supported cost basis accounting for investments, other than short-term trading securities. A primary concern has been volatility.[6] In a bank, total assets may be twenty times the amount of shareholders' equity. If investments are valued at market value, a decline of, say, 5 or 10% in value over a period could have a very significant effect on reported equity. Since market values can easily change by more than this over a one-year period, financial institutions fear that adoption of market value accounting could have a serious effect on depositor and investor confidence, which in turn could have various serious adverse economic consequences.[7] There is concern that the reported effect on equity may be misleading since liabilities, which may be an effective hedge against some significant investment risks, must be carried at cost under current GAAP. In addition, concern is expressed that estimates of current values for some types of investments could be quite speculative.

On the other hand there have been some strong supporters in recent years for working towards fair value accounting for all financial instruments held by financial institutions (including derivatives and mortgages and loans as well as stocks and bonds). These views were strongly expressed in the U.S. by the chairperson of the SEC among others.[8] Some believe that cost basis accounting was a major contributor to the massive order of the losses resulting from the failure of many savings and loan organizations in the U.S. in the late 1980s. They argue that it enabled these organizations to mask real losses and liquidity problems and so continue to invest recklessly, and ultimately multiply their losses.[9] As well, it is to be noted that some financial institutions now internally mark their balance sheets to market on a daily or weekly basis so as to better manage their overall risk positions.

Thus, in those industries characterized by large investment portfolios there are sharply divergent practices and views. Historically, "specialized" accounting for financial instruments developed within particular financial industry sectors. Life insurance companies, banks, securities brokers and dealers, pension funds, etc., each developed their own accounting for investments more or less in isolation from the others. But market forces, and the removal of many of the legal barriers separating financial sectors, have stimulated demands for improved comparability between the financial statements of all types of financial institutions. This gives rise to a fundamental question: Is there something of substance about the circumstances of particular types of financial activities, or the ways in which they are managed, that justifies different accounting for the same financial instruments? A particular debt or equity security has the same economic benefits whether held by an insurance company, a bank, or any business entity. Yet a strong belief persists among important segments of the financial community that fair value accounting is appropriate in some situations and cost-based accounting in others.

A popular argument is that the appropriate measurement depends on whether it is management's intent to hold securities for short-term or long-term investing objectives. If one accepts this, it follows that an entity may have two pools of investments accounted for differently. In fact it has been the general practice of banks and trust companies to segregate trading portfolios which are valued at market, and other investment portfolios which are accounted for on a cost basis. Some contend that management intent may be demonstrated where, for example, officers responsible for the trading portfolio are different from those responsible for long-term investment policy. Many are not convinced, however, that accounting on the basis of management intent can be made operational. Their concern is that it is open to earnings management—that an enterprise may select securities with unrealized gains in its long-term, cost-based portfolio to be sold, or to be transferred at market value to its trading portfolio, so as to improve reported income, while leaving securities with unrealized losses as long-term investments (what is known in the trade as "gains trading" or "cherry picking"). There is some evidence of this behaviour in practice.[10]

Several approaches have been put forward that attempt to overcome some of the disadvantages of cost-based accounting or mitigate the volatility of a straight fair value approach on periodic income reporting. We will discuss three of these—the "deferral and amortization" basis of accounting for fixed-interest securities, the "moving-average market value" basis for equity securities, and the use of fair values in the balance sheet with unrealized gains and losses being put in equity rather than included in income.

Deferral and Amortization

The amortized cost basis of accounting provides a smooth portrayal of investment income from debt securities, provided all securities are held to maturity. But even in portfolios held for the long term, some buying and selling before maturity usually takes place in the interests of improving investment performance. From the viewpoint of any individual security, recognition of gain or loss on disposal before maturity is necessary to complete the record of investment performance. From the perspective of a portfolio as a whole, when proceeds from sales are regularly reinvested a different view of performance is possible.

To illustrate, suppose a ten-year bond paying interest annually at 7% is purchased at par at the beginning of year one. Assume that five years later interest rates have increased, and that the bond is sold and the proceeds reinvested in another bond of equivalent risk to yield annual interest at 10% for a further ten years. Under standard cost-based accounting a loss will be recognized on the sale, because the market value proceeds of the sold bond (equal to its remaining cash flows discounted at 10%) will be less than its carrying value. The effect of recording the loss is to increase future expected income over the term to maturity of the security sold from 7% to 10%. Yet there has been no real change in the composition of the portfolio.

The purpose of the deferral and amortization approach is to avoid this discontinuity in income reporting. Proponents of this approach argue that the original investment has an influence on income right up to its maturity date regardless of whether the issue was sold or held. In the above example, a sacrifice of principal has to be taken that offsets the higher yield rate obtainable on reinvestment. To portray this in the accounting, it is necessary to defer the loss on the issue sold and amortize that loss so that it is fully absorbed by the time the issue would have matured had it been held. To be consistent with accounting on the effective-yield basis for amortization of premiums and discounts on securities purchased, the amortization of the loss should be on a sinking-fund pattern. (While this example describes deferment of a loss, the same principle holds in relation to a gain.)[11]

Deferral and amortization accounting does not take into account the possibility that a decline in value of a debt security may be specifically attributable to a decline in its quality, rather than to changes in the general level of interest rates. It is necessary, therefore, to have a safeguard that calls for direct write-down against income of securities when a decline in value is other than temporary. If the portfolio is sold out or shrinks significantly, it also would not seem reasonable to continue to carry forward the full amount of deferred gains or losses. This effectively means that the accounting approach is not appropriate for other than well-established portfolios with reasonable assurance of continuity.

Deferral and amortization accounting is accepted in accounting for fixed-term portfolio investments held by life insurance enterprises in Canada,[12] and has been adopted by some other long-term debt portfolios.

In summary, the approach may be described as an extension of cost-based accrual accounting that has fairly limited application. It does not satisfy advocates of fair value accounting. They argue that in the above example a real economic loss was incurred on the initial bond at the moment when interest rates went up. In their view, it is not appropriate to defer this loss over the remaining term of the bond, whether or not it is retained or replaced.

Moving-Average Market Values

The return expected from investment in equities comes partly from dividends and partly from increases in the market value of the stock. It is total performance that counts. The cost method of accounting for such investments, therefore, fails to recognize an intrinsic part of the investment performance until the stock is sold. Since stocks may be held for a long time, this is an important shortcoming. The solution is accounting that reflects fair values. However, some who stress the importance of long-term investment performance object to basing the accounting on short-term fluctuations in market values. They desire to record equity investments at values that are generally representative of market conditions without necessarily using the quoted market values that happen to exist on the last day of the reporting period. They desire to reflect as income a figure that shows the investment performance averaged out over a period, not a figure that would be materially influenced—some may say distorted—

by the fact that the market may happen to be unusually high at the beginning of the period and unusually low at the end, or conversely.

One suggested accounting method is based on the idea that market prices, although following a long-term upward trend, display a cyclical pattern around the trend line over approximately a five-year period in response to the business cycle. The idea, then, is that equity securities in the portfolio may be carried at a five-year moving average of market prices, and in this way fluctuations of balance sheet values and reported income will be dampened.[13]

The question that must be asked is whether moving-average or similar valuations are merely for the purpose of smoothing income fluctuations, or whether they have any real economic significance. It was once commonly argued that a moving-average price is an estimator of future net realizable value from an investment and, on average, is superior for this purpose to spot market prices that are capricious in the short run.[14] This contention has been generally refuted on a priori grounds supported by empirical evidence. The evidence shows no clear correlation between past price movements in a stock and future price movements. Movements in stock prices from day to day form a "random walk." If prices go up for several days in a row there is no more reason to expect they will go up (or down) tomorrow than to expect that four heads shown on four tosses of a coin will be followed by another head (or a tail). The inference is that movements in prices respond to new information only and respond very quickly. At any given time, therefore, the current market price should be the best indicator of future realizable values discounted at the market's rate of return.[15]

Equity Adjustment

A compromise that permits the use of market values in the balance sheet but excludes market fluctuations from income was suggested by a CICA research study on portfolio investments.[16] Income would be reported on whatever long-term basis is selected. The balance sheet valuation of investments would be at fair value. The difference between that value and the carrying value that would be consistent with the long-term income recognition basis would be treated as a separate category of shareholders' equity. This idea has not been put into effect in Canadian GAAP, but we will see later that recent FASB and IASC standards have adopted a similar approach in respect of marketable securities that are considered to be "available for sale" but are not held for "trading purposes." These standards require that such securities be carried on the balance sheet at fair value, but that unrealized gains and losses be presented outside the regular income statement.

U.S. GAAP

Until the mid-1990s, accounting for portfolio investments in the U.S. was cost-based, with the exception of certain specialized industries (including brokers and dealers in securities and defined benefit pension plans). The application of cost-based accounting to marketable equity securities differed in some respects from normal practice in Canada, however. SFAS No. 12, issued in 1975, required different accounting for holdings of marketable equity securities classified as current assets and holdings classified as long-term assets. Both categories were to be valued at the lower of aggregate cost and aggregate market. Write-downs (and write-ups for subsequent recoveries not to exceed aggregate cost) had to be reflected in income for securities in the current-asset category, but were taken directly to shareholders' equity for long-term investments. If a decline in value of an individual long-term security was considered other than temporary, however, it was to be written down and the write-down charged to income.

All this changed in 1994. Several interrelated developments through the 1980s set the scene for re-examination of traditional cost-based accounting for financial instruments. This began with the renewed attention to the balance sheet and to reflecting "assets" and "liabilities" at relevant economic values. (We have discussed these developments in earlier chapters, particularly Chapters 4 and 9.) As well, during the 1980s the expansion of capital markets and the development of new risk management concepts had a significant effect on portfolio management practices.

In 1986, FASB began work on a project to re-examine all aspects of accounting for financial instruments. It initially focused on improving disclosures. The dramatic business failures in the savings and loan industry in the United States in the late 1980s provided graphic evidence of the weaknesses of historical cost accounting and related impairment standards. The FASB found itself under pressure from the SEC and others to give urgent attention to the measurement issues. As a result it gave high priority to a limited scope project to improve the measurement of investments in debt and equity securities. The result of this was SFAS 115.[17]

SFAS 115 applies to investments in equity securities that have readily determinable fair values and to all investments in debt securities. (Trade receivables and consumer and commercial loans are excluded because they are not securities.) Entities subject to specialized accounting practices, such as brokers and dealers in securities, defined benefit pension plans and investment companies, were exempted because they were already subject to standards requiring fair value accounting for their investment portfolios.

Under SFAS 115 debt and marketable equity securities are to be classified into three categories:

- Debt securities that the reporting enterprise has the "positive intent and ability to hold to maturity" are to be accounted for at amortized cost.

- Debt and equity securities that are acquired for short-term trading purposes are to be reported at fair value with unrealized gains and losses included in earnings.

- Debt and equity securities not classified in either of the above two categories are to be assumed to be available for sale, and are to be reported at fair value with unrealized gains and losses reported outside the statement of earnings in a separate statement of "other comprehensive income." Such gains and losses are to be transferred to earnings when realized.[18]

Thus the board accepted cost-basis accounting for debt securities to be held to maturity, but it defined this category in narrow terms. If a debt security would be available to be sold as part of an enterprise's portfolio management activities (for example, in response to changes in interest rates, foreign exchange risks, or changes in the availability or yield of alternative investments, or in response to liquidity needs), it must be classified in the available-for-sale category and reported at fair value. If management's intention to hold a debt security is uncertain, it would not be appropriate for it to be carried at amortized cost.

Transfers between categories are to be accounted for at fair value. For a security transferred from the trading category, any unrealized holding gain or loss would already have been recognized in earnings and is not to be reversed. For a security transferred into the trading category any unrealized gain or loss at the date of transfer will be immediately recognized in earnings. In the rare situation where a debt security is transferred from the hold-to-maturity to the available-for-sale category, the unrealized gain or loss will be classified in "other comprehensive income." Finally, if a debt security is transferred to the hold-to-maturity category from the available-for-sale category, any unrealized gain or loss will continue to be reported in "other comprehensive income," but it will be systematically amortized to earnings over the security's term to maturity as an adjustment of its yield.

The standard represented an important step. It replaced historical cost accounting with fair value accounting for a substantial portion of portfolio investments. Not surprisingly, it is open to criticism on several counts. In particular, for many enterprises that manage financial risk, particularly interest rate risk, on an overall basis for all financial assets and liabilities, SFAS 115 results in some mismatching of cost and fair values. The board determined, however, that it could not require fair value accounting for all financial instruments without further research, and it was unable to develop an operational approach for identifying and fair valuing specific liabilities that could be considered to be related to investments required to be carried at fair value. This difficulty was an important factor in the board's decision to require unrealized gains or losses on securities in the available-for-sale category to be excluded from the earnings statement.

Two board members dissented to the issuance of the standard on the grounds that it leaves too much room for classification on the basis of management intent and does not resolve the problem of "gains trading." In their view these problems can only be resolved by requiring fair value accounting for all debt and marketable equity securities, and including all unrealized gains and losses in earnings. Only this accounting would result in "reflecting the consequences of economic events (price changes) in the periods in which they occur rather than when managers wish to selectively recognize those consequences in earnings" (SFAS 115, page 11).

The board was of the view that this standard is only an interim solution (paragraph .87). It indicated that it would reassess the use of fair values for financial instruments when it addressed other related issues, particularly those relating to derivatives and hedging. (In 1998 the FASB issued a standard on accounting for derivatives and hedging activities, which is discussed in a subsequent section.) In the meantime, it was the hope of the board that the compromises made would be mitigated by the standards' disclosure requirements. These disclosures include information on any sales or transfers of securities in the available-for-sale and held-for-maturity categories.

IASC – IAS 39

In December 1998, the IASC issued a standard (IAS 39) on accounting for primary and derivative financial instruments. It includes provisions that are similar to SFAS 115.[19] These provisions have a somewhat wider scope, however, in that they apply to all financial assets (not just debt and marketable equity securities), with the exception of loans and receivables originated by the enterprise and financial assets that cannot be reliably measured on a fair value basis. (These exceptions, which are to be accounted for on a cost basis, probably have the practical effect of making the scope not much different from that of SFAS 115.) IAS 39 sets out essentially the same three categories of investment as in SFAS 115. However, for those financial assets in the "available-for-sale" category, an enterprise can make a one-time election to present unrealized gains and losses in the statement of income or in the statement of equity (to be transferred to the statement of income when realized). IAS 39 is effective for years beginning on or after January 1, 2001, with earlier adoption permitted.

Primary Financial Liabilities

FASB and IASC standards, and Canadian practice, call for primary financial liabilities to be carried on an amortized cost basis. Recent U.S. and IASC standards allow one exception to this, however—the carrying value of debt that is the subject of a "fair value hedge" is to be adjusted for unrealized gains and losses attributable to the hedged risk. This exception will be considered in the discussion of SFAS 133 later in this chapter.

Implementation Guidance

Following are some of the more significant considerations arising in applying cost and fair value bases of accounting.

The Cost Basis

As is true for monetary assets generally, income is recognized on fixed-term interest-bearing securities on the basis of their "effective yield." The effective yield is a calculated figure for each such security that represents a constant periodic rate of return on its carrying value over its entire life. To be conservative, the effective yield is generally calculated to the call date when a premium is paid and to the maturity date when a purchase is made at a discount.

To recognize the effective yield in income, it is necessary to amortize any difference between the original purchase price of a debt security and its ultimate redemption price in such a way that the sum of the cash yield and amortization in each period equals the income figure produced by applying the effective yield rate to the opening carrying value of the investment. Thus, when it is said that such securities are carried at cost, it must be understood that cost means amortized cost. An exception may be made for temporary holdings, since amortization for the short holding period is likely to be immaterial in relation to the ultimate gain or loss recorded on disposal.

The use of a constant yield rate to govern recognition of income is arbitrary, and gives no recognition to the term structure of interest rates—that is to the fact that normally short-term interest rates in the market tend to be lower than long-term rates. However, the accepted constant return assumption is convenient and corresponds with the normal way that investment yields are quoted in the marketplace.

The application of the effective interest method to indexed debt securities gives rise to some questions. The straightforward case is a debt instrument with floating interest payments that are calculated by reference to current interest rates. These are commonly tied to a bank's prime rate in Canada, or to the "London Inter-Bank Offered Rate" (LIBOR). In this case, changes in interest rates directly affect the future interest cash flows of the debt security, and thus its effective interest rate. This has no effect on the cost basis carrying value of the security, because the present value of its contracted cash flows discounted at the current effective interest rate will always be equal to its carrying value.

Questions arise when future payments of a debt security are indexed to prices that are not directly related to interest rates. A monetary asset or liability contract may base future cash flows on a wide variety of formulas or indices—for example, the price of some commodity, or a published cost-of-living or composite stock price index. In practice, the carrying value of such instruments is normally adjusted to reflect the current price of the governing index, with the adjustment being charged or credited to income. The 1994 CICA re-exposure draft on financial instruments proposed that the effect of a price change of an indexed bond be amortized over the remaining term to maturity as an adjustment of its effective interest yield (pars. .092–.094). This proposal seems misguided. Such adjustments are not the equivalent of a floating interest rate, but rather reflect the effects of assuming other price risks. The issue is whether the right to receive, or the obligation to pay, a cash amount in the future that is dependent upon the price of some commodity or index should be reflected at the time the price changes. It is worth noting that a directly equivalent issue is the accounting for monetary items denominated in a foreign currency. Here such items are to be translated at the current exchange rate (see discussion of this issue in Chapter 21).

When a particular security in a portfolio has been acquired in several lots at different times at different costs and subsequently part but not all of the holding is sold, the question arises as to what cost should be assigned to the part of the holding sold. The *CICA Handbook* recommendation in this case is to apply the average unit cost of all purchases in costing the securities sold (paragraph 3050.27). Since all securities are identical no matter when acquired, this is obviously the sensible answer.

As noted earlier, provision must be made to write down or provide allowances against cost values that are considered impaired. There are some difficult issues in determining these provisions, and they are ultimately highly subjective decisions. Discussion of asset impairments is deferred to Chapter 18.

The Fair Value Basis

There is not a great deal of authoritative literature on the determination of fair values of financial instruments.[20] Clearly quoted market prices, where available, provide the most reliable measure. Where a reliable quoted market value is not available, various estimation techniques may be used. For debt securities reasonable estimates may be based on discounting cash flows at current interest rates reflecting the term to maturity and specific credit risks.

One concern with accounting on the basis of fair values is that, even where there is a market price for a security, it may not be fully indicative of the realizable value of a large block of that security. Valuation based on the quoted market price in such a case presumes that it will not be sold as a block, which may be the most reasonable assumption. The concern here may be ameliorated by disclosure of investment concentrations, along with an explanation that quoted market prices of larger blocks of securities may not be representative of realizable value.

One might expect that the fair value of an investment should take into account transaction costs that would be incurred in an actual transaction. This is not the normal practice, however.

It is generally considered important to distinguish interest and dividend income from market appreciation and depreciation. Interest income is normally computed on the historical cost-based effective interest method, although there is no conceptual logic to determining interest on this basis within a fair value model.

It may be reasoned that, if a portfolio of securities is actively managed against market values, there is little information value in distinguishing realized from unrealized gains and losses. The *CICA Handbook* Section 4100 recommendations on pension plan investments do not require any distinction, thus simplifying the bookkeeping. However, with the exception of short-term trading portfolios, the normal practice has been to report separate figures for realized and unrealized gains and losses.

DERIVATIVES, FINANCIAL RISKS AND HEDGING

Derivatives

In general terms a derivative provides the holder (writer) with the right (obligation) to receive (pay) cash or other financial instrument in an amount determined by reference to price changes in an underlying asset(s) or index. Derivatives fall into two broad classes, options and forward contracts.

- The holder of an *option* has the right, but not the obligation, to buy or sell a specific property at a given price. The seller or "writer" of the option has the obligation to deliver or purchase the property in question, but only if the optionee demands it. Options can take many forms, and be combined with forward-type contracts. Guarantees may be considered to be a form of option.

- In contrast with an option, a *forward contract* represents a firm commitment on the part of the buyer and seller of the contract to purchase or sell the subject of the contract at a future date specified in the contract. Standardized forward contracts that are traded on an exchange are known as "future contracts." A number of other derivative products take the general form of forward contracts. These include swaps and a variety of commitments to purchase stocks, bonds and other instruments and indices.

There has been an explosive growth in the use of derivative financial instruments during the past two decades. Several factors may be cited. Primary among these have been the volatility of interest rates, foreign exchange rates and market prices of securities and commodities, and an increased global competitiveness for capital. As a result, businesses have been very vulnerable to financial risks, and much attention has been given to possibilities for hedging these risks. The rapid development of innovative financial instruments and risk management strategies has been enabled by developments in finance theory and by revolutionary improvements in computer and communication technologies.

These activities have opened new possibilities for investment, speculation, and hedging of risks. It is instructive to provide some discussion of risks and hedging before considering the accounting for these instruments.

Risks and Hedging

In general terms, exposure to risk is the condition of being unprotected against the possibility of adverse consequences, that is, of the possibility of incurring a loss. Risk is related to the potential to earn income, because as a general rule, to have prospects for earning a higher rate of return (interest in excess of the "risk-free" rate achievable on government bonds, for example) one must take higher risks. In efficient capital markets it can be expected that there will be a direct relationship between the extent of risk taken and the potential for gain—the greater the potential for gain, the greater the risk that must be taken.

All property is at risk of some sort. There is the risk of physical loss through fire, theft or accident. The risk of such losses can be lessened by preventive measures, and, to the extent it cannot be avoided completely, it may be shared through insurance. Property is also exposed to the risk of change in value over time. Risk is not simply confined to assets owned. There are risks in liabilities undertaken to finance assets as well, and in commitments to acquire assets or to undertake obligations.

A financial asset or liability will be exposed to one or more financial risks, which include interest rate risk, foreign currency risk, market risks (such as the risks of changes in commodity or specific equity prices), credit risk, and liquidity risk.[21]

These financial risks give rise to two types of risk exposure: (1) fair value exposure, and (2) cash flow exposure.

- *Fair value exposure.* The fair value of a financial instrument (primary or derivative) will be exposed to changes in the prices of one or more of the above financial risks. As an example, the fair value of a loan asset that requires repayment of principal and fixed-interest coupon payments at specified times will vary with changes in the current market rates of interest. To generalize, the fair value of a financial instrument is exposed to changes in the prices of those financial risks that are the basis of its contractual rights or obligations.

- *Cash flow exposure.* An asset or liability is exposed to cash flow risk if changes in the price of a financial risk factor result in changes in the expected future cash flows to be received or paid. For example, the cash to be received or paid under a contract to purchase a quantity of a commodity at a specific price on a specific date will vary with changes in the price of the commodity. For all financial risks *except* interest risk the effects of fair value and cash flow risks are directly consistent with one another—because the change in price of the risk factor will affect the future cash flows to be received or paid, and the change in the present value of those cash flows (discounted at a current market interest rate) will be equal to the change in the fair value of the instrument. However, interest risk behaves differently. In the case of a floating rate loan, (a loan contract that calls for interest coupon payments to be tied to the current market rates of interest—for example, to be based on the current "LIBOR" rate or the current "prime rate of interest"), a change in the market rate of interest has no effect on the fair value of the loan (so there is no fair value exposure). But a change in the market rate of interest changes the interest coupon payments and, therefore, the amount of future cash flows payable under the loan (so there is a cash flow exposure).

An enterprise may reduce its exposure to risk in a number of ways. It may do so by diversification. Diversification is achieved by investing in several different investments of different entities in different industries, so as to mitigate risk of loss from events particular to one company or one industry. In a broad sense, diversification is a hedging strategy, since hedging may be broadly defined to mean taking actions to avoid or reduce particular risks. Hedging is typically thought of in a more specific sense, however. In this sense, a risk position is considered to be hedged if changes in its fair value and/or cash flows are expected to move inversely with changes in the fair value and/or cash flows of some other position of the enterprise. A fair value risk exposure may be considered to be hedged when the same cause that triggers an unfavourable change in its fair value will cause an offsetting favourable change in the fair value of some other position.

In some situations an enterprise can arrange its affairs to be in a naturally hedged position, for example, when an enterprise's fixed-interest coupon loan investment is financed by fixed-interest coupon debt of the same amount and duration. In this case, a rise (or fall) in the general level of interest rates will decrease (increase) the fair value of both the asset and liability positions by equal amounts. In other cases, an enterprise will acquire a financial instrument, such as a futures contract, whose fair value and/or cash flows can be expected to vary in the opposite direction to the fair value and/or cash flow changes in the position that it is designed to hedge.

Risk reduction has a price however. In addition to direct costs for brokers' commissions, etc. to arrange hedging transactions, accepting less risk will generally mean accepting less potential for gain. Thus an enterprise may elect to take certain risks in order to increase its prospects for gain. As an example, it may elect to have a somewhat unbalanced interest risk position in the hope of profiting from future changes in interest rates. Derivatives may be used to pursue a risky strategy in order to increase the potential for gain (i.e., speculate), or to hedge or contain risks. As well, a company may have to accept some risks in order to eliminate others. An enterprise must, for example, assume some counterparty credit risk in arranging an interest rate swap to eliminate fair value interest risk on its fixed-rate debt. In developing a risk management strategy one must determine what risks one is willing to take and what risks one may want to take steps to reduce or avoid. Different strategies may be appropriate at different times depending on expectations and economic conditions.

Accounting—Stages of Development

Accounting for derivatives cannot be considered in isolation from other financial instruments. It has, like the colour of a chameleon, tended to be adjusted to try to blend in with the surroundings. More precisely, accounting for derivatives, or gains and losses thereon, have tended to be adjusted to be consistent with the accounting for the risk positions that are indicated to be the purposes of acquiring or issuing the derivatives. This has led to a mixture of fair value and cost-based accounting, and to various forms of "hedge accounting" adjustments to reflect gains and losses on derivatives used as hedging instruments in the same period(s) as the gains and losses are reflected on the designated hedged items.

There have been virtually no standards or authoritative guidance on accounting for derivatives and hedges in Canada, apart from CICA recommendations on hedging of foreign currency items (see discussion in Chapter 21). Canadian practice has its basis in standards and practices developed in the U.S. on accounting for futures contracts, foreign exchange contracts, and options.[22] These were developed in the 1980s, and suffer from a number of significant problems.

In 1998, the FASB issued a controversial and highly complex standard (SFAS 133), designed to address a number of the problems.[23] It is effective for fiscal years beginning after June 15, 2000, although earlier application is encouraged. SFAS 133 requires that all derivatives be measured at fair value, and it sets out conditions under which specified forms of "fair value" and "cash flow" hedges may be designated, and it specifies the accounting for these hedges. The FASB sees this standard as a step towards fair valuing all financial instruments, and it has indicated that it plans to re-address the need for hedge accounting within that context.

We will examine the standards and practices for derivatives and hedge accounting, and their broader implications for financial instruments generally, in three stages. First, we will review standards and practices as they have existed before SFAS 133, because these continue to comprise the basis for Canadian GAAP at the present time. We will then turn to overview the major provisions of SFAS 133, and consider their implications. Finally, we will consider the case for what some, including the FASB, believe to be the ultimate solution—measuring all financial instruments at fair value.

Accounting Prior to SFAS 133

Futures Contracts

Although it is to be superseded by SFAS 133, it is instructive to examine the FASB standard (SFAS 80) on futures contracts, because it set out an accounting approach which has been used as the model, with some adjustments, in accounting for derivative and hedging arrangements. The basic requirements of SFAS 80 are outlined below.

- An initial decision must be made whether a futures contract is considered to be a hedge. If it is not considered to be a hedge, it would be accounted for at fair value with gains and losses being taken directly to income.
- To be a hedge the following criteria are to be met:
  - The position (asset, liability, or commitment) deemed hedged must be exposed to price risk and contribute to the overall risk of the entity. That is to say, the risk could not already be hedged by the existence of other assets, liabilities, or commitments.
  - The futures contract must be designated as a hedge of a specific risk exposure at the inception of the hedge—and the designation and basis of the hedge should be documented.
  - There must be a clear economic relationship between the subject of the futures contract and the item hedged. At the outset of the hedge, past experience must indicate that high correlation of price change between the hedge and hedged item is probable.
- If a contract is considered a hedge, it would be accounted for on a fair value basis if the asset or liability or commitment hedged is also accounted for at fair value. Gains or losses recognized on one position would then offset losses or gains recognized on the other, which faithfully represents the purpose and economics of a hedge.
- When a contract hedges a position not accounted for at market, changes in the market value of the futures contract would be recognized as an adjustment of the carrying value of the hedged item.
- The price of a future contract may include a premium or discount equal to the difference between the futures contract price and the fair value of the item hedged at the date of the contract. Such premium or discount could be amortized to income over the life of the contract if the commodity or instrument being hedged was deliverable under the contract and it was probable that the hedge would remain in place until the specified delivery date.
- Futures contracts not related to existing asset, liability, or firm commitment positions could be accounted for as hedges of future positions (i.e., anticipatory hedges) if they meet the hedge qualification criteria referred to above, and if

- the significant characteristics of the anticipated future position (expected dates of transactions, type of commodity or financial instrument involved, expected quantity involved, and term to maturity (if a financial instrument)) are identified; and

- there is a high level of assurance that the anticipated transactions will occur.

• The market value of a futures contract designated as a hedge should continue to exhibit a high correlation with the market value of the item hedged throughout the period of the hedge. If it fails to do so, hedge accounting should be discontinued, and any difference between price changes on the futures contract and market value changes on the items hedged is to be written off.

• Disclosure would be made of the nature of assets, liabilities, firm commitments, or anticipated transactions hedged and the method of accounting for the futures contracts.

Foreign Currency Transactions

A separate FASB standard (SFAS 52) has dealt with hedging of foreign currency risks. In general, the concepts of hedging are very similar to SFAS 80. However, SFAS 80 has allowed more flexibility in some respects and has been more restrictive in others. For example, as noted above, SFAS 80 has generally required that the assessment of exposure to risk, as a condition for hedge accounting, be made at the overall enterprise level (although it has allowed an entity that managed risk on a more decentralized business unit basis to evaluate risk at that level). SFAS 52 has provided that risk exposure be assessed at the transaction level, so that a contract entered into to hedge the currency risk inherent in a particular transaction could duplicate other positions that already offset the exposure. On the other hand, SFAS 52 has generally not allowed anticipatory hedges. (Further analysis of hedging in relation to foreign exchange accounting is deferred to Chapter 21.)

Options

An option's value may be considered to consist of two parts: its "intrinsic value" and its "time value." Intrinsic value is the difference between the market price of the underlying instrument that is the subject of the option and the option's strike price. It is commonly known as the amount by which the option is "in-the-money." For a call option, the intrinsic value is the amount by which the market price of the underlying instrument exceeds the strike price. Conversely, for a put option it is the amount by which strike price exceeds the market price of the underlying instrument. Obviously, an option that is "out-of-the-money" will have no intrinsic value.

The time value is the portion of an option's value attributable to the time remaining before the option expires. It consists of the effect of discounting (the value that arises because the strike price does not have to be paid until a future date) and its volatility value. The greater the volatility of the price of the underlying instrument, the more valuable the option will be, since the chance of significant gain as a result of the price of the underlying instrument rising above the exercise price (for a call) or falling below it (for a put) is thereby enhanced. Because of the interaction of these factors, the value of an option can change substantially over its lifetime.

There has been little authoritative literature directly addressing the accounting for options. As a result practice has been somewhat diverse and it has drawn heavily on analogies to

SFAS 52 and SFAS 80. In 1986 the AICPA published an issues paper.[24] While not author- itative, most of its conclusions tended to become common practice in the U.S., and Canadian accountants have looked to U.S. practice for guidance. The AICPA issues paper was devel- oped within the general approach outlined above with respect to futures contracts. Its guid- ance has differed in some respects, however, as it attempted to take into account the unique one-sided risk and return nature of options.

The issues paper concluded that options that do not qualify for hedge accounting should be carried at their fair values by both the holder and the writer, with gains and losses being put directly through income. For commonly traded securities with readily observable mar- ket prices, the determination of the fair values of options is straightforward. For nontraded or thinly traded instruments an estimate must be made. While some have expressed con- cern about the reliability of estimates in these cases, option pricing models and other tech- niques are now well established and widely available at low cost. Many entities regularly use them for the purposes of portfolio management.

The criteria for determining whether an option qualified as a hedge have been generally the same as outlined above for futures contracts (SFAS 80), except that an option hedge could be assessed on the basis of matching transactions rather than on an overall enterprise risk basis. As well, contrary to SFAS 80, the AICPA issues paper concluded that hedge accounting using options was not appropriate if the item being hedged was carried on a cost (rather than on a LOCAM or market basis). The rationale for this is that changes in market values do not affect cost basis values and therefore items carried at cost cannot be con- sidered to be fair value risk exposures.

Of course, if an option is considered to be a hedge of a position that is accounted for on a fair value basis, there is no question but that the option position should also be valued at fair value. It is only when hedged positions are not accounted for at market with gains and losses recognized in income that questions arise. The AICPA issue paper determined that the accounting for options as hedges must be examined separately from the viewpoints of the option holder and the option writer.

- From the holder's perspective, it concluded that the intrinsic value and the time value com- ponents of a purchased option should be split and accounted for separately if the option qualified for hedge accounting. The time value portion would be amortized to income over the term of the option "using a rational and systematic method" (usually straight-line) except that, where the hedged position is an unrecognized future transaction (e.g., an anticipatory hedge), the time value portion would be deferred and included in the mea- surement of that future transaction. Changes in the intrinsic value were to be treated as adjustments of the carrying value of the underlying hedged item.[25]

- The fair value of an option as determined by an option pricing model will not include the risk of default by the option writer. Where the holder must look to an option writer, rather than an exchange, for collection, an assessment of collectibility must be made.

- The writer of an option must initially record an option as a liability at an amount equal to its fair value, which will generally be equal to its proceeds. There are situations, how- ever, where the proceeds received on issuing a derivative instrument may exceed the estimated cost of the writer to settle the obligation at that date, in which case a profit might be recognized.[26]

- It may be reasoned that a written option could never qualify as an effective hedge because it holds the possibility of unlimited loss to the option writer, with a possible gain being limited to the amount of the premium received. Thus it would not seem to meet the basic purpose of a hedge—that it mitigate risk. However, in practice it has been accepted that a written call option could qualify as a hedge if the writer owns the underlying instrument that is the subject of the hedge. As well, it has been accepted that written options used in certain combinations of options, such as interest rate collars, could qualify if other conditions are met.

- The AICPA Issues Paper concluded that where a written option qualifies for hedge accounting, its time and intrinsic values should not be split. It reasoned that it does not make sense for the writer of an option to separate out the time value and amortize it to income, because such amortization implies that the transaction's purpose was to earn income, and not to hedge. Further, it concluded that a written option can qualify for hedge accounting only to the extent of the amount of the premium received.

Guarantees

A guarantee may be considered to be of the general nature of an option. The guarantor is in a position analogous to the issuer of an option, and is exposed to risk of loss if certain future events occur (a third party defaults on its debt payments, for example). A party holding a guarantee is in a position similar to that of the holder of an option, and may be expected to exercise his/her right to receive the benefits set out in the guarantee agreement if certain events occur. There is generally no market for guarantees, but the accounting by the guarantor may be considered to be generally parallel to that of tradable options. Any amount received for a guarantee (which must generally all be attributable to its "time value") will be treated as a liability and may be amortized to income over the term of the guarantee. Provision would be made (in accordance with the provisions of the contingency standard discussed in Chapter 8) for the best estimate of any claim that is considered probable. Conversely, the holder of a guarantee would generally amortize any premium to expense over its term, but would likely recognize any benefit only when the event giving rise to a guarantee claim has occurred and the benefit is realized.

Swaps

A swap is a bilateral agreement between counterparties to exchange cash payments at specified future dates. In an interest rate swap the future payments are tied to differences between a stated fixed interest rate and the current floating rate as defined by "LIBOR" or the prime rate. In the simplest type of swap two counterparties agree to swap fixed for floating interest payments on an identical principal amount of debt.

In practice, swap contracts are likely to be arranged with a bank or other financial intermediary. An interest rate swap to exchange a fixed-rate interest obligation for a floating-rate interest obligation might reduce risk for both parties. For example, the party with a fixed-interest obligation might have assets producing income tied to floating rates, while the other party may be in the opposite situation. The number of possible advantages expands when obligations in different currencies are swapped. For example, a company may be able to borrow more cheaply for the long term in a foreign currency, and then use a swap to cover its foreign currency risk exposure.

A swap contract may be used to speculate as well as to shed risk. For example, although uncommon, a company with no debt or interest-bearing assets might agree to receive floating-rate interest based on a specified principal amount in return for an obligation to pay fixed-rate interest on that amount, if it thought interest rates were likely to increase. It would be expected that such swaps would be measured at their fair value.[27] A swap is most likely, however, to be acquired to match offsetting payments of existing assets or liabilities. For example, when a swap contract effectively converts interest payments of an identified existing primary asset or obligation from fixed to floating or floating to fixed, the swap is said to be matched. If one were to follow the criteria for qualification as a hedge in SFAS 80, a matched interest rates swap would qualify for hedge accounting if it reduced the enterprise's exposure to risk. To take an example, an enterprise would be exposed to interest rate risk if it had floating-rate assets financed by fixed-rate debt. If, however, the enterprise had fixed-rate assets, this swap would not qualify as a hedge because it would expose the enterprise to interest rate risk that did not before exist. In practice, however, consideration has not normally been given to the effects of a swap on enterprise risk, and all matched swaps have been treated as though they were hedges. Typically the matched debt or asset and the swap have been accounted for on a net cost basis as though the swap changed the interest rate characteristics of the asset or liability.[28]

Synthetic Instruments

The discussion of accounting for swaps serves well to introduce a broader set of considerations—accounting for so-called synthetic instruments. An entity may find it to its apparent advantage to acquire or issue two or more separate instruments that are collectively expected to replicate the essential characteristics of another instrument. In so doing, the entity may be considered to have constructed a "synthetic instrument." Interest rate swaps are commonly used to construct synthetic fixed-rate, or floating-rate debt. For example, an entity that wishes to issue fixed-rate debt may realize apparent cost savings in issuing floating-rate debt and simultaneously arranging a swap in which it agrees to receive floating-rate interest and to pay fixed-rate interest. Other examples in practice have included synthesizing forward contracts using options and synthesizing options by combining long positions in stocks with borrowings of appropriate amounts.

Some have argued that the individual financial instruments that effectively replicate another instrument should be recognized and measured on a combined basis as if they were the instrument being synthesized. Through such accounting, then, a single asset or liability would be recognized rather than separate assets and liabilities for the individual instruments. Advocates of this accounting argue that anomalous reported results may occur if the parts are accounted for separately. Suppose, in the synthetic fixed-rate debt example above, the swap did not meet conditions for hedge accounting in relation to the debt. In this case it might be reasoned that the swap would have to be considered speculative and measured at fair value while the debt would be accounted for on a cost basis.

The arguments for synthetic instrument accounting are difficult to sustain on close inspection, however. To begin with, skeptics caution that the apparent cost savings between a synthetic instrument and the instrument it is emulating may be largely illusionary, and that the differences in price are more likely to indicate subtle but important differences in risks. It may be reasoned that, since each component has its own risk and reward characteristics, it should be accounted for separately in accordance with those characteristics. The result of separate accounting would be that the individual instruments would not necessarily be measured on the same basis except as hedging conditions are met, and the balance sheet amounts would not be offset unless appropriate conditions for offsetting have been met (see discussion regarding offsetting of assets and liabilities at Chapter 9).

The 1994 CICA re-exposure draft on financial instruments took the position that the individual instruments should be accounted for separately. However, it then rationalized that the measurement of the separate instruments is likely to be consistent. This is because, under the re-exposure draft, measurement of individual financial instruments would be based on whether management intended to hold them for trading purposes or for the long term or to maturity, and one could expect that this intention would be the same for all investments held as part of a synthetic instrument.[29] Some have been highly critical of this result, feeling that this idea of measurement based on management intent would effectively permit management to override hedging conditions by designating instruments to be held as part of a synthetic instrument.

Compound and Embedded Financial Instruments

A compound financial instrument contractually combines two or more fundamental instruments. Complexities arise principally in respect of heterogeneous compound financial instruments, that is, instruments that are a combination of more than one type of fundamental instrument. These take a variety of forms, ranging from the comparatively simple (for example, a callable zero-coupon bond), to highly complex instruments that may contain various forms of forward commitments and embedded options. Some contracts include financial and nonfinancial elements—for example, debt might be repayable in cash or in ounces of gold at the option of the issuer or the holder. Compound instruments may be contrasted with synthetic instruments discussed in the preceding section. While the components of a synthetic instrument are independent contracts negotiated with different parties, in a compound instrument the components are bound together by contract with the same parties, and are interdependent.

As explained in Chapter 9, the *CICA Handbook* (Section 3860) now requires that the issuer of a financial instrument that has both a liability and an equity component split the instrument at its inception into its two components, and account for each separately. A common example is debt convertible at the option of the holder into common shares of the issuer. This split accounting is required to achieve a proper distinction between debt and equity. In other situations, however, compound instruments are generally accounted for based on the identified predominant component. For example, an investor in a debt security convertible into common shares will probably account for it as an investment in debt on the assumption that, until such time as the option to convert is exercised, its predominant characteristic is debt. This accounting is open to question. The conversion right clearly has value, which is evidenced by the fact that the convertible security will be issuable at a higher price (i.e., at a lower yield) than would debt that is similar in all respects except for the conversion privilege. However, some object to the idea of accounting separately for the components on the grounds that the conversion right is not separable from the security, that is, the exercise of one right extinguishes the other.

Primary Financial Instruments as Hedges

U.S. GAAP have not envisaged using primary financial assets and liabilities as hedging instruments, with the exception that SFAS 52 has allowed nonderivatives to be designated as hedges of certain foreign currency exposures. There is no conceptual basis for this position. Primary financial instruments, such as securities, loans and debt, may be just as effective as derivatives in offsetting other risk positions, and there may be valid reasons for acquiring or designing such instruments for hedging purposes. It would appear that the FASB has been reluctant to sanction hedge accounting beyond derivatives, because it has been concerned that this could result in more widespread use, and abuse, of an accounting practice that is, at best, of dubious merit. Practice in Canada, however, and in a number of other countries, has allowed some use of primary instruments as hedges beyond that permitted under U.S. GAAP.

Hedges of Commitments and Anticipated Transactions

In logic, for there to be a hedge, there must be an existing position exposed to risk. An entity may be exposed to risk as a result of commitments as well as positions in presently owned assets or liabilities. For example, a financial intermediary under some conditions might be willing to make mortgage loan commitments at fixed interest rates several months before the money is to be advanced. By so doing it exposes itself to the risk that the mortgages receivable may not be worth face value at the time they are originated because interest rates have increased in the intervening period. An interest rate futures contract can hedge this risk. Any gain or loss on such hedge contracts has typically been treated as an adjustment to the carrying value of the mortgages, to be amortized to income over the period the mortgages are outstanding.

Likewise, an operating business may undertake commitments for various reasons. For example, to assure supply a business may place fixed-price orders for crucial raw materials for future delivery. If the business does not have equivalent fixed-price sales orders for the product that is to be produced with the raw material, there is a risk that the sales market price will fall so that it will not adequately cover the fixed raw material price. To offset this risk the business might sell a futures contract for the commodity in question. Any gain or loss on the futures contract would then be deferred and treated as an adjustment of the purchase cost when delivery is taken.

If a fixed-price commitment to buy can be hedged, what about a situation in which future purchases are certain or probable but there is no commitment? A going concern manufacturing enterprise may be virtually certain to be buying its basic raw materials on a regular basis. Some financial intermediaries such as life insurance companies are virtually assured of a regular inflow of funds requiring investment. In these situations, an enterprise may wish to "lock in" current prices for future material prices or "lock in" current yields on expected future interest-bearing investments.

In such situations, an enterprise might try to accomplish this locking in by acquiring commodity futures or interest rate futures. The futures contracts in such a situation would then be designated as an "anticipatory hedge." It is argued that, when a business is highly likely to buy the item in question because of the circumstances of the business, it is very little different from a fixed-price commitment which may be hedged by a futures contract. As a result, the argument goes, no gain or loss on such futures contract should be recognized in

income. Rather, changes in the value of the futures contract would be deferred and ultimately treated as an adjustment to the cost of the item deemed hedged.

This accounting lacks conceptual validity. What exactly is the position at risk that is
being hedged? The manufacturing enterprise is not locked into any fixed-price commitment
for the commodity to be purchased in the future period, and whatever price is paid may or may
not be covered by product sales revenues at that time. Are these not simply future events
that should be accounted for in the future period? Hedge accounting results in any gain or loss
on the futures contract being carried forward as part of the value of a future transaction that
has no basis for recognition in the current period. Such deferred gain or loss cannot qualify
as a "liability" or "asset."[30] It would appear that the futures contract in this case is simply a
speculative future commitment rather than a hedge of a position at risk.

This lack of validity can also be demonstrated in the financial intermediaries example.
Certainly, such companies may wish to lock in interest rates for future purchases by buying
interest rate futures contracts. When the future arrives, however, the investment in the securities previously intended may well not be the best choice available out of the spectrum of
possible investments, (and would be rendered even less attractive if the recorded cost figure
is to be current market price plus a deferred loss on the futures contract).[31]

GAAP, as defined by SFAS 80, has not made these distinctions. All it has required is a
highly assured future transaction. SFAS 52, on the other hand, has required a fixed-price commitment.

In Canada, as in most countries, anticipatory hedge accounting has been a common
practice, and contrary to SFAS 52, the practice has been extended to anticipated transactions
involving foreign currency risk (see discussion in Chapter 21).

The Problems with Traditional Accounting

The world of financial instruments, and risk management practices, has undergone revolutionary change. The above review of accounting standards and practices for primary and
derivative financial instruments gives evidence of piecemeal efforts to adapt and modify traditional historical cost-realization principles to try to cope with a changing capital markets environment. The result is well described as a "mixed-attribute" system—a mixture of cost and
fair value, supplemented by hedge accounting adjustments. As we have seen, the FASB
attempted to instill some discipline to this mixed-measurement model by defining rules for
distinguishing when marketable securities should be carried at cost or fair value, and how gains
and losses should be treated, as well as defining some standards for hedge accounting.

Despite the FASB efforts, this accounting has been subject to a number of interrelated
problems. Certain of these are very briefly highlighted below:

- The inevitable result of a mixed measurement model is that financial assets and liabilities representing offsetting risk exposures may be recognized and measured on different bases, so that gains and losses are recognized in income in different periods. This
  mismatching has led to the demand for special hedge accounting adjustments. It is apparent from the preceding analysis that hedge accounting has serious shortcomings. To
  begin with, management's ability to decide whether or not to designate qualifying situations as hedges is troubling. Further, the criteria for determining what qualifies as a
  hedge is complicated, incomplete and inconsistent in some significant respects. Finally,
  hedge accounting is completely lacking in conceptual justification in respect of hedges
  of anticipated transactions.

- The result of hedge accounting as applied has been that many derivatives are effectively off-balance sheet. Most derivatives have little or no initial cost. Therefore, if no recognition is given to changes in their fair values, or such gains and losses are deferred from earnings recognition and reported as part of the carrying value of designated hedged items, then they are effectively invisible. Thus users of financial statements have found it very difficult to determine what derivatives an enterprise has, and the risk exposures and income effects of these derivatives. Many derivatives (for example, certain interest rate swaps discussed earlier) have been carried off-balance sheet even though they may not meet formal hedge accounting criteria.

The previously noted Joint CICA/IASC 1994 re-exposure draft on accounting for financial instruments proposed hedge accounting that essentially attempted to build on the then existing U.S. model. Many respondents disagreed with this approach, although there seemed to be no consensus on how the proposed rules could be improved. The CICA has not proceeded to develop any hedge accounting standards (apart from those in place in respect of foreign currency transactions), and the IASC determined that the whole approach to financial accounting for financial instruments, including hedge accounting, needed to be rethought.

SFAS 133—Derivatives and Hedging

SFAS 133 is seen by the FASB as an intermediate step in its long-term project on accounting for financial instruments. This standard "… is intended to address the immediate problems about the recognition and measurement of derivatives while the Board's vision of having all financial instruments measured at fair value in the statement of financial position is pursued" (paragraph 216). We will overview the major provisions of this standard, and comment briefly on the issues it has addressed, the problems it has left outstanding, and the new issues that it has created. SFAS 133 is a highly complex and detailed standard, perhaps the most difficult accounting standard yet issued. Readers are therefore cautioned that they must carefully study the standard and supporting appendices and guidance, in order to understand it fully.

SFAS 133 supersedes SFAS 80, the AICPA guidance on options, parts of SFAS 52 dealing with hedge accounting, and a number of EITF abstracts. The major provisions of SFAS 133 may be summarized as follows:

- An enterprise is required to recognize almost all free-standing derivatives, as well as certain derivatives embedded in other contracts, and measure them at fair value.
- The accounting for gains and losses on measuring derivatives at fair value depends on their intended use. If certain conditions are met, a derivative may qualify for designation as one of three possible types of hedges, each with different accounting for the gains and losses or for the hedged item. If a derivative is not designated as a hedging instrument, gains and losses thereon are recognized directly in income.

Derivatives at Fair Value

The FASB concluded that the only relevant measure for derivative instruments is fair value. It reasoned that cost is not a relevant measure for derivatives because the cost of a derivative is often zero, which does not fairly reflect its subsequent value, since it can often be effectively settled for its fair value at any time, and such fair value can be volatile and differ significantly from zero.

A few derivatives have been exempted (see paragraph 10). These include certain derivatives based on physical conditions, such as the weather, or based on the price of certain nonfinancial assets or liabilities that cannot be readily converted to cash, and certain insurance contracts. Guarantees are also excluded. All included derivatives are presumed to be capable of reliable fair value measurement.

The requirement to fair value virtually all derivatives gives rise to some difficult definitional issues. Derivatives must be distinguished from other financial instruments that may be accounted for differently. As well, derivative instruments are sometimes embedded in other contracts, such as bonds, insurance policies and leases. The board considered it important that an enterprise not be able to avoid the requirements of SFAS 133 merely by embedding a derivative in another contract. Thus it requires that an embedded derivative be separated from the host contract and accounted for as a derivative, if its economic characteristics and risks are not "clearly and closely related" to those of the host contract, the overall contract that embodies both the embedded derivative and host contract is not already accounted for on a fair value basis, and a separate investment with the same terms as the embedded derivative would be accounted for as a derivative under the standard. A set of detailed rules and voluminous guidance is provided to implement these conditions.

The Continued Need for Hedge Accounting

The demand for hedge accounting is reinforced by the requirement to measure derivatives at fair value, but not other major categories of financial instruments (including loans, debt securities that meet the "held-to-maturity" condition of SFAS115, and primary financial liabilities). Indeed, new measurement mismatches are created. For example, interest rate swaps are to be measured at fair value while debt continues to be carried on a cost basis.

An objective of SFAS 133 that has driven its hedge accounting provisions is that "only items that are assets or liabilities should be reported as such in financial statements" (paragraph 217). Losses and gains arising from measuring derivatives at fair value clearly cannot qualify as assets or liabilities merely because the derivatives are designated as hedging instruments. With this objective in mind, the standard provides for the following three forms of hedge accounting, where specified qualifying conditions are met:

- *"Fair value" hedges.* A derivative may be designated as a hedge of the exposure to changes in the fair value of a qualifying recognized asset or liability carried on a cost basis, or of an unrecognized firm commitment. Such a hedged item is to be remeasured at its fair value to the extent of the risk that is the subject of the hedge. Losses or gains arising on this remeasurement are then reflected in income, as is the gain or loss on the hedging derivative instrument. The result is that income will reflect an effective matching, and will record a net gain or loss to the extent the hedge is not fully effective.

  While this accomplishes an income matching for designated hedges of existing risk exposures, it has the anomalous effect that identical assets or liabilities or firm commitments may be recognized and measured at partial or full fair value or cost, or not recognized at all (in the case of commitments), depending on whether or not they have been designated as partially or fully hedged items.

- *"Cash flow" hedges.* A derivative may be designated as a hedge of an exposure to variability in cash flows either of a recognized asset or liability (a floating-rate debt instrument), or of a forecasted transaction to take place in a future period. To the extent that the hedge is considered effective, the gain or loss on the derivative is initially reported outside regular income as a component of "other comprehensive income." The gain or loss is subsequently transferred to regular income when the hedged transaction affects income. A gain or loss relating to an ineffective portion of a hedge is to be immediately reflected in income.

This, then, continues the conceptually indefensible practice of hedge accounting for forecasted transactions, but it does so without deferring losses and gains on hedging instruments as assets or liabilities on the balance sheet. Instead it passes them through a second performance statement ("other comprehensive income"). This may seem to be a slight-of-hand, but it does have the very significant effect of making the gains and losses on hedges transparent, because the adjustments in and out of other comprehensive income are to be disclosed.

The FASB continues to allow hedge accounting for forecasted transactions despite its firm belief that it has no conceptual justification (see paragraphs 326–329). It has accommodated it for purely pragmatic reasons. It recognizes that the practice has become entrenched and that any attempt to prohibit it at this stage would be very strenuously opposed, and might well endanger its ability to achieve the other provisions in the standard.

- *Hedges of net investments in foreign operations.* The FASB elected not to change the accounting for foreign currency adjustments arising on the translation of self-sustaining foreign operations. Such adjustments are to be excluded from the income statement and presented as a separate component of other comprehensive income. In Canada, they are classified as a separate component of equity (see Chapter 21). To avoid mismatching, the FASB continues to provide for gains and losses on designated, qualifying hedges of these net investments to also be presented in other comprehensive income.

- *Derivatives not designated as hedges.* Where derivatives are not designated as hedges, gains and losses are recognized directly in income, as under pre-existing practice.

The qualifying conditions for hedge accounting generally reflect the model set out in SFAS 80, described earlier. Some modifications have been made, however, to try to ensure rigorous application, reasonable consistency, and effectiveness (see detailed requirements in paragraphs 20–21, 28–29, and 36–42). The following are among the more significant modifications:

- At the inception of a hedge, formal documentation of a hedging relationship is to include the basis for how the enterprise plans to assess the hedge's effectiveness. Disclosure is required of the enterprise's hedging objectives and strategies, to provide a context for statement reader evaluation of the hedge and its gain and loss effects.

- An enterprise must have good reason to expect that a hedge will be "highly effective" in achieving the offsetting changes in the fair value or cash flows of the risk being hedged. This provision is intended to be essentially the same notion as that of "high correlation" in SFAS 80. SFAS 133 does not specify how high effectiveness is to be assessed, except that assessment is to be based on, and consistent with, the objectives of the enterprise's risk management strategy. It does not require that exposure to risk on an enterprise-wide basis be justified as the basis for designating a hedge.

- The hedged item(s) must be specifically identified, and there are rules with respect to when a range of similar items may qualify for hedge accounting, and when a portion of a risk exposure may be hedged.

- The standard continues to prohibit the use of nonderivatives as hedging instruments, except that, consistent with SFAS 52, it allows nonderivatives as hedges of unrecognized foreign currency commitments attributable to foreign currency exchange rates and of the foreign currency exposure of the net investment in a foreign operation.

To summarize, it may be concluded that SFAS 133 has taken a significant positive step in requiring that all derivatives be recognized and measured at fair value, and in improving the consistency and visibility of hedge accounting. A high price is paid, however, in terms of the effects of dealing with the difficulties caused by measuring derivatives at fair value while certain other significant financial instruments continue to be measured on a cost basis. To operationalize this part-way position, SFAS 133 has had to construct highly complex and intricate rules for distinguishing derivatives from other financial instruments, and for developing hedge accounting compromises that remove deferred gains and losses from the balance sheet while not unduly upsetting traditional income reporting. The result calls out for a more rational long-term solution.

IASC Developments

Like Canada, the IASC has had virtually no standards in place on the recognition and measurement of financial instruments. We have observed that its joint project with the CICA, begun in 1989, was successful only in developing a general disclosure and balance sheet presentation standard (*CICA Handbook* Section 3860 in Canada, and IAS 32 in the IASC).

The IASC has had a major incentive to develop a comprehensive standard for accounting for financial instruments sooner rather than later. In an agreement with the International Organization of Securities Commissions (IOSCO), the IASC committed to put in place a core set of standards by the end of 1998. IOSCO agreed that it would then consider endorsing IASC standards as the benchmark standards to be used by companies with cross-border exchange listings. The IASC urgently needed a standard on financial instruments to complete the core set. An IASC/ CICA discussion paper issued in 1997 recommended that all financial instruments be measured at fair value and that significant constraints be placed on hedge accounting.[32] It was clear that it would be unrealistic to expect to incorporate such far-reaching changes in IASC accounting standards within the IOSCO timetable. Thus the IASC board set out to construct an acceptable compromise standard. IAS 39 was issued at the end of 1998, effective for financial years beginning on or after January 1, 2001, with earlier application permitted.

The basic measurement and hedge accounting provisions in IAS 39 are very similar to those of SFAS 115 and SFAS 133, but they are set out in much less specific terms. In our earlier discussions of portfolio investments, we briefly compared IAS 39 provisions with those of SFAS 115. The more significant areas of difference between IAS 39 and SFAS 133 on accounting for derivatives and hedges are as follows:

- IAS 39 provides for a derivative, or other financial instrument that would otherwise be measured at fair value, to be exempted from fair value measurement if there is no quoted market price for it in an active market, and its fair value cannot be reliably measured.

- A hedge of an unrecognized firm commitment is to be accounted for under IAS 39 as a "cash flow" hedge, rather than as a "fair value" hedge.

- Under IAS 39 the portion of a gain or loss on a hedging instrument that is effective as a "cash flow" hedge is initially recognized as a separate component of equity (rather than in "other comprehensive income"). Further, gains and losses on cash flow hedges of a future asset or liability are transferred from equity to adjust the initial measurement of the hedged asset or liability at the time it is acquired or incurred (rather than being amortized to income as the asset or liability is reflected in income as under SFAS 133).

Canada

There are, at present, no specific plans for the development of standards in Canada on accounting for derivatives and hedges. As noted earlier, practice in Canada has been based, for the most part, on U.S. GAAP as it existed prior to the development of SFAS 133. There is a very significant question as to what extent, if any, the new provisions of SFAS 133 could be considered to be acceptable under Canadian GAAP without the due process of standard setting in this country. In particular, there has been no precedent in practice in Canada for measuring all derivatives at fair value, except in investment enterprises and pension funds that, as explained earlier in this chapter, carry all financial instruments at fair value. Neither has there been any precedent for the application of "fair value" hedge accounting, or for the classification of gains and losses on "cash flow" hedges outside regular income.

On the one hand, there is likely to be significant pressure from some Canadian companies that raise capital in the U.S. for the U.S. standard to be accepted in Canada. On the other hand, other enterprises may resist the complex and restrictive U.S. accounting, and some may wish to pick and choose which parts of SFAS 133 they would like to adopt.

Thus, the CICA Accounting Standards Board must step in, and quickly, to rule on these issues.

THE ULTIMATE SOLUTION—FAIR VALUE MEASUREMENT OF ALL FINANCIAL INSTRUMENTS

A compelling case can be made for the superior relevance of a comprehensive fair value measurement system for financial instruments over cost, or mixed cost and fair value systems. Certain of the more prominent arguments are summarized below.[33]

- It is well accepted that market values in an efficient market impound all publicly available information pertaining to a security's value. These market values thus reflect the effects of changes in economic conditions as they take place. Cost-based figures reflect only the effects of conditions as they were when the transactions took place. Thus, cost can be misleading as a basis for assessing value in making decisions to sell, settle or hold existing financial instrument positions. As well, with the passage of time, historical prices of financial instruments become increasingly irrelevant to assessing present liquidity or solvency.

  It is true that cost-based financial asset values are written down to reflect impairment conditions, but this is only part of the story of the effects of changing economic conditions. Further, as we will see in more depth in Chapter 18, the historical cost model has no inherent basis for measuring impairment and, as a result, accounting for impairment has been lacking in consistency and clear criteria.

- It is also well accepted that capital markets price financial instruments by discounting expected future cash flows using the current rate of return available in the marketplace for cash flows of commensurate risk. These pricing principles can be applied to instruments that do not have actively traded market values. In other words, it may be presumed that, within open market-based economies, the fair value of nontraded instruments (i.e., the amount at which they would be exchanged between knowledgeable, willing parties at arm's length) will be the present value of their expected future cash flows to yield the current available market rate of return for equivalent risk.

- Increasingly, as we have seen, enterprises and investors manage their financial instruments together, so as to control exposure to key financial risks on an enterprise-wide basis. These risk management practices call out for a uniform fair value measurement system as the basis for assessing and controlling fair value price risks.

- A basic objective of financial accounting is that like things be measured in like ways. The measurement of all financial instruments at fair value would do this. It would improve comparability by pricing currently expected future cash flows for all financial instruments at their present values using the same current market rate of return appropriately adjusted for risk. Cost values, in contrast, impede comparability because like things may look different and different things may look alike. For example, two entities holding identical investments, with identical future contracted cash flows, could report them at very different amounts because they were purchased at different times when interest rates were at different levels.

- Since fair values can be expected to embody current information about current economic conditions and market expectations, they can be expected to provide a more superior basis for prediction than out-of-date cost figures.

- It has been commonly argued that fair value is not relevant for debt-type instruments, such as loans, that management intends to hold to maturity. We have seen efforts to develop mixed measurement models based on this presumption—in particular, SFAS 115. There is reason to doubt this argument. First, the contracted rights and obligations, and risks and value characteristics, of a financial instrument do not depend on management's intention to hold or trade. An enterprise is made better or worse off by a change in the fair value of a financial instrument, whether it chooses to realize the value change immediately or over its term to maturity. As well, in volatile capital markets, rational managers may change their intentions. They may rebalance risks and realize gains and losses often by a simple phone call.

- Fair value accounting measures performance on the basis of holding management accountable for the current effects of its decisions to hold positions. Historical cost accounting reflects only the effects of management's decisions to realize gains and losses by sale or settlement. As we have noted, this cost-realization model is open to "cherry picking" unrealized gains and losses, and consequently to the management of reported income.

- We have seen the complexity of hedge accounting standards that are designed to try to correct for the income effects of measuring some financial instruments in hedging relationships at market and others at cost. Comprehensive fair value accounting for financial instruments would eliminate the demand for hedge accounting for this purpose.

- There is an increasing body of empirical evidence that supports the superiority of the information value of fair value measurements over cost and over mixed cost–fair value systems for financial instruments.[34]

The above arguments and evidence may seem convincing. There are, however, some additional considerations.

- There are some significant unresolved questions of principle with respect to the measurement of fair values for certain types of financial instruments and situations. These include questions relating to the appropriate basis for measuring complex financial instruments such as bank demand deposits and credit card receivables. These issues pertain to whether fair value measurement should be based on immediate or expected future settlement, on entrance or exit markets, and on prices for individual items or for groups of similar instruments. The differences between these bases are potentially very material. Other issues include the fair valuation of large holdings, valuing illiquidity, and the implications of bid-ask spreads and transaction costs. (The FASB is currently studying these issues.)

- Many have doubts about the reliability of fair value estimates of financial assets and liabilities for which there are no ready market values. Particularly troublesome are untraded or thinly traded equity securities and related derivatives. Such problems of reliability of fair value estimates should be put in perspective, however. There are many cases within current GAAP where cost or value must be estimated, and the use of reasonable estimates is an essential part of the preparation of financial statements. Nevertheless, it may be that some exceptions would have to be made for situations in which reasonable fair value estimates may not be feasible on a cost-effective basis. Valuation difficulties may be expected to diminish as markets continue to develop and as experience is gained. There have been significant advances in estimation methodology, based on developments in finance theory and computer technology.

- Some have expressed concern that it is inconsistent to adopt fair value accounting for financial instruments but not for nonfinancial assets and liabilities. Fair value advocates respond that financial instruments are distinctly different from most nonfinancial assets and liabilities. Nonfinancial assets, such as plant and equipment, are inputs to a process for generating goods or services for sale. They must be used with other inputs to be "transformed" into goods and services that can be sold to generate cash flows. Under the current accounting model, these nonfinancial assets are carried on a cost basis until they are transformed into financial instruments (generally cash or receivables). The value of a financial instrument, on the other hand, is linked to future cash flows by contract. No manufacturing transformation or significant value adding effort is required of the holder of a financial asset to obtain its value. Certainly a collection process is involved in obtaining the cash flows from loans receivable, but this may be considered to be of a different order than the transformation of nonfinancial inputs into goods and services. In summary, it may be argued that cost basis accounting for nonfinancial assets is not necessarily inconsistent with fair value accounting for financial instruments. Regardless of one's position on this matter, however, it may be reasoned that improved accounting for financial instruments should not be constrained by existing accounting for nonfinancial assets and liabilities.

- Some of those who may support the case for fair valuation of financial assets are uneasy about measuring debt on a fair value basis. A common concern is that a debtor is likely to have limited prospects for settling its debt before maturity and realizing any gain or loss. This is not a valid concern, because the logical case for fair value does not depend upon immediate realizability. An enterprise with fixed coupon debt is made better or worse off by changes in interest rates, whether or not gains or losses are realized by immediately settling the debt or by incurring uneconomic interest costs in future periods.[35] As well, we have noted the inconsistencies of reflecting the effects of changes in interest rates in fair valuing derivatives, but not debt, when they are used together to manage interest risk.

Some have difficulty with the idea of fair valuing debt for changes in interest rates because they believe that fixed coupon debt is not risky (because the interest rate coupons are fixed), and that floating rate debt is risky (because floating rate debt payments will increase with increases in interest rates) so that the enterprise with floating rate debt is subject to "cash flow" risk. It seems anomalous to them that, on a fair value basis, the fixed coupon debt value changes with changes in the general level of interest rates (i.e., is considered risky), while the value of floating-rate debt is unaffected (i.e., is not considered risky). There is a logical explanation. There is no "cash flow risk" in a floating-rate loan within the capital markets pricing model. The general market level of interest rates indicates the rate of return that can be expected to be obtained in the marketplace at that time. If the general market level of interest rates increases from, say, 6% to 10%, one should expect to be able to earn 10% on the funds obtained by issuing the debt. Thus, a floating rate loan is not risky because the increased interest cash outflows should be recoverable by investing the funds at equivalent current achievable market rates of return. The only reason why an entity may not be able to recover that higher market rate of interest is if it has locked its assets into a lower fixed rate of return. In this case, it is the asset values that are impaired, and require write-down.

Perhaps the major underlying concern with fair valuing debt is that it would result in an enterprise reflecting gains or losses on its debt as a result of changes in its own credit quality. In other words, a company with a deteriorating financial condition would show a decreasing fair value for its debt. This seems difficult to accept intuitively, although the effect is explainable in economic terms. A company that is able to fix its interest coupon payments on long-term debt before its creditworthiness deteriorates has achieved a gain.[36]

- Many are concerned about the volatility of fair values. Fair value advocates argue that this should be a concern only if this volatility is not representative of real changes in underlying price-risk conditions. If the underlying economic conditions are volatile, they reason, the financial reporting objectives of representational faithfulness and neutrality require that accounting should reflect this volatility. If an enterprise wishes to mitigate the effects of volatility on its financial position, it must adopt appropriate hedging strategies.

- Related to the above concern is the presentation of gains and losses in the income statement. Some who may be prepared to accept fair value measurement of financial assets and liabilities on the balance sheet have significant reservations about reflecting unrealized gains and losses in the income statement. As we have seen, the FASB and IASC have bent to these pressures by providing for the initial classification of unrealized gains and losses on "held-for-sale" marketable securities outside regular income. It is difficult to defend this on conceptual grounds.

- There has, to date, been strong opposition to a full fair value model for financial instruments from many preparers and accountants. In particular, it is notable that banks argue that their "banking book activities," largely loans financed by deposits, are appropriately managed on a "net gap" basis. This basis focuses on comparing the expected timing and amounts of cash inflow streams to result from banking book assets with the expected timing and amounts of cash outflow streams to result from banking book liabilities, and managing the net cash flow effects. The claim for this traditional approach to banking is that it works well within a cost-based accounting system and requires no fair value calculations.

A number of accounting standard-setting bodies are actively engaged in addressing these issues. The FASB has observed in SFAS 133 that:

> The Board is committed to work diligently toward resolving, in a timely manner, the conceptual and practical issues related to determining the fair values of financial instruments and portfolios of financial instruments. Techniques for refining the measurement of the fair values of all financial instruments continue to develop at a rapid pace, and the Board believes that all financial instruments should be carried in the statement of financial position at fair value when the conceptual and measurement issues are resolved (paragraph 334).

The FASB is currently considering the conceptual and measurement issues that it believes must be resolved, and it is intending to issue a statement of the board's "preliminary views" for comment in late 1999.

Other standard-setting bodies, notably those of the U.K. and Australia, have expressed the view that the objective should be to put in place a full fair value model for financial instruments.[37] The IASC/CICA sponsored discussion paper has proposed that:

> ... there is a powerful logic for adopting an integrated set of principles based on recognition of financial assets and financial liabilities at their fair value at the time that an enterprise becomes party to a contract and ongoing measurement at fair value. It is proposed that these principles reflect the realities of capital markets, rational financial risk management practices and investor decision processes.[38]

In 1997 an international Joint Working Group on Accounting for Financial Instruments was set up. It consists of representatives of ten accounting standard-setting jurisdictions (Australia, Canada, France, Germany, the IASC, Japan, New Zealand, the Nordic Federation, the U.K., and the U.S. (FASB)). This group is carrying out a series of projects to address the key accounting and disclosure issues, with a view to recommending a proposed standard for consideration by the represented standard-setting bodies, and for distribution for public comment. This group has adopted as its working premise the conclusion of the IASC/CICA discussion paper, that fair value measurement of all financial instruments should be the ultimate objective of financial accounting.

DISCLOSURES

As a result of its joint project, the CICA and IASC adopted virtually identical disclosure standards in 1995.[39] These disclosures are similar to the requirements of the FASB at that time. The CICA standard requires:

- Information about the extent and nature of financial instruments at the reporting date (both recognized and unrecognized), including significant terms and conditions.

- Information on the enterprise's exposure to interest rate risk, including contractual repricing and maturity dates, and effective interest rates.

- Information on credit risk, including the amount that represents the enterprise's maximum credit exposure at the balance sheet date, and significant concentrations of credit risk.

- The fair value of both recognized and unrecognized financial instruments by representative classes. (Where it is not considered practicable to estimate fair value of a particular instrument with sufficient reliability, that fact is to be disclosed together with information about the instrument's principal characteristics.)

- When financial instruments are carried at amounts in excess of fair value, their carrying amounts and fair value by appropriate groups, and the reasons and nature of the evidence that are the basis for not writing them down.

- A description of anticipatory hedges, including the hedging instruments, the future hedged transactions, and the amount of any deferred or unrecognized gain or loss and the expected timing of its recognition in income.

These disclosures represent a significant step towards improving the visibility of financial instruments. However, they provide an incomplete picture. They do not, for example, require any specific disclosures of currency risk or commodity or other market risks. More generally, there has been an increasing demand for expanded disclosures of risk profile information by types of financial risk and risk sensitivities. As well, it has become recognized that information on an enterprise's financial risk management objectives, policies and strategies is important in providing a context for evaluating information on risk exposures, income results and hedging activities.

CICA Handbook paragraph 3860.43 encourages, but does not require, a discussion of management policies for controlling the risks associated with financial instruments. Recent FASB and IASC standards require information on management's objectives and strategies for holding hedging instruments, and they also provide for some expanded information about hedging transactions.[40]

Much attention is currently being given to the development of quantitative information about the market risks of financial instruments, not only at a point in time, but over periods of time. FASB standards (SFAS 119 and SFAS 133) have encouraged disclosures of this type. One such class of measures is generally described as "value at risk" (VAR). Value at risk measures are designed to estimate the susceptibility to loss of an entity's financial exposures. They are developed by using historical market movements of the financial assets held to estimate the range of possible changes in the fair value of the portfolio. A confidence interval is selected, so an entity might report the estimated maximum potential for loss in fair value from adverse market movements covering 95% of market movements over a specified time period. These figures might be reported in the form of a graph of daily or weekly determinations. These measures attempt to factor in the risk mitigating effects of portfolio diversification and hedging practices. Such measures were originally developed for internal risk management purposes, but some financial institutions have been providing VAR information in their published financial reports. There is as yet no clear consensus on methods and assumptions for determining VAR. Thus calculations may lack consistency and comparability, and they are relatively costly to compute.

The SEC has issued requirements for disclosure of qualitative and quantitative information about market risks inherent in derivatives and other financial instruments and derivative commodity instruments. An enterprise is to choose between three methods for disclosure of quantitative information, which is to be reported outside the financial statements: (1) a tabular presentation of expected cash flow amounts and related contract terms, by maturity dates, (2) a sensitivity analysis (such as the effects of a one percentage point change in interest rates), or (3) VAR-based analysis. Additional qualitative disclosures are also required about primary risk exposures, how they are managed, and actual or expected changes in these exposures.[41]

SUMMARY

Accounting for financial instruments has attracted much attention in recent years, as it has become evident that GAAP have not kept pace with developments in the capital marketplace. The debate has focused mainly on three issues: (1) measurement (the extent to which a fair value basis should replace traditional cost-based accounting), (2) hedge accounting, and (3) presentation and disclosure of financial risk exposures and sensitivities, gains and losses arising from changes in fair value, and hedging activities.

Traditionally, accounting practices and standards have dealt separately with particular classes of primary instruments (receivables and loans, temporary and long-term portfolio investments, and debt). Loans and receivables are generally carried on a cost basis with allowance for impairment. Under Canadian GAAP, temporary investments are not to be carried above market value, and a number of enterprises carry them at market value. There is, in Canadian practice, much flexibility in determining whether a marketable security is to be classified as a temporary or trading investment, or as a long-term investment. In the end, the decision will tend to reflect management's short-term trading or long-term investment intentions.

The CICA standard on long-term portfolio investments requires cost-based accounting, but it exempts organizations that account for security holdings at market value in accordance with practice in their industry. In practice, long-term portfolio investments are accounted for on a fair value basis by some major classes of financial and investment enterprises, including some not-for-profit organizations. Clear criteria have not been developed to distinguish the substance of these situations from those in which portfolio investments are carried on a cost basis. The chapter demonstrates that there are strongly divergent practices and views in those industries characterized by large investment portfolios.

It seems clear that GAAP have been evolving towards fair value accounting for at least portfolio investments that are actively traded. On the other hand, there continues to be strong support for cost basis accounting for financial instruments that are intended to be held for the long-term or to maturity.

One of the strongly held traditional objections to fair value accounting for long-term investments has rested on the contention that, when the intention is to hold a financial investment for the long term or to maturity, fair value fluctuations introduce erratic gains and losses that it is argued are essentially meaningless. Several approaches have been advanced to try to address some of the disadvantages of historical cost accounting or to smooth out the volatility of fair value accounting. These have included the deferral and amortization of realized gains and losses on fixed-term debt securities, the use of moving-average market values, and the classification of unrealized gains and losses outside the regular statement of income, as a separate component of equity or in a second performance statement. Each of these approaches has its advocates, and may be reasoned to ameliorate some concerns. However, they do not resolve the cost versus fair value debate.

In the U.S., an FASB standard requires fair value accounting for investments in all marketable equity securities and many debt securities. Only debt securities that meet strictly defined conditions evidencing management's positive intent to hold them to maturity are to be accounted for at amortized cost. The rest are to be accounted for at fair value. Unrealized gains and losses are included in earnings for trading securities, but are initially classified outside regular earnings (in "other comprehensive income") for other securities that are considered to be held-for-sale. Such gains and losses are then transferred to earnings upon realization. The IASC has recently adopted very similar requirements.

The use of derivatives has greatly expanded in recent years. They are used both for speculative and hedging purposes. It has been generally accepted that derivatives that are held for speculative purposes should be accounted for at their fair values with gains and losses put through income. More commonly, derivatives are intended to hedge other risk positions.

A risk position may be considered to be hedged when the same cause that triggers an unfavourable change in its fair value or cash flows will cause a favourable change in the fair value or cash flows of some other position. Under existing GAAP, the application of normal recognition and measurement practices can result in a hedging instrument being recognized at a different time or measured on a different basis than the position being hedged. Traditional hedge accounting has attempted to adjust for these mismatches by deferring gains or losses on hedging instruments to the periods when the offsetting losses or gains are recognized on the position being hedged.

There have been no standards or authoritative guidance in place on accounting for derivatives or hedges in Canada, with the exception of some general provisions for hedge accounting for foreign currency transactions. Practice in Canada has tended to be based on accounting standards and practices developed in the U.S. in the mid-1980s.

Accounting for hedges and derivatives has become increasingly unsatisfactory as the array of derivative products and risk management strategies has grown. Most derivatives have little or no initial cost. Thus, when accounted for as hedging instruments on a cost basis, they effectively have no recognized presence in an enterprise's financial statements. Further, hedge accounting practices have been inconsistent, open to abuse, and their effects have not been transparent. In particular, the practice of hedge accounting for forecasted transactions is conceptually unsupportable.

An FASB standard (SFAS 133), issued in 1998, has been designed as an intermediate step to address a number of the problems. It requires that virtually all derivatives, including those embedded in other contracts, be recognized and measured at fair value. The standard sets out conditions under which specified forms of "fair value" and "cash flow" hedges may be designated, and it specifies accounting for, and expanded disclosure of, these hedges. It continues to allow a form of hedge accounting for forecasted transactions. The gains and losses on hedges of forecasted transactions cannot be deferred on the balance sheet, but rather are required to be presented in "other comprehensive income," to be transferred to income when the hedged transactions are reflected in income. The provisions of this standard are highly complex and detailed. The IASC has adopted a standard that includes provisions that are similar to those of SFAS 133 in most respects, but it is much less detailed and rigorous.

A strong case can be made that the ultimate solution lies in measuring all financial instruments at fair value, with all gains and losses recognized directly in income. The FASB, and representatives of a number of other standard-setting bodies, including Canada, are committed to work towards resolving certain conceptual and practical issues to enable this objective to be achieved. There has been much opposition to this proposed solution, however, on the part of many preparers and accountants. Particular concerns have focused on the reliability of fair value estimates of untraded instruments (such as loans and private equity securities), the very idea of fair valuing debt and particularly with recognizing gains and losses resulting from a debt issuer's credit quality, and the volatility of reported income. Underlying this opposition is a strongly entrenched belief held by many that fair value is not relevant to financial instruments that management intends to hold for the long-term or to maturity, despite strong arguments and empirical evidence to the contrary.

Disclosures of financial instruments have been significantly improved in recent years. The CICA now requires fairly extensive disclosures of financial instruments, their terms and conditions, information on interest and credit risks, as well as their fair values. It has become recognized, however, that these disclosures are incomplete, and need to be expanded. The new FASB and IASC standards will require additional information on management's hedging objectives and policies, and the effects of hedging transactions.

Currently considerable attention is being given to the development of qualitative and quantitative information on financial risk exposures and risk sensitivities. The SEC has recently required extensive disclosures of this nature.

REFERENCES

[1]   The term "financial instrument," is defined in CICA, "Financial Instruments—Disclosure and Presentation," *CICA Handbook*, Section 3860 (Toronto: CICA), par. .05. This definition is generally consistent with those of the FASB and IASC.

[2]   CICA, "Temporary Investments," *CICA Handbook*, Section 3010 (Toronto: CICA), pars. .01 and .02.

[3]   CICA, "Life Insurance Enterprises—Specific Items," *CICA Handbook*, Section 4210 (Toronto: CICA).

[4]   However, Canada is participating in an IASC project addressing accounting for insurance contracts, which is considering fair-value based measurement methods.

[5]   See CICA, "Pension Plans," *CICA Handbook*, Section 4100 (Toronto: CICA). Section 4100 permits a plan obligation to be determined using a long-run approach with the added requirement that, in the case where a plan obligation figure is inconsistent with valuing investment assets at fair value, the amount of "actuarial asset values" that is considered to correspond with the pension obligation figure should also be disclosed (see par. 4100.17).

[6]   See M.E. Barth, W.R. Landsman and J.M. Wahlen, "Fair Value Accounting: Effects on Banks' Earnings Volatility, Regulatory Capital, and Value of Contractual Cash Flows," *Journal of Banking and Finance*, 1995, pp. 577–604. This empirical study of approximately 140 U.S. banks over a twenty-year period through 1990 found that fair value estimates of investment securities gains and losses were significantly more volatile than earnings calculated using historical cost gains and losses and that, had fair value accounting been used to determine regulatory capital, violations of regulatory capital would have been more frequent. The incremental volatility seemed not to be reflected in stock prices, however, and the study (being restricted to investments) did not reflect the possibility of offsetting volatility in the fair value of other financial instruments (i.e., hedging).

7   Many bankers in the U.S. have expressed concern that adoption of fair value accounting for "banking book" investment portfolios could have serious adverse economic consequences. See, for example, Ernst & Young, *Fair Value Accounting Study: A National Survey of Chief Financial and Chief Investment Officers in 216 Financial Services Institutions* (New York: Ernst & Young, 1994).

8   See, for example, A. Wyatt, "The SEC Says: Mark to Market!" *Accounting Horizons*, March 1991, pp. 80–84.

9   See, for example, G.J. Staubus, "Cherry Pickers' Friend—FASB Proposal Caters to Banks, Insurers," *Barron's*, December 7, 1992, pp. 16–17.

10 See, for example, M.E. Barth, W.H. Beaver, and M.A. Wolfson, "Components of Earnings and the Structure of Bank Share Prices," *Financial Analysts Journal*, May–June 1990, pp. 53–60.

11 For a fuller illustration, see R.M. Skinner, "Accounting for Profits and Losses on Investments," *Canadian Chartered Accountant*, April 1961, pp. 327–33; and M. Moonitz, "Accounting for Investments in Debt Securities," in *Essays in Honor of William A. Paton*, ed. S.A. Zeff, J. Demski, and N. Dopuch (Ann Arbor, Mich.: Division of Research, Graduate School of Business Administration, University of Michigan, 1979), pp. 57–72. It should be added that, although Moonitz agreed that no profit or loss occurs at the date one debt security is exchanged for another, he advocated market value based accounting rather than "deferral and amortization" accounting.

12 See CICA, "Life Insurance Enterprises—Specific Items," *CICA Handbook*, Section 4210 (Toronto: CICA), pars. .08–.14.

13 The operation of moving-average methods is more fully explained in the CICA Research Study, *Accounting for Portfolio Investments* (Toronto: CICA, 1984).

14 See, for example, W.J. Morris and B.A. Coda, "Valuation of Equity Securities," *Journal of Accountancy*, January 1973, pp. 48–54.

15 W.H. Beaver, "Reporting Rules for Marketable Equity Securities," *Journal of Accountancy*, October 1971, pp. 57–61; and "Accounting for Marketable Equity Securities," *Journal of Accountancy*, December 1973, pp. 58–64.

16 CICA, *Accounting for Portfolio Investments*.

17 FASB, *Accounting for Certain Investments in Debt and Equity Securities*, Statement of Financial Accounting Standards No. 115 (Norwalk: FASB, 1993).

18 See FASB, *Reporting Comprehensive Income*, Statement of Financial Reporting Standards No. 130 (Norwalk: FASB, 1997).

19 IASC, *Financial Instruments: Recognition and Measurement*, IAS 39 (London: IASC, 1998), pars. 68–92 and 95–102.

20 For proposed guidelines based on referenced sources, mostly in the U.S., see IASC, *Accounting for Financial Assets and Financial Liabilities*, a discussion paper (London: IASC, 1997), pp. 101–107.

21 These risks are defined at IASC, *Accounting for Financial Assets and Financial Liabilities*, pp. 36–37.

[22] FASB, *Accounting for Futures Contracts*, Statement of Financial Accounting Standards No. 80 (Stamford: FASB, 1984); FASB, *Foreign Currency Translation*, Statement of Financial Accounting Standards No. 52 (Stamford: FASB, 1981); and AICPA, Accounting Standards Division, *Accounting for Options*, Issues Paper 86-2 (New York: AICPA, 1986).

[23] FASB, *Accounting for Derivative Instruments and Hedging Activities*, Statement of Financial Accounting Standards No. 133 (Norwalk: FASB, 1998).

[24] AICPA, *Accounting for Options*, Issues Paper 86-2.

[25] An Appendix to AICPA, *Accounting for Options*, Issues Paper 86-2 contains examples of typical situations.

[26] CICA Emerging Issues Committee, *Accounting for the Issue of Certain Derivative Instruments*, EIC 39 (Toronto: CICA, 1992). For a good discussion of the factors that a derivative writer should take into account in pricing its products and determining its profit on issuance, see R.D. Reading and J.C. Lam, "Managing a Derivative Products Business from a Risk-Adjusted Return Perspective," in *Advanced Strategies in Financial Risk Management*, ed. R.J. Schwartz and C.W. Smith, Jr. (Englewood Cliffs, N.J.: New York Institute of Finance, 1993), pp. 553–76.

[27] For a discussion of issues involved in measuring the fair value of swaps, see W.C. Rupert and W.N. Oakes, "Interest-Rate Swap Accounting: What Is Market Value?" *Bank Accounting and Finance*, Summer 1990, pp. 1–14.

[28] See R.D. Nair, L.E. Rittenberg, and J.J. Weygandt, "Accounting for Interest Rate Swaps—A Critical Evaluation," *Accounting Horizons*, September 1990, pp. 20–30.

[29] CICA, *Financial Instruments*, Re-exposure Draft (Toronto: CICA, 1994), pars. A67–A69.

[30] See discussion at FASB, *Accounting for Derivative Instruments and Hedging Activities*, pars. 322–27.

[31] For an analysis of hedge accounting issues, see J.B. Adams and C.J. Montesi, Principal Authors, *Major Issues in Hedge Accounting* (Norwalk: FASB, 1995).

[32] IASC, *Accounting for Financial Assets and Financial Liabilities*, 1997. This discussion paper was jointly sponsored by the IASC and CICA.

[33] Ibid., chap. 5. This discussion paper contains a comprehensive analysis of the arguments.

[34] See American Accounting Association's Financial Accounting Standards Committee, "Response to a Discussion Paper Issued by the IASC/CICA Steering Committee on Financial Instruments, 'Accounting for Financial Assets and Financial Liabilities'," in *Accounting Horizons*, March 1998, pp. 90–97. The paper overviews and cites empirical and conceptual research on the relevance and information value of fair values of financial instruments.

[35] For a demonstration of the fundamental arguments using simple examples, see D.W. Willis, "Financial Assets and Liabilities—Fair Value or Historical Cost?" *FASB Status Report*, August 18, 1998, pp. 5–10.

[36] See discussion of the arguments for and against fair value measurement of an enterprise's own credit risk component of its debt at IASC, *Accounting for Financial Assets and Financial Liabilities*, pp. 110–13.

[37] In particular, see Accounting Standards Board, *Derivatives and Other Financial Instruments*, A Discussion Paper (London: The Accounting Standards Board Limited, 1996).

[38] IASC, *Accounting for Financial Assets and Financial Liabilities*, p. 13, par. 1.4.

[39] CICA, "Financial Instruments—Disclosure and Presentation," Section 3860 (Toronto: CICA, 1995), pars. .43–.95; and IASC, *Financial Instruments: Disclosure and Presentation*, IAS32 (London: IASC, Revised 1998), pars. 42–44.

[40] FASB, *Accounting for Derivative Instruments and Hedging Activities*, SFAS 133, pars. 44–45; and IASC, *Financial Instruments: Recognition and Measurement*, IAS 39, par. 169.

[41] SEC, *Disclosure of Accounting Policies for Derivative Financial Instruments and Derivative Commodity Instruments and Disclosure of Quantitative and Qualitative Information about Market Risk Inherent in Derivative Financial Instruments, Other Financial Instruments, and Derivative Commodity Instruments*, SEC Release No. 33-7386 (Washington: SEC, 1997).

RECOGNITION OF ASSET IMPAIRMENT;

STATEMENT PRESENTATION OF ACCOUNTING ADJUSTMENTS AND EXTRAORDINARY, UNUSUAL AND PERIPHERAL GAINS AND LOSSES

Previous chapters have dealt with the recognition and measurement of normal recurring operating and investment activities and, in Chapter 8, we discussed the recognition of contingencies (with particular reference to contingent loss liabilities). Within this framework we will now give consideration to asset impairment issues, and then turn our attention to adjustments resulting from various types of events or transactions that lie outside usual recurring operating activities. These include extraordinary and unusual gains and losses, discontinued operations and restructurings, prior period adjustments, and accounting changes.

ASSET IMPAIRMENT

In this part we will address losses to be recognized with respect to financial and operating assets when the normal revenue and expense recognition rules are inadequate (e.g., write-downs of inventory). These issues might have been addressed in earlier chapters dealing with individual assets. Discussion has been consolidated here, however, to see to what extent existing standards and practices in recognition of losses are consistent, one with another.

When, as often happens, the current fair value or value in use of an asset appears to be less than its carrying value on the books, what should be done? The question arises in respect of assets carried on a cost basis, because the regular allocations and amortizations of cost basis accounting do not factor in adjustments for possible impairments in value arising from unanticipated events or changes in conditions.

Some have argued within traditional historical cost accounting theory that no write-downs for impairment should be made on the grounds that realized income is most accurately portrayed simply by matching costs actually incurred with resulting proceeds. On the other hand, it can be argued that expense recognition is essentially a process of writing off costs whose benefit has expired. If a cost incurred cannot be recovered from future revenue, its benefit has clearly expired and it should be written off.

The historical development of accounting has supported the latter point of view from an early date for assets held as part of working capital. The nineteenth-century dividend cases (discussed in Chapter 3) suggested that circulating capital should not be valued above realizable value. The use of financial statements for credit purposes made lower of cost and market (LOCAM) a widely accepted basis of asset valuation. The advent of the income tax established the principle of realization for income tax (meaning that assets could not be valued above cost before realization). It also provided an incentive to write down assets below cost when possible. Thus, LOCAM became well established as the basis for valuation of working capital. The need for provision for impairment of investment in capital assets remained more doubtful until quite recently, however.

In analyzing asset impairment issues, we might begin with the general principles for the recognition of contingent losses developed in Chapter 8—that best estimate provisions should be made when it becomes likely that a loss will be sustained as a result of events that have taken place. Several issues require clarification in applying this thinking to recognition of losses on assets held.

- How is a deterioration in the value of an asset to be determined? More precisely, how is "value" (fair value or realizable value or value in use) to be interpreted? Should such values be discounted for the time value of money and, if so, how should the interest rate be determined and should the effects of changes in interest rates be reflected?

- Has a loss event necessarily taken place when the market or fair value of an asset has declined below its cost-based carrying value?

- Must there be an examination of the relationship between cost and recoverable value for each individual asset or may it be accomplished by groups of assets?

- Once assets have been written down, may they be written up again if their value recovers?

These issues will be discussed in the context of individual asset categories.

Inventories

The Meaning of "Market"

In Canada, there have been no CICA recommendations as to the meaning of "market" in the phrase "lower of cost and market." Practice is fairly well established, however, and there have been few developments over the past thirty or more years.[1] Since inventory is acquired for resale, the relevant market price is a selling price. Also, the price that is relevant is not necessarily the quoted selling price for goods at the financial reporting date, but rather the realizable price that will be achieved on sales. Market is thus taken as realizable value less costs that would directly and necessarily be incurred to effect a sale. Because of this emphasis on an actual cash value for the inventory, it would be logical to discount the estimated net proceeds should realization be likely to be delayed. For inventory that will turn over within a normal short period, however, this refinement is ignored.

Inventory held that is not ready for sale, such as work in process and raw materials, is more difficult to value at net realizable value because both the ultimate sales price and costs to complete and sell are less certain. For these reasons, the interpretation of the term "market" may shift to replacement cost for raw materials, plus manufacturing costs incurred to date for work in process in the early stages. Reliance on replacement cost is based on an expectation that selling prices will tend to move in step with replacement costs. When that is not a reasonable expectation a write-down to replacement cost may not be required. Conversely, a write-down may be required when ultimate realizable value has obviously declined even though replacement costs have not declined.

In a majority of business situations a profit margin over replacement cost is available, so that inventory written down to replacement cost will normally yield a margin. Inventory written down just to realizable value, however, will not yield a margin. One could therefore argue that the use of realizable value as a test for market for one section of inventory and replacement cost for another is inconsistent. In practice, however, that inconsistency exists. The accepted idea is that inventory need not be written down so far as to assure a profit in the following accounting period. The use of replacement cost for valuation of raw materials and work in process in its early stages is merely an expedient.

The valuation of inventory of retailers represents an exception to the statement that the term *market* ordinarily means net realizable value. In many retail enterprises it would be an unreasonably onerous task to price all items of inventory on hand at their specific cost. It is therefore accepted that cost or LOCAM may be estimated by the "retail method" of inventory valuation. Under this method, inventory is first priced on the basis of selling prices marked on the product, and a percentage deduction is made from the total selling price for the inventory (or for major groupings of inventory) to reduce to cost or LOCAM.

The percentage deduction is developed from stock purchase records priced at both cost and retail. If the retail prices used in this calculation are modified to allow for mark-ups and mark-downs subsequent to purchase of the stock, the percentage arrived at will represent the average gross profit realized on sale. Application of this percentage to inventory priced at retail at any particular date should reduce it to approximate cost. On the other hand, if retail prices in the calculation are not adjusted for subsequent mark-downs, a larger percentage will be developed that represents a normal or target gross profit. If this percentage is applied to items in inventory that have been marked down from their original selling price, those items will be priced below cost, and the inventory as a whole can be described as being priced, on average, at the lower of cost and selling price less a normal percentage margin. That percentage must cover selling costs. Since these represent a much higher proportion of total cost in a retailer than in most other industries, this departure from the use of straight net realizable value is less important than it might seem at first sight.[2] While the retail inventory method is still the most commonly used approach by retail enterprises, advances in computer technology are enabling more precise item-by-item inventory management and LOCAM valuations.[3]

In the United States, in contrast to Canada, replacement cost is taken as the dominant interpretation of market price. This is qualified by a provision that an inventory item need not be written down as far as replacement cost if that would yield more than the normal profit margin on estimated selling price. On the other hand, if replacement costs remain equal to or above historical cost but selling prices decline, the inventory must be written down if historical cost exceeds net realizable value.[4] Thus, for much of the time the American rule will cause write-downs to allow a profit margin in the next accounting period, but that will not always be the case.

Application of the Market Test

In both countries the most common practice is to compare cost and market prices for individual inventory items in applying the LOCAM test. When this is done, the figure to which an inventory item is written down is assumed to be its "cost" so long as the item continues to be held. That is to say, an item cannot be written down in one period and then, if still on hand at the end of the next, be written back up. A less common practice is to compare the aggregate cost of inventory with aggregate market value for each natural product division in the inventory rather than item by item. If this is done, the net write-down is not attributed to specific products, and it is therefore more difficult to prevent a write-down in one period being offset by a recovery in net realizable value in the next.

Although purchase commitments for inventory are not recorded in the formal accounts, they do constitute a position at risk, and the tradition of conservatism calls for a provision for loss on the same basis as would be required if the goods on order had been received. Similarly, when a contractor estimates that losses will be incurred on a contract in hand, a full provision for the estimated loss on the total contract is to be made even though the contract is incomplete at the reporting date.

Loans Receivable

Loans receivable are financial assets that consist of promises by borrowers to pay specified or determinable amounts on specified dates or on demand, usually with interest. They comprise a broad class of assets and include consumer installment and credit card loans, residential mortgages, business loans and commercial mortgages of all types, and direct financing leases.

It is possible that certain loans or portfolios of loans may be sold or held for sale. For example, a financial institution might sell a block of mortgages to a pension fund. The "securitization" of receivables, permitting unit interests to be sold to private investors, has become more common in recent years, although it has gone further in the U.S. than in Canada. By and large, however, loans are intended to be held until they are repaid. Loans intended to be held to maturity are generally carried on a cost as opposed to a fair value basis, so that their collectibility rather than their current market value is the dominant factor to be considered in assessing the appropriate carrying value for them. (Some advocate that all financial instruments, including loans, should be measured at fair value. See discussion at Chapter 17.)

A Historical Perspective

Until recently the only *CICA Handbook* standard was a simple requirement to provide adequately for uncollectible accounts and notes receivable (*CICA Handbook* Section 3020, since revised). In practice, providing for loan impairment had usually been thought to call for examination of loans individually and an estimate of amounts not recoverable based the current condition of the debtor. Sometimes reference was made to the accounting standard on contingencies (see Chapter 8) to justify making provisions for losses on individual loans only when they were both likely and considered reasonably capable of estimation. This approach was not satisfactory, particularly for financial organizations with large loan portfolios. Its practical effect was that loan losses tended to be recognized late. To begin with, if the contingencies standard was followed literally, no provision for loss would be made when a loss with respect to a given account was reasonably possible but yet could not be called likely. Likewise provision could be avoided if the amount was not considered capable of reasonable estimation. Yet, from the viewpoint of a loan portfolio taken as a whole, a reasonable possibility of loss on a number of loans may add up in a statistical sense to virtual certainty of some loss for the group of existing loans. It may be some time after loans are made before losses on individual accounts are evident. It could be reasoned, then, that a lending organization should make specific provision for uncollectible loans based on individual examination of the accounts in a portfolio *plus* a general provision with respect to the portfolio as a whole based on experience and judgment of current conditions. But there was little precedent for this.

Beyond this, the time value of money was generally not taken into account. The traditional assessment of collectibility of a loan looked only to the recovery of the amount recorded on the books; the collectibility of future interest was not considered. Thus, if a loan was expected to yield collections just equal to its principal amount over a period of time, even a very long period, no provision for loss would be required. This accounting seemed to be sanctioned in the U.S. by an FASB standard on "troubled debt restructurings," that is, situations in which a creditor granted concessions to a debtor in financial difficulties that would not be made to financially sound debtors. That standard required that in a troubled debt restructuring situation a loan asset should be written down only to the extent that future receipts are estimated to be less than the asset carrying value. [5]

This traditional accounting for loan losses enabled lending institutions significant flexibility in reporting. There was considerable support on the part of financial institutions and some regulators for judicious smoothing of loan losses over time. As well, it was often argued that losses in a financial institution engaged in commercial lending tend to be cyclical. The conventional reasoning was that loan losses are likely to be bunched when business conditions are bad, and the need to maintain public confidence in such times was considered to justify various expedients to smooth reported losses and income over a cycle. This concern to maintain public confidence has been particularly evident in respect of banks and other deposit-taking institutions.

The traditional accounting by banks and other lending organizations was to identify "nonperforming loans" and make no interest accruals on these loans. In principle, such categorization has been judgmental but, for convenience, some institutions adopted a standard rule, or some regulators required a rule, such as that no interest be capitalized with respect to loans on which principal or interest payments were more than ninety days overdue. In the banking industry in particular, charges to income for impairment of principal of nonperforming loans was based on the idea of "working out" loss situations in bad times by charging them off over a period of years, perhaps based on average losses over a presumed normal business cycle. This effectively resulted in carrying forward losses to be absorbed in years when it was expected that higher operating profits could reasonably absorb them. Consistent with this, in the United States empirical evidence suggests that stock prices of banking institutions behaved as though the writing off of loan losses was good news causing stock prices to go up. In other words the actual charging of losses to income may have been interpreted by investors as a signal of strength—that the lending institution's earning power was considered sufficiently strong so as to be able to absorb large loss hits to earnings. On the other hand, the evidence also seems to indicate that capital markets tended to respond negatively to banks reporting of increases in the amounts of nonperforming loans, as perhaps, a lead indicator of real likely loss experience.[6]

Some may argue that this approach to accounting for loan impairment was justified on the grounds that it helped to preserve an aura of smooth earnings and financial stability of banking institutions, and thus helped maintain public confidence. But the presumptions on which it was based—of well-diversified loan portfolios and recurring business cycles in relatively stable times—came to be increasingly out of joint with the reality of loan portfolios and business and interest rate volatility. In Canada, the unsatisfactory nature of accounting for impaired loans was underlined by the failure of two banks in Western Canada in the early 1980s. Their loan portfolios were not well diversified, and were of above-average risk and vulnerable to a downturn in the price of oil and real estate values. A high-profile inquiry into their failure was very critical of the accounting, and in particular of the smoothing out of provisions for loan losses over time and the basing of loss provisions on optimistic expectations of future recovery of business conditions.[7]

Current Standards

Standards put in place in Canada and the U.S. in the mid-1990s go quite a way to addressing the major criticisms of traditional practices.[8] The CICA requirements go further in certain significant respects than those of the FASB. We will review the *CICA Handbook* recommendations and note the major areas of difference from the FASB standard.

- A loan or portfolio of loans is to be considered impaired if the lender does not have reasonable assurance of "timely collection" of the full amount of both principal and interest. The standard sets out various indicators of the deterioration in the creditworthiness of a borrower or guarantor that should cause the lender to evaluate whether a loan is impaired.

- In addition to evaluating impairment of individual loans, the CICA standard requires that the lender stand back and assess whether collective provisions for impairment should be made against any groups of loans with similar risk characteristics. Particular events or changes in economic conditions may indicate impairment in groups of loans to borrowers in a particular industry or geographic region that is not yet evident in individual loans. To illustrate, perhaps a sharp decline has occurred in the price of a commodity, such as oil or lumber, that can be expected to have a serious adverse effect on the loan paying ability of borrowers in regions that are dependent on the oil or lumber industry. In this case, an additional provision should be made against the group of loans for impairment that cannot be identified on a loan-by-loan basis. The FASB standard deals only with impairment at the level of individual loans.

- The CICA standard states that a lender's assumptions as to future economic conditions should be "realistic and conservative" in relation to the conditions existing at the time the financial statements are prepared. Specifically, one should not assume that current conditions will improve unless there is persuasive, independent evidence to support the assumption. This is not an explicitly stated condition of the FASB standard, although it requires "the creditor's best estimate based on reasonable and supportable assumptions and projections" (SFAS 114, par. 15).

- Impaired loans are to be measured at their estimated realizable amounts. The determination is to be made by discounting expected future cash flows at the effective interest rate inherent in the loans, that is, at the rates at which interest is accrued on the amortized cost basis. On this basis there is no adjustment of the discount rate for changes in the general level of interest rates except for floating rate loans. In other words, the provisions for impairment are not intended to recognize the economic loss that occurs when interest rates increase causing the fair value of fixed-rate loans to decrease. Nor is there any adjustment of the rate for changes in the credit risk of the borrowers. This is considered to be consistent with the historical cost basis of accounting in the sense that the interest rate used to determine the present value of an impaired loan reflects the risk premium inherent in the original loan transaction. It may be argued that failure to reflect changes in the interest rate credit risk premium will result in overstating the real value of an impaired loan, since a loan to a debtor encountering financial difficulties is likely to be more risky than it was considered to be at its inception.

    An exception is made to this historical cost-based measurement approach, however, in situations in which the amounts and timing of future cash flows cannot be reliably estimated. In this case, they may be measured based on either the fair values of the security underlying the loans or, where they exist, on observable market prices for the loans.

- The CICA standard requires that changes in the estimated realizable values of loans in periods subsequent to initial recognition of impairment be reflected in income in the periods in which the changes take place. When measured on the cost basis, two sources of changes may be distinguished. The estimated timing or amounts of future cash flows may change and, where this occurs, the present value of the adjustments is to be charged or credited to the income provision for impairment. The other source of change in realizable value results from the accretion of the discounted present value of an impaired loan over time to its estimated future value. Under the CICA standard, this accretion is to be accrued each period at the effective interest rate inherent in the loan, and reported either as interest income or as part of the income charge or credit for loan impairment. The initial FASB statement had a similar requirement, but the board subsequently backed away, under pressure from the financial institution preparer community, from requiring accrual of the interest discount on an impaired loan.[9] As a result, under U.S. GAAP, an impaired loan may be carried at less than the discounted present value of its expected cash flows in periods subsequent to the recognition of impairment.

    If the realizable value is based on the fair value of the underlying security or on observable market prices, changes in value are to be reflected in income as part of the provision for impairment in the period of change.

- If a loan in financial difficulties is restructured, its recorded amount is to be adjusted to the present value of the cash flows receivable under the modified terms discounted at the rate of interest inherent in the original loan. Such adjustment is to be treated as part of the charge or credit for impairment in the period. In most cases, a restructured loan will previously have been recognized as impaired so that an adjustment on restructuring could be either positive or negative.

- When a lender forecloses on a loan, the assets acquired should be valued initially at the lower of the recorded amount of the loan and the estimated net proceeds to be received from the sale of the assets (or, in the rare case where the assets are not to be held for sale, at the lower of the recorded value of the loan and the assets' fair value).

- Disclosure of impaired loans is much expanded from that of previous practice. The more significant CICA disclosures are the following:

  - The total recorded investment in individual impaired loans and in each group of loans against which a collective allowance for impairment has been made, along with the amounts of the related allowances. This information is to be set out by groups of loans with similar characteristics.

  - The net charge or credit to income in respect of impaired loans.

  - The amount of interest income represented by interest accrued on impaired loans.

  - The basis of determining the amount of the allowance for impairment and an explanation of the events and conditions considered in determining the impairment charge to income in the period.

Investments

Chapter 17 has discussed accounting for portfolio investments. In brief, it may be stated here that temporary investments are not to be carried at amounts in excess of their current market value. Where investments are classified as long-term, however, an individual investment holding carried on a cost basis is to be written down only when its realizable value has suffered a decline below carrying value that is considered to be "other than temporary." A *CICA Handbook* standard dating back to 1973 sets out some conditions that may indicate a decline in value that is other than temporary.[10] These include the following:

- Severe losses incurred by the investee and/or continued losses over a period of years.

- A prolonged period in which the quoted market value of the security is less than its carrying value. (Declines in value of fixed-maturity securities need not be taken into account if the decline is the result of general market conditions—e.g., a rise in interest rates—and it is expected that the security will be held to maturity.)

- Financial difficulties suffered by the investee.

This list is not all inclusive. The standard states that when indicators of impairment persist for three or four years, there is a presumption that a value decline is other than temporary which may be rebutted only by persuasive evidence. As well, if management intends to sell a security in the near future, or if it may be required to liquidate its portfolio because of needs for cash, it may be necessary to write down the security or portfolio if recovery cannot be expected before realization.

The concept of an "other than temporary" decline is open to wide interpretation, and this has enabled some organizations to delay write-downs well beyond when loss events have occurred. The CICA standard does not allow a write-down to be reversed if there is a subsequent recovery of value before its disposal, and this, some feel, has served to inhibit write-downs.

When a write-down is considered necessary a further judgment is needed as to the amount of the write-down. The CICA standard is silent on this, but practice has accepted recoverable value based simply on the cash that can be got out of the asset with no regard to the length of time taken to recovery. This nondiscounted approach is, of course, inconsistent with the loan impairment standard discussed above.

Clearly the standard of *CICA Handbook* Section 3050 for impairment of investments carried on a cost basis is overdue for review. The 1994 CICA re-exposure draft on financial instruments, discussed in the preceding chapter, proposed impairment standards for debt securities along the lines of those discussed above with respect to loans. It further proposed that equity securities be written down when fair values are lower than cost except if there is persuasive evidence that carrying amounts will be recoverable within the intended holding period.[11] This would seem to carry a strong presumption of write down where fair value is less than carrying value, as it would presumably be rare for there to be persuasive evidence that current reductions in fair values will reverse. There are no current plans to implement these proposals and the old *CICA Handbook* Section 3050 provisions remain in place. Progress of these proposals seems to have become stalled in a larger debate on whether cost or fair values should be used as the basic measure of financial instruments (see discussion in Chapter 17).

In the United States, SFAS 115 (discussed in Chapter 17) deals with impairment of securities classified as either available-for-sale (which are carried at fair value with unrealized gains and losses reported outside regular income in a statement of other comprehensive income) or held-to-maturity (carried on cost a basis). It requires that a provision be made through income for any decline in fair value below the amortized cost base that is other than temporary (see paragraph 16).

Capital Assets

Declines in value expected to result from the use of capital assets should be allowed for by systematic depreciation provisions over their estimated useful lives. Unanticipated events may take place or conditions may change, however, causing unamortized carrying values of capital assets to become impaired. In other words, in some situations it may become unlikely that unamortized capital asset carrying values will be recovered from net revenues to be generated over their estimated remaining useful lives.

Historically, accounting literature has been ambivalent on the question of accounting in these situations. On the one hand, the accountant's conservative instinct urges recording of all losses even though realization has not taken place. On the other hand, some have argued that, as long as a capital asset remains in use, no write-down for impairment needs to be made—that depreciation accounting does not embody any valuation but simply calls for systematic allocation of unamortized cost, less estimated residual value, over expected remaining useful life. Accountants generally came to reject this argument as accounting began to embrace more of a balance sheet orientation. Within this orientation it may be reasoned that it is fundamentally inconsistent with the concept of an asset (reflecting expected future benefits) to carry forward an unamortized cost in excess of its recoverable value. From this perspective, the chief problem is to estimate a reliable figure of value recoverable from a capital asset. Unless it is near the end of its physical life, one often cannot be very sure of projections of future net revenues, or that economic conditions will not change. In addition, since future cash flow is the product of many resources working together, it is hard to assign impairment of value to specific assets. (For example, it might be that a whole plant or division is obsolete.) In view of the subjectivity of estimates of recoverable value, there could be abuses. For example, a management, particularly one newly placed in charge, might wish to write down assets sharply (the so-called "big bath" treatment) to relieve future reported income of some of the burden of depreciation.

The consequence of these conflicting views and concerns was that for many years accounting practice could be well summarized by the following excerpt from a 1970 AICPA statement on basic accounting concepts and principles:

> *In unusual circumstances* persuasive evidence may exist of impairment of the utility of productive facilities indicative of an inability to recover cost although the facilities have not become worthless. The amount at which those facilities are carried is *sometimes* reduced to recoverable cost and a loss recorded prior to disposition or expiration of the useful life of the facilities.[12] (emphasis added)

In addition, there has been debate over the years as to what may constitute the appropriate basis for determining the recoverable cost or value of an impaired capital asset. An estimate of the net amount realizable on disposition may not seem appropriate if the asset is to continue in use, and particularly if its "value in use" (the estimated net present value of future cash flows from the asset) is higher. A reduction to value in use, however, means that (if the new valuation is accurate) future operations can be expected to show a profit after depreciation on the new carrying value. Moreover, the amount of that profit will be determined by the discount rate assumed in the calculation of net present value. Many accountants have felt it to be improper to charge operations today to allow a profit to be recorded in future. They have argued that the reduction in carrying value need only be to the amount of cash that actually will be recovered from use (or sale) of the asset in future, without any discounting.

The practice of providing for capital asset impairment was, thus, quite mixed, ranging from no provision until virtual realization on abandonment or disposal of the assets to "big bath" accounting. These inconsistencies began to attract significant critical attention in the 1980s.[13]

In 1990 the CICA issued a standard on capital assets (and we discussed its provisions relating to capitalization and amortization in Chapters 11 and 12). It requires that when the carrying value of a capital asset, less provision for future removal and site restoration costs and deferred taxes, exceeds "recoverable amount," the excess should be charged to income.[14] It lists conditions that "may indicate" the need for a write-down, advising that "the persistence of such conditions over several successive years increases the probability that a writedown is required unless there is persuasive evidence to the contrary" (paragraphs 3060.46 and .47).

The determination of the net recoverable amount of an impaired capital asset is to be based on estimated future net cash flows to result from its use together with its residual value. The future net cash flows are not to be discounted, but they are to be reduced by directly attributable general and administrative costs, including carrying costs. Thus, if the asset is directly financed by debt, its interest costs must be deducted. This was presumably required to avoid the prospect of expecting to report losses in future periods from operating impaired assets that are debt financed. On the other hand, some may think it incongruous that the same impaired asset may be written down to different amounts depending on how it happened to be financed.

When it is not practicable to identify the net cash flows attributable to a single capital asset, because a number of assets work together, the net recoverable amount is to be calculated for the group of assets as a whole. Once written down, the new value is considered to be the asset's new cost base and the write-down cannot be reversed if net recoverable amount subsequently increases.

How might one evaluate this standard? Clearly, it took an important step in asserting the principle that provision be made for impairment of capital assets when conditions indicate that carrying values will not be recovered. It leaves much room, however, for variability in assessing whether an impairment condition exists and in making what must generally be highly subjective estimates of future cash flows. The lack of discounting for the time value of money seems inconsistent with the more recent CICA standard on impaired loans discussed in an earlier section of this chapter.

A separate CICA recommendation, dating back to the mid 1970s, deals with goodwill impairment. *CICA Handbook* paragraph 1580.62 says simply that where there has been "permanent impairment in value" of the unamortized portion of goodwill, it should be written down by a charge to income. This is a prescription for waiting too long to recognize impairment, and it leaves management open to choose its concept of discounted or undiscounted recoverable value. It is not surprising that widely different approaches are being taken in practice. Clearly this standard is out of date and overdue for review. An Emerging Issues Committee Abstract (EIC 64) calls for disclosure of how an enterprise determines whether there is permanent impairment of goodwill, and information about any write-downs in the reporting period.

The FASB has recently taken quite a different approach.[15] It calls for a review for impairment of long-lived assets (including identified intangibles and related goodwill) that will be held and used by an entity. A review is to take place whenever events or changes in circumstances indicate that their carrying amounts may not be recoverable. The standard sets out several examples of situations that indicate that a review for impairment should be undertaken. These include:

- A significant decrease in the market value of an asset (which may indicate that the asset has been adversely affected by new technology).
- A significant physical change in an asset or in the extent or manner in which it is used (for example, if an asset is maintained only as a standby).
- A significant change in legal requirements or in the business environment that could adversely affect an asset's value (for example, if major environmental remediation is required by new legislation).
- A projection or forecast indicates continuing losses associated with an asset.

In performing a review for recoverability, an entity would estimate the future net cash flows expected to result from the use of the asset and its eventual disposition. If the sum of these cash flows, without any discounting or interest charges, is less than the carrying value of the asset, an impairment loss is to be recognized. In carrying out this analysis assets are to be grouped at the lowest level for which there are identifiable cash flows that are independent of other groupings.

When this test for the existence of impairment is met, an impairment loss is to be measured as the amount by which the carrying value of the asset exceeds current fair value. The difference is to be charged to income.

It is important to understand the thinking underlying the FASB approach. The board reasoned that, when an entity determines that an asset in use is impaired, (that is when the sum of future cash flows to result from using the asset is greater than its carrying value), management must decide whether to continue to use it in its operations, or whether it should sell it. A decision to continue to use an impaired asset is economically equivalent, in the board's view, to a decision to invest in the asset anew at its fair value, with the result that the fair value is considered to represent a new cost base for the asset. Based on this reasoning, the board believes that using fair value to measure an impairment loss is not a departure from the historical cost principle and that, accordingly, the new cost should be amortized over the asset's remaining useful life and not written up to reflect any recovery of value in subsequent periods.

Quoted market prices in active markets are considered the best evidence of fair value, if available. Otherwise, estimates may take into account prices for similar assets and/or employ various valuation techniques. These include the present value of estimated future cash flows using a current interest rate commensurate with the risks involved.

The standard deals separately with long-lived assets that are to be abandoned or held for disposal, or just do not have any future service potential to the entity. These are to be reported at the lower of their carrying amounts and fair value less any costs to sell. The FASB has a project in process to address implementation issues that have arisen with respect to assets to be disposed of and the consistency of the impairment standard with other standards relating to provisions for disposal of business segments and restructurings.

Certain disclosures are required by the FASB standard. These include the amounts of recognized losses and descriptions of the underlying facts and circumstances.

A recent IASC standard has taken still another approach.[16] It requires that a determination of the recoverable values of long-lived assets (including intangibles and related goodwill) be made if there are indications that they may be lower than their carrying amounts. It lists possible external and internal indicators. Recoverable value is defined as the higher of net selling price and value in use. Value in use is to be determined by discounting expected net cash flows to be generated by the use of the assets plus any residual value at a current risk-adjusted interest rate. Where recoverable value is less than carrying amount, the difference is to be written off by a charge to income. In contrast with the CICA and FASB standards, reinstatement of a previously recorded impairment write-down would be made when an asset's recoverable amount rises above its written down carrying amount as a result of changes in economic conditions.

Special Situations

Disposal of Part of a Business

Occasionally an enterprise sells or plans to sell the assets and undertaking of a substantial portion of its business as a unit, or discontinues a substantial division. This unusual event raises several questions as to recognition, measurement, and reporting.

The first question relates to the recognition date. What is the past event that would trigger the recognition of a disposal or discontinuance of part of a business? The CICA has adopted the date at which management approves a formal plan of disposal.[17] This is generally consistent with U.S. GAAP. Some argue, however, that the adoption of a formal plan of disposal does not absolutely obligate management, and that a later point in the process should be taken, for example, when plans are publicly announced or when effective agreement is reached with a third party.[18] Prior to the recognition date no accounting action is to be taken except in the case where assets in use should be written down for impairment.

On the adoption of a formal plan of disposal, an estimate needs to be made of the gain or loss. In that estimate it is necessary to consider not only the probable net proceeds of asset disposal but also the possibility of cash operating losses for the period until the disposal can be concluded. More or less consistent with the general treatment of contingencies (see Chapter 8), recognition of loss is required when it is anticipated; recognition of gain is delayed until realization. This approach is applied to disposal proceeds of assets and prospective operating results taken together. That is to say, losses on asset disposal may be offset by expected profits during the period up to disposition, and conversely.[19] The income statement presentation of gains or losses on disposal of part of a business will be discussed in a subsequent section.

Restructurings

Throughout the late 1980s and early 1990s many enterprises found it necessary to undertake major programs to restructure certain of their operations to try to improve their cost effectiveness so as to maintain or regain their competitive position under difficult economic conditions. A restructuring might or might not involve the disposition of a part of a business, but it generally results in downsizing and integrating existing operations and in reducing employee workforces. There is no question but that these costs should be expensed, i.e., that they do not represent capitalizable values. One would expect that the recognition, measurement and presentation issues should be similar to those relating to the disposal or discontinuance of part of a business. Some additional questions have arisen in practice, however. Securities regulators in Canada and the U.S. became concerned that abuses were occurring and, in particular, that a number of companies were being tempted to overstate restructuring costs so as to improve reported ongoing operating earnings. This was being done in several ways, including treating costs incurred to achieve expected future benefits (retraining costs for example) as restructuring expenses, providing for future costs to carry through existing restructuring plans that really related to future activities, and labelling certain ongoing operating expenses as "restructuring" costs. Several pronouncements have been issued to try to rule out these perceived abuses.[20]

Reorganizations and Quasi-Reorganizations

On rare occasions a company that is in financial difficulties may go through a reorganization in which creditors and shareholders may accept a reduction in their rights and claims upon the company, and assets are written down to values considered more realistic in the situation. The *CICA Handbook* requires that a financial reorganization that does not result in the same party controlling the enterprise before and after be accounted for on a basis analogous to that of a business acquisition. The identifiable assets and liabilities of the enterprise are comprehensively revalued effectively establishing a new starting point. Such values should reflect fair values as of the date of the reorganization that are consistent with the bargaining of new rights and claims between the creditor and equity interests. No value is to be assigned to goodwill, however. The *CICA Handbook* sets out specific accounting and disclosure requirements.[21]

A quasi-reorganization is similar except that it does not involve the creditors. Instead, it takes place after formal approval by the shareholders, usually involving a reduction of legal capital.

In both reorganizations and quasi-reorganizations, any write-down of assets is applied first to eliminate retained earnings (if any). Thereafter, the write-downs (plus any existing deficit) are reclassified to contributed surplus, share capital or a separately identified account within shareholders' equity. To show that the enterprise has had a "fresh start," disclosure is made, for a period of at least three years after the readjustment, that the balance in retained earnings account (or deficit) was accumulated since the date of the reorganization.

PRESENTATION OF EXTRAORDINARY AND UNUSUAL ITEMS AND OTHER ADJUSTMENTS

The special situations just discussed result in losses or gains that lie outside the normal course of operations or that arise from incidental and possibly nonrecurring activities. There is naturally a question as to how such gains and losses can best be reported in financial statements to assist readers in assessing just what has happened. The same question arises with respect to various other adjustments, including adjustments to correct errors, adjustments of past figures in the light of new information, or adjustments resulting from changes in estimates or in accounting policies. These matters are considered in this section.

Extraordinary Items

From the early development of income measurement there existed a strong tradition, derived from English law, of a distinction between capital gain and income. The classic example is that of the tree and its fruit. The tree is a capital asset and the fruit the income derived from it. Correspondingly, proceeds from sale of fruit were considered income but from the sale of the tree capital, i.e., not income. Following this legal precedent, accounting reports often excluded so-called capital gains or losses from the figure of income reported and, instead, charged or credited them directly to "capital reserves" or simply to the earned surplus account.

This legally derived point of view was quite acceptable to accountants at the time. The accountant's interest in income measurement stemmed from its usefulness in indicating the earning power of a business—the source of capital value. Accordingly, many accountants felt that it was important that the reported income figure be normal, not "distorted" by unusual events or transactions. Under this view not only capital gains or losses could be excluded from income, but also gains and losses from windfalls, casualties, or other unexpected events. This "current operating performance" viewpoint on income measurement was completely acceptable in the 1930s and 1940s when the historical cost theory gained its ascendancy.

At the same time, an opposing viewpoint was held that subsequently gained strength. Under the "all-inclusive" view, emphasis was laid upon the idea of the statement of income as providing a complete historical record, year by year, of the results of operations. It was considered fruitless, and possibly misleading, to filter out gains and losses thought to be nonoperating or nonrecurring. It was argued that if gains and losses can happen once, they can happen again. In any event, their existence is part of the record of performance. Given adequate disclosure, statement readers can make their own decisions as to whether a gain or loss should be considered a factor in recurring earning power.

The passage of time disclosed the weakness in the notion of current operating performance. Its implementation required a decision in every unusual case whether a gain or loss should be reported as part of income or not. Such classification distinctions are always difficult at the borderline. In practice, the result of the classification uncertainties was that losses excluded from income tended to far exceed gains so excluded.

This suggestion of bias in the accounting was naturally disturbing. In an effort to rectify the situation, the U.S. Committee on Accounting Procedure in 1947 attempted to define and limit the items that could be excluded from reported income.[22] The committee's advice was as follows. First, capital transactions *must* be excluded from reported income. Second, material extraordinary items – defined as being items which in the aggregate are clearly not identifiable with or do not result from the usual or typical business operations of the period— *ordinarily* should also be excluded. Examples of such items were set out.

Inconsistent practice continued. The Accounting Principles Board addressed the question again in 1966 and moved further towards the all-inclusive position, although with some compromises.[23] One compromise was that "prior period adjustments" (a relatively new term) were to continue to be excluded from reported income. Other extraordinary items, although now to be included in net income reported for a year, were to be identified and reported on an after-tax basis at the end of the statement of income, clearly segregated from ordinary income for the year. An attempt was also made to provide a more rigorous definition of both prior period adjustments (see further discussion below) and extraordinary items. In 1969, the CICA adopted the American recommendations with only minor changes in wording.

The basic criterion of an extraordinary item was that a reasonable person would not take it into account as a recurring factor in evaluating the operations and worth of an enterprise. To meet this criterion, an item should be not typical of normal business operations and not expected to recur regularly over a period of years. Both these characteristics were required. In practice, however, the concept of risks outside normal business operations was rather loosely interpreted in both the U.S. and Canada, and frequency of occurrence seemed to be the real operational test. For example, if an enterprise with a limited number of major customers suffered a significant bad debt loss on the bankruptcy of one of them, management might regard that as extraordinary, regardless of whether some bad debt losses are typical of normal business operations.

The result was that these accounting standards did not succeed in eliminating criticisms about inconsistency in the treatment of extraordinary items.[24] Whereas formerly the criticisms mainly concerned their total exclusion from income, now the criticism lay in their classification. The underlying cause, however, was the same. Where there is a continuous shading from white at one end to black at the other, it is notoriously difficult to express in words just where in the grey area white should be deemed to have become black.

The U.S. Accounting Principles Board tried again in 1973.[25] The board emphasized that an event or transaction had to meet *both* the test of abnormality in relation to the ordinary activities of the enterprise and the test of infrequency of occurrence to qualify as extraordinary. Only three examples of extraordinary items were mentioned. These were gains or losses resulting from (1) a major catastrophe such as an earthquake, (2) an expropriation, or (3) a prohibition under a new law or regulation. The board also removed one of the events previously most frequently classified as extraordinary by prescribing separate accounting for gain or loss on disposal of a segment of a business. (See the following section on presentation of discontinued operations.)

The result of these new recommendations, together with indications of close monitoring of extraordinary items by the Securities and Exchange Commission, was a sharp reduction in the number of extraordinary items reported.[26] In 1990 the CICA amended its standard on extraordinary items to make it, if anything, even more restrictive than that in the U.S. In addition to being expected to occur infrequently and not to typify normal business activities of the entity, an extraordinary item must not depend primarily upon decisions or determinations by management or owners.[27] Thus extraordinary items have become rare indeed.[28]

Discontinued Operations

The U.S. standard adopted in 1973 ruled that when a complete segment of a business is discontinued, ordinary income is to be subdivided between income from continuing operations and income from the discontinued segment.[29] The following is to be shown separately in respect of the discontinued segment (on an after-tax basis, with disclosure of the tax effects):

• Gain or loss from operations in the reporting period up to the date of the formal decision to discontinue or dispose of the segment (the measurement date).

• The net gain or loss resulting from disposal of the segment, including any expected profit or loss on operations subsequent to the measurement date (to the extent operating profit/loss can be estimated with reasonable accuracy—ordinarily expected to be for a period no longer than one year). A net loss on disposal of the segment is to be provided for at the measurement date, while a net gain is to be recognized only when it is realized.

Other disclosures include information about the segment being discontinued and the plan of disposal, the measurement date and the disposal date or period expected for disposal, a description and the carrying value of major classes of assets and liabilities of the discontinued business still on hand at the balance sheet date, and revenue of the discontinued operations for the reporting period. Previous years' operating figures are to be restated to break out the profit or loss on the segment for comparison.

The results of disposals of assets or an undertaking constituting less than a line of business cannot be treated as either a discontinuance of business or an extraordinary item. They may, if material, be given special disclosure as a component of ordinary continuing income before tax.

The CICA adopted this presentation and accompanying disclosures of discontinued operations in 1990.[30] Until then, gain or loss on sale or discontinuance of a plant or a significant segment of a business was reported as extraordinary. In 1998 the IASC issued a standard requiring disclosures of discontinuing operations (IAS 35).

Unusual Items

Both in Canada and the United States, items forming part of ordinary operations that are "unusual" in nature or infrequent in occurrence are to be reported as separate components of ordinary income or given special footnote disclosure.[31] This reflects recognition that it is of significance for investors to be able to separate out the effects on income of the unusual— nonrecurring, atypical gains and losses—and that this is not fully enabled by the separation of "extraordinary items." Financial analysts stress the importance of information that helps them estimate the "core earnings" of an enterprise.[32] This is consistent with empirical evidence cited in Chapter 4 that securities prices act as though they reflect the present value of expected sustainable earnings.

One would not think it should be difficult for management of an enterprise to identify material unusual items, although judgment is required. Generally, any revenue or expense that stands out from a trend established over the most recent years should be reviewed for special disclosure. In addition, all material gains or losses on peripheral activities should be reviewed for frequency of occurrence. If there is adequate disclosure of all unusual items, one may question whether there is any great advantage to the segregation of defined extraordinary items, particularly if the definition of "extraordinary" does not coincide with what the ordinary financial statement reader would understand by that word.

Disclosure of unusual items has often not been well done in practice, however. Accounting authorities and securities regulators in Canada have expressed concern that some enterprises have developed an "operating income" classification within their income statement that includes some revenues and gains that may not be typical of normal operating activities while placing certain recurring-type charges below the operating line. As well in a few cases companies have accorded some unusual items a separate classification in the income statement that has looked very much like "extraordinary" treatment. The OSC issued a staff accounting communiqué addressing these perceived abuses.[33] The concept of "income from operations" has not been well defined in accounting literature,[34] and the old debate on distinguishing current operating performance seemed to be re-emerging.

Prior Period Adjustments

In spite of the shift toward the all-inclusive income statement in the 1960s, prior period adjustments continued to be excluded from reported income. The intention was that items excluded from current year's income should be restricted to the results of events that not only had their roots in the past but also were not attributable to any business done in the current year. The CICA put a standard in place in 1971 (*CICA Handbook* Section 3600). To qualify for treatment as a prior period adjustment, an item

- had to be specifically identified with and directly related to business activities of particular prior periods,
- could not be attributable to economic events occurring subsequent to those periods,
- must depend primarily on decisions or determinations by persons other than management, and
- could not reasonably be estimated prior to such decisions.

The standard suggested that true prior period adjustments should be rare. Two examples in Canadian practice were nonrecurring settlements of income taxes, and settlements of claims arising from litigation. The criteria proved incapable of being consistently applied, even to these situations. In some cases where a litigation claim settlement or tax judgment was a "surprise," it was treated as an economic event of the current period. As well, some adjustments of estimated provisions for a tax or litigation uncertainty were viewed simply as corrections of estimates in the periods of settlement rather than as prior period adjustments. It was also argued by some that out-of-court settlements did not qualify as a prior period adjustments, because settlement required the active involvement of management, while others thought that this distinction made no sense. Overall, there was evidence indicating that more debits were accorded prior period treatment than credits.[35]

In 1977 the FASB moved even further toward the all-inclusive income concept by restricting prior period adjustment treatment to two items: (1) corrections of errors of prior years, and (2) specific adjustments related to recovery of preacquisition tax loss carryforwards of subsidiary companies.[36] (The latter adjustment was subsequently removed.) In 1991 the CICA removed *CICA Handbook* Section 3600, so that prior period adjustments now apply only to corrections of errors and changes in accounting policy (see *CICA Handbook* paragraph 1506.31).

Error Corrections

In Canada, the correction of an error from previous years is treated as a prior period adjustment. An error may be purely mechanical in nature, such as an error in arithmetic, or may be a bad estimate based on ignorance or misinterpretation of information available at the reporting date. The availability of information is crucial. Accounting estimates are continually revised in subsequent periods based on new information. Such revisions are not considered corrections of errors, because the original estimates were not in error if they were based on all the information available at the time.

Corrections of errors are treated as follows:

- The adjustment is charged or credited to retained earnings.
- Income and retained earning balances for all prior years presented are restated for the adjustment.
- Adequate explanations are given of the adjustment or correction.[37]

Accounting Changes

Accounting changes may be classified as (1) changes in accounting estimates, (2) changes in accounting policies, and (3) changes in the definition of the accounting entity covered by the financial report.

Changes in Accounting Estimates

Many estimates are required in accounting because of the uncertainty inherent in the real world—such as estimates of the service lives of capital assets, of salvage values, of realizable values of inventory, of recoverable values of accounts receivable, and of amounts that will be payable under warranties. No matter how careful these estimates, revisions to some of them will prove necessary from time to time. If the estimates were originally made in an unbiased fashion, revisions must be the result of subsequent experience, new developments, or new information. It is accepted, therefore, that revisions should not give rise to restatement of results previously reported.

If the estimate relates to a specific amount receivable or payable, the effect of the changed estimate is absorbed immediately in the income of the year of change. On the other hand, if the estimate has to do with amortization of a long-lived asset, the effect of a correction is spread over the current and future periods. The difference in treatment is probably pragmatic. Estimates of the duration of a long-lived asset may well be uncertain even when updated, and may be subject to additional revisions in future. It is thought best to mitigate the effect of such uncertainties by spreading any adjustments so far as possible. (This represents the authors' interpretation of the rather uninformative, if not circular, advice given in paragraph 25(b) of Section 1506 of the *CICA Handbook*.)

Broadly speaking, a similar treatment is adopted for estimates of long-term liabilities. Changes in actuarial assumptions in determining pension obligations, for example, are commonly carried forward to future periods (see Chapter 14). On the other hand, increases in a provision for estimated losses should not be delayed when there is little continuing uncertainty as to their amount. If, for example, early losses on a product with a five-year warranty indicate much poorer expectations than were originally anticipated, the required increase in provision should be recognized immediately, not be phased in. Similarly, provisions for contingent losses, where made, are regularly revised based on best estimates.

Changes in accounting estimates are sufficiently common that there is no general rule requiring their disclosure. If a change qualified as an "unusual item," however, or if the change could have a material effect on reported results in future years, it should be disclosed.

Changes in Accounting Policies

Changes in accounting policies are less frequently encountered than changes in accounting estimates. Where more than one accounting policy is possible in given circumstances, an entity is expected to have chosen that which seems most suitable to it. The term "accounting policies" is interpreted broadly to include methods of application.

When an accounting policy is changed, should it be adopted prospectively with no change to previous accounting or should it be made retroactive? Two possibilities are conceivable if adjustment is retroactive. The amount of the adjustment could be taken to retained earnings without restatement of prior years' earnings figures. Alternatively, previous years' earnings could be restated so far as they are presented, with consequential adjustment of balances of retained earnings for each year presented.

The primary argument against restatement is that it may reduce public confidence in the financial statements. On the other hand, on the assumption the new accounting policy is considered preferable, it seems more useful to readers of financial statements to report figures for all years on the new basis, so that comparisons between years are facilitated and distortion of trends is prevented. This position is accepted in Canada and restatement is recommended (*CICA Handbook*, Section 1506).

Exceptions are made on practical grounds in two situations. First, it may be impossible to know what the figures would have been at the beginning of the year of change if the new accounting policy had been effective. Second, there may be situations where the amount of the adjustment at the beginning of the year of change is known, but limitations in the accounting records make it very difficult or impossible to reconstruct figures on the new basis beyond that point. For example, a manufacturer switching from a direct costing inventory method to one that includes certain fixed overheads might find that records required to assess these overheads were unavailable earlier than the first of the year of change.

U.S. requirements differ from those of Canada. Adjustments caused by accounting policy changes are, with a few exceptions, to be included in income of the year of change as a "catch-up" adjustment. Figures for prior years reported for comparative purposes would not be restated, but additional pro forma figures of net income and earnings per share would be supplied to show what the figures would have been had the new accounting policy been in effect previously.[38]

In both countries, when new standards have required changes in established policies, they have sometimes permitted or required different treatments. For example, prospective adjustment has been permitted in some new pronouncements to ease transitional difficulties.

Canadian practice can be summarized as follows:

- Voluntary changes in accounting policy that concern assets or liabilities on hand before the effective date of change should be applied retroactively if possible. If so applied, reported financial statement figures presented for years before the year of change should be restated, again if possible. When new standards are required, prospective treatment has sometimes been permitted or required.

- The nature of any change in accounting policy is to be described. This should be supplemented by disclosure of its impact on figures presented which, depending upon the case in hand, can usefully be crystallized in terms of its after-tax impact on net income, earnings per share, or on working capital. In all cases, the disclosure of impact should deal with the impact on the current period (indicating, for example, whether and by how much the net income for the year has been increased or decreased by the change compared with what it would have been under the previous policy). Where previous years' figures have been restated, that fact should be made clear along with similar disclosure of the impact.

- Where a change in accounting policy has *not* been applied retroactively, that fact should be disclosed. Where it has been applied retroactively but previous year's figures have *not* been restated, that also should be disclosed. In that case the cumulative adjustment to the opening balance of retained earnings should be clearly disclosed.

- Disclosure of changes in accounting policy should not be confined to those that have a material effect in the year of change if the effect is likely to be material in future.

  This practice requires interpretation in a number of areas.

- An entity may be accounting for certain items of revenue or cost on a simple basis (such as the cash basis) because they are immaterial. If they subsequently become material, adoption of a more careful accounting policy is not regarded as a change in accounting policy. In general, adoption of a new accounting policy because of new conditions or because of entry into a new line of business is not considered a change in accounting policy.

- It is sometimes argued that an accounting change is not a change in accounting policy, or even a change in method of application of an accounting policy, but is merely a "refinement" introduced in the interests of more accurate accounting. For example, suppose overhead in inventory has been calculated heretofore on the basis of a plant-wide allocation rate but departmentalization now permits a more accurate assignment of overheads to various product lines. It might be argued that there is no change in accounting objective or principle here, but that the calculation has simply been refined. However, one may prefer the simple viewpoint that any change in figures reported that is not caused by real changes in the business done, but merely by changes in the way it is accounted for, should be described as a change in accounting policy. The term "refinement" should be reserved for an immaterial change.

- Not infrequently, changes in the classification of assets, liabilities, revenues, or expenses in the financial statement are made from one period to another. On the theory that accounting includes recording, classifying, reporting, and interpreting the results of economic events it can be argued these classification changes are also changes in accounting policy. Certainly rules for classification of current assets and current liabilities are conventionally considered to be accounting principles. Nevertheless, it has been accepted that a distinction may be made between recording and measurement on the one hand and presentation in the financial statements on the other. Thus, reclassification is not normally regarded as a change in accounting policy. To improve comparability, however, previous years' financial statements are reclassified to conform with the latest year reported where possible, and the figures are labelled "reclassified."

- Occasionally, there can be difficulty in distinguishing between accounting policy changes and changes in estimates. Indeed, an accounting policy change can substitute for a change in estimate. It is generally considered that, where there is doubt, its treatment as a change in estimate should be preferred to treatment as a change in policy. This preference is presumably based on the desire to make sure that current income reported includes all the effects of changes triggered by current experience. In individual cases, however, judgment may well be difficult. (See *CICA Handbook* paragraph 1506.23.)

In view of the potential difficulties for users in sorting out changes in financial reporting, there is a general presumption that accounting policies should be applied without change year after year. American standards go further and provide that a change in policy may only be made to a policy considered preferable in the circumstances, and that the auditor should specifically state his or her approval of the change. This requirement is supplemented by an SEC requirement that registrants file notice of accounting policy changes accompanied by the audit firm's statement that it considers the change to be preferable. This counsel of perfection is well intentioned but of doubtful effectiveness. As an example, many accountants consider LIFO accounting to be fundamentally inconsistent with the historical cost accounting model. Yet it is not known that any auditor withheld approval of the many changes to LIFO accounting that have occurred since the date of APB Opinion No. 20. The reason is simple. The very existence of alternative accounting policies is prima facie evidence that standard setters are unable to specify the circumstances in which each of the competing policies is applicable. If standard setters cannot accomplish this task, it is unreasonable to expect individual auditors or members of management to succeed where they have failed.

There is some evidence that managements' motivations in making discretionary accounting changes may often relate more to managing reported earnings than to improving statement representational faithfulness.[39] The most practical answer to this may be appropriate full disclosure of changes, so that readers may be able to assess something of their merit, and perhaps possible motivations, as well as their effects.

Changes in Reporting Entity

The third category of accounting change—namely, a change in the reporting entity—occurs much less frequently. Such a change may be caused by a change in circumstances. For example, when two entities combine in a pooling of interests, the new entity is deemed a continuation of both of the preceding entities; their histories should therefore be combined. A change in entity resulting from a change in accounting policy or judgment is not supposed to be possible for commercial enterprises, since all subsidiaries must now be consolidated (see Chapter 20). (There is still some possibility of this for not-for-profit organizations, however, since consolidation of controlled entities continues to be a policy choice of management. See discussion in Chapter 27).

Some questions may arise in the applications of consolidation accounting.

- Suppose an investment in a 40% owned company has been carried on the equity basis of accounting and this year is consolidated because acquisition of additional shares has given the parent company control. Should the consolidation be given retroactive treatment? The answer is no since equity accounting was, and continues to be, appropriate for the position as it was at the previous year-end. It might be useful, however, to present supplementary pro forma consolidated figures for purposes of comparison as a aid to reader comprehension.

- Consider also a situation where a previously consolidated subsidiary is sold during the year. In this case the change in entity is not an accounting change but a real event. Nevertheless, it would be useful to restate the previous years' figures so that the subsidiary is removed from the consolidation and recorded on the basis of equity accounting, so as to make clear the effect of removing the subsidiary on the ongoing revenues, expenses and assets and liabilities of the continuing entity.

Performance Reporting—Recent Developments

Some significant exceptions to the all-inclusive concept of income appeared in U.S. GAAP when some FASB standards provided that certain gains and losses be reported within a separate component of equity, rather than in the statement of income. The first of these pronouncements was SFAS 12 issued in 1995 (since superseded). It required that lower-of-cost-and-market adjustments to long-term investments be taken directly to shareholders' equity. Subsequently, FASB standards have required that the following items be presented in equity:

- Certain foreign currency adjustments relating to net investments in foreign entities, and gains and losses on hedges thereof (SFAS 52).

- Unrealized holding gains and losses on available-for-sale securities (SFAS 115).

- Certain net additions to pension liabilities that were not considered appropriate to be recognized as pension costs (SFAS 87).

SFAS 133 on accounting for derivatives and hedges gives rise to some additional gains and losses to be classified outside the statement of earnings.

Thus far the only adjustment required under Canadian GAAP is in respect of adjustments relating to net investments in foreign entities, which are explicitly required to be taken directly to equity (see Chapter 21)—but CICA standards have yet to address issues relating to accounting for financial instruments that have given rise to some of the FASB equity adjustments.

There has been no conceptual basis provided for these adjustments. The decisions to report them in equity appear to be pragmatic responses to concerns of many preparers and accountants that reporting these gains and losses in income would upset conventional earning, realization and/or matching concepts, and would create an undesirable level of volatility in reported income. In essence, then, provision for their presentation in equity could be interpreted as simply compromises to achieve sufficient consensus for the recognition of gains and losses that had not previously been recognized in financial accounting. Their presentation in equity has been defended on the grounds that the adjustments must be clearly disclosed, so that they will be transparent to the discerning reader.

There has been a growing uneasiness with these equity adjustments. The demand for some gains and losses to be reflected outside regular income has stimulated international efforts to reconsider the reporting of financial performance.

The U.K. Accounting Standards Board took the first step in 1992, when it required the presentation of a second performance statement as part of the full set of financial statements.[40] This new statement, called the "Statement of Total Recognized Gains and Losses" (STRGL), was established to report certain components of general financial performance that were permitted or required by U.K. law or accounting standards to be presented outside the statement of profit and loss. Primary among these items are unrealized gains and losses arising on revaluations of capital assets, which revaluations are permitted in the U.K. The

STRGL is to be presented as a primary financial statement, and the total STRGL is to be added to the statement of profit and loss results to report a total measure of financial performance.

In 1997, the FASB moved further towards an all-inclusive approach to income reporting by applying the concept of "comprehensive income" to encompass all recognized changes in equity other than those resulting from investments by, and distributions to, owners.[41] SFAS 130 divides comprehensive income into two parts: (1) income, and (2) other comprehensive income. The latter includes the foreign currency adjustments, unrealized gains and losses on marketable securities, and additional pension liability adjustments noted above. It now also includes gains and losses arising from "cash flow" hedges provided for by SFAS 133 on accounting for derivatives and hedges (see Chapter 17). SFAS 130 requires that other comprehensive income be reported with the same prominence as other financial statements, and that an amount representing total comprehensive income for the period be reported. Enterprises are permitted to present other comprehensive income as part of an expanded income statement, as a separate statement, or, less desirable, as a separate component of the statement of changes in equity.

In 1997, the IASC opted for an approach that is less consistent with the all-inclusive income approach.[42] It provides that other IASC standards may specify that certain gains and losses be presented within the statement of changes in equity. There is no requirement that a total be presented that reflects the sum of these items and the net profit or loss for the period.

To date, the CICA has not addressed the issues, and there is no provision under Canadian GAAP for the presentation of a second statement of financial performance.

In all three of the U.K., FASB and IASC standards, the items to be presented in the second performance statement are restricted to items specified for this treatment by other standards. None of these standards provides any conceptual justification for why certain items of financial performance are to be reported outside the regular income statement.

Perhaps the most contentious presentation issue relates to whether gains and losses presented in the second performance statement should be transferred to regular income when they are deemed to have been earned, realized or matched under traditional income reporting conventions. Under SFAS 130 all items reported in other comprehensive income are eventually reported in net income. To illustrate, unrealized gains and losses on held-for-sale investments initially reported in other comprehensive income, are transferred ("recycled") to income when they are realized. This requires a disclosed reversing entry in other comprehensive income at the time of the transfer, which some find to be a rather confusing item. In contrast, the U.K. standard does not provide for recycling of items from STRGL to the statement of profit and loss. It takes the view that gains and losses should be reported only once, in the period they arise, in the appropriate statement of performance. The IASC standard accepts recycling for some items, but not others, reflecting whatever is provided for in the specific IASC standards pertaining to the particular items.

Thus there is much inconsistency internationally, and a lack of conceptual basis, for reporting "other comprehensive income." A recent G4+1 paper reviewed current developments and put forward the working group's views as to how performance reporting should develop in the future.[43] It proposed that "the ideal long-term goal would be for all financial performance to be reported in a single statement of financial performance, such as an expanded income statement, rather than in two statements of performance or in a statement of performance and a statement of changes in equity" (paragraph 3.19). The majority of the working group supported reporting income in three broad categories—operating/trading activities, financing activities, and other gains and losses. The G4+1 is continuing to consider how these categories might be developed and interpreted.

SUMMARY

This chapter deals with two broad subject areas: (1) standards for recognition of loss resulting from asset impairment and certain special situations (disposal of part of a business, restructurings and reorganizations), and (2) statement presentation of gains and losses and adjustments of all types.

Modern accounting theory holds that the cost basis carrying value of an asset should be represented by future benefits expected to result from its use or sale or from the receipt of cash flows representing principal, interest or dividends. Normal expense recognition conventions are supposed to allow for the write-off of costs of assets in use as benefits are consumed. But not infrequently losses must be recognized in situations where the expected recoverable values of assets are less than their cost-based carrying values. The basis of that recognition differs to some extent from one category of asset to another.

- It is accepted that inventory, as a current asset, should not be carried at an amount above its net realizable value. For practical reasons, replacement cost is taken as a proxy for realizable value for raw materials and work in process at early stages of production. The exact manner of application of the lower of cost and market rule may vary to some extent.

- In the past provisions for impairment of receivables tended to be based on assessing individual accounts for likely measurable losses with no consideration of the time value of money. Lending institutions commonly smoothed out loan loss provisions for periods of up to five years, with the object of reflecting average losses over a presumed normal economic cycle. This practice was defended on the grounds that it helped to preserve an aura of financial stability and public confidence in these institutions. These practices have come to be recognized as unsatisfactory in the contemporary volatile business and investment environment. Standards in Canada and the U.S. now require full and immediate provision against income for loan impairment based on the discounted present value of realistic estimates of future principal and interest cash flows. The new standards also require expanded disclosures of impaired loans and loan loss provisions.

- Marketable securities carried as temporary investments must be written down when market value is below cost. Long-term portfolio investments carried on a cost basis are required to be written down only if a decline in value is considered to be other than temporary. The test is applied by individual security. The CICA standard is silent as to how to determine recoverable value, but practice has accepted a nondiscounted interpretation. Written-down values are considered to represent a new cost figure and write-downs cannot be reversed before realization.

- Historically, the theory of providing for capital asset impairment has been quite mixed, and practice ranged from no provision until virtual realization on abandonment or disposal of assets to "big bath" accounting. In 1990 the CICA took a step towards addressing the evident deficiencies of practice. It issued a standard requiring provision against income where an asset's net recoverable value is estimated to be less than its carrying value. Recoverable value is defined as the sum of estimated undiscounted future cash flows to result from the use of a capital asset, reduced by directly attributable general, administrative and interest costs. When it is not practicable to identify cash flows attributable to a single asset, net recoverable value is to be determined for groups of assets that work together. Once made, write-downs are not to be reversed. In the U.S. a FASB standard takes a different, two-step approach. First, capital assets and any related goodwill are considered impaired if the sum of future cash flows, without discounting or interest charges, is less than carrying value. If this test is met, an impairment loss is measured as the amount by which the carrying value exceeds fair value, which is considered to represent a new cost base for the asset. A recent IASC standard requires assessment of possible impairment where certain indications are present. It requires write-down to a lower recoverable value, which is defined as the higher of net selling value and value in use.

Some substantive questions arise in accounting for certain special situations involving the disposal of part of a business, the restructuring of certain business operations, and relatively rare situations in which an entity is forced by financial difficulties to undergo a reorganization. During the past few years standard setters and securities regulators have given considerable attention to better defining exactly when these events should be given accounting recognition, how provisions for losses should be measured, and what may constitute appropriate presentation and disclosure.

At one time, under the "current operating performance" idea, it was thought that the results of a variety of capital and other nonrecurring transactions should be excluded from the report of income for a period in order to enhance its usefulness as an indicator of operating results ordinarily to be expected. Faced with great difficulty in making a clean distinction between ordinary and other transactions and events, accounting standards have, over a long period of time, moved away from the current operating performance concept toward the "all-inclusive" concept. The latter concept holds that virtually every transaction or event other than transactions with owners is part of the income history of an enterprise and should be reported through income sooner or later. The present position is as follows:

- Gains and losses in capital transactions—nonreciprocal transactions with owners—continue to be excluded from income. Depending upon the situation, they may be credited or charged directly to a capital surplus account.

- Income reported is to be all-inclusive with a few exceptions.

  - Errors in previous years' accounts discovered in a current year require adjustment of prior period figures.

  - Changes in accounting policies, if applied retroactively, also produce prior period adjustments. Special disclosure is to be given to emphasize the effect of the change in policy on the current year and on restated figures for prior periods. Some changes in accounting policy standards are applied prospectively, and these too require special disclosure. In the U.S., voluntary accounting policy changes are treated as special "catch-up" adjustments in income.

  - There has been an increasing tendency internationally for some standards to provide for certain gains and losses to be presented outside the statement of income. The only instance in Canada at present is the requirement that certain foreign currency adjustments relating to investments in foreign entities, and to hedges thereof, be reported in equity. However, there can be expected to be pressures for such adjustments in other developing areas not yet addressed in CICA standards. A FASB standard requires presentation of such gains and losses within a broad concept of "comprehensive income." U.K. and IASC standards have taken somewhat different approaches to defining presentation within a second performance statement. There is no provision under Canadian GAAP for presentation of a second performance statement.

- "Extraordinary items" and gains and losses arising from discontinued operations are each to be shown separately, net of tax, at the foot of the income statement. In order to avoid abuse, the term "extraordinary item" has been defined so narrowly that the categorization is of questionable value.

- Unusual income items that do not qualify for "extraordinary" treatment are to be presented as separately disclosed components of ordinary income before tax. Evidence indicates that there is room for improvement in the presentation and disclosure of unusual items. There have been demands for better information to help users distinguish "core" earnings.

REFERENCES

1   A research study published in 1963 still reasonably reflects the issues. See G. Mulcahy, *Use and Meaning of "Market" in Inventory Valuation* (Toronto: CICA, 1963).

2   For a more complete description of the finer points in the retail method of inventory valuation, see B.J. Bunton and R.J. Sycamore, "What's Wrong with the Retail Method," *CA Magazine*, October 1981, pp. 40–47.

3   See, for example, G.J. Switzer, "A Modern Approach to Retail Accounting," *Management Accounting*, February 1994, pp. 55–58.

4   See American Institute of Accountants, Committee on Accounting Procedure, *Restatement and Revision of Accounting Research Bulletins*. Accounting Research Bulletin No. 43 (New York: AIA, 1953), chap. 4, Statement 6.

5   FASB, *Accounting by Debtors and Creditors for Troubled Debt Restructurings*, Statement of Financial Accounting Standards No. 15 (Stamford: FASB, 1977).

6   See, for example, W. Beaver, C. Eger, S. Ryan, and M. Wolfson, "Financial Reporting, Supplemental Disclosures, and Bank Share Prices," *Journal of Accounting Research*, Autumn 1989, pp. 157–78; P.A. Griffin and S.J.R. Wallach, "Latin American Lending by Major U.S. Banks: The Effects of Disclosures about Nonaccrual Loans and Loan Loss Provisions," *The Accounting Review*, October 1991, pp. 830–46; and J.M. Wahlen, "The Nature of Information in Commercial Bank Loan Loss Disclosures," *The Accounting Review*, July 1994, pp. 435–78.

7   See W. Z. Estey, *Report of the Inquiry into the Collapse of the CCB and Northland Bank* (Ottawa: Minister of Supply and Services Canada, 1986), in particular, pp. 300–304, and Appendix F.

8   CICA, "Impaired Loans," *CICA Handbook*, Section 3025 (Toronto: CICA, 1994); CICA, "Accounts and Notes Receivable," *CICA Handbook* Section 3020 (Toronto: CICA, Revision 1994); and FASB, *Accounting by Creditors for Impairment of a Loan*, Statement of Financial Accounting Standards No. 114 (Norwalk: FASB, 1993).

9   FASB, *Accounting by Creditors for Impairment of a Loan—Income Recognition and Disclosures: An Amendment of FASB Statement No. 114*, Statement of Financial Accounting Standards No. 118 (Norwalk: FASB, 1994).

10 CICA, "Long-Term Investments," *CICA Handbook*, Section 3050 (Toronto: CICA), pars. 20–26.

11 CICA, *Financial Instruments*, Re-exposure Draft (Toronto: CICA, April 1994), pars. .097–.129.

12 AICPA, APB, *Basic Concepts and Accounting Principles Underlying Financial Statements of Business Enterprises*, APB Statement No. 4 (New York: AICPA, 1970), par. 183, principle M-5C.

13 See, for example, D.R. Beresford and R.D. Neary, "Impairment of Value of Long-Lived Assets," *Financial Executive*, July 1985, pp. 5–8.

14 CICA, "Capital Assets," *CICA Handbook*, Section 3060 (Toronto: CICA), par. 42.

15 FASB, *Accounting for the Impairment of Long-Lived Assets and for Long-Lived Assets to Be Disposed Of*, Statement of Financial Accounting Standards No. 121 (Norwalk: FASB, 1995).

16 IASC, *Impairment of Assets*, IAS 36 (London: IASC, 1998).

17 CICA, "Discontinued Operations," *CICA Handbook*, Section 3475 (Toronto: CICA). See also CICA Emerging Issues Committee, *Liability Recognition for Costs to Exit an Activity (Including Certain Costs Incurred in a Restructuring)*, EIC 60 (Toronto: CICA, Revised 1995).

18 See discussion of these issues in L.T. Johnson, *Future Events: A Conceptual Study of Their Significance for Recognition and Measurement* (Norwalk: FASB, 1994). The IASC has recently issued a standard that requires not only a formal plan, but also that "valid expectations" have been raised in those affected, by either starting to implement the plan or announcing its principal features. See IASC, *Provisions, Contingent Liabilities and Contingent Assets*, IAS 37 (London: IASC, 1998), pars. 72–77.

19 See *CICA Handbook*, Section 3475, pars .08–11.

20 See CICA Emerging Issues Committee, *Liability Recognition for Costs to Exit an Activity (Including Certain Costs Incurred in a Restructuring)*, EIC 60 (Toronto: CICA, Revised 1995); Ontario Securities Commission, *Restructuring and Similar Changes (Including Writedowns of Goodwill)*, Staff Accounting Communiqué No. 10 (Toronto: OSC, December, 1994); and FASB, Emerging Issues Task Force, *Liability Recognition for Certain Employee Termination Benefits and Other Costs to Exit an Activity (Including Certain Costs Incurred in a Restructuring)*, EITF Abstract No. 94-3 (Norwalk: FASB, 1994).

21 See CICA, "Comprehensive Revaluation of Assets and Liabilities," *CICA Handbook*, Section 1625 (Toronto: CICA), pars .05, .15–.16 and .39–.54.

22 See American Institute of Accountants, Committee on Accounting Procedure, *Income and Earned Surplus*, Accounting Research Bulletin No. 32 (New York: AIA, 1947), subsequently consolidated in *Restatement and Revision of Accounting Research Bulletins*, Accounting Research Bulletin No. 43 (New York: AIA, 1953), chap. 8.

23 AICPA, APB, *Reporting the Results of Operations*, APB Opinion No. 9 (New York: AICPA, 1966).

24 See, for example, L.A. Bernstein, "Extraordinary Gains and Losses—Their Significance to the Financial Analyst," *Financial Analysts Journal*, November–December 1972, pp.

49–52, 88–90; M.J. Amenta, "Unsettled Issues and Misapplications of APB Opinion No. 9 as to Treatment of Extraordinary Items," *The CPA Journal*, August 1972, pp. 640–43, 664; and W. Langdon, "Abuse of the Extraordinary Item," *Cost and Management*, November–December 1973, pp. 53–55.

25   AICPA, APB, *Reporting the Results of Operations—Reporting the Effects of Disposal of a Segment of a Business, and Extraordinary, Unusual and Infrequently Occurring Events and Transactions*, APB Opinion No. 30 (New York: AICPA, 1973).

26   Other U.S. accounting standards, however, required certain items to be classified as extraordinary that did not meet the basic criteria of APB Opinion 30—notably the realization of the benefit of an income tax loss carryforward [which was finally removed in 1992 by FASB *Accounting for Income Taxes*, Statement of Financial Accounting Standards No. 109 (Norwalk: FASB, 1992)]; and gains or losses on the extinguishment of debt, see FASB *Reporting Gains and Losses from Extinguishment of Debt: An Amendment of APB Opinion No. 30*, Statement of Financial Accounting Standards No. 4 (Stamford: FASB, 1975).

27   CICA, "Extraordinary Items," *CICA Handbook*, Section 3480 (Toronto: CICA).

28   A CICA survey of 300 public Canadian companies indicated only three reported extraordinary items in 1992. Eighty-one of these companies reported extraordinary items in 1989, the year before the change to the *CICA Handbook* standard. See CICA, *Financial Reporting in Canada 1993*, 20th ed. (Toronto: CICA, 1993), p. 187. See also note in CICA, *Financial Reporting in Canada*, 23rd ed. (Toronto: CICA, 1998), pp. 431–32.

29   AICPA, APB, *Reporting the Results of Operations* (1973).

30   CICA, "Discontinued Operations," *CICA Handbook*, Section 3475 (Toronto: CICA).

31   With respect to Canada, see CICA, "Extraordinary Items," *CICA Handbook* Section 3480, par. 12, and CICA, "Income Statement," *CICA Handbook*, Section 1520 (Toronto: CICA), par .03(l).

32   See AICPA, Special Committee on Financial Reporting, *Improving Business Reporting—A Customer Focus* (New York: AICPA, 1994), pp. 79–84. This was a conclusion of this U.S. study of investor and creditor information needs in the U.S. It recommended more information on unusual or nonrecurring items, and elimination of the "extraordinary items" classification on the grounds that the concept is too narrow to be useful.

33   Ontario Securities Commission, "Income Statement Presentation," Staff Accounting Communiqué No. 6, July 1992, in *Consolidated Ontario Securities Act and Regulation 1996 with Policy Statements, Blanket Orders and Notices*, 25th ed. (Scarborough, Ontario: Carswell Thomson Canada Ltd., 1996).

34   See, for example, J.E. Ketz and J.A. Largay III, "Reporting Income and Cash Flows from Operations," *Accounting Horizons*, June 1987, pp. 9–17.

35   See CICA, *Financial Reporting in Canada 1993*, p. 203.

36   See FASB, *Prior Period Adjustments*, Statement of Financial Accounting Standards No. 16 (Stamford: FASB, 1977).

37   CICA, "Accounting Changes," *CICA Handbook*, Section 1506 (Toronto: CICA), pars. .26–.30.

38   See AICPA, APB, *Accounting Changes*, Opinion No. 20 (New York: AICPA, 1971).

[39] See, for example, G.S. May and D.K. Schneider, "Reporting Accounting Changes: Are Stricter Guidelines Needed?" *Accounting Horizons*, September 1988, pp. 68–74; and S. Lilien, M. Mellman and V. Pastena, "Accounting Changes: Successful Versus Unsuccessful Firms," *The Accounting Review*, October 1988, pp. 642–56.

[40] Accounting Standards Board, *Reporting Financial Performance*, FRS 3 (London: Accounting Standards Board, Inc., 1992).

[41] FASB, *Reporting Comprehensive Income*, Statement of Financial Accounting Standards No. 130 (Norwalk: FASB, 1997). This standard implemented the concept of "comprehensive income" defined in FASB, *Elements of Financial Statements*, Statement of Financial Accounting Concepts No. 6 (Stamford: FASB, 1985), pars. 1, and 70–77.

[42] IASC, *Presentation of Financial Statements*, IAS 1 (Revised) (London: IASC, 1997), pars. 86 and 88–89.

[43] L.T. Johnson and A. Lennard, Principal Authors, *Reporting Financial Performance: Current Developments and Future Directions* (Norwalk: FASB, 1998).

BUSINESS COMBINATIONS

At some point in their history many enterprises unite with or obtain control over the assets and undertakings of other business entities. These are known as "business combinations." A business combination may be accomplished by the direct purchase of the assets of an operating enterprise or, indirectly, by the purchase of a majority of the controlling shares of the other entity. The consideration given may be cash, other monetary assets, or the acquiring entity's shares. Some enterprises are involved in many business combinations over a period of years.

A Historical Overview

The appropriate approach to accounting for business combinations was a matter of great debate in the late 1960s and early 1970s. It had been common for a purchaser to record the assets and liabilities of the entity purchased at their carrying value in the books of the latter. The difference between the aggregate of those carrying values and the purchase price was recorded as a separate asset (often called goodwill) or, if negative, as a separate component of shareholders' equity. Thereafter, this "purchase discrepancy" might or might not be amortized to income. Alternatively, the purchase discrepancy could be written off to retained earnings at the time of acquisition.

This accounting for acquisitions had no theoretical justification. The purchaser's cost had no necessary relationship to book values of the vendor. What was relevant to the purchasing entity was the cost of what it had acquired. It came to be accepted that this cost is best represented by the fair values of the assets and liabilities of the acquired entity at the date of acquisition. Moreover, the accounting profession in North America ultimately agreed that it made no sense to write off the "goodwill" part of the cost paid in an arm's-length transaction immediately the deal was consummated. Rather, it was accepted that any excess of the purchaser's cost over the amounts assigned to the acquiree's assets and liabilities at the date of acquisition should be treated as a separate "goodwill" asset to be amortized to income over future periods. These concepts were embodied over time in standards, culminating in the U.S. with APB Opinion No. 17 issued in 1970,[1] and in Canada with CICA recommendations effective in 1974.[2]

Beginning in earnest in the 1960s it became popular in the U.S. for business combinations to be based on exchanges of common shares and accounted for as "poolings of interests." The essential idea was that where two (or more) companies are combined through an exchange of voting shares, one entity should not be considered to have acquired the other. Rather the two (or more) groups of owners could be viewed to have simply pooled their resources, with the result that no new basis of accounting should be considered to arise. The carrying value of the assets and liabilities of the combining entities are simply added together, and the financial statements of the combined entity presented for prior periods to reflect the financial position and results of operations as if the companies had been combined since their inception.

Many U.S. companies found pooling-of-interests accounting attractive because it enabled them to report higher income and return on investment figures as a result of not revaluing assets to higher fair value amounts at the date of the combination, and thereby avoiding charging subsequent periods' income with amortization of those higher values. It is generally acknowledged that pooling-of-interests accounting was widely abused in U.S. practice in the 1960s, and stretched beyond any justifiable interpretation of the concept. Ultimately, after much debate, APB Opinion No. 16 was issued in 1970 and it continues to be in force.[3] It requires that purchase accounting be followed except where pooling-of-interests conditions are met. In essence, the U.S. standard is based on the idea that a combination should be treated as a pooling of interests only if it is effected through an exchange of voting shares and there are no direct or collateral arrangements to bail out the shareholders of one or other of the constituents. This general idea is supported by detailed rules. It is an extremely complex standard which did not succeed in clarifying the concept, or in entirely eliminating abuses.[4] It did, however, significantly restrict the application of pooling-of-interests accounting.[5]

Pooling-of-interests accounting was never as prevalent in Canada as in the U.S., perhaps because through the 1960s it was not necessary to resort to pooling in order to understate assets acquired and hence future charges against income. Effective in 1974 the *CICA Handbook* prescribed a much more straightforward standard than that of the U.S. It requires that business combinations be accounted for as purchases whenever one of the constituencies entering into a combination can be identified as the acquirer. Only in rare cases where a business combination is effected by an exchange of shares and it is not possible to identify one of the parties as the acquirer, is pooling-of-interests accounting to be followed.[6] As a result, pooling-of-interests accounting in Canada is very rarely seen.[7] The Canadian principle has subsequently been adopted in a number of other countries, and by the IASC.[8]

Accounting for business combinations has recently re-emerged as a controversial issue. Over the past few years powerful Canadian business interests, led by the banks, have alleged that the inability to use pooling-of-interests accounting except in very rare cases under Canadian GAAP has put them at a severe competitive disadvantage with U.S. companies in growing their businesses within North America and internationally. They have brought pressure to bear on the CICA to allow pooling-of-interests accounting under U.S. rules. The Office of the Superintendent of Financial Institutions has backed the banks and it has taken the unprecedented step of threatening to use its powers to override Canadian GAAP on this issue, if discrepancies between Canadian and U.S. rules are not removed within a short time frame. The controversy has received considerable press coverage.[9]

These pressure tactics have put Canadian GAAP in a precarious position. Even though the *CICA Handbook* standard is generally regarded around the world as superior to that of the FASB, the CICA Accounting Standards Board would not seem to be in a very strong position to resist the formidable forces arrayed against it. It became clear that it would have to reconsider its standard and do so quickly.

Fortunately, the FASB itself, and the G4+1 group of standard-setting bodies added projects to their agendas to re-evaluate accounting for business combinations. In 1996, the FASB decided to re-evaluate its standards on purchase versus pooling, along with accounting for purchased goodwill and other intangibles. In late 1997, the CICA Accounting Standards Board and the FASB agreed to carry out their respective projects on a common timetable with the objective of issuing exposure drafts in 1999 proposing harmonized standards. These efforts are being carried out in coordination with the G4+1 standard setters, and the joint proposal is to rule out pooling-of-interests accounting altogether. At the time this is written, an invitation to comment has been issued, and deliberations are underway in Canada, the U.S. and other G4+1 jurisdictions.[10]

Through the balance of this chapter we will first examine the logical basis for purchase and pooling accounting, and then address issues related to the application of the purchase and pooling methods.

Purchase versus Pooling

When one entity pays cash or other monetary consideration for the assets or shares of another entity, the transaction is obviously a purchase by the entity paying the consideration. However, when a business combination is effected by an exchange of shares, it may be less clear whether one entity has acquired the other or whether the businesses have pooled or merged their resources. The following quotation from APB Opinion No. 16 summarizes a theory in support of pooling-of-interests accounting:

> Those who support the pooling of interests method believe that a business combination effected by issuing common stock is different from a purchase in that no corporate assets are disbursed to stockholders and the net assets of the issuing corporation are enlarged by the net assets of the corporation whose stockholders accept common stock of the combined corporation. There is no newly invested capital nor have owners withdrawn assets from the group since the stock of a corporation is not one of its assets. Accordingly, the net assets of the constituents remain intact but combined; the stockholder groups remain intact but combined. Aggregate income is not changed since the total resources are not changed. Consequently, the historical costs and earnings of the separate corporations are appropriately combined. In a business combination effected by exchanging stock, groups of stockholders combine their resources, talents, and risks to form a new entity to carry on in combination the previous businesses and to continue their earnings streams. The sharing of risks by the constituent stockholder groups is an important element in a business combination effected by exchanging stock. By pooling equity interests, each group continues to maintain risk elements of its former investment and they mutually exchange risks and benefits (par. 28).

APB Opinion No. 16 accepted this theory and concluded that pooling-of-interests accounting should be followed when the conditions implicit in this quotation are met—in particular, that the transaction reflect a straightforward exchange of voting common shares, there is no new invested capital and no significant withdrawals of assets from the group, and the shareholders of the continuing entity remain as shareholders of the combined entity with no significant changes in their proportionate rights and risks. The standard sets out twelve detailed conditions aimed at ensuring that this conceptual basis for pooling is met. The very need to develop such complex rules to apply a theory may cause one to question whether there may be something wrong with the theory, and certainly it has led to a narrow, rule-based approach to applying the standard.

Perhaps the most debatable aspect of the U.S. standard is its omission of any condition with respect to the relative size of combining entities that may be accorded pooling-of-interests accounting. Can there be a real marriage between a flea and an elephant? If one entity is 2% of the size of the other, can there be any meaningful decision by the shareholder groups to pool their interests? If one group ends up controlling the combined entity, it seems difficult to sustain an argument that a purchase (a transfer of control of the assets and undertakings of one entity to the other) has not taken place.

The Canadian standard has taken a different direction. Purchase accounting is considered appropriate whenever one of the constituents entering into a combination can be identified as the acquirer. In the case of a business combination effected by the exchange of shares one must then look to who ends up with control of the combined entity in order to identify the acquirer. If the shareholders of one of the combining entities end up with more of the voting shares than do those of the other entity, the former would normally be regarded as the acquirer. If, however, the balance is relatively even, other indicators should be considered. For example, if the smaller constituent is owned by a tightly knit group while the share ownership of the other is widely dispersed, the dominant interests in the smaller may end up effectively controlling the merged entity. Representation on the board of directors after the merger, and the holders of important management positions may also give a good indication of who was the influential party in the combination. In rare cases these indicators fail, and it is apparent that the combination is a true merger. In such cases "pooling-of-interests" accounting is followed.

In some cases a company issuing shares to acquire the outstanding shares of another company may issue so many of its shares that it has effectively given control over to the shareholders of the other company. For example, if a small company issued three times the number of its existing outstanding shares to acquire all the shares of a larger company, the former shareholders of the latter would end up with three-quarters of the voting shares of the combined entity. In this case the larger company is considered the acquirer for accounting purposes. This is known as a "reverse takeover," because the parent company in legal form is the acquired subsidiary from an in-substance accounting perspective. Reverse takeovers have been used on occasion to obtain stock exchange listings for nonpublic operating companies. This is done by having an inactive or dormant public company issue its shares for those of the operating enterprise. Certain unique aspects of the accounting for reverse takeovers are discussed later in this chapter.

PURCHASE ACCOUNTING

Purchase accounting simply follows the normal approach to accounting for a basket purchase (see Chapter 6), with refinements to allow for the complexities of a business combination. The main problems to be addressed in purchase accounting are (1) valuation of the consideration given for the business acquired, (2) allocation of its cost among the various assets and liabilities acquired, (3) treatment of the purchase discrepancy between the net aggregate value assigned to the assets and liabilities and the net cost, and (4) disclosure required in financial statements after the combination.

Valuation of the Consideration

The aggregate cost of the net assets acquired in a business combination accounted for as a purchase is the fair value of the consideration given. (Possible exceptions to this general rule are discussed under the headings "Non-Arm's-Length Business Combinations" and "Nonmonetary Consideration" later in this chapter.) A valuation problem may arise when the consideration given is in the form of assets other than cash. If securities are issued that provide a fixed yield in the form of interest or preference dividends and do not have other unusual characteristics, a valuation reflecting the market values of the securities about the time of issue or the current market values of similar securities should be reasonably satisfactory. It would be wrong to value the securities issued at their par or face value if their contractual interest or dividend rate is different from market yield rates.

Valuation of common stock issued to effect an acquisition may present more of a problem. To measure the sacrifice involved in the consideration given, one would ideally like to know the cash-equivalent value of the shares issued. The current quoted market price at the acquisition date may represent best evidence of current value, but there can be reasons for a somewhat different valuation. A large block of shares will not necessarily command the same price as smaller lots customarily traded on the market, especially if the shares are only thinly traded. The *CICA Handbook* advises that "the market price for a reasonable period before and after the date of acquisition ... should be considered in determining the fair value of the shares issued" (paragraph 1580.27). In subjective terms, the company's sacrifice can best be expressed as an estimate of what net consideration it could expect to receive either in a public or private issue of an equivalent number of shares. It was not uncommon in the past for large blocks of shares issued in a business acquisition to be discounted more or less arbitrarily by 15% to 30% or more from the current market price. Securities regulators may be expected to question such discounting in the absence of solid evidence of the effects of particular restrictions on the use of the shares or of a lack of a representative market.[11]

The situation is still more difficult if the shares of the acquirer are not quoted. Corporations law requires that the directors place a stated value on shares issued equal to the value of the consideration received for them. But valuing a business acquired may be difficult. The calculations and judgments made by the acquirer in deciding to make an offer may be helpful but such estimates are much less persuasive evidence than would be an agreed-upon cash price. Detailed evaluations of assets acquired will be required for the next step in the accounting, and may be helpful in giving some very rough indication of aggregate value. Since, however, the valuation of goodwill and most other intangible assets may be largely a matter of judgment, individual asset valuations may rarely produce a total figure acceptable as the total value to be applied to the deal.

In spite of all these difficulties, valuation of the consideration given is a necessary starting point in accounting for the purchase transaction.

Correlation of Valuation of Consideration and the Effective Accounting Date for an Acquisition

The determination of the effective date of a business acquisition is important because it is the date at which the amounts assigned to the business assets acquired and liabilities assumed are determined and from which the acquirer reports income from the business acquired. It would be misleading to start recognizing income from the business acquired before recognizing any interest expense or dilution of earnings per share resulting from the consideration given up, or vice versa. Care must be taken in the accounting to avoid this lack of coordination.

As with any asset acquisition, the effective date in economic terms is the date upon which the acquirer takes control of the property and is in a position to enjoy its rewards. Depending on the terms and conditions of the underlying sales agreement, it may be difficult to determine exactly when this happens in the typical case where the acquiree's operations continue on uninterrupted. From the purchaser's point of view, it may be convenient to pick a month-end or quarter-end as the effective date of acquisition for accounting purposes, so as to minimize the work involved in cutting off and verifying the asset position in the midstream of operations. When the effective date of acquisition is somewhat arbitrarily set, however, it is important that other aspects of the transaction be selected or calculated so as to be consistent with it. For example, if the consideration payable under the purchase agreement varies with the amount of working capital or equity reported by the acquiree at a given date, it is usually logical that that date should be selected as the effective date of acquisition for the acquirer's accounting. As another example, sometimes the agreement prohibits payment of dividends or adjusts the purchase price for any dividends paid after a given date. Such terms suggest that the purchase is effective by that date. If the effective date chosen for accounting precedes the record date of a dividend going to vendor shareholders, that dividend must be treated as a liability when the purchaser allocates the purchase consideration among the assets and liabilities of the business acquired (for the purpose of consolidation accounting). The effective acquisition date may be delayed in cases where an acquisition is subject to serious conditions that are other than remote, such as, for example, regulatory approval that is not assured and could prevent the acquirer from exercising control.

Once the effective date of acquisition for accounting purposes is determined, it is necessary to achieve logical consistency with the valuation of the consideration (see *CICA Handbook* paragraph 1580.39). Thus (subject to materiality considerations), if the consideration takes the form of a cash payment made before the effective accounting date, the out-of-pocket acquisition cost should be increased by capitalization of actual or imputed interest between the payment date and the effective accounting date. Likewise, if payment is not made until after the effective accounting date, the payment should be allocated partly to imputed interest expense, with the remainder being treated as the acquisition cost. Equivalent accounting is required if the consideration takes the form of an interest-bearing security that does not bear interest at a current competitive rate, or the date upon which interest begins to accrue on the security does not coincide with the effective accounting date for the acquisition. Finally, if the consideration given is in the form of common shares, the calculation of earnings per share for the issuer in the period of acquisition should assume that the shares were issued at the effective accounting date for the acquisition.

Contingent Consideration

Sometimes the consideration promised in an acquisition is adjustable depending upon future events. The *CICA Handbook* (paragraph 1580.33) suggests that, if the outcome of such contingencies can be determined "beyond reasonable doubt," the acquisition should be recorded on the expected outcome basis. Since the adjustment clause in the contract probably reflects different views by the vendor and purchaser as to the probable future outcome, it is likely that the criterion "beyond reasonable doubt" will rarely be fulfilled at the acquisition date. In that case the accounting, when the outcome of the contingency is known, depends upon the type of adjustment clause.

- An adjustment clause may provide that additional consideration shall be given if earnings are maintained or increased in a specified future period. Such a clause probably indicates some doubt as to the earning power of the business acquired. When that doubt is resolved, any additional consideration under the adjustment clause is regarded as part of the payment for the acquisition, and therefore requires adjustment of the values recorded for the net assets acquired in the combination (frequently an addition to the figure of goodwill).

- In some situations contingent consideration is in-substance compensation for services to be received in subsequent periods and, if so, it should be treated as compensation expense in those periods rather than as additional consideration related to the cost of the business acquisition. Treatment as compensation expense may be called for when recipients of contingent compensation based on earnings are employees, officers or others who are providing ongoing services to the acquired company.[12]

- An adjustment may depend upon the future market price of the shares issued by the acquirer. For example, assume an acquirer issued 100,000 shares at a time when the value of the shares issued was $40 each, with a guarantee of a share price of $45 one year later. If the market price does not reach $45 at the specified date, more shares will be issued to make the value $4.5 million. That is, if the market price remains at $40 a share it will be necessary to issue another 12,500 shares. In such a case the guaranteed value is regarded as the value of the acquisition ($4.5 million in this example). Therefore, the acquisition should be recorded originally at that cost and resolution of the contingency should merely require a change in the number of shares recorded as issued, not a change in the value placed on the acquisition. Questions can arise, however, where the acquirer agrees to issue additional shares in future based on stated minimum share prices that do not guarantee the full fair value of the consideration at the acquisition date. These are discussed in a FASB Emerging Issues Task Force Abstract (EITF 97-15).

Allocation of Cost of an Acquisition

The valuation of the consideration establishes the aggregate cost of the assets less the liabilities acquired or assumed in a business acquisition. It is then necessary to allocate that cost to individual assets and liabilities. This is not an easy task. Acquirers rarely make valuations of individual assets and liabilities in arriving at their acquisition decision. Some business acquirers wonder why an allocation of purchase price is necessary, seeing that valuations of individual assets and liabilities did not enter into their decision process. The answer is simple. The accounting process depends on tracking individual assets and liabilities and changes in them. An investment in a going concern is an investment in assets having varying useful lives. Accounting must separate the future cash flow from the investment into the portion that represents recovery of investment and the portion that represents income, in order to measure the success of the investment and its financial position period after period.

The acquirer might then ask: Why do I need to change the valuations of assets and liabilities that were on the books of the acquiree? The answer again is simple. If the acquirer paid more for the acquired company's assets than the original owner, more of the future cash flow of the business will represent recovery of investment to the acquirer than it did to the original owner. If the acquirer entity wants to assess the result of *its* investment decision, then it must take into account the cost of the investment to *it*, not to the previous owner.

Allocation Bases

How should the acquirer's cost be assigned to the individual assets and liabilities acquired? The starting point assumption is that the purchase cost should be allocated to the identifiable assets and liabilities of the acquired entity on the basis of their fair values—that is, on the basis of the amounts that would be expected to be agreed upon by knowledgeable and willing transacting parties dealing at arm's length, with particular reference to factors that would be relevant to the acquirer. In other words, the object is to determine the fair values that the acquirer would reasonably have been expected to pay for each of the identifiable assets and to assume in respect of each of the identifiable liabilities.

It should be noted that under existing GAAP in Canada only *the acquiring company's interest* in the acquiree's identifiable assets and liabilities is based on their fair values at the date of acquisition. The interest of any noncontrolling (minority) shareholders in the identifiable assets and liabilities is reflected at their carrying values in the accounting records of the company acquired. Thus, if Company A acquired 80% of the shares of Company B, each of the identifiable assets and liabilities of B would be valued in A's consolidated accounts 80% based on fair values at the date of acquisition and 20% based on the carrying values in the accounts of B. (The accounting for noncontrolling interests in consolidated financial statements will be discussed and illustrated in the immediately following chapter, "Intercorporate Investments.")

As already noted, the amount of the consideration is unlikely to equal the sum of the fair values of the identifiable assets acquired less liabilities assumed. If the purchase price exceeds the estimated fair value of all the acquiree's identifiable assets less liabilities, the residual is assigned to goodwill.

Numerous issues arise in estimating the fair values of identifiable assets and liabilities, but the general principles may be summarized in a few statements.

- It is important that both liabilities and assets be fair valued. The overall acquisition cost is determined by the value of obligations assumed, as well as the amount of cash paid or value of common shares issued. Debt assumed should *not* be recorded at face value if it could be discharged for less or, if it could not be discharged, if it could be fully serviced (principal and interest) by purchasing safe investments at a cost lower than the face value of such securities.

- Monetary liabilities and assets are valued at the amount of future cash payable or receivable from them, discounted at an interest rate appropriate to the risk characteristics of the item. If the monetary asset or debt is marketable, the market price will provide direct evidence of the discounted present value.

- Nonmonetary assets and liabilities present more of a problem. Nonmonetary obligations require an estimate of the future cost of fulfilling the obligation. In theory, that future cost should represent an amount equivalent to that which would have to be paid to some other party in order to assume the obligation, and that amount should be discounted to present value at the acquisition date.

- Nonmonetary assets held for sale should be valued at estimated selling price, less allowance for any costs to be incurred in completing and selling the product, and less a reasonable allowance for profit with respect to effort required and delay in realization. The valuation should be such that the acquirer stands to recognize a profit on sale that is reasonable in relation to the value to be added subsequent to the acquisition date. Thus, in valuing inventories of finished goods, the manufacturing profit should be considered to have been earned by the vendor and included in the fair valuation of the inventory by the purchaser. This means that when the inventory is sold, the profit reported in the acquirer's consolidated financial statements will be the selling profit only. Current replacement costs are used for inventories of raw materials, since no value will have been added by the manufacturing process prior to the business acquisition.

- Nonmonetary assets not held for sale should be valued at estimated replacement cost for similar capacity.

These are the general principles, and they accord with the recommendations of *CICA Handbook* Section 1580. A number of issues are commonly encountered in making allocations of the cost of a business acquisition.

- To be truly realistic the allocation should identify and value assets or liabilities that are valuable but not on the books of the acquiree. For example, the going rental rate for rented premises may be substantially different than it was when the lease was initiated. If so, it may have acquired a considerable value or represent a considerable burden that should be taken into account in allocating the cost of an acquisition.

- In acquiring another company, the purchasing entity may well have to incur significant costs to integrate the acquired operations with its own. These may include severance indemnities for surplus employees and costs of closing duplicate facilities. The question is, when are such costs appropriately included as part of the cost of the business acquisition, and when may they represent costs to restructure inefficient operations that should be expensed? Some purchasers have been tempted to include as part of the cost of a business acquisition large accruals for restructurings that may not be a direct result of the acquisition. The EIC deliberated on this issue and concluded that costs of restructuring and integration may be recognized in the purchase cost allocation only when they would not be incurred absent the acquisition and they are specified in reasonable detail as part of a planned program at the date of acquisition.[13]

- Several questions come to mind when an acquiree has a defined benefit pension plan, or other post-employment benefit plan, that will continue after the acquisition. The accounting for a business acquisition should include the accrual of a liability to the extent that the projected benefit obligation exceeds the value of funded plan assets. Alternatively, a net asset should be recognized to the extent that the value of funded plan assets exceeds the projected benefit obligation, *if* the acquirer can expect to benefit from the surplus assets in the plan (see discussion of this issue in Chapter 14). Consistent with the *CICA Handbook* Section 1580 recommendations for fair value-based allocations to individual identifiable assets and liabilities of an acquired company, one would expect the determination of a net pension asset or liability to be a best estimate of its fair value as of the date of acquisition. This has several implications:

- Generally, the full amount of the projected obligation should be recognized at the acquisition date without any offset for prior period service costs or net experience gains or losses that have not yet been amortized by the acquiree.

- Sometimes a business combination results in an equalization of pension plan benefits offered to employees of the combined entities. If the acquiree is effectively obligated to such equalization and it will involve increased costs, the increase in obligation attributable to employees' services to the date of acquisition should be allowed for in the valuation.

- Plan assets should be valued their fair value and the projected benefit obligation should be discounted on a current settlement rate basis.

Although the above valuations of net pension obligations and assets are consistent with the principles of business combination accounting, they would not appear to be required by Canadian pension accounting standards. Rather, for reasons of expediency and convenience of future accounting, pension obligations and assets assumed in a business acquisition may simply be valued using methods and assumptions compatible with those used in the acquiring company's plans. *CICA Handbook* (paragraph 1580.45(g)) would seem to support this view. [Note: In 1999 the paragraph has been amended to incorporate the above implications, in conjunction with the adoption of a new standard on future employee benefits—*CICA Handbook* Section 3461.]

• The *CICA Handbook* suggests the valuation of intangible assets "which can be identified and named."[14] As is argued in Chapter 12, many more intangible factors can be identified and named than can be valued on any reasonable arm's-length equivalent basis. In logic, the valuation of specific intangible factors acquired in a business combination should be restricted to those assets whose utility can be transferred to other parties independent of the business and therefore have some hope of a value in exchange. Even for these, hard evidence should be available to justify the basis of valuation. But it is apparent that both the CICA and FASB business combinations standards contemplate the individual valuation of all "identified" intangibles regardless of whether they can stand separately from the business. Securities regulators have been active in encouraging this interpretation, presumably to try to achieve quicker amortization of intangibles by minimizing the amount of cost that is allocated to goodwill—since goodwill may be amortized over up to forty years while the justifiable useful lives for many specific intangibles may be considerably shorter.

In some situations a significant proportion of consideration paid for a company is in respect of intangibles such as R&D. As observed in Chapter 12, GAAP require that most R&D costs be expensed immediately when they are incurred. In the U.S., the acquirer must account for such costs arising in a business acquisition on the same basis it would have followed had they been incurred directly. Accordingly, the acquirer must assign a cost to the R&D, based on its fair value, and then immediately expense that amount.[15] Accounting in Canada is different. The EIC has interpreted *CICA Handbook*

Section 1580 to require that an acquirer treat the cost that is reasonably attributable to individual intangibles (including R&D and oil and gas and mineral exploration, etc.) acquired in a business combination as assets, regardless of whether the costs would have been expensed if incurred directly.[16] The Canadian accounting seems more consistent with the philosophy of business acquisitions accounting, which presumes that the fair value of intangibles acquired represents assets not expenses. On the other hand, the U.S. position holds that, if the cost of R&D does not meet the tests of technological and commercial feasibility or alternative use necessary to the capitalization of internally developed R&D, capitalization should not be warranted simply because the expenditures were made as part of a business combination.

- The values assigned by an acquirer to the assets and liabilities of an acquired company are likely to differ, in some cases substantially, from their tax bases. Clearly such differences affect the fair values of these assets and liabilities to the acquirer—for example, the value of an asset that is not fully deductible for tax purposes is less than the value of an identical asset that is fully deductible. In economic terms, the *after-tax* fair value of an asset or a liability is the fair value as it would be if the tax basis was the same amount, plus or minus the present value of the future tax effect caused by any difference in the tax base. It had been accepted in Canada that, in theory at least, the fair values of identifiable assets and liabilities of an acquired company should reflect their discounted after-tax fair values at the date of acquisition. However, the CICA has recently followed the FASB lead and put in place a standard that applies tax allocation accounting to virtually all temporary differences, including differences arising in a business acquisition (with the exception of goodwill that is not deductible for tax purposes). As explained in Chapter 16, differences between the tax and accounting bases of assets and liabilities are to be recorded as tax allocation balances in the balance sheet at current tax rates on a nondiscounted basis. Since these deferred tax balances are not computed on a present value basis, this means that the values assigned to the corresponding assets and liabilities will require adjustments if these values, net of the tax allocation balances, are to be equal to their after-tax fair values.

- Tax assets, including loss carryforwards and tax allocation benefits, are to be recognized under the new CICA income tax standard (see Chapter 16) if it is more likely than not that the enterprise will realize the future tax benefits. Such "future income tax" assets are not to be discounted, however, and therefore will not represent their fair value. (These requirements represent a change from the former income tax standard that allowed loss carryforwards of an acquired company to be set up on a discounted basis, and other tax allocation balances to be set up on a nondiscounted basis, if there was "reasonable assurance" of realization of their benefits.) The new CICA income tax standard also provides for the acquirer to include an income tax asset in respect of any of its own previously unrecognized tax benefits that are more likely than not to be realized as a result of the business acquisition. These are to be set up as one of the identifiable assets acquired in the acquisition, again on a nondiscounted basis (see *CICA Handbook*, paragraphs 3465.46 and .47). If not recorded at the time of acquisition because of lack of requisite assurance, any subsequent realization is to be applied to reduce goodwill, and then other intangibles related to the acquisition, to zero, with any remaining amount being applied to reduce income tax expense (see *CICA Handbook*, paragraph 3465.48).

These requirements are consistent with SFAS 109 in the U.S.

In view of the occasionally severe difficulties in valuation, it may take several months to a year before a cost can be allocated on the basis of reasonably satisfactory evidence. Initial allocations, therefore, may in some cases be tentative and subject to adjustment when all the necessary information is obtained.[17]

Accounting for Purchase Discrepancies

Purchased Goodwill

If any part of the purchase price remains unallocated to identifiable assets, that residual is assigned to goodwill. Chapter 12 has discussed the different possible ways to account for goodwill arising on acquisition. Present standards require that it be amortized over its estimated life, not to exceed forty years. In view of the nebulous nature of goodwill it is usually impossible to make any very close estimate of its reasonable life. Many acquirers use the maximum forty-year amortization period even though one's subjective opinion might suggest such a period is usually too long in our ever-changing business environment.

Negative Discrepancies

Where a negative purchase discrepancy falls out from the valuation of the net assets of the acquiree, the *CICA Handbook* directs that it be allocated so as to reduce the values assigned to individual nonmonetary assets. The selection of nonmonetary assets is to be based on judgment but usually would begin with the intangibles, followed by the capital assets. There have been cases where such application of a negative purchase discrepancy has produced patently absurd results. Capital assets and even inventory have been required to be written off, even though the previous operations of the acquiree have reported profits after normal charges for depreciation and cost of sales. Such cases represent true bargain purchases. The issues and other possibilities for accounting for "negative goodwill" are discussed in Chapter 12.

Acquisitions Disclosure

Accounting standards (*CICA Handbook* paragraph 1580.79) call for disclosure of pertinent details about business acquisitions, including a description of the business acquired and the percentage interest held in voting shares (where the acquisition is effected through a share purchase). The effective date of acquisition and the period for which the results of the acquiree are included in the income statement of the acquirer are also to be disclosed.

Financial details of the acquisition are to be disclosed, including (1) details of the fair value of the consideration given, (2) the total amount assigned to all assets excluding goodwill, (3) the amount assigned to goodwill and its proposed amortization period, (4) the amount assigned to total liabilities of the acquiree, and (5) the minority interest in net assets. For the purpose of tie-in with information in the statement of changes in financial position, it is useful to provide additional detail as to categories of assets acquired and liabilities assumed. All this information can be compactly presented in the so-called "acquisition equation," which details the assets acquired less liabilities and minority interest, if any, and balances them with the consideration given. A description of any contingent consideration and its amount is also to be disclosed.

Supplemental pro forma disclosure of results of operations on a combined basis from the beginning of the year of acquisition is also considered very desirable to aid investment analysis in the year of acquisition and comparison in the next year.

POOLING-OF-INTERESTS ACCOUNTING

As noted at the beginning of this chapter, pooling-of-interests accounting is followed in Canada only when none of the constituents entering into a business combination can be identified as the dominant party. The theory of pooling accounting, then, is that the former constituents have simply agreed to share their interests and therefore no new basis of accountability should arise. The mechanics are very simple. The accounting policies of the constituents entering into the combination should first be adjusted to reflect common bases where appropriate (see *CICA Handbook* paragraph 1580.63). After this is done, the balances of assets, liabilities, and equity of the constituents (as adjusted) are simply added together to form the balance sheet of the combined entity. Since the combination is deemed to be a continuation of the previous constituents, the income figures previously reported by the separate constituents (after restatement for accounting policy changes) are likewise added together to provide an earnings history for the combined entity.

In theory, the capital, contributed surplus, and retained earnings accounts of the constituents would also be added together to form the elements of shareholder's equity reported by the combined entity. Depending upon the way the combination is consummated, however, the legal capital of the continuing entity may be greater than the sum of the shareholder capital amounts previously reported by the constituents. If it is desired to report the amount of legal capital on the face of the balance sheet in such a situation, it is necessary to transfer contributed surplus (if any), and perhaps some retained earnings as well, to the capital account.

Initially, some accountants questioned the theory that there is no new basis of accountability in a true pooling of interests. They suggested that a pooling of interests is a significant event and should not be accounted for merely by carrying forward the reported accounting figures for the constituents of the combination. Instead, they advocated "new entity" accounting whereby all the assets and liabilities of the merged entities would be valued at fair value at the date of the combination.[18] This proposal has drawn little support. Although it may be at least as logical in theory as conventional pooling accounting, it would compound the valuation difficulties present in purchase accounting.

OTHER ISSUES RELATED TO BUSINESS COMBINATIONS

"Push-Down" Accounting

When an acquisition takes the form of a purchase of shares of an acquiree, the purchase accounting standard applies only to the valuation of assets and liabilities in the parent company's consolidated financial statements. Purchase accounting rules do not speak to the effect of the combination, if any, upon the accounting of the newly acquired subsidiary.

Suppose the new parent has acquired 100% of the voting common shares of the acquiree and no outstanding public interest remains in it in the form of debt securities, preferred shares, or other securities. It may well be convenient for the new parent to "push down" to its new subsidiary the values it has allocated to assets and liabilities in order to facilitate the future consolidation of financial statements. Beyond the question of convenience, however, there is a question of principle. Since evidence of the current value of the assets and liabilities of the subsidiary has been provided by an independently bargained exchange transaction, would it be better accounting to report on that basis in the subsidiary's financial statements for all public reporting purposes after the acquisition? The U.S. Securities and Exchange Commission has required push-down accounting by companies that become "substantially wholly-owned."[19]

Questions begin to arise when the acquiree is not wholly owned by its parent, or when there are publicly held securities in it that have priorities over its common shares. Why should the financial reports to the noncontrolling interests or to such security holders be influenced by a transaction in which neither they nor the reporting entity itself participated? Beyond this, there is a general question—if one type of transaction external to an entity causes an adjustment of the measurement basis of its assets and liabilities, are there other transactions that logically might have a similar result? Should there be a change in basis of measurement whenever there is a significant change in the controlling ownership of an entity, or is this merely a selective (and somewhat haphazard) application of current value accounting?

The CICA addressed these issues and developed a standard in 1992. It permits push-down accounting only where all, or virtually all, of the equity shares in an enterprise have been purchased by an acquirer who controls the enterprise after the transaction(s), and the values are reasonably determinable (see *CICA Handbook* Section 1625). An acquirer that holds at least 90% of the equity interest after the acquisition is presumed to have acquired virtually all of the enterprise's equity shares. Push-down accounting in this situation is not viewed as a departure from historical cost accounting, because the new pushed-down values reflect the cost to the new owners as a result of an arm's-length transaction(s). Push-down accounting is not required, as it is in the U.S. Rather it is left to the acquirer to decide whether it "would find the new costs more useful in evaluating investment returns and enterprise performance" (paragraph 1625.14).

In the U.S., the SEC requires that a parent company's debt assumed in connection with an acquisition be pushed down to the subsidiary's financial statements if the subsidiary is to assume the debt, or it offers its securities for sale to the public and the proceeds will be used to settle the debt, or it guarantees or pledges its assets as collateral for its parent's debt.[20] In Canada, it is not considered appropriate for the subsidiary to record its parent's debt except if it is a liability of the subsidiary (*CICA Handbook*, paragraph 1625.28).

Reverse Takeovers

As previously explained, a reverse takeover occurs when a company issues so many of its shares to acquire the outstanding shares of another company that the shareholders of the other company end up with control of the combined entity. In this case, the other company (the legal subsidiary) is considered to be the acquirer for accounting purposes. The accounting to reflect this fact can seem confusing, because of the upside down nature of the transaction. But the general principles of business acquisition accounting, previously discussed, apply. The key to the accounting is to keep clearly in mind who is the in-substance accounting acquirer. The accounting for reverse takeovers is well explained and illustrated in CICA

Emerging Issues Committee Abstract EIC-10. The following basic accounting and presentation considerations may be emphasized:

- The purchase cost is equal to the fair value of the business of the legal parent, because it is the acquired company for accounting purposes. EIC-10 discusses various possible approaches to estimating this purchase cost.

- As in any business combination, shareholders' equity of the continuing consolidated entity immediately after the transaction is equal to the book value of the equity of the acquirer (in this case, the legal subsidiary) plus the fair value/cost of the business of the acquiree (in this case, the legal parent). Since the legal subsidiary is the continuing entity, its retained earnings and other surplus accounts should be carried forward, and the amount recorded for share capital of consolidated equity on acquisition should be equal to the book value of its capital plus the fair value/cost of the acquired (legal parent) entity, excluding any part of that cost incurred in cash. However, the *legal* capital structure is that of the legal parent. The legal capital may simply be described in the notes to the financial statements. Alternatively, it may be considered necessary or desirable to record the legal capital on the face of the balance sheet, perhaps for example, where the companies are amalgamated. In such a case, as previously noted with respect to poolings of interest, adjustment may be made by a transfer from contributed surplus or retained earnings, or it may be set up as a separately disclosed item in shareholders' equity.

- The financial statements of the continuing entity must be issued in the name of the legal parent, which may be a source of confusion. In some cases, this confusion is reduced by changing the name of the company to be similar to that of the accounting acquirer. In any event, it is important that there be a clearly referenced explanation of the substance of the transaction.

- The comparative figures presented are, of course, those of the accounting acquirer (i.e. the legal subsidiary).

- Earnings per share calculations must be based on the legal shares outstanding. For calculations in respect of periods prior to a reverse takeover, the number of legal shares equivalent to the shares of the acquirer issued and outstanding in those periods must be computed. This will be the number of shares issued by the legal parent company to the shareholders of the legal subsidiary adjusted to take into account any shares issued or redeemed by the legal subsidiary in the relevant periods.

- It might be that some shareholders of the legal subsidiary do not exchange their shares for shares of the legal parent. Although they own a share of the accounting acquirer, they are minority interests in the legal subsidiary. Accordingly, they must be reported as minority interest in the consolidated financial statements at their proportionate interest in the book value of the net assets of the legal subsidiary.

Non-Arm's-Length Business Combinations

Sale of an unincorporated business by an individual to a wholly owned company, amalgamation of two companies wholly owned by another company or by an individual, or sale of an operating division by a parent company down to a wholly owned subsidiary all represent rearrangements of the legal interests of the controlling entity without significant economic substance. Because the rearrangements lack economic substance, a change in basis of measurement for assets and liabilities involved is generally not appropriate.

Instead, what has been called "continuity-of-interest" accounting is appropriate. The controlling entity carrying values of assets and liabilities transferred from one legal entity to another should not change. For example, an amalgamation of two companies under common control, although not technically a pooling of interests, would be accounted for using an approach similar to pooling of interests accounting.[21] Or, if shares of a wholly owned subsidiary corporation are issued to its parent in consideration for a business acquired from the parent, the shares issued should be recorded at an amount equal to the parent's carrying value of the net assets acquired.

Even if the consideration paid by the acquirer in such a case is cash, the transaction cannot, in logic, be accounted for based on the cash amount. Suppose, for example, a subsidiary 100% owned by another corporation buys a business for $150,000 cash from that other corporation, and the net assets transferred have a book value of $100,000. Continuity-of-interest accounting prevents the net assets acquired being accounted for at more than $100,000. To balance the transaction, the extra $50,000 should be treated by the acquiring subsidiary as a distribution of its equity, as though it were a dividend.[22] To see the sense in this note that the same end result could have been accomplished by having the acquiring subsidiary actually pay a dividend of $50,000 and then buy the net undertaking for its book value of $100,000. In other words, the common controlling interest could have dictated that the subsidiary pay any amount of cash to its parent.

Certain explanatory comments need to be added, however.

- When corporations legislation establishes the stated capital of a company as an amount equal to the fair value of consideration received, a problem will be encountered similar to that described above under pooling-of-interests accounting. If stated capital is to be reported in the equity section of an acquiring corporation, it may be necessary to capitalize surplus. Alternatively, note disclosure may be made that the legal capital is different from the amount reported as capital for accounting purposes.

- If the tax basis of net assets transferred remains the same as it was in the hands of the vendor, deferred tax accounts should be transferred unchanged. On the other hand, if the tax basis is changed as a result of the transaction, the deferred tax accounts may well need to be adjusted. Under continuity-of-interest accounting it is appropriate to look at tax allocation on a combined basis. That is to say, if one subentity reduces tax by selling assets below their previous tax basis, it would be appropriate for the buying subentity to recognize deferred tax accordingly in its accounts.[23]

- Disclosure is required of related party transactions (see Chapter 6). That disclosure would be a logical place to explain any accounting effects created by differences in the measurements used in the continuity-of-interest accounting and those applicable for taxation or for determining the amount of legal capital.

The foregoing description of continuity-of-interest accounting has been predicated on the assumption that there has been no change in the interests of the proprietors of the entities entering into the combinations. If that condition does not hold, the basis of continuity-of-interest accounting—no change in economic substance—may be overturned. For example, suppose a parent company sells an operating division to a 55% owned subsidiary. The existence of a significant outside interest (in this case, the 45% minority interest in the subsidiary) may be reasoned to give some arm's-length substance for reflecting the transaction at its agreed-upon exchange value.

The directors of the subsidiary would have a duty to be satisfied that the purchase price did not exceed fair value for the business acquired. Normal Canadian practice has long accepted recording a transaction where there is a significant noncontrolling interest, as in this example, at its exchange value, with the details to be provided in the disclosure of related party transactions. (In the parent company consolidated financial statements, profit recorded on the intercompany transaction would be eliminated, as will be described in the next chapter.) Until recently, however, no authority in Canada has stated how large an outside interest introduced must be to justify the abandonment of the continuity-of-interest principal.

In 1995 a new *CICA Handbook* Section 3840 was issued that addresses this question. It rules that related party transactions that are not in the normal course of operations should be measured at the agreed-upon exchange amount if (a) the change in ownership interests in the property is "substantive," and (b) the exchange amount is supported by "independent evidence." [24] A substantive change in ownership interests may be presumed generally when a transaction results in unrelated parties acquiring or giving up at least 20% of the ownership interest in the property (paragraph 31). Independent evidence of exchange value is to include "at least" one of the following—an independent appraisal by a qualified appraiser, recently quoted prices in an open and unrestricted market, comparable independent bids, or comparable amounts of similar arm's-length transactions (paragraphs 35–36). The section then states that formal bargaining with unrelated parties or their representatives also constitutes independent evidence (paragraph 37). No guidance or explanation is provided, and one might doubt whether "bargaining" with a minority interest, which may have little real bargaining power vis-à-vis the controlling interest, will necessarily provide evidence supporting the exchange value that is equivalent to an independent appraisal or a comparable arm's-length price.

One particular area of potential confusion as to the application of the measurement requirements of Section 3840 deserves mention. This relates to the transfer of a business to a wholly owned subsidiary under an arrangement which calls for the subsidiary to issue shares to outside interests. Suppose, for example, that an enterprise forms a new company, transfers a business to it, and immediately has the new company issue a 30% interest in its shares to unrelated parties, perhaps by way of a public share issue.

On the one hand, it could be argued that the transfer of the business to the new company should be accounted for under this section at its fair value, on the grounds that there is a substantive change in the ownership interest in the business (since unrelated parties acquire a 30% interest in it), presuming the fair value can be substantiated by independent evidence. On the other hand, fair value accounting for this transaction would seem to be in conflict with provisions of *CICA Handbook* Section 1625 on "Comprehensive Revaluation of Assets and Liabilities." Reasoning within it, the newly formed company would be expected to reflect the assets of the business at its carrying value in its parent's accounts, and these amounts could not be comprehensively revalued except if virtually all (90% or more) of its equity shares are acquired by a single acquirer (in which case, the acquirer's values may be pushed down to the subsidiary). In the above example, only 30% of the new company's shares would be acquired, and not by a single acquirer.

How are the provisions of these two sections to be reconciled? A somewhat uneasy distinction is put forward in paragraph 3840.33. It holds that a transfer of a business between controlling interests should not be considered to result in a substantive change in ownership interests unless the unrelated interests are in place prior to, and independent of, the transfer transaction. The transaction in the above example would not meet this test because no outside interest existed prior to, and apart from, the transfer. This interpretation treads a fine line. It may be effective in preventing direct abuses of the requirements of *CICA Handbook* Section 1625. However, suppose the example transaction is changed slightly. Suppose the outside 30% interest in the above example was to set up its own entity into which it placed its cash investment, and then had that entity directly acquire the business from the controlling enterprise for consideration consisting of 30% cash and 70% of the entity's own shares. Presumably this transaction would be recorded by the entity as a business acquisition at the fair value of the consideration given.

What this illustrates is the difficulty of developing effective standards that preclude an entity from writing up its business assets above their cost base, and yet allow related party transactions to reflect exchange values where there is some significant involvement by outside interests. (Reference should be made to Chapter 6 for a general discussion of the measurement and disclosure of related party-transactions.)

Nonmonetary Consideration

Many business acquisitions are accomplished by an exchange of shares; the acquirer issues its shares for the shares of the acquired company. In substance this is a nonmonetary transaction in the sense that the acquirer exchanges a share interest in its company for a controlling interest in the acquired company. In relatively rare cases the businesses of the acquirer and acquiree may be considered similar productive assets. For example, a company that consists solely of a specialty TV network in eastern Canada might issue its shares to acquire a company with a similar specialty TV network in western Canada. We have discussed in Chapter 6 a standard, *CICA Handbook* Section 3830, which requires that a nonmonetary exchange of similar productive assets be accounted for at book value rather than fair value. The thinking is that the mere exchange of interests in similar productive assets is not a value-adding event (i.e., does not result in the "culmination of the earnings process") since the transacting enterprises can only expect to realize an increase in value if the assets can be successfully used to generate income in future periods. Should this also apply to business combinations in which an acquirer issues its shares for a business consisting of similar productive assets? *CICA Handbook* paragraph 1580.29 may seem to indicate "yes"; it provides that the cost to purchase a business should be determined by the fair value of the consideration given *except* as specified in paragraph 3830.08. However, the Emerging Issues Committee has ruled that the issuance of an entity's own shares for another entity consisting of similar productive assets does not meet the definition of a "nonmonetary exchange" as contemplated in Section 3830 and should, therefore, always be measured at fair value.[25]

SUMMARY

A business combination occurs when an existing entity, or a new entity, acquires control over one or more other existing entities. In Canada, whenever a dominant party in a combination can be identified (the acquirer), a business combination is accounted for by the "purchase" method. In essence, the purchase method simply spells out how this particularly complex form of "basket purchase" of assets (and assumption of liabilities) is to be accounted for.

The application of purchase accounting presents several problems.

- The first problem is that of measurement of the purchase consideration. The basic accounting principle, that a transaction should be measured at its cash-equivalent value at the transaction date, is applicable. This means that a fair value must be assigned to non-cash consideration. Depending on the circumstances, contingent consideration may require assignment of additional cost to the purchase at the time of the transaction or, more likely, at some later date.

- The second problem, and a major one, is that of assignment of the value of the consideration to the various assets acquired and liabilities assumed. In this connection, it is necessary to take into account the possible existence of assets and liabilities that are not on the books of the acquiree. A fair value must be assigned to any liabilities assumed. Then, a fair value is estimated for the assets—a difficult problem for assets not regularly traded in a market. A fair value that would be arrived at in an ordinary exchange should be adjusted to allow for any difference between the tax basis of assets and liabilities and the fair values so estimated. A new tax accounting standard now in place in Canada, patterned on that of the U.S., requires that a separate tax asset or liability will be recorded for any such difference.

- When the sum of estimated fair values is compared with the gross purchase consideration, there usually will be a "purchase discrepancy"—a difference, plus or minus, between the sum of fair values and the gross cost. If the gross cost is greater than the identifiable assets, the positive purchase discrepancy is considered to be goodwill. If the purchase discrepancy is negative—that is, the sum of the estimated fair values of assets exceeds the gross cost—the discrepancy is judgmentally applied so as to reduce the cost assigned to identifiable assets.

A purchaser's first financial statements after an acquisition are expected to provide information on the acquisition and its manner of accounting.

A simpler accounting approach known as "pooling-of-interests accounting" is followed when an acquirer cannot be identified in a business combination. This approach simply calls for adding together the assets, liabilities and equity of each of the combining entities (after any adjustments necessary to make their accounting policies conform). In effect, the entities combined are treated as though they always had been combined. Consistent with this, the historical earnings records of the combining entities are added together to provide an earnings history for the newly combined entity.

After a purchase of another company, the new parent company's costs (as determined by the allocation process) may be "pushed down" onto the books of the subsidiary where virtually all of the equity of the subsidiary is owned by the parent.

The combination of businesses under common control is a frequently encountered example of a "related-party transaction." If no new stakeholders are being brought into the picture, the fact of the combination does not justify the use of a new basis of accounting. Instead, the use of "continuity-of-interest" accounting—a method similar to pooling-of-interests accounting—is appropriate. If there are substantive new outside ownership interests in the combining entities, however, there is more rationale for a new basis of accounting.

A CICA recommendation now provides a standard for determining when related-party transactions of this nature should be accounted for at their agreed-upon exchange values.

REFERENCES

1   AICPA, APB, *Intangible Assets*, Opinion No. 17 (New York: AICPA, 1970).

2   CICA, "Business Combinations," *CICA Handbook*, Section 1580 (Toronto: CICA).

3   AICPA, APB, *Business Combinations*, Opinion No. 16 (New York: AICPA, 1970).

4   Some examples are given in S.P. Gunther, "Lingering Pooling Problems," *The CPA Journal*, June 1973, pp. 459–64. See also J.C. Anderson and J.G. Louderback, III, "Income Manipulation and Purchase-Pooling: Some Additional Results," *Journal of Accounting Research*, Autumn 1975, pp. 338–43.

5   The AICPA annual survey of 600 companies, *Accounting Trends and Techniques*, 48th ed. (Jersey City, N.J.: AICPA, 1994), p. 58, reported that in 1993 only 21 poolings were reported in comparison with 200 instances of business combinations accounted for as purchases.

6   CICA, "Business Combinations," *CICA Handbook*, Section 1580, pars. .12–.21.

7   Only two instances of pooling-of-interests accounting were reported in 1997 by the CICA survey of 200 public Canadian companies, in comparison with 84 instances of purchase accounting. See CICA, *Financial Reporting in Canada 1998*, 23rd ed. (Toronto: CICA, 1998), p. 130.

8   IASC, *Business Combinations*, IAS 22 (revised 1998) (London: IASC, 1998).

9   See, for example, S. Craig, "OSFI Drafts Accounting Rule Change for Mergers," and E. Reguly, "Bankers Suffering from Pooling Envy," *Globe and Mail*, July 23, 1998; A. Tovlin, "Other Sectors Support OSFI's Pooling Proposal," *The Financial Post*, August 4, 1998; and "Accounting for Takeovers Should Tell the Whole Story," editorial, *The Financial Post*, August 7, 1998.

10 CICA, Accounting Standards Board, *Methods of Accounting for Business Combinations: Recommendations of the G4+1 for Achieving Convergence*, Invitation to Comment (Toronto: CICA, 1998).

11 The Emerging Issues Committee has underlined that, when the market for the class of shares issued to effect a business acquisition is active and liquid and the shares are not restricted, there should not be any adjustment to quoted market prices determined over a reasonable period before and after the date of the acquisition. CICA, Emerging Issues Committee, *Fair Value of Shares Issued as Consideration in a Purchase Business Combination*, EIC 76 (Toronto: CICA, 1996).

12 This possibility is not noted in *CICA Handbook* Section 1580 but it is acknowledged in AICPA, APB *Business Combinations*, par. 86. Factors to be considered in evaluating whether an arrangement for contingent consideration is, in substance, compensation for future services are set out in FASB, Emerging Issues Task Force, *Accounting for Contingent Consideration Paid to the Shareholders of an Acquired Enterprise in a Purchase Business Combination*, EITF No. 95–8 (Norwalk: FASB, 1995).

13 CICA, Emerging Issues Committee, *Costs Incurred on Business Combinations*, EIC 42 (Toronto: CICA, 1992).

14 *CICA Handbook*, Section 1580, par. 45(e).

15 See FASB, *Applicability of FASB Statement No. 2 to Business Combination Accounting by the Purchase Method*, FASB Interpretation No. 4 (Stamford: FASB, 1975); and FASB, Emerging Issues Task Force, *Purchased Research and Development Projects in a Business Combination*, EITF No. 86–14 (Norwalk: FASB, 1986).

16 CICA, Emerging Issues Committee, *Identifiable Assets Acquired in a Business Combination*, EIC 55 (Toronto: CICA, 1994).

17 See CICA, Emerging Issues Committee, *Adjustments to the Purchase Equation Subsequent to the Acquisition Date*, EIC 14 (Toronto: CICA, 1990).

18 See, for example, A.R. Wyatt, *A Critical Study of Accounting for Business Combinations*, AICPA Accounting Research Study No. 5 (New York: AICPA, 1963), pp. 81–86. For a more recent discussion of the issues related to "the fresh-start method," see CICA, *Methods of Accounting for Business Combinations: Recommendations of the G4+1 for Achieving Convergence*, especially pp. 22-23.

19 See SEC, *The Application of the "Push Down" Basis of Accounting in the Separate Financial Statements of Subsidiaries Acquired in Purchase Transactions*, Staff Accounting Bulletin No. 54, (Washington: SEC, November 3, 1983).

20 SEC, Staff Accounting Bulletin No. 73 (Washington: SEC, December 30, 1987).

21 One difference should be noted, however. In "continuity-of-interest" accounting the earnings history of the combined entities would include the income figures for each constituent company only from the respective dates that each has been part of the corporate group.

22 See CICA, "Related Party Transactions," *CICA Handbook*, Section 3840, pars. .09 and .16–.17.

23 This is illustrated in Appendix C to *CICA Handbook* Section 3840.

24 The Emerging Issues Committee has confirmed that these conditions are applicable to the transfer of businesses between entities under common control. See CICA, Emerging Issues Committee, *Transfer of a Business Between Entities Under Common Control*, EIC 66 (Toronto: Canada, 1995).

25 CICA, Emerging Issues Committee, *Measurement of the Cost of a Business Acquisition Effected by Issuing Shares*, EIC 62 (Toronto: Canada, 1995).

INTERCORPORATE INVESTMENTS

In many business combinations the acquiring company does not buy the assets of the business acquired directly but rather buys a majority of the shares of the company holding the assets. In addition, many companies choose to set up separate subsidiaries to carry on various aspects of their business or to operate in different geographical regions. Some companies, indeed, may be purely holding companies with little in the way of assets outside their investments in subsidiary or affiliated companies.

CONSOLIDATED FINANCIAL STATEMENTS

How should a parent company report its investment in one or more subsidiaries in its financial statements? Conceivably it might record such investments at a figure representing the cost invested in them and report as income from them merely the amount of dividends received. Such a basis of accounting was widely used some decades ago. The objections to it are obvious from a simple example. Suppose an operating company took a major division of its business and sold it to a subsidiary company in return for all its shares. Nothing would have happened in substance. Yet, if the investment in the subsidiary were accounted for on the cost basis, the financial statements of the parent would lose a great deal of information. The individual assets, liabilities, revenues, and expenses of the subsidiary would no longer be reported in the financial statements of the parent. Income reported from the subsidiary could be varied almost at will merely by the parent company's decision to cause its subsidiary to declare or withhold the declaration of dividends. The idea of consolidated financial statements to overcome these disadvantages was adopted by some North American companies even before 1900 and was widespread before there were any accounting standards on the subject.

The Concept of Consolidation

A consolidated basis of accounting has been said to be desirable when a group of companies constitutes an economic unit. Just what constitutes an economic unit is not entirely clear from the words themselves. The simple notion that an economic unit comprises a parent company and its subsidiaries does not take us very far without a clear answer to the question—what exactly is a "subsidiary"? As we shall see, this is not an easy question.

The idea of an economic unit seems to lead naturally to adoption of *control* as the primary criterion for consolidation. "Assets" are defined in terms of control over expected future benefits.[1] Thus it may be expected that a reporting enterprise should consolidate all assets, and liability claims against those assets, of entities that it controls.

A second reinforcing criterion is that of ownership. As a general presumption, if an entity owns a majority of the voting shares of a business enterprise, it would normally be expected to control it. There are, however, some conflicts and uncertainties.

- Suppose Company P owns 60% of the common shares of Company S which owns 60% of the common shares of Company A. The beneficial interest of Company P in the net assets and income of Company A is only 36%. That is, if all the income of Company A were distributed or all its assets were distributed in liquidation, and the amounts were paid on by Company S to its shareholders, Company P would receive only 36%. Yet there is no doubt that Company P is firmly in control of the management of Company A's resources.

- To make the example more extreme, suppose the capital structure of each of Company S and Company A consisted of voting common shares to the extent of 20% of the common equity and nonvoting shares to the extent of 80%. Suppose also that Company S owned all the voting shares and none of the nonvoting shares of Company A, and Company P's ownership of Company S was similar. Then Company P would have absolute control of the resources of Company A but only a 4% beneficial interest in them. Some accountants have been of the view that consolidation accounting is inappropriate in such a case.

- On the other hand, a subsidiary company might be wholly owned but be subject to debt covenants or other restrictions that might be so constraining that the exercise of parent company control is rather limited in scope.

Traditional Standards and Developing Issues

Rules governing consolidation practice were issued in the U.S. in 1959.[2] A standard generally consistent with that of the U.S. was issued in Canada in 1978.[3] These standards combined the criteria of control and ownership. A "subsidiary" was defined as a company in which another company *owned* directly or indirectly a majority of shares carrying the right to elect at least a majority of the members of the board of directors. This definition laid stress on control, but control exercised through the means of voting share ownership, not through other means. Two exceptions were made for situations in which the mechanical application of this rule would not accord with the basic criteria. A subsidiary would not be consolidated if (1) control was likely to be temporary because of a planned disposition of the subsidiary, or (2) increases in the subsidiary equity were unlikely to accrue to the parent or if the parent's control was seriously impaired, as when a subsidiary was in receivership or bankruptcy.

The rules requiring consolidation were also subject to exception on more pragmatic grounds. The CICA standard provided that a subsidiary need not be consolidated "when the financial statement components of a subsidiary are such that consolidation would not provide the more informative presentation to the shareholders of the parent company." [4] The intent of this vague wording was amplified by indicating that there may infrequently be circumstances where "a subsidiary's financial statement components may be so dissimilar to those of the other companies in the group that their inclusion in the consolidated financial statements would provide a form of presentation which may be difficult to interpret."[5] The concern was that consolidation of the balance sheet and income statement of two dissimilar entities (for example, a finance company and a manufacturing enterprise) makes it hard to apply the conventional tools of financial analysis that would be applied to either separately. Yet this problem is present to some degree in most consolidations. A consolidation of a manufacturing enterprise and a retail enterprise will also upset expected financial ratios. The *CICA Handbook* suggested that it would be rare that full consolidation of all subsidiaries would not be the more informative presentation. However, some argued to the contrary that a set of financial statements excluding some subsidiaries from consolidation, if accompanied by financial statements of the subsidiaries not consolidated, would often be more informative than a fully consolidated statement. Thus, it was far from clear how to interpret the CICA recommendation. Practice in both Canada and the U.S. permitted nonconsolidation of subsidiaries having nonhomogeneous operations or large minority interests.

The argument above suggests that consolidation has distinct disadvantages as well as advantages. It is not just that consolidation of components in different lines of business distorts financial ratios. Consolidation may also conceal aspects of the legal position that are significant to the financial position. Many writers have pointed out that creditors cannot depend on consolidated financial statements to indicate the safety of their position, since their claim (in the absence of cross guarantees) is restricted to the assets of the individual legal entity to which they have advanced credit. Shareholders may also be misled. For example, consolidation of healthy subsidiaries with a parent company in a weak working capital position may conceal the real risks of the latter, for assets of the subsidiaries may be tied up by contracts or debt covenants and thus may be unavailable at short notice to stave off insolvency of the parent. If earnings are mainly in the subsidiaries, it also may be difficult to pass cash up to the parent company to meet its interest or dividend requirements. [6]

Various possibilities have been put forward for overcoming these difficulties, but none is without some objection.

- Financial statements might be presented on a "consolidating" basis. Such statements look very like a consolidation worksheet, presenting in columns side by side the figures of the individual parent and subsidiary companies, adding across (after adjustments and eliminations) to the consolidated figures. Consolidating statements are highly revealing to a serious analyst, but the detail may be overpowering for the ordinary financial statement reader. [7]

- Financial statements might be presented on an unconsolidated basis (with the investment in subsidiaries accounted for on the equity basis) with supplementary statements provided for at least the major subsidiaries. To tie in with the parent company's figure of investment on the equity basis, it would be desirable that the figures of the subsidiary be stated on the "push-down" basis. To amplify the presentation, the main financial statements could also show fully consolidated figures side by side with the unconsolidated parent company figures. As with consolidating financial statements, a drawback to this solution is the increased complexity of the financial presentation. As well, the parent company's balance sheet would not present all the assets it controls, and all the liabilities against these assets.

- Reliance could be placed on "segment information" pertaining to the different lines of business carried on within the group to supply the additional information as to financial position and operations of components of the group. (See discussion of segment disclosure in Chapter 23.) This solution may be reasonably satisfactory only if different lines of business are generally carried on in different subsidiaries, and/or if lines-of-business disclosures are expanded to include information on the internal legal structure and financial positions and operations of key legal entities within a corporate group. Segment information is not normally provided on this basis.

Developments in Standards to Meet a Changing Environment

The business environment has much changed since the standards described above were issued. Enterprises have tended to become more diverse and complex. Increasingly, control may be achieved by means other than directly owning a majority voting interest—through various forms of contractual arrangements, options and business structures. These developments call for a broader concept of "control" in defining subsidiaries that should be considered part of an economic unit for consolidation purposes.

At the same time, accountants generally came to recognize that it is simply not possible to develop convincing operational criteria for consolidating some subsidiaries and excluding others. It began to be accepted that, for reasons of comparability and completeness, it may be better to require that all subsidiaries be consolidated, and that disaggregated information necessary to understanding the business segments and legal structure of a corporate group may be best provided in notes and schedules supplementing consolidated financial statements.

The first step was taken in 1987 in the U.S., when SFAS 94 eliminated the "nonhomogeneity" exception that had resulted in the exclusion of many finance, insurance and other subsidiaries from consolidation.[8] This statement requires that all subsidiaries be consolidated. It does not, however, redefine the concept of control, but continues to define subsidiaries as entities in which the parent owns the majority of the voting interest, except if control is likely to be temporary or does not rest with the owners of the majority voting interest.[9]

The CICA followed suit, in requiring the consolidation of all subsidiaries of business entities in 1991.[10] As with the FASB standard, the *CICA Handbook* section exempts from consolidation investments in which control is considered to be temporary at the date of acquisition. The CICA standard goes further, however, to require consolidation based on a broader concept of "subsidiaries" and "control." It defines "control" of an enterprise as the "continuing power to determine its strategic operating, investing and financing policies without the co-operation of others" (paragraph 1590.03(b)). A "subsidiary" is defined as "an enterprise controlled by another enterprise (the parent) that has the right and ability to obtain future economic benefits from the resources of the enterprise and is exposed to the related risks" (paragraph 1590.03(a)). At least two questions come to mind in respect of these definitions.

- How is one to interpret the phrase "without the cooperation of others" in applying the concept of control? Control is rarely absolute and without restrictions. A business enterprise needs the cooperation of employees, debt holders (particularly where an entity may be on the verge of financial difficulties), and suppliers and customers (particularly where there is some degree of economic dependence on a supplier of a vital resource or on a major customer). Presumably this is not what is meant, but rather that an enterprise lacks control over an entity if it must depend on another party not exercising a power it has to veto or override strategic management decisions. There is a real difference between the ability to exercise control subject to restrictions imposed by economic conditions and the need to meet legal obligations and the expectations of customers, debt holders, etc., and not having the essential power to direct the strategic investing, financing and operating activities of an enterprise.

* The definition of "subsidiary" seems to comprise two conditions—control *and* the right and ability to obtain future economic benefits along with exposure to related risks. When might control exist without the ability to obtain economic benefits? The standard does not elaborate on this.

The CICA standard explains that a subsidiary relationship should normally be presumed when there is ownership of a majority of voting shares sufficient to elect a majority of the board of directors. Supporting guidance briefly refers to types of circumstances in which an enterprise may have effective control over another entity with less than a majority voting interest. These include control by statute or contract, and control through the ownership of instruments that, if converted or exercised, would give the acquiring enterprise a majority voting interest.

It is not clear how the standard should be applied to "special purpose entities," which may be created to hold assets and incur liabilities on behalf of a reporting enterprise without being technically controlled by it. This is unfortunate, because this ambiguity is permitting such arrangements to be designed to achieve "off-balance sheet" financing. This issue is discussed later in this section.

What has this CICA standard achieved? On the one hand, it does clearly require the consolidation of all "subsidiaries." However, its broader requirements for determining what constitutes a "subsidiary" do not seem to have had a major impact on practice.[11] In an effort to provide information on borderline cases, disclosure is required of situations in which control is considered to exist with less than a majority interest, and where control is considered not to exist despite holding more than 50% of the voting shares (paragraphs 1590.22-.23).

The FASB issued an exposure draft in 1995 that would also broaden the concept of "control" in defining subsidiaries to be included in consolidated financial statements.[12] (It is to be noted that, as at the cut-off date for analysis in this book, the FASB was about to issue a revised exposure draft that would attempt to clarify the 1995 proposed definition of "control," and expand implementation guidance.) The 1995 FASB exposure draft proposed to define "control" somewhat differently from the CICA:

> Control of an entity is power over its assets—power to use or direct the use of the individual assets of another entity in essentially the same ways as the controlling entity can use its own assets (paragraph .10).

A "subsidiary" is defined simply as "an entity that is controlled by another entity" (paragraph 3(b)). These concepts would seem to have a simpler and sharper focus than those of the CICA. The FASB proposals reject the idea that any condition for consolidation is needed in addition to control. As with the CICA standard, an entity would not be consolidated if control is temporary at the date it is acquired.[13] Unlike the CICA standard, the FASB proposals would apply not only to business enterprises, but also to not-for-profit organizations. (Issues relating to defining the boundaries, and determining consolidation standards, for not-for-profit organizations are deferred to Chapter 27.)

The 1995 FASB proposals distinguish "legal" control from "effective" control. Legal control exists when the controlling party has an unconditional right to control that is enforceable at law. Effective control is control achieved by other than an unconditional legal right—for example, control resulting from owning a large minority voting interest where no other party or organized group of parties has a significant interest. The FASB proposals emphasize that determining whether effective control exists will require careful consideration of all the relevant facts and circumstances. It sets out some general presumptions of effective control (paragraph 14), and a listing of potential indicators of control (paragraph 158).

In assessing these CICA and FASB developments, three particularly difficult issues warrant attention.

- The Canadian standard and the FASB proposals both recognize that an enterprise may have effective control over another entity with a large minority interest. The FASB exposure draft suggests that a "large minority interest" might be as low as 35% to 40%. The essential question is how one determines whether a 40% investor has control. Might the investor be considered to have the ability to elect a majority of the investee's governing board simply because other shareholders are widely dispersed? The FASB exposure draft suggests that effective control could be demonstrated by a recent election to dominate the process of nominating candidates for the investee's governing board and to cast the majority of votes for the election of board members. But is this necessarily convincing evidence? Outside shareholders may not oppose the election of the investor's slate of directors as long as they agree with the investor's policies and direction. Just because they have supported the investor in the past does not mean that they are necessarily controlled. Guidance supporting the FASB proposal indicates that an investor may have effective control by being able "to persuade...other investors...to vote for its nominees" (paragraph 180). The CICA standard seems to be stricter than this. Specifically it states:

  > Control is not conferred by the holding of proxies or participation in a limited voting arrangement that is temporary in nature, provides for joint control or is cancelable by other parties to the arrangement. Such limited voting arrangements force an enterprise to rely on the continuing co-operation of other owners. (paragraph 1590.13)

- The CICA standard and FASB proposal both indicate that an enterprise that does not own a majority voting interest may have effective control over the other entity through owning securities or other rights that can be converted into a majority voting interest. Such rights may be in the form of options, warrants, convertible debt or convertible nonvoting equity. There is a nice question whether the holding of such rights constitutes a sufficient condition for consolidation. As a general point of principle, having an option to acquire an asset and actually owning that asset are two different things. In other words, the potential for obtaining control at some future date must be distinguished from existing control. Thus, it may be reasoned that some additional factors must be present in a situation which, taken together with the option, create the basis for existing effective control. The CICA standard and 1995 FASB proposals are not very clear on this point, although certain additional considerations are noted in supporting guidance discussions. These include the following:[14]

  - The ability to exercise the option should be unilateral and not dependent on uncertain future events or decisions of others.

- There should be no economic or legal impediment to the exercise of the option. For example, it should not involve incurring costs that are so high as to put conversion in any serious doubt.

- The FASB exposure draft emphasizes that control is "an exclusionary power"; for an entity to have effective control of a corporation through an option, it should be clearly evident that no other entity controls it.

The 1995 FASB exposure draft offers an example. Suppose that a Company F establishes Company G to develop a new product, and hires Mr. Smith to lead the development. Suppose that Mr. Smith invests a nominal amount for all of G's voting shares, while F provides the needed capital in the form of a debenture that is convertible at any time into a majority voting interest. In this situation, Mr. Smith may be an employee, under the control of Company F, in which case, Company G would clearly be a subsidiary of Company F. [15]

- An enterprise may create special purpose entity or trust which has no voting stock. Alternatively outside parties may contribute a nominal amount of equity capital with sufficient votes to elect a majority of directors, but the directors may have little or no real power. Such corporations may be set up to perform specific activities on behalf of the enterprise that created it (the "sponsor"). For example it may hold capital assets to be leased to the sponsor, and borrow money against those assets. The corporation's charter and objects may limit its activities so as virtually to predetermine how its assets are to be used.

It might be argued that, if the strategic activities of such a special purpose entity are effectively preprogrammed, then neither its creator nor anyone else can be said to have "the continuing power to determine its strategic operating, investing and financing policies ...." As noted earlier, the *CICA Handbook* Section 1590 does not give any direct guidance with respect to these arrangements, and it seems likely that special purpose entity arrangements can be designed to escape consolidation. The FASB exposure draft proposes that an enterprise should be considered to control any entity that it has established, even though it may have no voting interest in it, if the entity's charter, by-laws or trust instrument (1) cannot be changed by anyone other than the sponsor, and (2) limit the entity to activities that are substantially for the economic benefit of its creator. (Preparers' concerns with respect to the implications of these FASB proposals, and more generally, disagreements as to acceptable criteria for consolidation of special purpose entities, help to explain why the FASB has not yet finalized this standard, and is, instead, to issue a revised exposure draft.)

We may sum up as follows:

- Defining "control" is central to determining the assets of an organization and, therefore, to determining those entities ("subsidiaries") that should be considered part of the economic group that comprises a business enterprise. Although control normally exists through holding a majority equity voting interest, control may be exercised by other means. This presents a problem for financial accounting as modern businesses become more inventive in developing various forms of risk and control sharing arrangements that make it increasingly difficult to define the boundaries of a business entity. [16]

- The consolidation of all subsidiaries make much sense, but consolidated accounts can hide important information unless they are supplemented by improved disaggregated information on the business segments and legal entities that make up the business enterprise.

As a general point it may be noted that, unfortunately, there has been little interest in the theoretical issues related to consolidation policy and procedures in the past twenty to thirty years, and there is little empirical evidence on user preferences or on the comparative information value of alternative accounting approaches. For the most part developments in recent years in accounting thinking on these issues have come from the practicing profession and standard setters, notably the FASB.[17]

Possible Bases for Implementation of Consolidation

There are several conceivable ways of putting together figures in a consolidation. A choice is required whenever there is a noncontrolling interest in a subsidiary.[18] The choice affects two aspects of the consolidated financial statements: (1) the valuation of assets and liabilities of the subsidiary included in the consolidated statements, and (2) the figure ascribed to noncontrolling interests in the consolidation.[19] The differences will be illustrated by the following simple example. Company P buys 70% of the common shares of Company S for $84,000. The net asset position of Company S at the date of acquisition is summarized in Table 20-1.

Table 20-1	Net Assets of Company S at Acquisition		
	Book Value	**Fair Value**	**Excess of Fair Value**
Working capital	$50,000	$ 50,000	—
Capital assets	30,000	50,000	$20,000
	$80,000	$100,000	$20,000

Since 70% of the fair value of the identifiable net assets of Company S is $70,000, there is a purchase discrepancy of $14,000 inherent in the price of $84,000, and this is considered to be goodwill.

- Under an entity concept of accounting, the primary focus of interest is on the resources under the control of the entity. The objective of an entity concept of consolidation is to show the subsidiary assets in consolidation at a figure based on their fair value at the date of acquisition. Since the parent company paid $84,000 for a 70% interest, the fair value of all the assets might be assumed to be $120,000 [(100/70) × $84,000]. The identifiable assets would be included in the consolidation at $100,000, goodwill at $20,000, and noncontrolling interest at $36,000 (30% of $120,000). Consistent with the entity concept, the share of the noncontrolling interest in the earnings of the subsidiary would *not* be reported as a deduction in the consolidated income statement but rather as a distribution of consolidated income. Also the noncontrolling interest would be reported in the balance sheet as a form of equity, rather than something completely outside the consolidated equity.

- Under the proprietary concept of accounting, the primary interest lies in reporting to the shareholders of the parent company. (Noncontrolling shareholders in the subsidiary should refer to the financial statements of the subsidiary itself.) The 70% interest of the parent company in the assets of the subsidiary should therefore be recorded at the parent company's cost, and the 30% interest held by the noncontrolling shareholders recorded at the book values used in reporting to them. Thus the identifiable assets of the subsidiary would be included in the consolidation at $94,000 (70% of $100,000 plus 30% of $80,000), goodwill at $14,000, and noncontrolling interest at $24,000. This concept is also known as the "parent company" approach to consolidation. In the consolidated income statement, to be consistent with a strict proprietary viewpoint, the share of the noncontrolling interest is deducted in arriving at consolidated earnings and the noncontrolling interest itself is excluded from shareholders' equity in the balance sheet.

- A compromise approach, leaning rather more closely to the entity approach, has been known as the "parent company extension" approach. Under this basis the identifiable assets are included in the consolidation at their fair value of $100,000. Goodwill, however, is restricted to the excess of the parent company's cost over its share of fair value— i.e., $14,000—and the noncontrolling interest is reported at its share of the fair value of the assets excluding goodwill, namely $30,000. This approach may be rationalized in several ways. Since the statement is intended for the shareholders of the parent company and not for the shareholders of the subsidiary, there is no reason to base the noncontrolling interest figure on the book values applied in reporting to them alone. Instead it may be reasoned to be more logical to show their interest at values that are relevant to the parent company shareholders. Thereby one avoids the rather strange mixed asset carrying values, consisting of 70% at a current figure of cost and 30% at figures established in transactions by the subsidiary at earlier dates. The restriction of the reported goodwill to the parent company's cost may be justified by the argument that there may be a value to control as such which would be included in the parent company's cost, and it cannot be assumed that there is a corresponding value to the noncontrolling interest.

The *CICA Handbook* recommends the use of the parent company concept of consolidation—the second of the three described above.[20] This choice is explainable on practical grounds. The net assets included in the consolidation are reported at the parent company's cost, and the values assigned to the assets and liabilities of a subsidiary on acquisition simply reflect an allocation of that cost. As well, it may be argued that the "entity" and "parent-company-extension" approaches violate the concept of acquisition cost, because the part of the fair value allocation credited to the noncontrolling interest has not been purchased by the parent investor and, therefore, is not the direct result of a bargained arm's-length transaction.

The parent company approach has also been the prevailing practice in the U.S. However, the 1995 FASB exposure draft proposes to require the "parent-company-extension" concept (which it describes as the "economic unit" approach applied on the "purchased goodwill" method) (paragraphs 22–28 and 101–116). The board reasons that this approach logically follows from a consolidation concept based on the power to direct the use of the individual assets of a subsidiary. The transaction that gives a parent company control over a subsidiary is, it proposes, logically reflected at the full fair values of the underlying assets and liabilities over which control has been acquired. The exposure draft proposes that a noncontrolling interest is properly classified as equity because it represents a residual interest in a component of the consolidated enterprise.[21] In so concluding, the board rejects the proprietorship-based argument —which is that non-controlling interest should be classified between liabilities and equity on the grounds that, while it does not meet the definition of a liability, it is not part of the equity of the controlling interests. The FASB observed, in support of the economic unit approach, that recognition of the fair value of all identifiable assets and liabilities as of the date of the acquisition of a subsidiary is the standard in certain other jurisdictions, notably Australia and the United Kingdom.[22]

Still another possibility for consolidation remains. Consolidated statements could be prepared on a basis known as "proportionate consolidation" or "pro rata consolidation." Under this concept, the noncontrolling interest in assets and liabilities of the subsidiary is completely disregarded. If the parent company has a beneficial interest of 70% in the subsidiary, it merely takes up 70% of the valuation of the subsidiary's assets and liabilities, which is arrived at in the usual way by allocating the parent company's cost. Similarly, in the income statement 70% of the revenues and expenses of the subsidiary are included line by line in the consolidated figures. In this manner the noncontrolling interest does not appear anywhere in the consolidated financial statements. There is consequently no question as to how it should be valued. This pro rata concept is consistent with the overall proprietary approach to accounting, but it is criticized on the grounds that inclusion of only the parent company share of the subsidiary's assets, liabilities, revenues, and expenses in the consolidated financial statement conflicts with the idea of the entire group being one economic unit. The parent controls *all* of the assets and operations of a subsidiary, not just its 70% interest. That objection seems to be well founded and proportionate consolidation has no acceptance within GAAP, except in respect of jointly controlled entities (to be discussed later in this chapter).[23]

Accounting for Changes in the Parent Company's Interest

We shall now proceed to a brief discussion of some technical issues encountered in consolidation accounting. First we shall deal with changes in the investing company's interest in another company.

Step Acquisitions

Control may be acquired only after a series of acquisitions. A small interest in a company may be acquired initially simply as a portfolio investment. Subsequently more may be acquired so that the investor begins to have "significant influence" over the investee, even though outright control is not held. Further acquisitions may then push the interest to one of control, at which point consolidation is in order.

If majority control were acquired in one step, the procedure would be straightforward. As already described, the cost of the investment would be allocated taking into account the fair values of the subsidiary's assets and liabilities at date of acquisition. But in a step-by-step acquisition the cost of the investment has been incurred at several dates, and the fair values of the subsidiary's assets and liabilities will have been different at each date. How is the aggregate of such costs to be assigned to assets and liabilities and dealt with thereafter in the consolidation? Under the parent company concept (which as noted above is the basis of GAAP in Canada), the answer is simple in principle. The cost of a 20% acquisition (say) is dealt with in exactly the same way as the cost of a 55% acquisition. That is, a 20% cost is allocated taking into account fair values at the date the interest is acquired and enters into consolidation accounting based on those values. If fractional interests are acquired in several steps, each is dealt with in this way. Thus, in consolidation, the parent company's share of assets and liabilities of the subsidiary will be recorded based on allocations of costs incurred by the parent at several different dates, while the noncontrolling interest share of the subsidiary's net assets will always be based on the subsidiary's book values, as they exist from time to time.[24]

This general principle encounters some practical difficulties in application. As noted, before control is acquired blocks of shares may have given the investor influence but not control, and before that, blocks may have been acquired only for investment purposes. If shares acquired give the investor significant influence, "equity accounting" for them is required thereafter. As will be described subsequently, equity accounting is similar to consolidation in requiring allocation of the investment cost over the investee's net asset position at the date of acquisition. Thus, if equity accounting is already being performed for blocks of shares held, the acquisition of another block giving control creates no new problems with respect to previous holdings. But, if the first one or two blocks of shares acquired are accounted for as portfolio investments, there will have been no allocation of cost at their acquisition dates, and it rarely, if ever, will be possible to make a good allocation retroactively. In these circumstances, it is accepted that the cost of blocks of shares held before significant influence is acquired should be added to the cost of the newly acquired shares when equity accounting first becomes appropriate, and that such total cost be allocated based on fair values at that date.[25]

A different answer to accounting for step acquisitions may be reasoned under an entity or economic unit consolidation approach. Some believe that the transaction that results in acquisition of control of an entity is a significant event that changes the nature of previously acquired investments from portfolio or equity investments into part of a control position. They argue that the whole investment should be marked to fair value at the date control is achieved, with any differences between the carrying values and current fair values of earlier investments recognized as gains or losses resulting from the acquisition of control. Some members of the FASB believed this argument to have merit, but the board as a whole concluded that the fair values of earlier investments may not be reliably measured, and thus rejected this idea.[26]

Changes in a Parent Company's Interest Subsequent to Acquiring Control

Under Canadian GAAP, when a parent company sells some of its shares in a subsidiary but retains control, those shares will be costed at their average carrying value, and a gain or loss will be recorded by the parent accordingly. In the consolidated financial statements there is a rather peculiar result of such a sale. Although the consolidated balance sheet still includes *all* the assets and liabilities of the subsidiary, the values attaching to them will change. That is because of their mixed basis of valuation—part at the parent company's cost and part at the noncontrolling interest value (based on book values in the accounts of the subsidiary). If the balance between the parent company and noncontrolling interest share changes, the carrying values change in consolidation.

If the parent company sells enough shares to lose control, of course consolidation of the subsidiary ceases, and its assets and liabilities disappear line by line from the consolidated figures. If significant influence is retained, the remaining investment in shares reverts to the equity accounting basis. If the sale of shares drops the holding below the level at which equity accounting is appropriate, the carrying value of any remaining shares held is treated as though it represented "cost" and normal cost-based investment accounting follows from then on. (Note: in some situations the shares of passive equity investments will be carried at market or fair value, as discussed in Chapter 17.)

From a consolidated point of view, an issue of shares by a subsidiary company to the public has the same result as a sale by the parent company of some of its holdings in the subsidiary. After the issue there are more assets within the consolidated group, but the parent company's interest in the assets held by the subsidiary is decreased while that of noncontrolling shareholders is increased. The amount per share received by the subsidiary on the share issue may be more or less than the parent company's carrying value per share at the date of the subsidiary share issue. If it is more, the parent company will gain more from the increase in the subsidiary's total assets than it loses from the dilution of its equity in the subsidiary, and conversely. Thus it will have a gain or loss to record.

There is a debatable point here. If the parent company's invested cost is deemed to include a premium for control (accounted for as goodwill), that particular portion of the investment is not diluted by the subsidiary's share issue so long as control is retained. That suggests that the proceeds per share received by the subsidiary from the share issue to outsiders could actually be less than the parent company's carrying value per share without there being a loss to the parent. A similar point arises if the parent sells some shares in the subsidiary without selling control. Perhaps some proportion of the parent company's carrying value theoretically need not be costed out against the sales proceeds. The *CICA Handbook*, however, recommends the recognition of disposal of goodwill as an intrinsic part of the sale in this situation. (See paragraph 1600.43.)

When additional shares of a partly owned subsidiary become available for purchase, a parent company may be in a position to buy them itself or to cause the subsidiary to buy in those shares. From the group point of view, the effect is the same. Resources within the group are reduced by buying up the subsidiary shares, and the parent company's percentage interest is increased. Accordingly, a purchase of minority interest shares by the subsidiary itself is accounted for in consolidation just as though it were a step acquisition by the parent company. (See paragraph 1600.48.)

Existing practice in the U.S. is similar to that of Canada, except that the SEC permits a gain or loss arising from the issuance by a subsidiary of its own shares to be treated either in income or as an adjustment to paid-up capital.[27] However, as previously noted, a FASB exposure draft now proposes an economic unit approach to consolidation. Under this approach a noncontrolling interest in a subsidiary would be considered part of the equity of the consolidated reporting entity. It would follow from this that transactions in the shares of a subsidiary that do not change control are changes in the equity of the reporting entity, and accordingly would not result in the recognition of any income gain or loss.

Mechanics of Consolidation

Various technical problems occur in the mechanics of consolidation that will be touched on only briefly here.

- Ideally the fiscal period of a subsidiary to be consolidated will coincide with that of the parent. It has been accepted, however, that statements with fiscal period-ends up to three months apart may be consolidated.[28] If such a gap exists, intercompany transactions between the statement dates must be examined to ensure that appropriate eliminations, adjustments, and disclosures are made.

- Ideally, also, accounting policies of a subsidiary should be consistent with those of its parent. There may, however, be disadvantages to a newly acquired subsidiary in changing its policies to conform with the parent, especially if a noncontrolling interest exists or the subsidiary operates in a foreign country in which its accounting methods are the norm, or perhaps are legally required. It has, therefore, been accepted that a subsidiary's accounting policies need not be changed or adjusted for the purposes of consolidation so long as they are policies that would be acceptable in Canada. If not changed, however, disclosure of the accounting policies used in the consolidated financial statements will become more complex.[29]

- A number of adjustments are required in the consolidation process. There must be elimination of the balance representing the investment in the subsidiary in the books of the parent company, substituting for it the net assets of the subsidiary and the noncontrolling interest. In the course of the elimination, any differences between subsidiary asset and liability values and the allocation of the parent company's purchase cost at the time of acquisition must be allowed for, as well as amortization or write-off of these differences against earnings reported subsequent to the acquisition. Finally, since the consolidated financial statements treat the group of companies as one entity, there must be elimination of the effects of intercompany transactions upon figures in the financial statements of the individual entities being consolidated. All these types of adjustments are described in standard accounting textbooks.

- One conceptual issue must be resolved in relation to the treatment of profit on intercompany sales when a noncontrolling interest exists in one or the other of the parties to a transaction. In a "downstream" sale (from parent company to subsidiary) it could be argued that the parent company has realized profit to the extent of the noncontrolling interest's share of the transaction. Likewise, in an "upstream" sale (from subsidiary to parent) it could be argued that the noncontrolling interest, as an outside party to the transaction, should be credited with its share of the profit for purposes of its valuation in the consolidated financial statements. Both these views are rejected in practice. Since the parent company is considered in control of all transactions, all profit effects are to be eliminated. In the case of an upstream sale, the elimination carries through to the share of the noncontrolling interest in the profit that has been recorded in the subsidiary's accounts (see *CICA Handbook*, paragraphs 1600.30–.32.).

- Preferred shares of subsidiary companies that are held by outsiders are classified as part of the noncontrolling interest. Hence, preferred dividends paid to that noncontrolling interest should be deducted in the consolidated *income* statements as part of the noncontrolling interest entitlement. If a subsidiary has failed to pay dividends on cumulative preferred shares held by noncontrolling shareholders, provision for those dividends also should be deducted in the consolidated income statement, even though such a provision is not recognized in the income statement of the subsidiary (*CICA Handbook*, paragraph 1600.59).

- Upon occasion, operating losses or consolidation adjustments, if applied in the normal fashion, could turn the noncontrolling interest share of equity into a negative figure. Unless noncontrolling shareholders have given guarantees, they cannot be forced to contribute additional amounts to cover subsidiary losses. Accordingly, losses that are charged to the noncontrolling interest should ordinarily be limited to an amount that would reduce it to zero. Beyond that point, the parent company must recognize 100% of the losses as its own for purposes of consolidation (*CICA Handbook*, paragraphs 1600.57–.58). Of course, if the parent company decides it will not give further support to the subsidiary, it need not provide for the losses. In such a case it would remove the subsidiary from the consolidation, because its failure to give support will result in loss of control.

Consolidation Where Reciprocal Shareholdings Exist

Occasionally subsidiary companies hold common shares in their parent company. When they do, the preparation of consolidated financial statements becomes more complicated.

To begin with, the investment by a subsidiary in the shares of its parent company is treated in the consolidated balance sheet as a deduction from equity, just as if the parent itself had acquired its own shares (see *CICA Handbook* paragraph 1600.71). Thus consolidated equity is determined net of any subsidiary investment in the parent company, and consolidated income is calculated on a basis consistent with this. To achieve this, a special calculation of consolidated income is necessary because of the circularity of the income flow. This circularity may be best understood by an example. Suppose parent Company P owns 80% of subsidiary Company S, and that S in turn owns 20% of P. Consider the result that would follow if the two companies fully distributed their respective earnings. An initial distribution by P would go 80% to its outside shareholders and 20% to S. The latter portion would then be redistributed by S, 20% to its outside shareholders and 80% back to P. Upon receipt of that distribution (equal to 16% of the initial distribution) P would again pay it out, 80% to its outside shareholders and 20% to S, and so on.

The ultimate apportionment of income may be calculated by simultaneous algebraic equations. Suppose that P earns $300,000 and S earns $160,000 before taking into account the intercompany shareholdings. Two equations may be set up with two unknowns (P equal to the total income of P, and S equal to the total income of S):

$$P = \$300,000 + .8S$$

$$S = \$160,000 + .2P$$

Solving for P = $509,225, from which S's 20% interest in P is deducted to arrive at $407,620. This amount represents the consolidated within group income of P (i.e. the amount that is attributable to P's consolidated equity net of S's 20% investment in P). More complete calculations are demonstrated in the Appendix to *CICA Handbook* Section 1600 (Case Study E).

An alternative approach has sometimes been seen in practice. It is based on an implicit simplifying assumption that the subsidiary has paid a dividend in kind of its shareholdings in the parent company just before consolidation. In the above example this would result in an assumed transfer of 80% of the shares held by S to P and 20% to the noncontrolling interests of P. This effectively assumes away the interlocking share problem so that it is no longer necessary to calculate P's share of S's earnings through the use of simultaneous equations. Consolidated income is simply calculated as $428,000 (that is, P's income of $300,000 plus 80% of S's income ((.8)($160,000) = $128,000).

The essence of the difference between this alternative and the simultaneous equations approach lies in the number of shares considered to be outstanding. Under the simultaneous equations approach 100% of the shares held by S are treated as reacquired by P, while under the alternative only 80% are considered to have been reacquired, the other 20% being distributed to the noncontrolling interests. Each ends up with the same reported earnings per share. The alternative approach is inconsistent with the balance sheet presentation required by the *CICA Handbook*, however.

COMBINED FINANCIAL STATEMENTS

Our discussions have thus far been restricted to consolidated financial statements, which represent a parent company and its subsidiaries. We have seen that consolidated financial statements are justified by the parent's control over subsidiary entities.

A combined financial statement is different, in that it comprises the accounts of two or more organizations where one of the organizations does not control the other(s). There are no standards governing when combined statements may or may not be prepared. Combined financial statements may be judged to be more useful than separate financial statements of related entities in, for example, presenting the financial position and results of operations of a group of companies owned by the same individual, or of a group of subsidiaries in the same industry or geographic region, or that are under common management.

Generally speaking, where combined financial statements are prepared, similar principles to those used in preparing consolidated financial statements apply.

THE "EQUITY" BASIS OF ACCOUNTING

The equity basis of accounting began to become popular in the 1960s for investments that represented significant interests in other companies, but less than control warranting consolidation accounting. It was a result of dissatisfaction that the normal cost accounting basis for portfolio investments failed to portray the performance of investments in which an investor had some degree of participation and influence on the investee. Standards for equity accounting on the basis of "significant influence" were introduced in the U.S. in 1971, and in the *CICA Handbook* in 1977.[30] These standards remain in place, substantially unchanged from when they were issued.

The equity basis of accounting, like the cost method, records the investment as a single figure on the asset side of the balance sheet and income from the investment on a single line in the income statement. The basis of measurement of the investment is, however, changed. The income attributable to the investor following equity accounting is computed in the same way as is income for the majority interest in a consolidation.

Authoritative accounting literature has been largely silent on the conceptual basis for equity accounting. A few accountants have challenged its conceptual validity for significantly influenced, but not controlled, investees. The basis for this challenge is that accrual of the investor's proportionate interest in the equity earnings of a noncontrolled investee does not meet the concept of an "asset," defined as "economic resources controlled by an entity..." (*CICA Handbook*, paragraph 1000.29). If an investor does not control the investee, it does not have the power to have assets equal to its share of the investee's earnings remitted to it, or alternatively, to direct their use in the investee enterprise. Thus, the theoretical credentials for equity accounting on the basis of significant influence are open to question.[31] Some accountants defend the equity basis of accounting simply as a valuation, arguing that it results in a better measure of the value of the investment than does cost. In any event, the equity basis of accounting has become widely accepted as a useful part-way point between ordinary cost-based accounting and consolidation accounting when an investor does not have actual control but does have significant influence over the investee.

The equity method of accounting is firmly based on the concepts of consolidation accounting. The *CICA Handbook* requires that "investment income as calculated by the equity method should be that amount necessary to increase or decrease the investor's income to that which would have been recognized if the results of the investee's operations had been consolidated with those of the investor" (paragraph 3050.08).

Thus, an investor who uses equity accounting must make an allocation of investment cost on the basis of fair values of the assets and liabilities of the investee at the date of acquisition. Subsequently it adjusts its share of income reported by the investee to amortize any differences between the investee's book values for assets and liabilities and the allocation implicit in the investor's purchase price. The carrying value of the asset on the equity basis of accounting begins at cost, is increased by the investor's share of the profit or loss of the investee calculated as just described, and is reduced by any dividends paid by the investee. Occasionally, also, the investor may have to record its share of prior period adjustments or capital transactions reported by the investee. On this basis the carrying value of the investment is equal to the aggregate of the investor's net interest in the assets and liabilities of the investee after adjustments similar to those that would be made in consolidation.

The equity method of accounting is sometimes called "one-line consolidation." That description is apt, except that the investor's share of extraordinary items, discontinued operations, prior period adjustments, and capital transactions of the investee are not recorded on the same line as income from the investee but rather are reported according to their nature, as they would be if they were the result of the investor's own transactions.

The attempt to tie in with consolidation accounting has one anomalous result. A profit taken on a downstream sale (say, of inventory) from the investor to the investee will be recorded through the normal sales and cost of sales accounts of the investor. If the item sold is still in the inventory of the investee at the year-end, the profit will normally be eliminated through reducing the figure of income picked up with respect to the investee, even though the investee did not record that income. (*CICA Handbook*, paragraph 3050.15, provides some flexibility in this regard.)

As indicated, equity accounting is considered appropriate when the investor does not have actual control but does have significant influence upon the investee. The existence of significant influence may be indicated by representation on the board of directors, participation in policy-making processes, material intercompany operating links, and so on. An investor may take quite a passive interest in an investee and yet still be deemed to have significant influence because of the potential inherent in any large ownership interest. The authoritative standards suggest that there should be a presumption of significant influence when the shareholding is 20% or more and a presumption of lack of influence below that level. Both of these presumptions are open to rebuttal by other evidence. For example, even if a holding is over 20%, the existence of another investor having a large block of shares would create some doubt. That doubt might be set at rest by evidence of more active influence such as representation on the board. However, if an investor is frozen out by hostile interests or is unable to obtain any consideration greater than that to which any shareholder is entitled, a lack of significant influence would be demonstrated. One practical test of significant influence lies in the investor's ability to obtain sufficient information from the investee on a timely basis to perform equity accounting.

Reciprocal Shareholdings—Equity Accounting

There have been a number of cases in Canada where two companies each hold substantial blocks of shares in the other and it is clear that each has significant influence on the affairs of the other. Thus equity accounting seems appropriate for the interlocking shareholdings. The application of equity accounting in this case is based on the general principles already illustrated for consolidation accounting, but there are some new considerations.

As was described in the discussion of consolidation accounting, the cost of a subsidiary's shareholding in the parent is shown as a deduction from consolidated equity, on the basis that it is equivalent to the parent acquiring its own shares. Consistent with this, the simultaneous equation determination of consolidated earnings is reduced by the subsidiary's percentage interest in the parent company. However, in an equity-accounting situation, neither company will show its interest in its own shares held by the other company as having been reacquired. Thus it may seem appropriate to show earnings figures in relation to all the shares outstanding.

To illustrate, suppose the P − S example developed in our earlier discussion of consolidated reciprocal shareholdings is changed such that P owns only 30% of S, which interest is equity accounted. The other facts are unchanged, i.e., S owns 20% of P, P earns $300,000 and S earns $160,000 before accounting for the intercompany shareholdings. Solving the simultaneous equations, P = $370,212. On a consolidated basis, this amount would be reduced by S's 20% interest in P to $296,170. But, since S's share interest in P is not deducted from P's shareholders' equity, it might be argued that total earnings reported by P should be $370,212 (which would result in P showing equity earnings in S of $70,212—that is, $370,212 less P's operating income of $300,000).[32] This result is inconsistent with the strict requirements of *CICA Handbook* paragraph 3050.08 because it would report income in excess of what would be reported on a consolidated basis. In fact the total of the reported earnings of P and S on this gross basis would be greater than the total of their respective earnings before adjustment for their intercompany holdings.[33]

This problem is only an aspect of a larger problem in statement presentation. The bottom line figure of earnings represents a company's share of earnings on its own assets (a share which is less than 100% because of the interlocking shareholdings) plus its share of the other company's earnings. The income statement, however, will report 100% of the sales, expenses, and operating income of the company carrying on the activity, and the difference between that operating income figure and the bottom line of income reported (which difference could be negative) will be reported as though it were income attributable to the investment in the other company. This presentation is rather unsatisfactory and could be misleading to anyone trying to analyze and project the profitability of each company. It appears impossible to cure this deficiency without reporting the earnings of both companies in the financial statements of each company and indicating the significance of each earnings stream to the bottom line for each particular company based on the effect of the intercompany shareholdings.[34]

ACCOUNTING FOR JOINT VENTURES

An increasingly common form of business operation, especially in certain industries, is the joint venture. A joint venture often is incorporated but may also be a partnership or some other unincorporated arrangement. Hence this part of this discussion is not limited just to intercorporate investments.

In very broad terms, the business motivation for a joint venture is the desire to share the risks and rewards of the venture. In risky types of enterprise, joint ventures are one means whereby venturers can spread their risks rather than put all their eggs in one basket.

In other cases, venturers may pool resources in order to be able to afford a facility that none would find economical on their own.

From the accounting standpoint, the important characteristic of a joint venture is that it is under joint control.[35] Normally there will be a formal agreement that establishes that joint control. For operational purposes the agreement overrides differences in ownership interest. Thus, even if one venturer holds a majority share of a project, it still should be accounted for as a joint venture if the actual control is joint. As an investment, therefore, the joint venture falls somewhere between a subsidiary that is controlled by the investor alone and a large shareholding that gives the holder significant influence but not control.

Before there were any authoritative statements on joint venture accounting three bases of accounting for joint ventures were found in practice—the cost basis, the equity basis, and proportionate or pro rata consolidation. The last of these was common in certain industries where venturers held undivided interests in assets of the venture.

Equity accounting for joint ventures has been criticized on the grounds that it fails to show details of assets and liabilities over which the investor has (joint) control and of the revenues and expenses associated therewith. A company that carried on all its business in the form of joint ventures could have just one line in each of its financial statements—investment in joint ventures in the balance sheet and net income from joint ventures in the income statement. Proponents of proportionate consolidation argue that the real assets at work are those of the joint venture, and the venturer has the power to actively participate in their joint management.

On the other hand, the proportionate consolidation method has been criticized because it adds together the directly owned assets and liabilities of the investor with a pro rata share of indirectly controlled assets and liabilities of one or more joint ventures. There is an important point of principle here. It may be reasoned that the proportionate consolidation of a jointly controlled entity's assets is fundamentally inconsistent with the concept of an "asset" as "a resource controlled by an entity" because a venturer cannot control its pro rata share of individual assets in a joint venture. To report that the assets of an enterprise with, say, a 30% interest in a jointly controlled entity includes 30% of the venture's cash balance and 30% of its plant balance is, it is contended, a misrepresentation of the reality. It is argued that the venturer should account for only what it does control—its investment in the joint venture. Likewise it may be reasoned based on the concept of a "liability" that it is incorrect for a venturer to record a portion of a joint venture's debt where the venturer has no more than a secondary responsibility (if it has guaranteed payment of the debt).

In an attempt to mitigate this problem, the "expanded equity" basis of presentation has been proposed whereby the pro rata share of assets, liabilities, revenues, and expenses of joint ventures would be included in the financial statements but segregated from the corresponding items pertaining to the direct activities of the investor. Some compression would be required under this basis to avoid overly cumbersome financial statements. For example, the direct current assets of the investor could be set out in the normal fashion followed by one figure described as "investor share of net current assets of joint ventures."[36]

The CICA initially addressed this issue in 1977.[37] It recommended the equity basis as the basic method of accounting for investments in joint ventures. Proportionate consolidation was allowed, however, as an alternative when "a significant portion of the venturer's activities is carried out through joint ventures." The logic of this was not impressive, and opinions varied as to the meaning of "significant portion." The recommendation came to be interpreted in practice as permitting a free choice between the two methods. The section called for note disclosure in summary form of the venturer's share of the assets, liabilities, income, and expense of the joint ventures, (normally on a combined basis) where proportionate consolidation was followed, and separately for significant joint venture activities accounted for on the equity basis.

A new CICA standard (a replacement for *CICA Handbook* Section 3055) was issued effective for years beginning in 1995. It requires proportionate consolidation for all joint ventures, with supplementary disclosure of the major components of interests in joint venture assets, liabilities, revenues, expenses, cash flows, and related contingencies and commitments. In so doing it followed the lead of the IASC which sets out proportionate consolidation of all joint ventures as its benchmark standard, although it permits equity accounting as an allowed alternative.[38]

The governing U.S. standard, which dates back to 1971, requires the large majority of joint ventures to be accounted for on the equity basis. Proportionate consolidation may be followed in limited cases for some unincorporated joint ventures where the investor-venturer owns an undivided interest in each asset and is proportionately liable for its share of each liability, and where "it is the established industry practice (such as in some oil and gas venture accounting)."[39]

Venturer Transactions with a Joint Venture

The accounting by a venturer for transactions with a joint venture has given rise to many questions over the years. The *CICA Handbook* makes recommendations that differ in some important respects from transactions with equity accounted investees.

* It has long been held that, where assets are transferred to a joint venture in exchange for a capital interest in it, no gain should be recognized. The principle here has been that the capital contribution to a joint venture does not result in the culmination of an earnings process; the only way in which the venturer will realize income from its contribution is through the joint venture's subsequent income earning activities.

  This principle has been significantly "refined" in the new *CICA Handbook* standard:

  – It requires that a gain be recognized on a capital contribution to a joint venture to the extent of the interests of the other unrelated venturers, but it is to be shown on proportionate consolidation as a deferred liability to be amortized to income, normally over the life of the contributed assets (paragraphs 3055.27 and .29).

  – If a loss results on such a contribution, it is to be charged to income at the time of the transaction to the extent of the interests of other unrelated venturers. Further, the contributing venturer is to consider whether the transaction provides evidence that its proportionate share of the contributed assets is impaired and should be written down.

  – A further complication arises if the contributing venturer receives cash or other assets that do not represent a claim on the joint venture, in addition to an interest in the joint venture. This is viewed as a sale to the other unrelated venturers in the proportion of (1) the fair value of the cash or other assets received that are not a claim on the joint venture to (2) the fair value of total assets contributed by the venturer. This gain is recognized in income at the time of the transaction, except to the extent that the cash or other assets received represent the venturer's share of borrowings by the joint venture or if the venturer has undertaken an obligation to the joint venture or others that effectively negates the receipt (paragraphs 3055.28, .30 and .34).

- When an ordinary business transaction takes place, and the substance of the transaction is such that a gain or loss has occurred
  - a gain is recognized to the extent of the interests of other venturers not affiliated with the investor, and
  - a loss would normally be recognized in full. (The *CICA Handbook* provides that a loss would be recognized only to the extent of the interests of other unrelated venturers in the unlikely situation that the transaction does not provide evidence of a decline in the value of the relevant assets—see paragraph 3055.36.)

SUMMARY

When a parent and subsidiary company relationship is established, whether as a result of a business combination or otherwise, it is required that the parent company prepare its financial statements on a consolidated basis thereafter. The basic concept is that entities under common control form one economic unit, which should accordingly report on a unified basis. Traditionally, the primary criterion for consolidation was the existence of control effected through ownership, direct or indirect, of a majority of the voting shares of the subsidiary. The *CICA Handbook* now requires consolidation on the basis of a broader concept of "control." It recognizes that an enterprise may have effective control over another entity by other means than owning a majority of its voting shares, for example, by statute or contract, or in some cases, through the ownership of instruments that, if converted or exercised, would give the enterprise a majority voting interest. The CICA standard lacks clarity, however, in its application to special purpose entities and to situations in which an entity may have effective control as a result of options or conversion rights. The FASB has proposed a new standard that would also broaden the concept of "control," with some potential differences from that of the CICA.

There are different possible ways to apply consolidation accounting. The "parent company" concept is used in practice in Canada. Under that concept, when a noncontrolling interest exists, the figure attributed to the noncontrolling interest in the consolidation represents its percentage share of the book value of the equity shown by the subsidiary. As a result of this treatment, the net assets of the subsidiary included in the consolidation are valued on the basis of the parent company's cost determined at the time of the business combination (see Chapter 19) to the extent of the parent company's percentage interest in the net assets, and at the subsidiary company's book value to the extent of the noncontrolling interest percentage. Other concepts of consolidation base the valuation of the noncontrolling interest and of the subsidiary's net assets entirely (with the possible exception of goodwill) upon the parent company's acquisition cost and the distribution of that cost among the assets and liabilities. The FASB is proposing to adopt this latter concept.

Another conceivable basis for consolidation accounting is that of proportionate or pro rata consolidation. On this basis, the consolidated financial statements reflect only the parent company's share of the assets, liabilities, revenues, and expenses of the subsidiary, and the valuation of those items is determined initially by the allocation of the parent company's cost in the business combination. In this way, the issue of presentation of noncontrolling interest is avoided. The proportionate consolidation method is not used in consolidation practice today but is now required by the CICA in joint venture accounting.

While consolidated financial statements do present information in a compact form, they are not without disadvantages. When the asset and debt structures of the parent and one or more subsidiary companies are different, the act of adding them together in consolidation tends to average out ratios such as working capital or interest coverage and may obscure real financial weakness in the parent company. These problems may be overcome if consolidated financial statements are supplemented by appropriate disaggregated information on the business segments and legal entities that comprise the consolidated business enterprise.

There are a large number of technical questions that arise in the application of consolidation accounting. These are discussed in works devoted to the subject and are not dealt with in any great detail in this chapter.

Equity accounting is a derivative of consolidation accounting that was developed for cases where an investor had an investment position that gave it significant influence over another entity but not majority voting control. In this situation, it was considered that the normal accounting basis whereby an investment in equity shares is carried at original cost failed to portray the real performance of the investment satisfactorily. The equity method records such investments at their original cost to the investor increased by its share of earnings of the investee subsequent to the date of acquisition determined as they would be if the subsidiary's financial statements were adjusted for purposes of consolidation with the investor, and reduced by cash dividends paid by the investee. The investment is presented on one line in the investor's balance sheet, and its share of income for a period is reported on one line in the income statement (with the exception of its share of extraordinary items and any gain or loss on discontinued operations). For this reason, the method is sometimes known as "one-line consolidation."

The joint venture has become an increasingly common form of business operation as a vehicle for sharing risks and pooling resources. A joint venture is characterized by agreement among the venturers that gives them all a share in control. In most countries, including the U.S., the large majority of joint ventures are accounted for by the equity method. Recently the CICA took the somewhat debatable position that all joint ventures should be accounted for on the proportionate consolidation basis. This followed the lead of the IASC.

REFERENCES

1   See CICA, "Financial Statement Concepts," *CICA Handbook*, Section 1000 (Toronto: CICA), pars. .29–.31.

2   AICPA, Committee on Accounting Procedure, *Consolidated Financial Statements*, Accounting Research Bulletin No. 51 (New York: AICPA, 1959).

3   This was included in CICA, "Long-Term Investments," *CICA Handbook*, Section 3050 (Toronto: CICA), pars. .03–.14. These paragraphs were superseded and replaced by a new *CICA Handbook* section issued in 1991 (see note 10).

4   Ibid., par. 14. Another exception was made for entities that followed accounting that was inconsistent, and considered incompatible, with GAAP. For the most part, these entities were financial institutions, notably banks and life insurance companies that followed accounting practices permitted or prescribed by government regulation. This problem was removed when banks and insurance companies became subject to GAAP in 1992.

5   Ibid., par. 13.

6   For a detailed discussion and skeptical view of the advantages claimed for consolidation accounting, see R.G. Walker, "An Evaluation of the Information Conveyed by Consolidated Statements," *Abacus*, December 1976, pp. 77–115.

7   Consolidating financial statements have been advocated by the major interest group representing financial analysts. See P.H. Knutson, *Financial Reporting in the 1990's and Beyond*, a position paper of the Association for Investment Management and Research (Charlottesville, VA: Association for Investment Management and Research, 1992), p. 41.

8   FASB, *Consolidation of All Majority-Owned Subsidiaries*, Statement of Financial Accounting Standards No. 94 (Norwalk: FASB, 1987).

9   An EITF Abstract provides guidance on when minority interests may be considered to have "substantive participating rights" that would overcome the presumption that the majority voting interest should consolidate the investee. See FASB, Emerging Issues Task Force, *Investor's Accounting for an Investee When the Investor Has a Majority of the Voting Interest but the Minority Shareholder or Shareholders Have Certain Approved or Veto Rights*, EITF No. 96-16 (Norwalk: FASB, 1996).

10 CICA, "Subsidiaries," *CICA Handbook*, Section 1590 (Toronto: CICA).

11 The CICA survey *Financial Reporting in Canada 1998*, 23rd ed. (Toronto: CICA, 1998), p. 144, reported that six of the 200 Canadian public companies surveyed disclosed the consolidation of investees that were less than majority owned in 1997 (nine in 1996), and "in most of the cases there was majority ownership of the voting shares." Five companies in 1997 (two in 1996) excluded a majority owned investee from consolidation..

12 FASB, *Consolidated Financial Statements: Policy and Procedures*, Proposed Statement of Financial Accounting Standards (Norwalk: FASB, October 1995).

13 Unlike the CICA recommendations, however, the FASB proposals contain a clear definition of "temporary." Control would be considered to be temporary only if, at the date of acquisition, the parent is obliged to relinquish control, or parent management has a plan and reasonable expectation for the subsidiary's disposal, normally to take place within one year. Ibid., par. 16.

14 See, CICA "Subsidiaries," *CICA Handbook*, Section 1590, par. 13(b); and FASB, *Consolidated Financial Statements: Policy and Procedures*, pars. 10, 14c, 153 and 188–89.

15 See FASB, *Consolidated Financial Statements: Policy and Procedures*, Example 3, pars. 188–89.

16 Steven Wallman, SEC Commissioner, noted these possibilities:

> The concept of what we call the firm is … changing. For example, it is harder now to define the outer edges of the firm …
>
> We will reach the day in the not-too-distant future … where there will be "virtual firms" with hundreds or thousands of individuals networked together in combinations that form and dissolve as tasks are required to be performed. The key assets of this "virtual firm" may well be only human resources or intellectual capital, its outer edges will change daily, and its liabilities and cash flows will be sliced and diced as needed and as is efficient.
>
> It will be a challenge to determine how one is to account for these virtual firms in a timely way that accurately and fairly measures income, cash flows, and real assets and that makes the slightest sense from the perspective of a user of financial statements. Current

GAAP and SEC reporting requirements are struggling to keep pace with the rapid changes in firm structure and function already upon us. We hardly have begun the planning necessary to anticipate how to cope with these future developments.

S.M.H. Wallman, "The Future of Accounting and Disclosure in an Evolving World: The Need for Dramatic Change," *Accounting Horizons*, September 1995, p. 87.

[17] See American Accounting Association's Financial Accounting Standards Committee, "Response to the FASB Discussion Memorandum 'Consolidation Policy and Procedures'," *Accounting Horizons*, June 1994, pp. 120–25.

[18] The term "noncontrolling interest" has replaced the traditional term "minority interest," recognizing the broader concept of control in defining a parent-subsidiary relationship—i.e., that a parent may control another entity with less than a majority voting interest, so that the noncontrolling interest in the subsidiary may have the majority rather than minority interest share of the subsidiary.

[19] For a thorough development of the different concepts of consolidated financial statements, see J.R.E. Parker and G. Baxter, *Advanced Corporate Financial Reporting: A Canadian Perspective* (Homewood, Ill.: Richard D. Irwin Inc., 1990), pp. 273–96; and T.H. Beechy, *Canadian Advanced Financial Accounting*, 3rd ed. (Toronto: Harcourt Brace & Company, 1994), chaps. 7–13.

[20] CICA, "Consolidated Financial Statements," *CICA Handbook*, Section 1600 (Toronto: CICA).

[21] In so concluding the board is simply confirming a conclusion reached in the FASB Conceptual Framework Concepts Statements. See FASB, *Elements of Financial Statements*, Statement of Financial Accounting Concepts No. 6 (Stamford: FASB, 1985), par. 254.

[22] See FASB, *Consolidated Financial Statements: Policy and Procedures*, par. 111.

[23] For an interesting, different view that proportionate consolidation should be followed for all material common stock investments regardless of whether control may be said to exist, see H. Bierman, Jr., "Proportionate Consolidation and Financial Analysis," *Accounting Horizons*, December 1992, pp. 5–17.

[24] See CICA, "Consolidated Financial Statements," *CICA Handbook*, Section 1600, pars. .13 and .15.

[25] Ibid., par. .11.

[26] For a discussion of the issues, see FASB, *Consolidated Financial Statements: Policy and Procedures*, pars. 119–25.

[27] For a critical review of U.S. practice on this issue, see M.L. Davis and J.A. Largay III, "Reporting Consolidated Gains and Losses on Subsidiary Stock Issuances," *The Accounting Review*, April 1988, pp. 348–62.

[28] The FASB has proposed requiring that financial statements of subsidiary companies cover the same fiscal period as that of the parent company in consolidated financial statements unless conformity is "not practicable." See FASB, *Consolidated Financial Statements: Policy and Procedures*, pars. 33 and 133.

[29] The FASB has proposed that the accounting policies of a parent and its subsidiaries be consistent in consolidated financial statements except where GAAP permit a single

entity to use different accounting methods for the same type of transactions or events. Ibid., pars. 31–32 and 131–32.

30 See AICPA, Accounting Principles Board, *The Equity Method of Accounting for Investments in Common Stock*, Opinion No. 18 (New York: AICPA, 1971); and CICA, "Long-Term Investments," *CICA Handbook*, Section 3050 (Toronto: CICA, 1977), par. 23. (Section 3050 has been subsequently amended and the current paragraph is 3050.06.)

31 Little attention has been given to this conceptual issue in North America, but it has been the subject of some debate in other jurisdictions, notably Australia. For example, the Director of the Australian Accounting Research Foundation (AARF) has made these observations:

> ... our work on the conceptual framework and the parallel work on consolidations caused us to reconsider the conceptual validity of the equity method of accounting. With the concept of assets and the reporting entity ... all being built around the notion of control over economic benefits, it was difficult to see how an accounting methodology based on the concept of significant influence could fit neatly into the framework.

W.J. McGregor, *Directions For Australian Standard-Setters—A Personal View*, a paper presented at AARF Forum on Off-Balance-Sheet Structures Beyond Consolidations—What of Non-Subsidiary Arrangements? (Melbourne: November 1989), p. 7.

32 The supporting calculations:

$$P = \$300{,}000 + .3S$$

$$S = \$160{,}000 + .2P$$

$$\text{Solving for } P = \$370{,}212$$

P's within group consolidated income would be $370,212 less S's 20% interest in that income, or $296,170. Therefore, P might report income on a gross or net basis as follows:

	Gross Basis	**Net Consolidated Basis**
P's own operations	$300,000	$300,000
Equity interest in S	70,212	(3,830)
	$370,212	$296,170

The negative equity interest of $3,830 on the net consolidated basis arises because S's 20% interest in P's earned operating income (of $300,000) exceeds P's 30% interest in S's smaller operating income (of $160,000).

33 In the example, the operating incomes were P = $300,000 and S = $160,000, for a total of $460,000. Solving for P and S using simultaneous equations results in gross income of P = $370,212 and S = $234,042 for a total of $504,254. If these figures were reduced by the effect of the in-group holdings, the total would be equal to the sum of P and S operating incomes:

$$P = \$370{,}212 - 20\% \text{ owned by } S = \$296{,}170$$

$$S = \$234{,}042 - 30\% \text{ owned by } P = \$163{,}830$$

$$\$460{,}000$$

34 This issue has not received much attention in accounting literature, but see M.E. Bradbury and S.C. Calderwood, "Equity Accounting for Reciprocal Stockholdings," *The Accounting Review*, April 1988, pp. 330–47.

35 See CICA, "Interests in Joint Ventures," *CICA Handbook*, Section 3055 (Toronto: CICA), pars. .03–.08.

36 For a good discussion of these ideas, see D.L. Reklau, "Accounting for Investments in Joint Ventures—A Re-examination," *Journal of Accountancy*, September 1977, pp. 96–103; and R. Dieter and A.R. Wyatt, "The Expanded Equity Method—An Alternative in Accounting for Investments in Joint Ventures," *Journal of Accountancy*, June 1978, pp. 89–94.

37 CICA, "Investments in Corporate and Unincorporated Joint Ventures," *CICA Handbook*, Section 3055 (Toronto: CICA, 1977), par. 11. This section was superseded by a new section 3055 issued in 1994.

38 IASC, *Financial Reporting of Interests in Joint Ventures*, International Accounting Standard IAS 31 (London: IASC, 1991, reformatted in 1994).

39 See AICPA, Accounting Principles Board, *Investments in Partnership and Ventures*, Accounting Interpretation No. 2 of Opinion No. 18 (New York: AICPA, 1971). In addition, the following AICPA issues paper is still referred to as an important reference source in the U.S.: AICPA, Accounting Standards Executive Committee, *Joint Venture Accounting*, Issues Paper (New York: AICPA, 1979).

FOREIGN CURRENCY TRANSLATION

The history of accounting practice and accounting standards in relation to business done in foreign currencies has been confused and controversial. It has been difficult to understand the implications of the economic forces that determine exchange rates and the changes in those forces over time, and of recent developments in foreign currency risk management theory and practice.

Three sets of issues will be discussed in this chapter. The first set concerns the choice of reporting currency by an entity that conducts operations in more than one currency. The second concerns the accounting by an entity for transactions—purchases, sales, investments, and borrowing—conducted by it in a currency other than its reporting currency. The third concerns the translation for the purpose of incorporation in the parent entity's financial statements of the separate financial statements of a branch or subsidiary that are maintained in a different currency. (By extension, these same issues are applicable to equity accounting or proportionate consolidation for an investment in a foreign joint venture or other investee, since these methods are based on the same concepts as consolidation accounting.) Before discussing these accounting issues it may be helpful to provide some background on determinants of currency exchange rates.

BACKGROUND ON CURRENCY EXCHANGE RATES, RISKS AND FINANCIAL INSTRUMENTS

In the period since 1944 there have been two distinct international systems for managing currency relationships. In 1944, the Bretton Woods agreement produced a system whereby the governments of major trading nations undertook to maintain the price of their currencies in U.S. dollars at "pegged" or fixed rates, with narrow fluctuations permitted around those rates. The resultant stabilization of exchange rates simplified the accounting problem of translating amounts expressed in foreign currency and enabled simple solutions that would work most of the time.

There were two major accounting problems related to foreign currency in this era. First, the pegged rate for any particular currency might get out of line with basic economic conditions from time to time, eventually forcing a change in the official pegged rate—devaluation of currency downward or revaluation upward in terms of the U.S. dollar. Whenever such a change occurred, there was always some confusion and debate as to its accounting consequences, which would be settled one way or another (not necessarily consistently by all companies affected), and the accounting would then settle down again. Second, there was the ever-present question of how to translate currencies of countries outside the Bretton Woods system for the purpose of consolidation or equity accounting. This was particularly troublesome with respect to the currencies of those countries experiencing rapid inflation. Normally those currencies exhibited a progressive and often severe weakening trend against those of the more stable industrialized countries. The general solution in this case was to distinguish between assets and liabilities that were deemed to hold their essential economic value regardless of the value of the currency of the country of residence—to be translated at historical exchange rates, and other assets and liabilities that were assumed to be exposed to risk of changes in the currency value—to be translated at current rates.

In the early 1970s the Bretton Woods system collapsed. In essence, the underlying economic influences determining the relative values of currencies became too volatile and too strong to be confined within a system of government-determined, infrequently changed, pegged rates. Adjustments were made, first to a new schedule of fixed rates (the Smithsonian agreement) and then to a system of largely floating rates.

The increase in frequency and magnitude of changes in currency exchange rates thereafter triggered closer examination of accounting bases for translation and the reported gains and losses that resulted from exchange movements. The result was a widespread feeling that accounting did not properly portray the exposure to foreign exchange risk in foreign operations. Much study and debate ensued, resulting after some trial and error in revised standards in the early 1980s. For the most part these standards are still in place today. However, they are far from perfect. In Canada, the appropriate treatment of changes in foreign exchange rates on reported income and certain hedge accounting practices continue to be controversial, and proposals for revisions to the 1980s standards in these areas are yet to be acted upon.

There are two basic theories that suggest how exchange rates should be expected to change over time. The *purchasing power parity theory* argues that one country's currency should be expected to weaken in terms of that of another country if prices in its economy are rising faster than prices in the other country. The rationale is simple. If prices are rising rapidly in one country, that should tend to penalize its exports and encourage imports. Changes in the balance of trade would change the supply of and demand for its currency in the exchange markets and tend to drive its exchange rate down.

The *interest rate parity theory* is based on the connection between interest rates and exchange rates. If exchange rates were really expected to remain steady, it would pay investors to move funds from countries with low interest rates to those with higher rates (assuming the level of investment risk is perceived as being equal). That movement should tend to reduce interest rates in the recipient country and raise them in the country that is exporting capital. The movement should continue until an equilibrium position is reached. An ideal equilibrium would exist if risk-adjusted interest rates in each country were equal and their currency exchange rate steady. So far as capital movements are concerned, however, the situation would also be in equilibrium if relatively higher interest rates in one country were just sufficient to compensate for the rate of decline in the exchange value of its currency.

These are two different theories. The purchasing power parity theory concentrates on the current balance of trade as the primary influence on foreign exchange rates. The interest rate parity theory concentrates on capital flows. They have important common elements, however. Taken together they point to interrelationships between rates of inflation, interest rate levels (which impound inflation expectations) and currency exchange rates of different countries. The expectation must be that the interplay between these factors will be reflected in capital markets prices for interest rates and exchange rates. Structural factors, such as significant changes in prices of oil, primary metals, grains, etc., and changes in the international competitiveness of industry in individual countries, are also important. They can have major implications for the balance of international monetary flows, inflation rates, interest rates and the supply and demand for foreign currencies. A key question is whether all these factors are fairly and fully impounded in foreign currency prices at any given time, or whether governments at least temporarily influence them by strategic market interventions.

The multiplicity of influences on exchange rates makes it difficult to be sure what forces are responsible for changes in exchange rates from time to time. It is therefore difficult to be sure that accounting policies dependent on shifting exchange rates are always consistent with fundamental long-term economic forces. But, by the same token, if one cannot make other than highly subjective assessments of what may be the underlying long-term economic forces and their effects, what could be a better measure of fundamental currency value than the prices that are the result of actual transactions in the marketplace?

For a closer look at exchange rates as they exist from time to time we shall now turn to a brief discussion of the foreign exchange markets. Markets for currencies of important trading nations are well developed. The spot exchange rates are determined by demand and supply for the currencies in question which, as just discussed, result basically from trading transactions, capital movements, and occasional government intervention in the exchange markets.

Anyone who enters into commitments that will involve the purchase or sale of a foreign currency at some future date is exposed to the risk of loss if there is an adverse movement in exchange rates between the commitment date and the future settlement date. To limit the risk it is possible to enter into "forward" contracts, generally with a bank or other financial institution, to buy or sell the committed foreign currency amount at the future settlement date for a stated price. That forward exchange rate tends to be the spot rate plus or minus the interest differential between the interest rate available on the currency bought and that applicable on the currency sold over the period of the contract.

To understand why, consider a foreign currency debt payable six months hence. The debtor could buy the requisite foreign currency at the spot rate with funds borrowed in domestic currency. He or she could then make a six-month loan of the foreign currency. At the end of the six months, the loan proceeds would provide the foreign currency to repay the foreign currency debt. During the six months the debtor would have received interest on the foreign currency loan and paid interest on the domestic currency borrowing. Incurring this differential in interest would have enabled the debtor to cover the foreign currency debt without buying the currency forward. Because this possibility exists, arbitrage will tend to ensure that the forward contract will be priced on the basis of the spot currency price plus or minus the interest differential as described (together with any charge for service by the financial institution arranging the forward contract).

Since interest differentials tend to reflect the relative strength of the two currencies, there will be a general tendency for spot rates to move in the direction of the forward rates over a period. Because of the many factors that may influence an exchange rate in the short term, however, it is unlikely that the spot rate at the end of a forward contract will be exactly equal to the forward rate at the inception of the contract.

A foreign exchange risk exists whenever the domestic currency equivalent of a future cash flow in a foreign currency could be affected by exchange rate changes. Such future cash flow may result from an existing monetary asset or liability (such as an account receivable or payable) or from an existing commitment. In economic terms the exposure to risk is hedged if the loss from an adverse exchange movement on an existing monetary position or commitment is offset by gain on some other instrument or security resulting from the same exchange movement. Different types of instruments are available to hedge foreign exchange risk, each with its own characteristics and costs. Derivative instruments used to manage foreign currency risks fall into two broad classes, forward contracts and options. These basic instruments and their more significant variations and extensions have been explained in relation to managing financial risks generally in Chapter 17, and the reader is referred to that chapter. Following is a brief overview of these derivatives in terms of their use in managing foreign currency risks:

- As already noted above, a foreign currency forward contract is a contract to buy or sell a specified amount of foreign currency at a specified future date for a specified price in domestic currency.

- Foreign currency futures are essentially standardized forward contracts that are traded on an exchange. They are expressed in standard round amounts maturing after a preset time period. Futures contracts are regularly "marked to market." That is, as the foreign exchange rate changes from day to day, each contracting party pays or receives amounts to or from the exchange so as to make up the difference between the spot price and the contract price so long as the contract is outstanding. The contracts are usually closed out before their maturity date rather than being settled by actual receipt or payment of the foreign currency amount specified in the contract.

- Foreign currency options, like futures contracts, are traded on an exchange. Foreign currency options give the holder the right to "call" or "put" a specified amount of foreign currency for a specified price during the option period. A person wishing to hedge against loss on payment commitments in a foreign currency would buy a call option. A put option hedges against loss on amounts collectible in the foreign currency. An option, unlike a forward or futures contract, can prevent loss to the holder (beyond the premium amount) but does not preclude gain. Accordingly, as one might expect, the premium paid for an option is higher than the commission that would be payable on a futures contract of equivalent amount.

- Foreign currency options and futures are typically available only for relatively short periods. A foreign currency swap agreement, in contrast, may cover periods ranging from two to three years up to ten years or even longer. Swaps, which are essentially series of forward contracts, are commonly used to convert existing debt obligations from one currency to another. We have discussed interest rate swaps in Chapter 17. Foreign currency swaps differ from pure interest rate swaps in that they can offset the risk on principal payment as well as on interest payments. They can embrace interest rate risk protection as well as foreign currency risk protection, since the interest obligations exchanged can be from a fixed to a floating rate of interest as well as being from one currency to another. Thus, they are extremely flexible instruments. Swap contracts that represent mere exchanges of currencies today with an agreement to re-exchange at specified rates in future are also common. In substance these provide risk protection similar to a long-dated forward exchange contract. Swap contracts facilitate the exploitation of anomalies in the foreign exchange and capital markets. For example, a borrower may at times be able to get better interest rates in relation to its creditworthiness in the Eurocurrency market than at home. A swap contract can then shed the foreign currency risk taken on without necessarily wiping out all the interest rate advantage. A risk is assumed, however, that the other party to the swap may not perform if the exchange rate moves adversely to its interest. The reliability of that party is thus important. Swap contracts may also be helpful in overcoming other problems such as lack of available credit in local markets, foreign exchange controls, and taxation anomalies.

We turn now to a discussion of the accounting issues.

THE CHOICE OF REPORTING CURRENCY

Most people probably assume that an entity reports in the currency of the jurisdiction in which it is incorporated, or if not incorporated, where its management and control resides. That assumption is valid in the vast majority of situations. Yet a number of Canadian companies report in U.S. dollars,[1] and a limited number of multinational corporations report in a currency other than that of the jurisdiction in which the parent company is incorporated. There must be some justification for these departures from normal practice, but what is it? To date accounting standards have given no guidance on this subject, and accounting literature has been sparse.[2]

Consider these possible situations:

- A company is incorporated and majority-owned in Canada but carries on all its business operations in the United States. Apart from a bank account and a few investments, all assets and liabilities are held in the United States.

- A company incorporated and wholly owned in Canada carries on all its operations in Argentina and, as above, holds almost all its assets in that country. There is, however, a significant amount of debt payable in Canadian dollars.

- A multinational corporation is incorporated in Luxembourg, has business operations widely spread around the world outside North America, and is listed on all the major stock exchanges in the world. The nationality of its shareholders is also diverse, the largest single group being U.S. shareholders holding 39% of the outstanding common shares.

Opinions might well differ as to the most useful and understandable reporting currency in these situations. Following are some factors that would influence opinions.

- The starting point would be the country of incorporation. If substantial operations are carried on there or substantial ownership is located there, the jurisdiction of incorporation might well be decisive, all other factors being equal. But a company can be incorporated in a jurisdiction largely as a matter of legal convenience or for taxation reasons. These are factors that have little significance to the objective of useful and understandable financial reporting. Hence, one may conclude that the country of incorporation is not a significant consideration in itself. It may be used as a sort of "tie breaker" if the merits of the currency of the country of incorporation and one or more other currencies are evenly balanced.

- The currency in which transactions are denominated, in contrast, is a highly important factor. This factor, however, needs some interpretation. Consider a Canadian company in a resource industry conducting all its operations in Canada but selling virtually all its production abroad at prices set in U.S. dollars. The majority (in number) of its transactions are conducted in Canadian dollars—all its purchases and payroll—and basic records except for sales and accounts receivable are kept in Canadian dollars. That might suggest that the financial statements should be expressed in Canadian dollars. On the other hand, the ultimate source of profits is sales in U.S. dollars, and the company may even have a policy of paying dividends in U.S. dollars, to save conversion costs for those shareholders who wish to receive payment in that currency. In such a case, the choice of reporting currency as between the Canadian dollar and U.S. dollar may be relatively evenly balanced.

- If there is a significant amount of debt outstanding, the currency in which the bulk of the debt is denominated has some importance to the decision. Since coverage of debt interest is an important aspect of financial reporting, it may be less confusing to have the debt interest reported as an unchanging figure year by year so long as the debt itself is unchanged. This may be important not only to the debt holders themselves but also for analysts wishing to assess the financial risk of the company.

- A multinational company with operations scattered around the world may find that no one currency stands out as the one in which the majority of its operations are carried on. Various other considerations then receive added importance. For example, if many more shareholders reside in one of the countries in which there are significant operations than in any of the others, the currency of that country might well be a logical choice for the reporting currency.

- The choice of currency might also be strongly influenced by the relative strength and stability of each of the possible contenders. Where a choice exists, a country with restrictions on currency convertibility might be avoided. Also, the currency of a country with low, or no more than moderate, inflation is preferable. A currency suffering rapid depreciation in value represents a poor choice of reporting currency for anyone not familiar with its history.

- The U.S. dollar is a strong contender for selection by any multinational company where no other currency is the predominant choice. As a reserve currency, and one in terms of which most other currencies are quoted in the foreign exchange markets, the U.S. dollar is the best known of all the world currencies. It also has had the advantage historically of a low rate of inflation relative to many other countries. As an alternative it may be that, at some future date, multinational corporations will wish to report in an artificial currency that represents an average of a "basket" of currencies, such as the Special Drawing Rights established by the IMF. At present, however, these artificial currencies are not sufficiently well known to the public at large to serve as a satisfactory basis for financial reporting.

The foregoing suggests that there are times when the choice of reporting currency is not an automatic or mechanical choice. The currency in which most business is carried on by the entity must be a strong contender, but other factors are also important.

The CICA Emerging Issues Committee has addressed the question of changing the reporting currency. It makes the important point that the selection of the currency of measurement is not a matter of free choice, but should be based on the facts of the particular circumstances. Thus a change in reporting currency would normally be made only if the substance of a company's situation has changed. In this case, the committee concluded that comparative figures for prior periods should not be restated because this would imply that the new reporting currency had always been appropriate. Rather, prior period numbers should simply be recast through a "translation of convenience," that is simply by applying the exchange rate prevailing in that prior period to the previously reported numbers.[3]

One additional possibility might be noted. It could be that a Canadian company that prepares its accounts in Canadian dollars has securities listed on a foreign stock exchange. The company might elect to do a "translation of convenience" of its Canadian dollar accounts into the foreign currency in order to facilitate reporting to its foreign security holders. In this case the display currency is different than the underlying measurement currency.

Choice of Reporting Currency and Choice of GAAP

Is there any implication that accounting principles used in a financial report must be those of the country whose currency is adopted as the unit of measurement? For example, if a Canadian company reports in U.S. dollars, might readers assume that it follows U.S. generally accepted accounting principles? There is no recognized rule that the choice of accounting principles depends upon the choice of reporting currency, or vice versa. Nevertheless, in view of the possibility of confusion on this point, it is highly desirable, if not essential, that a company not reporting in the currency of its own jurisdiction should disclose very clearly that its accounting principles are determined by practice in its own country. This is particularly important when a substantial body of its shareholders resides in the country whose currency it uses as the unit of measurement.

TRANSACTIONS AND BALANCES IN FOREIGN CURRENCY

Any enterprise may have transactions denominated in a currency other than its reporting currency. (Hereafter such currencies will be referred to as foreign currencies. For a Canadian company using the U.S. dollar as its reporting currency, transactions in Canadian dollars would, by this definition, be regarded as foreign currency transactions.) Three issues will be discussed in relation to foreign currency transactions: (1) At what exchange rate shall these transactions be recorded initially in the accounts kept in the reporting currency? (2) What is to be the valuation basis of assets and liabilities denominated in foreign currency subsequent to the transaction date that gives rise to them? (3) On what basis shall exchange rate gains and losses on assets and liabilities denominated in foreign currency be recognized in income? For convenience, the discussion will initially be limited to unhedged positions in foreign currency and then will consider the effect of hedging.

Translation at the Transaction Date

The general rule is that a transaction denominated in a foreign currency should be translated at the spot rate when first recognized in the accounts. This will normally result in a satisfactory measure of cost equal to the fair value of consideration given. However, its application to transactions resulting from commitments made at an earlier date is open to some question.

Consider the accounting for a Canadian company's commitment, entered into on June 30, for a shipload of product from France with delivery scheduled for approximately November 30 and settlement in francs two months after delivery. It is assumed that the Canadian company is exposed to the risk of changes in the exchange rate for French francs as soon as it is committed to the purchase. Clearly, if the franc goes up against the Canadian dollar after the commitment date, the amount required to be paid for the product in Canadian dollars is increased, and vice-versa.[4] What might be the most appropriate accounting for this situation? The currency commitment might be recognized on June 30 as a forward currency contract at the forward currency exchange rate for settlement on November 30. At any financial reporting date prior to settlement the domestic currency equivalent of the foreign currency obligation would be measured by reference to the forward exchange rate prevailing on the reporting date. The difference between that amount and the commitment priced at the forward currency exchange rate at June 30 would be the gain or loss to be recognized in income.

Such early recognition of commitments subject to foreign exchange risk is not the norm under existing GAAP, however. Accounting standards have chosen to adhere more closely to the normal practice for domestic transactions. That is to say, the transaction is recognized at the performance date rather than the commitment date, except that the tradition of conservatism would call for a provision for loss if it is apparent that the amount to be paid for the product in Canadian dollars exceeds its recoverable value. In the above example, it may be expected that the transaction would be recognized at the delivery date (November 30), at which point there would be a debit to inventory and a credit to accounts payable, with the amount payable in francs translated at the spot exchange rate at that date (assuming no "lower of cost and market" provision for loss is necessary).

As we shall see later, the above foreign currency commitment may be hedged by a foreign currency forward contract or other monetary instrument that would be measured at the current exchange rate. This exposes a fundamental inconsistency with measurement of the foreign currency commitment at cost, and gives rise to a demand for special hedge accounting adjustments.

Assets and Liabilities Denominated in a Foreign Currency

At one time it was considered appropriate for foreign currency receivables and debt to be left on the balance sheet at their original transaction values without any adjustment for changes in exchange rates, at least until they became current assets or current liabilities. This was considered consistent with the cost basis of accounting, and increases or decreases in values subject to market fluctuations were recognized only when they were realized or when realization was imminent. Contemporary accounting standards have progressed far beyond this traditional accounting. It is now generally accepted that current exchange rates are more relevant than past rates, and that foreign currency denominated monetary assets and liabilities should always be measured at current exchange rates.

Thus, consistent with accounting standards in the U.S., the IASC, and virtually all developed countries, Canadian GAAP require monetary assets and liabilities denominated in foreign currencies, and nonmonetary assets carried at fair values determined in foreign currencies, to be measured at the exchange rates in effect on the balance sheet date.[5] This is, in essence, fair value accounting for the foreign currency component of these assets and liabilities. This accounting recognizes that when a company invests in a monetary asset or incurs a liability denominated in a foreign currency, it exposes itself to direct risk for changes in that exchange rate. (There can be questions with respect to determining the foreign currency component of some monetary assets and liabilities that have domestic and foreign currency denominated elements, for example, dual currency bonds, which are the subject of an EIC Abstract.)[6]

The cost of a nonmonetary asset acquired through a foreign currency transaction is established at the transaction date, by the Canadian dollar equivalent of the foreign currency paid at that date. However, if a nonmonetary asset is for some reason carried at fair value determined in a foreign currency (this might occur, for example, if foreign-sourced inventory is written down to market value, or a marketable security denominated in a foreign currency is carried at fair value), it must be translated at the current exchange rate in order to be measured at the Canadian dollar equivalent fair value.

Gains and Losses on Assets and Liabilities Denominated in a Foreign Currency

The measurement of monetary assets and liabilities denominated in foreign currencies at current exchange rates on the balance sheet leaves the question whether the consequential adjustments should be part of income in the periods when the exchange rates change. The United States position, and that of the IASC and standards in most countries, is that adjustments should be recognized in income immediately. The Canadian standard has compromised. That compromise may have been understandable at the time the CICA standard was issued in 1983. Foreign currency borrowings have been far more important to Canadian companies than to U.S. companies, in view of the smaller capital market in Canada. Given the volatility of foreign exchange rates under a floating-rate system, immediate recognition of unrealized gains or losses on adjustments of foreign currency debt to current rates could, in some companies, swamp reported operating income, especially in quarterly financial statements. Many apparently continue to believe that it is fundamentally misleading to permit what may be mere fluctuations in exchange rates to have this effect.

The Canadian compromise has taken this form (*CICA Handbook*, paragraph 1650.23):

- As noted already, monetary assets and liabilities are translated at the rate current at the financial reporting date since no other rate is considered equally relevant. If a monetary item has a "fixed or ascertainable life," resulting adjustments in carrying value are treated as deferred charges or deferred credits. Adjustments with respect to a monetary item that has no ascertainable life, or which is classified as a current asset or liability, are to be recognized in income immediately.

- Adjustments deferred are amortized over the remaining term of the receivable or debt if it has a fixed or ascertainable life extending beyond the end of the next fiscal year.

This compromise is much more difficult to justify now than it was in 1983 for the following reasons:

- Canada is now almost alone in the world in deferring and amortizing these adjustments. The IASC eliminated deferral and amortization of exchange differences as an allowed alternative in 1989.[7]

- The concern that foreign exchange gains and losses resulting from fluctuating exchange rates could swamp reported operating income has been lessened in the sense that companies can substantially reduce income volatility by sound foreign currency hedging practices. Capital markets for exchange rate instruments have developed to the point that most exchange risk exposures can be effectively hedged. Indeed, there is a strong counter argument that deferral and amortization accounting only serves to obscure an enterprise's foreign exchange risk management practices and the impact of unhedged foreign exchange positions.

- The increased attention to developing accounting standards from conceptual framework concepts has made it much more difficult to accept presenting deferred charges and deferred credits on the balance sheet that cannot be justified as real assets and liabilities.

- There has been mounting pressure in recent years from securities regulators and some preparers and analysts to reduce differences between Canadian and U.S. GAAP. The conflicting treatment of foreign currency gains and losses has been a primary source of differences, both in number and in dollar effect.[8]

- Finally, significant accounting problems arising from the deferral and amortization requirements would be eliminated if all foreign currency gains and losses, or at least those in respect of unhedged positions, were to be recognized in income immediately.

With respect to the latter point, the following have been the more significant implementation questions and anomalies.

- *Meaning of "ascertainable life."* The meaning of the term "ascertainable life" is obscure. It was probably inserted to take care of such situations as bank loans that, although in demand form, have a schedule for repayment that is understood between the borrower and the bank. To have any meaning, a stretch-out of amortization over a presumed ascertainable life should be based on some external evidence, such as an understanding with the borrower, and should not be based merely on management's expectations as to future availability of cash for debt reduction.[9]

- *Basis of amortization.* The precise method of amortization over the remaining term of a long-term monetary asset or liability is not specified. Various possible bases of amortization over the remaining lifetime have been explored in the literature.[10] Because these proposals are all based on prospective amortization, as required by the *CICA Handbook*, they all suffer from a fundamental flaw—the impact of a given change in exchange rates on amortization for the period, and thus on income, is much greater if it occurs near the end of the debt life than if it occurs near the beginning (because there is a much shorter period to absorb the effect).

- *Renegotiation of foreign currency debt.*[11] If foreign currency debt is settled before maturity, any unamortized balance of deferred debit or credit with respect to that debt is to be written off. The *CICA Handbook*, however, makes an exception in unspecified circumstances "when a renegotiation of the terms and conditions ... may not constitute a settlement ..." (paragraph 1650.27). In such a case the deferred charge or credit remaining is to be amortized over the life of the renegotiated debt.

  The first question is: What constitutes renegotiation? Can it be "renegotiation" if a new lender takes over the position of the lender being paid off? That might not seem unreasonable if, for example, it resulted simply from a company changing bankers without significant other changes in the debt characteristics. Can it be called renegotiation if debt in one currency is paid off with proceeds from borrowing in another currency? Some have argued that some currencies are so closely linked that substitution of one for the other without major change in terms of the debt can be regarded as a renegotiation rather than a settlement.[12] Is there any limit to changes in debt terms? For example, if the maturity date is extended from five years to ten or twenty years, or if there is a substantial change in the security supporting the debt, or if the interest rate is changed from fixed to floating or the reverse, can that still be regarded as renegotiation? Without a clear explanation of the meaning of the term "renegotiation," the answers to these questions are matters of opinion.

A second question concerns the merits of the instruction to amortize the deferred debit or credit remaining at the time of renegotiation over the duration of the renegotiated debt. If the new debt has a shorter maturity than that replaced, most would agree that the amortization should be revised so that any deferred debit or credit is fully amortized when the debt is retired. The position when the maturity date of debt is extended upon renegotiation is more debatable. At the time the original debt was issued the company undertook an exposure to foreign exchange risk for the original term of the debt. By extending the term to maturity by renegotiating debt, an entity assumes a *greater* exposure to foreign exchange risk than it had before. Clearly the exchange risk is greater when the borrowing is for five years (say) than for six months. It flies in the face of logic that by increasing its exposure to foreign exchange risk an entity should reduce its recognition of loss (or gain) with respect to past foreign exchange risk taking.

A Conceptual Evaluation of Canadian Treatment of Foreign Currency Gains and Losses

When a company invests in a foreign currency monetary asset or incurs a foreign currency monetary liability, it exposes itself to risk from changes in the exchange rate with respect to that currency. The result of that risk must be recognized in income at some time. One way to do so is to continuously restate the carrying value of the asset or liability to an amount equal to its face amount in foreign currency translated at the exchange rate current at the reporting date and recognize the adjustment in income immediately as a gain or loss.

The CICA has thus far rejected this treatment, largely because fluctuations in exchange rates could have a significant impact on periodic income reported and yet be meaningless if they were to cancel out over the term to maturity of the asset or liability. We must carefully trace where this line of thinking leads. If changes in foreign currency exchange rates are not recognized in income directly, then they must be carried forward to future periods. This immediately places the accountant on very shaky ground. If it is accepted that foreign exchange rates are determined in well-developed ("efficient") markets, then what can be the basis for deferring income recognition of the effect of changes in these prices? The accountant is unlikely to have information that is not available to the marketplace, i.e., that will not have been impounded in the market price. The accountant would thus seem to have no rational basis for "betting against the market" in deferring foreign exchange losses and gains; in other words, the resulting deferred debits and credits would not seem to be justifiable as real "assets" or "liabilities."

As an aside, if one accepts this "mark-to-market" reasoning, one would also expect to fair value monetary assets and liabilities for interest rate changes, and to put the resulting gains and losses through income. Given the interconnectedness noted earlier between interest rates and foreign currency rates, recognizing only foreign currency gains and losses on monetary items immediately in income may present only part of the picture.

Many accountants in Canada seem not to have been convinced by these "efficient market" arguments, however, and continue to see merit in amortization of foreign currency gains and losses on long-term monetary items. Therefore, let us pursue this possibility a bit further. The CICA considers that a foreign currency gain or loss is inherently part of the return on the monetary asset or the cost of the debt over its life, and therefore that it should be amortized in some way over that period. Unfortunately, even if it is conceded that gain or loss should be amortized, the approach taken by the CICA is severely flawed. If the ultimate foreign currency gain or loss is regarded as an adjustment of the yield on the investment or the effective cost of the debt, that adjustment applies over the whole contract period of the asset or liability. It does not just apply to the period remaining after a movement in the exchange rate occurs. Thus prospective amortization of the effect of exchange rate changes is inconsistent with the basic CICA rationale for amortization.

To see this, let us ask ourselves whether the probability of a future gain and the probability of a future loss on foreign exchange are evenly balanced when a Canadian company borrows abroad at a lower interest rate than that obtainable at home. The interest rate parity theory, referred to earlier, tells us that the risk expectation is that there will be foreign exchange losses on the debt. If the risk were evenly balanced, everyone (except those with a high aversion to risk) would borrow abroad to take advantage of the lower interest rate. That would result in a quick equalization of interest rates. If that equalization has not occurred, it must be presumed that the probability is that exchange losses will occur in the future. Forward exchange rates reflect this expectation; as noted earlier, a forward exchange rate tends to be the spot rate plus or minus the differential between the interest rate available on currency bought and that available on the currency sold.

How, then, might amortization be applied from the beginning? Consider a Canadian company borrowing abroad. At the time of borrowing it could be estimated what rate of interest would have had to be paid on borrowing on equivalent security at home. Interest expense might then be recorded at that estimated domestic rate, with the excess over the actual foreign interest rate being credited to the liability account. Then, to the extent that differences arose from time to time between that carrying value for the liability and its principal amount translated at current exchange rates, those differences could be amortized over the period to debt maturity. If the interest rate parity theory is broadly accurate, this treatment would reduce differences to be amortized and provide a better portrayal of annual debt cost. This possible approach has not been given serious consideration in accounting literature.

Seen in the light of the above analysis, the CICA treatment of deferred debits or credits seems particularly unfortunate. If the interest parity theory is correct, entities that borrow in a foreign currency principally to take advantage of lower interest rates will tend to find that those lower rates will be associated with future foreign exchange losses—i.e., there will be deferred exchange losses more often than deferred exchange gains. If this is so, the CICA standard is unconservative at every point. First, it has chosen not to recognize the loss in full when the exchange rate does change. Second, it does not provide from the inception of the borrowing for the probable strengthening of the foreign currency vis-à-vis the domestic currency that economic theory suggests is to be expected. Third, amortization of the deferred loss is prospective only and therefore tends to push off recognition of the loss so that it is piled on top of further losses that are likely to occur in future. Finally, companies are able to take advantage of an undefined notion of renegotiation to push loss recognition still further into the future.

Recent Developments

It seems clear that the existing *CICA Handbook* deferral and amortization standards cannot be sustained. The obvious choice to replace it, given acceptance by standard setters in other countries and the IASC, is immediate recognition in income of all gains and losses. Yet, there has continued to be significant opposition to this in Canada, particularly from within the preparer community.

A CICA task force was formed in 1989 to review the existing *CICA Handbook* requirements. It could not reach a consensus on this issue. It recommended that fundamental issues relating to accounting for financial instrument derivatives, hedge accounting, and risks and uncertainties needed to be resolved to provide the basis for developing a sound standard on foreign currency translation that would stand the test of time.[13]

The CICA Accounting Standards Board issued an exposure draft on foreign currency translation in 1993, and a revised re-exposure draft in 1996. Both documents proposed translation of monetary items denominated in foreign currencies at current exchange rates with immediate recognition of gains and losses in income, except for certain rate-regulated situations and where specified hedging criteria are met.[14] However, the current position of the CICA Accounting Standards Board is that the existing standard should be left in place until decisions are made with respect to the more general topic of accounting for financial instruments (see Chapter 17).

Speculative Foreign Currency Contracts

Foreign currency contracts (forward exchange contracts, currency futures contracts, and currency options) have been described earlier. These contracts may be used to hedge an existing exposure to foreign exchange risk. Accounting in that situation will be discussed subsequently. Equally, they may be used for speculation on foreign exchange movements.

When an entity has committed itself to a foreign exchange contract for speculative purposes, there is little doubt that the most informative accounting is to recognize gain or loss as the fair value of the contract changes. That accounting is required by U.S. standards. The *CICA Handbook* does not speak directly to the question of accounting for speculative foreign exchange contracts. The U.S. standard has become general practice in Canada and preferable to any other basis, such as one that recognizes losses immediately but defers gains until realization.

Hedges of Exposure to Foreign Currency Risk

Foreign currency risk is hedged in generally the same ways, involving the same basic types of primary and derivative financial instruments, as are other financial risks (interest and market price risks). It should not be surprising then that the fundamental issues of hedge accounting are not unique to foreign currency risk; we have already examined them in the broader context of financial instruments in Chapter 17. The following discussion will presume knowledge of that chapter and will address the issues and standards specific to foreign currency hedge accounting as an extension of that earlier discussion.

As explained earlier, an economic hedge exists when the foreign exchange risk on one position is offset by an equal and opposite risk on another position. That is, if a change in the exchange rate occurs, it will be favourable to one and adverse to the other with the net effect being zero. Positions exposed to foreign exchange risk include monetary assets and liabilities denominated in a foreign currency, nonmonetary assets carried at fair values determined in a foreign currency, firm commitments to pay or receive foreign currency in the future, and various types of foreign currency forward and option contracts.

Any position which, standing by itself, is exposed to foreign exchange risk can serve as a hedge of another risk in the same foreign currency that takes the opposite direction. For example, an entity can be naturally hedged if its activities are such that its accounts receivable and accounts payable in a particular foreign currency are approximately equal in amount most of the time. Or, if an entity has some positions at risk that are not naturally hedged, it can arrange one or more foreign currency contracts to accomplish a balanced risk position.

It is an objective of accounting standards to account for foreign currency positions that are fully hedged in such a fashion that no net foreign exchange gain or loss will be reflected in income. This objective would be accomplished if all foreign currency positions were to be recognized on a symmetrical basis and continuously revalued at current exchange rates, with the value adjustments taken immediately to income. The result would be that no *net* gain or loss would be reflected in income on foreign currency positions that are fully hedged (because gains on the one side would be offset by losses on the other), while the impact of changes in foreign currency rates for positions that are speculative or imperfectly hedged would be appropriately reported in income as they occur. This, then, is the ideal.

Unfortunately, in certain significant situations the recognition and measurement of foreign currency risk positions will not correspond with this ideal. The basic situations and the current CICA standards and practices accepted in Canada for dealing with these situations are outlined below.

- As noted earlier in this chapter, a commitment to make a purchase or sale is generally not recognized in accounting until performance. Accordingly, the treatment of the effect of exchange rate movements on a position hedging a foreign currency commitment must be made to conform. This might be done by making no adjustment for the effect of foreign exchange movements on the hedging medium before the commitment becomes a recognized transaction, or else the gain or loss resulting from such adjustment might be deferred until the transaction recognition date. The emphasis in the CICA accounting standards is on the latter treatment. In Canadian practice, however, a forward contract hedging a commitment might be left unrecognized until the commitment becomes a transaction, for reasons of convenience.

- The *CICA Handbook* visualizes situations in which a nonmonetary asset or a future revenue stream may be regarded as a hedge of an existing foreign currency risk exposure. In such a case, when the position at risk is a monetary asset or liability, it will be regularly revalued for the effects of changes in exchange rates, and the CICA standard provides that the resulting gains and losses be deferred to be recognized in the future period in which the nonmonetary asset is considered to be converted into the foreign currency or the revenues are recognized.

- The *CICA Handbook* allows that a net investment in a "self-sustaining" foreign operation of the reporting entity may be hedged against foreign currency risk. (This is discussed in the following section on translation of consolidated and equity accounted foreign operations.)

- The CICA requirement for deferral and amortization of gains and losses on foreign currency denominated long-term monetary assets and liabilities with fixed or ascertainable lives will require some modification to give effect to certain hedging relationships. If a long-term monetary foreign currency position is partially hedged, it will be necessary to apportion the adjustment to its carrying value so that only the hedged proportion is taken to income (to be matched with the offsetting gain or loss on the hedging instrument) while the remainder is deferred and amortized on a basis consistent with that previously described for unhedged positions. (Alternatively, some might interpret the *CICA Handbook* to suggest that the amount of the adjustment to a long-term monetary asset (or liability) and to a position identified as hedging it should be netted against each other and any net excess of the asset (or liability) adjustment should be deferred to be amortized to income in future. This would have the effect of including any differences resulting from imperfections in the hedge in the amount to be amortized in future.) In addition, there are questions with respect to the proper treatment of accumulated deferred translation gains and losses on a foreign currency denominated monetary asset or liability that is then hedged part way through its life by another foreign currency instrument.[15]

Because the above hedge accounting results in the deferral of gains and losses that could otherwise have to be reflected in income, accounting standards have sought to ensure that there is discipline in identifying a hedging relationship and that the hedge is genuine and will continue to be effective over the hedge period (see *CICA Handbook* paragraphs 1650.48–.50). To be considered effective, it must be probable at the outset that the value of the hedging instrument will change with changing exchange rates so as to offset the impact of those rate changes on the position hedged. If the hedging instrument is for a shorter period than the position hedged, the *CICA Handbook* seems to suggest that the management must have an intention of renewing the hedge up to the settlement date of the position hedged in order to justify deferment of gain or loss (*CICA Handbook*, paragraph 1650.44). The standards require that management identify the existence of the hedge prior to following hedge accounting.[16]

When gain or loss is being deferred on a presumed hedge, a problem may arise if hedge accounting must be discontinued before its originally expected date. The recommended treatment is as follows. If (1) a hedging instrument matures before settlement date of the position hedged and is not renewed, or (2) the hedging instrument is disposed of before that date, or (3) hedge accounting is discontinued because the hedge appears not to be effective, any cumulative gain or loss deferred up to the date of such event is to continue to be deferred until recognition date for the transaction hedged and then will be used to adjust the transaction measurement in the manner previously described (*CICA Handbook*, paragraph 1650.51).

These CICA foreign currency hedge accounting requirements are subject to the same serious shortcomings applicable to traditional hedge accounting generally that we examined in Chapter 17. Two particularly problematic applications of the CICA requirements in respect of foreign currency hedges involving nonmonetary assets and future revenue streams are discussed below.

Hedging with Nonmonetary Assets

The *CICA Handbook* indicates that a nonmonetary asset held that will (with reasonable assurance) be converted into sufficient foreign currency at the date of settlement of a liability in the same currency can be viewed as a hedge of that liability (*CICA Handbook*, paragraph 1650.48). It is hard to be sure what was meant by this. One may suppose that a situation was visualized in which an entity owns a piece of real estate located in the foreign country which it intends to sell and use the proceeds to liquidate the liability deemed hedged. Even if such a position could be identified, there is an accounting problem because the carrying value of the nonmonetary asset will not be continuously adjusted for exchange rate changes. Consequently, it is necessary to defer the gains or losses recognized on the regular adjustment to the current exchange rate of the liability deemed hedged. When the asset is sold, what is to become of that deferred gain and loss? The only apparent way to avoid reporting it as a foreign exchange gain or loss seems to be to treat it as an adjustment of the proceeds of sale from the asset and thereby as a factor in the net gain or loss reported on that sale.

The logic of all this is not supportable. The CICA recommendation overlooks the essential nature of a hedging instrument, namely that its value can be *relied upon* to fluctuate proportionate to changes in the foreign exchange rate. That simply cannot be said about a piece of real estate, or any other nonmonetary asset. The 1996 CICA re-exposure draft would not permit hedge accounting for nonmonetary assets.[17]

Revenue Stream Hedges

The *CICA Handbook* speaks of a future revenue stream in a foreign currency as a possible hedge of foreign currency obligations. Let us visualize a typical "revenue stream" hedging situation. Suppose a Canadian company borrows in U.S. dollars to finance its productive facilities which produce goods or services to be sold in the U.S. market. It is expected that the debt will be repaid with the U.S. dollars generated by those revenues. Management has determined that it makes much sense to borrow in U.S. dollars in this situation, because it can take advantage of lower U.S. interest rates while assuming no net exchange risk. If the U.S. dollar increases in value against the Canadian dollar, the increase in debt costs in Canadian dollars will, it is expected, be offset by increases in revenues in equivalent Canadian dollars. On the basis of this reasoning it is argued that any gains or losses on the translation of the debt into Canadian dollars should be deferred to be recognized at the time the future revenues are recorded. These arguments are seductive and the *CICA Handbook* has accepted them:

> When there is reasonable assurance that an enterprise will undertake the purchase or sale of goods or services in a foreign currency in a future period, it may choose to hedge the transaction so that it establishes the Canadian dollar price of those goods or services at the time of entering into the hedge. Since a subsequent change in exchange rates will not affect the Canadian dollar price of the related goods or services, there will be no exchange gain or loss. Any costs associated with the hedge would be included in the Canadian dollar price of the goods or services (paragraph 1650.51).

There are, however, many questions and the arguments do not stand up well under close scrutiny, reasoning within fundamental accounting principles.

Let us first examine the principle. This is fundamentally a recognition question. Can one justify the recognition of a future transaction as a hedge of, or as being hedged by, an existing asset or liability risk position (in this case foreign currency denominated debt)? This issue was analyzed in Chapter 17 (under the heading "Hedges of Commitments and Anticipated Transactions"). There we made the distinction between firm commitments to buy or sell goods or services at fixed prices and expected future purchases or sales. A fixed-price commitment, standing by itself, represents an existing risk position assuming the reporting enterprise has a present obligation to fulfill its side of the commitment at the fixed price and stands to gain or lose if the price changes.

But what of expected future sales or purchases for which the company has no existing fixed price commitment? It may be highly probable that the company will make some level of sales in U.S. dollars in the future. But such sales are treated as future events to be recognized in the future periods in which they take place. When the future arrives, conditions may have changed. The company may find that it is able to price its sales differently to compensate for U.S. dollar exchange rate changes, or it may modify its goods or services to sell profitably at lower Canadian dollar prices, etc. The point is that the possibility that future revenues in U.S. dollars may be affected by changes in exchange rates is not an existing foreign currency risk position in financial accounting. This is evident from the fact that no provision for impairment of future revenues will be made in this year's financial statements if the U.S. exchange rate decreases. The deferral of foreign currency gains and losses on existing U.S. dollar denominated debt to be carried forward as an adjustment of future revenues may be reasoned to misstate those revenues because they will then not be measured at exchange rates existing when they take place.

The second area of concern with the CICA's "revenue stream hedges" recommendations is practical. There is an undesirable degree of flexibility in the standard. This is directly related to concerns of principle because, when one has no clear principle to base accounting upon, it becomes very difficult to determine how and where lines should be drawn and the accounting is bound to become arbitrary. Examination of the implementation problems thus helps to illustrate problems of principle.

- To begin with, one needs to understand what is meant by a "revenue stream." The term "revenue" is by itself confusing in this context. Revenue is an accrual accounting term. Debt is not paid with revenue; it must be paid with cash. Thus the *CICA Handbook* must really mean cash flow from sales or services in this context. Consider a case in which cash from sales revenue in the foreign currency is partly used to cover operating expenses in that currency. It is obvious that only the *net* cash stream is available to meet the foreign currency obligation.

  The *CICA Handbook* is silent on this point. However, the general instruction is that there should be reasonable assurance that a hedge will be effective in order for hedge accounting to be applied. This could be taken to mean that there should be reasonable assurance that an adequate U.S. dollar cash flow, net of amounts needed to cover operating costs, will be available. In practice, this might well mean that the maximum that could be designated as a hedge is the net cash flow from operations available in U.S. dollars, regardless of where the operating costs were incurred. The vague CICA "effectiveness" rule leaves much to interpretation in this regard.

- Another problem with a hedge in the form of a revenue stream is that of timing. Cash flow from operations comes in a more or less continuous stream; debt is paid off all at once or in blocks at specific dates. One of the conditions for an *effective* hedge of this kind, then, might be that the cash flow in the foreign currency be accumulated in cash, or an asset easily convertible to cash, so that it is actually available to pay off the debt when required. The *CICA Handbook* makes no mention of this.

•   If it is probable that there will be a margin of net foreign currency receipts over debt requirements, it may be asked whether the entity can pick and choose which years' net cash flows shall be deemed to be hedged with the debt. To take an extreme case, suppose a debt matures five years hence and the forecast shows a net cash flow in foreign currency in each year, over and above the amount required to take care of the debt interest, that is sufficient to meet the requirement for retirement of debt principal. May the entity pick the revenue of the last year as the hedge of the debt principal? The *CICA Handbook* does not deal with this point, and some major concerns may be expressed.

First, the further into the future that the forecast extends, the less assurance there can be as to its accuracy. Thus, other things being equal, the margin for error allowed in the forecast should be much greater in the fifth year than in the first year. It may be that the uncertainty is sufficiently great that there cannot be reasonable assurance of the hedge effectiveness in that year almost regardless of the size of the future foreign currency cash flow that is forecast. Second, consider the effects of such a designation. Suppose a case where the foreign currency is strengthening at a rate of 10% a year over five years. If only the fifth year cash flow is designated as a hedge, the income figures for years one to four will all be translated at exchange rates current in those years, while some part of the revenue in the fifth year will be translated at an exchange rate in effect five years earlier. Not only will this distort the true trend in revenues, it will also, in effect, load the entire exchange loss with respect to the debt principal into just one year out of the five years that the debt is outstanding. This can hardly be said to be good accounting, and must lead one back to question the principle.

All in all, when the issues are weighed up, it is strongly arguable that leaving the accounting alone would provide a more faithful representation of what is actually occurring. The fact of the matter is that revenue in any year ought to be translated at the exchange rate in effect in that year, not a rate in effect some time earlier. The gain or loss on exchange rate movements occurs when the rate changes, not some years later when cash is collected to pay off the changed liability.

Yet business management has a case too. The strategy of issuing U.S. dollar debt to help mitigate a future risk of possible loss in revenues that could result from a decrease in the U.S. dollar exchange rate may be eminently sound. Management may argue that forcing recognition in income of exchange gains and losses on debt denominated in U.S. dollars is a misrepresentation when the expectation is that these gains and losses will be offset by compensating changes in the Canadian dollar value of future sales. Immediate income recognition is, it may be argued, inconsistent with management's purpose in undertaking the U.S. dollar borrowing, and is not reflecting the reality as management sees it.

It can be seen, then, that revenue-stream hedging, and more broadly hedging of future transactions, is a most vexing problem for accounting standard setters.

The task force commissioned by the CICA to review the *CICA Handbook* standard on foreign currency translation recommended that revenue-stream hedge accounting be eliminated.[18] The CICA Accounting Standards Board did not accept this advice, and the CICA re-exposure draft proposed to continue to permit it. It did, however, propose more stringent conditions, including that it be highly probable that the foreign currency net cash flows to result from the designated future revenue streams will match in both timing and amount those of the existing foreign currency denominated debt.[19] The main thrust of the re-exposure draft proposals is, as noted earlier, to eliminate deferral and amortization of foreign currency gains and losses arising on unhedged long-term monetary items with fixed or ascertainable lives. The continuation of revenue-stream hedge accounting may have been viewed by the CICA board as a political necessity to achieve this primary objective.

The CICA standard and proposals for its revision will have to be re-evaluated in light of major new FASB and IASC standards issued in 1998. The FASB standard deals broadly with derivatives and hedging activities. Its requirements in respect of hedges of foreign currency exposures may be summarized as follows:[20]

- The designation of a hedging relationship is subject to stringent conditions. As well, an enterprise must document its policies and establish at the inception of a hedge the methods it will use to assess its effectiveness.

- A hedge of the exposure to exchange rate changes of a recognized asset or liability or an unrecognized firm commitment is referred to as a "fair value hedge." Gains or losses on such hedges are to be recognized in income together with the offsetting gain or loss on the hedged item that is attributable to the foreign currency risk being hedged.

- A hedge of the foreign currency risk exposure of a qualifying anticipated future transaction (for example, a revenue stream hedge) is referred to as a "cash flow hedge." The effective portion of the hedge's gain or loss is initially to be reported as a component of "other comprehensive income" (i.e., outside the statement of regular income), and subsequently transferred into regular income when the hedged transaction affects earnings.

- The gain or loss on a hedge of the foreign currency exposure of a net investment in a foreign operation continues to be reported in other comprehensive income as part of the cumulative translation adjustment.

- This standard precludes the use of nonderivative financial instruments as hedges except that a nonderivative denominated in a foreign currency may be designated as a hedge of the foreign currency exposure of an unrecognized firm commitment denominated in the foreign currency, or a net investment in a foreign operation. Thus, the common practice in Canada of designating foreign currency denominated debt as a hedge of future revenue streams is not permitted under U.S. GAAP.

- More extensive disclosure is required of hedges, including a description of management's risk management policy for each type of hedge.

The FASB requirement for the classification of gains and losses of hedges of anticipated future transactions in "other comprehensive income," to be transferred to earnings when the hedged transaction affects earnings, is an uneasy compromise. It avoids deferral of gains and losses on the balance sheet, but effectively achieves the same result in reported earnings. However, these hedges and their effects will be much more transparent.

The FASB standard covers all derivatives and hedging relationships, not just those related to foreign currency exposures. Reference should be made to Chapter 17 for analysis of this FASB standard in relation to hedge accounting more generally.

The IASC also put in place a standard on accounting for financial instruments that is similar in many respects to that of the FASB, although it is developed in much less detail.[21]

TRANSLATION OF FOREIGN CURRENCY FINANCIAL STATEMENTS FOR CONSOLIDATION OR EQUITY ACCOUNTING PURPOSES

Many enterprises have investments in branches and subsidiaries that operate in foreign countries and prepare financial statements expressed in the foreign currencies. For purposes of preparing consolidated financial statements, it is necessary to "translate" those financial statements into the reporting currency of the parent. Likewise, when an entity has an investment position that gives it significant influence over a foreign company or when a entity is a participant in a joint venture operating abroad, it is necessary to translate the foreign currency statements of the investee for the purpose of performing equity accounting or proportionate consolidation in the financial statements of the investor. In each case, the translation procedure is governed by the same principles. For ease in explanation we shall concentrate on translation of the financial statements of subsidiary companies for incorporation in the consolidated financial statements of their parent. It should be understood that the same considerations apply to the translation of the financial statements of branches and investees.

Techniques for the translation of foreign currency financial statements developed over a long period of time without any very profound conceptual basis. It is clear that, from a parent company's point of view, operations abroad have risks not present in domestic operations. One risk is that of changes in the exchange rate for the currency of the country in which the subsidiary is situated. The questions pertinent to translation techniques are: (1) How should that risk exposure be measured? and (2) When should gains or losses from foreign exchange risks be considered realized?

In the turbulent state of the foreign exchange markets that developed after the collapse of the Bretton Woods system, the traditional bases for translation were seen to be inadequate. Today's accounting standards prescribe two different bases for translation to be applied in different circumstances—the temporal translation method and the current-rate translation method.

The Temporal Translation Method

The "temporal" approach to translation was developed in Accounting Research Study No. 12 published by the American Institute of Certified Public Accountants in 1972.[22] The study looked at the problems of translation very much from the perspective of the parent company. The logical translation method would be derived, it was argued, if one asked a simple question. What would the accounts show if (1) all the transactions of the foreign entity had been conducted by the parent company itself, (2) it had recorded them in its accounts in its domestic currency equivalent at each transaction date, and (3) it subsequently had modified carrying values of foreign currency assets and liabilities recorded following the rules of generally accepted accounting principles? The answer also was simple. Under generally accepted accounting principles some assets, such as inventory, fixed assets, or deferred charges, would be carried most of the time based on the historical cost established when they were acquired. For these, then, the appropriate translation rule was this: translate historical cost shown in foreign currency accounts at the historical exchange rate applicable at the transaction date. Other assets, such as accounts receivable in a foreign currency, would be carried under generally accepted accounting principles at realizable values at the financial reporting date. To express these at their equivalent realizable values in domestic currency, the current foreign exchange rate at the financial reporting date would be required.

From this the temporal principle was deduced. If an asset or liability is to be recorded under GAAP at historical cost, apply the historical exchange rate to its historical cost in foreign currency. If an asset or liability is to be recorded at a realizable value, apply the current exchange rate to its current value in foreign currency. The rule was to be applied rigorously. Thus, since the generally accepted accounting basis for inventory is lower of cost and market, the historical cost and current value, after translation into the domestic currency at the applicable exchange rate, should be compared to find the appropriate carrying value in the parent company's financial statements.

Under the approach as advocated, cash held by the foreign subsidiary was assumed always to be carried at current value and hence was to be translated at the current exchange rate. This thinking, however, was extended to all assets and liabilities denominated in foreign currency (that is, assets and liabilities customarily described as monetary). If the intention was not to change GAAP, this was an error. Generally accepted accounting principles do not require that monetary items such as long-term receivables or long-term bonds payable be carried at current fair value.

Two principal criticisms were made of the temporal method in the form in which it was implemented.

- Immediate recognition in income of the net gain or loss on translation of monetary items made net income reported very volatile under a floating rate exchange system. For example, if (1) short-term monetary assets and liabilities were in balance, (2) the long-term debt/equity ratio was one to one, and (3) the net income excluding foreign exchange translation adjustments represented 10% of shareholders' equity, a 5% movement in the foreign exchange rate from one fiscal period to the next could result in an increase or decrease in profit reported for shareholders by 50%. Research undertaken after the temporal method was adopted in the United States showed that some managements were engaging in costly transactions, so-called accounting hedges, to neutralize this accounting effect.[23] The many people who believed that the temporal method did not properly reflect a firm's exposure to foreign currency risk considered this uneconomic activity a particularly unfortunate result of the method.

- Many believed the method was often actually perverse in its accounting for the effects of foreign exchange movements. An illustration often cited was that of an American parent company with an investment in a self-contained German subsidiary. If monetary liabilities in the German subsidiary exceeded monetary assets, as was usually the case, a strengthening in the German mark vis-à-vis the American dollar would cause recognition of a loss on the net foreign currency debt exposure. Yet, since future earnings in German marks would now be more valuable in terms of American dollars, the real economic effect of the exchange rate change in most cases would be favourable. (It would not necessarily be favourable, however, if the German subsidiary exported much of its product and the strengthening of the mark left it less competitive in its markets.)

Such criticisms as these were so telling that the FASB standard relying on the temporal method had to be modified within a few years of its adoption. (A Canadian standard following and largely copying the U.S. standard had to be suspended even before it became effective.)

The Current-Rate Translation Method

The chief alternative proposed in the 1970s was the "current-rate" method. This method was widely used by British companies and some other multinational companies outside North America and was recommended (with modification in some situations) in a Canadian research study.[24] The method was simplicity itself. *Every* asset and liability item in the balance sheet of the foreign subsidiary would be translated at the year-end rate of exchange. Revenues and expenses recorded in the income statement were either translated at the same rate or at the average rate for the year (to approximate the rate prevailing at the transaction dates). The effect of the method was that a gain or loss would be shown in the translated accounts every time the exchange rate changed. The amount of gain or loss would be equal to the percentage change in the value of the foreign currency (in terms of the domestic currency) applied to the net reported assets of the foreign operation. The amount of such gain or loss for a year was included in income or, in British practice, was taken directly to retained earnings or treated as a capital transaction.

The focus of attention under the current-rate method was on the net investment in the subsidiary. To the parent, it was the net investment in the subsidiary that was at risk of changes in exchange rates, not just certain of the subsidiary's assets and liabilities. That overall risk, it was felt, could be properly portrayed by translating all assets and liabilities at the current exchange rate.

The current-rate method also had its critics.

- Many accountants did not like the idea that, in the parent company's statements, the same subsidiary nonmonetary asset would be shown at different amounts from one accounting period to the next. For example, a newly constructed building acquired by a foreign subsidiary and initially carried at $1 million in the parent company's statement would be stated at $1,100,000 the next year if the foreign currency appreciated by 10%. It was argued that this was fundamentally inconsistent with historical cost accounting.

- This characteristic of the current-rate method resulted, in extreme cases, in the "disappearing asset" phenomenon. In a foreign country with a high rate of inflation and consequently a rapidly declining exchange rate, use of the current-rate method rapidly reduced the carrying value, when translated into the parent company currency, of all assets held over a number of years. For example, if the foreign currency was weakening at the rate of 25% a year vis-à-vis that of the parent company, an investment in land by the subsidiary at a cost equivalent to $1 million in parent-company currency would be reduced to a carrying value of approximately $11,000 in the parent company's statements after twenty years. In fact, the land would not be diminishing in value if the revenues generated by it did not decline with the declining exchange rate but held their value in real Canadian dollar terms.

Clearly the current-rate method could also be inconsistent with economic reality. Where the temporal method assumed that the amount of foreign currency cash flows to be generated by nonmonetary assets would change so as to completely compensate for changes in the value of the currency, the current-rate method presumed that the amount of cash flows in foreign currency from nonmonetary assets would remain the same, no matter what changes occurred in the value of the foreign currency. In an economy suffering from rapid inflation, this latter assumption is clearly wrong.

The Canadian research study recognized this problem and suggested that the answer, where subsidiaries operated in a highly inflationary economy, would be to use price-level-adjusted accounts rather than historical cost accounts as the basic accounts for the subsidiary and translate them using the current-rate method.[25] This is the so-called "restate-translate" approach. The obvious difficulty lies in deciding where to draw the line between "highly" inflationary economies and economies with a more moderate rate of inflation.

The lesson that emerges from this discussion is that all inflexible rules for translation are likely to be in error at least some of the time. Ideally, what is required is a set of translation methods from which one method can be selected in each case to fit the real economic exposure of the consolidated entity to exchange risk of the entity whose financial statements are being translated. Consider the possible differences in circumstances of a German subsidiary of an American parent. If the subsidiary incurs all its costs in Germany and sells all its output in Germany with little competition from foreign suppliers, its business will be relatively unaffected by exchange rate movements. A weakening of the mark against the U.S. dollar would suggest that the investment in Germany will show lower returns in U.S. dollars. Suppose, instead, that the German subsidiary sold most of its output in the United States. With revenues in the stronger currency and costs in the weaker, the change in exchange rates would be highly beneficial to operating profits. Suppose, in the alternative, that the subsidiary sold most of its output in Italy in lira and that currency had weakened even more than the German mark. Then the subsidiary would be worse off even than it was in the first case.

This discussion far from exhausts the possible economic effects of exchange rate changes. One must also consider the cost performance of the subsidiary and its competitors. If, for example, the German subsidiary is competing with a Swedish company to sell its product in America and the Swedish costs have risen more slowly than the weakening of the krona against the U.S. dollar while German costs have risen faster than the rate of weakening of the mark, the loss in its competitive edge might well more than outweigh the apparent beneficial effect of the weakening of the mark against the dollar when viewed in isolation.

It seems that, in general, it will be hard to find a translation method that will regularly be consistent with the full economic impact of exchange rate movements. The reason is that the impact of movements in exchange rates between countries is interlinked with changes in exchange relationships with other countries and relative changes in prices in all countries concerned. This means there will be considerable ambiguity about the significance of "gains" and "losses" thrown up in translation of foreign currency statements, no matter what translation approach is utilized. Some writers believe that the problem of foreign currency translation cannot be solved without the adoption of current value accounting.[26] With current value accounting all assets and liabilities could be translated at current rates. Even this solution depends upon the current values reflected in the accounts being good estimators of future cash flows from the assets and liabilities, which will not always be the case.

The 1980s Standards for Foreign Currency Translation

As has been noted, a FASB standard put into effect in the mid-1970s (SFAS 8) and a Canadian standard, both based on exclusive adoption of the temporal method, failed to win support and acceptance. As a result, compromise standards were issued in both countries in the early 1980s (SFAS 52 in the U.S. and *CICA Handbook* Section 1650 in Canada). These standards attempted to be more responsive to differences in circumstances—adopting the current-rate method for one set of circumstances and the temporal method for other circumstances.[27]

The attempt was to base the choice of method on distinctions in the economic environment of the subsidiary. The FASB described the problem as one of determining the "functional currency" of the subsidiary, "the currency of the primary economic environment in which that entity operates." The CICA described it as distinguishing between "self-sustaining foreign operations," and "integrated foreign operations" by which is meant foreign operations whose exposure to exchange rate risk is similar to that of the parent company.

Considerable judgment is required in assigning foreign operations to one category or the other. The standards suggest these guidelines (see *CICA Handbook*, paragraph 1650.10):

- Sales prices of a self-sustaining foreign operation are responsive primarily to local conditions. They are not determined primarily by international prices or worldwide competition which would make them sensitive in the short run to exchange rate changes.

- A self-sustaining operation has an active local sales market and, to the extent it exports, its markets are primarily outside the parent company's country.

- The labour, material, and other costs of a self-sustaining operation are primarily local in origin rather than originating in the country of the parent company.

- Apart from the parent company's basic investment, financing of a self-sustaining operation is carried on primarily in its own currency and is capable of being serviced by its own operating cash flow.

- A self-sustaining operation has a low volume of intercompany transactions with its parent; neither is there any other extensive interrelationship of their operations.

- As a result of all these conditions, the cash flows of a self-sustaining entity are primarily not in the currency of the parent company and are insulated from the parent company on a day-to-day basis.

If these guidelines, taken together, do not indicate that a foreign operation should be considered to be self-sustaining, it is to be treated as an "integrated foreign operation"—that is, it is to be considered to be more in the nature of an extension of the parent company's own operations.

When a foreign operation is self-sustaining, only the parent's net investment is considered to be exposed to foreign exchange risks. Accordingly, the current-rate method of translation is to be used. Because of the ambiguous nature of the debit or credit arising on translation, however, it is considered best to exclude it from the income statement. Instead it is treated as a separate component of shareholders' equity.

Should the parent company sell or liquidate all or part of its investment in a self-sustaining foreign operation, a proportionate part of the translation adjustments accumulated in shareholders' equity would be transferred to income account and treated as part of the gain or loss recognized on disposition of the investment. (It would seem to follow in logic that, if the foreign subsidiary itself sold off its business operations and, say, reinvested its proceeds in securities, so that it was no longer a self-sustaining operation, the parent company should, in consolidation, transfer the accumulated deferred exchange gains and losses to income to be offset or grouped with the gain or loss on sale of its business operations shown by the subsidiary itself.) A reduction in the equity of the foreign operation as a result of dividends or other capital transactions is also to be accompanied by a transfer of a proportionate part of translation adjustments from shareholders' equity to income. (Under U.S. standards a transfer is made only when the investment is sold or liquidated.).[28] However, a write-down or a significant loss in the financial statements of a self-sustaining foreign operation would not by itself result in a reduction of the translation adjustment equity component.[29]

It may not normally make sense to hedge the exposure to foreign currency adjustments arising on translation using the current-rate method, since these may well not represent real economic gains or losses. However, there are situations in which it may be considered appropriate to arrange such a hedge (for example, a reporting enterprise may borrow in foreign funds to finance the net investment in a self-sustaining foreign operation). Accounting standards permit hedge accounting of self-sustaining operations where the general conditions with respect to identification and reasonable assurance as to effectiveness are met (see *CICA Handbook*, paragraph 1650.55). The gain or loss on the hedge would offset the adjustment from translation treated as a component of shareholders' equity.

As already described, the current-rate method of translation becomes unsatisfactory when a high rate of inflation in the foreign environment causes a rapid weakening in the exchange value of its currency. The *CICA Handbook* has followed the FASB lead in requiring that the temporal method be used in place of the current-rate method for self-sustaining operations in economies where the inflation rate is high relative to that in the economy of the parent company. It may be argued that the restate-translate approach, which adjusts the foreign operations accounts for the general purchasing power effects of inflation prior to translation, is the conceptually appropriate approach in these circumstances. It has been rejected by the CICA and FASB primarily because the reflection of general purchasing power adjustments does not accord with Canadian and U.S. GAAP—and the temporal method is seen to be an effective compromise in that it avoids the "disappearing assets" problem resulting from applying the current rate method under hyper-inflationary conditions (since the temporal method applies the historical exchange rate to all nonmonetary assets carried on a cost basis).[30] No specific guidance is given in the CICA standard as to the difference in inflation rates that would be considered high. The FASB suggests that the temporal method be used in place of the current-rate method when the cumulative inflation rate in the foreign economy (*not* the excess of the foreign inflation rate over that in the country of the parent) reaches approximately 100% over a three-year period.

The IASC has opted for a "restate-translate" approach for a foreign operation reporting in the currency of a hyper-inflationary economy. It requires that the primary financial statements of any enterprise reporting in the currency of a hyper-inflationary economy be restated for changes in the general purchasing power of the reporting currency. A parent company would then translate the accounts of such a foreign operation on the temporal or current-rate basis depending on whether it is an integrated or self-sustaining foreign operation.[31]

The temporal method of translation is to be used for integrated foreign operations as well as for self-sustaining operations in highly inflationary economies. Canadian practice has introduced one variation from the approach described earlier. Previously it was stated that all gains and losses on translation under the temporal method are recorded in income as they occur. To be consistent with its treatment of long-term foreign currency monetary items of a domestic enterprise, the *CICA Handbook* directs that gains and losses on translation of long-term monetary assets and liabilities of integrated foreign operations also be deferred and amortized over their remaining terms.

Other Issues

Certain countries have a variety of foreign currency controls and also may have a variety of official exchange rates at which businesses may acquire or sell foreign currencies arising from foreign operations. Unofficial or free market rates may also be in existence. Where this situation exists, any translations required to be made at the current rate encounter the problem of choosing which current rate is appropriate. The FASB suggests that, except in unusual circumstances, the rate selected should be that which would be available upon remittance of dividends to the parent company.[32]

Throughout most of the literature and throughout this discussion it has been assumed that an actual exchange rate—whether historical or current—must be used for translation. Some writers have suggested that this results from a fixation with currency and currency movements as though all the assets of a subsidiary were going to be returned to the parent company in the form of currency sooner or later. The fact is, to the contrary, that physical resources of the subsidiary are, in general, not going to be liquidated and the proceeds remitted but rather are going to be replaced. It has been suggested that actual current exchange rates may not be appropriate for measuring and translating the physical resources of the foreign operation because of the many erratic short-term influences upon them. These ideas have not received any very extensive exploration and development, however.[33]

DISCLOSURES

To the present, disclosures by Canadian companies of foreign currency transactions, balance sheet risk exposures and income effects have been sketchy and incomplete, rarely going beyond the following inadequate *CICA Handbook* requirements:

- The currency in which long-term debt is payable where it is payable in other than the reporting currency (paragraph 3210.06).
- The method of amortizing deferred gains and losses on long-term monetary items (paragraph 1650.23).
- Cumulative gains and losses arising from the translation of self-sustaining foreign operations presented as a separate component of shareholders' equity, and the significant elements giving rise to changes in the cumulative amount in the reporting period (paragraphs 1650.36 and .39).
- Reasons for any significant changes in translation methods for foreign operations (paragraph 1650.43).
- The translation adjustment in the cash flow statement for the effect of exchange rate changes during the reporting period on the opening cash equivalents balance and net changes in cash equivalents in the period (paragraph 1650.69).

Disclosure of the amount of exchange gains and losses included in income in the reporting period is indicated to be "desirable" (paragraph 1650.44), but it is provided by only a minority of companies with foreign currency transactions and risk positions.

Clearly one must have more information than is contained in the above disclosures to be in a position to fully understand an enterprise's balance sheet exposure to foreign currency risks and the impact of these risk positions and transactions on income and cash flows. The inadequacy of disclosure standards relating to this and other financial risks has become very evident in recent years. Chapter 17 has included an overview of developments in disclosure standards with respect to financial instruments generally. A more recent *CICA Handbook* section calls for expanded information about financial instruments, and its requirements for disclosure of the contractual terms and conditions of financial instruments and hedges of antic- ipated transactions (including the amount of any deferred or unrecognized gain or loss result- ing from such hedges) apply to financial instruments denominated in foreign currencies.[34]

The 1996 CICA re-exposure draft proposed requiring disclosure of the income impact of foreign currency gains and losses and the net amounts of unrealized exchange gains and losses on long-term monetary items and other deferred gains and losses.[35]

SUMMARY

The fact that an enterprise may conduct business in more than one currency results in sev- eral problems for accounting. First, when a significant proportion of the enterprise transac- tions is conducted in one or more currencies other than that of its country of domicile, the question is raised as to what currency the enterprise should adopt as a basis of expression in its financial statements. Once that is decided, it is necessary to consider how to account for transactions that are denominated in currencies other than the reporting currency and how to report gains and losses resulting from movements in exchange rates. Finally, when an entity has an investment in a branch, subsidiary, joint venture, or other investee over which it has significant influence and those entities report in a foreign currency, it is necessary to have a standard method for translating the statements of the other entities for the purpose of consolidation accounting, proportionate consolidation, or equity accounting.

The choice of reporting currency is only occasionally difficult. Important considera- tions are: In what currency is most business done? What currency will be familiar to users of the financial statements? What is the relative stability of the various currencies that seem to be possible contenders? These indicators need not point in the same direction, so that the choice among them ultimately comes down to a matter of judgment.

Numerous questions arise relating to accounting for transactions denominated in a for- eign currency. The general principles adopted to guide practice are set out below.

- A transaction denominated in a foreign currency is translated at the spot rate when first recognized in the accounts. This approach is generally satisfactory, but can be criticized when it is applied to transactions resulting from commitments made at a significantly ear- lier date. Once a commitment expressed in a foreign currency is made, an enterprise may be at risk of exchange rate movements from that date. That risk can be minimized by entering into a forward exchange contract or some other type of hedging instrument. In any event, it is strongly arguable that the change in the commitment price as a result of the exchange rate change over the period of the commitment ought to be reported as a gain or loss on foreign exchange, not as an adjustment of the cost reported in the ulti- mate purchase transaction or the revenue proceeds reported from the sale that was the sub- ject of the commitment.

- The carrying value of monetary assets and liabilities expressed in a foreign currency are continuously updated after their first recognition to their equivalent amount at report- ing-date exchange rates. The resulting adjustment is written off to income as a gain or loss on foreign exchange in the United States except that it may be initially classified in "other comprehensive income" in respect of qualifying hedges of forecasted future transactions. In Canada, an exception is made for gain or loss on long-term monetary assets and liabilities that have an ascertainable life, which is to be deferred and amortized over the remaining life of the asset or liability. This exception is open to serious criticism on both theoretical and practical grounds. It is evident that it is not sustainable in the modern world; in 1996 the CICA proposed to eliminate it, but the old standard remains in place.

- The foreign exchange risk with respect to a foreign currency contract—a forward, futures, option, or swap contract—also carries risk with respect to movements in the exchange rate. If the effect of foreign exchange movements on obligations under such a contract is in the opposite direction (i.e., favourable or adverse) to the effect of foreign exchange risk on an existing asset, liability, or commitment, the two positions are said to be hedged. If a foreign currency contract is not hedged, it is speculative in character. That speculative character should be recognized by continuously valuing the effect of exchange rate changes on the contract and recording an asset or liability as a result of that valuation, carrying the adjustment to income as gain or loss on foreign exchange.

- When a foreign currency contract hedges a foreign currency monetary asset or liability, the same accounting as just described for a speculative contract has the appropriate effect. When both positions are continuously revalued at current exchange rates, and value adjustments are recognized in income, the adjustments to income will offset each other to the extent that the hedge is fully effective. If it is not fully effective, the net adjustment will properly show as gain or loss on the exposed risk.

- When one or both sides of a balanced hedge position are not recognized as an asset or liability in the balance sheet, the question arises how to recognize the effect of exchange rate changes. It is not the practice (unfortunately) to recognize a change in the value of a commitment in a foreign currency as an asset or liability and carry the adjustment to income. Accordingly, if a foreign currency contract, or some other position, hedges a commitment, the accepted practice in Canada is to defer the foreign exchange gain or loss recognized on the hedging position. Because of the deferment of recognition of gain or loss in this situation, it is important that there be assurance that an effective hedge really exists. A new FASB standard calls for "fair value hedge accounting" (under which the hedged position is translated at current exchange rates with gains or losses recognized in income) in these situations, if certain qualifying conditions are met.

- The *CICA Handbook* contains ill-thought-through recommendations with respect to treatment of nonmonetary assets and future revenue streams as hedges of positions exposed to foreign currency risk. A strong case can be made that their treatment as hedges distorts reporting of future profit on sale of the nonmonetary asset or future revenues. The accounting is also open to manipulation to avoid current recognition of foreign exchange loss. A new FASB standard no longer permits deferral of gains and losses on hedging instruments in these situations, but does permit classification of gains and losses on qualifying hedges of forecasted future transactions outside regular income, to be transferred to income when the hedged transaction is reflected in income.

A third area of difficulty caused by business done in a foreign currency is that of translation of the statements of a subsidiary, branch or investee that are maintained in a foreign currency. Two approaches to translation on consolidation are: the temporal approach and the current-rate approach. Consolidation by the use of either method will result in net debits or credits appearing upon translation whose significance can be hard to interpret in particular circumstances. If the translation method were ideal, any such net debit or credit would represent a real economic loss or gain from movements in the exchange rates attributable to the exposure to currency risk of the subsidiary or investee. It is very doubtful, however, that any method of translation could be devised to measure these economic effects accurately in every situation. Certainly, it can easily be shown that both the temporal and current-rate methods are unrealistic in given situations.

Accounting standards have attempted to reach a compromise that will be broadly satisfactory, even though far from perfect. The basic idea is that, if a foreign operation is relatively self-contained, the exchange risk of the parent company does not pertain to the individual assets and liabilities of the subsidiary but rather to the fact that the future cash flows from the subsidiary available for dividends or further investment will be in the foreign currency. Application of the current-rate method to translate all the assets and liabilities reported by the subsidiary ensures that, if the foreign currency weakens vis-à-vis that of the parent, there will be a debit adjustment on translation and vice versa (assuming the parent has some positive equity in the subsidiary). In view of the fact that there is no assurance that a debit adjustment is a real loss or a credit adjustment a real gain, these translation adjustments are not reported as gains or losses in consolidated income but rather are accumulated as a separate component of shareholders' equity.

Where a foreign currency is rapidly weakening because of inflationary pressures, the current-rate method, in effect, writes down every asset and liability. This is unrealistic with respect to nonmonetary assets held for a significant period of time (such as plant) because increased prices in the foreign currency will usually maintain the real value of the asset or at least slow its loss. Accordingly, the temporal method is to be substituted for the current-rate method for translation of all self-sustaining operations in highly inflationary economies.

The theory underlying the temporal method, however, has nothing to do with inflation. The method takes the perspective of the parent company and seeks to achieve the same result through translation as would occur if the parent company conducted all the transactions abroad itself, rather than through a foreign subsidiary. Thus, nonmonetary assets and liabilities of the foreign operation are translated at the historical exchange rate applicable when the assets were acquired or liabilities incurred (unless it is necessary to record them at market values, in which case current-rate translation of their foreign market value would be required). Monetary assets and liabilities are translated at current rates just like monetary assets and liabilities of the parent company itself that are denominated in a foreign currency. The adjustments arising from such translations at current rates on short-term monetary assets and liabilities are taken directly to income and on long-term items are deferred and amortized. If the assets and liabilities of the foreign operation are hedged, however, the treatment of exchange adjustments would be consistent with that described above for hedges of foreign currency transactions by a domestic company.

REFERENCES

[1]   The 1998 CICA survey of annual reports of 200 Canadian public companies reports that the 1997 financial statements of 28 companies were expressed in U.S. dollars (23 in 1996). A number of these companies explained that a substantial proportion of their assets, liabilities and earnings are located or originate in the U.S. or that the U.S. dollar is the principal currency in which business is conducted. See CICA, *Financial Reporting in Canada 1998*, 23rd ed. (Toronto: CICA, 1998), p. 5.

2   A CICA re-exposure draft, *Foreign Currency Translation* (Toronto: CICA, 1996), par .003(b) proposed some general factors to be considered in selecting the "measurement currency" for a reporting enterprise.

3   CICA, Emerging Issues Committee, *Changes in Reporting Currency*, EIC 11 (Toronto: CICA, 1990).

4   Here it is assumed that the company is exposed to foreign currency risk upon entering into the purchase commitment. This will not always be the case. For example, suppose the Canadian company was committed to purchase an item denominated in, say, U.S. dollars and that the fair value of the item varies directly with changes in the U.S./Canadian dollar exchange rate. In this case the company would not be exposed to foreign currency risk on the commitment. If the U.S. dollar goes up against the Canadian dollar, the company will have to pay more for the item in Canadian dollars, but this would be compensated for because the fair value of the item would have increased commensurately. Thus, one must carefully assess the effect of foreign currency changes on the *net* commitment, and this may be difficult to assess in some situations. As will be seen, this is a very important issue because defining what constitutes existing risk exposures is central to determining when hedge accounting may be considered appropriate.

5   CICA, "Foreign Currency Translation," *CICA Handbook*, Section 1650 (Toronto: CICA), pars. .16 and .18.

6   CICA, Emerging Issues Committee, *Accounting for Dual Currency Bonds*, EIC 82 (Toronto: CICA, 1997).

7   IASC, *The Effects of Changes in Foreign Exchange Rates*, IAS 21 (London: IASC, revised 1993).

8   Office of the Chief Accountant of the Ontario Securities Commission, *Study of Differences Between Canadian and United States Generally Accepted Accounting Principles* (Toronto: Ontario Securities Commission, 1993).

9   The CICA Emerging Issues Committee dealt with general issues relating to *Short-Term Foreign Currency Obligations Under Long-Term Debt Facilities*, EIC 16 (Toronto: CICA, 1990). The abstract holds that, for such debt to be considered to have an ascertainable life beyond the end of the current year, there must be a "committed facility" with a scheduled maturity that the lender cannot unilaterally cancel unless the borrower has violated the terms of the facility.

10   See P.D. Jackson and M.B. Meagher, "The New Foreign Currency Recommendations," *CA Magazine*, December 1978, pp. 46–53.

11   See discussion of this issue at CICA, *Foreign Currency Translation Issues*, A Research Report (Toronto: CICA, 1989), pp. 19–20. It documents the wide range of flexibility and views on the issues.

12   The Emerging Issues Committee has concluded that, at least in respect of short-term foreign currency obligations under long-term facilities, a change in currency constitutes a settlement with consequent immediate recognition in income of any unrecognized foreign currency gains and losses. See EIC 16 (Toronto: CICA, 1990).

13   CICA, *Foreign Currency Translation Issues*, chap. 2.

[14] CICA, *Foreign Currency Translation*, Exposure Draft (Toronto: CICA, 1993); and CICA, *Foreign Currency Translation*, Re-exposure Draft (Toronto: CICA, 1996).

[15] See CICA, Emerging Issues Committee, *Mid-Term Hedging of a Long-Term Foreign Currency Denominated Monetary Item*, EIC 3 (Toronto: CICA, 1989).

[16] *CICA Handbook*, Section 1650, par. 50. This paragraph states only that, if a foreign currency contract, asset, liability or future revenue stream is to be regarded as a hedge, "it should be identified as a hedge of the item(s) to which it relates." The task force on foreign currency translation issues found the term "identify" ambiguous and recommended that it be replaced with an explicit, documented designation of a hedge with clearer implications that hedge accounting can only be applied prospectively from the date of designation. See CICA, *Foreign Currency Translation Issues*, pp. 66–67.

[17] CICA, *Foreign Currency Translation*, Re-exposure Draft (Toronto: CICA, 1996), par .018.

[18] CICA, *Foreign Currency Translation Issues*, chap. 3.

[19] CICA, *Foreign Currency Translation*, Re-exposure Draft, (Toronto: CICA, 1996). See in particular, par .028 which proposes the need to set aside funds from designated revenue streams to be able to demonstrate that the cash flows will match those of the existing debt in timing and amount.

[20] FASB, *Accounting for Derivative Instruments and Hedging Activities*, Statement of Financial Accounting Standards No. 133 (Norwalk: FASB, 1998).

[21] IASC, *Financial Instruments: Recognition and Measurement*, IAS 39 (London: IASC, 1998).

[22] L. Lorensen, *Reporting Foreign Operations of U.S. Companies in U.S. Dollars*, Accounting Research Study No. 12 (New York: AICPA, 1972).

[23] See T.G. Evans, W.R. Folks, and M. Jilling, *The Impact of Statement of Financial Accounting Standards No. 8 on the Foreign Exchange Risk Management Practices of American Multinationals: An Economic Impact Study* (Stamford: FASB, 1978).

[24] R.M. Parkinson, *Translation of Foreign Currencies* (Toronto: CICA, 1972).

[25] Ibid., chap. 10.

[26] See, for example, W. H. Beaver and M.A. Wolfson, "Foreign Currency Translation and Changing Prices in Perfect and Complete Markets," *Journal of Accounting Research*, Autumn 1982, Part II, pp. 528–50. The authors developed a formal analysis of the properties of the major foreign currency translation methods under assumptions of perfect and complete markets and perfect purchasing power parity between countries. Based on these assumptions they concluded that only comprehensive market value accounting with translation at current rates of exchange can possess both economic interpretability and symmetry. Elitzur attempted to extend this analysis to draw conclusions as to the "distortions" of accounting results rendered by the current rate and temporal methods under certain conditions of imperfect purchasing power parity. See R.R. Elitzur, "A Model of Translation of Foreign Financial Statements Under Inflation in the United States and Canada," *Contemporary Accounting Research*, Spring 1991, pp. 466–84.

[27] See D.W. Collins and W.K. Salatka, "Noisy Accounting Earnings Signals and Earnings Response Coefficients: The Case of Foreign Currency Accounting," *Contemporary*

Accounting Research, Fall 1993, pp. 119–59. The authors provide evidence that suggests that earnings reported under SFAS 52 may have been perceived by capital markets to be of higher quality than those produced by SFAS 8. However, the evidence is open to alternative explanations, and difficulties of research design—see discussant comments by J.L. Kao, pp. 161–66, and P.A. Griffin, pp. 167–78. Some other studies have found no significant differences in capital market price responses as between SFAS 8 and SFAS 52. See B.S. Soo and L.G. Soo, "Accounting for the Multinational Firm: Is the Translation Process Valued by the Stock Market?" *The Accounting Review*, October 1994, pp. 617–37.

28 The CICA 1996 re-exposure draft proposed to eliminate this difference. See CICA, *Foreign Currency Translation*, Re-exposure Draft, p. 2 and par .063.

29 See CICA, Emerging Issues Committee, *Reductions in the Net Investment in Self-Sustaining Foreign Operations*, EIC 26 (Toronto: CICA, 1991).

30 See explanation in FASB, *Foreign Currency Translation*, Statement of Financial Accounting Standards No. 52 (Stamford: FASB, 1981), pars. 106–107.

31 See IASC, *Financial Reporting in Hyperinflationary Economies*, IAS 29 (London: IASC, 1989 (reformatted in 1994)); and IASC, *The Effects of Changes in Foreign Exchange Rates*, IAS 21 (London: IASC, revised 1993).

32 FASB, *Foreign Currency Translation*, par. 27b.

33 See G.M. Scott, "Currency Exchange Rates and Accounting Translation: A Mismarriage?" *Abacus*, June 1975, pp. 58–70. Scott suggested several possible substitutes for actual exchange rates in a position paper presented at the FASB public hearings in December 1980 and urged further extensive research. One of these possibilities was advocated in D.H. Patz, "A Price Parity Theory of Translation," *Accounting and Business Research*, Winter 1977, pp. 14–24. The winter 1978 issue of the same journal contained rigorous criticism of Patz's ideas in J. Flower, "A Price Parity Theory of Translation: A Comment," pp. 64–65, and F.L. Clarke, "Patz on Parities, Exchange Rates and Translation," pp. 73–77. It also contained a lengthy reply by Patz to Flower's comment—"A Price Parity Theory of Translation: A Reply," pp. 66–72.

34 See CICA, "Financial Instruments—Disclosure and Presentation," *CICA Handbook*, Section 3860 (Toronto: CICA), pars. .52 and .92.

35 CICA, *Foreign Currency Translation*, Re-exposure Draft, pars. .100–.113.

CASH FLOW STATEMENTS

There are two, and only two, basic kinds of financial statements. There are statements reporting stocks of resources and claims upon them at a single point in time (such as a balance sheet). There are also statements reporting flows of resources, designed to explain changes in the amounts of net resources held between two dates. The income statement is a flow statement. It explains increases in resources and consumption of resources associated with the earnings activities of the entity.

The income statement, however, does not tell the whole story about resource flows. First, it deals only with those resource flows that are part of earnings activity. It does not report changes in resources and claims resulting from investment and borrowing or raising capital. Second, it deals with resource flows in general. It does not distinguish flows affecting the liquidity of a business. It does not distinguish, for example, between an expense consisting of consumption of cash and an expense consisting of the consumption of serviceability of capital assets. Thus, there is room for statements of resource flows other than the income statement. A financial statement focusing on changes in the liquid resources of an entity has a long tradition. The objectives of that statement have not always been clear, however, and there can be several variations in its form.

In the first part of this chapter we discuss the variety possible in statements of resource flows, and how thinking has evolved and standards developed. In so doing we identify and consider a number of presentation issues and technical problems. In the second part we discuss the proposals of some accounting thinkers for changing the present make-up of financial reports to make a cash flow statement the principal financial statement.

THE POSSIBLE VARIETY IN STATEMENTS OF RESOURCE FLOWS—AND THE EVOLUTION OF ACCOUNTING STANDARDS

Business is undertaken with the objective of making a return. The income statement is designed to measure the entity's success in doing so. But income, measured in accordance with accrual accounting principles, may not be accompanied by a corresponding net inflow of cash. For example, consider a manufacturer of complicated equipment, each unit of which costs $50,000 in out-of-pocket costs. If that equipment can be sold for $100,000 a unit, one might think, correctly, that the business is profitable. But, if the customary practice is to sell the equipment for only $10,000 down, with the remainder payable over ten years with interest, the entity will have paid out $40,000 more than it receives at time of sale for each unit. In the long run, the cash will be more than recouped. But in the short run, especially if sales are brisk, the entity has an ever-increasing need for cash and, if financing is not available, may become insolvent even though it is basically a sound business.

This is only one example among many possible causes of financial difficulty. A business may become unable to meet its debts as they fall due because it overexpands in relation to its capital base, because it assumes heavy fixed operating costs in a venture whose revenues are volatile, or because it invests in illiquid assets with only short-term financing, trusting to refinance the debt as it falls due. The moral is simple: It is not enough to be profitable; one must be solvent as well.

Objectives of Statements of Changes in Liquid Resources

Some of the objectives put forth for statements of changes in liquid resources are described briefly below.

- In the ultimate, the value of a business to an investor depends upon its ability to generate cash. Some think that an explanation of past cash or near cash flows, especially for a series of years, will be useful as a basis for predicting future cash flows. There is a source of possible confusion in this. Cash flows are irregular in their incidence over the lifetime of an enterprise. The purpose of accrual accounting in the measurement of income is precisely to eliminate confusion caused by these irregularities—to assign revenues and expenses to the period giving rise to them rather than the period when the cash flow occurs. Why then is it desired to get back to actual cash flows?

   One explanation lies in the possibility that prediction of future cash flows may best be made by a two-stage process. Past years' reported incomes, because they are determined by an orderly process, may form a good basis (along with other information) for predicting future years' incomes. Then a separate prediction can be made of future years' cash flows based upon analysis and projection of items that reconcile income and cash flows.

- A second explanation is that a comparison of funds flows from operations with the income reported for a year provides information about what is called "the quality of earnings." The simple thought is that if operations are producing a significant flow of liquid resources in relation to the income reported, there is less risk than when income reported is accompanied by very little current flow of usable funds. The explanation is related to the fact that some people mistrust accrual accounting. They feel that it is too flexible in its assumptions and requires too much judgment in its application to be reliable. Hard cash data are deemed less subject to errors in judgment and arbitrary procedures.

- A more obvious use of funds flow information is to assist in assessing the debt-paying capacity or solvency of an enterprise. Such an assessment requires information both from the financial position statement and a statement showing operating funds flows. The future cash requirements to meet existing liabilities and required future investment must be compared with projected realizations of existing resources and projected funds from operations within the forecast time frame. In tight situations, funds flow from operations may require prediction on a month-to-month or even day-to-day basis.

- Funds flow information is also one element in a somewhat broader assessment—that of financial flexibility. A firm may be able to pay its debts as they fall due but have little left over to expand or take advantage of opportunities to move in new directions. Financial flexibility comes not only from cash generated by the existing business and the ability to realize upon existing assets without disrupting the business, but also from the ability to raise new financing. Since the greater the amount of assets available to provide security the easier it will be to come by new financing, it is arguable that a somewhat broader definition of funds from operations than straight cash is appropriate for this purpose. Information as to unused lines of credit could also be pertinent.

This discussion of objectives suggests that a funds statements may need to be designed to perform more than a single function. The idea developed that the significance of the statement would be clearer if it distinguished three activities: investment activities, financing activities, and the effect on funds of operating activities. That solution still leaves open the nagging question of what is the most useful definition of funds. As well, it gives rise to some significant classification issues. Why should it be considered, for example, that a purchase of capital assets is an investing activity while purchase of inventory is an operating activity? These questions will be discussed subsequently.

Evolving Concepts and Standards

Statements of funds flows have undergone some significant changes in thinking over the years. These changes have involved the following issues:

- The definition of funds (e.g., whether working capital, net monetary assets, cash, or cash and cash equivalents) should be the measure of liquidity that is the basis of these statements.

- Whether such statements should endeavor to present all significant changes in financial position or only those that directly affect the chosen definition of funds.

- The format of the statement and the basis of classification within it.

- The direct versus indirect presentation of funds from operations.

We will examine each of these issues, and indicate how thinking has evolved and the issues addressed in a progression of accounting standards.

In Canada, the original *CICA Handbook* Section 1540, (entitled "Statement of Source and Application of Funds") was revised and expanded in 1974 (and renamed the "Statement of Changes in Financial Position"), again in 1985, and most recently in 1998 (when the title was changed to "Cash Flow Statements"). The 1998 revision did not initiate fundamental changes in objectives or approach, but rather expanded and clarified some matters, and it eliminated certain alternatives and some differences with current IASC and FASB standards (while creating a few additional differences). As will be seen, the Canadian standard is now consistent in most substantial respects with those of the IASC and FASB.[1]

The Definition of Funds

Early desires for a statement of flows of cash or near-cash resources were, no doubt, greatly influenced by the need for a solvency perspective. The actual format of such "funds" statements, as their use became more widespread, tended to be geared to explain changes in working capital, rather than some more narrowly defined group of liquid resources. In part this may have been because bankers relied heavily upon working capital and working capital ratios in assessing creditworthiness of prospective borrowers. Thus it was logical to account for changes in the resources that the bankers were looking at. In part, also, it may have been because it was easier to construct a statement using working capital as the definition of funds than it was to construct one focusing on movements in cash alone. The preparation of a statement of changes in working capital was taught in influential accounting texts from early in the twentieth century.

Provided all the elements of working capital will be turned into cash within a short period, it may serve as a satisfactory indication of liquidity and may provide a more stable basis for prediction than other measures of funds. It has, however, fallen into disfavour and it is open to criticism for several significant reasons. First, the inclusion of short-term borrowing under the conventional definition of current liabilities means that such borrowing does not appear as a financing activity—a suppression of information that some consider important. Second, inventory and prepayments are different in kind from other current assets. They do not represent cash or claims to cash; they represent outlays made with the hope of recoupment of their value. In a crisis there is considerably less assurance that they can be liquidated quickly for something near carrying value. Third, the inclusion of monetary assets and inventories in the definition means that under inflationary conditions the funds statement will conceal the squeeze on cash that may be extracted from operations. If prices are generally rising, the dollar amount of each of accounts receivable, accounts payable and inventory are likely to increase over a period of a year even though the volume of business done remains constant. As a result, much of the earnings shown by the historical cost accounting system may be represented by the net increase in investment in these resources, and not by cash available for distribution. A more narrow definition of funds would show this; the broader working capital definition would not.

Finally, because of differences in accounting conventions, the comparability of funds flow figures between companies is reduced if this definition is used. For example, apparent funds flow for a period may be very different depending upon whether inventory is costed on a direct-costing or absorption-costing basis, or whether the FIFO or LIFO convention is used. Many people are attracted to the funds statement precisely because it need not be contaminated by the flexibility in accepted accounting principles. Achievement of that objective, however, requires that the definition of funds include only items that are measured on a consistent, unambiguous basis.

Some have advocated defining "funds" as net short-term monetary assets. This definition would mitigate some of the problems of working capital while reducing some erratic effects of irregularities in straight cash flow, including irregularities possible as a result of a deliberate delay in making payments of accounts payable. Its usefulness depends on an assumption that accounts receivable and payable will be liquidated over a short period. Accordingly, longer-term accounts—say in excess of 30 or 60 day terms—would be excluded. However, under conditions of economic stress, sales may be made to less creditworthy customers and it may be more difficult to collect them in full on a current basis. In other words, the inclusion of short-term monetary assets that cannot be readily converted into known amounts of cash may serve to mask a real deterioration in a business' liquidity.

Over the years a trend developed to present statements of changes in financial position that focus on cash or near cash. CICA, FASB and IASC standards have all adopted "cash and cash equivalents" as the concept of funds to be reported. The FASB standard reasons in support of this definition that cash flow effects are the focus of decisions of investors, creditors and others, but "... whether cash is on hand, on deposit, or invested in a short-term investment that is readily convertible into a known amount of cash is largely irrelevant to users' assessments of liquidity and future cash flows" (SFAS 95, paragraph 51).

The 1998 CICA standard tightened up its definition to be consistent with those of the FASB and IASC. It defines "cash equivalents" as "short-term, highly liquid investments that are readily convertible to known amounts of cash and which are subject to an insignificant risk of changes in value" (paragraph 1540.06). Equity investments are explicitly excluded (paragraph 1540.08). (While publicly traded equity investments may be highly liquid, their values are subject to risk of changes in market prices.) To qualify as a cash equivalent, an investment must have a short maturity, not exceeding three months.

But an enterprise still has considerable flexibility within this definition. It can elect to classify some or all investments qualifying as "cash equivalents" as trading or other investments rather than as cash equivalents (see paragraph 1540.09). Also, there is room for judgment in assessing whether bank borrowings payable on demand, for example bank overdrafts, should be treated as cash equivalents (see paragraph 1540.10). As well, the CICA standard excludes "cash subject to restrictions that prevent its use for current purposes" citing as an example compensating balances required in accordance with lending arrangements (paragraph 1540.07). It then goes on to try to distinguish situations in which cash or equivalents may be available for current purposes but on a restricted basis (paragraph 1540.52). Clearly, this is open to interpretation.

Since there is flexibility in the concept of "cash equivalents," it is highly desirable that financial statement preparers give careful consideration to the interpretation that is most suitable to their circumstances. Disclosure is required of the components and policy for determining the components (paragraphs 1540.48 and .49).

Nonfund Transactions

A funds statement that fails to report financing and investing transactions that do not involve a source or use of the defined fund resource (be it working capital, net monetary assets or cash equivalents) is considered unfortunate by some accountants. The result is that changes over a period in balance sheet figures for long-term assets and liabilities would not always be fully explained. Moreover, it could be deemed to be misleading, since a purchase of capital assets in consideration for direct assumption of debt, for example, is hardly different in economic effect from a purchase of capital assets for cash coupled with a replenishment of cash by borrowing. Other examples of noncash investing and financing transactions include converting debt to equity, obtaining an asset by entering into a capital lease, and exchanging noncash assets or liabilities for other noncash assets or liabilities.

A sentiment grew up in favour of including a report of all investing and financing activities in the statement, not just those that had an immediate impact on funds. This was accomplished by treating such transactions as though they involved a simultaneous source and use of funds. Thus a purchase of capital assets financed by a long-term liability could be treated as a deemed use and source of funds.

Under this total resource perspective it was considered more descriptive to entitle the statement "Statement of Changes in Financial Position" rather than "Statement of Funds." In the United States, the stated purpose of the predecessor to SFAS 95 (APB Opinion 19) was to explain all significant changes in financial position regardless of whether they directly affected cash or working capital.[2] SFAS 95 reversed this position. It holds that including noncash transactions in the body of a statement of cash flows would unduly complicate the statement and detract from its purpose of providing information about an enterprise's cash receipts and payments. SFAS 95 does, however, require separate disclosure of information about the effects of noncash investing and financing transactions that affect an enterprise's financial position.[3] The 1985 *CICA Handbook* standard did not rule out inclusion of noncash transactions in the statement itself, but it did require separate disclosure of their investing and financing aspects indicating the nature of their relationship. The 1998 CICA standard adopted the U.S. position (paragraphs 1540.46 – 1540.47).

Format and Classification Issues

At one time the most common format for a statement of changes in liquid resources was one divided into two categories—sources of financial resources and uses of financial resources. Under this structure the focus of interest—the bottom line—was on the net change in liquid funds (however they were defined). This simple split does not provide for any classification of funds flows by their nature or type of activity. The idea began to take hold that the statement would have increased information value if it distinguished operating, investing and financing activities.[4] This three-way classification would then reflect the three basic financial decision areas of a business. CICA, FASB and IASC standards have all adopted this classification. While the general nature of operating, investing and financing activities may be reasonably clear, significant areas of ambiguity become apparent when one attempts to apply the classification scheme.

One of the most troublesome sources of confusion has been the difficulty in interpreting what is meant by "operating." In previous practice it was customary to calculate funds from operations as being funds resulting from all transactions other than those that involved noncurrent borrowing or the acquisition of noncurrent assets. Compare this with some other concepts of the term "operating." In the classification of accountable events in Chapter 5, a distinction was made between purchases and sales occurring in the conduct of the principal business carried on (called operating transactions) and passive investment transactions or financing activities. Under this definition, the purchase of a capital asset required for the business carried on would be an operating transaction just like the purchase of inventory. On the other hand, receipt of income from investments would be an investment transaction, and payment of interest on borrowing would be a financing transaction.

The 1985 CICA standard stated that "... some may prefer to classify certain items, such as regular replacements of fixed assets, as an operating activity rather than an investing activity."[5] Nothing was said directly about interest receipts and interest payments, although it could be inferred that they were not regarded as investing and financing activities. As to dividends paid, it said: "With regard to payment of dividends, while some view this as a financing activity, others view it as a normal part of operating activities; still others may prefer to classify dividends separately."[6] It would appear then that "as you like it" was the order of the day.

The 1998 CICA standard is more specific, and is now generally consistent with SFAS 95. Operating activities are defined as the "principal revenue-generating activities of the enterprise" (paragraph 1540.06), and are presumed to include the cash effects of events and transactions entering into the determination of income (paragraph 1540.16). In cases of doubt operating activities is considered the residual category to include generally all cash flows that do not specifically fall into the investing or financing classes. Investing activities are considered to include making and collecting loans, and acquiring and disposing of debt and equity investments and capital assets. Financing activities include borrowing and repaying debt and obtaining and redeeming capital of owners.

Following is a discussion of certain of the more significant areas of classification difficulty.[7]

- As noted above, the purchase and sale of both inventories and plant and equipment could be considered either operating or investing activities. The description of investment activities as "expenditures ... made for resources intended to generate future income and cash flows" (paragraph 1540.18) would encompass most assets. In practice, however, it is accepted that cash payments for inventories should normally be classified as operating outflows, whereas payments for capital assets are to be considered an investing activity.

- A similar issue arises with respect to the distinction between purchases on account from suppliers of goods and services and debt arising from money borrowing. Both could be considered financing, but the former are generally classified as operating because they are normally considered to be related more to an enterprise's ongoing operations than to its capital structure.

- There are some difficult classification issues on the margins of the above two generalizations, however. An example is provided by installment sales and installment purchases of inventory where the cash flows extend out over several reporting periods. Such transactions have attributes of both operating and investing activities in respect of installment sales, and operating and financing activities in respect of installment purchases. SFAS 95 has ruled, basically on pragmatic grounds, that the classification of all cash flows related to installment sales or purchases should be determined by the original purpose for which the cash flows are to be received or paid, with the result that they would all be treated as operating regardless of when they are received or paid. The practical difficulty with the alternative treatment of installment sales as an investing activity is that an enterprise financing most of its sales under installment sales plans could find itself regularly reporting negative cash flows from operations. But the FASB classification is open to criticism because it is inconsistent with its required treatment of the receipt of principal payments on other investments in debt instruments as an investing activity, and with its treatment of cash outflows to repay other long-term debt used to acquire inventories as a financing activity.[8]

- The classification of interest and dividends received and interest paid has been particularly controversial. SFAS 95 requires that they be treated as cash flows from operating activities. Three of the seven board members dissented, arguing that interest and dividends received should be treated as cash inflows from investing activities, and that interest paid is a cost of obtaining financial resources that should be treated as cash flows from financing activities. The FASB standard acknowledges that a reasonable case could be made for this view, but it notes that there has been substantial support in practice for the view that "... in general, cash flows from operating activities should reflect the cash effects of transactions and other events that enter into the determination of net income."[9]

  As noted above, the 1985 CICA standard did not speak to the treatment of interest and dividend receipts and payments (although in practice they were generally included in operating activities). The 1998 CICA standard explicitly requires interest and dividends received and interest paid be treated as operating items, assuming they entered into the determination of net income (paragraph 1540.34).

  The treatment of interest on debt as an operating cash flow has an effect which may seem anomalous when the debt is issued at a premium or discount. Suppose, for example, that debt to be repaid in five years in the amount of $1,000,000 is issued for $800,000. The discount of $200,000 will be amortized as additional interest expense over the five-year term. But the cash outflow of this amount will not take place until the end of year five, with the result that the $200,000 will be included as a cash outflow from operations at that time, while the balance of the debt repayment of $800,000 will be treated as a financing activity outflow.[10]

- There has also been considerable debate with respect to the classification of dividends paid. As noted earlier, the 1985 CICA standard allowed treatment as financing, operating or classification as a separate item. The 1998 standard adopted the FASB requirement that they be treated as a financing item (paragraph 1540.35).

- The 1998 CICA standard holds that cash flows arising from the purchase and sale of securities and loans held for "trading purposes" should be classified as operating, rather than investing, activities. The rationale it provides is that they are similar to inventory acquired for resale (paragraph 1540.17). Thus, depending on management's intention to hold marketable securities for long-term investment or for trading purposes, they may be classified as investing or operating (or, as noted earlier, if they qualify as cash equivalents, they could be included as part of the cash fund itself). The analogy of trading securities with inventory held for sale would seem to lack credibility, except in specialized cases of enterprises acting in an investment dealer capacity.

- If a gain or loss is removed from operations and reported as an investment or financing activity, in principle any effect of that gain or loss on taxes payable should likewise be removed from the report of cash flow from operations. Ascertaining that effect on actual taxes payable, however, may require considerable effort in some cases because of its interaction with deferred taxes. That effort is likely to be rewarded by figures that have little information content. Consider, for example, disposal of some depreciable property for proceeds equal to its original cost. If that property constitutes the only depreciable property of the enterprise, all the capital cost allowance previously claimed for tax purposes will be recaptured and substantial actual taxes will be associated with the disposal. On the other hand, if the property belongs to the same class as other depreciable assets, the credit of the disposal proceeds against the class for tax purposes might result in a lesser amount of recaptured capital cost allowance or none at all. Hence, the immediate tax payable as a result of the property disposal might be substantial, something less than substantial, or nothing at all. Future capital cost allowance claims also will be affected by the fact situation, so that reported net cash flow from operations in future years after the adjustment for deferred tax will be correspondingly greater or less.

It is generally conceded that there is little value in making a careful computation of actual cash effects in such situations. A possible alternative would be to assume a notional tax charge that would be appropriate to the profit recognized (at normal tax rates to the extent the profit was represented by recaptured capital cost allowance, and at capital gains tax rates beyond that) and to offset the differences between that notional tax charge and the actual tax charge through the reconciling item for deferred taxes in the presentation of funds from operations. Alternatively, it might be arbitrarily decided that all income taxes actually paid should be shown as deductions from funds from operations except in individual cases where the effect on tax of a gain or loss reported in the investment or financing section of the statement of cash flows is both obvious and substantial.

SFAS 95 requires that all income taxes paid be classified as operating cash flows.[11] The 1998 CICA standard adopts a puzzling middle ground. It states that cash flows arising from income taxes should be classified in operating activities unless they can be specifically identified with financing or investing activities, "in which case they *may be* classified accordingly" (emphasis added) (paragraph 1540.38). Thus, an enterprise would seem to be able to follow SFAS 95, and classify income tax flows as operating activities, even if they could be clearly identified with a financing or investing activity.

Despite these classification difficulties, empirical evidence indicates that reported cash flows from operations under SFAS 95 have significant incremental information value.[12]

Statement Presentation of Funds from Operations

Cash from operations for a period is, of course, ultimately derived from collections of revenues. A positive net cash flow from operations is shown if such collections exceed the total amount of operating payments of all kinds and interest and taxes.

The direct way to report the elements of cash from operations, accordingly, would be to list these various amounts, classifying collections by source and payments according to their nature. This listing would look very much like a statement of income. The principal difference would be that the income statement figures are measured by accrual accounting while the funds statement figures would report actual cash flows. Collections from customers would replace sales revenue; payments to manufacturing labour and suppliers of materials would replace the cost of inventory sold, and so on.

In spite of its advantages, the direct method of presentation of funds derived from operations is hardly ever used. Instead, the traditional approach starts with the figure of reported income for the year and identifies elements therein that are not associated with funds flows, as well as gains and losses reported that should be classified as resulting from investment and financing activity rather than from operations. With this information in hand, the indirect method backs into a figure of net funds from operations by adding to or subtracting from the income figure those aspects of revenues, expenses, gains, and losses that should be classified as financing or investment or that do not represent funds flows at all.

This "indirect" or "reconciliation" approach has been sharply criticized. It is felt that a statement of operating funds flows should report actual flows, not consist of a reconciliation statement in which no single figure represents a funds flow. Beyond this, it is asserted (with considerable justification) that the format of the statement is positively misleading. For example, by starting with net income and adding back the depreciation and amortization figure, the statement makes it appear that depreciation is a source of funds or cash when it is nothing of the sort.

Against this criticism it has been strongly argued that the indirect form of presentation is valuable precisely because it highlights the difference between income and *cash* flow and because it pinpoints allocations (such as depreciation and deferred taxes) that represent somewhat arbitrary elements in the income statement. A further practical advantage, not often realized in practice, is that it permits reporting of different definitions of funds within one statement. For example, the reconciliation could be set up as shown in Table 22-1.

Current U.S. and Canadian standards encourage the direct method but allow either the direct or indirect approaches. Few companies have adopted the direct method. Financial analysts have generally expressed disappointment in this.[13]

When funds were defined as working capital, it was fairly easy to derive the figure of working capital from operations from the figure of net income for the period. Now that funds are defined as cash and cash equivalents, the indirect method is a more difficult calculation. It requires that examination be made of movements in current assets and liabilities that are not regarded as cash and cash equivalents, as well as in noncurrent assets and liabilities, in order to see whether they involve operating, investing, or financing activities. For example, suppose capital asset purchases in the year have been financed by accounts

Table 22-1	Explanatory Format for Reconciliation of Cash from Operations
Net income from operations	$ XXX
Add (deduct) expenses (revenues) not affecting working capital in the year	
Depreciation and amortization	XX
Increase in long-term deferred taxes	XX
etc.	XX
Net increase in working capital as a result of operations	XXX
Add (deduct)	
Increase in inventory	(XX)
Decrease in prepayments	XX
Net increase in short-term monetary resources as a result of operations	XX
Add (deduct)	
Increase in accounts receivable	(XX)
Decrease in accounts payable and accrued expenses	(XX)
Net decrease in cash and cash equivalents as a result of operations	$(XX)

payable that are still outstanding at the year-end. If the total of all accounts payable at the end of the year is merely compared with the total of all accounts payable at the beginning and the net change is treated as a reconciling item in arriving at cash from operations, the financing will be understated and cash from operations will be overstated. Similarly, an account receivable with respect to the sale of an investment can result in misstatement of funds from operations. To avoid these errors it is necessary to scrutinize the balances of current accounts receivable and payable at the end of each reporting period to identify any material amounts that do not arise from operating transactions.

Some Technical Problems

A number of technical problems encountered in the preparation of the cash flow statement are noted below.

- The use of absorption costing for inventory valuation can cause confusion when the indirect method of portraying funds from operations is used. Suppose, for example, that depreciation of manufacturing plant for a year is $100,000 but that depreciation included in closing inventory is $5,000 higher than in the opening inventory. Thus, the actual noncash charge against income for the year with respect to manufacturing depreciation is only $95,000. If in the cash flow statement the increase in inventory as shown by the balance sheet is treated as a use of cash, the actual use of cash to build inventory will be overstated by $5,000. To compensate, the add-back to income specifically with respect to depreciation must be stated at $100,000, not the $95,000 amount that was implicit in cost of sales for the year.

- Under equity accounting for an investment, the investor recognizes as income the increase in its equity in the investee. That income does not represent a cash flow. Some have advocated treating it as such in reporting cash flow from operations, compensating by recording a notional outflow of cash as an investment activity. On this basis, any actual cash inflow from dividends would be recognized as realization of the investment. Such a presentation is of dubious merit, since the investor does not make a conscious decision to reinvest in the investee and does not have control over the amount of dividends. The required treatment (see *CICA Handbook* paragraph 1540.40) is to recognize the equity in income of the investee as a noncash item and pick up any dividend received as a cash flow from operations (so long as the dividend together with dividends previously received does not exceed the investor's share of income subsequent to acquisition of the investment).

- Similarly, alternative treatments are conceivable with respect to the noncontrolling interest share of consolidated income. Some might advocate reporting that share as though it were a notional outflow of cash and a corresponding financing inflow of cash of that amount less dividends actually paid to the minority interest. The alternative is now required—to treat the noncontrolling interest share in earnings as a noncash item but treat actual dividends paid as a financing cash outflow (paragraph 1540.35).

- The reconciliation of net income and cash flow from operations begins with the figure of net income excluding extraordinary items. It is then necessary to ascertain the cash effects of any extraordinary items and report them as operating, investment, or financing cash flows according to their nature (paragraph 1540.32).

- Portraying the effect of business combination understandably in a cash flow statement presents a practical problem. The acquisition of another business will result in increases in virtually all the asset and liability categories in the balance sheet. As a result, net changes between opening and closing consolidated balance sheets will be affected by both the acquisition and by the regular activities of the reporting entity. If the cash from operations is calculated using the indirect method, the adjustments of net income for changes over the year in balances of monetary assets and liabilities and inventories (for example) must take into account only the net change in these items from regular activities. As a result, readers may be confused if they attempt to compare the net change figure described in the cash flow statement with the net change shown by the opening and closing balance sheets. To help readers understand the reason for this lack of correspondence, the investment in the business acquired could be shown by individual asset and liability categories in the section on investing activity. This, however, is a cumbersome presentation. To achieve a simpler presentation, the investment in the business acquired is to be shown as one figure of total cost less the cash and cash equivalents acquired. To help the reader to an understanding of how the acquisition affected individual balance sheet categories, an "acquisition equation" (setting out the amount of assets and liabilities other than cash equivalents in the business acquired summarized by major category) could be provided as supplementary note disclosure.[14]

- A sale of a segment of a business that has been included in the consolidated financial statements—a "decombination"—presents a similar problem in reverse, and is accommodated by the same presentation approach as for business acquisitions.

- There may be occasions when a significant build-up of inventory, and possibly monetary working capital, in anticipation of a business expansion or a new venture may be appropriately treated as an investing activity in the same way as cash invested in capital assets. It would obviously be necessary to have a clear and carefully controlled understanding of the basis for the build-up and the period over which it extends to avoid abuse of this presentation.

- A company may engage in a variety of transactions that give rise to monetary assets or liabilities denominated in foreign currency or may hold foreign currency cash balances. For accounting purposes these balances of foreign currency assets and liabilities will be continuously adjusted to current exchange rates, giving rise to the recognition of gains or losses in income if the assets and liabilities are current or to deferred gains and losses if the assets and liabilities are long-term (under Canadian practice). Such deferred gains and losses are subsequently amortized to income.

  With respect to accounts receivable and payable in foreign currency that are classified as current, gains and losses recorded must be eliminated from the statement of cash flow from operations because they do not represent a change in cash and cash equivalents. The indirect approach to the calculation of cash from operations achieves this elimination automatically by adjusting net income from operations for differences between the opening and closing reported balances of such monetary assets and liabilities.

  With respect to noncurrent monetary assets and liabilities in foreign currency, there is no such automatic adjustment. For these items, therefore, it is necessary to treat the amount of any amortization of deferred foreign currency gains or losses or any write-off on settlement of the asset or liability position as a noncash adjustment to net income. The cash received or paid on ultimate settlement of noncurrent foreign currency assets or liabilities would appear in the investment or financing activity sections. These same rules apply for a foreign operating unit that is included in the consolidated financial statement whose accounts are translated using the temporal approach (see Chapter 21).

With respect to foreign currency assets and liabilities that are included in the definition of funds (i.e., cash and cash-equivalents), gains and losses recognized as the result of exchange rate changes must be included as a net cash inflow or outflow in the statement of cash flows since they represent changes in the carrying amount of cash and cash equivalents. It is reasoned that, since this net gain or loss is not a cash receipt or payment per se, it should be reported as a separate item in the statement of cash flows.[15]

- Generally the gross amounts of cash receipts and payments should be reported. For example, cash holdings to acquire capital assets should be reported separately from the proceeds of sales of capital assets, and proceeds from borrowings should not be netted against debt repayments. Reporting only the net amounts for such items would limit a reader's basis for understanding the extent of investing and financing activities.

However, the nature, volume and turnover of some transactions is such that disclosure of gross cash inflows and outflows may not have additional information value, and might even serve to overwhelm and obscure the investing and financing activities of a business. Examples might include a portfolio of short-term receivables or a trading portfolio of marketable securities. SFAS 95 permits net reporting for such items where the turnover is quick, the amounts large and the maturities short. It also allows reporting on a net basis where an enterprise is considered to be substantively holding or disbursing cash on behalf of its customers, and it cites demand deposits of a bank and customer accounts payable of a broker-dealer as examples.[16] The FASB subsequently extended permissible netting to banks and similar organizations in respect of deposits with other financial institutions, term deposits and customer loans.[17] The CICA has now adopted similar provisions (see paragraphs 1540.25–.27).

- Chapter 20 referred to the weaknesses of consolidated statements for the purpose of revealing the creditworthiness of the parent company. Those observations are of particular importance for the cash flow statement because its use is so closely associated with the evaluation of solvency and financial flexibility. Developing problems in the cash position of a holding company or in any of the subsidiaries may be masked by strong operating cash flows in other components in the group. Debt covenants or other impediments may prevent the free transfer of cash between components. If this difficulty exists, the only real solution seems to be to present additional disclosure—possibly to the extent of providing an analysis of the cash flows by legal components. Present standards do not require reporting by legal components, but do require disclosure of cash and cash equivalents for which use is restricted, including legal restrictions on general use by the consolidated entity (paragraphs 1540.50 and 1540.52).

The best solutions to many of these, and other technical problems, are not readily deducible from a coherent theory underlying cash flow statements. The theory is rather vague, and limited by the varied and, in some respects, conflicting purposes of the statement. As noted in the above discussions, the CICA 1998 standard has introduced more specific guidance on a number of matters, mostly by adopting previously developed FASB positions. These may serve to improve Canadian practice, but in the U.S. published cash flow statements have been criticized as often being obscure, incomplete and internally inconsistent.[18] In view of these deficiencies, accounting standard setters may need to make additional efforts to develop and explain the theories underlying the cash flows statement and spell out their implications for specific issues.

Scope Considerations

A funds flow statement has come to be regarded as a basic financial statement for most types of enterprises—a statement that contains essential information that complements the balance sheet, income statement and statement of retained earnings. The *CICA Handbook* includes it in the general package that normally comprises "financial statements" of profit-oriented enterprises (see paragraph 1000.04). Nevertheless, Section 1540 provides that a separate statement is not necessary for nonpublic enterprises with "relatively simple operations" such that cash flow information is "readily apparent" from other financial statements or is adequately disclosed in financial statement notes (see paragraphs 1540.03 and .04).

Certain special characteristics of financial institutions, pension plans, investment enterprises and not-for-profit organizations have given rise to some questions as to the relevance of conventional cash flow statements to their situations. The discussion of not-for-profit organizations is deferred to Chapter 27.

Financial Institutions

It has been contended that the standard cash flow statement does not contain additional useful information in respect of many financial institutions, particularly banks. The following considerations may be raised:

- Financial institution operations, particularly those of banks, are such that their cash flows are different in nature from those of other nonfinancial enterprises. For example, it is claimed that cash may be viewed as a bank's "product," created through its leverage on capital and its lending activities. Some have held that cash is the equivalent of inventory of a manufacturing company, and that a statement of cash flows for a bank has no more meaning than would a statement of inventory flows for a nonfinancial company.

- The shareholders' equity in a financial institution will be small in relation to its deposit or policy liabilities, so that net income and related cash flows from operations are bound to be relatively small in relation to receipts and disbursements associated with financing and investing activities. In an important sense the receipt of funds from depositors and policy holders and the investment of those funds are operating activities. Thus, it may be claimed that attempting to classify funds between operating, investing and financing activities does not yield particularly useful information. It might be contended that a more appropriate classification of cash flows is one that corresponds with the two sides of the balance sheet—cash flows associated with financing activities (including flows of deposit money, money for policy reserves and debt and equity transactions), and cash flows associated with investment activities (including maturities, disposals and new investments).

- A substantial part of the assets of a financial institution will be monetary and reasonably liquid. A financial institution will hold a minimum of cash or cash equivalents because they are nonearning or low-earning assets (but might not the same be said of any rationally managed business?). The argument is that the concept of "cash and cash equiva-lents" is less distinct and useful in respect of a financial institution than for other non-financial enterprises. The real liquidity risks and dangers of insolvency in respect of a financial institution may lie less in cash flow information than in the risk quality of its assets (for example, some loans may be highly liquid and some highly illiquid, depend-ing on the health of the borrowers), and on mismatching of maturity dates of financial assets and liabilities, and risks of reduction in deposit support because depositors have more attractive opportunities for the use of their funds elsewhere.

Standard setters have not been persuaded by these arguments. They have concluded that, although financial institutions have unique characteristics, their essential needs for cash are substantially the same as for any business enterprise—to invest in its operations, to pay its oblig-ations and to provide returns to its investors. Like any profit-oriented enterprise it must gen-erate positive cash flows over the long run to survive and flourish. Cash flows of a bank, for example, may be larger and turn over faster, but this does not make them different in substance from those of a nonfinancial business. As well, many nonfinancial organizations have sig-nificant financial activities (for example, have a finance company or insurance subsidiary).

In sum, it is now well accepted that the particular characteristics of financial institutions can be accommodated within a statement of cash flows and the standards for classification of operating, financing and investing activities. In particular, as has been noted earlier, the con-cept of "cash equivalents" and standards allowing netting of certain types of cash receipts and disbursements have been made flexible to accommodate financial institution activities.

Certainly it is recognized that a cash flow statement cannot tell the whole story with respect to solvency and liquidity, and that there is a need for improved disclosures about the financial instruments held and issued by financial institutions and their financial risk expo-sures. (These matters are discussed in Chapter 17).

Investment Enterprises

Pension plans, and highly liquid investment funds that meet certain conditions, are exempted from requirements to present a cash flow statement (paragraph 1540.02).

Pension plans are subject to the provisions of another CICA standard that requires pre-sentation of plan investments at fair value and a statement of changes in net assets (*CICA Handbook*, Section 4100). The FASB had previously instituted a similar exemption which it extended to all employee benefit plans that present financial statements on the same basis as those required of defined pension benefit plans. While the FASB does not require the inclusion of a statement of cash flows for such plans, it does encourage its presentation, particularly where a plan's assets are not highly liquid.[19]

Consistent with the FASB, the CICA also concluded that investment funds that have highly liquid investments, that have little or no debt, that carry substantially all of their investments at market value, and that present a statement of changes in net assets, need not provide a statement of cash flows. Cash flow information is not considered to have signif-icant information value for these entities where their investments are readily convertible into cash at short notice. Open-ended investment companies (mutual funds) are expected to maintain portfolios that will enable them to redeem units in the funds within a few days. Sufficient information for users to assess liquidity and financial flexibility is considered to be provided in the balance sheet and statement of changes in net assets.

CASH FLOW ACCOUNTING MODELS

Some accounting theorists consider the statement of cash flow to be something more than a statement that complements and supplements an accrual accounting system. Rather, they consider it the preeminent flow statement that should be used to the exclusion of others, especially the income statement. They have two reasons for this, one positive and one negative. The positive reason rests upon the proposition that users of financial statements are interested in an entity's ability to generate cash. From this they reason that a statement focusing on cash will provide feedback on actual results achieved as compared with previous expectations and (possibly) will provide a better basis for assumptions as to the future. The negative reason rests upon their rejection of conventional income accounting because of its reliance upon allocations. Cash flow theorists believe accounting allocations are so arbitrary that measures of resource flows that are seriously affected by them must be meaningless.

The statement of cash flow (SCF) is advocated as a substitute for an income statement in significant part because it largely avoids the allocation problem. It does so, however, only at the expense of creating another problem—that of presenting information whose usefulness is limited because its proper interpretation is not clear. If the cash balance is reduced over a period, for example, one must ask whether this is because of lack of profitability of the business or because of increased investment in inventory and plant attributable to growth. Attempts to deal with this problem include (1) broadening the definition of "cash flow," (2) interpretive classifications within the SCF, (3) provision of multi-period data to reduce the impact of temporary fluctuations in cash flow, and (4) provision of supplementary information on assets and liabilities measured on an allocation-free basis.

Since the SCF dispenses with an income statement, it is clear that the indirect method of presentation, starting with net income and reconciling to a figure of cash flow from operations, cannot be used. The following comments should be considered in the context of a statement disclosing cash inflows and cash outflows directly.

The Definition of Cash Flow

Cash flow theorists face a question equivalent to that discussed earlier under the heading "definition of funds," namely, what shall be the definition of "cash flow?" Similar considerations apply. Straight cash is completely factual, but it may be unduly affected in any reporting period by leads and lags in the cash impact of other transactions. To mitigate this impact, some theorists have suggested that legal claims to receive or pay cash should be treated as "unrealized cash flows." In effect, a "cash flow" is something different from a flow of cash. From the standpoint of the information value of the SCF, this approach is probably an improvement over a statement tied to cash movements alone, but it is not without problems.

- It would seem foolish to report an extremely temporary investment of cash—say a purchase of a short-term deposit receipt—as a cash outflow. Yet, if one admits that some investment transactions should not be reported as cash outflows or cash inflows, the question arises as to what is the logical dividing line. It cannot be that no security investment transaction should be reported as cash outflow or inflow. An investment in a venture capital company, for example, might be as doubtful, if not more doubtful, of return as an investment in plant and equipment.

- If the creation of accounts receivable on sale is reported as unrealized cash inflow, should there be any limit to the maturity date of the receivable? As soon as an uncollected account receivable is recorded as a cash flow, a form of allocation has taken place. A future real cash flow has been allocated to the present period. An allocation process is even more evident if the account receivable is discounted. Then the future cash flow is being allocated part to the present and part (as interest) over the period until the account becomes collectible.

Classification within the Statement

The information value of any flow statement depends to a significant extent upon the classification of flows. For expenditures there are two fundamental bases of classification—by nature of expenditure and by purpose of expenditure. Thus expenditures may be classified as purchases of materials, merchandise, supplies, utilities, equipment, labour, and so on. Or they may be classified as spending on acquisition, manufacturing, and storage of goods, acquisition of equipment, repairs and maintenance, marketing, general and administration, research and development, and so on. To a considerable extent the latter classification system requires allocation. Labour and supplies, for example, may be manufacturing, marketing, administration, or research and development costs. Allocations are normally also required if there is any desire to report cash flows by different segments of a business.

A further type of allocation often suggested is that of partitioning expenditures for plant investment among costs of maintaining existing productive capacity, investment for growth, and other expenditures that neither add to capacity nor to growth—for example, for pollution control devices.[20] This partitioning, it is felt, would help the reader understand whether the business is consuming its capital base, something that is not apparent from a cash flow statement for short periods of time. Undoubtedly this would be valuable information if it could be obtained. Unfortunately it requires very uncertain estimates. If new plant substitutes for labour without any increase in physical output capacity, is that growth? Or if new plant can produce 150% of the capacity of plant replaced at a lower cost per unit, how is the replacement portion of the expenditure to be measured? The FASB considered expanding disclosures of SFAS 95 to require the classification of investment cash outflows between expenditures for maintenance of existing capacity and expenditures for new capacity. It concluded, however, that such an allocation would be arbitrary and that the cost of preparation would exceed any information value benefits.[21] These questions are essentially the same as those that have arisen under current cost accounting for the purpose of measuring depreciation on a current cost basis—and have proven very contentious. (See Chapter 24 for more complete discussion.)

It must be conceded that the SCF does eliminate certain types of allocations. Once cash outflows are reported and classified, there is no further allocation, such as allocation of inventory cost to cost of sales or of plant costs as depreciation. In addition, the extent of allocation can be reduced, for example by assigning variable costs only to described purposes. Thus, if allocation-free accounting is the goal, cash flow accounting achieves it to a considerable degree.[22] The key question is whether, in so doing, it destroys much of its usefulness.

Multiple-Period Cash Flow Statements

One suggestion for overcoming the limited significance of a SCF for a single period is that such statements should be presented as a series covering a number of years.[23] This suggestion has a degree of persuasiveness since, over a long enough period, any going concern must replace the investment it starts out with, and over a period of time net cash flows will tend to approach net income. There are some difficulties with the idea, however.

- Cash flows over a series of years will be reported in dollars of different purchasing power, so that the series as a whole lacks internal comparability. The solution suggested to this is to use an index to restate the series to a constant dollar basis.

- An entity that has been in operation for a limited number of years only and is still growing may not provide a history long enough to provide a representative picture of long-term cash flows. Even a long-established entity may be steadily growing or declining in real terms throughout the period covered by the series of cash flow statements. Since a cash flow statement, by definition, shows capital expenditures as an outflow and does not attempt to measure the growth or shrinkage in capital base, the proper interpretation of a series of cash flow statements, even for an extended period, may be in doubt.

Lawson proposes to meet the latter difficulty in the following fashion. First, he assumes that the market value of a company's securities should reflect its expectations for future cash flows. Thus, a statement that shows how that market value has changed in total over a period (when measured in constant dollars) should show whether the real capital base is increasing. If the capital base is relatively constant, then it may be assumed that the average net cash flows after capital expenditures, when expressed in real terms, fairly represent the basic profitability of the business. This test may be supplemented by examination of the real rates of return over a period on the debt and equity securities of the company based on their market prices. Inadequate rates of return would reinforce the implications of declining real net cash flows over the period, and vice versa. Egginton criticizes Lawson's proposals on the grounds that, if the cash flow information is inadequate in itself to inform investors and creditors, the difficulty cannot be cured by introducing investor valuations based upon the presumably inadequate information.[24]

Supplementary Information on Assets and Liabilities

A more direct way to cope with the failure of cash flow statements to disclose growth or shrinkage in the capital base is to provide supplementary information about assets and liabilities that are not treated as part of the cash position. Cash flow adherents take it as given that this information cannot be based upon conventional historical cost accounting valuations because such valuations depend upon allocations—the very procedures that cash flow accounting is trying to avoid. The only alternative is to adopt a market valuation approach to measures of assets and liabilities. Once the historical cost accounting model has been abandoned, it seems obvious that those market values must be values current at the reporting date. Moreover, to be consistent with cash flow accounting theory the valuations too must be allocation-free.

The most obvious allocation-free market values are exit prices—estimates of net amounts realizable for the assets.[25] Entry values—estimates of current costs of acquisition—can be allocation-free as well, but only if they are based upon second-hand market prices. In contrast, the usual approach in current cost accounting is to estimate the values for property, plant, and equipment by obtaining replacement costs new and deducting accrued depreciation therefrom. Since depreciation is an allocation, this approach is unacceptable.

Cash Flow per Share

In the U.S., SFAS 95 forbids the presentation of cash flow per share, precisely because the board does not accept that cash flow can be an effective measure of enterprise performance. In its view only an appropriate measure of earnings can fulfill that role. The board concluded that reporting cash flow per share "… would falsely imply that cash flow, or some component of it, is a possible alternative to earnings per share as a measure of performance" (paragraph 122).

The CICA has no prohibition on reporting cash flow per share; the *CICA Handbook* is silent on the subject. A number of Canadian companies disclose cash flow per share information, some in their financial statements and some elsewhere in their annual reports. An Emerging Issues Committee Abstract has indicated that cash flow per share should not be presented on the face of the income statement in case it may seem to be a surrogate for earnings per share. The abstract goes on to state the view that, where a cash flow per share figure is disclosed, it should be accompanied by sufficient information to enable readers to see how the numerator is derived from the statement of changes in financial position. As well, the description of the cash flow figure should be consistent with that of the items in the funds statement on which it is based, and the number of shares entering into the calculation should be consistent with the determination of earnings per share.[26]

SUMMARY

A financial statement focusing on changes in the liquid resources of an entity has a long tradition. Unfortunately, the objectives of that statement have not always been clear and there can be several variations in its form. The following are some of the statement's objectives:

- The statement may help assess the financial flexibility of an entity, its creditworthiness, and whether its operations are contributing to its solvency.

- The statement may help predict future cash flows by showing how past operations have affected the liquid position of the enterprise.

- The statement, by reporting investing and financing transactions, helps explain changes in resources and claims that are not explained by the income statement.

- By reconciling net income with liquid funds from operations, the statement helps to enlighten the reader as to the extent to which profits are represented by liquid resources and also the significance of some accounting allocations to the figure of net income reported.

The idea developed that these objectives may be best served by dividing the statement into three parts, each focusing on different activities—one on the effects of financing activities and increases or decreases in capital employed, one on the effects of management decisions on investment and disinvestment, and one on the effects of operations.

Several major questions must be addressed in settling the presentation of the statement and thinking with respect to them has evolved over the years.

- What is the best definition of liquid funds for the purposes of the statement? Standards have moved away from a broad definition such as working capital to cash and cash equivalents. The term "cash equivalents," however, is used with some flexibility.

- Should the statement strive to include all significant changes in financial position (including, for example, the exchange of capital assets for debt, and the conversion of debt) or only those that directly affect cash and cash equivalents? CICA standards now require the latter, but they also require disclosure of significant noncash financing and investing transactions.

- Just what activities should be classified as "operating?" This has been a troublesome area and accounting theory provides no clear answers to a number of questions bearing on this issue, including whether the purchase of plant and equipment should be classified as an operating or investing activity, whether the repayment of amounts owing to suppliers is an operating or financing activity, whether interest and dividends received are operating or investing activities, and whether interest paid on debt is an operating or financing activity. The U.S. standard has specified more or less arbitrary treatments for these items, and a recent revision to the Canadian standard has adopted positions that are generally consistent with them.

- Should liquid funds from operations be computed directly by reporting sources of cash inflows and objects of cash expenditures, or indirectly by reconciliation of funds from operations with reported net income? Either approach is considered acceptable, but a large majority of statements adopt the indirect method.

In addition, there are numerous technical problems in drawing up cash flow statements. Authoritative literature now provides guidance on most of these, but there is still considerable room for inconsistent variability. In particular, the flexibility possible in the choice of definition of liquid funds and in the division between operating and other activities, means that statements prepared by different enterprises will be lacking in comparability.

The relevance of conventional cash flow statements to financial institutions, pension and similar plans, and investment enterprises is open to question. Standard setters have not been persuaded by arguments that financial institutions should be exempted from providing cash flow statements. Rather it has become reasonably well accepted that their particular characteristics can be accommodated by providing some flexibility in interpreting the definition of "cash equivalents," in classifying cash flows to activities, and in allowing some netting of cash receipts and disbursements in respect of certain investing and financing transactions involving high volume and quick turnover.

Pension plans and highly liquid investment enterprises (for example, mutual funds) are allowed to provide a statement of changes in net assets rather than a cash flow statement, provided certain conditions are met.

A small number of accounting theorists advocate cash flow accounting not as one component of accrual financial statements but as a substitute for them. The problem for a reporting system focusing on cash flows is to make the statement of cash flow provide more information than one would obtain merely from reading a bank passbook. To achieve this objective, cash flow theorists have had to address many of the questions discussed earlier—how to define cash flows, how to classify them in an illuminating fashion, and how to give a clue as to expectations of future cash flows beyond those that are implicit in the balances of cash and cash equivalents reported.

Consideration of these questions leads to a conclusion that some disclosure of values of assets and liabilities that do not represent cash and cash equivalents is necessary. As a result, cash flow accounting cannot be looked upon seriously as a separate accounting model. It can be used as a means of providing a different perspective from the income statement in accrual accounting, or it can be used as a component of a current value system. But a statement of cash flow cannot stand alone as an adequate financial report for any complex business.

REFERENCES

1 See FASB, *Statement of Cash Flows*, Statement of Financial Accounting Standards No. 95 (Norwalk: FASB, 1987); and IASC, *Cash Flow Statements*, IAS 7 (London: IASC, revised 1992).

2 AICPA, APB, *Reporting Changes in Financial Position*, APB Opinion No. 19 (New York: AICPA, 1971).

3 See FASB, *Statement of Cash Flows*, pars. 6, 10 and 70–74.

4 See L.C. Heath, *Financial Reporting and its Evaluation of Solvency*, Accounting Research Monograph No. 3 (New York: AICPA, 1978), chap. 7.

5 CICA, "Statement of Changes in Financial Position," *CICA Handbook*, Section 1540 (Toronto: CICA, Superseded in 1998), par. 17.

6 Ibid.

7 For a discussion of a number of these issues, and a critical assessment of SFAS 95, see H. Nurnberg, "Inconsistencies and Ambiguities in Cash Flow Statements Under FASB Statement No. 95," *Accounting Horizons*, June 1993, pp. 60–75.

8 See FASB, *Statement of Cash Flows*, pars. 93–95 and the dissent of the three board members to this FASB position.

9 Ibid., pars. 88–90. Some claim that this principle is not rigorously applied in SFAS 95, noting that gains and losses on capital asset disposals are excluded from cash flows from operations. See H. Nurnberg, "Inconsistencies and Ambiguities in Cash Flow Statements Under FASB Statement No. 95," p. 65.

10 See CICA, Emerging Issues Committee, *Interest Discount or Premium in the Statement of Changes in Financial Position*, EIC 47 (Toronto: CICA, 1993).

11 See FASB, *Statement of Cash Flows*, pars. 91–92. See criticism of this treatment at H. Nurnberg, "Inconsistencies and Ambiguities in Cash Flow Statements Under FASB Statement No. 95," pp. 67–69. Note that the author cites evidence that some U.S. companies have been allocating income taxes in cash flow statements despite the FASB prohibition.

12 See C.S.A. Cheng, C. Liu and T.F. Schaefer, "The Value-Relevance of SFAS No. 95 Cash Flows from Operations as Assessed by Security Market Effects," *Accounting Horizons*, September 1997, pp. 1–15.

13 See, for example, P.H. Knutson, *Financial Reporting in the 1990s and Beyond*, a position paper of the Association for Investment Management and Research (Charlottesville, V.A.: Association for Investment Management and Research, 1993), pp. 65–67.

14 See *CICA Handbook*, pars. 1540.42–.45. It is to be noted that it requires disclosure of only the amount of total assets, net of cash equivalents, and the total liabilities of the acquired enterprise, not the composition of its major assets and liabilities.

15 See FASB, *Statement of Cash Flows*, par. 101. The calculation of the adjustment is illustrated in Example 2 of Appendix C to this standard. (The revised 1998 CICA standard also requires this presentation. See par. 1540.31.)

16 Ibid., pars. 11–12, 31 and 75–80.

[17] FASB, *Statement of Cash Flows—Net Reporting of Certain Cash Receipts and Cash Payments and Classification of Cash Flows from Hedging Transactions*, Statement of Financial Accounting Standards No. 104 (Norwalk: FASB, 1989).

[18] "... the imprecision with which FAS 95 appears to the applied, and the need... to resolve a variety of ambiguous situations as well as to forestall the many detectable errors ..." are concerns put forward in the U.S. by the financial analyst community. See P.H. Knutson, *Financial Reporting in the 1990's and Beyond*, pp. 44, and 46-47.

[19] FASB, *Statement of Cash Flows—Exemption of Certain Enterprises and Classification of Cash Flows from Certain Securities Acquired for Resale*, Statement of Financial Accounting Standards No. 102 (Norwalk: FASB, 1984).

[20] See, for example, R.G. Stephens and V. Govindarajan, "On Assessing a Firm's Cash Generating Ability," *The Accounting Review*, January 1990, pp. 242–57.

[21] FASB, *Statement of Cash Flows*, pars. 97–99.

[22] For a more extended discussion, see B.A. Rutherford, "The Interpretation of Cash Flow Reports and the Other Allocation Problem," *Abacus*, June 1982, pp. 40–49, and T.A. Lee, "Cash Flow Accounting and the Allocation Problem," *Journal of Business Finance & Accounting*, Autumn 1982, pp. 341–52.

[23] A concise explanation of the suggestion may be found in G.H. Lawson, "The Measurement of Corporate Performance on a Cash Flow Basis: A Reply to Mr. Egginton," *Accounting and Business Research*, Spring 1985, pp. 98–108. A similar idea in concept is outlined in Y. Ijiri, "Recovery Rate and Cash Flow Accounting," *Financial Executive*, March 1980, pp. 54–60.

[24] See D.A. Egginton, "Cash Flow, Profit and Performance Measures for External Reports: A Rejoinder," *Accounting and Business Research*, Spring 1985, pp. 109–12.

[25] See T.A. Lee, "Reporting Cash Flows and Net Realizable Values," in *Cash Flow Accounting*, ed. B.E. Hicks and P. Hunt (Sudbury, Ontario: International Group for Cash Flow Accounting, and Research and Publication Division, School of Commerce and Administration, Laurentian University, 1981), pp. 215–37.

[26] CICA, Emerging Issues Committee, *Presentation of Cash Flow Per Share Information*, EIC 34 (Toronto: CICA, 1991).

DISCLOSURE
ISSUES

The objective of financial statements is to present fairly the financial position and results of operations of an enterprise. The accounting recognition and measurement principles and the fundamentals of balance sheet, income and cash flow presentation discussed in previous chapters provide the base for this. The classification of assets and liabilities in the balance sheet and of items of revenue, expense, gain and loss in the income statement should enhance information. The description of each line item is itself information, and information may also be provided parenthetically. Through the decades since the 1960s the financial statement base has come to be augmented with increasingly extensive supporting and elaborating disclosures in notes and supplementary schedules.

Financial statements are useful if they provide the fundamental data for financial analysis. Diligent users of financial statements will take the data presented therein and analyze them, possibly calculate ratios and percentages considered significant, perhaps rework and project the data in various ways, integrate these calculations with other economic data outside the organization, examine trends, and make comparisons with other enterprises. There is some overlap of functions that may be performed by the accountant and by the financial analyst in developing, segmenting and calculating financial data to facilitate financial analysis. It is not clear just where the responsibility of the one ends and the other begins.

Our current times have been described as an "information age," meaning that a key commodity has become information. Those who are the first to have it, understand it, and exploit it, have an edge in today's fast-paced global marketplace. Capital markets seem to have an almost insatiable appetite for more and more financial information, and there is a competitive interest in it. Financial statements of public enterprises have evolved from a balance sheet and income statement supplemented by a few explanatory notes into annual and interim reports in which the space devoted to footnotes and supporting schedules and analyses typically far exceed that of the basic statements themselves.

Some have been questioning whether this is getting out of hand. How much is enough, and is there a problem of "information overload"? How much and what kinds of disclosures should be required by accounting standards and securities regulators? Unfortunately, there has been no clearly enunciated theory of financial disclosure. Rather, there has been a series of cost-benefit considerations.

The logical beginning point for delineating and analyzing these questions is to identify the users of financial information and the information that may be considered pertinent to their decisions. Taking a user's perspective helps to draw out the potential purposes of financial disclosures, and helps to explain disclosure standards that have developed and are under development. But one must also assess potential limiting factors reflecting proprietary interests, and whether the costs of disclosures may exceed their benefits. These factors are notoriously difficult to evaluate because they involve largely subjective considerations. In addition, the ground is continually shifting as, for example, advances in information technology reduce information preparation and analysis costs, and as the relative positions and expectations of competing interests in financial information change. Accounting disclosure issues may be viewed within a broad societal context, which involves balancing the public interest and external stakeholders' "rights to know" information that is relevant to their welfare, against enterprises' right to withhold information that may be considered proprietary or too costly to provide.

In this chapter we first consider basic classes of financial disclosure from an external user purposes perspective, and then examine potential constraints on disclosure, cost-benefit considerations, and materiality. Finally, we will turn to examine several significant areas of disclosure: interim financial statements, segmented reporting, and earnings per share.

TOWARD A FRAMEWORK FOR DISCLOSURE— AN EXTERNAL USER PERSPECTIVE

Financial accounting conceptual frameworks generally identify two basic purposes of financial information: (1) information for decision making, which would suggest reference to assumptions as to users' economic purposes and the information needs of rational decision models relative to those purposes, and (2) stewardship information, that is information that is needed to hold enterprise management accountable for managing a business in the best interests of its stakeholders. This latter purpose gives rise to "agency theory" considerations discussed in Chapter 4.

These purposes provide a starting point. They point to the need for information that is relevant to user decision models, and information that can be used to assess whether management of business enterprises is fulfilling its contracts with its external stakeholder interests. But to take this further, and deduce what would be useful disclosure, one must have some mental image of the users of financial reports. It is logical to try to put oneself in the shoes of the user and ask oneself what information is pertinent to his or her economic purposes. To do this we must first ask who are the users?

We have noted in previous chapters that GAAP financial statements are intended to be "general purpose" financial information, meaning that they are intended to meet the general financial information needs of all external stakeholders. However, investors and credit grantors are considered to be the primary users (see *CICA Handbook* paragraph 1000.11). It is their decision usefulness and accountability interests that are the basic focus of financial reporting for business enterprises. If we were to take a broader view of stakeholder interests, to include employees, government, environmentalists and other public/society interests—some additional areas of disclosure could be expected to emerge.[1]

In assessing disclosures one must also consider that different users will have different abilities to understand them. It may be that some potential readers will never understand financial statements, no matter how much effort is made to present them clearly. The *CICA Handbook* states that "users are assumed to have a reasonable understanding of business and economic activities and accounting, together with a willingness to study the information with reasonable diligence" (paragraph 1000.19). The conceptual frameworks of the FASB and IASC make similar assumptions. The image is that of an intelligent and motivated lay person, not that of a professional financial analyst. A difficult question is whether disclosure standards should go beyond this and require additional information that can be used only by a sophisticated analyst. In the following discussion our central concern is with what is *potentially useful*. For this purpose it is appropriate to take the perspective of a skilled analyst so as to probe the limits of disclosure.

Many academics and others argue that it is a mistake to worry about any particular class of investment user or level of expertise. They point to the large body of "efficient markets" research that indicates that there is a close to instantaneous reaction of securities prices to information in well-developed capital markets. It may then be fruitless for individual investors to attempt their own analyses of public information as a basis for investment decisions, because by the time they do so it will already have been impounded in security prices. The important objective is to make information available to the markets and, in general, the more information made available and the faster it is disseminated, the more efficient the markets will be. This would lead to reasoning that information should be provided to enable serious analysis by those who, effectively, make the markets. But not all markets are efficient and many enterprises do not have publicly traded securities.

We have noted that there is no clearly enunciated theory of financial disclosure. However, if we take as given the primacy of investor and capital market interests, we may then consider what may be the properties of information that are relevant to rational investor/capital market decision models and contractual accountability.

The FASB concepts statements, upon which the much briefer *CICA Handbook* Section 1000 financial statement concepts are based, are reasoned from this premise:

> People engage in investing, lending and similar activities primarily to increase their cash resources .... A successful investor or creditor receives not only a return *of* investment but also a return *on* that investment ... commensurate with the risk involved.[2]

In other words, it may be presumed that the economic purpose of investors is to achieve a return on investment commensurate with the level of risk involved. This is entirely consistent with capital markets thinking.

The FASB reasons further as to the purpose of financial reporting—that it "... should provide information to help investors, creditors and others assess the amounts, timing and uncertainty of prospective net cash inflows to the related enterprise."[3] The *CICA Handbook* framework reflects similar conclusions (see, for example, paragraph 1000.12).

It may be distilled from this that investors, and capital markets participants generally, are interested in financial information that helps them predict an entity's future earnings (its source of "prospective net cash inflows"), and identify and understand the uncertainties of these prospective cash flows (the particular risks and sources of volatility, as well as measurement uncertainties).

These two investor purposes—prediction and assessment of risk/uncertainty—may be reasoned to provide the primary impetus for most financial statement disclosures supplementing the basic figures in the financial statements themselves. They provide the conceptual anchor points for assessing particular disclosures. The usefulness of a possible disclosure may be evaluated in terms of how it may be reasoned to contribute to one or both of these basic purposes—that is, for theorizing how it may be expected to have information value. Empirical research on, for example, stock market price effects of particular disclosures may then help confirm or refute these expectations.

We have noted that financial accounting conceptual frameworks identify a further purpose—stewardship information. Investors may be expected to want information on a business's past financial performance in order to assess management and hold it accountable. The question is whether the accountability/stewardship purpose of financial information gives rise to additional disclosures.

Following is a discussion of disclosures under these broad purposes.

Disclosures with Expected Predictive Value

The usefulness of many disclosures lies in helping provide a basis for prediction of future earnings and future net cash inflows.

Assessment of Sustainable Earnings

An analyst's forecast of the future will usually begin with a review of the past. That analysis forms one input to a judgment as to the extent to which future events are likely to resemble past events. Financial reporting of past income figures may be helpful in predicting future earnings or cash flows of an entity if it has "feedback value," that is, if it can "confirm, or correct, previous evaluations" (*CICA Handbook*, paragraph 1000.20).

The analyst will be assisted in his or her analysis if published financial reports clearly identify various components of the income reported. First, there should be clear disclosure of any amounts that may have little significance for future cash flows but rather represent adjustments of the past record—such as the effects of changes in accounting policy. It would then be useful for there to be disclosure of gains and losses that may be expected to be unique and nonrecurring. Some, but not all, of these may be characterized in financial statements as "unusual" or "extraordinary" items (see discussion in Chapter 18).

The general aim should be to distinguish between the regular and irregular in revenue and expense flows. It will be helpful to distinguish between the results of the core business carried on and peripheral or incidental activities, including holding gains, because the latter may be more prone to irregularity. Even within core operations, items that are inherently unstable should be identified, such as gains and losses on foreign exchange. Other items may need special disclosure because they occur infrequently or, in a particular year are significantly different from their usual amount. The analyst is interested in trying to estimate sustainable earnings as the basis for making predictions of future cash flows.

As we have noted in Chapter 18, the separation of recurring from nonrecurring items, and sustainable from nonsustainable earnings, is no easy task. The question is whether the separation of core or sustainable earnings is the role of accounting or financial analysis. A special committee on financial reporting was set up in the U.S. to address increasing concerns about the relevance and usefulness of financial reports. It conducted extensive research into the information needs of modern users of financial reports. One of its key recommendations was that users do not believe that sufficient information is provided about nonrecurring and unusual items to enable them to determine core earnings.[4]

Identification of Key Variables

Simple projections of past trends and earnings are unlikely to produce satisfactory forecasts of the future. Every business is subject to a variety of influences, the effect of which can be estimated more reliably by looking at their impact on various types of revenues or costs individually. Some aspects of a business are more important than others to its overall success, so that a decomposition of figures to permit concentration on these key variables will be helpful. The following may be expected to be useful in this task:

- A basic classification of the balance sheet components as (1) operating assets and liabilities, including plant and equipment, (2) more or less passive investments, and (3) financing liabilities, would assist in an appreciation of the basic structure of the enterprise. Segregation of revenues and costs by these same categories would assist in an appreciation of the key variables, especially if the regular and irregular were differentiated in each category as suggested above.

- Within the operating category it would be useful if changes in revenue from year to year were explained as resulting from changes in price, changes in volume, and the introduction of new products.

- Similarly, explanation of the behaviour of costs could be useful. A separation of expenses between those that vary with changes in production volume and those that are relatively fixed in amount would greatly assist user forecasts. It needs to be appreciated, of course, that it is rarely possible to make a clean categorization of costs as being one or the other, so that any overall division must be somewhat subjective and approximate.

- Classification of expenses by function served—as cost of sales, marketing, administration, and so on—is generally more useful for forecasting than classification by object of expenditure.

- Disclosure of amounts of expense in categories that are subject to a degree of management discretion could assist in assessing whether management is expanding, maintaining, or neglecting key contributors to its future earning capacity. Such expenses would include, for example, costs of repairs and maintenance, advertising costs, and research and development costs.

- Similarly, disclosure of expenses that are incurred largely for future benefit even though written off currently would be useful. These would include, for example, costs of research and development and major product launch costs.

- Disclosure of some nonmonetary indicators could also be useful, such as the percentage of capacity utilization in the period, and order backlog at the end of the period.

Accounting Variability and Comparability

Comparability of reported financial information is vital if it is to have feedback value and provide a valid basis for predicting future cash flows or earnings. Users will want to compare financial information as between entities and over time. Comparability is considered one of the principal attributes of financial information that makes it useful to users (see *CICA Handbook*, paragraphs 1000.18 and 1000.22). Following are basic areas of disclosure related to comparability and accounting variability:

- To be able to make relevant comparisons between entities, an analyst needs to understand the possible impact on reported figures of different available methods of reporting. Disclosure of significant accounting policies is accepted as a required accompaniment of financial statements. Of particular importance is the disclosure of policies selected from permissible alternatives, policies followed that are peculiar to an industry, and policies adopted with respect to significant situations that are peculiar to the entity itself and are not clearly governed by a general accounting standard (see *CICA Handbook* Section 1505) .

- Obviously, disclosures should be made of changes in accounting policies that have a material effect on figures presented or that potentially could have a material effect on future years. The disclosures should, where possible, indicate what revisions have been required to previous years' figures presented for comparison as a result of adoption of a new accounting method, and the effect on the financial statements of the current period (see *CICA Handbook* Section 1506, and discussion in Chapter 18).

- The international comparability of financial information has become important. Many enterprises now carry on business and raise capital outside their home countries, and most Canadian investors no longer invest only in Canadian companies but rather seek international investment opportunities and diversification. The problem is that accounting standards and practices can differ markedly between countries, so that investors have difficulty in comparing financial statements of companies domiciled in different countries. Disclosure of accounting policies followed is not considered to be enough. Investors want to see numerical reconciliations of at least reported income figures with some common, understandable set of accounting principles. Canadian companies that have their securities traded in the U.S. have long been required by the SEC to include a reconciliation of reported Canadian GAAP income to U.S. GAAP income where there are significant differences.

  This issue is affecting more and more Canadian companies as the North American Free Trade Agreement and other factors lead them to seek capital and do business in the U.S., as well as in other countries. (These concerns for comparability have given rise to pressures for international harmonization of accounting standards, which have major implications for the future of Canadian GAAP—see discussion in Chapter 26.)

- Related party transactions may also be a source of accounting variability, with implications for comparability. The measurement and disclosure of related-party transactions have been discussed in Chapter 6.

Aids to Analysis and Forecasting

Summaries of past earnings and other selected figures may facilitate analysis of trends. As well, key statistics may be computed on a standardized basis to enable valid comparisons between enterprises and within an enterprise over time.

One of the most widely quoted statistics in financial analysis is that of earnings per share. The complexities of share capital, and in particular securities that have some form of contingent claim upon present or future earnings, give rise to potential inconsistencies in these calculations. It is therefore considered to be important that these calculations be standardized, or at least that the bases of their determination be evident, so as to enable meaningful comparisons between entities and over time. Standards for the calculation of earnings per share are discussed in a later section of this chapter.

More could be done along these lines. Standards or guidelines could be developed for calculations of return on assets, debt/equity ratios, coverage of interest and preferred dividend requirements by earnings, and so on.[5] Cooperation between accounting standard setters and financial analysts would be desirable if extensions of disclosures in this way were contemplated.

Recurring suggestions have been made over many years that management should provide short-term forecasts of revenues and earnings. Professional analysts make forecasts on their own account but may welcome the check on their opinions provided by management forecasts. It has also been noted by some that management makes forecasts, and that there may be a concern that such forecasts are known to insiders, and may be disclosed selectively to favoured analysts. Thus, general disclosure of management's forecasts has been urged by some to provide a fair game for all. Against this, there is concern that management forecasts could be biased and misleading or that unsophisticated readers might place too much faith in them. The *CICA Handbook* has established some standards for the measurement, presentation and disclosure of future-oriented financial information when presented for external users in the form of general purpose financial statements.[6] Some enterprises prepare future-oriented financial information in connection with securities offerings, but it has not been the practice to do so in periodic financial reporting.

Pro forma financial statements are financial statements for a past period adjusted to give effect to one or more significant events or transactions that have occurred subsequent to the date of the financial statements or are pending. Examples of transactions for which pro forma statements may be appropriate include securities offerings and the use of the proceeds therefrom, corporate acquisitions, a major investment in capital assets, a divestiture of a business segment, and the retirement of debt or other outstanding securities. The nature and effect of such transactions may be well illustrated by showing how they would have affected the historical financial statements if they had taken place at the beginning or end of the reporting period. Pro forma financial statements are commonly presented in prospectuses and information circulars offering securities or dealing with amalgamations, mergers or corporate reorganizations. Such pro forma financial statements are not forecasts or projections because they simply recast historical financial statements to reflect the effect of a particular transaction or event.

Pro forma financial statements are to be clearly labelled as such, and the adjustments and their effects are to be disclosed and explained. It would generally be expected that pro forma financial statements will be presented only where the transactions or events are reasonably assured and their effects are capable of reliable quantification and clear presentation.[7] However, securities commissions and others have expressed concerns with respect to inconsistent practices and inadequate disclosures in some situations. Questions have arisen with respect to the presentation of what may amount to forecasts in the guise of pro forma adjustments, and whether pro forma financial statements may be issued in combination with forecasts or projections. It is generally acknowledged that the very general guidance provided in *CICA Handbook* Section 4000 (paragraphs 4000.18–.25) needs to be updated and expanded. The CICA has indicated that it plans to withdraw Section 4000, because it has largely been superseded by developments in practice. It has begun a project to assess developments and issue a new standard on pro forma financial statements.

Disclosure of Uncertainties and Risk Exposures

Investors can be expected to be interested in the extent to which reported values may be subject to variability as a result of uncertainties and risk exposures. We may distinguish two classes of variability.

- The first is *measurement uncertainty*, including estimation variability. Measurement uncertainty has been defined to exist "when there is a variance between the recognized amount and another reasonably possible amount" (*CICA Handbook* paragraph 1508.03). As we have observed in previous chapters, many financial statement figures are dependent upon estimates of future outcomes which, by necessity, are subjective. As well, when an enterprise can choose between accounting policies, there will be more than one way to measure an item.

- The second class comprises *volatility and risk*. The reported value of an item is volatile if it is highly susceptible to significant increases or decreases as a result of changes in future conditions. Risk is the potential for loss as a result of adverse consequences of changes in future conditions. The reported value of a particular item may have no measurement uncertainty, and yet be volatile and risky. For example, there is likely to be little or no measurement uncertainty as to a foreign exchange rate at a given date, as there will be a readily observable market price. However, that rate is constantly changing and is, therefore, volatile. As a result, the carrying value of a monetary asset denominated in a foreign currency is subject to risk, that is, it is susceptible to loss in value should the rate decrease.

Measurement Uncertainty and Estimation Variability

The principles of statistical probability tell us that a numerical representation of some uncertain state requires more than a single value estimate of its most likely (best estimate) or mean ("expected value"). It also requires depiction of the size and shape of the probability distribution about that value. Accounting estimates rarely, if ever, permit precise statistical depiction, but this does not preclude providing some useful information as to significant measurement/estimation uncertainties.

Estimation variability is a significant element of the application of many accounting policies that require judgment involving future expectations. General standards of fair presentation require disclosure of significant estimates of this kind. For example, estimates of useful lives and salvage value that are used as a basis for depreciation rates, or of the rates themselves that result from such estimates, are required to be disclosed. Unfortunately, these disclosures are often too imprecise to be very useful. It does little good to know that the useful life of equipment has been estimated in the range of five to thirty years, unless one knows what type of equipment is being depreciated and what is the dollar amount of investment depreciated over each different period.

A CICA commission on the public's expectations of audits singled out the paucity of disclosure with respect to measurement uncertainties as a potential cause of public misconceptions and unfulfilled expectations. It recommended that the *CICA Handbook* standards for disclosure of accounting policies be amplified to require "… full but compact disclosure of all the areas in which judgments have been required that have a significant effect on the financial statements." [8]

In 1995, partially in response to this recommendation, the CICA issued a standard on measurement uncertainty. It requires disclosure of the nature of a measurement uncertainty that is material (see paragraphs 1508.06 and 1508.11). This is intended to include a description of the circumstances giving rise to the uncertainty. As well, the recorded amount of an item subject to measurement uncertainty is to be disclosed, except where the disclosure would have a significant adverse effect on the entity (paragraph 1508.08). The extent of a material uncertainty is to be disclosed "when it is reasonably possible that the recognized amount could change by a material amount in the near term" (paragraph 1508.07).

This standard is, perhaps too general and weakly worded to be very effective. Disclosures made in response to the standard have largely been general statements about the areas in which judgments and estimates are necessary, and assertions that actual results could differ from estimates. Areas noted have included depreciation and depletion, environmental and site restoration provisions, and useful life estimates of capital assets.

Volatility and Risk

Risk is a key factor in any evaluation of an enterprise's prospects. Familiarity with a company's products and services provides an analyst with a basic understanding of its risks. That understanding can be enhanced by key income and balance information broken down by segments of the business that may be subject to significantly different risks and different rates of profitability and growth. Segmentation by geographical areas provides another helpful perspective on political, economic, and foreign currency risk. (See further commentary on segmented reporting later in this chapter.) Improved assessment of risk and uncertainty is also the principal justification for disclosure of an enterprise's contingencies.

In recent years there has been an emphasis on improving disclosures of financial risk exposures and of management's policies for managing interest, foreign currency, commodity and other market price risks. This emphasis is the result of the expansion of global capital markets, and the use of derivatives and other financial instruments to hedge, or in some cases, greatly magnify exposure to financial risks. These concerns for better disclosures have been stimulated by some sudden and spectacular corporate failures attributable to assuming huge financial risks, which were generally not clearly evident from the financial statements. Significant developments in financial risk disclosure standards have taken place, and are continuing (see discussion in Chapter 17).

More broadly, some have argued for the development of standards for the disclosure of what may be described as "risk profiles" of business enterprises. This would include descriptions of both operating and financial risks facing an enterprise, and how they are being managed.[9]

Liquidity, Insolvency and Going Concern Risks

Liquidity is commonly thought of as the ability of an enterprise to turn assets into cash. Liquidity is obviously also affected by liabilities to pay cash over the short term, and by the cash generating capability of an entity's operations. Solvency is the ability of an enterprise to pay its debts when they become due.

One might generally assume that financial statement users should be able to judge an enterprise's liquidity and solvency risks from financial statements that meet reasonable standards of fair presentation—that is, from the descriptions and classifications of reported assets and liabilities on the balance sheet, and by disclosures of, for example, the maturities of its monetary assets and liabilities, its commitments and contingencies, and its operating cash flows. Financial statements prepared in accordance with GAAP should be expected to provide this basic information. However, in Chapter 9 we examined some significant limitations in the effectiveness of the balance sheet to fully depict the financial condition of an enterprise. It noted, for example, the inadequacies of the current asset-current liability classification, and the potential problems of "off-balance sheet" items.

If an entity is at significant risk of becoming insolvent, the validity of the basic "going concern" assumption may be called into question. Financial statements are generally prepared on the assumption that an entity will continue to be solvent—more precisely, that "it will continue in operation for the foreseeable future and will be able to realize assets and discharge liabilities in the normal course of operations" (*CICA Handbook*, paragraph 1000.58). It is on the basis of being a going concern that capital assets can be amortized over potentially long periods reflecting their expected value-in-use lives to the business. The measurement and presentation of assets and liabilities could be very different if an entity cannot be expected to continue to be a going concern.

In an uncertain world there is virtually always some risk that a given entity could become insolvent in the future. Of course some businesses are in better financial condition, with better prospects for the future, than others. Insolvency can occur as a sudden bolt from the blue, as a result of some unforeseeable catastrophic event. But more likely there will be indications of the existence of conditions that may jeopardize the continuance of an enterprise as a going concern. These may include recurring operating losses, serious deficiencies in working capital, excess of liabilities over liquid assets, fixed-term borrowings approaching maturity without realistic prospects for repayment or renewal, negative cash flows from operations, violations of long-term debt covenants, etc. In most cases, the key signs of potential problems should be evident from the financial statements. A considerable body of empirical research exists on the ability to predict business failures from financial statement information.[10]

It has long been accepted, however, that readers of financial statements should not be left to read the signs by themselves, but should be provided with an explicit warning where there is substantial doubt that an entity will be able to continue as a going concern. However, the only reference to this financial reporting responsibility in the *CICA Handbook* appears in an auditing standard. It indicates that adequacy of financial statement disclosure should be assessed in terms of whether "the information explicitly draws the reader's attention to the possibility that the enterprise may be unable to continue realizing its assets and discharging its liabilities in the normal course of business" (paragraph 5510.53). It contains a list of some conditions that may indicate cause for concern (paragraph 5510.52). There has been no authoritative accounting guidance on what constitutes appropriate disclosure, and practice has been rather uneven. Pressures for improved CICA guidance and expanded disclosure requirements arose in the late 1980s, as a result of public concern following a number of major business failures.[11] The development of clear and useful guidance is easier said than done, however. The main difficulty is that it is virtually impossible to design truly objective criteria for determining how serious the risk of failure should be before a going concern uncertainty disclosure should be provided. Also, there is the problem of setting the length of the future period for which the risk of failure should be evaluated. As well, enterprise managements tend to resist going concern uncertainty disclosures in most situations. Such disclosures may reflect badly on their stewardship, and there is a fear that premature disclosure of going concern uncertainty could precipitate a business' failure.

A CICA research study on the accounting and auditing implications of the going concern assumption published in 1991 recommended a set of disclosures.[12] The nature and extent of these disclosures would depend upon the degree of doubt about the validity of the going concern assumption. The CICA Accounting Standards Board finally issued an exposure draft in 1996. It proposed prominent note disclosure in situations "when known events and conditions cause significant doubt about an entity's ability to continue as a going concern for a period of twelve months from the date of completion of the financial statements ...."[13] Proposed disclosures included descriptions of the underlying events and conditions and management's plans for dealing with them.

The CICA seems to have lost its momentum on this project. At the time of writing, it seems unlikely that a *CICA Handbook* standard will be issued in the near future.

Other Perspectives

Financial statement disclosures are not fully explained by the predictive and risk and uncertainty information needs. Another class might be generally described as disclosures that attempt to compensate for inadequate accounting. Several examples may be cited.

- As will be discussed in Chapter 24, the historical cost accounting model has severe deficiencies under conditions of rapidly changing prices and inflation. Supplementary disclosures of current cost and general price level accounting information were called for in the late 1970s and early 1980s, to try to help users compensate for these deficiencies.

- Similarly, supplementary disclosure of the fair value of financial instruments is required to help users evaluate the effects of changing market conditions and financial risk exposures, because such effects and exposures are not well reported by historical cost-based measures. These issues are discussed in Chapter 17.

- The CICA has been urged to provide expanded disclosures of unrecognized commitments. Examples include operating lease commitments, long-term product purchase and sale agreements (common in the resource sector), take-or-pay commitments (often entered into by pipelines and public utilities), and sales of assets with repurchase options or obligations.[14] In previous chapters, we have discussed the challenges these complex arrangements pose for accounting recognition and measurement. In many situations the substance of these arrangements may seem to be assets and liabilities that should be recorded in an enterprise's balance sheet, even though the traditional tests for recognition are not technically met. The problem is intensified when transactions are carefully structured to achieve off-balance sheet treatment. In particular, see the discussion of lease accounting (Chapter 13), asset transfers and securitizations (Chapter 7), and the general discussion of off-balance sheet items in Chapter 9.

As a general rule, disclosure is not a substitute for proper accounting, but in the above situations it is better than nothing. It may be that disclosure is the best possible first step in respect of difficult areas that require further study and familiarity before they can be reliably recognized and measured within the financial statements themselves.

A further class of possible disclosures relates generally to accountability. One might ask whether the basic contracting/stewardship purposes of financial accounting give rise to any disclosures that are distinct from predictive and risk evaluation purposes. In the not-for-profit sector, presentations and disclosures of the discharge of stewardship responsibilities are evident in fund accounting and information on the use of donations that have been designated for specific purposes (see Chapter 27). However, it seems difficult to identify additional disclosures in respect of contracting/stewardship for business enterprises that are not called for by predictive and risk and uncertainty information needs.

CONSTRAINTS ON DISCLOSURE

Proprietary Information

Even though external user interests are seen to be paramount in designing disclosure standards, most would concede that they are not absolute. An enterprise may suffer competitive disadvantage from too much disclosure. Knowledge that a business is exceptionally profitable in some areas may attract new entrants to those areas. Knowledge of the cost structure of a successful enterprise may guide competitors to improvement of their own operations. Knowledge that an enterprise is weak in some area may lead to a vigorous competitive attack to force it out of business. From capital markets and general society perspectives such information may be viewed as beneficial, because it may be expected to result in better bases for investor decisions, in more quickly weeding out uneconomic operations, and in stimulating better productivity and efficiency.

It is generally recognized, however, that some measure of confidentiality should be respected in establishing disclosure standards. Yet it is difficult to decide where to draw the line. The general rule may be stated to be that an enterprise should not be compelled to disclose information that will jeopardize its competitive position or otherwise bring a serious adverse affect upon it, unless the better interests of fairness of disclosure require it. But how are standard setters supposed to trade off the interests of society with the rights of an enterprise to confidentiality? Enterprises often argue that new disclosures will hurt their competitive position. The argument was made fifty years ago against disclosure of revenue figures and twenty-five years ago against disclosure of information about separate segments of a company's business. Companies have survived the imposition of both these disclosures and many others as well. It seems impossible to provide any specific guidance in this area.

The line defining proprietary financial information which need not be disclosed has been drawn differently in different societies and at different times. It will tend to depend on the relative power positions of particular interests. A recent example of the difficulties that standard setters can have is the recent attempt to update and improve the CICA standard on the measurement and disclosure of contingent liabilities. The standard was ultimately withdrawn because powerful representatives of the legal profession contended that disclosures of possible outcomes of litigation in process could be harmful to their clients' interests (see Chapter 8).

Information Overload

Studies of "human information processing" seem to suggest that people are limited in the amount of information they can use as an aid in arriving at a decision. Beyond a certain point, more information seems not to improve decisions—in fact, it may make them worse.

What implications may this have for financial statement disclosures, which have very substantially increased in quantity and complexity? This has been the subject of heated debate, particularly in the U.S., where financial disclosure requirements have been more extensive than in Canada and the rest of the world. Some accountants and managers have claimed that information overload has set in—that "users are overwhelmed," and that "the sheer quantity of financial disclosures has become so excessive that we've diminished the overall value of these disclosures."[15] But there does not seem to be any clear, hard evidence of this overload effect. Although financial statement disclosures have increased very significantly, the costs of information technology have decreased, and user accessibility to information processing technology has improved. Information overload has not been a concern voiced by representatives of financial analysts. The Association for Investment Management and Research has noted that "the need for information to compare investment opportunities of disparate character is greater than ever", and that "the accessibility of computing power continues to rise as rapidly as its cost falls …. Quantitative analysis becomes practicable to an extent never dreamed of previously."[16]

The full implications of technological developments for financial analysis and ability to process increased quantities of complex information have yet to unfold. It may be that there is virtually no limit to the amount of information that may be assimilated by the capital markets as a whole, but it seems likely that, even with vastly improved technology, individuals do have significant limits in their ability to understand and use it.

In the U.S., the FASB and SEC have initiated efforts to try to simplify disclosures and eliminate those that are not useful. To date, they have not achieved major reductions.[17] In Canada, information overload concerns have been expressed mostly in respect of smaller private organizations. With respect to Canadian capital markets, some have voiced the opposite concern —that the extent and timeliness of disclosure requirements of Canadian companies has been lagging behind investors' needs and expectations.[18]

One set of suggestions has focused, not on reducing information, but rather on improving the ability of users to navigate through data. Some have suggested "two-tier" or "differential" disclosure. That is, financial information in addition to that deemed necessary in published financial reports may be made accessible upon request for more in-depth analysis purposes. Such an approach is, in effect, supported by the U.S. Securities and Exchange Commission, which requires financial reports filed with it to be supplemented by more detail than is customarily given in reports to company shareholders.

As well as making extensive additional information available to the professional analyst, it could be desirable to move in the other direction and present simplified accounts. These may well have merit from a public relations viewpoint, but they have their own pitfalls in terms of selection of information to be highlighted and changes required in terminology to make the simplified statements understandable.[19]

Another possibility for reducing disclosures is to eliminate some of the inadequacies of financial accounting recognition and measurement, and so reduce the need for disclosures discussed earlier that attempt to compensate for these inadequacies.

Cost/Benefit Trade-Offs

In general terms, constraints on disclosure rest on the proposition that costs of disclosure should not exceed benefits. It is difficult to make this advice specific. Benefits from additional financial disclosure may be small if the information disclosed is available in other ways. Even if it is not, it is notoriously difficult to measure the benefits of additional information. Direct costs of disclosure may be capable of estimation, but secondary effects are hard to identify, and it is often not known what the result would have been without disclosure. Further, the benefits and costs accrue differently to different parties. Managements have commonly claimed, for example, that corporations bear the costs of preparing and distributing financial reports while analysts and investors obtain most of the benefits. However, as to be discussed below, this may be a shortsighted view. In the end, the balance between cost and benefit can be very much a matter of opinion.

How one balances the costs and benefits of financial disclosures will depend upon the extent to which one accepts a capital markets, versus a paternalistic, role for financial information. The capital markets vision is evident in the objectives of securities commissions and stock exchanges. For example, the introduction to the Toronto Stock Exchange's Timely Disclosure Policy contains the following statement:

> Public confidence in the integrity of the Exchange as a securities market requires timely disclosure of all material information concerning the business and affairs of companies listed on the Exchange, thereby placing all participants in the market on an equal footing.

It is the mission of securities commissions to try to ensure a "fair game." It is reasoned that if investors have the information they need to assess risks and make informed decisions, they are then in a position to assume full responsibility for their decisions and to accept the results of their actions.

It must be recognized, however, that this vision is not fully shared by some other regulatory authorities. In particular, the traditional mission of bank regulators has led them to lean towards some careful management of financial information about the financial condition of financial institutions, especially at key times when an institution may be in financial difficulties. Bank regulators, and governments themselves, may be concerned not to cause undue anxiety on the part of investors and depositors, which they fear could trigger over-reactions and unjustified loss of public confidence in the banking system, and in government monetary policies. This view seems to presume that investors, depositors and the public cannot be trusted to properly assess complex information, and act rationally. This view would seem to be declining in influence with the globalization of capital markets, but it is still present.

Voluntary Disclosures

Some reason that financial disclosures do not need to be legislated. They argue that business managements will have powerful natural motivations to provide disclosures that will balance benefits and costs in the best interests of all parties. They believe that securities regulators and accounting standard setters have underestimated the incentives for companies to provide needed information voluntarily. If certain information is important to investors, enterprises that fail to provide it can expect to find that they must pay a higher cost of capital, and that their stock prices will be depressed by a discount for "information uncertainty." In support of this view, there would seem to be signs of increased recognition within enterprises of the benefits of full and timely disclosure.[20]

On the other hand, many would seem to believe that many business enterprises are motivated to take narrow, short-term perspectives on disclosure. A growing body of academic research on voluntary financial disclosures focuses on the tension that exists between a manager's desire (1) to communicate good news to, and withhold bad news from, capital markets; and (2) to hide or play down good news from competitors in the enterprise's product lines.[21] Empirical evidence seems to indicate that, on balance, business managers may be reluctant to reveal the full extent of bad financial news as quickly and reliably as good financial news. It is suggested that management's predisposition in this regard may be affected by its compensation plans that are tied to earnings or stock prices, but may be expected to be countered by concerns with respect to loss of credibility in the capital marketplace and possible lawsuits, if information is unduly repressed.

These conflicting factors are difficult to sort out. Also, much of this research has been carried out within the U.S. environment, which environment may differ from that of Canada in some respects (differences in the extent of management stock options, and the extent of required disclosures, SEC enforcement, and risk of litigation, for example).

On balance it would seem to be naïve to rely on voluntary disclosures. If one could do so, then one might expect that disclosures in Canadian company financial statements would be the equal of those of U.S. companies, despite the fact that Canadian standards have required a lesser level of disclosure in many areas (as has been documented in earlier chapters). However, this seems not to be the case.[22]

Materiality

The concept of materiality is a practical tool to assist in the selection of information to be disclosed in financial statements, as well as the precision with which it need be measured. The concept is firmly based in the orientation of financial statements to user needs. That is to say, there will be a failure in communications if statements contain a material error, misrepresentation or omission. The financial statement preparer uses the materiality criterion in fulfilling its reporting obligation, but it must be understood that the criterion is derived from user needs.

The accepted concept of materiality is that some information or some aspect of statement presentation is material if its omission or misrepresentation could affect a decision of a reasonably intelligent and rational reader of financial statements. Although logical, this concept presents considerable difficulty in implementation. How can we know what may be expected to influence decisions? In theory, reference would be made to statistical confidence levels in rational investment decision models. However, unfortunately, we do not have such well-defined models to work from, and we do not have any very concrete evidence explaining how people make investment or credit decisions. Most accounting definitions of the materiality concept refer to decision making by "a reasonable person," or "the average prudent investor."

The FASB issued a comprehensive discussion paper on criteria for determining materiality in 1975.[23] On the basis of responses to it, and further deliberations, it decided to discontinue the separate study of materiality, and the matter was subsumed within its concept statement on the qualitative characteristics of accounting information. This concept statement adopted the position that, "no general standards of materiality could be formulated to take into account all the considerations that enter into an experienced human judgment." [24]

Research and practice suggests that (1) there can be a considerable dispersion in opinions held by various observers as to what is or is not material, (2) enough consensus exists that some guidance can be given in broad quantitative terms, and (3) there are some factors that can only be expressed in qualitative terms.[25]

Quantitative Criteria

To make the concept of materiality operational, it has been necessary to adopt a number of quantitative rules of thumb. These tend to be modified to fit particular circumstances, based on judgment. For the most part, materiality is judged in relative, rather than absolute, terms. If a piece of financial information is small relative to its setting, it is not material just because it might be an enormous amount in relation to the wealth of an average individual.

Net income is, not surprisingly, the most commonly used reference base against which materiality is judged. The normal rule of thumb is that an item over 10% of normal net income before income tax should be considered material, while an item under 5% need not be regarded as material—subject to the possibility that other factors may provide more important reference points than net income in some situations (as will be discussed below).[26]

It is generally felt that an income reference base should be a normal, representative income figure. Thus it may be necessary to eliminate the effects of abnormal income, such as unusual nonrecurring gains or losses, or unusual amounts of management fees or bonuses, or the effects of related-party transactions that are not in the normal course of operations. It makes little sense, assuming the business remains essentially the same, that the reference base should vary significantly from year to year. Representative income might be best indicated by an average of net income for several years, rather than the current year's figure if it is abnormally low or high. If an enterprise has just broken even, or suffered losses for several years, the quantification of materiality may be based on a notion of a normal level of profitability, which may be derived by applying a conservative target percentage return on equity to the amount of shareholders' equity reported in the balance sheet. A CICA Audit Guide suggests that, when income is not considered to be an appropriate base, materiality might be judged in terms of percentage ranges applied to gross profit, revenues, assets or equity. The guide provides examples of percentage ranges that might be considered appropriate.[27]

Bases other than income may be logical in certain circumstances. For example, suppose a question concerns disclosure of a possible contingent loss which, if it occurred, would not be considered a recurring factor in any evaluation of the earnings prospects of a business. A comparison of the possible loss with the amount of shareholders' equity rather than with income for a single year, might well be an appropriate measure from a knowledgeable user's perspective. In another situation, if a company were suffering a liquidity problem, one might judge the materiality of a particular item by the impact its treatment would have on the total liquid assets disclosed, or on net working capital.

The income rule of thumb has been developed in the context of annual financial statements. Interim financial statements can present a problem. An item that represents only 4% of normal net income for a year is likely to be a much higher percentage of net income for the quarter in which it occurs. It may not seem reasonable that an item that is immaterial in the context of annual reporting should become material just because the report is only for part of the year. On the other hand, the possibility of giving a misleading impression of interim results and trends is increased if the base is annual income. In the end, if reported interim income results are to have significance in and of themselves, it would seem that materiality should be assessed in relation to interim period income.[28]

Qualitative Criteria

In assessing materiality, a number of considerations exist that cannot be expressed in quantitative terms. These considerations influence decisions when the quantitative tests fall in the intermediate zone, and they may on occasion be sufficient to suggest that an item should be considered material even when it falls below the customarily recognized minimum level of materiality.

- Accounting measurements in certain types of industries are inherently less precise than in others. As a result, reported earnings may well fluctuate widely from period to period as specific uncertainties become resolved and settlements take place. It may well be felt that the materiality of an uncertainty requiring disclosure in such a situation may be higher than in an enterprise in a more stable type of industry.

- The precision with which assets and liabilities may be measured varies substantially according to their nature. Cash may normally be measured within narrow tolerances, while estimation of cost or realizability of inventory, or realizability of capital assets, may often be very difficult. It is generally felt that the materiality test may be less stringent in the latter cases than in the former.

- A particular type of event or contingency may have an isolated impact upon an enterprise or may promise a continuing impact. More stringent materiality levels apply in the latter situation than in the former.

- A business may have a weak financial structure or be experiencing liquidity problems. Materiality is interpreted more stringently in such a case when considering known errors or questions of statement presentation. Indeed, if a particular item in question could mean the difference between signalling or not signalling default on a debt covenant, the leeway for materiality consideration with respect to known errors virtually disappears.

Finally, there are a limited number of situations in which quantitative criteria for materiality may not be relevant. There are certain conditions or transactions that a user of financial statements is entitled to know if they exist. A good example is provided by transactions with related parties. These may be immaterial in their financial effect, but the statement reader is entitled to know that they have taken place.

In applying the above quantitative and qualitative factors, it is important to remember that there are inherent limits as to the level of precision that financial accounting information can reasonably be expected to achieve in given circumstances at a manageable cost. Materiality might then be equated with measurement uncertainty discussed earlier in this chapter. We have noted efforts to improve the disclosure of measurement uncertainty. A CICA research study advocated disclosure of assumed materiality levels to financial statement users, either by management in the notes to the financial statements, or by the auditors as part of the auditors' report.[29] While the idea seems to have merit, it has not achieved any acceptance in practice, and no standard-setting authority has seriously considered requiring it. This position may be understandable if one accepts the FASB conclusion, noted earlier, that no general standards of materiality can be formulated.

INTERIM REPORTING

The usefulness of financial reports depends significantly upon their timeliness. Although annual reporting is the traditional norm, public companies have been required to provide interim reports to shareholders for some three decades, and many public companies voluntarily supplied quarterly or semiannual reports long before that time.

The timeliness of financial information has been increasing in importance as global capital markets seek information on the effects of events when they happen. There has been pressure for earlier release of more extensive quarterly information. Some question whether, with the shrinking of product cycles and the rapidity with which financial position and income earnings prospects can change, even quarterly reports may be insufficient.[30]

Previous chapters have revealed the problems in assigning revenues and costs to annual periods for the purpose of measuring income. These problems are even more severe when the reporting period is shorter. In annual reports, many costs are treated as expense when incurred, even though known to benefit the future, because expectations of the amount and timing of future benefit are too uncertain to permit reliable allocation. In the more confined perspective of interim reporting, the nonallocation is perceived to involve an even greater distortion of income measurement. The question is, should something be done about it?

Two Different Concepts of Interim Reports

The answer to the preceding question may depend upon one's concept of an interim report and its objectives. Under one concept, the description "interim report" is considered to be a misnomer. A report for a three-month period ought not to be considered interim. It is a report for a self-contained or "discrete" period of three months. As such, there should be no difference in accounting principles and procedures between a report for a quarter and a report for a full year. If certain procedures are not satisfactory for quarterly reporting, they should be changed—but the same changes should be made in annual reporting. The perspective of a short period provides a good test whether accounting procedures are satisfactory.

Under a completely different concept, a financial report for less than a year is considered an interim report on part of the year, not an independent report in its own right. The main idea underlying the so-called "integral" concept is that an interim report should help the reader predict what the annual report will show. It is appropriate to allocate the results of events between interim periods if, by so doing, prediction of the annual figures will be assisted, even though such allocation would not be permitted between annual periods.

The limits of the integral concept should be understood. It is not intended that the net income reported for three months should be one-quarter of the net income expected to be reported for a full year. Operating revenues for the quarter, for example, will be measured on the same basis as for a full year and thus will vary from period to period. Rather, the general idea is that some operating expenses will be allocated in proportion to revenues so that the margin on sales for the interim period should be a better estimate of the margin obtainable for the full year. Thus, it remains necessary for the statement user to predict revenues for the full year in order to predict the year's net operating income. In addition, allocations are restricted to ordinary operating costs. Gains and losses on disposal of capital assets and investments, or any items that would be classified as extraordinary or unusual in annual reporting are to be reported in the period when they occur, not "smoothed" over several interim periods within the fiscal year.

It is far from clear that the objective of assisting the prediction of annual results necessarily requires adoption of the integral concept. The integral method requires that both revenue and costs for the remainder of the year be accurately forecast by management in order that costs may be allocated so as to result in approximately level margins of operating profit in all periods. If a business is volatile, not only may interim figures determined by the integral method be poor predictors of annual results, they could also be a poor record of actual events, having been contaminated by the effect on allocations of estimation errors.

Neither has it been established that the discrete concept provides a poor basis for prediction. A policy of reporting expenses largely as costs are incurred, together with a history of quarterly experience in previous years, might well provide a serious analyst with a good basis for prediction.

On the surface, Canadian and U.S. standards are at odds as to the preferable concept. The *CICA Handbook* states: "Interim financial reports should present information with respect to the results of operations of a company for a specified period rather than a proration of expected results for the annual period." [31] In contrast, the U.S. standard says, "... each interim period should be viewed primarily as an integral part of an annual period." [32] Examination of the actual recommendations in the two standards, however, indicates that neither rigorously adheres to a single concept and they are not seriously at odds with each other. Each might be described as taking a compromise or "combination" approach.

These standards permit considerable latitude in allocating certain types of costs between periods. Some have expressed concern that reported interim earnings may be open to an unreasonable degree of discretionary allocation and income smoothing. In particular, the leading association representing financial analysts has strongly urged the FASB to revise its standard (which, like the Canadian standard, is now twenty-five years old) and require a clearly defined discrete approach.[33] Some academic research seems to indicate that capital market prices behave as though investors attempt to remove the effects of annualizing adjustments—more precisely, that U.S. stock prices largely fail to reflect the extent to which reported quarterly earnings series differ from a seasonal random walk effect.[34] A recent IASC standard (IAS 34) has adopted an approach that is, in most respects, consistent with the discrete model.[35]

It must also be recognized that interim financial reports are generally subject to greater estimation variability than annual reports, for two reasons. First, in the interests of achieving timeliness, most enterprises do not apply the same extent of closing procedures as for annual financial statements. For example, estimates of allowances for asset impairment and contingent losses, and physical verification of inventories, are likely to be less rigorous and detailed. Second, the relative effects of imprecision on interim information is greater because the numbers associated with shorter periods are smaller. (As noted earlier, this latter fact has implications for interpreting what should be considered to be material. An integral approach would suggest that materiality be defined in relation to expected annual results, while a discrete approach would define materiality by reference to interim results standing alone.)

Some Specific Allocation and Estimation Issues

The trade-offs involved in developing operational methods for allocation and estimation in interim reporting are best appreciated in considering some common applications.

Inventories and Cost of Goods Sold Expense

The general requirement is that enterprises should measure inventories and cost of goods sold expense by the same principles for both interim and annual reporting. However, approximations and estimations based on annual expectations are accepted in practice.

- As described in Chapter 10, enterprises may have absorption costing systems under which overhead costs are allocated to inventories on some predetermined, or standard costing, basis. Since production activities may fluctuate for seasonal or other reasons, this process will tend to result in underabsorption or overabsorption of overheads. At a fiscal year-end unabsorbed amounts are not carried forward. For interim reporting purposes, however, it has been accepted that such variances that are reasonably expected to be absorbed by the year-end may be deferred at an interim reporting date. Other unanticipated variances not due to seasonal effects that can be expected to reverse by year-end are expensed in the interim period in which they arise. If, for example, there is a significant underabsorbed balance at a period-end because of low production attributable to slack economic conditions, that balance should be written off. It is to be noted that IAS 34 does not permit deferral of variances in interim reports merely because they are expected to be absorbed by the year-end (see Appendix 2, paragraph 28).

• LIFO inventory calculations are normally carried out on an annual basis, so that the effect of a reduction in inventory quantities is not reflected in an inventory valuation at an interim date if that reduction is expected to be restored by year-end.

• Inventories are represented in annual financial statements at the lower of cost and market, and a write-down to market value is considered to establish a new cost base which is not adjusted for subsequent recoveries. It has been accepted, however, that no provision is needed in an interim report if the loss can be reasonably expected to be recovered before it is sold, or by the year-end, if it remains unsold. An example might be a situation in which there is an established pattern of seasonal price fluctuations. One might be skeptical that such a situation could arise very often, and IAS 34 seems not to permit the practice (see Appendix 2, paragraph 26).

The *CICA Handbook* has a brief paragraph on the determination of interim inventories, which seems open to a wide range of interpretation on these issues.

Costs Determined at the Year-End

Certain costs incurred by a company (or cost reductions) may be based on formulas that are calculated only annually. In such cases, it may be necessary to make estimates of the formula for the year in order to make accruals at interim period ends. Such cases include nondiscretionary expenditures that benefit the whole year, but may be incurred in single or lump sums during a year. Insurance premiums and normal recurring fees (such as audit fees) are examples. They may also include expenditures for which a liability is incurred late in the year, but that relates to activities during the year. Possible examples include sales discounts based on minimum annual sales volumes, contingent lease payments based on achievable annual sales levels, and certain bonus plans. In these situations it may be necessary to estimate the annual amount and accrue a reasonable portion of it at each interim period end. However, certain of these costs require careful assessment as to the extent to which a company may be considered to be obligated at the interim period-end. For example, it has been common in North America for companies to accrue in interim financial statements estimates for normal recurring repairs and maintenance. IAS 34 takes a more rigorous position consistent with the discrete concept. It states that planned periodic maintenance costs should not be anticipated "unless an event has caused the enterprise to have a legal or constructive obligation" (Appendix 2, paragraph 2). It reasons that the intention to carry out future maintenance is not sufficient to give rise to a liability at an interim date. Likewise, IAS 34 states that a bonus should be anticipated only if there is a legal or constructive obligation at the interim date, and the amount can be reasonably estimated (Appendix 2, paragraphs 5-6).

The CICA standard would seem to allow for interim depreciation provisions to be based on expected year-end balances (see paragraph 1750.24). There would seem to be little justification for this, and IAS 34 makes it clear that depreciation should be based only on assets existing in the interim period.

Income Taxes

Income taxes represent a special case of a cost determined by a formula at the year-end. The general objective is to calculate an effective rate of tax for the year and apply it to the pre-tax income as reported for the interim period. The rate should reflect the company's budget and intentions for the year, and should be re-evaluated and adjusted prospectively at each interim reporting date in the light of current information. Some questions arise in applying this general objective.

- If the business is eligible for the small business tax credit or the manufacturing and processing credit, the effective tax rate will be sensitive to the proportion of profit for the year not qualifying for the credit. The estimate, therefore, needs to be kept under review as the year progresses so that the assumed rate can be adjusted if conditions change.

- Suppose different types of income are taxed at different rates. For example, suppose capital gains are included in income, or suppose income contains foreign source income taxed at different rates than domestic income. Should the pre-tax income reported at each interim period be disaggregated and different effective rates be applied to each component, or should the average effective tax rate for the year be calculated on a global basis and that rate applied to the pre-tax reported income of the interim period regardless of its components? A disaggregation of rates so as to deal separately with each class of income taxable at different rates would be the better answer.

- If a business shows a loss in one or more interim periods at the beginning of the year and that loss is expected to be offset by profits in the remainder of the year, and if a taxable profit also existed in previous years within the loss carryback period, an assumption must be made as to whether the interim period loss should be deemed to be carried back to previous years or offset by profits of future periods within the current year. The rate of tax applied in calculating the tax recovery might differ depending upon this choice. The *CICA Handbook* recommends assuming a tax recovery as though the loss were carried back to previous fiscal year(s) (paragraph 1750.20). If there is no taxable profit within the loss carryback period or if its amount is not sufficient to fully absorb the interim period loss of the current year, a potential tax recovery is to be assumed from profits that are considered to be more likely than not to be achieved in the remainder of the current fiscal year or in future years.

Presentation and Disclosure

The original CICA standard concentrated on income statement data. A few supplementary disclosures were required of significant changes since the last annual financial statements in contingencies and commitments and capital structure, and in accounting methods. The standard has been expanded in recent years to provide for key information on significant cash flows and certain information about business segments.

No balance sheet is required by the CICA standard, although many companies do voluntarily provide a condensed balance sheet and statements of cash flows and retained earnings. Such statements are required by the SEC, and are now required by IAS 34.

In 1991, a CICA-commissioned research study concluded that the *CICA Handbook* standard had become out of date and was urgently in need of significant revisions.[36] It recommended that all enterprises that are legally required to issue interim reports prepare such reports on a quarterly basis, and that these reports include the same financial statements presented in annual reports and in the same level of detail. It did allow, however, that notes could be presented on a condensed basis. Presumably these notes should be sufficient to enable readers to understand significant changes in financial position and financial performance since the last annual reporting date. It further recommended that a fourth quarter report should be provided. It also concluded that interim financial statements should be based on accounting principles and practices consistent with those used in the annual financial statements.

To date, apart from modifications to require certain cash flow and segmented information, the CICA has not yet addressed these recommendations. [Note: A CICA project to improve interim reporting was initiated in 1999.]

SEGMENTED REPORTING

Historical Overview

Segmented reporting had its genesis in the early 1960s with concerns over the trend among corporations towards diversification into a number of lines of business. With diversification it became less easy for financial analysts to make an intelligent assessment of a company's prospects, since distinctly different risks and prospects for growth and profitability among various segments of the business carried on could be concealed within consolidated financial statements. After much debate the U.S. Securities and Exchange Commission imposed requirements for "line of business" reporting in filings by registrants with the commission in 1969 and 1970. These were followed in 1976 by FASB requirements for segmented disclosure in financial statements (which requirements were restricted within two years to enterprises with publicly traded securities). In 1979, Canadian accounting standards were changed to follow the United States' lead, with application restricted to public companies.[37]

The objective of these standards was to identify segments subject to different risks and with different growth and profitability prospects. Two bases for disaggregating consolidated data were specified—by industry and by geographic area. Specific definitions of "industry" and "geographic area" were not provided, leaving management with much flexibility.

- Segmentation by industry could be based on the nature of the product, the nature of the production process, or the nature of the market served. Profit centres defined for internal purposes might be useable, but the organizational structure was not supposed to determine the definition of segments if the resulting segmentation would not be considered to meet the test of distinguishing segments by similarity of risks and growth prospects.

- Geographic segmentation was to be based on the location of the enterprise's operations. Each enterprise was to determine by common sense tests what groupings of countries would constitute natural geographic segments of its operations, based on such factors as the proximity of operations, interrelationships of operations between countries, and the degree of commonality of economic and political conditions.

The standards provided quantitative guidelines to be applied so that only material segments would be reported and, conversely, to try to ensure that enough segments would be reported to account for at least 75% of an enterprise's revenues.

The standards required a general description of the products and services of each industry segment, and identification of the countries included in geographic segments. For each reported industry segment disclosure was required of revenues (subdivided between sales to outsiders and sales to other industry segments), operating profit or loss, identifiable net assets, depreciation, capital expenditures, and certain supporting disclosures. Guidance was provided on what should and should not be included in the measure of operating profit or loss. The total of segmented operating profit or loss was to be reconciled with net income reported in the income statement.

With respect to operations in different geographic areas, disclosures were required of revenues (subdivided between sales to outsiders and other geographic segments of the enterprise), a company-chosen measure of profit or loss ranging from operating profit to net income, identifiable assets, and certain supporting disclosures. Revenues from sales to foreign customers were also to be disclosed if they exceeded 10% of sales to domestic customers.

Empirical research has indicated that the resulting segmented reporting disclosures produced benefits in improving analysts' forecasts, although it appeared that disclosure of segment sales was more useful for this purpose than disclosure of profits. Segment information has apparently had an impact on the market's assessment of enterprise risk, and there is some evidence that the perceived riskiness of companies has been reduced more frequently than it has been increased as a result of this information.[38]

There were a number of problems with the standards, however. The most significant of these related to the segment definitions. In particular, analysts complained that a number of companies provided no segmentation, because they could claim, under the flexible provisions of the standard, to be in only one industry. Analysts believed that a number of other companies showed segments that were too broad to provide very useful information.

The CICA and FASB undertook independent research studies to review the adequacy of segment reporting requirements, to document the perceived problems, and to consider the need for changes. Each study concluded that there were serious inadequacies in the standards, and each identified similar issues that needed to be addressed.[39]

Redeveloping Segmented Reporting Standards

In 1993, the CICA and FASB agreed to jointly pursue the development of improved segmented reporting standards. The two boards worked together, and in 1997 were successful in putting in place standards that reached the same conclusions.[40]

These new standards require that segmented information be provided on the basis that management of the enterprise has organized its segments for making internal operating and performance decisions. The basic provisions of the CICA standard follow.

- The requirements apply to public companies, cooperative businesses, deposit-taking institutions and life insurance enterprises. Other entities are encouraged to provide these disclosures.

- An *operating segment* is defined as a component of an enterprise about which separate financial information is available that is regularly reviewed by the enterprise's chief operating decision maker in deciding how to allocate resources and assess performance. The "chief operating decision maker" refers to a function, which may be carried out by a group of executives or, in some organizations, by an individual. If the chief operating decision maker uses more than one set of segment information, other factors such as the structure of management responsibility centres, and the basis of segment information reporting to the board of directors, may be determining. An enterprise could be organized by its products and services, by geography, by some mixture of both, or on some other basis, such as customer type. In a few situations businesses may be structured on the basis of over-lapping responsibilities —for example, when certain managers are responsible for different product lines worldwide, while others are responsible for specific geographic areas. In such a case, the components based on products would constitute the operating segments. An enterprise is required to disclose information about its basis of organization.

Components of an enterprise that sell primarily or exclusively to other operating segments of the enterprise (vertically integrated operations) qualify as operating seg-ments if they are managed as such. As an example, oil companies commonly treat upstream activities (exploration and production) and downstream activities (refining and marketing) as separate segments, even though most or all of the upstream product (crude oil) is transferred to its refining operations.

- The standard sets out aggregation and quantitative thresholds for determining which operating segments should be reported separately, that is, should be identified as *reportable segments*. It permits combining of segments that meet criteria for being con-sidered to have similar economic characteristics. Operating segments that constitute 10% or more of reported revenues, assets or profit or loss must be reported separately, and reportable segments must account for at least 75% of an enterprise's external rev-enues. Disclosure is required of the factors used to determine reportable segments and whether operating segments have been aggregated.

- Disclosure is to be made of a measure of the profit or loss for each reportable segment and total assets, as well as certain specific revenue and expense items that are included in the measure of segment profit or loss reviewed by the chief operating decision maker. Disclosure is also to be made of expenditures for additions to capital assets and goodwill for each reportable segment to the extent that they are included in the determination of reported segment assets.

- Each of the above amounts is to be measured on the basis reported to the chief operat-ing decision maker, even if the measurement methods are not in accordance with GAAP or are not consistent with methods used in measuring consolidated financial statement figures. Explanations of the measurements are to be provided, along with reconcilia-tions of the totals of significant reported segment amounts (including revenues, profit or loss, and total assets) to corresponding amounts in the enterprise's financial statements.

- Certain basic information about products and services and foreign country activities is to be disclosed if it is not disclosed as part of its reportable segment information, unless it is impracticable to do so. This information includes external revenues for each prod-uct or service (or groups of similar products or services) and external revenues attributed to foreign countries, and capital assets and goodwill located in foreign countries (with such amounts to be disclosed separately for individual countries where the amounts are mate-rial). As well, information about the extent of an enterprise's reliance on major cus-tomers is to be given.

In summary, these standards represent an attempt to improve segment reporting by align-ing it with an enterprise's internal organizational structure. The CICA AcSB and FASB con-cluded that this "management approach" should result in a number of enterprises reporting a greater number of segments, and in most enterprises providing more useful information about each segment. An enterprise will not be able to claim that it has only one segment based on the subjective "risk and return" criteria, if it is effectively managed otherwise. The expectation is that this approach will enable readers to see an enterprise's operating results "through the eyes of management," and in so doing, gain insights into the risks and returns implications of the components of an enterprise's activities that management believes are important.

The reporting should be consistent with how management explains and analyzes enterprise performance in other parts of the annual report, which was often not the case under the old standards. As well, it is believed that the cost of providing segmented information will be reduced for many entities, since the information is largely based on what is prepared for internal use.

While users have been generally supportive of the approach, many preparers and some others have had reservations.[41]

- Many who have reservations with respect to the new standards believe that the management approach will decrease comparability between enterprises. Two companies could be in the same industries and geographic areas and yet have very different segment reporting because they are organized differently. As well, operating profit or loss figures may be reported at different levels as between enterprises and even within operating segments of the same enterprise. The reply to this is that a trade-off is necessary to have information that is consistent with how a business is organized and managed. As well, it should be recognized that there was really little comparability between enterprises under the alternative "risks and returns" approach of the old standards, because the concepts of "industry" and "geographic area" have proved to be open to wide interpretation.

- Another common concern is that using internal measurements that may not be GAAP reduces representational faithfulness. For example, depreciation expense might be allocated to segments while the corresponding assets are not, resulting in a lack of symmetry between reported measures of profit and loss and total assets. Other examples: pension expense may be allocated to segments on a cash basis, and inventory costs might be allocated differently than they are in the consolidated accounts. However, there has been no agreement on what constitutes GAAP for many allocations at the segment level (for example, allocations of joint costs, and transfer pricing), and the CICA and FASB concluded that many allocations that are inherently arbitrary may not be meaningful if they are not used for management purposes. Thus the boards decided to not try to draw lines and instead rely on disclosures of measurement bases used.

- There is some cause for concern that segmented results of companies with organizational structures that are not based on products/services or geographic areas will not provide information that is very useful in understanding its risks and return opportunities. For example, a business might be structured on the basis of competing submanagement empires that put disparate units together. Some believe that knowledge of this, and of the results of such a structure, will be useful and that capital markets will judge the enterprises accordingly. Nevertheless, the standards provide for fall-back secondary level disclosures (as noted above) about products and geographic areas if such information is not provided in the basic segmented disclosures.

- A number of preparers have expressed concern that the disclosure requirements could cause information to be revealed about corporate structure and results of components that would be competitively harmful to the reporting enterprise. The boards decided, however, not to provide for any exemptions, believing that the information required is not more detailed than that due to be provided by a company with a single operation, and that any exemptions would undermine the standard by providing the means for broad noncompliance.

In evaluating these concerns, one must keep in mind that determination of business components and measures of their profit or loss are inherently subjective, and arbitrary in some degree. Also, based on experience with the old standards, it seems unlikely that prescriptive rules defining industries and geographic areas could be successful.

The Canadian and U.S. standards are based on the reasonable presumption that the most useful information may be expected to result from management's judgments and allocations used for their own internal purposes, accepting that this involves some potential disadvantages which may be largely compensated for by requiring certain basic fall-back information and supporting disclosures of methods and bases.

One of the major disappointments to some is that these standards address only business operating segment information. They do not require broader disaggregations and, in particular, do not provide for information sought by lenders and creditors to help them assess risks and returns related to individual borrowing units within an enterprise. Borrowing units are often individual legal entities within a consolidated enterprise, and such legal entities may not be consistent with an enterprise's business segments. Borrowing risks may differ significantly as between borrowing units. Lenders, as well as other users, have expressed a desire for separate information on borrowing units, including, perhaps, multicolumn consolidated financial statements. To date, accounting standard setters have not rigorously addressed these possibilities.

The IASC Standard—Some Differences

The IASC also revised its standard on segmented reporting, effective in 1997.[42] It applies to public enterprises. While the U.S. and Canadian standards have fully embraced the "management approach," the IASC standard has modified it in some significant respects. IAS 14 (revised) requires that a company look to its internal organizational structure for reporting to its chief executive officer to identify reportable segments. However, if it happens that internal segments are not organized on either product/service or geographic lines, one must look to the next lower level of internal segmentation that does report on one of these lines. Thus the IASC standard requires primary reporting of segmented information either on a product/service or geographic area basis. It requires reduced ("secondary") segment information on whichever of these two bases is not reported as primary information.

There are also some differences in the items to be disclosed under the IASC standard. As well, reportable segments must earn a majority of their revenues from outside customers; thus, unlike the Canadian and U.S. standards, a vertically integrated activity is not a reportable segment (although the IASC standard encourages its reporting).

Perhaps most important, there are some significant differences in the measurement of segment data. The IASC standard does not rely on internal management measures, but prescribes measures of operating income before corporate expenses, taxes and financing costs. It requires that segment measurement methods be consistent with those applied in determining consolidated enterprise figures.

Significant efforts were made by representatives of the IASC, FASB and CICA to try to harmonize the standards, but, as can be seen, some significant differences exist.

THE CALCULATION OF EARNINGS PER SHARE

The calculation and interpretation of earnings per share (EPS) is straightforward if a company has only common shares outstanding and is under no obligation to issue further shares at less than their fair value. However, in the 1960s, many companies began issuing a variety of securities that provided contingent interest in or claims upon present or future earnings that otherwise would accrue to the existing common shareholders. These have included options, warrants, convertible debt and preferred shares, and other agreements under which common shares are contingently issuable at potentially dilutive prices.

Securities authorities became alarmed by the possibilities of misleading computations of EPS that did not recognize these potentially dilutive effects. The accounting profession was initially reluctant to become involved in what was essentially not a question of financial reporting, but rather one of determining a statistic based on financial reporting. However, it was soon persuaded that a standardized calculation of EPS as part of financial statements would be constructive.

The essence of the challenge in computing EPS is to present fairly the impact of contingent rights on the numerator and denominator of the EPS statistic. U.S. and Canadian standards issued in 1969 and 1970, respectively, attempted to address this matter.[43] Both standards required that companies report two fundamental EPS amounts—one reflecting a basic or primary figure and the other the effects of potential dilution. The Canadian and U.S. standards differed in their bases for determining these two figures.

The standards were frequently criticized (particularly in the U.S.) as being arbitrary, overly complex, and of questionable usefulness.[44] The 1969 U.S. standard was the subject of nearly 120 formal interpretations and amendments.

In 1994, the FASB undertook a project on EPS to be pursued concurrently with a similar project of the IASC. Its objective was to improve and simplify its standard and make it compatible with international standards. In 1997, the FASB issued a new standard (SFAS128).[45] Its provisions are substantially the same as an IASC standard issued at the same time.[46]

To date the CICA has made no significant changes to its old standard, but the AcSB has recently decided to undertake a project to re-examine it with a view to harmonizing it with those of the FASB and IASC. The basic requirements of the existing CICA standard are reviewed below, and compared with those of the old and new FASB standards. In the process several of the more contentious issues are identified and briefly considered.

The Calculation of Basic EPS

The *CICA Handbook* standard requires that "basic EPS" be based upon the hard facts as they exist at the financial reporting date – that is, based on the weighted average of fully participating shares actually outstanding during the financial reporting period and the actual earnings reported as reduced by interest or preferred dividends actually paid or accrued with respect to other senior securities.

Matters of application are reasonably straightforward. They relate to the following:

- The treatment of undeclared dividends on preferred shares (the only undeclared dividends to be deducted from earnings (or added to a loss) are dividend entitlements for the period on cumulative preferred shares).
- The use of a weighted average of shares outstanding, where shares have been issued or reacquired during the period.
- The retroactive adjustment of EPS for stock dividends and stock splits.
- The calculation of separate basic EPS for fully participating preferred shares that have different dividend rates from the common shares.

The 1969 U.S. standard required a different calculation. It was felt that some contingent equity securities were so likely to be exercised that it would be misleading to calculate a basic EPS figure leaving them out. Accordingly, tests were designed for identifying securities that should be regarded as "common stock equivalents," and these were included in the denominator in the basic EPS statistic, which was called "primary earnings per share."

This U.S. modification was heavily criticized over the years in American literature, in particular for its highly arbitrary basis for determining when convertible bonds should be considered to be common share equivalents (based on whether the yield was less than two-thirds of the yield of Aa-rated corporate bonds at the time of issuance). The significance of the resulting primary EPS figure was open to some question. It appears that the Canadian standard setters were wise to avoid the complications and arbitrariness of the U.S. standard in this aspect. The new U.S. standard adopts a basic EPS calculation that is essentially the same as that of the Canadian standard.

The Calculation of Dilutive Effects

A "fully diluted" figure of EPS is determined on a "what if" basis. The objective is to show the effect of the maximum dilution of EPS which potential conversions, exercises, and contingent issuances would have caused if they had taken place at the beginning of the reporting period (or the date at which these other securities were issued, if later). To do this, the calculation of basic EPS is revised to increase the number of residual equity shares deemed outstanding in the denominator, and to increase the reporting earnings in the numerator for the estimated impact on earnings if the contingent equity claims had been exercised. In keeping with the objective of showing the worst case scenario from the standpoint of existing shareholders, a contingent claim is not included if it would have an anti-dilutive effect—raising EPS rather than reducing it.

If a number of potentially dilutive securities exist, the sequence in which they are considered may affect the amount of the dilution effect. Unless one security must be exercised before another or at the same time, the calculation should begin with the security that has the most dilutive effect, and the calculation should proceed, security by security, to the least dilutive. Although this matter is not explicitly addressed in the CICA standard, it may be reasoned to follow from the objective of showing the maximum dilution effect. This sequencing is explicit in SFAS 128 (paragraph 14).

SFAS 128 requires that the "control number" for determining whether potential issues of common shares are dilutive is income from continuing operations (that is, income before discontinued operations and extraordinary items). This is to avoid the situation where there is positive income from continuing operations but a loss on discontinued operations or from an extraordinary item that results in an overall net loss. If the net loss were the control figure, the potential issuance of contingent common shares would be considered anti-dilutive and excluded, although there would be a dilutive effect on income from operations (see SFAS 128, paragraph 15). The CICA standard does not address this issue.

When common shares are contingently issuable based on the attainment or maintenance of a specified amount of earnings, SFAS 128 requires that the additional shares shall be included in determining diluted EPS, assuming the effect is dilutive, if current reported earnings are at that level. If the number of shares contingently issuable is based on some external factor, such as the market price of the common shares at some future date, the number of contingent shares deemed issued is to be based upon the share price at the end of the reporting period. The general rule, then, is to base the calculation of diluted EPS on the level of earnings, or market price, or other external condition, as at the end of the reporting period, and assume that it will be maintained in future periods (see SFAS 128, paragraphs 30–34). The CICA standard is silent on this point.

The appropriate approach to calculating the dilutive effect of outstanding warrants or options has been the subject of debate over the years. Under the Canadian approach, the diluted EPS figure is calculated by (1) adding to the reported earnings for the year a notional return on the money that would be received upon exercise of the securities, and (2) dividing the total by the total number of shares that would be outstanding after exercise. The notional return represents a conservative estimate of the after-tax income that would be earned or the costs that could be avoided through the use of the funds received from exercise. The U.S. basis of calculation has been the so-called treasury stock method. Under the treasury stock method, it is assumed that the cash proceeds on exercise of the warrants or options are used to acquire treasury shares. Only the net assumed issuance of shares (the common shares that would be issued on exercise, less the treasury shares that would be acquired) is reflected in the denominator of the diluted EPS calculation. Although there has been criticism of this method,[47] the FASB decided to retain it (and the IASC agreed), primarily because of its use in U.S. practice, its relative simplicity, and its objectivity.

The imputed earnings method in place in Canada was rejected by the FASB and IASC because it requires subjective assumptions about the appropriate rate of earnings, and because it may be considered to treat anti-dilutive potential common shares in some situations as if they were dilutive (see discussion of this and other methods considered by the FASB and IASC at SFAS 128, paragraphs 100–108). SFAS 128 requires that the average stock price of the period be used in determining the number of treasury shares assumed purchased (see explanation at SFAS 128, paragraph 107).

One issue of debate between the IASC and the FASB was whether the objective of diluted EPS should be to indicate the potential effect of dilution on the reported basic EPS calculation *or* act as a warning signal of the potential dilution of basic EPS. Following from the latter objective, diluted EPS would be computed at end-of-period share balances and stock prices (rather than on the weighted-average method that is the basis of determining basic EPS). The IASC initially preferred this latter approach, while the FASB preferred the former. After much discussion, the IASC accepted the former approach, influenced in part by respondents to the exposure draft, most of whom indicated that they did not believe that the warning signal objective was relevant or useful.

The Significance of Calculated Dilution

Concerns have been expressed about the significance of fully diluted EPS figures. Some find fault with the calculation because it makes no attempt to estimate the probability that contingent claims will, or will not, be exercised. The FASB and IASC considered and rejected the idea that diluted EPS should be a predictor of dilution. It was reasoned that whether options or conversion rights will be exercised is usually not reliably determinable at an entity's reporting date—but that it is possible to make a reasonable estimate of what EPS would have been if they had been exercised.

In addition, some have expressed concern that the calculation of diluted EPS gives no recognition to the timing of possible exercise of the rights—other than, under the CICA and old FASB standards, rights need not be taken into account if they are not exercisable within ten years of the reporting date. This ten-year condition has been dropped from SFAS 128. The question is: given the time value of money, how useful is a calculation of dilution based on existing earnings in portraying an effect that may not occur for several years? Specifically, consider the case of a company that pays out a high proportion of its earnings in dividends to common shareholders. There is little dilution of current earnings from common shareholders since they are paid out in dividends. In reply to this criticism, it may be pointed out that attempting to factor in a time element would introduce considerable subjectivity and complexity to the calculations. As well, disclosures of the terms of securities and contingencies, and the reconciliation required under SFAS 128 (see following section) should enable readers to at least identify the timing implications.

Presentation and Disclosure

SFAS 128 requires presentation of EPS by enterprises with publicly held common shares or publicly held potential common shares. The CICA standard has broader application to all enterprises with share capital except government owned companies, wholly owned subsidiaries, and companies "with few shareholders."

The FASB requires that basic, and where applicable, diluted EPS for income from continuing operations and net income be presented on the face of the income statement, with equal prominence. Companies reporting an extraordinary item, a discontinued operation, or a cumulative accounting change adjustment, may present related EPS figures in the notes to the financial statements. The CICA standard provides for similar disclosures, except that it indicates that diluted EPS be provided in the notes to the financial statements, and that basic EPS may be disclosed in the notes or on the face of the income statement. Fuller disclosure is to be made, under the Canadian standard, of both basic and fully diluted EPS, on a pro forma basis if contingent equity is issued after the end of the reporting year but before the financial statements are issued.

SFAS 128 requires additional disclosures, including a reconciliation of the numerator and denominator of basic and diluted per share computations for income from continuing operations. The reconciliation is to include the income and share amount effects of each security that affects diluted EPS. There is also to be disclosure of securities that could be dilutive, but that were not included in the computation of diluted EPS because they were anti-dilutive in the period(s) presented. The CICA standard does not require these disclosures.

Evaluation of EPS Accounting Standards

The merit of an accounting standard on the calculation of EPS is that it requires disclosure of a standardized calculation that is indicative of the potential dilution in the interests of common shareholders in a company's earnings (even if the manner of calculation is not completely free from question). There is some research that indicates that mandatory reporting of diluted EPS appears relevant to investors.[48]

The new FASB and IASC standards have developed some improvements in the calculations, and some additional useful disclosures reconciling individual dilutive effects. As a result, the CICA standard is now somewhat outdated, and it lacks comparability in respect of certain aspects of the calculation of fully diluted EPS with the FASB and IASC required determinations.

SUMMARY

The primary criterion for information to be presented in financial reports is that it be helpful to users, with a particular focus on investors. User needs, however, are not the sole consideration. Most would agree that reporting entities have rights to some degree of confidentiality, that some information may be considered proprietary. Also, one ought to consider whether costs of providing information may exceed possible benefits. Unfortunately, there is rarely proper evidence or clear criteria to guide decisions as to how much financial reporting is enough, and the ground has been shifting as information technology has been improving and the relative positions and expectations of competing interests have been changing. In practice, accounting standard setters must grapple with these issues almost on a situation-by-situation basis.

Some have suggested that disclosure standards do not need to be legislated because business managements have powerful natural motivations to provide disclosures that will balance benefits and costs in the best interests of all parties. However, a growing body of empirical research suggests that managements may be reluctant to reveal the full extent of bad news as quickly and reliably as good news, and that the tension between opposing motivations is complex and may be expected to differ from situation to situation. On balance, it seems naïve to rely on voluntary disclosures.

The natural starting point in addressing what may be considered useful disclosures is to examine user decision models. However, we do not know a great deal about how investors and others make decisions. We might expect to find that different people make decisions differently, depending in part upon their degree of technical sophistication. There is a good argument that financial information should be aimed at sophisticated users, because it is they who make the capital markets efficient. But that argument is limited by the fact that many enterprises are not public companies, and all markets are not efficient.

If it is accepted that investors and capital markets are the primary user interests, then two principal questions help direct the identification of useful information: Would the information help to predict the future net cash inflows of an enterprise, and/or would it help in the assessment of the risks and uncertainties of those cash flows? The chapter discusses the broad nature of disclosures that may assist in prediction: Information that aids in assessing sustainable earnings, and in separating out nonrecurring effects; information that exposes key variables and their behaviour; information on accounting variability and that enhances comparability; and, possibly, information on management's expectations. The chapter also discusses attempts to improve disclosures of measurement uncertainties and risk exposures.

With some limitations, financial statements meeting GAAP should be expected to provide significant information that is helpful in assessing the liquidity and solvency of an entity. However, beyond this, there has been an expectation that readers of financial statements should be provided with a specific warning where there is substantial doubt that an entity will be able to continue as a going concern. There are, unfortunately, major problems in developing workable criteria for implementing such disclosure, and authoritative guidance is very limited. The CICA studied the issues in the late 1980s and early 1990s, but did not progress to the development of a standard.

The concept of materiality is a practical tool to assist in the selection of information to be disclosed in financial statements. The usual definition of materiality states that an item of information is material if it has the potential to affect a decision by an average prudent investor. To make the concept operational, it has been necessary to adopt some quantitative rules of thumb. There seems to be a consensus that, in most cases, an item will be considered material if it is over 10% of a representative net income figure, it will be considered immaterial if less than 5% of that figure, and possibly material depending on the circumstances if it falls in between. This rule is amplified and modified to fit special circumstances, based on judgment.

Timeliness in financial reporting is assisted by interim financial reports. There are two theories as to the nature of interim reports. One holds that each period's report should stand on its own feet (the "discrete approach"); the other is that accounting allocations should be managed so that the interim report helps the users forecast what will be the financial results for the full year (the "integral approach"). Present Canadian and U.S. standards represent a compromise, and financial analysts have criticized them for permitting too much latitude in allocating costs between interim periods. In 1991, a CICA research study concluded that the *CICA Handbook* standard was out-of-date and urgently in need of significant revisions. It strongly recommended improvements in disclosures, including the presentation of a full balance sheet, cash flow statement, and fourth quarter reports. The IASC has recently issued a standard that is, in most respects, consistent with the discrete approach, and it meets the basic presentation and disclosure recommendations of the CICA research study. The CICA has recently taken on a project to improve its standard.

With the diversification of many businesses, beginning in the 1960s, it has become important that enterprises present financial information disaggregated by business segments that are subject to different risks and prospects for growth and profitability. Standards put in place in the early 1970s have had information value, but analysts and others complained that they were far from adequate. The main problem was with the concept of business segments. A number of enterprises were able to claim, under the flexible provisions of the standards, to be in only one industry, and some others showed segments that were too broad to provide very useful information. The CICA and FASB entered into a joint project to address the issues, and this resulted in basically identical standards in 1997. The standards reflect a "management approach"—that is, segments are to be defined, and segmented information measured, on the bases reported to top management of an enterprise. An enterprise will, therefore, not be able to claim that it has only one segment based on subjective "risk and return" criteria, if it is managed otherwise. Most businesses may be expected to be structured on product/service and/or geographic lines. However, unless it is impracticable, some basic fall-back information is required about product/service and geographic activities, if it is not otherwise disclosed.

The IASC has also issued a new standard on segmented reporting. It has adopted what might be described as a modified management approach. It requires segmentation on the basis of internal information provided on either product/service or geographic lines, and it does not fully rely on internal management methods for measuring segmented information. It requires that certain segment data be provided and prepared on methods that are consistent with those applied in determining consolidated enterprise figures. Thus, despite significant efforts to harmonize them, CICA and FASB standards differ from IASC standards.

Earnings per share is so widely quoted and used a statistic that it has been considered useful to provide standards for its consistent presentation within financial statements. It is also considered important to put common shareholders on notice of possible dilution of their interest in a company's earnings, even though the basis for determination of a diluted EPS figure is open to some question. The CICA standard is now somewhat outdated, in light of recent improvements made to FASB and IASC standards.

REFERENCES

1   For one view of the implications for disclosure of a broad public interest perspective, see The Institute of Chartered Accountants in England and Wales, Accounting Standards Steering Committee, *The Corporate Report*, A Discussion Paper (London: Institute of Chartered Accountants in England and Wales, 1975). This report and possible broader purposes for financial reporting are considered in Chapter 25 on conceptual frameworks for financial accounting.

2   FASB, *Objectives of Financial Reporting by Business Enterprises*, Statement of Financial Accounting Concepts No. 1 (Stamford: FASB, 1978), par. 38.

3   Ibid., p. viii.

4   The AICPA Special Committee on Financial Reporting, *The Information Needs of Investors and Creditors* (New York: AICPA, 1993).

5   CICA, *Using Ratios and Graphics in Financial Reporting*, Research Report (Toronto: CICA, 1993).

6   CICA, "Future-Oriented Financial Information," *CICA Handbook*, Section 4250 (Toronto: CICA, 1989). A review of the issues and problems with respect to published management forecasts may be found in R.H. Kidd, *Earnings Forecasts* (Toronto: CICA, 1976).

7   See *Pro-Forma Financial Statements*, Staff Accounting Communiqué No. 9 (Toronto: OSC, 1994).

8   *Report of the Commission to Study the Public's Expectations of Audits* (Toronto: CICA, 1988), par.5.73.

9   See, for example, J.E. Boritz, *Approaches to Dealing with Risk and Uncertainty*, CICA Research Study (Toronto: CICA, 1990), chap. 5.

10 For a review of this literature, see J.E. Boritz, *The "Going Concern" Assumption: Accounting and Auditing Implications*, CICA Research Report (Toronto: CICA, 1991), chap. 7.

[11] See *Report of the Commission to Study the Public's Expectations of Audits*, pars. 5.11–5.19 and Recommendation 10.

[12] J.E. Boritz, *The "Going Concern" Assumption: Accounting and Auditing Implications*.

[13] CICA, *Going Concern*, Exposure Draft (Toronto: CICA, 1996), par. 04. It is notable that a CICA auditing exposure draft issued in 1995 proposed a different position. It proposed that the evaluation period should be one year from the date of the financial statements, rather than from the date they were completed. CICA, *Auditor's Responsibility to Evaluate the Going Concern Assumption*, Exposure Draft (Toronto: CICA, 1995), par. .07.

[14] See *Report of the Commission to Study the Public's Expectations of Audits*, pars. 5.29–5.31 and Recommendation 13.

[15] R.J. Groves, "Financial Disclosure: When More Is Not Better," *Financial Executive*, May/June 1994, pp. 11–14.

[16] P.H. Knutson, *Financial Reporting in the 1990s and Beyond*, a position paper of the Association for Investment Management and Research (Charlottesville, VA.: The Association for Investment Management and Research, 1993), p. 2.

[17] See SEC, *Report of the Task Force on Disclosure Simplification* (Washington: SEC, 1996). FASB considerations with respect to disclosure overload issues were reviewed in D.R. Beresford and J.A. Hepp, "Financial Statement Disclosures: Too Many or Too Few?" *FASB Status Report*, May 25, 1995, pp. 7–10; and L.T. Johnson, "Research on Disclosure," *Accounting Horizons*, March 1992, pp. 101–03.

[18] See Toronto Stock Exchange, "Corporate Disclosure Survey" in *Toward Improved Disclosure*, Background Papers of the Committee on Corporate Disclosure (Toronto: The Toronto Stock Exchange, 1995) pp. 3–32.

[19] For a review of the difficulties in preparing simplified financial statements, see P. Bird, "The Complexities of Simplified Accounts," in *External Financial Reporting: Essays in Honour of Harold Edey*, ed. B. Carsberg and S. Dev (Englewood Cliffs, N.J.: Prentice-Hall International in cooperation with London School of Economics and Political Science, 1984), pp. 16–24.

[20] See, for example, M. Gibbins, A Richardson, and J. Waterhouse, "The Management of Corporate Financial Disclosure: Opportunism, Ritualism, Policies, and Processes," *Journal of Accounting Research*, Spring 1990, pp. 121–43.

[21] See, for example, G.A. Feltham and J.Z. Xie, "Voluntary Financial Disclosure in an Entry Game With Continua of Types," *Contemporary Accounting Research*, Fall 1992, pp. 46–80; T.W. Scott, "Incentives and Disincentives for Financial Disclosure: Voluntary Disclosure of Defined Benefit Pension Plan Information by Canadian Firms," *The Accounting Review*, January 1994, pp. 26-43; D.J. Skinner, "Why Firms Voluntarily Disclose Bad News," *Journal of Accounting Research*, Spring 1994, pp. 38–60; and F. Gigler, "Self-Enforcing Voluntary Disclosures," *Journal of Accounting Research*, Autumn 1994, pp. 224–40.

[22] A Survey of Canadian financial analysts revealed that nearly 90% of respondents believed that financial disclosure is better in the United States than in Canada; see Toronto Stock Exchange, "Corporate Disclosure Survey."

23 FASB, *Criteria for Determining Materiality*, A Discussion Memorandum (Stamford: FASB, 1975).

24 FASB, *Qualitative Characteristics of Accounting Information*, Statement of Financial Accounting Concepts No. 2 (Stamford: FASB, 1980), par. 131.

25 Much of the research in this area is now quite old. See M.C. O'Connor and D.W. Collins, "Toward Establishing User-Oriented Materiality Standards," *Journal of Accountancy*, December 1974, pp. 67–75; and J.W. Pattillo, *The Concept of Materiality in Financial Reporting* (New York: Financial Executives Research Foundation, 1976). See also research reviewed in D.A. Leslie, *Materiality: The Concept and its Application to Auditing*, CICA Research Study (Toronto: CICA, 1985), pp. 17–19.

26 CICA, "Applying Materiality and Audit Risk Concepts in Conducting an Audit," *CICA Handbook*, AuG-7 (Toronto: CICA, 1990), pars. 4–8.

27 Ibid., par. 8.

28 While there is nothing specific on this point in Canadian authoritative literature, the IASC has recently adopted this position, see IASC, *Interim Financial Reporting*, IAS 34 (London: IASC, 1998), pars. 23–25.

29 D.A. Leslie, *Materiality: The Concept and its Application to Auditing*, pp. 39–40, 45–47 and 142–49.

30 See, for example, S.M.H. Wallman, "The Future of Accounting and Disclosure in an Evolving World: The Need for Dramatic Change," *Accounting Horizons*, September 1995, pp. 81–91, especially pp. 86–87.

31 CICA, "Interim Financial Reporting to Shareholders," *CICA Handbook*, Section 1750 (Toronto: CICA), par. .13.

32 AICPA, APB, *Interim Financial Reporting*, APB Opinion No. 28 (New York: AICPA, 1973), par. 9.

33 P.H. Knutson, *Financial Reporting in the 1990s and Beyond*, pp. 57–58.

34 S. Rangan and R.S. Sloan, "Implications of the Integral Approach to Quarterly Reporting for the Post-Earnings-Announcement Drift," *The Accounting Review*, July 1998, pp. 353–71.

35 IASC, *Interim Financial Reporting*, IAS 34 (London: IASC, 1998), pars. 37–39 and Appendix 2.

36 CICA, *Interim Financial Reporting: A Continuous Process*, Research Report (Toronto: CICA, 1991).

37 FASB, *Financial Reporting for Segments of a Business Enterprise*, Statement of Financial Accounting Standards No. 14 (Stamford: FASB, 1976) as amended by SFAS No. 18 (1977), SFAS No. 21 (1978), SFAS No. 24 (1978), and SFAS No. 30 (1979); and CICA, "Segmented Information," *CICA Handbook*, Section 1700 (Toronto: CICA).

38 For a review of empirical and analytical research on the benefits and costs of providing disaggregated disclosures, see R.M. Mohr and P. Pacter, "Review of Related Research" in P. Pacter, *Reporting Disaggregated Information*, Research Report (Norwalk: FASB, 1993), chap. 6.

[39] J.M. Boersema and S.J. Van Weelden, *Financial Reporting for Segments*, A Research Study (Toronto: CICA, 1992); and P. Pacter, *Reporting Disaggregated Information.*

[40] CICA, "Segment Disclosures," *CICA Handbook*, Section 1701 (Toronto: CICA); and FASB, *Disclosures About Segments of an Enterprise and Related Information*, Statement of Financial Accounting Standards No. 131 (Norwalk: FASB, 1997).

[41] D. Herrmann and W.B. Thomas, "Reporting Disaggregated Information: A Critique Based on Concepts Statement No. 2," *Accounting Horizons*, September 1997, pp. 35–44.

[42] IASC, *Segment Reporting*, IAS 14 (Revised) (London: IASC, 1997).

[43] AICPA, APB, *Earnings per Share*, APB Opinion No. 15 (New York: AICPA, 1969) as amended by APB Opinion No. 30 (1973), SFAS No. 21 (1978), SFAS No. 55 (1982), and SFAS No. 85 (1985); and CICA, "Earnings per Share," *CICA Handbook*, Section 3500 (Toronto: CICA).

[44] See, for example, R.D. Mautz, Jr. and T.J. Hogan, "Earnings Per Share Reporting: Time for an Overhaul?" *Accounting Horizons*, September 1989, pp. 21–27.

[45] FASB, *Earnings per Share*, Statement of Financial Accounting Standards No. 128 (Norwalk: FASB, 1997).

[46] IASC, *Earnings per Share*, IAS 33 (London: IASC, 1997).

[47] For an interesting discussion with some debatable points, see B. Barlev, "Theory, Pragmatism and Conservatism in Reflecting the Effects of Warrants on Diluted EPS," *Abacus*, June 1984, pp. 1–15. See also L.W. Dudley, "A Critical Look at EPS," *Journal of Accountancy*, August 1985, pp. 102–11.

[48] S. Balsam and R. Lipka, "Share Prices and Alternative Measures of Earnings per Share," *Accounting Horizons*, September 1998, pp. 234–49.

ACCOUNTING FOR CHANGING PRICES

In the preceding chapters we have described the accrual accounting system as it has evolved to date, which is based on concepts, standards and practices customarily known as generally accepted accounting principles (GAAP).

In general (with some exceptions) under GAAP the value added by an enterprise's productive activity and the effects of price changes on the value of its nonfinancial assets (inventories, capital assets, etc.) are not given recognition in the accounts until they are realized. Realization is normally considered to take place when there is a sale to an outside party. The objective of this accounting is to match the costs incurred with revenues, so as to determine realized income. Unrealized holding gains (and occasionally holding losses) are ignored. As a result, when prices change between the time that factors of production are acquired and the time they are sold, the costs that are matched with revenues are outdated.

For many years accounting theorists have criticized this lack of realism in historical cost-matching accounting. However, it has only been when price changes have become widespread and the rate of change has become extreme—that is under severe inflation or deflation—that business people have joined in this criticism. Under inflation, historical cost accounting generally reports profits that are higher than the cash available for distribution, because of the need to buy replacement factors of production at higher prices. The business community finds this disturbing, especially if the reported profits form the basis of income taxation.

Through the high-inflation period of the 1970s there was intense interest in finding a solution to the inadequacies of historical cost-based accounting. In the early 1980s that interest evaporated as the rate of inflation declined. In Canada, CICA recommendations for supplementary disclosure of the impact of changing prices were made just as interest died away. The recommended disclosures were not made mandatory and were widely ignored. Ultimately, they were withdrawn. The lack of general interest in the issues has continued to this day, as inflation rates have continued to be low.

Nevertheless, it would be rash to predict that significant inflation or deflation will never recur. Also, specific prices are always changing, even though there is no general price trend, and these changes may be important to some enterprises. It is still pertinent, therefore, to investigate the shortcomings of historical cost-based accounting and consider what might be done about them.

CONCEPTS OF INCOME AND CAPITAL

Since dissatisfaction with conventional cost-based accrual accounting under inflation largely stems from a popular perception that accounting income is overstated under inflation, it is pertinent to inquire into the ordinary person's understanding of what income is. In general usage, capital and income are interrelated concepts. Capital is the invested resource that is used to achieve future economic benefits. To determine income it is necessary to distinguish between benefits that represent a return *on* capital (that is, income) and those that represent a return *of* capital (that is, repayment of principal). Income is restricted to that portion of the return that can be consumed without reducing capital.

The idea that capital should be maintained is deeply rooted in human experience. To consume the "seed corn" would be disastrous for expectations of future crops. That, in essence, is why the proper measurement of income—the amount consumable while maintaining capital—has traditionally been regarded as very important.

Capital maintenance may be easy to visualize when we talk in elementary physical terms such as that of seed corn. It becomes more difficult to interpret when we think of the wide variety of business activities. Some general concept of capital that can be applied across the board is required. In view of the immense variety of productive assets, it is obvious that the omnibus term "capital" has to be expressed on a common money basis, so that different compositions of capital can be compared one with the other and from one time period to another. The key question is what the amount of money to be maintained is supposed to represent. Thus, instead of asking what is income, we have to ask ourselves what is the capital to be maintained?

Two basic elements or attributes of capital to be maintained must be specified in order to define an income measurement system:

- The basis of valuation of the stock of assets and liabilities that comprise the net assets (capital) of the business enterprise.
- The capital maintenance concept itself.

In addition, an income measurement model must specify whether income should be measured for the entity as a whole or only for the proprietary interest in it. Finally, a decision must be made whether gains to be reported in income should be subject to a test of realization.

Valuation of Assets and Liabilities

Under historical cost accounting, an enterprise's assets that are inputs to a revenue production process (inventories, property plant and equipment, intangibles, etc.) are stated at cost (or at the lower of cost and estimated recoverable value). Increases in the value of these assets are not recognized as increases in capital, and therefore income, of the enterprise until they are realized (with some exceptions when revenue is recognized before complete realization).

If the carrying value of such assets were to be restated to some more current basis of valuation, income reported would be affected because the expense recorded when the assets are sold or consumed in operations would be different. Holding gains or losses resulting from changes in their current values would also be recognized in some form, although whether they are reported as part of income will depend on the particular model of income (the capital maintenance model) that is adopted.

Several approaches to the valuation of assets may be considered. One approach is market value—that value at which an asset may be exchanged in the marketplace. Such market value may be taken from the buying side of the market—an "entry value"—or the selling side—an "exit value"—or a valuation might be based on the average of the two. Another approach might be to value an asset on the basis of discounting its future expected cash flows. Such a discounted cash flow (DCF) valuation of productive assets is sometimes described as "value in use," or "economic value." A DCF valuation can be quite subjective because it depends on uncertain expectations of future cash flows and a judgmental selection of an appropriate discount rate. This valuation approach is likely to be more feasible for financial assets (as discussed in Chapter 17), than for productive assets.

A given income accounting model may or may not apply a single basis of valuation to all assets. Some researchers believe that only one basis of valuation is appropriate for all assets based on the argument that one cannot add apples and oranges and get a total that has real world significance. Others argue that in differing circumstances different measurement bases may be the most reliable and effective way to arrive at useful values. In large measure the difference of opinion stems from differences in fundamental concepts.

For example, R.J. Chambers stresses the adaptivity of an enterprise as a fact of supreme importance to readers of its financial reports. He argues that the enterprise's ability to adapt advantageously (to new opportunities or challenges) depends upon the *current cash equivalent* of its resources, and thus the financial characteristic that is of the greatest importance to an asset is its realizable value—an exit price. *All* assets must be measured at their current exit prices to arrive at a measure of the total adaptivity of the enterprise.[1]

Other writers contend that an important purpose of financial reports is to help readers *predict* future cash flows of the enterprise. It is not helpful for this purpose to report the current realizable value of an asset such as a special purpose piece of heavy equipment if that asset is not going to be sold but rather will continue in use with far different consequences for future cash flow. Thus, some argue that different bases of valuation may be appropriate to indicate the *desired* asset attribute—the present value of future cash proceeds expected to result from its possession.

Having described three possible bases of valuation (entry price, exit price and value in use), we can expand the number of possibilities by adding a time dimension. Values under any of three bases of valuation may conceivably be derived from information as to conditions existing in the past or the present or expectations of conditions in the future. Thus, we can discern nine valuation possibilities (even though some are rather unlikely choices) as set out in Table 24-1.

Note that the accrual accounting model that is the basis of existing GAAP is among those models that use different bases of valuation in different situations. It is, in fact, commonly referred to as a "mixed" measurement model. Those bases differ not only in

Table 24-1	**Possible Approaches to Asset Valuation**		
		Valuation Basis	
Time of Valuation	**Past**	**Present**	**Future**
Entry price	Historical cost (HC)	Replacement cost (RC)	Future estimated buying price
Exit price	Past net selling price	Current net realizable value (NRV)	Future estimated net proceeds
Value in use	Past estimate of DCF	Present estimate of DCF, known as "economic value" (EV)	Future estimate of DCF

approach—entry value or exit value—but also in the time dimension. Historical acquisition cost is a past entry value, but, in particular circumstances, certain assets may be valued at a present entry value (replacement cost), a present exit value (net realizable value), or a future exit value (recoverable value).

Value to the Firm Valuation Approach

Considerable thought has been given to the creation of a decision rule for the selection of asset valuation bases that would correspond to the intrinsic value of assets to the enterprise. The resulting valuation approach has been variously called "deprival value," "opportunity value," or "value to the firm" (VF).[2] The reasoning underlying this approach runs as follows:

- The future cash consequences of any asset owned will be (1) the net proceeds from its sale, (2) the cash inflow attributable to its value in use, or (3) the amount collected if it is merely an account receivable.

- The present value of the higher of (1) the net proceeds available from disposition and (2) the cash inflow available from use represents the benefit accessible by the firm from possession of the asset. In the case of assets held for use in the business, this higher value is normally EV. In the case of goods to be sold, the higher value is almost always NRV.

- Another way to measure the benefit from possession of an asset is to look at the sacrifice a firm would have to make were it deprived of the asset and wished to restore its position. If RC is lower than one of the other two measures, it would pay the firm to replace the asset if it did not have it. Thus, RC becomes the appropriate basis of valuation. If RC is higher than both of the alternative measures, the asset would not be replaced if lost. In those circumstances, the higher of the other two measures indicates what probably will be done with the asset and the appropriate basis of valuation.

The great majority of valuation situations can be covered by two simple valuation rules derived from the above. These are: value assets held for sale at RC unless NRV is lower; value assets held for use at RC unless EV is lower.

This "value-to-the-firm" approach is subject to some practical problems, particularly relating to the ability to reliably estimate EV of capital assets when replacement is no longer considered to be worthwhile.

Valuation of Liabilities

The implications of the above valuation bases for the measurement of liabilities are open to some debate. First, there is a question whether an "entity" or a "proprietary" theory of accounting should be applied (see Chapter 5).

Some current value accounting models espouse the entity theory of accounting. Under the entity theory, all liabilities are treated equally with the equity interest as claims on entity resources, and interest payments are regarded equally with dividends as distributions of entity income earned, not as deductions to be made in the measurement of income. An entity theorist, therefore, is interested in the current value of assets but not nearly so much in the current value of liabilities. Since liabilities and equity are both viewed as claims on assets, it is considered the function of the marketplace, not of accounting, to estimate their value. If the current value of the equity claim is not recorded in the financial statements, it is considered equally logical, by this way of thinking, not to record the current value of the debt claim.

The proprietary approach, in contrast, focuses on the claim of the equity, the residual left over after deducting liabilities from assets. If it is important to the portrayal of the net equity position to report assets at current values, one would think that the same would be true of liabilities. Some arguments are made, however, for differentiating the position of the liabilities. There has been some discussion of these arguments in Chapter 17, in its discussion of the measurement of financial liabilities as part of accounting for financial instruments. In general, those opposing revaluation of liabilities may be expected to argue along the following lines:

- Price changes have little relevance to debt. A debt obligation is usually taken on as part of the financing plan of the enterprise with the intention of maintaining the debt to maturity. There is normally no intention to trade in debt. Thus, introducing changes in the value of debt would simply confuse the picture of management performance.

- There is a difference in the flexibility of action available with respect to assets and liabilities. Whether to sell or hold an asset is a perfectly unfettered decision (except when the asset is specifically mortgaged). Typically, an enterprise will not have the same ability to settle its debt. An enterprise may be effectively constrained in its ability to do so by a lack of available cash, or by the terms of the debt instrument and the need to negotiate any early settlement with the holder of the debt. Thus, it may be reasoned, that the current value of debt is irrelevant to any possible decisions that management could take. Many feel uncomfortable with treating any holding gain or loss on an entity's own debt as a part of income because such gains or losses may not be realizable by the entity.

- The market value of an entity's debt is influenced by the market's perception of the particular risks attached to the entity itself. Thus, if the entity is perceived to have become riskier, the market value of its debt securities will decline. Many find it intuitively repugnant that a decline in debt from this cause should be reported as an increase in equity.

Each of these arguments is open to debate, and at least the first two have become less compelling with the development of modern capital markets and derivative financial instruments. To start with, it may be noted that decisions are required as to the timing of debt issuance, whether to take interest rate risk (i.e., whether to issue floating or fixed rate debt), whether borrowing should be for the long-term or short-term, what collateral should be given, etc. It may be reasoned that the current value measurement of the effects on debt of good or bad judgments on these matters can be just as relevant as the current value effects of asset acquisition decisions. On a going forward basis, it has become common for business enterprises to alter the interest or foreign currency risk exposures on debt by using swaps or other derivative instruments. Thus, even if a debt obligation cannot be easily settled prior to its maturity, its interest and foreign currency risk exposures may be effectively settled using derivatives. Further, management may be expected to manage financial risks, such as interest and foreign currency risks, of assets and liabilities together—so that recording current values of assets but not of liabilities can lead to serious measurement and income reporting inconsistencies. As well, it is always possible that the business as a whole may be sold. If it is, the price arrived at by a rational buyer and seller will take into account the question whether debt assumed by the purchaser carries a favourable rate of interest.

Those who favour recording debt at current values must be prepared to answer a second question: On what basis is the current value to be determined? The possibilities may be listed as a sort of mirror image of the possibilities for assets, for example:

- Entry price—the amount that could be borrowed currently to replace the existing outstanding debt.

- Exit price—the amount required currently to pay off the loan. In the case of debt, two exit prices are possible:
  - the amount that would have to be paid in the market to buy in the outstanding debt in an orderly fashion; and
  - the contractual redemption price, if the borrower has the right to call the debt.
    Reasoning within a "value-to-the-firm" philosophy, the appropriate exit price would be the lower of these two amounts.

- Economic value—the present value of the payments that have to be made by way of interest and principal at maturity on the existing debt if it is not redeemed or replaced. This present value, of course, would depend on the discount rate assumed. Presumably the discount rate would be the current cost of debt funds to the entity, and thus the present value of existing debt would be the same as the amount that could be raised currently by committing the entity to the same schedule of debt payments (the entry-price alternative above).

The valuation alternatives for debt thus appear to be narrower than those available for assets.

In summary, various attributes of assets and liabilities could be measured. These include original exchange value (cost), current replacement cost, current exit value, the present value of expected future cash flows, some measure of future value, and various mixed models that use different values in different circumstances (such as the value-to-the-firm model).

Capital Maintenance Concepts

We have noted that the common notion of income is that of an amount that can be distributed without infringing on capital, that is, an amount that can be paid out while maintaining the value of net resources (capital) held by the enterprise. Capital maintenance models are divided into the following three basic groups in accounting literature:

- *Financial capital maintenance—money basis*. Capital to be maintained may be conceived of as simply the monetary value of net resources, with the value determined in accordance with whatever basis is used for valuing the assets and liabilities of the enterprise (i.e., historical cost, current cost, net realizable value, value-to-the-firm, etc.).

Income, then, is the increase in the monetary value of net resources over the period after allowing for any increase received by way of capital contributions or any decrease caused by dividends, capital withdrawals, or other distributions in the period. On this basis any change in asset and liability values that are recognized in the accounts, whether they result from productive activities or holding gains or losses, form part of income reported. Because the accounting is conducted strictly in terms of units of money, a dollar of reported income is worth less and less under inflationary conditions, and the reverse holds true under deflation.

- *Financial capital maintenance—purchasing power basis.* A second concept of capital retains the basic idea of capital as a monetary measure of net resources, but it defines capital to be maintained in terms of its purchasing power. Income for a period is simply the gain in purchasing power of net resources over the period (again excluding the effects of capital contributions or withdrawals during the period). Changes in purchasing power are measured by reference to a general index of prices. On this basis, any change in valuation of an asset or a liability within a period is compared with the change in the price index from the beginning of the period or from the time the asset or liability was acquired, if later, in order to measure the gain or loss in purchasing power.

- *Physical/productive capacity capital maintenance.* A third concept of capital maintenance visualizes capital not as a stock of money equivalents but as a pool of productive capacity. This is the concept that is closest to the notion of seed corn. It is based on the idea that income cannot be earned until capital is maintained in physical, productive capacity, terms.

    The question is, how to measure physical, or productive capacity, capital in monetary terms? One possibility is to develop a price index of physical resources making up the productive capital of the entity. Then the dollar amount of capital reported at the beginning of the period would be restated up or down by the *specific* price index, and the amount of that adjustment would be a charge upon income otherwise reported from productive activities and from price changes of assets and liabilities held. A more widely advocated approach seeks to ensure physical capital maintenance through the matching process in income determination. This is accomplished by expressing cost of goods sold and other expenses of earning income in terms of their replacement costs at the time of sale or consumption. The excess of revenues over replacement costs should be distributable while still leaving capital intact in physical terms (because it presumes replacement at current prices of factors of production used up in earning income). The difference between replacement costs of resources consumed in operations and their original acquisition costs (elsewhere called holding gains and losses) is excluded from income and, in effect, treated as a revaluation of invested capital.

Another possibility, which has not been seriously considered in authoritative accounting literature to date, is to define capital in terms of its earning power. The common objective of all profit-oriented enterprises is to use resources to generate cash flows sufficient to achieve the return of capital plus an appropriate income return to justify the effort and risk. Reasoning from this objective, it may be proposed that the value of an entity's capital to be maintained is the amount that maintains the capacity of the entity's capital to generate an appropriate return.

The question is, how to define capital in terms of its earning power? It is suggested that the answer is provided by modern capital markets theory. It is well accepted that a security traded in an active and open market will have a market value equal to its expected future cash flows discounted at the current market rate of return for assets of equivalent risk. The current market rate of return for various levels of risk can be readily observed from quoted market prices of government and corporate securities. This rate of return effectively defines the earning power of investments of different levels of risk. Within this capital markets concept, then, an enterprise's net resources (capital) may be defined as the present value of expected future cash flows discounted at the rate of return that is currently available in the capital market place for investments of similar risk. This value will generally be the fair value of financial instruments and a current market rate EV-based determination for productive assets in use. This measure of capital may be defined in either nominal or real (general price level adjusted) dollars.

This concept will be referred to as the *capital markets earning power basis* of capital maintenance. It may be considered a variation of financial capital maintenance, although it might also be considered to have some resemblance to productive capital maintenance where "productive capacity" is visualized in terms of earnings capacity. This concept of capital maintenance was not identified in accounting literature during the period of active study of capital maintenance and valuation concepts through the early 1980s—and it would probably have been summarily rejected as lacking in practical operationality if it had. But times have changed since then, particularly in respect of the development of capital markets. Thus what was unthinkable then, may warrant consideration now.

Other Elements in Income Accounting Models

As indicated earlier, the old debate between the proprietary and entity viewpoint carries over into income measurement models not based on historical cost. In some contexts the attraction of the entity viewpoint is enhanced. For example, if the objective in measuring income is to maintain the physical capital of the enterprise, it may seem somewhat artificial to consider only the maintenance of physical capital attributable to the equity investment in the enterprise, rather than the total productive capacity of the enterprise.

Finally, there has to be a decision whether a realization test has any place in income reporting. It may seem that an answer will be implicit in the choice of a basis of valuation for assets and liabilities. For example, if all assets are recorded at current realizable values, the realization test may seem to have been bypassed. But this is not necessarily so. It is always possible to identify and segregate from reported income those gains and losses attributable to value changes in assets and liabilities still on hand.

Thus, there are four elements to any accounting model that aims to report income for a period: (1) the measurement of assets and liabilities that make up aggregate capital, (2) the concept of capital to be maintained, (3) the entity/proprietary viewpoint assumed, and (4) whether income reported is to be subject to a test of realization.

A very large number of accounting models could be built up depending on the decisions made as to these specifications. This fact contributed greatly to the confusion and controversy in the period from 1970 to the early 1980s over the modifications that might be made to historical cost accounting to better depict the consequences of changing prices.

The succeeding sections of this chapter will discuss various models that have been suggested for the purpose of accounting for changing prices and indicate what choices have been made in these models with respect to the basis of valuation of assets and liabilities, capital maintenance, entity or proprietary approach, and recognition of a realization test.

GPL ADJUSTMENTS TO GAAP FINANCIAL STATEMENTS

In the 1970s, when inflation became too serious and too persistent to be ignored, the initial proposal of the accounting profession was to adopt general price-level accounting (GPL accounting).[3] The techniques of this system of accounting had been fairly well worked out by 1970. It involved the adjustment of figures arrived at under the familiar historical cost system by a single well-established index, published independently by some authority.

The crucial thing to appreciate about this application of GPL accounting is that it aims to change GAAP in one respect and one respect only. That is, it aims to substitute a unit of common purchasing power for money as the unit of account. The adjustments to the nominal dollar figures in the accounts are *not* revaluations of the assets, liabilities, or other figures affected. They are simply adjustments so that all dollar figures shown will be expressed in terms of a dollar with a consistent purchasing power. The adjustments thus do not represent changes in the asset and liability attributes measured. If an asset is shown at historical cost before adjustment, it continues to be shown at historical cost, but that cost is expressed in terms of dollars having a base-date purchasing power. If the asset is shown at market value, it continues to reflect market value.

The grafting of the GPL concept onto GAAP accounting involves two sets of issues: (1) those relating to the price index to be used (i.e., defining the unit of purchasing power), and (2) those relating to the restatement process itself.

Defining the Purchasing Power Unit

Money is the accepted unit of account because all economic assets and liabilities can be expressed in terms of their exchange values in monetary units. The trouble is that the purchasing power of money changes over time. If we do not change the monetary amount recorded as the purchasing power of money changes, we are not using a consistent standard of measure. Because the standard is not consistent, addition of two different money amounts—say, adding the nominal dollar cost of an asset bought in 1970 to that of one bought in 1985—tends to become meaningless given the effects of inflation on the purchasing power of the dollar between those two dates. It is for this reason that GPL accounting seeks to transform dollar measures made at different times into measures expressed in a unit of constant purchasing power.

The problem is that general purchasing power is an abstract concept. None of us buys or sells things in general. We buy or sell specific goods and services, and for this we pay or receive money or promises to pay money. Thus, it appears we must start with prices for specific commodities in any attempt to measure purchasing power in general. In essence, the general purchasing power of a dollar is estimated by constructing a price index of a representative basket of goods and services. The aggregate of the value of the basket of goods and services at a base date is set at 100, and differences in aggregate values at different dates are expressed as higher or lower index figures correlating with the change from the base-date values. Some of the more commonly referred-to indexes in Canada are: the consumer price index (CPI)—an index of prices of goods and services bought by individuals and families for personal consumption; the industry selling price index (ISPI)—an index of prices of Canadian manufacturing output; and the Gross National Expenditure deflator—an index of changes in the prices of all goods and services produced in Canada.

There are problems in constructing an index that purports to measure pure changes in prices. The more major of these are as follows:

- *Substitution.* When relative prices of commodities change, people change their spending habits. Thus, if butter becomes more expensive some people will switch to margarine. If beef prices go up, more chicken will be consumed. Thus, a price index that traces the changes in price of a "fixed basket" of goods with "fixed weights" assigned to the goods in the basket (as does the CPI, for example) may become less representative of prices of goods actually produced or consumed and overstate the rate of price change of goods actually being produced or consumed.

- *Quality changes.* Over time, technological innovation increases the quality or desirability of many products. (In some cases the quality of a commodity can decline over time—consider local postal service, for example.) Some attempt is made in the construction of price indexes to factor out the cost of quality improvements, but it is admitted that no price index adequately adjusts for quality changes.

Because of these difficulties, it may be that some price indexes tend to overstate the real rate of price change. Thus, although price indexes offer a means of estimating changes in the level of prices, they are not perfect tools for that purpose.[4]

Some people argue that an index of prices in general has no meaning. It is well known, for example, that it can cost more to live in one locality of a country than it does in another, even though the same currency is used as a medium of exchange in both places. The best answer to this is that if a country itself has any meaning and if its currency is freely exchangeable, the concept of general purchasing power is useful, just as an average can be a useful measure in many contexts.

Despite these objections to the relevance of price indexes, it is strongly arguable that price-level adjustments for financial reporting purposes are likely to improve the relevance of figures based on prices established at different dates, especially in times of significant price volatility and inflation. Once this is acknowledged, it is necessary to choose the index to be used as a measure of the change in general purchasing power of money. It has been noted that the objective of price-level accounting is simply to correct our measuring unit. Therefore, since money is exchangeable for any commodity, changes in its value should be measured in relation to changes in the prices of all commodities. That is to say, a broadly based price index, such as the GNE deflator, should be used. There are, however, some different views.

- Some have contended that it may be assumed that a business should maintain the purchasing power committed to it for business investment purposes. Therefore, an index of prices of goods in which the business customarily invests would be preferable to a completely general index for measuring the progress of that business.

- Others have argued that the index should be the CPI, since an important objective is that of reporting to shareholders, and shareholders are ultimately interested in the success of an enterprise in maintaining the purchasing power of the dollar for consumption purposes.

The GPL Restatement Process

Technical details on how to calculate GPL financial statements may be found in standard works on the subject and will not be reviewed here.[5] Rather the following discussion is aimed at identifying and commenting upon the key principles.

In principle, the procedures to restate the unit of account to a unit of constant purchasing power are as follows:

- The purchasing power of the dollar at a specific date must be selected as the standard of general purchasing power. GPL-adjusted statements can be presented either in dollars having the purchasing power they possess at the current reporting date, or in constant dollars of any earlier base date. The advantage of the former is that readers of financial statements are likely to understand better the value of the dollar (its purchasing power) at the date of the report than at some arbitrary earlier date. On the other hand, the use of the purchasing power equivalent at the end of the current reporting period has the disadvantage that comparative figures from previous years' financial statements have to be updated every time a new financial report is prepared. That is to say, when the 2000 balance sheet and income statement are published, the 1999 figures previously published have to be revised to be comparable in terms of the 2000 purchasing power of the dollar. This may be confusing to an unsophisticated reader. Either way, care needs to be taken to explain the concept of purchasing power units and how it is being applied.

- All dollar amounts in the accounts are translated for reporting purposes into their equivalents in terms of the purchasing power of the dollar at the selected date.

The basic requirement of GPL accounting is to restate all money figures presented in financial statements in terms of their equivalent in the purchasing power that the unit of money had at the selected base date. To accomplish this restatement it is necessary to distinguish between monetary and nonmonetary assets and liabilities. There is a simple reason for this. The purchasing power of monetary assets and liabilities is directly affected by a change in the purchasing power of the monetary unit. Consider money on deposit in a bank in Canadian dollars. When the purchasing power of the dollar changes, there is an immediate gain or loss in the purchasing power of that bank deposit. The same is true of all other assets and liabilities that are monetary in nature, i.e., that are money or claims to be received or paid in fixed amounts of money. Thus, if a bond is acquired at par for $1,000 and is held to maturity, the purchasing power invested in it will decrease or increase over that time directly with the change in the purchasing power of money. In contrast, the purchasing power obtainable from a nonmonetary asset is not governed by the purchasing power of money, at least not nearly to the same extent, because it does not consist of a claim to a fixed amount of money.

The GPL restatement process is, therefore, considered separately for nonmonetary and monetary items. (To simplify the discussion we will be assuming statements presented in terms of purchasing power at the end of the current reporting period.)

Nonmonetary Items

Historical cost figures for nonmonetary assets and liabilities at the end of a reporting period will require an index adjustment to restate them into dollars of current purchasing power. If, for example, an item of inventory was bought for $100 when the GPL index stood at 200, and the index at the date of the balance sheet was 210, the item of inventory would be reported at $105. The other side of the entry effectively goes to equity, so as to restate equity to dollars of current purchasing power.

When the inventory is sold, its cost will be further restated into dollars of purchasing power at that date so that cost of goods sold expense will be matched against revenues of equivalent purchasing power at the date of sale. Similarly, depreciation and other expenses will be restated in terms of the purchasing power of the dollar at the time they are charged to income. These figures will then be updated to reflect all revenues and expenses in purchasing power units as at the financial reporting date. Thus, a major criticism of historical cost accounting (that it matches out-of-date costs against revenues, resulting in understating income under inflation) would seem to be addressed.

Two general implementation considerations may be noted:

- To accomplish this restatement of financial statement figures, it is necessary to trace the dates of transactions that gave rise to the assets and liabilities. (In the above inventory example, one would need to know when the inventory was acquired in order to establish the change in GPL index from that date.) Where there are many transactions in a period, reasonable assumptions are made. For example, if inventory turns over every three months, it may normally be a fair approximation to assume that the inventory on hand at December 31 was acquired on average on the preceding November 15.

- Because the carrying value of nonmonetary assets is adjusted upward under inflationary conditions, the chances that carrying values will exceed recoverable values are greater than they are under historical cost accounting. Thus, greater attention must be paid to the possible need for write-downs when GPL accounting is used.

Of course, if a nonmonetary item is carried on the balance sheet at its current value (for example, if inventory is written down to its market value), it is then represented in dollars of current purchasing power and needs no GPL restatement.

Monetary Assets and Liabilities

If the GPL balance sheet is expressed in terms of the purchasing power of the dollar at the year-end balance sheet date, it follows that cash balances at that date are translated at parity. On the other hand, the balance of cash at the beginning of the current reporting period must be translated in terms of the purchasing power of the dollar *at the end of the year*. This reflects the fact that, under inflationary conditions, a dollar would buy more at the beginning of the year than at the end. To illustrate the principle here, assume a company held $100 of cash throughout a reporting period when the inflation index increased from 200 to 210. The opening cash balance would be restated to its purchasing power equivalent at the end of the year—that is $(210/200 \times \$100) = \$105$. The closing cash balance of $100 requires no adjustment as it reflects the purchasing power of the dollar at that date. Thus, the company would report a purchasing power loss of $5 due to holding an asset (cash) that declined in purchasing power during the period.

The same is true of all monetary assets. The basic principle is that general purchasing power is lost by holding monetary assets during a period of inflation. To accurately determine the amount of this purchasing power loss in a period, it will be necessary to trace the timing and amount of monetary transactions. (This will result in the restatement of figures for revenues, dividends, wages and other monetary transactions.)

Conversely, holding monetary liability positions during a period of inflation produces purchasing power gains. This is because outstanding debt represents less of a burden in terms of the purchasing power to be given up if the value of the dollar has declined during the period that it is outstanding.

Proponents of GPL accounting believe that the disclosure of the gain or loss on purchasing power associated with monetary assets and liabilities is one of the most important bits of information emerging from GPL accounting. However, many have been uncomfortable with reflecting a purchasing power gain on debt as a result of inflation. Is it really income? Is it realized or realizable? The following reflects the variety of arguments that have been made concerning the purchasing power gain on debt under inflation.

- First of all, some proponents of the entity theory would not dispute that some sort of gain is associated with the debt but argue that it should not be recorded in net entity income. In contrast, the purchasing power loss on cash held would be considered to belong in income because the cash is an asset of the entity required for its operation. Entity theorists argue that the purchasing power gain on debt is not a gain to the entity but rather a transfer of purchasing power from the debt holders to the shareholders. The assets for which the entity is accountable are not increased in either monetary or purchasing power terms because of the debt. Instead, the claim on entity assets by the debt holders has been decreased in purchasing power terms, and consequently the shareholders' claim has increased.

- Many people think that purchasing power gains and losses are unreal because they cannot perceive cash flows associated with such gains and losses. The concern of such people is that a gain in purchasing power cannot be spent. It seems irrational that the higher the debt position (which is often evidence of a shaky company), the greater will be the reported purchasing power gain on debt. As some have put it, a company could be showing substantial gains all the way into bankruptcy.

- Many people also are concerned that in some sense the gain is not "realized" until the debt is paid off. The general price level could reverse itself before the maturity date of the debt so that the present gain might be cancelled out by a loss.

- In contrast, the position of GPL theorists is that the concept of realization has no meaning in relation to changes in purchasing power of *monetary* assets or liabilities. Such changes, by definition, occur when the price level changes and are measured by it. There can be no justification or rationale for assigning the result of a change in price level occurring in one period to some other period. The simple fact is that, if the value of the dollar decreases, the burden of an obligation expressed in dollars decreases at the same time.

The purchasing power gain on debt may be viewed as an offset against interest expense, so as to show the net cost of debt in real terms in the period. The contracted interest rate on an entity's debt will reflect inflation expectations at the date it was issued (if it is fixed rate debt) or throughout the life of the debt (if it is floating rate debt). In other words, it is well recognized that market rates of interest include a premium sufficient to compensate a lender for the expected reduction in the purchasing power of cash flows when they are to be received. Thus, netting the purchasing power gain on debt against interest expense may be considered to show the net interest cost to the entity in the period—the net of the actual effect of inflation in the period on the purchasing power of the debt against the inflation premium that is included in the interest expense in the period. (It may be argued that a better measure of this effect is determined if debt is measured at its fair value, because its fair value represents its future cash flows discounted at the current market interest rate reflecting the market's current expectations of future inflation rates.)

In sum, it may be concluded that, if the essential premise of GPL accounting is accepted, gains and losses on monetary assets and liabilities should be recognized as income. This said, it must be recognized that these gains and losses may be hard to understand, particularly since they cannot be directly associated with cash flows. Thus it is important that their effects on GPL-restated income be clearly disclosed and explained. As well, a clear statement of changes in financial position that focuses on operating cash flows and liquidity is all the more necessary, to overcome the danger that inclusion of purchasing power gains on debt under inflationary conditions may obscure whether an enterprise has maintained its business liquidity.

Some Implementation Problems

The problems in implementing GPL accounting include: (1) determining the appropriate index, (2) distinguishing monetary from nonmonetary items, (3) translation of foreign operations for consolidation purposes, and (4) tax provisioning. The first of these has been discussed earlier in this section. Following is a brief discussion of the latter three problem areas.

What Is Monetary?

It is evident that the distinction between monetary and nonmonetary assets and liabilities is very important in GPL accounting. Published descriptions of GPL accounting have accepted the concept of "monetary" that is used in GAAP—that is, to include all assets and liabilities as monetary that represent claims that are fixed or determinable amounts of money. The essential characteristic for GPL accounting purposes is that the carrying values of monetary assets and liabilities in GAAP financial statements are already expressed in terms of the purchasing power of money at the financial statement reporting date. For certain types of assets and liabilities it may not be entirely clear whether this is the case. Some of the potential areas of uncertainty are discussed below:

- Debt that is convertible into common shares and certain preference shares may have some monetary and some nonmonetary characteristics. The recent *CICA Handbook* (Section 3860) requirement for classification by an issuer of financial instruments as between debt and equity, addresses this issue. One would expect that those items classified as financial liabilities under Section 3860 would be considered monetary for GPL restatement purposes, while those classified as equity would be considered nonmonetary. (The requirements of *CICA Handbook* Section 3860 in this regard are discussed at Chapter 9.)

- There may be some question with respect to unearned income. If payments received in advance of providing goods or services are mere deposits, and the actual prices or quantities of goods or services can vary, then the unearned income liability would seem to be similar to a negative receivable or a form of temporary financing, and thus monetary in nature. Otherwise, if the obligation is to deliver specific quantities of goods or services at specified prices, they should be treated as nonmonetary, and restated in terms of equivalent purchasing power from the date they originate, in order to be properly matched with related costs to be incurred in future periods.

- Deferred income tax balances arising under the "deferral" concept do not meet the definition of a monetary item; yet many have not considered treatment as nonmonetary to be satisfactory, and it may often be impracticable to break down deferred tax balances by year of origin in order to restate them. Some argue that, in a fundamental sense, tax allocation procedures represent expectations of future cash flows, so that there may be some justification for treating deferred tax balances as monetary. Of course, if deferred taxes are measured on the accrual basis (as is now to be required by the CICA, see Chapter 16) they clearly become monetary in nature.

- Receivables and payables in foreign currency are considered under GAAP to be monetary items, although some have argued that they do not represent claims that are fixed in terms of the reporting currency. Foreign currency denominated receivables and payables are, of course, translated at the current exchange rate, and thus may be considered to represent the purchasing power of the reporting currency at the balance sheet date.

Translation of Foreign Subsidiaries or Branches for Consolidation

Chapter 21 has described the two methods of translation of financial statement figures included in consolidated financial statements of subsidiaries or divisions whose accounts are kept in a foreign currency. The "current-rate" method is to be used for self-sustaining foreign operations. The "temporal method" is used when operations of the foreign unit are interdependent with the parent company.

GPL accounting introduces an additional step to be completed in the process of consolidating the foreign unit. Its historical cost figures must be restated in GPL terms. The question is whether this restatement should take place before the translation of its figures into the currency of the parent company—the so-called "restate/translate" approach—or after—the "translate/restate" approach. Under the restate/translate approach the purchasing power index used in the restatement process is that applicable in the foreign country. Under the translate/restate approach, the purchasing power index used is that applicable for the parent company's currency since the foreign unit's figures would have been translated into that currency before GPL adjustments are made.

The merits of each approach must be considered in conjunction with the method of translation (whether current rate or temporal method). It must be remembered that inflation (or deflation) in a country will have an impact on the exchange rate for its currency with other currencies as well as show up in the purchasing power index. One could argue, therefore, that if a current exchange rate is used for translation, it should be associated with price-level-adjusted figures at the reporting date, and if a historical exchange rate is used for translation, it should be associated with historical cost figures. Thus, where the assets and liabilities of a self-sustaining foreign operation are translated at current rates, the argument just made suggests the use of the restate/translate sequence in these circumstances.

It may be noted that if GPL accounting is applied, it is no longer necessary to have a rule that investments in "highly inflationary" economies should be translated using the temporal method even though the unit is self-sustaining. This exception under historical cost accounting to the standard treatment for self-sustaining investments is only an expedient to avoid the "disappearing asset" phenomenon (as discussed in Chapter 21). As soon as GPL accounting is adopted, this expedient becomes unnecessary, because nonmonetary assets are restated upwards to reflect their cost in current units of purchasing power in the foreign country before being translated at current rates.

Tax Provisions When the Accounts Are Restated

When GPL-adjusted financial statements are presented in terms of purchasing power current at the reporting date, the carrying values of all nonmonetary assets are restated in terms of their equivalent purchasing power at that period-end. Suppose an entity was formed to buy and hold a piece of property in expectation of its appreciation over a period of years. Assume further that the initial balance sheet was as follows: Land at cost—$500,000; Equity—$500,000. Assume further that the land was leased out for five years at a rental equal to municipal taxes, and that the general price level rose by 100% in that period. A GPL-adjusted balance sheet, expressed in terms of purchasing power at the end of the five years would show: Land—$1,000,000; Equity—$1,000,000. Then suppose, one day later, that the land was sold for $1,000,000. Immediately after the sale a balance sheet would show: Cash—$1,000,000; Liability for taxes (assuming a 23% capital gains rate)—$115,000; Equity—$885,000. The question is, was the GPL-adjusted balance sheet one day earlier, which showed an equity of $1,000,000, fairly presented?

- Traditional deferred tax accounting theory states that income tax is a cost that should be recognized as expense in the period when accounting income equivalent to taxable income is reported. That is, if accounting income is reported before being taxed, deferred taxes should be provided. In this case, however, the GPL restatement of asset cost is never credited to income but rather to capital. Thus there is no accounting income equivalent to the taxable income, and therefore it has been argued this is a "permanent difference" which should not be subject to allocation.

- Under the "temporary difference" approach to tax allocation, which is in place in the U.S. and has recently been adopted in Canada (see Chapter 16), the liability for taxes would be accrued at 23% of the asset restatement in each year. It would seem that the amount would be charged to reduce the capital maintenance credit to equity. It may be questioned, however, whether the tax might be better charged against income, notwithstanding that the asset restatement was credited to equity. If this was done, then, year by year there would be a charge to income without any compensating revenue or gain being reported. It might look odd to see a regular tax provision year by year when no net income or gain was showing. Yet this presentation would report an important reality. An income tax system that is based on historical cost is, in effect, a tax on capital during periods when the general price level is rising.

Evolving Views of GPL Accounting

The adoption of general price level restatement of historical cost-based (i.e., GAAP) financial statements represented the solution preferred (with some lack of enthusiasm) by practising accountants to the problem posed by inflation in the early 1970s. It addresses a major criticism of historical cost-matching accounting under inflation, in that it results in an up-to-date matching of costs and revenues in terms of equivalent units of general purchasing power. It is important to note that in countries experiencing very high rates of inflation (for example, Mexico until recent years) some form of general price level accounting has invariably been applied. (In such highly inflationary circumstances, contractual arrangements for the payment of services or financing will normally be price level indexed, so that GPL accounting becomes a natural choice.) The IASC standard (IAS 29) on *Financial Reporting in Hyperinflationary Economies* observes that:

> In a hyperinflationary economy, financial statements, whether they are based on a historical cost approach or a current cost approach, are useful only if they are expressed in terms of the measuring unit current at the balance sheet date ... (par. 7)

However, as the 1970s developed, many people criticized GPL accounting because the figures it produced for assets and liabilities did not represent values current at the financial reporting date. The feeling seemed to be that if historical cost figures were to be revised, the revision ought to be based on current values.

Most academic accountants did not support GPL accounting. Even though its basic ideas had been largely worked out in academic literature years earlier, by the 1970s academic accountants were interested in a more fundamental restructuring of the accounting model. Unfortunately, they were by no means unanimous as to the manner in which current values for assets and liabilities could or should be integrated with concepts of income. The plethora of ideas, each with its vociferous proponents, hindered general acceptance of any single proposal.

Finally, governments and government agencies played a part in the developing controversy. Just as accounting standard setters were on the point of adopting GPL accounting, the United Kingdom government announced a committee of inquiry into inflation accounting, and the United States Securities and Exchange Commission pre-empted the FASB by requiring companies to publish certain information based on replacement costs. Subsequently, government-sponsored reviews were initiated in Australia, New Zealand, and in Canada (by the Ontario government).[6] The effect of the government interventions was to preclude the adoption of GPL accounting in the mid-1970s and, in effect, force accounting standard setters to pursue accounting models directed to the valuation of assets and liabilities at current prices. Unfortunately, the government reviews were no more successful than academic studies in achieving consensus.

We shall now proceed to a description of a variety of accounting models based upon the use of current values.

CURRENT VALUE MODELS

The case for current values in accounting rests upon the simple idea that a user of financial statements will be better equipped with current value information to estimate amounts and timing of future cash flows and to evaluate management performance than he or she would be with information based on outdated historical costs.

It is agreed that the only possible objective for current value accounting is to value individual assets and liabilities of an enterprise, or in some cases groups of similar assets and liabilities, rather than the entity as a whole. The valuation of an enterprise as a going concern requires subjective estimates of future cash flows for the entity as a whole and a judgmental choice of discount factors to be applied to arrive at their present value. The job of financial reporting is to provide information about assets, liabilities, and equity, revenues, expenses, gains and losses and cash flows that will assist investors in making their subjective estimates of the value and prospects of a business.

An important corollary, which is not always appreciated, follows from the conclusion that it is not the purpose of financial accounting to value an entity as a whole. It is that a current value accounting system cannot be expected to value goodwill on a current basis—because the current value of goodwill can only be arrived at by subtracting the fair value of other assets less liabilities from the value of the enterprise as a whole.

Earlier in this chapter it was indicated that there are three possible bases for the valuation of assets and liabilities—discounted cash flow (DCF), an entry market price, or an exit market price. A current value accounting model may choose one of these. Alternatively, a model may choose a different valuation basis in different situations, in which case it must specify a decision rule for making the choice, such as value to the firm (VF).

DCF has generally been considered to be impracticable as a basis that could be applied across the board. (However, it may be used as a proxy to estimate current market value when a reliable market price is lacking.) Current value accounting models have thus generally been classified on the basis of whether they rely on entry values, exit values, or a situation-specific basis of valuation such as VF. The latter basis of valuation will use replacement cost most of the time, so that it is commonly considered to be largely equivalent to an entry-value system. Hence, we can say that current value accounting systems are basically of two types—entry value systems, which are widely known as current cost accounting (CCA), and exit value systems, which we shall call current realizable value accounting (CRVA).

CURRENT COST ACCOUNTING SYSTEMS

Simple Replacement Cost Accounting (RCA)

CCA has several versions. The simplest form of CCA is one in which amounts charged against income for assets sold or consumed in use are stated at their current replacement cost. Changes in asset prices while held (holding gains or losses) are treated as direct credits or debits to equity. This accounting model is based on the physical capital maintenance concept. It adopts the realization convention, and it adopts the entity concept since the capital maintained pertains to all the physical assets of the entity without any adjustment for debt financing. The thinking is that any income reported after absorbing a charge sufficient to replace the assets used or given up in the earnings process represents a genuine improvement in well-being. Such income can be distributed without infringing on the amount that must be invested in physical capital necessary to sustain the current level of operations.

Supporters of RCA in its physical capital maintenance form believe that reporting income only after full provision for physical maintenance of the resources of the entity provides a good measure of performance—that the resulting income figure shows whether the enterprise is able to recoup its costs from revenues when prices change. Further, they contend that it provides a good basis for prediction of future profitability of the enterprise, by excluding non-repeatable holding gains and losses from reported income.

However, supporters of RCA must answer some very significant challenges to these claims, challenges that go to the root of the conceptual defensibility and practical operationality of RCA and physical capital maintenance. Many have come to believe that the concept of physical or operating capital is so seriously flawed that it cannot stand as a legitimate, implementable general income measure.

What Is Replacement Cost of Productive Assets?

The Measurement Objective

The crucial starting point issue in the application of RCA is that of interpreting the meaning of replacement cost. The most serious question in this regard is whether the RC assumed is to be that of an identical asset or is to be based on the cost of replacing the asset service in the most favourable way. Business conditions change and technology improves. Thus, we cannot assume that resources consumed will be replaced with identical assets when the time comes for replacement. This problem is particularly acute with respect to capital assets.

- Notwithstanding the possibility of changes in business conditions and technology, the simplest approach is to interpret RC to mean the replacement cost of an asset identical to that which is being sold or consumed. Such RC may be more descriptively called "reproduction cost." Such an approach has the merit that expenses will be reported on an internally consistent basis. We will not, for example, report expenses for labour, supplies, power, etc., as actually incurred in the operation of the existing "old-tech" machine but report a cost for consumption of the machine service based on the cost of a different "new-tech" machine. Thus, the use of reproduction cost could be said to report performance on a factual basis. Income reported will be the result of the investment and operating decisions actually made in the past. By the same token, however, the reported income statement may be less useful as a predictor of what may be expected in future. More specifically, it may be considered to seriously misstate capital that needs to be maintained if replacement, when it occurs, will be based on a different configuration of factors of production at a different cost. On top of this, there is the practical point that reproduction cost for existing capital assets may be hard to find where the identical assets are no longer being made and markets for used assets of the same type are not active.

- The alternative is to estimate RC in terms of the replacement cost of equivalent capacity for physical service. This could be argued to be more relevant in that it does not base a charge to income for resource consumption on the RC of assets that will not be replaced. On the other hand, it can also be accused of being "what if" accounting—basing the allowance for resource consumption on costs of assets not even owned. In addition, it encounters the problem that actual operating expenses reported will have been incurred in conjunction with the use of the old-tech, presumably less efficient, assets. To cure this, it is accepted that if RC is based on an assumption of replacement with a more efficient asset, an estimate of the operating cost savings to result from the use of that asset must be made, and the capitalized value of those savings must be deducted from the RC of the asset.

- There is one further question on the basis of estimating RC. Should it be assumed that whole plant will be replaced in one stroke assuming the most efficient replacement configuration currently achievable, or should it be assumed that the replacement decision will be looked at on an individual asset basis? The sum of the cost of replacement of individual assets in a plant will probably not equal RC for the whole plant replaced at one time. There is no universal answer to this question. The common-sense solution is to choose one or the other basis of estimating RC in accordance with the way in which replacement is likely to take place in practice.

It can be seen that there is a certain ambiguity in the concept of physical capital maintenance in situations in which productive assets in a going concern enterprise are not likely to be replaced with identical assets. It is to be noted that this issue may not be a major problem if satisfactory used market prices are available for the asset actually owned. In that case, RC can be taken simply as the buying price of assets of the same age and condition in the market. Even if technologically advanced assets are available, it may be presumed that the used market price will compensate for any operating advantages held by them.[7] But active efficient markets for used capital assets are the exception rather than the rule.

Practical Estimation Issues

Estimation of the RC of inventories and capital assets may present considerable practical difficulties.[8] "Direct pricing," under which current buying prices of actual existing or replacement assets are determined, is the most accurate technique but is expensive. If the RC of technologically improved plant is to be estimated, it may be possible to take shortcuts based on generally known costs for units of size (for example, cost per square foot of buildings) or units of capacity for certain processing industries. Otherwise, estimation of the current cost of a modern equivalent plant and adjustments to allow for differences in capacity and efficiency of existing owned plant can be arduous.

The alternative is to rely on indexes applied to historical cost to produce current cost figures. When indexes are used, care needs to be taken that they are appropriate for the type of asset to which they are applied. In particular, inquiry should be made as to the extent to which the index makes an allowance for technological change. If such an allowance is made, the application of the index to the historical cost of the asset will not yield reproduction cost (if that is the figure desired). On the other hand, if such an allowance is not made or is made to an insufficient degree, the application of the index to historical cost of the asset held will not yield a figure appropriate as an estimate of RC of service capacity.

Some Evaluative Considerations

In general, we can say that the physical capital maintenance concept becomes more ambiguous and difficult to implement the greater the difference between the existing productive assets and the assets that will replace them. Physical or operating capital maintenance is essentially a static concept founded on an implicit assumption of continuing replacement of productive assets. When an entity is likely to replace existing productive assets with improved assets, most could accept that the concept requires allowances for differences in the "service capacity" between the existing assets and their likely replacements. In the modern age, enterprises are continually changing their business operations, so that it can become hard to know what maintenance of physical or productive capacity means. This problem is demonstrated in the following types of situations:

- Industries in which the product line is constantly changing. For example, when inventory consists of fashion goods, replacement with identical goods may not be planned even if the goods are available. In such circumstances the concept of current replacement cost becomes problematic if not imaginary. To achieve the aim of holding back enough from revenue to finance restocking in such situations, one might construct an index that reflects the annual rate of change in prices of the underlying factors of production that determine the cost of goods dealt in by the enterprise, and then use this index to revise the historical cost figures for cost of goods sold. This may seem rather crude and artificial, but it may be the only way to approximate the RCA objective.

- Industries that are undergoing fundamental technological change. An old example may illustrate this point. At one time most people crossed the Atlantic by ship. A company that wishes to be in the transatlantic transportation business has long since had to replace ships with planes. A physical maintenance concept based on ships for this business became irrelevant over time, no matter what technological improvements had been made to ships. (Had it been possible to instantly convert ships to cruise traffic, this would not have been true, but that development came later.) A farsighted company, considering itself in the transportation business rather than the shipping business, might have converted itself into an airline. But it would have required a considerable feat of imagination to visualize an income statement reporting the results of operations of the last remaining ships based on the replacement and operating costs of airplanes.

- Extractive industries. The principal assets of oil and gas and mining companies consist of reserves of oil and gas and mineral deposits and rights to share additional reserves that may be discovered on certain lands. Estimates of the replacement cost of such irreproducible assets is extremely difficult, and the worth of the information is questionable. One might attempt to estimate RC on the basis of current market prices for the existing assets or some indexing of historical costs actually incurred. Market prices for individual properties are likely to be of limited relevance to physical capital maintenance because they do not necessarily relate to the cost to replace existing resources. The costs of finding new properties can be expected to be highly variable from one region to another and estimates of such costs would not seem to be capable of providing a sound foundation for measuring income. Updated historical costs may be considered to be essentially meaningless if the assets cannot be reproduced.

Other Problems with Simple RCA

Monetary Assets

A further difficulty with the concept of physical capital maintenance lies in the fact that the total investment in any going concern is likely to contain nonphysical as well as physical assets (trade accounts receivable as an example) and will be financed in part by trade credit. Thus, the net investment in a business entity is likely to be different from the sum of its physical assets. Simple RCA has no concept for maintenance of the net investment in nonphysical assets, because it is implemented by means of replacement costing of assets consumed, and monetary assets are not consumed.

It has been argued that for certain purposes this is unimportant.[9] A different response is to broaden the concept of physical capital maintenance to that of maintenance of "operating capacity." Thus, if the actual operations of a firm depend upon investment in monetary assets as well as physical assets, we must take into account a requirement to maintain the capacity of the monetary assets as well. This leads to the idea of an allowance for maintenance of monetary working capital to be discussed in a subsequent section.

Portfolio Investments

Although the concept of operating capacity maintenance can solve some problems, it leaves others unsolved. The capital dedicated to portfolio investments has no device to ensure maintenance when prices change. Some proponents of physical capital maintenance have conceded this point.[10] They suggest that nonoperating capital be treated differently. Holding gains and losses on such capital would not be excluded from income, and thus a financial capital maintenance concept should be adopted for them. This is effectively an admission that operating capacity maintenance cannot be a comprehensive income measurement system. Rather, it is seen to be situation-specific—different applications are considered appropriate for measuring income from different segments of the entity.

Commodity Trading

For commodity traders or dealers, buying prices and selling prices are equal apart from transaction costs. Thus, RCA applied literally will always show zero profit. This anomaly is recognized by most writers. The solution usually proposed is to include gains and losses in income and to adjust them by a capital maintenance allowance. This may be achieved directly by factoring up their historical cost by a general price index in calculating gain and loss or indirectly by recording gains and losses on the basis of historical cost but treating the balance sheet carrying value of such inventories as though they were part of monetary working capital subject to an allowance to maintain its operating capacity.

The problem under RCA in dealing with the commodity trader is similar to a problem often raised in relation to an ordinary business. It is not uncommon for a business to vary its buying patterns for basic materials with the aim of buying at the most advantageous price. Good buying, in effect, is a managerial skill that is rewarded by holding gains. If a business speculated by buying or selling commodity options or futures contracts, there would be no doubt that gains would be part of operating income. If it takes equivalent risks through its purchasing policies for materials, however, any gain or loss is excluded from income by virtue of the fact that replacement cost is charged against revenue when revenue is recognized. Although this anomaly is widely recognized, no practical solution has been suggested to the problem of separation of gains and losses attributable to good buying and holding gains and losses from fortuitous price changes.

Debt Financing

Some argue that the complete exclusion of holding gains from income understates the amount that can safely be distributed to shareholders in times of rising prices when productive assets are financed in part by debt. They argue that the portion of holding gains on assets financed by debt is properly reported as income accruing to equity. If these holding gains are excluded from income and treated as a capital maintenance adjustment to equity capital, the existing level of debt in nominal dollars will form an ever-shrinking percentage of the total debt and equity capital of the entity (assuming the entity's revenues are sufficient to cover the current cost of assets sold or consumed in the earnings process). A reasonable assumption may be that the entity will finance increases in the RC of its assets in the proportion of its pre-existing debt to equity ratio, in which case it will not need to maintain equity capital for the proportion of the increase that it is assumed will be financed by debt. The so-called "financing" or "gearing" gain to be discussed subsequently attempts to provide for this.

Some oppose such an adjustment. Those who believe the entity theory should be applied naturally believe that the benefits that accrue to shareholders from holding gains on assets financed by debt should not be reflected in entity income. They will agree that in some circumstances an entity may properly borrow and use the borrowed money to increase shareholders' distributions. But they do not agree that this justifies treatment of such distributions as entity income. Others argue that when replacement costs are rising, an entity may be unable to maintain its percentage margins over RC. This possibility provides a different reason for exclusion of holding gains from income.[11]

Backlog Depreciation

Many writers have talked about the "backlog depreciation" problem. Backlog depreciation may be illustrated as follows. A three-year life capital asset is bought for $100 and is expected to have no salvage value. During its three years of service, average RC is $120, $150, and $180, so that current cost depreciation is reported at $40, $50, and $60 in successive years. When the time comes for replacement, the RC of the asset is $195. Accumulated depreciation written is only $150. The total "backlog" over the period is $45. The problem is that a charge against income based on RC is sufficient to replace the portion of the asset expensed at that date, but if the replacement is not made immediately and prices go on rising, the amount will be insufficient when the asset comes to be replaced.

It must be recognized, however, that the RC depreciation charge has the effect of holding in the entity cash generated from operations in an amount equal to the depreciation charge, assuming capital is maintained. In other words, the charge reduces the amount of income that can be distributed while maintaining capital. If the cash held back is invested in assets that are carried at replacement cost, and if there are holding gains on those assets equivalent to the increase in RC of the asset to be replaced, the exclusion of those holding gains from income will maintain the physical capacity of capital in the aggregate and there will be no backlog depreciation problem.[12] A number of writers have proposed to cure the apparent problem by calculating backlog depreciation regularly and charging it against income. For reasons just indicated, this is in error. The best answer to this problem may be to make sure some capital maintenance allowance is provided with respect to *all* the assets of the entity on hand whether they be operating or nonoperating, monetary or nonmonetary.

Some Proposed Modifications to Simple RCA

Certain ideas have been put forward in the literature to try to address certain of the above-noted problems with RCA. These are briefly discussed below.

The Monetary Working Capital Adjustment (MWCA)

It was noted above that if operating capacity is to be maintained, one must also adjust the profit reported for changes in the monetary working capital required by the business on account of changes in prices.

This idea is not easy to understand intuitively. The explanation commonly given is that, under conditions of rising prices, a given amount of monetary working capital loses part of its "operating capacity"—its capacity to finance a given volume of business. The more straightforward explanation is that cash flows tend to lag accruals. If income is defined as *cash distributable while maintaining capacity to operate at the same physical volume of business* (and it is assumed that credit terms must be maintained to do that volume of business), then this monetary working capital adjustment to the reported profit figure must be made.

There is a superficial similarity between the concept of the MWCA and the idea of purchasing power gains and losses on monetary items in GPL accounting. In fact, if specific selling and purchasing prices of an enterprise were changing at a rate identical to the general price level, the MWCA would be exactly the same in amount as the GPL gain or loss computed with respect to the assets and liabilities defined to be part of monetary working capital. The basic rationales of the two adjustments, however, are quite different. The MWCA proceeds from a physical capital maintenance perspective and applies only to monetary items required to conduct operations. The other proceeds from a financial capital maintenance perspective and applies to all monetary items.

Calculation of the MWCA, in theory, requires application of different rates of price change according to the particular item of monetary working capital involved. For example, the adjustment of accounts receivable should be based on the rate of change in selling prices, while the adjustment for accounts payable should be based on the rate of price change for goods and services purchased.

There has been some difference of opinion as to just what should be treated as operating monetary working capital. For example, some would treat all bank loans as a part of the financial structure of the entity. Others regard short-term bank loans as so intimately related to accounts receivable and inventory as to represent part of the *net* operating investment in the business. Thus, the concept of the MWCA has proved to be somewhat fuzzy.

The Financing Adjustment

As already indicated, many writers conclude that, to the extent holding gains have occurred on assets financed by debt whose claim on the assets is fixed in nominal dollars, that portion of the holding gains may properly be reported as income to the equity. The amount of the financing adjustment may be calculated by applying (a) the proportion at the beginning of the accounting period of debt on a historical cost basis to the aggregate of equity on a current cost basis and debt to (b) either realized, or realized and unrealized, gains or losses. Thus, the calculation reflects the continuation of the past proportion in which assets have been financed by debt.

There has been some debate as to whether the financing adjustment should be restricted to realized gains. If one accepts the view that increases in current cost of assets held do represent real gains (i.e., that the current cost asset values are recoverable from future revenues), then it may be reasoned that it is inconsistent not to recognize the income element of these gains. This argument is reinforced by the observation that the realization restriction distorts the timing of recognition of holding gains. The debt-related portion of increases in the replacement cost of land held for productive purposes, for example, would never get recognized in income unless the land is sold.

There has also been some debate with respect to whether bank overdrafts or short-term bank financing should be treated as debt or as part of monetary working capital. Obviously, both the figures for the monetary working capital adjustment and the financing adjustment are affected by the decision on this point and the final income figure reported is affected as well.

Use of the "Value to the Firm" Approach

Most people feel uncomfortable with the idea of reporting RC figures in financial statements that exceed the current economic or realizable values for the assets in question. For these reasons, current cost accounting advocates have virtually universally embraced the concept of "value to the firm." As stated earlier, the valuation approach boils down in most situations to two rules:

- Value assets held for sale at the lower of RC and NRV.
- Value assets held for productive use at the lower of RC and economic value (EV).

There are problems in fitting VF concepts into CCA theory, quite apart from the subjective character of estimates of EV. In the first place, consider the practical problem of separating the change in EV from one year to the next into something equivalent to depreciation and price change elements. Since EV is not a market price, it is impossible to measure any price change effect. Since this is so, there can be no amount credited to capital maintenance with respect to assets valued at EV, and the notion of maintenance of operating capacity is simply nonoperative.

A similar statement can be made for inventory carried at NRV. When NRV is below RC, it will no longer be profitable to replace the goods in question. Once NRV is adopted, changes in NRV before sale will presumably be reflected in the operating profit figures. But there will be no revaluation of the inventory item to reflect changing costs of production. Hence, the notion of maintenance of operating capacity is nonoperative in this case also.

The conclusion from the foregoing is that the adoption of the VF basis of asset valuation has serious consequences for the basic objectives of physical or operating capacity maintenance. In simple terms, capital maintenance is supposed to be achieved under CCA by charging income with the RC of assets sold or consumed. If something less than RC is charged, clearly capital is not maintained in any meaningful sense. An alternative approach, however, is conceivable. The problem may be addressed by applying a current cost price index to the aggregate asset value of the firm's assets, as explained in the following paragraphs.

Current Cost Accounting with Capital Maintenance Based on a Price Index

Under this approach the idea of maintaining capital by excluding holding gains and losses from reported income is abandoned. Instead, gains and losses are included in income, but a one-line capital maintenance adjustment is charged, calculated by applying an appropriate specific price index to the current value of the capital recorded as invested in the entity. A price index appropriate to the business of the particular entity might be constructed on the basis of a representative collection of productive assets used by the entity, or perhaps a published index of relevant product prices might be used. That index would be applied to the aggregate value of a firm's assets at the beginning of a period (valued on the VF approach or any other approach considered relevant). Income reported would include all holding gains and losses, and would deduct the increase in value that the index indicates was required to maintain the productive capital at the beginning of the year.

This expedient would solve more than the problem caused by the adoption of the VF valuation basis. It would also allow for maintenance of the net investment in monetary working capital, and would make provision for maintenance of capital invested in nonoperating assets (assuming the index is designed to encompass these assets). As well, if it is desired to adhere to the proprietary point of view, the capital maintenance adjustment would be applied to the equity capital only, thereby obviating the need for the financing adjustment.

The principal problem with the use of the one-line capital maintenance adjustment lies in the selection of an appropriate price index. The objective is to find or devise an index that reasonably reflects the changes in prices of assets specifically held by the entity, in line with the idea of maintenance of operating capacity. Many, however, may feel that the use of a general price index, as is called for by the objective of maintaining the general purchasing power of financial capital, is likely to be more suitable. If this is done, then one crosses the line from an operating capital maintenance to a financial capital maintenance purchasing power model.

To be logically consistent, the income figure against which a one-line capital maintenance adjustment is charged should include unrealized as well as realized holding gains and losses.

For example, if a company's sole asset were its investment in land, it would be illogical to charge a capital maintenance adjustment of, say, 10% against income from the land and yet ignore an unrealized gain in land value of an equivalent or larger percentage. Alternatively, if it is desired to exclude unrealized holding gains from income, consideration must be given to reducing the capital maintenance adjustment on some reasonable basis.

An Evaluation of Current Cost Accounting

The above analysis strongly suggests that the concept of maintenance of physical or operating capacity is seriously inadequate as a foundation for measuring enterprise income. First, it is difficult to implement because it is founded on the concept of continuing replacement of productive assets. In the common case where an enterprise will replace its existing productive assets with improved assets, it becomes difficult, and some cases impossible, to define productive capacity in a meaningful, operational sense.

Second, the basic concept does not address the problem of maintenance of capital in nonoperating assets, such as portfolio investments, and it requires the development of somewhat artificial expedients to adjust for the effects of changing prices on monetary working capital and holding gains financed by debt. It is to be noted that these issues pose a particular problem for the applicability of current cost accounting and operating capital maintenance to financial institutions. A major portion of their resources are financial assets, and issues relating to accounting for liabilities loom large for financial institutions because of their highly leveraged structures and the unique characteristics of deposit liabilities of banks and actuarial obligations of insurance companies. The physical operating capacity concept clearly has little relevance, and the broader idea of operating capacity seems difficult to define in a meaningful way for financial institutions. (It is notable that, as will be seen in a later section, the *CICA Handbook*'s 1983 standard on reporting the effects of changing prices within a current cost accounting framework exempted banks, trust companies and insurance companies.)

Finally, most authorities believe that, when a productive asset is not to be replaced because its recoverable value is less than its replacement value, it should be written down and charged against income on the basis of its recoverable value. There is no way in which the recoverable value of an obsolete asset can serve as a standard that shows whether productive capacity has been maintained.

An alternative approach would recognize all holding gains in income, but deduct a one-line allowance for capital maintenance based on changes in prices shown by an index that reflects a weighted average of prices of operating assets held by the entity. If the index were broadened to be representative of price changes in the broader categories of business investment, it would help to meet the objections that physical capital maintenance is too tied to the operating assets of the business. However, major conceptual and practical problems remain in this alternative; these come down to defining the operating capacity of a business and embodying it in a reliable index.

At the most fundamental level, the idea that a company has not earned income unless it has maintained its ability to replace its existing operating capacity is open to challenge. It may be argued that reinvestment in operating assets in the future is a future decision and that these future costs should not determine whether income has been earned by past investments and operations. Some reason that attempting to measure income on the basis of current replacement costs is confounding the measurement of this period's income with next period's investments. From a slightly different perspective, would a consumer agree that he or she should pay more for a company's product because the company will have to invest more in the future to manufacture the product in the future? This line of reasoning suggests that the fundamental premise of replacement cost accounting is open to question.[13]

But perhaps the ultimate test of current cost accounting is whether it can be demonstrated to have superior information content for users—in particular, whether it can provide a better basis than GAAP income or GPL-restated GAAP income for the prediction of future cash flows. Some empirical studies have been done on the incremental information content of changing prices disclosures that were required in the U.S. (under FASB Statement No. 33) and of current cost information provided by U.K. companies under its standard (SSAP 16). The results of this research have been mixed, and in general, inconclusive. A research report commissioned by the CICA reviewed this evidence up through 1989, and it cautioned that it would be premature to draw any definite conclusions from the body of studies done to that time.[14]

CURRENT REALIZABLE VALUE ACCOUNTING (CRVA)

The CRVA model adopts exit value as its sole basis of valuation, sees capital maintenance in financial terms, has a proprietary perspective, and does not embody a realization constraint. CRVA has received significantly less attention from accounting practitioners and standard setters than have various versions of CCA.[15]

The Merits of CRVA

On the practical side, it is argued that exit value is virtually the sole value attribute that is capable of being independently observed. Discounted cash flows cannot be observed because the cash flows lie in the future. Historical cost can be verified by observation at the time of acquisition, but in subsequent periods the costs of such assets as inventory and capital assets are subject to allocations and reallocations that result in carrying values that cannot be related to any real world evidence. Replacement costs based upon replacement costs new, possibly with estimated deductions for capitalized operating cost savings, and with an allowance for depreciation, may not be related to real world phenomena either. (It is conceded, however, that if replacement cost is estimated on the basis of used market prices, it will be based upon the same quality of evidence as exit values.)

In addition, CRVA proponents may stress the importance of "additivity." They argue that the total of entity wealth shown on a balance sheet is meaningless unless the individual measurements of assets are homogeneous, so that any addition is of like to like. This means, they reason, that an accounting model must select a single asset attribute to be measured in monetary terms and reported on the balance sheet. CRVA arguably has this attribute, and it can be applied to all assets and liabilities of an enterprise (although there are some ambiguities as regards the level of aggregation of assets to which CRVA should be applied which, some will argue, limits this claim of additivity). As well, if so desired, the CRVA figures may be general-price-level adjusted.

The conceptual justification for the use of exit values lies in their claimed significance for decision making. Decision making involves a choice between alternative courses of action based upon prediction of the consequence of each course of action and the preference of the decision maker for one consequence over the other. Many business decisions relate to buying, selling or holding assets. As an example, if one is considering selling an asset rather than holding it, the relevant comparison is between the estimated discounted value of future cash flows if the asset is held and the present realizable value (and perhaps also the discounted value of reinvestment opportunities). The exit value is pertinent to that decision.

In general, it is argued that the sum of realizable values for a firm's assets is a measure of its "adaptivity"—its ability to take a variety of beneficial actions. A decline in that total realizable value means that an entity is subject to greater risk, and this is of significance in assessing its solvency. An increase in realizable value gives the entity the flexibility to pay off debt, to increase borrowing, to switch from one business to another, and to take advantage of new opportunities to increase profitability. The argument is not that other value information would not be relevant — especially the discounted cash flow of various possibilities. Rather, the contention is that realizable values are relevant to most decisions and therefore should take priority as the basis for financial reporting.

Questions of Application

There are some unclear points in the application of CRVA. Two principal issues will be mentioned here.[16]

- Chambers has described exit values as "current cash equivalents"—a description that is appropriate to the objective of CRVA, namely, to display the ability of the entity to adapt. Sterling interprets an exit value as an immediate market selling price. Since it is immediate, that selling price must necessarily be for the asset "as is." Thus, for example, the exit value for a retailer's inventory is not the sum of the amounts for which the company would sell its goods individually, but rather the price it could obtain for quick disposition of the whole inventory—which may be approximated by the wholesale price in carload lots less incidental costs.[17] Chambers, on the other hand, speaks of resale prices in the short run and in the ordinary course of business. In this way he attempts to avoid the charge that his system is liquidation accounting rather than accounting for a going concern. His concept, however, does seem to introduce some ambiguities. For example, there are some assets whose sale is simply not in the ordinary course of business. Work in the course of manufacture is an example. Chambers' reply to this objection would probably be that if there is no such thing as a sale in the ordinary course, no sale price can be found and the asset must be valued at zero.

- What is the current cash equivalent for debt? Sterling regards debt as a negative asset to be recorded at the amount required to discharge it at the reporting date. That amount may be market value if the firm is permitted to buy in its own debt.[18] Chambers, in contrast, would show debt at the amount legally recoverable by the creditor, usually its nominal face amount. This hardly seems consistent with the notion of a current cash equivalent.[19]

Principal Criticisms of CRVA

The exit-price model was everywhere rejected in favour of entry-price models when standards for the publication of price-change-adjusted information were issued in several countries in the late 1970s and early 1980s. The principal criticisms made of CRVA are as follows:

- The sum of exit values of individual assets will be less than the selling price of the firm itself in a very large number of cases. The question then is asked whether exit values based on individual assets are relevant information for external investors of a company who are not in a position to make sell-or-hold decisions with respect to individual assets. The answer is likely to be pragmatic. As we have previously observed, any estimate of the exit value of an enterprise as a whole is likely to be too subjective to be used in financial reporting. However, the sum of exit values will indicate a floor value of the firm, which has some significance. Proponents of CRVA also point out that the sum of replacement costs of assets will not equal the replacement cost of the firm either, so that both current value models suffer from this defect.

- A second basis of criticism often takes the form of a question: Why should balance sheets report selling prices of assets that are not going to be sold? In essence, the question asks why exit values should take priority as the sole basis of valuation. That question reflects a lack of acceptance of "adaptivity" and changes in adaptivity as the primary objective for balance sheet and income statement measurements. Some charge that to take the measurement of exit values as an objective is to assume liquidation—an assumption that is unwarranted unless there are indications that liquidation is in prospect.

- A third criticism of exit-value accounting is that it may anticipate income not yet earned as a result of using sale prices as a basis of valuation for assets not yet sold.

- Another major source of disagreement with exit-value accounting usually comes to a head in a dispute over the balance sheet valuation of "nonvendible durables." The CRVA model works on the presumption that if a selling price cannot be found for an asset in its present form, it should be reported at zero in the balance sheet. Thus, work in progress inventory would often be carried at no value. Any capital assets that do not have a resale market—for reasons such as that they were built to the special specifications of the purchaser or that it would cost too much to rip them out and sell them would also be reported at no value. CRVA theorists readily concede that such assets may have a very substantial "value in use"—as measured by discounting expected cash flows from their use. They do not accept this as a measure of the asset value, however, because it is not a resale value and therefore is not a cash equivalent. The CRVA view is that the difference between acquisition cost of an asset and its resale value is a "sunk cost" that has no significance to the solvency or adaptivity of an enterprise. To the extent that an enterprise has taken cash or cash equivalents and sunk them into assets that are not salable, it has taken on risk. This, they argue, should be evidenced by writing off the sunk costs.[20] This result is unacceptable to most accountants and business people.

Although CRVA has generally been rejected as a comprehensive income measurement model, it is evident that exit values can play a crucial role in financial analysis in particular situations. For example, there is some evidence in the U.S. that the reporting of supplementary current value data by real estate companies is regarded as important by analysts, and that such disclosures may reduce the possibility that these companies' shares will be undervalued.[21]

It is also to be noted that modern finance theory can be interpreted to put exit values of use assets in a different context within a current value system. It has been suggested that the exit value of a productive asset in use be factored into its value as an abandonment option. In other words, in concept, the asset might be valued at its use value plus a put option with an exercise price equal to the asset's exit value.[22]

A CAPITAL MARKETS EARNING POWER APPROACH

It was noted earlier in this chapter that another possible model of accounting is suggested by modern capital markets theory. It is based on the premise that securities markets define the rate of return that can be expected for a given level of risk at any particular moment in time. This return effectively defines the earning power of investments. In brief, the argument is as follows. Given the pervasiveness of developed capital markets, rational investors can be expected to price any asset or liability at the present value of its expected cash flows at the current market rate of return for assets or liabilities of similar risk. Competitive market forces can be expected to drive the market value of an asset or liability to this present value. Any abnormal return expectation will be quickly arbitraged away. For example, suppose that information available to market participants indicates that a particular security is under-priced, i.e., that it is priced to earn a return that is superior to the current market rate available for assets of similar risk. It can be expected that buyers will immediately enter the market to acquire this asset until the price is bid up to where it is equal to the present value of expected future cash flows at the current market risk-adjusted rate of return.

This leads to the idea that an enterprise should be considered to have earned income in a period only after maintaining the earning power of its capital—more specifically, only when its capital has been maintained in value equal to the expected cash flows to be generated by its net resources discounted at the current risk-adjusted market rate of return. The following example illustrates this concept.

Suppose a company bought a zero coupon bond of $10,000 due in three years. Suppose that the current market rate of interest on three-year bonds of this risk is 8%, so that the company paid $7,938 for the bond (the present value of $10,000 due in three years at 8%). At the end of one year this would have accrued to $8,573 at 8%. But suppose the market rate of interest for two-year bonds of this risk at the end of year one is 10%. If the company recognized income of $635 (i.e., $8,593 – $7,938) for year one, it would not have maintained its capital in terms of its ability to earn the current market rate of return, because, at $8,573, its investment can only expect to earn 8%. Rational investors would not accept an 8% rate of return at the end of year one. To restate its capital in terms of earnings capacity relating to the rate currently available in the capital markets place, the company would have to write down its bond investment to the present value of expected cash flows at 10% (which present value is $8,264).

This capital maintenance model would seem to have a very attractive theoretical economic basis. In concept, it would result in all enterprises measuring capital to be maintained, and therefore income, against capital market expectations. Concerns with this model could be expected to focus on the potential volatility of income and underlying asset and liability values, and on doubts with respect to the practical, reliable measurability of assets and liabilities on this basis.

The model would require fair valuation of all financial assets and liabilities. This would be the quoted market values for all actively traded financial instruments. For nontraded instruments, fair value (the amount at which an item could be expected to be exchanged between knowledgeable willing parties in an arm's-length transaction) would be the value that could be expected to yield the return of principal plus the currently available market return for equivalent risk. As observed in Chapter 17, there is increasing acceptance of the possibility of moving towards measuring all financial assets and liabilities at their fair values.

The more difficult problem is the measurement of nonfinancial assets and liabilities (inventories, property, plant and equipment and other productive assets). The capital markets-based earning power model may be interpreted to call for productive assets to be carried at EV based on current interest rates. Most would probably reject EV because of the inherent subjectivity of its cash flow estimates. However, consideration might be given to a *realized* income variation of this approach. This might be reasoned along the following lines:

- The initial purchase cost of any productive asset may be assumed to be its fair value at the date of acquisition. Within a capital market context this fair value (cost) may be interpreted to reflect the present value of the future cash flows that will be generated by its use over its expected useful life, discounted at the current market risk-adjusted rate of return at that date. Within this EV perspective, this cost should be allocated over its useful life on the present value depreciation basis reflecting current interest rates and the pattern of expected future cash flows (that is, on the time-adjusted amortization basis illustrated in Chapter 11). If the cash flow expectations implicit in its cost are correct, this will result in the enterprise reporting an annual income return on the asset equal to the market rate of return.

- When expectations are not met, such that the asset carrying value cannot be expected to be recoverable from future cash flows, the carrying value would be expected to be written down to its estimated recoverable value. Recoverable value would be defined as its EV calculated current market interest rates if the asset is to continue in use, or as its NRV if it is to be sold. It may be noted that this recoverable value determination is not far off recoverable value tests that have been proposed for capital assets in recent years (see discussion at Chapter 18).

- When expectations change, such that a rate of return in excess of the current market rate is expected, the excess return would not be recognized until it is realized by future earning efforts. In other words, as within the existing historical cost-based accrual model, holding gains on productive assets would not be recognized in income until they are realized through their use or by their sale.

- When expectations change such that the expected pattern or period of future cash flows to be generated by the use of the asset changes, or the current market rate of return changes, these effects would be recognized by changing the amortization pattern or period of amortization.

There are obviously many questions in this suggested approach. The capital markets-based earnings power idea has yet to be given significant consideration in accounting literature.[23]

Ronen and Sorter propose an external reporting system based on computing the "market risk determined" value of an enterprise. This would be management's estimate of prospective cash flows incorporating its plans within market and industry forces, discounted at a market rate. The authors suggest that an appropriate discount rate would be that which could be earned on the portfolio of all securities listed on the New York Stock Exchange. This value would be compared with the exit value of the enterprise's net assets. The difference is the "specific advantage" of the entity, reflecting that part of expected cash flows that cannot be realized unless the enterprise continues its specific operations. The authors reason that there is significant information value in this system. It puts exit value in a context; the larger the amount of assets' exit value, the more flexible the enterprise and the less dependent it is on its specific operations.[24]

THE STANDARD-SETTING "EXPERIMENT"

As noted earlier, high inflation rates during the 1970s led to widespread criticism of historical cost-matching accounting, and GPL-adjusted historical cost accounting was not considered to be an adequate answer. There was a feeling that historical cost-based financial statements should be replaced, or at least supplemented, by current value information. Unfortunately, there was little agreement on which among many possible income models should be selected. Interest focused on current cost accounting, but there were diverse views on how it should be defined and applied.

The CICA offered, in *CICA Handbook* Section 4510, a smorgasbord of supplementary current cost and general price level disclosures that could be combined in various ways to construct different concepts of current cost-operating capacity, and current cost-general price-level-adjusted, income. In this it followed the lead of the FASB (in SFAS 33), although the items of disclosure recommended in Section 4510 differed in some respects from those of SFAS 33.

The data recommended for disclosure in Section 4510 included current costs for inventory, capital assets, cost of goods sold and depreciation. The section also called for disclosure of a financing adjustment, the gain or loss in general purchasing power resulting from holding net monetary items, and the changes in the current cost of inventory and capital assets attributable to general inflation.

These recommendations were applicable only to large companies with publicly traded securities, and they specifically exempted income-producing real estate assets, banks, trust companies and insurance companies.

These disclosures were billed as an "experiment," and companies were encouraged to adapt and expand upon the disclosures to fit their particular circumstances. The disclosures were intended to supplement rather than replace traditional historical cost-based GAAP financial statements. Unlike the U.S. and the U.K., the CICA disclosures were voluntary.

The Section 4510 recommendations were not a success. A number of reasons for this may be cited, and these are briefly summarized below. A more complete analysis of Canadian experience with the changing prices disclosures of Section 4510 is contained in a 1990 Research Report commissioned by the CICA.[25]

- The CICA recommendations did not become effective until 1983, by which time the rate of inflation had dropped significantly. While many may be concerned that inflation impairs traditional GAAP financial statements, few were very concerned with the levels of inflation that existed after the recommendations were issued.

- Most preparers did not well understand the current cost disclosures, did not find them useful, and generally did not believe that analysts and investors used the information. Accordingly, since the disclosures were voluntary, it is not surprising that few companies provided them—only about 20% of companies to whom the recommendations applied made the disclosures in 1983, and this dropped off to less than 5% in 1986.

- Most analysts found the information of limited usefulness, in part because the low company participation rate severely limited intercompany comparisons.

- There were concerns about the reliability of the data. Empirical research in the U.S. indicated that most U.S. companies used more easily applied, less expensive means to approximate current costs of their productive assets, and that these measures may not have accurately depicted the effects of specific price changes, and in particular, that they tended to understate adjustments for technological change. Interestingly, a Canadian study suggested that this may not have been as big a problem in Canada.[26]

The CICA-commissioned research report concluded that, based on the evidence it had gathered, Section 4510 was "beyond repair." It recommended that the section should be removed from the *CICA Handbook* and that resources should not be invested to improve it.[27] It cautioned, however, that it believed that the issue of changing prices was not dead.

Some argue that the "experiment" in Canada and the U.S. was not a valid test of the usefulness of CCA, because the measurement methods commonly applied by most companies were not rigorous and did not yield appropriate, reliable current cost measures, so that "despite several years of experimentation, we still do not know the extent to which current cost data can be useful."[28] Research on Australian companies that have revalued long-lived productive assets (a practice long permitted in that country) suggests that the resulting revaluation of equity is a significant explanatory variable for stock market prices for industrial companies with a high debt-to-equity ratio.[29]

Section 4510 was withdrawn from the *CICA Handbook* in 1992. This followed abandonment of SFAS 33 in the U.S. as a required standard in 1986,[30] and suspension of the current cost standard in the U.K. in 1985.

SUMMARY

The common notion of income for a period is that of an amount that can be paid out without infringing on capital—that is, that maintains the value of capital (net resources) held by the enterprise. Four elements or attributes of capital to be maintained must be specified in order to define an income measurement system: (1) a choice of the basis of valuation (historical cost, current cost, the present value of future cash flows (value in use), current exit values, or models that use different values in different circumstances (such as value-to-the-firm)); (2) a choice of capital maintenance model (financial capital based on monetary units, financial capital expressed in constant purchasing power, physical or operating capital, or perhaps, earning power capacity); (3) a choice of focus of interest (entity or proprietary); and (4) a decision whether to include unrealized holding gains and losses on asset and liability positions in income. Many different proposed models have been founded on different combinations of these elements. This diversity engendered much controversy in the 1970s when inflation ran high, and standard setters were unable to achieve general acceptance of one current value model.

In this chapter we reviewed various models that have been suggested for the purpose of accounting for changing prices, and we have discussed the choices that have been made in these models with respect to the above four dimensions.

GPL Restatement of GAAP

The almost instinctive reaction of the accounting profession to the short comings of historical cost accounting under conditions of high inflation has been to consider adoption of GPL restatement of that accounting. Its only change in concept is the substitution of a unit of general purchasing power as the unit of accounting in place of a unit of money. A strong argument can be made that GPL restatement improves the relevance of historical cost-based accounting in times of inflation. It reports a more up-to-date matching of costs and revenues as a result of restating old costs by an index of general purchasing power. Countries experiencing very high rates of inflation have invariably applied some form of GPL accounting. The notion of inflation is generally well understood and the rate of inflation is a well monitored aspect of most countries' economies.

The construction of price indexes contains some inherent problems, however. These include difficulties in factoring in the effects of changing consumption patterns and changes in the quality of goods and services whose prices enter into a general purchasing power price index. As well, a number of issues arise in the restatement process itself. These include the following:

- The classification of assets and liabilities as monetary or nonmonetary is critical to GPL restatement accounting. Unfortunately the basis for definition of items as monetary is not absolutely clear in all cases.

- Because the carrying values of nonmonetary items are adjusted upwards under inflationary conditions, the chances that carrying values will exceed recoverable values are greater than under historical cost accounting, and thus there is a greater reliance on recoverable value tests.

- GPL accounting results in recording gains on liabilities under inflation, and there has been much disagreement as to the nature of these gains and whether they should be considered to be income.

- Some technical issues are encountered. One example is the translation and restatement of foreign operations.

Current Cost Accounting

The efforts of accounting standard setters in the 1970s and early 1980s focused on current cost accounting and the maintenance of operating capacity. In essence, the results of these efforts demonstrated that the concept of maintenance of physical or operating capacity is seriously inadequate as a foundation for measuring income of enterprises across the board. First, it is built on the premise of continuing replacement of productive assets. In the common case where an enterprise can be expected to replace its existing productive assets with improved assets, it becomes difficult, and in some cases impossible, to define operating capacity in a meaningful, implementable sense. The basic idea that a company measure this period's income based on the cost of next period's inputs is open to serious question. From a purely practical perspective, the operating capacity maintenance concept does not address the problem of maintenance of capital invested in nonoperating assets, such as portfolio investments. As well, it is difficult to apply when operating assets are of a financial nature (monetary working capital) and thus are not sold or consumed in the course of operations. Since financial assets comprise virtually all the assets of financial institutions, it seems particularly hard to apply the operating capacity maintenance concept to them.

Another problem arises when an existing productive asset is not to be replaced. It is commonly suggested that such assets should be written down to their recoverable value, and the recoverable value charged against income. This "value-to-the-firm" accounting approach loses contact with the notion of productive capacity and whether it has been maintained.

Some of these problems are removed if the common approach to implementing the operating capacity maintenance concept (of charging the replacement cost of resources sold or consumed in measuring income and excluding all holding gains and losses from income) is abandoned. The alternative approach is to recognize all holding gains and losses in income and deduct a one-line allowance for capital maintenance based on an index of price changes appropriate to the particular operations of the enterprise. However, this alternative substitutes the problems of developing an appropriate index for the problems that it resolves.

Current Realizable Value (Exit Value) Models

Exit value accounting has been advocated by some academics. They argue that exit value is virtually the only value attribute that is capable of being independently observed and measured by reference to real world phenomena. As well, it may be claimed that the measurement of all assets and liabilities at their exit values will result in a homogeneous measure of an entity's wealth, i.e., that individual asset and liability exit values are truly additive. Conceptually, current realizable value accounting is reasoned to have decision usefulness as a measure of an enterprise's adaptivity.

Current realizable value accounting is, however, subject to overwhelming deficiencies in the eyes of most accountants. Their major criticisms may be captured in this question: Why should selling prices be reported for assets that are to be used, not sold? Special purpose assets, work in process, etc. may have no selling value, and thus would be reported as having zero value in an exit value balance sheet. Most accountants and business people do not accept that a business is worse off as soon as it acquires such assets. Some critics believe that exit value accounting assumes liquidation, which they feel is not appropriate for normal, going concern enterprises. Exit value accounting has everywhere been rejected by accounting standard setters as a general purpose accounting model.

The dominant conclusion that might be drawn from the analyses of the above alternatives is that all current value accounting models are significantly flawed, and that none is suitable for all purpose financial reporting.

Current value accounting, and accounting generally for changing prices and inflation, has received little attention since the mid 1980s. Interest declined when the rate of inflation declined. A major development since that time has been the emergence of global capital markets. Capital markets theory suggests a different approach to the definition of capital maintenance—one based on maintaining the earning power of capital as measured against the current risk-adjusted rate return available in the capital marketplace. This, however, is an idea that has yet to be rigorously examined.

REFERENCES

[1] See R. J. Chambers, *Accounting, Evaluation and Economic Behavior* (Englewood Cliffs, N.J.: Prentice-Hall, 1966; reprint ed., Houston: Scholars Book Co., 1974), especially chap. 9.

[2] This concept has been traced to J.C. Bonbright, *Valuation of Property* (New York: McGraw-Hill, 1937). It has also been propounded by (among others) D. Solomons, "Economic and Accounting Concepts of Cost and Value," in *Modern Accounting Theory*, ed. M. Backer (Englewood Cliffs, N.J.: Prentice-Hall, 1966), pp. 117–40, and E. Stamp, "Income and Value Determination and Changing Price-Levels: An Essay towards a Theory," *The Accountant's Magazine*, June 1971, pp. 227–92.

3   A number of other names have been applied to this accounting model. They include Constant Purchasing Power (CPP) accounting, Price-Level-Adjusted (PLA) accounting, and Constant Dollar (CD) accounting.

4   It is beyond the scope of this book to discuss differences in methods of construction of price indexes and problems with each method. If GPL accounting were to be used generally, the advice of experts in the design of price indexes would be desirable as to the best choice among those available. For some discussion of the use of price indexes in accounting, see R.R. Sterling, *Theory of the Measurement of Enterprise Income* (Lawrence, Kan.: University Press of Kansas, 1970), pp. 331–50; G. Whittington, *Inflation Accounting: An Introduction to the Debate* (Cambridge: Cambridge University Press, 1983), chap. 4; and *Reporting the Financial Effects of Price-Level Changes*, Accounting Research Study No. 6 (New York: AICPA, 1963), App. A.

5   For professional statements on the subject see AICPA, APB, *Financial Statements Restated for General Price-Level Changes*, APB Statement No. 3 (New York: AICPA, 1969), and Accounting Standards Steering Committee, *Accounting for Changes in the Purchasing Power of Money*, Provisional Statement of Standard Accounting Practice No. 7 (London: Institute of Chartered Accountants in England and Wales, 1974). Exposure drafts were also issued but never finalized by the FASB and CICA. For a more detailed "how-to-do-it" treatment, see A.D. Stickler and C.S.R. Hutchins, *General Price-Level Accounting: Described and Illustrated* (Toronto: CICA, 1975).

6   The several government-sponsored studies in order of publication are: *Inflation and Taxation: Report of Committee of Inquiry* (Canberra: Australian Government Publishing Service, 1975); *Inflation Accounting: Report of the Inflation Accounting Committee* (London: Her Majesty's Stationery Office, 1975); *Report of the Committee of Inquiry into Inflation Accounting* (Wellington, N.Z.: Government Printer, 1976); and *Report of the Ontario Committee on Inflation Accounting* (Toronto: Ministry of Treasury, Economics and Intergovernmental Affairs, 1977).

7   See L. Revsine, "Technological Changes and Replacement Costs: A Beginning," *The Accounting Review*, April 1979, pp. 306–22.

8   Detailed investigation of these difficulties is beyond the scope of this book. For a more complete discussion see *Estimating Current Values: Some Techniques, Problems and Experiences* (Toronto: CICA, 1979), and C.S.R. Drummond and A.D. Stickler, *Current Cost Accounting: Its Concepts and Its Uses in Practical Terms* (Toronto: Methuen, 1983).

9   For example, Revsine argues that a capital maintenance concept appropriate for national policy decisions need be concerned only with physical assets because only "real" assets are of significance to the welfare of the nation as a whole. See L. Revsine, "Physical Capital Maintenance: An Analysis," in *Maintenance of Capital: Financial Versus Physical*, ed. R.R. Sterling and K.W. Lemke (Houston: Scholars Book Co., 1982), pp. 75–94. Revsine argues that different capital maintenance concepts are legitimate for different purposes. This contention, however, suggests that either financial reports should present a variety of income measures deemed appropriate for different purposes or we must pick the most widely useful basis for general purpose reporting. Revsine stopped short of making such a choice.

10   For example, see Revsine, "Physical Capital Maintenance: An Analysis," p. 91.

[11]   Merrett and Sykes argue this point vigorously, citing a study showing that expenditures at higher replacement costs in Britain in years prior to 1975 earned no additional return compared with the lower price assets they replaced. See A.J. Merrett and A. Sykes, "Seven Answers Looking for a Question," *Accountancy*, December 1979, pp. 74–78. See also Revsine, "Physical Capital Maintenance: An Analysis."

[12]   This was demonstrated in the so-called Sandilands Committee report, *Inflation Accounting: Report of the Inflation Accounting Committee*, pp. 142–45.

[13]   See, for example, comments by J.A. Milburn in *Maintenance of Capital: Financial Versus Physical*, ed. Sterling and Lemke, pp. 97–103.

[14]   See, J.R. Hanna, D.B. Kennedy and G.D. Richardson, *Reporting the Effects of Changing Prices: A Review of the Experience with Section 4510*, CICA Research Report (Toronto: CICA, 1990), chap. 2.

[15]   For a more complete understanding of CRVA and its rationale, the reader is referred to the works of Chambers and Sterling cited in the bibliography.

[16]   For more complete description of the points of debate that have existed even among supporters of the general concept of CRVA, see E.R. Iselin, "Chambers on Accounting Theory," *The Accounting Review*, April 1968, pp. 231–38; R. Ma, "On Chambers' Second Thoughts," *Abacus*, December 1974, pp. 124–28; and R.J. Chambers, "Third Thoughts," *Abacus*, December 1974, pp. 129–37.

[17]   See R.R. Sterling, *Toward a Science of Accounting* (Houston: Scholars Book Co., 1979), pp. 111, 117, and 220n.

[18]   Ibid., p. 159n.

[19]   Chambers' view has had its vigorous supporters. See, for example, S. Henderson and G. Peirson, "A Note on the Current Cash Equivalent of Liabilities," *Abacus*, June 1980, pp. 61–66. See also Chambers' own defence in "Edwards and Bell on Income Measurement in Retrospect," *Abacus*, June 1982, pp. 3–39.

[20]   Sterling devotes an appendix of his book to the case of the nonvendible durable. See Sterling, *Toward a Science of Accounting*.

[21]   See, for example, E.P. Swanson and F. Niswander, "Voluntary Current Value Disclosures in the Real Estate Industry," *Accounting Horizons*, December 1992, pp. 49–61.

[22]   See J.K. Cheung, "The Valuation Significance of Exit Values: A Contingent-Claim Analysis," *Contemporary Accounting Research*, Spring 1990, pp. 724–37.

[23]   A capital maintenance model that defines capital in terms of capacity to earn the current market rate of return is proposed in IASC, *Accounting for Financial Assets and Financial Liabilities*, A Discussion Paper, (London: IASC, 1997), chap. 6, in the context of proposals for measuring financial assets and liabilities at fair value. There is some development of the basic ideas and their implications for nonfinancial assets and liabilities, in J.A. Milburn, *Incorporating the Time Value of Money Within Financial Accounting* (Toronto: CICA, 1988).

[24]   J. Ronen and G.H. Sorter, "Relevant Accounting," *The Journal of Business*, April 1972, pp. 258–82.

[25]   Hanna et al., *Reporting the Effects of Changing Prices: A Review of the Experience with Section 4510*.

26 See D.B. Thornton, "Capital Values in Use Versus Replacement Costs: Theory and Canadian Evidence," *Contemporary Accounting Research*, Fall 1988, pp. 343–70. Contrary to Thornton's findings, however, the 1990 CICA Research Report survey of preparers suggested most Canadian companies presenting current costs did not factor technological change into their estimates.

27 Hanna et al., *Reporting the Effects of Changing Prices: A Review of the Experience with Section 4510*, p. 96.

28 E.P. Swanson and K.A. Shriver, "The Accounting-for-Changing-Prices Experiment: A Valid Test of Usefulness?" *Accounting Horizons*, September 1987, pp. 69–77.

29 P.D. Easton, P.H. Eddey, and T.S. Harris, "An Investigation of Revaluations of Tangible Long-Lived Assets," *Journal of Accounting Research*, Supplement 1993, pp. 1–38. See also V.L. Bernard, "Discussion of an Investigation of Revaluations of Tangible Long-Lived Assets," *Journal of Accounting Research*, Supplement 1993, pp. 39–44.

30 See FASB, *Financial Reporting and Changing Prices*, Statement of Financial Accounting Standards No. 89 (Stamford: FASB, 1986).

A CONCEPTUAL FRAMEWORK AND STANDARD SETTING

A CONCEPTUAL FRAMEWORK FOR FINANCIAL REPORTING

In Chapter 4 we traced the development of accounting theory and standard setting in the U.S. and Canada, with some reference to the IASC and the emerging international dimension. We noted that by the end of the 1960s significant weaknesses in the classical historical cost-matching model had become apparent. Some academics were arguing that the weaknesses were fatal, and we noted the developing influence of an "informational value" perspective, which originated in the efficient markets literature emanating from finance economics. Academics advocating this perspective have tended to downplay accounting as a measurement discipline with any effective conceptual framework. Some have envisaged accounting standard setting as essentially a social welfare optimization exercise to be achieved through political processes.

While admitting serious weaknesses in historical cost-matching accounting, standard setters have continued to work in the belief that the model is capable of being developed and extended beyond its traditional base to meet the demands of a changing business and capital markets environment. A key presumption in this is that an improved model can be reasoned forward from conceptual foundations based on accepted economic principles and rational decision models.

In addition we have seen that financial accounting has been, and is continuing to be, severely challenged by revolutionary advances in information technology, and the emergence of global capital markets which have featured increased volatility and the development of derivatives and new risk management concepts. These have had profound effects on business and investment practices which, in turn, have served to heighten demands for changes in historical cost-based accounting. The analyses of Part II bear witness that in many areas of accounting, accountants and standard setters have had to address complex issues arising in the modern world of business and finance that simply were not contemplated by traditional accounting concepts and conventions.

In the U.S. we have seen that the FASB has responded with a profusion of standards, interpretations and guidance on many issues. An inevitable consequence of issue-by-issue standard setting has been inconsistencies between standards, and it is increasingly difficult to detect a coherent underlying theory. Existing accounting has been described as a "mixed attribute" model. All this gives evidence of an accounting model in the process of change.

Canadian experience has been subject to the same influences, and there has been the same tendency towards the development of new standards. This has not taken place on the same scale as in the U.S., however, and Canadian standards are now lagging U.S. GAAP in some areas, and more recently, lagging some IASC standards. Some very difficult questions are being posed as to the role of Canadian accounting standards and standard setting. Some have even been questioning the need for separate Canadian accounting standards given the dominance of U.S. capital markets and demands for harmonized international accounting standards.

These challenges have led some thoughtful accountants to want to re-examine the relevance of the conceptual foundation on which accounting measurement and recognition principles have been based, as well as the standard-setting process itself. In this chapter we will examine the nature, purpose and importance of a sound conceptual framework. We will then consider the existing framework and its limitations, and in what ways it may need to change to meet the above-noted challenges. Certain changes in basic concepts of accounting can be discerned from changes in standards and practices examined in the preceding chapters.

In the following chapter we will consider pressures on the Canadian standard-setting process in light of developments in business and finance and the pull of U.S. capital markets and international harmonization objectives.

THE NATURE, PURPOSE, AND NECESSITY OF A CONCEPTUAL FRAMEWORK

Much has been written about conceptual frameworks for financial reporting. And much effort has been expended, particularly by the FASB, to discover and propound such a framework. However, most of the serious effort took place some time ago. The FASB framework, consisting of six concepts statements was largely developed in the late 1970s through the mid 1980s. A number of other jurisdictions, including Canada and the IASC, adopted conceptual frameworks several years later.[1] But these are much briefer and less rigorous documents, and for the most part, they have been modelled on that of the FASB. There have been no significant innovations in these adaptations. As we have seen in Part II, some elements of these frameworks (notably the concepts of "assets" and "liabilities") have proved to be very useful. However, as reported in Chapter 4, there has been some disappointment that the FASB, despite its prodigious efforts, was unable to achieve agreement on fundamental recognition and measurement concepts. Existing conceptual frameworks have largely left open questions as to the relative merits of different capital maintenance systems, and historical cost versus current cost, current value and present value measurement attributes. In short, developed conceptual frameworks have been incomplete, and consequently of limited value in the development of accounting standards.

The FASB concepts statements, and similar frameworks in other jurisdictions, have remained basically unchanged since their adoption. (Recently, however, the FASB has proposed the integration of some important present value and cash flow concepts within its framework.) The following discussion will focus on the conceptual framework for accounting for business enterprises, and then briefly note its extension to include not-for-profit organizations.

The Nature and Purpose of a Conceptual Framework

What exactly is a conceptual framework? Essentially it is an interrelated structure of propositions and observations that provides a logical foundation for deducing what accounting principles ought to be. While seemingly simple, this definition embodies two important presumptions:

- First, it presumes that a conceptual framework has a normative purpose, that is, it is intended to provide a basis for determining what accounting principles ought to be.
- Second, in defining a conceptual framework as a logical foundation, it presumes that it involves a process of deduction, or reasoning forward, within a rational structure of propositions and evidence. Within this context, accounting may be considered to be, potentially at least, more of an applied science than an art, and its conceptual basis much more than a generalization of existing conventions and practices.

Typically, such a framework begins with an examination of the objectives of financial accounting. From these it attempts to reason forward based on observations and postulates as to such matters as the domain of financial reporting, the nature of the phenomena to be reported, user information needs, qualities of useful financial information, and limitations on what it is possible to know and practical to report. Such a framework is intended to be prescriptive rather than descriptive.

Descriptive approaches to the development of accounting theory were normally taken by accounting writers up to about 1960.[2] Accounting practices were observed and hypotheses developed as to why they took the form they did. Some generalizations were then made about the goals of accounting that were consistent, as far as possible, with observed practices and the hypotheses explaining them. A purely descriptive framework has inherent limitations. If some established practice is inconsistent with the hypothesized framework, there is always a basic question whether it is the practice that is at fault or the framework. Should the practice be prohibited, or should be framework be patched to rationalize the practice? Too much of the latter can lead to a formless structure that not only loses its power to guide practice, but also loses respect. Moreover, a descriptive conceptual framework suffers from too great a reliance on the existing environment. If economic and social conditions change, the existence of a framework tied to practice under previous conditions may reinforce resistance to needed change to accounting practice. It has been observed that, in these changing times, "it is not enough to do what was possible, expected and accepted in the past."[3]

The great virtue of a prescriptive approach, and at the same time a potential source of weakness, is that it is not bound by existing practice or existing ideas.[4] Ideally, each building block in the framework is researched and discussed on its own merits. Each block is logically interrelated with the previous one. There are potential difficulties with this. If one goes astray at an early stage in building the framework, that fact may not become apparent until anomalies arise in attempting to apply it to real world situations. Perhaps because of this, many are uncomfortable about agreeing to generalized statements—for example, about objectives—unless they can see what accounting conclusions will be drawn from them.

Modern attempts of the FASB and others to construct a conceptual framework have been prescriptive rather than descriptive. This does not mean that the framework is wholly normative. On the contrary, like any good theory, it must be firmly grounded in factual premises. Empirical evidence is required to ensure the basic premises accord with observable facts. A fundamental premise underlying the existing conceptual framework is that "accounting principles rest on principles of economics".[5] By this it is meant that accounting principles should be expected to be based on rational economic purposes of business enterprises. Accounting standards should at least seek to separate the rational from irrational economic decision models and concentrate on the former. For this purpose, attention needs to be paid to the findings of economics, and in particular to accepted theories of finance as evident in the capital marketplace. This is a theme that will be pursued later in this chapter.

Is a Conceptual Framework Necessary?

Conceptual Considerations

Some researchers argue that there is no need for either a conceptual framework or accounting standards. The content of financial reports could, they assert, be the subject of private contract between those who manage entities and interested parties outside the entities, such as investors and creditors. This content would then be governed by what the contracting parties decide they want in their own best interests and are prepared to pay for.[6]

This proposal would seem not to be viable, except in respect of limited situations in which special purpose information is contracted for as a part of a private arrangement between an entity and another party (for example, some special accounting is sometimes contracted by parties to private financings).[7] The sheer numbers of organizations and investor interests, and the transient nature of many of these interests, render private contracting uneconomical. Contracting intermediaries would have to be formed to buy the information and resell it. It would be very difficult to control the dissemination of such information, and if it could not be controlled, few would be prepared to pay for it. As well, modern capital markets require information that is readily available and comparable between entities and over time.

Another argument is that the development of an agreed conceptual framework that is specific enough to enable accounting standard setters to reach clear and convincing conclusions on particular issues is a political impossibility. This argument stems from the observation that accounting standards have economic, social and political consequences. Accounting policies can make some people better off and others worse off. As a simple example, it is often argued that additional disclosure requirements impose costs on preparers of financial statements, with the benefit, if any, being received by those who use the information. Changes in the assessment of a business by users of financial statements may increase the cost of capital for some entities and lower it for others. Some argue that accounting is essentially a social choice mechanism, involving trade-offs between constituent interests, and that such trade-offs will be settled by a political process rather than a process of reasoning within a logical framework. Those whose welfare is affected by accounting information will be motivated to take political action to influence accounting standards in directions that they perceive will benefit their interests. As noted in more depth in Chapter 4, some conclude that self-interest driven political activities must dominate the development of accounting standards. Their research purports to offer evidence that leads to the relatively cynical conclusion that there will never be agreement on a comprehensive theory of accounting . In their view, the search for a conceptual framework is a waste of time.

There is just enough evident truth in this to give one pause for thought. Certainly it must be accepted that the selection of accounting standards can have economic, social and political effects. But this simply demonstrates that financial accounting has information value and affects user decisions. It may be reasoned that the very fact that accounting standards are important to business and investor interests (so that they may be expected to try to influence them) serves to underline the need for a well thought through conceptual framework.

Affected interests may be expected to try to influence the selection of accounting standards when there is perceived to be a range of choice. An effective conceptual framework should result in standards that at least eliminate choices that can be demonstrated to have no rational basis for support. The more fully developed and effective a conceptual framework, the narrower the range of choice that may be open to political pressures and influence by management and /or investor and other stakeholder interests. We have seen a good example of this in the development of the FASB standard on post-employment benefits. As observed in Chapter 14, the first reaction of managements of business enterprises was to strongly resist a new requirement to accrue for these costs, but their efforts were ineffectual when it became clear that that there could be no logical basis for objection, because the case that they are liabilities that enterprises should be recognizing and managing could not be challenged on any rational grounds.

In developing its concepts statements, the FASB concluded that "accounting did possess a core of fundamental concepts that are neither subject to nor dependent upon the moment's particular, transitory consensus," and that it was "imperative and proper to place before its constituents a definitive statement of its fundamental principles."[8] In other words, it must be concluded that financial accounting has a rational economic foundation. If it has no economic substance, wherein can lie its information value and its social significance? The information value of financial accounting must be presumed to lie in its ability to represent, within reasonable and understandable limits, the true and fair financial position, income and cash flows of business enterprises on a basis that is consistent with accepted economic principles. This is the expectation for financial accounting that is provided for in securities and corporations legislation.

The challenge for the accounting profession is to further develop and improve its conceptual foundation so as to better reflect the underlying economics of business enterprises in the face of major changes in business and investment practices that are rendering aspects of the traditional accounting model obsolete. As a noted accounting scholar observed, "our traditional accounting methods have been deficient and their deficiencies give rise to conflicts that could be avoided if accounting's theoretical foundations were more soundly based." [9]

It must be conceded, however, that financial accounting's conceptual basis must be set within the overarching values or norms of a society that define various stakeholders' "rights to know" and how these trade off against business' rights to privacy of information (so as to protect competitive position, for example). To illustrate, an accounting standard that requires contingent liabilities to be disclosed, even though disclosure may increase the likelihood of a claim being asserted against the enterprise, favours the interests of potential investors in the enterprise over those of existing investors and management.

The broader social value questions involve who should be accountable to whom, and for what, and who should have the primacy of right of selecting from among accounting alternatives—in other words, how to balance the rights and powers of competing interests? Accounting standard setters are not well placed to make social welfare decisions. Rather they must do the best they can to interpret, and work within, the social values framework defined by corporations and securities laws, business and investment practices, and customs of a society. Presumptions as to these values must be incorporated within accounting's conceptual framework.

In summary, the mission of the accounting standard-setting function may be defined as follows: to develop and maintain a system of financial accounting standards that provides for the fair presentation of financial position and results of operations of enterprises—on the basis of a conceptual framework that is sound and rational in relation to accepted concepts of economics, and that make trade-offs between competing interests that are consistent with information values defined by the laws and customs of the particular society.

Practical Considerations

From a purely practical point of view, the plain fact of the matter is that accounting standard setters must have a framework of fundamental concepts to reason within so as to be able to arrive at conclusions on accounting issues. Without a conceptual framework, standard setters have no agreed basis for their reasoning, with the result that their decisions on various issues are likely to lack cohesiveness. In this case a void is created that gives rise to conflicts, confusions and the potential for abuse. As business complexity increases, accountants and business persons will be uncertain as to what principles should govern the accounting recognition of important transactions and events. Different accounting methods will proliferate for the same transactions. It should not be surprising, given the advantages accruing to statement preparers of an optimistic report on operations, that practice will be something less than even-handed.

The reaction of standards setters and securities regulators to this situation may be standards overload. In the absence of clear principles, many questions arise that have to be dealt with by detailed rule making. In the presence of diverse practice and vested interests in particular practices, any standard method prescribed has to be buttressed by highly specific instructions to try to ensure that the standard is applied in accordance with its intent. Auditors add to the demand for specific instructions, partly because of genuine uncertainty as to the intent of a standard, but more to minimize the possibility of conflicts with clients over the interpretation of standards. Highly specific instructions, however, invite legalistic structuring of transactions to evade the intent of the standard. Such evasions lead, in turn, to further detailed standards and technical interpretations. These contribute to the burden of standards overload and, incidentally, increase the likelihood that literal interpretation of the rules will, in particular cases, produce results that do not pass a common sense test.

It is often suggested that the solution to these problems lies in the substitution of professional judgment for detailed rule making. Standards should be couched in general terms indicating the objectives sought by the standard in each problem area and the criteria that govern how the accounting should be performed. Professional judgment should then be applied in particular cases in determining the application of the criteria. This suggestion has much to commend it. It must be recognized, however, that professional judgment cannot be exercized in a vacuum. There must be a broadly agreed conceptual framework if there is to be any hope that individual issues can be settled by judgment that will yield other than random results or, more likely, results reflecting the beliefs and desires of preparer interests. The broad principles of that framework need to be stated in explicit terms if it is to be effective in guiding practice.

In summary, it is evident that a conceptual framework is essential. It is important to the process of standard setting that fundamental principles do not have to be thought through afresh, and more than likely inconsistently, each time a problem is considered. An agreed framework should help those making representations on a proposed standard to identify and address issues that ought to be considered. In other words, it should help to provide the basis for productive and relevant debate. Standards arrived at that have been considered and tested against the background of an agreed framework should be internally consistent. A well thought through conceptual framework that is reasoned within rational economic premises should give accounting standards external validity and thus make them more defensible against political pressures. Finally, an agreed conceptual framework should reduce the need for detailed standards. If the logical basis is apparent, it may be hoped that practice will often adapt to it without the need for detailed guidance.

One final caveat, it is only if standards setters are prepared to take a conceptual framework seriously and allow it to guide their resolution of individual issues, that it can be expected, little by little, and from precedent to precedent, to gain power and utility.

The Limitations of a Conceptual Framework

An accounting theorist's dream might be that a process of rigorously reasoning forward from firmly based propositions and observations reflecting rational economic purposes should produce a financial accounting system that is both *internally consistent* (that is, always recognizes, measures and presents like things in like ways), and *externally valid* (that is, results in values of assets, liabilities, revenues and expenses of business enterprises that represent relevant economic realities).

Of course the reality must fall short of this ideal. There are significant limits as to how far reasoning within a conceptual framework can be expected to take us. Even a prescriptive conceptual framework must factor in limitations as to what it is possible to know and practical to report. To be truly comprehensive, a conceptual framework should give explicit consideration to these limitations and their implications for financial accounting recognition, measurement, and disclosure.

Recognition and measurement limitations may be due to incomplete markets, pervasive uncertainties and allocation problems that cannot be resolved by nonarbitrary means. These effective economic indeterminacies give rise to potentially wide ranges of measurement/valuation alternatives in various circumstances that cannot be eliminated by reasoning from economic premises or estimation processes. Economic indeterminacies are much more than uncertainty. For example, they include the fundamental "allocation problem" which was discussed in Chapter 5. Indeterminacies may be dealt with in financial accounting in one of two ways:

- No recognition and measurement may be attempted; rather the area may be declared outside the realm of financial accounting. This is the case, for example, with internally generated goodwill; financial accounting makes no attempt to measure or account for it. Instead there is a shift from a goal of measuring the wealth of an entity as a whole to the lesser goal of measuring identifiable assets and liabilities.

- Alternatively, a more or less arbitrary measurement, estimation or allocation may be made, in which case the rule in accounting is to follow a consistent procedure. In some situations, nonrecognition may not be an option. Examples include depreciation allocation and pension obligation estimations. The accounting model demands reasonable determinations in these cases, on consistent and disclosed bases, even though the range of indeterminacy may be wide.

Accounting selections from ranges of defensible possibilities can have significant social welfare implications. To illustrate, suppose one is accounting for a hydroelectric company whose revenue rates are regulated on the basis of the utility's accounting expenses plus a rate of return to equity. A major element of these expenses will relate to the cost of its plant, so it is necessary to determine how this cost should be allocated to periods of use. The estimation of useful life and the selection of the pattern of benefit on which to base the depreciation method are subject to a considerable range of indeterminacy (see discussion at Chapter 11). At the same time, the choice of depreciation method has significant intergenerational equity implications. Should all users of electricity over the life of the plant pay the same price per kilowatt-hour with respect to the plant and, if so, should this be determined in real or nominal dollars? Alternatively, might future generations be expected to pay more or less (perhaps on the basis of some assumptions with respect to possible changes in technology and possible partial obsolescence of the plant over time)? A decision on these issues is implicit in whatever allocation method is chosen, and some allocation must be made if revenue rates are to be based on accounting expenses.

It should not be for accountants alone to make such policy decisions. However, it may be reasonable to expect that accountants should have some responsibility for defining the possibilities and their implications so that, in this case, the rate regulating authority and the stakeholders to which it is accountable, will be fully informed in making the revenue rate decision.

A fully developed conceptual framework would not sweep economic indeterminacies under the carpet with the all-too-typical advice that "professional judgment should be applied." Efforts to build a more complete conceptual framework may be usefully focused on examining the limits, and on defining the nature and range of economic indeterminacy in basic circumstances. Through such efforts it might be possible, for example, to develop bases for reporting ranges or other representations of the extent of indeterminacy, and for identifying and disclosing assumptions. An entity's financial position and income are not fully and fairly represented if pervasive uncertainties or fundamental indeterminacies are not disclosed.

One further point may be made. The nature and extent of economic indeterminacies in financial accounting can only be understood and assessed within a conceptual framework that has developed its rational economic basis as far as it reasonably can be. This is another way of expressing the idea, noted earlier in this chapter, that the better that financial accounting's concept statements can define its fundamental principles, the narrower will be the range of choice that is open to legitimate political and vested interest influences (which range is ultimately defined by economic indeterminacies).

Time and Place Validity

One might think that a conceptual framework for financial accounting, once established, should be fixed and stable—since it is based on fundamental objectives, business purposes and economic principles. But this is not the case. Any conceptual framework is valid only for its time and place. A highly socialized country, for example, may not place much emphasis on the importance of providing information to facilitate private investment decisions. If social values relevant to the trade-offs between the public's right to know and businesses' rights to privacy change, the conceptual framework may also change. As well, advances in information technology and capital markets may enable cost-effective measurements and complex calculations that previously were not practicable, and developments in economic thinking and business and investment practices may have implications for accounting theory. These developments may result in some reduction in economic indeterminacies.

In order to demonstrate how conceptual foundations may evolve and change, we might visualize three different economic orientations that could be expected to give rise to somewhat different conceptual frameworks.

- A free enterprise economy dominated by business enterprise management and private lenders and investors.
- A free enterprise economy within open and developed capital markets and extensive public investor interests.
- A free enterprise economy in which enterprises are considered to have broad accountability to external stakeholders beyond investors.

In the first orientation, business enterprise management, which may have a significant equity stake in the business, and private capital providers, including banks and other financial institutions and, perhaps, government, are the dominant interests in financial information. These groups might be expected to have protectionist and paternalistic attitudes towards the dissemination of financial information to external interests. Business managers and their accountants may take a conservative, stewardship attitude, assuming it is important for external investors and the public to see their enterprises as secure and stable, so that volatility in reported financial results should be smoothed out, and perhaps undisclosed reserves set aside in good times against the possibility of drawing these back to augment reported income in times that are not so good.

The second orientation features developed and open capital markets. The accounting and disclosure requirements of securities regulators and accounting standard setters are aimed primarily at providing "full and fair" disclosure to investors. Trading on the basis of inside information is illegal. The basis of this capital markets-driven economy is that extensive and timely financial information on business enterprises lays the groundwork for a "fair game" for investors and, in so doing, provides for the efficient pricing of securities and allocation of resources. In this case a conceptual framework gives primacy to investors and the decision usefulness of information for their purposes. Following from these purposes, it may be expected that the primary objective of financial accounting measurement should be to reflect best estimates, without modification to smooth out volatility, so that investors can see things as they are. Other stakeholders (including employees, suppliers, competitors, and the general public) may also be expected to benefit from this information, but their rights are considered to be secondary to those of the investors.

A third possible orientation may be characterized by a broad public accountabilty that goes beyond capital markets and investors. One interpretation would envisage a public reporting responsibility for every enterprise that "… commands human or material resources on such a scale that the results of its activities have significant economic implications for the community as a whole."[10] Such organizations would be accountable for a wide range of matters to those whose welfare is significantly affected by their activities. It has been suggested that, in addition to conventional financial statements, corporate reports should include a statement of value added, an employment report, and statements of money exchanges with government, transactions in foreign currency, future prospects, and corporate objectives.[11] A report on environmental impacts might also be added to this list. The philosophy of this orientation has been stated to be that "business enterprises can survive only with the approval of the community in which they operate and they have an interest in revealing information which displays how differing interests are being balanced for the benefit of the whole community." Further, "it is important to keep in mind the pervasive influence on management attitudes. Managements naturally respond to those indicators by which they consider their performance judged."[12]

It would seem that the history of financial accounting in the twentieth century in North America has been one of an evolution from the first to the second orientation. More recently this has taken on accelerating international dimensions with the globalization of capital markets. However, there continue to be significant vestiges of the first orientation even within the U.S., the bastion of capital markets.

THE EXISTING CONCEPTUAL FRAMEWORK—AN EVALUATION

The Asset and Liability View

We have seen that the FASB has been the leader in the development of the explicit conceptual framework that exists today. Its efforts resulted in a set of concepts statements that have been the model for others, including Canada and the IASC. This framework has provided a very important foundation for standard setters. In particular, it fundamentally changed the focus of accounting—from a revenue-expense matching perspective to a more disciplined and realistic approach founded on real-world concepts of "assets" and "liabilities." These concepts have been the building blocks for implementing a decision usefulness objective that extends beyond the traditional stewardship objective of accounting. In so doing, the "asset and liability view" has helped facilitate the evolution from the first (management-private investor dominated) orientation towards the second (capital markets-dominated) orientation.

The "asset and liability view" has proved to be superior in both concept and practice to the revenue-expense matching view that had previously dominated financial accounting. The traditional revenue-expense matching principle resulted in deferred balance sheet debits and credits that did not require any justification as economic assets or liabilities. They could simply be balances awaiting future allocation. This revenue-expense matching view, while useful and sufficient in a simpler time, was seen under rigorous analysis to be an inadequate foundation for the development of accounting. The FASB concepts statements conclude that it is essentially unworkable because it cannot be grounded in any theory that is not ultimately open ended and circular.[13]

The *CICA Handbook* framework adopted similar concepts of "assets" and "liabilities."[14] Interestingly, however, it has not been prepared to go all the way to preclude recognition of balance sheet debits and credits that do not meet these definitions. *CICA Handbook*, paragraph 1000.26 states that:

The existence of other items is not precluded. In practice, a balance sheet may include, as a category of assets or liabilities, items that result from a delay in recognition of revenue, expenses, gains and losses.

The CICA Accounting Standards Board has continued to be reluctant to fully accept the "asset and liability view"—as we have seen, for example, in its continuing to require the amortization of foreign currency gains and losses on long-term monetary items (see Chapter 21). Nevertheless, it is fair to say that the "assets and liabilities view" has significantly influenced the development of financial accounting in Canada in many other areas.

The conceptual framework's emphasis of the "asset and liability view" may be its main contribution. But its formal adoption of a decision usefulness objective with primacy given to external investor (capital markets) interests, and its descriptions of the qualitative characteristics of useful information, have also undoubtedly provided valuable reference points for the development of financial accounting.

The Insufficiency of the Stated Conceptual Framework

Overall then, it may be concluded that the conceptual framework has proved to be useful. However, at the same time, it must be recognized that the framework, as it has been developed so far, is incomplete and insufficient in some significant respects. In particular, as we have previously observed, it does not effectively address recognition and measurement principles. For example, it makes only general assertions that stress traditional conventions for recognition on the basis of reasonable measurability, conveyance of significant risks and rewards of ownership, and the probability of future benefits or sacrifices. We have seen these to be inadequate in respect of provisions and contingencies in Chapter 8, complex asset transfer transactions such as securitizations in Chapter 7, lease accounting in Chapter 13, as well as other areas. These conventions are, if anything, being used as reasons for resisting change rather than pointing the way towards clearly needed changes in accounting standards. As a result, the framework has been of limited assistance to standard setters in their efforts to extend, and in some cases, replace certain aspects of traditional recognition and measurement practices to meet the changed conditions and expectations of the capital marketplace.

We have briefly noted earlier in this chapter two other areas in which the framework may be considered to be incomplete: (1) insufficient definition of the limitations of financial accounting, and (2) lack of development of the implications of social value trade-offs between competing user interests. As well, there is the lack of a coherent theory of disclosure (as discussed in Chapter 23).

Developments beyond the Formal Framework

Progress on the development of a formal conceptual framework stalled in the mid 1980s when the FASB failed to achieve agreement on meaningful recognition and measurement principles. The FASB may have advanced the framework as far as it was possible at that time. Significant changes have taken place since then, however. In Chapter 4 we briefly noted certain of the major areas of change in the external environment that have profound implications for financial accounting. Generally these emanate from advances in computer and information technologies and the emergence of global capital markets. These have been matched by developments in finance theory and in the innovative use of derivatives, securitizations, leases, joint ventures and various other transactions and arrangements designed to segregate and manage risks, raise capital, restructure businesses and their assets and liabilities, and to achieve off-balance financing.

That these developments have very significant implications for financial accounting and its conceptual foundation is hardly news. Nevertheless, the nature and extent of these implications are still far from clear, and many accountants seem reluctant to accept that there is any need for basic changes in traditional accounting, even while major new standards are debated and issued all around them. The analyses of Part II demonstrate the extent of recent changes, and pending and proposed changes, in accounting standards. It may be difficult to see the forest for the trees, however—that is, to see the common themes that are running through the individual issues and standards. Fundamental developments in accounting concepts are evident in the following changes in accounting standards examined in earlier chapters:

- Extensions in the use of present value theory (in loan and capital asset impairment determinations (Chapter 18) in liability provisions (Chapter 8), and in the measurement of financial instruments (Chapter 17)).

- Acceptance of fair value measurement for at least some financial instruments (Chapter 17).

- Increased recognition of the concept of expected values in liability provisioning (Chapter 8).

- More rigorous attention to the central concept of control in defining assets, in determining the boundaries of consolidated reporting entities, and in unsorting the effects of transactions which result in separating risks and benefits, such as some forms of leases and securitizations (Chapters 7, 13 and 20).

- Extension of disclosure to enable users to better understand the risk and uncertainty dimensions of reported financial statement figures (for example, segment reporting (Chapter 23) and disclosures of financial risks as discussed in Chapter 17).

These and other areas of change in financial accounting demonstrate that the *real* underlying framework of accounting theory has been developing beyond the formal stated conceptual framework. It has been changing on a piecemeal, issue-by-issue and standard-by-standard basis. The result has been an uneven development. As an example, present value principles have been put in place in some areas of accounting but not in others in which they may be just as applicable. We have, as a consequence, an inconsistent "mixed attribute" model. The general principles underlying these developments in individual standards and their broader implications for the conceptual foundation of accounting, have not been addressed—with the notable exception of the FASB's proposed statement on cash flows and present value measurements.[15] Several conclusions may be drawn from these developments.

- They demonstrate change by adaptation, modification or extension of the traditional accounting model—rather than wholesale rejection of the old model to be replaced by something entirely new. Proposals for replacing historical cost accounting with current cost or current value accounting in the early 1980s did not succeed (for various reasons discussed in Chapter 24). Currently, standards setters are implicitly presuming, as evidenced by their actions, that the deficiencies of traditional accounting can be effectively addressed by changing or extending parts of the old model. This presumption is consistent with the general idea expressed in the earlier section on "time and place validity," that an accounting conceptual framework is not static but must evolve to reflect changes in economic/finance theories, capital markets, and society values.

- An effect of advances in capital markets and information technology has been to increase demand for, and at the same time better enable, recognition and measurement of certain assets and liabilities at earlier stages in the accounting process. The demand comes from increasing pressures in more volatile, fast-paced global financial markets for financial information to reflect the effects of changes in economic conditions when they take place. The improved ability to do so results from the expansion of active markets and the availability of reliable current prices for an increasing number of commodities and financial instruments. This has been abetted by the development of sophisticated measurement models for financial instruments and pension obligations, for example, and by the vastly improved ability of computers to handle masses of data and complex calculations.

  We have seen evidence of the accounting effects of these developments in the expansion of accounting accruals to reflect earlier recognition of rights and obligations (as discussed in Chapter 4). More specifically, we have observed standards in some jurisdictions for the earlier recognition of asset impairment (Chapter 18), and of recognition of value added and revenues at earlier stages in the earnings process (the most dramatic changes being in relation to financial instruments, Chapter 17). As well, increasingly complex and sophisticated transactions have demanded more precise and rigorous approaches to the recognition and derecognition of assets and liabilities where risks and benefits are "debundled" and "rebundled" by use of derivatives (Chapter 7). These external developments have also fundamentally changed thinking about disclosures, in particular with respect to the idea that the full depiction of the measure of an economic asset or liability includes its risk and uncertainty attributes (as discussed in Chapter 23). In all these areas, the old is being transformed to the new by piecemeal standard-by-standard extension of the old model. Ultimately some aspects of the old model may be barely recognizable, but it is a process of gradualism, rather than wholesale change. The presumption is that the traditional accounting model has the resilience to be expanded and developed.

- This process of piecemeal change has made it difficult to appreciate the extent and direction of change and its implications. The principles underlying the above-noted changes in specific standards have not been generalized and incorporated within the conceptual framework itself.

The Importance of Continuing to Develop the Formal Framework

Certainly there are difficult questions as to how far it is possible and appropriate to develop the formal statement of accounting's conceptual framework. In particular, it is difficult to determine when a conceptual development (for example, the concepts of present value and expected value) is sufficiently advanced to be incorporated in the foundations of accounting. As well, it may not seem desirable for the fundamentals of a framework to appear to be continually changing. Nevertheless it may be proposed that the case for extending and updating the framework now far outweighs these concerns. We have discussed earlier in this chapter why a clear statement of the defining premises and principles of accounting is necessary in the first place. An incomplete framework that has not evolved with the times does not meet this need. The following comments underline and extend the earlier discussion.

- The importance of a fully developed, and clearly stated, conceptual framework is closely related to the information needs of capital markets. The evidence seems clear that, in many recent instances of financial difficulties and economic crises, deficiencies of financial information and lack of confidence in, and perhaps poor understanding of, available economic data have seriously exacerbated the instability of capital markets. These informational insufficiencies can carry very high costs to society, often borne disproportionately by taxpayers and the general public.

- If financial information on public enterprises is not trusted, or its basis is not well understood, confidence in capital markets themselves may be undermined. The efficiency and equity of capital markets can be no better than the relevance, reliability and understandability of its information base. Accounting information that lacks credibility or is poorly understood can be expected to result in investors demanding high "information risk" premiums as the price for committing their resources. This increases the cost of capital to enterprises and makes capital allocation less efficient. Information uncertainty can also be expected to heighten volatility of market prices where markets may be driven more by rumours than facts.

- An incompletely developed and explained theory of financial accounting that seems to lack external validity and to be marred by internal consistencies, will not contribute to user confidence in financial information or capital markets. On the other hand, a well explained, reasonably complete and internally consistent framework that is convincingly reasoned from rational economic decision models will stand to enhance investor understanding and confidence. Such a framework is not only valuable for standards setters but also, in a less detailed and technical form, for all who are affected by the financial results of business enterprises.

The FASB experience has indicated that setting out accounting's conceptual foundations is not easy. There can be expected to be significant resistance and disagreement with concepts that represent a significant change from traditional thinking. Thus the process of developing a conceptual framework, and the standards within that framework, involves not only technical research to develop and validate the concepts, but also requires working to help affected interests understand its implications.

Many disagreements in financial accounting have their roots in different views of the purposes of financial accounting and its economic premises. The starting point for addressing these disagreements is to identify the underlying premises, assumptions and reasoning processes, as well as concerns with respect to their possible effects, so that they may be held up for examination. To enable this, all significant aspects of a conceptual framework need to be made explicit and thoroughly researched and debated, and their implications developed and explained.

A Drawing Together—Some Observations on Possible Future Directions

The essential building blocks of a typical prescriptive conceptual framework include:

- A statement of the objectives of financial accounting, including presumptions as to users and user information needs;

- Business purposes and the nature of the economic phenomena related to those purposes that comprise the subject matter of financial accounting; and

- Qualitative characteristics and limitations of financial information, and the balancing of conflicts between desirable characteristics.

In this final section we will comment on the development of each of these three areas within the existing conceptual. In so doing, we will briefly explore some considerations relating to possible future directions.

The Objectives of Financial Reporting

Every conceptual framework begins with a statement of objectives, and every statement of objectives comes to the conclusion that financial reports are intended to be useful. It is hardly debatable that accounting should be useful, but there are many questions as to who uses accounting information and how it is used—or, even more important, would be used if better information were available. The answers to these questions conceivably could suggest such a multiplicity of possible uses that it might be considered that general purpose financial reporting is impossible, at least in the absence of a hierarchical ordering of user needs. But let us look at the main use objectives identified in accounting literature to see if we can assess something of their implications for general purpose financial statements.

- In Part I we have noted the strong tradition in accounting history to the effect that the purpose of accounting is to report on the stewardship of management. That purpose implies the use of accounting to assist in the assessment of the performance of management. As an extension of this we observed (in Chapter 4) that some suggest that such information is vital to facilitate contracting and the operation of control devices to ensure the enforcement of contracts. These include contracts between owners of an entity and its management, between the entity and creditors, and between management and subordinates. We have also discussed in Chapter 4 the comparatively recent adaptation of this reporting objective (of control over the stewardship of management) provided by "agency theory."

    It has commonly been advocated that a reporting system suitable for stewardship and contracting must have certain characteristics; it should be predictable, it should be well understood by the contracting parties, and it should not be open to wide variation depending on individual judgment. In other words, it requires highly structured accounting rules. The difficulty is that hard-and-fast accounting rules may produce unintended results if the economic environment changes. Consider a management incentive contract based on reported historical cost profits. Such a contract might be satisfactory while price levels are stable, and absurdly unfair and unreasonable under conditions of rapid inflation. In the end, it would seem that any report for financial stewardship and contracting purposes must trade off the need for hard data with the need for a good correspondence with the actual economic outcomes; that is, it must have an objective of fair presentation.

    A narrow interpretation of stewardship responsibility is that it is merely an obligation to report on safe custody or proper disposition of assets entrusted. This is often taken to justify continued reliance on historical costs in financial statements. However, this interpretation has given way to a broader concept of "accountability"—that is, for reporting on the efficient, economic and effective use of resources and, even more broadly, to require reporting on the entity's (management's) success in achieving the goals of an enterprise. This broader accountability concept may be considered to embrace reporting on changes in the value of assets and liabilities. In order to assess an accountability objective, one must define those to whom the entity is accountable. As we have previously observed, who should be considered to be accountable to whom (and for what) is a matter to be defined by law and custom, and may be expected to change over time. Thus an accountability interpretation of stewardship becomes a very broad and expandable concept that, as we will see, has much in common with decision usefulness and social welfare objectives.

- The goal of decision usefulness has been accepted as the primary objective in many works on possible conceptual frameworks. This immediately suggests two questions: who are the users, and what financial information is relevant to their decisions? The FASB, CICA and IASC concepts statements all concentrate on the use of business financial reports for investment and credit decisions. These statements suggest, plausibly but without definite evidence, that information for these purposes will serve most other purposes as well. To the extent it does not, however, a value judgment has been made to give primacy to the decision needs of capital market participants.[16] This is consistent with the second (capital markets) orientation identified earlier in this chapter.

- We have also noted the objective of promotion of social welfare. The difficulty with this objective stems from doubts as to its feasibility. Measurement of costs and benefits are notoriously difficult to make. Attempts to combine individual preferences into an expression of social preference are generally considered to be impossible.[17] However, if one believes that social welfare considerations are effective in guiding legislative and government actions, it may be argued that a clear signal has been given to guide accounting standards. Corporations and securities legislation in Canada and the U.S. requires that financial statements be fairly presented. This implies a conclusion that social welfare is served by unbiased financial disclosure, even though the disclosure may not benefit all individual interests. The existence of securities legislation, in particular, attests to the importance of the belief that efficient capital markets will be socially beneficial, and therefore should be a fair game.

One might well conclude that the above financial reporting objectives do not provide much guidance for the resolution of specific accounting issues and for the development of accounting standards. It might also be observed that the above objectives are not fundamentally in conflict with one another. For each of these purposes, users have an interest in financial statements of business enterprises that have the same basic qualities of relevance and reliability. The FASB framework proposes as a working supposition that most users are interested in financial information that will help them in assessing the amounts, timing and uncertainty of prospective net cash flows to the entity.[18] The CICA and IASC frameworks have taken a similar line.

Economic Purposes, Capital Markets and Rational Expectations

One cannot define a financial reporting framework without first delineating the economic purposes of business enterprises that should be the object of this reporting. It is indisputable that the primary purpose of any profit-oriented entity is to create wealth, which is expressed in terms of money and is ultimately conceived as command over cash, or claims to future cash or cash-equivalent flows. Thus an enterprise may be presumed to invest in assets, regardless of their form, for the future net cash-equivalent flows they are expected to generate. There is nothing new in this. The FASB, CICA and IASC frameworks all indicate this.

This is not to suggest that the ability to generate net cash flows is the only objective of business enterprises that might be usefully accounted for. Many stakeholders are interested in other outputs and effects of business enterprise activities (such as is suggested by the third public accountability orientation discussed earlier). But information that bears on the amounts, timing and uncertainty of cash-equivalent flows is considered to be the primary purpose of financial accounting.

Thus economic resources (assets), claims upon these resources (liabilities and equity contracts), and changes in them (income) are the basic subject matter of financial accounting. Since it is the cash-equivalent expectation attribute of assets, liabilities and equity that is the primary objective of business activities, it seems appropriate to conclude that this attribute should be the focus of accounting recognition, measurement and disclosure.

The cash flow generation objective that is central to financial accounting has a powerful connection with a fundamental premise of capital markets. This is that rational investors price assets and liabilities by discounting expected future cash flows to yield the current rate of return for equivalent risk. Financial accounting has been slow to recognize the fundamental measurement implications of this well-accepted principle. The conceptual framework in the *CICA Handbook* classes present value measures with bases of measurement that are used "only in limited circumstances" (paragraph 1000.54). This reflects traditional historical cost thinking, which no longer accords with modern financial accounting as is demonstrated by the following present value applications.

- Going back to 1971, U.S. GAAP have required, with some exceptions, that a transaction involving the exchange of a note receivable or payable bearing a noncompetitive interest rate should be reflected at the fair value of the good or service received in the exchange, or the present value of the cash flows of the note discounted at the current rate of interest appropriate to the terms of the note at the date of the transaction, whichever is more clearly evident. This principle is also recognized in Canadian GAAP (see Chapter 6).

- Pensions and other post-employment benefit obligations are required by FASB and IASC standards to be measured on the basis of best estimates of the future cash flows discounted at a current, low-risk, rate of interest. The existing CICA standard is about to be amended to be very similar to that of the FASB. See discussion at Chapter 14.

- Loan impairment standards in the U.S. and Canada require a discounted measure of expected cash flows (see Chapter 18).

- A recently issued IASC standard will require that impaired capital assets be written down to the higher of their current net selling value or a value-in-use amount that is to be determined by discounting expected cash flows to be generated through the use of the assets using a current risk-adjusted rate of interest. An FASB standard requires a current present value measurement if an undiscounted determination of future cash flows is less than the capital asset's carrying value, while the Canadian standard is still essentially an undiscounted cash flow determination (see Chapter 18).

In addition to the above examples of standards in place, consideration is being given to the application of present value principles in a number of other areas. These include the application of present value methods to determine the fair value of financial instruments for which there is no ready market value (see Chapter 17), and the suggestion (in Chapter 11) that depreciation of capital assets should be based on present value principles, and that so doing would enable a logical basis for a present value measure of deferred income taxes (Chapter 16).

It has become apparent that the capital markets' present value premise has far reaching implications for financial accounting. Some advocate that it is a fundamental building block for asset and liability measurement that should be incorporated within the conceptual framework. Certainly there are major issues to be resolved before it could be fully applied in the measurement of all assets and liabilities. But the very definitions of "assets" and "liabilities," as expected future economic benefits and sacrifices (ultimately envisaged as cash or cash equivalents), implies the comprehensive relevance of the present value principle. In Chapter 24 we noted that the measurement of assets and liabilities on the basis of their expected ability to yield the currently available market rate of return, appropriately adjusted for risk, holds some interesting possibilities for defining a capital maintenance concept in terms of market capital return expectations.

To this point, however, there is no explicit accounting framework for the incorporation of present values and expected cash flows within the accounting model. However, a CICA research study developed some basic ideas with respect to a comprehensive present value framework, although essentially within a cost-based model,[19] and the FASB has made a promising start on a proposed concepts statement.[20]

Finance theories and capital markets practices have other important implications for the development of basic financial accounting concepts. Two areas may be noted, one relating to the recognition of financial assets and liabilities, and the other to defining the risk and uncertainty dimensions of accounting measurements.

• Existing conceptual frameworks hold that an essential condition for the recognition of assets and liabilities is that it be probable that future economic benefits will be obtained or given up (*CICA Handbook*, paragraphs .44–.45). This is a general long-standing convention that has been accepted, for example, in determining whether costs incurred to acquire nonmonetary inputs should be recognized as assets or simply expensed. Accounting for R&D costs, examined in Chapter 12, illustrates an attempt to apply this principle. It has also been accepted as a fundamental condition for the recognition of revenues on the sale of goods and services (see Chapter 7). However, we have observed that, for financial instruments, the probability of future benefit inflow or outflow is generally considered to be a matter affecting their measurement rather than their recognition. In a fair market the probability of receipt or payment of a benefit simply affects the price. A written option or credit guarantee may be "out of the money" (that is, it may be unlikely that any payment will be required). Yet such instruments have values at which they will trade in the financial marketplace. If the traditional conceptual framework probability condition were to be applied, these instruments would not be recognized. We have also discussed the relevance of probability ("expected value") theory to the recognition and measurement of liability provisions and contingencies (see Chapter 8). These developments demonstrate an ongoing evolution of standards and practices beyond the recognition convention embodied in the existing formal conceptual framework.

• Developments in financial risk management theories and derivatives, and increased market volatility in recent years, have given rise to demands for expanded quantitative and qualitative information about enterprise risk exposures. This has served to emphasize that it is not enough to report single value measures of assets and liabilities. A complete accounting measurement model would encompass operational concepts for reporting the significant statistical properties of accounting numbers (information on the dispersion about the reported value due to estimation uncertainties and other economic indeterminacies) as well as their risk attributes (see discussion at Chapter 23).

Qualitative Characteristics of Useful Financial Information

The CICA, FASB and IASC conceptual frameworks identify and describe a similar list of characteristics of accounting information that contribute to its usefulness.. The *CICA Handbook* concepts statement states that the four main characteristics are understandability, relevance, reliability, and comparability.[21]

The characteristic of *understandability* is defined by reference to users who "have a reasonable understanding of business and economic activities and accounting, together with a willingness to study the information with reasonable diligence" (paragraph 1000.19). The primary quality of *relevance* emphasizes the decision usefulness objective. To be relevant, financial information should be capable of influencing decisions in one of two ways. It should help users to evaluate the financial impact of past transactions or events so as to confirm or correct previous evaluations (that is, have "feedback value"), or to estimate an entity's future income and cash flows (that is, have "predictive value") (paragraph 1000.20). The predictive value of information trickles away as time passes, so that timeliness is considered to be an important attribute of relevance.

Reliability is considered to embody the concepts of representational faithfulness, verifiability, and neutrality (paragraph 1000.21). The *CICA Handbook* also includes "conservatism" in making judgments under conditions of uncertainty, while emphasizing that this should not encompass the deliberate understatement of assets, revenues and gains or the deliberate overstatement of liabilities, expenses and losses. The final primary characteristic is that of *comparability* of financial information between entities and over time (paragraph 1000.22).

These qualities expand upon the basic decision usefulness objective and, for the most part, they are self-explanatory. However, one very important point that is made in all existing conceptual frameworks does warrant some additional attention. This is the need for trade-offs between these desirable characteristics of financial information. As an example, additional relevance will frequently be achievable only by sacrificing some timeliness and/or verifiability. No operational principles are provided in existing conceptual frameworks for making these trade-offs. The *CICA Handbook* simply states that:

> Generally, the aim is to achieve an appropriate balance among the characteristics in order to meet the objective of financial statements. The relative importance of the characteristics in different cases is a matter of professional judgment (paragraph 1000.24).

This advice seems naïve and inadequate in light of our earlier discussions of social values and political pressures. What should be the basis for determining the "appropriate balance" and for making sound "professional judgments"? The quality of "neutrality" provides a focus for considering these questions. The CICA conceptual framework holds that financial statements should be neutral, that is should be "… free from bias that would lead users towards making decisions that are influenced by the way the information is measured or presented" (paragraph 1000.21(c)). It further notes that "… bias may occur when the selection is made with the interests of particular users or with particular economic or political objectives in mind." Some argue that it is impossible for accounting standards to be neutral, given the role that social values and political pressures play in their development.[22] They advocate, as we have noted earlier, that economic consequences be taken into account in establishing accounting standards—that accounting standard setting must be prepared to modify or override the conceptual framework to achieve desirable social goals. The framework quality of "neutrality" does not accept this, but stresses the primacy of representational faithfulness of financial information. In essence, it holds that accounting should not be open to bias or manipulation to favour the interests of one party at the expense of others. To tolerate such actions would misinform markets and in short order destroy the credibility of accounting standards and financial accounting, which could serve no one's long-term best interests.[23] Misinformed markets are likely to misallocate and misprice capital, to the detriment of almost everyone.

Of course, in an uncertain and imperfect world financial information cannot be perfect, and standard setters must make cost-benefit trade-offs between representational faithfulness, practical measurability, timeliness, etc. Thus it is important that standard setters be aware of the potential economic consequences of their standards and monitor actual consequences. If some interests may be disadvantaged by a new standard, it had better be defensible. It was suggested earlier in this chapter that a prescriptive conceptual framework should incorporate society values. Further, in making sensitive cost/benefit trade-offs between competing preparer and user interests, accounting standard setters must strive to reflect the society's information values as these are evidenced by its laws and customs. This is no easy task, however, especially since laws and customs are changing and evolving. There may be inconsistencies as between laws and regulatory authorities. For example, the objectives of securities regulators are consistent with full financial disclosure in the best interests of investors. On the other hand, banking regulators may desire some limits on disclosure and prefer a conservative accounting bias in some situations in the interests of maintaining the confidence of depositors and financial stability.

It is apparent that such trade-offs cannot be expected to be worked out by reference to a conceptual framework alone. Rather, emphasis must be placed on a fair and open standard-setting process that can be relied upon to make reasonable decisions in the public interest. The standard-setting process is the subject of the following chapter.

NOT-FOR-PROFIT AND GOVERNMENT ORGANIZATIONS

To this point we have considered the conceptual framework for business enterprises, whose economic purposes revolve around the profit motive and the creation of wealth. These motivations are not the focus of not-for-profit and government entities. For business enterprises the future benefits that are the primary objective of investing in resources are ultimately cash or cash equivalents. For not-for-profit entities the future benefits to be derived from investing in resources are defined in terms of the capacity to render services in the furtherance of the entities' programs.

As observed in Chapter 27, some argue that these fundamental differences in purposes should lead to a different conceptual basis for reporting not-for-profit financial activities. But this is not the conclusion reached by the CICA and FASB. While they accept that business and nonbusiness entities have different purposes, and that some different decisions are assisted by their financial reports, these two standard-setting bodies have come to the view that their financial statements should be based on substantially the same foundation. They reason that their financial resources and claims on those resources, and their transactions and events, are subject to the same economic forces. Not-for-profit organizations buy and sell resources in the same markets as business enterprises, and the rights conveyed by assets and the obligations imposed by liabilities are the same for all entities. In the case of non-business organizations, financial reports ideally should be supplemented with information about service accomplishments, but their financial statements should not reflect different financial accounting concepts.

As a consequence of this thinking, in both countries the concepts statements initially developed for business enterprises were subsequently supplemented and extended to incorporate not-for-profit organizations.[24] Government enterprises continue to be the subject of separate standards and separate standard-setting processes, but the reasons for this are likely founded more in practical considerations and traditions than in logical bases.

The unique aspects of not-for-profit and government activities and their implications for the application of the conceptual framework are discussed in Chapters 27 and 28.

REFERENCES

1   CICA, "Financial Statement Concepts," *CICA Handbook*, Section 1000 (Toronto: CICA); and IASC, *Framework for the Preparation and Presentation of Financial Statements* (London: IASC). The CICA section was issued in 1988 and the IASC framework in 1989.

2   Significant examples of attempts to build conceptual frameworks that describe and explain practice include W.A. Paton and A.C. Littleton, *An Introduction to Corporate Accounting Standards*, Monograph No. 3 (AAA, 1940); *Accounting and Reporting Standards for Corporate Financial Statements and Preceding Statements and Supplements* (AAA, 1957); P. Grady, *Inventory of Generally Accepted Accounting Principles for Business Enterprises*, Accounting Research Study No. 7 (New York: AICPA, 1965); AICPA, APB, *Basic Concepts and Accounting Principles Underlying Financial Statements of Business Enterprises*, APB Statement No. 4 (New York: AICPA, 1970); and R.M. Skinner, *Accounting Principles: A Canadian Viewpoint* (Toronto: CICA, 1972).

3   R. Lauver, "Accountant—Be a Measurer," *The CPA Journal*, January 1991, pp. 12–14.

4   Examples of attempts to propound this type of conceptual framework or elements of it include the AICPA Accounting Research Studies Nos. 1 and 3: M. Moonitz, *The Basic Postulates of Accounting* (New York: AICPA, 1961), and R.T. Sprouse and M. Moonitz, *A Tentative Set of Broad Accounting Principles for Business Enterprises* (New York: AICPA, 1962); *A Statement of Basic Accounting Theory* (AAA, 1966); W.J. Kenley and G.J. Staubus, *Objectives and Concepts of Financial Statements* (Melbourne: Accounting Research Foundation, 1972); *Objectives of Financial Statements*, vol. 1 (New York: AICPA, 1973); *The Corporate Report* (London: Accounting Standards Steering Committee, 1975); *Corporate Reporting: Its Future Evolution* (Toronto: CICA, 1980); and the six Statements of Financial Accounting Concepts published by the FASB from 1978 to 1985. Some of the proposals for changes in accounting to better reflect the impact of changing prices also effectively represent normative conceptual frameworks, although their authors pay relatively less attention to discussions of objectives and premises and relatively more to the practical working out of their proposals. See especially the works by Chambers, Edwards and Bell, and Sterling cited in the bibliography for Chapter 24.

5   G.J. Staubus, "The Market Simulation Theory of Accounting Measurement," *Accounting and Business Research*, Spring 1986, p. 118.

6   For a review of the arguments supporting this point of view, see E.R. Brownlee, II, and S.D. Young, "Financial Disclosure Regulations and Its Critics," *Journal of Accounting Education*, Spring 1986, pp. 113–26.

7   For a Canadian study of the choice between GAAP and tailored accounting principles in lending agreements, see D.A. Thornton and M.J. Bryant, *GAAP vs. TAP in Lending Agreements: Canadian Evidence* (Toronto: The Canadian Academic Accounting Association, 1986).

8   R.K. Storey, "The Framework of Financial Accounting Concepts and Standards," in D.R. Carmichael, S.B. Lilien and M. Mellman, *Accountants' Handbook*, 9th ed., Vol. 1 (Somerset, NJ: John Wiley & Sons, Inc., 1999), pp. 1.46 and 1.47.

9   D. Solomons, *Making Accounting Policy: The Quest for Credibility in Financial Reporting* (New York: Oxford University Press, 1986), p. 246.

10   The Institute of Chartered Accountants in England and Wales, Accounting Standards Steering Committee, *The Corporate Report*, A Discussion Paper (London: The Institute of Chartered Accountants in England and Wales, 1975), par. 1.2.

11   Ibid., Section 6.

12   Ibid., pars. 4.29 and 4.33.

13   See R.K. Storey, "The Framework of Financial Accounting Concepts and Standards," pp. 1.44–1.45.

14   CICA, "Financial Statement Concepts," *CICA Handbook*, Section 1000 (Toronto: CICA), pars. .29–.34.

15   FASB, *Using Cash Flow Information in Accounting Measurements*, Proposed Statement of Financial Accounting Concepts (Norwalk: FASB, 1997).

16   For a criticism of this approach, see N.Dopuch and S. Sunder, "FASB's Statements on Objectives and Elements of Financial Accounting: A Review," *The Accounting Review*, January 1980, pp. 1–21.

17   See, for example, J.S. Demski, "The General Impossibility of Normative Accounting Standards," *The Accounting Review*, October 1973, pp. 718–23; and R.G. May and G.L. Sundem, "Research for Accounting Policy: An Overview," *The Accounting Review*, October 1976, pp. 747–63.

18   FASB, *Objectives of Financial Reporting by Business Enterprises*, Statement of Financial Accounting Concepts No. 1 (Stamford: FASB, 1978), par. 37.

19   J.A. Milburn, *Incorporating the Time Value of Money Within Financial Reporting*, Research Study (Toronto: CICA, 1988).

20   FASB, *Using Cash Flow Information in Accounting Measurements*.

21   CICA, "Financial Statement Concepts," pars. 1000.18–.23.

22   L.A. Daley and T. Tranter, "Limitations in the Value of the Conceptual Framework in Evaluating Extant Accounting Standards," *Accounting Horizons*, March 1990, pp. 15–24.

23   The argument here could not be better expressed than they are in FASB, *Qualitative Characteristics of Accounting Information*, Statement of Financial Accounting Concepts No. 2 (Stamford: FASB, 1980), pars. 98–110.

24   *CICA Handbook* Section 1000, "Financial Statement Concepts," was expanded to incorporate not-for-profit organizations in 1991.

26

THE ESTABLISHMENT OF ACCOUNTING STANDARDS

In the preceding chapter, we made the case for a sound and well-articulated conceptual framework as the basis for financial accounting. We observed, however, that a conceptual framework is not enough—that no theory can provide answers to all the questions that can arise in attempting to faithfully represent the economic results of business activities in a highly complex and uncertain world. We also observed that a conceptual framework is not static but must evolve and adapt to changing business and investment environments, social values, and expectations for accountability. More specifically, we noted the need for cost/benefit trade-offs between relevance and reliability, and the challenge to develop accounting standards that effectively reconcile competing interests and at the same time are free of bias.

Standard setting in financial accounting thus involves difficult choices. The history of financial reporting for the last two centuries is the history of the evolution of ways of making these choices and of the standardization of financial reporting practices, at first through custom, and increasingly over time through a formal standard-setting process. It may be suggested that, to be successful, such process must have, and be seen to have, expertise, public responsibility, and independence from special interests. In this chapter we consider the process, how it has evolved, and the pressures for further development.

THE NATURE AND GOALS OF ACCOUNTING STANDARDS

The word "standard" can be used in several senses. In one meaning it refers to agreed-upon or legislated units of measure or specifications which, when applied to describe an object, provide assurance that it is what it is represented to be. Thus, because a standard description has been provided for a kilogram and a metre, we can know what we are getting when we buy something measured in those units. Or if we buy some piece of mechanical equipment approved by a standards association, we are provided with some assurance that it will perform in accordance with the specifications (or standards) of that association. In a similar way, the purpose of accounting standards is to provide the reader of a financial report with some assurance as to the significance and reliability of the information conveyed in the financial statements. Unfortunately, because of the uncertainty inherent in economic affairs, it is much more difficult to create effective accounting standards than it is to define physical measurement standards or standards of physical performance.

Goals of Standard Setting

The primary goal of standard setting is to facilitate achievement of the goals of financial reporting. These were discussed in the previous chapter. There it was concluded that faithful representation of relevant economic phenomena and events in a cost-effective manner provides the most satisfactory goal for financial reporting.

Also discussed in that chapter was the more ambitious goal of promotion of social welfare, and it is important to consider the implications of that goal for standard setting. The social welfare argument runs as follows. An accounting standard may be expected to favour some parties in society and harm the interests of others. Therefore the imposition of a standard is, in effect, a social choice. Some reason from this that standards should be consciously selected so as to promote social welfare, or that accounting standards should be appraised in terms of their probable economic consequences. This, however, merely leads to more questions. Since an important purpose of accounting is to give assistance in decision making, an effective standard ought to be expected to have economic consequences. The real question is whether the consequences are good or bad. That is a value judgment that few, if any, are qualified to make. Moreover, one should be skeptical of one's ability to truly assess economic consequences. In general, it appears that judging specific accounting standards by a social welfare criterion is likely to be impossible or completely lacking in objectivity.

An alternative conclusion drawn from the social choice line of thinking is that standard setting should be a political process. Those interested in or affected by proposed standards would lobby for their own interests. In the narrow interpretation of this view the test of a good standard would not lie primarily in its relevance to users or its faithful portrayal of economic events but simply in whether the appropriate political voting process was achieved. It is not hard to see that under this philosophy the wishes of organized forces with power behind them would prevail.

Acceptance of the conclusions from either of these two lines of thinking would be disastrous. Nothing could undermine the credibility of financial reporting among users more than knowledge that the amount of information released in financial reports has been determined by political horse trading or that the information itself may have been biased by some standard setters' opinions as to what is good for people to know.[1]

However, to say that accounting standards should not be politically motivated is far from saying that standard setters should not be aware of potential economic consequences and political influence. On the contrary, standard setters must be concerned that full and fair consideration has been given to the views and cost/benefit claims of all interested parties. In a broad sense, standards must rest upon general acceptance. But this acceptance should reflect the informed public interest. The achievement of fair financial presentation is a demanding technical process that must give consideration to the full range of interests, experience and knowledge that is relevant to the issues being addressed.

How does a standard-setting body balance these considerations? A former FASB member observed:

> The FASB has attempted to strike this balance by giving paramount consideration to agreed concepts, principles, and logical consistency in setting accounting standards. The answer produced by following this process is presumptively adopted, absent compelling evidence that cost/benefit and economic consequences would make the solution unacceptable.[2]

To achieve acceptance the process must be seen to be conducted in an unbiased fashion. Otherwise it may lack credibility. It is essential that a standard-setting body have enough authority and independence without, in the process, becoming an insensitive, bureaucratic structure. If standard setters do not explain the standards sufficiently to make them defensible against attack, and ensure that supporters of the standards as well as detractors are heard from, there is danger that particular standards or the standard-setting authority itself may be upset.

The question then is how to structure a standard-setting process to achieve these mixed goals? The following attempts a listing of certain basic elements that may be considered necessary for a standard-setting activity to be able to develop competent standards that can command broad acceptance.

- A persuasive conceptual framework with which individual standards can be shown to be consistent is essential, for all the reasons discussed in the preceding chapter.

- The body that is entrusted with the responsibility for standard setting should have sufficient independence and authority so as to be free from undue political influence. This would require that members of the body be selected through an unbiased process on the basis of their independence and competence, and that the body as a whole should contain, or have on staff, the necessary expertise. It must also must be sufficiently resourced to be able to fulfill its responsibilities on a timely basis.

- The standard-setting body must have an accountability to the public interest, and its standards must have a status that compels compliance with them. Effective public accountability requires that the process be open and that there be an independent monitoring of compliance.

- Thorough research of all aspects of an issue and publication of the results helps prepare the way for a standard. In particular, there is a need to learn from and integrate the implications of other disciplines for accounting. For example, economic theory concerning currency exchange rates is relevant to an accounting standard on foreign currency transactions and translation. Finance theory dealing with the valuation of options can help accounting measurements related to risk bearing. Research in human information processing may help with questions relating to the display of financial information. The challenge is both to make clear the practical application to accounting standards of such theory and research and to make that application known to those responsible for accounting standards.

- Standards should be issued only after "due process" allowing ample opportunity for interested parties to submit their views.

- The reasoning underlying standards arrived at and the reasons for rejecting major alternatives should be explained clearly and incisively. On those occasions when a standard prescribes some degree of arbitrariness in measurement in the interest of greater comparability, that should be frankly admitted. Where a standard requires complicated procedures unfamiliar to present practice, illustrations should be provided. Briefings and educational seminars may also be necessary.

Certain models for standard-setting have been proposed for achieving these ends. These are considered in a subsequent section.

The Scope of Accounting Standards

Accounting Standards and Professional Judgment

In the presence of uncertainty, the application of judgment is inevitable. But since accounting standards are intended to minimize uncertainty in accounting presentation, there must be a question where the boundary lies between those matters that are best covered by a standard and those that are best left to professional judgment.[3]

We may begin by observing that every accounting standard is a substitute for individual opinion or judgment. That is the point of having a standard. It is to get away from a chaotic situation in which each person's opinion is as good as the next person's. It is an attempt to substitute the *collective* judgment of the standard setters (who, it is to be hoped, will reflect the best thinking and evidence available) for that of individuals. The key question is: When should a collective judgment be embodied in a standard and when should the matter in question be left to the judgment of preparers and auditors?

To cast light upon this question, let us consider several possible applications of judgment in financial reporting.

- We talk in accounting about "measurement." As we use the term, measurement can rest upon factual information such as original cost or a current market quotation or upon an estimate involving the future such as that of an asset's economic life. Ordinarily a judgment estimate is highly dependent upon the facts of the situation in which it is made. There is a very strong case that situation-specific estimates should be left to the individual judgment of preparers and their auditors. There may, however, be exceptions. For example, suppose it were observed that, within a particular industry, estimates of useful lives of similar depreciable assets varied quite widely. Suppose, also, that investigation revealed little or no evidence of differences in circumstances justifying the differences in estimates. The varying estimates simply reflected varying degrees of optimism on the part of those making the estimates. In such a case, it would not be unreasonable for standard setters to demand that individual estimates be based on better evidence or, failing that, that some consensus or average estimate be used.

- Often accounting standards call for action based on such words as "likely," "reasonably estimable," or "significant." These words imply that an estimation judgment is to be made. They also require an additional judgment, however. The preparer or auditor must come to a conclusion as to what the words themselves mean before they can be applied. The requirement for the latter type of judgment is questionable. Statement preparers and auditors are not expert in semantics. Every effort should be made in accounting standards to avoid the necessity for readers to guess at the meaning of words. In practice, this suggests that the estimates called for should be described in more concrete, quantitative terms.[4]

- Occasionally standards may use such words or phrases as "meaningful," "proper accounting treatment," "most appropriate in the circumstances," or "which most fairly match revenue." Phrases such as these call for a judgment as to what are GAAP or what is in accordance with accounting theory (for example, the references to proper accounting or to fairly matching revenue). Such calls for judgment are essentially circular. It is the function of accounting standards to indicate what is good financial reporting. To instruct that preparers or auditors should exercise judgment as to what is acceptable or fair says nothing and, in effect, negates the objective of standard setting.

What do these examples tell us? They tell us that the primary role of accounting standards is to express a collective judgment as to the best accounting theory and its practical application. Standards for application are developed chiefly for accounting problems that can be categorized as having common characteristics. The more individual the characteristics of a problem, the less likely it is that standards, inevitably worded in general terms, can deal with it. The pre-eminent role of individual judgment lies in making estimates under uncertainty that are applicable in a specific situation. Standard setters often signal an intention that individual judgment be used through their choice of words. While this is legitimate, care is necessary to see that the objective sought by the standard is clearly specified. There may be some temptation for standard setters to avoid controversy by failing to make clear the objective of the standard and by using wording vague enough to admit several interpretations, under the guise of allowing individual judgment.[5]

Broad versus Detailed Standards

Often the issue of the role of professional judgment is stated in terms of making a choice between broadly stated standards—assumed to leave room for the exercise of professional judgment—and highly detailed rule making. In view of the immediately preceding discussion, such a statement can be seen to be a vast oversimplification. We have observed that, given the inherent uncertainties of future economic events that are at the basis of accounting, judgment can never be eliminated by detailed accounting rules. The hope is that the exercise of professional judgment will be enhanced by sound standards. It may be suggested that judgment in applying standards can be improved by taking steps to ensure that the goal of fair presentation is not lost sight of, working to clarify the principles on which standards are based, enriching measurements with supporting information, and providing a facility for interpretation of standards.[6]

In recent years both measurement and disclosure standards have been issued at an increasing pace and in increasing detail. Standards have tended to become more complex, mirroring the complexities in the transactions and the events they have to deal with. Some have complained that accounting standards are imposing an unreasonable burden on financial statement preparers. These complaints tend to be directed at the standards, not the underlying conditions that give rise to them. For example, accounting standards did not cause exchange rate instability; rather they had to adjust so as to try to provide realistic figures under the unstable conditions. A complaint concerning increased complexity in accounting standards is not logical unless the standards themselves fail to capture the essence of the economic phenomena being accounted for (as sometimes they do). Nevertheless, exasperation with the detail and complexity of accounting standards is real.

Some may advocate trying to simplify the standards notwithstanding the more complex economic environment. A movement toward simplification of standards probably would mean a movement away from accrual accounting and toward cash accounting. Such a movement may seem to have some attraction in the face of uncertainty. For example, the difficulty of dealing with uncertainty was a motive in the standard for expensing most R & D costs (see Chapter 12). Unfortunately, in a complex economic environment such simplification tends to run counter to faithful representation of economic events. Thus there are likely to be distinct limits to such simplification, and opinions are likely to differ sharply on how far it can be carried.

Differential Standards

The charge that accounting standards are unnecessarily complex is pressed most vigorously in relation to small business.[7] It is argued both that (1) the relative cost of complex accounting standards is greater for small business than for large because the small business may not have the skills in-house to make the computations necessary to implement complex standards, and (2) the benefit from complex standards is less or even nonexistent for small business because owner-managers do not understand them. What are the possibilities for differential standards—standards that are different for different classes of entity? The immediate problem is that of providing defensible criteria for distinguishing between different classes of reporting entity. One possible criterion could be that of size. But, quite small entities may enter into complex transactions that require careful accounting. Also, there is no strong evidence that users of financial statements of small entities do not need the same quality of information as is required from larger entities, and the existence of differential standards might well be confusing to some users.

Another possible criterion might be based on the degree of outside interest in the entity. Thus entities that do not have publicly traded securities outstanding might be permitted to follow less onerous standards than companies with a public interest. This proposal could also be questioned on the grounds that users of the financial statements of closely held companies, if not insiders, may well have a need for information of the same quality as that provided by public companies. In addition, some argue that the financial health and performance of large, closely held entities is of such importance to society that their financial reports should meet accepted standards for public reporting and be freely available even though a widespread ownership interest is lacking.

If a satisfactory basis for distinguishing between classes of entity were found—perhaps based upon a combination of size and public involvement—it would still be necessary to decide which standards should apply to each class of entity. It is often argued that disclosure standards should be less demanding for closely held entities where financial statement users may be more closely familiar with the entity or may be in a better position to obtain information from management as needed. On these grounds, for example, it is felt that such entities may be released from the necessity of providing a cash flow statement or supplementary information on segments of the business.

Some feel that there is no justification for different measurement standards between classes of entity. If, for example, the standards are well designed to measure the performance of a large entity, it is not obvious why different standards should be selected for another entity simply because it is small. There is some suggestion that cost/benefit considerations may justify the distinction. If the small entity is not already making the calculation on its own account and needs to obtain outside help to implement a standard, the relative cost of so doing may be considerably greater than for a larger entity. If, in addition, there are few report users for whom the information would make a difference, it may carry little benefit. This thinking has been followed to suggest that tax allocation accounting and lease capitalization might not be required for smaller entities.

It may be that it is not necessary to specify different standards for smaller, nonpublic, companies. The key problem is to arrive at some practical definition of entities whose financial reporting is unimportant from the standpoint of society at large. If such a definition can be framed, it would be possible to dispense with all but a very minimum financial reporting responsibility for such entities. It would then be up to those having financial or other dealings with such entities to contract with them for financial reports in whatever form is mutually satisfactory. For example, a bank extending credit might require a financial report prepared so as to meet normal standards, might be satisfied with a simplified statement, or might accept the statements prepared for taxation purposes. If the public interest in the financial report is minimal, there is no reason why the contracting parties should not make their own decisions on the form and extent of reporting. For this approach to be feasible in Canada, it would, of course, be necessary for corporations legislation to permit such freedom for defined classes of entity.

MODELS FOR STANDARD SETTING

In this section we consider possible mechanisms for arriving at financial accounting standards. This involves consideration of who should be entrusted with the responsibility for setting standards and the ultimate source of legitimacy for the standards.

We suggested, in Chapter 25, a progression of three broad scenarios in discussing the development of a conceptual framework for financial accounting: (1) private sector dominated, (2) capital markets dominated, and (3) a broad public stakeholder orientation. We posited that the primary thrust over the past several decades has been towards a more fully developed capital markets-driven orientation. We may consider possible models for accounting standard-setting within this context.

Voluntary Free-Market Standards

Let us consider how voluntary standards would be arrived at. This is, in fact, the situation that prevailed up until the 1930s in the United States and until still later in other English-speaking countries.

The foundation of recognized standards would be practice. Preparers of financial statements would be influenced in their choice of accounting method by observation of what other reporting entities were doing. The law might require that financial statements be "fairly presented" or give "a true and fair view." If not required by law, an assertion of fairness could be inferred from the very fact that a financial report is published. (To deliberately publish a misleading financial report could be considered fraud.) It would be believed that (1) the overriding requirement of fairness, (2) the power of precedent, and (3) the guidance given in accounting literature by authorities on the subject would combine to produce a consensus or "general acceptance" as to best methods of accounting in given circumstances.

A control over misleading reporting could be considered to exist through the medium of the audit. The auditor would be guided by the same understanding of theory and accepted practice as management. If the auditor were unable to issue an unqualified report, the financial statement reader would be made aware of possible questions concerning the integrity of management's representations. Associations of auditors might stimulate the process of general acceptance by providing studies of difficult questions and publishing recommendations as to best practice.

Certain advantages may be claimed for this model.

- Management would have considerable latitude for selecting accounting methods it considered best suited to its circumstances. Accordingly, there would be little likelihood that management would be forced to use different methods for external reporting than those it considered best for internal management reporting. In this way, accounting costs would be minimized.

- Enterprises would be free to experiment with new methods of accounting in new or changed economic circumstances. General acceptance would not become an inhibiting factor until such time as it became apparent that other entities did not consider the innovative accounting to be appropriate.

In support of this model it may be contended that the managements of reporting entities have an interest in providing sufficient information to satisfy those who provide resources needed by the enterprise. It is important to ask whether the preparers' self-interest in rendering financial reports is sufficient to result in satisfactory reports without outside intervention or the imposition of standards.[8]

Successful enterprises would be expected to have some incentive to encourage full disclosure because efficient capital markets should reward them with a lower cost of capital relative to their less successful brethren. One might think, then, that competition for capital would tend to force all enterprises to match the standards of the more successful.

However, even successful enterprises have some reasons to limit disclosure. Too much flaunting of success may attract competition and possibly unwelcome attention from government regulatory agencies. Also, it is commonly thought that a smooth record of progress is preferable to the ups and downs of normal business, so that even the managements of successful companies have some incentive to retain flexibility in financial reporting—which effectively means something less than full and unbiased reporting of events as they occur. Managements are also judged (sometimes unfairly) on results shown by financial reports in the short term. It is, therefore, quite natural for them to wish to retain some degree of control over how information is reported.

It must also be remembered that financial reporting is not without cost. External reporting of information that is routinely available from the accounting records or that is developed for purposes of internal reports to management does not entail significant incremental cost. Going beyond this may do so. This fact may help to explain managements' resistance to standards that require additional computations or valuations such as those involving tax allocation accounting, lease capitalization, and fair value measurement of financial instruments.

In the final result, it is observable that those responsible for financial reports generally desire that accounting standards be flexible and be stated in general terms, leaving considerable scope for judgment in the precise method of application of the general principles.[9]

Experience has shown serious problems with this model.

- General acceptance has not emerged in the absence of mandatory standards. Conflicting accounting practices among entities have been much in evidence when there are no obvious differences in economic circumstances to justify the different accounting. In fact, it would seem that the bad will tend to drive out the good. The abusive spread of pooling-of-interests accounting in the U.S. in the late 1960s and recent pressures from business interests in Canada for more extensive use of this accounting (see Chapter 19), and the continuance of cash basis accounting for post-employment benefits until standards were put in place (see Chapter 14), are two prominent examples of the tendency to poor accounting practices lacking externally imposed standards.

- Even when accounting measurements are not in dispute, the degree of disclosure can vary with substantial impact on the significance of the financial statements. The strong resistance encountered from time to time to proposals for disclosure of important information (such as the resistance over several decades to disclosure of sales and, later, to segment reporting) suggests that optimal financial reporting is unlikely to be achieved when responsibility is left solely in the hands of statement preparers.

It may be expected that the auditor would exert some control over misleading reporting. However, it seems clear from experience that, in the presence of wide diversity in generally accepted practice and the absence of mandatory standards, the auditor has little ability to impose improved accounting methods and disclosure upon clients.

Certainly auditors stand between the preparers and users of financial reports. They are charged with the responsibility of attesting to the fair presentation of financial statements. It is in their self-interest that the financial statements be fairly presented and be seen to be so presented, because otherwise their attestation loses credibility. But they can face great difficulties in achieving this objective. In particular, there is the difficulty of judging what is fair presentation when well-established practice does not clearly cover a particular situation. As well, there is the fact that the audit appointment is usually greatly influenced by management even when it is nominally made by the shareholders. The auditor is thus subject to contradictory forces. A well-understood conceptual framework for financial reporting and well-recognized broad principles of application are clearly in the self-interest of auditors. In general, auditors may be expected to feel a need for a detailed formulation of accounting standards in view of the possibilities for differences of opinion on complex issues and the consequent inevitability of inconsistent practice without rigorously defined rules of application. In the absence of a high degree of underlying consensus, auditors will be unable to discriminate between acceptable and unacceptable practice within quite a wide range.

The ultimate conclusion is that voluntary accounting standards are an unrealizable dream. Standards must be backed up by some authority.

Government-Mandated Standards

At the other extreme lies the possibility that accounting standards might be legislated by a government or a government agency. This would be a dramatic contrast to the situation in which accounting standards are controlled largely by those who have the obligation to report. A simple line of argument could be proposed in favour of such a shift. The reason for government involvement in the first place would be the belief that fair financial disclosure is in the public interest (for reasons such as promotion of efficiency of the capital markets or the importance of reliable financial information for public policy). It would be further believed that a government body could be independent of preparers and other vested interests.

The possible objections to government-established standards include the following:

- While a government may be independent of excessive influence from financial statement preparers, it might be open to pressures from other sources. The government itself might wish to bias accounting standards to attain certain ends and it may be susceptible to political pressures. To avoid these pressures, it would be necessary to give a governmental standard-setting agency the sort of independence that is granted to such bodies as the Bank of Canada and the Auditor General of Canada.

- There would be considerable danger that the standard-setting function would be underfunded and, as a result, would fail to command the best talents available. The status and independence of the agency would be factors in determining the importance of this difficulty.

- In maintaining its independence from pressures from the private sector, the staff of a government agency might tend to become cut off from first-hand experience with accounting issues, thereby losing some degree of competence.

- A bureaucratic organization might fail to be sufficiently sensitive to the costs associated with its reporting requirements and to the possibility that costs exceed benefits.

- A bureaucratic organization might tend to protect itself through the adoption of rigid rules, thereby limiting innovation and the exercise of judgment. It might also be reluctant to change a position once taken and might leave rules outstanding that have outlived their usefulness.

These outcomes are possible but not inevitable, especially if a conscious effort were made to guard against them. In Canada, there appears to be little support for the setting of accounting standards by government at the time of writing. A cost to the government would be involved that is now borne by the private sector. In addition, if the responsibility for standard setting were split among the provinces, as is securities administration at this time, the danger of underfunding and its attendant evils would be greatly multiplied.

Private Sector Standard-Setting Models

There are various possible private sector models. In Canada, standard setting has continued to rest with the accounting profession, more specifically with the CICA. A number of other countries, including the U.S., once had similar standard-setting bodies, but most have now replaced them with organizations that are independent of the accounting profession. In the U.S., the FASB replaced the APB, which was a creature of the public accounting profession, in 1973. More recently, in the U.K., the professional standard-setting body was replaced by an independent Accounting Standards Board.

In assessing private sector models, it is important to recognize that they are almost never fully private. Most have some working relationship with government to give them legitimacy and authority.

Mixed Government/Private Sector Standards

Various compromises are feasible by which responsibility for establishing accounting standards might be shared by the government and the private sector. One such compromise is found in the United States. The Securities and Exchange Commission is empowered by law to establish accounting standards for companies whose securities are publicly traded. It has never exercised that power to the full. It has directly established standards for disclosure in financial statements required to be filed with it. But, by and large, it has relied upon the private sector—first the accounting profession and latterly the FASB—to establish standards for accounting measurement. The distinction between disclosure and measurement does not have a great deal of intrinsic logic since both are necessary for fair presentation of financial information. Neither is the distinction inviolable in practice. The SEC has on occasion provided its interpretation of what accounting measurements ought to be or has indicated that it does not support standards for measurement arrived at in the private sector.

There are practical advantages to this sharing of responsibility. The SEC is relieved of a great deal of cost and gains access to a great deal of expertise through its reliance upon the private sector. For its part, the private sector is able to feel that accounting standards are, for the most part, set in a forum in which the interests of all are represented, rather than being handed down by fiat from an autocratic authority.

There are also disadvantages. Chief among these is the fragility of the arrangement. The FASB must obtain its funding from parties interested in financial reporting. Effectively, its efforts must satisfy most contributing parties most of the time. In view of the substantial differences of opinion possible over accounting standards, that is not easy to do. Indeed, one suspects that it is only by persistent reference to the need to retain standard-setting in the private sector that support is maintained. Moreover, the FASB's efforts can be undermined in other ways. Those dissatisfied with standards or proposed standards have sometimes been able to lobby the SEC or U.S. Congress for relief—a process that is inordinately harmful to orderly standard setting. The result has been politicization of the United States process for establishing accounting standards.

The Evolution of Private Sector Standards in Canada

In common with a number of countries, a private sector standard-setting body in Canada evolved out of efforts by the accounting profession to encourage good reporting. The difference between standards set by such bodies and those described earlier as voluntary or free-market standards lies solely in the greater authority of the standard-setting bodies. The development can be a gradual one, as epitomized by the Canadian experience.

Early Canadian accounting recommendations purported to be no more than guides to good practice. Unless a recommendation became accepted as the sole accounting method to fit the circumstances, a recommendation might have little practical influence. Chapter 4 has recounted how that condition gradually changed. The most notable event was the adoption of National Policy No. 27 by Canadian Securities Administrators in 1972. Under that policy and subsequently under corporations legislation of the federal and several provincial governments, the term "generally accepted accounting principles" is interpreted to mean the recommendations in the *CICA Handbook*. The recommendations thereby became accounting standards required by law for most public corporate financial reports.

The resulting position cannot be described simply as a state in which accounting standards are set in the private sector, since the support rendered by the governmental recognition is an essential element. Nevertheless, the formulation of the standards themselves has remained the prerogative of a private sector institution—the CICA. There have been several advantages to this situation. Standards have been established without cost to the government. Standard setting has been largely free from political interference. The CICA has had access through its membership to the advice and service of volunteers with a wide range of experience in financial reporting problems. The CICA budget, financed by its membership, has permitted funding of research and employment of staff.

This historical development in Canada has occurred without a great deal of conscious thought as to its implications. In their early days, the membership of provincial institutes of chartered accountants and of the CICA consisted largely of *public* accountants. The institutes were formed to create qualifying standards for service to the public and to promote recognition of the special skills of their members. There was a strong tendency to equate accounting as a profession with public accountancy. It was natural for an association largely composed of auditors, much of whose work lay in giving opinions on fair presentation of financial statements, to be especially concerned with criteria for fair reporting. And it was well within the rights of the members to consult together and provide recommendations or even rules binding on the membership as to the terms upon which members should be prepared to express unqualified opinions on financial statements presented to them for audit.

In short, the auditing profession has a major stake in the fairness and usefulness of financial reports. The auditing profession's livelihood depends upon its reputation for being able to add credibility to the financial statement assertions of management, so that they are relevant and reliable for external user purposes. Thus there is a natural correspondence between the interests of the auditing profession and users.

We have noted that, when the auditor deals with the management of his or her client directly, the possibility of pressing the user viewpoint vigorously is limited by the fact that the auditor has a practical need to retain the goodwill of the management. When auditors act together through their professional association, however, a better balance is possible. It is arguable that a strong motivation behind the formation of the professional standard-setting body was the desire of auditors to find some way to counterbalance preparer control of financial reports and the resulting potential bias.

On balance, recommendations made in the *CICA Handbook*, largely upon the initiative of auditors, have been reasonably evenhanded in reflecting the views and needs of both statement preparers and users. It is this fact that justified securities administrators and legislators in giving special place to the *CICA Handbook* in the scheme of regulation of financial reporting. Such reliance implies that it must be acknowledged by the CICA and its membership that the standard-setting function entrusted to it is in the public interest. That means that the function must be performed efficiently. It also means that the self-interest of members must be subordinated should it conflict with the public interest in standard setting.

THE FORCES OF CHANGE

The Existing System

At the time this is written, the basic features of the Canadian process may be summarized as follows:

- The thirteen member complement of the Accounting Standards Board are all unpaid volunteers reflecting a variety of backgrounds. Practising public accountants no longer constitute a majority of the board.

- The board is supported by professional staff of the CICA, all of whom have public accounting or business accounting experience, but for the most part, staff have had little or no academic accounting or finance theory or research backgrounds.

- Most significant projects have been developed by separate task forces, whose members are unpaid volunteers selected to provide a variety of backgrounds and experience relevant to the subject areas of the project. The research and analysis support for task forces is provided by CICA professional staff. The CICA also has a separate research department that commissions studies in accounting, auditing and other areas. In recent years, it has allocated much of its limited resources to nonaccounting areas.

- When the necessary majority of the board is prepared to endorse a proposed standard, an exposure draft is published, which is widely disseminated for comment. Comment letters are carefully considered, and in recent years, a special effort has been made to reach individuals and entities that may be assumed to have a special interest in the subject. Invariably, changes are made as a result of comments received. If these changes represent changes to important principles proposed in the exposure draft, or new principles are introduced, a revised exposure draft may be issued. A final standard is adopted with the approval of at least two-thirds of the board members.

- The board has been advised by a Standards Advisory Board which includes representatives of major stakeholder interests, including securities and bank regulators, the legal and actuarial professions, and the financial analyst community. This advisory group has not met during the past few years, however.

- A separate Emerging Issues Committee, consisting of fourteen unpaid volunteers, drawn mainly from expert accountants in the major accounting firms and business and financial enterprises, considers matters requiring interpretation of CICA standards and emerging issues. It issues brief "abstracts" outlining its judgment on these issues. These are included in a separate section of the *CICA Handbook*. In order to issue an abstract, twelve of the fourteen members must agree.

This process has served the Canadian public interest reasonably well, but recently several developments have given rise to a need to rethink the purposes and process of accounting standard-setting in Canada. The following problem areas may be singled out for attention:

- Increasingly, there have been questions as to the independence of a standard-setting body that is controlled by one professional accounting body, and there have been some pressures for a more widely representative process.

- Some have urged a more open process that provides better opportunity for interested parties to be heard and consulted. At the same time, there is concern that provisions for "due process" be better balanced with the need for more timely standards.

- There are grounds for concern that vital standard-setting support activities, including research, monitoring, enforcement and education activities are inadequate, given the extent of change and the complexity of accounting issues.

- The internationalization of business and investment activities, and demands for harmonization of accounting standards internationally, and more specifically, with the U.S., are seriously challenging the purpose of Canadian standards and their long-term viability.

- The costs of independent standard setting and related activities have greatly increased in recent years, while at the same time, CICA professional staff resources and the commitment of volunteers have been declining. Thus, there are major concerns whether the CICA can continue to take full responsibility for the process, or whether a more broadly financed authority should be established.

We will briefly discuss each of these areas, and indicate changes that have been proposed and that are scheduled for implementation at the time this is written.

Issues of Independence and Representation

In the U.S., a major reason for the demise of the APB, and its replacement by the FASB, was a perception that the APB lacked independence. It appeared to cynical observers that APB members, the majority being partners of public accounting firms, were open to pressures from important clients that could result in standards being biased toward preparer interests. Although there was no solid evidence of this, the potential for bias was seen to be real enough to seriously damage the credibility of the APB as a standard-setting body. Concerns with respect to undue preparer influence have continued to arise periodically with respect to the process of appointing FASB members.[10] The relative independence of the FASB in comparison to the APB has been achieved by highly paying board members for significant (five-year) terms and by requiring them to sever relationships with their former businesses or firms.

In Canada, members of the CICA Accounting Standards board continue to be unpaid volunteers. We noted earlier the suggestion that a board with a significant number of its members from public accounting practice may be expected to have a natural tendency to counter potential preparer bias, because auditors have a major stake in ensuring that accounting standards are well defined and provide reliable bases for giving opinions on the fairness of financial statements. However, this argument appears to have lost much of its force in recent years. Public accounting practitioners no longer dominate the board and, more important, the business of major public accounting firms has become increasingly focused on management consulting activities, with auditing declining in importance. Board members from public accounting firms thus have a greater incentive to see issues from the perspective of business management rather than user interests.

Some argue that concerns about preparer bias are overstated—that a responsible person should be able to separate the role of standard setting in the public interest from his or her position as a preparer, auditor or user. Certainly competent standard setting requires a variety of expertise and experience, so that it makes sense to ask a variety of organizations to nominate "representatives," with the proviso that they should be chosen for the wisdom they can bring to the standard-setting process, not as representatives sent to bargain for a particular point of view. Nevertheless, the perspective a business person, public accountant, or user brings to standard setting may be expected to be coloured by his or her background and work setting. In any event, in the end it is the perception of the public as to the possibility of bias (whether conscious or not) that could damage the credibility of the standard-setting function.

In addition, other accounting associations in Canada have their own qualifying requirements and regard their members as professionals. These associations complain that they are unreasonably excluded from the standard-setting process controlled by the CICA. Sensitivity to these concerns has led the CICA to reserve some positions on its Accounting Standards Board for nominees of other bodies, including representatives of accounting academia and financial executives as well as other accounting associations. These moves have not fully satisfied other accounting associations.

The CICA Board of Governors recently commissioned a task force to review the CICA's standard-setting activities. Its report, issued in May 1998, concluded that the accounting standard-setting function should remain in the private sector and that the CICA should continue to assume the leadership role, while securing additional funding from external sources.

It recommended a smaller board of not more than nine members, selected to ensure an appropriate balance of competencies and experience. The members would continue to be unpaid volunteers, except for a full-time paid chair. It further recommended establishing an Accounting Standards Oversight Council, to replace the Standards Advisory Board. It would be broadly representative of significant interest groups. Rather than simply providing advice, it would take an active role in determining the board's priorities, in appointing board members, and in reviewing and reporting to the public on the board's performance.[11] It is expected that changes along these lines will be implemented in late 1999, although the sources of additional funding seem yet to be well defined.

Due Process and Timeliness Issues

At one time the making of accounting recommendations was regarded very much as a technical matter. However, once *CICA Handbook* recommendations became virtually binding standards and their public interest character recognized, the need for "due process" in setting standards came to be accepted. Due process means simply that adequate publicity has been given to the deliberations and intentions of the standard setters and all interested parties have had an opportunity to be heard. A primary objective is to make sure that all information and data relevant to an issue is available to the standard setters.

A large measure of openness in the standard-setting process is desirable, for the simple reason that it may result in eliciting information bearing on the subject under consideration that otherwise would not be available. From a political standpoint, emphasis is placed on providing for free expression of all opinions, and having an open decision-making process to avoid suspicion that the conclusions of the decision makers are subject to undue influence.

In the past, due process has largely centred on developing and giving wide dissemination to exposure drafts reflecting the board's considered proposals for *CICA Handbook* standards. A most important question for the standard-setting process is whether an exposure draft is successful in eliciting responses that are (1) sufficiently representative of all points of view, and (2) likely to uncover all potential pitfalls and problems not foreseen by the standard-setting board. It has become apparent that, while the exposure draft process is very important, it cannot be relied upon in itself to achieve these purposes. Experience with standards on contingencies (Chapter 8) and on the presentation and disclosure of financial instruments (Chapter 9) well illustrate this. In both cases, exposure drafts were issued, and significant consultations carried out. But it was not until standards were developed that key constituencies fully focused their attentions on them, and they then voiced significant opposition to them. In the one case (contingencies) the standard ended up being withdrawn and in the other case (disclosure and presentation of financial instruments) some significant interpretation questions were raised that required further analysis. These incidents may have served to damage the credibility of the board, despite its significant efforts to elicit responses through the exposure draft process.

If it is the case that most respondents, including public accounting firms (who had been counted upon to carry out thorough analyses of CICA proposals) are not prepared to analyze proposed standards in depth, then additional procedures must be undertaken. These should include rigorous field testing by CICA staff (who need to improve their expertise in field test research) in cooperation with key affected interests. Increased use of focus groups of affected interests, public meetings and the Internet may also help. The possible additional cost should be balanced against the possible gain in information.

The FASB extends its public exposure two ways. For major projects a discussion memorandum may be prepared by the staff with the assistance of an advisory task force and made public. This discussion memorandum provides an organized and comprehensive review of issues relating to the particular topic and permits a linkage of possible provisions in the standard with underlying theory or reasoning that is much better than that found in the typical exposure draft. Public hearings are held after the issuance of discussion memorandums, and as part of the exposure draft process, to increase the dialogue between standard setters and interested parties. By these means the FASB unquestionably broadens its exposure to different points of view.

It is to be noted that CICA staff have been attempting to improve awareness of board activities and proposals, for example, through its "FYI" publication and the CICA web site. As well, it has carried out some field studies and consultations with key interests to try to uncover potential problems on certain issues. However, these efforts have been constrained by cost and staff resource limitations (to be discussed in a subsequent section). The CICA Task Force on Standard Setting advocated "outreach programs," to identify those individuals and organizations that should be heard from on a particular issue and elicit information directly from them.[12]

Another significant question is whether board meetings should be open to the public. The FASB has open board meetings, and the IASC will open its board meetings to the public beginning in 1999. The FASB's experience has been largely positive, although there have been some potential drawbacks. What exactly constitutes a board meeting has had to be carefully defined, along with rules on how many board members can be in the same place at the same time without having to give due notice of a public meeting. A practice has developed of holding "pre-board" meetings of small groups of board members to prepare for public meetings. Some have expressed concern that open meetings of a volunteer board may lead to posturing by members, who may be reluctant to take public positions on controversial issues that may not be popular with their business colleagues and clients.

On the other hand, the benefits of openness include increased public awareness and, potentially at least, increased public confidence in the fairness and credibility of the standard-setting process. Certainly, there is a strong case that a process that develops standards that are effectively embodied in the law should be an open one. The CICA Task Force on Standard Setting, however, believes the Canadian board's decisions should continue to be made in private.[13]

Emerging Issues

The trade-off between due process and timeliness warrants careful attention. The development of a standard takes time, often in excess of two or three years. The extension of due process has served to lengthen the time frame. It has been recognized that there needs to be a quicker process for dealing with emerging and interpretive issues. Such issues often arise suddenly. For example, a government action or change in legislation may give rise to questions that need quick answers. Undesirable accounting practices with respect to novel types of transactions can take root and can be difficult to eradicate subsequently. However much we may deplore the fact, in the real world statement preparers on occasion have powerful reasons for preferring one treatment over another, and these reasons may have nothing to do with what is sound accounting in a technical sense. In such situations, any ambiguity in the wording of a standard, or any wording that seems to offer a loophole for arguing the merits of a particular position, may be exploited. Such ambiguities or loopholes will often exist, since no board can write flawless standards, nor is it possible to foresee every situation to which a standard may be applied.

The CICA has two means of addressing emerging and interpretive issues:

- Following the lead of the FASB, the CICA established an Emerging Issues Committee in 1989. To date it has issued over ninety abstracts.

- The Accounting Standard Board can issue guidelines. These have been issued rather sparingly in recent years.

The issuance of EIC abstracts and guidelines do not involve the extent of due process required to issue a *CICA Handbook* standard. Thus, there is some potential for abuse in subverting the normal procedures for openness, exposure of proposals for public comment and opportunity for all interested parties to respond and have their views considered. There can be a rather fuzzy line between an emerging or interpretive issue and a standard-setting issue requiring full due process. Further, while EIC interpretations and guidelines may be said to have less authority than standards, in practice they become presumptive standards. Securities commissions, for example, view guidelines and abstracts as defining GAAP.

On balance, it is accepted that there must be a facility for providing timely authoritative guidance on emerging and interpretive issues. The broad framework or theory governing present accepted accounting practice is sufficiently well established that EIC abstracts and guidelines can be provided even where a specific standard governing the issue is not stated in the *CICA Handbook*. It is very important, however, that there be clearly defined terms of reference and controls over these interpretive processes. The EIC process, for example, calls for a super majority (twelve of fourteen members) to approve an abstract, and it is ultimately accountable to the board, which could overrule it. The limits on the issuance of guidelines by the board is not so well defined, but there have been no obvious instances of abuse. If significant external interests object to a lack of due process on issues that may be considered to go beyond mere interpretations, the board would presumably have to address them as full standard-setting issues.

Necessary Supporting Activities

The standard-setting process does not operate in isolation. It is but one part of a larger system. Achieving fair financial reporting requires that each of the activities described below be in place and operate effectively. The complexity of accounting issues and the extent of changes in underlying concepts and technology (discussed in preceding chapters) have put immense pressures on these supporting activities.

Research

Since standards should be based on informed judgment of the standard setters, it is natural to consider what research support should be available. Research for this purpose may take several forms. First, there is descriptive research designed to discover and report factual information on how business is carried on, how calculations are made, or how the economy works. For example, considerable factual knowledge of leasing arrangements, the working of options and futures markets, actuarial methods of calculation of pension costs and accrued liabilities, and the operation of foreign exchange markets are necessary before accounting standards in these areas can be intelligently considered.

Second, there is what may be called analytical research. The relationship between the problem area under consideration and general accounting and economic theory is traced. Based on this and on the specific characteristics of the problem, issues are identified, and possible paths of reasoning are worked out leading to possible solutions.

Third, there is research into the costs and benefits of standards and their possible economic impact and information value. Much accounting research carried out in universities is empirical research of this nature (see discussion in Chapter 4). While this research is important, there has been criticism that financial accounting has been lacking an adequate academic base in sound analytical research.[14]

In practice, effective research is time-consuming and expensive. Identifying and resolving accounting issues requires a mix of descriptive, analytical and empirical research. Frequently it must draw on evidence and theories outside the discipline of accounting per se. In previous chapters we have seen the influence of finance economics, statistical probability, and other behavioural disciplines on the development of accounting thinking. The extent and sophistication of research necessary to support effective standard-setting requires a substantial investment. Increasingly, accounting standard setters are joining forces to share the load and work together towards internationally agreed-upon solutions. Examples include the G4+1 series of studies, the joint project between the FASB and CICA on segment reporting (see Chapter 23), and between the FASB and IASC on earnings per share (Chapter 23), and joint efforts of standard setters to address accounting for financial instruments (Chapter 17) and business combinations (Chapter 19).

Monitoring the Effectiveness of Standards

It is important that there be a systematic monitoring for compliance with standards, both as the basis for an enforcement function (see below) and to bring to light any need to modify standards, or to provide additional interpretation or guidance. The standard-setting body should also periodically review standards to identify those that are obsolete or no longer required. Rigorous monitoring and updating has become more onerous (and more important) as the body of standards has grown in size and complexity, and as the effects of change have multiplied and intensified. A responsibility to monitor standards has long been recognized.[15] However, the CICA, in common with standard-setting authorities in most other countries, has not devised a systematic monitoring activity.

Enforcement of Standards

Without enforcement of compliance with standards, the process may be undermined. The tradition in this country has been largely to rely on self-regulation by the professional institutes of chartered accountants. This is a quiet process that is not widely observable by the public, and it has been suggested that professional accountants may be reluctant to criticize their peers. Enforcement by the courts has tended to be uneven, and too late. In the U.S., the SEC plays a powerful role in policing U.S. accounting standards in respect of public enterprises. In Canada, provincial securities commissions, led by the OSC, have this role, but they have not had the resources to do as effective a job as the SEC. It may be time for a thorough review of the enforcement of Canadian accounting standards in the public's interest.

Education

Perhaps the most important of all the support activities is that of continuing education, particularly for the accounting profession, but also for users, preparers and regulators. It is disturbing to note the paucity of in-depth courses and guidance material on new accounting standards and developing accounting theories and issues—and the general lack of informed debate of accounting matters within the accounting profession in Canada. In these times of major change, there is a danger that the critical mass of practising public accountants will lose its expertise and knowledge base in its essential financial accounting discipline.

The best of standards will not be effective if they are not well enough understood to be reasonably applied as intended. It has been a major thesis of this book that a good working understanding of individual accounting standards requires a thorough grounding in accounting theory and its genesis in economics, capital markets practices and academic research. It is not enough just to read the standards. The report of the CICA Task Force on Standard Setting has noted the importance of education and training, but it made no specific recommendations.

In summary, a combination of supporting activities must be present to make the accounting standard-setting process effective. The above analysis suggests that there are strong grounds for believing that these functions need to be upgraded and revitalized in Canada.

The Challenge of International and U.S. Accounting Standards

The IASC and the Internationalization of Standard Setting

Accounting standards have traditionally been developed in national settings. The need for national standards has often been stimulated by government pressures and local laws and institutions. Users of financial reports, however, are not confined within national borders. In particular, capital flows across boundaries. It is obviously in the interests of efficient allocation of capital that reporting standards be harmonized internationally.

The globalization of capital markets and business and investment practices has profoundly accelerated the demand for convergence between national accounting standards and for a common international base of standards. Investors do not confine their investments to enterprises within their national jurisdictions but seek international diversification. Their efforts to compare the reported financial results of enterprises located in different countries can be confounded by different accounting practices. Business enterprises seeking to raise capital internationally face the costs and complications of preparing their financial statements to meet, or reconcile with, several different bodies of national standards. This is necessary in order to conform to particular national securities or corporations laws, or simply to provide financial information on bases that will be familiar to foreign investors.

The goal of developing a common base of international accounting standards is not new. The International Accounting Standards Committee (IASC) was formed in 1973, and it has issued a series of international standards. Until recently, its standards accommodated a large number of alternatives. This resulted from a desire to avoid significant conflicts with standards of influential participating countries. This tended to dilute their impact, although they did make a worthwhile contribution to improving financial reporting in many countries. In recent years, the IASC has made a concentrated effort to eliminate alternatives, and to develop a set of standards that could be sufficiently robust and comprehensive to be suitable for cross-border capital raising and listing purposes in all global markets.

In 1995, it was agreed with the International Organization of Securities Commissions (IOSCO) that the IASC would carry out a very ambitious series of projects to complete a mutually agreed upon core set of standards. IOSCO would then consider endorsing these standards for use in cross-border listings. The program was completed at the end of 1998, and IOSCO is now going through an evaluation process. The OSC and the SEC are important members of the IOSCO working party that is conducting this evaluation.

There is growing international support for IASC standards. Among other developments:

- IASC standards have been adopted voluntarily by some large multinational companies.

- Belgium, France, Germany and Italy, among other countries, have recently decided that certain significant companies within their jurisdictions can base their consolidated financial statements on IASC standards in place of existing national requirements.

- The Australian Accounting Standards Board is currently working towards eliminating differences between its national standards and those of the IASC.

The IASC is currently considering major structural changes to its standard-setting process. Its present board, comprising sixteen delegations and a number of observers, is cumbersome. As well, national delegations tend to be appointed by professional accounting associations which may not represent their national accounting standard-setting authorities. For example, the FASB has only observer status on the IASC Board. The U.S. delegation is appointed by the AICPA.

A strategic working party, chaired by a Canadian, has recommended that a smaller technical body be set up on which national standard setters would play the major role. This body would be overseen by a larger board that would have a wider, more representative membership than at present. This board would be responsible for final approval of IASC standards and exposure drafts.[16] These recommendations are controversial as they strive to strike a balance between the objectives of (1) technical competence (based on a partnership with major national standard setters), and (2) a political process that will give representation to major affected interests. There is concern in some quarters that the IASC standard-setting process not be dominated by the U.S., or G4 standard setters. On the other hand, there are concerns that the IASC process not be open to being undermined by political compromise.

Canada has been represented on the IASC board since the beginning.[17] For many years, compliance with Canadian GAAP would, with few exceptions, mean compliance in significant respects with IASC standards, since the latter allowed many alternatives. However, there are now a number of significant differences between Canadian and IASC standards, as IASC standards have been expanded and improved.[18]

Although Canada has played a prominent role at the IASC, for the most part the impact of international standards on Canadian practice has not been very noticeable.[19] To date there has been little interest in IASC standards on the part of most Canadian companies.[20] Canadian companies looking to raise capital outside Canada have most often gone to the U.S. When they have gone abroad, they have, for the most part, been able to raise money on the strength of Canadian GAAP. But this is in the course of change. If the IASC achieves the leadership role in global standard setting, Canadian enterprises could be disadvantaged if Canadian standards are inconsistent with IASC standards and could expect to have to present reconciliations of differences between IASC and Canadian standards in the notes to their financial statements.

There are other important international activities. As previously noted, national standard setters in Australia, Canada, New Zealand, the U.K. and the U.S. have formed a group (on which the IASC has observer status) (called the "G4+1"). Its objective is to seek common solutions to difficult financial reporting issues and to promote these solutions in a series of studies. As well, an American organization of standard setters (including Chile, Canada, Mexico and the U.S.) was formed in the early 1990s. Thus far its primary focus has been on understanding and reconciling differences in accounting practices between the member countries.[21]

There is clearly an increasing tendency for major accounting issues to be addressed in an international context.

The Pull from the U.S.

A more immediate challenge to Canadian standards is presented by U.S. accounting standards. Historically (as we have seen throughout this book), U.S. accounting literature and practice have had a substantial influence on the development of Canadian GAAP. Indeed, many innovations in Canadian accounting have had their origins south of the border. The CICA board has, nevertheless, maintained its independence to determine for itself what should be required by Canadian standards. As demonstrated in the preceding chapters, it has not infrequently chosen a different direction from that of the U.S. on particular issues, although its basic framework and fundamental concepts are the same. This has served Canada well, by and large, over the years. However, some significant cracks have been appearing in the support for this independence.

In the past few years pressures from some large business interests in Canada for increased harmonization with, or even adoption of, U.S. GAAP have been all but overwhelming. At the root of these pressures is the very extensive "North Americanization" of business, presumably stimulated in significant part by the North American Free Trade Agreement. Some claim that Canadian enterprises are put at a competitive disadvantage with U.S. enterprises by being required to report on the basis of accounting standards that differ from U.S. GAAP. Business combination accounting provides a specific example; the Canadian standard severely restricts an enterprise's ability to account for business combinations by the "pooling-of-interests" method. Canadian banks and high-tech companies claim that this has put them at a serious disadvantage with U.S. competitors. They have requested that the CICA abandon its standard for that of the U.S., even though the Canadian standard has been in place for almost twenty-five years, and its restriction of pooling-of-interest accounting is widely acknowledged (even by the FASB) as superior in concept and information value to U.S. GAAP (see discussion of this issue at Chapter 19).

Some Canadian companies that issue securities in the U.S. have requested permission from provincial securities commissions to adopt U.S. GAAP for reporting in Canada, in order to simplify their reporting and reduce costs. It is to be noted that the SEC has always accepted Canadian company registrants financial statements prepared on the basis of Canadian GAAP, but it requires a note explaining and reconciling the income effects of significant differences with U.S. GAAP. Some claim that these reconciliations have become increasingly costly to prepare and that they tend to confuse rather than enlighten investors on both sides of the border.

In 1993, the OSC carried out a survey of the differences reported in these GAAP reconciliation notes.[22] It confirmed that there were many reported differences between U.S.

and Canadian GAAP and that they could have material effects on reported net income. This was hardly news, but at the same time it cited an empirical study that indicated that the U.S./Canadian GAAP reconciliation note disclosures provide no incremental information value to investors.[23]

It is difficult to interpret these seemingly contradictory findings. Some might believe this demonstrates that Canadian GAAP has no information value over U.S. GAAP, thus perhaps supporting the case for allowing Canadian companies the option of reporting in U.S. GAAP. Alternatively, the findings might be interpreted to mean that the GAAP differences reflect real differences in circumstances between Canada and the U.S., that is, that there is no incremental information value in a Canadian GAAP reconciliation to U.S. GAAP because U.S. GAAP give the wrong answers in a Canadian context. Or it might be that there is information content in the disclosures, or some portions of them, but that the testing methodology was not extensive or powerful enough to detect it.[24]

The OSC solicited comments on its survey report. It subsequently indicated that it had no plans to change its existing policies, which require Canadian company registrants to report on the basis of Canadian GAAP, except in a few rare cases where an enterprise's operations, resources and security holders are essentially based in the U.S.

In 1994, the CICA Board of Governors established an Inter-Institute Vision Task Force (VTF) to articulate a vision for the chartered accountancy profession for the twenty-first century. The impetus for this initiative was concern that the traditional areas of accounting and auditing have seemed to be declining in importance. One of the VTF conclusions was that the profession could no longer afford to focus on Canadian-based standards for accounting and auditing in a global marketplace. It suggested that efforts be made to eliminate differences in accounting with the U.S. Specifically it recommended that the CICA "harmonize accounting and auditing standards globally, with a particular focus on developing common standards on an integrated basis ..., first in North America and then internationally."[25] The VTF expressed the view that such harmonization should enable a re-allocation of significant CICA funding from the accounting standard-setting function to other areas of "strategic importance to the profession's pre-eminence." The previously noted CICA Task Force on Standard Setting was established by the board of governors to review all the CICA standard-setting activities in response to the VTF report. The CICA Task Force on Standard Setting reached quite different conclusions with respect to accounting standard setting from that of the VTF. While it strongly supported the principle of international harmonization of accounting, it proposed a broader view of "harmonization":

> Our Task Force views standards as being harmonized when they have been arrived at following
> a process of input and negotiation among the relevant standard-setting bodies ... (page 12).

It concluded that Canada should not confine itself to a regional North American orientation, but should continue to play a significant role on the broader international scene and retain its ability to set unique Canadian accounting standards where circumstances warrant.

> ... we see harmonization as involving a two-pronged approach focusing on eliminating differences between existing standards and on working jointly with other major national and international standard-setting bodies to ensure that, in developing future standards, differences do not occur (page 12).

The task force thus envisaged an active role, which it acknowledged would require significantly more, not less, resources.

The essential question is how should Canadian standards be set in the future? This question might be best approached by asking, first, why should there be any differences between Canadian and U.S. GAAP? Certainly, Canada and the U.S. have much in common. They have very similar capital markets-based, free enterprise economies. Capital and goods move fairly easily between the two countries. Preparer and user interests in accounting information in each country may be expected to see enterprise assets and liabilities and profits and losses measured and presented in like ways. As we observed in Chapter 25, the two countries have essentially the same conceptual accounting frameworks. However, there are, as our analyses of earlier chapters attest, many difficult accounting issues on which different answers may be justified within this common framework. Can there be any valid basis for different answers to these issues between Canada and the U.S.? On the one hand, it might be contended that differences are likely to be more the result of there being two standard-setting bodies than any in-substance reasons. Any two different bodies operating independently are almost sure to arrive at somewhat different conclusions on complex issues. This problem is compounded because the style, wording and detail of the U.S. and Canadian standards differ. As a result, even if the fundamental principles of a Canadian and U.S. standard on a particular matter are the same, differences in the way the standards are expressed will tend to lead to the presumption that they are different—especially if the words are literally interpreted.

One may be tempted to conclude from this that there should be one North American standard setter, and that the Canadian authority could take a reduced role, perhaps even become a "free rider" on the back of FASB standards. But the reasons for some U.S.–Canadian GAAP differences may lie more deeply.

- Canadian enterprises face some significant differences in economic circumstances from those typically faced by U.S. enterprises. For example, the U.S. dollar is a dominant currency while the Canadian dollar is a secondary one. Many Canadian enterprises borrow in the dominant U.S. currency as a natural hedge against exchange risk on future expected sales in U.S. dollars. This has given Canadians a different perspective on foreign currency and foreign currency hedging issues (see Chapter 21). Other examples where the Canadian position may give rise to some differences in perspective on accounting issues include the following:
  - differences in tax laws and tax and government grant incentives (the *CICA Handbook* has a different position on investment tax credits than the U.S.—see Chapter 15);
  - less developed markets for certain financial instruments (giving rise to differences in the use of nonderivatives for hedging purposes (see discussion of this issue at Chapter 17);
  - greater concentrations in certain industries (for example, in the extractive industries, giving Canada some different perspectives on what accounting priorities should be); and
  - differences in the banking system.
- U.S. and Canadian standard setters are subject to different political systems and vested interest pressures that may shape choices on difficult accounting issues differently. Underlying the balancing of competitive interests in financial information may be some differences in the two societies' values (embodied in laws and practices) with respect to trading off the public's "right to know" with businesses' rights to privacy and protection of information from competitive adversarial interests. The question—who is accountable to whom and for how much?—might be answered somewhat differently in the two countries.

Thus, while the U.S. and Canadian general environments are very similar, there may be some subtle, and perhaps not-so-subtle, differences which may lead to different conclusions on accounting issues, and accounting priorities.

Viewed in this broader perspective there may be some cause for concern about the VTF's suggestion to integrate standard setting on a North American basis. It is hard to see how such a basis would not be dominated by the U.S., especially if there were to be a reduced allocation of CICA resources. The FASB and SEC have no mandate to consider the Canadian public interest as it may differ from that of the U.S. The view of the U.S. is undoubtedly influenced by its position as a dominant world economic power, and by its unique political institutions. It could not be relied upon to appreciate the issues and priorities as seen from a Canadian perspective. Canadian interests may have much more in common with a number of other smaller countries, and it may benefit from the broader, more representative constituency of the IASC. The real test may be to ask informed Canadians whether they would be prepared to accept whatever accounting and disclosures the FASB and SEC determine to be appropriate. It is crystal clear, however, that the days when Canada could have unique standards without consideration of U.S. and international implications are over. Canada cannot afford to have unnecessary differences with U.S. standards, or IASC standards.[26]

In an ideal world there would be one internationally agreed-upon set of accounting standards, and like circumstances would be accounted for in like ways no matter where the reporting enterprise is domiciled. But this is not an ideal world.

Over the long term, national standards may be expected to give way to international standards, with national standard-setting bodies largely concentrating on interpreting international standards to fit the legal and economic circumstances of their particular jurisdictions. However, for the present, the best course for Canada may be, as the CICA Task Force on Standard-Setting has recommended: (1) to maintain its independence to make its own standard-setting determinations, (2) to actively participate in the international standard setting, and (3) to work to eliminate differences with U.S. and IASC standards that cannot be justified.

But the course proposed by the task force is not an easy one. It will require a firm line if it is to be successful. There would seem to be considerable dangers that, without a strong Canadian standard-setting authority and strong supporting activities (with respect to research, monitoring, compliance enforcement and education), Canadian standard-setting will be eroded by the influence of U.S. GAAP.

The practical situation is that any new U.S. standard is likely to automatically become acceptable in Canada unless the area covered by the standard has already been dealt with within the *CICA Handbook* and the Canadian standard clearly precludes the American position. A good test of this is provided by SFAS No. 133 on the fair value measurement of derivatives and hedge accounting. Many of the requirements of this standard (relating to embedded derivatives and "fair value" hedging, for example) are new and not addressed even indirectly in CICA standards, and they have no precedent in Canadian practice. Such standards could lead to an increase in the diversity of accepted accounting practice in Canada. Worse, unless strong direction is provided by the standard-setting authority (including the EIC), entities may be able to pick and choose which parts of the U.S. standards they will adopt and which they will reject.

This is not a new problem, although its effects are intensifying with each new FASB standard. It is long past time that Canadian standard setters addressed it. Managing this problem will require case-by-case examination of U.S. standards as they are issued to determine the best possible Canadian reaction. Based on such an examination, the Accounting Standards Board might make one of several possible statements:

- The subject of the U.S. standard is on the agenda of the Canadian board or will shortly be placed upon it. No change should be made in Canadian accounting practice until a Canadian standard is issued.

- The U.S. standard provides a reasonable interpretation of accepted accounting theory, and its recommendations may be regarded as being within generally accepted accounting principles in Canada. (On occasion it might be advisable to state that the U.S. recommended position should be adopted only if it is adopted in its entirety, including the required disclosures.)

- The U.S. recommendations are too different from generally accepted accounting principles in Canada and should not be adopted.

The last of these statements is the one most likely to draw criticism. However, if the Canadian board is to control its own agenda and priorities, some such action must be considered. It goes without saying that Canadian standard setters should keep fully informed of work proceeding in the United States and should consciously try to tailor their own projects so as to avoid unnecessary conflicts with American standards.

Cost and Commitment

A final question concerns who should cover the cost of standard setting. Even with a substantial amount of voluntary effort, establishing accounting standards in a modern economy is costly. Research, staff support, and extensive exposure of the process to the views of interested parties is required. The membership of the CICA bears virtually the whole cost of this work now. This is a historical accident. As has been noted, accounting standards are of direct assistance to auditors. Thus, when the CICA was dominated by auditors, it was entirely natural to devote some of its resources to the encouragement of improvements in financial reporting. Governmental reliance on CICA efforts represents a form of free ride that continues to be possible only so long as the membership continues to consider the burden worthwhile. With a steady or increasing demand for accounting standards in an ever more complex economy, and the declining percentage of auditors in the membership (who have the greatest stake in good accounting standards), there are indications that the membership at large is unwilling to continue to bear the entire cost of what needs to be done. This condition calls for reconsideration of the place of the standard-setting function within the CICA or even within the private sector.

A SUMMARY EVALUATION

It is clear from the preceding analysis that the achievement of an effective independent standard-setting process that would accomplish the recommendations of the CICA Task Force on Standard-Setting represents a very demanding challenge. It would envisage an expansion of activities beyond those assumed by the existing board. And it must be recognized that the existing CICA standard-setting activity is significantly underresourced at present. The task force noted the considerable strains on existing CICA resources:

It is increasingly difficult to obtain volunteers due to conflicting demands on their time. In addition, because of reallocation of resources within budget constraints, there is a lack of staff support to cope with project demands on a timely basis (page 27).

The question must then be raised: Is it reasonable to expect that an effective CICA accounting standard-setting process, and related supporting activities, can be adequately resourced? Consideration may be given to the following:

- In the past the high quality of volunteer support of CICA standard-setting has been its life blood. But at least two factors would seem to have substantially reduced this resource and its effectiveness. First, the increased commitment required of volunteers to master highly complex issues and the extent of change is more than most individuals are able to give. Second, as we have noted earlier, there has been a reduced willingness on the part of major public accounting firms, who have been the backbone of support in the past, to commit significant expert resources to CICA standard-setting efforts. In a sense this is puzzling, because of the very significant stake these firms have in sound accounting standards. Several years ago, a high profile enquiry into the "audit expectations gap" noted that many believe that "the auditor is in a weak position vis-à-vis management." It concluded:

  > In these circumstances the quality of accounting standards is most important. A well-reasoned and established accounting standard can give the auditor leverage in disputes with management ... we believe shortcomings in accounting standards are or can be important contributing factors in expectation gaps." [27]

  It has been suggested that the reasons for reduced commitment from major public accounting firms relates to the increasing importance to these firms of management consulting. But whatever the reasons, it may be very important to achieve their recommitment, if Canadian accounting standard setting is to be able to survive as a private sector function.

  In any event, it is questionable whether all that needs to be done can be accomplished by volunteers, assisted by CICA staff. A number of accounting standard-setting bodies in other jurisdictions have, or are contemplating having, at least some full-time standard setters. The CICA Task Force on Standard-Setting has recommended a full-time chair for the CICA board. As well, it has recognized the need for a substantial increase in staff resources.

- There may be some significant efficiencies that could be achieved by a well-focused standard-setting program, with clearly established priorities, and coordination and pooling of resources with other national and international accounting standard-setting bodies. It would seem unwise for Canada to be pioneering new accounting standards that have not been well tested by, or with, other standard-setting bodies. As well, considerable benefits could be achieved if the *CICA Handbook* could adopt the style and wording of the FASB and/or IASC standards, where possible. The difficulty here is that the IASC and FASB styles and degree of detail are very different. *CICA Handbook* standards are much closer in style to those of the IASC, than those of the FASB.

- Even if significant efficiencies could be achieved, a broader funding basis for Canadian standard-setting is needed. CICA members cannot be expected to foot the full bill. This has been recognized by the task force but it has proposed no clear plan. In this, the CICA faces a basic dilemma. It cannot realistically expect to maintain control over the standard-setting process if others are expected to contribute significant amounts to it. Other contributors will likely want direct representation in the process. This, in turn, gives rise to the need to carefully balance interests to ensure independence of the standard-setting process. Some possible sources of funding that are being tapped by other countries include:

— securities commissions levies on securities registrants,

— trading fees levied by stock exchanges,

— government subsidies, and/or

— private company donations.

The rationale for such funding sources is that they are among the primary beneficiaries of effective standard setting.

REFERENCES

1   See D.J. Kirk, "Concepts, Consensus, Compromise and Consequences: Their Roles in Standard Setting." *Journal of Accountancy*, April 1981, pp. 83–86. See also two articles by D.Solomons. "The Politicization of Accounting," *Journal of Accountancy*, November 1978, pp. 65–72 and "The Potential Implications of Accounting and Auditing Standard Setting," *Accounting and Business Research*, Spring 1983, pp. 107–18.

2   V.H. Brown, "Accounting Standards: Their Economic and Social Consequences," *Accounting Horizons*, September 1990, pp. 89–97. This article provides an insightful perspective on the nature of economic and social costs and benefits, and on considerations relating to how they may be evaluated.

3   A CICA Research Study has examined the meaning and role of professional judgment in financial reporting, with particular attention to judgments required in CICA accounting standards. M. Gibbins and A.K. Mason, *Professional Judgment in Financial Reporting* (Toronto: CICA, 1988).

4   An experimental study set in a tax context suggests, however, that replacing the latitude in verbal thresholds with numerical thresholds may not diminish preparer ability to manipulate results where there is latitude available in assessing the evidential support for numerical thresholds. A.D. Cuccia, K. Hackenbrack, and M.W. Nelson, "The Ability of Professional Standards to Mitigate Aggressive Reporting," *The Accounting Review*, April 1995, pp. 227–48.

5   For an evaluative analysis of the interaction between judgment and U.S. accounting standards, see A.K. Mason and M. Gibbins, "Judgment and U.S. Accounting Standards," *Accounting Horizons*, June 1991, pp. 14–24.

6   See R.M. Skinner, "Judgment in Jeopardy," *CA Magazine*, November 1995, pp. 14–21.

7   The CICA has recently established a study group to consider financial reporting for small business enterprises. It is to consider how financial information needs of those providing capital to small business might be more effectively met, and the degree to which reporting in accordance with GAAP might be modified to meet those needs. It is expected to report in 1999.

8   Some scholars believe that statement preparers' needs to retain the confidence of the capital markets provide sufficient incentive for the provision of adequate financial

reports. See, as an example, H. Kripke, "Would Market Forces Cause Adequate Securities Disclosure Without SEC Mandate?" in *Government Regulation of Accounting and Information*, ed. A.R. Abdel-khalik (Gainesville, Fla.: University Presses of Florida, 1980), pp. 202–24. See also discussion in Chapter 4 of academic research involving "signalling theory" that is concerned with understanding the sources that may determine when management will be motivated to disclose information voluntarily.

9   The generality of this observation may be illustrated by literature from two countries. See E.H. Flegm, *Accounting: How to Meet the Challenges of Relevance and Regulation* (New York: A Ronald Press Publication, John Wiley & Sons, 1984) and I.N. Tegner, "British Accounting Standards—A Finance Director's Assessment," in *British Accounting Standards: The First 10 Years*, ed. Sir R. Leach and E. Stamp (Cambridge: Woodhead-Faulkner, 1981), pp. 223–30. C.T. Horngren, a one-time APB member once said "...financial executives in the aggregate will oppose almost anything that a standards group comes out with." See R.R. Sterling, ed., *Institutional Issues in Public Accounting* (Lawrence, Kan.: Scholars Book Co., 1974), p. 309.

10   For a chronicle of the FASB's ongoing struggle with preparer interests who have sought to constrain the standard-setting process, see R. Van Riper, *Setting Standards for Financial Reporting: FASB and the Struggle for Control of a Critical Process* (Westport, CT: Quorum Books, 1994).

11   *CICA Task Force on Standard Setting: Final Report* (Toronto: CICA, 1998).

12   Ibid., p. 46.

13   Ibid., p. 29.

14   See *Measurement Research in Financial Accounting*, Workshop Proceedings, University of Waterloo School of Accountancy (Toronto: The Ernst & Young Foundation, 1994).

15   A CICA commissioned review of standard-setting procedures in 1980 recommended that standards be reviewed every five years to evaluate their continuing acceptability and usefulness. CICA Special Committee on Standard Setting, *Report to CICA Board of Governors* (Toronto: CICA, 1980), pp. 106–107.

16   IASC Strategy Working Party, *Shaping IASC for the Future*, A Discussion Paper (London: IASC, 1998).

17   The Canadian delegation presently consists of two persons, one appointed by the CICA and the other appointed alternately for two and one-half year terms by the Certified General Accountants' Association of Canada and the Society of Management Accountants of Canada.

18   *CICA Handbook* Section 1501, "International Accounting Standards," contains a comparison of Canadian and IASC standards, but it is at present out of date.

19   There have two notable exceptions to this in recent years. First, the *CICA Handbook* Section 3860, "Financial Instruments – Disclosure and Presentation," was developed in a joint project with the IASC, and is virtually identical to the IASC standard (IAS 32). Second, recent revisions to the *CICA Handbook* Section 1540, "Cash Flow Statements," were much influenced by the IASC standard (IAS 7).

20   The CICA survey of financial statements of two hundred Canadian public companies reported that only nine made reference to conformity with IASC standards in their 1997

financial statements, while eighty-three included notes on differences between U.S. and Canadian GAAP. CICA, *Financial Reporting in Canada 1998*, 23rd ed. (Toronto: CICA, 1998), pp. 67–68.

21 CICA, *Significant Differences in GAAP in Canada, Chile, Mexico and the United States* (Toronto: CICA, 1998).

22 Office of the Chief Accountant of the Ontario Securities Commission, *Study of Differences Between Canadian and United States Generally Accepted Accounting Principles* (Toronto: Ontario Securities Commission, 1993). This study examined the financial statement notes reconciling Canadian and U.S. GAAP differences of sixty-eight Canadian companies listed on the Toronto Stock Exchange and one or more U.S. exchanges for the five-year period 1987–1991.

23 S.P. Bandyopadhyay and G.D. Richardson, "Academic Perspectives on the OSC Report on the Study of Differences Between Canadian and American GAAP," in Ontario Securities Commission, *Study of Differences Between Canadian and United States Generally Accepted Accounting Principles*, pp. 43–50. See also S.P. Bandyopadhyay, J.D. Hanna, and G.D. Richardson, "Capital Market Effects of U.S.–Canada GAAP Differences," *Journal of Accounting Research*, Autumn 1994, pp. 262–77.

24 A subsequent study did find some evidence that U.S. GAAP reflects information investors use in establishing share prices beyond that reflected in Canadian GAAP. M.E. Barth and G. Clinch, "International Accounting Differences and Their Relation to Share Prices: Evidence from U.K., Australian, and Canadian Firms," *Contemporary Accounting Research*, Spring 1996, pp. 135–70.

25 See *CICA Task Force on Standard Setting: Final Report*, p. 12.

26 It is currently not possible to conform with both U.S. and IASC standards on many issues. See FASB, *The IASC–U.S. Comparison Project: A Report on the Similarities and Differences Between IASC Standards and U.S. GAAP*, ed. C. Bloomer (Norwalk: FASB, 1996).

27 *Report of the Commission to Study the Public's Expectations of Audits* (Toronto: CICA, 1998), pars. 4.31-4.32.

Part

NOT-FOR-PROFIT ORGANIZATIONS AND GOVERNMENTS

4

Chapter 27

NOT-FOR-PROFIT ORGANIZATIONS

The financial accounting model that we have been addressing to this point was developed with profit-seeking enterprises in mind. It has laid so much emphasis on the measurement of income that one could easily believe that it has no relevance for organizations that are not seeking profit. Indeed, it has been frequently asserted by accountants and managers in the not-for-profit sector that these entities are different, and therefore that their accounting and reporting should be different. It is undeniable that they have different characteristics from profit-oriented entities. Whether this requires a different set of accounting principles is another question.

To answer this question we may look to whether there is a body of theory upon which separate and distinct not-for-profit sector accounting principles could be constructed. Unfortunately, until quite recently, accounting theory and accounting standards have largely ignored not-for-profit entities. As a result, their accounting practices developed from a mixture of influences which have included internal budgeting, legal compliance, and various situational factors. Such practices have been very diverse. They have differed from one segment of not-for-profit activity to another—for example, hospital accounting has been different from university accounting. Substantial differences have also existed between individual entities within a segment, with major differences in such fundamental areas as the activities included in the reporting entity, the extent to which accrual accounting was followed, whether capital expenditures were expensed or capitalized and amortized, whether fund accounting was followed and, if so, how it was applied.

In recent years accounting standard setters in Canada and the U.S. have come to the conclusion that an independent conceptual framework is not necessary for any particular category of entity.[1] Consistent with this conclusion, their concept statements contain definitions of the elements of financial statements that pertain to both not-for-profit and profit-oriented entities. The economic essence of "assets" and "liabilities" is considered to be fundamentally the same whether they are owned by commercial businesses or not-for profit enterprises. The view then is that the differences between these enterprises can be reasonably accommodated within the same framework. This has, not surprisingly, been controversial, and there has been considerable resistance in some quarters to the implications of the framework concepts for accounting by not-for-profit entities.

It has been widely accepted, however, that traditional not-for-profit accounting practices have needed to be substantially improved to be more consistent and to provide a more complete picture of financial position and financial activities. A CICA research study published in 1980 made many recommendations, including advocating full accrual accounting and capitalization of capital expenditures.[2]

Certainly there are important unique issues arising from not-for-profit purposes and activities. The starting point for identifying and addressing them is to have a clear definition of what distinguishes a "not-for-profit organization." The definition that has been developed has three main elements:

- *Purpose of the organization.* The organization is operated exclusively for social, educational, professional, religious, health, charitable or other not-for-profit purposes. There is no direct profit motive.

- *No financial return.* The organization's members, contributors and other resource providers do not, in these capacities, receive any financial return directly from the organization. Members, contributors and resource providers may benefit economically from their involvement with a not-for-profit organization. (For example, consider a professional association. Members, by virtue of belonging to the professional association, can enhance their ability to earn income.) However, the key point is that any financial return related to membership dues or contributions paid to the organization does not come directly from the organization itself.

- *No ownership interest.* Not-for-profit organizations *normally* have no transferable ownership interests. This part of the definition is more of a description of how most not-for-profit organizations are organized, rather than a necessary condition. Some not-for-profit organizations do have transferable ownership interests. For example, some golf and country clubs have transferable memberships. The existence of such transferable interests in an organization does not preclude it from being a not-for-profit organization if the other elements of the definition are satisfied.[3]

This description of "not-for-profit" organizations might be considered to embrace governments as well. Indeed, the two sectors have important characteristics in common, including that they do not have owners that benefit directly from their activities, and that earning a profit is not a primary goal. However, there are some important differences and accounting standards for these sectors have developed separately and from somewhat different perspectives. This chapter will address not-for-profit organizations, and the following chapter will focus on the unique aspects of governments.

HISTORICAL PERSPECTIVE ON ACCOUNTING BY NOT-FOR-PROFIT ORGANIZATIONS IN CANADA

Prior to 1988, there were no formal accounting standards for not-for-profit organizations. In that year, not-for-profit organizations were brought within the scope of the *CICA Handbook*, the intent being that existing accounting standards would apply to not-for-profit organizations unless otherwise specified.[4] This was a controversial move; many argued that it was inappropriate to force not-for-profit organizations into the accounting model that had evolved for profit-oriented enterprises.

At the same time a brief *CICA Handbook* section was issued to provide limited guidance on some of the issues that were considered to be unique to not-for-profit organizations, such as donations in kind, pledges and restricted donations.[5] Perhaps of most significance in this section was the requirement for not-for-profit organizations to follow accrual accounting. Much of the not-for-profit sector had been following various modified cash bases of accounting. Accrual accounting meant that some expenses would have to be recognized in periods before the related funding would be received. One example was vacation pay. Many government-funded organizations, such as hospitals, were opposed to recognizing such obligations since they are normally funded when they are paid, not when the entitlement is earned.

Apart from accrual accounting, the section dealt mainly with disclosure while leaving important recognition decisions up to the individual organization, such as how to account for capital expenditures. Some critics of the new section argued that it left too many important issues open. It enabled organizations in the sector to ostensibly report in conformity with generally accepted accounting principles while still exhibiting much of the diversity in practice that had existed previously. For example, capital assets could be expensed on acquisition or capitalized, either with or without being amortized, all under the guise of generally accepted accounting principles.[6]

Then in the early 1990s, the CICA undertook to consider those areas that had been left open in 1988. The first step, taken in 1991, was to establish the conceptual basis for the development of accounting standards for not-for-profit organizations. This was accomplished by formally incorporating not-for-profit organizations within the *CICA Handbook* statement of fundamental financial reporting concepts that had originally been developed for business enterprises. The *CICA Handbook* Section 1000 on "Financial Statement Concepts" was modified to recognize the unique purposes of not-for-profit organizations, and to affirm the relevance to these purposes of the basic elements of financial reporting (assets, liabilities, revenues, expenses, gains and losses), the general concepts of recognition and measurement (including accrual accounting), and the qualitative characteristics of useful financial information.

These concepts have had a significant impact on the development of accounting standards for not-for-profit organizations. A task force, which included representatives of key not-for-profit sectors, was established to work within this framework to propose accounting standards on issues of particular significance to not-for-profit organizations. After a period of deliberation and consultation, exposure drafts were issued by the CICA Accounting Standards Board, comments considered, and a final set of standards put in place in 1996.[7] These standards address the major areas of accounting that may be considered unique to not-for-profit organizations—the recognition of contributions, the treatment of resource restrictions, accounting for capital expenditures, financial statement presentation, fund accounting and the definition of the reporting entity.

In the U.S., the FASB also undertook a major project on accounting for not-for-profit organizations in the 1980s. As we will see, the FASB adopted markedly different positions on some significant issues.[8]

BASES OF ACCOUNTING—TRADITIONAL PRACTICES

Examination of the financial reports of not-for-profit organizations before the introduction of the conceptual framework and accounting standards for not-for-profit organizations demonstrates that different entities had widely different accounting bases, and rationales for these bases. Many not-for-profit entities adopted a narrow view of stewardship and accountability. It is helpful to explore some reasons for this diversity.

Extent and Complexity of Activities

To some extent different bases of accounting simply reflected differences in size and complexity of reporting organizations. We should not be surprised if an entity follows a cash basis of accounting if cash is its primary asset and it has no significant liabilities. For many entities the question as to basis of accounting arose when they began buying on credit. Often they would remain with cash accounting for a time because it was less work. Sometimes such an entity would receive an unpleasant surprise because bills accumulated unnoticed. As a result, it might adopt a "modified cash" basis of accounting, accruing for liabilities unpaid but continuing to recognize revenues on a cash basis.

Once accounts payable are recognized, however, it is hard to resist the argument that accounts receivable should be recognized as well. Sometimes only certain accounts receivable and payable would be recognized and other assets (for example, inventories, property, plant and equipment) and other liabilities (for example, accruals for vacation pay) would be ignored.

It is probably not difficult to get agreement that a not-for-profit organization should be responsible for reporting all material financial claims and the net change in them in its financial statements. (There could, however, be some differences of opinion as to what qualifies as a financial claim.) The real arguments began when it was suggested that organizations ought to be accountable for assets and liabilities beyond those that could be categorized as simple financial claims (in particular, accruals for future employee benefits related to services that had been provided, and capitalization of nonfinancial assets).

Some organizations that charged a fee for service, or received grants based on the cost of service, or simply wanted to track the cost of services being provided, followed the practice of recording prepayments and inventories of major supplies, and capitalized and depreciated capital expenditures. The statement of operating activity would record expense as the benefit from these assets was consumed, rather than when they were acquired.

The Influence of Sources of Funding

In several types of not-for-profit organizations there was a strong tradition of separate accounting according to the source of funds—in particular, a distinction was made between funds received for "capital" and "operating" purposes.[9] Sometimes this separation would reflect external restrictions requiring that certain grants or donations be used for capital purposes. In other cases, it merely reflected the entity's own view as to how it should finance its activities. Two examples may be cited:

- A private club may have a policy that the cost of club premises and major renovations should be financed out of initiation fees from members so far as possible. Accordingly, initiation fees would be excluded from the report of operating activity, as would the related capital expenditures. Other capital expenditures of a more minor nature, however, may have been written of as operating expenses when incurred. Depreciation on expenditures capitalized may or may not have been recognized as operating expenses depending upon the directors' policy decision on whether depreciation should be recovered from annual fees, a decision which could change from time to time.

•   A university, public art gallery, museum or similar institution may have an understanding that major building projects would be financed by capital campaigns. Accordingly, capital campaign donations and the projects financed by them may have been excluded from operating activities.

Accounting for major capital expenditures in such situations varied. In some situations, for example most universities, they were capitalized in a separate capital fund and not depreciated. Alternatively, they may have been depreciated but depreciation recorded in a capital fund rather than the operating statement. The argument usually made for these treatments was that, since campaign contributors donate these assets, depreciation should not be recognized because it is not to be recovered from service fees and operating grants. In some cases capital expenditures would simply be charged to equity when incurred, offset by capital donations and other revenues allocated to their purchase.

The Influence of the Spending Budget

In a not-for-profit organization, a budget adopted for a year may have been used as a device to control expenditures. Every purchase order placed or other commitment reduces the amount authorized, and a commitment can be made only if it does not exceed the remaining limit. With such a system in force, an organization may have argued that amounts authorized by the budget for spending out of current year's resources should be reported as liabilities at a period-end, so long as purchase orders have been placed with suppliers. Thus, amounts reported as liabilities could have included both actual accounts payable and "encumbrances"—that is, unfilled commitments. As a result, expenditures reported would have included intended expenditures as well as actual. This accounting basis could be used to manage results reported merely by varying the decision as to the extent to which unspent budgetary authority was deemed to have lapsed.

From the foregoing paragraphs we can see that, without a governing framework and explicit accounting standards consistent with that framework, organizations could choose to account for financial claims only, or also to account for various other assets such as prepayments and supplies; they could choose to capitalize some or all capital expenditures and record depreciation on some or none of them; and they could even recognize liabilities for commitments placed from which no benefit had yet been obtained. Rationalizations were given for these various treatments, usually based on their usefulness for internal policy decisions. What was lacking was any theory of what represents relevant reporting to users external to the organization.

FUNDAMENTAL CONCEPTUAL ISSUES

We will begin by considering the users of not-for-profit financial reports, and what may be considered to be the objectives of financial reporting for these users. We will then assess the implications of these objectives for determining appropriate bases of accounting and accountability, and whether the concepts of assets, liabilities, revenues and expenses developed for business enterprises have relevance to not-for-profit organizations. Finally, we will address issues related to defining the boundaries of the not-for-profit reporting entity—and consider the principles that should determine those activities to be included in the reporting entity.

Conceptual Framework

Before specific accounting standards could be developed for not-for-profit organizations, it was necessary to settle on an appropriate conceptual framework. As noted, standards setters in the U.S. and Canada concluded that the starting point should be to examine the conceptual framework adopted for business enterprises and modify it, as needed, to incorporate not-for-profit organizations.

The conceptual framework that was adopted for not-for-profit organizations has been criticized by those who believed that the standard setters had simply taken the framework developed for profit-oriented enterprises, changed a few words, and forced it inappropriately on not-for-profit organizations. It is true that relatively minor changes were made in adapting the existing framework to not-for-profit organizations. However, standard setters reasoned that this conceptual framework flows logically from the needs of the users of not-for-profit financial statements and objectives that are consistent with those needs.

Users of Financial Reports

Since the basic objective of financial reports is to provide information that is useful to users of those reports, it is important to identify who the users are and to consider what basis of accounting is most consistent with their rational decision purposes. It is possible to draw up a lengthy list of potential users of the financial reports of not-for-profit organizations. The following covers the main categories:

- *The operational management of the organization.* Management uses financial information in their evaluation of the results of past efforts, in the control of resources, in planning for the future and in developing budgets, and in advising governing bodies on these matters. Thus, financial accounting information, and the basis on which it is prepared, is of fundamental importance to not-for-profit organization management. Of course, management can command internal information pertaining to the organization's financial position and results of operations on whatever basis, and in whatever form, it finds useful. Internal financial reports need not be constrained by *CICA Handbook* accounting standards. Nevertheless, for basic reasons of efficiency and consistency of perspective, one might expect that it would be desirable that the principles of accounting recognition and measurement not be fundamentally inconsistent as between internal and external financial reports.

  In the final analysis, however, the primary focus of financial reporting should not be dictated by management's perceived internal needs, but rather should be governed by the evident needs of the external stakeholders to whom management is accountable.

- *Governing bodies.* These include members of the organization's board of directors. Such bodies have a fiduciary duty to make sure that the organization is managed in a sound and responsible manner. As part of the management of the organization, these groups are insiders with access to more information than normally appears in financial reports. However, these groups may consist largely of volunteers who need an efficient way of gaining information about the organization's financial position and results of operations to help ensure they have met their fiduciary duties.

- *Resource providers.* Individuals, corporations, governments and other not-for-profit organizations provide resources to not-for-profit organizations in order to support their activities. In addition, some not-for-profit organizations, such as associations and clubs, have members who pay membership fees. Resource providers, who are usually separate from management and are thus external users, need financial information in order to help evaluate an organization's performance and financial needs, and ultimately to assess whether the organization continues to merit their support or continued membership. Resource providers use financial information in considering whether the organization is being managed in a responsible manner and is making appropriate use of the resources provided to it.

- *Lenders and creditors.* Although investor interest is absent in not-for-profit organizations, lenders and creditors require financial information to assess an organization's solvency and to evaluate its ability to meet its obligations.

A comparable list of users of financial statements of business entities could be drawn up. As with the above list, it includes internal and external stakeholders who may have different and sometimes conflicting needs. For business enterprises financial accounting has focused on a particular class of user— investors and creditors and the expectations of capital markets. We have considered the implications of this investor-capital markets orientation for financial accounting's conceptual framework in Chapter 25.

Is there any parallel user group for not-for-profit organizations? Specifically can we identify a class of external user (as has been done in the case of business enterprises) to provide a logical focus for developing a financial accounting framework appropriate to not-for-profit organizations? One group stands out that is analogous to investors in business enterprises—the external resource providers to not-for-profit enterprises. The *CICA Handbook* concepts statement reasons that members of and contributors to not-for-profit organizations, like investors in business enterprises, are "often segregated from management creating a similar need for external communication of economic information about the entity to members and contributors" (paragraph 1000.10). It also observes that creditors can be expected to have similar needs.

Objectives of Financial Reporting

Stewardship

The *CICA Handbook* concepts statement emphasizes financial information about how management of a not-for-profit organization has discharged its stewardship responsibilities:

> Information regarding discharge of the stewardship responsibilities is especially important in the not-for-profit sector where resources are often contributed for specific purposes and management is accountable for the appropriate utilization of such resources (paragraph 1000.14).

An organization is entrusted with resources by contributors or members. It is accountable for demonstrating that it has spent the resources in accordance with its basic purposes in a properly authorized fashion. This proposition was traditionally interpreted to mean that

(1) cash basis accounting for contributions and revenue should be appropriate because the entity cannot be accountable for resources it has not yet received, (2) expenditure in accordance with proper authority represents a discharge of the entity's responsibility, and (3) financial reports must demonstrate accountability for restricted-purpose funds by reporting them separately from unrestricted funds.

These interpretations of the stewardship concept are very narrow. Since the goal of every not-for-profit organization is to provide some service, accountability does not end when cash resources are spent. Full accountability requires a broader reporting of performance. Ideally, to discharge its accountability obligation an entity should report its progress, both in quantitative and qualitative terms, in achieving its service delivery objectives.

There are major difficulties in achieving this ideal, however. First, it is very difficult to measure and communicate the quality of service. Second, one might question what such information has to do with a financial report. The answer is that, if the goal of a financial report is to report on performance, it must provide some indicators of the entity's output. In a business entity the revenue of the enterprise from outside parties provides a positive indicator of whether its output is satisfactory. The same is not true of not-for-profit organizations, except for those that operate on a fee-for-service basis. Therefore, indicators of services output are needed. But those indicators by themselves will also be insufficient. To enable proper assessment, indicators of quantity and quality of service output need to be compared with the cost of providing the service. Only in this way can a judgment be made as to the organization's performance and whether the service was worthwhile and cost effective.

We are a long way from having reports of stewardship that meet the ideals just expressed. Nor does it appear, in view of the intangibles in assessment of service quality, that we will ever reach that ideal. Experimentation is required to discover what is possible, and efforts are made from time to time to that end.[10] It may be noted that financial statements prepared under generally accepted accounting principles can be supplemented with detailed information about individual programs, information about the qualitative aspects of the services delivered and comparisons of actual results with those budgeted.

While fully informative reporting of service outputs may not be achievable at present, one important but limited measure is possible. It is presumably a goal of every service enterprise to maintain its financial ability to serve. To do so the entity must maintain its long-run financial health. It must raise enough money to cover its program costs, or else it must tailor its programs to the resources available. A financial report can inform its readers whether this goal has been achieved. That is why we have seen a shift beyond the traditional narrow stewardship approach to accounting, which could be described as: What funds did the organization raise and on what did it spend those funds? Stewardship remains an important financial reporting objective. However, its focus has changed to a broader accountability and can now be described as: What were the costs of services provided, how were those costs funded, and does the entity have the ability to meet its obligations and sustain its service delivery objectives? The *CICA Handbook* concepts statement has concluded that this latter interpretation is the primary interest of members, contributors and creditors of not-for-profit organizations.[11]

Long-Term Cost of Service

It was suggested above that simply reporting how resources were spent is too narrow a concept of accountability. The statement reader should be expected to be interested in the full cost of operations, not mere expenditure of cash. Full accrual accounting including allocation of all costs incurred to the particular periods in which their benefits are consumed, tends to show the long-term cash demands of the program carried on rather than short-term cash demands. We say "long-term" because in some cases—for example, buildings and equipment—the current period feels the benefit of cash paid long ago, and in others—for example, employee pensions—the current period benefits because of promises to pay cash that will mature many years into the future. If one assumes that the entity will continue to serve indefinitely, with replacement of assets as needed, such a portrayal of long-term cash demands may be very significant. (We also say "tends to show" because an allocation of costs incurred some time ago provides only an imperfect measure of cash required at current prices to replace assets consumed.)

Often those who advocate full accrual accounting for not-for-profit organizations are accused of wishing to impose business accounting principles upon not-for-profit organizations without understanding their special nature. Some argue that the nature of individual not-for-profit organizations needs to be considered in order to assess whether full accrual accounting is appropriate. One distinction proposed is between "club" and "non-club" organizations. (Some describe the distinction as being between "transactions/private service"-type and "collective/public service"-type not-for-profit activities.) Members of clubs pay membership fees and require information about the full cost of services provided in the period; they are concerned that one year should not bear the cost of assets that will be used in future years. It is argued that non-clubs providing services that are fully funded or subsidized by resource providers other than those benefiting from the organization's services do not need full accrual information because these resource providers are only interested in the organization's effective cash expenditure control.[12] Accounting standards setters in Canada and the U.S. do not support this view. Underlying the accounting standards in both countries is the belief that the full accrual perspective is relevant to all not-for-profit organizations, regardless of funding sources or the nature of their activities.

The expectation may be that both long-term cost of service and short-term cash flow information are useful. If so, an argument in favour of full accrual accounting is that it is relatively easy to convert a statement based on full accruals into a statement portraying flow of cash or liquid resources. (In fact, accounting standards for not-for-profit organizations now require that most organizations provide a statement of cash flows in addition to the full accrual financial statements.) In contrast it is impossible to determine the organization's results of operations and financial position on a full accrual basis from financial statements prepared on a cash basis.

In summary, a measure of full accrual cost of service is important for two reasons.

- First, the full accrual cost of service can be compared with contributions and other revenue for the period to assess whether the current generation of contributors is absorbing the full cost of service, or whether an organization is running down capital provided by previous generations or passing on a burden to future generations. In other words, knowing whether capital has been maintained in a not-for-profit organization—that is, whether it has operated on a break-even basis—requires full accrual accounting.

- Second, a full accrual basis of accountability is more relevant than cash accounting to resource providers, because it facilitates evaluation of whether the service is worthwhile. It is true that measuring the cost of the services provided deals only with the cost side of any cost/benefit analysis. As discussed above, indicators (usually nonmonetary) of service outputs need to be provided as well, to permit informed judgments as to the value of the service and the entity's effectiveness in meeting program objectives. Nevertheless, provision of cost data is the starting point if a valid program evaluation is to be made.

Financial Position

We should also not forget the importance of reporting the organization's financial position. As observed in Chapter 25, one of the major contributions of the developed conceptual framework for financial accounting has been its "asset and liability view," supported by rigorous economic definitions of these key elements. These definitions have proved to be fundamental building blocks for the development of accounting standards for business enterprises, and the adoption of parallel definitions for not-for-profit organizations provides an important part of the basis for the rational development of accounting standards for them as well.

Assets are defined as economic resources that are controlled by the organization as a result of past transactions or events. Consistent with the fact that a not-for-profit organization's main objective is to provide some service, one of the modifications of the *CICA Handbook* conceptual framework is to recognize that assets of a not-for-profit organization generally embody the capacity to provide services (while assets of a business enterprise embody the capacity to generate cash flows) (paragraph 1000.30). This clearly extends the concept of assets beyond financial claims, and the concept is consistent with the broad accountability objective for reporting long-term costs of services on a full accrual basis.

With the extension of the conceptual framework to not-for-profit organizations, the definition of a liability (as an obligation arising from a past event or transaction that will entail a future outflow of resources) now applies to all types of entities. There would seem to be no logical basis for arguing that the existence of a liability may depend somehow on the profit or nonprofit purposes of the enterprise.

The Reporting Entity

A key conceptual issue concerns criteria for determining the not-for-profit reporting entity. We have to define the boundaries of the entity before we can know what it should be reporting.

As we saw in Chapter 20, it is accepted in accounting for profit-oriented entities that the objective is to report on the economic unit. The boundaries of a business economic unit are established by control relationships, which are normally the result of ownership of a majority of voting shares. In not-for-profit organizations we lack the test of share ownership. What, then, is the operational concept of a not-for-profit organization economic unit? The concept of control in a not-for-profit context and two competing concepts are discussed below.

Control

The concept of control may be reasoned to be just as applicable to defining a not-for-profit organization as it is for a business enterprise. This conclusion is implicit in accepting the relevance to not-for-profit organizations of the conceptual framework definition of "assets," as resources *controlled* by the entity. Whether assets are controlled directly or through control of another entity is of little consequence. As well, from an accountability standpoint, it may be reasoned that a not-for-profit organization should be held responsible for the activities it controls.

It is not surprising then that the CICA has concluded, as has the FASB, that a not-for-profit reporting entity includes all the entities controlled by it. There are, however, some difficulties in determining when control exists in the not-for-profit sector.

The CICA accounting standard adopts the same definition of control for not-for-profit organizations as for profit-oriented enterprises. Control is considered to be the continuing power to determine another entity's strategic operating, investing and financing policies without the cooperation of others (paragraph 4450.02). Since these strategic policies are usually set by an entity's board of directors, control is generally presumed to exist when the organization has the right to appoint the majority of the other organization's board of directors. However, it is considered that there may be situations in which control over another organization exists even though the reporting entity does not have the right to appoint the majority of its board. For example, a fund raising foundation may be set up with the sole purpose of raising and holding funds for the organization, with little or no scope for any other activities. It may be reasoned that the foundation's resources should be included with those of the reporting organization, even if it does not elect the majority of the board.[13]

Therefore, in addition to the right to appoint the majority of another organization's board of directors, the CICA's Accounting Standards Board concluded that there are other indicators that need to be considered. Other possible indicators of control include a significant economic interest in the other organization, provisions in the other organization's bylaws that limit its activities to providing benefits to the reporting organization, or integrated purposes such that the organizations have common or complementary objectives. A significant economic interest may exist when the other organization holds resources for the benefit of the reporting organization or when the reporting organization is responsible for the other organization's liabilities (see paragraphs 4450.06-.12).

The Core Activity

Some have argued that the concept of control for defining the reporting entity is of secondary importance to reporting based on the "core activity." Consider a university that carries on a large number of ancillary activities ranging from printing and publishing and the operation of hospitals and medical and dental clinics to the operation of athletic stadiums and parking lots. There is little doubt that the core activities of a university are teaching and research. A possible basis for financial reporting, therefore, is to include only the assets, liabilities, revenues, and expenses of those core functions in the financial statements of the university and treat the ancillary activities as separate entities, each of which would have its own financial report. Such a reporting basis may fit in well with the organizational structure, since it is quite likely that the ancillary activities will be administered in a decentralized fashion and will usually have their own accounting records. In addition, proponents of this approach argue that resource providers are often only interested in the particular segment of the organization that they support.

However, there are significant reasons for rejecting the core activity concept.

- First, there almost inevitably will be situations in which the boundaries of the core activity are uncertain. Such uncertainty may enable the exclusion of some activities from a financial report so as to "manage" results reported.

- Second, it may well be asked whether a not-for-profit organization is fulfilling its accountability obligation if significant activities for which it is responsible are excluded from its external financial report. Proponents of the core activity approach will argue that this objection is unimportant if separate financial reports for the excluded activities are readily available. However, it is only when a financial report covers all the activities for which the organization is responsible that the full financial significance of the entity can be appreciated.

- Third, understandability of core activities can be achieved by careful design of the report, providing additional detail as to segments of activity. In addition to the full financial statements of the reporting entity, separate financial reports for each significant ancillary activity could be provided for those who have an interest in only that activity.

Restricted-Purpose Resources

Many not-for-profit organizations receive contributions that are subject to restrictions imposed by the contributor specifying how a contribution is to be used. In some cases, the restrictions may lead to the creation of a legal trust. In other cases, there may be no trust, but the circumstances in which the money is collected—for example, a capital campaign for specific building purposes—create an implicit trust that the recipient must respect.

Some hold that such restricted funds are separate reporting entities. Those who hold this view are doubtful of the propriety of presenting a combined statement of funds and especially presenting combined totals of all the funds. Others strongly believe that some combining or aggregation of all the funds is necessary to provide an understandable picture of the activities and resources of the whole organization. The CICA accounting standard takes this latter view, and concludes that information about restrictions can be provided through presentation and disclosure. These issues are discussed further in a subsequent section on restricted purpose contributions.

In summary, alternative bases for defining the reporting entity, based on core activities or setting aside restricted-purpose funds as separate reporting entities, are rejected because (1) they provide an incomplete picture, and (2) information on these activities and resource restrictions can be provided within consolidated financial statements prepared on the basis of control.

The CICA Standard

Thus the CICA standard defines the not-for-profit economic entity in terms of control. Unfortunately, it does not follow through and require that all controlled entities be consolidated. Rather, it permits either their consolidation or note disclosure of summary financial information about controlled entities in lieu of consolidation (paragraphs 4450.14 and .22).

A further concession is made for organizations that control large numbers of individually immaterial organizations (for example, an association that controls a large number of local chapters). Such organizations need neither consolidate the individually immaterial organizations nor disclose summary financial information about them. They need only note why they are not consolidated and why no financial information is provided about them. In these cases the expense of preparing consolidated financial statements or providing summary information is considered to exceed the benefits. The basis for this contention may be questioned if the controlled entities are material in aggregate to the reporting organization, because the result is incomplete accounting. The *CICA Handbook* suggests that "the reporting organization may choose not to exercise financial control over these small organizations" (paragraph 4450.27). Does an organization have this choice? It would seem likely that either it controls these smaller organizations, and has responsibility for their financial activities, or it does not. It is to be remembered that "control" is defined as the "continuing power" to determine strategic activities, not whether one decides to exercise its power.

In summary, the ability of not-for-profit enterprises to omit significant controlled resources and obligations from its financial statements leaves the potential for seriously incomplete reporting. Not-for-profit organizations can, therefore, report in conformity with GAAP on the basis of a significantly less stringent standard for reporting financial position and activities than that required of business enterprises.

SPECIFIC ISSUES IN ACCOUNTING FOR NOT-FOR-PROFIT ORGANIZATIONS

We have noted that the CICA Accounting Standards Board has determined, after considerable deliberation and due process, that not-for-profit organizations should prepare general purpose financial statements on the basis of generally accepted accounting principles as defined by the *CICA Handbook*—that is, that the *CICA Handbook* should apply to both for-profit and not-for-profit organizations.

One might first ask what authority this determination may have. Corporations acts and other legislation applicable to not-for-profit entities have generally not required that they prepare financial statements in accordance with the *CICA Handbook* standards. As a result, a not-for-profit organization might prepare its financial statements on some basis other than GAAP. However, if it did purport that its financial statements conformed with GAAP, it would be expected that these statements should meet *CICA Handbook* standards, since they define GAAP. Further, an auditor or accountant with a professional accounting designation may be in contravention of professional codes of conduct if he or she were to be associated with financial statements of a not-for-profit organization that could be considered inadequate because they did not meet professional (CICA) standards.[14]

In bringing not-for-profit organizations within the ambit of the *CICA Handbook*, it was recognized that some standards developed for profit-oriented enterprises have little or no applicability to them (for example, standards on income taxes and capital shares), or only apply in limited circumstances. These areas of inapplicability are fairly obvious and, for the most part, uncontentious.[15] Of more significance are issues that are unique to not-for-profit organizations, or where the needs of these entities, and users of their financial statements, may be considered to be different from those of profit-oriented enterprises. A separate (Section 4400) series of *CICA Handbook* standards was established to address these matters.

We will now turn to consider the issues that are commonly raised in accounting and reporting for not-for-profit entities, and examine how CICA standards have addressed these issues.

Contributions

Although some not-for-profit organizations receive fees for service, much of the support for this sector comes from nonreciprocal transactions—that is, from contributions rather than from revenues earned as a result of consideration received in exchange for goods or services. Contributions may be from the private sector (from individuals, corporations or other not-for-profit organizations) or from the public sector (government grants of various types).

The following basic questions arise in respect of the recognition, measurement, and presentation of contributions and related income.

- Should contributions be recognized only on receipt of cash or tangible goods or services, or are there situations in which contributions that are promised but not yet received should be recognized as assets (contributions receivable)? Examples include pledges and bequests.

- How should contributions that are subject to externally imposed restrictions be recognized and presented?

- What standards are appropriate for the recognition and measurement of donations in kind (for example, contributed materials or services of volunteers)?

- Are there special considerations with respect to the recognition and measurement of investments and investment income related to contributed resources?

Different not-for-profit entities had developed widely different answers to these questions. *CICA Handbook* standards, effective for the most part in 1997, now address each of these areas.

Contributions Receivable

The large majority of contributions are recognized when cash (or in some cases other tangible assets or services) are received, because it is then that the transactions take place and recognition criteria are met. But questions arise in respect of pledges and bequests, where contributors may have provided the organization with a formal promise to pay fixed or determinable amounts at future fixed or estimable dates. Does the organization have an asset that should be recognized in its accounts in these situations?

The *CICA Handbook* rules that a contribution receivable should be set up when the amount can be reasonably estimated and its ultimate collection can be reasonably assured (paragraph 4420.03). This provision simply restates the general recognition criteria in the conceptual framework (paragraph 1000.44). While this provision may seem to be a significant step towards recognition of contributions receivable, supporting guidance as to acceptable levels of uncertainty suggests that pledges and bequests will not often qualify for recognition before cash is received. The following comments may be made with respect to its application:

- The recognition criteria as stated above are incomplete in and of themselves. They need to be considered in relation to the concept of an asset. Specifically, it is not enough that an amount to be received can be reasonably estimated and its ultimate collection reasonably assured. It must also meet the vital test of being an "asset," that is, a resource "controlled by an entity *as a result of past transactions or events*" (emphasis added) (paragraph 1000.29). To illustrate, an organization may be able to make a reasonable estimate of next year's operating grant that it can expect to receive from a government agency, but the amount cannot be set up as an asset in the current year's statement of financial position because the past event entitling the organization to the grant has not yet occurred.[16]

- Some dispute whether a compelling past event has taken place with respect to a pledge of a future donation, justifying recognition of an asset, because it may not be clear that pledges are legally enforceable. However, legal enforceability is not set out as a necessary condition of an asset. The CICA standard emphasizes collectibility and cautions that "factors outside the organization's control, such as current economic conditions and the continued goodwill and ability to pay" would mean that, "in many cases" pledges would not meet the conditions for recognition (paragraph 4420.05). It observes that organizations with large annual fund raising campaigns may be able to estimate the realizable value of pledges from recurring sources accurately enough to warrant recognition. However, it notes that the uncertainty of pledges due more than one year from the reporting date "would normally be so great as to preclude their recognition" (paragraph 4420.06). It also observes that in many cases bequests would not be sufficiently certain to warrant recognition (but no other guidance is provided). In practice, bequests are normally not recognized until received. Disclosure is to be provided of the amounts of any pledges and bequests recognized as assets (paragraph 4420.08).

• If pledges or requests are recognized as receivables on the balance sheet, there is a question as to whether they are revenues of the current period or are, by the very fact that they are not received, more properly treated as deferred revenues or contributions restricted for use in the future periods in which they are to be received. Restricted contributions are discussed in the following section.

The FASB standard requires that an unconditional promise to make a contribution to a not-for-profit organization be recognized as revenue by the organization at its fair value in the period when the promise is received. The FASB distinguishes an unconditional right to receive promised assets from external restrictions as to how contributed assets are to be used by the organization. A restriction as to use does not preclude recognition where the organization has an unconditional right to receive the assets. This would seem to be a clearer basis for recognition than the CICA standard. The FASB standard notes, however, that determining whether a promise is unconditional, or whether receipt depends on some more-than-remote condition being met, can be difficult in some situations.[17]

Restricted-Purpose Contributions

Perhaps the most difficult issue unique to not-for-profit organizations involves contributions that are subject to externally imposed restrictions that specify how contributed assets are to be used. The challenge is to properly recognize and disclose restricted-purpose contributions, and how the funds have been used, without destroying the understandability of the financial statements.

It is first important to distinguish externally restricted contributions from internal designations. In the past, there has been some practice of earmarking some unrestricted donations and treating them as restricted. For example, when support is received of a type that cannot be counted upon on a regular basis—for example, large bequests—some governing boards are concerned about the effect on the bottom line of reporting the support as current revenue. There had been a tendency in such cases to wish to designate the support for a specific purpose (there may even be a stated policy that all bequests shall be treated as endowments) and exclude the proceeds from current revenues in the regular statement of activity. The CICA standard now requires that all contributions that are not restricted by the donor be reported as current revenues when received (paragraph 4410.47 and .68). An organization may, however, make voluntary appropriations of unrestricted resources for restricted purposes, by separately disclosed transfers presented outside the revenue and expense statement.

When restricted-purpose funds are received, the accounting records must be set up so as to make sure the restrictions are observed. That means that the initial receipt must be credited to an identified account, and the funds appropriately segregated from unrestricted resources. Thereafter, there must be a system to keep track of segregated assets and the fulfilment of restrictions as obligations for spending on the restricted purposes are met. In some cases an entity may have received contributions for hundreds of separate special purposes. Although the accounting records must account individually for each one, it is accepted that they may be classified into a number of natural groupings for the purpose of financial reporting so that only the totals for each group are reported. Common groupings are, (1) endowments (funds whose capital may not be spent); (2) resources for the acquisition or construction of capital assets (contributions received for the acquisition of buildings and equipment); and (3) groupings of resources received for various types of restricted purposes (separate groupings may include scholarships, specified research, and amounts to be used for future operations).

In most situations, restrictions are clearly indicated by the donor in the terms of the contribution, but in some cases they may be specified by some other source, for example, legislation.[18] Restrictions may also be implied, such as when an organization solicits funds for a specific purpose (for example, a campaign for funds to acquire or build a capital asset). The important point is that there is a basis for expectation on the part of the contributor that the funds are restricted for use for a specified purpose (see *CICA Handbook*, paragraph 4410.06).

The practical importance of a restriction may vary. The purposes of some restricted donations may be so much a part of the normal operations of the entity that the restriction is purely a matter of form. The entity meets the restriction simply by doing what it intended to do anyway. At other times, contributions may be received for spending on a specific subset of an organization's activities (a particular research project, for example), or on purposes that the entity would not undertake were it not for the special funding. These variations in circumstances and in possible types of restrictions make it difficult to draw hard-and-fast rules as to how restricted-purpose contributions should be recognized and reported.

It has been previously noted that some think that funds received for restricted purposes should be excluded from the reporting entity, or at least separated from its accounting for unrestricted funds. Some argue that the entity does not have full control of these resources. Such a legalistic point of view must be rejected if it is accepted that an entity should be accountable for all resources for which it has responsibility. If an entity accepts funds for restricted purposes, it may be assumed that those purposes are compatible with the service objectives of the entity. Usually a restricted gift enhances the capacity of the entity to undertake or expand programs that it wants to do. In any event, in accepting restricted funds, the entity assumes control over them, and has a responsibility to use them in accordance with the restrictions. It would hamper the portrayal of the activities of the entity if spending on a particular program would be only partly recorded, or recorded in two different places, depending on whether the spending was funded by unrestricted or restricted resources. Thus it is important to report restricted resources within the body of the financial statements of the reporting entity. (We have noted, however, in the earlier discussion of the reporting entity that, unfortunately, the CICA standard allows an organization to place assets in a separate legal entity with summary information disclosed in footnotes rather than consolidated within the reporting entity.)

The *CICA Handbook* defines two fundamentally different approaches that not-for-profit organizations may adopt for recognizing and presenting restricted resources: (1) the deferral method, and (2) the restricted fund method. The standard permits both methods and combinations of these methods.

The Deferral Method

The essential principle of the deferral method is that contributions are recognized as revenue when restrictive conditions are fulfilled. Thus unrestricted donations are recognized as revenues currently, while temporarily restricted contributions are deferred on the balance sheet until the restricted conditions are met. Endowments—that is, contributions that may not be spent, but must be invested to produce income for the entity—are credited directly to an endowment capital account, a separate component of "net assets" (the not-for-profit equivalent of equity in a profit-oriented enterprise).

Some have argued that support received in respect of nonreciprocal transactions—that is, from contributions including government grants and private donations—is not revenue at all, since it is not earned. They would not include nonreciprocal support in the entity's statement of activity, but in a separate capital account. The CICA has concluded that contributions, other than endowment-type contributions that are treated as capital under the "deferral method," do become revenue (paragraph 1000.37).

The basic idea of the deferral method is to match contributions revenue with the expenses of providing services that were funded from the contributed resources, so as to help users assess the extent to which an organization has been able to obtain resources to cover the cost of its services (paragraph 1000.28).

There are some major conceptual and practical issues relating to the application of the deferral method.

- The amount of a restricted-purpose contribution awaiting the fulfillment of its conditions (for example, a grant for next year's operations, or a contribution for research that is yet to be undertaken) is to be deferred on the balance sheet. Does this deferred contribution meet the conceptual framework definition of a liability? Some may reason that it does— that it represents an unavoidable obligation to provide future services resulting from a past transaction (the past transaction being the acceptance of the restricted-purpose contribution). The FASB does not agree. It has rejected the deferral method because it has concluded that restricted-purpose contributions involve only a fiduciary duty, which does *not* result in a liability (or in permanent capital in respect of endowments)—but is simply revenue in the period received.[19] It is notable that the CICA standard does not describe deferred contributions as liabilities, but states only that "deferred contribution balances should be presented in the statement of financial position outside net assets" (paragraph 4410.52). Thus, it may be argued that the CICA has compromised its conceptual framework in accepting the deferral method.

- Contributions for the purpose of acquiring depreciable capital assets are to be deferred and recognized as revenue in step with the depreciation expense related to the capital asset (paragraph 4410.33). This, then, achieves a matching of the revenue (the amortization of the capital contribution) with the related cost (the amortization of the capital asset). It may be reasoned in support of this treatment that the organization fulfills its obligation under a capital contribution not when it acquires the asset, but only as it keeps the asset and uses it throughout its useful life. A contribution that funds a nondepreciable asset (such as land) is treated as analogous to an endowment, as part of the capital (net assets) of the organization.

- It is possible that a contribution could be designated by a donor for the repayment of the organization's debt. The CICA standard requires that the not-for-profit organization should attempt to assess whether the debt was incurred to fund costs of future periods. If this is determined to be the case, then the contribution is to be deferred and spread over the future periods as those expenses are recognized. For example, if the contribution was for the full repayment of a mortgage on a building, it would be amortized as revenue over the remaining life of the building. If the debt was incurred to acquire a nondepreciable asset, such as land, the contribution would be treated as capital (that is, as a direct increase in net assets). If the debt cannot be related to the incurrance of costs in respect of future activities, it is to be recognized as revenue currently (see paragraphs 4410.38–.44).

Disclosure is required of deferred contribution and endowment balances, and of the nature of restrictions and amount of changes in these balances during the reporting period. These disclosures are to enable users to see the amount of restricted contributions received in the period, and how they have been applied during the period.

The Restricted Fund Method

Under a pure restricted fund method separate funds would set up for one or more classes of temporary and permanently restricted funds. All unrestricted revenues and all expenses are recorded in the general (unrestricted) fund. The general fund may be segregated by activities. Restricted contributions are recorded immediately upon recognition as revenue in the appropriate restricted fund. When temporary restrictions are satisfied, the amounts are transferred from the restricted fund to the general fund.

The FASB has adopted this objective, although it does not require fund accounting to achieve it. It requires that all contributions be recognized as revenues, to be classified as permanently restricted, temporarily restricted, or unrestricted net assets.[20] The CICA standard permits a much looser application, including combinations of restricted fund and deferral methods. Following are the main areas of difference between the CICA standard and a pure restricted fund approach:

- The CICA standard permits a not-for-profit organization to appropriate funds from unrestricted general fund resources to restricted or endowment funds, through the use of interfund transfers. Thus reported restricted and endowment fund balances may include amounts that have no externally imposed restrictions, but are simply the result of decisions of the board of the organization to designate funds for particular purposes. This practice is not allowed under the FASB standard; it requires a strict segregation of permanently restricted, temporarily restricted, and unrestricted net assets based on externally imposed restrictions.

It is important to clearly distinguish between externally and internally restricted resources. The latter are voluntary designations under the control of the organization, and can be reversed or increased at the whim of its board. As noted earlier, in the past some entities have reported voluntary appropriations of funds to restricted purposes as though they were expenditures of the general fund, and did not distinguish the receipts in the restricted funds from externally restricted contributions. This practice has long been criticized. The CICA standard requires that transfers to and from restricted funds be disclosed, and presented outside the revenue and expense statement (paragraphs 4400.12 and .13). As well, the amount of net assets attributable to external restrictions is to be disclosed (paragraph 4400.28).

- Under Canadian GAAP an entity may adopt the restricted fund method for certain types of restrictions (for example, contributions restricted for the purpose of acquiring capital assets) and elect to use the deferral approach for some other types (for example, a grant received in respect of next year's operating expenses may be recognized as a deferred contribution in the general fund) (see paragraphs 4410.65-.67).

- Expenses related to the use of restricted resources are generally to be reported in the statement of revenue and expense of the restricted fund (see paragraph 4400.36). However, an entity with a capital asset fund may elect whether to charge depreciation to that fund or to the general operating fund (paragraph 4430.22). Under the FASB standard, all expenses are presented in the unrestricted statement of activities, because restricted amounts are transferred to unrestricted net assets when the restricted purposes are fulfilled. Under the CICA approach, some expenses related to a particular operating activity (for example research) could be reported in the general fund statement of revenues and expenses (to the extent they are funded by unrestricted resources) and some in a separate restricted fund revenue and expense statement (to the extent they are funded by restricted contributions). (An entity could overcome this problem by appropriating sufficient unrestricted resources to the restricted fund to cover all expenses of that type.)

- The CICA permits "fund accounting" for other than restricted-purpose contributions. Organizations that adopt fund accounting are to provide a brief description of the purpose of each fund, including "the extent to which the particular fund is used to report restricted resources and the types of expenses that are reported in the fund" (paragraphs 4400.06–.07).

There may be a question under both the deferral and restricted fund methods as to when a temporary restriction has been fulfilled. Suppose funds are received and set aside for a given purpose in the amount of $100,000. Suppose further that the entity spends $150,000 for that purpose in a year, but finances that spending entirely out of unrestricted funds rather than using any of the funds set aside. One school of thought is that the donation of restricted funds should not be reported as having been met in the year because the money set aside has not been used. Another school argues that once sufficient expenditures have been made to meet the restriction, there is no longer an outstanding unfulfilled condition. The latter point of view is preferable, and is required by the FASB.[21] The CICA standard is silent on this issue, but a CICA guide indicates that the latter approach is appropriate.[22] The former basis is open to manipulation whenever an entity is in a strong enough financial position to pick and choose when it will use restricted-purpose money to meet its program costs.

Summary Evaluation

The CICA standard thus provides not-for-profit organizations with a complex range of choices. It is unfortunate that the CICA could not settle on one system of accounting for restricted-purpose contributions, as has been done in the U.S. Rather, it has attempted to construct a difficult compromise that gives not-for-profit organizations the ability to select which of two different systems it will apply to each of a number of possible types of restricted contributions. In addition, it can appropriate unrestricted resources and transfer them to restricted funds.

Depending on how a not-for-profit organization elects to apply the standard, its financial statements may be difficult to understand and lack comparability with other not-for-profit organizations. One or more classes of temporarily and permanently restricted contributions can be recognized immediately as revenue, if placed in restricted funds. Alternatively, some or all restricted contributions may be deferred until the restriction is satisfied (if temporarily restricted) or treated as permanent capital (if permanently restricted). Thus different organizations may recognize and present the same types of contributions in very different ways.

This compromise was fashioned, in part, to try to accommodate the opposing views of some larger not-for-profit organizations—in particular universities (which had traditionally accounted on complex fund accounting bases) and hospitals (which had tended to apply deferral-type accounting to restricted contributions).

The standard may be considered to be an improvement over pre-existing practices in Canada, because it defines and places some parameters on the application of the two basic methods. As well, it provides for extensive disclosures of the accounting, so that it should be transparent, at least to reasonably knowledgeable and diligent users. It is to be noted that not-for-profit organizations can choose to implement the standard in relatively easy-to-understand ways by selecting a straightforward deferral or fund accounting method that is clearly disclosed. Many resource providers to not-for-profit organizations are volunteers from the private sector who are presumably accustomed to business enterprise accounting. It may be that they relate more easily to the deferral method than fund accounting, because it may seem to be more consistent with business enterprise accounting.

Contributions in Kind

Some organizations receive contributions of capital assets. A contribution of a capital asset is to be recognized at its fair value at the date of the contribution, except in unusual circumstances when the fair value cannot be reasonably determined. In this latter case it is to be recorded at nominal value and information about the asset is to be disclosed (paragraphs 4430.06 and .38-.39).

The standards allow, but do not require, an organization to recognize contributed materials and services if fair value can be reasonably estimated and if the materials and services are used in the normal course of operations and would otherwise have been purchased. Recognition of contributed materials and services is not required when these criteria are met principally because of the concern that determining fair value, especially of volunteer services, could be onerous (paragraphs 4410.16-.17). U.S. standards are again more demanding of a full accounting of resources that meet general recognition conditions. The FASB requires organizations to recognize contributed materials at fair value. Contributed services are to be recognized if the services received (a) create or enhance nonfinancial assets or (b) require specialized skills, are provided by individuals possessing those skills, and would typically need to be purchased if not donated.[23]

Investment Income and Investment Valuation

Some not-for-profit organizations receive investment income that is externally restricted. For example, a contribution for endowment may be invested and earn investment income that must be used for a purpose specified by the contributor. The accounting standards treat such externally restricted investment income in the same way as a restricted contribution. As a result, restricted investment income will be deferred or recognized as revenue of a restricted fund, depending on the nature of the restriction, if any, and on whether the organization elects to use the deferral method or the restricted fund method.

Many not-for-profit organizations that receive substantial restricted and endowment contributions may build up large pools of investments. In 1988, when not-for-profit organizations were brought within the scope of the *CICA Handbook*, not-for-profit organizations were expected to follow essentially the same accounting for investments as for-profit enterprises, which meant accounting for most long-term portfolio investments at cost. However, there are two provisions in the scope of *CICA Handbook* Section 3050 on long-term investments (paragraph .01) that provide for the possibility of market value accounting.

The first relates to companies that account for security holdings at market value in accordance with accepted practices in their industry. As noted in Chapter 17, investment companies commonly mark investments to market. Some draw an analogy between investment companies and certain not-for-profit foundations, whose primary purpose is to manage large investment portfolios and distribute their income to one or more not-for-profit organizations. They argue that such foundations are similar to investment companies and some carry their investments at market value.

The second is a scope provision introduced into Section 3050 at the time not-for-profit organizations were brought within the scope of the *CICA Handbook*. Under this provision, pooled investment funds of not-for-profit organizations that allocate income and value contributions and withdrawals on a market value basis are permitted to follow market value accounting for their investments. The intended meaning of a "pooled fund" is not clear, however. Some interpret it to enable virtually any investment in a pooled investment fund of a not-for-profit organization to account for portfolio investments at market value—regardless of whether the pool relates only to a single organization that has pooled its investments. Others believe that, in order to be a pooled fund under Section 3050, an investment fund must be one in which two or more arm's-length organizations hold investments.

We have seen that the accounting for financial instruments has been undergoing rapid changes (see Chapter 17). It appears that the CICA has decided to leave these grey areas in accounting for investments by not-for-profit organizations until the larger issues are resolved. The differences between not-for-profit and for-profit enterprises would not seem to justify different investment accounting standards. The CICA research study published in 1980, indicated a preference for not-for-profit organizations to carry portfolio investments at market value. The reasons cited for this position would seem to apply equally to for-profit enterprises.[24] It appears that most not-for-profit organizations are carrying portfolio investments using the cost method.

Under U.S. GAAP, not-for-profit organizations are to carry equity securities with readily determinable fair values and all debt securities at fair value with gains and losses reported in a statement of activities.[25]

Capital Assets

Reference has already been made to the wide variation in accounting for capital expenditures that existed among not-for-profit organizations. Capitalization of capital expenditures was strongly resisted in some quarters. Many not-for-profit organizations routinely expensed all capital items. This practice was argued to be justified, in part, on the basis of a very narrow interpretation of stewardship—accountability for reporting only on how cash resources were expended. Some, for example, expressed concern that an organization that paid for a capital asset out of a special fund raising would show a surplus if it recorded the asset, although it had spent all its cash. We have noted earlier in this chapter that a broader concept of accountability for a wider set of resources was recognized in the extension of the *CICA Handbook* conceptual framework to not-for-profit entities.

It was also noted earlier that the CICA conceptual framework recognizes that an asset of a not-for-profit organization embodies the capacity to provide services. In both the not-for-profit and the for-profit sector capital assets are acquired with the intention of being used. However, for not-for-profit organizations, capital expenditures are considered to be assets if they can be expected to be used to provide future services, rather than to generate future cash flows.

Having determined that capital expenditures should be recorded as assets, the question is whether to amortize these capital assets. The following arguments have commonly been made against amortization of capital assets by not-for-profit organizations:

- It is difficult to estimate capital assets' useful lives. Whether this is true may depend upon the particular situation. In general, since obsolescence may be less likely to be a factor affecting the assets of not-for-profit organizations, one may expect that estimation of useful lives would be easier than it is in business accounting, not harder.

- A charge for amortization should not be made with respect to contributed capital assets or capital assets purchased using resources restricted for that purpose because that would imply that the amortization should be covered out of current contributions or other operating revenue. A variation of this argument is that amortization is meaningless unless it is an operating cost to be recovered from current revenues. As discussed previously, reporting the full cost of services provided has been identified as a fundamental objective of not-for-profit organizations' financial statements. Regardless of how a capital asset is funded, there is a cost associated with its use.

- A figure for amortization based on the historical cost of assets will be meaningless because of changes in replacement cost of asset capacity and the purchasing power of the dollar. This objection has some merit, as it has in business accounting as well. Nevertheless, a basic presumption of the historical cost model, which would seem to be just as applicable to not-for-profit as for for-profit entities, is that cost-based amortization of capital assets has information value, in measuring cost of services, and there are no demonstrably superior measurement alternatives (see discussion in Chapters 11 and 24).

- Recording amortization will cost more than it is worth. This is a matter of opinion. Normally, calculating and recording amortization for external reporting is inexpensive. Greater costs would be involved if amortization figures were to be allocated to programs for internal management purposes, but conceivably more value would be derived from such use. Initial conversion to a system of amortization entails some cost, which might or might not be significant depending upon the individual situation and the degree of insistence on precision in the figures. (Some have suggested that accommodations should be made for smaller organizations that might find it particularly onerous to capitalize and amortize capital assets. This is discussed further below.)

The CICA and FASB have each concluded that standards for accounting for capital assets by not-for-profit organizations should be similar to those required for for-profit enterprises. However, some accommodations and adaptations for not-for-profit organizations have been made as outlined below.

- Items forming part of a "collection" are excluded from the definition of capital assets. A collection is defined as works of art, historical treasures and similar assets that meet certain criteria (paragraph 4440.03(b)). Original proposals were issued in both Canada and the U.S. that would have treated collections in effectively the same way as capital assets. However, standard setters in both countries have now concluded that there are important differences between collection items and capital assets and that the cost of capitalizing and amortizing these items may, depending on the collection, far exceed any benefits. As a result, organizations are not required to capitalize collections (as defined), although they are not precluded from doing so. An organization is to describe its collection and disclose its accounting policies, significant changes to the collection, expenditures on it, and proceeds of any sales of items in the collection (paragraph 4440.07).

- Certain works of art and historical treasures that are not part of a collection require capitalization but need not be amortized on the grounds that they have expected lives that are so long as to be virtually unlimited. The criteria for excluding such items from amortization are that they have cultural, aesthetic, or historical value that is worth preserving perpetually. The organization must also have the technological and financial ability to continue to preserve them (paragraph 4430.21). The same approach is taken under U.S. standards.

- Capital assets of business enterprises may require write-down under CICA standards when there are indicators that the estimated future net cash flows expected to result from their use may be less than the assets' carrying amounts (see Chapter 18). Because the capital assets of not-for-profit organizations usually embody the ability to provide services, rather than generate cash flows, the profit-oriented approach to capital asset impairment is not relevant. CICA accounting standards require that a capital asset of a not-for-profit organization be written down only if the asset no longer has *any* long-term service potential (paragraph 4430.28).

- As mentioned above, there have been significant concerns that the cost of capitalizing capital assets in the not-for-profit sector may exceed benefits. Standard setters concluded that, in most cases, the benefits can be expected to exceed the cost because of the importance of providing information about the full cost of services provided. However, an exception is made in the CICA standard for small organizations where the capitalization of capital expenditures may be quite onerous because of the lack of qualified staff in volunteer-run organizations. As a result, a cut-off was established and organizations with average annual revenues for the current and preceding year of less than $500,000 can choose to expense expenditures on capital assets, as long as they disclose certain information about them (paragraph 4430.40). Organizations qualifying for this exemption are considered likely to have smaller, more defined user groups who will have greater access to information about the organization. As a result, reporting the full cost of services provided for these organizations was considered less important from an accountability standpoint.

Financial Statement Presentation

Financial statements for a not-for-profit organization would normally consist of a statement of financial position, a statement of operations (reporting revenues and expenses), a statement of changes in net assets, and a statement of cash flows, as well as note disclosure. There are several financial reporting issues related to how these financial statements should be presented, especially when the organization uses fund accounting and has restricted resources.

Fund Accounting Issues

Fund accounting can be confusing, especially when numerous funds are reported. We have previously noted that CICA accounting standards take a permissive view of fund accounting, neither encouraging nor prohibiting it. The standards attempt to place some parameters on fund accounting presentation, and require some basic disclosures, to improve its effectiveness and reduce the potential for confusion.

- An organization must include a description of the purpose of each fund reported, including the extent to which it is used to account for restricted resources and the types of expenses it reports (paragraphs 4400.06-.07).

- Each fund is to be presented on a consistent basis from year to year. A change in the revenues or expenses reported in a particular fund would usually represent a change in accounting policy to be applied retroactively (paragraph 4400.08).

- Transfers between funds are to be clearly presented after the presentation of revenue and expenses, as appropriations of net assets. Their amounts and purposes are to be disclosed (paragraphs 4400.12-.13).

- A problem with fund accounting has been its tendency to be applied so as to report an organization's operations in a fragmented way. The accounting standards have attempted to deal with this problem by requiring all the funds' assets, liabilities and net assets to be reported in a single statement of financial position with a total column, adding up all the financial statement items for the organization as a whole (paragraph 4400.18). In addition, all the funds' revenues and expenses are to be reported together in a single statement of operations (see paragraphs 4400.35-.36). These requirements effectively reduce the number of funds that can be easily reported in the main financial statements. It has been suggested that additional fund detail can be provided, if needed, in supplementary schedules.

Restricted Resources

As discussed previously, the presentation and disclosure of restricted and unrestricted amounts in an understandable manner is an important goal of not-for-profit financial reporting. Depending on the method used to account for contributions, the amount of accumulated resources for which restrictions remain unfulfilled at the end of the period appear in the statement of financial position as either deferred contributions (under the deferral method) or restricted net assets. The following information is to be provided to help readers understand the nature and amounts of restricted balances:

- The nature of restrictions imposed on both deferred contributions and restricted net assets must be disclosed, including a brief description of the purposes for which the restricted amounts are to be used.

- The statement of financial position must show the amounts of net assets that are invested in capital assets, subject to permanent restrictions (i.e., endowments), subject to other restrictions, and unrestricted (paragraphs 4400.26-.28).

- A statement of changes in net assets during the reporting period is also to be provided (paragraph 4400.41), and disclosure is to be made of the nature and amount of changes in deferred contribution balances (paragraph 4410.53).

- As observed earlier in the chapter, the CICA standard permits restricted and endowment net asset balances to include amounts for internally, as well as externally, imposed restrictions. Because internal restrictions can be removed at the organization's discretion, they do not impose the same limitations on the organization's financial flexibility as do external restrictions. As a result, the externally restricted portion of the organization's restricted resources is to be disclosed (paragraph 4400.28).

Netting Revenues and Expenses

Not-for-profit organizations are to disclose the gross amount of revenues and expenses (paragraph 4400.37). In the past, some organizations have offset some expenses against revenues and reported only the net amount. For example, only the net amount achieved from fund raising activities might be reported, thus avoiding disclosure of the costs of raising the funds. The CICA standard attempts to rule out this possibility. It recognizes, however, that in some circumstances an organization may receive only the net proceeds from a fund raising event and have no control over, or perhaps even knowledge of, the gross amounts involved. In such a case revenue to the organization is the net amount received.

Statement of Cash Flows

The adoption of full accrual accounting, including capitalization and amortization of capital expenditures, has increased the importance of the statement of cash flows for not-for-profit entities. All but the simplest organizations are now required to provide separate statements of cash flows (paragraphs 4400.44-.53). The standards for the presentation of the statement are similar to those for business enterprises. However, there are some differences:

- *Noncash financing and investing activities.* It was noted in Chapter 22 that recent changes to the standards for cash flow statements prepared by business enterprises have required that noncash financing and investing activities, such as the acquisition of an asset under a capital lease, be excluded from the statement. This requirement was not adopted for not-for-profit organizations. Not-for-profit organizations commonly receive contributions in kind and the Accounting Standards Board concluded that including information about these contributions in the cash flow statement provides important information. Thus, not-for-profit organizations are required to include a noncash financing and investing transaction, such as the receipt of a contributed capital asset, as if it were a receipt and disposition of cash in the statement of cash flows.

- *Presentation of financing and investing activities.* Because of the importance of showing resource providers how the organization has used the resources it has been provided, accounting standards allow not-for-profit organizations to show financing and investing activities together in the statement of cash flows. For example, the receipt of a contribution restricted for the purchase of a capital asset can be grouped with the outflow of cash related to the purchase of the asset in the statement of cash flows.

Related Party Transactions

Standards are also provided for the disclosure of related-party transactions. Related parties are defined in essentially the same manner as for profit-oriented enterprises and the disclosures are the same. However, unlike the for-profit accounting standards, the standards do not deal with the measurement of related-party transactions in a not-for-profit organization's financial statements (see Section 4460).

SUMMARY

Until quite recently there has been no coherent theory of financial reporting for not-for-profit organizations. Accounting practices had tended to be influenced by the thinking of preparers of financial statements and had been little influenced by the perceived needs of external users. In particular, the use of financial statements to assist in the preparation of budgets and to evidence compliance with spending restrictions tended to bias financial reports towards the short-term objective of reporting the flows of cash or of financial claims. Many not-for-profit organizations had a narrow view of external financial accountability, and adopted a "modified cash" basis of accounting.

Accounting practices were very diverse. Some organizations accounted only for financial claims; others recognized some asset prepayments. Capital expenditures might be expensed or capitalized in whole or in part. Recognized capital assets could be depreciated or not. Many organizations did not accrue for all liabilities (for example, for earned future employee benefits). On the other hand, some organizations recognized liabilities for portions of unspent budget allotments. Financial accounting was further complicated by diverse fund accounting practices followed by some organizations. These practices were supported by various rationales.

In recent years more attention has been paid to the uses of financial information by parties outside the not-for-profit entity—in particular by resource providers. The idea of stewardship reporting has been expanded to suggest that financial reports should account for resources consumed in programs, not just money spent. In this way, a better perspective may be provided upon the long-term financial requirements of the entity than is offered by figures of short-term spending. Of course, program expenses do not provide much indication of program effectiveness unless some information is provided as to specific outputs of programs. The development and reporting of performance indicators is in its infancy, but is necessary if financial reports of not-for-profit entities are to tell the whole story. It is clear, however, that performance indicators ought to be compared with accounting measures of resources consumed, rather than resources acquired, to permit a proper judgment of stewardship. This broader concept leads to full accrual accounting and away from a short-run cash-based perspective. However, a statement of flows of cash or liquid resources has value in its own right.

Projects to address the issues of accounting for not-for-profit organizations were initiated in earnest in the 1980s in both Canada and the U.S. In Canada, the first tangible step was to expand scope of the *CICA Handbook* to encompass not-for-profit organizations. It did so while allowing them to continue most of their traditional practices. Next, the conceptual framework was amended to incorporate these entities. Most recently a set of accounting standards was issued that covers the major areas that are considered to be of special significance to not-for-profit organizations.

The conclusion that not-for-profit accounting standards should be reasoned from an adapted conceptual framework developed for business enterprises has been a most important one. This framework has been resisted in some quarters, on the grounds that it does not adequately take into account the unique nature of not-for-profit activities. However, there is a strong case that it does provide a relevant unifying framework that flows logically from the evident information needs of external users of not-for-profit financial reports. Particularly important is its emphasis on the same basic objective of broad accountability for resources and obligations that is required of business enterprises—and for its emphasis on providing information on the full cost of services.

The new series of accounting standards put in place in the *CICA Handbook* reflect the influence of this framework, but with some major compromises.

- A fundamental issue is that of defining the not-for-profit reporting entity. The CICA has concluded, as has the FASB, that the not-for-profit economic unit should be defined in essentially the same way as that of business enterprises—that is, the reporting entity is considered to include all entities controlled by it. Guidance is provided on some questions of determining when control exists within a not-for-profit context. Most unfortunately, the CICA standard does not follow through and require that all controlled entities be consolidated. It permits disclosure of summary financial information in lieu of consolidation. It further allows an organization that controls a large number of individually immaterial organizations to neither consolidate them nor disclose information about them.

- Perhaps the most difficult technical issue that is unique to not-for-profit organizations involves the recognition and presentation of restricted-purpose contributions. The CICA standard enables not-for-profit organizations to select between two very different methods—the "deferral" method and the "restricted fund" method. An organization can choose to apply one or other of these methods to different types of restricted contributions. Under the deferral method a contribution is recognized as revenue when the restriction has been met, while under the restricted fund method contributions are recognized as revenues on receipt in the appropriate unrestricted, temporarily restricted, or permanently restricted fund. Thus reported results can be very different depending on the combination of methods selected. As well, the CICA allows an organization to appropriate unrestricted resources to restricted funds. The standard provides for extensive disclosures to help users understand the accounting. In contrast, the FASB has instituted a more rigorous single method that requires organizations to recognize revenues currently and classify them as between permanently restricted, temporarily restricted, and unrestricted activities.

- Capital expenditures are to be capitalized and amortized in accordance with principles that are basically the same as those applied to business enterprises. However, collections of works of art and historical treasures (as defined) are exempted. As well, small organizations can choose to expense capital expenditures. In both cases certain disclosures are required.

- Not-for-profit organizations are to provide a statement of financial position (that reports totals of all funds' assets and liabilities), a statement of operations (that requires all funds' revenues and expenses to be reported in a single statement), a statement of changes in net assets (that is, equity), and, normally, a statement of cash flows. The standard provides guidance on a number of presentation issues, and requires fairly extensive disclosure.

REFERENCES

[1] See CICA, "Financial Statement Concepts," *CICA Handbook*, Section 1000 (Toronto: CICA), especially pars. .07–.14; and FASB, *Objectives of Financial Reporting by Non-Business Organizations*, Statement of Financial Accounting Concepts No. 4 (Stamford: FASB, 1980), par. 1.

[2] *Financial Reporting for Non-Profit Organizations* (Toronto: CICA, 1980).

[3] CICA, "Financial Statement Presentation by Not-For-Profit Organizations," *CICA Handbook*, Section 4400 (Toronto: CICA), par. .02(a).

[4] CICA, "Introduction to Accounting Recommendations," *CICA Handbook* (Toronto: CICA), par. .2.

[5] CICA, "Non-Profit Organizations," *CICA Handbook*, Section 4230 (Toronto: CICA). This section was superseded and replaced by "Not-For-Profit Organizations," *CICA Handbook*, Sections 4400, 4410, 4420, 4430, 4440, 4450, and 4460 in 1996.

[6] For a description of deficiencies in this section, see E. Paquin and S. Morin, "Coming Up Empty Handed?" *CA Magazine*, June 1989, pp. 38–45.

[7] CICA, "Not-For-Profit Organizations," *CICA Handbook*, Section 4400 Series (Toronto: CICA).

[8] FASB, *Accounting for Contributions Received and Contributions Made*, Statement of Financial Accounting Standards No. 116 (Norwalk: FASB, 1993); and *Financial Statements of Not-for-Profit Organizations*, Statement of Financial Accounting Standards No. 117 (Norwalk: FASB, 1993).

[9] For a discussion in favour of this viewpoint, and a criticism of the FASB framework, see R.N. Anthony, "The Non Profit Accounting Mess," *Accounting Horizons*, June 1995, pp. 44–53.

[10] Recent interest in nonfinancial performance measures fits in with this concern for reporting not-for-profit organization service outputs.

[11] See CICA "Financial Statement Concepts," par. 1000.13.

[12] For a discussion of these arguments, see H. Falk, "Towards a Framework for Not-For-Profit Accounting," *Contemporary Accounting Research*, Spring 1992, pp. 468–99; T.M. Beechy and B.J. Zimmerman, "Costs and the Collective Good," *CA Magazine*, November 1992, pp. 44–49; and J.C.C. Macintosh, "Finding the Right Fit," *CA Magazine*, March 1995, pp. 34–38.

[13] Note the similarity of such foundations and the preprogrammed "special purpose enterprises" established by some business enterprises, and the difficulties in determining whether they should be treated as subsidiaries (as discussed in Chapter 20).

[14] See, for example, Institute of Chartered Accountants of Ontario, "Rules of Professional Conduct," in *ICAO Member's Handbook* (Toronto: Institute of Chartered Accountants of Ontario) par. 206.

15 An appendix to the Introduction to the *CICA Handbook* Section 4400, "Not-For-Profit Organizations" provides guidance on the applicability of other *CICA Handbook* standards to not-for-profit organizations.

16 See CICA, Emerging Issues Committee, *Accounting for Government Funding to Non-Profit Organizations*, EIC 36 (Toronto: CICA, 1992). It concluded that expected future government funding should not be accrued in the current period to offset an accrued vacation pay liability, because it is not directly linked to the vacation pay accrual and is not currently receivable.

17 See FASB, *Accounting for Contributions Received and Contributions Made*, SFAS 116, pars. 22–23, and 57–66.

18 For example, condominium corporations are required by law to allocate a certain amount of their resources to a reserve for capital maintenance.

19 FASB, *Accounting for Contributions Received and Contributions Made*, SFAS 116, pars. 67–68.

20 See FASB, *Financial Statements of Not-for-Profit Organizations*, SFAS 117.

21 See FASB, *Accounting for Contributions Received and Contributions Made*, SFAS 116, par. 17.

22 K. Danyluk, *Not-for-Profit Financial Reporting Guide* (Toronto: CICA, 1998), p. 27.

23 FASB, *Accounting for Contributions Received and Contributions Made*, SFAS 116, pars. 8–10.

24 CICA, *Financial Reporting for Non-Profit Organizations*, p. 79.

25 FASB, *Accounting for Certain Investments Held by Not-for-Profit Organizations*, Statement of Financial Accounting Standards No. 124 (Norwalk: FASB, 1995).

C h a p t e r **28**

GOVERNMENT

The goals of government are different from those of a business enterprise. The principal objectives of a business enterprise are to earn profit and maximize the return on investment and the business' resources are employed for those purposes. Governments, on the other hand, have multiple social and economic objectives. They spend money to provide public services and to implement a variety of social, political, and economic policies.

In a business, revenues are typically derived from the sale of goods or services in direct exchange for cash, receivables or other consideration. In addition, there is a very direct relationship between costs and revenues since costs are incurred with the direct goal of increasing revenues. Conversely, in a government, the delivery of a service does not normally give rise to revenue, and the payment of taxes does not necessarily directly entitle a taxpayer to any particular public service or benefit. Because governments have the power to tax, their revenues are not dependent upon voluntary contributions or on the profitable sales of goods and services in the marketplace. Thus, the relationship between revenues and costs in any given period is not the same in government as it is for business.

Governments spend almost half of the national gross domestic product in Canada. They need financial information for good decision making and accountability. That financial information needs to be relevant, reliable, consistent and comparable. A 1981 CICA research study on financial reporting by governments found that government financial statements were none of these things. The study noted that "the financial statements for Canadian governments are now so complex and varied on presentation and terminology that even persons familiar with government accounting have difficulty in appreciating the significance of information conveyed."[1] After the study was completed, the CICA's Public Sector Accounting Board (PSAB) was created in 1981 to develop accounting and auditing recommendations for federal, provincial and territorial governments. In 1986 the scope of the Public Sector Accounting Board was extended to include accounting recommendations for local governments.

The responsibilities and authorities of the federal and provincial governments are set out in the constitution of Canada. These governments are sovereign entities and cannot be required to comply with PSAB's recommendations. Yet, there is a need for generally accepted accounting principles for governments that are independent and objective and that are developed with the key stakeholders, i.e. taxpayers, in mind. Governments comply with PSAB's recommendations voluntarily because they are persuaded that the result is better management information and a full accounting for their use of the public resources. With few exceptions, governments at the federal and provincial levels in Canada substantially comply with the accounting recommendations set out in the *Public Sector Accounting Handbook,* a vast improvement from the diversity that existed in 1981.

Local governments operate under different guidelines. Local governments are required by provincial legislation to issue financial statements to help demonstrate accountability and to help users understand and assess a local government's management of the public resources entrusted to it. In some jurisdictions provincial legislation requires local governments to prepare financial statements in accordance with PSAB. In other cases, local governments comply because of their need for better information.

The CICA's *Public Sector Accounting Handbook* defines "public sector" as including federal, provincial territorial and local governments, government organizations, organizations jointly owned or controlled by two or more governments, and school boards. To understand this definition it is necessary to understand the components. Government organizations are organizations that are accountable to the government for the administration of their financial affairs and resources and are owned or controlled by the government. There are different types of government organizations with different characteristics. *Government business enterprises* are separate legal entities with the authority to carry on a business. They sell goods and services to individuals and organizations outside the government and can maintain their operations and meet their liabilities through such activities. In other words, they are self-sufficient organizations.

Government business-type organizations also sell goods and services and conduct activities that are business-like. However, a government business-type organization may sell goods and services within the government or may rely on government subsidies to survive. Since they are not self-sufficient, they are different from government business enterprises. Finally, *government not-for-profit organizations* are those organizations within government that meet the definition of a not-for-profit organization in the CICA Handbook[2] and which have counterparts outside government.

Most government organizations are directed to follow the *CICA Handbook* unless otherwise directed to a section of the *Public Sector Accounting (PSA) Handbook.*[3] Other government organizations may choose to follow either the *PSA Handbook* or the *CICA Handbook,* selecting the basis that is most appropriate to their objectives and circumstances. The chart on page 655 summarizes the types of public sector entities and the appropriate accounting recommendations.

When the *Public Sector Accounting Handbook* does not provide specific guidance on accounting principles, a government would consider generally accepted practice in the public sector for guidance. Other sources that might be useful include analogous *CICA Handbook* material, other authoritative pronouncements, accounting literature and published financial statements in the private sector.

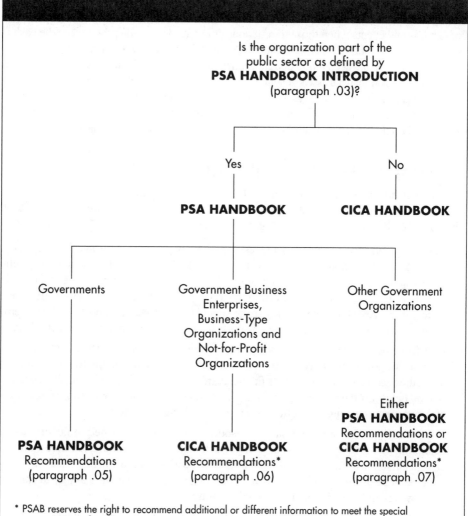

Is the organization part of the
public sector as defined by
PSA HANDBOOK INTRODUCTION
(paragraph .03)?

Yes   No

PSA HANDBOOK   **CICA HANDBOOK**

Governments   Government Business   Other Government
Enterprises,   Organizations
Business-Type
Organizations and
Not-for-Profit
Organizations

Either
PSA HANDBOOK
Recommendations or
PSA HANDBOOK   **CICA HANDBOOK**   **CICA HANDBOOK**
Recommendations   Recommendations*   Recommendations*
(paragraph .05)   (paragraph .06)   (paragraph .07)

* PSAB reserves the right to recommend additional or different information to meet the special
circumstances of government organizations.

FUNDAMENTAL CONCEPTUAL ISSUES

Basis of Accounting

A financial report demonstrates stewardship or accountability. Taxpayers, legislators, investors and other users of government financial statements need information that will help them assess the government's performance in the management of financial affairs and resources. In addition, financial information helps determine whether the financial resources entrusted to the government were administered appropriately. The conceptual framework set out in the *Public Sector Accounting Handbook* establishes a basis of accounting that considers the users and objectives of government financial statements as key in understanding the financial information.

The recommendations in the handbook are currently established using a general framework of a modified accrual basis of accounting. The modified accrual basis of accounting recognizes transactions and events when those transactions or events occur rather than when the cash is paid or received. Unlike full accrual accounting used in the private sector, financial performance under modified accrual accounting does not reflect the cost of nonfinancial asset consumption since the cost of nonfinancial assets acquired is expensed. The financial position focuses on financial assets (i.e., excluding capital assets) and liabilities. Virtually all other assets and liabilities are recognized in the same manner as under the accrual basis. Moreover, the modified accrual basis is evolving as governments move towards adoption of a full accrual basis of accounting.

Users of Government Financial Statements

Government financial statements help users understand and assess the state of a government's finances and its accountability for the administration of the resources entrusted to it. The following list covers the main categories of users:

- *The Public.* Taxpayers, ratepayers and residents directly provide the revenues and resources necessary for government operations. They are also the beneficial owners of the public money and property for which legislatures, councils and governments are responsible and are also the recipients of government services. Members of the public will have a variety of interests and views. They are or should be interested in reports on the government's finances and information on the costs of government programs and activities.

- *Governing bodies.* These include legislatures, local government councils and boards of directors of government organizations. These bodies are accountable to the public and are authorized to administer public financial affairs and resources. Financial statements will be helpful if they assist these governing bodies to evaluate the results of past policies and predict the possible effect of present and future policies.

- *Investors.* Investors provide financial resources. They are interested in government's economic performance since its impact on such matters as inflation and interest rates is significant to the attractiveness of government securities as investments. Financial statements will be useful if they provide information about government's ability to finance its activities and meet its liabilities and commitments.

- *Analysts.* Government's social and economic impact is of considerable interest to economists, sociologists, experts in public finance and the like. Senior governments, particularly, have such an impact on employment, interest rates, and exchange rates that reliable and timely financial reports are of considerable significance.

- *Regulators.* These include provincial governments and their commissions and boards, which have authority over local government activities. Regulators seek assurance that those activities are carried out in a fiscally responsible manner.

Objectives of Government Financial Statements

The objectives of government financial statements are based on the information needs of users. The *PSA Handbook* articulates five specific objectives of government financial statements. It is worth spending some time on these objectives since they have had and will continue to have a significant impact on the development of accounting standards for the public sector. These financial reporting objectives were established before any more specific accounting recommendations were developed. In contrast, the conceptual framework for profit-oriented enterprises was developed after a significant body of accounting standards had already evolved.

Function of the Financial Statements

> Financial statements should communicate reliable information relevant to the needs of those for whom the statements are prepared, in a manner that maximizes its usefulness. As a minimum, this requires information that is clearly presented, understandable, timely and consistent.[4]

This first objective requires reliable and relevant financial information, presented in a manner that maximizes its usefulness. It also emphasizes that the information should be clearly presented, understandable, timely and consistent. These qualities have long been recognized as important in financial reporting by profit-oriented enterprises. They are equally valid for government.

Scope of Government Financial Accountability

> Financial statements should provide an accounting of the full nature and extent of the financial affairs and resources for which the government is responsible including those related to the activities of government agencies and enterprises.[5]

The position taken with this objective sets the stage for defining the reporting entity, which we will discuss shortly. In this objective we see the link between financial reporting and areas of responsibility. Governments carry out policies and deliver programs and services through a variety of entities and organizations. While the objective does not say anything about how separate entities for which the government is responsible should be accounted for and does not address the issue of consolidation, it clearly establishes responsibility as the basis for government accountability.

Demonstrating Government Financial Accountability

> Financial statements should demonstrate the accountability of a government for the financial affairs and resources entrusted to it.
>
> a) Financial statements should provide information useful in evaluating the government's performance in the management of financial affairs and resources.
>
> b) Financial statements should provide information useful in assessing whether financial resources were administered by the government in accordance with the limits established by the appropriate legislative authorities.[6]

This objective states the importance of demonstrating the government's financial accountability. One aspect is to provide information that is useful in evaluating the government's performance in the management of financial affairs and resources. In this regard financial statements should provide information that facilitates the comparison of budget to actual results, the establishment of trends in spending, revenues, investing and borrowing, cost of operations and key relationships such as debt or debt-servicing costs to revenue. Another aspect of demonstrating government's accountability is to provide information that is useful in assessing whether financial resources were administered in accordance with the limits established by legislative authorities. Admittedly, financial statements by themselves cannot provide such assurance. However, it is important that they be presented with the right level of detail to show that financial activities were within the established limits with respect to spending, borrowing and investing activities, for example.

Reporting Government Financial Activities

> Financial statements should account for the sources, allocation and use of the government's resources in the accounting period and how it met its cash requirements.[7]

This objective sets out the importance of reporting the sources, allocation and use of the government's resources and of showing how the government financed its activities and met its cash requirements. This is useful information in understanding and assessing a government's resource requirements, the use of resources and revenue raising activities. The financial statements also inform users about the extent to which resources will be required from future revenues and borrowings to pay for spending of the period and how the government financed its activities in the period. In order to show the allocation and uses of a government's resources, financial statements report the nature and purpose of a government's expenditures or expenses. A government finances its activities and meets its obligations by revenue-raising, incurring debt payable in the future, or using existing cash. Financial statements should show how a government financed its activities and met its cash requirements.

Reporting Financial Condition

Financial statements should present information to display the state of a government's finances.

a)   Financial statements should present information to describe the government's financial condition at the end of the accounting period.

b)   Financial statements should provide information that is useful in evaluating the government's ability to finance its activities and to meet its liabilities and commitments.[8]

In the private sector, the main goal is profit and annual results are measured and reported in terms of annual profit and loss. Financial position is measured by adding or deducting the profit or loss from the owner's investment but, by and large, the focus of the financial statements is on annual results. Government is different. To adequately portray the state of the government's finances, statements provide information that will describe financial condition in terms of a government's liabilities and assets at the end of the period. Financial statements need to include indicators that can be used to determine whether the financial condition has improved or deteriorated. One important indicator of financial condition, particularly at the federal and provincial levels, is the difference between the government's liabilities and its financial assets, called net debt. We will discuss this indicator in some detail shortly. Government financial statements should also report information about a government's physical assets and we will consider later what this has meant for the development of reporting standards related to such assets. Finally, users expect financial statements to disclose the nature and term of liabilities and assets and of potential liabilities represented by commitments and contingencies such as guarantees and indemnities.

Government Reporting Model

The government reporting model is fundamentally different from the reporting model used for businesses and even for not-for-profit organizations. We have seen that users of government financial statements have different needs from users of private sector statements. One of the key indicators for Canadian governments, particularly federal and provincial, is net debt—the difference between a government's liabilities and its financial assets. Net debt measures the future revenues that need to be raised to pay for past transactions or the net financial assets that are on hand to finance future operations. Net debt is a relevant measure for governments because it shows the cumulative effects of deficit financing. At present, the levels of debt in Canada are high, despite recent progress by many governments in eliminating annual deficits.

Focusing on the importance of net debt has been a key factor in the success of improving the state of government finances. Net debt ensures that all of a government's liabilities, both short-term and long-term, are reported in the financial statements. As an example, provincial governments now report tens of billions of dollars of previously unrecorded employee pension obligations.

While net debt indicates the government's future revenue requirements, it does not describe the financial health of that government. Many of the benefits created from a government's financial activities go to society and will not be fully recorded on government financial statements. So, "assets" a government creates, like investments in education and health, will never show up on its financial statements. Financial statements also do not reflect the effectiveness of government spending and revenue decisions although there are demands for reports that provide evidence that good value for money is being achieved from public resources used.

Now that most governments are complying with generally accepted accounting principles for governments, there is an increased focus on performance measurement and accountability. Realistic, measurable objectives or targets that can be used to demonstrate performance are key elements in the accountability framework. The private sector has traditionally depended mainly on financial indicators to establish objectives and demonstrate performance. In contrast, government systems have focused on nonfinancial indicators. The shift now is towards government systems that show the costs of objectives and that match nonfinancial indicators with costs to determine financial performance against these objectives. Governments need information on the cost of services in order to assess the dual expectations of fiscal economy and improved delivery of public services.[9]

One of the major costs of providing government services is related to the acquisition of capital assets. We will discuss detailed accounting recommendations for capital assets later. For now, what is important to know is that traditionally most governments have charged the cost of acquiring capital assets to operations when the assets were purchased. But, without accounting control over the assets, comprehensive financial information that is essential for stewardship and accountability may be missing. Accounting for capital assets is therefore key in determining the full costs of government programs and services and in performance measurement. Allocating the cost of the assets to programs and services as the assets are used up rather than writing them off as purchased is a major step in moving governments towards a full accrual basis of accounting. For capital assets this means recording depreciation as a program cost. If capital assets are depreciated, government services and activities will be measured on a basis consistent with that of the private sector and this means better information to assess the relative efficiency of government programs and activities and to make informed decisions about outsourcing and privatizing operations. Although the benefits are substantial, capitalizing assets is a major undertaking for a government in terms of time, effort and cost.

General Standards of Financial Presentation

The general standards of government financial presentation build on many of the concepts set out in the objectives and translate those objectives into a sort of blue print for government financial statements. The general standards ensure full and fair disclosure of information in government financial statements. There are two main areas: general reporting principles and standards of presentation and disclosure.[10]

General Reporting Principles

The general reporting principles provide guidance on the reporting of financial information in financial statements to communicate information to users. Familiar issues include the role played by notes to the financial statements, the presentation of prior year comparative amounts, and the importance of consistency in financial reporting. In addition, since financial statements should present the substance of transactions and events, it is necessary to address the situation where legislation might require certain transactions or balances to be reported in a way that does not reflect their substance. As long as the legislative requirement can be met by special purpose financial statements or reports or by notes or schedules to the financial statements, presentation in the general purpose financial statements that reflects the substance of the transaction should prevail. Otherwise, the financial statements would be prepared in accordance with the legislation and note disclosure of this fact would be provided.[11]

Standards of Presentation and Disclosure

Among other areas, the standards in this area deal with reporting financial condition/position and financial activities. The most significant requirements are discussed below:

- *Reporting financial condition.* Financial statements need to provide information that will describe a government's financial condition in terms of its assets and liabilities at the end of the accounting period. They should include indicators that can be used to assess whether the government's financial condition has improved or deteriorated. The difference between liabilities and financial assets, net debt, emerges as an important financial statement measure for federal, provincial and territorial governments as well as local governments. Liabilities and financial assets are required to be included in the statement of financial position and the difference between a government's liabilities and financial assets at the end of the reporting period is to be reported. For local governments another indicator of financial condition may include fund balances (the difference between short-term assets and short-term liabilities). In order to provide an adequate description of a government's financial condition, information about tangible capital assets, such as land, buildings, equipment, roads and bridges, is important since these represent significant resources with which the government has been entrusted. Information about material financial commitments and contingencies would be disclosed in the notes to the financial statements since it is useful in assessing revenues that may be required in the future.

- *Reporting financial activities.* The main goal here is to report the government's revenues, expenditures (or expenses) and surplus or deficit for the period. For federal, provincial and territorial governments there are two basic ways that this can be done, depending on the government's approach to accounting for tangible capital assets, as will be discussed later. Revenues are to be segregated by different types (e.g., taxes, nontax sources, transfers from other governments). Expenditures or expenses are to be reported by function or major program. For local governments a statement of financial activities should account for all revenues by source and types, for all expenditures by function and the extent to which revenues were sufficient to meet expenditures.

- *Reporting legislative control and financial accountability.* Financial statements are used to provide information about the extent to which financial resources entrusted to the government are administered within provincial and local government legislative and regulatory authorities. One of the recommendations in this area deals with the presentation of planned or budgeted results along with actual results. This is an area that is unique to governments and reflects the fact that the budget is an essential part of the government financial planning process. Comparison of actual results to those budgeted demonstrates legislative control and responsibility since a government's governing body is accountable for departures from budget. Another element of reporting financial accountability is the recommendation that a government present information to show where a government has exceeded its borrowing, investing or expenditure authority limits.

Defining the Financial Reporting Entity

Defining the reporting boundaries of the government reporting entity presents more problems than it does for any other type of entity. Governments use a variety of ways to structure their activities, such as "special funds," Crown corporations and boards and commissions. While these organizations may issue separate financial statements, they provide only a fragmented view of the government as a whole. Users, on the other hand, need aggregated information that shows the position and operations of the government as a whole. Therefore, it is important to have criteria for deciding which organizations should be included in the government reporting entity if government financial statements are to be comparable and consistent.

If we wish to formulate criteria for determining what activities should be included or excluded from the government entity, the key question is whether any organization under the responsibility of the government is properly excluded from the government entity. If a government activity is accounted for outside its reporting boundaries the revenues and expenditures of the activity will not be included in government revenues and expenditures. In addition, advances a government makes to the organization will be treated as third party transactions and the assets and liabilities attributable to the activity will not appear in the government's statement of financial position. How a government chooses to provide programs or services should not alter the information reported in the government's financial statements. These financial statements need to properly represent the full range of government activity. While a summary report cannot be expected to provide much detail about individual activities of the government, supplementary notes and schedules can provide more detailed information. The potential confusion caused by aggregation of results of dissimilar activity could be mitigated by supplementary reports of segments of activity.

The Concept of Control

If it is acknowledged that an entity should provide information in its summary financial report for all activities for which it is responsible, some clarification of the idea of responsibility may be necessary. One might begin by suggesting that an entity is responsible for activities it controls. But there are some difficulties with defining the concept of control.

From a government viewpoint, having the authority to control can be interpreted broadly. Control might be interpreted in an administrative or financial sense or both. Governments have the authority to control a wide variety of activities and organizations through financial support or regulation. For example, suppose a government sponsors a charitable organization and, to this end, it provides an initial grant and appoints the first board of directors. Thereafter, the organization raises its own funds and a mechanism is in force for election of the governing board that does not provide or require that a majority be government appointees. Should that organization be included within the government entity up to the time that government funding no longer forms a majority of its revenues, up to the time that government nominees no longer control the board, or never?

Consider an even more significant example. Municipalities are, in law, "creatures of the province," notwithstanding that municipal governing bodies are elected by their residents. It seems unlikely that many people would argue that details of the operations and financial position of these bodies should be included in the financial reports of the provinces.

Combination of Accountability and Control or Ownership

Realistically, the power of the purse is the power of control. Consequently, reliance on the concept of control alone to define the reporting entity might result in all sorts of organizations being included in governments' financial statements simply by virtue of the funding relationship. The difficulty is distinguishing between organizations that are financially dependent on or regulated by the government and one that should be in the government reporting entity. It seems unlikely that many would argue that the details of all organizations receiving significant government funding should be included in governments' financial statements. To avoid such an impractical result, the government reporting entity has been defined to include those organizations that are (1) accountable for the administration of their financial affairs and resources either to a minister of the government or directly to the legislature or local government council and (2) owned or controlled by the government.[12]

- *Accountability.* In this context, accountability refers to the organization's accountability to the government for management's overall actions, operations and administration. In other words, organizations that are simply accountable to the government for the government funding that they receive would not be considered to be part of the government reporting entity.[13] For example, organizations that are only regulated by or financially dependent on government are are accountable to the government only for demonstrating compliance with regulations or funding arrangements. They are not accountable for their management's overall actions, operations and administration.

- *Ownership.* A government owns an organization when it has created or acquired the organization and, directly or indirectly, holds title to the majority of the organization's shares that carry the right to appoint at least a majority of the members of the board of directors or to the organization's net assets. Evidence that the organization holds title to an organization's net assets may appear in the form of legislation that allows the transfer of the organization's net assets (or net liabilities) to the government at the government's discretion or legislation that designates the organization as a Crown corporation or a government agency. Legislation allowing the transfer of an organization's net assets to a government only on dissolution of the organization is not evidence of government ownership since it would only be when the organization is dissolved that the government gains ownership of any residual interest.[14]

• *Control.* The definition of control has some similarities with that used for not-for-profit and profit-oriented entities. A government is considered to control an organization when it has the authority to determine the financial and operating policies of that organization, without requiring the consent of others or changes to existing legislative provisions. Evidence of control may be found in the legislation, regulations and bylaws that give the government the authority to determine the revenue-raising, expenditure and resource allocation policies of the organization or appoint a majority of the organization's governing board or its senior management. As with not-for-profit organizations, the presumption of control through appointment of the majority of the organization's governing board can be overcome by other factors. For example, control may not exist when the government's appointment of nominees selected by other groups is only a formality because the government does not have the right to refuse or remove nominees. Another example is an organization with a publicly elected board. If this board exists only to implement and administer the government's operating policies, rather than to determine those policies, the government could still be considered to control the organization even though its board is not appointed by the government.[15]

Thus, the government reporting entity is defined to include organizations which are both accountable to the government and owned or controlled by the government. Government financial statements should consolidate the financial statements of all organizations that are part of the reporting entity, with the exception of government business enterprises. Consolidation was considered to be the most appropriate course in most instances because it meets the financial statement objective to account for the financial affairs and resources for which the government is responsible.

The conclusion was somewhat different for government business enterprises, however. A government business enterprise has the following characteristics:

• it is a separate legal entity which has the power to contract and can sue or be sued;

• it has been delegated the financial and operational authority to carry on a business;

• it sells goods and services to individuals and organizations outside of the government reporting entity as its principal activity; and

• it can maintain its operations and meet its liabilities from revenues received from sources outside of the government reporting entity.[16]

Government business enterprises are different from other government organizations. They differ in their relationship to the government, their objectives and their operations. Examples of government business enterprises are public utilities, insurance corporations and provincial workers' compensation boards. A government business enterprise represents a financial asset of the government and, because of its business-oriented objectives, the *PSA Handbook* takes the view that equity accounting is more appropriate than consolidation for such enterprises.

Equity accounting avoids commingling the business enterprise's budget and actual results with those of other government organizations. It also avoids including the business enterprise's debt with that of other government organizations, which is appropriate since the business enterprise is expected to repay its debt from its own revenues. Because the government business enterprise carries on a business, it follows the same accounting policies as a private sector business. As a result, a government business enterprise is accounted for using the modified equity method, which differs from the equity method in that the business enterprise's accounting policies are not conformed to those followed by the government.[17]

The Government Reporting Entity—The Practical Reality

In addressing the government reporting entity the focus of PSAB has been on whole of government financial statements, i.e., financial statements that reflect the full nature and extent of the financial affairs and resources the government is responsible for. Putting the recommendations into practice has been a somewhat different story. Determining which entities the government is responsible for can be a difficult matter that requires the exercise of professional judgment. For example, there is currently considerable debate about the status of Workers' Compensation Boards (WCB's). In some provinces the Workers' Compensation Board is consolidated as part of the government reporting entity whereas in other provinces it is not. Decisions about accountability ownership and control are made based on existing legislation and other factors that are open to some degree of interpretation.

An additional complication is that in different jurisdictions the structure of government may vary. For example, in some provinces hospitals and universities are clearly part of the government reporting entity. The government is directly responsible for the organizations and appropriately consolidates them in the summary financial statements. In other provinces, hospitals and universities are definitely not part of the government reporting entity. While financially dependent on the government for funding, they are not owned nor controlled by the government and are not accountable for the administration of their financial affairs. In such cases, these organizations are appropriately excluded from the government reporting entity.

What is important to appreciate is that it can be difficult at times to draw the boundaries around the government reporting entity. The criteria are stringent but in practice professional judgment may be needed to decide on the relationship between the government and certain public sector organizations.

SPECIFIC ACCOUNTING ISSUES FACING GOVERNMENT

In this section, we will look at some specific accounting issues facing governments.

Revenues—Self-Assessed Taxes

Revenues include taxes, user fees, investment and natural resource revenue, grants and other transfers. Revenues would be accounted for in the period the transaction or event giving rise to the revenues occurred. This ensures that related financial assets are accounted for in the period they are created. The estimation of income taxes receivable presents a problem unique to governments since income taxes are self-assessed. Amounts owing from self-assessed taxes, such as personal and corporate income taxes, are determined by the taxpayer and are not normally estimated by the government at the end of the accounting period. The government may not have good evidence of amounts due for the period until tax returns are filed, and even then changes occur when returns are assessed. Governments have traditionally accounted for such tax revenue on a cash basis rather than make an estimate of the taxes receivable. As reliable methods are developed to estimate self-assessed tax revenues such amounts will be accounted for at the end of the accounting period to ensure that a complete measure of revenue is reported.

Tangible Capital Assets

Tangible capital assets are a significant economic resource managed by governments and a key component in the delivery of many government programs. Tangible capital assets in the public sector include items as diverse as roads, water systems, aircraft, dams, canals and bridges. Traditionally, practice in the government sector has been to write off capital property as expenditures at the time of acquisition. The reason for this was that total expenditures, including the cost of capital property, are an important factor in the assessment of future revenue requirements, which has been an important focus of government.

However, given the need to report government financial accountability and financial condition as set out in the objectives of financial reporting according to the *PSA Handbook,* the CICA's Public Sector Accounting Board began to consider how capital assets should be accounted for by governments. Scarce resources have led governments to focus increasingly on determining the cost of programs and services, and on performance measurement. When a capital asset is written off on acquisition, it is exempted from accounting controls and from future accountability. Evaluations of the cost of programs may not take into account the consumption of the capital assets used in delivering programs. Inappropriate allocations of government resources may result because the true cost of providing services is not known. Also, it may be difficult to determine whether a government is maintaining its asset base. For example, continual decreases in the carrying value of capital assets may indicate that a government is not maintaining or enhancing its asset base. Eroding the asset base can lead to increased financial burdens on future taxpayers and the associated cost of restoring the asset base could impair a government's ability to maintain other services.

There were also concerns that writing off capital assets on acquisition can lead to uneconomic practices. For example, a government may be more inclined to lease capital assets in order to spread the cost of those assets over the terms of the leases, rather than absorb the full cost in the year of acquisition. Such an approach may be more costly in the end if the present value of the lease payments is greater than the cost to purchase an asset outright.

A potential concern related to changing how capital assets were accounted for related to the reporting of government's financial condition or net debt. For example, if capital expenditures are capitalized, would they be deducted from the government's total liabilities reducing the net debt and making the government's financial picture look healthier? Would readers of the financial statements understand the change and its impact on traditional financial statement indicators?[18]

Consistent with the stated objectives of government financial statements, the PSAB concluded that, for federal, provincial and territorial governments, tangible capital assets should be reported as assets in the government's statement of tangible capital assets and amortized over their useful lives. Comprehensive financial information about tangible capital assets is essential for stewardship, accountability and security purposes. For example, providing such information will help governments identify and account for assets on hand, new acquisitions and disposals. By reporting information on capital assets, governments will be better able to demonstrate their accountability for those assets and the public will have a clearer picture of how its tax dollars are being used. Since the PSAB has not yet completed a project on accounting for tangible capital assets for local governments, the following discussion relates to the senior level of government.[19]

Reporting Expenditures versus Expenses

As noted earlier, governments are gradually shifting from a modified accrual basis of accounting towards full accrual accounting. The biggest difference in these two bases is the accounting for capital assets and whether capital assets are treated as expenditures (i.e., written off when purchased) or capitalized as assets and depreciated. This is the debate between an expenditure or expense basis of accounting. A government must choose whether to use an expense or expenditure basis of accounting for its capital assets. Expenditures are the cost of goods and services acquired in the period whether or not payment has been made whereas expenses are the cost of resources consumed in and identifiable with the operations of the accounting period. For both methods, a government prepares a statement of tangible capital assets which reports the net book value of a government's tangible capital assets and how it has changed in the period. The statement provides stewardship information, such as the types of assets, additions, disposals, consumption and valuation adjustments to help users in assessing a government's accountability. A government reporting on the expense basis also includes capital assets in its statement of financial position and reports depreciation in the operating statement. Net debt and the change in net debt are key measures of the state of a government's finances. Therefore, a government is required to report liabilities, financial assets and net debt on the statement of financial position. Net debt is then divided into its capital and operating components, with the capital component being equal to the net book value of the government's tangible capital assets. This presentation is aimed at ensuring the appropriate reporting of net debt such that it represents liabilities less financial assets. In other words, net debt should not be artificially reduced by the capitalization of capital assets. Also, under the expense basis of accounting, the statement of operations includes amortization as an expense in arriving at the surplus or deficit for the period. Similar to the situation with net debt, the statement of operations explains both the change in net debt and the change in the operating component of net debt. Overall this approach is similar to that related to not-for-profit organizations, which are required to separately identify the amount of net assets invested in capital assets.

Under the expenditure basis of accounting, the cost and amortization of capital assets only appears in the statement of tangible capital assets. Capital assets are not included in the statement of financial position, nor is amortization expense reflected in the statement of revenues and expenditures. It is not necessary to divide net debt into operating and capital components since the total net debt reflects only the operating component.[20]

Under both bases, the statement of tangible capital assets is provided to track the cost and amortization of these capital assets. Thus, both methods result in information about the government's tangible capital assets being presented in the financial statements. In addition the statement of financial position continues to account for net debt as a principal measure of financial condition. The reason for allowing a choice was to ease governments into the tracking of capital assets. Under the expenditure basis, a government can provide the necessary information without affecting the traditional reporting of net debt and surplus where capital assets are expensed as acquired. This methodology is a major step in moving governments towards full accrual accounting. Not only will this provide better information about the use of capital assets, but also, full accrual accounting means that the cost of government activities and services will be measured on a basis consistent with that of the private sector. So better information will be available to assess the relative efficiency of government programs and activities and to make informed decisions about whether outsourcing or privatizing operations is appropriate.

Restricted Assets and Revenues

Similar to not-for-profit organizations, governments have resources with varying degrees of restrictions. Restrictions limit the government's accessibility to resources.

External Restrictions

Resources subject to external restrictions (i.e., imposed by agreement with an external party or by legislation of another government) are the least accessible. They cannot be used for any purposes other than those stipulated, unless the government obtains approval from the external party or the relevant legislation changes. External restrictions are often associated with the inflow of resources received from external parties who specify how the resources are to be used. In addition, external restrictions may be imposed on the government's own assets, as is the case with sinking fund investments.

Internally Restricted Entities

Another category of restriction is referred to as internally restricted entities, which are separate legal entities within the government reporting entity, created by the government's own legislation. This legislation establishes an accountability relationship with parties external to the government reporting entity to use the entity's assets or net assets as specified while the legislation is in effect. The entity is considered restricted either because the legislation stipulates that the entity's revenues, which are derived principally from parties external to the government reporting entity in exchange for goods or services, can only be used to provide those goods or services or because the government cannot use the assets or net assets of the entity for a purpose other than providing the goods and services for which the resources were received. The restrictions placed on these assets are different from externally imposed restrictions since the government can change its legislation and effectively remove the restrictions. An example of such an entity is a provincial Crown corporation that provides insurance protection, such as automobile insurance. These entities receive insurance premiums from participants that are intended to pay the costs of the corporation and provide the insurance benefits to plan holders.

Designated Assets

These assets have been formally designated by the government to indicate its intention to use the assets for a specific purpose. Such designations of assets may be achieved through government legislation, by-law or resolution that limits the use of assets to specified purposes. Governments can readily change the legislation, by-law or resolution and use the designated assets for a different purpose if necessary.

Recognition and Disclosure of Restricted Resources

Similar to not-for-profit organizations, governments need a means of reporting so that the amount of restricted resources and the nature of restrictions are clear. The reporting requirements that have evolved vary depending on the degree of accessibility to the restricted or designated amounts. Externally restricted resources are the least accessible since they are not available for use at the government's discretion without the intervention of an external party or another government. Therefore, the accounting standards require that restricted inflows be deferred and recognized as revenue of the period in which they are used for the purposes specified. Disclosure of the nature and source of any external restrictions is also required. This approach to the recognition of externally restricted inflows is essentially the same as the deferral method for accounting for contributions discussed in the previous chapter.

Internally restricted entities are fully integrated in the government's financial statements (either through consolidation or the modified equity method, which would be used for government business enterprises). However, the government maintains a direct accountability to external parties to use the resources of the entity as specified as long as the legislation is in effect. The accounting standards require disclosure of summary financial information related to internally restricted entities, including total assets and liabilities, net assets or liabilities, total revenues and expenditures (or expenses) and net operating results for the period. In this way users can understand the extent to which the government's resources can only be used to finance the operations of internally restricted entities. A description of the nature of the internal restriction should also be provided.

Designations of assets do not really restrict the government's financial flexibility much, if at all. Governments can readily change the legislation, by-law or resolution used to designate assets. Therefore, disclosing information about designated assets is optional. Any information provided is to appear in the notes to the financial statements and, in fact, cannot be provided on the statement of financial position.[21]

Comparing these standards with those related to not-for-profit organizations discussed in the last chapter, we can see some similarities. The approach taken for government financial reporting of restricted amounts is very similar to the deferral method of accounting for contributions, which can be followed by not-for-profit organizations.

Government Transfers

One of the major ways that governments meet their objectives and carry out programs is through transfers to individuals, organizations or other governments. For example, the federal government provides transfers payments to the provinces for carrying out education and health care programs. Such transfers are akin to contributions in the not-for-profit sector since the government making the transfer does not receive any goods or services or a financial return. The *CICA Handbook* provides guidance to private sector recipients of such government assistance.[22] The *PSA Handbook* deals with the accounting for government transfers by the transferring government and any recipient government.

There are three major types of transfers:

1. Entitlements are transfers a government must make if the recipient meets specified eligibility criteria. Generally the terms are prescribed in legislation, by-law or regulation and the government has no option of opting out as long as the criteria have been met. In addition, there are no conditions on the recipient as to how the money is to be spent. Entitlements may be provided to individuals or to other governments. An example of an individual entitlement is old age security benefits. Canadians who reach the age of 65 and meet residency requirements are entitled to receive these benefits.

2. Transfers under shared cost agreements are reimbursements of eligible expenditures as a result of an agreement between the government and the recipient. To be entitled to reimbursement the recipient must spend money. Once eligible expenditures are incurred the recipient is entitled to the transfer. Generally the terms are negotiated in a signed contract.

3. Grants are transfers that are made at the discretion of the government. The government making the transfer decides whether or not to make the transfer, any conditions to be complied with how much will be transferred and to whom. Generally recipients must apply for the grant or meet some criteria. In contrast to entitlements, meeting eligibility criteria does not guarantee that the recipient will receive the money. The government still has discretion to decide and is not obligated until the grant has legislative approval. Only at the point when the government is committed to make the transfer does it become nondiscretionary.[23]

The issue in accounting for government transfers relates primarily to determining when recognition criteria have been met. As a general principle government transfers are recognized in a government's financial statements as expenditures or revenues in the period the events giving rise to the transfers occurred, providing the transfer is authorized, any eligibility criteria have been satisfied and the amount can be reasonably estimated. Applying the criteria will depend on the characteristics of the particular transfer.

Loans Receivable

Governments lend money to achieve policy objectives. For example, they may lend at concessionary terms in order to support regional development or give economic assistance. Such concessions might include low interest rates, extended repayment terms and forgiveness clauses. In this regard these special characteristics distinguish some government loans receivable from most commercial loans made in the private sector. Businesses are not typically in the practice of providing forgivable loans as a matter of policy. For the most part, the types of concessionary loans governments make will be more in the nature of grants rather than true loans receivable and would be reflected as such in the financial statements. For example, a forgivable loan is one that includes, in the terms of the loan agreement, conditions under which the principal and interest would be forgiven. When an amount is advanced with forgivable conditions, it would be accounted for as a grant unless it meets the definition of a loan receivable and there is evidence of recoverability. This would relate to the government's expectation of recovery of funds issued. Governments also sometimes make "loans" to borrowers that will be recoverable only through future appropriations from the government to the borrower. If there is a direct relationship between the assistance provided by the government to the borrower and repayment of the loan then the loan is more in the nature of a grant and would be accounted for as such. Finally, a loan may be provided with terms that are so concessionary that the substance of the transaction is more in the nature of a grant, for example when the interest rate is significantly below the government's average cost of borrowing at the date of issue. Loans with significant concessionary terms would be accounted for based on the substance of the transaction, which will likely be in the nature of a grant.

Loan Guarantees

Governments also achieve policy objectives through loan guarantees. A loan guarantee is a promise to pay all or part of a debt obligation in the event that the borrower defaults. When a government makes a loan guarantee it is a contingent liability and the normal business accounting principles for contingent liabilities would apply, namely disclosure in the financial statements and recognition of liabilities when the losses are likely. The key issue in accounting for loan guarantees is assessing when a contingent liability becomes an accounting liability to be recognized in the financial statements. Losses are recognized when it is determined that they are likely, which is generally prior to a government actually making a payment on the guarantee.

A similar issue to that discussed with respect to loans receivable arises, i.e., guaranteed loans expected to be repaid from future government funding are also to be recognized as liabilities or expenditures when a direct relationship can be established between the funding and the borrower's ability to repay the loan.

Pensions and Other Employee Future Benefits

Pension obligations arise from a promise by a government to provide pension benefits to employees in return for their services. So, they are a form of compensation offered for services rendered and accrue over the years employees render those services. In the context of the public sector, obligations for employee future benefits like pensions are typically fairly significant. It is therefore important that the unfunded liability be recorded in the financial statements.

Until the release of the Employee Future Benefits section of the *CICA Handbook* in 1999, PSAB's pension recommendations were similar to the private sector standards for pensions. Two key differences existed to reflect the unique characteristics of governments. The first difference relates to the accounting treatment of past service costs arising from plan amendments. A plan amendment occurs when a pension plan is changed or initiated and employees are given credit for services rendered in the past. PSAB recommends that these costs should be expensed immediately in the period of plan amendment, which is different from the private sector recommendation to amortize these costs over a future period. PSAB's rationale is that accounting for these costs immediately ensures that the effect of a decision to amend a plan is recognized in the period the liability is incurred. This is important in the framework of the government reporting model whereby the emphasis is on recording all liabilities in the balance sheet so that future revenue requirements can be assessed.

This emphasis on recording all liabilities also leads to the other major difference in pension accounting from the private sector. This difference relates to the unrecorded pension liability arising on implementation, i.e., the transitional balance. While the private sector standards have traditionally allowed amortizing such amounts over future periods, public sector recommendations advocate treating the transaction as a change in accounting policy applied retroactively. This means that accumulated surplus/deficit is adjusted to reflect the cumulative effect of implementing the recommendations and that the full liability for the pension obligation is recorded in the financial statements upon implementation.

While no specific recommendations exist at the present time for other employee future benefits, the Public Sector Board has a workplan in place to reconsider pensions and address these other areas, with an underlying goal of harmonizing where appropriate with the private sector standards for employee future benefits.

Indicators of Government Financial Condition

To date, the focus of government accounting has been on getting governments to report complete and consistent financial statements that provide an overview of the government as a whole. While the government reporting standards have been developed with the needs of the taxpayer in mind, it is difficult for the average person to assess whether a government is better or worse off based on the financial statements alone. Legislators and other decision makers also need to be able to consider key relationships and ratios in order to evaluate fiscal policies. In 1997 the CICA published a research report that identified a set of understandable financial indicators that are relevant for assessing the financial condition of governments.[24] The report defined financial condition as the government's financial health and established three components to measure that— sustainability, vulnerability and flexibility. *Sustainability* is the extent to which a government can maintain existing programs and meet existing debt requirements without increasing the debt burden on the economy. *Vulnerability* reflects the degree to which a government becomes dependent on sources of funding outside its control or influence, both domestic and international. *Flexibility* is the degree to which a government can increase its financial resources to respond to rising commitments either by expanding its revenues or increasing its debt burden.

Based on these components there are ten core indicators that measure financial condition and allow judgments to be made about the overall state of the government's financial health. By comparing trends in these indicators, users should be able to assess whether or not the financial condition of the government has improved or deteriorated. Examples of key indicators include the ratio of deficit to Gross Domestic Product (GDP), debt to GDP, public debt charges to revenues and total external debt to GDP.

SUMMARY

Financial reporting practices for governments have evolved considerably over the past few years. From a starting point of disarray less than twenty years ago, most senior (i.e., federal, provincial and territorial) governments are preparing financial reports on a consistent and comparable basis in accordance with the recommendations established by the Public Sector Accounting Board of the CICA. Governments have found themselves struggling in recent years with spending that has exceeded revenues year after year, and increased debt burdens and mounting interest charges on the debt. As a result, governments have been increasingly restrained by their financial situations and have found their flexibility in generating new programs significantly constrained. Gradually governments have been persuaded that there is a need for accounting and reporting standards that are appropriate for governments and that compliance with such standards results in better information.

Governments previously reported on a cash basis of accounting and have made the shift to a modified accrual basis whereby all long-term liabilities (like pension obligations) and all financial assets are recorded. The accounting for capital assets has been controversial and difficult as governments attempt to determine their full stock of capital assets and make assessments about allocating the costs of such assets to government programs. While there currently exists a state of flux as governments make this move gradually, there is agreement that the cost of capital assets is a cost of providing services and that these costs need to be captured in order for a government to maintain its asset base and the level of services provided.

Accounting for capital assets is the biggest step governments are taking towards a full accrual basis of accounting, which is essentially consistent with the private sector. While this will mean that the underlying accounting basis for governments is the same as for the private sector, the challenge remains to find a reporting model that reflects the uniqueness of governments. Governments are different from business in both their objectives and their financing. The needs of the users of government financial statements likewise are different.

While governments have made significant progress in controlling spending and improving service delivery, there is work to be done in lifting the debt burden and decreasing net debt of the government. The impact of significant government budget cuts in recent years has created a greater public awareness of the importance of efficient and effective service delivery. This new focus on service delivery and accountability for performance is driving governments to look at the management of public resources, including consideration of alternative ways of providing and financing services, eliminating services that are not core to a government's role and enhancing accountability for service delivery. In this context there is a continuing challenge to ensure that accounting and reporting standards provide better financial information for government decision making and accountability.

REFERENCES

[1]   *Financial Reporting by Governments* (Toronto: CICA, 1981).

[2]   CICA "Financial Statement Presentation by Not-For-Profit Organizations," *CICA Handbook—Accounting*, Section 4400 (Toronto: CICA), par. .02(a).

[3]   See CICA, "Introduction to Public Sector Accounting Recommendations," *Public Sector Accounting Handbook* (Toronto: CICA) for a discussion of how to distinguish these different types of government organizations, especially paragraphs .09–.12.

[4]   CICA, "Objectives of Financial Statements—Federal, Provincial and Territorial Governments," *Public Sector Accounting Handbook*, Section PS 1400 (Toronto: CICA), par. .23.

[5]   Ibid., par. .29.

[6]   Ibid., par. .34.

[7]   Ibid., par. .39.

[8]   Ibid., par. .46.

[9]   For an in-depth discussion of performance measurement and accountability, see *Costing Government Services for Improved Performance Measurement and Accountability*, (Toronto: CICA, 1999).

[10] General standards of financial statement presentation are set out in CICA, "General Standards of Financial Statement Presentation—Federal, Provincial and Territorial Governments," *Public Sector Accounting Handbook*, Section PS 1500 (Toronto: CICA) for federal, provincial and territorial governments. General standards for financial statement presentation of local governments are substantially the same and are set out in CICA "Objectives of Financial Statements—Local Governments," *Public Sector Accounting Handbook*, Section PS 1700 (Toronto: CICA) and in CICA, "General Standards of Financial Statement Presentation—Local Governments," *Public Sector Accounting Handbook*, Section PS 1800 (Toronto: CICA).

[11] CICA, "General Standards of Financial Statement Presentation," *Public Sector Accounting Handbook*, Section PS 1500 (Toronto: CICA), par. .23–.27 and CICA, "Objectives of Financial Statements," *Public Sector Accounting Handbook*, Section PS 1700 (Toronto: CICA), par. .56–.58.

[12] CICA, "Financial Reporting Entity," *Public Sector Accounting Handbook*, Section PS 1300 (Toronto: CICA), par. .07.

[13] Ibid., par. .09–.10.

[14] Ibid., par. .11–.13

[15] Ibid., par. .14–.17.

[16] Ibid., par. .21.

[17] Ibid., par. .21–.32.

[18] For a further discussion of the issues surrounding the PSAB project, see M. Jones, "Invisible Assets," *CA Magazine*, January–February 1994, pp. 65–67.

[19] See CICA, "Tangible Capital Assets," *Public Sector Accounting Handbook*, Section PS 3150 (Toronto: CICA).

[20] The reporting requirements under the expense and expenditure bases of accounting are presented in CICA, "General Standards of Financial Statement Presentation," *Public Sector Accounting Handbook*, Section PS 1500 (Toronto: CICA).

[21] CICA, "Restricted Assets and Revenues," *Public Sector Accounting Handbook*, Section PS 3100 (Toronto: CICA), par. .30.

[22] See CICA, "Accounting for Government Assistance," *CICA Handbook—Accounting*, Section 3800 (Toronto: CICA).

[23] CICA, "Government Transfers," *Public Sector Accounting Handbook*, Section PS 3410 (Toronto: CICA), par. .04.

[24] CICA, *"Indicators of Government Financial Condition"* (Toronto: CICA, 1997).

SELECTED

BIBLIOGRAPHY

PART I: THE HISTORICAL DEVELOPMENT OF ACCOUNTING

Chapter 2—The Record-Keeping Function of Accounting

Brown, R., ed. *A History of Accounting and Accountants.* London: Frank Cass & Co., 1905; reprint ed., New York: Augustus M. Kelley, 1968.

Chatfield, M. *A History of Accounting Thought.* Rev. ed. Huntington, N.Y.: Robert E. Krieger Publishing Co., 1977.

Littleton, A.C. *Accounting Evolution to 1900.* New York: American Institute Publishing Co., 1933.

Littleton, A.C., and Yamey, B.S., eds. *Studies in the History of Accounting.* London: Sweet & Maxwell, 1956.

Scott, W.R. *The Constitution and Finance of English, Scottish and Irish Joint-Stock Companies to 1720.* 3 vols. Cambridge: Harvard University Press, 1912; reprint ed., New York: Peter Smith, 1951.

Chapter 3—Emergence of the Financial Reporting Function

Brief, R.P. *Nineteenth Century Capital Accounting and Business Investment.* Ph.D. dissertation, Columbia University, 1964. New York: Arno Press, 1976.

_____. ed. *The Late Nineteenth Century Debate over Depreciation, Capital and Income.* New York: Arno Press, 1976.

Chatfield, M. *A History of Accounting Thought,* Rev. ed. Huntington, N.Y.: Robert E. Krieger Publishing Co., 1977.

_____. ed. *Contemporary Studies in the Evolution of Accounting Thought.* Belmont, Calif.: Dickenson Publishing Co., 1968.

French, E.A. "The Evolution of the Dividend Law of England." In *Studies in Accounting*, pp. 306–31. 3rd. ed. Edited by W.T. Baxter and S. Davidson. London: Institute of Chartered Accountants in England and Wales, 1977.

Hunt, B.C. *The Development of the Business Corporation in England, 1800–1867*. Harvard Economic Studies, vol. 52. Cambridge: Harvard University Press, 1936.

Littleton, A.C. *Accounting Evolution to 1900*. New York: American Institute Publishing Co., 1933.

Littleton, A.C., and Yamey, B.S., eds. *Studies in the History of Accounting*. London: Sweet & Maxwell, 1956.

Wells, M.C. *Accounting for Common Costs*. Monograph 10. Urbana, Ill.: Center for International Education and Research in Accounting, 1978.

Yamey, B.S. "Some Topics in the History of Financial Accounting in England, 1500-1900." In *Studies in Accounting*, pp. 11–34. 3rd ed. Edited by W.T. Baxter and S. Davidson. London: Institute of Chartered Accountants in England and Wales, 1977.

Chapter 4—Financial Accounting in the Twentieth Century

American Accounting Association, Executive Committee. "A Tentative Statement of Accounting Principles Underlying Corporate Financial Statements." *The Accounting Review*, June 1936. Reprinted in *Accounting and Reporting Standards for Corporate Financial Statements and Preceding Statements and Supplements*, pp. 59-64, AAA, 1957.

American Institute of Accountants, Committee on Accounting Procedure. *Restatement and Revision of Accounting Research Bulletins*, Accounting Research Bulletin No. 43. New York: AIA, 1953.

American Institute of Certified Public Accountants, Accounting Principles Board. *Basic Concepts and Accounting Principles Underlying Financial Statements of Business Enterprises*, Accounting Principles Board Statement No. 4. New York: AICPA, 1970.

Beaver, W.H. *Financial Reporting: An Accounting Revolution*. 2nd ed. Englewood Cliffs, N.J.: Prentice Hall, 1989.

Bernard, V.L., and Thomas, J.K. "Evidence that Stock Prices Do Not Reflect the Implications of Current Earnings for Future Earnings." *Journal of Accounting and Economics*, 1990, pp. 305–40.

Boland, L.A., and Gordon, I.M. "Practice in a Positive Light." *CA Magazine*, July 1992, pp. 37–41.

Canadian Institute of Chartered Accountants. *CICA Task Force on Standard Setting —Final Report*. Toronto: CICA, 1998.

Chatfield, M., ed. *Contemporary Studies in the Evolution of Accounting Thought*. Belmont, Calif.: Dickenson Publishing Co., 1968.

Feltham, G.A., and Ohlson, J.A. "Valuation and Clean Surplus Accounting for Operating and Financial Activities." *Contemporary Accounting Research*, Spring 1995, pp. 689–731.

Lev, B. "On the Usefulness of Earnings and Earnings Research: Lessons and Directions from Two Decades of Empirical Research." *Journal of Accounting Research*, 1989 Supplement, pp. 153–92.

May, G.O. *Twenty-Five Years of Accounting Responsibility, 1911–1936*. Edited by B.C. Hunt. 2 vols. New York: Price Waterhouse & Co., 1936; reprint ed. (2 vols. in 1), Houston: Scholars Book Co., 1971.

Miller, P.B.W., and Redding, R.J. *The FASB: The People, the Process and the Politics*. 2nd ed. Homewood, Illinois: Irwin, 1988.

Murphy, G.J., ed. *A History of Canadian Accounting Thought and Practice*. New York: Garland Publishing, Inc., 1993.

Paton, W.A., and Littleton, A.C. *An Introduction to Corporate Accounting Standards*. Monograph No. 3. American Accounting Association, 1940.

Previts, G.J., and Merino, B.D. *A History of Accounting in America*. New York: John Wiley & Sons, 1979.

Report of the Commission to Study the Public's Expectations of Audits. Toronto: CICA, 1988.

Richardson, G.D., "Signals and Signs." *CA Magazine*, March 1998, pp. 37–39.

Ripley, W.Z. *Main Street and Wall Street*. Boston: Little, Brown & Co., 1927.

Solomons, D. *Making Accounting Policy: The Quest for Credibility in Financial Reporting*. New York: Oxford University Press, 1986.

Storey, R.K. "The Framework of Financial Accounting Concepts and Standards," in Carmichael, D.R., Lilien, S.B., and Melman, M. *Accountants' Handbook*. 7th ed. New York: John Wiley and Sons, Inc. 1991.

_____. "Revenue Realization, Going Concern, and Measurement of Income." *The Accounting Review*. April 1959, pp. 232–38.

_____. *The Search for Accounting Principles: Today's Problems in Perspective*. New York: American Institute of Certified Public Accountants, 1964.

Thornton, D.B. "A Look at Agency Theory for the Novice." *CA Magazine,* November 1984, pp. 90–97 and January 1985, pp. 93–100.

Watts, R.L., and Zimmerman, J.L. *Positive Accounting Theory*. Englewood Cliffs, N.J.: Prentice Hall, 1986.

PART II: ACCOUNTING STANDARDS TODAY

Chapter 5—Accrual Accounting

Alexander, S.S. "Income Measurement in a Dynamic Economy," Revised by D. Solomons. In *Studies in Accounting Theory*, pp. 126–200. Edited by W.T. Baxter and S. Davidson. Homewood, Ill.: Richard D. Irwin, 1962.

Alexander, S.S., Bronfenbrenner, M., Fabricant, S., and Warburton, C. *Five Monographs on Business Income*. New York: American Institute of Accountants, 1950; reprint ed., Houston: Scholars Book Co., 1973.

Anthony, R.N. *Tell It Like It Was: A Conceptual Framework for Financial Accounting*. Homewood, Ill.: Richard D. Irwin, 1983.

Beaver, W.H. *Financial Reporting: An Accounting Revolution*. 2nd ed. Englewood Cliffs, N.J.: Prentice Hall, 1989.

Bevis, W.H. *Corporate Financial Reporting in a Competitive Economy*. New York: Macmillan Co., 1965.

Bird, F.A., Davidson, L.F., and Smith, C.H. "Perceptions of External Accounting Transfers Under Entity and Proprietary Theory." *The Accounting Review*, April 1974, pp. 233–44.

Hicks, J.R. *Value and Capital: An Inquiry into Some Fundamental Principles of Economic Theory*. 2nd ed. Oxford: Oxford University Press, 1946.

Johnson, L.T., and Storey, R.K. *Recognition in Financial Statements: Underlying Concepts and Practical Conventions*. Stamford: FASB, 1982.

Lee, T.A. "The Accounting Entity Concept, Accounting Standards, and Inflation Accounting." *Accounting and Business Research*, Spring 1980, pp. 176–86.

_____. *Income and Value Measurement: Theory and Practice*. Baltimore: University Park Press, 1975.

May, G.O. *Financial Accounting: A Distillation of Experience*. New York: Macmillan Co., 1943; reprint ed., Houston: Scholars Book Co., 1972.

Meyer, P.E. "The Accounting Entity." *Abacus*, December 1973, pp. 116–26.

Schrader, W.J., Malcom, P.E., and Willingham, J.J. "A Partitioned Events View of Financial Reporting." *Accounting Horizons*, December 1988, pp. 10–20.

Sprouse, R.T. "Accounting for What-You-May-Call-Its." *Journal of Accountancy*, October 1966, pp. 45–53.

Sterling, R.R., and Thomas, A.L., eds. *Accounting for a Simplified Firm Owning Depreciable Assets: Seventeen Essays and a Synthesis Based on a Common Case*. Houston: Scholars Book Co., 1979.

Study Group on Business Income. *Changing Concepts of Business Income*. New York: Macmillan Co., 1952; reprint ed., Houston: Scholars Book Co., 1975.

Thomas, A.L. *The Allocation Problem in Financial Accounting Theory*. Studies in Accounting Research No. 3. American Accounting Association, 1969.

_____. *The Allocation Problem: Part Two*. Studies in Accounting Research No. 9. American Accounting Association, 1974.

Chapter 6—Initial Recognition and Measurement

American Institute of Certified Public Accountants, Accounting Principles Board. *Interest in Receivables and Payables*, Opinion No. 21. New York: AICPA, 1971.

Canadian Institute of Chartered Accountants. "Non-Monetary Transactions." *CICA Handbook*, Section 3830. Toronto: CICA.

_____. "Related Party Transactions." *CICA Handbook*, Section 3840. Toronto: CICA.

_____. "Subsequent Events." *CICA Handbook*, Section 3820. Toronto, CICA.

Ijiri, Y. *Recognition of Contractual Rights and Obligations: An Exploratory Study of Conceptual Issues*. Stamford: FASB, 1980.

Johnson, L.T. *Future Events: A Conceptual Study of Their Significance for Recognition and Measurement*. Norwalk: FASB, 1994.

Johnson, L.T., and Storey, R.K. *Recognition in Financial Statements: Underlying Concepts and Practical Conventions*. Stamford: FASB. 1982.

Mason, A.K. *Related Party Transactions*. Toronto: CICA, 1979.

Chapter 7—Recognition of Revenues and Peripheral Sales and Realizations

American Institute of Certified Public Accountants, Construction Contractors Guide Committee. *Construction Contractors*. Audit and Accounting Guide. New York: AICPA, 1981.

American Institute of Certified Public Accountants. *Software Revenue Recognition*. Statement of Position 97-2, New York: AICPA, 1997:

_____. *Modification of SOP 97-2, "Software Revenue Recognition," With Respect to Certain Transactions*. Statement of Position 98-9. New York: AICPA, 1998.

Canadian Institute of Chartered Accountants. "Revenue." *CICA Handbook*, Section 3400. Toronto: CICA.

Canadian Institute of Public Real Estate Companies. *Recommended Accounting Practices for Real Estate Investment and Development Companies*. Toronto: CIPREC, 1998.

Financial Accounting Standards Board. *Accounting for Certain Service Transactions*. FASB Invitation to Comment. Stamford: FASB, October 23, 1978.

_____. *Accounting for Leases: Sale-Leaseback Transactions Involving Real Estate; Sales Type Leases of Real Estate*. Statement of Financial Accounting Standards No. 98. Norwalk: FASB, 1988.

_____. *Accounting for Sales of Real Estate*. Statement of Financial Accounting Standards No. 66. Stamford: FASB, 1982.

_____. *Accounting for Transfers and Servicing of Financial Assets and Extinguishments of Liabilities*. Statement of Financial Accounting Standards No. 125. Norwalk: FASB, 1996.

_____. *Recognition and Measurement in Financial Statements of Business Enterprises*. Statement of Financial Accounting Concepts No. 5. Stamford: FASB, 1984.

International Accounting Standards Committee. *Accounting for Financial Assets and Financial Liabilities*. A Discussion Paper. London: IASC, 1997, chap. 3.

Chapter 8—Expense Recognition; Losses and Contingencies

American Accounting Association's Financial Accounting Standards Committee. "Response to IASC Exposure Draft, 'Provisions, Contingent Liabilities and Contingent Assets'." *Accounting Horizons*, June 1998, pp. 192–200.

American Institute of Certified Public Accountants, Accounting Standards Executive Committee. *Disclosure of Certain Risks and Uncertainties*. Statement of Position 94-6. New York: AICPA, 1994.

Barth, M.F., and McNichols, M.F. "Estimation and Market Valuation of Environmental Liabilities Relating to Superfund Sites." *Journal of Accounting Research*, Supplement 1994, pp. 177–209.

Brown, C.S., and Wyatt, A.R. "Liabilities Belong in the Footnotes—Or Do They?" *Georgia Journal of Accounting*, Spring 1983, pp. 1–15.

Canadian Institute of Chartered Accountants. "Contingencies." *CICA Handbook*, Section 3290. Toronto: CICA.

_____. "Employees' Future Benefits." *CICA Handbook*, Section 3461. Toronto: CICA.

_____. *Environmental Costs and Liabilities: Accounting and Financial Reporting Issues*. A Research Report. Toronto: CICA, 1993.

Cormier, D., and Magnam, M. "Investors' Assessment of Implicit Environmental Liabilities: An Empirical Investigation." *Journal of Accounting and Public Policy*, Summer 1997, pp. 215–41.

Financial Accounting Standards Board. *Accounting for Contingencies*. Statement of Financial Accounting Standards No. 5. Stamford: FASB, 1975.

International Accounting Standards Committee. *Provisions, Contingent Liabilities and Contingent Assets*. International Accounting Standard 37. London: IASC, 1998.

Moonitz, M. "The Changing Concept of Liabilities." *Journal of Accountancy*. May 1960, pp. 41–46.

Ross, J.A. "Accounting for Hazardous Waste." *Journal of Accountancy*. March 1985, pp. 72–82.

Thornton, D.B. "Green Accounting and Green Eyeshades." *CA Magazine*, October 1993, pp. 34–40.

Chapter 9—Financial Position and Capital

Canadian Institute of Chartered Accountants. "Financial Instruments – Disclosure and Presentation." *CICA Handbook*, Section 3860. Toronto: CICA.

Financial Accounting Standards Board. *Distinguishing Between Liabilities and Equity Instruments and Accounting for Instruments with Characteristics of Both*. Discussion Memorandum. Norwalk: FASB, 1980.

Heath, L.C. *Financial Reporting and the Evaluation of Solvency*. Accounting Research Monograph No. 3. New York: AICPA, 1978.

_____. "Is Working Capital Really Working?" *Journal of Accountancy*, August 1980, pp. 55–62.

Ma, R. "Liability Measurement: The Case of the Lessee's Obligation." In *External Financial Reporting: Essays in the Honour of Harold Edey*, ed. Carsberg, B., and Dev, S. Englewood Cliffs, N.J.: Prentice-Hall International in cooperation with London School of Economics and Political Science, 1984, pp. 81–89.

Sheldahl, T.K. "Reporting Treasury Stock as an Asset: Law, Logic and Economic Substance." *The Accounting Historians Journal*, Fall 1982, pp. 1–23.

Chapter 10—Inventory and Cost of Sales

American Institute of Certified Public Accountants, Task Force on LIFO Inventory Problems. *Identification and Discussion of Certain Financial Accounting and Reporting Issues Concerning LIFO Inventories*. New York: AICPA, 1984.

Barden, H.G. *The Accounting Basis of Inventories*. Accounting Research Study No. 13. New York: AICPA, 1973.

Bar-Yosef, S., and Sen, P.K. "On Optimal Choice of Inventory Accounting Method." *The Accounting Review*, April 1992, pp. 320–36.

Cushing, B.E., and LeClerc, M.J. "Evidence on the Determinants of Inventory Accounting Policy Choice." *The Accounting Review*, April 1992, pp. 355–66.

Fremgen, J.M., and Liao, S.S. *The Allocation of Corporate Indirect Costs*. New York: National Association of Accountants, 1981.

Liao, S.S. "The Matching Concept and Cost Allocation." *Accounting and Business Research*, Summer 1979, pp. 228–35.

Shank, J.K., and Govindarajan, V. "The Perils of Cost Allocation Based on Production Volumes." *Accounting Horizons*, December 1988, pp. 71–79.

Sorter, G.H., and Horngren, C.T. "Asset Recognition and Economic Attributes—The Relevant Costing Approach." *The Accounting Review*, July 1962, pp. 391–99.

Staubus, G.J. "The Dark Ages of Cost Accounting: The Role of Miscues in the Literature." *The Accounting Historians Journal*, Fall 1987, pp. 1–18.

Wells, M.C. *Accounting for Common Costs*. Monograph 10. Urbana, Ill.: Center for International Education and Research in Accounting, 1978.

Chapter 11—Tangible Capital Assets and Depreciation

Baxter, W.T. *Depreciation*. London: Sweet & Maxwell, 1971.

Bennett, A.H.M. "Depreciation and Business Decision Making." *Accounting and Business Research*, Winter 1972, pp. 3–28.

Biedleman, C.R. *Valuation of Used Capital Assets*. Studies in Accounting Research No. 7. American Accounting Association, 1973.

Bierman, H., Jr., and Dyckman, T.R. "Accounting for Interest During Construction." *Accounting and Business Research*, Autumn 1979, pp. 267–71.

Brief, R.P. "A Late Nineteenth Century Contribution to the Theory of Depreciation." *Journal of Accounting Research*, Spring 1967, pp. 27–38.

Canadian Institute of Chartered Accountants. "Capital Assets." *CICA Handbook*, Section 3060. Toronto: CICA.

_____. *Environmental Costs and Liabilities: Accounting and Financial Reporting Issues*. Research Report. Toronto: CICA, 1993.

Egginton, D. "Fixed Assets: Costs, Lives and Depreciation." *Accountancy* (England), November 1984, pp. 138–44.

Johnson, O. "Two General Concepts of Depreciation." *Journal of Accounting Research*, Spring 1968, pp. 29–37.

Lamden, C.W., Gerboth, D.L., and McRae, T.W. *Accounting for Depreciable Assets*. Accounting Research Monograph No. 1. New York: AICPA, 1975.

Milburn, J.A. *Incorporating the Time Value of Money Within Financial Reporting*. Research Study. Toronto: CICA, 1988.

Morrison, R.M., and Shultz, R.J., eds. *Regulation and Inflation: An Evaluation of Tariff Levelling*. Montreal: National Energy Board and the Centre for the Study of Regulated Industries, 1983.

National Association of Accountants, Committee on Management Accounting Practices. *Fixed Asset Accounting: The Capitalization of Costs*. Statement on Management Accounting Practices No. 4. New York: NAA, 1972.

_____. *Fixed Asset Accounting: The Allocation of Costs*. Statement on Management Accounting Practices No. 7. New York: NAA, 1974.

Peasnell, K.V. "Capitalization of Interest." *British Accounting Review*, 1993, pp. 17–42.

Wright, F.K. "Towards a General Theory of Depreciation." *Journal of Accounting Research*, Spring 1964, pp. 80–90.

_____. "An Evaluation of Ladelle's Theory of Depreciation." *Journal of Accounting Research*, Autumn 1967, pp. 173–79.

Chapter 12—Intangibles

American Institute of Certified Public Accountants, Accounting Standards Executive Committee. *Accounting for Costs of Computer Software Developed or Obtained for Internal Use*. Statement of Position 98-1. New York: AICPA, 1998.

_____. *Reporting on Advertising Costs*. Statement of Position 93-7. New York: AICPA, 1993.

Bierman, H., Jr., and Dukes, R.E. "Accounting for Research and Development Costs." *Journal of Accountancy*, April 1975, pp. 48–55.

Brennan, B.A. "Mind Over Matter." *CA Magazine*, June 1992, pp. 21–24.

Canadian Institute of Chartered Accountants. *Accounting and Reporting for Enterprises in the Development Stage*. Research Report. Toronto: CICA, 1996.

_____. "Research and Development Costs." *CICA Handbook*, Section 3450. Toronto: CICA.

Catlett, G.R., and Olson, N.O. *Accounting for Goodwill*. Accounting Research Study No. 10. New York: AICPA, 1968.

Courtis, J.K. "Business Goodwill: Conceptual Clarification via Accounting, Legal and Etymological Perspectives." *The Accounting Historians Journal*, Fall 1983, pp. 1–38.

Financial Accounting Standards Board. *Accounting for the Costs of Computer Software to be Sold, Leased, or Otherwise Marketed*. Statement of Financial Accounting Standards No. 86. Stamford: FASB, 1985.

_____. *Accounting for Research and Development Costs*. Statement of Financial Accounting Standards No. 2. Stamford: FASB, 1974.

Gellein, O.S., and Newman, M.S. *Accounting for Research and Development Expenditures*. Accounting Research Study No. 14. New York: AICPA. 1973.

Gynther, R.S. "Some Conceptualizing on Goodwill." *The Accounting Review*, April 1969, pp. 247–55.

Hughes, H.P. *Goodwill in Accounting: A History of the Issues and Problems*. Research Monograph No. 80. Atlanta: Business Publishing Division, College of Business Administration, Georgia State University, 1982.

International Accounting Standards Committee. *Intangible Assets*. International Accounting Standard 38. London: IASC, 1998.

Johnson, L.T., and Petrone, K.R. "Is Goodwill an Asset?" *Accounting Horizons*, September 1998, pp. 293–303.

Lee, T.A. "Goodwill: An Example of Will-o'-the-Wisp Accounting." *Accounting and Business Research*, Autumn 1971, pp. 318–28.

Sougiannis, T. "The Accounting Based Valuation of Corporate R&D." *The Accounting Review*, January 1994, pp. 44–48.

Stivers, B.P., Kertz, C.L., and Beard, L.H. "What's Proper Accounting for Software Development?" *CA Magazine*, January 1985, pp. 28–33.

Chapter 13—Leases

Abdel-khalik, A.R. *The Economic Effects on Lessees of FASB Statement No. 13, Accounting for Leases*. Stamford: FASB, 1981.

Basu, S. *Leasing Arrangements: Managerial Decision-Making and Financial Reporting Issues*. Hamilton, Ont.: Society of Management Accountants of Canada, 1980.

Canadian Institute of Chartered Accountants. "Leases." *CICA Handbook*, Section 3065. Toronto: CICA.

Canadian Institute of Chartered Accountants. *Leasing Issues*. Research Report. Toronto: CICA, 1989.

Ely, K.M. "Operating Lease Accounting and the Market's Assessment of Equity Risk." *Journal of Accounting Research*, Autumn 1995, pp. 397–415.

Financial Accounting Standards Board. *Accounting for Leases: FASB Statement No. 13 as Amended and Interpreted*. Norwalk: FASB, 1998.

International Accounting Standards Committee. *Leases*. International Accounting Standard 17. London: IASC, Revised 1997.

McGregor, W. *Recognition by Lessees of Assets and Liabilities Arising Under Lease Contracts*. Norwalk: FASB, 1996.

Thornton, D.B. "An Application of Current Value Accounting to Lease Assets." CA M*agazine*, June 1976, pp. 32–41.

Chapter 14—Employee Compensation—Pensions and Other Post-Employment Benefits; Stock-Based Compensation

American Institute of Certified Public Accountants, Accounting Principles Board. *Accounting for Stock Issued to Employees*. APB Opinion No. 25. New York: AICPA, 1972.

Archibald, T.R. *Accounting for Pension Costs and Liabilities (A Reconciliation of Accounting and Funding Practice)*. Toronto: CICA, 1980.

Barth, M.E. "Relative Measurement Errors Among Alternative Pension Asset and Liability Measures." *The Accounting Review*, July 1991, pp. 433–63.

Barth, M.E., Beaver, W.H., and Landsman, W.R. "A Structural Analysis of Pension Disclosures Under SFAS No. 87 and Their Relation to Share Prices." *Financial Analysts Journal*, January–February 1993, pp. 18–26.

Canadian Institute of Chartered Accountants. "Employee Future Benefits." *CICA Handbook*, Section 3461. Toronto: CICA.

Ezra, D.D. *The Struggle for Pension Fund Wealth*. Toronto: Pagurian Press, 1983.

Financial Accounting Standards Board. *Employers' Accounting for Pensions*. Statement of Financial Accounting Standard No. 87. Stamford: FASB, 1985.

_____. *Employers' Accounting for Post-Retirement Benefits*. Statement of Financial Accounting Standards No. 112. Norwalk: FASB, 1992.

_____. *Employers' Accounting for Settlements and Curtailments of Defined Benefit Pension Plans and for Termination Benefits*. Statement of Financial Accounting Standards No. 88. Stamford: FASB, 1988.

_____. *Accounting for Stock-Based Compensation*. Statement of Financial Accounting Standards No. 123. Norwalk: FASB, 1995.

Foster III, T.W., Kouglev, P.R., and Vickrey, D. "Valuation of Executive Stock Options and the FASB Proposal." *The Accounting Review*, July 1991, pp. 595–610.

Gerboth, D.L. "Accruing the Costs of Other Post-Employment Benefits—The Measurement Problem." *The CPA Journal*, November 1988, pp. 36–44.

Mittelstaedt, M.F., and Regier, P.R. "The Market Response to Pension Plan Terminations." *The Accounting Review*, January 1993, pp. 1–27.

Pesando, J.E., and Clarke, C.K. *Economic Models of the Labour Market: Their Implications for Pension Accounting*. Studies in Canadian Accounting Research. Canadian Academic Accounting Association, 1983.

Robertson, D.A., and Archibald, T.R. *Survey of Pension Plans in Canada*, 9th ed. Toronto: Financial Executives Institute of Canada, 1993.

Schipper, K., and Weil, R.L. "Alternative Accounting Treatments for Pensions." *The Accounting Review*. October 1982, pp. 806–24.

Scott, T.W., "Costing the Gold Watch." *CA Magazine*, September 1992, pp. 39–45.

Skinner, R.M. *Pension Accounting: The Problem of Equating Payments Tomorrow with Expenses Today*. Toronto: Clarkson Gordon, 1980.

Chapter 15—Accounting for Government Assistance

American Institute of Certified Public Accountants, Accounting Principles Board. *Accounting for the "Investment Credit."* APB Opinion No. 2. New York: AICPA, 1962.

_____. *Accounting for the "Investment Credit."* APB Opinion No. 4. New York: AICPA, 1964.

_____. *Acceptable Methods of Accounting for Investment Credits Under 1971 Act*. Accounting Interpretations of APB Opinion No. 4, Interpretation No. 3. New York: AICPA, 1972.

Canadian Institute of Chartered Accountants. "Accounting for Government Assistance." *CICA Handbook*, Section 3800. Toronto: CICA.

_____. "Investment Tax Credits." *CICA Handbook*, Section 3805. Toronto: CICA.

Crandall, R.H. "Government Intervention—The PIP Grant Accounting Controversy." *Cost and Management*, September–October 1983, pp. 55–59.

Chapter 16—Income Tax

Ayers, B.C. "Deferred Tax Accounting Under SFAS No. 109: An Empirical Investigation of its Incremental Value-Relevance Relative to APB No. 11." *The Accounting Review*, April 1998, pp. 195–212.

Bains, R.A., Dieter, R., and Stewart, J. "Tax Allocation Revisited." *CA Magazine*, March 1984, pp. 69–73.

Beaver, W.H., and Dukes, R.E. "Interperiod Tax Allocation and Delta-Depreciation Methods: Some Empirical Results." *The Accounting Review*, July 1973, pp. 549–59.

Beechy, T.H. *Accounting for Corporate Income Taxes: Conceptual Considerations and Empirical Analysis*. Toronto: CICA, 1983.

Beresford, D.R., Best, L.C., Craig, P.W., and Weber, J.V. *Accounting for Income Taxes: A Review of Alternatives*. Stamford: FASB, 1983.

Bierman, H., Jr., and Dyckman, T.R. "New Look at Deferred Taxes." *Financial Executive*, January 1974, pp. 40–49.

Black, H.A. *Interperiod Allocation of Corporate Income Taxes*. Accounting Research Study No. 9. New York: AICPA, 1966.

Bullock, C.L. "Reconciling Economic Depreciation with Tax Allocation." *The Accounting Review*, January 1974, pp. 98–103.

Canadian Institute of Chartered Accountants. "Income Taxes." *CICA Handbook*, Section 3465. Toronto: CICA.

Cheung, J.K., Krishnan, G.V., and Min, C. "Does Interperiod Tax Allocation Enhance Production of Cash Flows?" *Accounting Horizons*, December 1997, pp. 1–15.

Drummond, C.S.R., and Wigle, S.L. "Let's Stop Taking Comprehensive Tax Allocation for Granted." *CA Magazine*, October 1981, pp. 56–61.

Financial Accounting Standards Board. *Accounting for Income Taxes*. Statement of Financial Accounting Standards No. 109. Norwalk: FASB, 1992.

Givoly, D., and Hayn, C. "The Valuation of the Deferred Tax Liability: Evidence from the Stock Market." *The Accounting Review,* April 1992, pp. 394–410.

Institute of Chartered Accountants in England and Wales. *Accounting for Deferred Tax*. Statement of Standard Accounting Practice No. 15, rev. London: Institute of Chartered Accountants in England and Wales, Revised 1985.

International Accounting Standards Committee. *Accounting for Taxes on Income*. International Accounting Standard 12. London: IASC, Revised 1996.

Milburn, J.A. "Comprehensive Tax Allocation: Let's Stop Taking Some Misconceptions for Granted." *CA Magazine*, April 1982, pp. 40–46.

Rosenfield, P., and Dent, W.C. "No More Deferred Taxes." *Journal of Accountancy,* February 1983, pp. 44–55.

Watson, P.L. "Accounting for Deferred Tax on Depreciable Assets." *Accounting and Business Research*, Autumn 1979, pp. 338–47.

Chapter 17—Financial Instruments

Accounting for Portfolio Investments. A Research Study. Toronto: CICA, 1984.

Adams, J.B., and Montesi, C.J., Principal Authors. *Major Issues in Hedge Accounting*. Norwalk: FASB, 1995.

American Institute of Certified Public Accountants, Accounting Standards Division. *Accounting for Options*. Issues Paper 86-2. New York: AICPA, 1986.

American Accounting Association's Financial Accounting Standards Committee. "Response to a Discussion Paper Issued by the IASC/CICA Steering Committee on Financial Instruments, 'Accounting for Financial Assets and Financial Liabilities'." *Accounting Horizons*, March 1998, pp. 90–97.

Barth, M.E., Beaver, W.H., and Wolfson, M.A. "Components of Earnings and the Structure of Bank Share Prices." *Financial Analysts Journal*, May–June 1990, pp. 53–60.

Barth, M.E., Landsman, W.R., and Wahlen, J.M. "Fair Value Accounting: Effects on Banks' Earnings Volatility, Regulatory Capital, and Value of Contractual Cash Flows." *Journal of Banking and Finance*, 1995, pp. 577–604.

Beaver, W.H. "Reporting Rules for Marketable Equity Securities." *Journal of Accountancy*, October 1971, pp. 57-61.

_____. "Accounting for Marketable Equity Securities." *Journal of Accountancy*, December 1973, pp. 58-64.

Canadian Institute of Chartered Accountants. *Financial Instruments*. Re-exposure Draft. Toronto: CICA, 1994.

_____. "Financial Instruments—Disclosure and Presentation." *CICA Handbook*, Section 3860. Toronto: CICA.

_____. "Pension Plans." *CICA Handbook*, Section 4100. Toronto: CICA.

_____. "Temporary Investments." *CICA Handbook*, Section 3010. Toronto: CICA.

Financial Accounting Standards Board. *Accounting for Certain Investments in Debt and Equity Securities*. Statement of Financial Accounting Standards No. 115. Norwalk: FASB, 1993.

_____. *Accounting for Derivative Instruments and Hedging Activities*. Statement of Accounting Standards No. 133. Norwalk: FASB, 1998.

_____. *Accounting for Future Contracts*. Statement of Financial Accounting Standards No. 80. Stamford: FASB, 1984 (Superseded 1998).

_____. *Foreign Currency Translation*. Statement of Financial Accounting Standards No. 52. Stamford: FASB, 1981.

International Accounting Standards Committee. *Financial Instruments: Recognition and Measurement*. International Accounting Standard 39. London: IASC, 1998.

_____. *Accounting for Financial Assets and Financial Liabilities*. A Discussion Paper. London: IASC, 1997.

Nair, R.D., Rittenberg, L.E., and Weygrandt, J.J. "Accounting for Interest Rate Swaps—A Critical Evaluation." *Accounting Horizons*, September 1990, pp. 20–30.

Reading, R.D., and Lam, J.C. "Managing a Derivative Products Business from a Risk-Adjusted Return Perspective." In *Advanced Strategies in Financial Management*. ed. Swartz, R.J., and Smith, Jr., C.W. Englewood Cliffs, N.J.: New York Institute of Finance, 1993, pp. 553–76.

Rupert, W.C., and Oakes, W.N. "Interest-Rate Swap Accounting: What is Market Value?" *Bank Accounting and Finance*, Summer 1990, pp. 1–14.

Skinner, R.M. "Accounting for Profits and Losses on Investments." *Canadian Chartered Accountant*, April 1961, pp. 327–33.

Willis, D.W. "Financial Assets and Liabilities—Fair Value or Historical Cost?" *FASB Status Report*, August 18, 1998, pp. 5–10.

Chapter 18—Recognition of Asset Impairment; Statement Presentation of Accounting Adjustments and Extraordinary, Unusual and Peripheral Gains and Losses

American Institute of Certified Public Accountants, Accounting Principles Board. *Accounting Changes*. Opinion No. 20, New York: AICPA, 1971.

_____. *Reporting the Results of Operations—Reporting the Effects of Disposal of a Segment of a Business, and Extraordinary, Unusual and Infrequently Occurring Events and Transactions*. Opinion No. 30. New York: AICPA, 1973.

American Institute of Certified Public Accountants, Special Committee on Financial Reporting. *Improving Business Reporting—A Customer Focus*. New York: AICPA, 1994.

Beaver, W., Eger, C., Ryan, S., and Wolfson, M. "Financial Reporting, Supplemental Disclosures and Bank Share Prices," *Journal of Accounting Research*, Autumn 1989, pp. 157–78.

Canadian Institute of Chartered Accountants. "Accounting Changes." *CICA Handbook*, Section 1506. Toronto: CICA.

_____. "Capital Assets." *CICA Handbook*, Section 3060. Toronto: CICA.

_____. "Comprehensive Revaluation of Assets and Liabilities." *CICA Handbook*, Section 1625. Toronto: CICA.

_____. "Discontinued Operations." *CICA Handbook*, Section 3475. Toronto: CICA.

_____. "Extraordinary Items." *CICA Handbook*, Section 3480. Toronto: CICA.

_____. "Impaired Loans." *CICA Handbook*, Section 3025. Toronto: CICA.

_____. "Long-Term Investments." *CICA Handbook*, Section 3050. Toronto: CICA.

Financial Accounting Standards Board. *Accounting by Creditors for Impairment of a Loan*. Statement of Financial Accounting Standards No. 114. Norwalk: FASB, 1993.

_____. *Accounting for Impairment of Long-Lived Assets and for Long-Lived Assets to be Disposed Of*. Statement of Financial Accounting Standards No. 121. Norwalk: FASB, 1995.

_____. *Reporting Comprehensive Income*. Statement of Financial Accounting Standards No. 130. Norwalk: FASB, 1997.

International Accounting Standards Committee. *Impairment of Assets*. International Accounting Standard 36. London: IASC, 1998.

Johnson, L.T., and Lennard, A., Principal Authors. *Reporting Financial Performance: Current Developments and Future Directions*. Norwalk: FASB, 1998.

Ketz, J.E., and Largay III, J.A. "Reporting Income and Cash Flows from Operations." *Accounting Horizons*, June 1987, pp. 9–17.

Lilien, S., Mellman, M., and Pastena, V. "Accounting Changes: Successful Versus Unsuccessful Firms." *The Accounting Review*, October 1988, pp. 642–56.

May, G.S., and Schneider, D.K. "Reporting Accounting Changes: Are Stricter Guidelines Needed?" *Accounting Horizons*, September 1988, pp. 68–74.

Wahlen, J.M. "The Nature of Information in Commercial Bank Loan Disclosures." *The Accounting Review*, July 1994, pp. 435–78.

Chapter 19—Business Combinations

American Institute of Certified Public Accountants, Accounting Principles Board. *Business Combinations*, Opinion No. 16. New York: AICPA, 1970.

Anderson, J.C., and Louderback III, J.G. "Income Manipulation and Purchase-Pooling: Some Additional Results." *Journal of Accounting Research*, Autumn 1975, pp. 338–43.

Byrd, C.E. *Business Combinations and Long-Term Intercorporate Investments: The Canadian View*. 2nd ed. Hamilton: Society of Industrial Accountants of Canada, 1976.

Canadian Institute of Chartered Accountants. "Business Combinations." *CICA Handbook*, Section 1580. Toronto: CICA.

_____. *Methods of Accounting for Business Combinations: Recommendations of the G4+1 for Achieving Convergence*. Invitation to Comment. Toronto: CICA, 1998.

International Accounting Standards Committee. *Business Combinations*. International Accounting Standard 22. London: IASC, Revised 1998.

Chapter 20—Intercorporate Investments

American Institute of Certified Public Accountants, Committee on Accounting Procedure. *Consolidated Financial Statements*. Accounting Research Bulletin No. 51. New York: AICPA, 1959.

American Institute of Certified Public Accountants, Accounting Principles Board. *The Equity Method of Accounting for Investments in Common Stock*, Opinion No. 18. New York: AICPA, 1971.

Bierman, Jr., H. "Proportionate Consolidation and Financial Analysis," *Accounting Horizons*, December 1992, pp. 5–17.

Bradbury, M.E., and Calderwood, S.C. "Equity Accounting for Reciprocal Stockholdings." *The Accounting Review*, April 1988, pp. 330–47.

Canadian Institute of Chartered Accountants. "Consolidated Financial Statements." *CICA Handbook*, Section 1600. Toronto: CICA.

_____. "Investments in Joint Ventures." *CICA Handbook*, Section 3055. Toronto: CICA.

_____. "Long-Term Investments." *CICA Handbook*, Section 3050. Toronto: CICA.

_____. "Subsidiaries." *CICA Handbook*, Section 1590. Toronto: CICA.

Dieter, R., and Wyatt, A.R. "The Expanded Equity Method—An Alternative in Accounting for Investments in Joint Ventures." *Journal of Accountancy*, June 1978, pp. 89–94.

Financial Accounting Standards Board. *Consolidation of All Majority-Owned Subsidiaries*. Statement of Financial Accounting Standards No. 94. Norwalk: FASB, 1987.

_____. *Consolidated Financial Statements: Policy and Procedures*. Proposed Statement of Financial Accounting Standards. Norwalk: FASB, 1995.

Neuhausen, B.S. "Consolidation and the Equity Method—Time for an Overhaul." *Journal of Accountancy*, February 1982, pp. 54–66.

Parker, J.R.E., and Baxter, G. *Advanced Corporate Financial Reporting: A Canadian Perspective*. Homewood, Illinois: Richard D. Irwin Inc., 1990.

Walker, R.G. "An Evaluation of the Information Conveyed by Consolidated Statements." *Abacus*, December 1976, pp. 77–115.

Chapter 21—Foreign Currency Translation

Aliber, R.Z., and Stickney, C.P. "Accounting Measures of Foreign Exchange Exposure: The Long and Short of It." *The Accounting Review*, January 1975, pp. 44–57.

Beaver, W.H., and Wolfson, M.A. "Foreign Currency Translation and Changing Prices in Perfect and Complete Markets." *Journal of Accounting Research*, Autumn 1982, Part II, pp. 528–50.

Canadian Institute of Chartered Accountants. *Foreign Currency Translation Issues*. Research Report. Toronto: CICA, 1989.

————. "Foreign Currency Translation." *CICA Handbook*, Section 1650. Toronto: CICA.

Collins, D.W., and Salatka, W.K. "Noisy Accounting Earnings Signals and Earnings Response Coefficients: The Case of Foreign Currency Accounting." *Contemporary Accounting Research*, Fall 1993, pp. 119–59.

Elitzur, R.R. "A Model of Translation of Foreign Financial Statements Under Inflation in the United States and Canada." *Contemporary Accounting Research*, Spring 1991, pp. 466–84.

Financial Accounting Standards Board. *Foreign Currency Translation*. Statement of Financial Accounting Standards No. 52. Norwalk: FASB, 1981.

Godfrey, J.M. "Foreign Currency Accounting Policy: The Impact of Asset Specificity." *Contemporary Accounting Research*, Spring 1994, pp. 643–71.

Goldberg, S.R., Titschler, C.A., and Godwin, J.H. "Foreign Reporting for Foreign Exchange Derivatives." *Accounting Horizons*, June 1995, pp. 1–16.

Hall, T.W. "Inflation and Rates of Exchange: Support for SFAS No. 52." *Journal of Accounting, Auditing & Finance*, Summer 1983, pp. 299–313.

Heywood, J. *Foreign Exchange and the Corporate Treasurer*. London: Adam & Charles Black, 1978.

International Accounting Standards Committee. *The Effects of Changes in Foreign Exchange Rates*. International Accounting Standard 21. London: IASC, Revised, 1993.

Jacque, L.L. "Management of Foreign Exchange Risk: A Review Article." In *International Accounting and Transnational Decisions*, pp. 361–84. Edited by S.J. Gray. London: Butterworth, 1983. (First published in *Journal of International Business Studies*, Spring–Summer 1981, pp. 81–101.)

Lorensen, L. *Reporting Foreign Operations of U.S. Companies in U.S. Dollars*. Accounting Research Study No. 12. New York: AICPA, 1972.

Parkinson, R.M. *Translation of Foreign Currencies*. Toronto: CICA, 1972.

Patz, D.H. "A Price Parity Theory of Translation." *Accounting and Business Research*, Winter 1977, pp. 14–24.

————. "The State of the Art in Translation Theory." *Journal of Business Finance & Accounting*, Autumn 1977, pp. 311–25.

Rodriguez, R.M. "Measuring and Controlling Multinationals' Exchange Risk." *Financial Analysis Journal*. November–December 1979, pp. 49–55.

Scott, G.M. "Currency Exchange Rates and Accounting Translation: A Mismarriage?" *Abacus*, June 1975, pp. 58–70.

Soo, B.S., and Soo, L.G. "Accounting for the Multinational Firm: Is the Translation Process Valued by the Stock Market?" *The Accounting Review*, October 1994, pp. 617–37.

Vézina, P. *Foreign Currency Translation—An Analysis of Section 1650 of the CICA Handbook.* Toronto: CICA, 1985.

Chapter 22—Cash Flow Statements

Cheng, C.S.A, Liv, C., and Schaefer, T.F. "The Value-Relevance of SFAS No. 95 Cash Flows From Operations as Assessed by Security Market Effects." *Accounting Horizons*, September 1997, pp. 1–15.

Canadian Institute of Chartered Accountants. "Cash Flow Statements." *CICA Handbook*, Section 1540. Toronto: CICA.

International Accounting Standards Committee. *Cash Flow Statements.* International Accounting Standard 7. London: IASC, Revised 1992.

Egginton, D.A. "Cash Flow, Profit and Performance Measures for External Reports: A Rejoinder." *Accounting and Business Research*, Spring 1985, pp. 109–12.

Financial Accounting Standards Board. *Statement of Cash Flows.* Statement of Financial Accounting Standards No. 95. Norwalk: FASB, 1987.

Heath, L.C. *Financial Reporting and the Evaluation of Solvency.* Accounting Research Monograph No. 3. New York: American Institute of Certified Public Accountants, 1978.

Hicks, B.E., and Hunt, P., eds. *Cash Flow Accounting.* Sudbury, Ont.: International Group for Cash Flow Accounting and Research and Publication Division, School of Commerce and Administration, Laurentian University, 1981.

Ijiri, Y. "Recovery Rate and Cash Flow Accounting." *Financial Executive*, March 1980, pp. 54–60.

Lawson, G.H. "The Measurement of Corporate Performance on a Cash Flow Basis: A Reply to Mr. Egginton." *Accounting and Business Research*, Spring 1985, pp. 98–108.

Lee, T.A. *Cash Flow Accounting.* Wokingham, Eng.: Van Nostrand Reinhold (U.K.), 1984.

Nurnberg, H. "Inconsistencies and Ambiguities in Cash Flow Statements Under FASB Statement No. 95." *Accounting Horizons*, June 1993, pp. 60–75.

Rosen, L.S., and DeCoster, D.T. "Funds' Statements: A Historical Perspective." *The Accounting Review.* January 1969, pp. 125–36.

Rutherford, B.A. "The Interpretation of Cash Flow Reports and the Other Allocation Problem." *Abacus*, June 1982, pp. 40–49.

Seed, A.H., III. *The Funds Statement: Structure and Use.* Morristown, N.J.: Financial Executives Research Foundation, 1984.

Stephens, R.G., and Govindarajan, V. "On Assessing a Firm's Cash Generating Ability." *The Accounting Review*, January 1990, pp. 242–57.

Chapter 23—Disclosure Issues

American Institute of Certified Public Accountants, Accounting Principles Board. *Interim Financial Reporting*. Opinion No. 28. New York: AICPA, 1973.

_____, Special Committee on Financial Reporting. *The Information Needs of Investors and Creditors*. New York: AICPA, 1993.

Balsam, S., and Lipka, R. "Share Prices and Alternative Measures of Earnings per Share." *Accounting Horizons*, September 1998, pp. 234–49.

Barlev, B. "Theory, Pragmatism and Conservatism in Reflecting the Effects of Warrants on Diluted EPS." *Abacus*, June 1984, pp. 1–15.

Bird, P. "The Complexities of Simplified Accounts." In *External Financial Reporting: Essays in Honour of Harold Edy*, ed. Carsberg, B., and Dev, S. Englewood Cliffs, N.J.: Prentice-Hall International in cooperation with London School of Economics and Political Science, 1984, pp. 16–24.

Bloom, R. "Functional Fixation and Information Overload Applied to Financial Statement Users." *Cost and Management*, July–August, 1980, pp. 43–45.

Boersema, J.M., and Van Weelden, S.J. *Financial Reporting for Segments*. Toronto: CICA, 1992.

Boritz, J.E. *Approaches to Dealing With Risk and Uncertainty*. Toronto: CICA, 1990.

_____. *The "Going Concern" Assumption: Accounting and Auditing Implications*. Toronto: CICA, 1991.

Canadian Institute of Chartered Accountants. "Applying Materiality and Audit Risk Concepts in Conducting an Audit." *CICA Handbook*, AuG-7. Toronto: CICA, 1990.

_____. "Earnings per Share." *CICA Handbook*, Section 3500. Toronto: CICA.

_____. "Future-Oriented Financial Information." *CICA Handbook*, Section 4250. Toronto: CICA.

_____. *Interim Financial Reporting: A Continuous Process*. Toronto: CICA, 1991.

_____. "Interim Financial Reporting to Shareholders." *CICA Handbook*, Section 1750. Toronto: CICA.

_____. "Segment Disclosures." *CICA Handbook*, Section 1701. Toronto: CICA.

_____. *Using Ratios and Graphics in Financial Reporting*. Toronto: CICA, 1993.

Dudley, L.W. "A Critical Look at EPS." *Journal of Accountancy*, August 1985, pp. 102–11.

Financial Accounting Standards Board. *Criteria for Determining Materiality*. FASB Discussion Memorandum. Stamford: FASB, 1975.

_____. *Disclosures About Segments of an Enterprise and Related Information*. Statement of Financial Accounting Standards No. 131. Norwalk: FASB, 1997.

_____. *Earnings per Share*. Statement of Financial Accounting Standards No. 128. Norwalk: FASB, 1997.

Feltham, G.A., and Xie, J.Z. "Voluntary Financial Disclosure in an Entry Game with Continua of Types." *Contemporary Accounting Research*, Fall 1992, pp. 46–80.

Gibbins, M., Richardson, A., and Waterhouse, J. "The Management of Corporate Financial Disclosure: Opportunism, Ritualism, Policies, and Processes." *Journal of Accounting Research*, Spring 1990, pp. 121–43.

Gigler, F. "Self-Enforcing Voluntary Disclosures." *Journal of Accounting Research*, Autumn 1994, pp. 224–40.

Groves, R.J. "Financial Disclosure: When More Is Not Better." *Financial Executive*, May–June 1994, pp. 11–14.

Herrmann, D, and Thomas, W.B. "Reporting Disaggregated Information: A Critique Based on Concepts Statement No. 2."' *Accounting Horizons*, September 1997, pp. 35–44.

Hicks, E.L. "Materiality." *Journal of Accounting Research*, Autumn 1964, pp. 158–71.

International Accounting Standards Committee. *Earnings per Share*. International Accounting Standard 33. London: IASC, 1997.

_____. *Interim Financial Reporting*. International Accounting Standard 34. London: IASC, 1998.

_____. *Segment Reporting*. International Accounting Standard 14. London: IASC, Revised 1997.

Johnson, L.T. "Research on Disclosure." *Accounting Horizons*, March 1992, pp. 101–103.

Kidd, R.H. *Earnings Forecasts*. Toronto: CICA, 1976.

Knutson, P.H. *Financial Reporting in the 1990s and Beyond*. A position paper of the Association for Investment Management and Research. Charlottesville, Va.: The Association for Investment Management and Research, 1993.

Landsittel, D.L., and Serlin, J.E. "Evaluating the Materiality of Errors in Financial Statements." *Journal of Accounting, Auditing & Finance*, Summer 1982, pp. 291–300.

Leslie, D.A. *Materiality: The Concept and Its Application to Auditing*. Toronto: CICA, 1985.

Mautz, Jr., R.D., and Hogan, T.J. "Earnings Per Share Reporting: Time for an Overhaul?" *Accounting Horizons*, September 1989, pp. 21–27.

Mohr, R.M., and Pacter, P. "Review of Related Research," in Pacter, P. *Reporting Disaggregated Information*. Norwalk: FASB, 1993, chap. 6.

O'Connor, M.C., and Collins, D.W. "Toward Establishing User-Oriented Materiality Standards." *Journal of Accountancy*, December 1974, pp. 67–75.

Pacter, P. *Reporting Disaggregated Information*. Norwalk: FASB, 1993.

Pattillo, J.W. *The Concept of Materiality in Financial Reporting*. New York: Financial Executives Research Foundation, 1976.

Rangan, S., and Sloan, R.S. "Implications of the Integral Approach to Quarterly Reporting for the Post-Earnings-Announcement Drift." *The Accounting Review*, July 1998, pp. 353–71.

Scott, T.W. "Incentives and Disincentives for Financial Disclosure: Voluntary Disclosure of Defined Benefit Pension Plan Information by Canadian Firms." *The Accounting Review*, January 1994, pp. 26–43.

Skinner, D.J. "Why Firms Voluntarily Disclose Bad News." *Journal of Accounting Research*, Spring 1994, pp. 38–60.

Wallman, S.M.H. "The Future of Accounting and Disclosure in an Evolving World: The Need for Dramatic Change." *Accounting Horizons*, September 1995, pp. 81–91.

Chapter 24—Accounting for Changing Prices

American Institute of Certified Public Accountants, Accounting Standards Board. *Financial Statements Restated for General Price-Level Changes*. Statement No. 3. New York: AICPA, 1969.

Baxter, W.T. *Accounting Values and Inflation*. London: McGraw-Hill, 1975.

Bell, P.W. *CVA, CCA and CoCoA: How Fundamental Are the Differences?* Accounting Theory Monograph No. 1. Melbourne: Australian Accounting Research Foundation, 1982.

Carsberg, B., and Page M., eds. *Current Cost Accounting: The Benefits and the Costs*. 4 vols. Englewood Cliffs, N.J.: Prentice-Hall International in association with the Institute of Chartered Accountants in England and Wales, 1984.

Chambers, R.J. *Accounting, Evaluation and Economic Behavior*. Englewood Cliffs, N.J.: Prentice-Hall, 1966; reprint ed., Houston: Scholars Book Co., 1974.

_____. *Accounting for Inflation*. Exposure Draft. Sydney, New South Wales: Department of Accounting, University of Sydney, 1975.

_____. "Edwards and Bell on Income Measurement in Retrospect." *Abacus*, June 1982, pp. 3–39.

Chasteen, L. "A Taxonomy of Price Change Models." *The Accounting Review*, July 1984, pp. 515–23.

Cheung, J.K. "The Valuation Significance of Exit Values: A Contingent-Claim Analysis." *Contemporary Accounting Research*, Spring 1990, pp. 724–37.

Easton, P.D., Eddey, P.H., and Harris, T.S. "An Investigation of Revaluations of Tangible Long-Lived Assets." *Journal of Accounting Research*, Supplement 1993, pp. 1–38.

Edwards, E.O., and Bell, P.W. *The Theory and Measurement of Business Income*. Berkeley and Los Angeles: University of California Press, 1961.

Hanna, J.R., Kennedy, D.B., and Richardson, G.D. *Reporting the Effects of Changing Prices: A Review of the Experience with Section 4510*. Toronto: CICA, 1990.

Inflation Accounting: Report of the Inflation Accounting Committee. London: Her Majesty's Stationery Office, 1975.

International Accounting Standards Committee. *Financial Reporting in Hyperinflationary Economies*. International Accounting Standard 29. London: IASC, Reformatted 1994.

Iselin, E.R. "Chambers on Accounting Theory," *The Accounting Review*, April 1968, pp. 231–38.

Lemke, K.W. "Asset Valuation and Income Theory." *The Accounting Review*, January 1966, pp. 32–41.

Ma, R. "On Chambers' Second Thoughts," *Abacus*, December 1974, pp. 124–28.

Report of the Ontario Committee on Inflation Accounting. Toronto: Ministry of Industry, Economics and Intergovernmental Affairs, 1977.

Revsine, L. *Replacement Cost Accounting*. Englewood Cliffs, N.J.: Prentice-Hall, 1973.

_____. "Technological Changes and Replacement Costs: A Beginning." *The Accounting Review*, April 1979, pp. 306–22.

Rosenfield, P. "A History of Inflation Accounting." *Journal of Accountancy*, September 1981, pp. 95–126.

Ronen, J., and Sorter, G.H. "Relevant Accounting." *The Journal of Business*, April 1972, pp. 258–82.

Seed III, A.H. *Inflation: Its Impact on Financial Reporting and Decision Making*. New York: Financial Executives Research Foundation, 1978.

Skinner, R.M. *Memorandum on the Significance of Debt Financing During an Inflationary Period and the Implications Thereof to a System of "Inflation Accounting."* Supplementary Paper No. 2 prepared for the Ontario Committee on Inflation Accounting. Toronto: Ministry of Treasury, Economics and Intergovernmental Affairs, 1977.

Solomons, D. "Economic and Accounting Concepts of Cost and Value." In *Modern Accounting Theory*, ed. Backer, M. Englewood Cliffs, N.J.: Prentice-Hall, 1966, pp. 117–40.

Stamp, E. "Income and Value Determination and Changing Price Levels: An Essay Towards a Theory." *The Accountants' Magazine*, June 1971, pp. 227–92.

Sterling, R.R. *Theory of the Measurement of Enterprise Income*. Lawrence, Kan.: University Press of Kansas, 1970.

_____. *Toward a Science of Accounting*. Houston: Scholars Book Co., 1979.

Sterling, R.R., and Lemke, K.W., eds. *Maintenance of Capital: Financial versus Physical*. Papers from the Clarkson Gordon Foundation Symposium held under the auspices of the Faculty of Business Administration and Commerce, University of Alberta, August 1981. Houston: Scholars Book Co., 1982.

Sterling, R.R., and Thomas A.L., eds. *Accounting for a Simplified Firm Owning Depreciable Assets: Seventeen Essays and A Synthesis Based on a Common Case*. Papers from Accounting Researchers International Symposium held at Jesse H. Jones Graduate School of Administration, Rice University, May 1978.

Stickler, A.D., and Hutchins, C.S.R. *General Price-Level Accounting: Described and Illustrated*. Toronto: CICA, 1975.

Swanson, E.P., and Shriver, K.A. "The Accounting-for-Changing-Prices Experiment: A Valid Test of Usefulness?" *Accounting Horizons*, September 1987, pp. 69–77.

Thornton, D.B. "Capital Values in Use Versus Replacement Costs: Theory and Canadian Evidence." *Contemporary Accounting Research*, Fall 1988, pp. 343–70.

Whittington, G. *Inflation Accounting: An Introduction to the Debate*. Cambridge: Cambridge University Press, 1983.

PART III: A CONCEPTUAL FRAMEWORK AND STANDARD SETTING

Chapter 25—A Conceptual Framework for Financial Reporting

Accounting and Reporting Standards for Corporate Financial Statements and Preceding Statements and Supplements. Evanston, Ill.: AAA, 1957.

American Accounting Association, Committee on Concepts and Standards for External Financial Reports. *Statement on Accounting Theory and Theory Acceptance*. Sarasota, Fla.: AAA, 1977.

American Institute of Certified Public Accountants, Accounting Principles Board. *Basic Concepts and Accounting Principles Underlying Financial Statements of Business Enterprises*. APB Statement No. 4. New York: AICPA, 1970.

Amernic, J.H., and Lemon, W.M. "Do We Need a Canadian Conceptual Framework?" *CA Magazine*, July 1984, pp. 22–27.

A Statement of Basic Accounting Theory. Evanston, Ill.: AAA, 1966.

Brownlee II, E.R., and Young, S.D. "Financial Disclosure Regulations and Its Critics." *Journal of Accounting Education*, Spring 1986, pp. 113–26.

Canadian Institute of Chartered Accountants. "Financial Statement Concepts." *CICA Handbook*, Section 1000. Toronto: CICA.

Carsberg, B. "The Quest for a Conceptual Framework for Financial Reporting." In *External Financial Reporting: Essays in Honour of Harold Edey*, pp. 25–39. Edited by B. Carsberg and S. Dev. Englewood Cliffs, N.J.: Prentice-Hall International, in cooperation with London School of Economics and Political Science, 1984.

Corporate Reporting: Its Future Evolution. Toronto: CICA, 1980.

Cramer, J.J., Jr., and Sorter, G.H., eds. *Objectives of Financial Statements*. Vol. 2. New York: American Institute of Certified Public Accountants, 1974.

Daley, L.A., and Trantner, T. "Limitations in the Value of the Conceptual Framework in Evaluating Extant Accounting Standards." *Accounting Horizons*, March 1990, pp. 15–24.

Demski, J.S. "The General Impossibility of Normative Accounting Standards." *The Accounting Review*, October 1973, pp. 718–23.

Dopuch, N., and Sunder, S. "FASB's Statement on Objectives and Elements of Financial Accounting: A Review." *The Accounting Review*, January 1980, pp. 1–21.

Financial Accounting Standards Board. *Objectives of Financial Reporting by Business Enterprises*. Statement of Financial Accounting Concepts No. 1. Stamford: FASB, 1978.

————. *Qualitative Characteristics of Accounting Information*. Statement of Financial Accounting Concepts No. 2. Stamford: FASB, 1980.

————. *Objectives of Financial Reporting by Nonbusiness Organizations*. Statement of Financial Accounting Concepts No. 4. Stamford: FASB, 1980.

————. *Recognition and Measurement in Financial Statements of Business Enterprises*. Statement of Financial Accounting Concepts No. 5. Stamford: FASB, 1984.

————. *Elements of Financial Statements: A Replacement of FASB Concepts Statement No. 3 (Incorporating an Amendment of FASB Concepts Statement No. 2)*. Statement of Financial Accounting Concepts No. 6. Stamford: FASB, 1985.

————. *Using Cash Flow Information in Accounting Measurements*. Proposed Statement of Financial Accounting Concepts. Norwalk: FASB, 1997.

Grady, P. *Inventory of Generally Accepted Accounting Principles for Business Enterprises*. Accounting Research Study No. 7. New York: AICPA, 1965.

Institute of Chartered Accountants in England and Wales, Accounting Standards Steering Committee. *The Corporate Report*. A Discussion Paper. London: The Institute of Chartered Accountants in England and Wales, 1975.

International Accounting Standards Committee. *Framework for the Preparation and Presentation of Financial Statements*. London: IASC, 1989.

Kahn, N., and Schiff, S. "Tangible Equity Change and the Evolution of the FASB's Definition of Income." *Journal of Accounting, Auditing & Finance*, Fall 1985, pp. 40–49.

Macve, R. *A Conceptual Framework for Financial Accounting and Reporting: The Possibilities for an Agreed Structure*. London: Institute of Chartered Accountants in England and Wales, 1981.

May, R.G., and Sundem, G.L. "Research for Accounting Policy: An Overview." *The Accounting Review*, October 1976, pp. 747–63.

Milburn, J.A. *Incorporating the Time Value of Money Within Financial Reporting*. Toronto: CICA, 1988.

Moonitz, M. *The Basic Postulates of Accounting*. Accounting Research Study No. 1. New York: AICPA, 1961.

Objectives of Financial Statements. Vol. 1. New York: American Institute of Public Accountants, 1973.

Paton, W.A., and Littleton, A.C. *An Introduction to Corporate Accounting Standards*. Monograph No. 3. Evanston, Ill.: AAA, 1940.

Solomons, D. *Making Accounting Policy: The Quest for Credibility in Financial Reporting*. New York: Oxford University Press, 1986.

Sprouse, R.T., and Moonitz, M. *A Tentative Set of Broad Accounting Principles for Business Enterprises*. Accounting Research Study No. 3. New York: AICPA, 1962.

Storey, R.K. "The Framework of Financial Accounting Concepts and Standards." In Carmichael, D.R., Lilien, S.B., and Mellman, M. *Accountants' Handbook*, 9th ed. Vol. 1. Somerset, N.J.: John Wiley & Sons, Inc., 1999.

Chapter 26—The Establishment of Accounting Standards

Abdel-khalik, A.R., ed. *Government Regulation of Accounting and Information*. Gainesville, Fla.: University Presses of Florida, 1980.

Bandyopadhyay, S.P., Hanna, J.D., and Richardson, G.D. "Capital Market Effects of U.S.–Canada GAAP Differences." *Journal of Accounting Research*, Autumn 1994, pp. 262–77.

Barth, M.E., and Clinch, G. "International Accounting Differences and Their Relation to Share Prices: Evidence from U.K., Australian, and Canadian Firms." *Contemporary Accounting Research*, Spring 1996, pp. 135–70.

Brown, V.H. "Accounting Standards: Their Economic and Social Consequences." *Accounting Horizons*, September 1990, pp. 89–97.

CICA Special Committee on Standard-Setting. *Report to CICA Board of Governors*. Toronto: CICA, 1980.

CICA Task Force on Standard Setting: Final Report. Toronto: CICA, 1998.

Cuccia, A.D., Hackenbrack, K., and Nelson, M.W. "The Ability of Professional Standards to Mitigate Aggressive Reporting." *The Accounting Review*, April 1995, pp. 227–48.

Flegm, E.H. *Accounting: How to Meet the Challenges of Relevance and Regulation*. New York: A Ronald Press Publication, John Wiley & Sons, 1984.

Gibbins, M., and Mason, A.K. *Professional Judgment in Financial Reporting*. Toronto: CICA, 1988.

IASC Strategy Working Party, *Shaping the IASC for the Future*. A Discussion Paper. London: IASC, 1998.

Kirk, D.J. "Concepts, Consensus, Compromise and Consequences: Their Roles in Standard Setting." *Journal of Accountancy*, April 1981, pp. 83–86.

Leach, Sir R., and Stamp, E., eds. *British Accounting Standards: The First 10 Years*. Cambridge: Woodhead-Faulkner, 1981.

Mason, A.K., and Gibbins, M. "Judgment and U.S. Accounting Standards." *Accounting Horizons*, June 1991, pp. 14–24.

Measurement Research in Financial Accounting. Workshop Proceedings, University of Waterloo School of Accountancy. Toronto: The Ernst & Young Foundation, 1994.

Mosso, D. "Standards Overload—No Simple Solution." *The CPA Journal*, October 1983, pp. 12–22.

Office of the Chief Accountant of the Ontario Securities Commission. *Study of Differences Between Canadian and United States Generally Accepted Accounting Principles*. Toronto: OSC, 1993.

Skinner, R.M. "Judgment in Jeopardy." *CA Magazine*, November 1995, pp. 14–21.

Solomons, D. "The Politicalization of Accounting." *Journal of Accountancy*, November 1978, pp. 65–72.

_____. "The Potential Implications of Accounting and Auditing Standard Setting." *Accounting and Business Research*, Spring 1983, pp. 107–18.

Van Riper, R. *Setting Standards for Financial Reporting: FASB and the Struggle for Control of A Critical Process*. Westport, CT.: Quorum Books, 1994.

PART IV: NOT-FOR-PROFIT ORGANIZATIONS AND GOVERNMENTS

Chapter 27—Not-for-Profit Organizations

Anthony, R.N. *Financial Accounting in Nonbusiness Organizations: An Exploratory Study of Conceptual Issues*. Stamford: Financial Accounting Standards Board, 1978.

_____. "The Non Profit Accounting Mess." *Accounting Horizons*, June 1995, pp. 44–53.

Beechy, T.M., and Zimmerman, B.J. "Costs and the Collective Good." *CA Magazine*, November 1992, pp. 44–49.

Canadian Institute of Chartered Accountants. "Financial Statement Concepts." *CICA Handbook*, Section 1000. Toronto: CICA.

_____. "Not-for-Profit Organizations." *CICA Handbook*, Section 4400 Series. Toronto: CICA.

Falk, H. "Towards a Framework for Not-for-Profit Accounting." *Contemporary Accounting Research*, Spring 1992, pp. 468–99.

Figlewicz, R.E., Anderson, D.T., and Strupeck, C.D. "The Evolution and Current State of Financial Accounting Concepts and Standards in the Nonbusiness Sector." *The Accounting Historians Journal*, Spring 1985, pp. 73–98.

Financial Accounting Standards Board. *Accounting for Certain Investments Held by Not-for-Profit Organizations*. Statement of Financial Accounting Standards No. 124. Norwalk: FASB, 1995.

_____. *Accounting for Contributions Received and Contributions Made*. Statement of Financial Accounting Standards No. 116. Norwalk: FASB, 1993.

_____. *Financial Statements of Not-for-Profit Organizations*. Statement of Financial Accounting Standards No. 117. Norwalk: FASB, 1993.

_____. *Objectives of Financial Reporting by Non-Business Organizations*. Statement of Financial Accounting Concepts No. 4. Stamford: FASB, 1980.

Financial Reporting for Non-Profit Organizations. Toronto: CICA, 1980.

Macintosh, J.C.C. "Finding the Right Fit." *CA Magazine*, March 1995, pp. 34–38.

"Report of the Committee on Nonprofit Organizations, 1973–74." *The Accounting Review*, Supplement 1975, pp. 1–39.

Chapter 28—Government

Beedle, A. *Accounting for Local Government in Canada: The State of the Art.* Research Monograph No. 2. Vancouver: The Canadian Certified General Accountants' Research Foundation, 1981.

Canadian Institute of Chartered Accountants. *Public Sector Accounting Handbook.* Toronto: CICA.

Federal Government Reporting Study: Detailed Report. Ottawa: Office of the Auditor General of Canada, and Gaithersburg, Md.: U.S. General Accounting Office, 1986.

Financial Reporting by Governments. Toronto: CICA, 1980.

Indicators of Government Financial Condition. Toronto: CICA, 1997.

Jones, M. "Invisible Assets." *CA Magazine*, January–February 1994, pp. 65–67.

Local Government Financial Reporting. Toronto: CICA, 1985.

McCrindell, J.Q., Principal Author. *Costing Government Services for Improved Performance Measurement and Accountability.* Toronto, CICA, 1999.

Index